BRITISH
COMPANY CASES
1993

CCH EDITIONS LIMITED

TAX, BUSINESS AND LAW PUBLISHERS
TELFORD ROAD, BICESTER
OXFORDSHIRE OX6 0XD

Telephone: Bicester (0869) 253300
Facsimile: Bicester (0869) 245814
DX: 83750 Bicester 2

ABOUT THE PUBLISHER

CCH Editions Limited is the UK affiliate of Commerce Clearing House Inc, a publishing company which provides leading tax and business law reporting services in the US.

Other CCH affiliates provide similar authoritative services in Australia, Canada, New Zealand, Asia, Japan and Europe.

A highly qualified editorial staff and many years of experience stand behind all CCH publications.

Disclaimer

This publication is designed to provide accurate and authoritative information in regard to the subject matter covered. It is sold with the understanding that the publisher is not engaged in rendering legal or other professional service. If legal advice or other expert assistance is required, the services of a competent professional person should be sought.

Ownership of Trade Marks

The Trade Marks

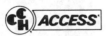 

CCH ACCESS, COMPUTAX and **COMMERCE CLEARING HOUSE, INC.** are the property of Commerce Clearing House, Incorporated, Chicago, Illinois, USA

ISBN 0 86325 348 2

ISSN 0269–0535

FOREWORD

British Company Cases 1993 reproduces the full text of British company law cases heard in the High Court, Court of Appeal, House of Lords, Judicial Committee of the Privy Council, Scottish Court of Session, Northern Ireland High Court, and reported during the year. Each case has a headnote outlining the facts, the decision and the reasons for the decision.

The decisions reproduced are listed alphabetically by name in the Cases Reported list. Cases and legislation referred to in the judgments are included in the Cases Cited list and the Legislation Finding List. The decisions are indexed by subject matter in the Topical Index.

Cases in this volume of *British Company Cases* should be cited as follows: [1993] BCC page. Thus the case of Portbase (Clothing) Ltd which appears at page 96 would be cited —

Re Portbase (Clothing) Ltd [1993] BCC 96.

The cases in this volume were reported by DSP Barbour, Barrister and E O'Grady, Barrister.

FOREWORD

TABLE OF CONTENTS

CASES REPORTED IN 1993

This table lists all cases reported in British Company Cases 1993.
References are to pages.

COURTS

The following is a list of members of the judiciary in order of seniority
as at 31 December 1993

Appellate Courts

House of Lords

The Lord High Chancellor: Lord Mackay of Clashfern

Lords of Appeal in Ordinary

Lord Keith of Kinkel
Lord Templeman
Lord Goff of Chieveley
Lord Jauncey of Tullichettle
Lord Lowry

Lord Browne-Wilkinson
Lord Mustill
Lord Slynn of Hadley
Lord Woolf
Lord Lloyd of Berwick

Court of Appeal

The Lord High Chancellor: Lord Mackay of Clashfern
The Lord Chief Justice of England: Lord Taylor of Gosforth
The Master of the Rolls: Sir Thomas Henry Bingham
The President of the Family Division: Sir Stephen Brown
The Vice-Chancellor: Sir Donald James Nicholls

Lords Justices of Appeal

Sir George Brian Hugh Dillon
Sir Brian Thomas Neill
Sir Martin Charles Nourse
Sir Iain Derek Laing Glidewell
Sir Alfred John Balcombe
Sir Ralph Brian Gibson
Sir Thomas Patrick Russell
Dame Ann Elizabeth Oldfield
    Butler-Sloss
Sir Murray Stuart-Smith
Sir Christopher Stephen Thomas
    Jonathan Thayer Staughton
Sir Michael Mann
Sir Donald Henry Farquharson
Sir Anthony James Denys McCowan

Sir Alexander Roy Asplan Beldam
Sir Andrew Peter Leggatt
Sir Michael Patrick Nolan
Sir Richard Rashleigh Folliott Scott
Sir Johan Van Zyl Steyn
Sir Paul Joseph Morrow Kennedy
Sir David Cozens-Hardy Hirst
Sir Simon Denis Brown
Sir Anthony Howell Meurig Evans
Sir Christopher Dudley Roger Rose
Sir Leonard Hubert Hoffmann
Sir John Douglas Waite
Sir John Ormond Roch
Sir Peter Leslie Gibson
Sir John Stewart Hobhouse
Sir Denis Robert Maurice Henry

High Court of Justice

Chancery Division

The Vice-Chancellor: Sir Donald James Nicholls

Sir John Evelyn Vinelott
Sir Jean Pierre Frank Eugene Warner
Sir Jeremiah LeRoy Harman
Sir John Leonard Knox
Sir Peter Julian Millett
Sir Robert Andrew Morritt
Sir William Aldous
Sir Donald Keith Rattee
Sir John Frank Mummery

Sir Francis Mursell Ferris
Sir John Murray Chadwick
Sir Jonathan Frederic Parker
Sir John Edmund Fredric Lindsay
Dame Mary Howarth Arden
Sir Edward Christopher
  Evans-Lombe
Sir Robert Raphael Hayim Jacob
Sir William Anthony Blackburne

Queen's Bench Division

The Lord Chief Justice of England: Lord Taylor of Gosforth

Sir Hadyn Tudor Evans
Sir Ronald Gough Waterhouse
Sir Frederick Maurice Drake
Sir Christopher James Saunders French
Sir Iain Charles Robert McCullough
Sir Oliver Bury Popplewell
Sir William Alan Macpherson of Cluny
Sir Philip Howard Otton
Sir Michael Hutchison
Sir Mark Oliver Saville
Sir Swinton Barclay Thomas
Sir Richard Howard Tucker
Sir Robert Alexander Gatehouse
Sir Patrick Neville Garland
Sir Michael John Turner
Sir John Downes Alliott
Sir Harry Henry Ognall
Sir Konrad Hermann Theodor
  Schiemann
Sir John Arthur Dalziel Owen
Sir Francis Humphrey Potts
Sir Richard George Rougier
Sir Ian Alexander Kennedy
Sir Nicholas Addison Phillips
Sir Robin Ernest Auld
Sir Malcolm Thomas Pill
Sir Stuart Neil McKinnon
Sir Mark Howard Potter
Sir Henry Brooke
Sir Thomas Scott Gillespie Baker
Sir Igor Judge
Sir Edwin Frank Jowitt

Sir Michael Morland
Sir George Mark Waller
Sir Roger John Buckley
Sir Anthony Brian Hidden
Sir John Michael Wright
Sir Charles Barrie Knight Mantell
Sir John Christopher Calthorpe Blofeld
Sir Peter John Cresswell
Sir Anthony Tristram Kenneth May
Sir John Grant McKenzie Laws
Dame Ann Marian Ebsworth
Sir Simon Lane Tuckey
Sir David Nicholas Ramsay Latham
Sir Christopher John Holland
Sir John William Kay
Sir Richard Herbert Curtis
Sir Stephen John Sedley
Dame Janet Hilary Smith
Sir Anthony David Colman
Sir Anthony Peter Clarke
Sir John Anthony Dyson
Sir Thayne John Forbes
Sir Michael Alexander Geddes Sachs
Sir Stephen George Mitchell
Sir Rodger Bell
Sir Michael Guy Vicat Harrison
Sir Bernard Anthony Rix
Dame Anne Heather Steel
Sir William Marcus Gage
Sir Jonathan Hugh Mance
Sir Andrew Centlivres Longmore
Sir Thomas Richard Atkin Morison
Sir Richard Joseph Buxton

Court of Session

The Court of Session, which is the highest civil tribunal in Scotland, consists of twenty-five judges four of whom, the Lord President and three judges, sit in the First Division, and the Lord Justice-Clerk and three other judges sit in the Second Division, the two Divisions together comprising the Inner House; the remaining judges officiate in the Outer House as Lords Ordinary.

Inner House Judges

First Division

Lord Hope (The Rt Hon J A D Hope PC), Lord President
Lord Allanbridge (W I Stewart)
Lord Cowie (W L K Cowie)
Lord Mayfield (I MacDonald)

Second Division

Lord Ross (The Rt Hon D M Ross), Lord Justice-Clerk
Lord Murray (The Rt Hon R King Murray)
Lord Davidson (C K Davidson)
    (*seconded to the Scottish Law Commission*)
Lord McCluskey (The Rt Hon Lord McCluskey)
Lord Morison (A M Morison)

Outer House Judges

Lord Sutherland (R I Sutherland)
Lord Weir (D B Weir)
Lord Clyde (J J Clyde)
Lord Cullen (W D Cullen)
Lord Prosser (W D Prosser)
Lord Kirkwood (I C Kirkwood)
Lord Coulsfield (J T Cameron)
Lord Milligan (J G Milligan)
Lord Morton of Shuna (H D B Morton)
Lord Caplan (P I Caplan)
Lord Cameron of Lochbroom (The Rt Hon the Lord Cameron of Lochbroom)
Lord Marnoch (M S R Bruce)
Lord MacLean (R N M MacLean)
Lord Penrose (G W Penrose)
Lord Osborne (K H Osborne)
Lord Abernethy (J A Cameron)

ABBREVIATIONS

AC	Law Reports, Appeal Cases, 1891–current
ACLC	Australian Company Law Cases, 1982–current (CCH)
ACT	Advance corporation tax
A & E	Admiralty and Ecclesiastical Cases, 1865–1875
Ad & E	Adolphus & Ellis's Reports, King's Bench, 1834–1840
A-G	Attorney-General
ALJR	Australian Law Journal Reports, 1958–current
All ER	All England Law Reports, 1936–current
App Cas	Law Reports, Appeal Cases, 1875–1890
Atk	Atkyn's Reports, Chancery, 1736–1755
B & CR	Bankruptcy and Companies Winding up Cases, 1915–1942
BCC	British Company Cases, 1983–current (CCH)
BCLC	Butterworths Company Law Cases
Beav	Beavan's Reports, Rolls Court, 1838–1866
Bligh	Bligh's Reports, House of Lords, 1818–1821
BR	Bankruptcy Reports (US)
B & S	Best & Smith's Reports, Queen's Bench, 1861–1870
BTC	British Tax Cases, 1982–current (CCH)
CA 1948	Companies Act 1948 (repealed)
CA 1985	Companies Act 1985
CA 1989	Companies Act 1989
CA	Court of Appeal
CB	Common Bench Reports, 1845–1856
CCC	cwmni cyfyngedig cyhoeddus (public limited company);
CEC	Cox's Criminal Cases, 1843–1941
CC(CP)A 1985	Companies Consolidation (Consequential Provisions) Act 1985
CCH	CCH Editions Limited
CEC	European Community Cases, 1989–current (CCH)
cf.	(confer) compare
ch. (Ch.)	chapter, Chapter (of Act)
Ch	Law Reports, Chancery Division, 1891–current
Ch App	Law Reports, Chancery Appeals, 1865–1875
ChD	Law Reports, Chancery Division, 1875–1890
CJ	Chief Justice
Cl & Fin	Clark and Finnelly's Reports, House of Lords, 1831–1846
CLC	Company Law Cases (Australia), 1971–1981 (CCH)
CLR	Commonwealth Law Reports, 1903–current (Australia)
Cmd, Cmnd, Cm	Command Paper
CMLR	Common Market Law Reports, 1962–current
Cr App R	Criminal Appeal Reports, 1908–current
Cr App R (S)	Criminal Appeal Reports (Sentencing), 1979–current

Crim LR	Criminal Law Review, 1954–current
CS(ID)A 1985	Company Securities (Insider Dealing) Act 1985
Ct Sess	Court of Session (Scotland)
cyf	cyfyngedig (limited)
D	Dunlop (Session Cases, 2nd Series) (Scotland), 1838–1862
De G M & G	De Gex, Macnaghten & Gordon's Reports, Chancery, 1851–1857
DLR; (2d); (3d); (4th)	Dominion Law Reports (Canada), 1912–1922; (Second Series), 1923–1968; (Third Series), 1969–1984; (Fourth Series), 1984–current
DTI	Department of Trade and Industry
E & B	Ellis & Blackburn's Reports, Queen's Bench, 1851–1858
ECR	European Court Reports, 1954–current
EEC	European Economic Community
EG	Estates Gazette, 1858–current
Eq	Equity Reports, 1853–1855; Equity Cases, 1866–1875
ER	English Reports, 1220–1865
ExD	Law Reports, Exchequer Division, 1875–1880
F	Federal Reporter (US); Fraser (Session Cases, 5th Series) (Scotland), 1898–1906
Fam	Law Reports, Family Division, 1972–current
F2d	Federal Reporter (Second Series) (US)
ff.	following
FLR	Family Law Reports, 1980–current; Federal Law Reports (Australia), 1956–current
FSR	Fleet Street Reports, 1963–current
F Supp	Federal Reporter Supplement (US)
FTLR	Financial Times Law Reports, 1986–1988
Hare	Hare's Reports, 1841–1853
HC	High Court
HL	House of Lords
HLCas	House of Lords Cases, 1846–1866
HMIT	Her Majesty's Inspector of Taxes
ICR	Industrial Cases Reports, 1972–current
IH	Inner House (Court of Session, Scotland)
IR	Irish Reports, 1894–current
IR 1986	Insolvency Rules 1986
J	Mr Justice
JBL	Journal of Business Law
JC	Justiciary Cases (Scotland)

KB	Law Reports, King's Bench Division, 1900–1952
LC	Lord Chancellor
LCJ	Lord Chief Justice
LJ	Lord Justice of Appeal;
	Law Journal Reports, New Series, 1831–1949
LJ (OS)	Law Journal Reports, Old Series, 1822–1831
Ll Rep	Lloyd's Reports, 1951–current
LR	Law Reports, from 1865
LT	Law Times Reports, 1859–1947
LTJo	Law Times Newspaper, 1843–1964
Law Soc Gazette	Law Society's Gazette
Ltd	Limited
M	Macpherson (Session Cases, 3rd Series) (Scotland), 1862–1873
Macq	Macqueen's Reports (Scotland), House of Lords, 1851–1865
Mer	Merivale's Reports, Chancery, 1815–1817
Moore Ind App	Moore's Indian Appeals, Privy Council, 1836–1872
Mor	Morison's Decisions, 1540–1808
MR	Master of the Rolls
M & S	Maule and Selwyn's Reports, King's Bench, 1813–1817
M & W	Meeson & Welsby's Reports, Exchequer, 1836–1847
My & Cr	Mylne & Craig's Reports, Chancery, 1835–1841
Myl & K	Mylne & Keen's Reports, Chancery, 1832–1835
n.b.	(nota bene) note well
ND	North Dakota
NI	Northern Ireland
	Northern Ireland Law Reports, 1925–current
NLJ	New Law Journal, 1965–current
NSWLR	New South Wales Law Reports, 1880–1900; 1971–current
NSWR	New South Wales Reports, 1960–1970
NW	North Western Reporter (US)
NZLR	New Zealand Law Reports, 1883–current
O.	Order
P	Law Reports, Probate, Divorce and Admiralty Division, 1891–1971
PC	Privy Council
P & CR	Property and Compensation Reports, 1950–current
PD	Law Reports, Probate Division, 1875–1890
plc	public limited company
PLR	Pension Law Reports, 1989–current
Price	Price's Reports, Exchequer, 1814–1824
Pt.	Part
Pty	Proprietary
P Wms	Peere Williams' Reports, Chancery and King's Bench, 1695–1735

QB	Law Reports, Queen's Bench Division, 1891–1900; 1952–current
QBD	Law Reports, Queen's Bench Division, 1875–1890
QC	Queen's Counsel
R	(regina) queen; (rex) king
	Rettie (Session Cases, 4th Series) (Scotland), 1873–1898
RSC	Rules of the Supreme Court
S	Shaw (Session Cases, 1st Series) (Scotland), 1821–1838
SA	South African Law Reports, 1948–current
SALR	South Australian Law Reports, 1866–1892, 1899–1920
SASR	South Australian State Reports, 1921–current
SC	Court of Session Cases (Scotland), 1906–current
Sch.	Schedule
Sel Cas t King	Selected Chancery Cases, 1724–1733
SI	Statutory Instrument
SIB	Securities and Investments Board
Sim	Simons' Reports, Chancery, 1826–1852
SJ	Solicitors' Journal, 1857–current
SLT	Scots Law Times, 1893–current
SRO	Self-regulating Organisation
SR & O	Statutory Rules and Orders
SSAP	Statement of Standard Accounting Practice
Swan	Swanston's Chancery Reports, 1818–1819
TC	Tax Cases, 1875–current
TLR	The Times Law Reports, 1884–1952
TMA	Taxes Management Act (1970)
TPD	Transvaal Provincial Division Reports, 1902–1946
UK	United Kingdom
US	United States of America
	United States Reports
USM	Unlisted Securities Market
v	versus
VAT	value added tax
V-C	Vice-Chancellor
Vern	Vernon's Reports, Chancery, 1680–1719
Ves Jun	Vesey junior's Chancery Reports, 1789–1817
VLR	Victorian Law Reports, 1875–1956
VR	Victorian Reports, 1870–1872; 1957–current
WLR	Weekly Law Reports, 1953–current
WN	Law Reports, Weekly Notes, 1866–1952
WN (NSW)	Weekly Notes, New South Wales, 1884–1970
¶	Paragraph

FOREIGN WORDS AND PHRASES

The following is a list of Latin and other words and phrases frequently found in decisions of the courts.

ab initio	from the beginning
ad hoc	arranged for this purpose
ad infinitum	to infinity
ad litem	for the law-suit
ad valorem	according to value
a fortiori	with stronger reason
alio intuitu	with a motive other than the ostensible and proper one
aliter	otherwise
a priori	deductively
bona fide	in good faith
caveat	warning, proviso
cadit quaestio	admitting of no further argument
certiorari	a writ, replaced by judicial review
cestui que trust	a person for whom another is trustee
contra	against
coram	before, in the presence of
corpus	the capital of a fund, as contrasted with the income
ejusdem generis	of the same kind
et al.	and others
et seq. (et sequens)	and the following
ex abundanti cautela	from excess of caution
ex debito justitiae	a remedy applicable as of right
ex gratia	as a favour
ex parte	an application in a judicial hearing made by one party in the absence of the other
hic	this, here
ibidem (ibid.)	in the same place
infra	below
in limine	at the outset
in loco parentis	in the position of parent
in re	in the matter of
in situ	in place
in specie	in its actual state, in kind
inter alia	among other things
inter partes	between or among the parties
inter se	among themselves
inter vivos	during lifetime
in toto	entirely
intra vires	within the powers of, e.g. a company
lis	legal action
locum tenens	a substitute
mandamus	a writ
modus operandi	a plan of working

mutatis mutandis	in the same manner with appropriate changes for the context
nisi	unless
nisi prius	unless before
obiter dictum	a judicial expression of opinion on a matter, not essential to the decision, and therefore not a binding authority
pari passu	rateable
passim	in various places
per alium	by means of another
per curiam	by the court
per diem	daily
per se	by itself, taken alone
prima facie	at first sight
pro rata	in proportion
quantum	a concrete quantity
quantum meruit	as much as he deserved
quid pro quo	consideration
re	in the matter of
res judicata	an issue already decided judicially
semble	it appears
sc. (scilicet)	namely, understand
sic	thus
simpliciter	without addition or qualification
sine qua non	an indispensable condition
stricto sensu	in its strict meaning
sub judice	in course of trial
sub nom	under the name of
sub voce	under a specified word
supra	above
ultra vires	beyond the powers, e.g. of (the directors of) a company
vide	see
viz. (videlicet)	in other words, namely

1993

BRITISH COMPANY CASES

Cited [1993] BCC

R v International Stock Exchange of the UK and the Republic of Ireland Ltd, ex parte Else (1982) Ltd & Anor.

Queen's Bench Division and Court of Appeal.
Popplewell J; Sir Thomas Bingham MR, McCowan and Leggatt L JJ.
Judgment delivered 20 July 1992 and 16 October 1992.

> *Admission of securities to listing — Delisting of shares — Whether shareholders could challenge delisting decision — EC Directive 79/279 (admission directive) (OJ 1979 L66/21), art. 15.*

This was an application by shareholders for judicial review of a decision of the International Stock Exchange to delist the shares of Titaghur plc.

The company's shares were suspended on 29 June 1988. On 23 November 1990 there was a hearing before a panel of the Stock Exchange which decided that the company should be delisted ("the panel decision"). On 7 December 1990 there was an appeal hearing before a committee: they made the decision that the company should be delisted ("the committee decision"). The company was party to those proceedings and made representations. None of the applicants nor any other shareholders were invited to that meeting, nor were they invited to make representations. It was not the practice of the Stock Exchange when considering the suspension or delisting of a company to accord a hearing to anyone other than the officers of the company.

The issues were whether (1) the applicants had standing to apply for judicial review, (2) they had any right to be heard before the committee, (3) there were any special circumstances justifying the committee's decision, (4) the committee's decision was irrational and (5) the decision to delist was necessary and proportionate to the damage which it was designed to prevent. The applicants submitted that if the committee's decision was set aside they were entitled to damages.

The judge decided that the committee's decision was not irrational or disproportionate but referred to the Court of Justice of the European Communities a question on the interpretation of art. 15 of Directive 79/279 on admission of securities to official stock exchange listing, which the applicants argued gave them rights in relation to delisting and to challenge the committee's decision. The Stock Exchange appealed.

Held, allowing the appeal:

The right to apply to the courts contained in art. 15 was conferred on the company or issuer alone.

The following cases were referred to in the High Court judgment:

Associated Provincial Picture Houses Ltd v Wednesbury Corp [1948] 1 KB 223.
Bulmer (H P) Ltd & Anor v J Bollinger SA & Ors [1974] Ch 401.
Cheall v Association of Professional Executive Clerical and Computer Staff [1983] 2 AC 180.
Council of Civil Service Unions & Ors v Minister for the Civil Service [1985] AC 374.

C & E Commrs v ApS Samex (Hanil Synthetic Fiber Industrial Co Ltd, third party) [1983] 1 All ER 1042.

Prudential Assurance Co Ltd v Newman Industries Ltd & Ors (No. 2) [1982] Ch 204.

R v Independent Television Commission, ex parte TSW Broadcasting Ltd [1992] TLR 155.

R v IR Commrs, ex parte National Federation of Self-Employed and Small Businesses Ltd [1982] AC 617.

R v LAUTRO Ltd, ex parte Ross [1993] QB 17 (DC and CA).

R v Monopolies and Mergers Commission, ex parte Argyll Group plc (1986) 2 BCC 99,086; [1986] 1 WLR 763.

R v Secretary of State for the Environment, ex parte Rose Theatre Trust Co [1990] 1 QB 504.

R v Secretary of State for the Home Department, ex parte Brind & Ors [1991] 1 AC 696.

Salomon v A Salomon & Co Ltd [1897] AC 22.

Shaw (John) and Sons (Salford) Ltd v Shaw & Anor [1935] 2 KB 113.

The following cases were referred to in the judgment of Bingham MR:

Bulmer (H P) Ltd & Anor v J Bollinger SA & Ors [1974] Ch 401.

CILFIT Srl & Anor v Ministry of Health [1982] ECR 3415.

R v Pharmaceutical Society of Great Britain, ex parte Association of Pharmaceutical Importers [1987] 3 CMLR 951.

Roger Henderson QC, Adrian Brunner and John Cone (instructed by the Solicitor to the Stock Exchange) for the Stock Exchange.

Stuart Isaacs QC and Monique Allan in the High Court and Monique Allan and Marc Rowlands in the Court of Appeal (instructed by Arnold Deacon Greene & Co, Sleaford) for the applicants.

AMENDED NOTICE OF APPLICATION

1. This application for leave to apply for judicial review is made by Else (1982) Ltd . . . (the first applicant) and by Leonard Brearley, trustee of Vale Private Pension Trust . . . (the second applicant).

2. Relief is sought in respect of . . .

    (iii)   the decision taken by the Committee on Quotations of the International Stock Exchange on 7 December 1990 to uphold the decision of the Quotations Panel taken on a date prior to 7 December 1990 to delist the shares of Titaghur.

3. The applicants seek the following relief:

    (i)   an order of certiorari quashing the decision(s) of the panel and/or of the committee delisting Titaghur's shares; further or alternatively,

    (ii)   a declaration that:

        (a)   the delisting of Titaghur's shares was unlawful as being contrary to the provisions of sec. 145(1) of the *Financial Services Act* 1986, further or alternatively, contrary to r. 520.7 of the Stock Exchange Rules; further or alternatively,

        (b)   in any proceedings before the panel or committee for the purposes of deciding whether Titaghur's shares should continue to be listed, the applicants shall be entitled to be given the opportunity to make representations and have their views taken into consideration; further or alternatively,

A   (iii) an order of mandamus, ordering

(a) the committee to reinstate Titaghur on the official list; further or
alternatively,

(b) ordering the lifting of the suspension on dealings in Titaghur's shares
which was imposed on 29 June 1989; further or alternatively,

B   (c) that in any renewed proceedings before the panel or committee for
the purposes of deciding whether Titaghur's shares should continue
to be listed, the applicants should be given the opportunity to make
representations and have their views taken into consideration; further
or alternatively,

(iv) damages for such loss in value of the shares as the court shall find has been
occasioned by the removal of the shares of Titaghur from the official list.

C
The grounds upon which relief is sought

4. The decisions were made contrary to natural justice in that the applicants who are
shareholders in Titaghur and have thereby a substantial interest in the decisions, were
not notified of the matters under consideration by the panel and the committee and/or
were not given the opportunity to make representations prior to any decisions being

D taken or reconsidered.

Particulars

(i) Official notification of the delisting was not given to the applicants until
shortly after 30 January 1991 on the publication of the chairman's statement
with Titaghur's interim figures for the six months to 30 September 1990.

E   (ii) At no time after the suspension of Titaghur's shares on 29 June 1989 until
receipt of the interim figures over 18 months later were the applicants
notified of any of the investigations concerning Titaghur's affairs.

(iii) Neither of the applicants was therefore given the opportunity to present its
views or make submissions during this period in respect of the matters
apparently being considered by the ISE authorities, whether by the panel

F   or by the committee.

5. Further or alternatively, the decisions taken by the panel and/or the committee to
delist Titaghur's shares were unreasonable.

Particulars

(i) All the information requested by the ISE subsequent to the suspension of
G   Titaghur's shares had been supplied prior to the decision of the committee
to uphold the decision of the panel delisting Titaghur's shares.

(ii) No correspondence from the ISE identifies any outstanding requests for
financial information.

(iii) The reason given for the decisions was that Titaghur had failed to provide
adequate financial information to the ISE whereas the accounts of Titaghur
H   for the period ending 31 March 1990 which were placed before the panel
and committee could not be described as amounting to "inadequate financial
information".

(iv) The qualifications which the accounts contained did not give rise to a
presumption that there were special circumstances which would preclude
normal regular dealings in the shares of Titaghur.

(v) There was no other basis on which a reasonable panel or committee for the   A
purposes of sec. 145(1) of the FSA could conclude that the shares of
Titaghur should be delisted.

(vi) The chairman's shareholding amounted to only about 29 per cent of the
issued share capital of Titaghur.

(vii) There are approximately 950 different registered shareholders in Titaghur,
of which 430 are UK based; 70 per cent of the shares are held in blocks of   B
between 500 to 50,000 shares.

(viii) The financial affairs of Titaghur were at the relevant time up to date for the
first time for some years.

6. There was therefore no basis on which the panel or the committee could conclude
that there was insufficient information on Titaghur, further or alternatively, that the
criminal prosecution of Titaghur's chairman required them to take steps to delist   C
Titaghur's shares.

7. Further or alternatively, the panel and/or the committee failed to take into account
relevant considerations in deciding to delist Titaghur's shares.

Particulars

(i) The panel and the committee should have taken into account the position   D
of small shareholders.

(ii) Even if there had been some deficiency in the information supplied by
Titaghur, by delisting its shares rather than continuing the suspension until
such time as the ISE's questions had been dealt with, the ISE have abrogated
their responsibilities to the majority of small shareholders and have handed
the running of Titaghur to large shareholders who can now act outside the   E
rules and protection of the ISE under which small shareholders made their
investment.

(iii) Further, the decisions taken by the panel and the committee to delist
Titaghur's shares have seriously jeopardised the invested capital of the
applicants (as well as other holders of Titaghur's shares) in that by delisting
Titaghur's shares they are each of them unable readily to find a market in   F
which to sell them.

8. Further or alternatively, the decisions of the panel and committee were invalid by
reason of their failure to comply with their own procedures.

Particulars

The best particulars the applicants can provide are as follows: G

(i) It was only open to the panel or committee to consider delisting Titaghur's
shares once information required by them was not forthcoming.

(ii) All information requested by the Quotations Department of the ISE had
been provided by Titaghur's brokers, Keith Bayley, Rogers & Co.

9. Further or alternatively, the panel and/or the committee took into account irrelevant
matters in coming to their decision to delist.   H

Particulars

The best particulars the applicants can provide are as follows:

(i) All the information which was requested by the ISE had been supplied.

A
    (ii) Even if there had been information supplied to the ISE which was not in their view in compliance with the requirements of the "Yellow Book", any non-compliance could have been dealt with by an extended suspension pending resolution of the problem and did not warrant action as disproportionate as the delisting of Titaghur's shares.

    (iii) The chairman of Titaghur was at the material time facing criminal prosecution for insider trading.

B
    (iv) At a meeting which took place some time between 17 July and 17 September 1990 at which it would appear that *suspension* of Titaghur's shares was discussed, two investigation officers from the surveillance department of the ISE were present who seemed principally to be concerned with lack of notification of the chairman's share dealings rather than the provision of financial information on Titaghur.

C
    (v) Numerous requests were made in writing by the ISE for information on the chairman's share dealings and *not* for financial information on Titaghur . . .

10. Further or alternatively, the decisions of the panel and committee were unlawful and ultra vires.

D
Particulars
    (i) The reason for the decision was given as the failure of Titaghur to provide adequate financial information. This is not sufficient ground for discontinuing the listing of a security under sec. 145(1) of the FSA.

    (ii) The committee and the panel failed to consider the question as to whether they were satisfied that the financial information was so inadequate as to amount to special circumstances precluding normal regular dealings in the shares of the company as required by sec. 145(1) of the FSA.

E
    (iii) The panel did not have authority to cancel the listing of Titaghur's shares under r. 520.7 of the Stock Exchange Rules.

11. By reason of the matters aforesaid, the decisions by the panel and/or the committee were perverse and unreasonable in that no reasonable panel or committee properly directing themselves as to the relevant and material matters could possibly have decided to delist the shares of Titaghur.

F

HIGH COURT JUDGMENT
(20 July 1992)

Popplewell J: The parties

G
    These are two associated applications. In the first Else (1982) Ltd and Leonard Brealey (trustee of Vale Private Pension Trust) seek judicial review of the decision by the committee on quotations of the International Stock Exchange on 7 December 1990 to delist the shares of Titaghur plc. In the second application Mr Thomas has an identical claim. The applicants in the first application are shareholders in Titaghur. So too is Mr Thomas. Titaghur ("the company") is in the jute business employing some 18,000 in India.

H

The brief facts

    The company had its shares suspended on 29 June 1988. One of its directors was accused of insider trading. He was subsequently tried and acquitted. On 23 November 1990 there was a hearing before a panel of the Stock Exchange which decided that the company should be delisted ("the panel decision"). On 7 December 1990 there was an

appeal hearing before a committee: they made the decision that the company should be   A
delisted ("the committee decision"). The company was party to those proceedings and
made representations. None of the applicants nor indeed any other investors were
invited to that meeting, nor were they invited to make representations. It is not the
practice of the Stock Exchange when considering the suspension or delisting of a
company to accord a hearing to anyone other than the officers of the company. The
company has not sought to challenge the committee decision.

B

The issues

(1)   It not being in contention that the respondent's decision is susceptible to judicial
review, do the applicants have any locus standi?

(2)   Did the applicants have any right to be heard before the committee?

(3)   Were there any special circumstances justifying the committee's decision?
C
(4)   Was the committee's decision irrational?

(5)   Was the decision to delist necessary and proportionate to the damage which it was
designed to prevent?

Additionally there were two other issues which arose during the hearing before me.
First, the applicants submit that if the committee's decision is set aside they are entitled
to damages. That matter, it is agreed, must await the outcome of my decision.   D

The other issue arose from the original pleading and from a re-amendment that was
sought during the trial. That allegation was an allegation of actual bias against
Mr Pickles and a reasonable suspicion of bias against him, Mr Lyons, and Mr Westall.
I declined to allow the amendment which made the allegations against Mr Lyons and
Mr Westall and the allegation which was of actual bias against Mr Pickles. The allegation
that there was a reasonable suspicion of bias against Mr Pickles remained and was not
abandoned until Mr Isaacs rose to reply. I need say no more than that. It was very   E
unfortunate that the allegations were ever made. They were totally devoid of any
substance. No one reading the documents upon which reliance was placed could possibly
have had the remotest suspicion of bias, let alone of any actual bias. The allegations
should never have been made, let alone pursued. I need say no more.

Locus standi   F

I turn now to the issue of locus standi and the right to be heard. It has been faintly
argued by Mr Henderson that, even if these applicants had a right to be heard by the
committee, they have no locus standi before the court. It was a subsidiary argument.
I say no more than that it has no substance. In my judgment the two questions go hand
in hand. Mr Isaacs has contended that, even if the applicants have no right to be heard
by the committee, nevertheless they have a right to come to court to challenge the   G
decision, in the same way as an ex parte injunction. I allowed the case to proceed and to
hear argument on the merits before determining this issue.

At the leave stage *Auld* J was satisfied that the applicants had arguably a sufficient
interest within O. 53, r. 3(7). My attention was drawn to the decision of the House of
Lords in *R v IR Commrs, ex parte National Federation of Self-Employed and Small
Businesses Ltd* [1982] AC 617, to *R v Monopolies and Mergers Commission, ex parte
Argyll Group plc* (1986) 2 BCC 99,086; [1986] 1 WLR 763 and to *R v Secretary of State*   H
for the Environment, ex parte Rose Theatre Trust Co [1990] 1 QB 504. The general
principles are not in doubt; their application to the variety of circumstances which arise
in judicial review proceedings can cause difficulties; in the instant case I am quite
satisfied that, if the investors have no right to be heard before the committee, they
equally have no right to be heard by the court.

A   **The right to be heard by the committee**

This depends on the interpretation of art. 15 of Council Directive of 5 March 1979 coordinating the conditions for the admission of securities to listing (79/279, OJ 1979 L66/21), "the admission directive". It is submitted on behalf of the applicants that the article itself makes it abundantly clear that these investors do have such a right. Alternatively Mr Isaacs contends that this is a matter of Community law where the domestic court should seek under art. 177 of the Treaty of Rome the assistance of the

B   European Court in interpreting art. 15 if this matter is not otherwise clear. Mr Henderson contends that the practice of the Stock Exchange is not to allow anyone other than the company to be heard either in suspensions or in delisting. Given the wording of art. 15, he submits the result must necessarily be resolved in his favour.

It seems to me logical first to decide whether the committee's decision *can* be challenged on the not unfamiliar grounds either of irrationality, or of failure to take into

C   account matters which should be taken into account, or finally of imposing a penalty which was unnecessary and out of proportion to the damage which it was designed to prevent.

I have therefore decided to resolve those questions first, before approaching the knotty question of the interpretation of art. 15.

D   **Special circumstances**

The committee's powers to delist a company are contained both in domestic law and in Community law. In Community law it is contained in art. 14 of the admission directive and reads as follows:

"(1) . . .

E   (2) The competent authorities may decide that the listing of the security be discontinued where they are satisfied that, owing to special circumstances, normal regular dealings in a security are no longer possible."

Section 145(1) of the *Financial Services Act* 1986 reads:

"The competent authority may, in accordance with the listing rules, discontinue the listing of any securities if satisfied that there are special circumstances which

F   preclude normal regular dealings in the securities."

It is accepted that there is no practical difference in interpretation between the directive and the Financial Services Act.

It is important to set out something of the discussion at the committee meeting so that the decision of the members can be seen in its proper perspective. Mr Elwes was in the chair. He was a qualified chartered accountant. He became finance partner of Rowe

G   & Pitman, a member of the Stock Exchange Council and of the quotations committee, and was responsible for a report to the Stock Exchange on the effect of Big Bang. Ms Heaton, who is a member of the Bar, joined the Department of Economic Affairs in 1967, was transferred to the Treasury and after ten years joined Lazard Brothers where she became a director. Mr Douglas Mann was the managing director of the Primary Markets division. Mr Legge-Bourke had been a member and partner of Grieveson Grant and subsequently director of Kleinwort Benson. He had been involved in the

H   unlisted securities market. Mr Ross Russell was senior partner of John Prost & Co, a firm of stockbrokers who had been concerned with the primary market, advising companies on listing or raising funds through the issue of shares, and is currently deputy chairman of the committee on quotations. Mr Smith had to leave the meeting before it ended. The final member was Mr Webster, who is a fellow of the Institute of Actuaries and has been involved with the investment operations of Sun Life for the past 25 years.

Currently he is the managing director of Sun Life Asset Management Ltd, the holding   A
company for all the group's investment operations.

Apart from Mr Douglas Mann and Mr Smith, they have all deposed in affidavits as to
the reason for their conclusion. There is also before the court a six-page document
setting out the discussions which took place at the committee meeting.

Some comment was made by Mr Thomas at the absence of an affidavit from
Mr Douglas Mann. However, as I observed to him during the course of argument, it is   B
not always the case that every member of a body whose decision is impugned will swear
an affidavit. See, for instance, *R v ITC, ex parte TSW*. Nothing sinister is to be implied
from the absence of an affidavit from Mr Douglas Mann. The reason why the committee
came to their decision emerges from these affidavits and from the minutes of the
meeting. In simple terms it was the inadequacy of the company's accounts. That is
reflected in the announcement made by the Stock Exchange after the meeting of the
committee, which reads as follows: C

"At a meeting held on Friday, 7 December 1990 the Committee on Quotations of
The International Stock Exchange ('the committee') decided to cancel the listing
of the securities of Titaghur plc.

The auditors' report on the accounts of Titaghur plc for the year ended 31 March
1990 contains numerous qualifications. In the opinion of the committee therefore
there is inadequate financial information available concerning this company.   D

Following the committee decision, Titaghur plc's listing will be cancelled on
Thursday, 13 December 1990."

It is equally clear that the committee took into account the previous history of the
company and more particularly that there was no assurance for the future as to the
financial position.

Ms Heaton said: E

"So far as the accounts were concerned . . . they were clearly seriously defective.
Mr Drummon's explanation of the qualified audit reports, and the apparent
failure of the management to tackle the problem, gave me no comfort that things
would improve. I did not believe that, based on the published accounts,
shareholders could make any informed decisions about the company's worth as
an investment and it appeared that this situation was likely to continue for the   F
foreseeable future."

Mr Legge-Bourke said:

"I have seldom seen a set of company accounts with such a combination of
qualifications in them. With such qualifications it would be very difficult for there
to be an orderly market in the shares because investors would not have adequate
information to form a judgment as to the company's real financial position and   G
prospects.

The qualifications in the accounts, the history of the accounts of the company and
the fact that Mr Drummon could give us no comfort that future accounts would be
unqualified, very strongly influenced my judgment in the appeal . . .

I was satisfied that the state of the accounts were special circumstances precluding
normal regular dealings in the shares and even Mr Drummon agreed that the   H
company would not be suitable as a new applicant for listing."

Mr Drummon deposed in an affidavit filed shortly before the hearing:

"The final point was the quality of financial information and I advised the directors
that our position on this was weak. The result I hoped for, and believed I had a
chance of achieving, was for the company to remain suspended and for it to be

A given a reasonable time to get its accounts in order and up to standard, even if this meant changing the auditor."

Mr Ross Russell said:

"In view of Mr Drummon's statement that the company would not be suitable for listing as a new applicant and having regard to the heavily qualified auditors' report I concluded that it would be inappropriate to restore the listing of Titaghur
B plc.

My decision to recommend cancellation of the Titaghur listing was correct. It was my expressed opinion that the question for the committee centred upon the accounts of Titaghur. I was satisfied that there were special circumstances which precluded normal regular dealings in the company shares, and took account of the following factors namely:

C (1) The 1990 accounts of Titaghur plc were qualified to a degree that made them of doubtful value as a basis for valuing the shares.

(2) A company with accounts qualified to that extent would not be allowed to get a listing if it was applying for the first time.

(3) The Quotations Department staff had given the company considerable latitude in not requesting suspension of Titaghur plc shares earlier, and by
D doing so gave the company an opportunity to produce unqualified accounts.

(4) However, despite an assurance that the 1990 accounts when available would not be heavily qualified this did not turn out to be so.

(5) We were told by the company's broker at the meeting on 7 December 1990 that there was no assurance that future accounts would not also be qualified.

(6) There was no indication when unqualified accounts would be available.
E Furthermore, there was no indication as to when the qualifications would be removed and it therefore was apparent that the suspension could continue for a long period without the issuer taking the necessary action, i.e. the production of unqualified audited accounts necessary to obtain the restoration of listing."

Mr Webster said:

F "To my mind the inadequacy of the company's accounts was the central issue and the main factor which led me to decide that the listing of the company's securities should be cancelled. I have seen numerous accounts over the last 25 years and I cannot recall seeing a set of listed company's accounts with so many qualifications contained in them. I did not and do not consider that normal regular dealings in the company's shares are possible because of the inadequacy of the accounts.

. . . there did not seem that there was any possibility of the company improving
G its accounts in the near future."

Finally Mr Elwes said:

"I do not believe that I have ever seen another set of audited accounts for a UK company which contained so many audit qualifications and apparent errors. The accounts were difficult to interpret or follow. My views as to the accounts were supported by Mr Drummon who said during his submission that there was no
H doubt that the company would not be suitable for listing as a new applicant and he was unable to give any assurance that the next accounts would be unqualified. The committee had to take into account the long period during which the Titaghur listing had already been suspended, the unsatisfactory financial information available about Titaghur and the absence of any undertaking that this situation would improve. I concluded that there was, and for the foreseeable future would

be, inadequate information available to investors to enable them to make an
informed assessment of the assets and liabilities, financial position, profits and
losses, and prospects of Titaghur. I was satisfied therefore that there were a
number of circumstances which would preclude normal regular dealing in Titaghur
shares."

Mr Isaacs contends that the reason given by the respondents was not a ground for
delisting in that it did not constitute special circumstances. He submitted that the
question of special circumstance was an objective one and that the views of the
committee were irrelevant. He instanced insolvency and failing to meet requirements of
the listing by a company which had no prior record as being special circumstances,
whereas delisting because of takeover or rumours would not. Mr Thomas instanced a
situation where insider dealing was proved which could constitute special circumstances,
but they both agreed that in the instant case they did not.

It is accepted that there are three elements involved: (1) the existence of special
circumstances; (2) the impossibility of normal regular dealings; and (3) the causation of
(2) by (1). Mr Isaacs contended that as at the material time the listing of the company
shares was suspended normal regular dealings were already impossible and therefore
there was no causal connection between the special circumstances and the impossibility
of normal regular dealings. I do not believe that that is a correct argument. It would
otherwise deprive the Stock Exchange of the right ever to delist a company whose shares
were suspended. If there is an impossibility of normal regular dealings over and above
the fact that the shares are suspended and there are special circumstances, it seems to
me open to the Stock Exchange to delist. Additionally he observes that a number of the
deponents make no mention of special circumstances and that the minutes of the
committee make no mention of it. The decision letter dated 7 December 1990 simply
reads:

". . . the listing of the company's securities will be cancelled in view of the
inadequacy of the financial information currently available concerning the
company."

He contends that the view expressed by Mr Drummon is immaterial and that the
qualifications in the accounts had existed since 1983; many of them had continued to
appear since June 1984, and that the absence of information was relatively insignificant.
To this end he relied on an affidavit from Mr Kabraji, who is a partner in the firm of
Grant Thornton. He is obviously very experienced in investigations and corporate
finance acquisitions and mergers, takeover bids etc. No one could criticise his expertise.
This was his view:

"I would disagree in most respects with Mr Elwes that the accounts do not provide
adequate information . . .

My analysis of the views expressed by the committee, best summarised by
Mr Elwes's affidavit, would suggest that only superficial consideration was given
to whether or not the information given in the accounts was adequate. In my
opinion, as explained at para. 182 and 183 above, the information was not so
inadequate as to give rise to a fear that an investor would be seriously misled or to
justify the cancellation of the listing."

He added:

"In fact the accounts appear to provide all the information required by statements
of standard accounting practice and the *Companies Act* 1985 with three exceptions"
[which he named].

A   The effect of Mr Kabraji's evidence is that there were no circumstances which entitled the committee to come to the conclusion which they did, let alone there being any special circumstances.

In reply to Mr Kabraji's affidavit the respondents put in evidence an affidavit of Mr Kellas, who is a partner in KPMG Peat Marwick, whose qualifications are not dissimilar to those of Mr Kabraji's. Mr Kellas did not agree with Mr Kabraji's view. It

B   was pointed out by Mr Isaacs that he had not deposed that there were special circumstances. Mr Henderson replied that it was not part of his function so to depose.

I hope I may be forgiven for not entering into a dispute between two very distinguished accountants. It is quite impossible to determine on affidavit who is right and who is wrong. It is necessarily a matter of opinion. But in any event it is in my judgment quite irrelevant to the issue which I have to decide. That question is: were there special circumstances in this case which were capable of justifying the committee's decision?

C   While Mr Isaacs is quite right to say that this is an objective test, the court is entitled to look at the experience and expertise of the committee who made the decision in helping them to decide whether they were right to consider that there were special circumstances.

A further point was made, which was this. The "Yellow Book", *Admission of Securities to Listing*, produced by the Stock Exchange Council, Section 1, Ch. 4, at para. 2, says:

D
        "The continuation of a suspension for a prolonged period without the issuer taking adequate action to obtain restoration of listing is likely to lead to the Council cancelling the listing. There may also be cases where a listing should be cancelled without suspension intervening (for example a significant change in the company rendering it unsuitable for listing)."

It is argued that that does not set out the position under the directive or under the

E   Financial Services Act. It is in my judgment a perfectly proper element to be taken into account, namely, that where the issuer has failed to take action to deal with the problem that has arisen after suspension that may constitute a special circumstance justifying delisting. There is nothing in the minutes of the committee which is not consistent with the evidence deposed to in the affidavits of the members. I can find nothing to fault the decision of the committee on this aspect of the case.

F
Irrationality

The way that this is put is as follows:

        "No committee properly directing itself on the relevant law and acting reasonably could have made the decision. The alleged inadequacy of the financial information available to the committee at the time concerning the company could not properly

G   have led to the decision."

To this end Mr Isaacs put in a document containing 38 separate matters which he contended supported the allegation that there was irrationality. It is headed "Annex on irrationality of the decision". In addition he relied on matters deposed to by Mr Brealey. Mr Brealey is a director and chairman of the first applicant, Else (1982) Ltd, and is a trustee of the second applicant. He says:

H   ". . . I am told by Mr Drummon of Keith Bayley and verily believe that all the information requested by the ISE subsequent to the suspension of Titaghur's shares had been supplied prior to the decision of the committee to uphold the decision of the panel delisting Titaghur's shares. There is no correspondence of which I am aware which identifies any outstanding requests for financial information.

Secondly, all accounts of Titaghur had been brought up to date and complied, so far as I am aware, with the requirements of the 'Yellow Book'. Third, the decision to suspend Titaghur's listing, after a period in which its accounts had not been filed, at a time when its financial affairs had finally been put on a proper footing, was, in all the circumstances, perverse and unreasonable.

. . . in addition to considering whether or not all the financial information requested by the ISE had been supplied by Titaghur, the panel and the committee should also have taken into account the position of small shareholders. Even if there had been some deficiency in the information supplied by Titaghur, by delisting its shares rather than continuing the suspension until such time as the ISE's questions had been dealt with, I believe that the ISE have abrogated their responsibilities to the majority of small shareholders and have handed the running of Titaghur to large shareholders who can now act outside the rules and protection of the ISE under which small shareholders made their investment."

He added:

". . . a chairman of such an important committee would have sought answers to the points raised before taking a vote to uphold the decision to delist a public company and disenfranchise the investments of several hundred people. The obvious persons to give those answers were the company's accountants.

. . . The committee of 7 December merely rubber-stamped the panel's decision and acted in bad faith."

Mr Kabraji said:

"With one exception, that relating to the revalued amount of the fixed asset disposals, the qualifications were due either to facts beyond the control of the directors or to disagreement between the directors and auditors on the appropriate accounting policy."

I turn now to the detail of the "Annex on irrationality" of the decision. I do not propose to deal with them all because some of them seem to be either irrelevant or to have such marginal relevance as not to be worth considering.

"No warning was given that the respondents were concerned about qualifications or inadequacy of financial information in the accounts when the shares were suspended on 29 June 1989."

This is factually true. However it is clear from the second affidavit of Mr Pickles that the company either was aware or must have been so aware.

"The company, therefore, had no opportunity to rectify the position because it was not aware of the possibility of its shares being delisted."

This, in the light of Mr Pickles's second affidavit, cannot be supported and in any event, even if there had been no warning, there was no reason why the accounts should have continued to be qualified. It is equally clear from Mr Drummon's affidavit that he was under no illusion when he went before the committee what the issue was.

"Since 1983 all the accounts of Titaghur had been qualified . . . but no concern was expressed by the respondents in relation to the 1985 accounts at the time of publication . . . no action was taken by the respondents to suspend the shares or impose conditions for continued listing . . ."

The answer to this is given by Mr Douglas Mann. It would have been open to the Stock Exchange to have taken earlier steps to suspend the listing of these shares, but quite clearly the fact that they acquiesced in this situation cannot assist the applicants in the instant argument.

A

> "At no time was [Mr Drummon] or the company told that the suspension was due
> to anything in the company's accounts . . ."

On 28 March 1990 the brokers wrote to the Stock Exchange asking for restoration of
the listing of the company's shares. On 17 July they wrote again after a meeting on
9 April 1990. It ended:

B

> "The directors are confident . . . that the accounts for the year to 31 March 1990
> will be in much better shape and hopefully unqualified . . .
>
> I believe that I have addressed all your concerns and it is important that the 600
> shareholders on the UK register obtain a market for their shares and I hope you
> will now agree to remove the suspension."

It is quite clear from what appears earlier that it was contemplated that clear accounts
would be provided. There was a meeting between Mr Drummon and Mr Pickles on

C

2 August 1990. That letter was discussed and Mr Pickles says:

> "It reflects Mr Drummon's clear understanding that Titaghur had to put its house
> in order particularly in respect of reducing if not removing qualifications from the
> audited accounts and it was agreed that the listing of Titaghur would be referred
> to the Quotations Panel when the audited accounts to 31 March had been received
> by the Stock Exchange. When the audited accounts were received it was apparent

D

> that they were still heavily qualified."

In the end none of this in my judgment is of very great significance because when
Mr Drummon went to the meeting of the committee he knew perfectly well that the
question of delisting was the matter in issue. The appearance before the committee was
an appeal from the panel. The panel, true it is, had taken into account as one of the
factors the charge against Mr Brealey but that delisting because of the company's

E

position was at issue cannot be doubted. The notification of the result reads as follows:

> "The panel therefore decided to cancel the listing of the securities of Titaghur plc
> for the following principal reasons:
>
> (1) continuing uncertainty about the company's financial position . . .
>
> No proper consideration was given to the fact that the qualifications contained in
> the 1990 accounts were material but not fundamental."

F

Mr Kabraji at para. 193 has so deposed; that was Mr Kabraji's opinion; it was not the
opinion of the committee. Nor in so far as it is relevant was it the opinion of Mr Kellas.

Paragraphs 27 and 28 relate to an interpretation of the company's financial position.
This was a matter for the judgment of the committee.

> "The relevant papers relied on by the company were supplied to the committee

G

> 15 minutes before the start of the meeting at approximately 12 o'clock pm on
> 7 December 1990. . . . This was insufficient time to understand the company's
> explanations in relation to the accounts."

Of all the matters set out as constituting irrationality, this seemed to me initially at
any rate to have the most substance.

The factual position appears to be this. The documents which are in bundle 5,

H

section 2, were before the committee in good time. The bundle of documents which are
bundle 5, section 3, were before the committee some 15 minutes before they sat. The
full accounts were handed in by Mr Drummon during the course of the meeting.

The documents relating to the company's financial affairs which were before the
committee in proper time were extracts from the accounts for the year ended 31 March
1990, that is the consolidated profit and loss account, the consolidated balance sheet,

the statement of source and application of funds and most particularly the report of the   A
auditors with the qualifications.

Included in the documents handed in just before the meeting were the auditors'
reports for the accounts to June 1986, June 1987, June 1988, March 1989 and March
1990. The document handed in by Mr Drummon was the full report and consolidated
accounts for the year ended 31 March 1990. That contained over and above what the
committee already had, the chairman's statement, the accounting policies, and the notes
to the financial statements.   B

It is clear from the notes of the committee meeting that after Mr Drummon had
handed in the full copy of the accounts there was a discussion about them. There appears
this note:

> "The chairman referred to the company's accounts for the year ended 31 March
> 1990 and said that it was difficult to reconcile the balance sheets and the source
> and application of funds statement. He asked Mr Drummon for an explanation.   C
> Mr Drummon made no reply. The chairman said that the report of the auditors
> referred to the writing back of exceptional items of £1.66m without having
> identified what it was for. Mr Drummon said that a note appeared in the chairman's
> statement that explained the item."

The only note in the chairman's statement relating to this item reads as follows:

> "*Finance*   D
>
> The in-depth investigations into the creditors' lists has continued throughout the
> year and I am pleased to report further reductions amounting to £1,655,786. This
> work will continue until every pound of over-provision has been identified. As
> mentioned previously, new finance is required to provide for the basics of this
> business, viz. stocks of raw jute and finished goods. The recapitalisation was and
> is still necessary in order to retain the full benefits of profits from our product.   E
> I am hoping that within the present financial year recapitalisation will be
> completed."

It is clear from the notes of the meeting that there was further discussion about the
inadequacy of the accounts.

I have already set out the view that each member of the committee took of these
accounts. In my judgment the committee had ample opportunity to consider them. They   F
had the basis of the accounts together with the auditors' qualified report. They were
presented at the hearing with the full accounts. They are experienced readers of
accounts. There was a discussion about the accounts. This meeting is said to have lasted
an hour to an hour and a half. It is impossible to conclude that these very experienced
members were not fully aware of what the accounts said and the difficulties facing
Mr Drummon. There was in my judgment ample time to understand the company's
somewhat inadequate explanations in relation to the accounts.   G

The final matter under this heading is the allegation:

> "The committee were unreasonable in coming to the decision which they did at a
> meeting which was not attended by the company's auditors and which did not
> include a detailed discussion about the true effect and reason for the
> disqualification."

The presence or absence of the auditors was entirely a matter for the company. Their   H
absence cannot vitiate the committee's decision. There was in my judgment a proper
discussion about the reason for the qualification and about its effect and there is nothing
in that point.

Finally I have stood back and looked at the allegations which were put forward to
suggest irrationality. I look at them individually. I look at them as a whole and ask

A   myself: was this decision, taking also into account both the special circumstances and proportionality in domestic law, *Wednesbury* unreasonable? I conclude that it is simply not possible to make a finding that the committee's decision was unreasonable.

Proportionality

It is accepted that in the light of the decision of the House of Lords in *Council of Civil
B   Service Unions v Minister for the Civil Service* [1985] AC 374 that so far as English domestic law is concerned it is not a free-standing principle, nor is it appropriate for a judge at first instance to take the first step to incorporate the doctrine. See also Lord *Lowry* in *R v Secretary of State for the Home Department, ex parte Brind* [1991] 1 AC 696 at p. 766.

It is not in dispute equally that it is a matter to be taken into account as an aspect of irrationality, which I have done.
C
Mr Isaacs however further contends that proportionality is a well known concept of European law and that any decision to delist pursuant to the power conferred by art. 14(2) of the directive had to have been proportionate. Put in its simplest terms, it is that the committee could have just as well extended the suspension which then existed pending resolution of the problem without taking the drastic step of delisting.

It is accepted by the respondents that suspension was an option which was open to
D   them. Indeed the members of the committee refer to the matter specifically in their affidavits and set out the reasons why in fact they decided to take the decision to delist. Among the arguments which they considered was that, as no action had been taken against the company in the past when they had defaulted on providing financial information, was it right now to suspend or delist? That argument was clearly debated at the committee meeting and it was pointed out by Mr Douglas Mann that the company's listing should have been suspended in the past.
E
The history of suspension is this. On 9 May 1988 the listing of Titaghur was first suspended due to non-payment of annual listing charges. That suspension was lifted on 9 June 1988 as a result of listing charges being paid and registration problems rectified. On 28 June 1989 Reginald Brealey was arrested for suspected insider dealing offences, and on 29 June 1989 suspension in dealing with Titaghur shares occurred "pending an announcement". That suspension has continued until this delisting. It is clear however
F   from the correspondence dealing with applications for the suspension to be lifted that the continuation of the suspension no longer depended solely on Mr Brealey's position but now encompassed the failure by the company to put its financial house in order.

It is quite clear from all the affidavits and from the minutes that the committee took into account that not only had there been a period of suspension but that the company had continued to fail to put its house in order. It is equally clear that the committee took
G   into account the position of shareholders. They had to do a balancing exercise. They were entitled to take into account what appears in the Yellow Book, Section 1, Ch. 4, at para. 2:

> "The continuation of a suspension for a prolonged period without the issuer taking adequate action to obtain restoration of listing is likely to lead to the Council cancelling listing."

H   Mr Leonard Brealey said in his affidavit:

> ". . . even if there had been information supplied to the ISE which was not in their view in compliance with the requirements of the 'Yellow Book', any non-compliance could have been dealt with by an extended suspension pending resolution of the problem and did not warrant action as disproportionate as the delisting of the Titaghur shares."

Mr Kabraji said this:

> "In my opinion, it would have been proper and reasonable and in the interests of
> the shareholders, present and future, for the Stock Exchange to have given a
> warning to the company that it considered the financial information available to
> be inadequate. The company could have been given a specified continued period
> of suspension, from the date of notification of the concern, within which to rectify
> the position on the understanding that failure to do so would result in cancellation
> of the listing. It was unreasonable of the Stock Exchange to conclude that the
> information in the accounts was inadequate to the extent that the only option
> available was immediately to cancel the listing without giving the company a
> reasonable opportunity to rectify the position."

That was certainly a view which could be properly put forward and was indeed put
forward by Mr Drummon at the committee hearing. If they had decided to continue
suspension, it was undoubtedly an option open to them. But the fact they choose a
different option does not of itself invalidate it, nor give rise to a legitimate complaint so
as to enable a successful application for judicial review.

What was the effect of the delisting? If the company was still listed, it had all the
protection provided by the Yellow Book. Interim audited accounts would be provided
for six months. Explanations of failure to meet public forecasts would have to be given.
Where there is qualification to the accounts the directors have to explain why. Any
price-sensitive information has to be reported. There is a restriction of the directors'
dealings on shares. The directors of a private company are not accountable to anyone
and directors can deal at any time.

True it is, that there may be some small protection under sec. 459 of the Companies
Act because delisting of a company does not remove the protection of the Companies
Act. As Mr Thomas pointed out, a shareholder looks to the Stock Exchange to protect
him against majority shareholders or against manipulation by the directors. As he
observed, if the company is listed he can control the officers of the company; otherwise
officers can withhold information and are not publicly accountable.

These are all perfectly valid points of which the committee could scarcely have been
unaware.

I have considered all these arguments with considerable care. But I have been left in
no doubt that the decision of the committee was not disproportionate to the damage
which it was designed to prevent within the doctrine of proportionality either at common
law or under Community law. It was a decision in my judgment to which they were
perfectly entitled to come. If I were minded to take a view contrary to theirs (which I am
not) it was not a decision in my judgment which can be properly challenged in judicial
review proceedings.

Right to be heard by the investors before the committee

As I have indicated, this depends upon the effect of art. 15. There is no dispute that
art. 15 has a direct effect and can be relied upon by individuals before national courts.
Article 15(1) confers a right to apply to the courts in clear and unconditional terms. The
question therefore is not whether there is a right to apply to the courts but upon whom
that right is bestowed. It is contended by the respondents that in domestic law that right
cannot be bestowed upon a shareholder, that the same applies in interpreting art. 15,
and that because the matter is so clear it is not a matter which should be referred to the
European Court. Mr Isaacs contends that, whatever may be the position in English
domestic law, it is irrelevant because art. 15 is the governing piece of legislation. He
submits that the matter is so clear from the article itself that I should give effect to his

A   submission; alternatively, that if it is not clear, I should make a reference under art. 177 of the Treaty of Rome.

The Council Directive of 5 March 1979 is a directive which is for the purpose of "coordinating the conditions for the admission of securities to official Stock Exchange listing". The preamble in its material form reads:

B   "Having regard to the Treaty establishing the EEC, and in particular Articles 54(3)(g) and 100 thereof,

. . .

Whereas the coordination of the conditions for the admission of securities to official listing on stock exchanges situated or operating in the Member States is likely to provide equivalent protection for investors at Community level, because of the more uniform guarantees *offered to investors* [emphasis added] in the

C   various Member States; whereas it will facilitate both the admission to official stock exchange listing, in each such State, of securities from other Member States and the listing of any given security on a number of stock exchanges in the Community; whereas it will accordingly make for greater interpenetration of national securities markets and therefore contribute to the prospect of establishing a European capital market;

D   . . .

Whereas there should be the possibility of a right to apply to the courts against decisions by the competent national authorities in respect of the application of this directive, although such right to apply must not be allowed to restrict the discretion of these authorities;

. . .

E   Whereas, for this reason, coordination should first be limited to the establishment of minimum conditions for the admission of securities to official listing on stock exchanges situated or operating in the Member States, without however giving issuers any right to listing;

Whereas, this partial coordination of the conditions for admission to official listing constitutes a first step towards subsequent closer alignment of the rules of Member

F   States in this field."

Article 9(3) reads:

"Without prejudice to the other powers conferred upon them, the competent authorities may reject an application for the admission of a security to official listing if, in their opinion, the issuer's situation is such that admission would be detrimental to investors' interests."

G   Article 11 reads:

"The competent authorities may refuse to admit to official listing a security already officially listed in another member state where the issuer fails to comply with the obligations resulting from admission in that Member State."

Article 13 reads:

H   "1. An issuer whose securities are admitted to official listing shall provide the competent authorities with all the information which the latter consider appropriate in order to protect investors or ensure the smooth operation of the market.

2. Where protection of investors or the smooth operation of the market so requires, an issuer may be required by the competent authorities to publish such information in such a form and within such time limits as they consider appropriate.

Should the issuer fail to comply with such requirement, the competent authorities   A
may themselves publish such information after having heard the issuer."

Article 14 reads:

"1. The competent authorities may decide to suspend the listing of a security
where the smooth operation of the market is, or may be, temporarily jeopardised
or where protection of investors so requires.

2. The competent authorities may decide that the listing of the security be   B
discontinued where they are satisfied that, owing to special circumstances, normal
regular dealings in a security are no longer possible."

Article 15 reads:

"1. Member States shall ensure decisions of the competent authorities refusing
the admission of a security to official listing or discontinuing such a listing shall be
subject to the right to apply to the courts.   C

2. An applicant shall be notified of a decision regarding his application for
admission to official listing within six months of receipt of the application or,
should the competent authority require any further information within the period,
within six months of the applicant's supplying such information.

3. Failure to give a decision within the time limit specified in paragraph 2 shall be
deemed a rejection of the application. Such rejection shall give rise to the right to   D
apply to the courts provided for in paragraph 1."

Article 16 reads:

"Where an application for admission to official listing relates to certificates
representing shares, the application shall be considered only if the competent
authorities are of the opinion that the issuer of the certificates is offering adequate
safeguards for the protection of investors."   E

Domestic law

Although I accept the argument that Community law is the law which is decisive on
this matter, in deference to the arguments which have been put forward I give my
considered views on the position in domestic law.

The *Financial Services Act* 1986 by sec. 188(1) provides: F

"Proceedings arising out of any act . . . of

. . .

(d) the competent authority in,

the discharge or purported discharge of any of its functions under this Act may be
brought in the High Court . . ."   G

It is the applicants' further contention that the respondents were in breach of natural
justice in failing to notify shareholders of the fact that delisting was under consideration
by the committee and in failing to give shareholders the opportunity to make
representations and to have those representations considered before a decision was
taken. The practical objections which the respondents rely on are said to be the costs
and administrative burden of identifying and communicating with shareholders.

It is said that the competent authority would on occasions have to evaluate, reconcile   H
and adjudicate between a possible multitude of differing views and that the identities of
shareholders and their views would be continually changing as the shares were traded.
The requirement to consult could be detrimental to the business interests of the company
because, for instance, of time delays which would inevitably result from consultation;
uncertainty affecting the decision-making process where shareholders' views differed

A   from those of the company; and because confidential information given to the authority
to enable it to come to an informed decision might have to be disclosed to shareholders
which might be in breach of the Financial Services Act.

Additionally, say the Stock Exchange, if shareholders are to have a right to be
consulted in delisting, so too should they have a right to be heard when suspension is
contemplated. A further argument which was put forward on behalf of the Stock
Exchange was where the "interest" was to stop. Thus if shareholders were alleged to
B   have a sufficient interest, others such as banks who grant loans on the security of shares
or persons interested in acquiring shares at the time of listing could similarly have
sufficient standing. I confess that that argument did not appeal to me at the time it was
put forward and further consideration has not improved its quality. Registered
shareholders are a definable class who are notified of shareholders' meetings, receive
dividends and other communications required under the Companies Act. Persons
C   outside that category in my judgment are not entitled in any event to be consulted.

In essence it is the contention of the Stock Exchange that they never have invited or
allowed shareholders to take part in discussions on delisting or suspension, and that the
company who is the subject of the inquiry is the proper body to be represented. It does
that through its board of directors. If a company is suspended or delisted, the remedy
for the shareholder is to bring pressure to bear upon the company through its directors
D   to apply for a suspension to be lifted or for re-listing.

My attention was drawn to a number of authorities illustrating the position of a
company and its directors in English domestic law of which *Salomon v A Salomon & Co
Ltd* [1897] AC 22 is the foundation. That decision decided that a company is a separate
legal entity from its members and its directors. I was referred to further authorities of
which it is only necessary to make passing reference. In *John Shaw and Sons (Salford)
Ltd v Peter Shaw* [1935] 2 KB 113, *Greer* LJ at p. 134 said:
E

"A company is an entity distinct alike from its shareholders and its directors.
Some of its powers may, according to its articles, be exercised by directors, certain
other powers may be reserved for the shareholders in general meeting. If powers
of management are vested in the directors, they and they alone can exercise these
powers. The only way in which the general body of the shareholders can control
the exercise of the powers vested by the articles in the directors is by altering their
F   articles . . ."

In *Prudential Assurance Co Ltd v Newman Industries Ltd (No. 2)* [1982] Ch 204 at
p. 224A the Court of Appeal said:

"A personal action would subvert the rule in *Foss v. Harbottle* and that rule is not
merely a tiresome procedural obstacle placed in the path of a shareholder by a
legalistic judiciary. The rule is the consequence of the fact that a corporation is a
G   separate legal entity. Other consequences are limited liability and limited rights.
The company is liable for its contracts and torts; the shareholder has no such
liability. The company acquires causes of action for breaches of contract and for
torts which damage the company. No cause of action vests in the shareholder.
When the shareholder acquires a share he accepts the fact that the value of his
investment follows the fortunes of the company and that he can only exercise his
H   influence over the fortunes of the company by the exercise of his voting rights in
general meeting. The law confers on him the right to ensure that the company
observes the limitations of its memorandum of association and the right to ensure
that other shareholders observe the rule, imposed upon them by the articles of
association. If it is right that the law has conferred or should in certain restricted
circumstances confer further rights on a shareholder the scope and consequences

of such further rights require careful consideration. In this case it is neither   A
necessary nor desirable to draw any general conclusions.

The rule in *Foss v Harbottle* is founded on principle but it also operates fairly by
preserving the rights of the majority."

The respondents point out that the shareholders have some rights under the Companies
Act and I was referred to sec. 459–461, sec. 368, and sec. 431–432 of the *Companies Act*
1985.   B

Two further authorities were drawn to my attention. The first is *R v Monopolies and
Mergers Commission, ex parte Argyll Group plc* (1986) 2 BCC 99,086. In that case the
applicants Argyll were bidding in competition with Guinness to take over Distillers.
Guinness's bid was referred to the Monopolies Commission under sec. 75 of the *Fair
Trading Act* 1973. For reasons which are immaterial the chairman recommended and
the Secretary of State agreed to give his consent to the reference being laid aside.
Guinness then made a revised bid for Distillers, which was not referred to the Commission,   C
and the applicants as minority shareholders in Distillers sought judicial review by way of
certiorari. *Donaldson* MR said at p. 99,095:

> "Argyll are minority shareholders in Distillers and they aspire to become sole, or
> at least majority, shareholders. Their interest may not represent a pure and
> burning passion to see that public law is rightly administered, but that could be
> said of most applicants for judicial review. Indeed, if it were the case that that was   D
> their only real interest, they would risk being branded as high-minded busybodies,
> which they are not either adjectivally or substantively.
>
> . . .
>
> Good public administration requires a proper consideration of the legitimate
> interests of individual citizens, however rich and powerful they may be and
> whether they are natural or juridical persons. But in judging the relevance of an   E
> interest, however legitimate, regard has to be had to the purpose of the
> administrative process concerned. Argyll has a strong and legitimate interest in
> putting Guinness in baulk, but this is not the purpose of the administrative process
> under the *Fair Trading Act* 1973. To that extent their interest is not therefore of
> any great, or possibly any, weight."

In *R v LAUTRO Ltd, ex parte Ross* [1993] QB 17 (DC and CA) the applicant was   F
finance director and a shareholder of Winchester Group ("Winchester"). LAUTRO
was the recognised self-regulating organisation for the purposes of the *Financial Services
Act* 1986. The decision which was attacked was a decision by the board of LAUTRO to
exercise its intervention powers so as to prohibit Norwich Union Life Insurance Society
("Norwich") and three associated companies from accepting any new investment
business from Winchester. Norwich terminated its agency with Winchester which, since
it no longer had any status as an authorised representative of the life assurance society,   G
could not thereafter conduct investment business.

The main thrust of Mr Ross's argument was that he should have been given the right
to be allowed to make representations before the service of a notice. The Court of
Appeal decided that that was not required; it would have been sufficient for Mr Ross to
have the opportunity after the notice to be allowed to make representations.

Mr Ross's interest was not challenged and the parties quite rightly treated Mr Ross as   H
Winchester's representative for this purpose. At p. 48D *Glidewell* LJ said:

> "I find much more difficulty with the second proposition advanced by Mr. Collins.
> In effect this raises the question, to whom is the duty of fairness owed? Is it owed
> to persons and bodies who are not members of Lautro? None of the authorities to
> which I have so far referred dealt with a situation in which a decision was made

A   which directly affected one party, A, and at the same time indirectly affected a second party, B, so as to raise the question: is there any duty in the decision-making authority to be fair towards B?

In support of his proposition, Mr. Collins quotes a short passage from the judgment of Lord Denning, M.R. in *Reg. v. Liverpool Corporation, Ex parte Liverpool Taxi Fleet Operators' Association* [1972] 2 Q.B. 299, a decision of this court. In that case the corporation was considering increasing the maximum number of licensed taxis in its area. The association objected. During the course of discussion, the chairman of the relevant committee publicly undertook that the number of licensed taxis would not be increased until a private Bill which contained relevant provisions had been enacted and come into force. Despite that undertaking, before the legislation was enacted, the committee and the council decided to increase the number of licensed taxis.

On a renewed application for leave to move for what would now be called judicial review, this court granted the application. All three members of the court took the view that the corporation was bound by its undertaking and could not resile from it without at least giving the association an opportunity to make representations. This was therefore the reason for the decision. However, in the course of his judgment Lord Denning said, at p. 307:

'when the corporation consider applications for licences under the Town Police Clauses Act 1847, they are under a duty to act fairly. This means that they should be ready to hear not only the particular applicant but also any other persons or bodies whose interests are affected.'

Mr. Collins argues that this applies in the circumstances of the present case. However, the question whether, apart from the undertaking, the association had a right to make representations was not in issue in that case. Indeed, it was a question about which, at p. 311B, Roskill L.J. expressed doubts. I cannot therefore regard the two sentences from the judgment of Lord Denning, which I have quoted, as being an authority on the question which we have to consider."

Glidewell LJ made reference to *Cheall v Association of Professional Executive Clerical and Computer Staff* [1983] 2 AC 180, where at p. 190A, Lord *Diplock* said:

"Decisions that resolve disputes between the parties to them, whether by litigation or some other adversarial dispute-resolving process, often have consequences which affect persons who are not parties to the dispute; but the legal concept of natural justice has never been extended to give such persons as well as the parties themselves rights to be heard by the decision-making tribunal before the decision is reached."

At p. 191E Lord *Diplock* said:

"Different considerations might apply if the effect of Cheall's expulsion from A.P.E.X. were to have put his job in jeopardy, either because of the existence of a closed shop or for some other reason. But this is not the case."

Glidewell LJ said at p. 50E:

"I accept that very frequently a decision made which directly affects one person or body will also affect, indirectly, a number of other persons or bodies, and that the law does not require the decision-making body to give an opportunity to every person who may be affected however remotely by its decision to make representations before the decision is reached. Such a principle would be unworkable in practice. On the other hand, it is my opinion that when a decision-making body is called upon to reach a decision which arises out of the relationship between two persons or firms, only one of whom is directly under the control of the decision-making body, and it is apparent that the decision will be likely to affect the second person adversely, then as a general proposition the decision-making body does owe some duty of fairness to that second person, which, in appropriate circumstances, may well include a duty to allow him to make representations before reaching the decision. This will particularly be the case when the adverse effect is upon the livelihood or the ability to earn of the second person or body.''

In the result the Court of Appeal decided that there was no requirement of fairness requiring LAUTRO to accord Winchester the opportunity to make representations as to why an intervention notice should not be served before deciding whether or not to serve such a notice. The extent of the duty owed must vary from case to case.

In the result, while I accept the proposition that the shareholders as a group are readily identifiable, having regard to the general position of a shareholder vis-à-vis the directors of a company, I do not accept that they have any right to be notified so as to have their representations heard or to be considered. That right is a right of the board of directors and theirs alone. Nor I do accept the proposition that, even if they are not entitled to be heard before a decision, they have a right to be heard after.

Community law

It was suggested that as this was an ''approximation'' in some way the directive did not need to be treated as having uniform application. I reject that argument and say nothing more about it. Secondly, reliance was placed in the preamble on the phrase ''although such right to apply must not be allowed to restrict the discretion of these authorities''. I do not treat that as authorisation by the directive to allow the authorities to act entirely as they like.

It is clear from the preamble and from what appears in the article that the protection of investors is what the directive has in mind. Equally it is clear from the various articles that different considerations are to be given to (1) listing, (2) suspension and (3) delisting. Emphasis was put on art. 15(2) and (3) in relation to an application for listing so that a failure to give a decision shall be a deemed rejection, which can only be a rejection of an applicant, who in turn must be the company. There is a strong argument that the position of those applying for an original listing is to be treated differently from those in the case of delisting. By art. 13 the issuer has to provide information which is in order to protect investors. An applicant before listing may indeed already have investors who need protecting. Article 15, which gives the right to apply to the courts, does not define the person or persons who has that right.

The applicant's submission is in a sense a simple one. The whole of this article is designed to protect investors. An investor in this case is a shareholder. If that is the case, then the persons who have the right to apply to the courts must include the investors.

It is pointed out that there are no express words giving the investors a right to apply to the courts. It is implicit that it is the company who has a right to apply for an official listing. Thus it is submitted that it alone must have the right to apply to the court in relation to a delisting. Article 13 makes reference to hearing the company should they fail to comply with the publication of information, but nowhere is there reference to hearing the investors. It is conceded by the applicants that art. 15(2) and (3) may relate to the company as the applicant for admission. But it is argued that it does not follow that the same is true in relation to decisions discontinuing such a listing. It is submitted that art. 15(1) must be interpreted in the light of the intention and purpose of the provisions of which it forms part, namely, to provide investor protection.

Some reliance was placed by Mr Henderson upon art. 58 and 54(3)(g) of the treaty. Article 58 puts companies and firms in the same position as natural persons. But it has

A no relevance in my judgment to any question relating to the relationship of a company and its shareholders. Article 54(3)(g) reads:

> "The Council and the Commission shall carry out the duties devolving upon them under the preceding provisions, in particular:
>
> . . .
>
B
> (g) by coordinating to the necessary extent the safeguards which, for the protection of the interests of members and others, are required by Member States of companies or firms within the meaning of the second paragraph of Article 58 with a view to making such safeguards equivalent throughout the Community;"

That is the article upon which the directive is based. It is further submitted that shareholders in a company seeking admission to listing stand to gain by a company being listed; they are not in a worse position by not being listed than they were in anyway,

C whereas shareholders in a listed company which is delisted stand in a worse position than they were when the company was listed.

Does the question admit of only one possible answer? My mind has fluctuated during the course of the arguments (which were skillfully developed) and since. Should I then make up my own mind and decide that the point is reasonably clear and free from doubt and not, as some would have it, shirk my responsibilities. I have to say that if I had no

D doubt I would not hesitate to express my view.

Reference under art. 177

Mr Henderson argues that the point is quite clear that there is no need for any reference to be made; that it is important that the matter should be speedily resolved because there are a number of these decisions both of delisting and suspension which regularly occur; and that if the practice of the Stock Exchange is to be challenged it is

E important that the procedure should be rectified at the earliest time.

Mr Isaacs, while arguing that the matter was clear and free from doubt, nevertheless as a secondary submission urged upon me that if I were unsure then clearly this was a matter for the European Court.

Article 177 reads:

F
> "The Court of Justice shall have jurisdiction to give preliminary rulings concerning:
>
> (a) the interpretation of this Treaty;
>
> (b) the validity and interpretation of acts of the institutions of the Community;
>
> (c) the interpretation of the statutes of bodies established by an act of the Council, where those statutes so provide.
>
> Where such a question is raised before any court or tribunal of a Member State,

G
> that court or tribunal may, if it considers that a decision on the question is necessary to enable it to give judgment, request the Court of Justice to give a ruling thereon.
>
> Where any such question is raised in a case pending before a court or tribunal of a Member State, against whose decisions there is no judicial remedy under national law, that court or tribunal shall bring the matter before the Court of Justice."

H In *C & E Commrs v ApS Samex (Hanil Synthetic Fiber Industrial Co Ltd, third party)* [1983] 1 All ER 1042 *Bingham* J gave his reasons why in that particular case he thought there should be a reference.

He observed at p. 1054f that guidelines were given by the Court of Appeal in *H P Bulmer Ltd v J Bollinger SA* [1974] Ch 401 at p. 422ff. where Lord *Denning* drew attention to four points relevant to the question whether a decision was necessary.

(1)   The point must be conclusive.

(2)   Previous ruling (irrelevant to the instant case).

(3)   Is it *acte claire*?

(4)   Decide the facts first.

So far as the exercise of discretion is concerned, Lord *Denning* said the following matters were to be considered:

(1)   the time to get a ruling;

(2)   the undesirability of overloading the Court of Justice;

(3)   the need to formulate the question clearly;

(4)   the difficulty and importance of the point;

(5)   the expense;

(6)   the wishes of the parties.

In the instant case the point will in my judgment be conclusive. Secondly, I do not regard the matter so free from doubt as to render the points *acte claire*. Thirdly, the facts are not in dispute.

So far as the discretion is concerned, I respectfully adopt and repeat what *Bingham* J said at p. 1055g:

"In endeavouring to follow and respect these guidelines I find myself in some difficulty, because it was submitted by counsel on behalf of the defendant that the issues raised by his client should be resolved by the Court of Justice as the court best fitted to do so, and I find this a consideration which does give me some pause for thought. Sitting as a judge in a national court, asked to decide questions of Community law, I am very conscious of the advantages enjoyed by the Court of Justice. It has a panoramic view of the Community and its institutions, a detailed knowledge of the treaties and of much subordinate legislation made under them, and an intimate familiarity with the functioning of the Community market which no national judge denied the collective experience of the Court of Justice could hope to achieve. Where questions of administrative intention and practice arise the Court of Justice can receive submissions from the Community institutions, as also where relations between the Community and non-member states are in issue. Where the interests of member states are affected they can intervene to make their views known. That is a material consideration in this case since there is some slight evidence that the practice of different member states is divergent. Where comparison falls to be made between Community tests in different languages, all texts being equally authentic, the multinational Court of Justice is equipped to carry out the task in a way which no national judge, whatever his linguistic skills, could rival. The interpretation of Community instruments involves very often not the process familiar to common lawyers of laboriously extracting the meaning from words used but the more creative process of supplying flesh to a spare and loosely constructed skeleton. The choice between alternative submissions may turn not on purely legal considerations, but on a broader view of what the orderly development of the Community requires. These are matters which the Court of Justice is very much better placed to assess and determine than a national court.

It does not follow from this that a reference should be made by a national court of first instance wherever a litigant raises a serious point of Community law and seeks a reference, or wherever he indicates an intention to appeal, even if he announces an intention to appeal, if necessary, to the highest court which is effectively bound to refer the question to the Court of Justice . . . Other considerations may affect the exercise of discretion. Sometimes no doubt it may

A   appear that the question is raised mischievously, not in the bona fide hope of success but in order to obstruct or delay an almost inevitable adverse judgment, denying the other party his remedy meanwhile. In my judgment none of these contra-indications obtains here."

(I interpolate nor do they in the instant case.)

B   "While I think the defendant unlikely to succeed, I do not regard its arguments as hopeless and they are of potential importance. . . . The reference to the Court of Justice would be unlikely to take longer than appeals have normally taken to reach the Court of Appeal, at least until recently, and unlikely to cost much more. If, at the Court of Appeal stage, a reference were held to be necessary, the delay and expense would be roughly doubled."

Everything there said seems to have application to the instant case.

C   In my judgment a decision on the question of Community law is necessary to enable the court to come to a proper and determinate conclusion in this case. I therefore propose to submit the question of the interpretation of art. 15 to the European Court. I shall invite counsel to agree a draft of the appropriate question or questions to be answered.

(*Proceedings stayed in relation to matter referred*)

D

COURT OF APPEAL JUDGMENT
(16 October 1992)

Bingham MR: This appeal concerns a company named Titaghur plc. The company (as I shall call it) was incorporated in Scotland in 1883. It runs a substantial jute business in India, where it has some 18,000 employees. The shares of the company were first

E   listed by the Stock Exchange in London in 1912 and continued to be so listed until 1988.

In May 1988 the International Stock Exchange of the UK and the Republic of Ireland (which I shall for brevity call "the Stock Exchange") suspended the listing of the company's shares because annual listing charges had not been paid. This omission was rectified and the listing was restored after one month's intermission.

On 28 June 1989 the listing of the company's shares was again suspended by the Stock
F   Exchange. The immediate cause of this suspension was the arrest of the chairman of the company on suspicion of insider-dealing offences. (He was later prosecuted on a number of counts and, after the events giving rise to this appeal, acquitted.) The suspension of the listing continued, partly because of uncertainty concerning the chairman's position, partly because the Stock Exchange was concerned about possible failures to notify dealings in the company's shares and partly because the Stock Exchange was concerned about the adequacy of the financial information provided by the company and about its
G   accounts. There were meetings between representatives of the company and the Stock Exchange concerning these matters, which were also raised in correspondence. It was made clear that the company wished the suspension to be ended, but it appears that in November 1990 the company's broker was told that the Quotations Department of the Stock Exchange had decided to take the matter of the listing of the company to the Panel of the Quotations Committee with a recommendation that the listing be cancelled. The broker indicated that he would probably not attend the Quotations Panel but might
H   appeal against any cancellation decision to the Quotations Committee. The case was duly referred to the panel, which on 23 November 1990 concluded that the listing should be cancelled.

The company (by its broker) was informed of this decision and exercised its right to appeal to the committee. The committee met on 7 December 1990 to hear the appeal. A director and two representatives of its brokers attended on behalf of the company.

The committee decided to uphold the decision of the panel and accordingly directed that   A
the company's listing should be cancelled in view of the inadequacy of the financial
information currently available concerning the company.

The company itself has taken no formal step at any time to challenge the decisions of
the panel or the committee. It is not a party to these proceedings and has played no part
in them.

The proceedings arise out of applications for judicial review made by three applicants.   B
All of the applicants are shareholders in the company, having bought shares off-market
during the period when the listing was suspended and before it was cancelled. Two of
the applicants (Else (1982) Ltd and Leonard Brealey as a trustee of a private pension
trust) sought leave to challenge the panel's decisions to suspend the company's listing in
June 1989 and to cancel the listing in November 1990 and the committee's decision to
cancel the listing in December 1990. They were granted leave to challenge the committee's
decision, but refused leave to challenge the panel's decisions. Following this refusal, no   C
renewed application for leave to challenge the panel's decisions was made until, during
the hearing of this appeal, application was made to this court for leave to move to
challenge the panel's cancellation decision. We refused that application. The third
applicant, Gerard Patrick Thomas, is a Scottish solicitor. He sought and obtained leave
to move to challenge the committee's cancellation decision. He has not sought to
challenge either of the panel's decisions.
                                                                                              D
Following an order for expedition, the hearing of these substantive applications took
place before *Popplewell* J in June 1992. At that hearing the applicants attacked the
committee's decision as irrational, disproportionate and tainted by bias or the appearance
of bias. The judge rejected these criticisms. His decision in rejecting them is the subject
of appeal, but has not formed part of this appeal hearing.

Before the judge an issue of European Community law arose on which the judge held
it necessary to seek a ruling from the Court of Justice of the European Communities   E
under art. 177 of the EEC Treaty to enable him to give judgment. Although the
applicants in the court below contended that the issue should be decided in their favour,
they did not resist the course adopted by the judge if he was left in doubt on the issue,
subject to settling appropriate questions. The Stock Exchange, on the other hand,
contended below that the issue should be decided in their favour and opposed a
reference. The judge having decided to refer, they appeal against his decision to do so.   F
They continue to argue that the Community law issue should be resolved in their favour.
As an authority responsible for regulating an important international market, they have
further urged the practical importance of knowing where they stand as quickly as
possible. The apparent cogency of that consideration has caused the hearing of this
appeal, on the Community law issue, to be expedited. It has proved convenient also to
consider an issue of domestic law closely related to the Community law issue. For the
avoidance of doubt I should make clear that by "domestic law" I mean, for present   G
purposes, the law of England not including that part of it which derives directly from the
law of the Community.

The issues

The central issues on this appeal are these:

(1)   Were the applicants as shareholders entitled to be notified of and given the   H
       opportunity to make representations (which should have been duly considered)
       about the committee's impending decision whether the company's listing should
       be cancelled

       (a) in Community law?

       (b) in domestic law?

A   (2)   Are the applicants as shareholders entitled to challenge the committee's decision
to cancel the company's listing

     (a) in Community law?

     (b) in domestic law?

In relation to questions such as (1)(a) and (2)(a), I understand the correct approach in
principle of a national court (other than a final Court of Appeal) to be quite clear: if the
B   facts have been found and the Community law issue is critical to the court's final
decision, the appropriate course is ordinarily to refer the issue to the Court of Justice
unless the national court can with complete confidence resolve the issue itself. In
considering whether it can with complete confidence resolve the issue itself the national
court must be fully mindful of the differences between national and Community
legislation, of the pitfalls which face a national court venturing into what may be an
unfamiliar field, of the need for uniform interpretation throughout the Community and
C   of the great advantages enjoyed by the Court of Justice in construing Community
instruments. If the national court has any real doubt, it should ordinarily refer. I am not
here attempting to summarise comprehensively the effect of such leading cases as *H P
Bulmer Ltd v J Bollinger SA* [1974] Ch 401, *Srl CILFIT v Ministry of Health* [1982] ECR
3415 and *R v Pharmaceutical Society of Great Britain, ex parte Association of
Pharmaceutical Importers* [1987] 3 CMLR 951, but I hope I am fairly expressing their
D   essential point.

It is convenient, with that point in mind, to turn to the Community law issue. This
arises, and arises only, from Council Directive of 5 March 1979 co-ordinating the
conditions for the admission of securities to listing (79/279, OJ 1979 L66/21), "the
admission directive". I shall refer to it as "the directive". Since its correct construction
lies at the heart of this appeal, the directive must be analysed in a little detail.

E   **The directive**

The directive was made under the EEC Treaty and in particular art. 54(3)(g) and 100
thereof. Article 54(3)(g) required the Council and the Commission to carry out their
duties under the Treaty in particular,

     "(g) by coordinating to the necessary extent the safeguards which, for the
     protection of the interests of members and others, are required by Member States
F   of companies or firms within the meaning of the second paragraph of Article 58
     with a view to making such safeguards equivalent throughout the Community."

The second paragraph of art. 58 contained a stipulative definition of "companies or
firms". Article 100 required the Council to issue directives for the approximation of such
provisions laid down by law, regulation or administrative action in member states as
directly affect the establishment or functioning of the common market.

G   The directive was intended, as its long title makes plain, to co-ordinate the conditions
for the admission of securities to official stock exchange listing. This was a step towards
establishment of a common market in securities. In other member states, as here,
conditions (imposed for the protection of investors) had to be met before a security was
admitted to listing. There could be no truly common market so long as different
conditions were imposed by the various member states. Still less could there be a truly
common market if it was open to national authorities, under the guise of protecting
H   investors, to make the admission of local securities to listing easier than that of foreign
securities. The policy objectives to be achieved by coordinating the listing conditions in
the various member states were outlined in the fifth recital to the directive: to provide
equivalent protection for investors at Community level, because of the more uniform
guarantees offered to investors in the various member states; to facilitate Community-
wide listing of member state securities; and to enable member states to penetrate each

other's securities markets so as to contribute to establishment of a European capital   A
market. The directive applied to entities not covered by the second paragraph of art. 58
of the Treaty and was acknowledged to go beyond art. 54(3)(g), but was seen as directly
affecting the establishment and functioning of the common market within the meaning
of art. 100.

The seventh recital to the directive is of such significance to this appeal as to justify
verbatim quotation: B

> "Whereas there should be the possibility of a right to apply to the courts against
> decisions by the competent national authorities in respect of the application of
> this directive, although such right to apply must not be allowed to restrict the
> discretion of these authorities;"

Co-ordination was in the first instance to be limited to establishing minimum conditions
for the admission of securities to official stock exchange lists in member states, but   C
issuers were to have no right to listing.

Section I of the directive contains general provisions. These prescribe minimum
conditions to be satisfied by securities admitted to official listing in member states and
minimum obligations to which issuers shall be subject. While member states may impose
conditions and obligations more stringent than the minimum, they may not (generally
speaking) discriminate in doing so. Member states may in accordance with applicable   D
national rules require issuers of securities admitted to official listing to inform the public
on a regular basis of their financial position and the general course of their business.

Section II of the directive concerns the authorities competent to admit securities to
official listing and contains the provisions most central to this appeal. Member states are
required to designate such competent authorities. It is common ground in this case that
the Council of the Stock Exchange is so designated and that the Committee on Quotations   E
is empowered to act on its behalf. Member states are to ensure that the competent
authorities have such powers as may be necessary for the exercise of their duties and, by
para. 3 of art. 9,

> "Without prejudice to the other powers conferred upon them, the competent
> authorities may reject an application for the admission of a security to official
> listing if, in their opinion, the issuer's situation is such that admission would be   F
> detrimental to investors' interests."

This is supplemented by art. 10:

> "By way of derogation from Article 5, Member States may, solely in the interests
> of protecting the investors, give the competent authorities power to make the
> admission of a security to official listing subject to any special condition which the
> competent authorities consider appropriate and of which they have explicitly   G
> informed the applicant."

Article 12 authorises competent authorities (in addition to any other sanction) to
publicise the fact that an issuer is failing to comply with its obligations. Article 13
requires an issuer whose securities are admitted to official listing to provide the competent
authorities with all the information they consider appropriate "to protect investors or
ensure the smooth operation of the market" and, by para. 2 of this article,   H

> "Where protection of investors or the smooth operation of the market so requires,
> an issuer may be required by the competent authorities to publish such information
> in such a form and within such time limits as they consider appropriate. Should
> the issuer fail to comply with such requirement, the competent authorities may
> themselves publish such information after having heard the issuer."

A   This section of the directive ends with art. 14–16, which I quote in full:

"Article 14.

1. The competent authorities may decide to suspend the listing of a security where the smooth operation of the market is, or may be, temporarily jeopardised or where protection of investors so requires.

B   2. The competent authorities may decide that the listing of the security be discontinued where they are satisfied that, owing to special circumstances, normal regular dealings in a security are no longer possible.

Article 15.

1. Member States shall that ensure decisions of the competent authorities refusing the admission of a security to official listing or discontinuing such a listing shall be subject to the right to apply to the courts.

C   2. An applicant shall be notified of a decision regarding his application for admission to official listing within six months of receipt of the application or, should the competent authority require any further information within the period, within six months of the applicant's supplying such information.

3. Failure to give a decision within the time limit specified in paragraph 2 shall be deemed a rejection of the application. Such rejection shall give rise to the right to

D   apply to the courts provided for in paragraph 1.

Article 16.

Where an application for admission to official listing relates to certificates representing shares, the application shall be considered only if the competent authorities are of the opinion that the issuer of the certificates is offering adequate safeguards for the protection of investors."

E   Section III of the directive covers the publication of information to be made available to the public. Section IV covers co-operation between member states. Our attention was drawn to art. 18, which requires member states to co-operate and communicate with each other. Article 19 imposes a duty of professional secrecy but provides that communication between the competent authorities of member states shall not be a breach of it. Section V made provision for a contact committee composed of

F   representatives of member states and the Commission to discuss implementation of the directive and practical problems arising from it and to advise the Commission.

At its request the court was referred to the proposal from the Commission, the opinion of the European Parliament and the opinion of the Economic and Social committee to which reference is made in the second, third and fourth recitals of the directive. These show, as one would expect, that the original draft of the directive was

G   modified before its final adoption, but they throw no definitive light on the issue between the parties in this court. It is, however, of interest that the proposed directive contained no precursor of the seventh recital in the directive, although it did provide in art. 10(2) that each member state should provide for a right of appeal to the courts against a decision to refuse an application for listing. The Economic and Social Committee criticised that proposal, suggesting that a right of appeal should be provided against any decision of the competent authorities and not just against a decision to refuse an

H   application for listing. The Parliament also felt that there should be greater rights of appeal against the decisions of the national authorities responsible for the admission of securities to quotation. It advised that there should be a right of administrative appeal against decisions to refuse listing, against decisions that information should be published, against decisions that listing be discontinued and against decisions by the competent authorities of their own motion to list a security (a power not in the event conferred by

the directive itself). There was no suggestion that the right of appeal should be conferred   A
on additional parties.

The parties to this appeal agree that the directive takes direct effect. We were told that
the researches of counsel had unearthed no relevant authority on its construction.

The applicants' argument on the directive

On behalf of the applicants, a long and detailed argument was advanced. I understood   B
the essential steps in the argument to be these:

(1)   The directive is a measure intended to protect investors, including shareholders
such as the applicants.

(2)   Shareholders such as the applicants are likely to suffer loss or prejudice if the
public listing of the company in which they hold shares is cancelled.

(3)   Shareholders such as the applicants cannot effectively resist a potentially damaging   C
cancellation unless they are notified of an impending decision, unless they are
informed of the grounds on which the decision may be taken, unless they have the
opportunity to make representations and unless the competent authority is bound
to consider these representations before making a decision.

(4)   The seventh recital of the directive and art. 15 impose no restriction upon the
parties granted a right to apply to the courts.   D

(5)   In the light of (1)–(4) above the intention of art. 15 is, or at any rate may be, to
confer rights on shareholders such as the applicants to be notified of an impending
decision whether a listing should be cancelled, to be informed of the grounds
relied on and to be given an opportunity to make representations and, after the
decision has been made, to challenge it.

(6)   The English court should accordingly seek a ruling from the European Court of   E
Justice on the correct construction of the directive, and the judge was right to
refer.

Each of these steps calls for careful consideration.

The conditions which national authorities impose on admission to listing are imposed
for the protection of investors. The body of investors includes existing shareholders. It
also includes, very particularly in this context, potential future investors. In dealing with   F
conditions imposed and obligations undertaken by companies whose securities are
admitted to listing, the directive expressly recognises the responsibility of the competent
authorities to protect the interests of investors, which must always be their overriding
concern when exercising their powers. But the primary purpose of the directive is to co-
ordinate the listing practice of competent authorities in the various member states with
a view to establishing a common market in securities and not, in any direct way, to
provide additional protection for investors.   G

I accept without question that shareholders such as the applicants are liable to suffer
loss or prejudice if the public listing of a company in which they hold shares is cancelled.
But so they may if the listing is suspended or, in a less obvious way, if an application for
listing is refused. The applicants accept that the directive does not, in either of these
situations, confer upon shareholders any right of recourse to the court.

I accept that in the ordinary way step (3) in the applicants' argument is likely to be   H
factually correct.

I accept that the seventh recital of the directive and art. 15 do not in express terms
define the parties upon whom a right to apply to the courts is conferred. But several
considerations compel me to what I regard as an inevitable conclusion that the right is
conferred on a company or an issuer alone:

A   (1)   In the proposed directive the right provided for was one of appeal. While the Economic and Social Committee and the Parliament favoured a wider right of appeal, there is no suggestion that they or anyone envisaged any right other than a right of appeal. In any ordinary situation, a right of appeal is accorded to the party who has been the subject of an adverse decision. There is nothing to suggest that any party other than a company or issuer was seen as potentially the subject of any adverse decision or as having any right of appeal.

B   (2)   The directive is concerned with relations between competent authorities (who are responsible for protecting the interests of investors) and companies or issuers. Nothing in the directive suggests that competent authorities may have direct relations with investors.

     (3)   Once it is accepted, as it must be, that the directive gives investors no right of recourse to the courts in respect of suspension and refusal of listing, it cannot
C   rationally be construed as conferring such a right on investors in respect of cancellation.

I cannot accept the soundness of step (5). In addition to reasons already given, I see powerful further objections, particularly to the rights the applicants claim before a cancellation decision is made:

     (1)   Such rights would in my view gravely restrict the discretion of the competent
D   authorities, which the seventh recital indicates must not be allowed. The applicants do not, I think, deny that the procedure for which they contend could substantially postpone the date at which a cancellation might become effective, but they suggest that only suspension need take place urgently; thereafter the rights of a company and investors are frozen and a delay in cancellation (they say) carries no risk. Often this may be so, but I do not accept it is necessarily so. Article 14 lays down different tests for suspension and cancellation. It is for the competent authority to
E   decide in the exercise of its informed judgment which of these courses, if either, is appropriate on given facts. Recent history in more than one field emphasises the need for regulatory authorities to take quick and decisive action where the situation requires it. The directive, in my view, recognises that need and gives effect to it. The applicants' argument subverts that intention.

     (2)   It is obvious that with a company of any size the task of circularising all shareholders
F   and giving them the information they need to make a decision is a substantial and expensive task. If the directive envisaged such a procedure it could scarcely avoid all reference to the questions: who is to carry out this task? And who is to pay? Spare though the style of Community draftsmanship may be, it would be surprising to find a lacuna as gross as this.

     (3)   There are deeply-rooted principles of company law that a company is a legal entity separate and distinct from its shareholders and that a shareholder may not as such
G   act on behalf of or enforce the rights of the company. On the applicants' argument, difficult questions would be bound to arise where, as here, a cancellation decision is accepted by a company but challenged by some (although only a small minority) of shareholders. It would arise even more acutely in the common case where cancellation is requested by a company, if resisted by a small minority of shareholders. These are, again, obvious problems posed by the applicants'
H   argument which the directive fails to address. This would be very surprising if that argument were right. If it is wrong, the directive does not give rise to these problems and they are rightly ignored.

     (4)   The directive does not define "investors". This is understandable if, as I hold, the directive confers no enforceable rights on investors. But on the applicants' argument, in an instrument having direct effect, it would be very important to

know who the class of "investors" included. A number of possible categories have been suggested, in addition to shareholders. But it is hard to suppose that potential buyers of securities, a class of much concern to the competent authorities, could enjoy the rights the applicants claim, and this lack of definition weighs powerfully against the applicants' argument, because an instrument of such uncertain scope cannot properly be given direct effect.

In the result, I feel able with complete confidence to reject the applicants' argument based on the directive. For reasons which I have tried to give, I do not share the doubts felt by the judge about the effect to be given to it. If I did, I would of course respect his exercise of discretion to refer, which would in any event have been the proper course. But taking the view I do, I do not find it necessary to seek a ruling on this question from the Court of Justice to enable me to give judgment. It follows that I would allow the appeal of the Stock Exchange on this point and quash the order made under art. 177 of the Treaty.

Domestic law

It was not suggested that the law of England, independently of Community law, permitted an affirmative answer to the question posed at (1)(b) above. Nor, I think, was it argued that domestic law, independently of Community law, conferred a right on shareholders as envisaged by question (2)(b). But the applicants argued (and the Stock Exchange broadly denied) that as shareholders they had a sufficient interest in the cancellation decision within the meaning of sec. 31(3) of the *Supreme Court Act* 1981 and O. 53, r. 3(7) of the Rules of the Supreme Court to enable a grant of leave to move for judicial review to be properly made, subject of course to the applicants meeting the other qualifying conditions.

On the facts here, no application for leave to move was made before the cancellation decision. I decline to speculate what the position would have been had the applicants been in a position to apply, and had they done so, at that stage.

When the applicants applied for leave to move, *Auld* J was tentatively of opinion that they could show a sufficient interest. He was no doubt mindful that they were not busybodies but claimed, as shareholders, to have a direct financial interest in the company which the cancellation decision affected. At the substantive hearing *Popplewell* J took a different view, ruling that the applicants had no sufficient interest. The applicants appeal against that decision. In the event, however, the judge did investigate and rule upon the various grounds relied upon to challenge the committee's cancellation decision (with the exception of additional grounds which he did not, quite rightly, allow the applicants to pursue). He rejected that challenge. It follows that whether the applicants had a sufficient interest to mount a retrospective challenge to the cancellation decision is strictly academic unless or until this court is persuaded that the judge was wrong to reject that challenge. The applicants do not appeal on that aspect. It is therefore undesirable to express a concluded view. I would simply observe that the problems facing any shareholder seeking to mount such a challenge are formidable in the extreme. In a highly sensitive and potentially fluid financial market, the factors listed in sec. 31(6) of the 1981 Act have a special significance. And the courts will not second-guess the informed judgment of responsible regulators steeped in knowledge of their particular market. But if, exceptionally, a shareholder were able to overcome these formidable problems, I question whether his claim to relief should fail for lack of sufficient interest.

The order resulting from this hearing is not entirely straightforward. I would be grateful if counsel could prepare draft minutes of order, which should be copied to Mr Thomas and, if agreed by all parties, submitted to the Associate.

A

McCowan LJ: I agree with the Master of the Rolls' judgment and would add only a few words of my own.

Miss Allan for the applicants conceded before this court that only the company in question, as the applicant for listing, has the right to apply to the courts in respect of a refusal of admission to listing. But, she argued, para. 1 of art. 15 only provides, as she put it, "a broad scenario", which is cut down in respect of a refusal of admission to listing by para. 2 and 3, but not in respect of discontinuance of listing, as to which the article is

B silent.

To my mind, however, it would be very odd if art. 15 contemplated that a wider class of persons than the company should have the right to apply to the courts in respect of discontinuance of listing than in respect of admission to listing but neglected to say so. Moreover, Miss Allan has been unable to point to anything in art. 15 to suggest that an application to the courts in respect of discontinuance can be made by a different body or class of persons than that which the article clearly says can make the application in

C respect of listing, namely the company.

In my judgment, therefore, the terms of art. 15 itself are plainly against her submissions.

Leggatt LJ: It is the policy of the EEC Treaty to abolish restrictions on freedom of establishment. One way of furthering this policy is to co-ordinate safeguards for the protection of individuals by rendering the safeguards "equivalent" throughout the Community. A series of directives has applied this principle to companies. But that does

D not detract from the distinction which English law recognises between a company and its members. The court cannot interfere with the internal management of a company acting within its powers. Although the court will interfere to prevent fraud on a minority of shareholders, it will not ordinarily recognise any independent right of action by an individual shareholder based on an allegation of damage to the value of his shareholding, whether caused by the directors or by third parties. Nothing in Community law departs from that principle unless the applicants' submission in the present case is correct that

E Directive 79/279 (OJ 1979 L66/21) accords to individual shareholders the right to apply to the court for the purpose of objecting to the discontinuance of the listing of the company of which they are members.

Community legislation about stock exchanges is mainly concerned with the listing of securities. Directive 79/279 has been followed by directives dealing with requirements for furnishing particulars of securities for which listing has been applied, and with

F information which must be published regularly by companies with listed shares. These directives are intended to protect investors as well as to facilitate access to the markets of the member states.

The scheme of the relevant Community legislation, and Directive 79/279 in particular, is to provide for the co-ordination of conditions for admission to listing by designating a competent authority in each member state to police the process. Ancillary provision is made for the suspension of listing and for discontinuance of listing. But although one of

G the main aims of controlling admission to listing is the protection of investors, the directive is concerned with the means of control by the competent authority rather than with conferring rights on investors so that they may look out for themselves.

The function of Directive 79/279, known as "the admission directive", is co-ordinating the conditions for the admission of securities to official stock exchange listing. The recitals show that this process is likely to provide protection for investors by rendering

H more uniform the practices in the member states. The general approach is prescribed by art. 3 which says:

"Member States shall ensure that:

— securities may not be admitted to official listing on any stock exchange situated or operating within their territory unless the conditions laid down by this directive are satisfied, and that

A

— issuers of securities admitted to such official listing, whether admission takes place before or after the date on which this directive is implemented, are subject to the obligations provided for by this directive."

Article 4 provides that the admission of securities to official listing is subject to the conditions set out in Sch. A and B relating to shares and debt securities, and that the issuers of listed securities must fulfil the obligations in the corresponding Sch. C and D. Schedule A therefore contains conditions for the admission of shares, and Sch. C deals with the obligations of companies whose shares are admitted. Paragraph 2 of Sch. C is concerned with treatment of shareholders. By subpara. (b):

B

"The company must ensure, at least in each Member State in which its shares are listed, that all the necessary facilities and information are available to enable shareholders to exercise their rights."

This includes information about shareholders' meetings and notices about dividends and new shares.

C

Section II of the directive is headed "Authorities Competent To Admit Official Listing". In that section art. 9 by para. (1) requires member states to designate the competent authority "to decide on the admission of securities to official listing". Paragraph 3 provides:

"Without prejudice to the other powers conferred upon them, the competent authorities may reject an application for the admission of a security to official listing if, in their opinion, the issuer's situation is such that admission would be detrimental to investors' interests."

D

Article 10 applies to any special condition to which the competent authority may make the admission of a security subject, and of which they have informed the applicant, that is, the person applying for the admission. Article 11 refers to a refusal to admit. Articles 12 and 13 apply to failure by the issuer to comply with obligations and to publish information. Article 14 is concerned with suspension and discontinuance of the listing. Finally, para. 2 of art. 15 relates to notification to an applicant of a decision regarding his application for admission, and para. 3 provides that a deemed rejection of the application "shall give rise to the right to apply to the courts provided for in paragraph 1". The would-be issuer is both the applicant for admission and the person with the right to apply to the courts. Paragraph 1 itself says that:

E

F

"Member States shall ensure decisions of the competent authorities refusing the admission of a security to official listing or discontinuing such a listing shall be subject to the right to apply to the courts."

"Decisions" are made under art. 9(1); "decisions refusing" may be made under art. 9(3) or under art. 11; and "decisions discontinuing" may be made under art. 14(2).

In my judgment as a matter of construction the fact that the decisions have to be "subject to the right to apply to the courts" means that as with a deemed rejection under art. 15(3), it is the giving to the applicant of an adverse decision by the competent authority that also gives to the applicant a right to apply to the courts. There is no other person to whom that right is given: it is given solely to the applicant. Miss Allan argues that because the directive is for the protection of investors it is they who must have a right to apply to the court. That is a non sequitur. Nothing in the language of the directive accords such a right to investors, actual or potential. I am fortified in this conclusion by the fact that, if the law were otherwise, the consequences of extending to persons other than the company the right to apply to the court would be commercially intolerable. If the number of shareholders was large, the process of identifying and communicating with them might be onerous, protracted and expensive. As Mr Henderson has pointed out, it might jeopardise confidentiality. It might even allow the will of a majority to be

G

H

A   thwarted, if not overcome, by the protestation of an individual shareholder. I therefore
conclude that the correct application of Community law in this case is so obvious as to
leave no scope for any reasonable doubt; that recourse to the European Court is
unnecessary; and that the appeal should be allowed.

(*Counsel to provide minutes of order*)

B

C

D

E

F

G

H

Downsview Nominees Ltd & Anor v First City Corporation Ltd & Anor.

A

Privy Council.
Lord Templeman, Lord Lane, Lord Goff of Chieveley, Lord Mustill and Lord Slynn of Hadley.
Judgment delivered 19 November 1992.

B

Receivership — Duties owed by first debenture holder and receiver and manager to second debenture holder.

This was an appeal from the Court of Appeal of New Zealand concerning the duties which a first debenture holder and a receiver and manager appointed by the first debenture holder owed to a second debenture holder.

The mortgagor company, "GEM", carried on business as new and used motor vehicle dealers. The principal shareholder and manager of the company was "P". GEM had issued a debenture ("the Westpac debenture") which secured the sum of NZ$ 230,000 in priority to a second debenture made in favour of the first respondent, "FCC".

C

GEM was trading at a loss and, the moneys secured by the second debenture having become due and payable, FCC appointed two accountants to be receivers and managers of GEM. The FCC receivers formed the provisional view that a sale of the assets of GEM would be necessary. They removed P from his position as manager of GEM. P consulted the appellant, "R", who controlled the appellant company, "Downsview". The Westpac debenture was assigned to Downsview and R was appointed receiver and manager under that debenture. R took over the assets and management of GEM from the receivers and managers appointed by FCC and restored P to the management of GEM. R announced that it was his intention to trade the company out of its financial difficulties. FCC offered to buy out the Westpac debenture or sell its debenture to Downsview. GEM continued to trade at a loss, incorporating a new subsidiary to receive the proceeds of sale of vehicles. FCC eventually obtained a court order for the Westpac debenture to be assigned by Downsview to FCC on terms and for R to cease to act as receiver and to transfer GEM's assets to receivers appointed by FCC.

D

E

The judge at first instance found that R and Downsview had employed their powers under the Westpac debenture for their own purposes and not for proper purposes, in breach of their duties to the subsequent debenture holder. The judge held that the respondents were entitled to damages on the basis of the difference between the loss that would have been incurred had the original receivership been allowed to proceed unimpeded, and the loss actually incurred as it emerged following the second receivership by the original receivers. In addition R was prohibited under sec. 189 of the New Zealand Companies Act without the leave of the court from being a director or promoter of or being concerned in or taking part in the management of any company for a period of five years.

F

G

The New Zealand Court of Appeal accepted that on the application of negligence principles a receiver and manager who elected to carry on the business of the company and to trade it out of receivership owed a duty of care to subsequent debenture holders to take reasonable care in dealing with the assets of the company. The Court of Appeal held that R was in breach of the duty of care to FCC, that Downsview was not in breach and that the court had no jurisdiction under sec. 189 of the Companies Act to prohibit R from being a director.

H

R appealed and the respondents cross-appealed.

Held, dismissing the appeal and allowing the cross-appeal, restoring the orders made by the first instance judge against R and Downsview (except the order under sec. 189):

A   1. **A mortgagee owed a duty to subsequent encumbrancers and to the mortgagor to use his powers for the sole purpose of securing repayment of the moneys owing under his mortgage and a duty to act in good faith. He also owed specific duties which equity imposed on him in the exercise of his powers to go into possession and his powers of sale. The same rules applied also to a receiver and manager appointed by the mortgagee. There was no general duty in negligence to use reasonable care in dealing with the assets of the company.**

B   2. **A dissatisfied second debenture holder could require the prior debenture to be assigned to him (it being well settled that the mortgagor and all persons having any interest in the property subject to the mortgage or liable to pay the mortgage debt could redeem). A dissatisfied company could raise the money to pay off the debenture holder. But if a receiver and manager decided at his discretion to manage and did manage in good faith with the object of preserving and realising the assets for the benefit of the debenture**

C   **holder, he was subject to no further or greater liability.**

3. **A receiver and manager committed a breach of his duty if he abused his powers by exercising them otherwise than for the special purpose of enabling the assets comprised in the debenture holder's security to be preserved and realised for the benefit of the debenture holder. (Re B Johnson & Co (Builders) Ltd [1955] Ch 634 approved.)**

D   4. **There was overwhelming evidence that the receivership of R was inspired by him for improper purposes and carried on in bad faith, ultimately verging on fraud. The liability of Downsview arose as a result of Downsview's breach of duty in failing to transfer the Westpac debenture to FCC.**

The following cases were referred to in the judgment:

Caparo Industries plc v Dickman & Ors [1990] BCC 164; [1990] 2 AC 605.

CBS Songs Ltd & Ors v Amstrad Consumer Electronics plc & Anor [1988] AC 1013.

E   *Cuckmere Brick Co Ltd & Anor v Mutual Finance Ltd* [1971] Ch 949.

Johnson (B) & Co (Builders) Ltd, Re [1955] Ch 634.

Murphy v Brentwood District Council [1991] 1 AC 398.

Tomlin v Luce (1889) 43 ChD 191.

Gary Judd and Robert Chambers (instructed by Alan Taylor & Co) for the appellants.

F   Rhys Harrison and Ralph Simpson (instructed by Wray Smith & Co) for the respondents.

JUDGMENT
(Delivered by Lord Templeman)

This appeal requires consideration of the duties, if any, which a first debenture holder and a receiver and manager appointed by a first debenture holder owe to a second debenture holder.

G   The mortgagor company, Glen Eden Motors Ltd (formerly Glen Eden Fiat Centre (1975) Ltd and hereafter called "GEM"), carried on business as new and used motor vehicle dealers and held Fiat and Mazda franchises for the sale of their vehicles and spare parts. The principal shareholder and manager of the company was Mr Pedersen.

On 11 August 1975 GEM issued a first debenture ("the Westpac debenture") which eventually secured the principal sum of NZ\$ 230,000 in priority to a second debenture.

H   That second debenture dated 18 September 1986 was made in favour of the first respondent, the First City Corporation Ltd ("FCC").

Each debenture created a fixed charge over certain assets of the company and a floating charge over the remainder. Each debenture contained power for the debenture holder to appoint a receiver and manager, who was to be deemed to be the agent of the company and was authorised to perform any acts which the company could perform.

For the six-months' period to 30 September 1986 GEM traded at a loss. On 10 March 1987, the moneys secured by the second debenture having become due and payable, FCC appointed two chartered accountants, Chilcott & Chatfield, experienced in receiverships to be receivers and managers of GEM. The FCC receivers formed the provisional view that a sale of the assets of GEM would be necessary. They removed Mr Pedersen from his position as manager of GEM.

Mr Pedersen consulted the appellant, Mr Russell, who controlled the appellant company, Downsview Nominees Ltd ("Downsview"). On 23 March 1987 the Westpac debenture was assigned to Downsview and Mr Russell was appointed receiver and manager under that debenture. Mr Russell took over the assets and management of GEM from the receivers and managers appointed by FCC and restored Mr Pedersen to the management of GEM.

On 25 March 1987 Mr Russell announced that it was his intention to trade the company out of its financial difficulties subject to a review in three months' time. On 27 March 1987 the solicitors for FCC wrote to the directors of Downsview. The letter contained the following:

"Our client informs us that you as first debenture holder have now appointed a receiver of Glen Eden Motors Ltd. As a consequence our client's receivers Chilcott & Chatfield have temporarily withdrawn to permit your receiver Mr Russell to take control of the company until such time as your debenture can be repaid in full.

Our client informs us that it is your receiver's intention to attempt to trade the company out of its present difficulties. Our client considers that any such attempt is extremely unlikely to improve the situation and indeed is highly likely to result in damage to the shareholders of the company and to itself as subsequent debenture holder.

To prevent any dispute developing our clients have instructed us to write to you and make the following offer on their behalf:

Our client will purchase your debenture at a price equivalent to all amounts outstanding and secured under your debenture at the date of settlement; or alternatively

Our client will sell to you its debenture for a price equivalent to all amounts secured and outstanding under its debenture at the date of settlement."

The letter added that $721,621.69 were then outstanding under the FCC debenture.

On 4 April 1987 GEM issued a third debenture in favour of Downsview and on 6 May 1987 Downsview advanced $100,000 to the company. Mr Russell claimed that the moneys raised by the third debenture were "receiver's borrowings" having preference to all other claims in the receivership, including the claims of FCC.

GEM continued to trade but paid no interest, let alone principal, due under the Westpac debenture or the FCC debenture.

At the end of three months Mr Russell had prepared no past accounts or future budgets but was aware that the company was trading at a loss.

On 13 July 1987 Mazda (New Zealand) Ltd gave notice to determine the company's Mazda franchise dealership. About the same time Mr Russell caused to be incorporated Gemco Motors Ltd ("Gemco") as a subsidiary of GEM.

By a letter dated 13 August 1987 the solicitors for FCC called upon Downsview to assign the Westpac debenture to FCC as a subsequent chargeholder. Mr Russell on behalf of Downsview refused, notwithstanding that Downsview would have been paid all the moneys secured by the Westpac debenture. These proceedings were instituted on

A   8 September 1987 and by an interlocutory application FCC sought an order directing Downsview to assign the Westpac debenture to FCC.

From 1 October 1987 proceeds of vehicles sold by the company were received by Gemco, which acknowledged a borrowing from GEM to the extent of the value of the vehicles sold.

B   On 24 November 1987 *Thorp* J heard the application by FCC for an order directing Downsview to transfer the Westpac debenture to FCC. On 5 December 1987 Gemco issued a debenture in favour of Downsview. On 23 December 1987 Mr Russell swore in an affidavit that the amount required to discharge the debt owing to Downsview, and the amount required to discharge the liabilities and charges of the receiver, amounted to $825,727. He subsequently increased this figure. On 11 January 1988 *Thorp* J ordered the Westpac debenture to be assigned by Downsview to FCC on terms. Downsview and Mr Russell appealed and sought a stay of execution of the order for assignment. On C   2 March 1988 *Thorp* J refused a stay on terms.

On 9 March 1988 Mr Russell borrowed from one of his other companies the sum of $272,000 and paid to Downsview the sum of $271,665.39 by way of repayment of the moneys secured by the Westpac debenture, so as to leave a balance outstanding of $1,000. FCC, in ignorance of these manoeuvres complied with the conditions imposed by *Thorp* J which obliged FCC to pay $130,000 to Downsview and to pay a further D $170,000 into court before receiving an assignment of the Westpac debenture. Downsview assigned the Westpac debenture to FCC but Mr Russell refused to relinquish control of GEM without a further payment to himself of $329,000 in cash. On 21 April 1988 *Smellie* J ordered Mr Russell to cease forthwith to act as receiver of GEM and to transfer GEM's assets to receivers appointed by FCC. He directed that the order was not to be sealed until FCC had deposited an additional $20,000 in court and had appointed E   receivers under its debentures. On the same day Mr Russell effected an assignment of a debenture issued by Gemco in favour of Downsview to another of his companies, Terocon Press Ltd. The following day Terocon Press Ltd made an advance under the debenture to Gemco of $190,000. This sum was immediately transferred from Gemco to GEM by way of reduction of the intercompany indebtedness. On the same morning Mr Russell as receiver of GEM paid to his company Corporate Enterprises Ltd the sum of $224,000 by way of reduction of his receiver's borrowings. Also on the same day Mr F   Russell caused certain new and used vehicles valued at $303,543 to be removed from the premises of GEM and Gemco and stored in a warehouse. On the same day Mr Russell caused Terocon Press Ltd, the holder of the debenture from Gemco, to make demand upon Gemco for repayment upon one hour and 25 minutes' notice of the amount owing under that debenture said to be $245,129. Mr Russell also wrote cheques on behalf of Gemco for sums in excess of $100,000 in favour of creditors of Gemco. He then gave G   notice to the registrar that he had ceased to act as the receiver of GEM at noon on 22 April 1988. FCC on 26 April appointed Chilcott & Chatfield, their original receivers, to be again the receivers and managers of GEM.

On 30 September 1988 FCC assigned to the second respondent First City Finance Ltd ("FCF") the FCC debenture together with all its rights, titles and interests in the moneys payable thereunder and all rights, powers and remedies thereunder.

H   These proceedings were continued by FCC and by FCF. The action came before *Gault* J who on 4 August 1989 delivered judgment. He summarised the relevant parts of the statement of claim as follows:

> "The plaintiffs, in the statement of claim, alleged that Downsview and Mr Russell, as prior debenture holder and receiver respectively, owed duties to FCC and/or FCF to—

'(1) Exercise their powers for proper purposes.

(2) Act honestly and in good faith.

(3) Exercise reasonable care, skill and diligence.

(4) Discharge the Westpac debenture immediately they were in a position to do so.

(5) Pay over or surrender to FCC the surplus assets of GEM after satisfaction of the Westpac debenture.'

They allege that Downsview and Mr Russell acted, or omitted to act, in a fraudulent, reckless or negligent manner in breach of these duties. The alleged breaches are particularised at length in the fourth amended statement of claim and may be summarised under three headings—

(a) Acquiring the Westpac debenture and carrying out the receivership thereunder for the improper purpose of preventing the plaintiffs enforcing their security.

(b) Conducting the receivership in a reckless or negligent manner.

(c) Failing to accept the plaintiffs' offer to discharge the obligations under the Westpac debenture and to assign the Westpac debenture to the plaintiffs."

The judge recorded the following allegations by FCC and FCF:

". . . that Downsview in the course of events I have described, acted in bad faith and other than as a prudent debenture holder would act in the exercise of its power by knowingly, and without any real intention of enforcing the security under the Westpac debenture, preventing enforcement of the plaintiff's security. This was effected by purchasing the Westpac debenture and appointing Mr Russell knowingly to act as he did as receiver and manager of GEM."

Gault J made the following findings:

"Mr Russell said he took the view his responsibility was to the company to do the best possible job he could and that this would have been ultimately to the benefit of everyone, including FCC. I do not accept that that was his approach at the time. He resolved to acquire the debenture, appoint himself receiver and permit the company to trade on under the same management, without taking the time to fully investigate the financial affairs of the company, the competence of its management or the basis upon which FCC was seeking to enforce its security. In my judgment his true motive was to involve himself in the affairs of GEM for the benefit of himself and his company while undertaking to assist Mr Pedersen and to 'save' GEM. His own brief of evidence reads—

'170. It is perfectly lawful for anyone to purchase a debenture. Downsview is in the business of acting as a nominee in the lending of money. The Westpac debenture was a good investment because it was a first charge over a long established company. There was no doubt that it would get its money back plus interest. Therefore, from Downsview's point of view, there was no downside risk in acquiring the debenture.

171. From my point of view, I saw it as a good and interesting job as receiver, for which I expected to be well paid.

172. It was an interesting job, because I saw the opportunity of preserving the company for the benefit of its unsecured creditors and shareholders, as well as for the secured creditors. Saving the company, in circumstances where it had been struck a severe blow by the appointment of the first receivers, was a challenge which I was happy to take up.'

A

In pursuit of his own objectives Mr Russell embarked upon a course, having as its first objective disruption of the receivership under the FCC debenture. His intention in urgently acquiring the Westpac debenture and accepting appointment as receiver was not for the purpose of enforcing the security under the Westpac debenture but for the purpose of preventing the enforcement by the plaintiffs of the FCC debenture. Further . . . in conducting the correspondence with the solicitors for FCC in the months immediately following his appointment as receiver, he had no genuine intention of either agreeing to assign the Westpac debenture to FCC, or of acquiring the FCC debenture. During that period, had he so wished, he could have facilitated the speedy acquisition of the Westpac debenture by FCC in a manner similar to its acquisition by Downsview. Subsequently his resistance to prompt assignment of the Westpac debenture, even in the face of a direction from the court, was prompted in part by his anxiety to secure any outstanding fees and liabilities and in part to secure the interests of his companies. I consider he was also motivated to a considerable degree by a determination simply to retain control of the business affairs of GEM to frustrate the enforcement by the plaintiffs of the security under the FCC debenture . . .

B

C

The decision to acquire the Westpac debenture and assume the office of receiver of GEM is inter-related with the determination by Mr Russell that the company should continue to trade . . .

D

In the circumstances I consider that Mr Russell and Downsview employed the powers under the Westpac debenture for their own purposes and not for their proper purposes. To use these powers as they did constituted a clear breach of each of their respective duties to the subsequent debenture holder . . .

E

I have no difficulty in reaching the conclusion that, taking office for the purposes he did and conducting his receivership in the manner I have outlined, constituted breach by Mr Russell of his duty to the holder of the FCC debenture. While I consider his conduct fell below the required standard, even in the initial period, I find that after July 1987 his conduct can be described only as reckless . . .

F

The plaintiff's claim for failure by Downsview to assign the Westpac debenture had two separate bases. The first was on the refusal by Downsview to accept FCC's offer to purchase the Westpac debenture when first made four days after Downsview acquired the debenture. It follows from the finding I have made already, that had Downsview acquired the debenture and exercised the powers under it for their proper purposes, the offer made on behalf of FCC would have been responded to . . .

G

The response by Mr Russell (for Downsview and I believe for himself) simply underscores the finding I have already made, that both defendants employed the powers under the Westpac debenture in breach of the duty they had to the subsequent debenture holder."

The judge held that FCC and FCF were entitled to damages on the basis of the,

"difference between the loss that would have been incurred had the first receivership of Chilcott & Chatfield been allowed to proceed unimpeded, and the loss actually incurred as it has emerged following the second receivership by those two accountants."

H

In the result judgment was entered in favour of FCC and FCF against Downsview and Mr Russell for $554,566.33. In addition Mr Russell was prohibited under sec. 189 of the Companies Act without the leave of the court from being a director or promoter of or being concerned in or taking part in the management of any company for a period of five years from the date of judgment. Downsview and Mr Russell appealed asserting over 30 grounds.

The Court of Appeal (*Cooke* P, *Richardson* and *Casey* JJ) in the judgment of the court delivered by *Richardson* J on 12 March 1990 accepted that:

A

". . . on the application of negligence principles a receiver and manager who elects to carry on the business of the company and to trade it out of receivership owes a duty of care to subsequent debenture holders to take reasonable care in dealing with the assets of the company."

The Court of Appeal held that Mr Russell was in breach of the duty of care to FCC, that Downsview were not in breach and that the court had no jurisdiction under sec. 189 of the Companies Act to prohibit Mr Russell from being a director or promoter or from being concerned with the management of a company.

B

Mr Russell appealed against the decision of the Court of Appeal against him; FCC and FCF cross-appealed against Mr Russell and Downsview for the reinstatement of the orders made by *Gault* J.

When the appeal and cross-appeal came before the board, it was apparent that the judgments of the courts below raised fundamental questions concerning the nature and extent of any liability by a mortgagee and by a receiver and manager to the mortgagor company or to a subsequent debenture holder for his actions. The statement of claim pleaded that Downsview and Mr Russell were in breach of a duty to exercise their powers for proper purposes, in breach of a duty to act honestly and in good faith and in breach of a duty to exercise reasonable care, skill and diligence. *Gault* J held that:

C

D

"the proposition that a receiver will not be liable in negligence so long as he acts honestly and in good faith no longer represents the law of New Zealand . . . The authorities clearly indicate that on an application of negligence principles, a receiver owes a duty to the debenture holders to take reasonable care in dealing with the assets of the company."

In the Court of Appeal it was accepted by the court without any argument to the contrary by counsel that *Gault* J was correct in his conclusion:

E

"that, if there were any duties on the part of Downsview and Mr Russell as receiver to a subsequent debenture holder, they would have to be based in negligence."

The appellants' case and the respondents' case as presented to the board did not challenge these conclusions. The board however were considerably troubled by the approach of the courts below and on terms gave leave to the respondents to raise the whole question of the foundation and extent of the duties owed by a first debenture holder and his receiver and manager to a subsequent debenture holder. An adjournment was granted so that both sides could reconsider the whole question and submit supplemental cases and arguments.

F

The first submission made on behalf of Downsview and Mr Russell is that they owed no duty to FCC because FCC was only a debenture holder and not a mortgagee. This submission is untenable.

G

A mortgage, whether legal or equitable, is security for repayment of a debt. The security may be constituted by a conveyance, assignment or demise or by a charge on any interest in real or personal property. An equitable mortgage is a contract which creates a charge on property but does not pass a legal estate to the creditor. Its operation is that of an executory assurance, which, as between the parties, and so far as equitable rights and remedies are concerned, is equivalent to an actual assurance, and is enforceable under the equitable jurisdiction of the court. All this is well settled law and is to be found in more detail in the textbooks on the subject and also in *Halsbury's Laws of England* (4th ed.), vol. 32, para. 401 et seq. The security for a debt incurred by a company may take the form of a fixed charge on property or the form of a floating charge which

H

A   becomes a fixed charge on the assets comprised in the security when the debt becomes due and payable. A security issued by a company is called a debenture but for present purposes there is no material difference between a mortgage, a charge and a debenture. Each creates a security for the repayment of a debt.

The second argument put forward on behalf of Mr Russell and Downsview is that though a mortgagee owes certain duties to the mortgagor, he owes no duty to any subsequent encumbrancer; so Downsview and Mr Russell owed no duty to FCC. This
B   argument also is untenable. The owner of property entering into a mortgage does not by entering into that mortgage cease to be the owner of that property any further than is necessary to give effect to the security he has created. The mortgagor can mortgage the property again and again. A second or subsequent mortgage is a complete security on the mortgagor's interests subject only to the rights of prior encumbrancers. If a first mortgagee commits a breach of his duties to the mortgagor, the damage inflicted by that
C   breach of duty will be suffered by the second mortgagee, subsequent encumbrancers and the mortgagor, depending on the extent of the damage and the amount of each security. Thus if a first mortgagee in breach of duty sells property worth £500,000 for £300,000, he is liable at the suit of any subsequent encumbrancer or the mortgagor. Damages of £200,000 will be ordered to be taken into the accounts of the first mortgagee or paid into court or to the second mortgagee who, after satisfying, as far as he can, the amount of any debt outstanding under his mortgage, will pay over any balance remaining
D   to the next encumbrancer or to the mortgagor if there is no subsequent encumbrancer. In practice the encumbrancer who first suffers from the breach of duty by the first mortgagee and needs the damages payable by the first mortgagee to obtain repayment of his own debt will sue the first mortgagee. If the encumbrancers do not suffer because they have been able to obtain repayment of their debts without recourse to the damages, then it will be the mortgagor who will sue. In *Tomlin v Luce* (1889) 43 ChD 191 the Court
E   of Appeal held that the first mortgagees were answerable to the second mortgagees for the loss caused by a misstatement made by the auctioneer appointed by the first mortgagees to sell the property comprised in their security. The court directed that there should be an enquiry as to damages and that the first mortgagees should be allowed in their accounts the amount of their debt less the actual proceeds of sale from the property and the amount of the damages.

F   The next submission on behalf of Mr Russell and Downsview is that, even if a mortgagee owes certain duties to subsequent encumbrancers, a receiver and manager appointed by a mortgagee is not under any such duty where, as in the present case, the receiver and manager is deemed to act as agent for the mortgagor. The fallacy in the argument is the failure to appreciate that, when a receiver and manager exercises the powers of sale and management conferred on him by the mortgage, he is dealing with the security; he is not merely selling or dealing with the interests of the mortgagor. He is
G   exercising the power of selling and dealing with the mortgaged property for the purpose of securing repayment of the debt owing to his mortgagee and must exercise his powers in good faith and for the purpose of obtaining repayment of the debt owing to his mortgagee. The receiver and manager owes these duties to the mortgagor and to all subsequent encumbrancers in whose favour the mortgaged property has been charged.

The next question is the nature and extent of the duties owed by a mortgagee and a
H   receiver and manager respectively to subsequent encumbrancers and the mortgagor.

Several centuries ago equity evolved principles for the enforcement of mortgages and the protection of borrowers. The most basic principles were, first, that a mortgage is security for the repayment of a debt and, secondly, that a security for repayment of a debt is only a mortgage. From these principles flowed two rules, first, that powers conferred on a mortgagee must be exercised in good faith for the purpose of obtaining

repayment and secondly that, subject to the first rule, powers conferred on a mortgagee   A
may be exercised although the consequences may be disadvantageous to the borrower.
These principles and rules apply also to a receiver and manager appointed by the
mortgagee.

It does not follow that a receiver and manager must immediately upon appointment
seize all the cash in the coffers of the company and sell all the company's assets or so
much of the assets as he chooses and considers sufficient to complete the redemption of   B
the mortgage. He is entitled, but not bound, to allow the company's business to be
continued by himself or by the existing or other executives. The decisions of the receiver
and manager whether to continue the business or close down the business and sell assets
chosen by him cannot be impeached if those decisions are taken in good faith while
protecting the interests of the debenture holder in recovering the moneys due under the
debenture, even though the decisions of the receiver and manager may be disadvantageous
for the company.   C

The nature of the duties owed by a receiver and manager appointed by a debenture
holder were authoritatively defined by *Jenkins* LJ in a characteristically learned and
comprehensive judgment in *Re B Johnson & Co (Builders) Ltd* [1955] Ch 634 at
pp. 661–662. The Lord Justice said that:

> ". . . the phrase 'manager of the company,' prima facie, according to the ordinary
> meaning of the words, connotes a person holding, whether de jure or de facto, a   D
> post in or with the company of a nature charging him with the duty of managing
> the affairs of the company for the company's benefit; whereas a receiver and
> manager for debenture holders is a person appointed by the debenture holders to
> whom the company has given powers of management pursuant to the contract of
> loan constituted by the debenture, and, as a condition of obtaining the loan, to
> enable him to preserve and realize the assets comprised in the security for the
> benefit of the debenture holders. The company gets the loan on terms that the   E
> lenders shall be entitled, for the purpose of making their security effective, to
> appoint a receiver with powers of sale and of management pending sale, and with
> full discretion as to the exercise and mode of exercising those powers. The primary
> duty of the receiver is to the debenture holders and not to the company. He is
> receiver and manager of the property of the company for the debenture holders,
> not manager of the company. The company is entitled to any surplus of assets   F
> remaining after the debenture debt has been discharged, and is entitled to proper
> accounts. But the whole purpose of the receiver and manager's appointment
> would obviously be stultified if the company could claim that a receiver and
> manager owes it any duty comparable to the duty owed to a company by its own
> directors or managers.

> In determining whether a receiver and manager for the debenture holders of   G
> a company has broken any duty owed by him to the company, regard must be
> had to the fact that he is a receiver and manager — that is to say, a receiver,
> with ancillary powers of management — for the debenture holders, and not
> simply a person appointed to manage the company's affairs for the benefit of the
> company . . .

> The duties of a receiver and manager for debenture holders are widely different
> from those of a manager of the company. He is under no obligation to carry on the   H
> company's business at the expense of the debenture holders. Therefore he
> commits no breach of duty to the company by refusing to do so, even though his
> discontinuance of the business may be detrimental from the company's point of
> view. Again, his power of sale is, in effect, that of a mortgagee, and he therefore
> commits no breach of duty to the company by a bona fide sale, even though he

A   might have obtained a higher price and even though, from the point of view of the company, as distinct from the debenture holders, the terms might be regarded as disadvantageous.

In a word, in the absence of fraud or mala fides . . . the company cannot complain of any act or omission of the receiver and manager, provided that he does nothing that he is not empowered to do, and omits nothing that he is enjoined to do by the

B   terms of his appointment. If the company conceives that it has any claim against the receiver and manager for breach of some duty owed by him to the company, the issue is not whether the receiver and manager has done or omitted to do anything which it would be wrongful in a manager of a company to do or omit, but whether he has exceeded or abused or wrongfully omitted to use the special powers and discretions vested in him pursuant to the contract of loan constituted by the debenture for the special purpose of enabling the assets comprised in the

C   debenture holders' security to be preserved and realized."

The duties owed by a receiver and manager do not compel him to adopt any particular course of action, by selling the whole or part of the mortgaged property or by carrying on the business of the company or by exercising any other powers and discretions vested in him. But since a mortgage is only security for a debt, a receiver and manager commits a breach of his duty if he abuses his powers by exercising them otherwise than "for the

D   special purpose of enabling the assets comprised in the debenture holders' security to be preserved and realized" for the benefit of the debenture holder. In the present case the evidence of Mr Russell himself and the clear emphatic findings of *Gault* J, which have already been cited, show that Mr Russell accepted appointment and acted as receiver and manager,

"not for the purpose of enforcing the security under the Westpac debenture but

E   for the purpose of preventing the enforcement by the plaintiffs of the FCC debenture."

This and other findings to similar effect establish that, ab initio and throughout his receivership, Mr Russell did not exercise his powers for proper purposes. He was at all times in breach of the duty, which was pleaded against him, to exercise his powers in good faith for proper purposes.

F   *Gault* J rested his judgment not on breach of a duty to act in good faith for proper purposes but on negligence. He said:

". . . on an application of negligence principles, a receiver owes a duty to the debenture holders to take reasonable care in dealing with the assets of the company . . . Downsview's position is merely a specific example of the duty a mortgagee has to subsequent chargeholders to exercise its powers with reasonable care."

G
    Richardson J, delivering the judgment of the Court of Appeal, agreed that duties of care in negligence as defined by *Gault* J were owed by Mr Russell as receiver and manager and by Downsview as first debenture holder to FCC and FCF as second debenture holders. *Richardson* J agreed that Mr Russell was in breach of his duty but, differing from *Gault* J, held that Downsview had committed no breach.

H   The general duty of care said to be owed by a mortgagee to subsequent encumbrancers and the mortgagor in negligence is inconsistent with the right of the mortgagee and the duties which the courts applying equitable principles have imposed on the mortgagee. If a mortgagee enters into possession he is liable to account for rent on the basis of wilful default; he must keep mortgage premises in repair; he is liable for waste. Those duties were imposed to ensure that a mortgagee is diligent in discharging his mortgage and returning the property to the mortgagor. If a mortgagee exercises his power of sale in

good faith for the purpose of protecting his security, he is not liable to the mortgagor
even though he might have obtained a higher price and even though the terms might be
regarded as disadvantageous to the mortgagor. *Cuckmere Brick Co Ltd v Mutual
Finance Ltd* [1971] Ch 949 is Court of Appeal authority for the proposition that, if the
mortgagee decides to sell, he must take reasonable care to obtain a proper price but is
no authority for any wider proposition. A receiver exercising his power of sale also owes
the same specific duties as the mortgagee. But that apart, the general duty of a receiver
and manager appointed by a debenture holder, as defined by *Jenkins* LJ in *Re B Johnson
& Co (Builders) Ltd* [1955] Ch 634 at pp. 661–662, leaves no room for the imposition of
a general duty to use reasonable care in dealing with the assets of the company. The
duties imposed by equity on a mortgagee and on a receiver and manager would be quite
unnecessary if there existed a general duty in negligence to take reasonable care in the
exercise of powers and to take reasonable care in dealing with the assets of the mortgagor
company.

Richardson J appreciated the contradictions and inconsistencies between the duties
of a receiver and manager as set forth by *Jenkins* LJ based on historical equitable
principles and the suggested additional or alternative duty of care based on negligence.
Richardson J said:

> "The existence, nature and extent of the receiver's duty of care must be measured
> in relation to the primary objective of the receivership which is to enforce the
> security by recouping the moneys which it secures from the income or assets of the
> company subject to the security, and for that purpose by exercising incidental
> powers of management, and when recoupment is complete to hand the remaining
> property back to the control of the company."

Their Lordships consider that it is not possible to measure a duty of care in relation to
a primary objective which is quite inconsistent with that duty of care.

There is a great difference between managing a company for the benefit of a debenture
holder and managing a company for the benefit of shareholders. If the debenture holder
is dissatisfied with the policy or performance of his appointed receiver and manager, the
appointment can be revoked. A dissatisfied second debenture holder may require the
prior debenture to be assigned to him or may put the company into liquidation. A
dissatisfied company may raise the money to pay off a debenture holder or put the
company into liquidation. But if a receiver and manager decides at his discretion to
manage and is allowed to manage and does manage in good faith with the object of
preserving and realising the assets for the benefit of the debenture holder, he is subject
to no further or greater liability.

In the UK the possible harsh consequences to a company of a receivership may be
averted by an administration order under the *Insolvency Act* 1986. Such an order may
be made if the company is or is likely to become insolvent and if the order will be likely
to achieve, inter alia, the survival of the company or any part of its undertaking as a
going concern. A petition for an administration order may be presented by the company
or the directors or by a creditor. The order appoints an administrator to manage the
affairs of the company with powers of sale and automatically prevents a receiver from
acting and prevents a creditor from enforcing any security without the consent of the
administrator or the leave of the court. The administrator may be removed if the
company's affairs are managed by him "in a way which is unfairly prejudicial to the
interests" of the company's creditors or members. Similar legislation is in force in the
US. In the absence of any such legislation, the only limitations on the exercise of power
by a receiver and manager are the requirements to act in good faith for the purpose of
preserving and realising the assets for the benefit of the debenture holder.

A   The House of Lords has warned against the danger of extending the ambit of negligence so as to supplant or supplement other torts, contractual obligations, statutory duties or equitable rules in relation to every kind of damage including economic loss; see *CBS Songs Ltd v Amstrad Consumer Electronics plc* [1988] AC 1013 at p. 1059, *Caparo Industries plc v Dickman* [1990] BCC 164 and *Murphy v Brentwood District Council* [1991] 1 AC 398. If the defined equitable duties attaching to mortgagees and to receivers and managers appointed by debenture holders are replaced or supplemented

B   by a liability in negligence the result will be confusion and injustice. A receiver and manager liable in negligence will be tempted to sell assets as speedily as possible for the purpose of repaying the mortgage debt, a decision which, whether negligent or not, does not expose him to a suit for damages but may be disadvantageous to the company. A receiver who is brave enough to manage will run the risk of being sued if the financial position of the company deteriorates, whether that deterioration be due to imperfect knowledge or bad advice or insufficient time or other circumstances. There will always

C   be expert witnesses ready to testify with the benefit of hindsight that they would have acted differently and fared better.

A receiver and manager is appointed when the mortgagor company is in financial difficulties. He may know nothing of the trade carried on by the mortgagor company and nothing about the individual affairs of the company. He is dependent on information furnished by the directors and managers who must bear some responsibility for the

D   financial difficulties of the company. *Richardson* J in the present case, in discussing the ambit of sec. 189 of the Companies Act, said:

> "There is a further justification for maintaining that clear distinction between the acts of the manager of the company and the acts of the receiver and manager of its property. The company has vicarious responsibility for the acts of the manager and in the exercise of those functions as manager the manager is not personally

E   liable to other parties except for misfeasance. In contrast the receiver is personally liable on any contract entered into by him in the performance of his functions, except in so far as the contract otherwise provides (sec. 345(2)). In policy terms it may be considered entirely appropriate to confine the external sanction under sec. 189(1)(c) to officers of the company, leaving errant receivers and managers to their personal liability in respect of contracts, and recognising too that in the

F   ordinary course poorly performing receivers are not likely to be given further assignments by debenture holders of other companies."

Similar considerations apply to Downsview. A mortgagee owes a general duty to subsequent encumbrancers and to the mortgagor to use his powers for the sole purpose of securing repayment of the moneys owing under his mortgage and a duty to act in good faith. He also owes the specific duties which equity has imposed on him in the exercise of his powers to go into possession and his powers of sale. It may well be that a mortgagee

G   who appoints a receiver and manager, knowing that the receiver and manager intends to exercise his powers for the purpose of frustrating the activities of the second mortgagee or for some other improper purpose or who fails to revoke the appointment of a receiver and manager when the mortgagee knows that the receiver and manager is abusing his powers, may himself be guilty of bad faith but in the present case this possibility need not be explored.

H   The liability of Mr Russell in the present case is firmly based not on negligence but on the breach of duty. There was overwhelming evidence that the receivership of Mr Russell was inspired by him for improper purposes and carried on in bad faith, ultimately verging on fraud. The liability of Downsview does not arise under negligence but as a result of Downsview's breach of duty in failing to transfer the Westpac debenture to FCC at the end of March 1987. It is well settled that the mortgagor and all persons

having any interest in the property subject to the mortgage or liable to pay the mortgage
debt can redeem. It is now conceded that FCC were entitled to require Downsview to
assign the Westpac debenture to FCC on payment of all moneys due to Downsview
under the Westpac debenture. On 27 March 1987 FCC offered to purchase the Westpac
debenture and to pay Downsview all that was owing to them. It was faintly argued that
Downsview were entitled to refuse the offer because at a later stage they reasonably
believed, so it was said, albeit wrongly, that the FCC debenture was void for non-
registration. There is nothing in this point. The reason given by Mr Russell on behalf of
Downsview for the refusal of Downsview to assign the Westpac debenture to FCC as a
subsequent charge holder was that,

> "we do not know of any right of assignment which subsequent charge holders
> have in respect of an earlier charge."

Mr Russell is now older and Downsview are now wiser.

Downsview were from the end of March 1987 in breach of their duty to assign the
Westpac debenture to FCC. If that debenture had been assigned, Mr Russell would have
ceased to be the receiver and manager and none of the avoidable losses caused by
Mr Russell would have been sustained.

Gault J decided that the damages payable by Mr Russell and Downsview were:

> "the difference between the loss that would have been incurred had the first
> receivership of Chilcott & Chatfield been allowed to proceed unimpeded, and the
> loss actually incurred as it has emerged following the second receivership by those
> two accountants."

Gault J found that Mr Russell accepted appointment as a receiver and manager for an
improper purpose, namely the purpose of disrupting the receivership under the FCC
debenture and for the purpose of preventing the enforcement of the FCC debenture.
He was therefore in breach of his duty from 23 March 1987 onwards. The measure of
damages decided by *Gault* J applies to this breach of duty just as it would have applied if
Mr Russell had been liable in negligence. The breach of duty of Downsview in refusing
to assign the Westpac debenture following the letter dated 27 March 1987 can be dated
from the end of March. There was no difference in the position of the company between
23 March 1987 when Mr Russell was appointed receiver and manager and the date when
Downsview received the letter dated 27 March and should have agreed to assign the
Westpac debenture and withdraw Mr Russell. Accordingly Downsview, by committing
a breach of duty in not accepting the offer of FCC to take an assignment of the Westpac
debenture, are liable with Mr Russell for the difference between the loss that would
have been incurred, had the first receivership of Chilcott & Chatfield been allowed to
proceed unimpeded, and the loss actually incurred as it emerged following the second
receivership by those two accountants. FCC accepted that if the first receivership
had continued it would not have been possible to get in all the assets of the company
until 31 August 1987. *Gault* J after hearing expert evidence, concluded that 31 August
1987 was "the date by which substantially all funds available from the disposal of assets
would have been paid over to FCC, the debenture holder". *Gault* J also found that
$898,461 was the amount that would have been recovered by the FCC debenture holder
at 31 August 1987. After making adjustments for interest, the amounts received by FCC
and other matters not in dispute, judgment was entered for $554,566.33.

The Court of Appeal held that *Gault* J lacked jurisdiction under sec. 189 to prohibit
Mr Russell from acting as a director or promoter or being concerned in the management
of the company. Their Lordships agree for the reasons given by *Richardson* J.

In the result their Lordships are of the opinion that the appeal ought to be dismissed
and the cross-appeal allowed and that the orders made by *Gault* J against Mr Russell

A and Downsview should be restored, save that the order against Mr Russell under sec. 189 of the Companies Act should be quashed. The costs of FCC and FCF in the courts below and the costs of the appeal and cross-appeal before the board should be paid by Mr Russell and Downsview subject to the conditions imposed by the board and accepted by FCC and FCF when, on 17 June 1992, the board granted leave for arguments to be advanced which had not been raised before the Court of Appeal. Those conditions were set forth in a letter dated 18 June 1992 addressed to the parties by the registrar of

B the judicial committee.

(*Order accordingly*)

_____

Re S H & Co (Realisations) 1990 Ltd.
Ellis & Anor v Nyckeln Finance Co Ltd.

A

Chancery Division (Companies Court).
Mummery J.
Judgment delivered 16 October 1992.

Financial assistance for acquisition of own shares — Private companies — B
Statutory declaration by directors — Whether directors' statutory declaration
contained sufficient particulars of form and principal terms of assistance —
Companies Act 1985, sec. 151, 155, 156.

This was an application by the receivers of S H & Co (Realisations) 1990 Ltd ("the
company") for directions whether a debenture granted by the company was void because
of a failure to comply with the prescribed procedures relating to the provision of financial C
assistance by the company for the acquisition of its shares.

The financial assistance was given in the context of a management buy-out of the
company in September 1989. A company, Rolelock Ltd, was formed and used as a vehicle
for the acquisition by the company's existing management of all the issued shares in the
company for £9.75m. As part of the buy-out, Nyckeln Finance Co Ltd provided financial
assistance to Rolelock in the sum of £8.25m for the acquisition of the shares in the D
company pursuant to the terms of a loan agreement, and the company executed a
guarantee and debenture in favour of Nyckeln.

The receivers (in the interests of the company's unsecured creditors) sought directions
whether the statutory declaration by the directors of the company pursuant to sec. 155(6)
of the Companies Act 1985 sufficiently contained the particulars required by sec. 156 of
the financial assistance to be given by the company. Although the declaration mentioned E
the Nyckeln debenture, there was no statement of the property charged, or the kind of
charge granted (i.e. fixed or floating), or the fact that a guarantee was given by the
company to Nyckeln in addition. Since "debenture" had no precise meaning, the
declaration failed to give the particulars prescribed by form 155(6)a of the form the
assistance would take and the principal terms on which it would be given.

Held, making an order in terms of the receivers' originating summons: F

The matters omitted from the particulars about the identity of the property charged,
the kind of charge granted, and the guarantee, did not prevent the particulars in fact
contained in the declaration from being reasonably and fairly described as particulars of
the form and principal terms of the financial assistance.

The following cases were referred to in the judgment:
G
De Courcy v Clement & Anor [1971] 1 Ch 693.
Knightsbridge Estates Trust Ltd v Byrne & Ors [1940] AC 613.
Pearl Assurance Co Ltd v West Midlands Gas Board [1950] 2 All ER 844.
Precision Dippings Ltd v Precision Dippings Marketing Ltd & Ors (1985) 1 BCC
99,539; [1986] Ch 447.
Royal Bank of Canada v IR Commrs [1972] Ch 665.
Yolland, Husson & Birkett Ltd, Re [1908] Ch 152. H

Mary Arden QC and Andrew Thompson (instructed by Edwards Geldard, Cardiff)
for the receivers.

Michael Crystal QC and Richard Sheldon (instructed by Wilde Sapte) for Nyckeln
Finance Co Ltd.

A

JUDGMENT

Mummery J: Introduction

This case is concerned with the construction and application of the provisions in Pt. V, Ch. VI of the *Companies Act* 1985 which prescribe the procedure to be followed by a private company wishing to take advantage of the relaxation of the general prohibition of financial assistance by a company for the acquisition of its own shares.

B

The application before the court is made under sec. 35 of the *Insolvency Act* 1986 which entitles receivers appointed out of court to apply to the court for directions in relation to any particular matter arising in connection with the performance of their functions. On such an application the court may give such directions, or may make such order, declaring the rights of persons before the court or otherwise, as it thinks just.

The applicants, Mr Robert Ellis and Mr Stuart Lindsay, both partners in Touche Ross and licensed insolvency practitioners, are joint administrative receivers of S H & Co (Realisations) 1990 Ltd (formerly called Shephard Hill & Co Ltd), which I shall refer to as "the company". They were appointed joint administrative receivers of the assets and undertaking of the company first on 27 November 1990 by Barclays Bank plc pursuant to the terms of debentures granted by the company to the bank on 26 September 1989 and on 31 July 1990. Secondly, they were appointed on 28 November 1990 by the respondent Nyckeln Finance Co Ltd ("Nyckeln") under a group guarantee and debenture ("the Nyckeln debenture") also granted by the company on 26 September 1989. The appointment of receivers by Nyckeln followed the making of a demand by Nyckeln on the company on 26 November 1990 for repayment of £5,228,500. The demand was not satisfied.

C

D

The receivers have realised the assets of the company. They have made arrangements for the discharge of the company's liability to Barclays Bank and have made provision for the costs and expenses of the receivership. A substantial surplus remains in the receivers' hands. Their question for the court is whether that surplus should be applied in discharge of the liability of the company to Nyckeln. The doubts in their minds about payment to Nyckeln rests on the possibility that the Nyckeln debenture was granted in circumstances in which there was a failure to comply with the prescribed procedures relating to the provision of financial assistance by the company for the acquisition of its shares.

E

F

It is common ground that, if there was a failure to comply with the formalities prescribed in sec. 155 and 156 of the *Companies Act* 1985,

(1)   there has been a breach of the general prohibition in sec. 151 on financial assistance by the company for the acquisition of its own shares; and

(2)   the consequence of that breach is that the Nyckeln debenture is void, both as to the security thereby granted and as to the liability to make payment under the covenant.

G

The specific question for decision is framed in the following terms in para. 1 of the application dated 14 May 1992:

"(1) Whether the statutory declaration made on 26 September 1990 by the directors of the company pursuant or purportedly pursuant to sec. 155(6) of the *Companies Act* 1985 sufficiently contained the prescribed particulars referred to in sec. 156 of the *Companies Act* 1985 of financial assistance proposed to be given by the company for the purpose of the proposed acquisition by Rolelock Ltd ('Rolelock') of the whole of the issued share capital of the company."

H

The answer to this question depends, first, on the contents of the statutory declaration, viewed in the circumstances in which it was made; secondly, on the construction of the

statutory provision which prescribes the form of the statutory declaration; and, thirdly,   A
on the application of those provisions of the statutory declaration itself. The decision on
that question will also resolve similar questions arising in connection with two wholly
owned subsidiaries of the company referred to later.

The rival arguments have been deployed with exceptional skill and lucidity by Miss
Mary Arden QC, who submitted that the statutory declaration did not contain the
prescribed particulars, and Mr Michael Crystal QC, who submitted on behalf of Nyckeln   B
(now in administration) that the statutory declaration did contain the prescribed
particulars.

I should explain that Miss Arden, as well as appearing for the applicant receivers of
the company, who were appointed by the secured creditors and who have no financial
interest in the outcome of the application, performed the necessary and invaluable
function of advancing to the court all possible arguments in the interests of the unsecured
creditors of the company. The applicants had, via the creditors' committee of the   C
company, invited those unsecured creditors, who wished to do so, to apply to be joined
in the application. No creditor accepted the invitation.

The factual background

The statutory declaration of 26 September 1989 was made in the context of a
management buy-out of the company in September 1989. The company had two wholly   D
owned subsidiaries: SH Realisations (1990) Ltd (formerly Shephard Hill Ltd) ("SH")
and Shephard Hill Mining Ltd (formerly Coal Trading Co (Opencast) Ltd) ("Mining").
Rolelock was formed and used as a vehicle for the acquisition by the existing management
of the company of all the issued shares in the company for £9.75m. As a result of the
buy-out, the company became a wholly owned subsidiary of Rolelock.

Finance came from two sources. Barclays Bank provided a short term facility of £1.5m   E
to the company for working capital. This was later increased to £2.5m and further
secured. Nyckeln provided financial assistance to Rolelock in the sum of £8.25m for the
acquisition of the shares in the company.

The Nyckeln facility was provided pursuant to the terms of a loan agreement made
between Rolelock and Nyckeln on 26 September 1989.

Only two provisions of the loan agreement are relevant: F

(1)   By cl. 5.02 it was a condition precedent to the obligation of Nyckeln to make an
         advance to Rolelock that Rolelock should have executed a debenture and a shares
         mortgage in favour of Nyckeln over the shares it acquired or was to acquire in the
         company;

(2)   By cl. 7(f) Rolelock undertook to,

         "procure, following completion of the acquisition of [the company], that [the   G
         company] and each subsidiary will comply with the procedures set out in sec. 155–
         158 of the *Companies Act* 1985 in respect of the financial assistance for the
         acquisition of the shares and all other legal requirements and that [the company]
         and each group subsidiary executes a group guarantee and debenture in the form
         set out in appendix E and [the company] executes the company's share mortgage
         and procures the registration of [Nyckeln's] nominees as shareholders as soon as
         legally permissible thereafter."   H

On 26 September 1989 further documents were executed; the Nyckeln debenture, a
company's share mortgage between the company, Nyckeln and Mining; two group
guarantees and debentures, one by SH in favour of Nyckeln, the other by Mining in
favour of Nyckeln; and, finally, a priority agreement made between Nyckeln, Barclays
Bank and the company, which was supplemented by a later deed dated 19 September

A   1990. The group guarantees and debentures and the share mortgages were all registered at Companies House on 10 October 1989 (the day after the registration of the bank's debenture) pursuant to sec. 395 of the *Companies Act* 1985.

For present purposes it is only necessary to refer to three of the terms of the Nyckeln debenture.

(1)   Clause 2.01 contained a covenant for repayment.

B
"The company hereby covenants duly and punctually to pay and discharge the secured liabilities as and when the same shall become due, owing or payable and whether at maturity, upon acceleration or otherwise."

"Secured liabilities" were defined as meaning all the liabilities of Rolelock under the loan agreement and the security documents to which it is a party and of the company or in respect of this debenture (whether in respect of principal, interest,
C   fees, taxes, costs expenses or indemnities).

(2)   Clause 2.02 was a charging clause by which the company, as beneficial owner, and as security for the payment when due of the secured liabilities mortgaged, charged and assigned and agreed to assign in favour of Nyckeln,

     (a) by way of first legal charge, all its estate and interest in all freehold and leasehold property;

D
     (b) by way of first fixed charge all its estate or interest in freehold or leasehold property hereafter acquired or belonging to the company, all plant and machinery now or in the future owned by the company and all present and future uncalled capital and goodwill of the company;

     (c) by way of first priority assignment the benefit of the contracts of the company specified in appendix B;

E
     (d) by way of first floating charge all the undertaking, property, assets and rights of the company, including specified items such as book debts, shares, insurance policies, contracts and so on.

(3)   Clause 5.01 contained a guarantee by the company in consideration of Nyckeln entering into the loan agreement with Rolelock and of making or maintaining loans available to Rolelock thereunder. The company guaranteed to Nyckeln
F   payment on the due date of all sums payable now or in the future to Nyckeln by Rolelock under the loan agreement or in connection therewith. The company also undertook with Nyckeln that, and whenever Rolelock should be in default in the payment of any sums whatsoever under or in connection with the loan agreement, the company would pay such sums on demand.

The statutory declaration

G
At a meeting of directors of the company on 26 September 1989 the directors made a statutory declaration which was filed at Companies House on 6 October 1989, along with the auditors' report and special resolution. The declaration was available at the meeting held to pass the special resolution approving the giving of financial assistance.

As the question for decision on this application depends on whether the contents of the declaration complied with the statutory requirements, it is necessary to examine
H   them in some detail.

The declaration is headed "Companies Form No. 155(6)a — Declaration in relation to assistance for the acquisition of shares".

It is stated to be pursuant to sec. 155(6) of the *Companies Act* 1985 and is addressed to the registrar of companies. The name of the company is given and the names and addresses of the directors are set out.

The directors solemnly and sincerely declare that the company is proposing to give financial assistance in connection with the acquisition of shares in the company and that the assistance is for the purpose of reducing or discharging a liability incurred for the purpose of the acquisition. The number and class of the shares to be acquired is stated to be 212,500 ordinary shares of £1 each. It is stated that the assistance is to be given to Rolelock Ltd, the person who has acquired the shares. Rolelock's address is given.

There are two boxes which have been completed. The first box is headed "The assistance will take the form of:". The second box is headed "The principal terms on which the assistance will be given are:".

It is submitted on behalf of the unsecured creditors of the company that the information given in the first entry of each of the two boxes is inadequate.

In the first box the form of financial assistance is stated to be:

"(i) the granting of a group debenture in favour of Nyckeln Finance Co Ltd."

There are references in para. (ii) and (iii) of the box to the shares mortgage and the priority agreement. No criticism is made of the adequacy of those particulars.

In the second box of principal terms on which assistance will be given it is stated:

"1. In terms of the said group debenture:

that the company

   (i) covenants to pay Nyckeln Finance Co Ltd ('Nyckeln') all liabilities of itself to Nyckeln, and all liabilities of Rolelock to Nyckeln under a loan agreement whereby Nyckeln agreed to make available a loan facility to Rolelock Ltd for the purpose of acquiring the whole issued share capital of the company and

   (ii) in security for such covenants, grants a debenture in favour of Nyckeln."

There are references in para. 2 and 3 to the principal terms of the shares mortgage and the priority agreement. No criticism is made of the adequacy of those particulars.

The directors conclude the statutory declaration by stating:

"We have formed the opinion, as regards the company's initial situation immediately following the date on which assistance is proposed to be given, that there will be no ground on which it could be then found to be unable to pay its debts.

We have formed the opinion that the company will be able to pay its debts as. they fall due during the year immediately following that date."

An auditor's report, as required by the statutory provisions, is annexed to the declarations and is to the effect that the auditors had enquired into the affairs of the company and are not aware of anything to indicate that the opinion of the directors as to the company's immediate and medium term solvency is unreasonable.

No point arises on the form, contents or adequacy of the auditors' report.

Part V, Ch. VI of the Companies Act 1985

Against that factual background, it is now necessary to consider the relevant statutory provisions. They are as follows:

(1) There is a general prohibition on the provision of financial assistance by a company or any of its subsidiaries for the purpose of an acquisition of its own shares. The prohibition applies to both public and private companies. It is in these terms:

"151(1) Subject to the following provisions of this Chapter, where a person is acquiring or is proposing to acquire shares in a company, it is not lawful for the

A   company or any of its subsidiaries to give financial assistance directly or indirectly for the purpose of that acquisition before or at the same time as the acquisition takes place.

(2) Subject to those provisions, where a person has acquired shares in a company and any liability has been incurred (by that or any other person) for the purpose of that acquisition, it is not lawful for the company or any of its subsidiaries to give

B   financial assistance directly or indirectly for the purpose of reducing or discharging the liability so incurred."

Contravention of the prohibition in that section by a company not only renders the security unenforceable, it also renders the company liable to a fine. It renders every officer of it who is in default liable to imprisonment or a fine, or both. The maximum term of imprisonment on indictment is two years: sec. 730 and Sch. 24.

C   (2) "Financial assistance" is defined in sec. 152(a). The relevant definitions state:

"(ii) financial assistance given by way of guarantee, security or indemnity, other than an indemnity in respect of the indemnifier's own neglect or default, or by way of release or waiver. . .

(iv) any other financial assistance given by a company the net assets of which are thereby reduced to a material extent or which has no net assets . . .''

D   There follows a definition of the expression "distributable profits" in relation to the giving of any financial assistance.

It is common ground that financial assistance in this sense was provided by the company for the acquisition of its own shares.

(3) The provisions of sec. 151 are relaxed in the case of private companies in a group of sections, sec. 155–158, subject to compliance with procedures prescribed for the

E   protection of creditors and minority shareholders of the company. Section 155(1) provides:

"Section 151 does not prohibit a private company from giving financial assistance in a case where the acquisition of shares in question is or was an acquisition of shares in the company or, if it is a subsidiary of another private company, in that other company if the following provisions of this section, and sections 156 to 158,

F   are complied with as respects the giving of that assistance."

(4) The relevant features of the scheme of relaxation for present purposes include the making of a statutory declaration of solvency in the prescribed form by the directors of the company proposing to give the financial assistance. Section 155(6) provides:

"The directors of the company proposing to give the financial assistance and, where the shares acquired or to be acquired are shares in its holding company, the

G   directors of that company and of any other company which is both the company's holding company and a subsidiary of that other holding company shall before the financial assistance is given make a statutory declaration in the prescribed form complying with the section next following."

(5) Section 156 contains the provisions relevant to the statutory declaration under sec. 155.

H   Section 156(1) is the crucial provision. It is necessary to read the whole section in order to see its context.

"(1) A statutory declaration made by a company's directors under sec. 155(6) shall contain such particulars of the financial assistance to be given, and of the business of the company of which they are directors, as may be prescribed and shall identify the person to whom the assistance is to be given.

(2) The declaration shall state that the directors have formed the opinion, as   A
regards the company's initial situation immediately following the date on which
the assistance is proposed to be given, that there will be no ground on which it
could then be found to be unable to pay its debts; and either—

    (a) if it is intended to commence the winding up of the company within 12
months of that date, that the company will be able to pay its debts in full
within 12 months of the commencement of the winding up, or   B

    (b) in any other case, that the company will be able to pay its debts as they fall
due during the year immediately following that date.

(3) In forming their opinion for the purposes of subsection (2), the directors shall
take into account the same liabilities (including contingent and prospective
liabilities) as would be relevant under sec. 122 of the Insolvency Act (winding up
by the court) to the question whether the company is unable to pay its debts.   C

(4) The directors' statutory declaration shall have annexed to it a report addressed
to them by their company's auditors stating that—

    (a) they have enquired into the state of affairs of the company, and

    (b) they are not aware of anything to indicate that the opinion expressed
by the directors in the declaration as to any of the matters mentioned in
subsection (2) of this section is unreasonable in all the circumstances.   D

(5) The statutory declaration and auditors' report shall be delivered to the
registrar of companies—

    (a) together with a copy of any special resolution passed by the company under
section 155 and delivered to the registrar in compliance with section 380, or

    (b) where no such resolution is required to be passed, within 15 days after the   E
making of the declaration.

(6) If a company fails to comply with subsection (5), the company and every
officer of it who is in default is liable to a fine and, for continued contravention, to
a daily default fine.

(7) A director of a company who makes a statutory declaration under section 155
without having reasonable grounds for the opinion expressed in it is liable to   F
imprisonment or a fine, or both."

(6) A form has been prescribed by the *Companies (Forms) Regulations* 1985
(SI 1985/854), reg. 4(1), Sch. 3 and Pt. II of Sch. 4. The particulars contained in the form
are the particulars prescribed for the purposes of the provisions of sec. 155(6) and
sec. 156(1) of the 1985 Act, as referred to in those forms. The relevant form is 155(6)a
with such variations as circumstances require.   G

The issue on this application is whether the statutory declaration made by the directors
contains the prescribed particulars of the financial assistance to be given. There is no
dispute on certain points.

It is agreed that non-compliance with the statutory requirements is not a mere
procedural irregularity capable of being waived or dispensed with and validated by
unanimous agreement of all members entitled to vote at meetings of the company. See,   H
for example, *Precision Dippings Ltd v Precision Dippings Marketing Ltd & Ors* (1985)
1 BCC 99,539 at p. 99,543 per *Dillon* LJ.

It is also common ground that, if there is non-compliance with sec. 155(6) and
sec. 156(1), the relaxation provisions do not apply and a breach of sec. 151 is committed
with all the consequences of unenforceability and liability to penal sanctions.

Submissions for unsecured creditors

It was submitted on behalf of the unsecured creditors that the statutory declaration was flawed because it did not comply with the statutory requirement that it should contain the prescribed particulars, that is particulars of the form (i.e. essential nature) of the assistance to be provided and particulars of the principal terms on which the assistance would be given. The particulars should have identified those aspects of the transaction which constitute the essential form and principal terms of the financial assistance. Neither box in the completed form contained a statement of

(1)   the property charged; or

(2)   the kind of charge granted (i.e. fixed or floating); or

(3)   the fact that a guarantee was given by the company to Nyckeln in addition to a covenant for payment.

Miss Arden illustrated her arguments on this point by producing a specimen completed form of prescribed particulars for the two boxes showing how it should be done. The first box of her draft refers not just to the grant of the debenture, but also to the agreement to pay, guarantee and the grant of fixed and floating charges over its assets. The specimen box of principal terms contains similar information as to the creation of various charges over various items of property and assets.

It was submitted that the reference to the grant of a "debenture" in favour of Nyckeln in the box for principal terms was insufficient to constitute the necessary particulars. This is because the word "debenture" has no precise meaning beyond referring to a document which either creates or acknowledges a debt. See *Knightsbridge Estates Trust Ltd v Byrne* [1940] AC 613 at pp. 621–622 per Viscount *Maugham*.

Section 744 of the *Companies Act* 1985 defines "debenture" as including "debenture stock, bonds and any other securities of a company, whether constituting a charge on the assets of the company or not". Thus a debenture does not necessarily mean a document which creates a charge, let alone a particular type of charge over any particular type of asset. It is, however, observed in *Gower's Principles of Modern Company Law* (5th ed.) p. 379 that:

"In practice, the absence of a precise definition has given rise to surprisingly few problems and to even fewer reported cases . . ."

—though the editors add that may change in view of the inventiveness of recent developments in banking and commercial circles, although they express the view that there will not be much trouble if the courts display the common sense which they displayed in the *Knightsbridge* case. It is also observed at p. 380 that the normal debenture,

"consists of one of the series of securities ranking *pari passu* with each other. The expression 'debenture' is applied indiscriminately to the instrument creating or evidencing the indebtedness and to the debt itself and the bundle of rights vested in the holder to secure its payment. These rights, as we have seen, may include a charge on all or some of the company's assets . . . When there is a charge, it will probably be a floating charge . . ."

See, for example, *Re Yolland* [1908] Ch 152 at p. 156 and *Pearl Assurance Co Ltd v West Midlands Gas Board* [1950] 2 All ER 844 at p. 845B.

It was also submitted that the use of the word "security" in the box for principal terms did not necessarily mean that a charge had been created by the debenture.

As there were no particulars in the statutory declaration showing the property charged, the kind of charge or the giving of the guarantee, the declaration did not reveal the nature and extent of the financial assistance to be given. A person looking at the

statutory declaration available for inspection at Companies House would not be in a
position to make an assessment of the impact on the company of the financial assistance
given. The fact that a person could find that information elsewhere, such as in the
charges register kept at the company's registry, did not constitute an excuse for failing
to comply with the requirements for the contents of the statutory declaration.

The result is that there has been no compliance with sec. 155(6). The general
prohibition on financial assistance in sec. 151 has been infringed and the security granted
by, and the covenants in, the Nyckeln debenture are unenforceable.

Conclusions

It is of course important that there should be compliance with procedures prescribed
by Parliament for the protection of the interests of those dealing with or concerned in a
company, whether they be creditors or shareholders. It is common ground in this case
that the statutory declaration was completed in good faith by an experienced firm of
solicitors, acting on behalf of the directors, in an honest attempt to ensure compliance
with the statutory requirements. Those facts would not, however, constitute an excuse
for non- compliance. The duty is to comply with the objective requirements, not simply
to use best endeavours to comply with them.

Looking at the general statutory requirements and at the particular statutory declaration
in this case, however, I have reached the conclusion that there has been compliance,
though it is a case close to the line.

In future solicitors responsible for completing such a statutory declaration should err
on the side of caution and include the fuller form of particulars as exemplified by
Miss Arden's specimen forms. Particulars in that form would remove any possible doubt
as to whether there had been compliance. Although the particulars in this case do not
match that standard they are, in my view, sufficient to satisfy the statutory requirements
for the following reasons.

First, I note that the legislation does not in terms state how detailed the particulars
must be. As a matter of ordinary English "particulars" consists of details, items or points
of information: see *Royal Bank of Canada v IR Commrs* [1972] Ch 665 at p. 675F per
Megarry J.

The legislation simply limits the scope of particulars to be contained in the statutory
declaration to,

> "such particulars of the financial assistance to be given, and of the business of the
> company of which they are directors, as may be prescribed and shall identify the
> person to whom the assistance is to be given."

See sec. 156(1) of the *Companies Act* 1985. Form 155(6)a refers to the form of assistance
and to the principal terms on which it will be given.

The question is, therefore, how detailed, how particularised do those particulars have
to be to comply with the prescribed form?

I accept Mr Crystal's submissions that, in answering the question, the court should
have two particular factors in mind.

(1) The principal purpose of requiring a statutory declaration is to ensure that
financial assistance provided by a private company satisfies the criteria in sec. 156(2).

The statutory declaration may at the same time provide information to those who
search the company file at Companies House where the statutory declaration and
auditors' report have been delivered pursuant to sec. 156(5). But it is not the principal
purpose of the statutory declaration to provide, for example, particulars of the property

A   charged or the kind of charges. There is no requirement for registration of the declaration by the registrar. The requirement is simply for delivery of the declaration to the registrar.

(2) The consequences of non-compliance are severe. It is not simply a question of making the security and covenant for payment unenforceable, though those are serious matters in themselves. Penalties are incurred under sec. 156(6) and, more seriously, under sec. 151(3).

B   Read in the light of those factors, I am satisfied that the statute does not require the provision of particulars in as much detail as Miss Arden contends. The statutory declaration, read as a whole, contains information which can fairly and reasonably be described, in ordinary language, as "particulars" of the form of assistance to be provided and of the principal terms on which the assistance will be given. The reader of the declaration is informed that the company is proposing to give financial assistance in connection with the acquisition of shares in it; the assistance is for the purpose of

C   reducing or discharging a liability incurred for the purposes of that acquisition; that the number and class of shares to be acquired is identified; that the assistance is to be provided to Rolelock; that Rolelock was acquiring the shares; that no cash was to be transferred to Rolelock; that the assistance was given on 26 September 1989; that the assistance took the form of a group debenture granted by the company in favour of Nyckeln; that the liability secured by the debenture was the company's covenant to pay

D   its liability to Nyckeln and the liability of Rolelock to Nyckeln under the loan agreement; and that the liability of Rolelock to Nyckeln arose by virtue of the provision of a loan facility by Nyckeln to Rolelock for the purpose of the latter's acquisition of the whole of the company's share capital.

Following an approach similar to that adopted by *Megarry* J, admittedly in a different context, in *De Courcy v Clement* [1971] 1 Ch 693 at pp. 698H–699B, I conclude that the

E   matters omitted from the particulars about the identity of the property charged, the kind of charge granted, and of the guarantee, do not prevent the particulars in fact contained in the declaration from being reasonably and fairly described as particulars of the form and principal terms of financial assistance.

For these reasons, I shall make an order in the terms of para. (1) of the originating summons.

(Order accordingly)

F

G

H

M S Fashions Ltd & Ors v Bank of Credit and Commerce International SA & Anor (No. 2).

A

Chancery Division.
Hoffmann LJ (sitting as an additional judge of the Chancery Division).
Judgment delivered 27 November 1992.

B

> *Liquidation — Set off — Plaintiff companies were indebted to bank in liquidation — Directors guaranteed companies' liabilities as "principal debtor" — Directors placed money on deposit with bank as security — Whether directors could set off deposits against companies' debts — Whether bank could demand full payment from companies — Insolvency Rules 1986 (SI 1986/1925), r. 4.90.*

These were three motions raising a point on the law of set-off in insolvency.

In M S Fashions, S and his brother executed a mortgage deed to secure advances by BCCI to their companies. The brothers, defined together with their companies as "the principal debtor", covenanted to pay on demand in writing all moneys owed by the principal debtor, i.e. each other and their companies. S later gave BCCI additional security by depositing money in an account with BCCI and signing a letter of charge charging the deposit to secure the liabilities of the companies, again as "principal debtor".

C

D

When BCCI was wound up in January 1992, S had about £300,000 in the deposit account with BCCI and his companies owed BCCI about £572,000. S claimed to set off his deposit against what he owed to BCCI under the mortgage and letter of charge, arguing that that would pro tanto extinguish the liability of the companies as well.

BCCI argued that before an account could be taken under r. 4.90 of the Insolvency Rules, S had either to file a proof or a defence to a claim by the liquidator; alternatively that S's liability was contingent upon the making of a demand and none had been made.

E

Held, **declaring that the companies' indebtedness at the date of the winding up had been extinguished or reduced by the amount of the relevant deposit:**

1. It was not right that there could be no set-off until BCCI sued S and he pleaded a set-off by way of defence. If there were existing cross-claims arising out of mutual dealings before the winding up, r. 4.90 took effect.

F

2. Under the instruments which deemed S to be a principal debtor, his liability was not contingent; it was either a joint and several liability with the companies or a several liability for the same debt. That liability could be set off against the liability of BCCI to S on the deposit.

The following cases were referred to in the judgment:

G

Barnett, Ex parte (1874) LR 9 Ch App 293.
Bradford Old Bank Ltd v Sutcliffe [1918] 2 KB 833.
Brown's Estate, Re [1893] 2 Ch 300.
Charge Card Services Ltd, Re (No. 2) (1986) 2 BCC 99,373; [1987] Ch 150.
Daintrey, Re. Ex parte Mant [1900] 1 QB 546.
Debtor, Re a, ex parte Peak Goldfield Ltd [1909] 1 KB 430.
Dynamics Corp of America (in liquidation), Re [1976] 1 WLR 757.
Esso Petroleum Co Ltd v Alstonbridge Properties Ltd & Ors [1975] 1 WLR 1474.

H

Farley v Housing and Commercial Developments Ltd (1984) 1 BCC 99,150.
Middleton v Pollock (1875) LR 20 Eq 515.
New Quebrada Co Ltd v Carr & Ors (1869) LR 4 CP 651.
Northern Counties of England Fire Insurance Co, Re. Macfarlane's Claim (1881) 17 ChD 337.

A
Owen v Wilkinson (1858) 5 CB (NS) 526; 141 ER 213.
Sovereign Life Assurance Co v Dodd [1892] 2 QB 573.
Stephens, Ex parte (1805) 11 Ves Jun 24; 32 ER 996.

Alan Steinfeld QC and Francis Tregear (instructed by Zaiwalla & Co) for the plaintiffs in *M S Fashions*.

Jonathan Sumption QC and Helen Davies (instructed by Slaughter and May) for the
B plaintiffs in *Impexbond* and (instructed by Glanvilles, Portsmouth) for the plaintiffs in *High Street Services*.

Neville Thomas QC and Robin Dicker (instructed by Lovell White Durrant) for BCCI.

JUDGMENT

C
Hoffmann LJ: There are before the court motions under RSC, O. 14A in three actions which raise a common point of principle on the law of set-off in insolvency. A bank advances money to a company. Repayment is guaranteed by a director who has a deposit account with the bank. As between himself and the bank, the director is expressed to be a principal debtor. On the insolvency of the bank, can the director set off his claim for return of his deposit against his liability to pay the company's debt, so that the debt is wholly or pro tanto extinguished? Or can the bank claim the whole debt
D from the company and leave the director to prove in the liquidation for his deposit?

I shall set out briefly the facts of the three cases. In *M S Fashions*, Mr Sarwar and his brother Mr Safdar executed a mortgage deed dated 30 May 1984 to secure advances by BCCI to their companies, M S Fashions Ltd and M S Fashions (Wholesale) Ltd. The main purpose of this document was to give BCCI a mortgage over a property which the brothers owned in Leeds. But it also contained a general covenant by which the brothers (defined, together with their companies, as "the principal debtor") covenanted to pay
E on demand in writing all moneys owed by all the persons defined as "the principal debtor", that is to say, each other and their companies.

On 9 December 1985 Mr Sarwar gave BCCI additional security. He deposited money in an account with BCCI and signed a letter of charge by which he charged the deposit to secure the liabilities of the companies. He agreed that the bank could at any time without notice apply the deposit towards satisfaction of the companies' indebtedness and that
F "the liabilities hereunder shall be as that of principal debtor". In addition, he signed two unlimited guarantees of the companies' liabilities in BCCI's standard form. These were expressed to be additional to any other security the bank might have.

In *High Street Services*, Mr Raees Ahmed on 24 April 1989 executed three separate documents each headed "Cash Deposit Security Terms — Third Party". Each was to provide security for advances to one of his companies: High Street Services Ltd, Portmaid Fashions Ltd and Cira Ltd. They were standard forms which contained both a
G guarantee of the company's liabilities and also "as a separate and independent obligation" a covenant that on demand in writing, the companies' liabilities would be recoverable from Mr Ahmed as principal debtor. It also gave BCCI a charge and other rights in respect of a deposit account in Mr Ahmed's name. In addition, Mr Ahmed signed separate guarantees of the liabilities of each company in BCCI's standard form.

In *Impexbond*, Mr Nasir Amir on 11 March 1985 deposited money with BCCI and
H executed a charge over the deposit to secure the liabilities of his company Impexbond Ltd. The document was similar to the letter of charge in *M S Fashions* and provided that "the liabilities hereunder shall be as that of principal debtor". On 29 May 1986 Mr Amir executed a charge in similar form over the same and another deposit account to secure the liabilities of Tucan Investments plc. He also executed standard form guarantees of the liabilities of both companies.

Thus a common feature of all three cases appears to be that the director signed a   A
document saying that his liability to pay the company's debts was to be as that of a
principal debtor. Mr Neville Thomas QC, who appeared for BCCI, questioned whether
this was entirely true. In *M S Fashions* he said that including Mr Sarwar and his brother
in the definition of the "principal debtor" was strange and possibly a mistake. But the
bank seems to have wanted to pile up as many cumulative rights as possible against the
directors and I cannot say that as a matter of construction it would make no sense to give
effect to the definition. There is no claim for rectification and I doubt whether it would   B
be possible to show the necessary contrary intent on the part of both parties. Mr Thomas
also said that the reference to liability being as that of principal debtor in the *M S
Fashions* and *Impexbond* letters of charge was odd because the letters did not expressly
create any liability. They merely constituted a charge over the deposit in favour of
BCCI. On the other hand, I think it is a tenable view that such charges over deposits can
be analysed as the creation of a liability on the part of the chargor for the company's   C
debt, not exceeding the amount of the deposit, which can be set off against BCCI's
liability to repay the deposit. It seems to me that the reference to the liability of the
depositor as being that of a principal debtor should, as a matter of construction, be taken
as having this effect. Whether or not this is the only way in which it can take effect (see
Re Charge Card Services Ltd (No. 2) (1986) 2 BCC 99,373 at p. 99,391) I think that the
principal debtor clause enables it to do so.
                                                                                              D
BCCI was compulsorily wound up on 14 January 1992. At that date, the state of
accounts between the parties in the three cases was as follows. In *M S Fashions*,
Mr Sarwar had about £300,000 in the deposit account with BCCI and his companies
owed it about £572,000. Mr Sarwar claims to set off his deposit against what he owes
BCCI under the mortgage deed and letter of charge and says that this will *pro tanto*
extinguish the liability of the companies as well. In *High Street Services*, Mr Ahmed had   E
about £426,000 on deposit and the companies owed BCCI over £1m. Mr Ahmed claims
to be able to set off BCCI's liability on the deposit against his liability in respect of the
companies' debts. In *Impexbond*, the companies owed BCCI about £3.3m and Mr Amir
had about £4.5m on deposit. He claims to be able to set part of this sum against his
liability to pay the companies' debts and to prove in the liquidation of BCCI for the rest.

The *M S Fashions* litigation was precipitated by BCCI (through its liquidators)   F
appointing administrative receivers of both M S Fashions companies on 20 May 1992.
On the following day the companies applied to *Millett* J for leave to bring proceedings
against BCCI and an order restraining the administrative receivers from acting. On the
following day *Millett* J refused relief on the ground that the claim to set-off was not
arguable. On the same day the Court of Appeal (*Woolf* and *Scott* L JJ) expressed a
provisional contrary view and gave leave to commence originating summons proceedings
against BCCI claiming a declaration that the companies' indebtedness had been partially   G
extinguished by the set-off of Mr Sarwar's deposit (see [1992] BCC 571). But the Court
of Appeal refused injunctive relief on the grounds that even after set-off, the companies
would still owe BCCI about £300,000. On 28 July 1992 Mr Sarwar paid the balance of
the indebtedness and costs and the administrative receivers were discharged by consent.
The set-off issue comes before the court on a motion to determine an issue of law under
RSC, O. 14A. Similar motions are brought in *High Street Services* and *Impexbond*.
                                                                                              H
Insolvency set-off has been a creature of statute since the time of Queen Anne (4 & 5
Anne, c. 17, sec. 11). The current provision applicable to companies is r. 4.90 of the
Insolvency Rules 1986:

> "(1) This Rule applies where, before the company goes into liquidation there
> have been mutual credits, mutual debts or other mutual dealings between the

A
company and any creditor of the company proving or claiming to prove for a debt in the liquidation.

(2) An account shall be taken of what is due from each party to the other in respect of the mutual dealings, and the sums due from one party shall be set off against the sums due from the other.

. . .

B
(4) Only the balance (if any) of the account is provable in the liquidation. Alternatively (as the case may be) the amount shall be paid to the liquidator as part of the assets."

This language is substantially the same as that used in earlier bankruptcy statutes going back to the *Bankruptcy Act* 1869. Between the *Judicature Act* 1875 and the *Insolvency Rules* 1986, the bankruptcy rule was also applied in company liquidations.

C
Certain principles as to the application of these provisions have been established by the cases. First, the rule is mandatory ("the mandatory principle"). If there have been mutual dealings before the winding-up order which have given rise to cross-claims, neither party can prove or sue for his full claim. An account must be taken and he must prove or sue (as the case may be) for the balance. Secondly, the account is taken as at the date of the winding-up order ("the retroactivity principle"). This is only one manifestation of a wider principle of insolvency law, namely, that the liquidation and distribution of the assets of the insolvent company are treated as notionally taking place simultaneously on the date of the winding-up order (see *Oliver* J in *Re Dynamics Corp of America (in liquidation)* [1976] 1 WLR 757 at p. 762). Thirdly, in taking the account the court has regard to events which have occurred since the date of the winding up ("the hindsight principle"). The hindsight principle is pervasive in the valuation of claims and the taking of accounts in bankruptcy and winding up. A good example of the principle being applied outside the context of set-off is *Macfarlane's Claim* (1881) 17 ChD 337 in which the value of a claim under a fire insurance policy was determined by reference to the loss suffered in a fire which occurred a month after the insurance company had been wound up.

In reading the cases, the interaction of these principles has to be borne in mind. Mr Neville Thomas QC, who appeared for BCCI, said that the right of set-off under r. 4.90 is procedural and that the mutual credits and debits of BCCI and the directors retain their separate existences until such time as the account is taken in the context of the director filing either a proof or a defence to a claim by the liquidator. This is of course true in the somewhat trivial sense that no account will be taken until something happens which makes it necessary to apply r. 4.90 and take one. But that cannot in my judgment affect the substantive rights of the parties which, whatever the context in which the question may subsequently arise, are treated as having been determined by an account taken at the date of the winding up. This is a consequence of the mandatory and retroactivity principles. Thus in *Farley v Housing and Commercial Developments Ltd* (1984) 1 BCC 99,150, Mr Farley was director of a building company engaged in erecting two buildings for a developer. On 5 February 1975 the building company resolved to go into creditors' voluntary winding up. At the date, the building company had a claim for money owing under the contract but the developer said it had a cross-claim for damages. Three years later, the liquidator of the building company assigned the benefit of its claim to Mr Farley personally. He argued that he was entitled to claim in full against the developer, leaving it to prove in his company's liquidation for its damages. But *Neill* J rejected this submission. He said that on the date of the winding up, sec. 31 of the *Bankruptcy Act* 1914 (in similar terms to r. 4.90) immediately took effect and "the balance of the account and no more became the sum thereafter owing to or from the respective parties" (at p. 99,156).

D

E

F

G

H

British Company Cases

Mr Thomas cited a number of cases which he said were at variance with the retroactivity   A
principle. But I think that on examination it will be found that none of them are
concerned with this principle at all. *New Quebrada Co Ltd v Carr* (1869) LR 4 CP 651
was decided on demurrer to a replication. A company made a call on the three joint
holders of shares. They pleaded a set-off. The company's replication alleged lack of
mutuality because after the commencement of the action and before the plea, one of the
three had been adjudicated bankrupt and his joint interest in the debt due from the
company had thereby vested in his assignees. The shareholders argued that nothing   B
passed to the assignees because on the bankruptcy, by virtue of the then equivalent of
r. 4.90, the bankrupt's share of the debt was automatically set off against the company's
claim for calls. The Court of Common Pleas held that there had been no bankruptcy
set-off: the bankrupt's individual interest in a joint debt could not be set off against the
company's joint claim against the three shareholders. None of this represents any
challenge to the retroactivity principle. It is true that *Brett* J went on to deal with what   C
the position would be if the set-off rule did apply and said (at pp. 653–654):

> "I think its only effect is to transfer the claim to the assignees, subject, when they
> seek to enforce it, to a right of the plaintiffs to deduct their debt. It does not,
> I think, extinguish the mutual debts, but if it did, I should have thought it would
> have answered the plea of set-off. In either view I think it does not leave a right of
> action in the bankrupt against the plaintiffs, and that he cannot, therefore, avail
> himself of his claim against the plaintiffs under an ordinary plea of set-off . . ."   D

This passage is not altogether easy because *Brett* J is mounting one rejected hypothesis
on another, but I take him to mean that the set-off rule does not mean that the debt owed
to the bankrupt does not pass to his assignees. It does, and is then subject to the account
taking procedure of the rule. So whether or not the set-off rule applies, the bankrupt no
longer retains a cause of action which can be used as non-bankruptcy set-off against the
company. *Brett* J is not in my view addressing himself to the retroactivity principle. In   E
Re a Debtor, ex parte Peak Goldfield Ltd [1909] 1 KB 430 the debtor owed the company
£1,453 in respect of the costs of unsuccessful litigation. The company presented a
bankruptcy petition. Two weeks before the hearing, the debtor bought £1,460 nominal
value of the company's debenture stock and claimed a set-off. But a couple of days
before the petition was heard, a judgment creditor of the debtor obtained the appointment
of a receiver of the debenture stock by way of equitable execution. The Court of Appeal
decided that the execution had deprived the debtor of his beneficial interest in the stock.   F
Accordingly there was no mutuality and a receiving order was made. *Fletcher-Moulton*
and *Farwell* L JJ, like *Brett* J in the *New Quebrada* case, thought that bankruptcy set-off
applied only after the debtor had become bankrupt and involved a taking of an account
with the trustee, not the bankrupt. Accordingly, the debtor could resist the receiving
order only by a valid plea of statutory set-off. This required mutuality at the date of the
hearing of the petition.   G

In *Sovereign Life Assurance Co v Dodd* [1892] 2 QB 573, Mr Dodd borrowed £1,170
from the Sovereign Life Assurance Co on the security of his life assurance policies.
Before the policies matured, the company was wound up. But Mr Dodd went on paying
his premiums until the policies became due. By this time there was a scheme of
arrangement under which policy holders were only entitled to substantially reduced
payments in respect of their policies. When the company sued Mr Dodd for repayment
of the £1,170, he pleaded a set-off of the full amount due on his policies. The company   H
said that he was entitled to set off only the reduced sum payable under the scheme of
arrangement. The Court of Appeal held that he was entitled to rely by way of set-off on
the full amount. This is a good example of the hindsight principle, by which account is
taken of the fact that the policies have actually matured after the winding-up date.
Bowen LJ expressly drew an analogy with *Macfarlane's Claim*.

A   Mr Thomas referred to several other cases which are also in my judgment illustrations of the hindsight principle and I do not think it is necessary to analyse them at length. In my judgment the retroactivity principle is firmly established. It follows that I reject the submission that there can be no set-off until such time as BCCI decides to sue the directors and they plead a set-off by way of defence. If there are existing cross-claims arising out of mutual dealings before the winding up, then I consider that r. 4.90 took effect.

B

This brings me to the question of whether such cross-claims exist. Mr Thomas said that with the possible exception of *M S Fashions*, in which a demand in writing was made in November 1991, BCCI had no claims against the directors, whether now or at the date of the winding up. The liability of the directors was contingent upon the making of a demand and none had been made. Since the liability of the directors was merely contingent, it could not form the subject of set-off. No doubt they would be entitled to

C   plead set-off if BCCI decided to make a demand and sue them on their guarantees, but this may never happen. In particular, it will not happen if BCCI can recover the advances from the companies themselves.

The problem of contingent claims can often be solved by the hindsight principle. *Macfarlane's Claim* was a case in which a subsequent event enabled the court for the purposes of proof to quantify a claim against the insolvent company which had been

D   contingent at the date of the winding up. The same would apply to quantification for the purposes of set-off. *Re Daintrey. Ex parte Mant* [1900] 1 QB 546 shows the hindsight principle applied to a contingent claim in favour of the insolvent. An extended discussion of this and similar cases can be found in *Re Charge Card Services Ltd* and it would be superfluous to cover the same ground. Sometimes, however, the insolvent estate needs to be wound up before it is known either that the contingency has occurred or that it will not occur. The court must then put some value on the contingent claim and it will do this

E   for the purposes of ordinary proof or the taking of an account under r. 4.90. There is no similar mechanism for valuing claims by the insolvent, but I am not sure that this is a real problem. Until the contingency occurs, the liquidator or trustee will not be able to use the claim as either a cause of action or a set-off. If the other party has a cross-claim, he will be able to prove for the full amount. I suppose it may happen that the contingency occurs long after the winding up has been completed and the company is then restored to the register and brings an action. The defendant may have proved for his cross-claim

F   and received a small dividend. Can he still rely on the full claim as a set-off, giving credit for the dividend? For my part, I do not see why not.

If the relationship between BCCI and the directors was governed only by the standard form guarantees, I think that there would be no answer to the submission that the liability of the directors remains contingent. All the guarantees in the BCCI standard

G   form require a demand in writing before any liability arises on the part of the guarantor. It is well established that in such a case, no cause of action arises until the demand is made: see *Bradford Old Bank Ltd v Sutcliffe* [1918] 2 KB 833. It would follow that (apart from the *M S Fashions* case) there is nothing due from the directors to BCCI and no basis for set-off against what is owed to them on the deposit accounts.

In fact, however, the directors are also liable to BCCI under the various instruments I have described and which deems them to be principal debtors. This liability is in my

H   judgment not contingent at all. It is either a joint and several liability with the companies or at any rate a several liability for the same debt. In *M S Fashions* and *Impexbond* the letters of charge made no mention of the need for any demand. In the case of the mortgage deed in *M S Fashions* and the charge on the deposit in *High Street Services* the obligation was to pay on demand in writing. However, in the case of primary obligations as opposed to secondary ones like guarantees, a provision for demand in writing is not

regarded as creating a contingency: see *Re Brown's Estate* [1893] 2 Ch 300. Thus in the
case of a promissory note payable "on demand", the debt, arises immediately the note is
given and is not contingent upon demand.

A

In my judgment the "principal debtor" clauses have the effect of creating primary
liability for the purposes of the rule that the debt is not contingent upon demand. This
was the provisional view of *Walton* J in *Esso Petroleum Co Ltd v Alstonbridge Properties
Ltd* [1975] 1 WLR 1474 at p. 1483 and I think it was correct. It is true that for some
purposes the courts will look to the underlying reality of the suretyship relationship
rather than the formal agreement that liability is to be as principal debtor. But this is
only for the purpose of protecting the surety's equitable rights against the principal
debtor and giving effect to such consequences as may affect the creditor, such as the
surety's right to take over securities and the rule against double proof. Otherwise there
is no reason why creditor and surety should not make whatever terms they choose. The
right to a demand before liability can accrue is not inherent in the nature of suretyship
and will not be implied unless expressly provided. There seems accordingly no reason
why the parties should not modify the effect of such a provision.

B
C

One therefore has on the one hand a liability of BCCI to the individual director
against a several liability of the director to pay the same debt as that for which the
company is liable. Such liabilities may be set off against each other. Outside the context
of suretyship this was regarded as beyond doubt in *Owen v Wilkinson* (1858) 5 CB (NS)
526; 141 ER 213. It was also applied in a suretyship context by Lord *Eldon* in *Ex parte
Stephens* (1805) 11 Ves Jun 24; 32 ER 996. This is not an easy case to interpret because it
involved a fraud by one of the parties and it is necessary to analyse, first, what part the
fraud played in the decision and secondly, whether it would still be a necessary element
today. Miss Stephens had entrusted some gilt-edged stock to her bankers, who collected
the dividends on her behalf. They dishonestly sold the stock and kept the £3,000
proceeds, but continued to make payments which they pretended were the dividends
they had received. Meanwhile, Miss Stephens's brother borrowed £1,000 from the
bankers on the security of a joint and several promissory note signed by himself and his
sister. The bankers were then adjudged bankrupt and Miss Stephens and her brother
petitioned Lord *Eldon* for an order that the £1,000 owed by Miss Stephens on the
promissory note be set off against the £3,000 which she had discovered that the bankers
owed her as damages for the conversion of her stock. The problem was therefore very
similar to that in the present case, because the alternative was to allow the bankers'
assignees to sue the brother for the full £1,000 and leave Miss Stephens to prove in the
bankruptcy for her £3,000.

D
E
F

Lord *Eldon* thought that this would be unfair. He said (at p. 28; 998):

> ". . . she had a demand against her brother for the sum of £1,000 as paid to his
> use; also upon the statute of mutual debts and credits; and they shall not be
> permitted to say she shall not, if she chooses, pay the debt; when the consequence
> is that she loses her money and they can call on him. If she had this equity before
> the bankruptcy, so she has it afterwards; and therefore she has a clear right to say
> they shall hold £1,000 of her money in discharge of the note, and shall deliver up
> the note."

G

In *Middleton v Pollock* (1875) LR 20 Eq 515, *Jessel* MR explained the basis of Lord
Eldon's decision (at p. 520):

H

> "If she had not by fraud been kept in ignorance of the facts, she would have known
> that the bankers had a £3,000 debt due to her and that she owed them £1,000 on
> the promissory note, and she would have said to them: 'Set one against the other,
> and pay as much of the balance as you can'; and in that case she would have paid
> £1,000 as the surety, and would have had a right to sue the brother from time to

A   time, and to stand in the place of the bankers as his creditor. After the bankruptcy the assignees could be in no better position: they only took what the bankrupts were entitled to, and they could not have been allowed to say: 'You had no right of set-off before action brought', because it was their own fraud which prevented her knowing the facts which gave rise to the set-off. *But the right of set-off was indisputable. There was a several demand on the one side and on the other;* and therefore the only relief that she got was relief against the neglect to assert that

B   right in due time, which was not really neglect, but rather omission — caused by the fraudulent concealment by the bankers of the true facts of the case: and neither they nor their assignees could take advantage of their fraudulent concealment to deprive her of that right of set-off."

    Jessel MR says, in the passage I have italicised, that the right to set-off was indisputable. The bankers were severally liable to Miss Stephens for £3,000 and she was severally

C   liable to them for £1,000. If one then applies the mandatory principle, one would think that there was nothing more to be said. Rule 4.90 applies. But the Master of the Rolls seems to be saying that in the ordinary way, Miss Stephens ought to have done something about asserting her right of set-off before the bankruptcy. The implication is that, but for the fraud which prevented her from knowing that she ought to do something, she would have been unable to assert the set-off once the bankruptcy had supervened. I am naturally nervous at finding that I do not fully understand the reasoning of *Jessel* MR,

D   but I cannot follow why it mattered that Miss Stephens had not asserted a right of set-off before the bankruptcy and therefore needed to be relieved, on the ground of fraud, against that omission. I can only think that the consequences of the mandatory principle (as illustrated by *Farley v Housing and Commercial Developments Ltd*) were not as fully appreciated in 1875 as they are today. In my view the fraud would not today be a material element in deciding whether r. 4.90 applied. All that is necessary is that there

E   should have been mutual dealings resulting in cross-claims and it does not matter that one of the parties was unaware of her cross-claim until after the relevant date. I therefore regard *Ex parte Stephens* as similar to *Owen v Wilkinson* and to this case.

    As I mentioned at the beginning of this judgment, the point at issue has already received interlocutory consideration by *Millett* J and the Court of Appeal in *M S Fashions*. *Millett* J refused interlocutory relief on the ground that there could plainly be no set-off. He said that it was elementary that set-off operated only by way of defence

F   and was not equivalent to payment. The bank could release its claims against the directors — even the director against whom a written demand had been made — and still enforce its claims against the companies. No question of set-off would arise until BCCI actually sued a director. Meanwhile, there was nothing to stop BCCI from suing the companies.

    In the Court of Appeal, *Scott* and *Woolf* L JJ disagreed. They said that the

G   mandatory principle applied to the directors' obligations as at the date of the winding up and that the effect of the set-off was to diminish or extinguish the debt owed by them and their companies. As will be apparent, I respectfully agree with this analysis.

    It remains to notice some subsidiary points taken by Mr Thomas on behalf of BCCI. He argued that because the deposits were charged to BCCI, the directors had no beneficial interest in the money and accordingly there was no mutuality between their

H   claims and those of BCCI. This is a pleasing paradox but in my view fallacious. Ignoring for the moment the question of whether such a charge is conceptually possible, the charge was of a debt owed by BCCI to secure a debt owed to BCCI. The account to be taken by r. 4.90 must require an unwinding of that arrangement so that the deposit is set off against the debt it was intended to secure. There is a similar answer to Mr Thomas's alternative submission that BCCI were entitled under their security documents to

transfer the deposit to a suspense account rather than applying it in discharge of the
debt. In my judgment this clause cannot survive the winding up of BCCI and the
application of the mandatory principle. It is designed to entitle BCCI to postpone the
taking of an account and inconsistent with taking one as at the date of winding up.

Finally, Mr Thomas said that although r. 4.90 might result in a set-off between BCCI
and the director, this did not amount to payment of the debt owed by the company. It
gave the director a complete or *pro tanto* defence but not the company. This, I think,
ignores the fact that the director's set-off operates in respect of *the same debt* as that
owed by the company. If, as I think it must be, the set-off is equivalent to payment by
the director (see *Ex parte Barnett* (1874) LR 9 Ch App 293) then I think it must operate
also to extinguish to the same extent the debt owed by the company.

I will therefore declare that the indebtedness of each of the companies as at the date
of the winding up has been extinguished or reduced by the amount which on that date
was standing to the credit of the directors on their respective deposit accounts.

(*Declaration accordingly*)

A

B

C

D

E

F

G

H

A
Re Rex Williams Leisure plc.

Chancery Division (Companies Court).
Sir Donald Nicholls V-C.
Judgment delivered 3 December 1992.

B
Directors — Disqualifying unfit directors of insolvent companies — Procedure — Whether evidence of DTI examiner should be struck out as hearsay — Whether respondents could file no evidence before hearing — Whether disqualification proceedings should be stayed pending outcome of litigation by company — Companies Act 1985, sec. 447; Company Directors Disqualification Act 1986, sec. 16; Insolvent Companies (Disqualification of Unfit Directors) Proceedings Rules 1987 (SI 1987/2023), r. 2–4, 6, 7.

C
This was an application by the respondents to an originating summons by the Secretary of State for Trade and Industry seeking their disqualification as directors.

The respondents were directors of Rex Williams Leisure plc which went into administration in April 1990. The company carried on a gaming and amusements business. The statement of affairs showed an estimated deficiency as to creditors of about £2.6m.

D
The disqualification proceedings were defended. Affidavit evidence was filed in support of the application by the Secretary of State. The directors then made an application raising three issues.

(1) The principal affidavit filed in support of the Secretary of State's application was by an examiner in the DTI's investigations division who had interviewed nine directors and employees of the company in exercise of powers conferred on him pursuant to sec. 447 of the Companies Act 1985. The interview notes were exhibited. The respondents submitted that the notes being put forward as evidence of the facts related to the examiner by the interviewees were hearsay. They also objected to the examiner's comments on the notes. They sought to have those parts of the evidence struck out.

E

(2) The respondents, in case they wished to submit at the hearing that on the admissible evidence there was no case to answer, sought a direction enabling them to file no evidence before the hearing and to give evidence orally at the hearing should they choose to do so. They argued that sec. 16(1) of the Company Directors Disqualification Act 1986, which provided that the person against whom a disqualification order was sought might "appear and himself give evidence or call witnesses", meant that a respondent could postpone adducing evidence until after the applicant had closed his case. Rule 6 of the Insolvent Companies (Disqualification of Unfit Directors) Proceedings Rules 1987, which required a respondent to file in court any affidavit evidence in opposition to the application he wished the court to take into consideration, within 28 days from the date of service of the summons, only specified a time-limit within which the respondent had to file evidence if he wished to do so.

F

G

(3) The respondents' conduct which formed the basis of the disqualification application was also the subject of a pending action brought by the company against one of the respondents who therefore sought an order staying the disqualification application until after the action had been disposed of.

H
Held, dismissing the respondents' application:

1. By analogy with the admissibility in evidence of the contents of reports made by inspectors appointed under sec. 431 of the 1985 Act, the court could take account of information or documents obtained under sec. 447, which formed the basis of a decision by the Secretary of State to apply for a disqualification order. The court would decide how much importance or weight to attach to the information in question and would be astute

to see that a respondent was not prejudiced by the hearsay nature of the information. The
court would have no difficulty when disputes of fact arose in identifying which parts of the
affidavits or the official receiver's report were comment as distinct from evidence of fact.

2. Exceptional cases apart, the rules required a respondent to adduce his evidence in
the form of affidavits which the applicant was to have the opportunity to consider and
refer to before the effective hearing of the summons. A respondent might still elect to
adduce no evidence and make a submission of no case to answer. But the effect of the rules
was that he must make his decision on that when he had seen and considered the
applicant's evidence. He could not postpone his decision until after the close of the
applicant's case at the effective hearing of the disqualification application.

3. There was a public interest in disqualification orders being made in respect of unfit
directors of insolvent companies. It could not, in general, be right that disqualification
proceedings should await the outcome of parallel private litigation. The protection
afforded to the public by a disqualification order should not have to wait on the
determination of other claims against a director and the speed at which the parties chose
to proceed with them.

The following cases were referred to in the judgment:

ABC Coupler and Engineering Co Ltd, Re (No. 2) [1962] 1 WLR 1236.
Alexander v Rayson [1936] 1 KB 169.
Allied Produce Co Ltd, Re [1967] 1 WLR 1469.
Armvent Ltd, Re [1975] 1 WLR 1679.
Koscot Interplanetary (UK) Ltd, Re [1972] 3 All ER 829.
Laurie v Raglan Building Co Ltd [1942] 1 KB 152.
St Piran Ltd, Re [1981] 1 WLR 1300.
SBA Properties Ltd, Re [1967] 1 WLR 799.
Travel & Holiday Clubs Ltd, Re [1967] 1 WLR 711.

John McDonnell QC and Clive Hugh Jones (instructed by D J Freeman, agents for
Garstangs, Bolton) for the applicants.

Guy Newey (instructed by the Treasury Solicitor) for the Secretary of State for Trade
and Industry.

JUDGMENT

Nicholls V-C: This appeal raises some points of importance on the procedure affecting
applications for company director disqualification orders. An administration order was
made in respect of a company, Rex Williams Leisure plc, on 30 April 1990. The company
carried on a gaming and amusements business. The statement of affairs showed an
estimated deficiency as to creditors of about £2.6m. An originating summons was issued
on 27 April 1992 whereby the Secretary of State for Trade and Industry is seeking a
disqualification order against two defendants: Mr Frank Warren and Mr Peter Sealey.
Mr Warren was a director of the company from October 1987 until October 1989. The
disqualification proceedings are being defended. Affidavit evidence was filed in support
of the application by the Secretary of State. In the normal course the next step would be
for the defendants to file affidavit evidence in answer. Subject to any further evidence
filed in reply by the Secretary of State, the case would then be heard and determined,
either by the registrar or the judge, after cross-examination of the deponents if necessary.

In the present case that normal course was not followed. Before me is an application
by the defendants raising essentially three issues. First, they object to much of the
evidence put forward on behalf of the Secretary of State in support of the disqualification
application. They say it is hearsay and inadmissible, and they seek to have those parts of
the evidence struck out at this stage.

A   Secondly, they wish to preserve their rights to submit to the court, when this matter comes on for hearing, that on the admissible evidence there is no case for them to answer. To this end they wish to file no affidavit evidence at all at this stage. They want to take that course because they cannot withdraw their evidence once filed. Even if at the hearing they make it plain that they themselves do not wish to present any evidence to the court, the Secretary of State will be entitled to rely on any affidavit evidence already filed on the defendants' behalf. Further, the defendants and the other deponents

B can be ordered to attend and be cross-examined on their affidavits even if the defendants do not rely on these affidavits at the hearing. Thus they, the defendants, will effectually lose their right to make a submission of no case to answer if they file evidence before the hearing of the originating summons. They seek now a direction enabling them to give their evidence orally at the hearing should they choose to do so.

     The third matter raised concerns the fact that the defendants' conduct which forms

C the basis of the disqualification application is also the subject of a pending action brought by the company against one of the two defendants. The defendants seek an order staying the disqualification application until after the action has been disposed of.

Submission of no case to answer

     I shall consider the second of the three issues first. In the ordinary course of a civil action tried without a jury, after the plaintiff has closed his case the defendant may, if he

D wishes, make a submission that he has no case to answer. In the usual case where the burden of proof rests on the plaintiff, the defendant may submit to the judge that having regard to the evidence adduced by the plaintiff the plaintiff's case must fail. When such a submission is made to a judge sitting alone, the judge will normally require the defendant to elect to call no evidence before ruling on such a submission: see *Alexander v Rayson* [1936] 1 KB 169 at p. 178 and *Laurie v Raglan Building Co Ltd* [1942] 1 KB 152

E at p. 155. The reason for this is that the judge should not be called upon to express an opinion on the evidence and its reliability until all the evidence is before him. If the defendant elects to call no evidence, he will then stand or fall with his submission of no case. If the submission fails, he cannot then change his mind and call evidence. But, and this is the important feature for present purposes, this normal method of conducting a trial with oral evidence means that it is not until after the plaintiff's evidence has been called and tested by cross-examination that the defendant has to decide finally whether

F to adduce evidence on his own behalf. Until then he can keep his powder dry. This is still so under the modern practice whereby witness statements are served in advance of the trial. If a defendant serves a witness statement but does not call the witness to whose evidence it relates, no other party may put the statement in evidence at the trial: see RSC, O. 38, r. 2A(4).

     It is against this background that Mr McDonnell called attention to sec. 16(1) of the

G *Company Directors Disqualification Act* 1986 ("the Disqualification Act"):

> "A person intending to apply for the making of a disqualification order by the court having jurisdiction to wind up a company shall give not less than 10 days' notice of his intention to the person against whom the order is sought; and on the hearing of the application the last-mentioned person may appear and himself give evidence or call witnesses."

H Mr McDonnell relied on the phrase "or call witnesses". The statute, he submitted, envisages that a defendant may call oral evidence.

     The next step in the defendants' argument was to turn to the *Insolvent Companies (Disqualification of Unfit Directors) Proceedings Rules* 1987 (SI 1987/2023), which I shall call "the disqualification rules". These rules cover applications made under sec. 7 and 8 of the Disqualification Act. The present case is such an application. Rule 2

provides that applications made in the High Court shall be made by originating summons
and that the Rules of the Supreme Court shall apply except where the disqualification
rules make provision to inconsistent effect. So before considering the disqualification
rules further, I turn to the Rules of the Supreme Court. Order 38, r. 2(3) provides that in
any cause or matter begun by originating summons evidence "may" be given by affidavit
unless the rules otherwise provide or the court otherwise directs. Order 28 is the
particular order concerned with originating summons procedure. Rule 1A(4) prescribes
the time-limit within which a defendant who "wishes to adduce affidavit evidence" must
do so. Rule 4(3) obliges the court, at an early stage of the proceedings, to consider:

> ". . . whether there is or may be a dispute as to fact and whether the just,
> expeditious and economical disposal of the proceedings can accordingly best be
> secured by hearing the summons on oral evidence or mainly on oral evidence and,
> if it thinks fit, may order that no further evidence shall be filed and that the
> summons shall be heard on oral evidence or partly on oral evidence and partly on
> affidavit evidence, with or without cross-examination of any of the deponents, as
> it may direct."

Further, O. 28, r. 8 gives the court power at any stage to direct that the proceedings shall
continue as if begun by writ. I pause to note the defendants' submission that, thus far,
the originating summons procedure is not inconsistent with a defendant retaining the
opportunity to postpone adducing any evidence until after the plaintiff's case has been
closed in a case where there are disputes of fact. In such a case the court can give
directions for oral evidence.

I should also note here an historical feature on which Mr McDonnell placed some
reliance. It is that before 1986 the procedure governing disqualification applications
was, likewise, not inconsistent with the defendant having the opportunity to postpone
adducing evidence until after the plaintiff's case was closed. Applications for
disqualification orders under the *Companies Act* 1948 were made either by an originating
summons in accordance with RSC, O. 102, r. 2 or, if the company was being wound up,
by a summons under r. 68 of the *Companies (Winding-Up) Rules* 1949. The latter rule
expressly envisaged that on the return of the summons the court would give directions
on whether points of claim and defence were to be served, whether the evidence should
be taken wholly or in part by affidavit or orally, and whether there should be
cross-examination.

I now return to the disqualification rules. This is the crucial phase in the defendants'
argument. Rule 3 of the disqualification rules regulates the manner in which the case
against a defendant shall be presented. Rule 3 prescribes that when the summons is
issued the evidence in support of the disqualification application shall be filed in court,
and copies shall be served on the defendant. The evidence is to be in the form of
affidavits, except that where the application is made by the official receiver it may be in
the form of a written report. Rule 6 of the disqualification rules deals with the defendant's
evidence and the plaintiff's evidence in reply, in these terms:

> "(1) The respondent shall, within 28 days from the date of service of the summons,
> file in court any affidavit evidence in opposition to the application he wishes the
> court to take into consideration and shall forthwith serve upon the applicant a
> copy of such evidence.
> (2) The applicant shall, within 14 days from receiving the copy of the respondent's
> evidence, file in court any further evidence in reply he wishes the court to take
> into consideration and shall forthwith serve a copy of that evidence upon the
> respondent."

Rule 7 governs the hearing of the application. As one would expect, the registrar has a
wide discretion to give directions. In particular, under r. 7(5)(c) he may give directions

A   for the filing in court and service of further evidence by the parties, and directions as to "such other matters as the registrar thinks necessary or expedient with a view to an expeditious disposal of the application".

      Mr McDonnell submitted that, properly construed, r. 6 of the disqualification rules does no more than specify a time-limit within which, if the defendant wishes to file affidavit evidence, he must do so. The rule does not detract from a defendant's statutory right to "call witnesses". Further, in giving directions under r. 7(5)(c) it would be a wrong

B   exercise by the registrar of his discretion for him to order the filing of affidavits if a defendant wishes to postpone adducing evidence until after the plaintiff has closed his case and the defendant has then decided whether he wishes to make a submission of no case to answer.

      I am unable to accept these contentions. The one matter which seems to me to shine clearly through all these provisions is that the disqualification rules envisage that a

C   defendant who wishes to oppose the making of a disqualification order must present his evidence in the form of affidavits. Rule 6 admits of no other construction. This is confirmed by r. 4. Rule 4 sets out details of matters which must be endorsed on the summons by way of information to the defendant. One of the matters of which the defendant must be told at the outset in this way is:

D   "(e)   that any evidence which the respondent wishes to be taken into consideration by the court must be filed in court in accordance with the time limits imposed under Rule 6 (the provisions of which shall be set out on the summons)."

      I recognise that, once filed, a defendant's affidavit is available to be referred to and relied on by a plaintiff. To that extent a defendant is not so well placed under this procedure as he is with a procedure for oral evidence. I am unable to find in that element of disadvantage for a defendant sufficient justification for reading r. 6 of the disqualification

E   rules in any other sense than I have just stated. A defendant may still elect to adduce no evidence, and make a submission of no case to answer. But the effect of the rules is that he must make his decision on that when he has seen and considered the plaintiff's evidence. He cannot postpone his decision until after the close of the plaintiff's case at the effective hearing of the disqualification application by the registrar or judge.

      I recognise also that in this respect the disqualification rules may represent a departure from the procedure followed before 1986. However, this is an argument which cuts both

F   ways. The framers of the disqualification rules must have had in mind that disputes of fact were likely to arise on disqualification applications. Despite this, and in contrast to the position under the 1949 winding-up rules and, indeed, under the *Insolvency Rules* 1986 (see r. 7.10), the disqualification rules do not countenance service of points of claim and defence and the giving of evidence in chief orally. No doubt there may be exceptional cases where it is appropriate for the court to give a direction that the evidence of a

G   particular witness should be given orally; for example, when a witness sought to be called by one party refuses to make an affidavit and his attendance and evidence have to be procured by subpoena. But exceptional cases apart, the rules require a defendant to adduce his evidence in the form of affidavits which the plaintiff is to have the opportunity to consider and reply to before the effective hearing of the summons.

      Mr McDonnell advanced an alternative submission that, if this is their correct interpretation, the disqualification rules are ultra vires. On this footing the rules purport

H   to take away from a defendant the right to "call witnesses" expressly given him by sec. 16 of the Disqualification Act. I do not agree. The rule-making power under the Disqualification Act is to be found in sec. 21. The effect of that section, for present purposes, is to confer on the Lord Chancellor, with the concurrence of the Secretary of State and after consultation with the insolvency rules committee, the like power of making rules with regard to sec. 6–10 of the Disqualification Act as is conferred by

sec. 411 of the *Insolvency Act* 1986. For this purpose those sections are deemed to be
incorporated in Pt. I–VII of the 1986 Act. Under sec. 411 rules may be made for
regulating the practice and procedure of any court exercising jurisdiction for the
purposes of Pt. I–VII of the 1986 Act on matters "concerned with or arising out of . . .
the insolvency or winding up of companies, being any provision that could be made by
rules of court" (sec. 411(2)(a) and Sch. 8, para. 2). In my view, r. 6–7 of the disqualification
rules fall within the ambit of the power even though, curiously, sec. 16 of the
Disqualification Act is not among the sections specifically mentioned in sec. 21(2) as
deemed included in Pt. I–VII of the Act of 1986 for the rule-making purpose. I cannot
read the phrase "call witnesses" in sec. 16 as giving a defendant an overriding right to
insist on the evidence of his witnesses being adduced orally. The statute provides that
the defendant "may appear and himself give evidence or call witnesses". In my view
rules of the court may properly be made regulating the manner in which the evidence of
the defendant and his witnesses is to be to be presented to the court.

Hearsay evidence

The principal affidavit filed in support of the Secretary of State's application is an
affidavit made by a chief examiner of the investigations division of the Department of
Trade and Industry. He interviewed nine directors and employees of the company, in
exercise of powers conferred on him pursuant to a direction given by the Secretary of
State under sec. 447 of the *Companies Act* 1985. He has exhibited the notes he made at
these interviews. In his affidavit he has made comments and submissions based on what
he was told at the interviews.

Mr McDonnell submitted, correctly, that these interview notes are being put forward
as evidence of the facts related to the examiner by those interviewed and that as such
this is hearsay evidence. He submitted that, save for the interviews with the two
defendants themselves, these notes are inadmissible in evidence and that the notes and
the comments based thereon should be struck out from the evidence. RSC, O. 41, r. 5
provides that, with certain immaterial exceptions, an affidavit "may contain only such
facts as the deponent is able of his own knowledge to prove". The general relaxation of
this rule for affidavits used in interlocutory proceedings is not applicable here, because
this disqualification application is not an interlocutory proceeding. Section 447(8) itself
provides that a statement made by a person in compliance with a requirement to provide
an explanation of documents may be used in evidence "against him". This does not
apply to the bulk of the statements, which were made by persons other than the two
defendants themselves.

Mr Newey's answer to this attack was to pray in aid by way of analogy the principle
that the court has developed regarding the admissibility in evidence of the contents of
reports made by inspectors appointed to carry out investigations under sec. 431. I was
referred to several authorities: *Re ABC Coupler and Engineering Co Ltd (No. 2)* [1962]
1 WLR 1236; *Re Travel & Holiday Clubs Ltd* [1967] 1 WLR 711; *Re SBA Properties
Ltd* [1967] 1 WLR 799; *Re Allied Produce Co Ltd* [1967] 1 WLR 1469; *Re Koscot
Interplanetary (UK) Ltd* [1972] 3 All ER 829; and *Re Armvent Ltd* [1975] 1 WLR 1679.
These decisions establish that the contents of inspectors' reports may properly be taken
into account by the court when considering a petition for the winding up of a company
brought by the Secretary of State in exercise of his powers under what is now sec. 124A
of the 1986 Act. The rationale of this principle is that an inspectors' report is not ordinary
hearsay evidence because inspectors act in a statutory fact-finding capacity. Further, it
would be nonsensical if the court could not take the report into consideration in deciding
whether it was just and equitable to wind up the company when the statute envisages
that it is from the report itself that the Secretary of State will reach his conclusion on
whether or not it is expedient in the public interest that the company should be wound

A
up and a petition should be presented accordingly. *Dillon* J observed in *Re St Piran Ltd*
[1981] 1 WLR 1300 at p. 1306D:

> "It would be strange . . . if Parliament had intended that the Secretary of State
> should have to rely on entirely fresh evidence and should not be able to present
> the report to the court and rely on the findings of the inspectors."

In the *St Piran* case, *Dillon* J went further and applied the same approach to a petition
presented by a contributory. He held (at p. 1306G):

B

> "If inspectors are appointed because there is ground for suspecting that material
> information has been withheld from shareholders in a company and the inspectors
> by questioning the directors and examining documents not available to the general
> body of shareholders establish that this is so and report accordingly, there may
> well be little public interest involved to make it expedient for the Secretary of
> State to present a petition. A minority shareholder aggrieved by consistent
C
> withholding of material information might, nonetheless, wish to petition, and it
> would to a considerable extent, as it seems to me, defeat the object of having the
> inspectors' inquiry if the aggrieved shareholder could not rely on their report.
>
> Accordingly, I see no valid reason why the inspectors' report cannot be used to
> support a contributory's petition to the same extent that it can be used to support
> a petition by the Secretary of State."

D
In my view the analogy between explanations furnished pursuant to a sec. 447
direction and a report prepared by inspectors appointed under sec. 431 is compelling for
present purposes. Part XIV of the *Companies Act* 1985 contains a series of powers given
to the Secretary of State. They form part of the armoury of powers created by Parliament
for the investigation and regulation of companies in the public interest. Under sec. 431
the Secretary of State may appoint inspectors, with wide powers of investigation. They
are required to make reports to the Secretary of State (sec. 437). As already noted,
E
Parliament envisaged that one of the consequences of an inspectors' report is that this
may form the trigger for the presentation of a winding-up petition by the Secretary of
State. Another consequence Parliament envisaged is that, based on such a report, the
Secretary of State may apply for a disqualification order against a person who is or was a
director of the company. So far as material, sec. 8 of the Disqualification Act provides:

> "(1) If it appears to the Secretary of State from a report made by inspectors under
F
> section 437 of the Companies Act . . . or from information or documents obtained
> under section 447 or 448 of the Companies Act . . . that it is expedient in the
> public interest that a disqualification order should be made against any person
> who is or has been a director or shadow director of any company, he may apply to
> the court for such an order to be made against that person.
>
> (2) The court may make a disqualification order against a person where, on an
> application under this section, it is satisfied that his conduct in relation to the
G
> company makes him unfit to be concerned in the management of a company."

In my view the approach adopted by the court to the use of the contents of an
inspectors' report on a winding-up petition is equally applicable on an application for a
disqualification order founded on such a report. That is so, because the rationale
underlying the use of the contents of an inspectors' report on a winding-up petition is
equally applicable to a disqualification application based on the contents of such a
H
report. In the latter case as much as the former Parliament must have intended that the
Secretary of State should be able to present a case to the court founded on the
information gathered by the inspectors and set out in their report. Indeed, sec. 441 of
the *Companies Act* 1985 as amended now provides expressly that a copy of an inspectors'
report is admissible on applications under sec. 8 of the Disqualification Act as evidence
of any fact stated therein.

What, then, of information garnered under sec. 447? Section 447 is another power　　A
conferred upon the Secretary of State by the same Part, Pt. XIV, of the *Companies Act*
1985. The Secretary of State may at any time, if he thinks there is good reason to do so,
authorise an officer of his or any other competent person to require a company to
produce to the officer or other person any documents which he, the officer or other
person, may specify: see sec. 447(3), as amended. This power includes authority, if the
documents are produced, to require any person who is a present or past officer or　　B
employee of the company to provide an explanation of the documents (subsec. (5)(a)(ii)).
Failure to comply with a requirement to produce documents or provide an explanation
is a criminal offence.

One then asks oneself: what use is the Secretary of State intended to make of
information so obtained? The answer is that Parliament envisaged that similar
consequences should flow from information obtained by an authorised person under
sec. 447 as apply in the case of information obtained by inspectors and set out in their　　C
report. In the former case as well as in the latter, the Secretary of State may act on this
information in deciding to present a winding-up petition on the ground that it is just and
equitable to wind up a company: see sec. 124A(1)(a) of the *Insolvency Act* 1986.
Likewise, as can be seen from sec. 8(1) of the Disqualification Act quoted above,
Parliament envisaged that information or documents obtained under sec. 447 may form
the basis for a decision by the Secretary of State to apply for a disqualification order on
the ground that it appears to him expedient in the public interest that such an order　　D
should be made.

I appreciate that a sec. 447 direction leads to a less formal and less elaborate
investigation than the appointment of inspectors under sec. 431. But under both sections
the information is being sought and provided pursuant to statutory powers and obligations.
The differences in the two procedures do not dictate that in the one case the court can
take into account the information obtained and in the other case it cannot. Rather, in　　E
both cases the evidence is admissible but the court should take the differences into
account when deciding, having regard to all the evidence and all the circumstances of
the particular proceedings, how much importance or weight should be attached to the
information in question. The court is well able to do this. The court will have due regard
to the source and nature of the information and also the circumstances in which it was
provided. The court will be astute to see that a company or a defendant is not prejudiced　　F
by the hearsay nature of the information. If the defendant's evidence raises an issue
which needs to be tried, the court will take appropriate steps to ensure that the issue is
justly and fairly resolved. *Templeman* J adverted to this in *Re Armvent Ltd* [1975]
1 WLR 1679 at p. 1685H, in the context of a winding-up petition:

> ". . . even if the report of the inspectors is challenged nevertheless it ought to be
> treated as prima facie evidence and . . . it ought to be left to a judge in any case　　G
> having read the report and having seen the witnesses to make up his own mind
> whether it is just and equitable to wind up the company. The whole machinery of
> the inspectors' report was evolved in order to enable the Secretary of State to
> present a winding-up petition where the Secretary of State considers the public
> interest so demands. It would be unfortunate if once the Secretary of State has
> reached that conclusion on proper grounds based on the inspectors' detailed
> report, that the court should be right back to square one and start against as　　H
> though the inspectors had never come on the scene at all. A great deal may depend
> on the contents of the report and the evidence set out in the report; but I would
> hope that a report of this nature would be accepted by the court as being prima
> facie evidence of the main conclusions drawn by the inspectors. Once evidence is
> sworn to the contrary then if the Secretary of State fails to support the report by

A   direct evidence which removes any doubt cast on the validity of the inspectors'
     conclusions the court would not be slow to dismiss the petition.''

     I shall therefore not strike out those passages in the chief examiner's affidavit
     concerned with the sec. 447 interviews.

     Nor shall I strike out the passages which consist of comments and submissions based
     on the exhibited interview notes. In a case such as this it can be helpful in practice for an
B   affidavit to spell out, concisely and lucidly, the inferences and conclusions a party will
     ask the court to draw from the evidence. Indeed, the disqualification rules require that
     the plaintiff's affidavits or the official receiver's report are to include a statement of the
     matters by reference to which the defendant is alleged to be unfit to be concerned in the
     management of a company (r. 3(3)). So the plaintiff's case must be stated clearly in the
     evidence. The defendant must know what case he has to meet. I do not see how the
     inclusion of this material in the plaintiff's evidence can prejudice the defendant. At the
C   hearing the court will have no difficulty, when disputes of fact arise, in identifying which
     parts of the affidavits or the official receiver's report are comment as distinct from
     evidence of fact. That is so in the present case.

     A further aspect of the evidence challenged by the defendants concerns documents
     which have been found in the company's records or produced pursuant to sec. 447.
     These have been exhibited to the affidavits. Some of the documents are, or may be, draft
D   documents such as accounts or reports which were never finalised and approved or draft
     minutes of meetings which were never circulated or approved, or drafts of letters which
     were never sent. Here also I do not think I should strike out the criticised material. The
     Secretary of State must be entitled to put such documents in evidence, for what they
     may be worth. At the hearing of the summons there may be argument about their
     evidential significance or even their relevance, but that does not mean they should be
     struck out from the affidavit evidence at this stage as inadmissible. Those are matters to
E   be looked into properly at the hearing of the disqualification application. Meanwhile, if
     the accounts or reports were never finalised or approved or the letters never advanced
     beyond the stage of drafts, the defendants can say so in their evidence and explain the
     position. This should not give rise to any embarrassment for them in this case. Nor is
     there any question of this course being oppressive to them because of the volume of the
     documentation or for any other reason.

F   I should add one final point before parting from the question of hearsay evidence.
     I appreciate that if affidavits containing hearsay evidence may be put before the court in
     support of a disqualification application, one result is to place on a defendant the onus
     of responding to hearsay evidence and showing cause why an order should not be made.
     I do not find this altogether surprising. I am mindful of the grave consequences a
     disqualification order can have. A disqualification order is a serious interference with
G   the freedom of an individual. I am also mindful that the Secretary of State or the official
     receiver will not usually have first-hand knowledge of the matters on which the
     disqualification application is founded but, and this is important, a defendant to a
     disqualification application inevitably will have such knowledge. Many disqualification
     applications are not defended. When they are, the facts which are seriously in issue may
     be very limited. It would be absurd, because it would be pointless, for the affidavit
     evidence in chief always to consist exclusively of matters within the personal knowledge
H   of the deponent. Frequently disqualification applications are based on a defendant's
     conduct as a director over many months or even years. There is a measure of practical
     good sense in a procedure whereby the plaintiff has first to set out his case, with sufficient
     clarity and identification of the evidence being relied on for the defendant to know
     where he stands. Then the defendant puts in his evidence. The plaintiff can see what
     factual issues there are, and he can then take steps and incur expense in adducing where

A

necessary first-hand evidence on these issues, before the hearing. In this way the genuine issues can be resolved properly and fairly in the interests of the defendant and in the public interest. This procedure does not prejudice a fair and just trial of the issues.

Staying the disqualification application

B

I turn to the third question. On 4 September 1990 the company, acting by the administrators, issued a writ against Mr Warren claiming repayment of £200,000 paid by the company in March 1988 to Mr Warren or a company owned by him in connection with a proposed share purchase. A statement of claim was served, followed by an application for summary judgment. Mr Warren made an affidavit explaining why no money was owed to the company even though the proposed share purchase did not proceed. On 9 January 1991 the application for summary judgment was adjourned to the judge. There the matter rests. The action has remained dormant ever since. The application has never been disposed of. Apparently there is a possibility that the company may be relisted on the unlisted securities market. If that happens, it will then be for the new management to decide whether to proceed with the action.

C

This disqualification application was launched in the following year on 27 April, just within the two year period prescribed by sec. 7(2) of the Disqualification Act. In the disqualification application the Secretary of State is relying mainly on the same matters as those in issue in the action. The defendants submitted that those matters should be determined in the action. The action was brought by administrators appointed by the court, and in the action Mr Warren will have the benefit of being able to require that the plaintiff company first prove its case by strictly admissible evidence before he is called upon to adduce any evidence in his own defence. Had it not been for the two-year limit, the Secretary of State would have awaited the outcome of the action before seeking a disqualification order. The court should exercise its discretion against duplication of proceedings.

D

E

I am not impressed by these submissions. The proceedings are brought by the Secretary of State in the public interest. There is a public interest in disqualification orders being made in respect of unfit directors of insolvent companies. Section 6(4) prescribes a minimum period of disqualification of two years. It cannot, in general, be right that disqualification proceedings should await the outcome of parallel private litigation. The protection afforded to the public by a disqualification order should not have to wait on the determination of other claims against a director and the speed at which the parties choose to proceed with them. Here there has been no movement in the administrators' action for almost two years. Mr Warren has taken no step to hasten on those proceedings. I can see no justification for staying the disqualification proceedings because of the existence of this presently dormant action. The disqualification proceedings may prove to be mistaken. The allegations of misconduct against the defendants may turn out to be without substance. That is a matter to be determined at the hearing of the disqualification application. The application should proceed to that hearing in the ordinary way.

F

G

Conclusion

For these reasons I shall not grant the relief sought in the defendants' summons.

(*Order accordingly*)

H

R v Secretary of State for Trade and Industry, ex parte Airlines of Britain Holdings plc & Anor.

Court of Appeal (Civil Division).
Neill, Beldam and Kennedy L JJ.
Judgment delivered 4 December 1992.

Mergers — Secretary of State decided not to refer proposed acquisition to Monopolies and Mergers Commission — Merger was not concentration with a Community dimension within EC merger control regulation — Whether Secretary of State had duty to consider implications of art. 86 of EEC Treaty — Fair Trading Act 1973, Pt. V; EEC Treaty, art. 86–88; EC Regulation 4064/89 (OJ 1990 L257/13), art. 1, 22.

This was a renewed application by two companies, Airlines of Britain Holdings plc and Virgin Atlantic Airways Ltd, for leave to apply for judicial review of decisions made by the Secretary of State for Trade and Industry and the Director General of Fair Trading relating to the proposed acquisition by British Airways plc of all the assets of Davies & Newman Holdings plc.

The Secretary of State decided not to refer the proposed acquisition to the Monopolies and Mergers Commission under the Fair Trading Act. The applicants then submitted to the Secretary of State that there was a duty under Community law to consider the applicability of art. 86 of the EEC Treaty to the proposed acquisition. The Fair Trading Act 1973 did not exclude the operation of art. 86, and the Secretary of State did not have power to clear a proposed acquisition under the 1973 Act where that acquisition also involved or might involve an infringement of art. 86 and 88. Council Regulation 4064/89 concerning the control of concentrations between undertakings did not apply because the scope of the regulation was limited by art. 1 to concentrations with a Community dimension. Accordingly, it fell to the UK authorities to give effect to art. 86 in accordance with the provisions of art. 88.

Held, dismissing the application:

The Secretary of State was right to conclude that he had no duty to have regard to art. 86 for the purpose of reaching a decision on the proposed merger. His duty was to apply UK competition law. Under the merger control regulation, concentrations with a Community dimension were handled by the Commission unless remitted to a member state. A concentration which fell short of having a Community dimension was dealt with by a member state applying its own national competition law, though a member state could refer the matter to the Commission (under art. 22, para. 3 of the regulation).

The following cases were referred to in the judgment of Neill LJ:

Ahmed Saeed Flugreisen & Anor v Zentrale zur Bekämpfung unlauteren Wettbewerbs e V (Case 66/86) [1989] 2 CEC 654; [1989] ECR 803.
Ministère Public v Asjes & Ors (Joined cases 209–213/84) [1986] ECR 1457.

Jeremy Lever QC and Michael Patchett-Joyce (instructed by the Treasury Solicitor) for the Secretary of State for Trade and Industry and the Director General of Fair Trading.

David Pannick QC and Paul Lasok (instructed by Harbottle & Lewis) for the applicants.

Michael Beloff QC, Richard Fowler QC and Paul Walker (instructed by Linklaters & Paines) for British Airways plc.

JUDGMENT

Neill LJ: This is a renewed application by the two applicant companies, Airlines of Britain Holdings plc and Virgin Atlantic Airways Ltd, for leave to apply for judicial review of decisions made by the Secretary of State for Trade and Industry and the Director General of Fair Trading relating to the proposed acquisition by British Airways plc of all the assets of Davies & Newman Holdings plc. The principal asset of Davies & Newman is Dan-Air Services Ltd.

The relevant decisions as set out in the notice of application were:

(1)   The decision of the Secretary of State made on or about 2 November 1992 not to refer to the Monopolies and Mergers Commission under the *Fair Trading Act* 1973 the proposed acquisition by British Airways of all the assets of Davies & Newman.

(2)   The decision made by or on behalf of the Secretary of State concerning the application of art. 86 of the Treaty of Rome to the acquisition.

(3)   The decision made by or on behalf of the Director General of Fair Trading concerning the application of art. 86 to the acquisition.

The application is renewed following the refusal of leave by *Schiemann* J on 23 November 1992. At the time of the hearing of the application by the judge the Secretary of State had not reached a final decision about the applicability of art. 86.

On Friday 23 October 1992 the Office of Fair Trading wrote to the applicants to inform them that British Airways had announced that it had reached conditional agreement to buy the assets of Davies & Newman. The letters to the applicants continued:

"The arrangements as described appear to constitute a merger situation falling within the merger provisions of the *Fair Trading Act* 1973 and the Director General of Fair Trading will, therefore, be advising the Secretary of State for Trade and Industry whether the merger should be referred to the Monopolies and Mergers Commission for investigation.

The purpose of this letter is . . . to invite [the applicants] to submit to the Office any views they wish the Director General to take into account in preparing his advice."

The applicants were asked to make any representations by 5 pm on Tuesday, 27 October, a deadline which was later extended to 8 am on Wednesday, 28 October.

The powers of the Secretary of State to make a reference to the Commission in anticipation of a merger are contained in sec. 75 of the 1973 Act. The applicants duly made representations within the prescribed time limit. On Monday, 2 November, however, the Secretary of State informed the applicants that he had decided not to make a reference, though he accepted that the proposed merger raised "competition concerns". The applicants, though they were disappointed by the decision of the Secretary of State not to make a reference under the provisions of the 1973 Act, accepted that the Secretary of State had a discretion which in the circumstances could not be challenged by judicial review.

The present case arises from a further submission which was made by the applicants to the Secretary of State on Friday, 30 October. By letters written on behalf of the applicants dated 30 October 1992 attention was drawn to art. 86. The letters contained this paragraph:

"The UK competent authorities are already seized of the proposed British Airways/Dan-Air transaction, and we submit it is their duty under Community law to consider the implications of art. 86 to that transaction. In our view the *Fair*

Trading Act 1973 does not, and cannot exclude the operation of art. 86, and the Secretary of State does not have power to clear a proposed acquisition under the 1973 Act where that acquisition also involves or may involve an infringement of art. 86 and 88 of the EEC Treaty."

On Monday, 2 November the applicants' solicitors were informed that the Secretary of State had considered the submissions with, regard to art. 86 and 88 and had concluded that no action was called for. On the hearing of the renewed application we were informed that the Secretary of State had now considered the matter further and had come to the conclusion on advice that art. 86 and 88 do not apply to the proposed merger.

The relevant EC provisions

Part III of the Treaty of Rome sets out the policy of the Community. Section 1 of Ch. I contains rules on competition applying to undertakings. It is necessary to set out art. 86–89:

"*Article 86*

Any abuse by one or more undertakings of a dominant position within the common market or in a substantial part of it shall be prohibited as incompatible with the common market in so far as it may affect trade between Member States.

Such abuse may, in particular, consist in:

(a) directly or indirectly imposing unfair purchase or selling prices or other unfair trading condition;

(b) limiting production, markets or technical development to the prejudice of consumers;

(c) applying dissimilar conditions to equivalent transactions with other trading parties, thereby placing them at a competitive disadvantage;

(d) making the conclusion of contracts subject to acceptance by the other parties of supplementary obligations which, by their nature or according to commercial usage, have no connection with the subject of such contracts.

Article 87

1. Within three years of the entry into force of this Treaty the Council shall, acting unanimously on a proposal from the Commission and after consulting the Assembly, adopt any appropriate regulations or directives to give effect to the principles set out in Articles 85 and 86.

If such provisions have not been adopted within the period mentioned, they shall be laid down by the Council, acting by a qualified majority on a proposal from the Commission and after consulting the Assembly.

2. The regulations or directives referred to in paragraph 1 shall be designed, in particular:

(a) to ensure compliance with the prohibitions laid down in Article 85(1) and in Article 86 by making provision for fines and periodic penalty payments;

(b) . . .

(c) to define, if need be, in the various branches of the economy, the scope of the provisions of Articles 85 and 86;

(d) . . .

(e) to determine the relationship between national laws and the provisions contained in this section or adopted pursuant to this article.

Article 88

Until the entry into force of the provisions adopted in pursuance of Article 87, the authorities in Member States shall rule on the admissibility of agreements, decisions and concerted practices and on abuse of a dominant position in the common market in accordance with the law of their country and with the provisions of Article 85, in particular paragraph 3, and of Article 86.

Article 89

1. Without prejudice to Article 88, the Commission shall, as soon as it takes up its duties, ensure the application of the principles laid down in Articles 85 and 86. On application by a Member State or on its own initiative, and in cooperation with the competent authorities in the Member States, who shall give it their assistance, the Commission shall investigate cases of suspected infringement of these principles. If it finds that there has been an infringement, it shall propose appropriate measures to bring it to an end.

2. If the infringement is not brought to an end, the Commission shall record such infringement of the principles in a reasoned decision. The Commission may publish its decision and authorise Member States to take the measures, the conditions and details of which it shall determine, needed to remedy the situation."

For the sake of completeness I should also set out the text of art. 235 of the Treaty:

"If action by the Community should prove necessary to attain, in the course of the operation of the common market, one of the objectives of the Community and this Treaty has not provided the necessary powers, the Council shall, acting unanimously on a proposal from the Commission and after consulting the Assembly, take the appropriate measures."

The case for the applicants in the present proceedings is that the Secretary of State remains under an obligation in accordance with art. 88 to consider the applicability of art. 86 because no regulations or directives adopted in pursuance of art. 87 have yet come into force to give effect to the principles set out in art. 86.

The first regulation implementing art. 86 was Council Regulation 17/62 (OJ 1962 L13/204) which was adopted on 6 February 1962. By art. 1 of Regulation 141/62 of 26 November 1962 (OJ 1962 L62/2751), however, it was provided that Regulation 17/62 should not apply in the transport sector.

The next regulation to which we were referred was Council Regulation 3975/87 (OJ 1987 L374/1) which came into force on 1 January 1988. This regulation laid down the procedure for the application of the rules on competition to undertakings in the air transport sector, but it was provided by art. 1 of the regulation that it should apply "only to international air transport between Community airports".

I come therefore to Council Regulation 4064/89 (OJ 1990 L257/13) which came into force on 21 September 1990. It is this regulation which is of crucial importance in the present case. I shall have to make a number of references to its terms.

Regulation 4064/89 is concerned with the control of concentrations between undertakings. The word "concentration" is defined in art. 3 as follows:

"1. A concentration shall be deemed to arise where:

(a) two or more previously independent undertakings merge, or

(b) — one or more persons already controlling at least one undertaking, or

(c) — one or more undertakings

acquire, whether by purchase of securities or assets, by contract or by any other means, direct or indirect control of the whole or parts of one or more other undertakings."

A   By way of preamble to the regulation it was recited that the Council of the European Communities had adopted the regulation having regard to a number of matters. The preamble is expressed in these terms:

"Having regard to the Treaty establishing the European Economic Community, and in particular Articles 87 and 235 thereof . . .

(1) Whereas, for the achievement of the aims of the Treaty establishing the European Economic Community, Article 3(f) gives the Community the objective of instituting 'a system ensuring that competition in the common market is not distorted';

. . .

(3) Whereas the dismantling of internal frontiers is resulting and will continue to result in major corporate reorganisations in the Community, particularly in the form of concentrations;

. . .

(7) Whereas a new legal instrument should therefore be created in the form of a Regulation to permit effective control of all concentrations from the point of view of their effect on the structure of competition in the Community and to be the only instrument applicable to such concentrations;

(8) Whereas this Regulation should therefore be based not only on Article 87 but, principally, on Article 235 of the Treaty, under which the Community may give itself the additional powers of action necessary for the attainment of its objectives, including with regard to concentrations on the markets for agricultural products listed in Annex II to the Treaty;

(9) Whereas the provisions to be adopted in this Regulation should apply to significant structural changes the impact of which on the market goes beyond the national borders of any one Member State;

(10) Whereas the scope of application of this Regulation should therefore be defined according to the geographical area of activity of the undertakings concerned and be limited by quantitative thresholds in order to cover those concentrations which have a Community dimension; whereas, at the end of an initial phase of the application of this Regulation, these thresholds should be reviewed in the light of the experience gained;

. . .

(15) Whereas concentrations which, by reason of the limited market share of the undertakings concerned are not liable to impede effective competition may be presumed to be compatible with the common market; whereas, without prejudice to Articles 85 and 86 of the Treaty, an indication to this effect exists, in particular, where the market share of the undertakings concerned does not exceed 25 per cent either in the common market or in a substantial part of it;

(16) Whereas the Commission should have the task of taking all the decisions necessary to establish whether or not concentrations with a Community dimension are compatible with the common market, as well as decisions designed to restore effective competition;

. . .

(29) Whereas concentrations not covered by this Regulation come, in principle, within the jurisdiction of the Member States; whereas, however, the Commission should have the power to act, at the request of a Member State concerned, in cases where effective competition could be significantly impeded within that Member State's territory;

. . ."

The scope of Regulation 4064/89 is prescribed in art. 1 as follows: A

"1. Without prejudice to Article 22 this Regulation shall apply to all concentrations with a Community dimension as defined in paragraph 2."

It is common ground in the present case:

(1)   that the proposed merger will result in a concentration within the meaning of art. 3; but

B

(2)   that the concentration is not of sufficient size to amount to a concentration with a Community dimension as defined in para. 2 of art. 1.

Article 2 of the regulation provides that concentrations with a Community dimension should be appraised by the Commission. The succeeding articles in the regulation lay down the procedure to be followed by the Commission and prescribe, inter alia, time limits for initiating proceedings and for the giving of decisions and also the investigative powers of the Commission. By art. 9 it is provided that the Commission may in certain   C
circumstances refer a notified concentration to the competent authorities of a member state with a view to the application of that state's national competition law.

I come next to art. 21 and 22. By para. 1 of art. 21 it is provided that, subject to review by the Court of Justice, the Commission shall have sole jurisdiction to take the decisions provided for in the regulation. By para. 2 of art. 21 it is provided that no member state shall apply national legislation on competition to any concentration that has a Community   D
dimension. Article 22 (so far as relevant) is in these terms:

"1. This Regulation alone shall apply to concentrations as defined in Article 3.

2. Regulations No. 17, No. 1017/68, No. 4056/86 and No. 3975/87 shall not apply to concentrations as defined in Article 3.

3. If the Commission finds, at the request of a Member State, that a concentration as defined in Article 3 that has no Community dimension within the meaning of   E
Article 1 creates or strengthens a dominant position as a result of which effective competition would be significantly impeded within the territory of the Member State concerned it may, in so far as the concentration affects trade between Member States, adopt the decisions provided for in Article 8(2), second subparagraph, (3) and (4)."

Article 8 contains provisions relating to the powers of decision of the Commission.   F

The effect of Regulation 4064/89

The argument on behalf of the applicants was developed on the following lines:

(1)   Regulation 3975/87 applied to air transport but only to a limited extent. By para. 2 of art. 22 of Regulation 4064/89 however, Regulation 3975/87 can no longer apply to a concentration as defined in art. 3. The proposed merger is such a concentration.   G
Accordingly Regulation 3975/87 does not apply even to a limited extent to the proposed merger.

(2)   Regulation 4064/89 does not apply to the proposed merger because the scope of the regulation is limited by art. 1 to concentrations with a Community dimension.

(3)   It follows therefore that there is in force no implementing measure which has applied art. 86 to the proposed merger. Accordingly it falls to the UK authorities   H
to give effect to art. 86 in accordance with the provisions of art. 88.

In the context of this argument we were referred to two cases in the European court which I can identify as the *Asjes* case [1986] ECR 1457 and the *Ahmed Saeed* case [1989] 2 CEC 654. These two authorities establish that where regulations or directives adopted in pursuance of art. 87 do not apply to the facts of the particular case the authorities in

A   member states continue to be under a duty under art. 88 to rule on any abuses of a dominant position as prohibited by art. 86.

As one would expect, this argument was presented attractively and with great skill. In my judgment, however, it is bound to fail.

Article 1 of Regulation 4064/89, which defines the scope of the regulation, provides that the limitation of the regulation to "concentrations with a Community dimension" is

B   "without prejudice to Article 22". It seems to me to be quite clear that Regulation 4064/89 has been adopted as an "appropriate" regulation "to give effect to the principles set out in Article 86". In other words, it is a regulation of the kind contemplated in art. 87 of the Treaty and applies generally to all concentrations as defined in art. 3 of the regulation. The effect of the regulation is to require the Commission to deal with all questions arising under art. 85 and 86 and to leave it to the national courts to apply their own domestic competition legislation to concentrations within their purview. This

C   division of work is apparent from the framework of the preamble. It is also apparent from the provisions of art. 21, art. 22, para. 3, and art. 9, para. 3(b). Article 9 empowers the Commission to refer a case downwards to a member state and in that event the member state applies its own national competition law. Per contra, it is provided in art. 22, para. 3 that a member state can refer a concentration upwards to the Commission so that the Commission may determine whether a concentration that has no Community dimension nevertheless may affect trade between member states.

D   It was submitted on behalf of the Secretary of State that Regulation 4064/89 creates a "seamless system for dealing with concentrations within the Community". Concentrations with a Community dimension are handled by the Commission unless remitted to a member state. A concentration which falls short of having a Community dimension is dealt with by a member state applying its own national competition law, though a member state can refer the matter to the Commission under art. 22, para. 3. I consider

E   these submissions to be correct.

It follows therefore that I consider that the Secretary of State was right to conclude that he had no duty to have regard to art. 86 for the purpose of reaching a decision on the proposed merger. His duty was to apply UK competition law.

In these circumstances it is unnecessary to deal separately with the other two decisions which are referred to in the notice of application.

F   I would refuse the application for leave to apply for judicial review.

Beldam LJ: I agree.

Kennedy LJ: I also agree.

(*Application dismissed with one set of costs in favour of the Secretary of State for Trade & Industry and the Director General of Fair Trading*)

G

H

Re Portbase (Clothing) Ltd.
Mond v Taylor & Ors.

Chancery Division (Companies Court).
Chadwick J.
Judgment delivered 15 December 1992.

Winding up — Preferential debts — Priorities — Expenses of winding up — Company executed debentures creating fixed and floating charges — Secured creditors executed deed of priority — Debenture creating fixed charge postponed to subsequent debenture creating floating charge — Company went into creditors' voluntary liquidation — Whether preferential debts payable in priority to secured debts — Whether expenses of winding up payable in priority to preferential debts — Insolvency Act 1986, sec. 115, 175.

This was an application by the liquidator of Portbase (Clothing) Ltd ("the company") for directions whether the claims of preferential creditors to be paid out of the proceeds of the realised book and other debts had priority over the claims of floating charge holders, who had priority over other fixed charge holders by virtue of a deed of priority.

There was a subsidiary question whether the costs and expenses of the winding up were to be paid out of the proceeds of the realised book and other debts in priority to the claims of the preferential creditors.

Before going into liquidation the company had given a debenture creating fixed and floating charges over all its property to the bank and a second debenture, secured by a floating charge, to its directors. At a time when the company's indebtedness to the bank amounted to some £350,000, the company obtained a loan of £200,000 from the trustees of its parent company's pension scheme (the trustees of the pension scheme included the company's directors). The company then executed a third debenture in favour of the trustees for the purpose of securing the £200,000 loan; and the company, the bank, the directors, as holders of the second debenture, and the trustees entered into a deed of priority postponing the bank's debenture and the directors' debenture to the new debenture in favour of the trustees. The trustees' debenture contained fixed and floating charges over all the company's property in substantially the same terms as those in the bank's debenture.

The total of realisations made by the liquidator and a receiver appointed by the trustees was £97,848. The liabilities of the company included £39,500 or thereabouts due to the Inland Revenue and to the Customs and Excise as preferential creditors. The payment of liquidation expenses and preferential creditors in priority to the claims of the secured creditors would leave little, if any, surplus. If the liquidation expenses and the preferential creditors did not rank ahead of the trustees, there would be insufficient to cover the liquidator's expenses and nothing for the preferential creditors. Whatever the position as between the trustees, the liquidator and the preferential creditors, there was no prospect of any payment to meet the secured claims of the bank and the directors under their debenture or the claims of the unsecured creditors.

The question whether the trustees' debenture created a fixed or a floating charge over the book and other debts was not argued (counsel reserving the point for argument in an appellate court). The priority question was therefore argued on the basis that the trustees' debenture created a floating charge, whereas the bank's debenture did create a fixed charge over the book and other debts.

Held, answering the liquidator's questions in the affirmative:

1. The effect of the deed of priority (as between the bank and the trustees) was that the bank's debenture had to be treated as if, when made, it had been expressed to be subject

A

to the trustees' debenture. The position as between the bank and trustees was that, upon crystallisation of the floating charge in the trustees' debenture, the book and other debts of the company were to be applied in satisfaction of the debt secured by that charge before they could be applied in satisfaction of the bank's debt. (Re Camden Brewery Ltd (1911) 106 LT 598 (note) applied.)

B

2. Where a subsequent fixed charge was made subject to a prior floating charge, the effect of sec. 175(2)(b) of the Insolvency Act 1986 was to give the preferential creditors priority over both the first and the second chargees. (Waters v Widdows [1984] VR 503 followed; Re Woodroffes (Musical Instruments) Ltd [1986] Ch 366 distinguished.)

3. "The company's assets" in sec. 115 of the 1986 Act out of which the liquidation expenses were payable included assets which were subject to a charge which as created was a floating charge but which had crystallised prior to the commencement of the liquidation. (Re Barleycorn Enterprises Ltd [1970] Ch 465 applied; Re Christonette International Ltd [1982] 1 WLR 1245 not followed.)

C

The following cases were referred to in the judgment:

Barleycorn Enterprises Ltd, Re [1970] Ch 465.
Brightlife Ltd, Re (1986) 2 BCC 99,359; [1987] Ch 200.
Camden Brewery Ltd, Re (1911) 106 LT 598 (note).
Cheah Theam Swee v Equiticorp Finance Group Ltd & Anor [1992] BCC 98; [1992] 1 AC 472.

D

Christonette International Ltd, Re [1982] 1 WLR 1245.
Company No. 005009 of 1987, Re a (1988) 4 BCC 424.
Fablehill Ltd, Re [1991] BCC 590.
Griffin Hotel Co Ltd, Re [1941] Ch 129.
Lewis Merthyr Consolidated Collieries Ltd, Re [1929] 1 Ch 498.

E

Siebe Gorman & Co Ltd v Barclays Bank Ltd [1979] 2 Lloyd's Rep 142.
Stephenson (Robert) & Co Ltd, Re (1912) 106 LT 595; [1913] 2 Ch 201 (CA).
Waters v Widdows [1984] VR 503.
Woodroffes (Musical Instruments) Ltd, Re [1986] Ch 366.

Simon Mortimore QC and Lexa Hilliard (instructed by Halliwell Landau) for the liquidator.

David Halpern (instructed by Baker & McKenzie) for the first, second and fifth respondents and (instructed by Pannone & Partners) for the sixth respondent.

F

JUDGMENT

Chadwick J: Portbase (Clothing) Ltd ("the company") is incorporated under the *Companies Act* 1985. On 9 May 1991 it was resolved that the company be placed into creditors' voluntary liquidation. This application has been brought by the liquidator for the purpose of having questions which arise in the winding up of the company determined by the court pursuant to sec. 112 of the *Insolvency Act* 1986.

G

The questions for determination arise in the following circumstances. On 21 June 1988 the company, by way of debenture, created fixed and floating charges over all its property in favour of Lloyds Bank plc ("the bank") as security for all moneys and liabilities then or at any time thereafter owing by the company to the bank. On 19 April 1989, the company granted a second debenture, secured by a floating charge, in respect of an advance of £82,787 made to it by its directors, William Thomas Taylor and Maureen Taylor.

H

On 16 January 1991 the company's indebtedness to the bank amounted to some £350,000. The company obtained a loan of £200,000 from the trustees of the Morrison Fashions Ltd Pension Scheme for the purpose of reducing its debt to the bank. Morrison Fashions Ltd was the company's immediate parent; and the trustees of the pension

scheme included Mr and Mrs Taylor. On the same day, 16 January 1991, the company   A
executed two documents: (1) a third debenture in favour of the trustees for the purpose
of securing the £200,000 loan and (2) a deed of priority. The other parties to the deed of
priority were the bank, Mr and Mrs Taylor as holders of the second debenture and the
trustees.

The purpose of the deed of priority was to postpone the bank's debenture of 21 June
1988 and the Taylors' debenture of 18 April 1989 to the new debenture created that day
in favour of the trustees. The trustees' debenture contained fixed and floating charges   B
over all the company's property in substantially the same terms as those in the bank's
debenture.

The company ceased to trade at or about the beginning of March 1991. On 13 March
1991 the bank closed the company's trading account; and opened a No. 2 account in the
company's name for the purpose of collecting book and other debts. The total of the
payments into that account has been £53,692: £19,252 of that sum represented moneys   C
collected since the commencement of the liquidation on 9 May 1991.

On 8 August 1991 the bank accounted to the liquidator for the moneys collected since
the commencement of the liquidation. On 25 September 1991 the trustees appointed a
receiver under the powers contained in the trustees' debenture. On 30 September 1991
the bank accounted to the receiver for the balance in the company's No. 2 account
(£34,440) representing moneys collected prior to the commencement of the liquidation.   D

The liquidator has himself collected further book debts, amounting to £31,815, and
made other realisations amounting together to £12,371. Taken together, and excluding
interest, the proceeds received from the realisation of the company's assets in the
liquidation and the receivership amount to £97,848.

The liabilities of the company include £39,500 or thereabouts due to the Inland
Revenue and to Customs and Excise as preferential creditors. The liquidator has   E
incurred substantial expenses in the liquidation; including expenses in relation to this
application. The payment of liquidation expenses and preferential creditors in priority
to the claims of the secured creditors — and, in particular, in priority to the claims of the
trustees who themselves have priority over the other secured creditors by virtue of the
deed of priority — will leave little, if any, surplus. On the other hand, if the liquidation
expenses and the preferential creditors do not rank ahead of the trustees, there will be
insufficient to cover the liquidator's expenses and nothing for the preferential creditors.   F
Whatever the position as between the trustees, the liquidator and the preferential
creditors, there is no prospect of any payment to meet the secured claims of the bank
(£154,000 and interest) and the directors under their debenture (£82,787 and interest)
or the claims of the other unsecured creditors, shown as £129,638 in the directors'
statement of affairs.

It is in these circumstances that the liquidator has made the present application. The   G
respondents to that application are Mr and Mrs Taylor, the other pension scheme
trustees, and the receiver appointed by the trustees under their debenture. Following
amendment and reamendment, the substantive relief now sought by that application is
the determination by the court of the following questions:

"(1)(a) . . . whether the company, by the [trustees'] debenture . . . created a
fixed or floating charge on (a) its book debts . . . and/or on (b) its other monetary   H
debts and claims [collectively 'book and other debts'];

(b) in the event that the trustees' debenture created a floating charge on the book
and other debts . . .

(i) whether the claims of the preferential creditors of the company, as defined
by sec. 386 of the *Insolvency Act* 1986, to be paid out of the proceeds of the

A   realised book and other debts have priority over the claims thereto of the trustees and/or the . . . receiver . . . pursuant to the terms of the trustees' debenture; and in that event;

    (ii) whether the costs and expenses of the winding up of the company must be paid out of the proceeds of the realised book and other debts in priority to the claims of the preferential creditors . . ."

B   The first of those questions — whether the trustees' debenture created a fixed or a floating charge over book and other debts — has not been argued before me. Mr Halpern, who appeared for the first, second and fifth respondents, accepted — in my view, quite properly — that, on the present state of the authorities, I would be unlikely to hold that the trustees' debenture created a fixed charge over book and other debts.

The difficulty, which Mr Halpern recognised, may be explained shortly. The property charged by the trustees' debenture includes:

C   "Secondly: All book debts both present and future due or owing to the company . . .

Thirdly: All other monetary debts and claims . . . both present and future (including things in action which give rise or may give rise to a debt or debts) due or owing to the company . . ."

D   The final paragraph in the charging clause is in these terms, so far as material:

"The charges hereby created . . . as regards all charged property secondly and thirdly described shall constitute first fixed mortgages by assignment subject to reassignment on redemption and as to the charged property sixthly described shall be a floating charge . . ."

The property "sixthly described" is described in these terms:

E   "The undertaking and all property and assets of the company both present and future including . . . the charged property first secondly thirdly fourthly and fifthly described (if and in so far as the charges thereon or any part or parts thereof herein contained shall for any reason be ineffective as fixed charges)."

Clause 4.2.4 of the trustees' debenture seeks to prevent the company from dealing with its book or other debts without the prior consent of the trustees "except by getting in and realising them in the ordinary and proper course of its business". That would, as it seems to me, necessarily include the payment of the proceeds of those book and other debts into the company's bank account. At the time when the debenture was granted the company's account with the bank was substantially overdrawn. Contemporary correspondence suggests that all those concerned — the trustees, the company and the bank — expected that situation to continue during the term of the loan which the trustees' debenture was intended to secure. In any event, the trustees' debenture contains no provision restricting the use which the company might make of any balance which might from time to time stand to the credit of its account with the bank. The purpose of the loan was to enable the company to continue trading. It could not sensibly have been contemplated that the trustees' consent would be required to the operation of the company's bank account in the ordinary course of business.

In these circumstances, to hold that the trustees' debenture succeeded in creating a fixed security over the book and other debts, I would have to be satisfied that the reasoning set out in the judgment of *Hoffmann* J in *Re Brightlife Ltd* (1986) 2 BCC 99,359 at pp. 99,362–99,363 was plainly wrong. Mr Halpern appreciated, realistically, that he would be unlikely to discharge the burden. He expressly reserved the point for argument in an appellate court.

I approach the second question, therefore, on the basis that the trustees' debenture created a floating charge, and not a fixed charge, on the company's book and other

debts. As I have already indicated, the charging provisions in the bank's debenture were   A
in substantially the same terms as those in the trustees' debenture. In particular, the
charging provisions in relation to book and other debts, which I have set out above, are
in identical terms in the two debentures. Nevertheless, for reasons which require a short
explanation, the second question was argued before me on the premise that the bank's
debenture did create a fixed charge over book and other debts.

The bank's debenture contains, at cl. 2(b)(i), a requirement that the company shall   B
not without the consent in writing of the bank,

> "sell assign discount factor charge or otherwise dispose of the charged property
> secondly or thirdly described or any part thereof save in accordance with cl. 9(d)
> hereof . . ."

Clause 9(d) required the company to,

> "pay into its account or accounts with the bank all moneys which it may receive in   C
> respect of the book and other debts and claims mortgaged (by way of assignment)
> or charged by it . . ."

Comparable provisions in the Barclays Bank standard debenture, at cl. 5(c), led *Slade* J
in *Siebe Gorman & Co Ltd v Barclays Bank Ltd* [1979] 2 Lloyd's Rep 142 to the
conclusion that that debenture had succeeded in creating a fixed charge over book debts
(see at pp. 158–159). The point was considered and explained by *Knox* J in *Re a
Company No. 005009 of 1987* (1988) 4 BCC 424 at pp. 432–434 — see, in particular, at   D
p. 434.

In these circumstances I have thought it right to accept, for the purposes of deciding
the second question raised by the liquidator's summons, that the bank's debenture did
create a fixed charge over book and other debts. Mr Halpern, for the trustees, is not
concerned to argue the contrary; indeed, his submissions in relation to the second
question are necessarily based upon the premise that the bank's charge is a fixed charge.   E
The liquidator has not thought it necessary to argue against that premise in the interests
of the preferential creditors. He may well have taken the view that I would regard myself
as bound to follow the reasoning of *Slade* J in *Siebe Gorman*; and that the present case is
not distinguishable from *Siebe Gorman* on the facts. I should, however, make it clear
that, in deciding the second question on this basis, I should not be taken to have formed
any view on arguments which might have been advanced by the preferential creditors,   F
who have not been represented before me.

The right of preferential creditors to have their debts paid in a liquidation or
receivership in priority to the claims of debenture holders under a floating charge was
introduced, almost one hundred years ago, by the *Preferential Payments in Bankruptcy
Amendment Act* 1897, sec. 2 and 3. The comparable provisions are now contained in,
respectively, sec. 175 of the *Insolvency Act* 1986 and sec. 40 of the 1986 Act and sec. 196
of the *Companies Act* 1985. Section 175(2)(b) of the 1986 Act is in these terms: G

> "(2) Preferential debts—
>
> (b)   so far as the assets of the company available for payment of general creditors
> are insufficient to meet them, have priority over the claims of holders of
> debentures secured by, or holders of, any floating charge created by the
> company, and shall be paid accordingly out of any property comprised in or
> subject to that charge."   H

For the purpose of that subsection a preferential debt is a debt listed in Sch. 6 to the 1986
Act (money owed to the Inland Revenue for income tax deducted at source; VAT, car
tax etc.; social security and pension scheme contributions; remuneration etc. of employees
etc.) — see sec. 386 of the Act; and a floating charge means a charge which, as created,
was a floating charge — see sec. 251 of the Act. Section 40 of the 1986 Act applies where

A   a receiver has been appointed on behalf of debenture holders secured by a charge which, as created, was a floating charge; but only if the company is not at the time in course of being wound up. Section 196 of the *Companies Act* 1985 applies where possession is taken, by or on behalf of debenture holders of property [comprised in or subject to a charge], which, as created, was a floating charge, and the company is not at that time in the course of being wound up. In the present case the relevant provisions are those contained in sec. 175 of the 1986 Act.

B   It is clear that, in the present case, the assets of the company available for payment of general creditors are insufficient to meet the preferential debts. On the figures which I have set out earlier in this judgment there are no assets available for payment of general, meaning unsecured, creditors. It is also clear that, on the basis that the trustees' debenture created a floating charge, and not a fixed charge, over the company's book and other debts, the trustees are holders of a debenture secured by a floating charge. It

C   is irrelevant, in that context, that the floating charge in the trustees' debenture crystallised in or about March 1991, prior to liquidation. In those circumstances sec. 175(2)(b) of the 1986 Act requires, in terms, that the preferential debts have priority over the claims of the trustees and "shall be paid accordingly out of any property comprised in or subject to that charge".

  Nevertheless, but for the deed of priority in the present case, the book and other debts
D   of the company would not be available to satisfy the preferential debts. That property would be taken out of sec. 175(2)(b) of the 1986 Act by the prior fixed charge in favour of the bank. That is because the property out of which the preferential debts are to be paid does not include property or assets which are never payable to the chargee (or any receiver for the chargee) as holder of the floating charge — see *Re Lewis Merthyr Consolidated Collieries Ltd* [1929] 1 Ch 498, per Lord *Hanworth* MR at p. 511 and per *Lawrence* LJ at p. 512. The basis for that view is, I think, that where property is
E   comprised in a prior fixed charge it is not that property, but only the equity of redemption in that property, that can be said to be comprised in or subject to the subsequent floating charge.

  The first point which I have to decide, therefore, is the true effect of the deed of priority. The purpose of the deed, as appears from the recital, is to record an agreement as to "the respective priorities as from the date hereof of the original first and second
F   debentures and the new first debenture". The "original first and second debentures" are, respectively, the bank's debenture and the Taylors' debenture and the "new first debenture" is the trustees' debenture. The operative clauses are in these terms, so far as material:

> "1. The original first debenture holder hereby agrees that the original first debenture shall be postponed to and rank in priority immediately after the new
G   first debenture to the limited extent of the loan as therein defined.
>
> 2. [a similar provision in relation to the original second debenture]
>
> 3. All parties agree that the new first debenture shall rank in priority to the original first and original second debentures to the limited extent of the loan as defined on the new first debenture.
>
> 4. The parties hereto agree that nothing herein contained shall as between the
H   company and the original first debenture holder affect or prejudice any of the rights or remedies of the said original first debenture holder which shall remain in full force subject only to the new first debenture and postponement of the security of the original first debenture to the extent aforesaid shall be deemed to relate only to the moneys secured by the new first debenture and shall not in respect of any further moneys advanced by the new first debenture holder to the company

be deemed to confer on them any like rights of priority over the original first   A
debenture holder.

5. [a similar provision in relation to the original second debenture] . . ."

"The loan" has the meaning given to that expression by cl. 1.1 of the trustees' debenture. It means the sum of £200,000 together with interest and the costs of perfecting or enforcing the trustees' debenture. It is, I think, synonymous with the expression "the moneys secured by the new first debenture" which is used in cl. 4 of the deed of priority.   B

In considering the true effect of the deed of priority, it is, I think, helpful to keep in mind that both the bank's debenture and the trustees' debenture contained fixed charges as well as floating charges. The position immediately before the execution of the deed of priority — ignoring for the purpose of this analysis the floating charge to secure the Taylors' debenture — was that, in relation to any asset subject to the fixed charges, the bank's charge had priority over the trustees' charge. There is no doubt that the bank and   C the trustees were entitled, by agreement between them, to alter the priorities of their respective charges — see *Cheah Theam Swee v Equiticorp Finance Group Ltd* [1992] BCC 98. That is to say, the bank and the trustees were entitled to agree that the proceeds of any realisation of any asset subject to both the fixed charges should be paid to the trustees rather than to the bank; and that the debt secured by the trustees' charge (or some defined part of that debt) should be satisfied out of the proceeds of the charged asset before any part of those proceeds was applied towards the satisfaction of the debt   D secured by the bank's charge. In my view, this is what they have done by the deed of priority. They have agreed that, instead of the proceeds of realisation of any charged asset being applied to the satisfaction of their respective secured debts in the order which would otherwise be determined by the terms of their charges and the dates upon which they were created, those proceeds should be applied first in payment of the moneys secured by the trustees' debenture. The effect, therefore, is that the bank's debenture has been made subject to the trustees' debenture — as cl. 4 of the deed itself records. It   E must follow, in my view that a fixed charge in the bank's debenture became subject to a floating charge in the trustees' debenture; as would have been the case if the bank's debenture had been made at the same time as (or after), and had been expressed to be subject to, the trustees' debenture.

On the basis that the effect of the deed of priority (as between the bank and the trustees) is that the bank's debenture must be treated as if, when made, it had been   F expressed to be subject to the trustees' debenture, the position as between the bank and trustees is that, upon crystallisation of the floating charge in the trustees' debenture, the book and other debts of the company must be applied in satisfaction of the debt secured by that charge before they can be applied in satisfaction of the bank's debt — see *Re Camden Brewery Ltd* (1911) 106 LT 598 (note). *Fletcher Moulton* LJ explained the principles in these terms at p. 599:   G

> "The language of the charging clause . . . states expressly that the charge created by the later deed comes after the charge created by the earlier deed. It follows, therefore, in my opinion, that the floating charge created by the earlier deed, which extends over the after-acquired properties, takes precedence as a charge over the specific mortgage of those properties created by the later deed.
>
> This creates a perfectly intelligible legal position, and there is no difficulty in   H deducing from it the rights of the respective parties. So long as the company is a going company and no default is made, the floating charges do not become affixed to any portion of the property of the company, and it can deal with any part of this property as it thinks best, subject, of course, to any specific mortgages which exist upon such part. If during this period any of these later acquired properties should be sold, the precedence would be effected by the specific mortgage given by the

A
later deed, but not by either of the floating charges, but if a winding up should
take place so that both floating charges crystallise, the earlier floating charge
would take effect on these after-acquired properties in priority to the specific
mortgage given by the later deed."

See also *Re Robert Stephenson & Co Ltd* (1912) 106 LT 595, per *Parker* J at pp. 597 and
598; and, in the Court of Appeal, [1913] 2 Ch 201 per *Farwell* LJ at p. 205.

B
    The liquidator submits that in such a case — that is to say in a case where a subsequent
fixed charge is made subject to a prior floating charge — the effect of sec. 175(2)(b) of
the 1986 Act is to give the preferential creditors priority over both the first and the
second chargees. It was so held in the Supreme Court of Victoria by *Nicholson* J in
Waters v Widdows [1984] VR 503. That was a decision on the provisions of sec. 331(1)
of the Companies (Victoria) Code — provisions similar to those now found in sec. 40 of
the *Insolvency Act* 1986 and sec. 196 of the *Companies Act* 1985 — but the reasoning by
C
which *Nicholson* J reached his conclusion would have applied with equal force to the
provisions in sec. 446 of the Code — that is to say provisions applicable in a winding up
which are in terms similar to those now in sec. 175(2)(b) of the 1986 Act. The judge
explained the question, and his answer, in these terms, at pp. 512–513:

> "The question is whether s. 331 [of the Code] operates to oblige the receivers to
> pay the employees in priority to the claims of the bank [the first chargee] pursuant
D
> to its floating charge and the claims of General Credits [the second chargee]
> pursuant to its charge having regard to the fact that the latter purports to have
> been a fixed charge from its inception. The section clearly has this effect in relation
> to the bank's charge so that again a strange result would enure if it does not have
> this effect in relation to the General Credits charge.

> In my view s. 331 on its proper construction has the effect of giving priority to the
> claims of the employee creditors . . ."

E
The judge reached his conclusion primarily on the basis that, upon its true construction,
the relevant statutory provision contained a clear legislative direction to the receivers
appointed by the bank to pay the preferred employee creditors in preference to the bank
out of such of the property coming into their control or possession as was subject to the
floating charge in favour of the bank — see [1984] VR 503 at p. 514, lines 48–52. But he
had regard, also, to the policy which, in his view, lay behind provisions favouring
F
preferential creditors at the expense of the holders of floating charges. He said (at
p. 513, line 51):

> "In arriving at this conclusion I have also had regard to the various expressions of
> judicial view as to the policy behind the section in question. In *Re Lewis
> Merthyr Consolidated Collieries Ltd*, Tomlin J said at [1929] 1 Ch p. 507: 'I quite
> understand that in regard to a floating charge there may be a reason for giving the
> priority, because until the receiver is appointed or possession is taken, the charge
G
> does not crystallise, and it may well be said that this particular class of debts
> (referring to employees) which may perhaps have contributed to produce the very
> assets upon which the floating charge will crystallise, are proper to be paid out of
> those assets before the debenture holder takes his principal and interest out of
> them. That seems to me to be a perfectly intelligible reason for the legislation, and
> is in accord with the view which I take of the section.'

H
Tomlin J's decision was confirmed on appeal: [1929] 1 Ch 510. Similar expressions
are to be found in the judgment of Barwick CJ in the course of his . . . judgment
in *Stein v Saywell* (1969) 43 ALJR 183 . . . His Honour said at p. 188: 'The policy
behind sec. 196 [of the New South Wales legislation — equivalent to sec. 40 in the
UK Act of 1986] and sec. 292(4) (which broadly corresponds to sec. 446 of the
Code) [equivalent to sec. 175(2)(b) in the UK Act] is, I think, quite plain.

A creditor who accepts a floating charge over a company's assets allows the
business of the company to be carried on and the assets of the company which are
subject to the floating charge to be altered, perhaps augmented, by the efforts of
the company and its employees. The holder of the floating charge is not to be to
able to displace the priorities which the legislation accords to certain debts which
accrue during the carrying on of the business; amongst those priorities is certain
remuneration of employees of the company. The method of ensuring that the
holder of such a charge does not compete with those creditors to whose debts
priority of payment is given is best seen, I think, in sec. 196 [of the New South
Wales Code]. Under that section, in the period prior to the actual commencement
of the liquidation of a company, a receiver for the debenture holder with funds in
hand which are the produce of the realisation of the charge created initially as a
floating charge is bound to pay out of those funds the debts of the preferred
creditors.'

In my view, these policy considerations as expressed by Tomlin J and Barwick CJ
have relevance to the present case. Although the General Credits security is
expressed in the form of a fixed charge and indeed of a conveyance of legal and
equitable estate, the fact that General Credits agreed with the bank that its
security should take in priority after the bank makes it clear that it was never the
intention of the parties that the company would do otherwise than carry on
business in the normal way until some further event occurred. In these
circumstances, I think that it would be unconscionable for the employees to be
deprived of the preferential rights unless the section makes it very clear that this is
the case. For the reasons already expressed, I think that the section makes it clear
that the employees are so entitled to preference and it is apparent that this result
is in accordance with the policy behind it."

Mr Halpern, on behalf of the trustees, attacked the reasoning which led *Nicholson* J
to reach the conclusion which he did in *Waters v Widdows*. He pointed out, correctly,
that the decision is not binding upon me. He submitted that the judge failed to give
proper effect to the principle that the finance company, General Credits, as the holder
of a fixed charge, was entitled to be paid out of the assets subject to that charge before
any part of those assets could be applied towards payment of the unsecured creditors,
including (in the absence of a statutory requirement to the contrary) preferential
creditors. There is, of course, no statutory provision which postpones the holder of a
fixed charge to the claims of preferential creditors.

The security position in *Waters v Widdows* was indistinguishable from that in *Re
Camden Brewery Ltd* and *Re Robert Stephenson & Co Ltd*. The principle to be derived
from those decisions of the Court of Appeal, as I understand it, is that holder of a
subsequent fixed charge which has been made subject to a prior floating charge — either
by express provisions in the fixed charge itself or by a restriction in the floating charge of
which the holder of the fixed charge had notice — takes his security upon terms that, if
before the charged property has been realised under that fixed charge events occur
which cause the floating charge to crystallise, then the proceeds of realisation must be
paid to the holder of the floating charge; the holder of the fixed charge can have no claim
upon those proceeds until the claims under the floating charge have been paid out. In
those circumstances, if the floating charge has crystallised prior to liquidation, the
position at the time when sec. 175(2)(b) of the 1986 Act comes to be applied will be that
the property in relation to which the successive charges have been created will be
property comprised in or subject to the floating charge for the purpose of that subsection.
It will not be taken out of that subsection by the rule in *Re Lewis Merthyr Consolidated
Collieries Ltd*. There is no basis upon which that rule can apply in the circumstances
postulated: first, because the charged property, or the proceeds of realisation, are

A   payable to the floating chargee and not to the fixed chargee: secondly, or alternatively, because the property subject to the floating charge is the charged property itself and not an equity of redemption associated with the fixed charge.

Section 175(2)(b) of the 1986 Act requires that preferential debts "shall be paid" out of property comprised in or subject to the floating charge. If, upon a true analysis, the property in relation to which the successive charges have been created is not taken out of that subsection by the rule in *Re Lewis Merthyr Consolidated Collieries Ltd* then it must be applied in payment of the preferential debts. The existence of the subsequent fixed charge is immaterial. For the reasons set out by *Nicholson* J in *Waters v Widdows*, the preferential creditors are not to be deprived of their rights to payment out of the property to which sec. 175(2)(b) applies unless the section so provides. It does not so provide.

C   Mr Halpern submits that I ought not to regard myself as free to adopt the reasoning which I have set out above; rather, I should follow the decision of *Nourse* J in *Re Woodroffes (Musical Instruments) Ltd* [1986] Ch 366. I should, of course, be very reluctant to adopt a view which was inconsistent with a decision of a judge sitting in this division on a point which had been properly before him.

The facts in *Woodroffes* were these. In 1980 the company created an all moneys debenture in favour of a bank. The bank's debenture contained (inter alia) a floating charge over all the company's undertaking and assets. The bank had the right, by giving notice under the debenture, to convert that floating charge into a fixed charge on any assets specified in the notice. On 9 August 1982 the company created a second debenture to secure £25,000 advanced by Mrs Woodroffe, a director of the company. That debenture was expressed to be subject to, and to rank immediately after, the bank's debenture. It, too, contained provision for conversion of the floating charge thereby created into a fixed charge by notice. On 27 August 1982 Mrs Woodroffe gave notice converting her security into a fixed charge on the whole of the company's undertaking and assets. The bank did not give a similar notice. On 1 September 1982 the bank served a formal demand for repayment and appointed joint receivers under its floating charge. On 28 November 1982 the company was ordered to be wound up by the court. The moneys collected by the joint receivers, after payment to the bank of amounts in respect of its fixed charges over specific assets under the 1980 debenture, amounted to £95,846; a sum that was insufficient to satisfy the balance of the bank's claim, Mrs Woodroffe's claim and the preferential creditors.

In order to understand the way in which the arguments were presented to the judge in *Woodroffes* it is necessary to keep in mind that the relevant section under which the preferential creditors in that case could claim payment out of assets coming into the hands of receivers appointed by the holder of a floating charge — sec. 94(1) of the *Companies Act* 1948 (the statutory successor to sec. 3 of the 1897 Act) — did not, in terms, apply to "a charge which, as created, was a floating charge" — compare sec. 40(1) of the 1986 Act and sec. 196(1) of the 1985 Act — and there was no statutory definition of "floating charge" in terms similar to those now found in sec. 251 of the 1986 Act.

In those circumstances the principal issue in the *Woodroffes* case was whether, at the date when the bank appointed joint receivers (1 September 1982) the bank was the holder of a debenture secured by a floating charge for the purposes of sec. 94(1) of the *Companies Act* 1948. That turned on the answer to one or both of the following questions: (1) whether the bank's charge had crystallised before 1 September 1982; and, if so (2) whether, for the purposes of sec. 94(1) of the 1948 Act, "floating charge" was to be construed in the sense now adopted in the 1985 and 1986 legislation — that is to say, a charge which, as created, was a floating charge — or had a more limited meaning — that is to say, a charge which was a floating charge at the relevant date on which the section fell to be applied, being the date of the appointment of a receiver or the date of taking possession of the charged property (as the case might be).

Nourse J held, on the facts, that the bank's floating charge did not crystallise before 1 September 1982. He took the view that that made it unnecessary for him to consider the second of the two questions which I have described above — see [1986] Ch 366 at p. 380C.

His decision on the first question led to what he described as "the rather odd result already indicated". On the basis of his finding, the position was that, at the date of the appointment of the joint receivers by the bank, Mrs Woodroffe's charge had become a fixed charge (on 27 August 1982) but the bank's charge, to which Mrs Woodroffe's charge was expressed to be subject, had remained a floating charge. The judge described the result in these terms at p. 375A–C:

> "If the bank's charge did not crystallise until 1 September, then the result, although rather an odd one, is not in dispute. The order of priority is (1) the bank to the extent of Mrs Woodroffe's £25,000 plus interest to date (about £9,500); (2) the preferential creditors; (3) the bank as to the balance of its claim; and (4) Mrs Woodroffe. The reason for this rather odd result is that the bank, although a floating chargee, ranks prior to Mrs Woodroffe who, as a fixed chargee, ranks prior to the preferential creditors. It would mean that the bank would get about £34,500, the preferential creditors would get about £61,346 and Mrs Woodroffe would get nothing."

In order to hold that "Mrs Woodroffe . . . as a fixed chargee, ranks prior to the preferential creditors" it was necessary to make the assumption that her charge — which, as created, had been a floating charge — was, as result of the conversion by notice which had occurred on 27 August 1982, not to be regarded as a floating charge for the purposes of sec. 94(1) of the 1948 Act. In other words, it was necessary to assume that sec. 94(1) of the 1948 Act did not extend to all charges which were floating charges as created. This was, of course, the issue raised in the second of the two questions which I have described above the question which the judge held that he did not need to decide. But the point had not been conceded. It was the point taken by the Crown in the context of its alternative submission (see p. 371E–F):

> "on the true construction of section 94 of the Companies Act 1948, the preferential debts owing to the commissioners should be paid in priority to the debts owing to the bank *and Mrs Woodroffe*. . ."(emphasis added)

Nevertheless, it seems that point was not pressed by the Crown in relation to the result that would follow if it were to succeed on its primary submission that the bank's debenture did not crystallise until 1 September 1982 (see p. 370G–H). The Crown's approach may be explained by the fact that, on the figures in that case, the preferential creditors would be paid substantially the whole of their debts if the Crown succeeded on its primary submission without it being necessary to challenge the priority of Mrs Woodroffe's charge.

Whatever the reason for the Crown's approach to this point, the fact that it was not addressed by the judge when explaining what the result would be if the bank's charge had not crystallised before 1 September 1982 suggests that, in the passage at p. 375A–C which I have set out above, he was really doing no more than record, as if it were a decision, a result which he thought was not in issue.

It appears from the report at [1986] Ch 366 that the point to which that passage is directed was never the subject of argument. In particular, the judge's attention was not drawn to the decision of *Nicholson* J in *Waters v Widdows*; nor was he taken to the

A statement of principle in *Re Camden Brewery Ltd* which I have set out above. The note of the submissions made by counsel for the bank contains the following passage at p. 368E–F:

> ". . . the notice given by Mrs Woodroffe on 27 August 1982 caused her debenture to become a second fixed charge instead of a second floating charge but which ranked subject to and immediately after the bank's debenture. However, the effect of Mrs Woodroffe's crystallising her own charge alters the priorities as
>
> B between the bank and preferential creditors: *In re Robert Stephenson & Co. Ltd.* [1913] 2 Ch. 201."

It is difficult to find any passage in the *Robert Stephenson* case which could be authority for the submission which counsel is there reported to have made. The position of preferential creditors does not appear to have been under consideration at all in that case. But, when that submission is put in the context of the bank's primary submission

C — which was that the bank's charge crystallised automatically upon the crystallisation of Mrs Woodroffe's charge — it may be that all that was being said was that, because the effect of Mrs Woodroffe crystallising her own charge was that the bank's charge crystallised at the same time, the priority between the bank and the preferential creditors was thereby altered.

I have examined, at some length, the arguments which were presented to *Nourse* J in

D *Woodroffes* in order to see whether the point which I now have to decide was really before him in that case. I take the view that he was not asked to decide the point; and that, in the passage on which Mr Halpern relies, the judge was doing no more than record, as a consequence which would follow from findings which he was about to make on other issues, a result which he thought was not in issue. That was, I think, the view which *Vinelott* J took of that passage, when he referred to it as "the solution to this puzzle that was agreed between counsel and accepted by *Nourse* J", see *Re Fablehill Ltd*

E [1991] BCC 590 at p. 600G. In these circumstances I think I can properly follow my own view; notwithstanding that it is inconsistent with the decision that was actually reached in *Woodroffes*.

The explanation which *Nourse* J gave for the "rather odd result" which, as he must have been told, was "not in dispute" is that which would follow from adopting a solution to the problem of circularity which had been advanced by Professor Goode and, at the

F date when *Woodroffes* was decided, appeared at pp. 54–55 in the first edition (1982) of his collected lectures on *Legal Problems of Credit and Security* — a source to which the judge expressly refers later in his judgment at p. 378B–C. The comparable passage now appears in the second edition (1988) at pp. 97–98.

The problem to which Professor Goode's solution is addressed is described in these terms:

G > "A fixed chargee, C, who would ordinarily have priority over an earlier floating chargee, F, in the absence of restrictions of which he has notice, may agree that his charge shall be subordinated to the floating charge. If the company subsequently goes into liquidation having preferential creditors (P), a neat circularity problem arises. The liquidator indicates that as there are insufficient free assets for the purpose, he proposes to pay P out of the assets comprised in the floating charge, pursuant to section 175(2)(b) of the *Insolvency Act* 1986. On the other hand he
>
> H must allow C first bite out of the assets comprised in the fixed charge (which are also within the floating charge), as a fixed charge has priority over preferential claims. F protests that this cannot be right, since he has priority over C by virtue of the agreement between them."

It can be seen from that description that the elements which are said to give rise to the problem of circularity are (1) that F has priority over C by virtue of the agreement

between them, (2) that C has priority over preferential creditors (P) and (3) that the   A
preferential claims have priority over F under the statute. Given those premises,
Professor Goode's view is that the problem of circularity is readily soluble through the
principle of subrogation:

> "Since F has priority over C by virtue of their agreement, so that C would be
> accountable to F for moneys received in the liquidation to the extent of C's
> subordination, all the interests are satisfied by treating F as subrogated to C to the   B
> extent necessary to give effect to the subordination agreement. That is to say,
> F will collect from the liquidator *in right of* C the amount due to C, or such part of
> that amount as is necessary to satisfy F's claim. As regards any balance due to F,
> this is postponed to the claims of P under section 172(2)(b)."

The question is whether, the elements which are said to give rise to the problem of
circularity are present on the facts which I have to consider.
    C
    In my view, in circumstances where F has priority over C independently of any
agreement between them (so that the first of those elements is not present), the solution
put forward by Professor Goode is not apposite. The holder of a fixed charge is, of
course, entitled to be paid in priority to unsecured or general creditors (including
preferential creditors) out of the assets which are subject to, and are available to satisfy,
his fixed charge. But if the assets subject to the fixed charge are also subject to a prior
floating charge, so that they are not taken out of sec. 175(2)(b) of the 1986 Act by the   D
rule in *Re Lewis Merthyr Consolidated Collieries*, then the assets available to satisfy the
fixed charge will be those assets remaining after, inter alia, the preferential creditors
have been paid. The assets subject to the fixed charge will not be taken out of
sec. 175(2)(b) of the 1986 Act in circumstances in which the fixed charge, as created, is
necessarily subject to the floating charge — for example, where the floating charge
contains an express prohibition against the creation of any subsequent charge, and the
holder of the subsequent charge had notice of that prohibition — for the reasons which I   E
have already explained. In these circumstances it would be wrong to regard the holder
of the fixed charge as having a priority over the preferential creditors in relation to the
assets which are subject to the floating charge. Accordingly, the second element in
Professor Goode's circle is also missing.
    The first of those elements was not present in the *Woodroffes* case. Mrs Woodroffe's
fixed charge was not subordinated to the bank's floating charge by virtue of any   F
agreement between them. The bank's floating charge had priority over Mrs Woodroffe's
charge for the reasons (1) that it was first in time and (2) that it contained an express
prohibition (of which Mrs Woodroffe had notice) against the creation of any subsequent
charge without the bank's consent, which was never obtained. The express provision, in
Mrs Woodroffe's charge, that it would be subject to and rank in priority after the bank's
charge acknowledged the position that existed by virtue of (1) and (2). There was no   G
agreement between the bank and Mrs Woodroffe. The bank was unaware of her charge
until some time after it had been created. For a statement of the relevant facts, see the
judgment of *Nourse* J at pp. 372E–373P. In those circumstances Mrs Woodroffe, as
holder of the fixed charge, could not claim to be paid out of the assets over which the
bank's floating charge subsequently crystallised until the claims under the floating
charge had been satisfied. It follows, in my view, that Mrs Woodroffe's fixed charge
could not properly be said, in the circumstances which existed at the relevant time, to   H
have priority over the preferential creditors.
    In the present case, however, the trustees, as the holders of the floating charge, do
have priority over the bank, as holder of the fixed charge, by virtue — and only by virtue
— of an agreement between them. That agreement is evidenced by the deed of priority.
But for the reasons which I have set out, I am satisfied that if the effect of the deed of

A

priority is that (as between the bank and the trustees) the bank's debenture must be treated as if, when made, it had been expressed to be subject to the trustees debenture — then the second of Professor Goode's three elements is not present. This is because, if the deed of priority does have that effect, the bank does not become entitled to payment out of the proceeds of realisation of any asset until after the debt secured by the trustees' floating charge has been satisfied; and the assets available to satisfy that debt are assets to which the provisions of sec. 175(2)(b) of the 1986 Act apply.

B

To meet the possibility that I might reach the same conclusion as *Nicholson* J in *Waters v Widdows*, Mr Halpern advanced an alternative submission as to the true effect of the deed of priority. He submitted that it is wrong to regard the deed of priority as having the effect that the bank's debenture must be treated as if, when made, it had been expressed to be subject to the trustees' debenture. The correct view, he submits, is that the deed of priority has the effect that the bank (or any receiver appointed by the bank under its debenture) is to be regarded as holding the proceeds of its security upon trust for the trustees — that is to say that the trustees are to be treated as having become entitled, by assignment or subrogation, to the security which the bank would otherwise have had as against the unsecured creditors.

C

D

I accept that it would be possible for two secured creditors to enter into an arrangement by which they exchanged the rights under their respective securities. In particular it would, I think, be open to a creditor secured by a prior fixed charge to assign to the holder of a subsequent floating charge some or all of his right to receive payment under the fixed charge. It may be that it was an arrangement of this kind that Professor Goode had in mind when he referred to F collecting from the liquidator in right of C the amount due to C. But this is not the arrangement which the parties have made under the deed of priority. That deed does not purport to effect any assignment or exchange of proprietary rights. All that it does is to provide, by way of contract, for the order in which the proceeds of realisation of the charged assets shall be applied in satisfaction of the secured debts. The trustees do not collect from the liquidator the proceeds of assets subject to their floating charge in right of the bank. They collect those proceeds from the liquidator because the assets were subject to their floating charge. They collect those proceeds in priority to the bank because they have agreed with the bank that the bank's claim to those assets will be subject to their claim.

E

F

The point can be tested in this way. Suppose that the trustees' floating charge were held to be invalid under the provisions of, say, sec. 245 of the *Insolvency Act* 1986. Would the trustees, nonetheless, be entitled to collect from the liquidator the proceeds of the book and other debts? If the trustees do, on a true analysis, collect those proceeds from the liquidator in right of the bank, the invalidity of their own floating charge would be irrelevant. Further, on that hypothesis, the bank would hold the proceeds of assets which it received from the liquidator under its fixed charge upon trust for the trustees, notwithstanding that the trustees' floating charge was invalid. But it could not sensibly be suggested that the deed of priority was intended to, or did, have that effect. The reason is that the deed was not intended to give to the trustees a security which they would not otherwise have. The deed does not effect any transfer inter se of the rights of the secured creditors to be paid out of the charged assets. It affects only the order in which payment out of those assets is made to creditors who are secured by virtue of their own charges.

G

H

For the reasons which I have set out in this judgment I answer question (1)(b)(i) of the reamended originating application in the affirmative: the claims of the preferential creditors to be paid out of the proceeds of the realised book and other debts do have priority over the claims thereto of the trustees and of the receiver whom they appointed.

Question (1)(b)(ii) of the reamended originating application must also be answered   A
in the affirmative. Rule 4.218 of the *Insolvency Rules* 1986 sets out, in order of priority,
the expenses of the liquidation which "are payable out of the assets". Section 115 of the
1986 Act requires that all expenses properly incurred in the winding up, including the
remuneration of the liquidator, are payable out of the company's assets in priority to all
other claims. If that were not a sufficiently clear direction that the expenses of the
liquidation are payable in priority to preferential debts, sec. 175(2)(a) of the 1986 Act
puts the point beyond doubt: B

"Preferential debts—

    (a) rank equally among themselves after the expenses of the winding up . . . ."

The only question is whether, in this context, "the company's assets" include assets
which are subject to a charge which, as created, was a floating charge but which has
crystallised prior to the commencement of the liquidation.

   C

In *Re Barleycorn Enterprises Ltd* [1970] Ch 465 the Court of Appeal held that the
company's assets, for the purpose of (inter alia) sec. 309 of the 1948 Act, included
property comprised in or subject to a floating charge. Section 309 of the 1948 Act has
been re-enacted in sec. 115 of the 1986 Act. But it is reasonably clear from the report at
[1970] Ch 465 that, in that case, the floating charge in the bank's debenture did not
crystallise until the winding-up order was made. It was on this basis that *Vinelott* J
distinguished *Re Barleycorn Enterprises* in *Re Christonette International Ltd* [1982] 1   D
WLR 1245: see in particular at p. 1250H. He followed the earlier decision of *Bennett* J
in *Re Griffin Hotel Co Ltd* [1941] Ch 129. *Bennett* J had held at p. 135:

"In my judgment, sub-s. 4(b) of s. 264 [of the *Companies Act* 1929] only operates
if at the moment of the winding up there is still floating a charge created by the
company and it only gives the preferential creditors a priority over the claims of
the debenture holders in any property which at that moment of time was comprised
in or subject to that charge."   E

Section 264(4)(b) of the 1929 Act was re-enacted, first, as sec. 319(5)(b) of the 1948 Act
and, now, as sec. 175(2)(b) of the 1986 Act. But, in the 1986 Act and for the purposes of
that section, a floating charge does include a charge which, as created, was a floating
charge notwithstanding crystallisation before the commencement of winding up — see
sec. 251 of the 1986 Act. The effect of that change, as it seems to me, is that the reasoning
upon which the decision of the Court of Appeal in *Re Barleycorn Enterprises Ltd* is   F
based must now lead to the conclusion that the company's assets, for the purposes of
sec. 115 of the 1986 Act, do include property comprised in or subject to a charge which,
as created, was a floating charge; and that *Re Christonette International Ltd* should not
be followed on that point. To hold otherwise would produce the result that, although (1)
preferential debts take priority over the claims of debenture holders secured by a charge
which, as created, was a floating charge and are to be paid out of property comprised in   G
that charge — sec. 175(2)(b) of the 1986 Act — and (2) preferential debts are to be paid
after the expenses of the winding up — sec. 175(2)(a) of that Act — nevertheless the
expenses of winding up cannot be paid out of some property — that is to say, property
which is comprised in a floating charge which has crystallised prior to the liquidation —
which is available to pay preferential debts. It is difficult to accept that that result could
have been intended when sec. 175 of the 1986 Act was enacted.

I will hear counsel's submissions on the orders, if any, which are required on the other   H
paragraph in the reamended originating application in the light of the answers which I
have given to the questions posed by para. (1).

(Order accordingly)

A **R v Monopolies and Mergers Commission & Anor, ex parte South Yorkshire Transport Ltd & Ors.**

House of Lords.

Lord Templeman, Lord Goff of Chieveley, Lord Lowry, Lord Mustill and Lord Slynn of Hadley.

B Judgment delivered 16 December 1992.

> *Mergers — Judicial review — Appeal — Local bus company mergers referred to Monopolies and Mergers Commission — Whether commission had jurisdiction in relation to "reference area" — Whether reference area was "a substantial part of the UK" — Fair Trading Act 1973, sec. 64(3).*

This was an appeal by the Monopolies and Mergers Commission from a decision of the Court of Appeal [1990] BCC 340 that a commission decision on a merger reference was unlawful and of no effect.

C

The merger reference was made by the Secretary of State for Trade to the commission under Pt. V of the Fair Trading Act 1973 in March 1990 and related to the acquisition by South Yorkshire Transport Ltd of various bus companies in a "reference area" consisting of South Yorkshire and parts of the counties of Derby and Nottingham. This comprised 1.65 and 3.2 per cent respectively of the area and population of the UK.

D

The commission's report was challenged on the ground that the commission lacked jurisdiction because the reference area was not "a substantial part of the United Kingdom" as required by sec. 64(3) of the Fair Trading Act 1973.

Otton J [1990] BCC 347 held that the reference area was not a "substantial part of the United Kingdom": "substantial" in the context was not to be equated with something greater than merely nominal; considering the extent, population and economic activity in the area, he held that the commission should have concluded that the reference area was not a substantial part of the UK. The Court of Appeal (by a majority) dismissed an appeal by the commission. Lord Donaldson of Lymington MR and Butler-Sloss LJ agreed with Otton J that the commission had erred in construing "substantial" in sec. 64(3) as meaning in effect "not insubstantial", whereas the word "substantial" required a comparative and test and the comparator was the whole of the UK. On that test the reference area was not a substantial part of the UK. Nourse LJ, dissenting, held that it was open to the commission to assume jurisdiction on the basis that "substantial" meant a part of such dimensions as to make it worthy of consideration for the purpose of the 1973 Act.

E

F

The commission appealed to the House of Lords.

Held, allowing the appeal:

G 1. The commission had not fallen into the error of assuming jurisdiction on the basis that it was enough for the reference area to be more than trifling.

2. The commission would have jurisdiction where the reference area was "of such size, character and importance as to make it worth consideration for the purposes of the Act". To that question an enquiry into proportionality would often be material but would not lead directly to a conclusion.

H 3. The approach of the commission was in general accord with that approach and the conclusion at which the commission arrived was well within the permissible field of judgment. Accordingly there was no ground for interference by the court.

The following cases were referred to in the speech of Lord Mustill:

Edwards v Bairstow & Anor [1956] AC 14.
Palser v Grinling; Property Holding Co Ltd v Mischeff [1948] AC 291.

Michael Beloff QC and William Charles (instructed by the Treasury Solicitor) for the appellants.

David Pannick QC and Mark Shaw (instructed by Simpson Curtis, Leeds) for the respondents.

SPEECHES

Lord Templeman: I have had the advantage of reading in draft the speech of Lord *Mustill*. I agree with it and, for the reasons given by him, I, too, would allow the appeal.

Lord Lowry: I have had the advantage of reading in draft the speech prepared by Lord *Mustill*. I agree with it and, for the reasons given by my noble and learned friend, I, too, would allow this appeal.

Lord Goff of Chieveley: I have had the advantage of reading in draft the speech of Lord *Mustill*. I agree with it and, for the reasons given by my noble and learned friend, I, too, would allow this appeal.

Lord Mustill: On 22 March 1990 the Secretary of State for Trade and Industry referred to the Monopolies and Mergers Commission for investigation and report the acquisition of the present respondents, South Yorkshire Transport Co Ltd, of certain companies operating local bus services in South Yorkshire and in parts of Derbyshire and Nottinghamshire. Upon the reference the commission had two distinct tasks. First, to decide whether the "merger situation", as it is known, was one which satisfied the criteria for investigation established by sec. 64(3) of the *Fair Trading Act* 1973. If it did not the commission had no jurisdiction to proceed. The commission decided that the criteria were satisfied, and went on to investigate the merger. On 1 August 1990 the commission published its report, to the effect that the merger might be expected to operate against the public interest, and that the most effective means to restore competition would be to require the respondents to divest themselves of the assets and businesses acquired. On the same day the Secretary of State announced that he had accepted the conclusions and recommendation of the report.

The respondents disagreed with the commission on both issues, but recognised that the conclusions and recommendations on the question of public interest were not open to effective challenge in the courts. They did however contest by judicial review the finding of the commission, crucial to its jurisdiction, that the geographical area by reference to which the existence of a merger situation had to be ascertained ("the reference area") was a "substantial part" of the UK, within the meaning of sec. 64(3) of the 1973 Act. The application for judicial review was heard by *Otton* J, who in a valuable and comprehensive judgment (see [1991] BCC 347), held that the respondents' challenge was well founded, that the commission had acted without jurisdiction, and that accordingly the conclusions and recommendations in the report, and the decision of the Secretary of State to accept them, were unlawful and of no effect. The commission appealed to the Court of Appeal ([1992] BCC 340) which by a majority (Lord *Donaldson of Lymington* MR and *Butler-Sloss* LJ, *Nourse* LJ dissenting) dismissed the appeal. The commission appeals to your Lordships' House.

I must now set out the relevant parts of the legislation, and describe the reference area to which the legislation must be applied. First, the legislation.

The crucial sections of the 1973 Act are as follows:

> "*Monopoly situation limited to part of United Kingdom*
>
> 9(1) For the purposes of a monopoly reference, other than a reference relating to exports of goods from the United Kingdom, the person or persons making the reference may, if it appears to him or them to be appropriate in the circumstances

A   to do so, determine that consideration shall be limited to a part of the United Kingdom.

(2) Where such a determination is made, then for the purposes of that monopoly reference the provisions of sections 6 and 7 of this Act, or such of those provisions as are applicable for those purposes, shall have effect as if, wherever those provisions refer to the United Kingdom, they referred to that part of the United Kingdom to which, in accordance with that determination, consideration is to be

B   limited.

(3) The preceding provisions of this section shall have effect subject to subsection (4) of section 50 of this Act in cases to which that subsection applies.

Merger situation qualifying for investigation

64(1) A merger reference may be made to the Commission by the Secretary of

C   State where it appears to him that it is or may be the fact that two or more enterprises (in this section referred to as 'the relevant enterprises'), of which one at least was carried on in the United Kingdom or by or under the control of a body corporate incorporated in the United Kingdom, have, at a time or in circumstances falling within subsection (4) of this section, ceased to be distinct enterprises, and that either—

D
(a) as a result, the condition specified in subsection (2) or in subsection (3) of this section prevails, or does so to a greater extent, with respect to the supply of goods or services of any description, or

(b) the value of the assets taken over exceeds [£30m].

(2) The condition referred to in subsection (1)(a) of this section, in relation to the supply of goods of any description, is that at least one-quarter of all the goods of that description which are supplied in the United Kingdom, or in a substantial

E   part of the United Kingdom, either—

(a) are supplied by one and the same person or are supplied to one and the same person, or

(b) are supplied by the persons by whom the relevant enterprises (so far as they continue to be carried on) are carried on, or are supplied to those persons.

F   (3) The condition referred to in subsection (1)(a) of this section, in relation to the supply of services of any description, is that the supply of services of that description in the United Kingdom, or in a substantial part of the United Kingdom, is, to the extent of at least one-quarter, either—

(a) supply by one and the same person, or supply for one and the same person, or

G
(b) supply by the persons by whom the relevant enterprises (so far as they continue to be carried on) are carried on, or supply for those persons."

Next, there is the reference area. This was delineated by the Secretary of State, when he referred the matter to the commission, as:

"The county of South Yorkshire, the districts of Bolsover, Chesterfield, Derbyshire Dales, High Peak and North-East Derbyshire in the county of Derby and the

H   district of Bassetlaw in the county of Nottingham."

This description in terms of local government boundaries lacks colour. It is easier to visualise the reference area as lying roughly between the Leeds/Bradford conurbation to the north, Lincolnshire to the east, Derby/Nottingham to the south and Greater Manchester to the north-west. More exactly, the spine of the area, some 45 miles long at its greatest extent, runs from just north of Derby through Matlock, and then continues

through Chesterfield, Sheffield and Barnsley to a point a few miles south of the line   A
joining Huddersfield, Wakefield and Pontefract. To the west the area encompasses the
Derbyshire Dales and the Peak District. On the eastern side of the spine there are found
at the northern end the industrial areas of Doncaster and Rotherham. Further south a
space of more open country extends to within about ten miles of Lincoln. The total
surface area is rather more than 1,500 square miles. About 1.8m people live there.
These figures represent 1.65 per cent and 3.2 per cent of the totals for the UK as a whole.

                                                                                         B
   I now turn to the decision under review. This was not the first occasion on which the
commission had occasion to consider the meaning of sec. 64(3) of the Act. In March
1989 the commission published its report (Cm 595, 1989) in another reference concerning
local bus services, where a similar challenge to the jurisdiction was made. The company
concerned was Badgerline Holdings Ltd. Since the reasoning which led the commission
to reject the challenge was adopted by the differently constituted group responsible for
the report in the present case, it is necessary to see how the commission arrived at its   C
conclusion. The discussion in ch. 2 of the Badgerline report is too long to set out in full,
but in summary it was as follows. First, the commission correctly stated that the words
"a substantial part of the United Kingdom" had to be considered in their statutory
context, and continued:

> "2.2 We had therefore to consider whether a merger situation qualifying for
> investigation had been created. This involved deciding whether there was a supply
> of the reference services (local bus services) in the UK or a 'substantial part of the   D
> United Kingdom'.
>
> 2.3 The relevant area for the supply of bus services in what is described in the
> reference as the 'specified area' (shown in the maps at Appendix 2.1), is defined
> as 'the County of Avon together with all parts of the Counties of Somerset and
> Wiltshire and of the County of Gloucester east of the River Severn which lie
> within 15 miles of the County of Avon'. If this area constitutes a 'substantial part   E
> of the United Kingdom' for the purposes of the Act we are required to consider
> whether the market share test, as described in para. 2.1 is in other respects
> fulfilled."

   The commission went on to describe the various quantitative and qualitative features
of the area in question which it considered relevant and concluded:

> "2.9 Thus although the specified area's population and land area represent   F
> relatively small proportions of the figures for the UK, in a number of respects the
> area plays an important part in the economic development and growth, and
> cultural life of the country. Taking all these factors into consideration, we found
> that the specified area played a significant part in the overall life of the UK and
> could not be regarded as not substantial. We therefore concluded that the area
> was of sufficient importance to the UK (considered as a geographical and economic
> unit) to be properly and correctly described as 'a substantial part of the United   G
> Kingdom' for the purpose of sec. 64(3) of the Act."

   A similar approach was adopted by the commission when, 17 months later, it published
the report now under review (Cm 1166, 1990). The following are the material paragraphs
of ch. 2:

> "2.5 We further consider that the phrase additionally involves both a quantitative
> and a qualitative assessment. In considering what quantitative and qualitative   H
> elements should be taken into account for this purpose, we had regard to the size
> of the reference area, its population; its social, political, economic, financial and
> geographic significance; and whether it had any particular characteristics that
> might render the area special or significant. These featured too in the previous
> reports and no additional relevant elements have occurred to us.

2.6 As to the quantitative elements relating to the reference area, it is roughly 1.65 per cent of the total area, and has a population of some 1.8m, or 3.2 per cent of the total population of the UK.

2.7 In considering the elements that give the reference area its particular characteristics, we noted that the area includes Sheffield, the third largest metropolitan district in England on the basis of population, one of the great cities of the UK, and the towns of Barnsley, Doncaster, Rotherham and Chesterfield. As well as traditional industries based on mining and steel, the area also has a range of other manufacturing and service activities, significant academic and sports facilities, and parts of the Peak District favoured for recreation.

2.8 Having taken into consideration the various factors, general and specific, mentioned previously and having done so in the context of the UK as a whole, we conclude that the area may be properly and correctly described as 'a substantial part of the United Kingdom', for the purpose of sec. 64(3) of the Act."

In the Divisional Court *Otton* J reached a different conclusion. After an extensive review of the authorities, in which he clearly demonstrated that the word "substantial" is (as he aptly put it) like a chameleon, taking its colour from its environment, he concluded that "substantial" in this context was not to be equated with something greater than merely nominal; and, that the right approach was to draw a contrast between the UK as a whole and the reference area, as regards the surface extent, the population and the relevant economic activity, here measured in terms of kilometres travelled by passenger buses. Inspecting the reasons given by the commission for assuming jurisdiction the judge found that it had misdirected itself by adopting the interpretation of substantial as meaning "more than de minimis" which he had himself rejected. He went on to hold that if the commission had applied the approach which he considered right the answer would inevitably have been that the reference area was not a substantial part of the UK.

In the Court of Appeal the majority of the court adopted a standpoint which, although rather differently expressed, was broadly the same as that of *Otton* J. By contrast, *Nourse* LJ held that the amount necessary to satisfy the test of substantiality depends on the purpose of the act in which the word is found; it is a variable, whose meaning expands or contracts so far as to give effect to that purpose. His Lordship saw no *a priori* reason for interpreting "a substantial part" in sec. 64(3) as meaning a big or large part of the UK; it means "a considerable part, that is, a part of such dimensions as to make it worthy of consideration for the purpose of the Act" (at [1992] BCC 340 at p. 347D). The percentages might not for other purposes be regarded as being substantial but in his opinion it was worthy of consideration for the purposes of the 1973 Act.

Arriving now at the present appeal I believe that the interpretation of sec. 64(3) must proceed by two stages. First, a general appreciation of what "substantial" means in its present context. Second, a consideration of the elements to be taken into account when deciding whether the requirements of the word, so understood, are satisfied in the individual case.

As to the first stage, in the field of common language no recourse need be made to [illegible] "substantial" accommodates a wide range of [illegible]. At the other, there is "nearly complete", as [illegible] agreement with what has just been said. In between [illegible] of meaning, drawing colour from their context. That the protean nature of the word [illegible] reflected in the decided cases is, I believe, made quite clear by the judgment of *Otton* J in which the authorities are so thoroughly discussed as to make it unnecessary to go through them again. It is sufficient to say that although I do not accept that "substantial" can never mean "more than de minimis", or

that in *Palser v Grinling; Property Holding Co Ltd v Mischeff* [1948] AC 291 at p. 317,   A
Viscount *Simon* was saying more than that in the particular statutory context it did not
have this meaning, I am satisfied that in sec. 64(3) the word does indeed lie further up
the spectrum than that. To say how far up is another matter. The courts have repeatedly
warned against the dangers of taking an inherently imprecise word, and by redefining it
thrusting on it a spurious degree of precision. I will try to avoid such an error.
Nevertheless I am glad to adopt, as a means of giving a general indication of where the
meaning of the word in sec. 64(3) lies within the range of possible meanings, the   B
expression of *Nourse* LJ, "worthy of consideration for the purpose of the Act". I will
later return to another aspect of the definition suggested by the Lord Justice.

Thus far, therefore, I accept the respondents' submission that if the commission
proceeded when examining its jurisdiction on the basis that it was enough for the
reference area to be more than trifling this was a radical misconception. At first sight it
appears that this gives them a powerful case, for we find in the report that the commission   C
calls up the idea of "something more than merely nominal". If this expression truly
reflects the basis of the decision there is reason for the court to interfere. Whilst
acknowledging the force of this argument, I have come to the conclusion that it gives too
little weight to the reasoning of the commission as a whole, and to the examination of
the facts which the commission deemed necessary in both the instant reference and in
the Badgerline case.

I begin with the latter, since the report in Badgerline was the point at which the   D
commission started to analyse its jurisdiction in the present case. It is interesting to note
that the commission in Badgerline adopted a turn of phrase not to be found in the report
on the present reference, namely (in para. 2.9) "could not be regarded as not substantial".
If the respondents are right, this expression would have been the symptom of an even
more explicit misdirection than in the present case. Yet when we look at the discussion
of jurisdiction as a whole it can be seen that the perspective is much wider. I will quote   E
the paragraph again:

> "2.9 Thus although the specified area's population and land area represent
> relatively small proportions of the figures for the UK, in a number of respects the
> area plays an important part in the economic development and growth, and
> cultural life of the country. Taking all these factors into consideration, we found
> that the specified area played a significant part in the overall life of the UK and   F
> could not be regarded as not substantial. We therefore concluded that the area
> was of sufficient importance to the UK (considered as a geographical and economic
> unit) to be properly and correctly described as 'a substantial part of the United
> Kingdom' for the purpose of sec. 64(3) of the Act."

As I read it this passage embodies an analysis much wider than the consideration simply
of whether the reference area was larger than de minimis; and the discussion in the
remainder of ch. 2 bears this out, for it would have been quite redundant if the   G
commission had been applying the de minimis test and nothing else, for this could have
yielded only one answer. Then, when one comes to study the reasons given in the present
case, which plainly intended to proceed on the same basis as in Badgerline we find the
commission equating "substantial" with "something real or important"; and although
this is linked to the expression "something merely nominal" by the expression "as
distinct from", I believe that this is employed as meaning "that is to say not" and does   H
not indicate that the two turns of phrase are the opposite sides of the same coin.

Beyond this, linguistic analysis is of little help. I prefer to look at what else the
commission has to say. In para. 2.4 the report adopts the respondents' contention that
the area is "important and substantive in relation to a larger whole". In para. 2.5 it is
said that the phrase involves both a quantitative and qualitative element. The commission

A   then continues by marshalling the facts which it considers relevant, including the "social, political, economic, financial and geographic significance" of the reference area. I cannot see why the commission should have taken all this trouble to examine the area's characteristics if it had thought that the simple test, admitting of only one answer, was whether the area was trivial.

B   Accordingly, although I appreciate the reasons why in the courts below it was held that the commission had entirely misunderstood the content of the words "a substantial part", I have come to the conclusion that the report does not disclose this fundamental mistake. There remains however the question whether, even if the commission had placed the test in broadly the right part of the spectrum of possible meanings it nevertheless failed to apply the test correctly. Here, the contest is between three methods of approach:

C   (1)   An arithmetical proportion should be struck between the reference area of the UK as a whole, as regards surface area, population and volume of the economic activity with which the reference is concerned. If the proportion(s) are too low, the area does not qualify.

(2)   An assessment in absolute terms of the size and importance of the area, independent of proportions.

(3)   A mixture of the two kinds of criterion.

D   The respondents contend for the first, proportionate, approach. At one stage of the passage of this case through the courts they placed the weight of their arguments on the collocation of "a substantial part" with "of the United Kingdom". On this view, one should look at the UK as a geographical feature of the map, and see how much of the map is occupied by the reference area. At other stages more significance was attached to the proportion which the economic activity in question (here, the operation of local bus services) in the reference area bore to the UK as a whole. Throughout, however, the

E   respondents relied on the fact that whatever comparison one chose to make the proportion was too low.

My Lords, although I agree that the relationship of the part to the whole is not to be ignored, I am unable to accept that proportionality is the beginning and end of the matter. As regards geographical extent the reference to a substantial part of the UK is enabling, not restrictive. Its purpose is simply to entitle the Secretary of State to refer to

F   the commission mergers whose effect is not nation-wide. Like the asset-value criterion of sec. 64(1)(b), the epithet "substantial" is there to ensure that the expensive, laborious and time-consuming mechanism of a merger reference is not set in motion if the effort is not worthwhile. The reference area is thus enabled to be something less than the whole. But I cannot see why its relationship to the whole is the only measure of the commission's jurisdiction. Nor does the contrast with sec. 9, which omits the word "substantial", yield any other result. As *Nourse* LJ pointed out the introduction of this new jurisdiction for

G   monopoly references in 1973 cannot have been intended to alter the meaning of an expression which had been in use since 1948. It may be that sec. 9 and 64 involve different tests. The question is not for decision here. What does seem to me clear is that there is no cut-off point fixed by reference to geography and arithmetic alone.

I have reached the same conclusion as regards the argument which came to the forefront of the respondents' case in this House, namely that the decisive factor consists

H   of a comparison between the number of bus miles run by the services under investigation and those in the country as a whole. I find this interpretation very hard to square with the words "part of the United Kingdom" which are surely intended to relate to the area itself, and not (at any rate primarily) to the market share of the area. Furthermore, the suggested criterion would produce odd practical results, for a sparsely populated area of great extent would automatically fail the test if poorly served by buses. Whereas, by contrast, a tiny area such as Inner London which would fail the respondents' test of geographical proportionality would easily qualify if bus mileage were the criterion. Moreover, as was pointed out in argument, since local bus services are by their nature both limited in their field of operation and in total mileage run, it is hard to see how on an uncritical application of an arithmetical test they could ever qualify for investigation under the Act. It seems to me that where the task is to interpret an enabling provision, designed to confer on the commission the power to investigate mergers believed to be against the public interest the court should lean against an interpretation which would give the commission jurisdiction over references of the present kind in only a small minority of cases. This is the more so in the particular context of local bus services, since the provision of adequate services is a matter of importance to the public, as witness the need felt by Parliament to make special provision for them in the *Transport Act* 1985.

Accordingly, although I readily accept that the commission can, and indeed should, take into account the relative proportions of the area by comparison with the UK as a whole, as regards surface area, population, economic activities and (it may be) in some cases other factors as well, when reaching a conclusion on jurisdiction, neither each of them on its own, nor all of them together, can lead directly to the answer. The parties could reasonably expect that since the test for which the respondents contend has been rejected another would be proposed in its place. I am reluctant to go far in this direction because it would substitute non-statutory words for the words of the Act which the commission is obliged to apply, and partly because it is impossible to frame a definition which would not unduly fetter the judgment of the commission in some future situation not now foreseen. Nevertheless I believe that, subject to one qualification, it will be helpful to endorse the formulation of *Nourse* LJ already mentioned, as a general guide: namely that the reference area must be of such dimensions as to make it worthy of consideration for the purposes of the Act. The qualification is that the word "dimensions" might be thought to limit the enquiry to matters of geography. Accordingly I would prefer to state that the part must be "of such size, character and importance as to make it worth consideration for the purposes of the Act". To this question an enquiry into proportionality will often be material but it will not lead directly to a conclusion.

Applying this test to the present case one will ask first whether any misdirection is established, and secondly whether the decision can be overturned on the facts. As to the first it is quite clear that the approach of the commission was in general accord with what I would propose. It is true that matters such as academic and sports activities, mentioned by the commission, are of marginal importance at the most, but I do not regard their inclusion in the list of features to which the commission paid regard as vitiating an appreciation of "substantial" which was broadly correct. On the second question the parties are at odds as to the proper function of the courts. The respondents say that the two stages of the commission's enquiry involved wholly different tasks. Once the commission reached the stage of deciding on public interest and remedies it was exercising a broad judgment whose outcome could be overturned only on the ground of irrationality. The question of jurisdiction, by contrast, is a hard-edged question. There is no room for legitimate disagreement. Either the commission had jurisdiction or it had not. The fact that it is quite hard to discover the meaning of sec. 64(3) makes no difference. It does have a correct meaning, and one meaning alone; and once this is ascertained a correct application of it to the facts of the case will always yield the same answer. If the commission has reached a different answer it is wrong, and the court can and must intervene.

I agree with this argument in part, but only in part. Once the criterion for a judgment has been properly understood, the fact that it was formerly part of a range of possible criteria from which it was difficult to choose and on which opinions might legitimately differ becomes a matter of history. The judgment now proceeds unequivocally on the

A basis of the criterion as ascertained. So far, no room for controversy. But this clear-cut approach cannot be applied to every case, for the criterion so established may itself be so imprecise that different decision-makers, each acting rationally, might reach differing conclusions when applying it to the facts of a given case. In such a case the court is entitled to substitute its own opinion for that of the person to whom the decision has been entrusted only if the decision is so aberrant that it cannot be classed as rational: *Edwards v Bairstow* [1956] AC 14. The present is such a case. Even after eliminating

B inappropriate senses of "substantial" one is still left with a meaning broad enough to call for the exercise of judgment rather than an exact quantitative measurement. Approaching the matter in this light I am quite satisfied that there is no ground for interference by the court, since the conclusion at which the commission arrived was well within the permissible field of judgment. Indeed I would go further, and say that in my opinion it was right.

C I would accordingly allow the appeal, and restore the decision of the commission and the Secretary of State.

Lord Slynn of Hadley: My Lords, I have had the advantage of reading in draft the speech prepared by Lord *Mustill*. I agree that, for the reasons he gives the appeal should be allowed.

(*Appeal allowed*)

D

E

F

G

H

Bishopsgate Investment Management Ltd v Maxwell.

A

Chancery Division and Court of Appeal.
Chadwick J; Ralph Gibson, Leggatt and Hoffmann L JJ.
Judgment delivered 21 December 1992 and 11 February 1993.

*Directors — Breach of duty — Appeal — Company sued former director
alleging misappropriations in breach of fiduciary duty — Whether company
was entitled to summary judgment — Whether there was causal link between
breach and company's loss — Whether there should be an interim payment.*

B

This was an appeal against an order for summary judgment and an interim payment,
in an action by Bishopsgate Investment Management Ltd, a company in liquidation,
against a former director, "IM", alleging that he was in breach of duties owed by him to
the company as a director in relation to certain transactions.

The company was the trustee of a common investment fund for the pension schemes of
various Maxwell group companies. It appeared that approximately £428m of the funds
which ought to have been under the company's control as trustee had been lent to or
misappropriated by companies or officers of companies within the Maxwell group and
that those moneys might never be recovered.

C

The company sought judgment pursuant to O. 14 of the Rules of the Supreme Court
against IM for compensation in equity alternatively for damages to be assessed in respect
of the relevant transactions set out in the statement of claim. Further, or in the alternative,
the company sought an order for interim payment pursuant to O. 29. In essence, the
company alleged that IM failed to take any or any adequate steps to ensure that assets
which were, or which should have been, vested in or under the control of the company as
trustee were dealt with with the due authority of the company acting by its board of
directors. However, in respect of a number of share transfers, the statement of claim
contained an allegation of positive conduct in effecting and/or agreeing to the share
transfers in breach of duty. The transfers were of quoted shares from the company for a
nil consideration to a company ("RMG") of which IM was also a director and which
controlled his late father's private interests. IM signed as a director beneath the signature
of his brother Kevin. At the same time, as a director of RMG, he also signed blank
transfers which enabled the shares to be pledged to Credit Suisse to secure advances for
the benefit of the private interests. When the shares were later sold the company received
nothing.

D

E

F

The judge held that there was a triable issue on causation in cases where IM's alleged
breach of duty was an omission, because it had not be shown that any steps which IM
could have been under a duty to take would have prevented the misappropriations.
However, he ordered IM to indemnify the company against the loss suffered by reason of
the transfers to Credit Suisse and made an order for interim payment in the sum of
£500,000. In those cases IM was in breach of fiduciary duty and the necessary causal link
was established.

G

IM appealed.

Held, dismissing the appeal:

1. It was not open to a director who chose to participate in the management of the
company and exercised powers on its behalf to argue that he was under no duty to act in
the first place. Nor could IM be excused on the ground that he blindly followed the lead of
his brother. If one signature was sufficient, the articles would have said so. The company
was entitled to have two officers independently decide that it was proper to sign the
transfers. IM was in breach of his fiduciary duty because he gave away the company's
assets for no consideration to a private family company of which he was a director. That
was prima facie a use of his powers as a director for an improper purpose and the burden
was upon him to demonstrate the propriety of the transaction.

H

A   **2. In the case of breach of the fiduciary duty, the cause of action was constituted not by failure to make inquiries but simply by the improper transfer of the shares to RMG. Even if IM had made inquiries and received reassuring answers from other directors whom he was reasonably entitled to trust, he would not have escaped liability for a transfer which was in fact for a purpose outside the powers entrusted to the board. The burden of justification was upon IM and he had adduced no evidence to raise a triable issue. It was the improper transfer which caused the loss and the necessary causal connection was**

B   **therefore established.**

The following cases were referred to in the High Court judgment:

Balli Trading Ltd v Afalona Shipping Ltd [1992] TLR 406.
Caffrey v Darby (1801) 6 Ves Jun 488; 31 ER 1159.
Clough v Bond (1838) 3 My & Cr 490; 40 ER 1016.
Dawson, Re. Union Fidelity Trustee Co Ltd v Perpetual Trustee Co Ltd [1966] 2
C   NSWR 211.
Miller's Deed Trusts, Re (1978) Law Society's *Gazette* 454.

The following case was referred to in the judgment of Hoffmann LJ:

McWilliams v Sir William Arrol & Co Ltd & Anor [1962] 1 WLR 295.

Philip Heslop QC, in the High Court, and John Brisby (instructed by Stephenson
D   Harwood) for the plaintiff.

V V Veeder QC in the High Court, Colin Rimer QC in the Court of Appeal, and Paul Girolami (instructed by Kingsley Napley) for the defendant.

HIGH COURT JUDGMENT
(21 December 1992)

E   **Chadwick J:** Bishopsgate Investment Management Ltd is a company in liquidation. This action was commenced, with the authority of the joint liquidators, by a specially endorsed writ issued on 8 May 1992. The defendant, Ian Robert Charles Maxwell ("Ian Maxwell"), was a director of the plaintiff company from 15 February 1988 until his resignation on 4 December 1991. The action is brought against him on the basis of allegations that he was in breach of duties owed by him to the company as a director in relation to certain transactions ("the relevant transactions") described in the statement
F   of claim.

The principal claim in the action is for a declaration that the plaintiff company is entitled to be indemnified against all claims that might be made against it in connection with the relevant transactions. By a summons issued on 11 June 1992 the company seeks judgment, pursuant to O. 14 of the Rules of the Supreme Court, for compensation in equity, alternatively for damages to be assessed in respect of each of the relevant
G   transactions. Further, or in the alternative, the company seeks an order for interim payment pursuant to O. 29 of the Rules of the Supreme Court. That summons is now before me. It is, perhaps, sufficient to mention, first, that the statement of claim endorsed on the writ extends to some 60 pages, second, that the amount sought by way of interim payment exceeds £400m and, third, that the matter was argued before me over a period of five days, in order to indicate that this is an application for summary judgment on an unusual scale.

H   The application is unusual in another respect. Ian Maxwell is the son of the late Ian Robert Maxwell ("Robert Maxwell"). Following the death of Robert Maxwell on 5 November 1991, the board of directors of the plaintiff company appointed the company's auditors and accountants, Coopers Deloitte, to carry out an investigation into its affairs; and, in particular, into moneys that might be due to it from Robert Maxwell Group plc ("RMG") and companies or organisations connected or associated

with RMG (together "the Maxwell group"). Coopers Deloitte presented a draft report
to the directors on 6 December 1991. On consideration of that report the then two
remaining directors of the company, Trevor Cook and Ronald Ernest Woods, formed
the view that approximately £428m of the funds which ought to have been under the
company's control as investment trustee of various pension schemes had been lent to, or
misappropriated by, companies or officers of companies within the Maxwell group; and
that there were substantial doubts as to the company's ability to recover those moneys.
In those circumstances the two directors petitioned the court for the winding up of the
plaintiff company and for the immediate appointment of a provisional liquidator. The
matters of concern were set out in an affidavit of Trevor Cook sworn on 8 December
1991. On the same day an order appointing Neil Hunter Cooper, a partner in the firm of
Robson   Rhodes,   as   provisional   liquidator   was   made   in   this   court   by
Morritt J.

The order of 8 December 1991 required Ian Maxwell to make an affidavit setting out
his knowledge of the affairs of the company. An affidavit in response to that order was
sworn by him on 16 December 1991. On 19 December 1991 Ian Maxwell was interviewed
by the provisional liquidator, acting through counsel, for the purposes of providing
information pursuant to sec. 235 of the *Insolvency Act* 1986. On 30 January 1992 an
order was made for his examination under sec. 236 of that Act. That private examination
took place on 24 and 28 February 1992. The statements which he made in his affidavit on
16 December 1991 and the answers given in his interview on 19 December 1991 and in
the course of his private examination on 24 and 28 February 1992 would be admissible as
evidence against Ian Maxwell in the present application by virtue of sec. 433 of the
Insolvency Act 1986; but it is unnecessary for the company or its liquidators to rely upon
that statutory provision. In an affidavit which he swore on 20 July 1992, in opposition to
the company's summons under O. 14, Ian Maxwell expressly adopts the statements
made in his December affidavit and the answers given in his interview and in his private
examination. Indeed, he has exhibited to that later affidavit not only the transcripts of
the interview and of the private examination but also copies of documents which were
put to him on those occasions.

The effect of the inquisitorial process under the insolvency legislation which I have
described above is that there is a great deal more material before the Court on this
application than would be usual on a summons under O. 14. In particular, I have the
advantage, which would not normally be available on a summons under O. 14, of
knowing the answers which Ian Maxwell has given on oath and under cross-examination
in relation to matters which now form the basis of the company's present claim. It is
against this background that I approach the question posed by O. 14, r. 3(1): namely,
has the defendant satisfied the court with respect to the claim to which the application
relates that there is an issue or question in dispute which ought to be tried or that there
ought for some other reason to be a trial of that claim.

The two principal issues which arise in the action may be stated shortly. First, whether
the acts or omissions of Ian Maxwell in relation to the relevant transaction constituted a
breach of his duties as a director of the plaintiff company. Second, whether it is necessary
for the plaintiff company to show a causal connection between his acts or omissions and
the loss which is said to have been suffered as a result of each of the relevant transactions.

Although I have used the phrase "acts or omissions" in stating the first issue, it is not
alleged by the plaintiff company that (save in relation to one particular matter) Ian
Maxwell was party to any acts of commission in relation to the relevant transactions; or
that he even knew of them. Save in one respect, the company's case, in essence, is that
Ian Maxwell ought to have known about the relevant transactions and ought to have
taken some steps to prevent them. Ian Maxwell accepts that, at the material times, he
took no, or no effective, part in the direction of the company's affairs in relation to the

A
relevant transactions or at all. His case is that he was entitled to, and did, leave the direction of the company's affairs in the hands of others whom he trusted. The second issue — which, at first sight, might appear beyond argument — arises in the circumstances that the plaintiff company has made little or no attempt in its statement of claim to assert that any step which Ian Maxwell could or might have taken as a director would or might have had the effect of preventing the loss which is said to have been suffered as a result of the relevant transactions.

B
The plaintiff company was incorporated on 14 October 1987 under the *Companies Act* 1985 as a company limited by shares. Its objects, set out in its memorandum of association as amended by special resolutions passed on 12 and 15 February 1988, include the following:

"(A)(i) To act either solely or jointly with others as trustee for any trust, pension or scheme, retirement benefit plan or otherwise . . .

C
(ii) To hold in trust as trustee . . . and deal with manage and turn to account any real and personal property of all kinds and in particular shares, stocks, debentures, debenture stock, bonds, securities and investments of all classes . . ."

On 31 March 1988 the trustees of three existing pension schemes — namely, the Maxwell Communication Pension Plan, the Maxwell Communication Works Pension Scheme and the Mirror Group Pension Scheme ("the original participating schemes")
D
— executed a deed to which the plaintiff company was party for the purpose of co-mingling certain of the assets of the original participating schemes in a common investment fund. The company was appointed trustee for the purpose of investing and managing the assets of the common investment fund in accordance with the terms of that deed. It is alleged in the statement of claim — and it is not in dispute — that from March 1988 the company's primary activity was to act as investment trustee to the common investment fund. From time to time in 1988 and 1989 other pension schemes
E
became participating schemes in the common investment fund. It is further alleged, and not disputed, that the company did from time to time act as investment manager in respect of other assets, not within the common investment fund, which were subject to the trusts of the individual participating schemes.

The relevant transactions are described in the statement of claim under the following heads : (1) Scitex, (2) LBI portfolio, (3) MCC shares, (4) TEVA, (5) Euris, (6) Lazards
F
Property Unit Trust, (7) other stock and (8) Banco Comercial Portuges. The allegations follow a common pattern; but it is, nevertheless, appropriate to examine the allegations separately in relation to each transaction. I set out below a summary of those allegations.

(1) *Scitex*

On or shortly after 29 June 1990 the plaintiff company purchased some 2.7m shares in Scitex Corporation Ltd, an Israeli corporation, on behalf of the common investment
G
fund. In or about December 1990 the company acquired a further 2.7m shares in Scitex by way of bonus issue, also on behalf of the fund.

At a board meeting of the company on or about 4 July 1991 it was agreed that the whole of the company's Scitex holding be sold to RMG. Under the terms of an agreement of that date, which was produced to the meeting, the consideration for the shares was to be fixed as at 4 July 1991 by a valuation to be provided by Goldman Sachs,
H
Lehman Brothers or another firm of similar standing. Beneficial ownership in the shares was to continue to belong to the company (*semble* as trustee of the common investment fund) until payment of the settlement price. Paragraph 3.7 of the statement of claim is in these terms:

"BIM [the plaintiff company] has not received any payment by RMG for the Scitex shares, further the Scitex shares are not registered in the name of BIM or

otherwise under its direction or control . . . The said proceeds of sale, which
ought to have been remitted to and received by BIM have been diverted by Kevin
Maxwell, further or alternatively by Robert Maxwell, to RMG without the
authority of BIM."

Kevin Maxwell is the brother of Ian Maxwell. He was also a director of the plaintiff
company between 15 February 1988 and 4 December 1991. There is no specific allegation
in the statement of claim as to what has happened to the Scitex shares formerly held by
the company. In the light of the allegations which are made, the inference which the
court is invited to draw is, I think, that those shares have been transferred out of the
name of the company, pursuant to the agreement of 4 July 1991, and have been disposed
of by RMG for its own benefit without payment to the plaintiff company of the
consideration fixed by that agreement. The value of the Scitex shares at the date of the
agreement is said to be approximately £103m.

The directors of the company who are shown in the relevant board minute to have
been present at the meeting on 4 July 1991 are Kevin Maxwell and Trevor Cook. It is not
suggested in the statement of claim that the defendant, Ian Maxwell, took any active
part in the disposal of the Scitex shares, or that he had actual knowledge at any relevant
time either that the transaction was about to take place or that it had taken place. The
relevant allegations against him are contained in para. 3.9–3.11 of the statement of
claim. Those allegations set a pattern which is followed in relation to other of the
specified transactions, and it is convenient to set them out:

"3.9 In breach of his fiduciary duties owed to BIM and/or the common law duty
of care owed by him to BIM, Ian Maxwell negligently failed to take any or any
adequate steps to familiarise himself as to and to take action in relation to the facts
and matters surrounding the Scitex shares . . .

3.10 Further or alternatively, in breach of his fiduciary duties owed to BIM and/
or the common law duty of care owed by him to BIM, Ian Maxwell negligently
failed:

3.10.1 To take any or any adequate steps to ensure that the proceeds of sale of the
Scitex shares were paid to BIM or were dealt with with the due authority of BIM,
acting by its board and/or in the best interests of BIM;

3.10.2 To take any or any adequate steps to warn BIM of the deteriorating
financial position of RMG, which he well knew;

3.10.3 To take any or any adequate steps to cause BIM to demand repayment of
such indebtedness and/or to demand and obtain security in respect of such
indebtedness;

3.10.4 To take any or any adequate steps to acquaint himself with the financial
position and state of affairs as between BIM on the one hand and RMG on the
other hand and/or the financial position of RMG and (as a consequence) thereafter
failed to take the steps that a reasonably competent director of BIM would have
taken as set out in para. 3.10.1–3.10.3 (inclusive) hereof.

3.11 By reason of the breaches of duty referred to above BIM has suffered loss
and damage being the value of the Scitex shares, further or alternatively the scale
price and proceeds of sale thereof, further or alternatively the value of any claim
that any pension scheme or schemes may have against BIM by reason of the
matters aforesaid."

(2) *LBI portfolio*

Clause 4 of the deed of 31 March 1988 empowered the plaintiff company to appoint
an investment manager to exercise the powers of investment delegated to the company

A   under that deed. By an agreement dated 31 January 1991 and made between the company and London & Bishopsgate International Investment Management PI ("LBI"), LBI was appointed investment manager in respect of the portfolio of investments then representing the investments which had been under LBI's management since 1 July 1988. It is alleged in the statement of claim that, in or about July 1991, LBI liquidated the whole or some part of that portfolio; and that the proceeds of such liquidation amounted to approximately £60m. Paragraph 4.3 of the statement of claim is in these
B   terms:

> "4.3 The said proceeds of the liquidation of the portfolio have not been received by BIM but such proceeds have been paid to RMG, further or alternatively for the benefit of LBG [London & Bishopsgate Group Ltd] and/or some other Maxwell company or Maxwell companies."

C   It is further alleged that that payment was not authorised by the plaintiff company and was of no benefit to the company.

Again, it is not suggested in the statement of claim that Ian Maxwell took any active part in the decision by LBI to liquidate the portfolio under its management; or in the decision to pay the proceeds of that liquidation to some company other than the plaintiff. Indeed, it is not suggested or alleged that Ian Maxwell knew of the arrangements (whatever they may have been) between the plaintiff company and LBI. What is alleged
D   in para. 4.1 of the statement of claim is that in breach of duty Ian Maxwell failed to take any steps to acquaint himself with the portfolio, the terms on which it was held by LBI, the proposal to liquidate the same or the manner in which the proceeds of liquidation were to be dealt with; that he failed to take any steps to prevent the proceeds of the portfolio from being paid away from the plaintiff company; or to ensure that it was dealt with in the best interests of the plaintiff company and with its authority. Paragraph 4.7 is
E   in similar terms to those of para. 3.11:

> "4.7 By reason of the breaches of duty aforesaid and the matters referred to in para. 1.6 hereof, BIM has suffered loss and damage of approximately £60m, further or alternatively, the value of (and the costs occasioned by) any claim that any pension scheme or schemes may have against BIM by reason of the LBI portfolio liquidation."

F   **(3) *MCC shares***

It is alleged in the statement of claim that, in or about April 1991, the plaintiff company held, or alternatively managed, 25m shares in Maxwell Communications Corporation plc ("MCC") — being 12.5m shares on behalf of Mirror Group Pension Scheme and 12.5m shares on behalf of Maxwell Communications Works Pension Scheme. It is said that, on or about 26 April 1991, Kevin Maxwell gave instructions to
G   Goldman Sachs, purportedly on behalf of the company and each of the two pension schemes, to sell those MCC shares. Neither the company, nor either of the two pension schemes, received the proceeds of such sale — amounting it is said, to approximately £54m. The allegation, made in para. 5.3 of the statement of claim, is that:

> "5.3 Such proceeds of sale were, on the instructions of Kevin Maxwell given on or about 29 May 1991 and confirmed by letter of that date signed by Kevin
H   Maxwell, diverted to BIT [Bishopsgate Investment Trust plc], an ultimate subsidiary of RMG, being remitted to BIT's bank account at National Westminster Bank plc, 41 Lothbury, London EC2."

It is further alleged that the payment of the proceeds of sale to BIT was neither authorised by the board of the company nor authorised by or on behalf of either of the two pension schemes.

Once again, it is not alleged that Ian Maxwell took any part in that transaction; or that A
he knew about the sale of the MCC shares either in April 1991 or at any material time
thereafter. The allegations, in para. 5.5 of the statement of claim, follow the same
pattern as those in para. 4.6: that is to say, it is alleged that Ian Maxwell failed to take
any steps to acquaint himself with the position or to protect the interests of the company.
Paragraph 5.6 of the statement of claim is in similar terms to those of para. 3.11 and 4.7.

(4) *TEVA*

It is alleged that, as at August 1991, the plaintiff company was the registered holder of
some 49m shares in TEVA Pharmaceutical Industries Ltd, an Israeli corporation. The
holding was comprised in three share certificates: No. 1568 in respect of 1,027,143
shares, No. 1155 in respect of 25,196,228 shares and No. 1165 in respect of 22,804,085
shares. The shares were assets of the common investment fund; alternatively belonged
to one or more of the individual pension schemes. On or about 8 July 1991 the certificates
and an executed stock transfer form were sent by Israeli lawyers to Kevin Maxwell at his
request.

The 25,196,228 shares comprised in certificate No. 1155 are said to have been charged
to National Westminster Bank plc in November 1991 to secure facilities made available
to RMG. No relief in respect of that transaction is sought on the summons which is
before me.

The 22,804,085 shares comprised in certificate No. 1165 are said to have been charged
to Lehman Brothers International Ltd on or about 12 July 1991. This is described in the
statement of claim as the "Lehman-TEVA" transaction. It is alleged that the transaction
was not authorised by the company; was of no benefit to the company; and was entered
into for the collateral purpose of providing security or funds for some other Maxwell
company.

Ian Maxwell is not said to have any part in the Lehman-TEVA transaction. The
allegations, as in the case of the transactions to which I have already referred, are that,
in breach of duty, he failed to take any steps to acquaint himself with the circumstances
in which the plaintiff company held the TEVA shares, the location of the share
certificates or the safeguards as to their custody. Loss and damage is alleged "in the
premises and by reason of the said breaches of duty in relation to the Lehman-TEVA
transaction" in the respects set out in para. 6.9 of the statement of claim.

The 1,027,143 TEVA shares comprised in certificate No. 1568 are said to have been
deposited with Credit Suisse as collateral for a loan or loans to RMG ("the Credit
Suisse-TEVA transaction"). The allegations against Ian Maxwell in relation to the
Credit Suisse-TEVA transaction are the same, mutatis mutandis, as those in respect of
the Lehman-TEVA transaction.

There is a further allegation in relation to the TEVA shares. It is said, in para. 6.20 of G
the statement of claim, that, if and in so far as the Lehman-TEVA transaction or the
Credit Suisse-TEVA transaction were effected pursuant to stock lending agreements
referred to under the heading "Other stock" in para. 9 of the statement of claim, then
Ian Maxwell was in breach of duty failing to acquaint himself with the terms of such
agreements or the operation of stock lending transactions. This allegation can
conveniently be analysed in conjunction with the other allegations relating to stock
lending.

(5) *Euris*

It is alleged that on or about 2 October 1989 the plaintiff company purchased
2,228,479 shares in Euris SA, a French investment trust, from Bishopsgate Investment
Trust plc. The shares were initially held in the name of Pergamon Media Trust plc,

A   subject to a declaration of trust in favour of the plaintiff company; but were, on or about 6 August 1990, transferred to and registered in the name of the plaintiff company. It is said that, by letter dated 3 September 1990, Kevin Maxwell purported to give instructions on behalf of the company for the transfer of 2.2m of the Euris shares into the name of Pergamon Holdings Ltd; and that those shares were then charged to Banque Nationale de Paris ("BNP") to secure a loan granted by that bank to Pergamon Holdings Ltd. It appears that BNP continues to claim the benefit of that security. The approximate value

B   of the Euris shares in November 1991 is said to have been £32m. It is not alleged that Ian Maxwell took any active part in the instructions given by his brother on 3 September 1990. But it is said that the decision to charge or pledge those shares was approved at a board meeting of Pergamon Holdings Ltd on 31 August 1990 at which Ian Maxwell was present. The breach of duty alleged includes failure to acquaint himself with the existence of the company's holding of Euris shares, and with the fact that the Euris

C   shares which were the subject of the proposed pledge approved by the Pergamon Holdings Ltd board on 31 August 1990 were the plaintiff company's shares. Paragraph 7.8 includes the following allegation:

> "7.8 In breach of his fiduciary duties and the duty of care owed by him (in each case to BIM), Ian Maxwell negligently:
>
> . . .

D
> 7.8.3 Effected and/or agreed to the Euris transactions (further or alternatively, as a director of HHL [meaning Pergamon Holdings], to the purported pledging of the Euris shares to BNP)."

The allegation as to loss and damage in para. 7.9 of the statement of claim is in terms similar to those in respect of the Lehman-TEVA transaction (para. 6.9) and the Credit Suisse-TEVA transaction (para. 6.19).

E   (6) *Lazards Property Unit Trust*

It is alleged that the plaintiff company holds or should hold 11,377 units in Lazards Property Unit Trust (having, as at October 1991, an approximate value of £29m) either as part of the common investment fund or, alternatively, on behalf of one or more of the individual participating pension schemes. It is said that Kevin Maxwell, alternatively Robert Maxwell, procured that some or all of these units be placed with Lehman

F   Brothers as security for facilities granted by Lehman Brothers to a company or companies within the Maxwell group. That was done without authority; was not bona fide in the best interests of the company; and was effected for a collateral purpose under which the company obtained no benefit. Lehman Brothers claim the benefit of the security.

It is not alleged that Ian Maxwell had any part in the transaction; or that he had any knowledge of it. The allegations against him, in para. 8.4 and 8.7 of the statement of claim are in similar terms to those made in para. 6.8 and 6.9 in relation to the Lehman-

G   TEVA transaction. There is a further allegation, in para. 8.6, which is equivalent to that in para. 6.20. This, too, can conveniently be analysed in conjunction with the other allegations relating to stock lending.

(7) *Other stock*

The other stock in respect of which claims are made under para. 9 of the statement of claim comprises (a) shares or stock having an approximate value as at December 1991 of

H   £3.8m which (in addition to the TEVA shares comprised in certificate No. 1165 and the Lazards Property Units) have been transferred to or deposited with Lehman Brothers; (b) shares or stock having an approximate value as at December 1991 of £61m which (in addition to the TEVA shares comprised in certificate No. 1568) have been transferred to or deposited with Credit Suisse; and (c) shares or stock having an approximate value as at December 1991 of £8m which are said to be "missing".

In relation to the £38m stock deposited with Lehman Brothers, Lehman claim security   A
over some £4m in value (in addition to the TEVA shares and the Lazards Property
Units). Lehman claims to have returned stock to the value of £5m or thereabouts; and
to have realised, pursuant to certain stock lending agreements, the balance amounting
in value to £29m. The relevant stock lending agreements are (a) an agreement dated
3 November 1989 between the plaintiff company and Shearson Lehman Hutton
International Inc (said to have been assigned to, or novated by agreement with, Lehman
Brothers pursuant to a letter dated 21 November 1990) and (b) an agreement dated   B
1 April 1991 between London & Bishopsgate Group Ltd ("LBG") and Lehman
Brothers International Ltd. The proceeds of the realisation of the £29m stock are said to
have been applied by Lehman in the reduction of liabilities incurred under those
agreements.

In relation to the £61m stock deposited with Credit Suisse, it is said that Credit Suisse
claim security over an amount of £22m in value (in addition to the TEVA shares); and   C
that Credit Suisse have realised the balance, amounting in value to £39m.

The allegation, made in para. 9.6 of the statement of claim in relation to each of the
categories of stock to which I have referred above, is that the transactions were not
entered into bona fide in the best interests of the plaintiff company; that the company
derived no benefit therefrom; and that they were entered into for this collateral purpose
of providing financial support to other companies in the Maxwell group — and, in   D
particular, in the case of stock deposited with Credit Suisse, to RMG.

Paragraph 9.7 of the statement of claim contains, in subpara. 9.7.1 and 9.7.2,
allegations in the familiar form to the effect that Ian Maxwell was in breach of duty in
failing to take adequate steps to acquaint himself with the identity of the stocks held by
the company, the proposals to transfer the same to Lehman or Credit Suisse, or the
circumstances in which they were transferred; and in failing to take adequate steps to
prevent the stocks from being dealt with without the authority of the board, or otherwise   E
than in the best interests of the plaintiff company. But that paragraph contains, also, an
allegation of positive conduct.

> "9.7 In the premises in procuring and/or permitting . . . the transactions or
> purported transactions referred to in this sec. 9 hereof, Ian Maxwell was in breach
> of his fiduciary duties and/or the common law duty of care owed by him to BIM
> . . .   F
>
> 9.7.3 Effecting and/or agreeing to individual transfers of shares or interests
> therein without taking any steps adequately or at all to ensure that such transfers
> were duly authorised by BIM, acting by its board of directors, and/or that they
> were in the best interests of BIM (and/or that they were duly authorised by any
> relevant pension scheme and in the best interests of such pension scheme)."

Paragraph 9.9 contains allegations of loss and damage in terms similar to those in   G
respect of the Lehman-TEVA transaction (para. 6.9) and the Credit Suisse-TEVA
transaction (para. 6.19).

(8) *Banco Comercial Portuges*

It is alleged that, by February 1990, the plaintiff company had 1,016,850 shares in
Banco Comercial Portuges ("BCP") as assets of the common investment fund. On or
about 7 October 1991, the BCP shares were sold and the proceeds of sale were diverted   H
to or for the benefit of LBG or of some other company or companies in the Maxwell
group. The sale of the BCP shares, and the diversion of the proceeds, was not authorised
by the board of the plaintiff company; nor was it in the best interests of the company.

It is not alleged that Ian Maxwell took any part in the transaction of October 1991.
The breaches of duty alleged are, as before, based on failure to acquaint himself with

A the position, and a failure to take adequate steps to protect the company's interests. In particular, it is alleged in para. 10.10.2 that:

> "Being aware of the existence of shares in Portuguese companies or entities owned by a Maxwell company or Maxwell companies (including for the purposes of this paragraph BIM) and knowing of proposals in or about the autumn of September 1991 to liquidate such holdings, fail to take any or any adequate steps
B to determine
>
> (i) whether or not BIM had any interest in any of such shares;
>
> (ii) whether or not BIM had authorised any such liquidation, or authorised any subsequent dealing with the proceeds of sale."

I have set out the allegations made in the statement of claim in summary but at some length, in order to demonstrate that it is not alleged (save in respect to the transfer of the
C shares referred to in para. 9.7.3) that Ian Maxwell was party to any acts of commission in relation to the relevant transactions. In essence, the complaint is that he failed to take any or any adequate steps to ensure that assets which were, or which should have been, vested in or under the control of the plaintiff company as trustee were dealt with with the due authority of the company acting by its board of directors — see, in particular, para. 3.10.1 (Scitex), 4.6.3 (LBI Portfolio), 5.5.3 (MCC shares), 6.8.3 and 6.18.3
D (TEVA), 7.8.2 (Euris), 8.4.2 (Lazards Property Unit Trust), 9.7.2 (other stock) and 10.10.3 (BCP).

Ian Maxwell's own approach to his responsibilities as a director of the plaintiff company can be seen from the following passages in his affidavit of 16 December 1991:

> "4 . . . it was resolved [at a meeting held on 15 February 1988] that I should be appointed a director of BIM. I was not aware in advance of that meeting that I was
E to be so appointed but it was consistent with the practice in the group that I and/or my father and brother be appointed to the board of group companies . . .
>
> 5 On the evidence of the board minutes my solicitors have received from Stephenson Harwood, it appears that I attended only the following meetings of the board, i.e. those held on 31 March 1989, 25 July 1990, 2 July 1991, 30 July 1991 [and five further meetings after the death of Robert Maxwell on 5 November 1991].
F
> 6 Reference to those minutes of the meetings which I attended gives a true impression of my limited involvement in the affairs of BIM. That is, I was not regularly deeply involved in the management of its affairs . . .
>
> 7 I received copies of the minutes of directors' meetings, and whilst I cannot always pretend I read them assiduously (they being but a tiny fraction of the paperwork with which I had to deal daily in my work) my reading of them and
G their very production showed there to be activity by Mr Cook and my fellow directors in whom I also had confidence, and with whom I would also meet frequently in the course of our working in group's publishing businesses.
>
> 8 I believe that I did on occasions sign documents as a director of BIM, such documents being:
>
> — authorisations/cheques for wages
H
> — authorisations/cheques for pensioners
>
> — transfer documents
>
> In relation to cheques or transfers I was, so far as I can recall, invariably the second signatory, the first signatory being either Mr Cook or another director. Consequently, I had no reason to doubt that I should countersign."

A

Ian Maxwell's knowledge of the affairs of the plaintiff company was limited; but he was aware that its primary, if not its only, function was to act as trustee of pension fund assets. This appears from answers given in his interview on 19 December 1991:

"Q. Is it not true that really BIM's only function was to act in connection with the pension funds? That is what its assets were, pension fund moneys?

A. I would say that is true.

Q. So, the company, BIM, did not really have any of its own assets. It only had other people's assets, namely pensions funds?

B

A. It may have managed other assets, I do not know.

Q. You do not know?

A. No.

. . .

C

Q. Were you aware that BIM was involved in stock lending?

A. No.

Q. Did you know BIM's almost sole function was to manage pension funds?

A. You asked me that before. I said that as far as I am aware that was the primary function of BIM. I did not know it did not have any money of its own. I did not know whether it had a bank account. Presumably it did . . .

D

Q. Do you know of any other assets that BIM had other than from pension funds?

A. No, I do not."

He was not aware of the trusts upon which the assets were held; nor was he aware of the investment objectives of the pension schemes or the common investment fund, the investments which were made, the basis upon which they were chosen or the advice which was taken from professional advisers. This appears from answers given in the course of his private examination on 24 and 28 February 1992:

E

"Q. Do you recall ever reading or being told about the terms of the underlying pensions schemes and in particular what was contained in their trust deeds?

A. No.

Q. Did you ask?

F

A. No.

Q. Do you remember ever reading or being told as to the terms of the instrument governing the common investment fund?

A. No.

Q. Did you ask?

G

A. No.

. . .

Q. Were you aware in your capacity as a director of BIM what the investment objectives of the schemes and the common investment fund were . . .

A. No, other than to say that logically it would be to maximise the investments in order to obtain the best possible return for BIM or for the underlying pension schemes.

H

. . .

Q. What did you think BIM was investing in?

A. I knew that BIM had investments, but I am afraid I could not tell you what those investments were in.

A

Q. Did you ever take the trouble to ascertain what BIM invested in?

A. No I did not.

Q. Were you ever curious?

A. I only attended nine meetings in five years. As far as I was concerned, this was not a subject of my expertise. I had so much else to be curious about . . . Mr Cook was in charge of BIM, in terms of the general manager. My father

B

was the chairman. They were better able to deal with that company's affairs than I was . . .

. . .

Q. As far as you were aware, who made the decisions as to invest this very substantial amount of money for the common investment fund and for the underlying schemes?

C

A. The professional manager, if I can call him that, in both of BIM and of the underlying schemes was Trevor Cook. My father was the chairman of BIM and of MGPT and MCC Works and would also have been involved in making investment decisions . . . I cannot give you any specific answer suffice to say we had a general manager, Cook, and we had a chairman who was very experienced in investment. They had access to any and all advice that they would have required to have taken

D

those decisions. To the extent that I was present at board meetings where such decisions were discussed they were discussed also with the directors.

Q. Although you say your father and Mr Cook would have had access to advice, so far as you were concerned as a director of BIM are you aware of any professional investment managers being engaged to advise the board on how best to invest it assets?

E

A. I just do not know I am afraid.

. . .

Q. What contribution did you, and indeed the board of BIM as far as you are aware, give to that consideration [of the relative risk between different investments]?

A. To the best of my recollection, I was not involved in any board meeting of

F

BIM at which the question of investments or risks of investments were discussed
. . .

Q. Are you aware of the board of BIM ever being given investment advice on matters of the risks of the investments and other matters of that kind?

A. I assumed it was, but not at meetings where I was present. As you know, I was only present, I think, at a total of nine board meetings, five of which were in the month of November 1991."

G

In considering the question posed by O. 14, r. 3(1) — that is to say, has this defendant satisfied me there is an issue or question in dispute which ought to be tried or that there ought for some other reason to be a trial — I must, as it seems to me, ask myself whether it is safe to proceed on the basis that those statements and answers do fairly reflect the evidence which Ian Maxwell would wish to give in relation to the first of the two principal issues raised by this action. I am satisfied that it is safe to proceed on that basis. In his

H

affidavit sworn on 20 July 1992, at para. 11, Ian Maxwell confirmed that the statements made in his December affidavit and the answers which he gave to the questions and documents put to him at his interview and in his private examination, as recorded in the transcripts, were then and remained true to the best of his recollection.

In those circumstances I take the view that, in relation to the first of the two principal issues raised by this action — that is to say, whether his acts and omissions in relation to

the plaintiff company constituted a breach of the duties which Ian Maxwell owed to the
company by virtue of his office as a director — there is no issue to be tried as to the extent
of his failure to act. In the light of the evidence which Ian Maxwell has already given, I
am unable to conceive that, following a trial, a court could come to any conclusion other
than that he did not take any positive steps to ensure that assets which were, or which
should have been, vested in or under the control of the plaintiff company as trustee were
dealt with with the due authority of the company acting by its board of directors.

    I have already indicated that, in relation to one particular transaction, the plaintiff
company's complaint includes an allegation of positive conduct. That is the allegation in
para. 9.7.3 that in connection with the transfer of stock to Credit Suisse, Ian Maxwell
was in breach of duty in "effecting and/or agreeing to individual transfers of shares".
The evidence in relation to this allegation may be summarised as follows.

(1)   On 27 September 1991 Larry Trachtenberg, as managing director of LBG sent to
    Credit Suisse a parcel of shares (represented by share certificates and stock
    transfer forms) "in exchange for sterling to be paid to the LBG account". The
    shares included the following:

Name	Quantity	Value
		£
Costain Group	35,000	104,000
BAT Industries	28,000	186,500
Legal & General Group	35,000	150,000
Smith & Nephew	25,000	32,250
Pentland Group	100,000	107,000
		579,750

    In each case the share certificate or certificates enclosed were in the name of the
    plaintiff company as registered owner. In the case of the Costain, BAT, Legal &
    General and Smith & Nephew shares, the certificate or certificates were
    accompanied by stock transfer forms in the corresponding amounts (a) for the
    transfer of the stock from the plaintiff company to RMG and (b) for the transfer
    of the stock from RMG to an innominate transferee. In the case of the Pentland
    Group shares there is a stock transfer form from RMG to an innominate transferee;
    but no transfer form (in evidence) from the plaintiff company to RMG. All the
    stock transfer forms (whether from the plaintiff company or from RMG) are
    undated and are signed by Ian Maxwell and Kevin Maxwell as directors. The
    inference that a transfer form from the company to RMG in respect of the
    Pentland Group shares was also signed by the two brothers is very strong.

(2)   On 18 October 1991 the Pentland, Legal & General and BAT shares were sold by
    Credit Suisse; and the proceeds of sale were credited to an account at Credit
    Suisse in the name of RMG. The Costain shares have also been sold and the
    proceeds held by Credit Suisse. The Smith & Nephew shares are thought to have
    been returned to Larry Trachtenberg at RMG on 1 November 1991; and
    subsequently sold by RMG. No part of the proceeds of any of these shares has
    been received by the plaintiff company.

(3)   The stock transfer forms relating to the Legal & General shares were put to Ian
    Maxwell in the course of his private examination on 28 February 1992. He
    accepted that the signatures on the transfer from the plaintiff company were those
    of himself and his brother; and that the signature on the RMG transfer was also
    his. He had no recollection of signing those transfers. He was then asked:

A

"Q. If you were invited to sign a share transfer form, which is an important document, because you are dealing then with assets, if the other signature is your brother, the question is, do you think it is likely your brother would have asked you to sign it, or somebody else?

A. No, you have to go back again to the custom and practice of the group. These forms would be originated by A, probably given to A's secretary, probably given to my secretary, probably arrived on my table and may have been signed, or the person who had drawn up the document or who had signed it might have come in. There are any number of ways these documents might have ended up being signed by me from time to time.

B

Q. Would you have signed a document like this without asking why it was necessary to sign it and the purpose behind the transaction?

C

A. I would not have signed a stock transfer form unless there was another signature which I recognised to be that belonging to an executive in the group who would know, in my view, what he would be doing . . ."

(4) Ian Maxwell's answer — that he would not have signed a stock transfer form unless there was another signature already on it — is borne out by the stock transfer forms themselves. On each form his signature appears below that of his brother.

D

In my view, in the light of the evidence which he gave on 28 February 1992 — which is consistent with that in para. 8 of his affidavit of 16 December 1991 and is confirmed in his affidavit of 20 July 1992 — I can proceed on the basis that there is no issue to be tried in relation to the circumstances in which Ian Maxwell signed the stock transfer forms which were sent to Credit Suisse on 27 September 1991. It seems to me inevitable that, following a trial, a court would reach the conclusion that Ian Maxwell added his signature below that of his brother without knowing, or making any inquiry, whether the transfers had been authorised by the board of directors or why the stock was to be transferred; but solely in reliance on the fact that Kevin Maxwell had already signed. At no stage was it suggested to me in argument that there were, or might be, grounds upon which, at a trial, Ian Maxwell could challenge that conclusion.

E

The questions in dispute, in relation to the first of the principal issues raised by this action, are:

F

(1) whether, as a matter of law, Ian Maxwell did owe to the plaintiff company a duty to take some positive step, in the context of each of the relevant transactions, to ensure that trust assets for which it was responsible as trustee were under the control of its board of directors; and

(2) whether, again as a matter of law, Ian Maxwell did owe to the plaintiff company a duty not to sign the stock transfer forms to which I have referred without first satisfying himself that the stock was to be transferred for some proper purpose of the company.

G

But those questions must be examined in conjunction with the second of the two principal issues — whether it is necessary for the plaintiff company to show a causal connection between Ian Maxwell's acts and omissions and the loss which is said to have been suffered as a result of each of the relevant transactions. The reason is that if the duty lies only in the tort of negligence, then it is beyond argument that some causal connection must be shown. Mr Heslop, who appeared for the plaintiff company, did not make a serious attempt to persuade me otherwise. His contention was, in effect, that I could infer that there was a sufficient causal connection between the act or omission and the loss to found a cause of action in tort.

H

British Company Cases

He urged me to find that Ian Maxwell ought to have known, in relation to each of the   A
relevant transactions, what was proposed or, at least, what had been done; and that,
with that knowledge, he should have been concerned that the interests of the plaintiff
company were being, or had been, disregarded. On that basis it was said that Ian
Maxwell could and should have taken one or more of the following steps:

(1)   he should have raised his concern with his father, Robert Maxwell,

(2)   he should have raised his concern at a properly convened meeting of the board of   B
       directors of the plaintiff company,

(3)   he should have reported his concern to the trustees of the pension funds,

(4)   he should have reported his concern to the statutory regulators (IMRO or SIB),

(5)   he should have drawn the attention of the Serious Fraud Office to the way in
       which the pension scheme assets were being used, and

(6)   he should have taken proceedings for an injunction in the name of the company.   C

I can see considerable force in the contention that Ian Maxwell ought to have made it
his business to know a great deal more about the affairs of the plaintiff company than he
appears to have done; and that, if he had known of the relevant transactions, he ought
to have been concerned for the plaintiff company's interests. I accept that the steps
enumerated above would have been open to him; although whether, in the particular
circumstances affecting this company, it would have been sensible in the interests of the
plaintiff company to take steps which might give publicity to the matters of concern   D
while there was any prospect of recovering trust assets is, I think, by no means self-
evident. But I am unable to accept that I ought to infer, at this interlocutory stage, that,
in relation to any one of the relevant transactions, there was some particular step which
ought to have been taken at a particular time; and which, if taken, would have prevented
the loss which is said to have been suffered as a result of that transaction. For example,
in the light of the evidence which has been filed on this application, I could not take the   E
view that, if Ian Maxwell had raised his concern with his father, or with his brother Kevin
Maxwell, or at a meeting of the board of directors, any one of the relevant transactions
would not, nevertheless, have been carried into effect or that assets already lost by, or
moneys due to, the plaintiff company would have been recovered. Whether, in relation
to each transaction, there were some steps which ought to have been taken by Ian
Maxwell — and which, if taken, would have prevented the loss — are questions which,
if they are to be investigated at all, ought to be investigated at a trial.   F

Faced with the suggestion that the statement of claim might have been more specific
in alleging what steps, if taken, would have prevented the loss alleged in relation to each
relevant transaction, Mr Heslop asserted that it was unnecessary for the plaintiff
company to plead a positive case alleging what ought to have been done. It was for the
defendant director to seek to excuse his failure to act by showing that no step which he
could have taken would have prevented the loss. Nevertheless he recognised, correctly   G
I think, that there were serious difficulties in the way of a successful claim founded in
tort if the plaintiff could not plead and prove the causal nexus between omission and loss
on which it relied.

In seeking to overcome — or, perhaps, to circumvent — these difficulties, Mr Heslop
urged me to hold that there was, on the facts admitted by Ian Maxwell, such an
abdication of his role as director as to amount to a breach of fiduciary duty; and that, in
those circumstances, it was unnecessary for the plaintiff company to establish that any   H
step that Ian Maxwell could or might have taken would have prevented the loss.

In support of the latter proposition, Mr Heslop sought to draw an analogy with the
position of a trustee. He relied on the decision of *Street* J in the Supreme Court of New
South Wales in *Re Dawson; Union Fidelity Trustee Co Ltd v Perpetual Trustee Co Ltd*
[1966] 2 NSWR 211. At p. 214, lines 51–52, the judge said:

A
> "The obligation of a defaulting trustee is essentially one of effecting a restitution to the estate. The obligation is of a personal character and its extent is not to be limited by common law principles governing remoteness of damage."

The judge then reviewed the nineteenth century English authorities on the nature of the obligation of the defaulting trustee; including, in particular, *Caffrey v Darby* (1801) 6 Ves Jun 488 and *Clough v Bond* (1838) 3 My & Cr 490. The conclusion which he
B reached is expressed at p. 215, lines 45–48:

> "The principles embodied in this approach do not appear to involve any inquiry as to whether the loss was caused by or flowed from the breach. Rather, the inquiry in each instance would appear to be whether the loss would have happened if there had been no breach."

It is not altogether easy to reconcile that approach with the views which appear to
C have been expressed by *Oliver* J in *Re Miller's Deed Trusts* (21 March 1978, reported in the Law Society's *Gazette* of 3 May 1978, p. 454). The note of his judgment contains this passage:

> "B was beyond doubt in breach in not keeping the other trustees informed of the company's progress, but his Lordship had no confidence that matters would have been significantly different so far as the beneficiaries were concerned had he done so. It was necessary to prove a causal connection between the breach of duty and
D the resulting loss. No principle could be extracted from the cases that once a breach of duty was shown the burden fell on the defaulting trustee to show that the loss did not result from the breach."

It is clear, in my view, that it is necessary to show, at the least, that the loss would not have occurred if there had been no breach of the fiduciary duty. It is also clear that *Oliver* J in *Re Miller's Deed Trusts* expressly rejected the suggestion that it was not for
E the plaintiff to establish, as an essential element in his cause of action for breach of fiduciary duty, the necessary causal link between the breach of duty and the loss which is said to have resulted from that breach.

I doubt whether the principle to be derived from the cases referred to by *Street* J in *Re Dawson* goes further than that a defaulting fiduciary will be liable for loss which is shown to result from his default, whether or not that loss would be regarded at common law as
F too remote to give rise to a cause of action in tort. In other words, that it is enough for the complainant to show that the default was causa sine qua non of the loss; he need not show that it was causa causans. But I do not think it appropriate to decide that question on the present application. In the light of the views expressed by *Oliver* J in *Re Miller's Deed Trusts* I am not prepared, on an application under O. 14, to hold — as Mr Heslop urges me to hold — that the burden falls on the defaulting fiduciary to show that the loss
G did not result from his breach. I keep in mind the admonition of the Court of Appeal in *Balli Trading Ltd v Afalona Shipping Ltd* [1992] TLR 406 that difficult questions of law are not suitable for determination on an application for summary judgment under O. 14 of the Rules of the Supreme Court.

On the basis that the burden does not fall on the defaulting fiduciary to show that the loss did not result from his breach, the difficulties which I have already identified in relation to the cause of action in tort cannot be overcome by treating Ian Maxwell's
H failure to act as a breach of fiduciary duty. Even accepting — as I do — that a defaulting fiduciary will be liable for loss which is shown to result from his default, whether or not that loss would be regarded at common law as too remote, the plaintiff company has not established the necessary causal link between the failure to act and the loss which is said to have been suffered. To put the point another way, I am satisfied that, in relation to claims based on Ian Maxwell's failure to act, there are issues or questions in dispute

which ought to be tried. The issue in relation to each of the relevant transactions is A
whether, but for Ian Maxwell's failure to act, the loss would not have occurred.

In those circumstances it is not necessary to decide whether Ian Maxwell's conduct in
relation to the plaintiff company constituted such an abdication of his role as director as
to amount to a breach of fiduciary duty; and it would be inappropriate to do so on this
application.

There remains, however, the claim based on the allegation in para. 9.7.3 of the B
statement of claim: that is to say, the claim based on the stock transfer forms which were
signed by Ian Maxwell and his brother, and sent to Credit Suisse on 27 September 1991.
In relation to this claim it does seem to me that the necessary causal link has been
established to found a cause of action for breach of fiduciary duty. But for Ian Maxwell's
signature on those transfer forms, those transfers would not have been effected. The
loss results from the transfer of the shares. The question is whether, in signing those
transfers forms without knowing, or making any inquiry in order to ascertain, whether C
the transfers had been authorised by the board of directors or why the stock was to be
transferred, Ian Maxwell acted in breach of his fiduciary duty as a director of the plaintiff
company. I have to decide whether that question ought to go to trial.

No one is obliged to accept office as a director of a company incorporated under the
Companies Acts. Those who do so undertake duties which are imposed by the company's
memorandum and articles of association, the provisions of the Companies Acts and the D
general law. In particular they must be taken to accept those duties which are ancillary
to the exercise of the powers conferred on directors by the articles of association. Those
are fiduciary powers; and, as such, are subject to the provisions of the general law
relating to the exercise of fiduciary powers. A proper starting point, therefore, is to
examine the position of the directors under the articles of association of the plaintiff
company.

The articles of association of the plaintiff company were in the form of Table A in the E
schedule to the *Companies (Tables A to F) Regulations* 1985 (SI 1985/805), with certain
modifications not here relevant. Regulation 70 in Table A provides that the business of
the company shall be managed by the directors. Regulation 72 empowers the directors
to delegate their powers to any committee consisting of one or more directors. They
may also delegate to any managing director or any director holding any other executive
office such of their powers as they consider desirable to be exercised by him. The minutes F
of the meetings of the directors of the plaintiff company are in evidence as exhibit
IRCM 1 to Ian Maxwell's affidavit of 16 December 1991. There is no resolution to be
found in those minutes by which the board delegated its powers generally to any
committee or to a single director. There are, of course, specific instances of delegation,
but those are not relevant to the question with which I am concerned.

A stock transfer in the form prescribed by sec. 1(1) of, and Sch. 1 to, the *Stock* G
Transfer Act 1963 is to be executed by a body corporate under its common seal. The
stock transfer forms with which I am concerned were in the prescribed form. Regulation
101 in Table A requires that the seal of the company shall only be used by the authority
of the directors or of a committee of the directors. The directors may determine who
shall sign any instrument to which the seal is affixed and unless otherwise so determined
it shall be signed by a director and by the secretary or by a second director. The stock
transfer forms with which I am concerned record that the common seal of the transferor H
company was affixed thereto in the presence of the two directors, Kevin Maxwell and
Ian Maxwell, who have signed each form. It is immaterial that, in fact, no seal was
affixed. Section 36A of the *Companies Act* 1985 (introduced by sec. 130(2) of the
Companies Act 1989 with effect from 31 July 1990) provides, by subsec. (4), that a
document signed by a director and the secretary of a company, or by two directors of a

A   company, and expressed (in whatever form of words) to be executed by the company has the same effect as if executed under the common seal of the company.

In those circumstances, in signing the relevant stock transfer forms, Ian Maxwell was exercising a fiduciary power, conferred by the articles, to alienate property of the company by an instrument which took effect as if executed by the company. In my view there is no doubt that in exercising that power Ian Maxwell was required to satisfy himself that the transfers were authorised by the board of directors or by a committee of

B   the directors; or, at the least, that the transfers could properly be ratified by the board. In the absence of board authority, Ian Maxwell was, at the least, required to consider and understand why the stock was being transferred to RMG — and thence from RMG to an innominate transferee — and to satisfy himself that the transfers were in the interests of the plaintiff company.

It must be kept in mind that the plaintiff company was, as Ian Maxwell knew, trustee

C   of investments representing pension scheme assets. In my view the duties of directors of a company in relation to the transfer of investments which the company holds as trustee ought to be closely analogous to those of an individual trustee in relation to the transfer of investments which are the subject of his trust. It could not, I think, be argued seriously that an individual trustee who signed a stock transfer form without considering whether the transfer was in the interests of his trust was not in breach of his fiduciary duty.

It is no answer for Ian Maxwell to say, as he does, that he signed the stock transfer

D   forms in reliance on his brother's signature. It is clear from his own evidence that he neither sought nor obtained any explanation from Kevin Maxwell. In particular he neither sought nor obtained any assurance that the transfers had been approved by the board. Where a document can take effect only on the basis that it has been executed by the company, it would make nonsense of the requirements in reg. 101 in Table A and sec. 36A of the 1985 Act if the second signatory (whether the secretary or another

E   director) were to add his signature on the sole ground that the document had already been signed by the first signatory. The requirement of two signatures must have some purpose. In my view the obvious purpose is that both signatories are required to address their minds to the question whether the execution of the document by the company has been properly authorised.

It follows, therefore, that I am not satisfied that there is an issue to be tried in relation to the stock transfer forms. In my view it is clear that, in signing those transfer forms,

F   Ian Maxwell was in breach of his fiduciary duty to the plaintiff company. I have already indicated that there is a sufficient causal link between that breach and the loss alleged in the statement of claim.

I will hear submissions from counsel as to the order which should be made on the plaintiff company's summons in the light of this judgment. My present view is that there should be no order under para. (1)–(9) and (11) of the summons. Paragraph (12) was not

G   argued before me; and is, I think, to be adjourned. Under para. (10) of the summons I propose, subject to hearing counsels' further submissions, to order that the defendant do indemnify the plaintiff company against all loss suffered by reason of the transfer of the five sterling investments referred to in the letter dated 27 September 1991 from LBG to Credit Suisse; and to order an inquiry into the amount of that loss. Paragraph (13) of the summons seeks an order for interim payment pursuant to O. 29, r. 10 of the Rules of the Supreme Court. I am satisfied that, if I have jurisdiction to do so, this is a proper case

H   in which to make such an order in an amount of £500,000; that being, as it seems to me, a reasonable proportion of the likely amount of the loss which is to be determined on the inquiry which I have proposed. In my view the case does fall within O. 29, r. 11(1)(b); and, accordingly, subject to hearing argument on the point, I propose to make that order.

(*Order accordingly*)

COURT OF APPEAL JUDGMENT   A
(11 February 1993)

Hoffmann LJ: Bishopsgate Investment Management Ltd ("the company") was trustee of the assets of a number of pension schemes for employees of companies controlled by the late Mr Robert Maxwell. After the death of Mr Maxwell on 5 November 1991 it was found that assets worth hundreds of millions of pounds held on behalf of the pension funds had been wrongfully sold or pledged for the benefit of Mr Maxwell's other   B
companies. The company was unable to meet its liabilities to the pension funds and was compulsorily wound up on 4 March 1992.

The defendant Mr Ian Maxwell was at all material times a director of the company. On 8 May 1992 the company commenced proceedings against him claiming that he was liable to make good the loss caused by a number of specified misappropriations on the ground they had been caused by breaches the fiduciary duty or duty of care which he   C
owed to the company. The company proceeded by summons for judgment under O. 14 of the Rules of the Supreme Court for damages to be assessed and also claimed an interim payment under O. 29, r. 11.

The summons was heard by *Chadwick* J over five days between 23 and 31 July 1992, when judgment was reserved. On 21 December he found in favour of the company on one set of misappropriations and ordered an interim payment in the sum of £500,000.   D
Against these orders Mr Maxwell now appeals. The claims in respect of the other misappropriations were dismissed and against that part of the order there is no cross-appeal.

Before dealing with the merits of the appeal, I feel I should say, having discussed the matter with my brethren, that we think the time taken to deliver judgment was excessive. We do not of course know why it took so long. The hearing was arranged at fairly short   E
notice to come on before the end of the summer term. The parties are entitled to feel that there was little point in exerting themselves if they were not going to have a decision for five months. There has also been inconvenience and additional expense arising out of a matter of which the judge could not at the time have been aware. Mr Maxwell gave his solicitors a second charge over his house to secure payment of their fees. It was registered on 31 July 1992. The plaintiff wants to apply under the provisions of the   F
Insolvency Act 1986 which give the court jurisdiction to set aside preferences given within six months before presentation of a bankruptcy petition. I say nothing about whether this charge even arguably satisfied the statutory criteria for a preference. But the time taken to give judgment used up five out of the six months and the statutory demand which must precede a bankruptcy petition requires another three weeks. The company was obliged to persuade this court to qualify its stay of the interim payment   G
order by allowing presentation of a petition provided that it was thereafter frozen pending this appeal.

A further difficulty was caused when Mr Maxwell then issued a summons to set aside the statutory demand: a step which ordinarily would have prevented presentation of a petition for some weeks until the summons could be heard: see sec. 267(2)(d) of the *Insolvency Act* 1986. *Chadwick* J was obliged to hear the summons as a matter of   H
urgency and dismissed it in time to enable the petition to be presented with three days to spare. All this expensive last-minute activity should have been unnecessary.

I return to the merits of the appeal. Mr Maxwell's evidence was that he knew that the company's business consisted principally, if not exclusively, of managing the assets of the pension funds. He knew that he was a director. Nevertheless, he took no interest

A   whatever in the management of the company. He attended few meetings and paid little attention to business when he did. He said he trusted and relied upon the other directors.

In relation to all but one of the misappropriations, his inactivity was total. The company does not allege he participated in or even knew of the relevant transactions. Its complaint is that he should as a director have taken enough interest to find out what was happening and prevent it.

B   The judge did not decide whether Mr Maxwell's failure to acquaint himself with the company's business was a breach of duty. In the older cases the duty of a director to participate in the management of a company is stated in very undemanding terms. The law may be evolving in response to changes in public attitudes to corporate governance, as shown by the enactment of the provisions consolidated in the *Company Directors Disqualification Act* 1986. Even so, the existence of a duty to participate must depend upon how the particular company's business is organised and the part which the director
C   could reasonably have been expected to play. The judge was right not to enter into these questions on a summons under O. 14.

The ground upon which he gave leave to defend was that there was a triable issue on causation. In cases in which the alleged breach of duty is an omission, the plaintiff must prove that compliance would have prevented the damage. If it would have happened anyway, the plaintiff has failed to prove his case. Thus in cases concerning safety
D   equipment such as *McWilliams v Sir William Arrol & Co Ltd* [1962] 1 WLR 295, to which Mr Rimer referred us, the plaintiff must show that the omission to provide the safety equipment caused the accident. He or his personal representative must therefore prove that he would have used the equipment and that it would have been effective. He may be assisted by presumptions which shift the duty to adduce evidence but the burden of proof is upon him. The judge gave leave because he was not persuaded to the necessary standard for the purposes of O. 14 that any steps which Mr Maxwell could
E   have been under a duty to take would have prevented the misappropriations. It seems to me that not only was the judge right, but the attempt to obtain judgment under O. 14 in respect of these transactions was misguided. It was inevitable that there would be triable issues on both liability and causation and the attempt to demonstrate the contrary on affidavit was a waste of time and money.

In the case under appeal, however, Mr Maxwell's breach of duty was not an omission.
F   The transaction involved the transfer of five parcels of publicly quoted shares from the company for a nil consideration to Robert Maxwell Group plc, a company of which Mr Maxwell was also a director and which controlled Mr Robert Maxwell's private interests. The company's articles required the transfer to be signed by a director and another director or the secretary. Mr Maxwell signed as a director beneath the signature of his brother Kevin. At the same time, as a director of Robert Maxwell Group plc, he
G   also signed blank transfers which enabled the shares to be pledged to Credit Suisse to secure advances for the benefit of Mr Robert Maxwell's private interests. Three of the five parcels of shares were sold on 18 October 1991 and the proceeds credited by Credit Suisse to the collateral account of Robert Maxwell Group plc. The bank claims to be entitled as bona fide pledgee to retain these proceeds. Another parcel was dealt with in the same way at a later date and one parcel may have been returned to Robert Maxwell Group plc and realised for the benefit of that company which is heavily insolvent. The
H   plaintiff company has received nothing.

The transfers by the company were not authorised by the board. Furthermore, no grounds have been put forward upon which it could honestly have been thought that the transactions were for the benefit of the company as trustee of the pension funds. Mr Maxwell made no enquiry about the transactions but signed them because Kevin had signed.

The judge said of these transfers (at p. 137A):

A

> ". . . in signing the relevant stock transfer forms, Ian Maxwell was exercising a fiduciary power, conferred by the articles, to alienate property of the company by an instrument which took effect as if executed by the company. In my view there is no doubt that in exercising that power Ian Maxwell was required to satisfy himself that the transfers were authorised by the board of directors or by a committee of the directors; or, at least, that the transfers could properly be ratified by the board. In the absence of board authority, Ian Maxwell was, at the least, required to consider and understand why the stock was being transferred to (Robert Maxwell Group plc) . . . and to satisfy himself that the transfers were in the interests of the plaintiff company."

B

In my judgment the contrary is unarguable. If a director chooses to participate in the management of the company and exercises powers on its behalf, he owes a duty to act bona fide in the interests of the company. He must exercise the power solely for the purpose for which it was conferred. To exercise the power for another purpose is a breach of his fiduciary duty. It is no answer that he was under no duty to act in the first place. Nor can Mr Maxwell be excused on the ground that he blindly followed the lead of his brother Kevin. If one signature was sufficient, the articles would have said so. The company was entitled to have two officers independently decide that it was proper to sign the transfer. Mr Maxwell was in breach of his fiduciary duty because he gave away the company's assets for no consideration to a private family company of which he was a director. This was prima facie a use of his powers as a director for an improper purpose and in my judgment the burden was upon him to demonstrate the propriety of the transaction.

C

D

Mr Rimer submits in this case too that the company has failed to show that these breaches of duty caused the loss. He says that the essence of the breach of duty was Mr Maxwell's failure to make proper enquiries before signing. The company must therefore demonstrate that proper enquiry would have prevented the loss. Mr Rimer says it will fail if the evidence shows that Mr Maxwell would have been fobbed off with some plausible explanation or, I suppose, if someone else would have been found to sign instead.

E

This is an attempt to characterise the breach of duty as an omission equivalent to Mr Maxwell's inactivity concerning the other transactions. But in my view it is fallacious. I say nothing about cases in which the breach of duty consists in doing an act without first making reasonable enquiries. Mr Rimer referred us to authorities which do not speak with one voice on whether it must be assumed that the defendant would have learnt the truth or whether he might have been told a plausible lie. In the case of breach of fiduciary duty, it seems to me that the cause of action is constituted not by failure to make inquiries but simply by the improper transfer of the shares to Robert Maxwell Group plc. Even if Mr Maxwell had made inquiries and received reassuring answers from other directors whom he was reasonably entitled to trust, he would not have escaped liability for a transfer which was in fact for a purpose outside the powers entrusted to the board. He may or may not have been entitled to relief under sec. 727 of the *Companies Act* 1985 but since in fact he made no inquiry, no reliance has — in my view rightly — been placed on this section. The burden of justification is upon Mr Maxwell and on this he has adduced no evidence to raise a triable issue. It was the improper transfer which caused the loss and the necessary causal connection is therefore established. I therefore think that the judge was right to hold there was no triable issue on the Credit Suisse transactions and the appeal should therefore be dismissed.

F

G

H

Mr Maxwell also asks for leave to appeal against the judge's order that he make an interim payment of £500,000 in respect of damage caused to the company caused by the

A   Credit Suisse misappropriations. To some extent this application was linked with the O. 14 appeal but it is also made upon independent grounds.

    The relevant provisions of O. 29, r. 10 and 11 are as follows:

> "10(1) The plaintiff may, at any time after the writ has been served on a defendant and the time limited for him to acknowledge service has expired, apply to the Court for an order requiring that defendant to make an interim payment.

B

> (3) An application under this rule shall be supported by an affidavit which shall—
>
> > (a) verify the amount of the damages, debt or other sum to which the application relates and the grounds of the application;
> >
> > (b) exhibit any documentary evidence relied on by the plaintiff in support of the application . . .

> 11(1) If, on the hearing of an application under rule 10 in an action for damages,

C

> the Court is satisfied—
>
> > (b) that the plaintiff has obtained judgment against the respondent for damages to be assessed . . .
>
> the Court may, if it thinks fit . . . order the respondent to make an interim payment of such amount as it thinks just, not exceeding a reasonable proportion of the damages which in the opinion of the Court are likely to be recovered by the

D

> plaintiff . . ."

    Mr Rimer says first that there was no sufficient evidence to verify the amount of the damages in accordance with r. 10(3)(a). This is he submits is a matter which, by analogy with the sufficiency of an affidavit complying with the rules under O. 14, goes to the jurisdiction of the court. It is true that the first affidavit in support of the summons does not ascribe any particular value to the claim in respect of the five transfers on which the

E   company succeeded. It merely verifies the statement of claim which includes the five parcels in stock pledged to Credit Suisse said in para. 9.5.2 of the statement of claim to have had a value about £61m. Paragraph 9.7.3 alleges that Mr Maxwell signed transfers of some of these shares but does not identify them or state their value. Finally, the statement of claim alleges that the company has suffered damage on various alternative bases, one of which is that it is liable to the pension funds to replace the value of the shares.

F   This omission was sought to be remedied by a further affidavit sworn by Mr Neil Cooper, the company's joint liquidator, in the course of the hearing on 27 July 1992. He exhibited the transfers signed by Mr Maxwell and a covering letter from Mr Larry Trachtenberg on behalf of London & Bishopsgate Group Ltd, another private Maxwell company, which says that the shares are enclosed and states their value. The total was £579,500. But Mr Rimer says that this did not amount to a verification on affidavit of the amount of the damages. There was no objection to Mr Cooper's affidavit and in my

G   judgment it provided evidence on which the judge could find that the value of the shares at the time of the transfer was £579,500. As they were quoted shares, it was a point which could easily have been checked if any one had thought it worthwhile to do so. Furthermore, it is clear from an exchange between Mr Veeder QC, who was appearing for Mr Maxwell, and the judge about Mr Maxwell's ability to pay £500,000 that everyone was proceeding on the assumption that Mr Trachtenberg's letter was evidence of the

H   value of the shares. After judgment on 21 December the judge heard further submissions from Mr Girolami as to why he should nevertheless not order an interim payment. There was no suggestion that he lacked evidence of the value the shares. I think it would be wrong to allow Mr Maxwell to take this point now.

    Secondly, Mr Rimer says it does not follow that the company's loss would be the full value of the shares. It might be able to get something back from Credit Suisse. But the

company held the shares as trustee for the pension funds and its liability as trustee was   A
to restore the fund. Prima facie, therefore, its loss was its liability to make good the
value of the shares. Credit Suisse appears to have taken the shares on the basis that they
were registered in the name of Robert Maxwell Group plc and claims to be bona fide
pledgees. I do not think that the judge was required to speculate on the possibility that
the company might be able to defeat this plea. It has no duty to engage in doubtful
litigation for the purpose of minimising the loss for which Mr Maxwell is liable. In my
judgment therefore the judge was acting within his discretion in deciding that £500,000   B
was a reasonable proportion of the damages which the company was likely to recover.

Finally, Mr Rimer says that the judge did not give any or sufficient consideration to
the evidence that Mr Maxwell could not pay £500,000. In his affidavit sworn on 20 July
1992 he said that he had no means sufficient to pay any of the claims against him or any
significant part of any of them. That was said when the claims exceeded £400m.
Mr Maxwell was nevertheless able on 31 July 1992 to provide his solicitors with security   C
over his house which has enabled them to receive £250,000. The defendant's lack of
means is something to which the judge should have regard but it is not, as in the case of
personal injury claims, a bar to the order: compare O. 29, r. 11(2)(c). Mr Rimer says
that the order in this case does not assist the company, because Mr Maxwell cannot pay,
and will cause him irreparable harm because it is likely to form the basis of a petition for
his bankruptcy. These points were put to the judge by Mr Girolami when he made the
order on 21 December and there is no reason to believe that the judge did not take them   D
into account. The transcript records him as saying that if Mr Maxwell would be
bankrupted by having to pay £500,000, it would be better to find this out as soon as
possible rather than after more expensive legal proceedings. This seems to me a practical
and sensible approach. The judge may also have taken the view that bankruptcy
proceedings might assist the company to discover exactly what assets Mr Maxwell did
have, whether he had given any away and to impose some control on his expenditure on
legal fees. None of this would have been unreasonable. In my judgment we should not   E
interfere with the judge's discretion. This application should therefore be refused.

Leggatt LJ: I agree that both appeal and application should be dismissed.

Ralph Gibson LJ: I also agree that the appeal from the order for summary judgment
should be dismissed. It has not been argued on appeal for Mr Ian Maxwell that he was
not in breach of the fiduciary duty which the judge held was owed by him to the plaintiff
company. He did fail before signing the transfer forms to make any enquiries in order to   F
consider and understand why the five sterling investments were being transferred. He
failed to satisfy himself that such transfers were in the best interests of the plaintiff
company.

It was acknowledged by the notice of appeal first filed that it was right to order Mr Ian
Maxwell to indemnify the plaintiff company against all loss suffered by reason of his
failure to comply with the duty upon him. But it was contended that it was necessary to   G
order an enquiry as to what if any loss had been thereby caused. An amended notice of
appeal presented to the court today in respect of which leave was given contends that
there should have been unconditional leave to defend.

The basis of these contentions was that the plaintiff company had failed either to
allege or to prove any causal connection between the breach of fiduciary duty and the
loss of the value of the shares transferred. In particular nothing was proved, it was said,   H
as to what would have occurred if Mr Ian Maxwell had made the inquiries which the
judge had held he should have made, or to show that, if he had made such enquiries, he
would not have signed the stock transfer forms for the sterling investments.

Further, it was said that Mr Ian Maxwell could not reasonably be expected, in
proceedings for summary judgment, before discovery or interrogatories, to adduce

A   evidence either as to what (if any) causal connection there was between the breach of duty found by the judge and the loss claimed, or as to what would have occurred if Mr Ian Maxwell had made the enquiries which he should have made.

The development of these contentions by Mr Rimer in argument, and the citation of authority, failed to persuade me that there was no sufficient allegation or evidence before the judge upon which his decision could be based. After reference to para. 9.7.3

B   of the statement of claim which in abbreviated form contained the allegation:

> "Effecting . . . individual transfers of shares . . . without taking any steps . . . to ensure that such transfers were duly authorised by (the plaintiff company), acting by its board of directors, or that they were in the best interests of (the company) . . . or . . . authorised by any relevant pension scheme . . ."

It was submitted that the allegation there pleaded is not that Mr Ian Maxwell was in breach of duty by merely signing the transfers: the breach alleged is signing without first

C   making proper enquiries. It did not follow, it was said, that any such breach of duty also caused the loss alleged to have been suffered by the plaintiff company in consequence of the share transactions. Further, the allegation in para. 9.9 was that "by reason of the said breaches of duty the plaintiff company has suffered loss and damage". There was no allegation that, had Mr Maxwell made proper enquiries, he would not have been justified in signing the transfers or that he would not have signed them, or that the

D   transactions with regard to the shares would not have taken place at all.

There is, in my judgment, no force in these submissions. It is, of course, true that the allegation made against Mr Ian Maxwell with reference to these transactions is not that he was in breach of duty by merely signing the transfers. The relevant allegations in the statement of claim include the following.

(1)   the shares had been purportedly disposed of to third parties;

E   (2)   the shares formed part of the property of the common investment fund or belonged to one or more pension schemes;

(3)   the transactions for which the transfers were used were not entered into bona fide in the best interests of the plaintiff company and the plaintiff derived no benefit therefrom, and they were entered into for a collateral purpose namely to provide financial support to other Maxwell companies including RMG;

F   (4)   therefore, by reason of Mr Ian Maxwell procuring the particular transactions (para. 9.7), by effecting the share transfers (para. 9.7.3) without making proper enquiries, the plaintiff company suffered loss and damage (para. 9.9) in the amount of the value of the missing shares (para. 9.9.2).

Those allegations can be summarised in the simple statement that Mr Ian Maxwell and Mr Kevin Maxwell by signing the share transfers as directors misapplied the property of the plaintiff company by applying it for a purpose to which the company

G   could not lawfully apply it. If that is proved, the directors responsible must replace the property or make good the loss and it matters not that in so acting they acted honestly: see *Halsbury's Laws* (4th ed.), vol. 7(1) (1988), para. 645 and the cases there cited.

The liability of directors participating in breaches of trust is joint and several. It might be that a director who signs a share transfer by which shares owned by the company are alienated for no consideration could show, or raise an arguable case to the effect, that

H   the transaction was for the benefit of the company and constituted no breach of trust. Upon the evidence before the judge it was, I think, clearly shown that the transfer of these shares constituted misapplication of the company's property and Mr Ian Maxwell has made no attempt to show that the transactions were even arguably for the benefit of the company. I agree also with the reasons give by *Hoffmann* LJ for dismissing the main appeal.

A

As for the application for leave to appeal, with reference to the interim payment, I agree that it also should be refused for the reasons given by *Hoffmann* LJ.

There are aspects of this litigation which give rise to concern. The obligation of Mr Ian Maxwell to make good the assets of the pension funds lost through his breach of trust is and was worth no more to the beneficiaries of the funds than his ability to pay. It is clear that a very large proportion of his assets are said to have been spent in legal costs before and after the commencement of these proceedings. There are many other legal proceedings with which we are not concerned and of which we have no knowledge. From the remaining assets of the pension funds, however, sums have been spent in seeking summary judgment for a vast amount of money which Mr Ian Maxwell could not possibly pay and part of those sums so spent in costs will not, by reason of the order for costs made by the judge, be recovered in any event. It would have been very much better for all concerned if the application for summary judgment had been limited in the first place to the matters in respect of which the order of the judge was made and which this court has upheld. The costs incurred in the application on the other matters would have been saved. No doubt the delay in the giving of judgment upon which *Hoffmann* LJ rightly commented would not have occurred and the added costs relating to the presentation of a bankruptcy petition would have been avoided. We know that our knowledge of the circumstances affecting these matters is incomplete. We have not heard Mr Brisby for the respondents because in our judgment it was not necessary to hear him for the disposal of the matters in issue. I make it clear, therefore, that I make no criticism of the conduct of these matters by any individual. Nevertheless, whatever the causes were, the outcome has been unsatisfactory. It would be wrong therefore for this court not to express concern about it, having regard to the number of persons interested in the funds.

B

C

D

(*Appeal dismissed*)

E

_____

F

G

H

A **Morgan v Morgan Insurance Brokers Ltd & Ors.**

Chancery Division (Companies Court).
Millett J.
Judgment delivered 20 July 1992.

B
> *Rectification of company's register of members — Proper parties to application — Costs — Directors wrongly refused to register transfer — Whether they should pay costs personally — Companies Act 1985, sec. 359; Rules of the Supreme Court, O. 102, r. 3(1)(g).*

This was a hearing on the costs of an application to rectify a company's register of members. The company was a small private company with 11 shareholders. The applicant held 76.93 per cent of the issued share capital. The other ten shareholders had small holdings ranging from one per cent to five per cent each. Nine of them were directors. The
C applicant attempted to transfer one share to his daughter but the directors refused to register the transfer. He then applied for rectification, joining the company and all ten other shareholders as defendants. The directors conceded that they had no right to refuse to register the transfer and agreed to do so. The applicant sought an order for his costs against the defendants personally. They sought an order that the costs of all parties be paid by the company.

D   *Held*, ordering the applicant's costs to be paid by the individual defendant directors:

1. The proper defendants to an application to rectify the register were the company and the registered holder or holders of the shares whose registration was in question if not the applicant. It was not necessary to join other shareholders who were registered in respect of shares other than those in respect of which rectification was sought; their interests were represented by the company.

E   2. Nor was it necessary to join the directors of the company where rectification of the register was sought unless an order for costs was sought against them. (Re Keith Prowse & Co Ltd [1918] 1 Ch 487 followed.)

3. The majority shareholder was blocked by the board from taking the only step open to him to put himself in a position of exercising the voting power to which his shareholding entitled him, and in blocking him the directors acted beyond their powers. The applicant had a strong case for seeking an order for costs against the directors. It was not necessary
F for him to establish bad faith before obtaining such an order.

The following case was referred to in the judgment:

Keith Prowse & Co Ltd, Re [1918] 1 Ch 487.

Catherine Roberts (instructed by Kent Jones & Done, Stoke-on-Trent) for the applicant.

G   Richard Gillis (instructed by Hacking Ashton Jervis & Co, Newcastle-under-Lyme) for the defendants.

JUDGMENT

Millett J: This is an application to rectify a company's register of members. The application has been disposed of by consent and I am left now only with the question of
H costs. The company is a small private company with 11 shareholders, one of whom, Mr Morgan, is the applicant. He holds 76.93 per cent of the issued share capital. The other ten shareholders have all very small holdings ranging from one per cent to five per cent each.

The articles of association confer no discretion on the board of directors to refuse to register a transfer. Mr Morgan appears to have been in dispute with his fellow

shareholders, nine of whom were members of the board of directors. He was unable to   A
obtain his way, in spite of the fact that he held a substantial majority of the issued shares,
because, by himself, he could not requisition a meeting of the company. Accordingly, he
attempted to transfer one share to his daughter and applied to register the transfer. The
directors refused to register the transfer for what they considered to be good reasons. It
is not suggested that they acted otherwise than bone fide in what they believed to be the
interests of the company. They were, however, wrong in their construction of the   B
articles. They were advised by the company's solicitor, and it was on his advice that they
refused to register the transfer. Hence the present application.

Mr Morgan is the applicant for rectification. He joined the company and all ten other
shareholders as defendants. Nine of them are directors, and the other, Mr Green, is not.
The application, no doubt, led the defendants to take further advice — they were all
represented by the same solicitors and counsel — and on reconsidering the articles of
association they conceded that the board had no right to refuse to register the transfer.   C
Accordingly, by Friday last, it was agreed that the defendants would register the
transfer; but the parties remained in dispute about costs. Mr Morgan sought an order
for his costs against the respondents personally. They sought an order that the costs of
all parties be paid by the company. Mr Morgan saw no reason why as majority he should
bear more than three-quarters of the costs of litigation which had been rendered
necessary by the directors' erroneous views of their own powers.
                                                                                            D
The first question is whether it was appropriate to join all the individual defendants.
They were joined as members of the company, apparently on a reading of O. 102, r. 3 of
the Rules of the Supreme Court and note 102/3/8 in vol. 1 of the *Supreme Court Practice
1993*, where it is said that a notice of motion for rectification of the register "should be
served on the company *and the registered holder of the shares* or such of them as is not
making the application". That sentence is not happily worded but in my judgment there
is little doubt as to what it means. The proper defendants to an application to rectify the   E
register are the company and the registered holder or holders of the shares whose
registration is in question if not the applicant. It is not necessary to join other shareholders
who are registered in respect of the shares other than those in respect of which
rectification is sought. Their interests are represented by the company. Mr Green,
therefore, who holds 30 of the shares in the company and who is not a director, ought
not to have been joined, for the application to rectify the register is not made in respect
of the shares which he holds.   F

Nor is it necessary to join the directors of the company where rectification of the
register is sought unless, of course, an order for costs is sought against them. In *Re Keith
Prowse & Co Ltd* [1918] 1 Ch 487, *Peterson* J held that where the board of directors
refused to register a transfer without justification, they were not properly joined as
defendants to an application for rectification. He said (at p. 491):
                                                                                            G
"The directors are the agents of the company, and in law it is the company which
is legally responsible for the unjustifiable acts of its agents, and the directors are
not to my mind necessary or proper parties to an application of this kind. If an
order on a company to rectify the register does operate, as in my view it does, as a
rectification of the register from the date when the order is made, then the only
object of joining directors as respondents to the motion is that a punitive order
may be obtained against them for payment of the costs. I do not think that, on   H
applications of this sort, directors ought to be joined as respondents . . ."

Accordingly, he refused to direct the respondent directors to pay the costs of the motion.

I would accept that as a statement of general principle and would agree that it is not
appropriate to join the directors to an application for rectification of the register unless
it is sought to make them liable for the costs. Nevertheless, it follows that it is appropriate

A to make them respondents where an order for costs is sought against them. Moreover, in my judgment, the court today is more ready than it was in former times to examine the true nature of the dispute between the parties and to make the order for costs reflect the true nature of the dispute. Here the applicant owned an overwhelming majority of the shares in the company. He wanted to transfer one share to his daughter in order to be able to requisition a meeting. I accept that the directors, on legal advice, acted in what they considered to be the best interests of the company in declining to register

B the transfer, but I cannot think it right that Mr Morgan ought indirectly to bear three-quarters of the costs of litigating the dispute that then ensued.

The position is that a majority shareholder was blocked by the board from taking the only step open to him to put himself in a position of exercising the voting power to which his shareholding entitled him, and that in blocking him the directors acted beyond their powers.

C In my judgment, Mr Morgan has a strong case for seeking an order for costs against the directors. I do not think it necessary for him to establish bad faith before obtaining such an order. By analogy with the cases of unfair prejudice where the court is very ready to make an order against individual shareholders who have acted unfairly, so, too, in this case, it appears to me unjust to the majority shareholder to order the company to pay Mr Morgan's costs.

D I will direct those costs to be paid by the individual defendants other than Mr Green.

(*Order accordingly*)

_____

E

F

G

H

A

Re Sibec Developments Ltd.
Barclays Mercantile Business Finance Ltd & Anor v Sibec Developments Ltd & Ors.

Chancery Division (Companies Court).
Millett J.
Judgment delivered 9 July 1992.

B

Effect of administration order — Release of administrators — Administrators retained creditors' goods in administration — Creditors sought leave to commence proceedings for damages for wrongful interference with goods — Creditors alternatively sought payment of hire/lease charges as administration expenses — Whether administrators were liable in conversion or to pay charges — Whether administrators' release should be postponed — Insolvency Act 1986, sec. 11(3), 20.

C

This was an application to postpone the release of administrators.

The administrators were appointed to Sibec Developments Ltd in June 1990. The company was then in possession of vehicles and computer equipment leased to the company by the applicants or the subject of hire-purchase agreements with the applicants. The leasing or hire-purchase agreements were terminated and the applicants asked the administrators to consent to the repossession of the goods. The administrators did not consent, and the applicants applied to the Companies Court for (1) leave to repossess the goods, under sec. 11(3) of the Insolvency Act 1986, and (2) delivery up of the goods by the administrators. The application sought alternatively (3) an order that notwithstanding the administration order the applicants might be at liberty to commence proceedings in the High Court against the company and/or the administrators for delivery up of the goods and/or damages for wrongful interference therewith; and, in the further alternative, (4) payment of hire and/or lease charges in respect of the goods as an expense of the administration.

D

E

In October 1990 the administrators agreed to let the applicants retake possession of the goods. Accordingly the court made no order on para. (1) or (2) of the application. Paragraphs (3) and (4) of the application were adjourned generally by consent with liberty to restore.

F

In February 1992 the administration order was discharged and a compulsory winding-up order was made. The administrators were appointed liquidators. The order provided in the normal way for the release of the administrators on the expiration of a specified period after they had filed their receipts and payments account. The applicants applied for an order postponing the administrators' release until after the claims under para. (3) and (4) of the adjourned application had been disposed of.

The administrators opposed the postponement of their release on the grounds that the applicants' claim against them personally for damages for wrongful interference with goods was bound to fail, and that the applicants had unreasonably delayed in prosecuting their claims whether for damages or for payment of hire or lease charges.

G

Held, postponing the administrators' release:

1. Section 11(3) imposed a moratorium on the enforcement of creditors' rights but did not destroy those rights. The section did not affect the applicants' immediate right to possession.

H

2. Whether or not the company, and possibly the administrators, might be liable to a claim for damages for conversion, the administrators, until their release, remained liable at the direction of the court to pay not only for the use of the goods of another, but also for compensation for having wrongfully refused leave to the owner to retake the goods.

A   **3. There was no difference in the quantification of loss arising from a wrongful refusal to comply with the owner's demand for delivery and loss arising from a wrongful refusal to consent to the owner taking possession.**

4. The administrators could not be released while there was a proper claim against them outstanding which ought to be tried. These questions should not have remained outstanding when the administration order was discharged. But there was no evidence that the delay had prejudiced the administrators.

B   **Per curiam: It was the more appropriate course that questions of this kind should be decided by the court having control of the administration.**

The following cases were referred to in the judgment:

Clayton v Le Roy [1911] 2 KB 1031.
Clough Mill Ltd v Martin [1985] 1 WLR 111.

C   Anthony Mann QC (instructed by Bond Pearce, Plymouth) for the applicants.

Patrick Howell QC and Edmund Cullen (instructed by D J Freeman & Co) for the administrators.

JUDGMENT

Millett J: On 25 June 1990 an administration order was made against Sibec

D   Developments Ltd ("the company"). Mr Jordan and Mr Addy ("the respondents") of Cork Gully were appointed administrators. The purposes for which the order was made were those contained in sec. 8(3)(a), (b) and (d) of the *Insolvency Act* 1986, that is to say:

"(a) the survival of the company, and the whole or some part of its undertaking, as a going concern;

E   (b) the approval of a voluntary arrangement under Part I [of the Act];

(d) a more advantageous realisation of the company's assets than would be effected on a winding up;"

At the date on which the administration order was made the company was in possession of a number of motor vehicles and computer equipment which were leased to the company by Barclays Mercantile Business Finance Ltd or Mercantile Credit Co Ltd ("the applicants") or were the subject of hire-purchase agreements with one or

F   other of the applicants. At the date of the order the company's rental payments were several weeks in arrears and in many, and perhaps all, cases the relevant leasing or hire-purchase agreement had been automatically terminated without notice to the company pursuant to the terms of the relevant agreement.

On 30 July 1990 the applicants' solicitors wrote to the respondents formally determining all agreements not previously determined, and in a separate letter of the same date they

G   invited the respondents to consent forthwith to the repossession of the goods which, they asserted, with the possible exception of a few of the vehicles, did not appear to be required for the purposes of the administration. (The motor vehicles in question had been used by the company's employees many of whom had been made redundant, and by 30 July 1990 many, and perhaps most, of the vehicles had been placed in storage.) The respondents did not consent to the applicants' repossessing any of the goods.

H   Accordingly on 25 September 1990 the applicants issued an application to the Companies Court for leave to repossess them. Leave was required because of the provisions of sec. 11(3) of the Act which provides:

"During the period for which an administration order is in force—

(c) no other steps may be taken to enforce any security over the company's property, or to repossess goods in the company's possession under any

A   hire-purchase agreement, except with the consent of the administrator or the leave of the court and subject (where the court gives leave) to such terms as the court may impose; and

(d) no other proceedings and no execution or other legal process may be commenced or continued, and no distress may be levied, against the company or its property except with the consent of the administrator or the leave of the court and subject (where the court gives leave) to such terms as aforesaid.''

Section 10(4) of the Act extends the meaning of hire-purchase agreement to include chattel leasing agreement.

The application sought an order:

(1) that notwithstanding the administration order the applicants might be at liberty to repossess the goods;

(2) delivery up of the goods by the respondents;

(3) alternatively an order that notwithstanding the administration order the applicants might be at liberty to commence proceedings in the High Court against the company and/or the respondents for delivery up of the goods and/or damages for wrongful interference therewith; and

(4) in the further alternative, payment of hire and/or lease charges in respect of the goods as an expense of the administration.

On 15 October 1990 the respondents agreed that the applicants could repossess all the goods but imposed a condition which was waived on 19 October. The application came before the court on 22 October 1990. By then the respondents had agreed to let the applicants retake possession of the goods, and accordingly the court made no order on para. (1) or (2) of the application. Paragraphs (3) and (4) of the application were adjourned generally by consent with liberty to restore. The applicants' application for costs was adjourned for evidence to be filed. It was restored before the court on 12 November 1990 when, by consent, the court ordered the respondents to pay the applicants' costs of the application personally.

The purposes for which the administration order was made were subsequently found to be incapable of achievement. On 11 January 1992 the respondents presented a petition for the discharge of the administration order and for a winding-up order. On 10 February 1992 the administration order was discharged and a compulsory winding-up order was made. The respondents were appointed liquidators. The order provided in the normal way for the release of the respondents as administrators on the expiration of a specified period after they had filed their receipts and payments account. They filed that account on 22 April 1992 and accordingly were due to obtain their release on 20 May.

In the meantime, on 15 April, however, the applicants applied for an order postponing the respondents' release until after the claims under para. (3) and (4) of their adjourned application had been disposed of and for directions as to the determination of those claims. That application is now before me. The respondents oppose it and press for their release to take effect. The release has not already taken effect because I made an interim order postponing the release pending the determination of this question.

The respondents oppose the postponement of their release on the ground that the applicants' claim (in para. (3) of the application) against them personally for damages for wrongful interference with goods is bound to fail; and that the applicants have unreasonably delayed in prosecuting their claims whether for damages or for payment of hire or lease charges.

A   I will deal first with the claim for damages against the respondents personally for wrongful interference with goods. The applicants case is as follows.

(1)   An officer of a company is liable if he procures the commission of a tort by the company.

(2)   On this basis a receiver may be liable in damages for conversion: see *Clough Mill Ltd v Martin* [1985] 1 WLR 111. That too is not in dispute.

B   (3)   It is implicit in sec. 234(3) and (4) of the Act that an administrator may be liable in tort.

(4)   There is no reason in principle why an administrator should not be liable for unlawful interference with goods if he procures the company to commit acts which amount to that tort.

Subject to the effect of sec. 11 of the Act, none of those contentions is challenged.

C   The respondents submit that the claim is doomed to fail because by virtue of sec. 11(3)(c) of the Act the immediate right to possession of the goods was no longer vested in the applicants after the making of the administration order. That submission treats sec. 11 as affecting substantive rights. In my judgment it does not have that effect. The section is couched in purely procedural terms:

> "(c) no other steps may be taken to enforce any security . . . or to repossess
D   > goods . . ."

Similarly para. (d):

> "no other proceedings . . . may be commenced or continued . . ."

Both paragraph presuppose that the legal right to enforce the security or repossess the goods and the cause of action remain vested in the party seeking leave. By giving leave, in my judgment, the court does not alter the parties' legal rights. It merely grants the
E   person having a legal right liberty to enforce it by proceedings if necessary. The section imposes a moratorium on the enforcement of the creditors' rights but does not destroy those rights.

     The applicants wish to sue the respondents for wrongful interference with goods, that is to say conversion, within the meaning of sec. 1(a) of the *Torts (Interference with Goods) Act* 1977. That tort covers the wrongful retention of goods in a manner which
F   is adverse to the rights of the owner. In *Clerk & Lindsell on Torts* (16th ed., 1989) at para. 22-24 (p. 1234) conversion by keeping is described as follows:

> "Mere unpermitted keeping of another's chattel is not a conversion of it. There must be some detention consciously adverse to the rights of the owner, such as an assertion of a lien that does not exist. The ordinary way of showing a conversion by unlawful retention of property is to prove that the defendant, having it in his
G   > possession, refused to give it up on demand made by the party entitled."

     Mr Mann, who appeared for the applicants, seized on the word "the *ordinary* way of showing a conversion" to submit that the making of a demand was not a precondition of the cause of action for damages in conversion. But in my judgment the use of that word was not intended to contradict the opening sentence, the "mere unpermitted keeping of another's chattel" is not a conversion of it. Demand is not an essential precondition of the tort in the sense that what is required is an overt act of withholding possession of the
H   chattel from the true owner. Such an act may consist of a refusal to deliver up the chattel on demand made, but it may be demonstrated by other conduct, for example, by asserting a lien. Some positive act of withholding, however, is required; so that absent any positive conduct on the part of the defendant, the plaintiff can establish a cause of action in conversion only by making demand. In my judgment so much is clear from *Clayton v Le Roy* [1911] 2 KB 1031 where the need for a demand in a simple retention

case is clearly stated. The reason for this is clearly stated by *Fletcher Moulton* LJ at p. 1048:

> "The question as to the exact moment at which a cause of action arises may seem a very technical one, but in my opinion it is a point of substance in this case, and for the following reason. In an action of detinue, as in other actions of tort, the Statute of Limitations runs from the time when the cause of action arose; consequently, if nothing has happened to give rise to an action of detinue, there is no period of time which can operate to extinguish the title of the real owner. He may have been deprived of control over his chattel for a hundred years, but it still remains his property, and an action will lie to recover it, unless there have been a demand and a refusal which would be sufficient to give rise to a cause of action. If there is a demand by the owner from the person in possession of a chattel and a refusal on the part of the latter to give it up, then in six years the remedy of the owner is barred; it is therefore very important for the owner that the law should lay down the principle that some clear act of that kind is required to constitute a cause of action in detinue."

And on p. 1050:

> ". . . the plaintiff must establish that at the moment of (issue of the writ) he was in a position to bring an action of detinue; in other words, that there had been a wrongful denial by the defendant of the plaintiff's title to the watch. At first the case was treated as though the question was as to the effect of a demand by the plaintiff of his watch and a refusal by the defendant to hand it over; but this point was practically abandoned, for there had been neither demand nor refusal. Then the question was treated, but rather vaguely, as one of conversion, and the defendant's letter of May 16 was said to be evidence of conversion. But the mere fact that there was evidence pro and con on such a point would not be enough; it is necessary to find as a fact that there was a demand and refusal before the issue of the writ."

In my judgment, that shows clearly that an overt act of withholding goods from the true owner is a condition precedent to the tort of conversion and that absent any overt act on the part of the party in possession the true owner must establish both demand and refusal before he can establish a cause of action.

In my judgment, therefore, to succeed in the present case where the respondents did nothing save retain the goods and decline to give their consent for the applicants' retaking possession, the applicants could not succeed in an action for conversion unless they were to establish: (1) an immediate right to possession, (2) a lawful demand for redelivery, and (3) unreasonable refusal to redeliver. In my judgment, sec. 11(3) does not affect the applicants' immediate right to possession. The question then arises whether para. (c) precludes the making of a demand, and, if it does not, whether the letter of 30 July constituted such a demand.

The construction of sec. 11(3) of the Act is not free from difficulty; the meaning and effect of the word "other" in both para. (c) and para. (d) in particular is obscure. One question of some difficulty is whether para. (c) is confined to extra-legal steps, that is to say, enforcing security without legal proceedings (for example, retaining possession under a lien or taking possession of goods) so that the taking of proceedings for the enforcement of a security or the repossession of goods is governed exclusively by para. (d); or whether there is an overlap between the two paragraphs.

The question whether the making of a demand necessary to constitute a cause of action in conversion is a step prohibited by para. (c) in a case where the proceedings would be for the enforcement of a security or the repossession of goods, is, I think, a difficult one and ought to be left to be decided in a case where it directly arises. It does

A not arise in the present case because the applicants wish to sue the respondents personally, not the company.

In my judgment, the administrators remain exposed to the claim so long as they have not been released, whether they committed the tort of conversion or not. That is because the respondents, as administrators, are officers of the court and at all times subject to the court's direction. If they wish to make use of another party's property for the

B purposes of the administration and cannot agree terms, they can seek the directions of the court. If administrators wrongly retain goods otherwise than for the proper purposes of the administration, for example, to use them as a bargaining counter, the owner can apply to the court to direct the administrators to hand over the goods without the need for action, and to pay compensation for having retained them in the meantime. Only in a case where there was a triable issue as to the ownership of the goods would the question of giving leave to take proceedings for possession arise. I can see no difference between

C the amount of compensation that the administrators should be directed to pay for having wrongfully retained goods properly demanded and for having wrongfully refused leave to repossess them.

Accordingly, in my judgment, whether or not the company, and possibly the administrators, may be liable to a claim for damages for conversion, the administrators, until their release, remain liable at the direction of the court to pay not only for the use of the goods of another, but also for compensation for having wrongfully refused leave

D to the owner to retake the goods.

In my judgment, it is the more appropriate course that questions of this kind should be decided by the court having control of the administration. In the present case the questions whether the company should pay rental for the period during which the respondents were properly retaining the goods for the purpose of the administration, or while they were considering whether or not they needed to do so, can be considered by

E the same court and at the same time as the claim for compensation for retaining the goods after the time when they ought to have consented to the applicants' retaking possession. There will be two advantages in this course. First the questions will be decided by the court which is seised of the administration and can give directions to the administrators who are its own officers. Secondly, the court will have a discretion to decide whether the administrators should be personally liable, should have a right of recoupment against the company's assets, or be released from liability.

F There is no difference in the quantification of loss arising from a wrongful refusal to comply with the owner's demand for delivery and loss arising from a wrongful refusal to consent to the owner taking possession, and there are considerable advantages in the claim being heard at the same time as the claim for rental. It is, in my judgment, unthinkable that the respondents should be released while there is a proper claim against them which is outstanding and which ought to be tried.

G I accept that it would have been better in the present case for the applicants to have proceeded more quickly against the respondents so that these questions should not have remained outstanding when the administration order was discharged. But there is no evidence that the delay has prejudiced the respondents. Accordingly I will accede to the application to postpone the release of the respondents, pending the determination of the applicants' claims for rental and for loss by reason of the respondents' failure to consent to the retaking of the goods earlier than was the case.

H I will give directions for the determination of both questions but I will leave it to counsel to formulate the directions that ought to be given. If they can agree, so much the better; if not, then I will rule.

(*Order accordingly. Applicants' costs to be expenses of the administration*)

A

Re Olympia & York Canary Wharf Ltd.
American Express Europe Ltd & Ors v Adamson & Ors.

Chancery Division (Companies Court).
Millett J.
Judgment delivered 24 July 1992.

B

Administration orders — Effect of administration order — Whether service of contractual notice was "other legal process" — Insolvency Act 1986, sec. 11(3)(d).

This application raised the question whether service by the applicants upon a company in administration of a contractual notice purporting to make time of the essence or to terminate the contract with the company by reason of the company's repudiatory breach, required the consent of the joint administrators of the company or the leave of the court as "other legal process" within sec. 11(3)(d) of the Insolvency Act 1986.

C

*Held***, declaring that service of a contractual notice did not require consent or leave under sec. 11(3)(d):**

"Legal process" in sec. 11(3)(d) meant a process which required the assistance of the court and did not extend to the service of a contractual notice, whether or not the service of such a notice was a precondition to the bringing of proceedings. (Dictum of Harman J in *Exchange Travel Agency Ltd v Triton Property Trust plc & Anor* **[1991] BCC 341 at p. 345H not followed.)**

D

The following cases were referred to in the judgment:

Birmingham and Staffordshire Gas Light Co, Ex parte. Re Fanshaw & Yorston (1871) LR 11 Eq 615.
Exchange Travel Agency Ltd v Triton Property Trust plc & Anor [1991] BCC 341.
International Tin Council, Re (1987) 3 BCC 103; [1987] Ch 419.
Paramount Airways Ltd, Re (Bristol Airport plc v Powdrill) [1990] BCC 130; [1990] Ch 744.

E

Robin Potts QC and Richard Snowden (instructed by Cameron Markby Hewitt) for the applicants.

Martin Pascoe (instructed by Allen & Overy) for the respondents.

F

JUDGMENT

Millett J: The question raised by this application is whether the intended service by the applicants upon the fourth respondent ("the company"), which is a company in administration, of a notice electing to treat a contract with the company as terminated by reason of the company's repudiatory breach, requires the consent of the joint administrators of the company or the leave of the court pursuant to sec. 11(3) of the Insolvency Act 1986.

G

Prior to the issue of the application, the applicants had served a notice purporting to make time of the essence of the performance of the company's obligations under the contract. A similar question arises whether the service of that notice required the prior consent of the joint administrators or the leave of the court.

The question can be formulated in more general terms as follows: whether the presentation of an administration petition or the making of an administration order operates to prevent a party to a contract with the company in question from serving notice making time of the essence, or accepting a repudiatory breach of contract, whether the breach was committed before or after the presentation of the petition or the making of the order.

H

A   Section 11(3) of the 1986 Act reads as follows:

"During the period for which an administration order is in force—

     (a) no resolution may be passed or order made for the winding up of the company;

     (b) no administrative receiver of the company may be appointed;

B   (c) no other steps may be taken to enforce any security over the company's property, or to repossess goods in the company's possession under any hire-purchase agreement, except with the consent of the administrator or the leave of the court and subject (where the court gives leave) to such terms as the court may impose; and

     (d) no other proceedings and no execution or other legal process may be commenced or continued, and no distress may be levied, against the company or its property except with the consent of the administrator or the leave of the court and subject (where the court gives leave) to such terms as aforesaid."

C

Section 10(1) of the 1986 Act contains like provisions in relation to the period beginning with the presentation of a petition for an administration order and ending with the making of such an order or the dismissal of the petition.

D   It has not been suggested that the service of either notice in the present case would constitute the taking of a step to enforce a security over the company's property or to repossess goods in the company's possession under any hire-purchase agreement. Whether the service of a demand or other notice which is a precondition for the enforcement of a security or the repossession of goods falls within sec. 11(3)(c) has not been argued, and nothing in this judgment should be taken as directed to any such question.

E   It will be observed that para. (d) divides into three parts. It prohibits (i) the commencement or continuation of "other proceedings"; (ii) the commencement or continuation of "execution or other legal process"; and (iii) the levying of any distress. It is not suggested that the service of either notice would constitute the levying of a distress.

F   In *Re Paramount Airways Ltd (Bristol Airport plc v Powdrill)* [1990] BCC 130, the Court of Appeal considered the meaning of the phrase "other proceedings" in subsec. (3)(d). At p. 153D *Browne-Wilkinson* V-C said:

". . . the natural meaning of the words 'no other proceedings . . . may be commenced or continued' is that the proceedings in question are either legal proceedings or quasi-legal proceedings such as arbitration . . . the reference to the 'commencement' and 'continuation' of proceedings indicates that what G   Parliament had in mind was legal proceedings. The use of the word 'proceedings' in the plural together with the words 'commence' and 'continue' are far more appropriate to legal proceedings (which are normally so described) than to the doing of some act of a more general nature."

The Vice-Chancellor contrasted the use of the word "proceedings" in para. (d) with the word "steps" in para. (c). He deprecated a wide formulation of the meaning of the H   word "proceedings" because such a construction would introduce great uncertainty as to what constituted commencement or continuation of proceedings, and asked—I think rhetorically—the question, "Would the acceptance of a repudiation of a contract by the company constitute a 'proceeding'?"

Counsel for the administrators has not contended that the service of either notice in the present case would constitute the commencement or continuation of proceedings.

The question which has been argued is whether the service of either notice would   A
constitute "execution or other legal process".

The question was considered by *Harman* J in *Exchange Travel Agency Ltd v Triton
Property Trust plc* [1991] BCC 341. That case was concerned with the peaceable
re-entry by a landlord after the tenant, which was in administration, had failed to pay
the rent. *Harman* J held that the landlord could not re-enter without the consent of the
administrator or the leave of the court because it was the taking of a step to enforce a   B
security over the company's property. I respectfully agree. However, *Harman* J gave a
second ground for his decision; namely, that the re-entry constituted the commencement
of legal process. In that case the company in administration was a tenant by assignment
which was not therefore in privity of contract with the landlord. In the course of his
judgment *Harman* J said (at p. 345H):

> "It seems to me that 'legal process' is exactly how one would describe the exercise   C
> of a right by a person not in a contractual relationship with his tenant but holding
> a relationship by privity of estate between them. In my judgment it is a correct use
> of words to describe a landlord who has legal rights, arising out of the privity of
> estate, which he exercises by the process of peaceable re-entry as exercising 'legal
> process'. It seems to me therefore that if this exercise of the right of re-entry be
> not a security, it is quite certainly the commencement of another legal process . . .

> It would be astonishing, in my mind, if Parliament has plainly prevented a landlord   D
> from issuing a writ for forfeiture or taking steps in the courts to effect a forfeiture
> and a re-entry, but has left entirely open and untouched the right to effect a
> peaceable re-entry. It must be obvious to all that the better realisation of the
> company's assets than in a winding up cannot be achieved if in a winding up
> peaceable re-entry is barred but in an administration peaceable re-entry is not
> barred."
>   E
I respectfully agree. In my judgment the peaceable re-entry is a step in the enforcement
of the landlord's security over the property of the tenant, and if the tenant is a company
in administration the taking of that step requires the prior consent of the administrator
or the leave of the court. The second ground of his decision, however, is a different
matter. It was unnecessary for the decision, and has wide implications, for no sensible
distinction can be drawn between the exercise of legal rights arising from privity of estate
and the exercise of rights arising from contract.   F

Harman J appears to have had little or no authority cited to him on the meaning of the
phrase "legal process". I have enjoyed the benefit of the citation of a considerable
amount of authority. The expression "legal process" is not a novel expression introduced
for the first time by sec. 10 and sec. 11 of the 1986 Act. Those sections have a long
history. Their immediate source is sec. 9 of the *Bankruptcy Act* 1914, which was based
on sec. 10 of the *Bankruptcy Act* 1883, which in turn was based on sec. 13 of the   G
Bankruptcy Act 1869. Section 9(1) of the *Bankruptcy Act* 1914 provided:

> "The court may, at any time after the presentation of a bankruptcy petition, stay
> any action, execution, or other legal process against the property or person of the
> debtor, and any court in which proceedings are pending against a debtor may, on
> proof that a bankruptcy petition has been presented by or against the debtor,
> either stay the proceedings or allow them to continue on such terms as it may think   H
> just."

In sec. 10 and sec. 11 of the 1986 Act, Parliament has effected certain modifications to
sec. 9 of the *Bankruptcy Act* 1914. The word "action" has been replaced by the more
compendious expression "proceedings" which is apt to denote any legal or quasi-legal
proceedings whether commenced by writ or otherwise; and a prohibition on the levying

A   of distress has been expressly included, thereby dealing with a question which had previously caused difficulty.

In *Stroud's Judicial Dictionary* (5th ed., 1986) it is said that the word "process" is:

> "the doing of something in a proceeding in a civil or criminal court, and that which may be done without the aid of a court is not a 'process'."

B   Therefore a distraint, whether for rent or any other payment, and whether the right of distress be given by common law, statute or, as it should seem, by any other authority was not a "process" nor was it an "execution, or other legal process" within the *Bankruptcy Act* 1869.

In *Ex parte Birmingham and Staffordshire Gas Light Co. Re Fanshaw & Yorston* (1871) LR 11 Eq 615, Sir *James Bacon* CJ held:

C
> ". . . a distress for rent cannot be considered to be included in the expression 'legal process,' in as much as no legal process whatever is necessary; and the landlord may, if he thinks proper, distrain with his own hands. As little can it be called an execution, for an execution is the result of a judgment which has been recovered in some Court of Law, but to a distress no legal proceedings whatever are necessary."

D   The presence of the word "stay" in sec. 9 of the *Bankruptcy Act* 1914, and the insertion of the word "legal" before "process" in sec. 11(3)(d) of the 1986 Act support the impression that the word "process" in each of the Acts means a process which requires the assistance of the court, and does not extend to the service of a contractual notice, whether or not the service of such a notice is a precondition to the bringing of legal proceedings.

In a different context, in *Re International Tin Council* (1987) 3 BCC 103, I had to consider the meaning of the phrase "immunity from suit and legal process" in the
E   *International Tin Council (Immunities and Privileges) Order* 1972. I held that it embraced all forms of the adjudicative and enforcement jurisdiction and included the winding-up process. In that enactment the phrase was a composite one, but in so far as it could be split into its component elements I expressed the view that "suit" extended to all forms of the adjudicative and "legal process" to all forms of the enforcement jurisdiction.

It is not necessary in this case to consider where the line is to be drawn between the
F   commencement or continuation of "proceedings" on the one hand or of "legal process" on the other. But in my judgment both concepts are well known. Together they embrace all steps in legal proceedings from the issue of initiating process, to their final termination in the process of execution or other means of enforcement of a judgment such as the appointment of a receiver by way of equitable execution or the making of a charging order or other steps for the enforcement of the court's judgment without execution. But
G   the phrase is not apt to describe the taking of non-judicial steps such as the service of a contractual notice in order to crystallise the liability of the party on whom the notice is served.

In my judgment, support for that conclusion can be derived from the use of the words "commenced or continued" in sec. 11(3)(d) of the 1986 Act. If the service of a contractual notice is part of a legal process, I am unable to understand what legal process it is supposed to commence or continue. The words "commence or continue" indicate a
H   process which has an independent existence of its own apart from the step by which it is commenced or continued; a process which either continues after or was in existence before the taking of the relevant step.

Further support for my conclusion, if it were needed, may be derived from a consideration of the legislative purpose for which sec. 10 and sec. 11 were enacted. They are intended to impose a moratorium upon the creditors of the company in order to

assist the administrator in his attempts to achieve the statutory purpose for which he was   A
appointed. They are couched in procedural terms and are designed to prevent creditors
from depriving the administrator of the possession of property which may be required
by him for the purpose of the administration.

Paragraphs (a) and (b) of subsec. 11(3) operate to prevent the replacement of the
administration by an alternative insolvency procedure before the statutory purpose for
which the administrator was appointed has been achieved. Paragraphs (c) and (d)
impose the moratorium. Their construction should be approached with that legislative   B
purpose in mind. They are not intended to interfere with the rights of creditors further
than is required to enable the administrators to carry out their functions, and in
particular they are not intended to interfere with the creditors' contractual rights to
crystallise their rights or discharge their own contractual liabilities.

Accordingly, I decline to follow *Harman* J's decision that a landlord's peaceable
re-entry amounts to the commencement or continuation of a legal process, though   C
I respectfully agree that it requires the consent of the administrator or the leave of the
court under sec. 11(3)(c) of the 1986 Act. I hold that the service of a contractual notice
purporting to make time of the essence or to terminate a contract by reason of the
company's repudiatory breach does not require the consent of the administrator or the
leave of the court under sec. 11(3)(d) of the 1986 Act, and I will so declare.

(Declaration accordingly)   D

A   # Re Olympia & York Canary Wharf Ltd (No. 2).
     # Bear Stearns International Ltd v Adamson & Ors.

Chancery Division (Companies Court).
Morritt J.
Judgment delivered 21 December 1992.

B   *Administration — Agreement to lease — Whether agreement to lease had been repudiated.*

By this application Bear Stearns International Ltd ("BSI") sought to establish that an agreement to lease made between BSI and Olympia & York Canary Wharf Ltd ("O & Y") and others had been discharged by the acceptance by BSI of the repudiation of the contract by O & Y, which was in administration.

C   **Under the agreement to lease BSI was to take a floor in Canary Wharf. Clause 6 provided for O & Y to take over the Bear Stearns group's liabilities under existing leases and, in cl. 6(c)(v), to indemnify Bear Stearns in respect of all reasonable costs and expenses incurred by Bear Stearns in respect of its continuing obligations as tenant under the leases. After the administration order had been made in respect of O & Y, BSI invoiced O & Y for sums due under the leases in respect of rent etc. BSI then demanded further sums due under the leases and the rent etc. already paid by BSI and invoiced to O & Y. In**

D   **the same letter BSI asked the administrators for confirmation that they would honour O & Y's obligations under the agreement to lease. When BSI did not receive the sums demanded nor the confirmation, it claimed that this constituted a repudiatory breach by O & Y of the agreement, which BSI had then accepted.**

The case for O & Y was that cl. 6(c)(v) was a warranty only so that its breach could not give rise to a repudiation capable of acceptance; alternatively that the circumstances were not such as to give rise to any repudiation even if the clause was an intermediate term. It

E   **was common ground that cl. 6(c)(v) was not a condition. BSI contended that its letter had made time of the essence in respect of the obligation to pay the rent demanded by invoice and that failure to comply with the requirement of the letter to pay was a repudiation which it was entitled to accept irrespective of whether cl. 6(c)(v) was an intermediate term.**

Held, **declaring that there was no repudiation which BSI could accept so as to discharge**
F   **it from further performance of the agreement to lease:**

1. Clause 6(c)(v) was an intermediate term and a breach might amount to repudiation. The failure to pay could not amount to a repudiation nor could the failure to give the confirmation sought. The administrators were under no obligation to provide any such confirmation as BSI sought.

2. The letter was effective to make time of the essence.

G   **3. Failure to comply with a notice making time of the essence did not itself constitute a repudiation irrespective of the consequences of the breach, and the failure of O & Y to comply with the terms of the letter did not go to the root of the contract.**

The following cases were referred to in the judgment:

Afovos Shipping Co SA v Pagnan & Anor [1982] 1 WLR 848.
Atlantic Computer Systems plc, Re [1990] BCC 859; [1992] Ch 505.
H   *Barr's Contract, Re* [1956] Ch 551.
Behzadi v Shaftesbury Hotels Ltd [1992] Ch 1.
Beswick v Beswick [1968] AC 58.
Bunge Corp v Tradax Export SA [1981] 1 WLR 711.
Collinge v Heywood (1839) 9 Ad & E 633; 112 ER 1352.
Decro-Wall International SA v Practitioners in Marketing Ltd [1971] 1 WLR 361.

Eshun v Moorgate Mercantile Co Ltd [1971] 1 WLR 722.   A
Federal Commerce & Navigation Co Ltd v Molena Alpha Inc & Ors [1979] AC 757.
Gibson v Goldsmid (1854) 5 De G M & G 757; 43 ER 1064.
Hongkong Fir Shipping Co Ltd v Kawasaki Kisen Kaisha Ltd [1962] 2 QB 26.
Hussein & Ors v Mehlman [1992] 32 EG 59.
Louinder v Leis (1982) 149 CLR 509.
Lowther v Heaver (1889) 41 ChD 248.
Scandinavian Trading Tanker Co AB v Flota Petrolera Ecuatoriana [1983] 2 AC 694.   B
United Scientific Holdings Ltd v Burnley Borough Council [1978] AC 904.
Universal Cargo Carriers Corp v Citati [1957] 2 QB 401.
Walsh v Lonsdale (1882) 21 ChD 9.

John Martin QC and Jonathan Simpkiss (instructed by Slaughter and May) for the
applicant.

Elizabeth Gloster QC and Martin Pascoe (instructed by Allen & Overy) for the   C
respondents.

JUDGMENT

Morritt J: By this application Bear Stearns International Ltd ("BSI") seeks to
establish that an agreement to lease dated 29 June 1990 made between BSI and Olympia
& York Canary Wharf Ltd ("O & Y") and others has been discharged by the acceptance   D
by BSI of the repudiation of the contract by O & Y. Initially BSI also sought to have
determined the basis on which it has occupied the premises, the subject-matter of the
agreement, both before and after the alleged discharge of the agreement.

The Bear Stearns group carries on the business of brokers, dealers and investment
bankers. The group includes three companies relevant to this application. The first is
Bear Stearns Companies Inc, a company incorporated in Delaware but based in New
York. This company is described in the evidence as the central corporate entity of the   E
group. The second is Bear Stearns International Corp, a company incorporated in the
Republic of Panama. This company was and is the lessee of premises situate on the first
floor of and known as No. 9 and 9A Devonshire Square, London EC2. The third
company is BSI. This company was incorporated in England. Formerly it occupied the
premises comprised in the Devonshire Square leases and now occupies floor 25 of
Canary Wharf. It is the proposed lessee of the latter premises pursuant to the agreement   F
to lease.

The Devonshire Square leases consist of two leases, one dated 14 October 1983 and
the other dated 24 June 1988. In each case the lessee was and is Bear Stearns International
Corp and the term was for 25 years from 29 September 1983 subject to determination at
the option of the tenant at the end of the tenth year by six months' previous notice in
writing. By the terms of the leases the tenant paid a rent, a service charge and an   G
insurance service charge. The premises comprised in the leases covered 19,156 square
feet. At the date of the agreement to lease the rent was at a rate per square foot of £46.50
for No. 9 and £38.63 for No. 9A.

O & Y has for some years been involved in the construction of a 50-floor tower block
at 1 Canada Square, London E14 5AB, known as Canary Wharf. The works of
construction were not complete when the agreement to lease was entered into on
29 June 1990. The parties to that agreement are expressed to be O & Y as the developer   H
and landlord, Olympia & York Canary Wharf Holdings as surety for the landlord, BSI
as the tenant, Bear Stearns Companies Inc as surety for the tenant and Bear Stearns
International Corp as the covenantee of a specific covenant to which I shall refer in due
course. The agreement was executed by the first four parties but not the fifth, Bear
Stearns International Corp.

A   The structure of the agreement to leases was as follows. Clause 2 provided for the completion of the works of construction so as to create the property to be leased by O & Y to BSI. The description in cl. 2.1 was subsequently amended. As so amended the premises to be demised were to consist of approximately 20,000 square feet of net internal area on floor 25 of the tower. Clauses 2.2–2.4 provided for certain works to be carried out by O & Y. Clause 2.5 provided for other works to be carried out by BSI as the tenant. The latter works, described as fitting out works, were to commence when the

B works to be carried out by O & Y had reached a sufficiently advanced stage, known as the access stage and to be identified by a certificate issued by O & Y. Such a certificate was issued on 23 January 1991 so that the provisions of cl. 2.6(b) never came into operation. But as that clause contains the covenant with Bear Stearn International Corp, which was given as the reason for that company being a party to the agreement, I should refer to it. It provides, in effect, that if the certificate had not been issued by

C 1 February 1991 O & Y should indemnify the covenantee from 1 August 1991 against any liability under the Devonshire Square leases, less any sums due in respect of the occupation of floor 25 during the same period. Clauses 2.7–2.13, 2.15 and 2.17 dealt with other matters which are not relevant. Clause 2.14 provided for the measurement of the net internal area on which the amount of the rent and other payments would depend. The agreed measurement was 19,888 square feet. Clause 2.16 provided for O & Y to make substantial payments to BSI. Paragraph (a) provided for O & Y to pay to BSI £55

D per square foot of net internal area towards the costs of fitting out the premises for the occupation of BSI. Paragraph (c) provided for a "reverse premium" of £25.32 per square foot of net internal area to be paid within five days of BSI going into occupation. Thus the agreement provided for £1,093,840 and £503,564 (in each case exclusive of VAT) to be paid by O & Y to BSI.

    Clause 3 dealt with the lease to be granted by O & Y to BSI. Clause 3.2 provided that,

E in the events which happened, the lease should commence on 23 July 1991 and be for a term of 25 years, with the rent being payable quarterly in advance. The rent was to be at the rate of £28.50 for the first five years and that amount plus the open market rent for certain car parking space referred to in cl. 3.1 for the next five years. In accordance with the provisions of cl. 3.5(a) and in the events which happened the rent became payable on 23 March 1992

F   Clauses 4 and 5 are not relevant to the issues before me, but cl. 6 is central to them. This clause provides for O & Y to take over the Devonshire Square leases and any liabilities thereunder. It starts by providing that any reference to "Bear Stearns" should be a reference to any company in the Bear Stearns group which was for the time being the tenant under the Devonshire Square leases. Paragraphs (a), (b) and (c)(i)–(iii) required O & Y to take an assignment of the leases if the landlord consented or unreasonably refused his consent. Consent was refused on 12 April 1991 and it is

G common ground that such refusal was reasonable. Thus those paragraph never came into effect. Paragraph (iv) provided that:

> "Failing such consent or determination by the court that consent has been unreasonably withheld Bear Stearns will continue as tenant of the Devonshire Square premises, but O & Y will have general and absolute control over Bear Stearns leasehold interest."

H Paragraph (v) provided:

> "From the takeover date [which was 8 October 1991] O & Y will indemnify Bear Stearns in respect of all reasonable costs and expenses incurred by Bear Stearns in respect of its continuing obligations as tenant under the Devonshire Square documentation [and the seeking to obtain any requisite consents to the assignment to O & Y]. O & Y shall reimburse the same to the tenant [sc. BSI as defined]

A

within ten days of demand. In consideration of that indemnity O & Y will receive from Bear Stearns on a 'flow through' basis all income derived from the Devonshire Square premises from time to time.''

Clause 7 provided for further confirmatory documentation consisting of an underlease of floor 25 of Canary Wharf and a takeover agreement relating to the Devonshire Square leases. Attached to the agreement were O & Y's standard forms which were to be used as the starting point ''for the documentation which is to be entered into . . . whereby for the avoidance of doubt the binding arrangements reflected in this agreement will be set out''; see cl. 7(c). The rest of cl. 7 contains a mechanism for the documents to be agreed on or before 30 September 1990 or thereafter to be determined by an independent person in default of agreement. It is accepted that the mechanism is contractually effective. The underlease was agreed and executed by O & Y on 27 April 1992. The takeover agreement was not agreed in all respects until 18 November 1992. All the drafts of the takeover agreement indicated that it was to be made between O & Y and BSI, not Bear Stearns International Corp which was the tenant under the Devonshire Square leases. Moreover, the drafts contained provisions which suggest that the draftsman thought that BSI was liable under the covenants contained in the Devonshire Square leases. Pursuant to cl. 7(h) completion was to take place ten days after the finalisation of the underlease and takeover agreement, namely, in the events which happened, 28 November 1991. Clauses 8–12 are not relevant.

On 13 May 1991 BSI appointed O & Y to be its project manager for the tenant's works to be carried out pursuant to the provisions of cl. 2.5 of the agreement to lease. This appointment gave rise to claims by O & Y against BSI.

On 4 October 1991 O & Y paid BSI £591,687 by way of reverse premium and £1,285,252 for fitting out costs as provided in each case by cl. 2.16. On 8 October 1991 BSI completed the tenant's works as provided for by cl. 2.5 and went into occupation of the premises agreed to be demised. Accordingly, that date is the takeover date for the purposes of cl. 6(a).

On 30 January 1992 O & Y paid to BSI a total of £483,812, being the sums paid or payable by Bear Stearns International Corp as the rent, service charges and insurance due under the Devonshire Square leases for the two quarters September 1991 to March 1992. Between 20 and 25 March 1992 BSI paid to O & Y the total sum of £186,188 due in respect of rent, service charge and insurance for floor 25 of Canary Wharf for the period 23 March to 30 June 1992. By this time there was a dispute between the parties as to the amount due by BSI to O & Y under the project management agreement. On 16 April 1992 O & Y claimed £159,510 inclusive of VAT.

On 28 May 1992 an administration order was made in respect of O & Y and O & Y Canary Wharf Holdings. The purposes for which such orders were made were those prescribed by sec. 8(3)(a) and (d) of the *Insolvency Act* 1986. One consequence of the orders is that no proceedings can be instituted against either company except with the consent of the administrators or the leave of the court: *Insolvency Act* 1986, sec. 11(3)(d). Another consequence is that debts and liabilities incurred during the course of the administration only obtain priority if they arise from contracts entered into by the administrator in carrying out his functions or are payable in respect of contracts of employment so entered into or adopted by the administrator: *Insolvency Act* 1986, sec. 19(5).

By invoices dated 5 and 19 June 1992 BSI claimed from O & Y the total sum of £252,155 in respect of rent, service charges and electricity due in respect of the Devonshire Square leases.

A   On 1 July 1992 solicitors for BSI wrote to the administrators of O & Y. They referred to the agreement to lease and enclosed a cheque for £175,497 in respect of the rent, service charge and insurance due in respect of floor 25. The letter continued as follows:

"Pursuant to Clause 6(C)(v) of the Agreement we hereby demand, on behalf of our clients reimbursement of the sum of £260,252.16 being rent, service charge and electricity (for the quarter 24th June to 29th September 1992) and insurance (for the year 15th May 1992 to 15th May 1993) paid by our client under the Devonshire Square lease. We also demand the sum of £252,155.91 being rent and service charges (for the quarter 25th March to 23rd June 1992) paid by our client under the Devonshire Square lease and invoiced to you on 10th March 1992. Such sums to be received by us on or before 13th July 1992.

In view of your appointment as administrators of O & Y and Holdings, our client has asked us to request that you confirm that you will honour the whole of the obligations of O & Y and Holdings under the Agreement. Please may we have this confirmation within the next 14 days i.e. on or before 15th July 1992.

Should we fail to receive the Devonshire Square Lease rent and the confirmation sought on the dates specified we will advise our client that this amounts to a repudiation by O & Y and Holdings of the Agreement entitling our client to rescind the Agreement. Our client will thereafter take such action as it considers appropriate."

Solicitors for the administrators and on their instructions for O & Y replied on 6 July in the following terms:

"Kindly note that although receipt of your clients' cheque is acknowledged our clients do not accept or acknowledge:

(i) that your clients are not obliged to make payments in respect of service charges, insurance and any other payments due under the Agreement (as defined in our letter);

(ii) that any purported failure to provide rent and other payments in respect of the Devonshire Square lease and the confirmations you have sought either constitutes repudiation by O & Y or Holdings or entitles your clients to rescind the Agreement.

Please also note that the joint administrators are not adopting any leases or agreements for lease so as to cause any liabilities to be incurred by them and that they are not causing either of O & Y or Holdings to become in breach of any such leases or agreements to lease."

On 10 July the solicitors for BSI wrote:

"In view of the contents of the final paragraph of your letter we await payment of the sums requested and the confirmation sought in our letter to your clients of 1st July 1992."

On 16 July 1992 the solicitors for BSI wrote again in the following terms:

"We have not received the sums demanded by us pursuant to cl. 6(c)(v) of the agreement to lease nor have we received the confirmation from your clients that they will honour the whole of the obligations of Olympia & York Canary Wharf Ltd ('O & Y') and ('O & Y Canary Wharf Holdings') under the agreement to lease.

We have advised our clients that this constitutes a repudiatory breach by your clients of their obligations under the terms of the agreement to lease. On behalf of our clients we accept your clients' conduct as such a repudiation and would inform

you that our clients regard their obligations under the agreement to lease as at an
end.

As a result, our clients intend to vacate the premises as soon as suitable alternative
accommodation can be found. We have advised our clients that they are entitled
to remain in the premises for so long as is reasonable to find such suitable
alternative accommodation and to fit them out to our clients' requirements.

For the avoidance of doubt our clients will not make any payment to your clients
in respect of any period after they have vacated the premises."

It is these four letters which BSI contends demonstrate the repudiation of the
agreement to lease by O & Y and the acceptance of that repudiation by BSI. It is
common ground that the validity or otherwise of that claim must be judged by reference
to the facts as they existed on 16 July 1992. Thus I can refer only briefly to the subsequent
events.

On 8 October 1992 Mr Bloom, one of the administrators, swore an affidavit in which
he stated that:

"Notwithstanding the inability of O & Y (because of its insolvency) to pay sums
which are presently payable, or will become payable, by O & Y in respect of the
Devonshire Square premises, such failure does not in the circumstances, amount
to a repudiatory breach of the agreement to lease. The administrators' position is
that BSI remains obliged to complete the agreement to lease notwithstanding
O & Y's failure to pay the said sums and that BSI will have to prove as an
unsecured creditor in the administration or eventual liquidation of O & Y."

On 26 October 1992 the solicitors for Bear Stearns International Corp gave notice to
the landlord of the Devonshire Square leases to determine them on 28 September 1993.
Whilst the precise figures are not agreed it is common ground that the outstanding
liabilities under the Devonshire Square leases will be of the order of £1.5m. On
20 November 1992 the solicitors for the administrators proposed to the solicitors for BSI
that the liability of O & Y to reimburse the amounts paid under the Devonshire Square
leases be set off against the liabilities of BSI to O & Y under the project management
agreement and in respect of floor 25 together with certain notional amounts of interest.
The consequence of this proposal if accepted would be that BSI would not have to pay
any rent for floor 25 until 15 January 1995.

The proceedings were commenced by an ordinary application in the administration
proceedings. The relief sought was for declarations that the agreement to lease had been
determined by the acceptance by BSI of the repudiation by O & Y to which I have
referred and for further declarations as to the legal nature of BSI's occupation of
floor 25, both before and after the alleged repudiation. These proceedings were
misconceived because the administration proceedings were not appropriate for the
determination of the substance of the dispute and because the administrators had not
consented, nor had the leave of the court been obtained, to the commencement of any
such proceedings.

Subsequently the administrators did give their consent but BSI did not institute any
other proceedings to determine the substance of the dispute. When the application came
on for hearing counsel for the administrators made it plain that although her clients were
concerned to have the dispute resolved on its merits she would contend that the
proceedings were misconceived if BSI sought to exclude from the court's consideration
points available to O & Y as opposed to the administrators. Such points included the
availability of the remedy of specific performance to enforce the agreement to lease and
questions of relief from forfeiture even if there had been the acceptance of a repudiation
as claimed by BSI.

A   It was manifest that the application then before the court was not adequate to deal with those points. In order not to waste the time already spent in arguing the repudiation point it was agreed that BSI would issue an originating summons raising the same points as in its ordinary application and that the affidavit evidence of both parties on the latter should stand as their evidence on the former. It was also agreed that O & Y should serve a counterclaim setting out their case on the further points I have mentioned. On this basis I will decide the question of repudiation and acceptance now and will leave for

B   subsequent argument after further evidence, if necessary, the remaining points raised by the originating summons and all the points raised by the counterclaim.

    The case for BSI, as opened, was that cl. 6(c)(v) of the agreement to lease was an intermediate term as described by Lord *Scarman* in *Bunge Corp v Tradax SA* [1981] 1 WLR 711 at p. 717, and that the test for determining whether the breach of that term constituted a repudiation of the contract was that stated by *Buckley* LJ in *Decro-Wall*

C   *International SA v Practitioners in Marketing Ltd* [1971] 1 WLR 361 at p. 380 which was approved by the House of Lords in *Federal Commerce & Navigation Co Ltd v Molena Alpha Inc* [1979] AC 757 at p. 779. That test is:

> "To constitute repudiation, the threatened breach must be such as to deprive the injured party of a substantial part of the benefit to which he is entitled under the contract . . . Will the consequences of the breach be such that it would be unfair

D   to the injured party to hold him to the contract and leave him to his remedy in damages . . . ?"

    BSI claims that the attitude of the administrators in the letter from their solicitors dated 6 July was as stated by Mr Bloom in his affidavit subsequently sworn on 8 October, which I have quoted. BSI claims that it is manifest that the test expressed by *Buckley* LJ is satisfied with the consequence that there was a repudiation by O & Y which BSI duly accepted by the letter dated 16 July.

E

    The case for O & Y is that cl. 6(c)(v) is a warranty only so that its breach cannot give rise to a repudiation capable of acceptance. Secondly, it was submitted that the circumstances of the case were not such as to give rise to any repudiation even if the clause was an intermediate term, and that there was no renunciation of the agreement to lease because, amongst other reasons, the letter of 1 July did not make time of the essence.

F

    In reply the case for BSI was expanded. It is contended that the letter of 1 July made time of the essence in respect of the obligation to pay the rent of £213,752 demanded by the invoice dated 5 June 1992 which was received by O & Y not later than 11 June. BSI contends that failure to comply with the requirement of the letter to pay by 13 July 1992 was a repudiation which it was entitled to accept irrespective of whether cl. 6(c)(v) was an intermediate term. Second, it is contended that the letter of 6 July is an anticipatory

G   breach or renunciation of the agreement to lease. Third, it is argued that cl. 6(c)(v) is an intermediate term which was broken by the letter of 6 July. In each of the second and third cases it is contended that the breach or renunciation was a repudiation which BSI was entitled to and did accept on 16 July as discharging it from any further obligation.

    I will deal first with the case for BSI as opened. It is common ground that cl. 6(c)(v) is not a condition. Thus it is necessary that it should be an intermediate term if its breach is to be capable of giving rise to a repudiation. For O & Y it was contended that the

H   subclause was a warranty only. It was submitted that the obligation on O & Y was only to enter into the covenant, that the liability under it is not coterminous with the duration of the underlease of floor 25 and that the underlease contains no provision enabling BSI to terminate if O & Y fails to perform its obligations under the subclause. It was pointed out that the subclause and the underlease deal with two separate properties and that the Devonshire Square leases are not vested in BSI but in its associated company,

Bear Stearns International Corp. Reliance was placed on *Gibson v Goldsmid* (1854)   A
5 De G M & G 757; 43 ER 1064 and *Lowther v Heaver* (1889) 41 ChD 248.

The question of whether cl. 6(c)(v) is an intermediate term or a warranty only is one
of construction of the agreement to lease. The question is whether breach of the term in
question may be attended by trivial, minor or very grave consequences (cf. *Bunge Corp
v Tradax SA* [1981] 1 WLR 711 at p. 717). It seems to me that the answer to that question
is obviously in the affirmative. Nevertheless, it would still be possible for the parties to   B
make it plain from the contract as a whole that the subclause is only a warranty.

In *Gibson v Goldsmid* (1854) 5 De G M & G 757 the parties had entered into a deed
of dissolution of their partnership. One term was an assignment in favour of the plaintiff
of certain shares thought to be transferable by delivery. In fact a formal transfer was
necessary. But the deed of dissolution contained a covenant for further assurance on
which the plaintiff sued the defendant because the latter had refused to execute the
transfer unless the plaintiff paid him sums alleged to be due under another term of the   C
deed. The court held that this latter liability was no defence to the obligation under the
covenant for further assurance as it applied to the shares. At p. 763; 1067, *Knight Bruce*
LJ said:

> "By executing the deed, Mr. Gibson and Mr. Grafton paid the price for the shares.
> The Defendant contends the Plaintiff's position to be that of a party to a contract
> who, having broken or omitted to perform a material term of it on his side, sues   D
> the other for specific performance of that other's part of the agreement. But I do
> not accede to this. The Plaintiff agreed to give a covenant of indemnity: he did so.
> His subsequent breach of it, if he has broken it, forms no breach of the agreement
> to give it. His covenant of indemnity and the Defendant's covenant as to the
> shares are legally independent of each other, it is certain. Lien, equally, and set
> off, appear to me to be out of the case; and a rule perhaps sometimes misunderstood,
> perhaps less wide in meaning than in expression — the rule namely — that a   E
> Plaintiff coming for equity must do equity, is without application in the present
> instance, as I view the matter. That unity of subject, or connection between
> subjects, which calls it into operation, is here, I think, wanting; and the Defendant
> must be left to sue upon his claim for indemnity. He cannot effectually set it up in
> this cause, at least according to my opinion."

I do not think that the principles there expressed have any bearing on this case. First,   F
it is a question of the construction of the agreement to lease whether cl. 6(c)(v) is
independent of the obligation to take the underlease of floor 25. In my view it is not; it is
further consideration. Second, on the question of repudiation the principle that he who
seeks equity must do equity has no application.

In *Lowther v Heaver* (1889) 41 ChD 248 a building agreement provided that the
builder should take from the defendant separate 99-year leases of each house built by   G
the builder when that house was roofed in. The draft lease entitled the defendant to
re-enter if works were not proceeded with for 21 days. Works were suspended and the
defendant declined to grant a lease of a house which had been roofed in before
suspension relying on the right of re-entry. The Court of Appeal held that he was liable
to do so because the house had been roofed in, that under the doctrine of *Walsh v
Lonsdale* (1882) 21 ChD 9 the plaintiff was in the position of an equitable tenant on the
terms of the draft lease and that that lease did not permit re-entry in the events which   H
had happened. Again I do not think that that decision has any application to the question
I have to decide or to the facts of this case. In *Hussein v Mehlman* [1992] 32 EG 59 it was
held that it is legally possible for a contract of letting to be repudiated. If it is repudiated
and the repudiation is accepted by the innocent party then it is at least doubtful whether
the contract can be specifically enforced, a condition on which the application of the

A   principle in *Walsh v Lonsdale* depends. Certainly the case throws no light on the question I am now considering whether cl. 6(c)(v) is an intermediate term or only a warranty.

     In my judgment it is plain that it is an intermediate term. It complies with the test to which I have referred, there is nothing in the agreement to indicate that it was intended to be a warranty only and neither of the cases relied on can produce a different result. Thus in principle a breach of cl. 6(c)(v) may amount to a repudiation. The question

B   whether it does so has been posed in a number of ways as shown by the speech of Lord *Wilberforce* in *Federal Commerce v Molena Alpha* [1979] AC 757 at p. 778 where he said:

> "Was this then such a threatened, or anticipatory breach as to entitle the charterers to put an end to the charters? It was argued for the charterers that clause 9 of the charters amounted to a condition of the contract, so that any breach of it automatically gave the charterers the right to put an end to it. I do not agree with
>
> C   this. The clause is not drafted as a condition, and on its face it admits of being breached in a number of ways some of which might be far from serious and would certainly not go to the root of the contract. I regard the clause as one, breaches of which must be examined on their individual demerits. Was this breach, or threatened breach, repudiatory or not? I shall not set out at any length the numerous authorities on anticipatory breach: this is one of the more perspicuous branches of the law of contract and the modern position is clear. The form of the
>
> D   critical question may differ slightly as it is put in relation to varying situations:
>
> > '. . . an intimation of an intention to abandon and altogether to refuse performance of the contract . . .' or 'evince an intention no longer to be bound by the contract . . .' (*Freeth* v. *Burr* (1874) L.R. 9 C.P. 208, 213, *per* Lord Coleridge C.J)
>
> E
>
> > 'I do not say that it is necessary to show that the party alleged to have repudiated should have an actual intention not to fulfil the contact. He may intend in fact to fulfil it, but may be determined to do so only in a manner substantially inconsistent with his obligations, and not in any other way (*Ross T. Smyth & Co. Ltd.* v. *T. D. Bailey, Son & Co.* [1940] 3 All E.R. 60, 72, *per* Lord Wright) such as to deprive 'the charterers of substantially the whole benefit which it was the intention of the parties . . . that the charterers should
>
> F
>
> > obtain from the further performance of their own contractual undertakings' (*Hongkong Fir Shipping Co. Ltd.* v. *Kawasaki Kisen Kaisha Ltd.* [1962] 2 Q.B. 26, 72, *per* Diplock L.J.).
>
> > 'To constitute repudiation, the threatened breach must be such as to deprive the injured party of a substantial part of the benefit to which he is entitled under the contract . . . Will the consequences of the breach be such that it would be unfair to the injured party to hold him to the contract and leave him
>
> G
>
> > to his remedy in damages . . . ?' (*Decro-Wall International S.A.* v. *Practitioners in Marketing Ltd.* [1971] 1 W.L.R. 361, 380, *per* Buckley L.J.).
>
> The difference in expression between these two last formulations does not, in my opinion, reflect a divergence of principle, but arises from and is related to the particular contract under consideration: they represent, in other words, applications to different contracts, of the common principle that, to amount to repudiation a
>
> H   breach must go to the root of the contract."

     In order to answer the question in whichever way it is posed it is necessary to analyse the breach relied on. On this part of its case BSI relies on the failure of O & Y to pay the sums or to provide the confirmation demanded in the letter dated 1 July by 16 July.

     So far as the failure to pay is concerned (subject to the later question of whether time was made of the essence) I do not think that such a failure can amount to a repudiation.

It deprives BSI of the amounts which should have been paid from the time when they   A
should have been paid down to 16 July. In no sense does this deprive BSI of the whole
benefit which the parties intended BSI should obtain from further performance of
O & Y's obligations under the agreement to lease. It has no effect as such on the
agreement to grant the lease of floor 25, which it was the principal purpose of the
agreement to provide for. Moreover BSI was not the tenant under the Devonshire
Square leases. Thus cl. 6(c)(v) did not benefit BSI. No doubt on the principle of *Beswick
v Beswick* [1968] AC 58 BSI could, subject to obtaining leave under sec. 11(3) of the   B
Insolvency Act 1986, have enforced the clause for the benefit of the tenant. But it could
not have obtained more than nominal damages for its breach. Thus the failure of O & Y
to pay sums due under cl. 6(c)(v) did not deprive BSI of anything of substance.

Then did the failure to give the confirmation sought constitute a repudiation? In my
judgment it plainly did not. The letter of 1 July 1992 was addressed to "The administrators"
of O & Y. The confirmation it sought was that "you (sc. the administrators) will honour   C
the whole of the obligations of" the companies in administration. The letter went on to
point out that the absence of such confirmation would be treated by BSI as a "repudiation
by (the companies) of the agreement entitling (BSI) to rescind the agreement".

In *Re Atlantic Computer Systems plc* [1990] BCC 859 at p. 867 the Court of Appeal
held that sec. 19(5) of the *Insolvency Act* 1986 did not impose personal liability on an
administrator in respect of contracts entered into by him in carrying out his functions.
Nevertheless it was considered by many insolvency practitioners as evidenced by   D
Gore-Browne on Companies, vol. 2, para. 31-11 and Totty and Jordan on *Insolvency*,
para. C5.29 that administrators might become personally liable on a collateral contract
or in tort in respect of contracts entered into by them on the company's behalf.

The reply dated 6 July says nothing about the liabilities or contractual obligations of
O & Y save that the administrators were not causing O & Y to become in breach of the
agreement to lease. Thus, if anything, the administrators were affirming the contractual   E
liability of O & Y to grant an underlease of floor 25. But the principal point was to make
quite clear that the administrators were not running any risk of becoming personally
liable. The administrators were under no obligation to provide any such confirmation as
BSI sought. BSI seeks to construe this letter in the light of the subsequent affidavit of
Mr Bloom which I have quoted. But I do not think that that is legitimate. The affidavit
came along after the critical date of 16 July and sets out the administrators' then position.   F
BSI did not read the letter of 6 July in that way at that time as is shown by the response
dated 10 July. As that letter shows, BSI expected O & Y to comply with its contractual
obligations because of the letter from the administrators. As far as the confirmation is
concerned nothing further happened before the letter of 16 July claiming that there had
been a repudiation.

These conclusions also dispose of the alternative contention raised by counsel for BSI
in his reply, namely, that the letter of 6 July was a renunciation or anticipatory breach.   G
In this connection I was referred to *Chitty on Contracts* (26th ed.), vol. 1, para. 1711,
1713 and 1717. As para. 1711 makes clear it is incumbent on BSI to establish that the
actions of O & Y at 16 July were such as to lead a reasonable person to conclude that
O & Y no longer intended to be bound by the provisions of the agreement to lease. At
that date O & Y had failed to pay the sums demanded, the administrators had failed to
provide confirmation that they would honour the obligations of O & Y but the   H
administrators had made plain that they were not causing O & Y to be in breach. In my
judgment that conduct does not satisfy the test to which I have referred and there was no
renunciation or anticipatory breach.

This leaves the question whether time was made of the essence in any respect and if it
was what effect that has on the question whether there was any repudiation. As I have

A   indicated, this point emerged at a late stage in the hearing during the reply of counsel for BSI. The point was raised in relation to the invoices dated 5 and 19 June 1992. It was not raised in relation to the invoice dated 10 March 1992 referred to in the letter dated 1 July 1992 until the conclusion of the rejoinder of counsel for BSI. In relation to the invoice dated 19 June an application to admit further evidence in relation to it was withdrawn. Thus the only evidence relates to the invoice dated 5 June 1992.

B   That evidence shows that the rent referred to in respect of the Devonshire Square leases was not due from Bear Stearns International Corp to the landlord until 24 June 1992. The invoice was rendered by BSI to O & Y on or before 11 June. It is dated 5 June and states "payment due by 24 June". It is one of the invoices which goes to make up the sum of £260,252 referred to in the letter dated 1 July. That letter demanded payment on or before 13 July. It is reasonable to assume that the tenant did not pay the rent to the landlord until 24 June. Thus at the time of the invoice Bear Stearns International Corp

C   had not paid and was not presently liable for the rent in question.

It is established by *Behzadi v Shaftesbury Hotels Ltd* [1992] Ch 1 that a party to a contract may make time of the essence in respect of a term by serving a notice to that effect immediately after the time for performing that term prescribed by the contract has passed. The time prescribed by the notice must be reasonable but there is no requirement that a reasonable time should have elapsed after the contractual date for

D   performance and before the service of the notice. The need for and effect of such a notice is graphically described by *Nourse* LJ at p. 12 in the following terms:

> "Before the Judicature Acts, equity's insistence that time was prima facie not essential to a contract for the sale of land was expressed either by granting specific performance to a party who was out of time or by restraining the other party from enforcing his consequential rights at law. Since the fusion of law and equity the view of equity has continued to prevail, but the authorities show that its patience

E
> is exhaustible. One example, a rare one, is where a party has delayed so long as to evince an intention not to be bound by the contract. In such a case the other party can without more treat the contract as repudiated: see *Farrant v. Olver* [1922] W.N. 47. More commonly, equity will not allow the contract to be so treated unless the party in default has been given an opportunity to mend his ways. The only way in which that can be done is by giving him notice to comply within a

F
> reasonable time. Such a notice is invariably described as one making time of the essence of the contract, although it has been justly observed that the description is not quite accurate. That is because one party cannot vary the terms of the contract on his own. In reality the notice is given in order to bring to an end, by equitable means, equity's interference with the legal rights of the parties."

BSI claims that the letter of 1 July was effective to make time of the essence in respect

G   of the obligation to pay the amount covered by the invoice dated 5 June so that O & Y's failure to pay by 13 July was, without more, a repudiation of the agreement to lease which BSI was entitled to and did accept by its letter of 16 July. O & Y disputes this submission on a number of grounds. One of those grounds is that one party cannot make time of the essence in respect of an inessential term. At a later stage in the argument O & Y contended that even if time may be made of the essence in respect of an inessential term failure to comply does not constitute a repudiation unless it goes to the

H   root of the contract. It seems to me that these two points are so closely related that it is convenient to deal with them together after I have considered the other objections raised by O & Y to the ability of the letter of 1 July to make time of the essence.

The first point relied on by O & Y is that the invoice dated 5 June was not a demand under cl. 6(c)(v) so as to fix a contractual time for payment, default in which entitled BSI to make time of the essence. It is contended by reference to *Collinge v Heywood* (1839)

British Company Cases

9 Ad & E 633; 112 ER 1352 that liability under an agreement to indemnify another A
against costs incurred or sustained does not arise unless and until the party to be
indemnified has paid the costs. Accordingly, it is submitted, when the invoice dated
5 June was rendered there was no liability for which O & Y was then liable to indemnify
BSI.

BSI accepted that *Collinge v Heywood* correctly states the rule at common law but
point out that in equity the person entitled to be indemnified was entitled to a *quia timet* B
order on the indemnifier to pay the amount in question as soon as the liability had been
incurred and ascertained. I was referred in this content to para. 1938 of *Chitty on
Contracts* (26th ed.). Clause 6(c)(v) refers to "reimbursement" of "costs and expenses
incurred". Thus it is plain that BSI cannot require O & Y to pay anything until the costs
etc. have been actually incurred by being paid. But I do not think that this precludes BSI
from demanding payment from O & Y before it has actually paid the landlord provided
that when the demand expires BSI has paid the landlord. Thus to this extent the C
provisions of cl. 6(c)(v) reflect the equitable rights of a person entitled to the benefit of
an agreement to indemnify. But there can be no breach of that provision by failing to
pay the sum demanded until BSI has paid the equivalent to the landlord. The letter of
1 July refers to the sum specified in the invoice as "paid by our client". It was not
suggested that I should not take that statement as showing that BSI had paid by 1 July
and I so hold. Thus on 1 July there was a breach of cl. 6(c)(v). Accordingly, BSI was
entitled to serve notice to make time of the essence in that respect. D

O & Y suggested that the letter of 1 July was not adequate for that purpose because it
merely demanded payment by 13 July. But it did more than that; it pointed out in
unmistakable terms the consequences as far as BSI was concerned of a failure to pay.
I do not think it is necessary for a notice to make time of the essence that it should use
those words. What is required is that the notice should state clearly what the other party
is required to do and the consequence if he fails (cf. *Afovos Shipping v Pagnan* [1982] E
1 WLR 848 at p. 854C).

Then it is objected that the letter did not allow a reasonable time within which to
comply. The letter was dated 1 July and in the ordinary course of post would have
reached the administrators on 2 July. It allowed until 13 July. Thus 11 days was allowed
for the payment of a sum £213,752. It was suggested that this was not reasonable because
in substance it gave no more than the ten days allowed by cl. 6(c)(v). I have already held F
that cl. 6(c)(v) did not require BSI to have paid the landlord before the invoice was
rendered; all that is required is that BSI should have paid before the ten days allowed by
the demand or invoice had expired or O & Y was sued for the amount claimed. Thus an
extra 11 days was allowed. There being no other objection to reasonableness I conclude
that the period allowed by the letter was reasonable.

O & Y's next objection is that any right to make time of the essence or to rescind was
waived by the payment of rent with the letter of 1 July. I reject this objection as well. As G
I have already held there was then no right to rescind capable of being waived. Moreover
the letter makes clear that far from BSI waiving the breach of contract which then
existed it was seeking to pursue it further.

The consequence is that in my judgment the letter of 1 July was, subject to the point
of law I mentioned earlier, capable of making time of the essence in respect of the
obligation of O & Y to pay to BSI the sum of £213,752 on or before 13 July 1992. The H
questions are did it do so and did the failure of O & Y to comply entitle BSI on 16 July to
treat such failure as a repudiation of the agreement to lease?

The submission of BSI is that time may be made of the essence in respect of any
contractual term by giving a notice requiring performance of that term within a reasonable
time and that failure to perform within that time constitutes a repudiation of the contract

A   whatever the nature of the term or consequence of the failure. O & Y submitted that this proposition could not be right because it would mean that the unilateral act of one party to the contract could give rise to legal consequences from the acts or omissions of the other party which could not flow from those acts or omissions alone. In other words one party could "put upon" the other party a repudiation which he had not committed; a result which a dictum of Lord *Denning* MR in *Eshun v Moorgate Mercantile* [1971] 1 WLR 722 at p. 726 said could not be achieved. The legal analysis of this objection is

B   clearly set out in para. 24 of the skeleton argument put in by O & Y. That paragraph reads as follows:

> "A notice seeking to make time of the essence for the performance of a particular contractual term must be in relation to a term that is essential to the non-performing party's obligations. Thus, for example, in cases concerning contracts for the sale of land, notice can be served making time of the essence in relation to completion or an intermediate (but essential) step towards completion, e.g.
C   deduction of title. However, if the notice is given in relation to a non-essential obligation, non-compliance with the notice does not permit an inference that such breach is repudiatory."

Thus there are the two points which I mentioned earlier, namely, whether there is any restriction on the type of term in respect of which time may be made of the essence and whether a failure to comply when time has been made of the essence is without more a

D   repudiation. On the first point O & Y relies on the statement of *Danckwerts* J in *Re Barr's Contract* [1956] Ch 551 at p. 556:

> ". . . at the time when the vendor purports to make time of the essence, the purchaser must be guilty of such default as to entitle the vendor to rescind the contract subject to its being done by a reasonable notice."

On the second point O & Y relies on a passage in Treitel, *The Law of Contract* (8th

E   ed.), p. 729 that:

> ". . . it does not follow that notice [making time of the essence] is in all cases sufficient to give rise to a right to rescind."

With regard to the first point BSI submits that the statement in *Re Barr's Contract* merely sought to summarise counsel's argument at p. 553 that "the purchaser must be in default to justify the vendor in rescinding". It was submitted that this submission merely

F   recorded what was then thought to be the law, namely that a reasonable time must elapse after the contractual time has passed before a notice making time of the essence could be served. It was common ground that that view had been shown to be wrong by the decision of the Court of Appeal in *Behzadi v Shaftesbury Hotels Ltd* [1992] Ch 1. I agree with this submission. First, if *Danckwerts* J had intended to refer to some limit on the nature of the term for which time could be made of the essence it is a surprisingly oblique way of expressing it. Second, the effect of making time of the essence, as

G   described by *Nourse* LJ in *Behzadi v Shaftesbury Hotels Ltd* at p. 12E is to bring to an end, by equitable means, equity's interference with the legal rights of the parties. I can see no reason why such interference should be so terminated in respect of some terms but not others, to be distinguished by whether or not the term is essential or inessential. Accordingly, I conclude that the letter dated 1 July 1992 was effective to make time of the essence in respect of the obligation to O & Y to pay the sum of £213,752.

H   Thus the second point is crucial. Is failure to comply of itself sufficient to constitute a repudiation or is it necessary that such failure should go to the root of the contract? In support of his argument for the first alternative counsel for BSI relied on a number of authorities which I shall deal with in turn.

First, reference was made to *Chitty on Contracts* (26th ed.) vol. 1, para. 1500. There it is stated that at common law performance of the contract had to be carried out upon

the exact date specified so that a party could treat the contract as repudiated if the other   A
party's performance was not completed on the fixed date. But it is plain that this passage
is dealing with conditions or intermediate terms which go to the root of the contract
otherwise some reference must have been made to *Federal Commerce v Molena Alpha*
[1979] AC 757.

Second, reference was made to *Behzadi v Shaftesbury Hotels Ltd* at p. 12 where
Nourse LJ stated that "it cannot be doubted that a failure to meet the time for the   B
performance of some other obligation has similar consequences". The similar
consequences referred to include treating the breach as a repudiation where time has
been made of the essence. But this does not assist BSI for it is clear from the passage at
p. 11H that *Nourse* LJ was considering contractual dates for completion or the
performance of some intermediate obligation.

Third, BSI relied on the passage from the judgment of *Mason* J in *Louinder v Leis*
(1982) 149 CLR 509 at p. 526 quoted by *Nourse* LJ in *Behzadi v Shaftesbury Hotels Ltd*   C
at p. 15 that:

> "The result of non-compliance with the notice is that the party in default is guilty
> of unreasonable delay in complying with a non-essential time stipulation. The
> unreasonable delay amounts to a repudiation and this justifies rescission."

This was said in reference to the completion of contracts for the sale of land. Thus   D
although the contractual date for completion may be inessential, failure to complete at
all will go to the root of the contact. Accordingly, *Mason* J was not considering the case
of a term which was inessential in that sense. What was initially non-essential was the
stipulation as to time not nature of the term, which plainly was a term breach of which
was capable of going to the root of the contract. I do not regard this statement as
supporting the case for BSI.

Fourth, in relation to the first point, BSI relied on passages in *United Scientific*   E
Holdings v Burnley BC [1978] AC 904 at pp. 928 and 946. But in so far as they deal at all
with the second point they are, in my judgment, in favour of O & Y. In the former
passage Lord *Diplock* summarised what he had said in *Hongkong Fir Shipping Co Ltd v*
Kawasaki Kisen Kaisha [1962] 2 QB 26. But the whole of the summary deals with the
question of terms going to the root of the contract. In the latter passage Lord *Simon of*
Glaisdale describes a notice making time of the essence as "evidence of the date by   F
which the promisee now considers it reasonable for the contractual obligation to be
performed". It seems to me that both passages at least leave open the question whether
non-compliance is per se a repudiation.

Thus I do not think that any of the authorities on which BSI relied supports the
proposition for which BSI contends. It is stated in *Chitty on Contracts*, para. 1502 that:

> "When a stipulation as to time is made 'of the essence' of the contract, a failure to   G
> perform by the stipulated time entitles the innocent party to elect to terminate the
> contract as for breach of a 'condition', with the consequences: (a) that the innocent
> party thereby puts an end to all primary obligations of both parties which have not
> already been performed . . ."

Thus *Chitty* is opposed to Treitel.

The authority cited by *Chitty* is *Scandinavian Trading Tanker Co AB v Flota Petrolera*   H
Ecuatoriana [1983] 2 AC 694 at p. 703. But that case dealt with the question whether
equitable relief from forfeiture was available in the case of a time charter where the ship
owner had exercised his right to withdraw the vessel. The point I am concerned with was
not in issue. The statement referred to in *Chitty* is the descriptive passage in the speech
of Lord *Diplock* at p. 703C:

A

"When time is made of the essence of a primary obligation, failure to perform it punctually is a breach of a condition of the contract which entitles the party not in breach to elect to treat the breach as putting an end to all primary obligations under the contract that have not already been performed."

Such a passage in a speech of Lord *Diplock* must be accorded the greatest respect even if the point was not in issue. Nevertheless, it seems to me that the description must be too wide if it is intended to state that a failure to perform a stipulation which does not go to the root of the contract is a repudiation merely because time has been made of the essence.

B

I prefer the submission of O & Y. First there is nothing in *Federal Commerce v Molena Alpha* [1979] AC 757 to suggest that the principles expressed, particularly by Lord *Wilberforce* at pp. 778–779, have no application to stipulations in respect of which time is originally, or is made, of the essence. Second, if the effect of making time of the essence is, as described by *Nourse* LJ in *Behzadi v Shaftesbury Hotels Ltd*, to remove equity's interference with the legal rights of the parties, the natural inference is that those rights arise from the ordinary principles of the common law and are not something special consequential on the removal of that interference. Third, and arising from the second consideration, if failure to comply with a notice making time of the essence of itself constitutes a repudiation irrespective of the consequence of the breach, then contrary to the statement of Lord *Denning* in *Eshun v Moorgate Mercantile* [1971] 1 WLR 722 at p. 726 it is possible to put upon another a repudiation which he has never committed. Fourth, there is no suggestion in *Universal Cargo Carriers Corp v Citati* [1957] 2 QB 401 that the delay in providing the cargo would have been a ground of rescission if notice had been given making time of the essence.

C

D

E

I consider for all these reasons that the submission of O & Y is correct in principle and consistent with such authorities as there are. Thus the last question is whether the failure of O & Y to comply with the terms of the letter dated 1 July and pay the sum of £213,752 specified in the invoice of 5 June went to the root of the contract as explained in *Federal Commerce v Molena Alpha*.

But the position in this regard on 16 July was the same in respect of the failure to pay £213.752 whereof time was of the essence as it was on BSI's case as opened. The failure to pay did not deprive BSI of anything of value to BSI. BSI was not and is not liable to the landlord under the Devonshire Square leases. The evidence of Mr Hacker, a director of BSI, pointed out that BSI was not the tenant but he provided no evidence to suggest that BSI is in any way liable to the landlord or to Bear Stearns International Corp by way of indemnity against the liabilities arising from the Devonshire Square leases. So far as BSI is concerned the unperformed obligations of the parties under the agreement to lease are the grant and acceptance of the underlease of floor 25. The underlease of floor 25 is the benefit to BSI to which it is entitled. The breach on which BSI relies does not affect these obligations and does not deprive BSI of this benefit. Thus, referring to the test as formulated by *Buckley* LJ in *Decro-Wall International SA v Practitioners in Marketing Ltd* [1971] 1 WLR 361 at p. 380, I do not think that the consequences of the breach of cl. 6(c)(v) are such as to make it unjust to BSI to hold it to the contract to take the underlease and leave it to its remedy in damages In a nutshell the submission that the underlease of floor 25 was to be swapped for the Devonshire Square leases is wrong because it ignores the separate legal existence of BSI and Bear Stearns International Corp and the absence of any evidence of a relationship whereby the former was or is directly or indirectly liable for the liabilities under the Devonshire Square leases of the latter.

F

G

H

In my judgment there was no repudiation on 16 July which BSI could accept so as to discharge it from further performance of the agreement to lease and I so declare.

A

For the reasons given in the written judgment I have handed down, in my judgment there was no repudiation on 16 July 1992 by Olympia and York Canary Wharf Ltd, which was capable of acceptance by Bear Stearns International Ltd so as to discharge the latter from all further performance in connection with the lease.

(*Order accordingly*)

B

C

D

E

F

G

H

A # Re David Meek Access Ltd.
Re David Meek Plant Ltd.

Chancery Division (Bristol District Registry).
His Honour Judge Weeks QC.
Judgment delivered 30 July and 24 September 1992.

B *Administration orders — Effect of order — Repossessing goods in company's possession under hire-purchase agreements — Companies leased construction plant and equipment from finance houses and sublet to end users — Hire-purchase agreements were terminated on or before presentation of administration order petitions — Whether plant and equipment remained "goods in the company's possession under any hire-purchase agreement" — Whether finance houses should have leave to repossess plant and equipment — Insolvency Act 1986, sec. 11(3)(c).*

C
These were judgments on applications by 11 creditors in the administration of two companies.

Both companies' business was hiring out equipment to the construction industry. They were in business on a large scale, and altogether the two companies either owned or had on hire purchase over 1,000 units and had an annual turnover of over £10m. The applicants were described as "leasing creditors" of one or both of the companies: that is, they were finance houses which let or sold to the companies under hire-purchase agreements items which the companies then let out to their customers, the end users of the equipment.

Before the administration order petitions were presented, some finance companies terminated the hire-purchase agreements, some sought to repossess their goods and were successful, others sought to repossess and failed, and others took no steps until the making of the orders. After the orders were made some leasing creditors sought the administrators' consent to repossession which was refused. The applicants then sought the leave of the court to repossess under sec. 11(3)(c) of the Insolvency Act 1986.

The hire-purchase agreements contained provisions for termination, either by way of acceptance of repudiation, or by way of giving notice in certain events, or in some cases by way of automatic termination on events which included the presentation or drafting of a petition for an administration order. The applicants contended that the termination of the hire-purchase agreements in any way before, or possibly on, the presentation of the petition for administration, meant that the goods subject to those hire-purchase agreements were not "goods in the company's possession under any hire-purchase agreement" within sec. 11(3)(c) of the Insolvency Act 1986. This was the preliminary issue.

G
The administrators' reasons for refusing consent were, first, that the companies' whole business was run with goods on hire purchase and unless the administrators kept those goods there would be no point in the administration and no proposals to present to the meeting of creditors. A subsidiary point was that if the administrators allowed one leasing creditor to repossess they would find it difficult or impossible to refuse others. The administrators also argued that at the time of the administration orders substantial sums were still due to the companies from end users, and that collection of those debts which were the companies' principal asset largely depended upon the continuation of the business. The final argument was that the creditors' meeting had approved proposals to hive down the business of the two companies to a new company. The plant and equipment of those finance companies which did not wish to participate in the hive down would be returned to them in an orderly fashion. The proposals included payment to the finance companies for use of their equipment since the date of the administration orders.

Held, ruling that leave was required under sec. 11(3)(c) and granting leave to repossess
to two only of the applicants:

1. Section 11(3)(c) extended to goods which were the subject of a hire-purchase
agreement, whether or not that hire-purchase agreement had been terminated before the
presentation of the petition for an administration order or on that event, provided the
goods remained in the company's possession.

2. The court had to balance any loss suffered by the applicant finance companies
against the administrators' reasons for refusing consent and the benefits to the other
creditors (including finance companies who had not applied for the return of their goods)
and to the companies as a whole arising out of the continued retention. (Re Atlantic
Computer Systems plc [1990] BCC 859 applied.)

3. The finance companies had not proved that they would suffer a significant loss
compared with the position they would have been in if they had been allowed to repossess
their goods when the administration orders were made.

4. There was good reason to believe that if the administrators allowed the finance
companies to repossess their goods at will, the administrations would have been abortive
and no proposals could have been presented to the statutory meeting. Equally there was
substance in the administrators' fear that the abrupt termination of trading would have
endangered the book debts which had been collected in an orderly fashion during the
continuance of trading. The administrators' proposals for the return of their goods to
those companies who did not wish to participate in the hive down were eminently sensible.
Thus, having regard to the parties' interests and the circumstances of the case, granting
leave would have impeded the achievement of the purposes of the administration orders.

5. Leave to repossess was granted to two creditors who had sought unsuccessfully to
repossess on the day before presentation of the administration order petitions.

The following cases were referred to in the judgments:

Astor Chemical Ltd v Synthetic Technology Ltd [1990] BCC 97.
Atlantic Computer Systems plc, Re [1990] BCC 439; [1990] BCC 859, [1992] Ch 505
(CA).
Meesan Investments Ltd, Re (Royal Trust Bank v Buchler) (1988) 4 BCC 788.
Paramount Airways Ltd, Re (Bristol Airport plc v Powdrill) [1990] BCC 130; [1990]
Ch 744.
Science Research Council v Nassé [1980] AC 1028.
Sibec Developments Ltd, Re [1993] BCC 148.
Smart Brothers Ltd v Holt & Ors [1929] 2 KB 303.

Anthony Mann QC and Stephen Davies (instructed by Meade King, Bristol) for the
applicants.

Patrick Howell QC and Ms M Maher (instructed by Osborne Clarke, Bristol) for the
respondents.

JUDGMENT ON PRELIMINARY ISSUE
(30 July 1992)

His Honour Judge Weeks QC: Over the last four days I have been hearing applications
by 11 creditors arising in the administration of two companies. The two companies are
David Meek Access Ltd and David Meek Plant Ltd. Both companies' business was
hiring out equipment to the construction industry. David Meek Plant hired out mobile
equipment in general, such as bulldozers, and David Meek Access hired out static
equipment, such as scaffolding. They were in business on a large scale, and altogether
the two companies either owned or had on hire purchase over 1,000 units.

Both companies were unable to pay their debts as they fell due. A petition for
administration order was presented on 3 April 1992 and an order was made by

A   His Honour Judge *Moseley* on 9 April 1992, giving as the grounds para. (a), (b) and (d) in sec. 8(3) of the *Insolvency Act* 1986.

     The present applications have been brought by 11 finance houses. They have all been described as "leasing creditors" of one or both of the two companies: that is, the finance houses let or sold to the companies under hire-purchase agreements items which the companies then let out to its customers, the end users of the equipment.

B   I have referred to hire-purchase agreements. This is intended to include the extended definition of hire-purchase agreement in the Act which includes conditional sale agreements, chattel leasing agreements and retention of title agreements.

     It has been agreed between counsel that it is appropriate at this stage for me to make a decision on one important issue which arises in most, if not all, of the 11 applications before me. The question turns on the construction of sec. 11(3) of the *Insolvency Act*
C   1986, in particular subsec. (c). I will read the whole of sec. 11(3):

     "During the period for which an administration order is in force—

       (a)   no resolution may be passed or order made for the winding up of the company;

       (b)   no administrative receiver of the company may be appointed;

       (c)   no other steps may be taken to enforce any security over the company's
D   property, or to repossess goods in the company's possession under any hire-purchase agreement, except with the consent of the administrator or the leave of the court, and subject (where the court gives leave) to such terms as the court may impose; and

       (d)   no other proceedings and no execution or other legal process may be commenced or continued, and no distress may be levied, against the company or its property except with the consent of the administrator or the
E   leave of the court and subject (where the court gives leave) to such terms as aforesaid."

     The factual background to the question is that the hire-purchase agreements under which the items of plant and equipment were let to the two companies contained provisions for termination, either by way of acceptance of repudiation, or by way of giving notice in certain events, or in some cases by way of automatic termination on
F   events which included, among other events, the presentation or drafting of a petition for an administration order.

     It is contended on behalf of the finance houses that the termination of the hire-purchase agreements in any way before, or possibly on, the presentation of the petition for administration, operated to take these goods subject to those hire-purchase agreements out of the phrase in sec. 11(3)(c) "goods in the company's possession under any hire-purchase agreement": so that sec. 11 does not bite on those goods during the
G   period for which the administration order is in force; nor did sec. 10, which is the section designed to apply during the period beginning with the presentation of a petition and ending with the making of an order for administration or the dismissal of the petition.

     Before I analyse the section there are two or three preliminary matters that I ought to mention. It is accepted on behalf of the finance houses that whether or not the agreements have been terminated before the presentation of the petition, if the finance
H   houses have to resort to law and take proceedings to repossess their goods, then such proceedings are caught by sec. 11(3)(d) and the consent of the administrator, or the leave of the court, is required to bring such proceedings. I am therefore only dealing with repossessions which can occur without the necessity for court proceedings.

     The second preliminary matter is that it is not accepted on behalf of the finance houses that the prohibition in sec. 11(3)(c) on steps being taken to enforce any security over the

company's property, would prevent the termination of a hire-purchase agreement, for A
example, by notice given during the period when the prohibition in sec. 11 or sec. 10
(as the case may be) is operative.

If it were the case that the question of whether "goods in the company's possession
under any hire-purchase agreement" has to be determined at a date later than the
making of the order for the purposes of sec. 11, or a date later than the presentation of
the petition for the purposes of sec. 10, and if it were the case that it was open for the
finance houses to serve notice of termination, then there may well be a very large lacuna B
in sec. 11(3)(c), because finance houses could then serve notices of termination after an
administration petition had been presented and repossess their goods on the basis that
they were then no longer in the company's possession under any hire-purchase agreement.
I do not propose to decide the question of whether serving a notice is any step to enforce
a security and I will attempt to disregard the lacuna that might otherwise arise.

The third preliminary matter is this. The phrase I have to construe is "goods in the C
company's possession under any hire-purchase agreement" specifically in section 11(3)(c).
The same phrase however occurs in sec. 10(1)(b) and sec. 15(2)(b) of the *Insolvency Act*
1986. It seems to me as far as is possible I ought to achieve a consistent construction in
the three sections.

A similar phrase occurs in the rules made under the Act at r. 2.27 of the *Insolvency
Rules* 1986 (SI 1986/1925) where there is reference to an owner of goods under a D
hire-purchase or chattel leasing agreement: the reference to chattel leasing agreement is
necessary because the rule goes on to refer to a seller of goods under a conditional sale
agreement, and all three types of agreement are dealt with compendiously under hire-
purchase agreements in the Act. I do not find any assistance from this particular phrase
in the rules.

I go back to the wording of sec. 11(3)(c) of the Act itself. The significant words are E
"goods in the company's possession under any hire-purchase agreement". It seems to
me that "in the company's possession" has to be given a temporal meaning in that when
one is seeking to apply the section one has to ask the question "when?" in relation to "in
the company's possession", because it would be nonsense to apply the section to goods
which long ago were in the company's possession but have long since ceased to have
anything to do with the company.

The natural time to apply a temporal test seems to me the time at which one is seeking F
to apply the section. Sections 10 and 11 apply during different periods. Section 10 applies
during the period beginning on the presentation of the petition and ending, in the
present case, on the making of the order. Section 11 applies during the period in which
the administration order is in force. So those two periods are different and do not
overlap.

Section 15 must apply during the period when the administration order is in force as G
well, because that deals with the powers of the administrator while he is in office. Within
these periods it seems to me natural to take the point when one is seeking to apply the
section to determine whether or not the goods in question are goods in the company's
possession.

It does not seem to me, however, to follow as of course, that one has to apply the same
temporal test to the following words "under any hire-purchase agreement". It is possible
on a strictly logical grammatical construction to require that the goods should not only H
be in the company's possession at the time when one is applying the section, but also
that they should be in the company's possession by virtue of a hire-purchase agreement
subsisting at the same time. But it seems to me to be equally possible, without distorting
the words, to construe the section as requiring, first, that the goods should be in the
company's possession at the relevant time, and, secondly, that that possession should be

A   attributable to, or derive its legal origin at some time from, a hire-purchase agreement, not necessarily a hire-purchase agreement still subsisting. This appears to me to be a legitimate construction of what is a compressed phrase "goods in the company's possession under any hire-purchase agreement".

I am faced with two possible constructions of the section. I have been referred to the case of *Astor Chemical Ltd v Synthetic Technology Ltd* [1990] BCC 97, for the proposition that an administrator is not in the same position as an administrative receiver

B   as regards compliance with contracts binding on the company. This proposition seems to me to beg the present question because the real point is how far sec. 11(3)(c) impinges on contractual rights.

I have also been referred to a short passage in the judgment of *Millett* J in *Re Sibec Developments Ltd* [1993] BCC 148 at p. 151C–E, where *Millett* J expressed the view that sec. 11 did not affect substantive rights and was couched in purely procedural terms

C   and imposed a moratorium on the enforcement of the creditors' rights but did not destroy those rights.

Accepting that in the full, I do not think that it assists me with the question which I have to decide, which, again, is the question of how far sec. 11(3)(c) affects those contractual rights.

I have also been referred to *Smart Brothers Ltd v Holt* [1929] 2 KB 303, which was a

D   decision on the meaning of sec. 4 of the *Law of Distress Amendment Act* 1908 which used the words "comprised in any hire-purchase agreement". I do not think that that section and its purpose are sufficiently close to the words used in the *Insolvency Act* 1986 and the purpose of that Act for me to be able to draw any useful conclusions from the judgments of the divisional court in *Smart Brothers v Holt*.

Where I do get assistance is from the judgment of the Court of Appeal in *Re Atlantic*

E   *Computer Systems plc* [1990] BCC 859. This was a case similar to the present in that the company in administration was a company which operated a business of hiring out computers. It did so with equipment which itself in turn had hired from finance companies.

One of the questions the Court of Appeal had to decide in that case was whether the equipment in the hands of the sub-hirers was within the wording of sec. 11(3)(c) "goods

F   in the company's possession". The relevant phrase was very close and included part of the words that I have to construe, but the problem confronting the Court of Appeal and *Ferris* J at first instance was not a temporal one. The argument was that the goods were in the possession of the end users — the sub-hirers — and not in the possession of the companies in administration.

Ferris J held that the goods were in the possession of the end users (see [1990] BCC

G   439). The Court of Appeal reached a different conclusion. One judgment was given, delivered by *Nicholls* LJ, who said on this question at p. 871H:

"In our judgment the answer emerges once one considers the purpose of sec. 11(3)(c). The paragraph is dealing with goods which, as between the company and its supplier, are in the possession of the company under a hire-purchase agreement. Those goods are to be protected from repossession unless there is either consent or leave. It is immaterial whether they remain on the company's

H   premises, or are entrusted by the company to others for repair, or are sub-let by the company as part of its trade to others. We do not see that such a construction does any violence to the language of the paragraph, or is more purposive than is warranted by the current approach of the English courts to statutes which are neither fiscal nor penal, even though it is said that a breach of the paragraph is a contempt of court."

I am encouraged by that paragraph to take a purposive approach to the construction A
of this section, as the Court of Appeal did in *Re Atlantic Computer Systems plc.*

For the purpose of sec. 11(3)(c) I derive help from an earlier passage in the judgment
delivered by *Nicholls* LJ at p. 867F where *Nicholls* LJ referred to:

> ". . . one of the primary functions of an administrator (being) that frequently, if
> not normally, he will continue to carry on the company's business and, hence, will
> continue to use the land and goods currently being used by the company for the B
> purposes of its business. Indeed, it is of the essence of his appointment that an
> administrator should do these very things in cases where the purpose sought to be
> achieved by the administration order is purpose (a) in sec. 8(3), viz. the survival
> of the company, and the whole or any part of its undertaking, as a going concern."

It seems to me more consistent with that purpose and more likely to promote that
purpose to give a wider construction to sec. 11(3)(c) if that can be done without distorting
its meaning. C

In my judgment that is possible in the present context by construing the reference to
"goods in the possession of the company" as applying a test of possession when the
section has to be considered but by not requiring any such temporal test to be applied to
the question of whether they are in the company's possession under any hire-purchase
agreement, and by including within the ambit of sec. 11(3)(c) and, also, within the ambit
of sec. 10(1)(b) and sec. 15(2)(b), goods which are in the company's possession at D
the relevant time and are, or have come into, the company's possession under a
hire-purchase agreement, as defined in the Act, whether or not that hire-purchase
agreement has been formally terminated or otherwise come to an end.

I think I can reach that conclusion without committing what *Nicholls* LJ referred to as
doing "violence to the language of the paragraph" or applying a more purposive
construction than is warranted by the current approach of the English courts.

Accordingly, I hold that sec. 11(3)(c) extends to goods which were the subject of a E
hire-purchase agreement, whether or not that hire-purchase agreement has been
terminated before the presentation of the petition for administration or on that event,
provided they remain in the company's possession.

(Ruling accordingly)

JUDGMENT ON APPLICATIONS
  F
(24 September 1992)

His Honour Judge Weeks QC: In the last week of July I heard applications by 11
creditors made in the administration of two companies. The two companies are David
Meek Plant Ltd and David Meek Access Ltd. On 30 July I gave judgment on one issue
which was common to most, if not all, of the applications, namely whether leave was
required to repossess goods which remained in the companies' possession although the G
relevant hire-purchase agreement had been terminated on or before the presentation of
the petition for administration. For the reasons already given I hold that leave was
required.

At the end of the hearing on 31 July I said that I would allow the applications made by
United Dominions Trust Ltd and Hill Samuel Leasing Co Ltd and grant them leave
under sec. 11(3)(c) of the *Insolvency Act* 1986 to repossess their goods but that I would
dismiss the applications by the other nine creditors. I now give my reasons for that H
decision.

The business carried on by the two companies was that of hiring out equipment to the
construction industry. David Meek Plant Ltd hired out mobile equipment such as
bulldozers, often with operators, and David Meek Access Ltd hired out static equipment
such as sophisticated forms of scaffolding. They were in business on a large scale, and

A   between the two companies had available for hire over 1,000 units and an annual turnover of over £10m. Nearly all the units were held by the companies under hire-purchase agreements as defined in sec. 10(4) of the Act, that is including conditional sale agreements, chattel leasing agreements and retention of title agreements. The owners of the units were some 45 finance companies, of which the 11 applicants form a minority, but a substantial minority, in number of items leased, capital value of the items and the amount of rental payments due.

B   Because of the recession in the building industry and a consequent fall in demand and hire charge rates, both companies got into financial difficulties. In the summer of 1991 an arrangement was made with the leasing creditors under which they agreed to take 80 per cent of the monthly sums which were then due under the various hire-purchase agreements. Unfortunately the companies were unable to meet even those payments, and in February 1992 a scheme was proposed under which £250,000

C   was to be paid into a trust fund and distributed pro rata so that effectively each leasing creditor would get about 59 per cent of his monthly debt.

   This scheme was approved with or without conditions by over 30 leasing creditors, but on 30 March 1992 the Inland Revenue, either deliberately or possibly inadvertently, caused to be advertised winding-up petitions against both companies, which they had issued the previous year but allowed to lie dormant, while arrangements to meet their

D   debts were made.

   The directors felt that the future of both companies was in imminent danger and petitions were presented on behalf of both companies for an administration order on 3 April. On 9 April, with the consent of National Westminster Bank and other companies with charges which entitled them to appoint an administrative receiver, administration orders were made in respect of both companies.

E   The affidavits in support exhibited a draft report by Ernst & Young which showed estimated total assets of £1.3m, preferential creditors of £660,000 and floating charge holders of £650,000, leaving £220,000 to be shared among the leasing creditors, who were owed £7.8m, and another £1m of trade and unsecured creditors.

   A forecast trading account for the months of April, May and June showed the companies as expected to be able to trade at a profit provided the leasing creditors received only an allowance for depreciation and interest and not their full charges of

F   some £450,000 per month. The orders were made for the purposes set out in para. (a), (c) and (d) of sec. 8(3), that is,

> "(a) the survival of the company, and the whole or any part of its undertaking, as a going concern;
>
> (c) the sanctioning under section 425 of the Companies Act of a compromise or arrangement between the company and any such persons as are mentioned in that

G > section; and
>
> (d) a more advantageous realisation of the company's assets than would be effected on a winding up."

   Before the petitions were presented, some finance companies terminated their hire-purchase agreements, some sought to repossess their goods and were successful, others sought to repossess and failed, and others took no steps until the making of the

H   orders. After the orders were made the joint administrators wrote to all the finance companies whose goods were still in the companies' possession, notifying them of the orders that had been made. Some then sought the administrators' leave to repossess and were refused. The ones who have applied to the court for leave are United Dominions Trust Ltd and Hill Samuel Leasing Co Ltd whose applications were made on 20 April, Westpac General Finance Ltd whose application was also made in April, Unibank plc

and Privatenbanken Leasing Ltd whose application was made on 22 May, Forward   A
Trust Ltd whose application was made on 10 June, Mercantile Credit Co Ltd and
Barclays Mercantile Business Finance Ltd whose application was made on 8 June,
Humberclyde Industrial Finance Ltd and UFB Asset Finance Ltd whose application
was made on 18 June 1992 and finally Midland Montagu Leasing Ltd who were joined in
the course of these proceedings. All seek leave under sec. 11(3)(c) to repossess their
goods and if leave be granted an order for delivery up.

Those who terminated their agreements on or before 3 April also sought a declaration   B
that the goods subject to those agreements are not within sec. 11(3)(c) and for the
reasons already given I have declined to make such a declaration.

At this stage I ought to explain the administrators' reasons for refusing consent
because the administrator is an officer of the court who, as the Court of Appeal has
stated, can be expected to make his decision speedily and responsibly.

The reasons given have been modified or extended in the course of time, and basically   C
there are four reasons for refusing consent. The first is that the companies' whole
business was run with goods on hire purchase and unless the administrators kept those
goods there would be no point in the administration and no proposals to present to the
meeting of creditors, which the administrators were required to summon under sec. 23
of the Act. The second is similar and has been called the floodgates argument; it is that if
the administrators allowed one leasing creditor to repossess they would find it difficult   D
or impossible to refuse others. This argument is, I think, no more than a reformulation
of the first and adds little or nothing. The third is different; the plant and equipment
were let to end users by the companies on contracts under which substantial sums were
still due at the time of the administration orders. If those contracts were broken by the
repossession of the goods hired, the administrators would face counterclaims for breach
of contract when they sought to recover the debts; even if there was no breach of contract
the repossession itself would make the debts more difficult to enforce. These three   E
reasons were referred to in the first affidavit which Mr Clapp, one of the administrators,
swore on 15 May. In para. 17 he said:

> "There were three purposes for which the administration orders were granted.
> These are the survival of the companies and the whole or part of their business as
> a going concern and/or the approval of a voluntary arrangement under Pt. I of the
> *Insolvency Act* 1986 and/or a more advantageous realisation of assets. The   F
> primary objectives are the survival of the companies and the implementation of a
> voluntary arrangement. In order to survive the companies must maintain their
> fleet of equipment which they have acquired from leasing creditors in order to
> maintain their existing contracts with customers. If I allowed all the equipment to
> be repossessed before putting proposals to creditors, there would be no business
> left and therefore no proposals to put. Thus the first two purposes of the
> administration orders would fail. I believe that the third purpose would also fail   G
> because the principal asset of the companies is their book debts and in practice
> their collection largely depends upon the continuation of the business. The plant
> and equipment supplied by UDT and HSL represents about six per cent of the
> fleet. Its removal would therefore be significant in itself. Moreover the knock-on
> effect would be enormous. If I either agreed to or am ordered to allow UDT and
> HSL to repossess their plant and equipment, it will not be possible to resist similar   H
> demands from other leasing creditors."

The fourth reason has emerged only after the statutory meeting which was held on
8 July. At that meeting a majority of creditors approved proposals, which may result
in hiving down the business of the two companies by transferring at least part of
their respective undertakings to a new company. This is not, as I understand it, within

A   para. (a) of sec. 8(3) because it is not intended that the companies themselves should survive, but it is within para. (d) because the proposals represent a more advantageous way of realising the companies assets.

The proposals do not anticipate any exercise of the administrators' powers in sec. 15 of the Act to dispose of property subject to hire-purchase agreements, and it is intended eventually to return the relevant plant and equipment to those finance companies who

B   do not wish to participate in the hive down.

Given that the administrators now admit they do not wish to retain the applicants' property indefinitely, Mr Mann for the applicant finance companies submits that sec. 11(3) of the Act is really dealing only with goods which the administrators propose either to retain indefinitely for the company's own business or to dispose of under sec. 15, and that consent should always be given when there are no long-term requirements for

C   the goods. I can find no such implication inherent in sec. 11(3)(c). Administration is intended as a temporary expedient, and there must be circumstances where administrators reasonably require goods for a limited period or a limited purpose. The court is specifically empowered to impose terms on giving leave and one of those terms might be that at the end of a given period or the cessation of a particular requirement the goods should he returned.

D   I revert now to events after the making of the orders on 9 April. The administrators at once appreciated that in order to have any chance of the approval of proposals at the statutory meeting it would be necessary to carry with them a large number of the finance companies who formed the vast majority of unsecured creditors. In May the administrators wrote round to the finance companies with a preliminary report. Draft proposals were then presented to an informal meeting of the leasing creditors held on 10 June. Those proposals contemplated an injection of some £1.05m of equity into the

E   companies, partly from an institutional investor and partly from new management, and they required the finance companies to write off 55 per cent of their accrued debts and convert a further 25 per cent into redeemable preference shares. These proposals were rejected at the meeting on 10 June but those present did not indicate to the administrators that they were not prepared to consider alternative proposals. The administrators therefore presented an alternative plan to the statutory meeting. The alternative plan was approved by a small majority at the statutory meeting held on 8 July and the

F   administrators are now bound by sec. 17 to manage the affairs of the company in accordance with the proposals approved at that meeting.

A report under sec. 24(4) was made to the court on 10 July and the approved proposals include the following:

"6. *Proposal to creditors*

G   6.1 Summary of proposal

The proposals envisage a new trading entity being formed to continue the business of Access and Plant. The administrators in conjunction with a committee of creditors are to assess whether the new business is viable. If the administrators conclude the business is not viable, they will market the assets of Access and Plant for sale as going concerns, failing which they will arrange the orderly return of the

H   finance equipment and the disposal of the premises and the unencumbered assets and the collection of the debts.

6.2 Formation of a new company

A new company will be incorporated to acquire the financed assets as well as the unencumbered assets. The proposal will involve the following main elements:

A

   (i) Full repayment of the capital element of the debts due to the finance companies whose equipment is to be utilised by the new company.

   (ii) The above repayment is to be phased over the remaining working life of the equipment.

  (iii) Interest on the outstanding capital is to be fixed over the period at 13 per cent.

B

  (iv) The finance companies are to grant a capital and interest holiday of four months from 1 August 1992 to allow the new company to generate working capital.

   (v) In addition to the existing management, new management will be recruited who will be prepared to make a cash investment into the new company.

  (vi) Working capital will be secured from a combination of bank borrowings and the factoring or discounting of the book debts.

C

  (vii) The new company will commence trading on 1 August 1992.

 (viii) Any unencumbered assets not acquired by the new company at the Henry Butcher & Co going concern valuations will be disposed of by the administrators.

6.3 Finance companies will be invited to terminate the existing agreements and to enter into new agreements with the new company.

D

6.4 It is proposed a committee of creditors be formed who, together with the administrators, can monitor the progress being made to secure the various elements of the proposed restructuring.

6.5 Trading projections and balance sheets for the new company for the eight months ended 31 March 1993 and years ended 31 March 1994 and 31 March 1995 are attached as appendix 2 to this report.

E

6.6 The trading projections anticipate profits of £43,177, £176,457 and £815,034 for the eight months ended 31 March 1993 and years ended 31 March 1994 and 31 March 1995 respectively.

6.7 The benefit of the formation of the new company will be the ultimate repayment to the finance companies, the disposal of unencumbered assets and the maximising of debtor collection. If by 1 August 1992 the administrators conclude that the restructuring proposals have failed or are likely to fail, or sufficient of the finance companies do not agree to the transfer of the financed equipment to the new company, the following phase will be implemented.

F

Sale of the operation as a going concern.

6.8 At the commencement of the administration procedure several approaches were made to us in which interest was expressed in acquiring some or all of the assets of the companies. This of course is not unusual but the concept of an asset sale to a party that would then continue a business operation may be feasible.

G

6.9 We would envisage a sale of the business would entail:

   (i) Preparation of an information pack for circulation to potentially interested parties. The information that would be required for this is already to hand.

H

  (ii) Agreeing and implementing an international marketing campaign with the first advertisement to appear in the financial and trade press as soon as possible.

  (iii) Offers to be invited.

A

6.10 Both we and our valuers believe a sale of the business as a going concern would achieve a significantly higher level of realisations than that likely to be achieved on a forced sale basis. It would therefore result in a mitigation of the losses that would otherwise be incurred.

6.11 The proceeds are to be divided by reference to the recent valuation undertaken by Henry Butcher & Co of the plant as a complete working hire fleet.

B

Repossession of the financed equipment and sale/realisation of other assets.

6.12 If both of the above phases fail there will be the orderly repossession of third party equipment and sale of the companies' assets. Any funds remaining after the costs and expenses of the administration will be distributed to creditors in their correct order of priority, subject to any court order obtained by the administrators or through the medium of liquidation.

C

6.13 If the proposals are approved the administrators will continue to monitor the running of the companies whilst the proposals are implemented.

6.14 BICF have indicated that they will continue to support the companies in administration.

7. *Payment to the finance companies for the use of the equipment since 9 April 1992.*

D

7.1 It has always been our intention that the finance companies should receive payment for the use of the equipment since the date of the administration orders. However, it is well known that neither Access nor Plant had been able to meet their full commitments in this respect for many months prior to the administration orders. No payments have been made to the finance companies during the administration.

E

7.2 We propose the basis to be used to calculate such payments is to deduct from the cash collections made for goods and services supplied since 9 April the associated costs of the invoice discount company, the costs of trading and £50,000 of the costs of the administration. The resulting balance should then be apportioned between the finance companies.

7.3 At appendix 1 are the consolidated profit and loss accounts for April and May and the projected account for June 1992. The statement indicates there will be surplus funds of £104,488, £161,970 and £161,872 for April, May and June 1992 respectively after paying the costs indicated. These sums, less £50,000 of the costs of the administration, will be available to make payments to the finance companies. Based on the full monthly rentals of £445,000, the above sum approximates to 28.4 per cent of this sum for the months of April, May and June.

F

7.4 The figures for June are best estimates and may vary, which may cause the anticipated payment to fluctuate.

G

7.5 The above computations assume irrecoverable debts are limited to 2.25 per cent and therefore presupposes the future obligations of Access and Plant to their customers are met for the provision of equipment under existing hire agreements. We will require the new company to meet the current obligations of Access and Plant in order to maximise recoveries from the sales ledgers by minimising counterclaims for breach of contract.

H

7.6 We propose to allocate the resulting balance as a proportion of the full monthly rental or hire/lease purchase instalments, which total £445,000.''

At the time of my decision the assessment of the viability of the new company had not been completed, but it has been decided that plan 2 (sale of the operation as a going concern) was not feasible.

I now turn to the question whether leave to repossess should or should not be granted,   A
and the leading case is *Re Atlantic Computer Systems* [1990] BCC 859, where the Court
of Appeal gave valuable guidance as to the general approach of the court to applications
under sec. 11. Before I read those guidelines I note that there is one strong similarity
between the present case and *Atlantic* and one significant difference. The similarity is
that the companies in administration were all conducting a business which consisted of
buying equipment on hire purchase and leasing it to end users. Section 11 and the
guidelines which the Court of Appeal formulated are intended to apply also to what   B
must be the more common situation where only part of the company's assets or stock-in-
trade is held on hire purchase. The significant difference is that the administrator in the
Atlantic case was seeking to use sec. 11 for what the Court of Appeal considered to be
an improper purpose. At p. 874, the court turned to the application for leave to repossess
and set out seven factors which the court considered to be of importance in that
particular case. The court's conclusions are stated under (8) at pp. 877–878.   C

"In this case it is for us sitting in the Court of Appeal to exercise our own
discretion. In so far as the question of granting leave arose at all before the judge
in view of his decision that the equipment was not in the company's possession,
the judge approached the question on the erroneous footing that Norwich and
AIB were entitled to be paid the rent due under the head leases, as an expense of
the administration.   D

Taking into account all the matters mentioned above, we are in no doubt that this
is a case in which we should exercise our discretion under sec. 11 to grant leave to
take steps to terminate the head leases and to repossess the goods and, in the case
of AIB, to enforce its security. The administration is a prelude to winding up the
company. In short, the administrators propose to negotiate benefits for the
unsecured creditors, who to a substantial extent are the end users and funders
themselves, by reducing the amount of the claims of the end users and funders.   E
End users will be asked to release their claims under the flex and walk options.
They may be asked to pay more, direct to the funders. Funders will be asked to
release their claims against the company under the head leases. The unsatisfactory
feature of these proposals is that the contemplated negotiations will take place at
the expense of the funders, in that the funders will be asked to agree to modify
their existing proprietary rights in a negotiation in which they will not be able to
rely on those rights. Their bargaining strength will be reduced to the prospect   F
that, if agreement is not reached after an indefinite period, the administrators
may give their consent under sec. 11. Or, presumably, Norwich and AIB could
embark on a fresh application to the court. This cannot be an acceptable basis on
which to conduct an administration. Norwich and AIB should not be compelled
to leave their property in such an administration against their will. The prohibitions
in sec. 11(3)(c) and (d) were not intended to be a means of strengthening an   G
administrator's position if he should seek to negotiate a modification of the
existing proprietary rights of the owner of the land or goods in question."

The ratio decidendi appears to me to be that it was not legitimate to refuse consent
under sec. 11(3)(c) in order to improve an administrator's bargaining position with one
particular class of creditors. The Court of Appeal however gave general guidance
starting at p. 879:   H

"*Leave applications: the general approach*

There is one final matter to which we now turn. In the course of argument we were
invited to give guidance on the principles to be applied on applications for the
grant of leave under sec. 11. It is an invitation to which we are reluctant to accede
for several reasons: first, Parliament has left at large the discretion given to the

A   court, and it is not for us to cut down that discretion or, as it was put in argument, to confine it within a straitjacket. However much we emphasise that any observations are only guidelines, there is a danger that they may be treated as something more. Secondly, sec. 11(3)(c) and (d) applies to a very wide range of steps and proceedings, and the circumstances in which leave is sought will vary almost infinitely. Thirdly, it is the judges who sit in the Companies Court who have practical experience of the difficulties arising in the working out of this new

B   jurisdiction, not the members of this court.

However, we have already drawn attention to the important role of the administrator in this field. He should respond speedily and responsibly to applications for consent under sec. 11. Parliament envisaged that in the first place sec. 11 matters should be dealt with by him. It is to be hoped, in the interests of all concerned, that applications to the court will become the exception rather than

C   the rule. But we recognise that for this to be so, authorised insolvency practitioners and their legal advisers need more guidance than is available at present on what, in general, is the approach of the court on leave applications. We feel bound, therefore, to make some general observations regarding cases where leave is sought to exercise existing proprietary rights, including security rights, against a company in administration.

D   (1)   It is in every case for the person who seeks leave to make out a case for him to be given leave.

(2)   The prohibition in sec. 11(3)(c) and (d) is intended to assist the company, under the management of the administrator, to achieve the purpose for which the administration order was made. If granting leave to a lessor of land or the hirer of goods (a 'lessor') to exercise his proprietary rights and repossess his land or goods is unlikely to impede the achievement of that

E   purpose, leave should normally be given.

(3)   In other cases when a lessor seeks possession the court has to carry out a balancing exercise, balancing the legitimate interests of the lessor and the legitimate interests of the other creditors of the company (see per *Peter Gibson* J in *Re Meesan Investments Ltd (Royal Trust Bank v Buchler)* (1988) 4 BCC 788 at p. 793).

F   The metaphor employed here, for want of a better, is that of scales and weights. Lord *Wilberforce* adverted to the limitations of this metaphor in *Science Research Council v Nassé* [1980] AC 1028 at p. 1067. It must be kept in mind that the exercise under sec. 11 is not a mechanical one; each case calls for an exercise in judicial judgment, in which the court seeks to give effect to the purpose of the statutory provisions, having regard to the parties' interests and all the circumstances of the case. As already noted,

G   the purpose of the prohibition is to enable or assist the company to achieve the object for which the administration order was made. The purpose of the power to give leave is to enable the court to relax the prohibition where it would be inequitable for the prohibition to apply.

(4)   In carrying out the balancing exercise great importance, or weight, is normally to be given to the proprietary interests of the lessor. Sir *Nicolas*

H   *Browne-Wilkinson* V-C observed in *Re Paramount Airways Ltd (Bristol Airport plc v Powdrill)* [1990] BCC 130 at p. 154 that, so far as possible, the administration procedure should not be used to prejudice those who were secured creditors when the administration order was made in lieu of a winding-up order. The same is true regarding the proprietary interests of a lessor. The underlying principle here is that an administration for the benefit of unsecured creditors should not be conducted at the expense of those who have proprietary rights which they are seeking to exercise, save to the extent that this may be unavoidable and even then this will usually be acceptable only to a strictly limited extent.

(5) Thus it will normally be a sufficient ground for the grant of leave if significant loss would be caused to the lessor by a refusal. For this purpose loss comprises any kind of financial loss, direct or indirect, including loss by reason of delay, and may extend to loss which is not financial. But if substantially greater loss would be caused to others by the grant of leave, or loss which is out of all proportion to the benefit which leave would confer on the lessor, that may outweigh the loss to the lessor caused by a refusal.

Our formulation was criticised in the course of the argument, and we certainly do not claim for it the status of a rule in those terms. At present we say only that it appears to us the nearest we can get to a formulation of what Parliament had in mind.

(6) In assessing these respective losses the court will have regard to matters such as: the financial position of the company, its ability to pay the rental arrears and the continuing rentals, the administrator's proposals, the period for which the administration order has already been in force and is expected to remain in force, the effect on the administration if leave were given, the effect on the applicant if leave were refused, the end result sought to be achieved by the administration, the prospects of that result being achieved, and the history of the administration so far.

(7) In considering these matters it will often be necessary to assess how probable the suggested consequences are. Thus if loss to the applicant is virtually certain if leave is refused, and loss to others a remote possibility if leave is granted, that will be a powerful factor in favour of granting leave.

(8) This is not an exhaustive list. For example, the conduct of the parties may also be a material consideration in a particular case, as it was in the *Paramount Airways* case. There leave was refused on the ground that the applicants had accepted benefits under the administration, and had only sought to enforce their security at a later stage: indeed, they had only acquired their security as a result of the operations of the administrators. It behoves a lessor to make his position clear to the administrator at the outset or the administration and, if it should become necessary, to apply to the court promptly.

(9) The above considerations may be relevant not only to the decision whether leave should be granted or refused, but also to a decision to impose terms if leave is granted.

(10) The above considerations will also apply to a decision on whether to impose terms as a condition for refusing leave. Section 11(3)(c) and (d) makes no provision for terms being imposed if leave is refused, but the court has power to achieve that result. It may do so directly, by giving directions to the administrator: for instance, under sec. 17, or in response to an application by the administrator under sec. 14(3), or in exercise of its control over an administrator as an officer of the court. Or it may do so indirectly, by ordering that the applicant shall have leave unless the administrator is prepared to take this or that step in the conduct of the administration.

Cases where leave is refused but terms are imposed can be expected to arise frequently. For example, the permanent loss to a lessor flowing from his

A   inability to recover his property will normally be small if the administrator
is required to pay the current rent. In most cases this should be possible,
since if the administration order has been rightly made, the business should
generally be sufficiently viable to hold down current outgoings. Such a term
may therefore be a normal term to impose.''

I omit para. (11) and (12) of the guidelines, which are of no relevance to the present
case. Mr Mann has relied strongly on para. (4), (5) and the last part of para. (10), for his
B   submission that leave should be granted in the present case.

It seems to me that taken in isolation some of the statements in those paragraph may
be putting the matter rather high: for instance, the statement at the beginning of
para. (5), that it will normally be a sufficient ground for the grant of leave if significant
loss would be caused to the lessor by a refusal. It appears to me almost inevitable in the
scheme of the Act that a refusal may cause the lessor significant loss. If the lessor is not
C   going to suffer significant loss by not repossessing (for example if the administrators are
continuing the full hire-purchase payments), then the lessor has no real incentive to
apply to the administrators for consent and still less reason for spending time and money
in applying to the court for leave.

I think the key is in para. (3) which requires the court to carry out a balancing exercise,
balancing the legitimate interests of the lessor against the legitimate interests of the
D   other creditors. Put like that, it appears that one is weighing like against like, but I think
what one really has to compare is the loss to the lessor (which is the measure of the
extent to which his legitimate interest is infringed) with the reasons for refusal, because
the other creditors have no legitimate interest as such under sec. 11(3)(c), only a hope
that the discretion conferred by Parliament will be exercised so as to promote the greater
good of the greater number.

E   As the Court of Appeal points out, the balancing exercise is not a mechanical one, but
one which requires an exercise in judicial judgment. On one side of the balance the most
important factor must be the likely loss to the applicant if consent is refused. In the
present case I do not think that this can properly be measured simply by taking the
current hire-purchase instalments.

Mr Clapp's evidence was that many of the agreements were at fixed interest rates of
F   up to 18 per cent per annum, whereas rates of 10–12 per cent were available in April
1992. The finance companies had already agreed to an across-the-board reduction of
20 per cent in the previous year and were contemplating a further reduction to 59 per
cent. Furthermore in the case of hire purchase each instalment includes an element of
payment for purchase of the capital asset and it is clear that the items subject to
hire-purchase agreements will never now be acquired by the companies in administration.
There is no evidence that the finance companies could have let second-hand equipment
G   on similar hire-purchase terms if they had repossessed. Nor do I think that the rental
payments made by the end users are any real guide to the finance companies' loss. The
arrangements with the end users were in the main short-term lets for a few weeks and
required constant administration and in some cases the services of operators. There was
no evidence that any of the finance companies had either the desire or the ability to
conduct this form of business on their own account.

H   The real loss to the finance companies can in my judgment be measured by the
difference, if any, in resale prices between April and August 1992 and the loss of interest
on the resale price that could have been achieved in April. There is little evidence to
guide me on this matter. The goods are items one would expect to depreciate in the
course of time, but over a period of a few months the price may be affected more
by market conditions. In May 1992 the administrators commissioned a report by

Henry Butcher & Co, international plant consultants, which is referred to in their   A
proposals to the statutory meeting.

In the report the consultants said:

> "In our opinion to mitigate potential losses it is essential and necessary for all
> financing parties involved to act together in either the restructuring and refinancing
> of the company, or in any future disposal.

> The open market value of the plant as a complete hire fleet is considerably higher   B
> than the open market value for removal and by retaining the plant as an operating
> unit should provide an overall higher realisation. The companies' owned and
> financed plant together forms a very significant package which if placed on the
> market would have to be undertaken with a good knowledge of that effect and a
> strategy of disposal. It could not be absorbed within the UK and any attempt to
> do so would have a massive downward effect upon the realisations and the market.

> In the event of a piecemeal disposal of the plant we would very strongly recommend   C
> a unified disposal strategy between all parties concerned. This would provide
> enough interest to market the assets properly in a competitive atmosphere
> throughout the UK, Europe and internationally to bring the maximum realisation."

Mr Clapp in cross-examination said that he was very concerned about the effect an
uncontrolled piecemeal sale would have on the market. He thought manufacturers
might go out of business and there would be massive write-offs. For example UDT had   D
on hire purchase to David Meek Access one year's entire production of scissor-lifts.

It seems to be probable that the hiving down arrangement, if it is feasible, will prevent
a flooding of the market and allow those finance companies who choose to sell to achieve
higher prices than would have otherwise been the case.

As to interest the only guidance I have are the administrators' monthly projections of
£47,000 for all the finance companies together, but that figure was not based on any   E
estimate of resale value. I can only say that I would expect the interest at ten or 12 per
cent on the retail price in April to be considerably less than tile £247,000 per month
which was the amount which the finance companies were expecting to take under the
arrangements proposed in March 1992.

At this stage I ought to say something about payment for retention of the goods,
because Mr Mann relies strongly on the observations in *Atlantic Computers* at p. 881H: F

> "Cases where leave is refused but terms are imposed can be expected to arise
> frequently. For example, the permanent loss to a lessor flowing from his inability
> to recover his property will normally be small if the administrator is required to
> pay the current rent. In most cases this should be possible, since if the administration
> order has been rightly made, the business should generally be sufficiently viable
> to hold down current outgoings. Such a term may therefore be a normal term to
> impose."   G

At p. 878E *Nicholls* LJ said:

> "This is not a case in which it is practicable to refuse leave on condition that the
> administrators pay all the current outgoings under the head leases. The rents from
> the sub-leases, even assuming the flow can be restarted promptly, are insufficient
> for this purpose."

In the present case the two companies had been unable for some time before the   H
administration petitions to hold down current outgoings. Their problem was that with
hiring rates current in 1991 and 1992 they could make a profit only if the finance
companies accepted a cut in their hire-purchase charges. Furthermore when the
administrators took office, they were faced with an immediate cash-flow problem. The
book debts had been factored to BI Commercial Finance Ltd, who allowed the companies

A   to draw up to £1.5m against unpaid approved invoices. Without this source of finance the administrators would have been unable to pay the wages and run the business. BICF insisted as a term of continuing the arrangement that the overdraft ceiling be reduced to £900,000 immediately, to £825,000 on 20 April and £625,000 by 18 May. The administrators accepted those terms, and the cash received from the end users was used to meet the running costs of the business and to reduce the overdraft with BICF which on 1 June 1992 stood at £331,637.

B

The administrators were throughout this period conscious of the need to make some payments to the finance companies, and before submitting their proposals to the informal meeting on 10 June Mr Clapp asked BICF to continue the overdraft and if necessary raise the ceiling to £900,000, so that a payment of £300,000 could be made immediately to the finance companies pro rata.

C   However, on 10 June the finance companies rejected the administrators' draft proposals and thereafter Mr Clapp as a "boring prudent accountant" did not feel able to use the BICF facility in case trading had to cease abruptly and he had borrowed money without being able to repay.

Since the beginning of July the companies have, however, been in credit with BICF and the approved proposals which I have read include a proposal to pay some £370,000 to the finance companies for the use of their equipment in the months of April, May and June.

D

Mr Clapp agreed in cross-examination that the only funds available at the end of July to make this payment was some £150,000 with BICF and the invoices due in August. On the basis, however, that the finance companies will eventually receive some £370,000 (which as the proposal says represents 28.4 per cent of their full monthly rentals for the months of April, May and June), I do not think that the finance companies have proved that they will suffer a significant loss compared with the position they would have been in if they had been allowed to repossess their goods at the beginning of April.

E

As against any loss suffered by the applicant finance companies, I have to set the administrators' reasons for refusing consent and the benefits to the other creditors (including those finance companies who have not applied for the return of their goods) and to the companies as a whole, arising out of the continued retention.

In my judgment there is substance in the reasons advanced by Mr Clapp in his first affidavit. There was good reason to believe that if the administrators allowed the finance companies to repossess their goods ad libidinem, the administrations would be abortive and no proposals could be presented to the statutory meeting. The creditors would thus have been deprived of the opportunity (which they have accepted) to approve proposals designed to achieve a more advantageous realisation of the companies' assets than would have been the case in a winding up. Finally I think there is substance in Mr Clapp's fear that the abrupt termination of trading would have endangered the book debts which at the beginning of April amounted to £1.8m and have been collected in an orderly fashion during the continuance of trading.

G

Next I have to consider the administrators' proposals for the return of their goods to those companies who do not wish to participate in the hive down. After the statutory meeting the administrators issued instructions that no item was to be let out for more than a month without specific authority. Some items were immediately available for collection at the end of July, but the scale of the companies' operations was such that some time-table was required to prevent too many collection vehicles arriving at the companies' depot at the same time. Those items on short-term hire were to be made available when they came off hire. Those items on long-term hire were to be replaced by other items hired specially by the administrators and made available accordingly. The anticipated result was that practically everything could be returned to the applicant

F

H

finance companies by the end of August. These seem to me to be eminently sensible   **A**
arrangements to meet a practical problem in returning the goods without upsetting the
end users or causing a jam at the places of collection.

In my judgment, having regard to the parties' interests and the circumstances of this
case, granting leave would have impeded the achievement of the purposes of the
administration orders. After carrying out the balancing exercise recommended by the
Court of Appeal I conclude that the administrators were right to refuse consent and   **B**
accordingly with two exceptions I dismiss the applications. The exceptions arise out of
circumstances peculiar to UDT and Hill Samuel. Both companies sought to repossess
on 2 April, that is the day before the presentation of the petitions. What happened is not
in dispute and is set out in the affidavits of Janet Trimmer for UDT and Lloyd
Meiklejohn for Hill Samuel. Ms Trimmer says in her affidavit:

> "On 1 April 1992, the day after the agreements had been terminated, letters of   **C**
> instruction were sent by facsimile transmission from my department to managers
> of UDT branches at Hatfield, Solihull, Reigate, Bristol, Bolton, East Midlands,
> Burnham and Leicester to attend at specified sites at which UDT's plant and
> equipment was located for the purpose of inspection, identification and arranging
> repossession. Each branch manager in turn arranged for a member of his staff to
> carry out these instructions and, at all eight locations, attempts to repossess were
> made on 2 April 1992.   **D**

Notwithstanding that the petition had not yet been presented I am advised and
verily believe that UDT representatives, namely Phil Kirkham and Paul Eshelby,
attending the companies' Liverpool depot on 2 April 1992, were told that, prior
to removal of any equipment, they should speak to 'the receiver'. Upon contacting
the companies' Bristol office the same day they were informed that an administrator
had been appointed and that, as a result, they should refrain from making any   **E**
mark of identification or repossessing the equipment in question. A UDT employee,
Tony Datko, attending at Milton Keynes, was advised similarly on the same day.
At other sites and in particular Bristol, Reigate and Solihull assurances were given
to Ian Houston and Tony Jones (Bristol), Rod Bridle (Reigate) and Mr I P Crane,
Mr A D Cooper and Ms A Parker (Solihull) that the items in question could be
collected by arrangement and, in the case of Bristol, it was agreed that the plant
and equipment would be delivered to UDT's depot at Yate during the weekend of   **F**
4–5 April. At other sites, for example Burnham, access to the plant and equipment
was denied on the basis that instructions were awaited from the companies' head
office at Bristol. In any event, UDT's representatives nationwide were unable to
secure the release of any of the plant and equipment notwithstanding that the
petition had not at that time been presented."

Mr Meiklejohn says in his affidavit: **G**

> "On 1 April 1992, the day after the agreements bad been terminated, a letter of
> authority was sent by facsimile transmission by my department to UDT authorising
> them to act on behalf of Hill Samuel in marking, labelling and arranging
> repossession of the plant and equipment at specified sites. I am advised and verily
> believe that Janet Trimmer, corporate credit executive with UDT, sent letters of
> instruction to managers of UDT branches to attend at sites at which Hill Samuel's   **H**
> plant and equipment was located for the purposes of inspection, identification and
> arranging repossession. Each branch manager in turn arranged for a member of
> his staff to carry out these instructions and, at all eight locations (at Hatfield,
> Solihull, Reigate, Bristol, Bolton, East Midlands, Burnham and Leicester),
> attempts to repossess were made on 2 April 1992.

A   Notwithstanding that the petition had not yet been presented, I am advised and verily believe that UDT representatives acting on behalf of Hill Samuel, namely Phil Kirkham and Paul Eshelby, attending the companies' Liverpool depot on 2 April, were told that, prior to removal of any equipment, they should speak to 'the receiver'. Upon contacting the companies' Bristol office the same day they were informed that an administrator had been appointed and that, as a result, they should refrain from making any mark of identification or repossessing the

B   equipment in question. A UDT employee, Tony Datko, attending at Milton Keynes was advised similarly on the same day. At other sites, and in particular Bristol, Reigate and Solihull, assurances were given to Ian Houston and Tony Jones (Bristol), Rod Bridle (Reigate) and Mr I P Crane, Mr A D Cooper and Ms A Parker (Solihull) that the items in question could be collected by arrangement and, in the case of Bristol, it was agreed that the plant and equipment would be delivered to the company's depot at Yate during the weekend of 4–5 April. At

C   other sites, for example Burnham, access to the plant and equipment was denied on the basis that instructions were awaited from the companies' head office in Bristol. In any event UDT's representatives nationwide were unable to secure the release of any of the plant and equipment notwithstanding that the petition had not at that time been presented."

petition were presented, and accordingly I will give them leave to repossess their goods

D   from 31 July 1992. I will hear submissions as to further directions, if any, to be given to the administrators and as to costs at a date convenient to all concerned.

(Order accordingly)

_____

E

F

G

H

Gamlestaden plc v Brackland Magazines Ltd & Ors.

A

Chancery Division (Companies Court).
Chadwick J.
Judgment delivered 13 November 1992.

> *Insolvency — Winding-up petitions — Provisional liquidators — Costs —*
> *Directors — Petitioning creditor applied for appointment of provisional*
> *liquidators — Companies obtained adjournment of applications — Applications*
> *unopposed at adjourned hearings and provisional liquidators appointed —*
> *Whether directors should pay costs personally.*

B

These were applications by a petitioning creditor, Gamlestaden plc, in relation to three companies against which winding-up petitions were pending. Provisional liquidators had been appointed to the companies, and Gamlestaden's application was for the individual directors of the companies and Brackland Publishing plc, a company with which the directors were associated, to pay the costs of the applications for the appointment of provisional liquidators.

C

When the applications for the appointment of provisional liquidators first came before the court the companies appeared by counsel and sought an adjournment, which was granted on certain undertakings being given. When the application came before the court again it was unopposed and the orders were duly made. Each of the companies had been the subject of more than one winding-up petition in 1992 and they appeared to be insolvent.

D

The companies' solicitors had come off the record. The directors and Brackland Publishing plc did not appear and were not represented on the costs applications.

Held, making costs orders against the directors personally and Brackland Publishing plc:

E

1. The costs thrown away by the adjournment were incurred by reason of the instructions which were given by the directors to their solicitors and counsel to the effect that there was some real matter to be investigated and some real prospect of being able to furnish material upon which the application to appoint provisional liquidators could be opposed. But not only was there nothing to investigate, but the directors of these companies must have been well aware that there was not the slightest chance that the position would look any more favourable after the adjournment. The adjournment was sought on a false basis, was wholly unnecessary, and arose from conduct by the directors which could not be regarded as being part of the proper exercise of their fiduciary duties in relation to the companies.

F

2. The circumstances which led to Gamlestaden's decision to apply for the appointment of provisional liquidators included, and to a very substantial extent were, the directors' conduct in relation to winding-up petitions which had been presented and paid off during the course of 1992. The number of petitions, and the number of substitutions, was not only strong evidence of inability to pay debts as they fell due, but also cogent evidence of questionable and dishonourable conduct on the part of the directors. The way in which the directors chose to conduct the affairs of the companies, in relation to the winding-up petitions which had been presented throughout 1992, gave rise to a wholly justifiable concern on the part of Gamlestaden that the assets of the companies could not properly be allowed to remain under the control of those directors for any longer than was necessary.

G

H

The following cases were referred to in the judgment:

Aiden Shipping Co Ltd v Interbulk Ltd [1986] AC 965.
Land and Property Trust Co plc & Ors, Re [1991] BCC 459; [1991] 1 WLR 601.

A *Record Tennis Centres Ltd, Re (Company No. 004055 of 1991)* [1991] BCC 509; [1991] 1 WLR 1003.
Scherer & Anor v Counting Instruments Ltd & Anor [1986] 1 WLR 615n.
Singh & Anor v Observer Ltd [1989] 2 All ER 751.
Taylor & Anor v Pace Developments Ltd [1991] BCC 406.

Gavin Lightman QC and Elizabeth Jones (instructed by Rowe & Maw) for the petitioning creditor.

B The respondents did not appear and were not represented.

JUDGMENT

Chadwick J: On 14 October 1992 orders were made in this court for the appointment of provisional liquidators of each of the three companies now known as Brackland Magazines Ltd, Brackland Holdings plc and FFC Construction Ltd. Winding-up orders
C have not yet been made in respect of those companies. The return date for the current petition to wind up Brackland Magazines Ltd is 18 November, and the return date for the current petitions to wind up the other two companies is 9 December 1992.

There are now before me applications by the petitioning creditor, Gamlestaden plc, in relation to each of the three companies for orders that the individual directors of those companies and Brackland Publishing plc, a company with which those directors are
D associated, do pay the costs of the applications for the appointments of provisional liquidators. When those applications for costs first came before me on 5 November 1992 the individual directors and Brackland Publishing plc were represented by solicitors and counsel. The applications were opposed. The hearing was not completed on 5 November. It was adjourned, and has now come back before me for further argument. In the meantime the solicitors formerly acting for the respondents have come off the record. The respondents are neither represented before me today nor do they appear in person.
E In the circumstances therefore I have not heard full argument on behalf of the respondents.

There is, in my view, no doubt that, in an appropriate case, the court has power to make an order against a person who is not a party to litigation requiring him to bear all or part of the costs of the litigation — see sec. 51 of the *Supreme Court Act* 1981, and the decision of the House of Lords in *Aiden Shipping Co Ltd v Interbulk Ltd* [1986] AC 965. In particular, the court has power to make such an order against the director of
F a company who improperly causes the company and the petitioner to incur costs in connection with a winding-up petition — see the observations of *Hoffmann* J in *Re Record Tennis Centres Ltd* [1991] BCC 509 at p. 516 — and to make such an order against an outsider who is funding the litigation on behalf of an unsuccessful party — see *Singh v Observer Ltd* [1989] 2 All ER 751.

Nevertheless the circumstances in which it will be appropriate to make such an order are rare. *Nicholls* LJ stated the principle in these terms in *Re Land and Property Trust*
G *Co plc* [1991] BCC 459 at p. 461H:

"... the circumstances in which it will be just to make a costs order against a person who is not a party to the proceedings will be exceptional. In the nature of things it will very seldom be right to order a person who is not party to proceedings to pay the costs of the proceedings."

There are observations to a similar effect in the decision of the Court of Appeal in
H *Taylor v Pace Developments Ltd* [1991] BCC 406. In particular, *Lloyd* LJ said at p. 409G:

"I do not say that there may not be cases where a director may not be properly liable for costs. Thus he might be made liable if the company's defence is not bona fide as, for example, where the company has been advised that there is no defence and the proceedings are defended out of spite, or for the sole purpose of causing

the plaintiffs to incur irrecoverable costs. No doubt there will be other cases. But
such cases must necessarily be rare. In the great majority of cases the directors of
an insolvent company which defends proceedings brought against it should not be
at personal risk of costs."

The question which I have to consider is whether in the circumstances of this case it
would be right to make the orders sought. That is to say, whether there are here such
exceptional circumstances as to make this one of those rare cases in which a person not
party to the litigation should be made to bear the costs.

The history of these matters may be summarised as follows.

(1) *Brackland Magazines Ltd*

There have been at least three petitions presented during the past year seeking the
winding up of the company now known as Brackland Magazines Ltd (formerly Newself
Ltd). The first of those petitions was presented on 15 October 1991 in the High Court. It
was withdrawn on 15 January 1992. A second petition, which is the petition now before
this court, was presented on 5 March 1992 in the Hertford County Court by Work
Station Solutions Ltd. On 8 May 1992 that petitioner was paid off and M P Byatt & Co
was substituted as petitioner. On 26 June 1992, M P Byatt & Co was paid off and Barnet
Alexander Chart was substituted as petitioner. On 16 August 1992, Barnet Alexander
Chart was paid off and Price Jamieson & Partners were substituted as petitioners. On
18 August 1992, a third petition was presented in the High Court by the Imagebank and
Stock Photos.

On 14 October 1992 Gamlestaden became aware of the petition pending in the
Hertford County Court. In due course, Price Jamieson & Partners having been paid off,
Gamlestaden were substituted as petitioning creditor on that second petition. The
second petition was transferred to the High Court. As I have said it is now due to be
heard on 18 November 1992. On that basis, the third petition was removed from the file.

(2) *Brackland Holdings plc*

In the case of Brackland Holdings plc, the present petition is the fourth that has been
presented this year. The first petition was presented on 2 February 1992. The petitioner
was paid off and the petition withdrawn on 27 February. The second petition was
presented on 10 March 1992. Again, the petitioner's claim was satisfied in part and the
petition was dismissed on 29 July. On 17 September a further petition was presented in
the Manchester District Registry; that was withdrawn on 1 October. The present
petition, in which Gamlestaden is petitioner, was presented on 7 October 1992.

(3) *FFC Construction Ltd*

In the case of FFC Construction Ltd a petition was presented on 20 July 1992, the
petitioner was paid off and the petition was withdrawn on 6 October. This present
petition was presented the following day on 7 October and, as I have said, it is due for
hearing in December.

A further part of the background against which an application for the appointment of
provisional liquidators was made was that the three companies with which I am now
concerned were associated — in the sense that they had common directors — with a
company known as Capital Expansion and Development Corp Ltd ("Capex"). The
petitioner, Gamlestaden, was also a creditor of Capex. On 2 October 1992 an application
to appoint a provisional liquidator of Capex came before *Millett* J. In a full judgment
given on that day, he reviewed the position in relation to that company. He said
(at p. 12D of his judgment):

A

"So far as jeopardy to the assets are concerned, I bear in mind these facts. The application is supported by a number of creditors and is not opposed by any. Capex appears to be continuing to trade and to employ staff while plainly insolvent. No application has been made for a sec. 127 order. There is no evidence before me of the source of finance, its quantum, or of the terms upon which it is being provided. There has, in my judgment, been a history of questionable conduct in the treatment of creditors by Capex and its directors but

B

I rely on one only: the way in which Holdings and Publishing [those are two of the three companies with which I am now concerned] have staved off creditors of winding-up petitions, paying off creditors at the last minute in order to get rid of a petition, and on occasion paying off the petitioning creditor but not a supporting creditor. The number of the petitions and the number of substitutions is not only strong evidence of inability to pay debts as they fall due but also cogent evidence of questionable and dishonourable conduct on the part of directors. In my

C

judgment, there is a strong public interest in the present case in ensuring that Capex should not continue to trade while hopelessly insolvent without the benefit of a sec. 127 order, without filed accounts, under the control of directors who are guarantors of the debt due to Gamlestaden, and with funds apparently obtained from other companies managed by them."

    In those circumstances the judge acceded to the application which was then before

D

him for the transfer of the Capex petition to the High Court and for the appointment of a provisional liquidator.

    That was the background to the application for a provisional liquidator in relation to the three companies with which I am now concerned. On 7 October 1992 the solicitors for the petitioner gave notice to the in-house solicitor acting for those companies of the intention to apply for the appointment of a provisional liquidator. The affidavit evidence

E

was supplied in the course of the following day, 8 October.

    On 9 October 1992 Gamlestaden made its application to me, ex parte, but on notice. The companies appeared and, through counsel, sought an adjournment for the stated purpose of enabling them to prepare their opposition to the applications for a provisional liquidator. An adjournment over until Wednesday, 14 October 1992 was granted upon certain undertakings being given. Those undertakings included undertakings not to

F

operate any bank accounts of the companies and to supply details of the companies' bank accounts to the petitioner by Monday, 12 October. There is no doubt in my mind that the adjournment was sought and granted on the basis that the protection which was being offered by the undertakings reflected that which would have been obtained if the petition had been advertised. In that event it is to be expected that the companies' bankers would have frozen the companies' accounts; and required the companies to obtain an order under sec. 127 of the *Insolvency Act* 1986 before allowing further

G

operation of those accounts. There is also no doubt in my mind that those undertakings were offered on the basis that counsel for the companies was instructed by those directors who were in court that there really were bank accounts to which the undertakings could apply and in relation to which the relevant details would be supplied. I was further assured, although not in the form of an undertaking, that management accounts were available and would be supplied to the petitioners and put before the court.

H

    When the matter had been considered by counsel and solicitors the decision was taken on 13 October 1992 — that is on the Tuesday before the adjourned hearing — not to oppose the application for the appointment of a provisional liquidator. That decision may, in part, have been the result of the discovery by those advising the companies that there were, in fact, no bank accounts of which particulars could be given and that there were no management accounts which could be put before the court. The undertakings

which had been offered on the previous Friday were illusory. There was nothing on
which they could bite. The matter came before me again on 14 October; the applications
were unopposed and the orders were duly made.

In those circumstances it appears to me that I ought to consider the exercise of my
discretion as to costs separately in relation to two distinct periods. I will deal first with
the later period. That is the period from 9 October until the making of the orders on
14 October. The costs thrown away by the adjournment on 9 October were, in my view,
incurred by reason of the instructions which were given by the directors to their solicitors
and counsel to the effect that there was some real matter to be investigated and some
real prospect of being able to furnish material upon which the application to appoint
provisional liquidators could be opposed.

In my view, not only was there nothing to investigate, but the directors of these
companies must have been well aware, on 9 October, that there was not the slightest
chance that the position would look any more favourable on 14 October. The adjournment
was sought on a false basis, was wholly unnecessary, and arose from conduct by these
directors which cannot be regarded as being part of the proper exercise of their fiduciary
duties in relation to these companies. In those circumstances I make an order that the
directors personally pay the costs thrown away by reason of the adjournment on
9 October.

The other period is the period leading up to the hearing on 9 October, including the
costs of obtaining the order for the provisional liquidator. In relation to that period the
costs incurred cannot be attributed to the directors' conduct on 9 October. The question,
therefore, is whether it would be just to require the directors, or the associated company,
Brackland Publishing plc, to bear the costs which the petitioner incurred in preparing to
apply, and in applying, for the appointment of a provisional liquidator.

I have been referred to a series of cases bearing on the question: what matters can be
taken into account in deciding how to exercise a discretion in relation to costs? The
following principles appear to me to be established. The court has an unlimited discretion
to make such order as to costs as it thinks the justice of the case requires; but that
discretion is to be exercised judicially and in relation to the facts of the case before it.
The grounds upon which that discretion is exercised must be connected with the case
before it; but may include any matter relating to the litigation, the parties' conduct in it,
or the circumstances which led to the litigation. A party who gives another party cause
to have recourse to the court will normally be required to compensate that other party in
costs.

The relevant proceedings with which I am concerned are the proceedings for the
appointment of a provisional liquidator. I am entitled, indeed required, to have regard
to all the circumstances which led to those proceedings. If authority be needed for that
proposition, it will be found in *Scherer v Counting Instruments* [1986] 1 WLR 615,
particularly at p. 618.

In my view, the circumstances which led to Gamlestaden's decision to apply for the
appointment of provisional liquidators included and, indeed, to a very substantial extent
were, the directors' conduct in relation to winding-up petitions which had been presented
and paid off during the course of 1992. I adopt the views expressed by *Millett* J, in the
related application in respect of Capex, that the number of petitions, and the number of
substitutions, is not only strong evidence of inability to pay debts as they fall due, but
also cogent evidence of questionable and dishonourable conduct on the part of the
directors. It seems to me that the way in which these directors chose to conduct the
affairs of these companies, in relation to the winding-up petitions which had been
presented throughout 1992, gave rise to a wholly justifiable concern on the part of

A   Gamlestaden that the assets of these companies could not properly be allowed to remain under the control of those directors for any longer than was necessary.

In those circumstances, I do think it just to make an order against the directors personally in relation to the costs which led up to the application and hearing for the appointment of provisional liquidators.

B   The position of the associated company, Brackland Publishing plc, is similar but not identical to that of the directors. The evidence which has been put before me shows that Brackland Publishing plc is the operating company amongst those companies under the control of these directors. The evidence shows that the course of conduct to which I have referred has been adopted by the directors with the assistance of, and for the benefit of, Brackland Publishing plc. It is that company which has provided funds to satisfy successive petitioners, and so to keep the three companies with which I am presently concerned — and, in particular, the first of those three companies, Brackland Magazines

C   Ltd — alive for its own benefit despite their obvious insolvency. It is Brackland Publishing plc which appears to have funded the opposition to the application for a provisional liquidator.

In those circumstances it seems to me right that the order for costs which I make should extend to Brackland Publishing plc.

(*Order accordingly*)

D

E

F

G

H

William Gaskell Group Ltd & Ors v Highley & Anor.

Chancery Division (Newcastle District Registry).
Morritt J.
Judgment delivered 25 November 1992.

Receivership — Debentures — Fixed or floating charges — Companies granted debentures to bank containing fixed charges on book and other debts and floating charges — Companies had to pay proceeds of debts into special account requiring bank's consent to drawings — Companies' business hived down and debentures transferred — Assignee of debentures appointed receivers — Whether fixed charges became floating as a result of assignment of debentures — Whether floating charge in debenture had crystallised before receivers' appointment — Companies Act 1948, sec. 94 (repealed; see Insolvency Act 1986, sec. 40).

These were applications in an action by three companies in liquidation against receivers of the companies.

The claim in the action was that the charges contained in the debentures under which the receivers were appointed, were floating and not fixed charges, and that accordingly the proceeds of realisations by the receivers, which were paid to the debenture holder or retained by the receivers in payment of their costs, charges and remuneration, should have been used to pay the preferential creditors of the companies in the receiverships pursuant to sec. 94 of the Companies Act 1948.

The debentures were granted to Midland Bank in 1982. In 1984 the bank demanded payment of the sums due. The companies' business was then hived down to a new company, and the bank was paid off and the debentures transferred to the new debenture holder which appointed the receivers.

The plaintiff companies applied for leave to add the liquidator of the companies as a plaintiff and the debenture holder as a defendant, and for leave to amend the indorsement on the writ. The receivers applied to strike out the plaintiffs' claim, alternatively for the determination of issues of law, alternatively for security for costs.

The plaintiffs accepted that the charges in the debentures, when the debentures were granted to the bank, were fixed charges. However, they argued that, after the assignment, a clause which required the companies to pay the proceeds of debts into a special account with the bank which the company could not draw on except with the prior consent of the bank, was commercially inoperable. The result was that on the transfer of the debenture the fixed charge on the companies' book and other debts ceased to be fixed and became floating.

There was a subsidiary question whether receipts in respect of two assets which were subject to the floating charge in one of the debentures were outside sec. 94 because the effect of the hive-down agreement and the other circumstances had given rise to an automatic crystallisation of the floating charge before the receivers were appointed.

Held, dismissing the plaintiffs' applications and acceding to the defendants' application to strike out the action, and ordering the liquidator to pay the defendants' costs of the plaintiffs' summonses:

1. The effect of the assignment was to divide the identity of the person whose consent was required to draw on the account. Previously the requisite consent was that of the bank as debenture holder and as the holder of the account. After the assignment the bank holding the account would have to decide as banker whether or not to pay a cheque when the account was in debit; the debenture holder (the assignee) had to decide whether or not to permit the special account to be drawn on at all and, if so, for what purpose.

A   Far from the restrictions falling away because they were commercially inoperable, they remained exactly the same as they were before but required the consent of the new debenture holder. There was nothing in the effect of the assignment, in its bearing on the effect of the restrictions, to create after the assignment a floating charge where, by definition and as admitted, before assignment it was a fixed charge.

2. The hive-down did cause the company to cease to carry on business and the floating
B   charge to crystallise. Alternatively, the assets concerned were transferred to the new company as part of the hive-down and there could therefore be no liability in respect of them under sec. 94.

The following cases were referred to in the judgment:

Aiden Shipping Co Ltd v Interbulk Ltd [1986] AC 965.
Armagh Shoes Ltd, Re [1982] NI 59.
C   *Brightlife Ltd, Re* (1986) 2 BCC 99,359; [1987] Ch 200.
Keenan Bros Ltd, Re (1986) 2 BCC 98,970; [1985] IR 401.
Miller (James) & Partners Ltd v Whitworth Street Estates (Manchester) Ltd [1970] AC 583.
Siebe Gorman & Co Ltd v Barclays Bank Ltd [1979] 2 Lloyd's Rep 142.
Woodroffes (Musical Instruments) Ltd, Re [1986] Ch 366.
Yorkshire Woolcombers Association Ltd, Re [1903] 2 Ch 284.

D   Jeffrey Littman (instructed by Hammond Suddards, Leeds) for the plaintiffs.

Peter Arden (instructed by Dibb Lupton Broomhead, Manchester) for the receivers.

Linden Ife (instructed by Parrott & Coales, Aylesbury) for the debenture holder.

JUDGMENT

[Nature of charge]
E
Morritt J: On 24 May 1982, William Gaskell Group Ltd, William Gaskell Upholland Ltd and William Gaskell Warehousing Ltd each granted to Midland Bank Ltd a debenture to secure an overdraft, a fixed loan and various guarantee liabilities in respect of other companies in the group.

On 21 June 1982, "Group", as I will call that company, gave a legal charge to the bank over certain property specified in the schedule to it.
F
On 1 June 1984, Midland Bank demanded from each of the three companies I have mentioned payment of the sum due.

There was then a period of some 12 days when negotiations took place, whereby the three companies sought to raise outside finance and, on 12 June 1984, two agreements were entered into.

By the first, made between Group and Upholland of the one part, and Lesley
G   Marketing Ltd, a company controlled by the controllers of Group and Upholland of the other part, the assets of Group and Upholland, relating to the haulage and warehousing business carried on by those companies, were hived down to Lesley Marketing Ltd. The price was the amount of an open market independent valuation; £75,000 was to be paid on 12 June 1984, and the balance of the valuation to be paid by three equal instalments in the following three calendar months.

H   By the second also on 12 June 1984, Waldis Investments paid to Midland Bank the sum of £281,000-odd and took a transfer from Midland Bank of the securities it held to secure the companies' indebtedness. Such securities included, but were not limited to, the three debentures I have mentioned.

On 13 June 1984, that is to say the following day, Mr Highley and Mr Venning were appointed receivers under the three debentures by Waldis. At that date there were, in

aggregate, £240,000-worth of preferential creditors of all or one or more of the three   A
companies I have mentioned.

The companies went into liquidation in October 1984 and between 1984 and 1988 the
receivers realised the assets subject to the debentures. They realised approximately
£250,000.

In due course, Mr Barry John Ward was appointed liquidator of each of the three
companies in question.   B

The amount raised by the receivers was paid either to Waldis Investments, or retained
by themselves in payment of their costs, charges and remuneration.

On 24 May 1990, proceedings were commenced by Barry John Ward against
Mr Highley and Mr Venning, the two receivers. The writ was indorsed with the following
claim:

> "Damages for loss and damage of the defendants suffered by William Gaskell   C
> Group Ltd (the company) as a result of the negligence and breach of statutory
> duty in their position as the joint receivers and managers of the company for which
> the plaintiff was liquidator."

On 20 May 1991, the writ was seemingly amended by deleting Mr Ward as the plaintiff
and inserting as the plaintiffs William Gaskell Group Ltd, William Gaskell Upholland
Ltd and William Gaskell Warehousing Ltd. There was no amendment to the identity of
the defendants and the indorsement on the writ remained the same. After a number of   D
false attempts at service of the writ, it was eventually served on the two defendants on
26 September 1991.

Following an application by the defendants to strike out the action on the grounds that
a statement of claim had not been served, a document purporting to be the statement of
claim was served on 19 December 1991. That document assumed in favour of the
plaintiffs, first, that Barry John Ward had been rejoined as a plaintiff; second, that   E
Waldis Investments, the assignee of the original debenture holder, had been joined as
the third defendant and, thirdly, that the writ had been duly amended so as to authorise
by the indorsement the claims made in the statement of claim on behalf of not only
Group but Upholland and Warehousing as well.

The claim made in the statement of claim is, in effect, that the assets of Group,
Upholland and Warehousing were subject to floating charges, pursuant to the three   F
debentures granted originally to Midland Bank and that, as such, the proceeds of sale of
those assets should have been utilised in discharging the preferential liabilities to which
I have referred.

The claim made by the plaintiffs is based on breach of a statutory duty alleged to arise
out of sec. 94 of the *Companies Act* 1948, in the case of the first two defendants, the
receivers, and in the case of the third defendant is based on a constructive trust alleged   G
to arise from knowledge of the statutory duty and the receipt, by Waldis, of the balance
of the proceeds of the realisation. It is asserted that Waldis thereby came under a duty to
apply the proceeds so received in satisfaction of the preferential liabilities.

The assets which are alleged to have been subject to the floating charges are referred
to in para. 18 of the statement of claim as being identified in the three schedules annexed
to it. The three schedules are, in effect, a summary of the receivers' receipts and
payments from 13 June 1984–12 June 1987 in respect of each of the three companies.   H
Schedule 1 relates to Group and indicates that the receipts were in respect of the sale of
property, rents, interest and insurance refund. In the case of Upholland, the receipts
were overwhelmingly book debts, but there was a little over £1,000 in relation to the sale
of a car and a vehicle licence refund. In the case of Warehousing, the receipts were, so
far as material, only book debtors.

A   The applications before me are two summonses by the plaintiffs for leave to join Mr Ward as an additional plaintiff and to join Waldis as the third defendant; and for leave to amend the indorsement on the writ.

This is opposed by the defendants, who claim that the statement of claim, even if leave were granted, does not disclose a cause of action so that, the various leaves sought should be refused. In addition, the defendants have, themselves, applied by summons for orders striking out the plaintiffs' claim, or specified parts of it, under RSC, O. 18,
B   r. 19, as being hopelessly bad claims or, alternatively, for the determination of various issues of law pursuant to O. 14A. If they fail on those two points, then they seek an order for security for costs.

One of the points raised by the defendants, in their application to strike out, is that there is no duty under sec. 94 of the *Companies Act* 1948 owed by receivers, or a debenture holder, to the company itself, or the liquidator of the company. It is said that
C   the duty is owed to the preferential creditors alone, who are, in effect, the beneficiaries under that section. To meet that point, on 16 November 1992, Mr Ward, on behalf of and as a liquidator of all three companies, took an assignment from the Customs and Excise of the benefit of a preferential debt due to Customs and Excise. Notice of that assignment was given to the defendants on 18 November 1992. That assignment has prompted a further application by the plaintiffs for further leave to amend the indorsement on the writ and in relation to the statement of claim which they otherwise seek to pursue.
D   Common to each application of either the plaintiffs or the defendants are a series of questions of law. The first in logical order arises from para. 12 of the statement of claim. Having set out the various provisions of the debentures, to which I shall return in a moment, para. 12 alleges:

"Upon the aforesaid transfer being executed . . ."

That is to say the transfer of the benefit of the debenture from Midland Bank to Waldis
E   Investments:

". . . the charges on the book and other debts of Group, Upholland and Warehousing, created by the said debentures, ceased to be fixed and became, at law, floating charges thereon."

That is the first point to be considered because, unless the charges were floating charges, sec. 94 can have no operation in relation to the assets referred to in certain parts of the
F   schedules to the statement of claim.

The debentures granted to Midland Bank by each of the three companies are in the same form. Clause 1 provides:

"This charge shall be security for the payment and discharge of the moneys and liabilities hereinafter defined."

Clause 2 defines the moneys and liabilities in wide terms so as to include any primary
G   liability as debtor, as well as a secondary liability as guarantor. Clause 3 contains an acknowledgement that I need not dwell on, and cl. 4 provides as follows:

"The company, as beneficial owner, hereby charges in favour of the bank:

(a) by way of first fixed charge, all book debts and other debts now and from time to time hereafter due, owing or incurred to the company, other than such of the said debts as the bank may have specifically agreed in writing to exclude from such first fixed charge (hereinafter collectively called 'debts'), and
H   and

(b) by way of floating charge, the undertaking of the company and all other its property whatsoever and wheresoever, both present and future, including its uncalled capital for the time being, and such of the book debts and other debts referred to in cl. 4(A) which are not charged hereunder by way of first fixed charged (hereinafter collectively called 'the assets')."

Thus, cl. 4 sets out a clear division between the first fixed charge on book debts, save those excepted by the bank, that is para. (a), and those debts are defined as "the debts", and para. (b) which confers a floating charge in respect of all other property of the company, such other property being defined as "the assets".

Clause 5 contains a number of restrictions, the first two of which relate to the debts, and the last three of which relate to the assets. Thus, it is only the first two which are relevant for present purposes. They are as follows:

"The company shall not, except with the prior written consent of the bank:

(a) purport to create. or permit to subsist over all or any of the debts, any mortgage, charge, lien, pledge or other security, other than this charge, or

(b) release, exchange, compound, set-off, grant time or indulgence in respect of or in any other manner deal with all or any of the debts, save as hereinafter expressly provided."

Clause 6 then contains a number of further restrictions, the first four of which relate to the debts as defined in cl. 4(a). The remaining ones relate to other assets and are not material. The material ones are as follows:

"Until this charge is discharged, the company will:

(a) get in and realise the debts in the ordinary course of its business, which shall not extend to the selling or assigning or in any other way factoring or discounting the same, and hold the proceeds of such getting in and realisation of the debts until payment to the special account, as hereinafter provided, upon trust for the bank,

(b) pay the proceeds of such getting in and realisation of the debts into such separate and denominated account with the bank (the special account) as the bank may require,

(c) not be entitled to withdraw from the special account all or any moneys standing to the credit thereof, except with the prior consent of the bank,

(d) if called upon so to do by the bank, execute a legal assignment of the debts to the bank in such terms as the bank may require, and give such notice thereof to the debtors from whom the debts are due, owing or incurred and take any such other steps as the bank may require to effect such legal assignment."

In the statement of claim, but not in argument, reference is also made to the provisions of cl. 7, which provide that:

"At any time before this charge is discharged (and whether or not the same shall become enforceable under the provisions hereinafter contained) the bank may, if and whenever and so often as it shall think fit, apply the whole or any part of the moneys from time to time standing to the credit of the special account in or towards the discharge of all or any of the moneys and liabilities and may pay the same to the credit of any other nominated account (including an account opened by the bank for the purpose) as security for any contingent or future liability of the company to the bank."

Clause 29, so far as material, provides:

"Where the context so admits;

(a) the expression 'the company' shall include its successors and permitted assigns, and the expression 'the bank' shall include its successors and assigns."

A   As I have indicated, the statement of claim in para. 12 accepts that the charge on the book debts, when the debenture was vested in the Midland Bank, was a fixed charge in accordance with the terms of the debenture. Thus, this is not a case in which the label the parties have chosen to put upon the charge is in any way incorrect. The question is whether the effect of the assignment by Midland Bank to Waldis Investments is, in law, to make what was previously a fixed charge a floating charge.

B   It is to be noticed, at the outset, that there is no allegation of fact, such as to give rise to any inference of a waiver of the rights arising under the debenture, or a variation of the terms of the debenture at the time of, or consequent upon, the assignment by Midland Bank to Waldis.

As stated in *Re Armagh Shoes* [1982] NI 59 at p. 62B, the contract constituted by the debenture must be construed by reference to the facts as they were, or might be foreseen to be, at the time it was executed and not by reference to the subsequent conduct of the

C   parties: see *James Miller & Partners Ltd v Whitworth Street Estates (Manchester) Ltd* [1970] AC 583.

For the plaintiffs it was contended that whilst the debenture itself envisaged the possibility of assignment and that the assignment might be to a person who was not itself a licensed bank, in such circumstances the restrictions imposed by cl. 6(b) could not be applicable and, therefore, I think the words used were, must "fall away".

D   The point is simply this: it is accepted that in most parts of the debenture it is perfectly possible to read into the debenture the name of "Waldis Investments" in place of the name of or reference to the bank, except in cl. 6(b). In cl. 6(a) one starts off with the proceeds of sale having to be got in and, until placed to the credit of the special account, being held in trust for — on this hypothesis — Waldis Investments. But then para. (b) provides:

E   "pay the proceeds of such getting in and realisation of the debts into such separate and denominated account with the bank (the special account) as the bank may require."

The point is that the first reference to the bank must remain a reference to Midland Bank plc because you can only have such an account with a licensed bank, whereas the second reference to the bank can perfectly properly be read as Waldis Investments. It is submitted that the result of so reading it is that on any subsequent operation of the

F   account, after the assignment, two consents are required. First, that of the bank where the account is held, because that is the person who will have to pay the cheque; but secondly, the consent of Waldis Investments because they are now, for that purpose, treated as being the bank, pursuant to the assignment. It is said that such a restriction is so onerous that it must be assumed that that cannot have been what the parties intended and that, therefore, there must have been some relaxation of the restrictions which were

G   previously applicable.

I have been referred to two passages in the judgment of *Farwell* J in *Re Yorkshire Woolcombers Association Ltd* at first instance. They are quoted in *Armagh Shoes* at pp. 69 and 72. At 69E, he is quoted as stating:

        "The very essence of a specific charge is that the assignee takes possession, and is the person entitled to receive the book debts at once. So long as he licenses the

H   mortgagor to go on receiving the book debts and carry on the business, it is within the exact definition of a floating security."([1903] 2 Ch 284 at p. 289)

Then, at p. 72G, *Farwell* J is quoted in another passage in his judgment in the *Yorkshire Woolcombers* case as follows:

        "Now it is quite plain on the construction of the deed itself, that it was not intended to stop the company; the company was clearly intended to go on. These

A

book debts are a considerable portion of the assets of the company and, at the date of the deed amounted to £71,000. If the assignment is to be treated as a specific mortgage or charge or disposition, then the company had no business to receive one single book debt after the date of it; but if, on the other hand, although not so called, the company was intended to go on receiving the book debts and to use them for the purpose of carrying on its business, then it contains the true elements of a floating security."([1903] 2 Ch 284 at p. 288)

B

It seems to me that it is necessary to trace the recent decision on the creation of fixed or floating charges in respect of existing or future book debts. For present purposes, it starts with the decision of *Slade* J in *Siebe Gorman v Barclays Bank* [1979] 2 Lloyd's Rep 142. In that case, the relevant debenture purported to charge all book debts by way of first fixed charge and provided that during the continuance of the security, the company should pay into an account with the bank all moneys etc. representing the book debts.

C

At p. 158, *Slade* J dealt with the question of whether it was possible, as a matter of law, to create a fixed charge on future book debts. He concluded that it was and that in that case the debenture was effective to do so. He said, at p. 159:

"If the debenture on its true construction had given the bank no rights whatsoever, at a time when the account of R H McDonald Ltd was in credit, to prevent the company from spending in the ordinary course of business all or any of the proceeds of book debts paid into its account, I would have been inclined to regard the charge, for all the wording of the debenture, as doing no more than 'hovering over and so to speak floating with' the book debts, within the words of Lord Macnaghten."

D

He then went on to conclude that:

"In my judgment, however, it is perfectly possible, in law, for a mortgagor, by way of continuing security for future advances, to grant to a mortgagee a charge on future book debts in a form which creates in equity a specific charge on the proceeds of such debts as soon as they are received and consequently prevents the mortgagor from disposing of an unencumbered title to the subject matter of such charge without the mortgagee's consent, even before the mortgagee has taken steps to enforce its security . . ."

E

F

The essential point of that case, therefore, was the existence of the account into which the proceeds of the book debt had to be paid. That was held by *Slade* J to be a sufficient restriction to remove the third characteristic of a floating charge, referred to by *Romer* LJ in the *Yorkshire Woolcombers Association* case [1903] 2 Ch 284 at p. 295, where he described it as follows:

"(3) if you find that by the charge it is contemplated that, until some future step is taken by or on behalf of those interested in the charge, the company may carry on its business in the ordinary way as far as concerns the particular class of assets I am dealing with."

G

Subsequent cases include *Re Keenan Bros Ltd* (1986) 2 BCC 98,970, in which it was held that it was possible, in law, for there to be a fixed charge on future book debts and that in that case there was such a fixed charge. The essential point was that the proceeds of the book debts had to be paid into a special account with the bank designated for that purpose.

H

Cases going the other way are *Re Armagh Shoes Ltd* [1982] NI 59 and *Re Brightlife Ltd* (1986) 2 BCC 99,359. In each case the result has depended on the proper construction of the debenture in question.

A   It seems to me that in this case it is plain from the restrictions imposed by cl. 6, para. (a) and (b), that the consent of the debenture holder was required for the use of the proceeds of the book debts in the continued operation of the companies' businesses. When the debenture holder was the bank, in effect, the consent of one person only was required, because the bank was the person holding the account and had to decide whether or not to pay the cheque drawn on that account, as well as the debenture holder having to decide whether or not to consent to the use of the money. But the requirement
B   for the bank's consent would, for example, have precluded the company from complaining if the bank refused to pay a cheque drawn on the denominated account when that account was in credit.

     The effect of the assignment has been to divide the identity of the person whose consent is required, in the sense that Midland Bank, or such other bank as holds the account, would have to make the decision as banker whether or not to pay the cheque
C   when the account was in debit, but the consent of the debenture holder continues to be required after the assignment. He has to decide whether or not to permit the special account to be drawn on at all and, if so, for what purpose. After the assignment, that person is Waldis Investments. Far from the restrictions falling away because they are, as alleged, commercially inoperable, it seems to me that they remain exactly the same as they were before but require the consent of Waldis. Previously the requisite consent was
D   that of the bank, which had to consent, anyway, because it was the holder of the account. But I see nothing whatever, in the effect of the assignment, in its bearing on the effect of the restrictions, to create after the assignment a floating charge where, by definition and as admitted, before assignment it was a fixed charge.

     I conclude, therefore, that in so far as the claim made by the plaintiffs is related to the allegation that the book debts coming within cl. 4(a) of the debenture executed by each
E   of the companies were assets in respect of which there was a duty imposed by sec. 94 of the *Companies Act* 1948, that allegation is wrong in law and that is a point which has to be taken into account in deciding whether to grant the relief sought by any and, if so, which of the parties' various summonses.

[Automatic crystallisation]

F   **Morritt J:** In the judgment I delivered about half an hour ago I concluded that on the transfer of the benefit of a debenture from the Midland Bank to Waldis Investments, the charge on the book debts remained fixed and did not become floating. The consequence was, that the whole of sch. 3 to the statement of claim had to be struck out, as did the claim made by William Gaskell Warehousing Ltd.

     The next point which would have arisen, had it not been conceded by the plaintiffs, was whether or not the proceeds of sale of the property comprised in the charge made by
G   William Gaskell Group Ltd in June 1982 contained a floating charge so as to raise the argument under sec. 94. That point was conceded, with the result that sch. 1 is also to be struck out.

     In sch. 2, the claim to be advanced by William Gaskell Upholland Ltd was in relation to receipts totalling £216,000-odd: £215,571 was in respect of book debts which, in accordance with my judgment, has to be struck out, leaving only receipts in respect of
H   the sale of a car, £750, and vehicle licence refunds, £408.32.

     Thus, the claim by Upholland in relation to the car and the vehicle licence refund, raises the question whether the effect of the assets sale agreement of 12 June 1984 and the facts as deposed to, give rise to an automatic crystallisation of the floating charge, to which the car and licence refunds were originally subject, so as to preclude the application of sec. 94.

As I have said, it is not in dispute that the vehicle and the licence refunds came within A
cl. 4(b) of the debenture so that the charge was a floating charge, unless and until crystallised.

It was decided by *Nourse* J in *Re Woodroffes (Musical Instruments) Ltd* [1986] Ch 366, that the cessation of business necessarily put an end to a company's capacity to deal with its assets and, therefore, automatically caused a floating charge to crystallise. This point is dealt with at pp. 376–378 of his judgment. After referring to the assumptions B made in all the reported cases as to automatic crystallisation, at p. 377G *Nourse* J said:

> "On that state of the authorities it would be very difficult for me to question it, even if I could see a good ground for doing so. On the contrary, it seems to me that it is in accordance with the essential nature of a floating charge. The thinking behind the creation of such charges has always been a recognition that a fixed charge on the whole undertaking and assets of a company would paralyse it and C prevent it from carrying on its business: see, e.g. *In re Florence Land and Public Works Co., Ex parte Moor* (1878) 10 Ch.D. 530, 541, *per* Sir George Jessel M.R. On the other hand, it is a mistake to think that the chargee has no remedy while the charge is still floating. He can always intervene and obtain an injunction to prevent the company from dealing with its assets otherwise than in the ordinary course of its business. That no doubt is one reason why it is preferable to describe the charge as 'hovering', a word which can bear an undertone of menace, rather D than as 'dormant'. A cessation of business necessarily puts an end to the company's dealings with its assets. That which kept the charge hovering has now been released and the force of gravity causes it to settle and fasten on the subject of the charge within its reach and grasp. The paralysis, whilst it may still be unwelcome, can no longer be resisted. For a more concise statement of this analysis I am indebted to Professor R. M. Goode in his collected lectures, *Legal Problems of* E *Credit and Security*, 1st ed. (1982), p. 57. I hold that the assumption correctly represents the law. Accordingly, if the company in fact ceased business on 27 August, or some other date before 1 September, the bank's charge crystallised then and not on 1 September."

That decision was referred to, without dissent, by *Hoffmann* J in *Brightlife* (1986) 2 BCC 99,359. Whilst not technically binding on me, I see no reason not to follow the F decision of *Nourse* J and have every reason to do so, in the light of the passage which I have read.

The question is, therefore, whether prior to the appointment of the receivers on 13 June 1984, Upholland had ceased business so as to cause a crystallisation of the floating charge, to which the vehicle and the licence refund was subject.

The evidence on this point consists of the agreement itself and the affidavit filed on G behalf of the defendants. So far as the agreement is concerned, it is dated 12 June 1984 and it recites wrongly, according to the evidence, that the purchaser is a wholly owned subsidiary of Waldis Investments, and it then provides in cl. 1:

> "The vendors shall sell and the purchaser shall purchase, as at the close of business on the date hereof, the haulage division of the vendors, comprising the following assets . . ." H

Paragraph (c) comprises:

> "All plant, machinery, furniture, fixtures, fittings, motor vehicles, trailers, tractors, units and other chattels used by the vendors in connection with the haulage business."

A   And para. (f):

> "Save as herein provided all other assets of the vendors owned by him in connection with the haulage business."

Clause 2 provided that:

> "The consideration should be the discharge of hire purchase and leasing liabilities."

B   Clause 3, excluding book debts and cash, and cl. 4 provided that the consideration should be the total of the valuation, which was provided for and subsequently carried out on 1 August.

Clause 6 provided:

> "Completion shall take place on 12 June 1984 when the vendors shall transfer all of the assets hereby agreed to be sold."

C   The evidence in this respect is contained in the affidavit of Mr McKendry, filed on behalf of the defendants, and in para. 14 he refers to the asset sale agreement. In para. 15 he states:

> "The result of the asset sale agreement was to cause Upholland to cease trading. In effect, the haulage business was hived down. I should mention one other matter which arises out of the agreement . . ."

And then he refers to the fact that Lesley Marketing was not a wholly owned subsidiary
D   of Waldis.

In para. 35, he states:

> "Upon completion of the asset sale agreement, Upholland ceased to trade. I understand this to be an event on which the Upholland floating charge had crystallised. This occurred prior to appointment of receivers, so that upon their subsequent appointment the floating charges were no longer floating but were instead fixed. If this argument is accepted, then in my respectful submission the claim filed in respect of Upholland should be struck out."

E

That affidavit and the passages that I have quoted was not challenged in any way in the evidence in answer sworn on behalf of the plaintiffs. There were, I think, two affidavits sworn on their behalf which did not take up that point at all.

It seems to me that on that state of the evidence, the only possible inference is that the asset sale agreement was completed as provided for, at the close of business on 12 June,
F   and that the necessary consequence of that was that Upholland ceased to carry on business on 12 June because it had no other business than the haulage business referred to. If it had been the case that there was any issue in this respect, then I would have expected that the liquidator, on behalf of Upholland, would have instructed solicitors, on Upholland's behalf, to put in issue the allegations made by Mr McKendry.

It seems to me, therefore, that on the evidence there is only one conclusion, namely
G   that Upholland ceased business on 12 June and that was, by definition, prior to the appointment of the receivers and the opening of business on 13 June.

There is also another reason why it seems to me that the claim in this respect, sought to be advanced by Upholland, is unsustainable. In the statement of claim, para. 14, Upholland, amongst others, asserts the provisions of the asset sale agreement of 12 June 1984 to which I have referred. Part of the allegation is that the sale included the plant, machinery, furniture, fixtures, fittings and motor vehicles and the full benefit of all
H   pending contracts in connection with the haulage business. There was, therefore, an assertion on behalf of Upholland that the car itself, and I would infer the licence refunds that seem to be attached to it, were sold on 12 June 1984 to Lesley Marketing. If that be the case, then, whether or not a charge crystallised on the cessation of business at the end of 12 June, the car itself had ceased to be an asset of Upholland and, therefore, was not subject to a floating charge which was capable of crystallising.

A

However, when it comes to para. 18 of the statement of claim, there the Upholland claim is maintained in relation to sch. 2 of the statement of claim, which sets out in terms the proceeds of sale of the car and the vehicle licence refunds.

It seems to me that on that alternative ground, Upholland's own claim shows that there can be no liability under sec. 94 in respect of the motor vehicle because, on the basis of its own assertions, the motor vehicle belonged not to Upholland but to Lesley Marketing. On that alternative ground as well, it seems to me that there can be no possible dispute or claim in relation to a duty under sec. 94 in respect of the car and vehicle licence refunds.

B

I think it follows from that — but I will hear counsel further — that I dismiss all the summonses issued on behalf of the plaintiffs and I grant the relief sought by the summons issued by the defendant, to strike out the action and dismiss it.

[Costs]

C

Morritt J: Having decided that the two summonses issued, as I stated earlier, by the plaintiffs should be dismissed and that I should make an order on the defendant's summons striking out the action, the question now arises as to what to do about the costs.

It appears from the affidavit of Steven Andrew Wyles — the date of swearing which is not apparent from the copy in the bundle — that the proceedings were commenced, on counsel's advice, and that they were funded, so far as the plaintiffs were concerned, by the preferential creditors, on whose behalf in substance the proceedings were commenced.

D

The application made by Waldis Investments and Mr Venning and Mr Highley is that I should order the liquidator to pay the costs personally.

It is necessary, I think, to treat each summons separately. In terms of time, the first one is the summons seeking leave to add Waldis Investments as the third defendant. That was issued on 1 April 1992. The title is expressed to be, "1. Barry John Ward . . .", then as (2), (3) and (4) the names of the companies are set out as plaintiffs, and the body of the summons says it is an application by the first plaintiff (referring back to Barry John Ward) for an order giving him liberty to join the third defendant. The summons is stated to have been taken out by Hammond Suddards, and the address is given, solicitors for the first plaintiff.

E

F

The second summons, dated 8 June 1992, is even clearer. In that case the title does not show Mr Ward to be a plaintiff, but in the body of the summons it states that it is an application by Barry John Ward, liquidator of the plaintiff companies, for an order that he be added as first plaintiff in these proceedings.

It is accepted by counsel for the plaintiffs that in that summons, at least, the liability for costs rests on Mr Ward personally, as being the applicant.

G

It seems to me that there is no distinction that can be drawn between the two of them. Both summonses are, in one description or another, applications by Barry John Ward. In each case the application has failed, and in each case I think that Barry John Ward should be ordered to pay the costs of the successful parties, being Mr Highley and Mr Venning, on the summons dated 8 June 1992, and Mr Highley, Mr Venning and Waldis Investments on the Summons dated 1 April 1992.

H

The third summons is a summons issued by Mr Highley and Mr Venning seeking an order striking out the statement of claim and dismissing the action, and various alternative forms of relief to which I have acceded. That summons was, as it was bound to be, addressed to the plaintiffs which were the three named companies. Mr Ward was not a party to that summons, nor was he, when the summons was issued, a party to the action in which the summons was brought. He was not, therefore, a party to either set of

A proceedings and the only jurisdiction to make an order for costs against him would arise under the *Aiden Shipping* decision and sec. 51 of the *Supreme Court Act* 1981. Under those provisions, it is plain that in what has been described in the subsequent cases as exceptional circumstances, it is open to the court to make a non-party pay the costs of the proceedings.

B I do not see any justification in this case for ordering the costs to be paid on that summons by Mr Ward. He is not a party. He has done nothing in the action, except as liquidator of the three plaintiffs. What he did as liquidator was done on the advice of counsel and though in other respects he has claimed to be a party already, that has not misled the defendants in any way. They have not, therefore, been in any way disadvantaged by any false representation made by the liquidator and I do not think the liquidator has himself been guilty of any misconduct.

C It would have been open to Mr Highley and Mr Venning either to seek an order for security for costs earlier or, alternatively, to have consented to Mr Ward becoming a plaintiff, which is what he asked for and which, at one stage, they appear to have consented to, but then withdrew their consent. Had that happened, then Mr Ward would have been personally liable as a plaintiff. As a third possibility, they might, but have not, have sought an order against the preferential creditors who, in accordance with the evidence, are the persons who are in fact funding or did fund this litigation.

D As I say, not one of those three courses has been adopted and I am, therefore, left with the position whereby the liquidator has commenced proceedings in the name of three companies of which he is liquidator, on the advice of counsel, which have failed. That is not, in my judgment, sufficient reason for making him liable to pay the costs personally.

(*Order accordingly*)

E _____

F

G

H

Re Kentish Homes Ltd.

Chancery Division (Companies Court).
Sir Donald Nicholls V-C.
Judgment delivered 29 January 1993.

> *Winding up — Whether post-liquidation community charges were provable —*
> *Whether payable as liquidation expenses — Insolvency Act 1986, sec. 115;*
> *Insolvency Rules 1986 (SI 1986/1925), r. 13.12.*

This was an application by the liquidators of Kentish Homes Ltd ("the company") to stay magistrates' court summonses issued by a local authority against the company for liability orders in respect of unpaid community charges, and for directions on how the company's liability for community charge ranked in the winding up.

The company, a property developer, went into receivership in July 1989 and into creditors' voluntary liquidation in August 1989. At the receivership date the company owed the charge holder, a building society, some £25.5m. The society advanced money to the receivers to complete blocks of flats which the company was developing. The proceeds of sale of flats were applied in development costs, receivership expenses and towards repayment of the post-receivership advances to the receivers. It appeared that the society would rank as an unsecured creditor for the original loans of £25.5m, with interest. There was little prospect of a significant dividend being paid to unsecured creditors.

The company, as freehold owner, was liable to pay standard community charges under sec. 3(3) of the Local Government Finance Act 1988 in respect of each flat from, in effect, six months after practical completion of the flat. The flats in question were completed after the company went into liquidation.

Held, declaring that the company was liable for standard community charges in the amounts in question for the relevant periods, but that the amount due was not provable as a debt in the winding up of the company, and refusing to direct the liquidators to pay the charges as an expense in the liquidation:

1. The liability was not a debt provable in the company's winding up under r. 13.12 of the Insolvency Rules 1986, because the liability did not exist at the date when the company went into liquidation and the liability which arose post-liquidation was not by reason of an obligation incurred before the commencement of the liquidation, but arose by reason of the company being the freehold owner of the empty but completed flats on each day throughout the relevant periods.

2. There was no scope for the court to direct payment of the liability by the liquidators as a liquidation expense on the basis of an obligation arising from property retained by the liquidators for the purposes of the liquidation. The liquidators did not remain in occupation of the flats. They had no hand in the completion of the building works, nor in the sale of the finished flats. The receiver took over the flats to the exclusion of the liquidators. He went into possession, and he was responsible for carrying out the work and then for marketing the flats.

3. Nor was there any special equity entitling the charging authority to be paid as a liquidation expense. It would be unfair to the proving creditors to prefer the charging authority ahead of all of them in a case where the liquidators had no use of or control over the flats in respect of which the charges arose.

4. It would be wrong to direct payment of the community charges as a liquidation expense, with a view to enabling the liquidators to have recourse against the receiver, because that would enable the charging authority to achieve indirectly via the liquidators what it could not achieve directly by a claim against the receiver.

A   The following cases were referred to in the judgment:

Atlantic Computer Systems plc, Re [1990] BCC 859; [1992] Ch 505.
Berkeley Securities (Property) Ltd, Re [1980] 1 WLR 1589.
Blazer Fire Lighter Ltd, Re [1895] 1 Ch 402.
Downer Enterprises Ltd, Re [1974] 1 WLR 1460.
Great Eastern Electric Co Ltd, Re [1941] Ch 241.
Islington Metal and Plating Works Ltd, Re (1983) 1 BCC 98,933; [1984] 1 WLR 14.

B   *Lancashire Cotton Spinning Co, Re* (1887) 35 ChD 656.
Lines Bros Ltd, Re [1983] Ch 1.
Liverpool Corporation v Hope [1938] 1 KB 751.
Mesco Properties Ltd, Re [1980] 1 WLR 96.
National Arms and Ammunition Co, Re (1885) 28 ChD 474.
Oak Pits Colliery Co, Re (1882) 21 ChD 322.

C   *Yourell & Anor v Hibernian Bank Ltd* [1918] AC 372.

Sarah Harman (instructed by D J Freeman & Co) for the liquidators.

Benedict Patten (instructed by the London Borough of Tower Hamlets legal department) for the charging authority.

Simon Mortimore QC (instructed by Hammond Suddards) for the building society and the receiver.

D

JUDGMENT

Nicholls V-C: Community charges, often referred to as poll tax, were created by the *Local Government Finance Act* 1988. The winding up of insolvent companies is governed by the *Insolvency Act* 1986. This case is concerned with the interaction of these two sets of statutory provisions. The problem concerns the remedies available for the recovery of community charges from a company when the liability arises after the company has

E   gone into liquidation. From April 1993 community charges are being abolished and replaced by council tax. Although community charges are nearing the end of their life, the relevant provisions in the *Local Government Finance Act* 1992 regarding council tax are in a similar form to the Act of 1988. So the issue raised in this case will arise equally under the legislation creating the new tax which is to replace community charges.

The history

F

In the late 1980s when the property market was still flourishing, the company Kentish Homes Ltd embarked on a major residential and commercial development on a site in London's docklands, in the London Borough of Tower Hamlets. The company planned to develop Burrells Wharf as 12 residential and commercial blocks, including four residential blocks to be given the nautical names of The Beacon, The Charthouse, The Platehouse and The Porthouse. The company owned the freehold of the site, and was

G   granted a facility of some £40m by Halifax Building Society. This facility was secured by a first legal charge dated 21 July 1988.

Work proceeded, but by the summer of 1989 the property market in the docklands area was beginning to wilt, and the company encountered serious financial difficulties. On 25 July 1989 the Halifax appointed receivers of Burrells Wharf under the legal charge. By that date the company's indebtedness to the Halifax, in respect of money drawn down plus interest, was about £25.5m. These receivers were later replaced by

H   another receiver appointed by the Halifax. On 3 August 1989 the company went into creditors' voluntary liquidation.

The Halifax was advised that a sale of Burrells Wharf in its then state would be likely to achieve a price of only about £3m. The society decided to complete the development of the four residential blocks I have mentioned, and to "mothball" the rest of the property until there were signs of a recovery in the property market. To achieve that end

a further £13m-odd was advanced by the Halifax to the receivers. Practical completion   A
of the construction of The Platehouse took place in June 1989, that is before the
appointment of the receivers. The other three residential blocks reached the stage of
practical completion in March and April 1990, some months after the receivers were
appointed and after the company went into liquidation.

The residential blocks comprise 151 self-contained flats. About 104 of these have now
been sold, by the granting of long leases. The sales have yielded almost £9m. To date the
receivers have spent about £17m on the further development of Burrells Wharf. The   B
proceeds of sale of the flats are being applied by the Halifax in further development
costs, receivership expenses and towards repayment of the £13m-odd advanced to the
receivers. The Halifax hopes the proceeds of sale of the remaining 47 flats will be
sufficient to repay the post-receivership advances with interest. It is unlikely that the
development of the remainder of Burrells Wharf will be completed for several years. As
matters now stand, it is likely that the Halifax will rank as an unsecured creditor for the   C
original loans of £25.5m with interest. There is little prospect of a significant dividend
being paid to unsecured creditors.

The company was also engaged in the development of a nearby freehold site known
as Bow Quarter, comprising 184 flats in five buildings. This was financed with money
advanced by Security Pacific National Bank on the security of a first legal charge dated
18 May 1989. Security Pacific appointed receivers over Bow Quarter on the same day as
the Halifax. These flats were later completed. All the flats have been sold by the   D
receivers, but there was no surplus available for payment to the company. I need not go
further into the facts regarding this development, because it is accepted that the relevant
facts and issues arising in respect of Bow Quarter stand on all fours with the Burrells
Wharf development.

The proceedings

Until sold the flats stood empty. No one was living in them. The company, as freehold   E
owner, was liable to pay standard community charges in respect of each flat from, in
effect, six months after practical completion of the flat. When a flat was sold and a long
lease was granted to a buyer, the company ceased to be liable. I shall refer to the periods
for which the company was liable to pay community charge in respect of the flats as "the
relevant periods". In consequence the company is liable to pay to the London Borough
of Tower Hamlets amounts of the order of £1,806 in respect of Bow Quarter and £65,920   F
in respect of Burrells Wharf. The latter sum will fall to be reduced if further flats are sold
before the end of the current financial year. The sums are approximate as the precise
amounts have not been finally agreed between the parties.

These amounts were, and are, payable by the company. Not having received payment,
in January and February 1992 Tower Hamlets caused 182 summonses to be issued in the
Inner London Thames area magistrates' court seeking liability orders. The summonses   G
were issued against the company even though the company was in the course of being
wound up as an insolvent company. The liquidators then made to this court the
application now before me. The liquidators seek, in short, an order staying the summonses
in the magistrates' court and directions on how the company's liability for community
charge ranks in the winding up, bearing in mind (1) that all the relevant periods
commenced after the company had gone into liquidation and (2) that throughout the
relevant periods it was the receivers, not the liquidators, who were in possession of the   H
flats and seeking to sell them.

The community charge legislation

Section 1 of the *Local Government Finance Act* 1988 conferred rights and imposed
duties on charging authorities in respect of personal community charges, standard

A community charges and collective community charges. Section 2 prescribed the circumstances in which a person is subject to a charging authority's personal community charge. Section 3 makes provision regarding standard community charge. Section 3(3) is the charging provision relevant in the present case. It provides that a person is subject to a charging authority's standard community charge on any day if he has at any time on the day a freehold interest in the whole of a self-contained part of a building which is situated in the authority's area, is not the sole or main residence of an individual, is a

B domestic property and is not subject to a lease for a term of six months or more. Thus liability to the charge accrues on a daily basis. Under sec. 6 the registration officer for a charging authority must complete and maintain a community charges register, containing an item in relation to each community charge to which a person becomes subject. The register must state, among other particulars, the name of the person subject to the charge and, in the case of the standard community charge, the address of the property by virtue of which the person is subject to the charge.

C
Section 14 prescribes how the amount payable as standard community charge is to be calculated. The amount set by the authority for its personal community charges for the financial year is to be multiplied by a multiplier fixed in accordance with sec. 40. Under sec. 40 the authority must determine a standard community charge multiplier for the properties in its area. The multiplier must be one of the following: 0, $\frac{1}{2}$, 1, $1\frac{1}{2}$ or 2. For each of the financial years in question Tower Hamlets fixed as 0 the multiplier for

D properties which were unoccupied and substantially unfurnished and whose erection was not substantially completed or in respect of which less than six months had elapsed since their erection was substantially completed. Once that period of six months had elapsed the multiplier, as fixed by the council, was 2 in respect of the flats with which this application is concerned. For the years 1991–92 and 1992–93, although not for the earlier year 1990–91, Tower Hamlets fixed as 0 the multiplier applicable to an unoccupied property where the person subject to the standard charge was a mortgagor and the

E mortgagee had taken possession under the mortgage.

The *Community Charges (Administration and Enforcement) Regulations* 1989 (SI 1989/438) contain provisions for the enforcement of community charges. It is common ground in the present case that the company is the chargeable person in respect of the flats for the relevant periods. Under reg. 29 the charging authority may apply to a magistrates' court for a liability order against a person who has failed to pay charges for which he is liable despite service of a demand notice and a reminder notice. The court is

F required to make the order if satisfied that the sum has become payable by the defendant and has not been paid. When such an order has been made against an individual, the authority may then make and serve an attachment of earnings order (reg. 32). Further, when a liability order has been made the authority may levy the appropriate amount by distress and sale of the goods of the debtor (reg. 39). If the debtor is an individual and the authority was unable to obtain payment in full by distress, the court may commit the debtor to prison if his failure to pay was due to his wilful refusal or culpable neglect

G (reg. 41). Regulation 43 deals with insolvency. Where a liability order has been made the amount due is deemed to be a debt, in the case of an individual, for the purposes of presentation of a bankruptcy petition under sec. 267 of the *Insolvency Act* 1986 or, in the case of a company, for the purposes of presentation of a winding-up petition under sec. 122(1)(f) of that Act. Finally, the court may make a charging order on the beneficial interest of the debtor in the property to which the charges relate (reg. 44). That remedy is applicable only where the community charge concerned was the collective community

H charge, which is not this case.

The winding-up legislation

I turn to apply these enforcement provisions to the case of a company. The provisions cause no difficulty if the period in respect of which the community charge is payable pre-dates the commencement of the winding up. They give the charging authority two

remedies: it may distrain, or it may present a winding-up petition. In the latter case the   A
amount due under the liability order will give the authority standing to present a petition
as a creditor. In the winding up the amount due will be provable as a debt. The
enforcement regulations do not expressly so provide but this follows, without the need
for express provision, from the fact that the company is obliged to pay the amount in
question to the charging authority. The amount due will be provable whether the
winding-up order was made on a petition presented by the charging authority or on the   B
petition of another creditor or, indeed, of the company itself. The authority will rank as
an unsecured creditor: in none of the legislation is there any provision giving any special
status, whether preferential or postponed, to community charge liability.

It is otherwise if the community charge liability arose only after the company had gone
into liquidation. Pursuant to the rule-making power contained in sec. 411 of the
Insolvency Act and para. 12 and 13 of Sch. 8 to the Act, the *Insolvency Rules* 1986
(SI 1986/1925) make provision for which debts are provable in a winding up. Rule 12.3(1)   C
provides:

> "Subject as follows, in both winding up and bankruptcy, all claims by creditors
> are provable as debts against the company or, as the case may be, the bankrupt,
> whether they are present or future, certain or contingent, ascertained or sounding
> only in damages."

This rule makes no express provision regarding the date at which claims, widely   D
defined, must exist. Rule 13.12 has the effect of making such provision by incorporating
a cut-off date into the definition of "debt". Rule 13.12(1) provides:

> " 'Debt', in relation to the winding up of a company, means (subject to the next
> paragraph) any of the following—
>
> (a)   any debt or liability to which the company is subject at the date on which it
>   goes into liquidation;   E
>
> (b)   any debt or liability to which the company may become subject after that
>   date by reason of any obligation incurred before that date; and
>
> (c)   any interest provable as mentioned in Rule 4.93(1)."

"Liability" includes a liability arising under an enactment (r. 13.12(4)).

In the present case the liability of the company in respect of the relevant periods
did not exist at the date when the company went into liquidation. So subpara. (a) does   F
not apply. Nor does subpara. (b) apply: the liability of the company which arose
post-liquidation was not by reason of an obligation incurred before the commencement
of the liquidation. The obligation arose by reason only of the company being the
freeholder owner of the empty but completed flats on each day throughout the relevant
periods. Hence in the present case the company's liability for these items of community
charge is not provable as a debt in the liquidation of the company.

I pause to note the incongruity of this conclusion in the case of community charges. It   G
is one thing to find that a debtor is unable to pay. The law provides creditors with
remedies, although it is a matter of everyday experience that in many cases creditors
find the remedies yield no fruit. That, unhappily, is a creditor's misfortune: the law
cannot produce money where none exists. It is an altogether different thing to find that
the law provides no remedy at all when an obligation to pay money is not met, even
though the debtor may have assets. Leaving aside distress, the long-stop remedy   H
provided for non-payment of community charges by a company is the right to present a
winding-up petition. The value of the latter remedy, for what it may be worth in the
particular case, lies in the ability of the charging authority to procure that if a company
will not pay, its assets are realised and the charging authority will share in the proceeds
with the company's other creditors. But the effect of the winding-up rules is that,

A   although the company is still in existence, if the liability to pay community charge arose only after the commencement of the winding up, the charging authority has no remedy at all, because it is not even permitted to prove in the winding up. The company may be declaring a handsome dividend, but so long as the company remains insolvent the charging authority, in respect of post-liquidation community charge liability, cannot share at all in the distribution of the proceeds of the company's assets.

B   The cut-off provisions may, in general, work reasonably satisfactorily in respect of claims based on contract. Claims arising under contractual obligations incurred before the date on which the company went into liquidation are provable. As to payments under contracts made with a company after it has gone into liquidation, for example, if goods are supplied to a company pursuant to arrangements negotiated with the liquidator, in general such payments will rank for preferential treatment as expenses incurred in the winding up. Unquantified claims for damages in tort are not so favourably treated. In

C   the past, if a company went into liquidation before a claimant had been able to quantify his claim by judgment or agreement he was left out in the cold. In *Re Berkeley Securities (Property) Ltd* [1980] 1 WLR 1589 the court struggled hard to avoid this injustice. *Vinelott* J held that a claim for damages in tort is excluded from proof only if it has not been liquidated at the time the claimant comes in to prove. He is not entitled to disturb prior distributions to other creditors but, as regards undistributed assets, he is entitled

D   to a dividend enabling him to "catch up" with distributions already made to other creditors. In *Islington Metal & Plating Works Ltd* (1983) 1 BCC 98,933, *Harman* J pointed out the difficulties with this solution having regard to the then statutory provisions and an established line of authority. The particular problem raised in those two cases has now been addressed by r. 13.12(2):

> "In determining for the purposes of any provision of the Act or the Rules about winding up, whether any liability in tort is a debt provable in the winding up, the
E   company is deemed to become subject to that liability by reason of an obligation incurred at the time when the cause of action accrued."

So far as it enables some liabilities in tort to be proved, this provision ensures justice to tort claimants. However, it still leaves a tort claimant without any remedy if his cause of action arose after the date when the company went into liquidation. In some instances it will be a matter of chance whether a cause of action in tort accrues before or after the date of the commencement of the liquidation. If a company sells and supplies dangerous

F   goods, it will be a matter of chance whether they cause injury and damage pre- or post-liquidation, and it is only when the damage is sustained that the cause of action in tort accrues.

The position in the present case is even more striking. After a company has gone into liquidation the charging authority has no option but to continue to supply the services which give rise to the community charge. Admittedly, when the flats are unoccupied the

G   benefits they enjoy from these services are much more limited than when someone is living there. Nevertheless, the flats continue to have the benefit of some of the services even though, because the company is already in liquidation, the authority for its part cannot share in the distribution of the company's assets so long as the company remains insolvent. (If, in the event, the company is able to pay all its debts in full, it may be that the charging authority will be entitled to be paid before any surplus is distributed to the shareholders: see *Re Lines Brothers Ltd* [1983] Ch 1 at p. 21, per *Brightman* LJ, the

H   *Islington Metal* case, mentioned above, at pp. 22–24, and *Simonds* J in *Re Great Eastern Electric Co Ltd* [1941] Ch 241 at p. 245. This must be a comparatively rare occurrence.)

Liquidation expenses

It is against this background that the court is being asked to direct that the amounts due from the company to Tower Hamlets should be paid by the liquidators as expenses

in the winding up of the company. The obligation to make these payments is an
obligation of the company, and it arose while the company was being wound up. If the
court directs the liquidators to discharge this obligation of the company out of assets in
their hands, the payment will constitute an expense properly incurred in the winding up.
It will rank for payment as a "necessary disbursement" by the liquidators in the course
of their administration (sec. 115 and r. 4.218(m)).

An interesting illustration of the court giving such a direction is to be found in *Re
Mesco Properties Ltd* [1980] 1 WLR 96. There several properties were sold after a
company had gone into liquidation. Some of the sales were by the liquidator, others by a
receiver appointed under legal charges, and one of the sales was by the mortgagee bank
itself. In consequence a liability to corporation tax in respect of chargeable gains arose.
In each case the tax liability was that of the company, even though some of the sales had
been made by a receiver or the mortgagee. The liquidator was under no personal
liability. *Brightman* J held that payment of the tax was a necessary disbursement which
the liquidator was bound to make. The liquidator appealed. The Court of Appeal
dismissed the appeal. *Buckley* LJ said (at p. 100):

> "It must, in my view, be open to a liquidator to apply to the court for guidance
> upon the question whether, if he discharges a certain liability of the company in
> liquidation, the payment will be a necessary disbursement within the meaning of
> rule 195. That is what the liquidator is doing in this case. The company is liable for
> the tax which is due. The tax ought to be paid. The liquidator is the proper officer
> to pay it. When he pays it, he will clearly make a disbursement. In my judgment it
> will be a necessary disbursement within the meaning of the rule. Moreover,
> common sense and justice seem to me to require that it should be discharged in
> full in priority to the unsecured creditors, and to any expenses which rank lower
> in priority under rule 195. The tax is a consequence of the realisation of the assets
> in the course of the winding up of the company. That realisation was a necessary
> step in the liquidation; that is to say, in the administration of the insolvent estate."

The court's discretion: retention of property by the liquidator

In that case the court held that justice required that the post-liquidation tax liability
should be paid as a liquidation expense. In *Re Atlantic Computer Systems plc* [1990]
BCC 859 at pp. 864–865, this court noted that in determining whether an obligation of
the company arising after the commencement of the winding up should be discharged as
a liquidation expense, the court is exercising a discretion, albeit the discretion is
exercised in accordance with established principles. One of the circumstances in which
the court will normally direct payment of such an obligation as a liquidation expense is
when the debt or obligation arises from property retained by a liquidator for the
purposes of the liquidation. For example, when a liquidator retains the property for the
purpose of selling it to best advantage, the post-liquidation rent will be payable as an
expense of the liquidation (see *Re Oak Pits Colliery Co* (1882) 21 ChD 322 at p. 330, and
Re Downer Enterprises Ltd [1974] 1 WLR 1460 at pp. 1465–1468). Similarly as to rates:
if the liquidator remained in beneficial occupation of the property for the purposes of
the liquidation, post-liquidation rates would be payable in full as a liquidation expense:
see *Re Blazer Fire Lighter Ltd* [1895] 1 Ch 402, applying the test enunciated by *Bowen*
LJ in *Re National Arms and Ammunition Co* (1885) 28 ChD 474 at p. 482. (I pause to
interpose that the problem raised by the present case does not arise in respect of rates.
Rates are still payable in respect of non-domestic property. In the distant past the
problem did not arise because if the liquidator was not in beneficial occupation of the
property, there was no rating liability on the company. That was so because liability to
be rated depended upon beneficial occupation. The *Local Government Act* 1966
departed from this traditional concept by empowering rating authorities to rate the

A owners of unoccupied property. That is still the position, under sec. 45 of the *Local Government Finance Act* 1988. However that liability is subject to exceptions, currently prescribed by the *Non-Domestic Rating (Unoccupied Property) Regulations* 1989 (SI 1989/2261). The exceptions include the case where the owner is a company in the course of being wound up.)

B On the facts of the present case there is no scope for the application of this "retention by the liquidator" principle. Here the liquidators did not remain in occupation of the flats. The liquidators had no hand in the completion of the building works, nor in the sale of the finished flats. The receiver took over the flats to the exclusion of the liquidators. He went into possession, and he was responsible for carrying out the work and then for marketing the flats. I note, for good measure, that in so acting after the liquidation of the company the receiver was not acting as agent of the company.

C *A "special equity"*

That, however, is not the end of the matter. The courts have recognised that, outside the recognised categories of case such as the one just mentioned, there may be other cases where it would be inequitable for the company or the liquidator to rely on the statutory bar which precludes a creditor from taking any steps against the company or its property once the company has gone into liquidation. The post-liquidation debt or liability may have arisen in circumstances where, in the words of *Cotton* LJ in *Re*
D *Lancashire Cotton Spinning Co* (1887) 35 ChD 656 at p. 662, there is some "special equity" which entitles the creditor to ask the court to relieve him.

Tower Hamlets submitted that, indeed, it would be inequitable here if the authority cannot look to the liquidators for payment of the community charges in respect of the flats as expenses of the liquidation: if it cannot do so, Tower Hamlets will have no remedy. Unlike a lessor who may put an end to the company's use of property leased to
E it by forfeiting the lease for non-payment of the rent, Tower Hamlets is obliged to continue to provide services throughout the winding up. Years may elapse before all these flats are sold. The statute imposes liability on the owner and, unlike rates, Parliament has provided no exemption from community charges in respect of unoccupied property belonging to a company in the course of being wound up. Further, and importantly, if the liquidators are directed to pay the community charges as expenses of the liquidation they will have a right of recourse against the receiver. Thus the burden
F will fall where broadly it ought to fall. It was the receiver who developed and then sold the flats, and it is fair and reasonable that the community charges payable on the flats pending sale should be paid out of money coming to the hands of the receiver.

Section 109(8) of the Law of Property Act 1925

On this line of argument one of the points in issue is whether, if they paid the community charges as liquidation expenses, the liquidators would have any right of
G recourse against the receiver. The Halifax denied that they would. I shall consider this point next. Under its legal charge the powers of the Halifax as mortgagee included the statutory power to appoint "a receiver of the income of the mortgaged property" (sec. 101(1)(iii) of the *Law of Property Act* 1925). In addition the Halifax was expressly authorised to appoint a receiver and manager, with wide powers to complete the development of the property and to sell the property or any part of it. Although the
H document appointing the present receiver is a little ambiguous, I am satisfied that his appointment is to be read as an appointment under both the statutory power and the express power.

Section 109 of the Act of 1925 makes provision for, amongst other matters, some of the duties of a receiver appointed under the statutory power. Section 109(8) provides that "the receiver shall apply all money received by him" in a stated order of priorities.

A

Item (i) in the list, and first in the order of priority, is "discharge of all rents, taxes, rates and other outgoings whatever affecting the mortgaged property". Item (ii) concerns annual sums and other payments having priority to the mortgage in right of which the receiver was appointed. Next come the receiver's remuneration, insurance premiums and the cost of repairs, followed by interest, and then the principal, due under the mortgage. Any residue of money received by the receiver is payable to the person who, but for the possession of the receiver, would have been entitled to receive the income of the property or who is otherwise entitled to the mortgaged property.

B

The Halifax advanced several arguments concerning the applicability and effect of sec. 109(8). The Halifax submitted that sec. 109(8) has no application in this case because one of the mortgage conditions, condition 15, made express provision for the application of money arising from any exercise by the Halifax of any of the statutory and other powers referred to in condition 13. This express provision in the deed displaced the statutory provision. I do not accept this construction of condition 15. I do not think that, fairly read, condition 15 applies to money received by a *receiver*, even though the receiver will have been appointed by the Halifax in exercise of one of its statutory powers as mortgagee. Condition 15 is concerned with how the Halifax shall apply money received by *it*.

C

The Halifax next submitted that the community charges payable by the company in respect of the flats are not within sec. 109(8)(i). They do not "affect" the property because non-payment of them by the receiver will not prejudice the receiver's possession of the flats. The receiver does not have to pay the community charges in order to preserve the property. do not think "affect" can bear this meaning. If it did, rates would fall within or without the paragraph depending on whether in the particular circumstances non-payment would prejudice the receiver's enjoyment of the property. On this argument rates payable by the owner when the property is unoccupied might not be payable by the receiver even though they are specifically mentioned in para. (i). That cannot be correct. In the present case the community charges are payable by the company by virtue of its being the owner of the flats. As such in my view they fall squarely within para. (i) as a tax affecting the property.

D

E

The Halifax further submitted that the company acting through the liquidators cannot compel the receiver to carry out his obligations under sec. 109(8). Section 109(8) is primarily for the benefit of the mortgagee. It is designed to preserve the mortgaged property while the receiver is in office and to ensure that the income, net of outgoings affecting the mortgaged property, is paid to the mortgagee rather than the mortgagor who is already in default. Just as the mortgagee can put his interests ahead of the mortgagor, so the receiver may give a higher regard to the interests of the mortgagee. The receiver owes no obligation to the mortgagor to make a payment under para. (i), by way of indemnity to the mortgagor ahead of payments to the mortgagee.

F

G

I do not agree. A mortgage deed is concerned to regulate the rights and duties of the parties: the mortgagor and the mortgagee. Subject always to contrary provision in the deed, sec. 101 and 109 of the Act of 1925 have the effect of incorporating into the relationship between the parties the powers and provisions set out in those sections. One of these, sec. 109(8), regulates the manner in which a receiver, appointed by the mortgagee pursuant to his powers, "shall" apply the income of the mortgaged property received by him. In the absence of authority I would have had no doubt that, when a mortgagor has agreed that a receiver may be appointed on these terms, he can require a receiver appointed pursuant to those provisions to comply with them. But authority is not lacking. In *Yourell v Hibernian Bank Ltd* [1918] AC 372, 386, Lord *Atkinson* expressed himself in terms to the effect that, although the receiver's statutory duties are

H

A   not owed more widely, they are owed to the mortgagor, the mortgagee and puisne encumbrancers.

The Halifax developed a further argument to the effect that the company could not compel performance of the receiver's statutory duty under sec. 109(8)(i) because it is in breach of its covenant contained in the mortgage deed to pay all rates, taxes and impositions payable in respect of the charged property and to keep the Halifax indemnified

B   against all claims arising from any breach of that covenant. Once again I am unpersuaded. Section 109(8) deals with a specific situation: how a receiver, if appointed, should apply money received by him. The company is as much entitled to enforce the receiver's duties under that subsection in a case where the company has covenanted to pay rates and taxes in respect of the mortgaged property as in a case where it has not.

The Halifax also submitted that the right to enforce the receiver's statutory duty is vested in the company. The company will suffer no loss if the receiver fails to pay the

C   community charges. If the receiver uses money in paying the community charges bill, there would be correspondingly less which he can pay to the Halifax. The overall liabilities of the company would remain the same; the only difference would be in the identity of the creditors. Once more I am unimpressed. The purpose of sec. 109(8) is to regulate the order in which money held by the receiver shall be applied. There cannot be room for doubt that a recalcitrant receiver could be compelled by the court specifically

D   to carry on his duties under that subsection and apply this money in accordance with the statutory order of priority, if necessary by granting appropriate injunctions against the receiver.

There was no evidence before me on precisely what money the receiver has or has had in his hands. I was told that the purchase price of the flats was paid directly to the Halifax by the buyers, although the position regarding the deposits was not clear. The Halifax contended that, moreover, sec. 109(8) only applies to income received by the receiver:

E   the subsection does not apply to capital. For a reason which will appear I need not pursue these points.

Exercise of the discretion

I turn now to consider whether indeed there is here a "special equity" which would require the court to direct that the community charges should be paid by the liquidators as a liquidation expense. In my view there is not. If I leave on one side for the moment

F   the liquidators' right of recourse against the receiver, the position is tolerably clear. The post-liquidation community charges are not provable as a debt, but that would not justify the court directing that they should be paid as a liquidation expense ahead of all the unsecured creditors whose debts are provable. That would be to go from one extreme to the other. It may be regarded as unfair to Tower Hamlets that it cannot prove for the post-liquidation charges even though it must still provide services. But it would

G   be equally unfair to the proving creditors to prefer Tower Hamlets ahead of all of them in a case where, as already noted, the liquidators have had no use of or control over the flats in respect of which the charges arose.

What, then, of the liquidators' right of recourse against the receiver? In my view it would be wrong for the court to direct payment of the community charges as a liquidation expense with a view to enabling the liquidators to have recourse against the receiver. If

H   a direction for payment as liquidation expenses were made in that circumstance, the purpose and effect would be to enable Tower Hamlets to achieve indirectly via the liquidators what it cannot achieve directly by a claim against the receiver. A taxing authority cannot compel a receiver to make payments in accordance with sec. 109(8)(i). That subsection does not create a statutory duty enforceable by a local authority: *Liverpool Corporation v Hope* [1938] 1 KB 751. It cannot therefore be right for the

court to order that the community charges should be paid as a liquidation expense, not
because it is genuinely intended that those charges should rank and be paid as a
liquidation expense in the winding up of the company, but as a stepping stone enabling
the local authority to reach the receiver and funds in his hands and be paid ahead even
of the mortgagees.

Accordingly I shall not direct the liquidators to pay the community charges in question
to Tower Hamlets as an expense of the liquidation.

No in-between course

I add a final observation. I have considered whether there is any way in which the
court, which is being asked to exercise its discretion, could achieve a result which lies
between the two extremes, the one being that Tower Hamlets has no remedy at all, and
the other being that Tower Hamlets is paid in full ahead of every one else. Counsel were
at one in submitting that no such way is open to the court. None has occurred to me.

My lack of enthusiasm for this result, that Tower Hamlets can claim nothing from
anybody, is a little countered by noting two points. First, as I have already mentioned,
from April 1991 onwards no community charges would have been payable in respect of
the flats for the relevant periods if the Halifax had gone into possession as mortgagee.
The policy underlying this is not easy to discern, given that a similar approach is not
applied when a company is in the course of being wound up as insolvent and the
liquidator is in possession. However, since there would have been no liability to
community charges if the Halifax had taken possession, it is perhaps not so unsatisfactory
as otherwise would be the case that Tower Hamlets has no remedy in respect of unpaid
community charges arising while the receiver appointed by the Halifax is in possession.

The second point turns on the facts of this particular case. Tower Hamlets' inability to
prove in the winding up of the company is unlikely to give rise to any injustice in this
case, for this reason: even if Tower Hamlets were able to prove as a creditor, there would
be little prospect of any significant dividend. Further, the remedy of distress would have
yielded nothing. Thus, although winding up had the effect of bringing down the shutters,
in practice this has not caused any substantial injustice to Tower Hamlets. Even if a
winding-up resolution had not been passed before the end of the relevant periods, Tower
Hamlets' remedies would have yielded little or no fruit.

Conclusion

In the course of the hearing before me Tower Hamlets made plain that it does not
intend to continue with the summonses in the magistrates' court and that it will withdraw
them. I shall therefore not make an order staying those proceedings. I shall make a
declaration to the effect that the company is liable to Tower Hamlets for standard
community charges in the amounts in question for the relevant periods, that the
obligation is an unsecured debt, but that the amount due is not provable as a debt in the
winding up of the company. I shall not direct the liquidators to pay these charges as an
expense in the liquidation.

(*Declaration accordingly*)

A
Runciman v Walter Runciman plc.

Queen's Bench Division.
Simon Brown J.
Judgment delivered 28 April 1992.

B
> *Directors — Disclosure of interest in contracts with company — Whether variation of director's service contract properly authorised — Whether director had properly disclosed interest in contract — Whether variation not made bona fide in interests of company — Whether extension of notice period invalid — Companies Act 1985, sec. 317.*

This was an action by a director for damages for wrongful dismissal. Liability was conceded. An issue remained whether the plaintiff's notice entitlement was three or five years. (There were other issues concerning the plaintiff's entitlement to ancillary benefits, his loss under the company's pension scheme, and mitigation of damage.)

C

D
The defendant company was a holding company whose principal subsidiaries were in the field of shipping and transport. The plaintiff was employed by the company from about 1964 until 12 November 1990. He was appointed chairman of the company by service agreement dated 22 June 1976. His dismissal followed the company's takeover by a Swedish company in May 1990. The 1976 agreement was terminable by the company on three years' notice. The company challenged the validity of a purported increase in the notice term to five years, contained in a letter written to the plaintiff by the company's deputy chairman in 1987. The company submitted, first, that there was no agreement at all between the plaintiff and the company with regard to the purported increase because nobody with authority agreed the increase on the company's behalf: there was no proper determination of the issue by the directors as required by the company's articles of association. Second, that even if there was such a determination it was in any event voidable by the company and unenforceable by the plaintiff because he failed to make a proper declaration of interest as required by the Companies Act 1985, sec. 317 and the articles. Third, that the company was also entitled to avoid the variation as not being made properly in the interests of the company.

E

Held, giving judgment for the plaintiff:

F
1. The articles said nothing as to how or when the directors were to arrive at their determination. Provided that by the time the term was sought to be enforced all the other directors could be shown to have concurred in the agreement of the term, it could then fairly and properly be said that they had determined it as the article required.

2. Section 317 applied to service contracts and to variations of them, but non-declaration of the plaintiff's interest in the variations in question was as purely technical as it could be, and to hold in the circumstances that that should render the extension of the notice term unenforceable would involve the most patent injustice.

G

3. Given the accepted bona fides of the directors, and given that it was essentially for them and not the court to decide what was in the company's interests, it was impossible to say that the board in 1987 reached a view of the matter which was not open to them.

The following cases were referred to in the judgment:

H
Bonelli's Telegraph Co, Re. Collie's Claim (1871) LR 12 Eq 246.
Charterhouse Investment Trust Ltd v Tempest Diesels Ltd (1985) 1 BCC 99,544.
Erlanger & Ors v New Sombrero Phosphate Co & Ors (1878) 3 App Cas 1218.
Foster v Foster [1916] 1 Ch 532.
Guinness plc v Saunders & Anor (1988) 4 BCC 377, [1988] 1 WLR 863 (CA); [1990] BCC 205, [1990] 2 AC 663 (HL).
Hely-Hutchinson v Brayhead Ltd & Anor [1968] 1 QB 549.

Lavarack v Woods of Colchester Ltd [1967] 1 QB 278.　　　　　　　　　　　　A
Lee Panavision Ltd v Lee Lighting Ltd [1991] BCC 620.
Richmond Gate Property Co Ltd, Re [1965] 1 WLR 335.
Smith (Howard) Ltd v Ampol Petroleum Ltd & Ors [1974] AC 821.

Patrick Elias QC and Michael Kay (instructed by Lovell White Durrant) for the
plaintiff.

Charles Falconer QC and Andrzej Kolodzies (instructed by Freshfields) for the　　B
defendant.

JUDGMENT

Simon Brown J: In this action the plaintiff claims damages for wrongful dismissal.
Liability for such wrongful (constructive) dismissal was conceded by the defendant some
two weeks before trial. But alas that concession by no means resolved all the difficulties
in the case. As will appear, many issues remain. Principally these concern:　　　　　C

(1)　The plaintiff's notice entitlement: was it three years or five?

(2)　The plaintiff's entitlement to ancillary benefits, the use of a motor car and so
　　　forth.

(3)　The plaintiff's loss under the defendant's pension scheme.
　　　　　　　　　　　　　　　　　　　　　　　　　　　　　　　　　　　　　D
(4)　Mitigation of damage: in particular what elements of the plaintiff's post-dismissal
　　　remuneration must now be brought into account in reduction of his claim?

The background to the claim is this. The defendant is a holding company ("the
company") whose principal subsidiaries are in the field of shipping and transport. The
plaintiff is now 57. He was employed by the company from about 1964 (when he ceased
full-time academic life) until 12 November 1990 — two days after his fifty-sixth birthday.
The plaintiff's family had been closely associated with the company for some 70 years.　E
Family members and related trusts owned very approximately 20–30 per cent of the
shares and throughout the great majority of the company's life time it had been chaired
successively by the plaintiff's grandfather, father and, from 1 July 1976, the plaintiff
himself — his appointment being by service agreement dated 22 June 1976. The
plaintiff's dismissal followed the company's takeover by a Swedish company (Avena) in
May 1990. That takeover had been hostile and resisted at first but ultimately recommended　F
to shareholders. Two years earlier the defendant had successfully resisted a hostile bid
from Telfos.

During the years with which this action is mainly concerned the company had seven
directors: the plaintiff himself as executive chairman; Donald Haley, the deputy chairman
and divisional chief executive; Michael Johnson, the managing director of the main
shipping line, reporting directly to Mr Haley; Roger McIntyre-Brown, the group　　G
financial director; Mr Bramall, chairman of an underwriting agency associated with the
group. Those were the five executive directors. And two non-executive directors: from
1971 until his resignation in June 1990, Mr Peter Grant, the present chairman of Sun
Life Assurance and until June 1988 deputy chairman of Lazards, the company's merchant
bankers; from 1976 until his retirement in June 1988, the plaintiff's father, the second
Viscount Runciman, who died in September 1989, and, from October 1988 onwards, his
replacement Sir Brian Shaw.　　　　　　　　　　　　　　　　　　　　　　　H

The 1976 service agreement provided so far as relevant:

(1)　That the plaintiff's employment as executive chairman (until 31 December 1999)
　　　was terminable by the company upon three years' notice, and by the plaintiff on
　　　six months' notice.

A (2)   That the plaintiff:

"shall devote the whole of his time and his attention to the proper performance of his duties hereunder and shall at all times use his best endeavours to promote the interests of the company and its subsidiaries from time to time . . . except that he may devote up to 80 working days in each year to other activities not competing with the business of the group."

B The plaintiff was further entitled to 21 working days' paid holiday per annum in addition to Bank Holidays (a further seven days).

(3)   That the company should pay to the plaintiff a basic salary of £15,000 per annum (the rate of such basic salary to be reviewed by the company at least once a year) and such fees as he might be entitled to as a director (£1,500 per annum throughout the relevant period).

C By letter dated 1 July 1987 Mr Haley wrote to the plaintiff on company writing paper as follows:

"*Re service agreement*

I am writing to advise you that (your 1976 agreement) is hereby amended so that the period of notice to be given by the company will be increased from three years to five years."

D The validity of that purported increase in the plaintiff's notice term is challenged by the defendant on three distinct grounds which at this stage I briefly indicate so as to highlight the significance of the further facts which follow. It is submitted, first, that there was no agreement at all between the plaintiff and the company with regard to the purported increase because nobody with authority agreed the increase on the company's behalf: there was, it is said, no proper determination by the directors as required by the company's articles of association. Second, that even if there was such a determination it was in any event voidable by the company and unenforceable by the plaintiff because he failed to make a proper declaration of interest as required by the articles. Third, that the company are also entitled to avoid the variation as not being made properly in the interests of the company.

What then is the evidence as to how and why the notice term contained in the 1976 agreement came to be varied in 1987? As to how, it is convenient first to indicate something of the practice followed within the company in respect of the executive directors' salary increases. What used to happen was this. The plaintiff, usually in consultation with Mr Haley, would annually formulate proposals for all executive directors (save Mr Bramall whose contractual arrangements were entirely separately agreed with the underwriting agency). The plaintiff would put those proposals to the two non-executive directors, always ensuring, so far as his own proposed increase was concerned, that Mr Haley would consult the non-executive directors separately about that. The plaintiff was, said Mr Haley and I accept, meticulous as to that. The plaintiff would also discuss the proposals with Mr Bramall; his disinterested views would have special value. Assuming, as seems invariably to have been the case, that the non-executive directors and Mr Bramall approved the proposals, they would then be notified to the other two executive directors, Mr Johnson and Mr McIntyre-Brown. Once all the directors had been thus informed of the position, the plaintiff would then instruct Mr McIntyre-Brown to implement the increases. There was no board meeting dealing with the increases, no discussion about them by the directors as a body. In large part the evidence as to that procedure was given orally: by the plaintiff, by Mr Haley and by Mr Grant. But to some extent it is borne out by such documents as relate to these annual salary increases. If one takes 1987, the year of the notice increase, the following documents are found.

(1)   A letter from the plaintiff to Mr Grant dated 4 November 1987 which includes   A
this:

> ". . . may I ask your independent advice about the appropriate salary levels
> for Donald, Roger and myself from 1 January 1988. As you know I have felt
> inhibited about putting through major increases until I felt that the company
> performance could justify it in the eyes of the shareholders . . . Although we
> have not made as much progress by now as I had hoped that we would, I do   B
> think (and hope that you agree) that the three of us ought now to start to be
> paid our market worth. My tentative thought is that Roger should go to
> £70,000, Donald £72,500, and myself a total of £500 higher than Donald at
> £73,000. How does that strike you?"

(2)   Mr Grant's reply to the plaintiff dated 11 November 1987 stated:

> "I am in full agreement with what you propose. The sums you suggest,   C
> I believe, are fully justified and could, indeed, be a little higher."

(3)   A memorandum from the plaintiff to Mr McIntyre-Brown (copied to Mr Haley)
dated 20 November 1987 said:

> "I have consulted Peter Grant and my father about remuneration for main
> board executive directors (excluding Bob Bramall, who will continue to be
> covered by his own arrangements . . .) with effect from 1 January 1988, and   D
> they agree that in addition to the extension of the service contract period from
> three to five years already decided, our basic salaries should be increased to
> the following levels:

WGR	£75,000
DJH	£72,500
RDMB	£72,500
MAJ	£58,000

> I will be writing individual letters confirming these figures in the normal way
> shortly."

As will be noted, the plaintiff's own salary was there being increased by £2,000
more and Mr McIntyre-Brown's by £2,500 more than had initially been proposed
to Mr Grant. It may well be that there had been further discussions following   F
Mr Grant's response to the initial proposal. I further note that apart from the
letter of 1 July 1987, that is the only document which mentions the increased
notice period.

(4)   A letter from Mr McIntyre-Brown to the plaintiff dated 30 November 1987
stating:

> "Further to the recent discussions with the non-executive directors I am   G
> instructed to increase your salary from 1 January 1988 to £75,000 per annum."

I think it unnecessary to refer to the equivalent correspondence regarding the salary
increases over the following two years save perhaps to note the non-executive directors'
responses to consultation. On 17 November 1988 Mr Grant acknowledged the plaintiff's
letter of proposal (which had invited views on both a higher and lower scale of increases)
and said: H

> "I would take the higher of the two possibilities. I believe an excellent job has
> been done by the team under your leadership both in the management of the
> business and in the management of the predator"

— a reference to the Telfos bid. And on 23 November 1989, Sir Brian Shaw responded
to that year's proposals as follows:

A   "I have no problems with the salary increases you are proposing for executive
directors from 1 January 1990, the percentages being much in line with what
seems to be happening elsewhere."

That proposal I may observe took the plaintiff up to his final salary level with the
company — £87,500, which, together with his director's fees of £1,500, made for total
remuneration of £89,000.

B   As stated, the bulk of the evidence regarding the procedures for varying the executive
directors' terms of employment related to salary increases — not, one may observe,
themselves put in issue in these proceedings. It is accepted, however, that a similar
procedure was followed with regard to the increase in the notice term. As to ancillary
benefits, the use of a motor car and the like, it appears that a somewhat more relaxed
procedure was followed. It omitted any specific consultation with the non-executive
directors; they merely came to learn of the variations in benefits, generally fairly
C   informally. The ancillary benefits, I may observe at this stage, are challenged on the
same grounds as the notice increase save only that no contention is advanced that these
benefits were conferred otherwise than in the interests of the company.

        As to the purpose for which the notice term was increased, the evidence is this. The
increase took place at the same time and to the same extent for all the working directors
(save Mr Bramall who, as stated, had special arrangements). What precipitated it was
D   the plaintiff's discovery from Mr Haley that both Mr Johnson and Mr McIntyre-Brown
had separately been approached by head hunters. And this at a time when it was known
that the John Govett Group had already built up a strategic 29.6 per cent stake in the
company, a stake highlighting the ever present possibility of a takeover bid, and which
indeed presaged Telfos's bid the following year. The matter was discussed with the non-
executive directors. The view taken was that, to secure Mr Johnson's and Mr McIntyre-
E   Brown's loyalty, their notice term should be increased. The logic is this. If a company is
faced with potential takeover (not in itself necessarily a bad thing), the directors may
regard themselves as under threat. If head hunted at that stage, the less secure they feel
under their existing contracts of service, the more likely they are to leave if a particular
opportunity presents itself. Recognising, as the company did, the excellence of the
existing group of working directors, both individually and as a team, it was thought
imperative to guard against the risk of Mr Johnson or Mr McIntyre-Brown leaving: their
F   security needed to be improved. And given that it was thought necessary to increase the
notice period for those two directors, so also was it thought appropriate to increase it
similarly for the other two — Mr Haley and the plaintiff himself. That, certainly, is what
all three of the witnesses called before me testified. True, they accepted that it was
unnecessary to secure Mr Haley's and the plaintiff's loyalty in this way. As for Mr Haley,
he was in 1987 already aged 59 and intent on leaving the company at 60 — although
G   prepared to carry on if needed, as in the event he was needed until 31 December 1990.
And so far as the plaintiff was concerned, he readily accepts that having spent his whole
commercial life with the company and having regard to his family's associations with it,
his loyalty was well nigh absolute: it was hardly conceivable that his decision whether to
remain would depend upon whether his notice term was three years or five. But
nevertheless, all three witnesses said, there was no good reason to differentiate between
the various executive directors. To have done so would have been invidious and
H   inappropriate. It was right that there should be equality between them in respect of their
notice term.

        Against that background of evidence let me now turn to deal in greater detail with the
legal arguments. The first two issues — as to whether there ever was any properly
authorised agreement to increase the notice term and as to whether the plaintiff was

required to declare an interest in this increase — require reference to the company's articles of association. Article 85 in particular is crucial:

> "(1) A director who is in any way, whether directly or indirectly, interested in a contract or proposed contract with the company shall declare the nature of his interest at a meeting of the directors in accordance with sec. 199 of the Act.
>
> (2) A director shall not vote in respect of any contract or arrangement in which he is interested, and if he shall do so his vote shall not be counted . . .
>
> (3) A director may hold any other office or place of profit under the company (other than the office of auditor) in conjunction with his office of director for such period and on such terms (as to remuneration and otherwise) as the directors may determine. No director or intending director shall be disqualified by his office from contracting with the company, either with regard to his tenure of any such other office or place of profit, or as vendor, purchaser or otherwise. No such contract, and no contract or arrangement entered into by or on behalf of the company, in which any director is in any way interested, shall be liable to be avoided, nor shall any director so contracting or being so interested be liable to account to the company for any profit realised by any such contract or arrangement by reason of such director holding that office or of the fiduciary relation thereby established.
>
> (4) A director, notwithstanding his interest, may be counted in the quorum present at any meeting whereat he or any other director is appointed to hold any such office or place of profit under the company or whereat the terms of any such appointment are arranged, and he may vote on any such appointment or arrangement other than his own appointment or the arrangement of the terms thereof."

Several other articles were discussed in course of argument but I have come to conclude that they bear only marginally on the points at issue. The defendant's first argument focuses essentially upon art. 85(3) and in particular its provision that an office held by a director — here the plaintiff's office of executive chairman — is held "on such terms (as to remuneration and otherwise) as the directors may determine". "The directors" are defined by art. 2 to be:

> "the directors for the time being of the company as a body, or a quorum of the directors present at a meeting of the directors."

I should perhaps note in passing art. 89(3), a provision complementary to art. 85(3), although in the end it adds little to the debate:

> "89(3) A managing director or any director holding any such other office or place of profit shall receive such remuneration or emoluments as the directors may determine."

Given that the relevant terms here were never decided at a directors' meeting, the critical question raised is, of course, this: did the directors as a body — i.e. all of them — determine that the plaintiff's notice term should be increased to five years? The plaintiff says "Yes", the defendant "No".

Let it be said at once that if the answer is indeed "No", then the purported agreement is clearly void. Many are the authorities and extensive the academic commentary establishing that. Prominent amongst the cases are *Re Richmond Gate Property Co Ltd* [1965] 1 WLR 335 and *Guinness plc v Saunders & Anor* [1990] BCC 205. Let this passage from Lord *Templeman*'s speech in *Guinness* (at p. 212H) suffice:

> "Equity forbids a trustee to make a profit out of his trust. The articles of association of Guinness relax the strict rule of equity to the extent of enabling a

A   director to make a profit provided that the board of directors contracts on behalf
         of Guinness for the payment of special remuneration or decides to award special
         remuneration. Mr Ward did not obtain a contract or a grant from the board of
         directors. Equity has no power to relax its own strict rule further than and
         inconsistently with the express relaxation contained in the articles of association.
         A shareholder is entitled to compliance with the articles. A director accepts office
         subject to and with the benefit of the provisions of the articles relating to directors
B   . . . A director who does not read the articles or a director who misconstrues
         the articles is nevertheless bound by the articles . . . At the board meeting . . .
         Mr Ward was present but he did not seek then or thereafter to obtain the necessary
         authority of the board of directors for payment of special remuneration. In these
         circumstances there are no grounds for equity to relax its rules further than the
         articles of association provide."

C   Was there then a failure here to determine the variation of the plaintiff's notice period
         in accordance with art. 85(3)? Contending that there was, Mr Falconer for the defendant
         submits that it would be wrong to conclude that when the plaintiff finally notified Mr
         Johnson and Mr McIntyre-Brown of the results of his (and Mr Haley's) consultation
         with the non-executive directors he was in any sense involving them personally in the
         decision-making process, wrong even to conclude that they were approving the various
         increases of pay or notice term. They never participated in the decision: they simply
D   took their own individual benefits from it. The reality, Mr Falconer submits, is to be
         found in the evidence: As Mr Haley put it:

         "Once the non-executives approved them, without more ado the increases would
         be put into effect."

         And as the plaintiff stated in his memorandum of 20 November 1987, after noting the
         non-executive directors' agreement to the increases:

E   "I will be writing individual letters confirming these figures."

         To similar effect is the plaintiff's letter to Mr Grant dated 21 November 1989:

         "I should like to let people know what has been decided early in December and
         should therefore be grateful if I could have your reaction by the end of this
         month."

F   And entirely consistently with all this, submits Mr Falconer, are the minutes of a board
         meeting of 24 May 1988 with regard to pensions:

         "Mr McIntyre-Brown stated that (the plaintiff) had advised him of his decision to
         amend the scheme after consultation with the non-executive directors and
         consideration of the actuary's report."

         Similarly the plaintiff's further and better particulars regarding the alleged basis of the
         agreed variation in the notice term:

G   "The agreement was made between the plaintiff on his own behalf and Peter
         Grant and the then Viscount Runciman, the non-executive directors of the
         defendant at that time, on behalf of the defendant. It was the defendant's practice
         at that time to agree changes to the directors' remuneration or terms and conditions
         of employment by the approval of the non-executive directors, who therefore
         acted as a subcommittee of the board of directors."

H   None of this, the argument runs, suggests that Mr Johnson and Mr McIntyre-Brown
         were themselves party to the determination of their colleagues' salary levels or other
         terms of contract. (They could not, of course, under the articles, determine their own
         terms.) The reality was rather that the decision was taken before ever these particular
         directors were notified of it. There was thus no unanimous determination by the board
         as a whole.

Powerfully although the argument was urged upon me, I have concluded that it fails.   A
And for this reason above all. The articles say nothing as to how or when the directors
are to arrive at their determination. In my judgment, therefore, provided only and
always that by that time the term relied upon is sought to be enforced all the other
directors can be shown to have concurred in the agreement of that term, it can then fairly
and properly be said that they have indeed determined it as the article requires. That
directors, provided they act unanimously, can act informally appears clearly established
— *Re Bonelli's Telegraph Co. Collie's Claim* (1871) LR 12 Eq 246 and *Charterhouse*   B
Investment Trust Ltd v Tempest Diesels Ltd (1985) 1 BCC 99,544 so decide, the latter
on the basis that informal acquiescence by other board members in an otherwise
unauthorised agreement by one of their number binds the company. So in my judgment
in the present case. And, indeed, I conclude that Mr Johnson's and Mr McIntyre-
Brown's involvement went beyond mere informal acquiescence. As the plaintiff told me
in evidence, when they were acquainted with the proposals following approval by the
non-executive directors they, as directors, had the opportunity to query them. The mere   C
fact that they never apparently did so and that their views were not more explicitly
canvassed seems to me nothing to the point: by the time of the implementation of the
various salary increases, and more obviously still by the time the plaintiff came to assert
his notice term, such terms were indeed "as determined" by the other board members,
and none of them could possibly have been heard to assert the contrary.

Mr Elias for the plaintiff put the case here in favour of my finding a binding agreement   D
in a number of different ways. These included the submission that the decision-making
process regarding a director's term of service can lawfully be delegated (see art. 89(4)
and 110) and that the company would be bound if all the directors acquiesced in such an
arrangement. Although having regard to my already stated conclusion it is unnecessary
to deal with these various alternative arguments in any detail, I should nevertheless
observe that there seem to me insuperable difficulties in the plaintiff here seeking to rely
on general powers of delegation under the articles — *Guinness* is to my mind   E
indistinguishable in this regard. What really serves to distinguish *Guinness* from this
case is not the different articles of association in play, not the different kind of
remuneration in question, not (on this issue) the absence of knowledge on the part of
the other members of the Guinness board, but rather that the decision there was taken
by a committee so that the matter was never determined by the board as a whole whereas
in the present case I have found that it was.   F

I pass to the defendant's second argument which centres on art. 85(1). Section 199 of
the Act (of 1948) there referred to, has been superseded by sec. 317 of the *Companies
Act* 1985 — as recognised in *Guinness*, not for present purposes significantly different.
The argument here is that the plaintiff was required by art. 85(1) to declare at a directors
meeting the nature of his interest in the relevant variations to his service agreement, that
he failed to do so, and that accordingly the variations relied upon, both as to the period
of notice and the fringe benefits (the salary increases, I repeat are not challenged in   G
these proceedings), are voidable at the suit of the company, unenforceable by the
plaintiff against it.

Once again there is ample authority for the proposition that non-compliance with a
requirement such as that imposed here by art. 85(1) leaves the contract voidable at the
option of the company: see most notably *Hely-Hutchinson v Brayhead Ltd & Anor*
[1968] 1 QB 549 and *Guinness*. But once again there is a dispute here as to whether the   H
article has in fact been breached. And even if it has, submits Mr Elias, there are
compelling reasons why the court should not permit the defendant now to avoid the
contract.

Four particular questions are raised upon this part of the case. First, as to whether
sec. 317 (and therefore art. 85(1)) has any application to service contracts between a

A   company and its own directors. Second, assuming it has, whether it applies to the variation of an existing contract. Third, again assuming it does, whether disclosure was made here by the plaintiff in conformity with the section. Fourth, assuming that the plaintiff was in breach of a duty to disclose, whether it is equitable to permit the defendant now to rescind.

B   Although these four questions were argued before me at very considerable length, I shall hope to be forgiven for dealing with them relatively shortly. The reason I do so is quite simply this. Whatever may have been the strict legal requirements of the position, on the particular facts of this case I am perfectly satisfied that for the plaintiff to have made a specific declaration of interest before agreement of the variations here in question would have served no conceivable purpose. It would have been mere incantation. Any non-compliance with art. 85(1) was accordingly wholly technical. Nothing could be less just than that the new owners of the company after takeover should now benefit from their adventitious discovery of such breach. To allow them to do so would be to sacrifice the plaintiff's legitimate interests on the altar of slavish adherence to ritualistic form.

C

To revert, however, to the questions. Does sec. 317 apply to service contracts? (Section 317 I propose to take as read rather than lengthen this judgment by its detailed recitation.) The plaintiff argues not, on the footing that self-evidently an executive director is interested in his own service contract so that it could never be necessary for him to declare that interest at a meeting. Mr Elias prays in aid in this regard sec. 317(3) which permits a director in certain circumstances to give a general notice which is then deemed a sufficient declaration of interest for future purposes. True, Mr Elias accepts, that subsection has no direct application to this case but, the argument runs, it appears at least to suggest that the legislation is concerned with realities rather than form. Compelling although at first blush I confess to have found this argument, I have regretfully come to reject it. Not only is it inconsistent with the plain language of the section, but there is ample authority for the proposition that the mere obviousness of a director's interest in a particular contract is no reason for non-compliance with the requirements of the section. That, indeed, is implicit in decisions like *Hely-Hutchinson* and *Guinness* each of which concerned contracts directly between a director and his company, contracts respectively of guarantee and for services. True, the contracts there in issue were made without knowledge on the part of some at least of the board's members. But that consideration cannot logically affect the question whether or not a particular type of contract falls within the legislation. And sec. 317(5), referring as it does to other transactions or arrangements in which a director is interested (such as loans to directors), points to the same conclusion. Furthermore, as Mr Falconer points out, to exclude service contracts from the ambit of sec. 317 would involve ridiculous and pointless distinctions being drawn (1) between the employed and the self-employed director; and (2) between benefits given to a director as part of his contract of employment and those given separately. Finally on this point the defendant drew my attention to *Foster v Foster* [1916] 1 Ch 532 a decision holding in terms that the statutory predecessor to sec. 317 applied to service contracts.

D

E

F

G

Does sec. 317 apply to variations? The plaintiff's contention that it does not again on analysis relies heavily on the apparent absurdity of requiring a declaration of interest in regard to such an agreement. Why declare an interest in the variation of a contract which the company already knows is one in which the director is interested? In addition, submits Mr Elias, if sec. 317 was intended to cover variations it would have said so expressly — in the same way that sec. 318(10) expressly applies subsec. (1) and (5) of that section to a variation of a contract of service as to the contract itself. But those arguments too must in my judgment fail. So far as the analogy with sec. 318 goes, I accept the defendant's submission that sec. 318(10) was necessary because

H

sec. 318(1) and (5) deal specifically with contracts of service — and a variation of such a   A
contract, albeit a contract, might well not in itself be regarded as a contract of service.
And I accept too the defendant's fundamental argument that a variation of contract is
itself a contract and that to construe sec. 317 otherwise would lead to pointless debate
about whether a given agreement constitutes a variation or a fresh contract. Looking
moreover to the purpose of the legislation and the mischief against which it is directed,
there will certainly be cases where it is as necessary for an interest to be declared in a
variation of contract as in the making of the contract in the first place: take *Guinness* and   B
suppose that the consideration for Ward's services had initially and in conformity with
the articles been agreed at £5,000 and only later varied to the eventual figure of £5.2m.

Was, then, disclosure made in the present case? Given as already stated that agreements
such as those here in question need not themselves be determined at a directors meeting,
there is, submits Mr Elias, implicit disclosure of an executive director's interest in his
service contract merely by the fact of his attendance at the first board meeting after his   C
appointment. And, the submission continues, that disclosure is implicitly made afresh
at every subsequent meeting which he attends, disclosure which would meet any
statutory requirement in regard to later variations. Mr Elias further submits that the
plaintiff here made in addition what was akin to express disclosure in that the company's
letters to shareholders, advising them to reject respectively the Telfos bid in 1988 and
the Avena bid (initially) in 1990, stated in terms that each of the four directors' contracts
"may be terminated by the company giving not less than five years' previous notice in   D
writing" — a statement expressly agreed (as were the letters as a whole) at board
meetings where the individual directors' interests in their contractual provisions were of
course obvious.

Not so, argues the defendant. There was never here anything said or done which even
purported to constitute a declaration of interest. To infer such declaration would involve
a fiction. Rather, Mr Falconer submits, for there to be compliance with the legislation all   E
contracts or arrangements between a company and one of its directors must at some
stage come before the board and a specific declaration of interest then be made in
respect of them. That is what sec. 317 on its proper construction and application
requires. Nothing short of it will do. And, counsel argues, there are good policy reasons
for this, amongst them these:

(1)   That a director with an interest is obliged to acknowledge formally his involvement   F
        in a transaction which may be inimical to the company and its shareholders.

(2)   The director's interest will then be considered by the board and other directors
        will be reminded of their duty to consider the company's interest as distinct from
        their colleague's.

(3)   Declarations of interest and their consideration will be minuted under the provisions
        of sec. 382 of the 1985 Act and a permanent record kept.   G

Support for such an approach appears to be found in the authorities. Mr Falconer
relies on two in particular. First the leading judgment of *Fox* LJ in the Court of Appeal
in *Guinness v Saunders* (1988) 4 BCC 377 which (at p. 382) includes this passage:

"It is said, as I understand it, on behalf of Mr Ward, that disclosure to the full
board would be an absurdity because the board, or at any rate the executive
committee of the board for the purpose of the bid, knew about the payment.   H
Assuming it were true that all the members of the board knew about the payment,
that does not alter the fact that the requirement of the statute that there be a
disclosure to 'a meeting of the directors of the company' (which is a wholly
different thing from knowledge by individuals and involves the opportunity for
positive consideration of the matter by the board as a body) was not complied

A

with. I conclude, therefore, that the statute required disclosure to a duly convened meeting of the full board of Guinness."

Albeit the House of Lords held that the Court of Appeal had proceeded on a wrong footing — their decision in particular being inconsistent with *Hely-Hutchinson v Brayhead Ltd* — that passage in *Fox* LJ's judgment was not itself criticised and remains, it is submitted, valid. Second, Mr Falconer invites my attention to *Lee Panavision Ltd v Lee Lighting Ltd* [1991] BCC 620, where at p. 627, *Harman* J adopted substantially the same approach.

B

I readily acknowledge the apparent weight of these arguments. And yet I remain profoundly reluctant to conclude that a director must solemnly declare an interest in his own service agreement — a contract which by its very nature involves his interest — before any variation is made concerning his salary or other terms of employment. Is there really, irrespective of the common sense of the position, a statutory requirement

C

for such formal declaration? I do not believe that the point is free from doubt. Lord *Goff*, for instance, spoke in *Guinness* (at p. 216E) of the "very serious difficulties arising upon the construction of sec. 317". And when *Lee Panavision* got to the Court of Appeal, *Dillon* LJ at p. 637 similarly recognised the problems in the legislation and, wisely as I believe, declined counsel's urgent invitation to express a view on the construction and effect of art. 85 in the light of sec. 317 despite blandishments that it was

D

necessary to do so to resolve difficulties for all practitioners. Against that background it would surely be rash indeed for me needlessly to venture a definitive view upon this troublesome issue.

As stated, it is upon the fourth question that I have reached the clearest conclusion. It is at this point that *Dillon* LJ's comments on sec. 317 (at p. 637D) become most pertinent:

E

". . . if the judge was entitled to make the findings of non-disclosure and non-declaration of interests that he did, the position is that each of the directors has failed to disclose formally at the board meeting an interest common to all the directors and, *ex hypothesi*, already known to all the directors. I would hesitate to hold that such apparently technical non-declaration of an interest in breach of sec. 317 has the inevitable result, as to which the court has no discretion, that the second management agreement is fundamentally flawed and must be set aside if

F

Lighting chooses to ask sufficiently promptly that it be set aside."

As it seems to me, the (assumed) non-declaration of the plaintiff's interest in the variations here in question was as purely technical as it could ever be. Whatever may be the suggested advantages of a strictly formal approach to the section — such as a record of the proceedings and a reduced risk of directors abusing their position — no such advantage would have accrued here. It is certainly not suggested in this case that the

G

plaintiff or his fellow directors in any way abused their position. Rather the basis of Mr Falconer's case for holding the plaintiff unable to enforce his increased notice term is the contention that the strict rule should invariably be applied save only where the right of rescission must in law be regarded as lost — by acquiescence, delay, the impossibility of making *restitutio in integrum*, or on some other similarly recognised ground. Here it is submitted that no such reason exists. In reality, submits Mr Falconer, there has been no delay and no acquiescence: it was not until after Avena's takeover that the new

H

management and shareholders learned of the circumstances in which the service agreements came to be varied, and in particular of the plaintiff's failure to disclose his interest. In this context he draws my attention to the decision of the House of Lords in *Erlanger & Ors v New Sombrero Phosphate Co & Ors* (1878) 3 App Cas 1218, and especially Lord *Blackburn*'s speech at p. 1280 where, dealing with the question of laches by a corporation, he said:

". . . it should be recollected that shareholders who seek to set aside a contract made by the governing body, have practically first to change that governing body, and must have time to do so."

A

The force of that observation is plain. But it must be read in the context of this earlier passage in the speech (at pp. 1279–1280):

". . . I think, from the nature of the inquiry, it must always be a question more or less, depending on the degree of diligence which might reasonably be required, and the degree of change which has occurred, whether the balance of justice or injustice is in favour of granting the remedy or withholding it. The determination of such a question must largely depend on the turn of mind of those who have to decide, and must therefore be subject to uncertainty; but that, I think, is inherent in the nature of the inquiry."

B

If then one poses the simple question: what does the balance of justice require in the present case, I am left in no doubt whatever as to the proper answer. The plain fact is that this plaintiff continued, from 1987 to 1990, to serve the company as its chairman understanding that his notice term had been increased to five years; that that equally was the understanding of all his fellow directors; and that Avena too, at the time of their takeover of the company, clearly understood that to be the position — an understanding in their case derived from the company's explicit letter published earlier in opposition to the bid. To hold in these circumstances that what was at most a merely technical breach of a statutory duty of disclosure should render that variation unenforceable would to my mind involve the most patent injustice.

C

D

I turn to the defendant's third argument, that the increase in the notice term should be set aside as having been made in breach of the directors' fiduciary duty , i.e. the duty of the plaintiff's fellow directors to exercise their powers bona fide in the interests of the company as a whole and for a proper corporate purpose. The principles of law here in play are not in doubt. They are stated in *Palmer's Company Law* (25th ed.), para. 8.508 as follows:

E

"The duty imposed upon directors to act bona fide in the interests of the company is a subjective one. As Lord Greene M.R. put it in *Re Smith & Fawcett Ltd.*, directors must act 'bona fide in what they consider — not what a court may consider — is in the interests of the company.' So long as the directors have correctly informed themselves as to how the company is defined in law (for this purpose, present and future shareholders), it is left to the directors in the exercise of their business judgment to decide how the interests of the company may best be promoted. The courts will interfere only if no reasonable director could possibly have concluded that a particular course of action was in the interests of the company."

F

In *Howard Smith Ltd v Ampol Petroleum Ltd & Ors* [1974] AC 821 Lord *Wilberforce* put it thus:

G

". . . it is then necessary for the court, if a particular exercise of (power) is challenged, to examine the substantial purpose for which it was exercised, and to reach a conclusion whether that purpose was proper or not. In doing so it will necessarily give credit to the bona fide opinion of the directors, if such is found to exist, and will respect their judgment as to matters of management; having done this, the ultimate conclusion has to be as to the side of a fairly broad line on which the case falls."

H

The defendant here argues that it was quite unnecessary for the plaintiff's and Mr Haley's notice terms to be increased merely because such variation was thought necessary for the other two directors. Mr Falconer points to various other very substantial

A   benefit increases conferred on the plaintiff in the 1987–88 period: an increase in salary from £48,000 to £75,000 with effect from 1 January 1988, an increased share option from 20,000 to 75,000 shares during 1987, and a reduction in the normal retiring age under the company's pension scheme from 65 to 60 at no additional cost to himself. Against that background, it is submitted, it was wrong to improve the plaintiff's notice term merely to achieve symmetry across the board. Mr Falconer does not suggest that the plaintiff's term was increased for any impermissible ulterior purpose; only that symmetry is not in

B   itself a proper or sufficient purpose — rather it needlessly burdens the company with high potential liability, just as has occurred.

This argument too I reject. Given the accepted bona fides of the directors, and given that it is essentially for them and not the court to decide what is in the company's interests, I find it quite impossible to say that this board in 1987 reached a view of the matter which was simply not open to them. Mr Grant told me in terms that he thought it

C   right to make no distinction between the four working directors, that it would have been invidious to have done so. Am I really to say that such a view was plainly wrong? On the contrary, in the context of this small and close knit executive team, the approach taken seems to me eminently understandable. As Mr Elias points out, the position is really not unlike that arising when salary increases are in question: merely because one particular director may have reached an age when his prospects of alternative employment have

D   faded would hardly be a sufficient, let alone a compelling, reason for denying him an increase otherwise required to maintain his appropriate position in the overall salary scale. Yet on Mr Falconer's argument, if there were no risk of his leaving the company, it would be unnecessary and therefore impermissible — in breach of his fellow directors' fiduciary duty — to pay him his increase.

It follows from all this that in my judgment the plaintiff is entitled to rely upon his five year notice term.

E   There remains this subsidiary issue: but for his dismissal would the plaintiff in fact have remained with the company for five years, until that is the age of 61, or would he rather, as the defendant contends, have retired a year earlier on his sixtieth birthday?

A letter written by the plaintiff to Mr Eliasson, Avena's controlling shareholder, dated 10 August 1990, setting out in broad terms his monetary claim upon dismissal suggests an intended retirement age of 60: commenting upon the difficulties of mitigating his loss

F   the plaintiff observed that he would soon be 56 and that:

"there is quite obviously no chance than anyone will offer me the executive chairmanship of a comparable company for the next four years."

In the light of the plaintiff's oral evidence, however, I have not the slightest doubt that the answer to this particular question is perfectly simple: he would probably have retired at 60 had he then become entitled to a pension under the revised pension scheme; if,

G   however, as the defendant contends, that revision is unenforceable whereby no pension is payable until the plaintiff attains the age of 65, he would in all likelihood have continued as the company's chairman at least until 61, quite possibly (although this is immaterial to his present claim) for longer still.

Both parties recognise that it is not possible within these proceedings to decide this and the other issues arising in regard to the pension scheme. At the outset of the hearing, indeed, it was agreed that the whole question of the plaintiff's loss of pension rights must

H   be left over for determination in a Chancery action to which other affected parties — not least the trustees of the scheme — will be party. In that action will be decided all the various questions raised as to the validity and true construction of certain deeds amending the pension scheme, and as to whether, the deeds apart, the plaintiff enjoys against the company any contractual right to enhanced pension benefits. The resolution of those issues will, therefore, incidentally resolve also the question whether the plaintiff

is to be compensated for his salary losses on the footing that he would have retired at 60   A
or later. All that I can and do determine for present purposes is that the plaintiff is
entitled to recover damages for loss of salary (and, as I shall shortly explain, loss of
ancillary benefits) for either four years or five depending upon the outcome of the
Chancery proceedings.

Coming then to the question of ancillary benefits, I record first my understanding of
what the parties now agree to be the precise extent of these heads of claim. They
comprise, I understand, the following losses, valued annually: B

(1)   use of motor car: £5,500,

(2)   permanent health insurance: £1,022,

(3)   private health insurance (BUPA): £844, and

(4)   telephone facility: £600.

There is, I repeat, no question but that such benefits are properly accorded to someone   C
in the plaintiff's position. But, as with the notice term, it is said that no agreement for
them was ever properly determined and that the required statutory declaration of intent
was never made. My conclusion upon the statutory declaration argument is a fortiori to
that already indicated regarding the notice term. So far as the question of authorised
agreement is concerned, however — the art. 85(3) point — the position is not quite so
straight forward. As indicated, the procedures for agreeing these particular elements of   D
the directors' emoluments were really rather informal. Yet here again I have concluded
that I can and properly should hold that, by at latest the time when this claim came to be
advanced, all the plaintiff's co-directors had at the very least acquiesced in the decision
to include these various benefits in the package of rewards due to the plaintiff under his
service agreement. Given the routine nature of these benefits — commonplace, as
Mr Grant agreed, for someone in the plaintiff's position — I see no reason to require
any degree of formality of determination on the part of the board as a whole in order to   E
satisfy the requirements of the articles. Realising indeed that these benefits were
enjoyed for many years to the clear knowledge, and with the manifest approval, of all
the directors, it would seem to me wholly unreal to regard them otherwise than as
determined by the plaintiff's colleagues, not to say unjust to deprive him of them for the
purposes of this claim.

I turn, therefore, to the final area of conflict between the parties, the issues raised in   F
regard to mitigation of damage. First the facts, as shortly and simply as may be although
they were explored in evidence at very considerable length.

At the date of his dismissal on 12 November 1990 the plaintiff was, as stated, being
paid by the company a total of £89,000 per annum. He was also at that time earning
£30,000 per annum as the joint deputy chairman of the Securities and Investments Board
(SIB). Shortly before leaving the company the plaintiff had set up a new company,   G
Runciman Investments Ltd ("Investments"), of which the shareholders were members
of his family and related trusts, for the purpose of reinvesting in shipping some of the
moneys received on the Avena takeover. For reasons which will appear, the plaintiff's
salary from Investments was at the rate of £25,000 per annum from 12 November 1990
until 11 February 1991, £20,000 per annum from then until 1 April 1991, and £7,500 per
annum from then onwards.

As all agree, the plaintiff's reputation in the shipping world and indeed in the wider   H
commercial world is of the highest. Perhaps, therefore, it was not altogether surprising
— although both the plaintiff himself and Mr Grant indicated some little surprise — that
very shortly after his dismissal he came to be offered the chairmanship of another
substantial shipping company, Andrew Weir & Co Ltd ("Weir's"). It was the plaintiff's
evidence that Weir's are one of only some half a dozen companies who might thus have

A   employed him and it was a happy chance that their existing chairman was retiring early in 1991. In the event the plaintiff accepted the appointment for not less than 18 months at a salary of £50,000 per annum payable as from 8 January 1991, his obligation being to devote to Weir's interests not less than two full working days per week with effect from 11 February 1991 (the date of his reduction in salary receivable from Investments). Having obtained that employment, and having shortly thereafter in March accepted appointment as chairman of the Royal Commission on Criminal Justice, the plaintiff

B   managed with effect from 1 April 1991 to secure Mr Haley's services to take over from him the executive direction of Investments. It was for that reason that the plaintiff's salary from Investments was substantially further reduced to £7,500 per annum. Since that date Investments has involved the plaintiff in no more than a half-morning meeting about every other month and an hour or so on the telephone with Mr Haley most Saturday mornings. Having accepted the chairmanship of the Royal Commission — an

C   appointment obviously of the very first importance and one which the plaintiff always recognised would involve his finding on average some two days a week over the two-year period of its work (commencing in earnest in June 1991), the plaintiff with effect from 30 June 1991 reduced his commitment to the SIB: he relinquished his place on two subcommittees thereby cutting time spent at SIB meetings roughly from two days a month to one. Consistently with that reduced commitment the plaintiff's salary from SIB was reduced from £30,000 to £20,000 per annum. Returning to the Royal Commission,

D   the plaintiff is remunerated for this work at the rate of £450 per full day, or £64.29 per hour (equating to £450 per day on the basis of a seven hour day), as appropriate. From April 1991 — when the plaintiff started to read himself into the task and, with his vice-chairman, Sir John May, to advise on the remaining membership of the Commission — until the end of February 1992, he worked the equivalent of 57 days and earned a total of £25,650 from this source. At an average of two days per week the plaintiff would receive

E   annually from the Commission £46,800.

     Before turning to the arguments arising, I should mention one other continuing demand upon the plaintiff's time: his senior research fellowship at Trinity College, Cambridge. This fellowship is renewable every five years and was last renewed as recently as March 1992. Under its terms the plaintiff is required to dine in college once a week during term time (therefore 24 nights a year); over the years it has been his practice

F   to remain in college for approximately half a day before or after such dinners. Because of his present commitment to the Royal Commission, however, the college well understand that until June 1993 the plaintiff will be unable to devote as much time as usual to his research work; at present he is really just keeping in touch with his subject — sociology — and writing very occasional learned articles. This fellowship, I should add, is unremunerated.

G   It is the plaintiff's case that he should only be required to give credit against his damages claim for such earnings as he receives from Weir's (and the value of his part-time use of their chauffeur driven motor car and, since 1 January 1992, private health insurance under the PPP). The defendants for their part contend that an altogether broader comparison should be made — between the plaintiff's overall earnings respectively before and after his dismissal — and that such comparison indicates that he is in fact financially better off now that he was with the defendant. Putting the ancillary

H   benefits aside, the plaintiff before dismissal earned £89,000 from the company and £30,000 from the SIB: £119,000 in total. He earns now £50,000 from Weir's, £46,800 per annum from the Royal Commission, £7,500 from Investments, and £20,000 from SIB: a total of £124,300 per annum. Furthermore, submits Mr Falconer, the plaintiff is additionally better off than before because, his employment with Weir's not being pensionable, he is entitled to and in fact does invest in a private pension scheme with the

favourable fiscal consequences flowing from that course — a benefit of £7,124 per annum   A
by way of the reduced incidence of taxation.

My conclusions upon this part of the case are these:

(1)   The defendants are not entitled to credit for the plaintiff's earnings from the
Royal Commission. I have not the least doubt that even had the plaintiff remained
with the defendant company he still could and would have accepted appointment
as chairman of the Royal Commission. I utterly reject Mr Falconer's argument   B
that had the company held the plaintiff to the strict letter of his service agreement
he would have been unable to honour his commitment to the Commission: as
Mr Elias points out, the plaintiff was left free under his 1976 agreement for a total
of 212 days a year (104 weekend days, 28 days holiday, and 80 'working days' for
which express stipulation was made freeing him for other activities). Moreover,
although the Royal Commission requires the equivalent of 104 days a year these
need not be whole days and they need not be 'working days'. As the plaintiff says,   C
one of the advantages of being chairman is that he controls the Commission's
timetable. He was therefore able to decide that a whole series of meetings should
be held on Saturdays. And, of course, it would have been perfectly open to the
plaintiff even had he remained with the defendant to devote himself to the Royal
Commission, as in fact he does, at either end of his normal City working day.

(2)   I reject too the defendant's contention that they are entitled to credit for the   D
plaintiff's earnings from the SIB. As stated, these earnings are reduced now below
their level at the date of dismissal. More important, however, I have no doubt that
the plaintiff, even had he remained with the defendant, could and would have
made time for his presently reduced level of commitment to the SIB as well as the
time necessary for the Royal Commission.

(3)   Nor in my judgment are the defendants entitled to credit for the plaintiff's   E
earnings from Investments save only to the limited extent that the plaintiff
between 12 November 1990 and 1 April 1991 was paid in excess of £7,500 per
annum. That excess ought properly to be regarded as earned in mitigation of the
plaintiff's damages and credited: after all, had he remained with the defendant,
I doubt whether he could properly have acted also as chief executive of another
company, even one devoted as Investments was to the intended investment of
family capital realised by the takeover and not in those early months actively   F
trading. I recognise that the plaintiff in fact combined the chairmanship of
Investments and exercised such executive direction as it required (albeit at a
reduced salary) with running Weir's from 11 February to 1 April 1991; I am not,
however, persuaded that he would have done so had he remained with the
defendant. To the extent of £7,500 per annum, however, I am satisfied that even
had the plaintiff not been dismissed he would still have set up Investments and
been entitled to play the chairman's role as presently he does, leaving executive   G
direction to Mr Haley. Although, moreover, Investments contemplate investment
in shipping, the plaintiff has no intention of competing with the defendant
company so that in my judgment the terms of his service contract (already cited)
would not have inhibited him in this additional employment.

(4)   So far as the plaintiff's research fellowship is concerned, nothing more need be
said than that I am satisfied that this would not have precluded his undertaking   H
those of his engagements that I have already concluded he would have pursued
even had he remained with the defendant, namely the Royal Commission, the
SIB and, to the present limited extent, Investments.

(5)   With regard to Weir's, although there can be no certainty that the plaintiff's
present engagement will continue beyond 8 July 1992 when it comes up for review,

A   I conclude that in all probability it will. True, the plaintiff's initial main task on
      appointment was to find a full-time chief executive and, that successfully achieved,
      he contemplates the possibility that Weir's may now need less of his own services.
      Given, however, that during most of last year the plaintiff was working for Weir's
      closer to three days per week than the two days contracted for, and given in
      addition the plaintiff's high standing not only in the shipping world generally but
      specifically with those about to decide his future at Weir's, I see every reason to
B   share his own expectation that he will be kept on. In the unlikely event that his
      chairmanship of Weir's were to cease, whether this July or otherwise earlier than
      he would wish, he could probably take up a fuller executive role in Investments
      and earn substantially more than his present £7,500 per annum from that source.
      Taking all things together and realising that the plaintiff received no salary
      increase from Weir's on the January 1992 review, I believe that the appropriate
      course is to impute to him a continuing income from Weir's for two days work per
C   week of £50,000 per annum until he would in any event have retired. The plaintiff
      must similarly give credit on a continuing basis for his private health insurance
      (which accordingly from 1 January 1992 extinguishes his BUPA loss) and for the
      partial use of a motor car. Precisely what sum is to be credited on this latter
      account is impossible to say on the present state of the evidence. I merely note
      that the plaintiff now has had to acquire a motor car for himself and has to meet its
D   running expenses for his private use whereas, during his employment with the
      defendant, the company car was entirely for his own use at all times and the
      company met all expenses upon it. If agreement cannot now be reached upon this
      slender issue, I shall refer it for further evidence and argument.

(6)   Mr Elias argues that some allowance should be made in the plaintiff's favour for
      possible salary increases pursuant to the defendant's obligation under his service
E   agreement to review his basic salary at least annually. Mr Falconer disputes this
      and argues on the contrary that the plaintiff should give credit for the tax benefit
      he obtains from now being able to invest in a pension scheme of his own — £7,124
      per annum as stated. I reject both these arguments: the answer to each is,
      I believe, to be found in *Lavarack v Woods of Colchester Ltd* [1967] 1 QB 278.

(7)   One final point arises, to my mind significantly the most difficult in respect of
F   mitigation. As stated, the plaintiff is now working two days a week for Weir's.
      Had he remained with the defendant, he would be working on average something
      over three days a week. Accordingly he now has spare at least one day a week
      which, if suitable work were available to him, he would be obliged to devote to
      earning further sums in mitigation of his loss. I do not doubt that he is in reality
      already an exceedingly busy man. But inexorably it follows from all that I have
      thus far found that this further day a week is indeed available to him: were it
G   otherwise, he could not have combined the Royal Commission, the SIB, and
      Investments with a continuation of employment by the defendant. Very little
      evidence was adduced as to the possibility of the plaintiff now seeking additional
      work and remuneration for a day a week or any such period: as indicated, the
      defendant's case was concentrated rather upon the contention that the plaintiff
      must now give credit for part at least of his present income from the Royal
      Commission. But does that mean that I must simply ignore the plaintiff's additional
H   earning potential in this regard? I believe not. Rather I must do my best to place
      some value upon the plaintiff's ability — and thus his duty in mitigation — now to
      seek further remunerative work for a day a week. The burden lies on the
      defendant to establish any failure by a plaintiff to mitigate his loss. So far as the
      past is concerned, I do not think that burden discharged. Henceforth, however,
      seeking to balance on the one hand the plaintiff's advantages in the way of

A

experience and reputation against on the other hand the difficulties that doubtless exist in the way of obtaining work of the sort I envisage — non-executive directorships, consultancy fees or whatever — I impute to the plaintiff a further earning potential in mitigation of his damages claim of £10,000 gross per annum.

That, I believe, at altogether too great length, concludes my findings on all outstanding issues. There will therefore be an order that the plaintiff recover damages to be determined in accordance with the terms of this judgment. I give both parties leave to apply lest any further difficulty arises, at the same time expressing my fervent hope that none will.

B

(*Order accordingly*)

C

D

E

F

G

H

A
Re Seagull Manufacturing Co Ltd.

Court of Appeal (Civil Division).
Lloyd and Hirst L JJ and Peter Gibson J.
Judgment delivered 3 February 1993.

B
> *Winding up — Public examination — Official receiver applied for public examination of director resident in Channel Islands — Whether court could order public examination of person out of jurisdiction — Insolvency Act 1986, sec. 133.*

This was an appeal by a director from a decision of Mummery J ([1991] BCC 550) restoring an order of the registrar for the public examination of the appellant in the compulsory winding up of Seagull Manufacturing Co Ltd.

C
The order for public examination was made ex parte on the application of the official receiver under sec. 133 of the Insolvency Act 1986. It was set aside by the registrar on the appellant's application on the ground that it was made without jurisdiction since at all material times the appellant was resident and domiciled out of the jurisdiction, since 1986 in Alderney.

The official receiver appealed on the ground that sec. 133 of the Insolvency Act 1986 empowered the court to order the public examination of a British subject notwithstanding his residence abroad, and Mummery J allowed the official receiver's appeal, holding that on its true construction sec. 133 applied to all who fell within the class of persons specified in subsec. (1)(a)–(c), whether they were British subjects or not and whether they were within the jurisdiction of the English court or not at the relevant time.

D
Held, dismissing the director's appeal:

E
Where a company had been wound up by the court, the obvious intention of sec. 133 was that those responsible for the company's state of affairs should be liable to be subjected to a process of investigation and that that investigation should be in public. Parliament could not have intended that a person who had had that responsibility could escape liability to investigation simply by not being within the jurisdiction. There was nothing in the legislation and no reasons of comity which indicated the contrary. Section 133 plainly did apply to the appellant.

F
The following cases were referred to in the judgment:

Bishopsgate Investment Management Ltd, Re [1992] BCC 222; [1993] Ch 1.
Blain, Ex parte. Re Sawers (1879) 12 ChD 522.
Clark (HMIT) v Oceanic Contractors Inc [1982] BTC 417; [1983] 2 AC 130.
Paramount Airways Ltd, Re (No. 2) [1992] BCC 416; [1993] Ch 223.
Theophile v Solicitor-General [1950] AC 186.
Tucker (R C) (a bankrupt), Re, ex parte Tucker (K R) [1990] Ch 148.

G
Paul Teverson (instructed by Rose & Birn) for the appellant.

Nigel Davis QC (instructed by the Treasury Solicitor) for the official receiver.

JUDGMENT

Peter Gibson J: This appeal raises a point of some importance in the compulsory
H
winding up of companies. On the true construction of sec. 133 of the *Insolvency Act* 1986, does the court have jurisdiction to order the public examination of an officer of the company when that officer is outside the jurisdiction of the court?

The company in question is Seagull Manufacturing Co Ltd ("Seagull"). It was incorporated in England as a private company on 17 March 1983. Its business was that of a computer utility organisation and it had its registered office in Dorchester.

The appellant, Mr Colin Slinn, was a director of Seagull from 27 January 1986 to 3 July 1988. He is a British subject but has since 1979 been resident out of the jurisdiction, first in the Isle of Man and, since July 1986, in Alderney in the Channel Islands.

On 30 May 1989 the Secretary of State for Trade and Industry instigated an inquiry under sec. 447 of the *Companies Act* 1985 into Seagull, following which he presented a petition under sec. 440 of that Act for the winding up of Seagull on the ground that that was expedient in the public interest.

In the petition it was alleged, amongst other things, that Mr Slinn had been obstructive in the sec. 447 inquiry, failing to produce books of accounts and financial records of Seagull, that Seagull was insolvent and unable to pay its debts, that Seagull's principal asset had been assigned first to himself and then to another company and that there was no record of any proper consideration being paid to Seagull, that there was no information on the payment and application of substantial funds subscribed and paid to Seagull by another company controlled by Mr Slinn, and no audited accounts had been filed by the company since those for the period ended 31 March 1986, which revealed a net loss of nearly half a million pounds. On 4 April 1990 a compulsory winding-up order was made on the petition which was unopposed.

On 11 April 1990, on the application of the official receiver an order was made by the Companies Court under sec. 426 of the *Insolvency Act* 1986, requesting the Insolvency Court in Alderney to act in aid by seizing documents of Seagull in the possession of Mr Slinn and by examining Mr Slinn. On 25 April of that year the Alderney court acting on that request ordered such seizure and the order was executed on 27 April. On 3 May 1990 the Alderney court in further compliance with the request made to it appointed an examiner. Mr Slinn appealed against both orders of the Alderney court but that appeal was dismissed by the Royal Courts of Guernsey on 8 November 1990 and a further appeal to the Court of Appeal in Guernsey was dismissed on 5 August 1991.

In the meantime, on 17 July 1990 the official receiver applied ex parte to Mr Registrar *Buckley* under sec. 133 for an order for the public examination of Mr Slinn at the Royal Courts of Justice. The registrar made that order and gave the official receiver leave to serve Mr Slinn at his address in Alderney. But on 25 September 1990 at an inter partes hearing Mr Registrar *Pimm* on Mr Slinn's application set aside those ex parte orders. The official receiver appealed and his appeal was allowed by *Mummery* J (see [1991] BCC 550) who restored the orders made by Mr Registrar *Buckley*. Before *Mummery* J there was affidavit evidence from the official receiver that creditors' claims against Seagull exceeded two million pounds, that Mr Slinn had not co-operated with the official receiver and that, despite being required by the official receiver to produce a statement of affairs for Seagull, no statement of affairs had been produced. The official receiver said that in the circumstances he wanted Mr Slinn examined in public where creditors and contributories could question Mr Slinn.

Mr Slinn now appeals to this court from *Mummery* J's decision. The only other fact which I need mention is that in January 1992 there was a private examination of Mr Slinn by the examiner appointed by the Alderney court.

I turn now to the statutory provisions. The *Insolvency Act* 1986 consolidates with amendments both the enactments relating to company insolvency and winding up and those relating to the insolvency and bankruptcy of individuals. It largely implemented the recommendations made in the *Report of the Review Committee on Insolvency Law and Practice* (Cmnd 8558, June 1982) of which the chairman was the late Sir Kenneth Cork (the "Cork Report"). It is obvious, not only from the report but also from the Act itself, that the intention was to harmonise the two systems as far as possible.

A   Part IV of the Act relates to the winding up of companies registered under the Companies Acts. Chapter VI in that part relates to winding up by the court and sec. 133 is in that chapter. But under Pt. V of the Act the court has jurisdiction to wind up not only companies registered in England and Wales but also unregistered companies, which include oversea companies, and Ch. VI of Pt. IV also applies to those companies (see sec. 221(1)). But the jurisprudence of the court has limited the exercise of the jurisdiction over oversea companies to companies which have a sufficient connection with England

B   and Wales and where there is a reasonable possibility of benefit for the creditors from a winding up (see *Re Paramount Airways Ltd (No. 2)* [1992] BCC 416 at p. 425).

Section 133 is one of a number of sections headed "Investigation procedures" and is in the following form:

"*Public examination of officers*

C   (1) Where a company is being wound up by the court, the official receiver or, in Scotland, the liquidator may at any time before the dissolution of the company apply to the court for the public examination of any person who—

(a) is or has been an officer of the company; or

(b) has acted as liquidator or administrator of the company or as receiver or manager or, in Scotland, receiver of its property; or

D   (c) not being a person falling within paragraph (a) or (b), is or has been concerned, or has taken part, in the promotion, formation or management of the company.

(2) Unless the court otherwise orders, the official receiver or, in Scotland, the liquidator shall make an application under subsection (1) if he is requested in accordance with the rules to do so by—

E   (a) one-half, in value, of the company's creditors; or

(b) three-quarters, in value, of the company's contributories.

(3) On an application under subsection (1), the court shall direct that a public examination of the person to whom the application relates shall be held on a day appointed by the court; and that person shall attend on that day and be publicly examined as to the promotion, formation or management of the company or as to

F   the conduct of its business and affairs, or his conduct or dealings in relation to the company.

(4) The following may take part in the public examination of a person under this section and may question that person concerning the matters mentioned in subsection (3), namely—

(a) the official receiver;

G   (b) the liquidator of the company;

(c) any person who has been appointed as special manager of the company's property or business;

(d) any creditor of the company who has tendered a proof or, in Scotland, submitted a claim in the winding up;

H   (e) any contributory of the company."

Section 134 relates to the enforcement of sec. 133. Amongst other things it provides:

"(1) If a person without reasonable excuse fails at any time to attend his public examination under section 133, he is guilty of a contempt of court and liable to be punished accordingly."

Various points are to be noted on sec. 133. First, in the case of an English winding up, as distinct from one in Scotland, the official receiver, and only the official receiver, has a discretion whether to apply to the court for the public examination of a person falling within the three categories mentioned in subsec. (1); and if he does so the court is required to direct a public examination. But where a substantial part of the creditors or contributories, that is to say one-half in value of the company's creditors or three-quarters in value of its contributories, so request, the official receiver must make the application, unless the court exercises its discretion to order otherwise.

Second, the class of persons who may be examined is a limited class of officers and other persons who, in the words of *Mummery* J (at p. 556D):

"have voluntarily concerned themselves in a specified capacity in the affairs of the company which is being wound up, i.e. as officer, liquidator, administrator, receiver or manager, or as participant in the promotion, formation or management of the company."

Third, the topics on which the examinee can be examined are limited to the promotion, formation or management of the company or the conduct of its business and affairs or the examinee's conduct or dealings in relation to the company.

Fourth, the persons who may take part in the public examination comprise those who might be expected to be most affected by the company being wound up by the court, including creditors and contributories.

On the face of sec. 133, it contains no territorial limitation. It is expressed to apply to "any person" who comes within any of the three categories in subsec. (1). But there is a well-established rule of construction that English legislation is territorial in effect in the sense that, in the absence of express enactment or plain implication, it is only to apply to British subjects or to foreigners within the jurisdiction (*Ex parte Blain* (1879) 12 ChD 522). For a recent statement of the rule I refer to *Clark v Oceanic Contractors Inc* [1982] BTC 417 at p. 422 where Lord *Scarman* described the general principle as being:

". . . that, unless the contrary is expressly enacted or so plainly implied that the courts must give effect to it, United Kingdom legislation is applicable only to British subjects or to foreigners who by coming to the United Kingdom, whether for a short or a long time, have made themselves subject to British jurisdiction."

That rule of construction is not of course entirely helpful to Mr Slinn as a British subject, but it exemplifies what might be thought to be a proper reluctance of the court to construe English legislation in such a way as to enable it to assert jurisdiction over those subject to another jurisdiction by their presence in that other jurisdiction, unless compelled to do so by the language of the legislation. The case before *Mummery* J and this court has been argued on the broad question whether the absence from the jurisdiction of a person otherwise within sec. 133(1) prevents the application of the section to that person; and that is a question of construction.

In the *Clark* case, which raised a question as to the liability to English tax of a non-resident corporation, Lord *Wilberforce* considered the rule of construction laid down in *Ex parte Blain* and said at p. 426 that it:

"requires an inquiry to be made as to the persons with respect to whom Parliament is presumed, in the particular case, to be legislating.

Who, it is to be asked, is within the legislative grasp, or intendment, of the statute under consideration? The contention being that, as regards companies, the statute cannot have been intended to apply to them if they are non-resident, one asks immediately — why not?"

A   In considering Lord *Wilberforce*'s question as to who comes within the legislative grasp of the section, one must look to the policy of the legislature in enacting the section in question.

     Where a company has come to a calamitous end and has been wound up by the court, the obvious intention of this section was that those responsible for the company's state of affairs should be liable to be subjected to a process of investigation and that that investigation should be in public. Parliament could not have intended that a person who

B   had that responsibility could escape liability to investigation simply by not being within the jurisdiction. Indeed, if the section were to be construed as leaving out of its grasp anyone not within the jurisdiction, deliberate evasion by removing oneself out of the jurisdiction would suffice. That seems to me to be a wholly improbable intention to attribute to Parliament.

     Further, sec. 133 must be construed in the light of circumstances existing in the mid-

C   1980s when the legislation was enacted. By use of the telephone, telex and fax machines English companies can be managed perfectly well by persons who need not set foot within the jurisdiction. There is no requirement that an officer of an English company must live in England, nor of course need an officer of an overseas company which may be wound up by the court. Such a company is very likely to have officers not within the jurisdiction.

D   I would emphasise that the question before this court is one of the scope of the Act and we are not concerned with whether the order for public examination can be effectively enforced against a person out of the jurisdiction (cf. *Theophile v Solicitor-General* [1950] AC 186 at p. 195).

     When Parliament enacted sec. 133, it is very likely that it did so against the background of what *Dillon* LJ in *Re Bishopsgate Investment Management Ltd* [1992] BCC 222 at

E   p. 232G, described as:

> "The public worry and concern over company failures on a large scale, and the need to safeguard the public against such failures . . ."

     Both public and private examinations have a significant role to play in the investigation of a company failure. The particular purposes that can be served by public examination were instructively set out in the Cork Report. After referring to the restricted scope of

F   the then operative provisions for public examination (which required the official receiver to express an opinion that there had been fraud in relation to the company) and to the fact that the provisions for public examination were no longer being used, the report continues at para. 654:

> "We believe that this approach to the public examination requires to be reviewed. If, as we recommend, the whole purpose of a Compulsory Winding Up Order is

G   > to deal with cases which are of sufficient gravity to justify a full investigation, then, we believe, a public examination has a role to play in the proceedings. We attach importance to a public examination for individual debtors in the event of a Bankruptcy Order being made and we consider that it would be undesirable if a similar provision was not available in the Compulsory Winding Up of an insolvent company, for use where the Court felt it to be appropriate.

H   > 655. A public examination during the course of Compulsory Winding Up proceedings should, as in Bankruptcy, be intended to serve three principal purposes:
>
>   (a) to form the basis of reports which the Official Receiver may have to submit to the Department concerning the affairs of the company; for example, concerning possible offences by officers of the company and others;

(b) to obtain material information for the administration of the estate which cannot as well be obtained privately; and

(c) to give publicity, for the information of creditors and the community at large, to the salient facts and unusual features connected with the company's failure.

656. We believe, as did the Jenkins Committee, that the revival of the public examination as a fact to be reckoned with in winding up proceedings is desirable. By exposing serious misconduct, it will help to promote higher standards of commercial and business morality and will also serve as a form of sanction against former officers of a failed company who have not adequately assisted the Official Receiver and the liquidator in the course of their respective investigations and administration of the company's affairs."

There is every reason to think that the provisions for public examination, now enacted in sec. 133, were intended by Parliament to serve those purposes. Moreover, the legislative intention, that there should be a proper and effective investigation through public and private examination, has been held to be so clear that even in the absence of express words this court has been able to hold in the *Bishopsgate* case that an examinee is not entitled to invoke the privilege against self-incrimination.

In answer to Lord *Wilberforce*'s questions, Mr Teverson (appearing for Mr Slinn) would seek to give a number of reasons why sec. 133 should not be construed to apply to those outside the jurisdiction. First, he submits that express words would be needed to make those not within the jurisdiction liable to public examination. He relied on the general practice of international law that courts of a country only have power to summon before them persons who accept service or who are present within the territory of that country when served with the appropriate process. Further, he submitted, the very fact that the court can wind up foreign companies means that without express words it could not have been Parliament's intention that sec. 133 did apply to any foreign officer of a company.

I am not persuaded by these contentions. I can see no reasons of comity which would prevent those who voluntarily were officers or otherwise participated in the formation or running of an English company being capable of being summoned by the English court for the purposes of public examination. The fact that Parliament has provided for the compulsory winding up of foreign companies, knowing that those companies would only be wound up when there was a sufficient connection with the jurisdiction, and the fact that Parliament provided that sec. 133 should apply in such a case, seem to me to indicate that the officers of such companies who may well not be within the jurisdiction should be examinable publicly.

Secondly, Mr Teverson based an elaborate argument on the judgment of this court in *Re Tucker (a bankrupt), ex parte Tucker* [1990] Ch 148. That was a decision on the construction of sec. 25 of the *Bankruptcy Act* 1914 relating to private examination as applied to a British subject resident in Belgium who was the brother of the debtor. Section 25(1) read:

"The court may, on the application of the official receiver or trustee, at any time after a receiving order has been made against a debtor, summon before it the debtor or his wife, or any person known or suspected to have in his possession any of the estate or effects belonging to the debtor, or supposed to be indebted to the debtor, or any person whom the court may deem capable of giving information respecting the debtor, his dealings or property, and the court may require any such person to produce any documents in his custody or power relating to the debtor, his dealings or property."

A   I should also read sec. 25(6):

> "The court may, if it thinks fit, order that any person who if in England would be liable to be brought before it under this section shall be examined in Scotland or Ireland, or in any other place out of England."

Dillon LJ, with whom *Lloyd* LJ and Sir *Nicolas Browne-Wilkinson* V-C agreed, placed particular reliance on the presence of that subsection in sec. 25, saying (at

B   p. 158G):

> "Finally, and to my mind conclusively, by section 25(6) the court is given a power . . . to order the examination out of England of 'any person who if in England would be liable to be brought before it under this section.' This wording carries inevitably, in my judgment, the connotation that if the person is not in England he is not liable to be brought before the English court under the section."

C   Mr Teverson points to the fact that the provisions for the private examination of a bankrupt are now contained in sec. 366 and 367 of the 1986 Act, and that subsec. (3) of sec. 367 is in a form very similar to sec. 25(6). The next stage of his argument is that by parity of reasoning, those private examination provisions are subject to the same territorial limitation as sec. 25 of the *Bankruptcy Act* 1914.

D   Next he draws attention to the fact that sec. 236 and 237 of the 1986 Act contain provisions for private examination in relation to companies in similar form to the provisions in that Act for the private examination of a bankrupt and that subsec. (3) of sec. 237 is in terms substantially similar to 367(3). So, he submits, the same territorial limitation applies to private examination in company cases.

The final stage of his argument is that there would be a surprising anomaly between public and private examinations relating to companies if a territorial limitation were not

E   implicit in sec. 133, given what he calls the substantial overlap between the persons expressed to be within sec. 133(1) on the one hand and sec. 236(2) on the other.

Mummery J was not convinced by this argument and neither am I. In my judgment the argument breaks down at a number of points. First, *Re Tucker* was a decision on a wholly different statutory provision, sec. 25 of the *Bankruptcy Act* 1914. It related to the private examination not of the debtor but of a person who came within the wide words:

F

> "any person whom the court may deem capable of giving information respecting the debtor, his dealings or property . . ."

Under sec. 1(2) of the *Bankruptcy Act* 1914, a debtor is defined as including any person who:

> "(c) was carrying on business in England, personally, or by means of an agent or

G   manager; or

> (d) was a member of a firm or partnership which carried on business in England."

It is not disputed by Mr Teverson that a foreign resident out of the jurisdiction can be a debtor for the purposes of the *Bankruptcy Act* 1914 and as such could be served with a bankruptcy notice. That being so, it seems to me that a debtor out of the jurisdiction could be examined privately under sec. 25 of the 1914 Act or publicly under sec. 15 of

H   that Act. Certainly *Re Tucker* does not decide the contrary.

Secondly, the class of persons who could, in *Dillon* LJ's phrase, be hauled before the court under sec. 25 was notably wider than the three categories of sec. 133. In particular it was not limited to the debtor but included anyone whom the court suspected might have relevant property or information. In contrast the class of persons in sec. 133 is limited to those who might be said to have had responsibility for the company.

Third, if it be right (1) that sec. 366 and 367 should be construed as subject to the same
territorial limitation as sec. 25 of the 1914 Act, and (2) that sec. 236 and 237 should
be similarly construed by reason of the inclusion of the subsection corresponding to
sec. 25(6) (and Mr Davis, appearing for the official receiver, whilst recognising the force
of an argument to that effect, does not concede that the relevant section should be
so construed), sec. 133 is plainly distinguishable by reason of the absence from it, or
sec. 134, of any provision corresponding to that in sec. 25(6), which was held to be so
determinative in *Re Tucker*.

Fourth, in any event I do not accept that a territorial limitation inferred from the
presence of a statutory provision in the form of sec. 25(6) in relation to a private
examination must be inferred in a section relating to a public examination without such
a statutory provision. Whilst there is some overlap between the classes of persons to
whom sec. 133(1) and 236(2) respectively apply, there are several important differences,
in particular in relation to the wide classes of person referred to in sec. 236(2)(b) and (c)
as compared with sec. 133(1)(b) and (c). Those classes comprise:

"(b) any person known or suspected to have in his possession any property of the
company or supposed to be indebted to the company, or

(c) any person whom the court thinks capable of giving information concerning
the promotion, formation, business, dealings, affairs or property of the company."

For my part I agree with *Mummery* J in holding that it is more appropriate to compare
the public examination provisions in the case of companies in sec. 133 with the public
examination provisions relating to individual debtors. As will have been seen from the
passage I have cited from the Cork Report, the committee considered that it would be
undesirable if a provision similar to that available in connection with the public
examination of individual debtors was not available in a compulsory winding up of an
insolvent company. When one compares sec. 133 with the provisions of sec. 290 of the
Insolvency Act 1986 relating to the public examination of a bankrupt, the similarity of
language is such that as *Stuart-Smith* LJ in the *Bishopsgate* case said at p. 249C:

"The effect of the change brought about in sec. 133 of the 1986 Act is to assimilate
public examinations of officers under that section with public examination of a
bankrupt."

In other words those within sec. 133(1) are the persons in a company context equivalent
to the bankrupt. Section 265 of the 1986 Act, containing provisions corresponding to
those in sec. 1(2) of the 1914 Act, in my view makes it impossible to contend that a
bankrupt who is out of the jurisdiction cannot be made subject to public examination. It
it would be a surprising anomaly if those within sec. 133(1) excluded persons out of the
jurisdiction.

Mr Teverson's third submission was based on the fact that the *Insolvency Act* 1986
provides an alternative procedure by means of orders in aid under sec. 426 which can be
used to cause the examination of persons in certain other jurisdictions. The *Bankruptcy
Act* 1914 had a provision for orders in aid and this was a point mentioned in *Re Tucker*
by *Dillon* LJ at p. 158G where he said the procedure, while taking advantage of the
jurisdictions of the bankruptcy courts of other countries, also respects those jurisdictions.

In the present case the official receiver has in fact been able to make use of the in aid
procedure to procure the private examination of Mr Slinn in Alderney. That the
Insolvency Act now provides for an in aid procedure in relation to company proceedings,
whilst a factor to be taken into account in construing sec. 133, seems to me to be one
only of slight weight. I cannot see that realistically Parliament could have intended that
procedure to be an adequate substitute for an ability to require an officer of a company
who is abroad to be subject to public examination, particularly when the procedure is
available in respect of persons present in so very few jurisdictions outside the UK.

A

Then Mr Teverson drew attention to the absence of any provision which dealt with administrative details affecting the public examination of someone abroad, such as the costs of attendance and travel arrangements, and he submitted that it should be inferred therefrom that Parliament did not intend that such a person should be summoned from abroad. I am not prepared to draw any such inference. It may be presumed that Parliament treated persons so summoned to be under a duty to attend the examination at their own expense.

B

Finally, Mr Teverson relied on r. 4.211(1) of the *Insolvency Rules* 1986 which requires service forthwith of a copy of the court's order for the public examination of a person. This, he submitted, showed that sec. 133 was not intended by Parliament to apply to persons outside the jurisdiction who could not be served forthwith. In my judgment there is nothing in this point either. It is impermissible to construe the Act by reference to the rules made under it, and in any event "forthwith" means no more than "as soon

C

as is reasonably practicable".

Mr Teverson also submitted there was an inconsistency between r. 4.211 with its mandatory requirement of service forthwith and r. 12.12(3) relating to service out of the jurisdiction of any process or order or other documents in insolvency proceedings. By that rule the court may order service to be effected "within such time, on such person, at such place and in such manner as it thinks fit". That rule applies to all insolvency proceedings, not just to public examination. I see no difficulty in construing the rule so

D

as to leave the court with a discretion as to matters such as the place and the manner in which service is to be effected whilst at the same time not affecting the requirement that there should be service on such person because of sec. 133 and r. 4.211.

For the sake of completeness I should mention two other matters. First, Mr Teverson sought leave to rely on the charter granted by Queen Elizabeth I to the residents of Guernsey, Alderney and Sark, granting immunity to such residents from process from

E

English courts concerning any matter in controversy arising in those islands. This was not a point taken below even though a letter from Mr Slinn to the official receiver on 25 June 1990 shows that Mr Slinn was aware of the point then. We refused leave to raise the point, which would have required evidence of Alderney law as well as evidence relating to whether matters in controversy did arise in the islands.

Second, Mr Davis by a respondent's notice sought to support the decision of the judge

F

on a further point based on the fact that Mr Slinn is a British subject and so, Mr Davis would have submitted, in any event sec. 133 applies to him. In the circumstances we did not find it necessary to call upon Mr Davis to argue the point.

For the reasons that I have given, it seems to me plain that sec. 133 does apply to a person such as Mr Slinn, notwithstanding his absence outside the jurisdiction. As Mr Davis submitted, the judge reached the right decision for the right reasons.

G

For my part I would dismiss this appeal.

Hirst LJ: I agree that the appeal should be dismissed for the reasons given by *Peter Gibson* J and I only wish to add a few words of my own.

In my judgment the key to this appeal lies in the determination of the question who is within the legislative grasp, or intendment, of sec. 133 of the *Insolvency Act* 1986, per Lord *Wilberforce* in *Clark v Oceanic Contractors Inc* [1982] BTC 417 at p. 426. This

H

section is headed "Public examination of officers" and each class of persons referred to in subsec. (1)(a)–(c) is or has been personally involved in that capacity in the direction or management of the company in liquidation.

The purpose of the public examination is to enable the official receiver in the fulfilment of his duty under sec. 132 to investigate inter alia the causes of failure of the company, and its business dealings and affairs, for which the officer in question is or may

have been wholly or partly responsible, and therefore personally and directly accountable
for what has gone wrong. The efficient and thorough conduct of such investigation by
the official receiver is of great public importance, as several recent notorious cases have
demonstrated. This process would be frustrated if, for example, a director, who had
with the aid of modern methods of communication run the company entirely from
abroad, was immune from public examination as he or she would be if Mr Teverson's
submissions were correct. The same applies to a director who has defrauded the
company in England and then absconded abroad shortly before the liquidation. These
are by no means fanciful illustrations in the world of the 1980s and 1990s, and many
similar ones could be given.

It follows that, in my judgment, all officers as described in sec. 133(1)(a)–(c), whether
inside or outside the jurisdiction, are within the legislative grasp and intendment of
sec. 133, which on its proper construction has no territorial limits.

I would add that I find no difficulty in distinguishing the *Tucker* case for the reasons
given by *Peter Gibson* J.

Lloyd LJ: I agree with both judgments.

(*Appeal dismissed. Leave to appeal to the House of Lords refused*)

A   # Re New Bullas Trading Ltd.

Chancery Division (Companies Court).
Knox J.
Judgment delivered 11 February 1993.

B
Receivership — Debenture — Debenture expressed to confer fixed charge over book debts — Debenture holder could give directions as to dealing with debts and proceeds — Materiality of restrictions on dealing with debts and proceeds — Whether charge was fixed or floating — Insolvency Act 1986, sec. 40.

This was an application by administrative receivers to determine whether a charge over the company's book debts contained in a debenture was a floating charge.

C
There were two debentures. The first debenture holder had been paid off. The second debenture was expressed to create a fixed charge over the book and other debts owing to the company. The debenture required the company to deal with the book and other debts in accordance with any directions from time to time given in writing by the debenture holder and in default of and subject to any such directions deal with the same only in the ordinary course of getting in and realising the same, and forbade selling, assigning, factoring or discounting the same in any way. It provided for the company to pay the

D
proceeds of book and other debts into a designated account and to deal with such moneys in accordance with any directions from time to time given in writing by the debenture holder, and, in the absence of any directions by the debenture holder, for such moneys to be released from the fixed charge on the debts and to become subject to a floating charge created by the debenture. No directions had been given by the second debenture holder pursuant to the provisions of the debenture. The preferential creditors argued that since the company was free, absent a direction by the debenture holder, to collect the book

E
debts, bank the moneys and spend them in the ordinary course of business, the charge was a floating charge at its creation (for the purpose of sec. 40 of the Insolvency Act 1986), notwithstanding the express terms of the debenture.

Held, declaring that the charge over the company's book debts was as created a floating charge:

F
Notwithstanding the parties' expressed intention to create a fixed charge, the extent to which the company was left free to deal with the book debts and the proceeds if and when collected compelled the court to conclude that there was a floating charge. The company was obliged to deal with the debts in accordance with the directions of the debenture holder if and when such directions were given, but as at the date when the charge was created that was a possibility and not an existing state of affairs. (Re Brightlife Ltd (1986) 2 BCC 99,359 followed.)

G
The following cases were referred to in the judgment:

Brightlife Ltd, Re (1986) 2 BCC 99,359; [1987] Ch 200.
Evans v Rival Granite Quarries Ltd [1910] 2 KB 979.
Governments Stock and Other Securities Investment Co Ltd v Manila Railway Co Ltd & Ors [1897] AC 81.
Illingworth v Houldsworth & Anor [1904] AC 355.

H
Keenan Bros Ltd, Re (1986) 2 BCC 98,970; [1985] IR 401.
Siebe Gorman & Co Ltd v Barclays Bank Ltd [1979] 2 Lloyd's Rep 142.
Street v Mountford [1985] AC 809.
Welsh Development Agency v Export Finance Co Ltd [1992] BCC 270.
Yorkshire Woolcombers Association Ltd, Re [1903] 2 Ch 284 (CA); [1904] AC 355 (HL).

Martin Pascoe (instructed by Clifford Chance) for the administrative receivers.

Jonathan Sumption QC and David Chivers (instructed by Lawrence Graham) for the debenture holder.

Christopher Tidmarsh (instructed by the Solicitor of Inland Revenue) for the preferential creditors.

JUDGMENT

Knox J: This is an application by administrative receivers of New Bullas Trading Ltd ("the company") asking that it may be determined whether on the true construction of a debenture dated 18 July 1989 made between the company and the first respondent, 3i plc ("3i"), the charge over the company's book debts created by cl. 3 thereof is a fixed or floating charge. I suspect that the wrong tense was used in that question because the issue that was argued before me was whether sec. 40 of the *Insolvency Act* 1986 applied. That section provides so far as relevant as follows:

> "(1) The following applies, in the case of a company, where a receiver is appointed on behalf of the holders of any debentures of the company secured by a charge which, as created, was a floating charge.
>
> (2) If the company is not at the time in course of being wound up, its preferential debts . . . shall be paid out of the assets coming into the hands of the receiver in priority to any claims for principal or interest in respect of the debentures."

Attention is firmly directed as a result of amendments introduced by the *Insolvency Act* 1985 to the time and the state of affairs when the charge was created rather than the time when the court has to look at the matter or the time when a crystallisation event occurred under the debenture.

There were in fact two debentures given by the company, one in favour of Lloyds Bank plc under which the plaintiffs, who are administrative receivers, were appointed to that position on 6 November 1991, and the second to 3i under which the plaintiffs were appointed six days later on 12 November 1991 as administrative receivers. The company went into creditors' voluntary liquidation on 28 September 1992.

The factual background is that the amounts due to secured creditors at the date of the appointment of the administrative receivers was £1.136m in favour of Lloyds Bank plc (and that except for a trivial sum has now been paid off), £100,000 to 3i, and to some minority shareholders, £37,500. The preferential creditors are estimated at slightly over £600,000 and there are four joined in the proceedings, the Commissioners of Inland Revenue, the Customs and Excise, the Department of Employment and the Department of Social Security. A representation order has been made for the Commissioners of Inland Revenue to represent the other respondents and there are, as usual, also some employees who rank as regards some of their claims as preferential creditors.

The proceeds now held of realisation of book debts are stated in evidence to be £459,714 with a further estimated £26,000 to come, but the total is obviously short of the claims of preferential creditors and, therefore, the order of priority which is regulated by sec. 40 of the *Insolvency Act* 1986 is likely to be critical. It was agreed before me that if the charge created by the debenture in favour of 3i over book debts was a fixed charge as created, 3i would rank ahead of the preferential creditors, but, conversely, if it was a floating charge the effect of sec. 40 would be to reverse that order of priorities.

The debenture was dated 18 July 1989 and it contains in cl. 1 a covenant for payment, the relevant passage being:

> "The company named in the second schedule hereto (hereinafter called 'the company') hereby covenants with 3i plc . . . that it will on such date or dates as

A   provided by cl. 2 hereof pay or discharge to 3i all moneys and liabilities now or at any time or times hereafter due or owing or incurred by the company to 3i in any manner whatever . . ."

Clause 2 so far as material said:

"All or any moneys and liabilities due or owing or incurred by the company to 3i shall be repaid or discharged by the company on demand unless otherwise agreed
B   in writing from time to time between the company and 3i . . ."

The charge is contained in cl. 3 which, again, so far as relevant reads as follows:

"The company as beneficial owner hereby charges with the payment and discharge to 3i of all moneys and liabilities hereby covenanted to be paid and discharged by the company and all other sums intended to be hereby secured . . ."

C   —and there follows a list of the property charged.

The first property charged was specific land and property specified in a schedule. The second charged property was all other freehold and leasehold property. The third was plant machinery and chattels which are defined as "the mortgaged chattels". The fourth was the goodwill and uncalled capital of the company.

The fifth is very material. It reads:

D   "The book debts and other debts due or owing to the company both present and future."

Sixth was stock-in-trade work-in-progress and such like. Seventh was a general sweeping up provision viz:

"All other the undertaking and all other property and assets of the company both present and future."

E   Clause 4 then defines the nature of the charges and, again, so far as relevant provides as follows:

"The charges on the property and assets first second third fourth and fifth described are created as fixed charges . . .
The charges on the property and assets sixth and seventh described . . . are created as floating charges until a demand has been made under condition 8 set
F   out in the first schedule hereto or until the provisions of condition 9 set out in the first schedule hereto become operative when the floating charges shall crystallise and become fixed charges.

The charges created hereby shall be a continuing security and shall unless otherwise agreed in writing by 3i be first charges. The company shall not without the previous written consent of 3i:

G   . . .

     (ii) create or continue any mortgage or charge upon any part of the other property or assets hereby charged which would rank either in priority to or pari passu with the charged hereby created;

     (iii) allow any lien to arise on or affect any part of the other property or assets hereby charged except in the case of a lien arising by operation of law in the
H   ordinary course of business."

Clause 5 I can pass over. Clause 6 so far as material reads:

"This debenture is issued subject to and with the benefit of the conditions set out in the first schedule hereto . . . The specifically mortgaged property and the property and assets third fourth fifth sixth and seventh described are therein together referred to as 'the mortgage property'. The bank specified in the fifth schedule hereto (or such other bank as 3i may agree to in writing) is therein referred to as 'the bank'."

Just following that through for a moment, the fifth schedule identifies Lloyds Bank plc and its address in Wolverhampton Road, Dudley.

Turning then to the conditions that are imported by cl. 6 of the main body of the debenture, the expression "subject to and with the benefit of the conditions set out in the first schedule" was not argued to give any priority over the main body of the deed to the schedule. It merely means that the two have to be read together.

Condition 8 contains the various events which caused the security to crystallise if and when a demand is made. So far as relevant it reads:

"In respect of any moneys or liabilities due or incurred by the company to 3i which by virtue of the agreement are to be discharged otherwise than on demand 3i shall nevertheless be entitled by notice to the company to demand the immediate payment and discharge thereof (or any part thereof) together with all interest and any other sums forthwith (or otherwise as 3i may require) at any time after the happening of any of the following events . . .."

Then there is a series of events such as the levying of distress which give rise to that state of affairs.

In condition 9 one gets the crystallisation events when no demand is needed and there is again a list of events such as an order for the winding up of the company or a petition being presented for an administration order which give rise to that state of affairs.

I turn now to the all important condition which is the one that deals with book debts. It reads as follows:

"(12) During the continuance of this security the company shall:

(A) pay into a current account or a separate designated account (as 3i may require) of the company with the bank all moneys which it may receive in respect of the book debts and other debts hereby charged and (subject to any rights of the bank in respect thereof) pay or otherwise deal with such moneys standing in such account in accordance with any directions from time to time given in writing by 3i; prior to any demand being made under condition 8 hereof or to the provisions of condition 9 hereof becoming operative in the absence of any directions from 3i any moneys received by the company and paid into such account in respect of the book debts and other debts hereby charged shall upon such payment in stand released from the fixed charge on such debts hereinbefore by this debenture created and shall stand subject to the floating charge hereinbefore by this debenture created over the other property and assets of the company; any such release shall in no respects derogate from the subsistence and continuance of the said fixed charge on all other book and other debts of the company for the time being outstanding;

(B) if called upon to do so by 3i execute a legal assignment of such book debts and other debts to 3i in such terms as 3i may require and give notice thereof to the debtors from whom the debts are owing or incurred and take such other steps as 3i may require to perfect such legal assignment;

(C) deal with such book debts and other debts in accordance with any directions from time to time given in writing by 3i (subject to any rights of the bank in respect thereof) and in default of and subject to any such directions deal with the same only in the ordinary course of getting in and realising the same (but not sell assign factor or discount the same in any way);

A   (D) permit the bank to furnish directly to 3i from time to time upon request full
              statements and particulars of all the company's accounts with the bank and
              such other financial statements and information respecting the assets and
              liabilities of the company as are from time to time available to the bank."

It was not contended before me that any other conditions in the debenture have any
material effect on what I have to decide. The evidence is that no direction was given by
B   3i pursuant to the provisions of that twelfth condition of the debenture.

There is, of course, the plainest possible expression of an intention to create a fixed
charge in the terms of the debenture. It could hardly be made clearer that that was what
the parties were intending to do in relation to the fifth charged assets, the book debts
and other debts due or owing to the company, both present and future; the contrary was
not contended. The question that was debated before me was whether in fact as a result
of the conditions and, in particular, condition 12 of the debenture, notwithstanding the
C   parties' expressed intention nevertheless what was at its creation brought about was a
floating rather than a fixed charge.

There are in principle two ways for a court to discard the parties' expressed description
of the nature of a transaction into which they enter. One is by a finding that some or all
of the agreement does not reflect what the parties in fact did agree. That is a state of
affairs which is commonly labelled a sham, although there are other words used. The
D   other separate means whereby the court discards the parties' expressed intention is by a
finding that the transaction entered into by the parties is on analysis of a different nature
from the description that they have given to it. If the transaction is a cow and has cloven
hooves, the parties cannot turn it into a horse by using equine terminology or saying that
it is a horse. That proposition was put somewhat more elegantly by *Staughton* LJ in
Welsh Development Agency v Export Finance Co Ltd [1992] BCC 270 at p. 301B when
E   he said:

     "There are in my opinion two routes by which this principle can be overcome. The
     first, which I will call the external route, is to show that the written document does
     not represent the agreement of the parties. It may, if one wishes, then be called a
     sham, a cloak or a device. The second is the internal route, when one looks only
     at the written agreement, in order to ascertain from its terms whether it amounts
     to a transaction of the legal nature which the parties ascribe to it."
F
And a little later on in dealing with that latter process he said (at p. 302B):

     "If one part of the agreement purports to create a particular legal transaction, it
     may happen that other provisions are inconsistent with such a transaction. The
     task of the court is then to ascertain which is the substance, the truth, the reality.
     That was plainly the approach of Lord *Herschell* LC in *McEntire v Crossley
     Brothers Ltd* [1895] AC 457 at pp. 463–466, where there are repeated references
G   to inconsistency. See also the speech of Lord *Watson* at p. 467:

          'The duty of a court is to examine every part of the agreement, every stipulation
          which it contains, and to consider their mutual bearing upon each other; but it
          is entirely beyond the function of a court to discard the plain meaning of any
          term in the agreement unless there can be found within its four corners other
          language and other stipulations which necessarily deprive such term of its
H   primary significance.' "

Staughton LJ then dealt with an argument that the court was free to disregard a label
which the parties have attached to a transaction and observed of that (at p. 302D):

     "If by label one means the description which is found on the backsheet, or even in
     a preamble or a recital, I can see that it should be given little if any weight. A label
     can also be found elsewhere. Thus in *Street v Mountford* [1985] AC 809,

Mrs Mountford agreed 'to take' a furnished room; the references to 'licence' in
the agreement were in truth labels and nothing more. 'Licence' was the name
by which the agreement described itself. And in *A G Securities v Vaughan* [1990]
AC 417 in the Court of Appeal at p. 444, *Bingham* LJ said that:

> '. . . the true legal nature of a transaction is not to be altered by the description
> the parties choose to give it.'

In my judgment the correct process, when one is following the internal route, is to
look at the operative parts of the document, in order to discover what legal
transaction they provide for. If some parts appear to be inconsistent with others in
this respect, a decision must be made between the two. That is what I understand
by ascertaining the substance of the transaction. The cases on whether an agreement
provides for a licence or tenancy — *Street v Mountford, A G Securities v Vaughan*
and *Aslan v Murphy* [1990] 1 WLR 766 — do not in my opinion overturn this
well-established doctrine.'"

In this case no sham is alleged. The question, therefore, is whether the characteristics
of the charge in particular as defined by condition 12 compel the court to arrive at the
conclusion that notwithstanding the parties' expressed and, it has to be assumed,
genuine intention to create a fixed charge, they nevertheless created a charge which
cannot operate as such a fixed charge, but is and can only be a floating charge at its
creation.

The provision for the express release in condition 12(A), if the money is paid into the
current or designated account in the absence of a direction by 3i, from the fixed charge
to the status of a floating charge, cannot in my judgment affect the proper analysis of the
nature of the charge as created. It was not argued that the charge was a floating charge
on the ground that it had the potential to become a floating charge or was what one could
perhaps call a fixed, but detachable charge.

The argument advanced on behalf of the preferential creditors was that as created this
was a floating charge and only a floating charge, notwithstanding the parties' expressed
intention to create a fixed charge. There is one point of construction of condition 12
which is not entirely clear and that is the question whether if sums were paid into the
current account or separate designated account by the company those sums (then by
definition in the bank account) were subject still to the potential right of 3i to give
directions on how to deal with such moneys.

If one takes the first part of condition 12(A) by itself the answer to that question would
appear to be yes. But if one has regard to the express release in the second of the two
parts into which condition 12 is broken by semi-colons, it is clear that once a payment in
has been made, in the absence of any directions from 3i it is released from the fixed
charge and becomes subject to a floating charge. In those circumstances one is faced
again with a question of reconciling two apparently conflicting provisions. In my
judgment it is the latter part of the clause that should be held to prevail, so that the
power to give directions in condition 12(A) would cease on the release from the fixed
charge which is provided for by the second part of that condition.

It is also to be observed that there is not, and was not argued to be, any particular
equity as between a fixed or a floating charge or any doctrine of public policy in relation
to such a distinction. In that respect the case is dissimilar from cases which arise under
Rent Acts, such as *Street v Mountford*, where there are considerations of public policy
as has been recognised by the House of Lords.

The submissions that were made on behalf of the preferential creditors were briefly as
follows: that the provisions of cl. 4 that the charge on book debts is a fixed charge is not
by itself conclusive. That is not seriously disputed, but, of course, what is said is that

A   clear evidence of the parties' intention is the point of departure for the court to adopt and the court before finding that that clear expression of intention has been frustrated, is obliged to find that what the parties have subsequently provided for is irreconcilable with what they say they are trying to do.

Secondly, and this was the sheet anchor of the argument as presented but not the only argument, Mr Tidmarsh for the preferential creditors submitted that if the charge had the characteristics identified in the well known judgment of *Romer* LJ in *Re Yorkshire Woolcombers Association Ltd* [1903] 2 Ch 284 at p. 295, then it was a floating charge and that was effectively an end of the matter. That was a decision on a somewhat less sophisticated instrument than this.

The mortgagor was the Yorkshire Woolcombers Association and they had borrowed money from a bank and that had been guaranteed by persons who included Mr Illingworth. Those guarantors were seeking security to cover their liability in respect of the Association's overdraft. With that in mind they executed the:

> ". . . indenture of October 25, 1902, was made between the association of the first part, Frederick Illingworth (the trustee) of the second part, and the said Frederick Illingworth and his co-guarantors of the third part. After reciting that the association had overdrawn their banking account to a considerable extent, and would from time to time require advances and accommodation from the said bank; that the guarantors had requested the association to discharge them from their liability under their respective guarantees, but the association had requested the guarantors not to take any immediate steps with a view to obtaining the discharge thereof, 'and the guarantors have agreed so to do on having such indemnity and specific security as hereinafter appearing,' the association covenanted to indemnify the guarantors as therein mentioned. The association as beneficial owners then assigned to F. Illingworth, his executors, administrators, and assigns, 'all and singular the book and other debts now owing to the association, and also . . . the book and other debts which may at any time during the continuance of this security become owing to the association (but not including uncalled capital of the association), and the full benefit of all of the securities for the said present and future book and other debts'—to hold the same unto the said F. Illingworth, his executors, administrators, and assigns, in trust for the guarantors in proportion to the amount of their respective liabilities, subject to redemption on discharge of the guarantors from all liability on account of their respective guarantees." (at pp. 285–286)

The transaction therefore was on its face an outright assignment.

Vaughan Williams LJ at p. 291 quoted one of the descriptions that had been given by Lord *Macnaghten* in the past of the expression "floating charge". The issue in the *Yorkshire Woolcombers Association* was whether the indenture from which I have read extracts was one which was liable to be registered under sec. 14(1) of the *Companies Act* 1900. That was a section which required such registration in respect of a floating charge. It was not a subsection like sec. 396(1) of the *Companies Act* 1985 that also required registration of charges over book debts. So there was a distinction which now no longer exists in the law so far as liability to registration was concerned. That was the context in which the issues arose and the deed in fact had not been registered. If it was a floating charge it was void as against the liquidator.

The definition that *Vaughan Williams* LJ quoted at p. 291 from Lord *Macnaghten*'s earlier judgment in *Governments Stock and Other Securities Investment Co v Manila Railway Co* [1897] AC 81 at p. 86 was as follows:

> "A floating security is an equitable charge on the assets for the time being of a going concern. It attaches to the subject charged in the varying condition in which

it happens to be from time to time. It is of the essence of such a charge that it
remains dormant until the undertaking charged ceases to be a going concern, or
until the person in whose favour the charge is created intervenes. His right to
intervene may of course be suspended by agreement. But if there is no agreement
for suspension, he may exercise his right whenever he pleases after default."

Of that *Vaughan Williams* LJ said:

"It will be seen, therefore, by that definition that even Lord Macnaghten, who is
remarkable for his accuracy of language, cannot succeed in defining a floating
security without using some terms which are not really applicable to the subject-
matter, but are only applicable by way of analogy. He talks of the charge as being
'dormant'. You want a definition of when and under what circumstances a charge
is properly spoken of as 'dormant'; but still, I shall take that as the definition for
the purpose of the present case . . ."

He then goes on to identify as the critical feature in this case that he was there dealing
with this feature (p. 293):

"But still . . . I do find, when I take the deed as a whole, clauses and arrangements
which, to my mind, are wholly consistent with it having been the intention of both
parties here that the association should be licensed to deal with these book debts
as they come into existence, just as if there had been no mortgage at all, unless
and until the mortgagee thought fit to intervene. Then when the mortgagees are
given by this deed, not the right to intervene upon any particular default happening,
but to intervene when they choose, still if they do intervene that does not give
them the right to complain of any appropriation of these book debts in the
meantime for purposes other than their security."

He then reads a passage which had frequently been mentioned in argument, making
the trustees not answerable for failing to receive debts or the proceeds of them and of
that he said:

"It is quite plain to my mind that there is a licence intended to be given to the
association to employ these book debts for any purpose it likes unless and until
the mortgagees intervene, and when the mortgagees have so intervened nobody
is to be held responsible for any appropriation of these book debts to purposes
other than those contemplated by the deed, which has taken place prior to the
intervention. There was a good deal of discussion in the course of the argument as
to what really is a 'specific security'. I do not think that for a 'specific security' you
need have a security of a subject-matter which is then in existence. I mean by
'then' at the time of the execution of the security; but what you do require to make
a specific security is that the security whenever it has once come into existence,
and been identified or appropriated as a security, shall never thereafter at the will
of the mortgagor cease to be a security. If at the will of the mortgagor he can
dispose of it and prevent it being any longer a security, although something else
may be substituted more or less for it, that is not a 'specific security'."

Romer LJ in his judgment, while first expressing a lack of intention to attempt an
exact definition of the term floating charge, went on to identify certain essential
characteristics and they have in fact been used in the past on numerous occasions as
constituting, if not a precise definition of the term "floating charge", at any rate, an
authoritative description of certain essentials. What he actually said at p. 295 was this:

"I certainly do not intend to attempt to give an exact definition of the term
'floating charge', nor am I prepared to say that there will not be a floating charge
within the meaning of the Act, which does not contain all the three characteristics
that I am about to mention, but I certainly think that if a charge has the three

A
characteristics that I am about to mention it is a floating charge. (1) If it is a charge on a class of assets of a company present and future; (2) if that class is one which, in the ordinary course of the business of the company, would be changing from time to time; and (3) if you find that by the charge it is contemplated that, until some future step is taken by or on behalf of those interested in the charge, the company may carry on its business in the ordinary way as far as concerns the particular class of assets I am dealing with.''

B
He then goes on to deal with the first two characteristics which he found were present in that case and I need not deal with that. The third characteristic, which was the one about which the debate principally arose (as indeed it is in this case) he dealt with in this way:

C
''. . . and, thirdly, in the present case, if I look at the deed which created the charge here, to my mind it is clearly contemplated that until some step is taken by or on behalf of those who are to have the benefit of the charge, the company would be able to receive the debts due to the company in its ordinary course of business, and to deal with them for the ordinary purposes of the business. In the first place, in considering that question, it is important to consider that a charge of debts is not completed until notice is given to the debtors, and you find by this deed that by express provision it is contemplated that the trustees need not, unless

D
they choose, give notice at all to the debtors, and more than that, there is an express provision that they cannot be compelled to do so, unless they have a request from those entitled to the charge — that is, the guarantors, or a majority of them. Then there is that further provision, to which my Lord has referred, that the trustees are not to be answerable for allowing the association to receive their debts, which I need not repeat. Treating this as a commercial document — as it is — what was the meaning of it? Did it not contemplate that until the trustees

E
thought it necessary to intervene, the charge should not be perfected by notice being given to the debtors, and that the business should be carried on in the ordinary way in regard to these debts, and that a debtor might go and pay to the company a particular debt, and the company might receive it, and deal with the cash in the ordinary way in which it would be dealt with in the ordinary course of business? I think that certainly is what is contemplated by this deed, and, indeed,

F
to hold otherwise would be to defeat, to my mind, the whole object and intent of the document . . .''

On that basis it was held to be a floating charge and therefore void for non-registration as against the liquidator. That case went to the House of Lords. The only passage that I need refer to is when Lord *Macnaghten* took up the implicit challenge in *Vaughan Williams* LJ's judgment of improving on what he had done previously in the *Government Stock v Manila Railway* case in the way of defining a floating charge. The decision in the

G
House of Lords is reported at [1904] AC 355 and the speech of Lord *Macnaghten*, which is very short (the whole case took only one day to be argued and decided), contains the following at p. 358:

''With regard to the criticism which Vaughan Williams L.J. passed, not I think unkindly, on some words of mine in the *Manila Case*, I only wish to observe that what I said was intended as a description, not as a definition, of a floating security.

H
I should have thought there was not much difficulty in defining what a floating charge is in contrast to what is called a specific charge. A specific charge, I think, is one that without more fastens on ascertained and definite property or property capable of being ascertained and defined; a floating charge, on the other hand, is ambulatory and shifting in its nature, hovering over and so to speak floating with the property which it is intended to affect until some event occurs or some act is

done which causes it to settle and fasten on the subject of the charge within its   A
reach and grasp."

The concept of a floating charge appears to defy judicial definition without the aid of
metaphor.

The question before me is whether the characteristics of the charge and, in particular,
those contained in condition 12, compel the court to arrive at the conclusion that
notwithstanding the parties' expressed intention there is a floating charge.   B

So far as the *Yorkshire Woolcombers* decision is concerned, the court was faced with
an outright assignment, subject to redemption, of both present and future book debts.
There was no attempt to create an equitable charge by imposing restraints upon the
mortgagor's ability to deal with book debts as they became subject to the "assignment".
It was a very simple and unsophisticated attempt to achieve by an assignment what was
not susceptible of a legal assignment. The conception of a legal assignment of a chose in   C
action was regulated then by statute as it is now in sec. 136 of the *Law of Property Act*
1925 and it was perfectly clear on the face of the transaction that no effective legal
assignment was being achieved and it was that as a step that *Romer* LJ was looking at to
see whether the event had occurred that would cause there to be a fixed rather than a
floating charge. In particular, the decision in *Yorkshire Woolcombers Association* is not
directed at the question how far a specific equitable charge can be created by a   D
diminution of the mortgagor's freedom of action in dealing with the book debts as and
when they arise because there was no such diminution of the mortgagor's freedom of
action involved in the case.

To return to the submissions made on behalf of the preferential creditors, it was
submitted that the position pending a direction by 3i exactly fitted what *Romer* LJ said
in the *Yorkshire Woolcombers* case, that the company was free, absent such a direction,   E
to collect the book debts and bank the moneys and spend them in the ordinary course of
business. That, it was submitted, was effectively the end of that. There was necessarily a
floating charge.

It was also submitted that the power to give a direction which was vested in 3i did not
prevent the charge from being a floating charge. This at the end of the day in my
judgment is the central question in the case. The admission was, however, made that, if   F
and when such a direction was given, it was possible, depending on the nature of the
direction, for the charge to become a fixed charge. An example that was taken in
argument was the possibility of a direction being given in the same terms as were
contained in the debenture that was in issue before the Supreme Court of Ireland in *Re
Keenan Bros Ltd* (1986) 2 BCC 98,970 at p. 98,973 where the deed of charge in favour
(it so happened) of a bank (Allied Irish Banks Ltd) contained the following two clauses: G

"The company shall pay into an account with the bank designated for that purpose
all moneys which it may receive in respect of the book debts and other debts
hereby charged and shall not without the prior consent of the bank in writing
make any withdrawals or direct any payment from the said account.

The company shall not without the prior consent in writing of the bank purport to
charge, waive, assign or otherwise deal with its book debts or other debts in favour   H
of any other person."

It was accepted by Mr Tidmarsh on behalf of the preferential creditors that if a
direction containing the effect of those two clauses had been given by 3i that would have
brought about a state of affairs where from then on there was a fixed charge rather than
a floating charge in existence.

A   *Henchy* J in the Supreme Court in Ireland said at p. 98,973:

> "As to the debenture deed . . . the company professed to charge in favour of the bank (AIB) its present and future debts as a first fixed legal charge. The extent to which this was to be in reality a fixed, rather than a floating charge, is shown by the following provisions in the deed:
>
>   (1) all moneys which were received by the company in respect of book debts were to be paid into a specified AIB branch and no withdrawals or payments from that account were to be made without the prior consent of the bank;
>
>   (2) the company was not, without the consent of the bank, to carry on its business otherwise than in the ordinary and normal course;
>
>   (3) the company was not, without the consent in writing of the bank, to diminish or dispose of its book debts otherwise than by collecting and lodging them in the specified account.
>
> It seems to me that such a degree of sequestration of the book debts when collected made those moneys incapable of being used in the ordinary course of business and meant that they were put, specifically and expressly, at the disposal of the bank. I am satisfied that assets thus withdrawn from ordinary trade use, put in the keeping of the debenture holder, and sterilised and made undisposable save at the absolute discretion of the debenture holder, have the distinguishing features of a fixed charge. The charge was not intended to fasten in the future on the book debts; it was affixed forthwith and without further ado to those debts as they were collected; so it did not in any sense float over those moneys. As I understand the law, assets the subject matter of a floating charge may be disposed of, at least in the ordinary course of business, by the maker of the charge without the consent of the chargee. That was not the case here."

E   Finally, Mr Tidmarsh submitted that the restraints in condition 12(C) on dealing with book debts did not prevent this debenture from being a floating charge. Although the submission was put in that way, that in my judgment is not quite the question. One is not in my view looking to see whether the provisions of condition 12 prevent this debenture from being a floating charge. What my task is, as I see it, is to see whether the provisions of condition 12 are irreconcilable with the parties identification of what they had done as the creation of a fixed charge. It is an important difference in approach to the problem.

F   There are in my view two English decisions which effectively govern these questions how far restraints on the power of a mortgagor to deal with book debts as and when received can constitute a fixed as opposed to a floating charge. The two decisions in chronological order are *Siebe Gorman & Co Ltd v Barclays Bank Ltd* [1979] 2 Lloyd's Rep 142 and *Re Brightlife Ltd* (1986) 2 BCC 99,359; [1987] Ch 200. The former is a decision of *Slade* J. The case was concerned with numerous issues, but the one which is significant for present purposes was the effect of a debenture which was executed by a company in favour of a bank, the respondent. In the debenture there were the following relevant clauses:

> "3. (The company) as beneficial owner hereby charges with the payment and discharge of all moneys and liabilities hereby covenanted to be paid or discharged by (the company) . . .
>
>   (d) by way of first fixed charge all book debts and other debts now and from time to time due or owing to (the company)."

There was also a clause numbered 5(c) which provided as follows:

> "5. During the continuance of this security (the company) . . .
>
>   (c) shall pay into (the company's) account with the bank all moneys which it may receive in respect of the book debts and other debts hereby charged

A

and shall not without the prior consent of the bank in writing purport to charge or assign the same in favour of any other person and shall if called upon to do so by the bank execute a legal assignment of such book debts and other debts to the bank."

Slade J at p. 158, having recorded the fact that there had been no dispute but that it was competent for anyone to whom book debts might accrue in the future to create for good consideration an equitable charge on those book debts which would attach as soon as they came into existence, went on to record the argument that notwithstanding the perfectly clear statement that what was being created was a first fixed charge on all book debts, what the result was, was, nevertheless, a floating charge and he cited the passage which I have already read from *Romer* LJ in the *Yorkshire Woolcombers* case stating the three characteristics of a floating charge. He went on to say:

B

"The charge on the book debts represented by the relevant bills in the present case clearly possesses the first two of these three characteristics. The dispute arises in regard to the third. The provisions of cl. 5(c) of the debenture obliged the debtor, even before the bank had taken any steps to enforce its security, to pay into the debtor's account with the bank all moneys which it might receive in respect of the relevant bills and not without the prior consent of the bank in writing to purport to charge or assign the same in favour of any other person. Notwithstanding these provisions, Mr Phillips, on behalf of Siebe Gorman, submitted that it was plain in the context of the debenture that (the company) was intended, until the bank took steps to enforce its security, to be free to continue trading and to use the proceeds of its future book debts, including the relevant bills for the purpose of such trading. He submitted that there were a number of forms of dealing with future book debts which were not precluded by the terms of cl. 5(c), for example, dealings by way of barter, exchange or set-off, and that the sub-clause necessarily implied that the debtor had the right to deal with future book debts, save as thereby expressly precluded. He emphasised that, while according to the terms of cl. 5(c) all the proceeds of future book debts would in the first instance have to go into the debtor's account with the bank, it must have been contemplated that (the company) would then be free immediately to draw out all those moneys for the ordinary purposes of its business, at least if such account was for the time being in credit."

C

D

E

F

In relation to that argument *Slade* J said:

". . . if I had accepted the premise that (the company) would have had the unrestricted right to deal with the proceeds of any of the relevant book debts paid into its account, so long as that account remained in credit, I would have been inclined to accept the conclusion that the charge on such book debts could be no more than a floating charge."

G

He then referred to what was said by Lord *Macnaghten* in relation to the definition of a specific charge, which I need not repeat. *Slade* J went on a little later to say (at p. 159):

"In my judgment, however, it is perfectly possible in law for a mortgagor, by way of continuing security for further advances, to grant to a mortgagee a charge on future book debts in a form which creates in equity a specific charge on the proceeds of such debts as soon as they are received and consequently prevents the mortgagor from disposing of an unencumbered title to the subject matter of such charge without the mortgagee's consent, even before the mortgagee has taken steps to enforce its security (compare *Evans Coleman & Evans Ltd. v. R. A. Nelson Construction Ltd.*, 16 D.L.R. (2d) 123). This in my judgment was the effect of the debenture in the present case. I see no reason why the court should

H

A
not give effect to the intention of the parties, as stated in cl. 3(d), that the charge should be a first fixed charge on book debts. I do not accept the argument that the provisions of cl. 5(c) negative the existence of a specific charge. All that they do, in my judgment, is to reinforce the specific charge given by cl. 3. The mere fact that there may exist certain forms of dealing with book debts which are not specifically prohibited by cl. 5(c) does not in my judgment turn the specific charge into a floating charge."

B
It will be noted that that approach of *Slade* J is in line with what I have said seems to me to be the proper approach, namely, to see whether the description of the transaction which the parties have adopted is necessarily to be departed from as a result of the terms of the transaction that they have provided for.

The authority of *Siebe Gorman* clearly shows that there is no legal impossibility involved in the creation of an equitable as opposed to a legal charge over future book debts and the *Yorkshire Woolcombers* decision is not an authority for any such wide proposition as that.

C

The authority the other side of the line to which I have earlier referred was *Re Brightlife Ltd*, a decision of *Hoffmann* J. Again, this was a case on a debenture which contained what was described as a first specific charge over all book debts and other debts at any time due or owing to Brightlife. The relevant clauses in that case were, first, cl. 3(B), which read as follows (and Norandex was the debenture holder):

D

"Norandex may at any time by notice to Brightlife (which was the company) convert the floating charge into a specific charge as regards any assets specified in the notice which Norandex shall consider to be in danger of being seized or sold under any form of distress or execution levied or threatened or to be otherwise in jeopardy and may appoint a receiver thereof."

E
Then there was a cl. 5(ii) which was a covenant by Brightlife that it (and I pass over (i) which was a covenant to conduct its affairs in a proper and efficient manner):

"(ii) shall not without the prior consent in writing of Norandex sell transfer or otherwise dispose of the whole or, except in the ordinary course of business, any part of its undertaking property or assets (being in the aggregate substantial) or deal with its book or other debts or securities for money otherwise than in the

F
ordinary course of getting in and realising the same which expression shall not authorise the selling, factoring or discounting by Brightlife of its book debts or other negotiable instruments held by it . . ."

In relation to those clauses *Hoffmann* J came to the conclusion that there was a floating charge. He said (at p. 99,362):

"Secondly, although cl. 3(A)(ii)(a) speaks of a 'first specific charge' over the book

G
debts and other debts, the rights over the debts created by the debenture were in my judgment such as to be characterised in law as a floating charge."

—and he refers to *Street v Mountford* and the passage in *Yorkshire Woolcombers* that I have quoted earlier and need not repeat. He went on to say:

"Counsel were agreed that the charge covered present and future debts and that such debts would in the ordinary course be changing from time to time. The first

H
two of the standard features are therefore present. But Mr Sheldon said that the charge did not allow Brightlife to deal with the debts in the ordinary way of business. Clause 5(ii) was highly restrictive of the company's power to deal with its debts.

It is true that cl. 5(ii) does not allow Brightlife to sell, factor or discount debts without the written consent of Norandex. But a floating charge is consistent with some restriction upon the company's freedom to deal with its assets. For example, floating charges commonly contain a prohibition upon the creation of other charges ranking prior to or pari passu with the floating charge. Such dealings would otherwise be open to a company in the ordinary course of its business. In this debenture, the significant feature is that Brightlife was free to collect its debts and pay the proceeds into its bank account. Once in the account, they would be outside the charge over debts and at the free disposal of the company. In my judgment a right to deal in this way with the charged assets for its own account is a badge of a floating charge and is inconsistent with a fixed charge."

He then refers to the fact that he had cited to him both the *Siebe Gorman* and *Keenan* cases. He says of *Siebe Gorman*:

". . . the debenture was in favour of a bank and not only prohibited the company from selling or charging its book debts but required that they be paid into the company's account with that bank. *Slade* J decided that as a matter of construction the bank would not have been obliged to allow the company to draw upon the account at a time when it still owed the bank money under the debenture. The company was not free to deal with the debts or their proceeds in the ordinary course of its business. Each debt as it accrued to the company could therefore properly be said to become subject to an equitable fixed charge."

Then he quotes a passage that I have read from *Slade* J's judgment about how he would have been inclined to accept the opposite conclusion if there had been an unrestricted power to deal with the proceeds. He says clearly rightly, if I may say so, that *Re Keenan Bros* was an even stronger case than *Siebe Gorman*. His conclusion, therefore, was that neither of those two cases were of assistance to the creditor (Norandex) in that particular case.

The question before me resolves itself into whether the terms of the charge are susceptible of creating a fixed charge or a specific charge and the touchstone for this is the extent to which the chargor is left free to deal with the book debts and the proceeds if and when collected. Fetters, or even a prohibition against factoring, assigning and selling, are plainly not enough (see *Re Brightlife*). An obligation to pay the debts into a particular account such as that contained in the *Siebe Gorman* case on the other hand has been held to be enough. In this case there is a power reserved to 3i to give directions which if given in a particular way are well capable of producing a fixed as opposed to a floating charge. The question is whether the existence of that right in the chargee suffices to make it possible to take the attitude of *Slade* J in *Siebe Gorman* that the limited restrictions in cl. 3(c) of that case were only reinforcing the specific charge given by the general words in the debenture.

In support of a submission that the existence of the right vested in 3i was consistent with the existence of a fixed charge as opposed to a floating charge, I was referred to *Evans v Rival Granite Quarries Ltd* [1910] 2 KB 979 in which *Buckley* LJ gave an analysis, by way I think of obiter dictum, of the nature of a floating charge. The actual decision was to the effect that neither a demand for payment nor a notice to bankers of the mortgagor company suffice to crystallise a floating charge and it is for that reason I say that what *Buckley* LJ said was strictly obiter, but with such an experienced judge in company law matters it obviously deserves great respect. At p. 999 he said:

"The nature of a floating security has been discussed and described in *In re Florence Land and Public Works Co.*, *Simultaneous Colour Printing Syndicate* v. *Foweraker*, *Government Stocks Investment Co v Manila Ry. Co.*, *Illingworth* v. *Houldsworth*, and other cases. The outcome of the decisions may be thus summarised. A floating security is not a future security; it is a present security, which presently affects all the assets of the company expressed to be included in

A   it. On the other hand, it is not a specific security; the holder cannot affirm that the assets are specifically mortgaged to him. The assets are mortgaged in such a way that the mortgagor can deal with them without the concurrence of the mortgagee. A floating security is not a specific mortgage of the assets, plus a licence to the mortgagor to dispose of them in the course of his business, but is a floating mortgage applying to every item comprised in the security, but not specifically affecting any item until some event occurs or some act on the part of the mortgagee

B   is done which causes it to crystallise into a fixed security. Mr. Shearman argued that it was competent to the mortgagee to intervene at any moment and to say that he withdrew the licence as regards any particular item. That is not in my opinion the nature of the security; it is a mortgage presently affecting all the items expressed to be included in it, but not specifically affecting any item till the happening of the event which causes a security to crystallise as regards all the

C   items. This crystallisation may be brought about in various ways. A receiver may be appointed, or the company may go into liquidation and a liquidator be appointed, or any event may happen which is defined as bringing to an end the licence to the company to carry on business. There is no case in which it has been affirmed that a mortgagee of this description may at any moment forbid the company to sell a particular piece of property or may take it himself and keep it, and leave the licence to carry on the business subsisting as regards everything else.

D   This would be inconsistent with the real bargain between the parties, which is that the mortgagee gives authority to the company to use all its property until the licence to carry on business comes to an end. It is impossible to evolve from the contractual relation between a company and its debenture-holders the proposition for instance that the latter may serve a notice on the company's bankers with regard to the honouring of the company's cheques and still say that, although he had stopped payment of the company's cheques, he was not interfering with the

E   carrying on of the company's business. Such a contention would be inconsistent with the true relation between the parties."

    That is an important dictum in that it analyses a floating charge as one which confers a right on the mortgagor to trade on unchecked and contemplates as a quite separate state of affairs a specific charge with a licence to deal with the specific asset in question.

F   Nevertheless, I have reached the conclusion that this case falls on the floating charge side of the line drawn between floating and specific charges, in that the mortgagor's ability to deal with book debts was *at the creation of the charge* (words which I emphasise because they are what sec. 40 points one to) were not subject to any greater fetters than *Hoffmann* J held were inadequate in *Re Brightlife*. Absent a direction from 3i there was a freedom of action conferred upon the company which was in my judgment inconsistent with the existence of a specific charge.

G   It was submitted to me by Mr Sumption that there were quite numerous reasons why the charge in this case was not a floating charge because it conferred on the chargee rights in respect of specific assets at a time when no sum was due and before the crystallisation had occurred. The limitations, which at the end of the day is the critical point in this case, on the company's freedom to deal with its debts were identified by him as follows.

H   First, the company's primary obligation was to deal with the debts in accordance with directions of 3i. That of course is true if and when such directions were given, but as at the date when the charge was created that was something that looked forward to a possibility and not an existing or determined state of affairs.

    Secondly, it was pointed out that under condition 12(A) once the proceeds of the debt had been collected they had to be paid into the designated account and, thereafter,

subject to the bank's rights had to be dealt with in accordance with 3i's directions. In fact   A
what the condition in terms says is:

> "The company shall pay into a current account or a separate designated account (as 3i may require) . . ."

I do not see any significant difference between that state of affairs, that is to say, the existence of a right in 3i to give a direction in relation to the account with, in the event, Lloyds Bank, from the right that was given to 3i to give directions how moneys from   B particular book debts were to be dealt with. It again requires a direction or a requirement by 3i.

The third point was that the circumstances in which the company was at liberty to deal with the proceeds of book debts in the ordinary course of business, was that no relevant directions had been given under condition 12(A), but it was submitted in that case the charge did not extend to the balance of the account at all because it had been expressly released and there was therefore no inconsistency in the liberty to deal with the   C subsistence of the charge. That I entirely accept as a submission, but it does not in my judgment touch the question which I have to decide, which is the adequacy of the fetters on the company's powers of disposal in relation to book debts.

The condition in cl. 12, subject to the one question of construction which I dealt with, is very skilfully put together and it does undoubtedly bring to a deliberate end what was hoped to be a specific charge on this event which is contemplated in this submission of   D payment in, absent a direction by 3i. There is no inconsistency at that end of the transaction, that is to say, once the payment in, absent a direction, has occurred. But that does not in my view touch the question of the nature of the restrictions placed on the company before such payment in.

Fourth it was said that 3i's directions could be given at any time, for example, at the inception of the agreement and that there was no necessity for default. This again I   E entirely accept, but it does not in my judgment touch the proposition that until the directions were given there was an inconsistent amount of freedom given to the company for there to be a fixed charge."

Finally, it was submitted that even when 3i has not intervened by giving directions, the company's rights to deal with the debts only extended to getting them in and that this did not involve parting with any interest in them. There is, one entirely sees, a provision   F preventing assigning, factoring or discounting, but that, in common with *Hoffmann* J in *Re Brightlife* I find to be inadequate. What there is not, but which would no doubt (had it been there) been adequate, was a restriction on the way in which the moneys could be dealt with, absent a direction by 3i. I find no such restriction and on that basis I have reached the conclusion that this was indeed necessarily a floating charge.

(Order accordingly)

  G

A
Re Northern Engineering Industries plc.

Chancery Division (Companies Court).
Ferris J.
Judgment delivered 12 February 1993.

B
Reduction of capital — Preference shares — Variation of class rights — Company proposed reduction of capital involving cancellation of preference shares — Articles required preference shareholders' consent to variation of rights — Articles deemed rights to be varied by "reduction of capital" — Whether cancellation of preference shares was a "reduction" — Companies Act 1985, sec. 135.

This was a petition seeking the court's approval of a reduction of capital. The petition was opposed by a preference shareholder.

C
The reduction involved paying off the preference shares and cancelling them. The question was whether the reduction which the company had resolved upon in general meeting also required the approval of preference shareholders. The company's articles required the preference shareholders' consent or the sanction of an extraordinary resolution passed at a separate class meeting for a variation of their rights (art. 6); a "reduction of the capital paid up on" such shares was deemed to be a variation

D
(art. 7(B)).

The company argued that art. 7(B) only applied where there was a reduction of the capital paid up on particular shares to a figure which exceeded zero. The preference shareholder argued that a cancellation of the preference shares was a "reduction" for the purpose of art. 7(B).

Held, declining to confirm the reduction:

E
Article 7(B) had the effect that the proposed cancellation of the preference shares in the company was to be deemed to be a variation of the rights attached to the preference shares and class meetings were therefore required by art. 6. As there had been no such class meetings the reduction of capital had not been carried out in accordance with the company's articles.

The following cases were referred to in the judgment:

F
House of Fraser v ACGE Investments Ltd & Ors (1987) 3 BCC 201; [1987] AC 387.
IR Commrs v Universal Grinding Wheel Co Ltd [1955] AC 807.
Prudential Assurance Co Ltd & Anor v Chatterley-Whitfield Collieries Ltd [1948] 2 All ER 593 (CA); [1949] AC 512 (HL).
Saltdean Estate Co Ltd, Re [1968] 1 WLR 1844.
Serpell & Co Ltd, Re [1944] Ch 233.

G
David Oliver QC and John Cone (instructed by Freshfields) for the company.

Richard Sykes QC (instructed by Herbert Smith) for the Commercial Union.

JUDGMENT

Ferris J: On this petition Northern Engineering Industries plc ("the company") seeks the approval of the court to a reduction of its capital pursuant to a special resolution of

H
the company passed on 6 January 1993. The petition is opposed by a company named NCB Trust Ltd which is the registered holder of two holdings of 11 per cent cumulative preference shares as nominee for two unit trusts managed by Commercial Union Investment Management Ltd which, in turn, is a subsidiary of Commercial Union plc. The Commercial Union companies have objected to the transaction on their own behalf and, at the prompting of the Association of British Insurers, on behalf of members of

the Association who invest in securities. I propose to refer to the opponents as "the Commercial Union".

The company was incorporated in 1977. Its principal object is to carry on the business of mechanical and electrical engineers. Its share capital has been altered from time to time, but it is unnecessary to go into the detail of these alterations. Immediately before the passing of the special resolution which I have referred to the authorised share capital of the company was £82,934,214 divided into:

(1)   320m ordinary shares of 25p each of which 247,134,492 have been issued and are fully paid up and the remaining ordinary shares are unissued;

(2)   709,600 5.375 per cent cumulative preference shares of £1 each all of which have been issued and are fully paid up;

(3)   1,460,000 three per cent cumulative redeemable preference shares of £1 each all of which have been issued and are fully paid up; and

(4)   764,614 11 per cent cumulative preference shares of £1 each of which 763,493 have been issued and are fully paid up, and the remaining 1,121 11 per cent cumulative preference shares are unissued.

The reduction of capital with which I am concerned affects the three classes of preference shares. The respective rights to income, capital and redemption attaching to the preference shares and ordinary shares of the company are set out in a new art. 3 of the company adopted by special resolution passed on 11 November 1988. I need not read its detailed terms. It will suffice to say that para. (A) of art. 3 prescribes the rights as regards income, which for present purposes are sufficiently apparent from the descriptions of the three classes of preference shares. Paragraph (B) states the rights as regards capital. It begins by providing that, "On a return of assets of the company available for distribution among the members shall be applied" in various ways. The amounts to be paid to the holders of preference shares include, in all cases, the amounts paid up on such shares and any arrears of dividend. In the case of the three per cent cumulative redeemable preference shares, a fixed premium of five pence per share is also payable. In the case of the 11 per cent cumulative preference shares a variable premium, the amount of which is to be calculated by reference to a complex formula, is payable. By para. (C) of art. 3 the three per cent cumulative redeemable preference shares (but not any of the other preference shares) are redeemable at the option of the company at the price of £1.05 per share on six months' previous notice in writing.

Since August 1989 the company has been a member of the Rolls-Royce group. All the 247,134,492 issued ordinary shares in the company are now owned beneficially by either Rolls-Royce plc or Rolls-Royce Finance Ltd. The preference shares are, I understand, held by a number of shareholders unconnected with the Rolls-Royce group, including, as I have mentioned, nominees for Commercial Union Investment Management Ltd. The directors of the company have, for some time, considered that the administration costs resulting from the maintenance of separate classes of ordinary and preference shares were not justifiable and they have sought to extinguish the preference shares. In October 1989 the company proposed a scheme of arrangement under which all the preference shares of each class would be cancelled in consideration of a payment, to be made by Rolls-Royce plc, of a fixed amount for each share. This amount was such as to provide a premium above the middle market price of the shares of each class on a specified day. However, when the scheme of arrangement was put to separate meetings of the holders of each class of preference shares it was rejected. It is said that a majority in number of the holders of each class voted in favour of the scheme, but that the vote was lost by "a small number of preference shareholders with large individual holdings".

A   The company now seeks to achieve substantially the same result by a different route, namely a reduction of capital, subject to the confirmation of the court, under sec. 135 of the *Companies Act* 1985. In summary, what is proposed is as follows:

(1)   All the authorised preference shares of each class are to be cancelled.

(2)   In consideration of the cancellation of the issued preference shares there is to be repaid to the holders of each class:

B   (a)   105 pence per share for each of the three per cent cumulative redeemable preference shares;

            (b)   100 pence per share for each 5.375 per cent cumulative preference share; and

            (c)   125 pence per share for each 11 per cent cumulative preference share;

C   together in each case with the amount of the accrued preference dividend up to the date of repayment.

The amounts to be repaid in respect of each preference share are those which are payable under para. (B) of art. 3 "on a distribution of assets of the company available for distribution among the members". It is accepted that the complex formula for ascertaining the premium to be paid to the holders of the 11 per cent cumulative preference shares has been correctly applied.

D   (3)   Consequential amendments are to be made to the company's articles.

(4)   The capital of the company is to be increased from £80m (at which it will stand by virtue of the cancellation of the preference shares) to £85m by the creation of 12m additional ordinary shares of 25 pence each.

(5)   The directors of the company will be authorised to allot unissued shares in the company, up to an aggregate nominal amount of £18,283,284. It is envisaged that

E   such allotment will be to one or more companies in the Rolls-Royce group and that part of the cash to be raised by such allotment will, directly or indirectly, be used to make the payments which are to be made to the holders of preference shares.

       Resolutions to implement these proposals were put to an extraordinary general meeting of the company held on 6 January 1993. Article 70 of the company's articles

F   permits the holders of preference shares to attend a general meeting at which certain specified business, including a resolution reducing the share capital of the company, is to be considered and to vote on any such resolution. The preference shareholders therefore had an opportunity to vote on the resolution reducing the capital of the company with which I am concerned. However the Rolls-Royce companies holding all the ordinary shares of the company were entitled together to over 247m votes against a maximum of some 2.9m votes exercisable by all the preference shareholders. As the

G   Rolls-Royce companies announced in advance that they intended to cast their votes in favour of the resolutions it is not surprising that all the resolutions put to the general meeting, including that for the reduction of capital, were duly passed as special resolutions. No separate meetings of the holders of any of the classes of preference shares were held.

       The question in this case is whether the capital of the company can, in the circumstances, be reduced by a special resolution of the company in general meeting without also being

H   approved by resolution of preference shareholders passed at separate class meetings.

       It is clear that, in the absence of an article which has a contrary effect, a cancellation of particular shares of a company on a reduction of capital is not something which requires the assent of the shareholders entitled to shares of the class which is to be cancelled if the reduction and cancellation is in accordance with the rights and liabilities attached to that class of shares. A reduction of capital by way of a cancellation of all of a

company's preference shares in consideration of a return of the proper amount due to   A
the holders of such shares is not an abrogation of the rights attached to these shares and
comes within the general principle that I have stated. This follows from the decision of
the House of Lords in *Prudential Assurance Co Ltd & Anor v Chatterley-Whitfield
Collieries Ltd* [1949] AC 512, and the analysis of the rights of preference shareholders in
this respect which was made by *Buckley* J in *Re Saltdean Estate Co Ltd* [1968] 1 WLR
1844, an analysis which has been described in the House of Lords as "an entirely correct
statement of law" (see *House of Fraser v ACGE Investments Ltd* (1987) 3 BCC 201 at   B
p. 206). When the *Chatterley-Whitfield* case was in the Court of Appeal, Lord *Greene*
MR referred to the recognised principle that, on a reduction of capital, a surplus is to be
applied in the first instance in the paying off of capital which is entitled to a priority in a
winding-up and said:

> "Every person who acquires shares in a company has only himself to blame if he
> does not know this, and I have no doubt that it is well recognised by business men"   C

(see *Re Chatterley-Whitfield Collieries Ltd* [1948] 2 All ER 593 at p. 596B).

None of this was disputed by Mr Sykes on behalf of the Commercial Union. His
contention was that, in this particular case, the company has an article which displaces
the general principle. The article he relied upon is art. 7(B), which has to be read in
conjunction with art. 6. The two articles are in the following terms:

> "*Variation of rights*   D
>
> 6. Whenever the capital of the company is divided into different classes of shares,
> the rights attached to any class may be varied or abrogated, either whilst the
> company is a going concern or during or in contemplation of a winding up, either
> (a) in such manner if any as may be provided by such rights or (b) in the absence
> of any such provision with the consent in writing of the holders of three-fourths in
> nominal value of the issued shares of the class or with the sanction of an   E
> extraordinary resolution passed at a separate meeting of the holders of the shares
> of that class, but not otherwise. To every such separate meeting all the provisions
> of these articles and of the Acts relating to general meetings of the company or to
> the proceedings thereat shall, mutatis mutandis, apply, except that the necessary
> quorum shall be two persons holding or representing by proxy at least one-third
> in nominal amount of the issued shares of the class and at any adjourned meeting
> shall be one person holding shares of the class in question or his proxy, and that   F
> the holders of shares of the class shall, on a poll, have one vote in respect of every
> share of the class held by them respectively.
>
> 7. (A) The rights conferred on the holders of the preference shares shall be
> deemed to be varied by the issue, except with the sanction of an extraordinary
> resolution passed at a single meeting of the holders of the preference shares, of
> any shares ranking as regards participation in profits or assets (or both) either: G
>
> (1) pari passu with the preference shares, if immediately after such issue the
>   total amount of the issued preference capital of the company ranking in
>   priority to or pari passu with the preference shares would exceed 50 per cent
>   of the total issued share capital of the company; or
>
> (2) in priority to the preference shares.
>
> (B) The rights attached to any shares shall be deemed to be varied by the   H
> reduction of the capital paid up on such shares and by the creation of further
> shares ranking in any respect in priority thereto, but shall not (except as otherwise
> expressly provided by the foregoing provisions of this article or by the conditions
> of issue of such shares) be deemed to be varied by the creation or issue of further
> shares ranking pari passu therewith or subsequent thereto."

A   The argument on behalf of the Commercial Union was that a reduction of capital by the cancellation of preference shares of the company is a "reduction of the capital paid up" on the preference shares for the purpose of art. 7(B). The counter-argument of Mr Oliver, on behalf of the company, was that art. 7(B) applies only where there is a reduction of the capital paid up on particular shares to a figure which exceeds zero. In other words "reduction" means something different from "cancellation" or "extinction".

B   Both sides prayed in aid what they respectively claimed to be the natural and ordinary meaning of the words "reduce" or "reduction". I was referred to the *Shorter Oxford English Dictionary* where a large number of meanings are given for "reduce", the most relevant being:

> "To bring down, diminish *to* a smaller number, amount, extent, etc., or *to* a single thing . . . To lower, diminish, lessen . . ."

C   Correspondingly the most relevant meaning of "reduction" is given as:

> "Diminution, lessening, cutting down."

Mr Oliver naturally emphasised the aspect of bringing down to a smaller number or a single thing. Mr Sykes suggested that the concept of bringing back or diminution from a particular state or condition was more apt. A person who, when told to reduce the amount of water in a bottle, empties the bottle completely could not be said to have disobeyed his instructions. This is so, he said, even though he might, in equal obedience,

D   have tipped out only half the contents.

I do not find the appeal of either side to the natural and ordinary meaning of "reduction" goes any distance towards providing a solution to the point of construction which faces me. Mr Oliver's preferred meaning is, no doubt, a natural and ordinary meaning of the word. Mr Sykes' preferred meaning is, it seems to me, a perfectly permissible one.

E   That this is so is illustrated by Section 135 of the *Companies Act* 1985, subsec. (1) and (2) of which are in the following terms:

> "*Special resolution for reduction of share capital*
>
> (1) Subject to confirmation by the court, a company limited by shares or a company limited by guarantee and having a share capital may, if so authorised by its articles, by special resolution reduce its share capital in any way.

F

> (2) In particular, and without prejudice to subsection (1), the company may—
>
> (a) extinguish or reduce the liability on any of its shares in respect of share capital not paid up; or
>
> (b) either with or without extinguishing or reducing liability on any of its shares, cancel any paid-up share capital which is lost or unrepresented by available assets; or

G

> (c) either with or without extinguishing or reducing liability on any of its shares, pay off any paid-up share capital which is in excess of the company's wants;
>
> and the company may, if and so far as is necessary, alter its memorandum by reducing the amount of its share capital and of its shares accordingly."

H   It was not disputed by Mr Oliver that subsec. (1) enables a company to which the section applies to reduce its share capital to nil, although other requirements of the Act have the effect that it must immediately increase such capital to a positive amount. This is confirmed by the terms of subsec. (2) which show that, among the modes of reducing capital permitted by subsec. (1), are the extinguishment of liability on any shares not fully paid up, the cancellation of certain paid-up share capital or the payment off of excess paid-up share capital. Section 135 thus illustrates the use of the word "reduce" or

its derivatives in both senses. In subsec. (1) "reduce" by itself includes reduction to
zero. In subsec. (2) "reduce" or "reducing" are used as an alternative to "extinguish"
or "extinguishing" and, by themselves, envisage something which falls short of
extinguishment.

Mr Oliver argued that the word "reduction" in the expression "reduction of the
capital paid up on such shares" in art. 7(B) has the more limited meaning illustrated
by the use of the same word in contrast to "extinguishing" in para. (b) and (c) of
sec. 135(2). Apart from relying on what he claimed to be the natural and ordinary
meaning of the word he put forward a number of arguments as suggesting this view.

First he contended that if "reduction" includes "extinction" in art. 7(B) there was no
real purpose in setting out in the articles the capital rights of preference shareholders, as
is done in some detail in art. 3. If preference shares can be cancelled on a reduction of
capital only if an extraordinary resolution is passed at class meetings of preference
shareholders, the preference shareholders can simply name their own price. I do not
accept this proposition. Apart from the fact that there are circumstances in which the
preference shareholders will have only the rights in respect of capital given by art. 3(B)
(which relates to Mr Oliver's next point), a definition of the capital rights of preference
shareholders, whether by giving express rights different from those of ordinary
shareholders or by leaving them to enjoy the same rights as ordinary shareholders, is an
inevitable feature of the constitution of a company which has preference shares and
ordinary shares. It is true that in the case of this company there is provision for the
payment of a premium in respect of two classes of preference shares, the provisions for
calculation of the premium being in one case detailed and complex, and that if the
company is to obtain an affirmative vote of its preference shareholders it may have to
offer an enhanced premium. But the starting point of any process of bargaining which
may be embarked upon will be the rights of the preference shareholders under the
article. Such bargaining will therefore build upon, rather than pass by, the provisions of
art. 3.

Mr Oliver's next point was that if "reduction" in art. 7(B) includes "extinction" then
the company cannot even procure a resolution of its shareholders for a voluntary
winding up without holding separate class meetings of the preference shareholders at
which there is an affirmative resolution for winding up. This would indeed be extraordinary
if it were true, but in my judgment it is not. A reduction in capital is one thing; a winding
up is quite another. When a liquidator in a solvent winding up makes a distribution to
the shareholders he makes a distribution in respect of the share capital of the company,
but he does not reduce the share capital of the company. The meaning of art. 7(B) which
is contended for by the Commercial Union does not, in my judgment, have the
consequence that a winding up of the company would be deemed to be a variation of the
rights attached to any shares of the company.

Thirdly Mr Oliver argued that his construction of art. 7(B) does not deprive the article
of purpose. It would continue to provide valuable protection to preference shareholders
if, for example, it were proposed to reduce capital without providing for a return of
assets to shareholders, as might be the case where capital has been lost. This, of course,
is true, but to my mind it is a minor point.

Next Mr Oliver suggested that the construction of art. 7(B) contended for by the
Commercial Union would, in practice, nullify the express right of the company to
redeem the three per cent cumulative preference shares pursuant to art. 3(C). In my
judgment this is not the case. I agree with Mr Sykes that a redemption of redeemable
shares (which is now governed by sec. 159 of the 1985 Act and which does not result in a
reduction of nominal capital — see sec. 160(4)) is different from a reduction of capital
under sec. 135 and that "reduction" in art. 7(B) refers only to a sec. 135 reduction. I do

A   not consider that a different view is required by the decision of the House of Lords in *IR Commrs v Universal Grinding Wheel Co Ltd* [1955] AC 807. That decision related to the meaning of a reference to a "sum applied . . . in reducing the share capital" of a business undertaking in legislation relating to profits tax. It was accepted that a sum equal to the nominal value of the preference shares was so applied. The dispute was only whether a premium which had been paid to the preference shareholders was likewise applied. Moreover the decision was before the effect of *Re Serpell & Co Ltd* [1944] Ch

B   233, on which the House of Lords relied in part for its analysis, was partially reversed by sec. 58(3) of the *Companies Act* 1948 (now sec. 160(4) of the 1985 Act).

Lastly Mr Oliver pointed out that if the draftsman of art. 7(B) had meant "reduction or repayment" instead of merely "reduction" in the sense contended for by the company, he could easily have done so. He produced extracts from the articles of a number of well-known companies. These showed that in many cases companies have sought to protect

C   their preference shareholders against redemption contrary to their wishes by means of a reduction of capital in accordance with the principle which I stated at an early stage of this judgment. In some cases the draftsman has indeed referred to "any reduction or repayment". In other cases the draftsman has used a form substantially the same as that of art. 7(B) of the company's articles. I can draw no significant conclusion from this.

I have dealt with most of Mr Sykes' argument on points of detail in discussing

D   Mr Oliver's contentions. Generally Mr Sykes argued that "reduction" in art. 7(B) has a meaning commensurate with that of "reduction" in sec. 135. As "reduce" is not a term defined in the 1985 Act Mr Sykes could not rely directly on that part of art. 2 of the company's articles which states that:

"words or expressions defined in the Acts shall if not inconsistent with the subject or context, bear the same meaning in these articles."

E   He submitted, nevertheless, that there ought to be a leaning towards construing the relevant part of art. 7(B) as covering the same ground as sec. 135. He pointed out that art. 49 of the company's articles, which contains the authorisation required if sec. 135 is to be applicable, permits the company "to reduce its share capital" in any manner authorised by the Act, which must be construed in the same sense as the equivalent words in sec. 135. It would be strange, therefore, if the reference in art. 7(B) to "the reduction of the capital paid up on [any] shares" were limited to a particular form of

F   reduction. Article 49 shows also that the draftsman was concerned to follow very closely what is now sec. 121 of the Act in relation to other alterations of capital. It would not be surprising, therefore, if in art. 7(B) he had intended to cover the same ground as sec. 135 in relation to reduction of capital.

Mr Sykes also relied upon an anomaly which would arise if Mr Oliver were right. If the company proposed to reduce its capital by writing down the nominal value of each

G   preference share from £1 to 1p in consideration of the return of 99 pence per share (together with all or a proportionate part of the premium which is payable to the holders of the three per cent and 11 per cent preference shares), then even on the construction of art. 7(B) favoured by the company there would have to be class meetings and class consents. But it is said that because the company actually proposes to cancel the preference shares altogether and return the extra penny art. 7(B) has no application. This cannot have been the intention when art. 7(B) was adopted and a construction of

H   the article which avoids this consequence without straining the language should be favoured. At the very least, Mr Oliver's acceptance that art. 7(B) would apply on a partial reduction in the nominal value of the preference shares, even where the reduction falls only fractionally short of extinction, deprives Mr Oliver's first contention (i.e. that the Commercial Union view virtually abrogates the capital rights prescribed by art. 3(B)) of much of its force.

A

In my judgment the arguments of Mr Sykes, as I have summarised them, have great force. As appears from my discussion of the contrary arguments, I consider that a number of them are ill-founded. The weight of those which I have not completely rejected is, in my view, much less than that of the arguments advanced on behalf of Commercial Union. In my judgment art. 7(B) has the effect that the proposed cancellation of the preference shares in the company is to be deemed to be a variation of the rights attached to the preference shares and class meetings are therefore required by art. 6. As there have been no such class meetings the reduction of capital which I am asked to confirm has not been carried out in accordance with the company's articles and I must decline to confirm it.

B

Mr Sykes briefly presented alternative arguments as to why I should decline to confirm the reduction even if I accepted the company's contention as to the construction of art. 7(B). In view of my conclusion on the construction point I do not think it necessary to consider these arguments.

C

(Order accordingly)

D

E

F

G

H

A # Zemco Ltd v Jerrom-Pugh.

Chancery Division (Bristol) and Court of Appeal.
His Honour Judge Weeks QC; Neill, Butler-Sloss and Hoffmann L JJ.
Judgment delivered 27 November 1991 and 2 November 1992.

B
> *Directors — Fiduciary duty — Whether payment to director was breach of duty — Whether director had to make repayment — Whether director could set off claim under contract.*

**This was an appeal against a judgment under O. 14. The defendant was a director of
the plaintiff company. In 1990 the defendant drew £36,800 out of the company's bank
account. The company's case was that the defendant had no right to take the money: the
payment was a breach of his fiduciary duty as a director and he therefore held it on
constructive trust for the company. The defendant claimed that he was or had become**
C **entitled to the money under his contract of employment with the company.**

Held, dismissing the appeal:

**It was clear that the payment was a breach of fiduciary duty on the part of the directors
and that accordingly the defendant held the money as constructive trustee for the
company. It remained in equity the company's money. The defendant had an arguable
claim for compensation under his terms of employment but he was not entitled to set off**
D **that subsequently acquired claim against his obligation as constructive trustee to restore
the company's money. (Dictum of Browne-Wilkinson V-C in Guinness plc v Saunders &
Anor (1987) 3 BCC 520 applied.)**

The following cases were referred to in the High Court judgment:

EVTR, Re (1987) 3 BCC 389.
Guinness plc v Saunders & Anor (1987) 3 BCC 520; (1988) 4 BCC 377, [1988] 1 WLR
E 863 (CA).
Taupo Totara Timber Co Ltd v Rowe [1978] AC 537.

Stephen Davies (instructed by Harrison Clark, Worcester) for the plaintiff.

Graeme Wood in the High Court and R S Levy in the Court of Appeal (instructed by
Geoffrey Parker Bourne) for the defendant.

F ### HIGH COURT JUDGMENT
(27 November 1991)

His Honour Judge Weeks QC: This is an appeal from an order made by District Judge
Bird on 28 August 1991. On an O. 14 application by the plaintiff, the district judge
ordered that judgment be entered for the plaintiff against the defendant in the sum of
£36,800 plus interest of £5,792, and gave leave to defend as to the balance of the claim.
The plaintiff has not appealed against that order; the defendant has, by notice given on
G 30 August 1991. The plaintiff is a company incorporated in the UK but since January
1983 has been a subsidiary of a company in California, Zemco Group Inc, which owns
999 of the 1,000 issued ordinary shares.

From February 1983 to November 1990 the only directors of the plaintiff company
were the defendant Mr Jerrom-Pugh and Mr W Zeigner. Mr Zeigner is also a shareholder
in the parent company and was a director of that company until 17 August 1990; he has
H also been described as chief executive or president of the parent company.

In August 1990 there was apparently a boardroom struggle within the parent company
and according to an affidavit of another director, Mr Romley, Mr Zeigner lost control of
the board on 6 August 1990. Whether Mr Pugh was immediately aware of this, I do not
know, but on 10 August 1990 he withdrew £36,800 from the plaintiff's account and paid
it into his own savings account at Lloyds Bank, Coventry.

It is pleaded in para. 10 of the statement of claim: A

"In breach of the aforesaid fiduciary duties, the defendant wrongly and without the knowledge or consent of the plaintiff's shareholders, converted to his own use the following moneys belonging to the plaintiff:

(a) on or about 10 August 1990, the defendant caused or procured the transfer of the sum of £36,800 out of the plaintiff's bank account into an account in his own name." B

In the defence, the introductory statement is denied but subpara. (a) is admitted. Mr Pugh's explanation for the transfer is that it was authorised by his only co-director and he relies on a document signed by himself which purports to be minutes of a telephonic meeting between the directors of the company Zemco Ltd at 5.30 am BST on Friday, 10 August 1990. The material part records that it was resolved that Mr Jerrom-Pugh should draw an advance of salary for the financial year 1990–91 totalling £36,800, subject to his ascertaining the facts and insurance implications from the company's auditors, Daffern and Co. C

I observe in passing that under sec. 311 of the *Companies Act* 1985 it is not lawful for a company to pay a director remuneration, whether as director or otherwise, free of income tax. D

The resolution referred to the company's auditors, who were Daffern and Co. On the same day Mr Pugh sent them a fax stating:

"From the attached minutes you will note that at a meeting of the directors it was resolved that I should draw an advance of salary totalling £36,800 for the financial year 1990–91.

This money is being withdrawn today. Will you kindly ascertain the amount of E income tax and national insurance contributions payable on this advance, in order that the appropriate remittance can be made to the Inland Revenue in September 1990."

Mr West, a partner in the auditor's firm at the time, says in an affidavit sworn on 15 August 1991:

"I recall receiving a fax message and enclosures from Mr Jerrom-Pugh on or F around this date (10 August), and although I cannot recall the dates and figures in the documents I received, the exhibited documents, so far as I can recall, are similar in context. However, within 24 hours of the message being received on the fax machine, I received a telephone call from Mr Jerrom-Pugh, who told me to destroy the minutes and the message as no action was to be taken upon it. He further told me that he had obtained a draft for £36,800 and that this would be G taken by him personally to Taiwan to be paid directly to Zemco Taiwan Ltd. On his instructions, I therefore destroyed and disposed of the fax message with the enclosed copy minutes."

Mr Pugh swore an affidavit on 13 February 1991, which says:

"On 10 August 1990 I withdrew the sum of £36,800 from a bank account belonging to the plaintiff and immediately deposited the same amount in an instant savings H account at Lloyds Bank, Earlsdon, Coventry.

On 13 August 1990 I instructed Lloyds Bank to convert the said sum of £36,800 into US dollars and to issue a banker's draft for the full amount in favour of Zemco Electronics, Taiwan, another subsidiary of the plaintiff's parent company. A draft for US$69,552 was issued on 16 August 1990.

A

On 15 November 1990 I instructed Lloyds Bank to cancel the draft and to pay the said sum of US$69,552 into a currency account to be opened in my own name. This account was numbered 12371618."

The plaintiff company's accounts for the year ended 31 August 1989 show the remuneration paid to Mr Pugh for the year ended 31 August 1988 as being £14,994, and for the year ending 31 August 1989 as £26,518. Accounts for the year ended 31 August 1990 show remuneration of £28,994 for that year. In August 1990 his normal monthly salary was £1,656.54 after deductions for tax and national insurance, and this continued to be paid to him after that month up to and including November 1990.

B

On 31 October 1990, Mr Pugh wrote to the chairman of the parent company:

"Following the defeat of Willard Zeigner's attempt, at the recent shareholders' meeting, to regain control of the board of directors, I have thought long and hard about my future with the company . . .

C

As you know, my service contract gives me the right to terminate my employment by giving three months' notice and to be entitled to one year's severance pay. This is to inform you, therefore, that I propose to resign from my position as managing director of Zemco UK and to terminate my employment with the company on 31 January 1991.

D

I confirm that my decision to terminate my contract is a direct result of the change in the management of the US parent company."

Paragraphs 10(b) and (c) of the statement of claim complain of sums admittedly received by Mr Pugh from the company of $9,000 on 11 October 1990 and $6,000 on 12 November. In November a repayment of $1,656 was made by Mr Pugh and he claims to be entitled to the balance of the $15,000 as part of his agreed salary in respect of the period to 31 January 1991. In these circumstances, it seems to me that the only lawful explanation of the receipt of £36,800 was that it was paid to the defendant on account of his 1991 salary entitlement and for no other purpose, to be returned by him to the company if and in so far as he received his 1991 salary by other means.

E

The counterclaim includes a claim for the balance of his net salary up to 31 January 1991, but this claim is not quantified and in view of the receipt of the two dollar sums, little if anything can be owing under that head. What is said by counsel is that Mr Pugh is entitled to retain the £36,800 on account of an entirely different debt, that is, the severance pay referred to in the letter of 31 October 1990, which I have read. I can see no foundation for this submission. The payment of £36,800 was authorised, if it was authorised, in August, for one particular purpose. At that time there was no question of severance pay because notice was not given until October of that year and Mr Pugh's employment did not cease until 31 January 1991. There is no evidence of any subsequent meeting of directors which authorised Mr Pugh to retain the money for any different purpose. In my judgment, he is clearly bound to repay it.

F

G

I must however consider the defendant's counterclaims for severance pay and for £9,993 in respect of hire-purchase payments on a company car. It is not, in my judgment, simply a question of legal or equitable set-off, because there is evidence that another subsidiary of the same American parent company has served a statutory demand for £732,992 on the parent company and proposes to petition for its winding up if the statutory demand is not met. There is therefore a possibility — I put it no higher than that — of the plaintiff company going into liquidation in the near future. If the defendant were entitled in a liquidation to set off either of his counterclaims against the debt of £36,800, I would regard it as unfair to order immediate judgment for that sum and would be minded to stay execution until the counterclaim had been determined.

H

The debt of £9,993 is said to arise because the terms of the defendant's employment   A
state that he should be provided with a motor car, and he says he paid nearly £10,000 to
the hire-purchase company in respect of the car. He claims for moneys paid on the
company's behalf.

The claim to severance pay arises in this way: on 31 January 1983, Mr Zeigner
apparently wrote to Mr Pugh as follows:

> "Dear Geoff,
>
> B
>
> Following our acquisition of Zemco (UK) Ltd, I have pleasure in confirming your
> appointment as managing director of the UK company at an initial salary of
> US$48,000 per annum.
>
> In consideration of your relocating to England and assuming full responsibility for
> the UK operation, this contract is for an initial period of five years and will be
> renewed, automatically, for further five-year periods unless either party gives   C
> written notice of their intention not to renew.
>
> The basic salary will be reviewed annually in the light of performance but, in
> addition, Zemco will provide you with a company car and pay all reasonable
> operating expenses thereof.
>
> As an employee of the UK company, you will be entitled to 20 working days'
> vacation per year plus statutory holidays. Furthermore, you will be entitled to   D
> payment for periods of sickness up to a maximum of 13 weeks in any calendar year
> less any social security benefits.
>
> If for any reason Zemco decides to terminate this agreement and discharge you
> from your role as managing director of the UK company, it is agreed that you will
> be given a minimum of three months' notice, in writing, and that you will be paid
> 12 months' severance pay from the end of that notice period.
>
> E
>
> Should you decide to terminate this contract, you will give us a minimum of three
> months' notice in writing. However it is expressly agreed that should your decision
> to terminate be as a direct result of a change in the management of the US parent
> company, 12 months' severance pay will be granted to you in compensation.
>
> I hope that this letter correctly sets out the terms and conditions agreed between
> us, and, on this assumption, would ask you to sign the enclosed copy and return it
> to me for safe-keeping."   F

Mr Pugh, in his letter of 31 October 1990, to which I have referred, claimed his
decision to terminate was a direct result of the change of management in the parent
company. It was at one stage suggested that such an agreement would contravene
sec. 312 of the *Companies Act* 1985, but in the light of the decision of the Privy Council
in *Taupo Totara Timber Co Ltd v Rowe* [1978] AC 537, this suggestion has not been
pursued.   G

I note however that another accountant, Mr Podesta, has deposed:

> "I clearly recall discussing with the defendant (Mr Pugh) the terms and conditions
> of his employment with the plaintiff company. At that time in 1987 the defendant's
> salary was paid through the plaintiff's parent company in the USA. Although I
> cannot recall the exact date on which the conversation took place, I do recall the
> defendant advising me that he did not have any written terms of his employment.   H
> In my subsequent report to my clients dated 13 July 1987, I recommended that the
> terms and conditions of the defendant's employment with the plaintiff company
> should be set out in a contract of service."

I note also that a copy of an Inland Revenue form has been exhibited in which
Mr Pugh apparently states that he was self-employed from May 1987 to March 1988, and

A   also that no contract of service with him was kept for inspection by the plaintiff company as required by the Companies Act. However, I accept that Mr Pugh has an arguable case in claiming the £9,993 and also one year's severance pay. Whether the latter should be paid gross or net of tax is not at all clear to me.

In a liquidation, the rules as to set-off are not the same as they are between solvent parties. However, what is clear is that there is a general rule that in both cases there can be no set-off for a simple debt against a proprietary claim. For example in *Guinness plc*
B   *v Saunders & Anor* at first instance, (1987) 3 BCC 520, the Vice-Chancellor said at p. 527:

> "The reference to equitable set-off applying to cross-claims which impeach the plaintiff's demand reflect older authorities on equitable set-off. The question therefore is whether the alleged cross-claim impugns Guinness' title to recover the £5.2m and whether, in all the circumstances, it would be just to permit a
C   > set-off.

> In my judgment, Mr Ward's cross-claims whether by way of quantum meruit or equitable compensation do not impugn Guinness' title to recover the £5.2m. That money has at all times been Guinness' money. From the date of its receipt by or on behalf of Mr Ward, he has held it on a constructive trust for Guinness. Guinness is now entitled to a judgment to recover its own property. The fact that, arising
D   > out of the same transaction, Mr Ward may be entitled to remuneration for his services, in no way impugns Guinness' right to recover its property from Mr Ward."

Similarly, in my judgment, the £36,800 is the plaintiff company's money, because it was paid for a specific purpose which has been satisfied or failed as in *Re EVTR* (1987) 3 BCC 389.

E   Mr Pugh may well be able to make good his counterclaims, but those counterclaims do not impugn the company's title to the £36,800. Accordingly, in my judgment he has no right of set-off and it would not be right to order any stay of execution. I also bear in mind what the Vice-Chancellor said in the Guinness case, at p. 527:

> "On wider principles, in my judgment it would be unfortunate if a director who has secretly received remuneration without proper authority is entitled to retain
F   > such remuneration until a possibly groundless claim on a quantum meruit has been determined. The first duty of directors and other fiduciaries who have procured that they receive money or property belonging to the company or their beneficiaries without due authorisation should be to repay what has wrongfully been abstracted. Their claim to receive some compensation on a basis different to that on which they took the money should stand as a cross-claim, not a set-off."

G   This may not be a case where a director has secretly received remuneration without proper authority. It is, however, a case where a former director is seeking to retain company money without due authorisation and in breach of the terms on which he says he received it.

In my judgment, his claims to severance pay and reimbursement are on a different footing to his duty to repay company money and should equally stand as counterclaims
H   and not a set-off.

Finally, some reliance has been placed on sec. 727 of the *Companies Act* 1985. A similar plea was rejected in the *Guinness* case in the court at first instance, for reasons set out at p. 527 of the report, and in the Court of Appeal for the reasons given at (1988) 4 BCC 377 at p. 384. In my judgment, there is even less justification for applying sec. 727 to the present case. Mr Ward, after all, had not been paid for his services other than by

the money which he was ordered to repay. Mr Pugh has been paid for the services for   A
which he drew the £36,800.

I see no prospect of his being allowed to retain this money under sec. 727, and
accordingly I dismiss the present appeal.

(*Order accordingly*)

COURT OF APPEAL JUDGMENT
(2 November 1992)

Hoffmann LJ: This is an appeal against a judgment under O. 14 given by His Honour
Judge *Weeks* QC sitting as a judge of the Chancery Division at Bristol. The plaintiff
("Zemco") is an English subsidiary of a US corporation called Zemco Group Inc
("Inc"). The defendant, Mr Jerrom-Pugh, was between April 1983 and 1 November
1990 the managing director of Zemco. The only other director was Mr W Zeigner, a US   C
resident who was until August 1990 the president of Inc and controlled the board of that
company. He and Mr Jerrom-Pugh had a close business relationship.

On 6 August 1990 Mr Zeigner was ousted from control of Inc by his colleagues on the
board. He appealed to the stockholders, but a general meeting in October 1990 declined
to reinstate him. This boardroom struggle has rather complicated the story as presented
in the evidence in this summons, but for the purposes of this claim the essential facts are   D
very simple.

On 10 August 1990 Mr Jerrom-Pugh drew £36,800 out of Zemco's bank account. He
did so by ordering a banker's draft in his favour and paying it into his personal bank
account. The plaintiff's case is that he had no right to take this money. The payment was
a breach of his fiduciary duty as a director and he therefore held it on constructive trust
for the company.

Mr Jerrom-Pugh claims that he was or has become entitled to the money under his
contract of employment with Zemco. He has produced a letter from Mr Zeigner dated
in London on 31 January 1983. This provides for the termination of the employment by
Mr Jerrom-Pugh on three months' notice but says that if his decision to terminate is,

"a direct result of a change in the management of the US parent company,
12 months' severance pay will be granted to you in compensation."

There is a dispute over the validity of this agreement, but, for the purposes of a
summons under O. 14, I think it should be assumed that Mr Zeigner was then entitled to
speak on behalf of the holders of the entire issued share capital of Zemco, namely Inc,
and enter on behalf of Zemco into an agreement with Mr Jerrom-Pugh. On 31 October
1990, after the failure of Mr Zeigner's attempt to regain control of Inc, Mr Jerrom-Pugh
gave written notice terminating his employment as from 31 January 1991. On
14 November he wrote an important letter in which he explains the purpose of the   G
August payment to himself. He says:

"You should be aware that, with Will Zeigner's approval and in anticipation of
my employment becoming untenable, I took the liberty to draw my agreed annual
salary for 1990–91 on 10 August of this year. Strictly speaking this amount does
not fall due until the end of my period of notice on 31 January 1991 but, in the
present circumstances, you will understand my unwillingness to repay the money   H
now. However, if you can suggest ways in which my severance pay can be
guaranteed, the money could be put to good use by (Zemco)]] in the intervening
period."

In support of his claim that Mr Zeigner had approved the payment, Mr Jerrom-Pugh
has produced minutes of a board meeting of Zemco held on the telephone at 5.30 am

A   BST on 10 August 1990 at which he and Mr Zeigner were present. This resolves that Mr Jerrom-Pugh should draw an advance of salary for the financial year 1990–91 totalling £36,800. Again, therefore, for the purposes of O. 14, it must be accepted that the making of that payment was authorised by the board.

B   The board of directors of a company are, however, under a fiduciary duty to the company to exercise their powers of management bona fide in the interests of the company. What this payment was doing was to put into Mr Jerrom-Pugh's hands a sum of money which on no view was then due, which might or might not become due at some date in the future, if Mr Jerrom-Pugh chose to avail himself of the severance pay provision in his contract, and which in the meanwhile, in his own words, "could be put to good use by" Zemco.

C   It seems to me quite impossible to justify such a payment as being in the interests of Zemco. Zemco's interests do not enter into it at all. The only purpose of the payment, as is apparent from Mr Jerrom-Pugh's request for a guarantee in substitution, was to secure Mr Jerrom-Pugh against the possibility that when the money actually fell due either the new management of the company might be reluctant to pay or, alternatively, the company might then be in insolvent liquidation. Accordingly it seems to me that, even for the purposes of O. 14, it is clear beyond doubt that the payment was a breach of fiduciary duty on the part of the directors and that accordingly Mr Jerrom-Pugh held the money as constructive trustee for the company. It remained in equity the company's money. Since then Mr Jerrom-Pugh has, as I have said, terminated his employment and he has, by virtue of the lapse of time, an arguable claim (I say no more than that) for compensation in the sum of a year's salary.

D

  The question then is whether he would be entitled to set off that subsequently acquired claim against his obligation as constructive trustee to restore the company's money. It is on that point the judge expressed his view in a way which I think it would be very difficult to improve upon. He said:

E

> ". . . what is clear is that there is a general rule that in both cases there can be no set-off for a simple debt against a proprietary claim. For example in *Guinness plc v Saunders & Anor* at first instance, (1987) 3 BCC 520, the Vice-Chancellor said . . ."

F   He then set out the facts of that case in which it was decided that Mr Ward had been wrongfully paid £5.2m which he held as constructive trustee for Guinness, but that he had an arguable claim for a quantum meruit for remuneration. The Vice-Chancellor went on to say (at p. 527):

> "In my judgment, Mr Ward's cross-claims whether by way of quantum meruit or equitable compensation do not impugn Guinness' title to recover the £5.2m. That money has at all times been Guinness' money. From the date of its receipt by or
G   on behalf of Mr Ward, he has held it on a constructive trust for Guinness. Guinness is now entitled to a judgment to recover its own property. The fact that, arising out of the same transaction, Mr Ward may be entitled to remuneration for his services, in no way impugns Guinness' right to recover its property from Mr Ward."

  As the judge goes on to say, that analysis applies precisely to this case.

H   The skeleton argument, which was put before us by Mr Levy, also contains reliance upon sec. 727 of the *Companies Act* 1985 which gives the court a jurisdiction to relieve fiduciaries from liability for breach of trust if they have acted honestly and reasonably and ought fairly to be excused.

  This defence was not urged in argument, and I think rightly so, because there seems to be no possibility of such a defence succeeding at trial. That, too, is a matter which was

A

dealt with by the Vice-Chancellor where he pointed out that the effect of such an order is to relieve the fiduciary from any obligation to pay the money back. In this case, if Mr Jerrom-Pugh succeeds in his cross-claim at the trial, which of course he may still bring, notwithstanding the subject-matter of the present claim, he will not need relief under sec. 727 and, if he fails in his cross-claim, it would obviously be quite wrong for him to be entitled to repayment of the money. On either view, therefore, sec. 727 is of no use to him. For those reasons I would dismiss the appeal.

B

Butler-Sloss LJ: For the reasons given in the judgment by *Hoffmann* LJ, I agree this appeal should be dismissed.

Neill LJ: I agree.

(*Appeal dismissed*)

——————————

C

D

E

F

G

H

A
Caledonian Produce (Holdings) Ltd v Price Waterhouse.
Court of Session (Inner House).
Lord McCluskey, Lord Kirkwood and Lord Caplan.
Judgment delivered 5 January 1993.

B
Caution for costs — Scotland — Noters granted authority to bring proceedings in name of company in insolvent liquidation — Defenders sought caution for costs — Whether noters were in same position in relation to action as liquidator — Whether Lord Ordinary was right to ordain caution — Companies Act 1985, sec. 726(2).

This was a reclaiming motion against an interlocutor of the Lord Ordinary ordaining the pursuers, Caledonian Produce (Holdings) Ltd ("the company"), to find caution in the sum of £50,000 for the expenses of the action pursuant to sec. 726(2) of the Companies

C
Act 1985.

The company was in insolvent liquidation and in the insolvency process the court had granted authority to four named persons ("the noters") or any of them to bring an action in the name and on behalf of the company against the defenders (conditional on indemnifying the company and the liquidator for their costs).

The action was then raised in the name of the company and of the four noters as

D
pursuers. It was an action of damages seeking payment of the sum of £6m by the defenders to the pursuers. Subsequently one of the noters withdrew. Later, the instance, conclusion and condescendence were amended so as to make it clear both that the company were the only pursuers and also that the three remaining noters were the persons who were using the company's name to pursue a claim which, if successful, would benefit the company and, perhaps, ultimately and indirectly, those who had an interest in any assets of the company.

E
The noters argued that the relationship between them and the action was, for all material purposes, to be equiparated with the relationship between the liquidator of a company and an action raised by the company in liquidation; that it was no more appropriate to order the noters to find caution than it would be to order a liquidator to find caution; and that the Lord Ordinary misdirected himself in his conclusion that, for the purposes of an application under sec. 726 of the Companies Act 1985, the position of

F
the individuals granted said authority was not, in so far as material, in pari casu with that of a liquidator.

Held, refusing the reclaiming motion:

The Lord Ordinary, faced with the fact that the nominal pursuer was plainly insolvent, was well entitled to hold that the appropriate order to make was one for caution. The overall judgment of the Lord Ordinary that there were marked differences, in relation to

G
the matter of liability for expenses, between the position of a liquidator and the position of the noters was plainly correct. It had not been shown that the Lord Ordinary misdirected himself in any material respect.

Arthur Hamilton QC (instructed by Anderson Strathern WS) for the company.

R L Martin QC (instructed Brodies WS) for the defenders.

H
OPINION OF THE COURT
(Delivered by Lord McCluskey)

This is a reclaiming motion by the pursuers against an interlocutor of the Lord Ordinary (*Penrose*) dated 2 December 1992. In that interlocutor the Lord Ordinary ordained the pursuers to find caution to the satisfaction of the clerk of court in the sum of £50,000 sterling for the whole expenses of the action both to date and to be incurred

A

in the future, pursuant to sec. 726 of the *Companies Act* 1985. The Lord Ordinary granted leave to reclaim.

The background to this litigation and the relevant history of the pursuers are set forth fully in the opinion of the Lord Ordinary bearing the date of the interlocutor. It is unnecessary for this court to repeat that narrative, the accuracy of which was not challenged before us. All that we need say is that the court ordered the company to be wound up in 1987 and appointed AWT Wight, chartered accountant, liquidator of the company. The whole assets of the company have subsequently been applied in the discharge of the claims of priority creditors. An estimated statement of affairs as at 24 November 1992 disclosed that the company had no assets and had substantial liabilities, resulting in a very substantial total deficiency. The company was and remains insolvent.

B

On 5 September 1991, in the insolvency process, the vacation judge, Lord *Kirkwood*, granted authority to four named persons (hereinafter referred to as "the noters") or any of them to bring an action in the name and on behalf of the company against the present defenders but made such authority conditional on the production in the liquidation process of a bond of caution or a letter of guarantee of a Scottish clearing bank or similar institution indemnifying the company and the liquidator personally:

C

> "against any liability in expenses incurred by it or him in the proposed litigation against Messrs Price Waterhouse and against any reasonable costs incurred by him as liquidator by reason of the dependence of said litigation, all as the same in case of dispute may be taxed by the auditor of the Court of Session, said bond of caution or letter of guarantee being in the amount of twenty thousand pounds (£20,000) but with leave to the liquidator on cause shown at any time after the first to occur of (1) any allowance of proof in the proposed action or (2) the appointment of the proposed action to the procedure roll or (3) the enrolment of a reclaiming motion in the proposed action to make further application in this process in respect of the sufficiency of the foregoing indemnity . . ."

D

E

The present action was then raised in the name of the company and of the four noters as pursuers. It was an action of damages seeking payment of the sum of £6m by the defenders to the pursuers. Subsequently one of the noters withdrew from the action by minute of abandonment and the Lord Ordinary dismissed the action by him against the defenders. Later, the instance, conclusion and condescendence were amended so as to make it clear both that the company were the only pursuers and also that the three remaining noters were the persons who were using the company's name to pursue a claim which, if successful, would benefit the company and, perhaps, ultimately and indirectly, those who had an interest in any assets of the company.

F

The Lord Ordinary wrote a substantial opinion explaining precisely the basis upon which he was granting the defenders' motion for caution. Mr Hamilton, for the reclaimers, submitted that although the decision whether or not to grant caution in circumstances such as obtained in the present case was a matter that fell within the discretion of the Lord Ordinary, it was open to an appellate court to review and reverse the Lord Ordinary's decision if it appeared that he had misdirected himself. It was submitted that he had done so and the grounds of attack upon the Lord Ordinary's opinion are to be found in the grounds of appeal.

G

The first ground of appeal is in the following terms:

H

> "The Lord Ordinary misdirected himself in his construction of the interlocutor by the honourable Lord *Kirkwood* dated 5 September 1991 in the liquidation process. The condition adjected to the authority granted by that interlocutor was designed to protect not the present defenders but the liquidator and the company."

We can deal with this matter shortly. In our view the Lord Ordinary's summary of the purpose and effect of the interlocutor of 5 September 1991 in the liquidation process is,

A   as submitted, open to some criticism. The words he used seem to suggest that the purpose of the vacation judge in imposing a condition in the terms specified above was to afford a degree of protection or security to the present defenders. We recognise that the imposing of the condition contained in the interlocutor of 5 September 1991 was likely to have the effect, at least indirectly, of affording some security to the present defenders in the event of an action being raised against them by the company acting under the authority contained in that interlocutor; but we do not consider that the

B   vacation judge imposed the condition in order to provide security for the present defenders; they after all were not represented in the liquidation process and made no representations to the vacation judge. The clear purpose of the vacation judge's interlocutor was to afford protection to the company and the liquidator against any potential liability for expenses etc. incurred in the proposed litigation. The fact that the present defenders might well derive some indirect benefit from the imposing of that

C   condition would not be enough in itself to warrant the Lord Ordinary's statement that:

> "the action against the present defenders had been raised on a conditional authority from the court which sought to protect *the defenders* against loss in the event that the action against them failed" (emphasis added).

It may be that the reference was intended to be to the liquidator and the company rather than to the defenders in this action. But while we consider that what was said was not an

D   accurate description of any purpose contained in the vacation judge's interlocutor we do not consider that the Lord Ordinary's decision was based to any material extent upon that reading of the condition imposed in the vacation judge's interlocutor. His consideration of the purpose and effect of the interlocutor of 5 September 1991 in that respect was, in our view, essentially part of a preliminary narrative.

In our view, the Lord Ordinary clearly decided in the defenders' favour not upon the basis of his finding such a purpose in that interlocutor but upon the basis that it was

E   appropriate in an application made under sec. 726 of the *Companies Act* 1985, in circumstances where the action was brought by a company in liquidation without the authority of the liquidator, to seek caution from those who were responsible for raising the action. It is plain from the Lord Ordinary's opinion that the principal argument that was presented to him, and repeated to this court, was to the effect that the relationship between the remaining noters and the present action was, for all material purposes, to be equiparated with the relationship between the liquidator of a company and an action

F   raised by the company in liquidation. The submission was that the Lord Ordinary's attempts to distinguish between an action brought by a liquidator and an action brought by others who had obtained the authority of the court failed and that, therefore, it was no more appropriate to order the noters to find caution than it would be to order a liquidator to find caution.

The arguments advanced were in support of the second ground of appeal which was in

G   the following terms:

> "The Lord Ordinary misdirected himself in his conclusion that, for the purposes of an application under sec. 726 of the *Companies Act* 1985, the position of the individuals granted said authority was not, in so far as material, *in pari casu* with that of a liquidator."

The Lord Ordinary found some ten grounds of distinction between the position of a

H   liquidator in relation to an action brought by him and the position of noters pursuing an action such as the present one. Each of these points of distinction was subjected to careful analysis and it was submitted that none of them was valid or, in so far as valid, was material.

In relation to these grounds of distinction Mr Hamilton submitted first that although, as the Lord Ordinary had stated, one of the noters might withdraw without prejudice to

the right of the remainder to proceed that was an unimportant matter given that each
was empowered by the interlocutor of 5 September 1991 to proceed on his own and it
was not suggested that none of the noters currently behind the action would be able to
meet a claim for expenses. Secondly, while it was also true that the noters might not
have total control over the action, that was true of the liquidator also and reference was
made to sec. 167 of the *Insolvency Act* 1986. The Lord Ordinary's statement that it must
be doubted whether the vacation judge in granting the authority contained in the
interlocutor had in mind any situation other than that four men of substance would be
instructing the action was not a view that he was entitled to take given that the
interlocutor permitted the noters "or any of them" to bring the action. It was also true
that none of the noters was a party to the litigation whereas the liquidator invariably was
in Scottish practice; however this was a matter of form rather than of substance. It was
also true that a solvent liquidator conjoined as pursuer with an insolvent company would
be directly responsible to the defender in respect of an adverse award of expenses; but
there was no difficulty in pronouncing a decree for expenses against an individual such
as any of the noters if their association with an action made that appropriate. There was
no direct precedent on this matter but having regard to the principles set forth in
Maclaren on Expenses, at p. 149, there should be no problem in obtaining an award of
expenses against the noters and making good that award.

It was also true, as the Lord Ordinary had observed, that the individuals authorised to
raise these proceedings had no access to the funds of the company nor to any other funds
from which to reimburse themselves. That, however, was often true of the liquidator as
well, so this was not a valid point of distinction.

On the next point of distinction noted by the Lord Ordinary, counsel suggested that
there was a distinction between directors who were agents of the company and a
liquidator who in a proper sense represents the company in liquidation. The noters
acting in an avowed representative capacity were not agents; they were also representing
the company in liquidation. In this respect also it was submitted there was no material
distinction between the position of a liquidator and the position of the present noters. It
was also suggested that the Lord Ordinary was mistaken in holding that a good ground
of distinction was that the liquidator was answerable to the whole body of creditors and
contributories of the company of which he was liquidator. The noters would be
accountable in respect of any sums awarded to the company in the action. It was
accepted that they were not accountable in respect of particular decisions in the litigation
but that was a point of no substance; the liquidator would not normally account in
respect of his day to day conduct of the litigation either.

The Lord Ordinary's next point, to the effect that the noters were seeking to avoid the
spirit of the undertaking to provide security given in the liquidation process, was, it was
submitted, simply a repeat of his misunderstanding of the vacation judge's interlocutor.
The last point was a repetition of the mistaken view that the individuals concerned could
not be made directly liable to the defenders in expenses in the present case. On the
authority of the passage quoted from *Maclaren on Expenses* it was reasonable to expect
that such an award could be made.

In our view, however, the Lord Ordinary did not misdirect himself in reaching the
conclusion that the requirements of sec. 726(2) were met and that there was no
alternative source of funds directly available to the defenders to meet any award of
expenses made in their favour against the company.

The correct starting point is, as the Lord Ordinary identified, sec. 726(2). This is the
modern version of a provision which has been in force for over a century. It reads as
follows:

A

"Where in Scotland a limited company is pursuer in an action or other legal proceeding, the court having jurisdiction in the matter may, if it appears by credible testimony that there is reason to believe that the company will be unable to pay the defender's expenses if successful in his defence, order the company to find caution and sist the proceedings until caution is found."

B

This was a case where a limited company was the pursuer in an action of damages. Mr Hamilton accepted that there was material before the court entitling the court to conclude that the company would be unable to pay the defenders' expenses if the defenders were successful in their defence. Thus it is plain that the conditions for ordering the pursuers to find caution existed here. But of course, this subsection applies to any limited company whether or not it is in liquidation. Its effect is to put a limited company in the same position as an individual in relation to the ordinary power of the court to order caution where there is good reason to believe that a pursuer will be unable

C

to meet a successful defender's expenses. Plainly where an individual pursuer is bankrupt the court is likely to consider favourably a motion to ordain caution to be found. In our view, where the pursuers are an insolvent limited company without any assets and with a substantial total deficiency, the court would want some good reason for not ordering caution if the defenders sought such an order.

D

In the normal case, namely where an insolvent company sues with the authority of the liquidator, and he appears in the instance as pursuer, the court is likely to accept that the liquidator will be able to meet any award of expenses made against him and/or the company in the litigation. The liquidator is an officer of court, he is expected to act responsibly and he is subject to supervision not only by the court but by the creditors, and he has or may have rights of relief against the body of creditors or other assets of the company. Thus his position is a special one and the court, knowing that an award of expenses can be made against him directly and even personally, might well have little

E

difficulty in holding that ordering him to find caution would be to place an unnecessary obstacle in the way of his pursuing an action.

But the noters in the present case are not in these respects and others identified by the Lord Ordinary in the same position as the liquidator. In particular, they are not officers of the court. They have no recourse against other assets of the company or any other persons such as creditors. They are subject to little if any control by any person and are

F

certainly free of some of the controls that in practice would apply to a liquidator. They are, in the conduct of the litigation itself, to all intents and purposes not accountable to anyone. They are effectively sheltering behind a nominal pursuer, even although they are perfectly open about doing so. Nonetheless they are necessarily rather more shadowy figures than a court-appointed liquidator. They may withdraw from the proceedings, as one of them did in the present case. They are manifestly less accessible for expenses or for other procedural purposes than is an officially appointed liquidator

G

who must always remain subject to the jurisdiction of the court. Plainly any award of expenses against a liquidator could be made good against the liquidator. It is by no means clear that in practical terms any award of expenses could be made good against any of the noters, particularly if at some stage he were to cease to be within the jurisdiction of the Scottish courts. If a court-appointed liquidator got into personal financial difficulties that circumstance would be likely to become known quickly and widely; that would not necessarily be the case with a person in the position of the three

H

noters, only one of whom is said to be a man of substance.

Although it was a matter of concession that none of the noters could properly be regarded as a *dominus litis* — because none had a direct interest in the subject-matter of the action — we consider that the position of the present noters is analogous to that of a *verus dominus litis*. In discussing the responsibility of a *verus dominus litis* for expenses, *Maclaren on Expenses* at pp. 149–150 envisages that the *dominus litis* may be made liable for expenses by one of various methods. Decree for expenses may be obtained against him in the action; a separate action for expenses might be brought; the other party might move that the *dominus litis* be sisted as a party; in some cases the nominal pursuer may be ordered to find caution for expenses before being allowed to proceed. The course to be chosen will depend upon the known circumstances. In our opinion, the analogy with the *verus dominus litis* is sufficiently strong to warrant the view that the court, when invited to consider making an order for caution in circumstances such as those that obtain here, can consider which, if any, of these options would be appropriate to give adequate protection to a defender who is facing an insolvent pursuer, being a company whose name is being used by others. The present noters are not parties to this action and indeed have caused their names to be removed from the instance. It may well be that the court in the present action could, if circumstances warranted it, make an order for expenses directly against the noters, or some of them, but that would not afford any protection unless there was good reason to believe that the order for expenses could be made good.

The Lord Ordinary, faced with the fact that the nominal pursuer is plainly insolvent, was well entitled, in our view, to hold that the appropriate order to make was one for caution. It is unnecessary for us to deal in detail with each of the criticisms made of the detailed distinctions which the Lord Ordinary set forth as bearing upon the distinction between a liquidator and a person in the position of the noters. No doubt some of the points of distinction are of less significance than others but the overall judgment of the Lord Ordinary is, in our view, plainly correct, that there are marked differences, in relation to the matter of liability for expenses, between the position of a liquidator and the position of those who are responsible for the current litigation. In our view it has not been shown that the Lord Ordinary misdirected himself in any material respect.

It was further submitted that, in any event, the amount of £50,000 was excessive, particularly having regard to the fact that in the interlocutor of 5 September 1991 the noters had been compelled to obtain a bond of caution or letter of guarantee in the amount of £20,000. However this is a matter which the Lord Ordinary plainly had before him; his decision as to the amount of caution derived from his view that the information placed before him by counsel for the defenders was soundly based upon a supportable calculation of the expenses liable to be incurred in the period for which caution was ordered. In our view, the determination of the amount of caution was not flawed by any misdirection. In these circumstances we refuse the reclaiming motion.

Council for the reclaimers finally invited the court, if the reclaiming motion were refused, to extend the period for lodging caution by 14 days. That was unopposed and the extension was granted.

We were due to hear on the summar roll a second reclaiming motion against the interlocutor pronounced by Lord *Morton of Shuna* in the liquidation process. However, counsel for the liquidator who was present throughout the hearing of the reclaiming motion in the action at the instance of the company indicated that, in the light of the court's decision on the reclaiming motion, he did not propose to proceed with his own appeal. Accordingly we heard no submissions on that matter.

(Order accordingly)

A   # Boocock v Hilton International Co.

Court of Appeal (Civil Division).
Neill, Mann and Hoffmann L JJ.
Judgment delivered 22 January 1993.

*Oversea company — Service — Whether writ properly served on oversea
company — Companies Act 1985, sec. 695.*

B
**This was an appeal against an order setting aside service of a writ and dismissing the
plaintiff's application for leave to extend the validity of the writ.**

**The questions on the appeal in relation to service were, first, whether the writ was
effectively served on the defendant which was a foreign company with a place of business
in Great Britain which had delivered to the registrar of companies a return in the
prescribed form containing the name and address of a person resident in Great Britain**
C   **authorised to accept service on the company's behalf (under sec. 691(1)(b)(ii) of the
Companies Act 1985). Secondly, whether, in the exercise of its discretion under O. 2, r. 1
of the Rules of the Supreme Court, the court could allow the service to be treated as good
service notwithstanding failure to effect service in accordance with sec. 695 of the
Companies Act 1985.**

Held, allowing the plaintiff's appeal:

D   **1. The Rules of the Supreme Court excluded the possibility of any form of service other
than those prescribed by the relevant enactment and the Companies Act 1985, sec. 695
contained a complete code as to the manner in which process could be served on an
oversea company. Service of the writ was not effected in accordance with sec. 695(1).**

**2. However, in the interests of justice the court's power under O. 2, r. 1 to cure an
irregularity should be exercised.**

E   The following cases were referred to in the judgment of Neill LJ:

Camera Care Ltd v Victor Hasselblad AB & Anor [1986] 1 FTLR 347.
Goldean Mariner, The [1990] 2 Lloyd's Rep 215.
Kleinwort Benson Ltd v Barbrak Ltd [1987] AC 597.
Leal v Dunlop Bio-Processes International Ltd [1984] 1 WLR 874.
Singh v Atombrook Ltd [1989] 1 WLR 810.
F   *Theodohos, The* [1977] 2 Lloyd's Rep 428.
Waddon v Whitecroft Scovell Ltd [1988] 1 WLR 309.

Michael Brent QC (instructed by Robin Thompson & Partners) for the plaintiff.

Andrew Phillips (instructed by Jarvis & Bannister) for the defendants.

JUDGMENT
G
Neill LJ: This is an appeal by Mrs Mary Boocock from the order of His Honour Judge
Lever QC sitting as a judge of the High Court whereby it was ordered, inter alia,

(1)   that the order of Master *Turner* dated 24 June 1991 granting leave to amend the
writ be set aside;

(2)   that the order of Master *Hodgson* dated 7 August 1991 extending the validity of
H   the writ be set aside; and

(3)   that service of the amended writ be set aside.

Before turning to the questions which arise in this appeal it is necessary to set out the
history of the action in some detail.

On 9 December 1987 Mrs Boocock attended a dinner and dance at the Hilton Beach
Club in the Hilton Hotel, Dubai in the United Arab Emirates. While she was on the

premises she was struck on the head by a large piece of timber which was supporting a
wind break. As a result she suffered serious injuries.

A

It appears that following the accident Mrs Boocock had to resign from her employment.
Shortly afterwards she returned to England. But she notified the hotel of her claim and
it was passed to the hotel's insurers, American International Underwriters (UK) Ltd in
Croydon. Correspondence between Mrs Boocock and the insurers continued into 1989.
On 11 November 1989 a firm of solicitors in Dubai wrote to American International
stating that they had been instructed to call upon the insurers to settle the compensation
due to Mrs Boocock immediately, failing which they were instructed to institute
proceedings against their insured. Further correspondence with the insurers, however,
proved inconclusive and on 2 May 1990 Mrs Boocock wrote to the chairman of Hilton
International in Watford. She stated that the management and staff at the hotel had
been very sympathetic and helpful towards her but that the insurers appeared to be
"hostile" to her claim. On 11 May the chairman's secretary replied as follows:

B

C

> "Michael Hirst [the chairman] is at present abroad on business. However, as he is
> particularly keen that this matter is dealt with expeditiously, I have passed a copy
> of your letter to Mr Geoffrey Chester, legal counsel, based here in Watford, who
> will personally investigate your comments and write to you further."

Also on 11 May 1990 Mr Geoffrey Chester, who described himself as "solicitor,
general counsel and secretary of Hilton International", wrote to Mrs Boocock:

D

> "A copy of Mrs Tayler's [the chairman's secretary] letter to you has been referred
> to me. I have duly written to our insurance department to expedite this matter and
> I trust your claim will shortly be dealt with."

A week later on 18 May Mr Paul Chambury, the head of group risk and insurance
services, wrote to Mrs Boocock stating that her case was not known to him. His letter
continued:

E

> "I should explain that Hilton International Co was acquired by the Ladbroke
> Group plc approximately two years ago, after the date of your accident. In these
> circumstances, I am unaware of your particular case and it could be that file notes
> are still being retained in their previous head office, situated in New York.

> On receipt of your further advices, I will look into matters as quickly as possible."

F

On 5 July 1990 Mrs Boocock's solicitors in Dubai wrote to Underwriters Adjustment
Co in Saudi Arabia. It would appear that Underwriters Adjustment Co were agents
acting for the insurers, American International Underwriters. In this letter the solicitors
referred to Mr Chambury's letter of 18 May to Mrs Boocock and asked Underwriters
Adjustment Co to forward to Mr Chambury copies of all expense statements and
documents which had been sent to them.

G

Further correspondence followed and eventually on 13 October 1990 Underwriters
Adjustment Co sent Mrs Boocock's solicitors in Dubai a fax containing an offer of
settlement in the sum of US$20,000.

On 6 November 1990 Mrs Boocock instructed her present solicitors. At about the
same time she went to see her local Member of Parliament who wrote to the chairman of
Hilton International on 16 November 1990. On 19 November 1990 Mr Hirst replied.
I should refer to part of this letter:

H

> "All insurance claims are dealt with by our group insurance department in
> conjunction with our insurers, American International Underwriters. However,
> I have contacted our director of insurance today to ascertain the position with
> regard to Mrs Boocock's claim.

A

I believe that Mrs Boocock was to undergo a medical examination within the last few weeks and that the report was to be forwarded to the insurance company for evaluation. Our insurance department are well aware of this claim but will contact American International Underwriters in order to ascertain the latest situation.

Thank you for bringing this matter to my attention. However, I am sure you will appreciate that matters are taken out of our hands somewhat when a case is referred to the insurers."

B

By now of course nearly three years had elapsed since the accident in December 1987.

On 7 December 1990, just before the expiration of the period of limitation, the plaintiff's new solicitors issued a writ claiming damages for personal injuries and consequential loss. The defendants named in the writ were Ladbroke Group plc (trading as Hilton International Hotels (UK) Ltd). On 27 February 1991 a copy of the writ was sent to Ladbroke Group plc. On 13 March 1991 solicitors acting for Ladbroke Group plc and Hilton International Co sent a fax message to the plaintiff's solicitors stating that the Ladbroke Group plc had purchased the assets and liabilities of all the Hilton International companies on 11 April 1988 but that Hilton International Hotels (UK) Ltd had never been either the owners or the occupiers of the Hilton Hotel in Dubai. Other errors in the writ were pointed out, but it is to be noted that the fax did not state the name of the owners, occupiers or managers of the Hilton Hotel, Dubai at the relevant time.

C

D

On 27 March 1991 the plaintiff's solicitors wrote to say that they had issued a summons to amend the writ and that if necessary they would seek leave to serve the writ out of the jurisdiction. On 23 May 1991 the solicitors acting for the Ladbroke Group plc and Hilton International Co (I shall call them "the defendants' solicitors") informed the plaintiff's solicitors, in response to a further enquiry, that they were instructed to accept service of proceedings on behalf of Hilton International Co.

E

On 24 June 1991 the plaintiff's solicitors obtained an order from Master *Turner* granting leave under the Rules of the Supreme Court, O. 15, r. 6 to amend the writ "by changing the defendants to read Hilton International Co notwithstanding the limitation period". It is common ground that following the order of Master *Turner* the amendment should have been made within 14 days in accordance with O. 15, r. 8(1). The amendment was not made, however, within that time limit.

F

On 6 August 1991 the defendants' solicitors sent a fax message to the plaintiff's solicitors stating that they were no longer instructed to accept service of proceedings on behalf of Hilton International Co. On the same day the defendants' solicitors served a defence on behalf of Ladbroke Group plc, being the defence to the original statement of claim which had been served on 1 March 1991.

On 7 August 1991 the plaintiff's solicitors obtained an order from Master *Hodgson* extending the time for the amendment of the writ. There is an issue between the parties as to whether the master's order also extended the validity of the writ for a further four months. On 14 August 1991 the copy of the amended writ together with a copy of the original statement of claim dated 1 March 1991 was received at the offices of Hilton International Co at International Court, 2–3 Rhodes Way, Watford.

G

On 29 August 1991 the defendants' solicitors wrote to the plaintiff's solicitors to say that they had received a copy of the amended writ dated 7 August 1991. The letter continued:

H

"It appears that the validity of the original writ, dated 7 December 1990, has been extended pursuant to the leave of Master *Hodgson*, once again obtained on 7 August 1991.

Would you please confirm whether a formal order was given by Master *Hodgson* or whether he merely endorsed the original writ.

We are far from satisfied that the extension of the validity of the writ is appropriate.   A
We take the view that you have not correctly addressed the amended writ. Hilton
International Co have no registered office within the English jurisdiction, a fact of
which we thought you were aware."

It was also pointed out in this letter that the statement of claim which had been served
was in the original form naming Ladbroke Group plc as the defendants.

On 9 September 1991 the plaintiff's solicitors replied: B

"The statement of claim clearly was served incorrectly, and I have accordingly
taken steps to serve a further statement of claim properly amended together with
a copy of the order of the master made on 7 August 1991.

I am a little concerned at the remainder of your letter. You have been throughout
well aware of the situation. Proceedings were issued originally against Ladbroke
Group plc in view of correspondence that had been received. The plaintiff placed   C
reliance upon those letters. That in the event turns out to be incorrect and
accordingly an application for leave to amend the defendants' title was made. You
were aware of this application and also aware of its return date. You indicated that
you were prepared to accept service of the proceedings against Hilton International
Co. That authority to accept was withdrawn on 6 August 1991.

As to service the company search that I have made shows Hilton International Co   D
as the registered office of Mr John Geoffrey Chester, International Court, 2–3
Rhodes Way, Watford, Hertfordshire WD2 4WY. In those circumstances service
was effected from the information that I had, correctly. If however you are stating
that there is a different Hilton International Co, and that leave is required to serve
out of the jurisdiction, perhaps you could advise as quickly as possible so as to
minimise any further delay.

For the record, I would be grateful if you could confirm that you do at least act for   E
Hilton International Co whether or not you retain instructions to accept service of
the proceedings.

As the proceedings have been formally amended proceedings no longer exist
against Ladbroke Group plc."

The defendants' solicitors replied at once on 11 September.   F

"As matters presently stand you do not have leave to serve an amended statement
of claim, and we take the view that you cannot now do so bearing in mind that our
clients have already pleaded to the statement of claim addressed to Ladbroke
Group plc.

The pre-proceedings correspondence makes it quite clear that your client has
been aware, from the outset, that Hilton International Co were the proper
defendants. That company has not ceased to exist and the mere fact that Ladbroke   G
Group plc happens now to own Hilton International Co is irrelevant.

With the greatest of respect it seems that the truth of the matter is that the wrong
defendant was named on the original writ . . .

The amended writ was not served upon Mr J Geoffrey Chester, and indeed is not
addressed to him.

We are seeking instructions to apply to the court to set aside service of the   H
amended writ."

It was at this stage that both parties made applications to the court. The matter came
before Master *Hodgson* on 19 February 1992. I have not seen a copy of the master's
order but it appears that he dismissed the summons issued by the defendants seeking
the setting aside of the service of the amended writ. The defendants then appealed.

A   The appeal was heard by His Honour Judge *Lever* QC sitting as a judge of the High
Court on 2 April 1992. He allowed the defendants' appeal and set aside service of the
writ and at the same time dismissed an application by the plaintiff for leave to extend the
validity of the writ by a further four months from 7 December 1991. The application for
leave to extend the validity of the writ had been made by the plaintiff at the hearing
without notice but with the consent of the defendants. The judge granted leave to appeal
from his order to this court.

B   I can now turn to the questions which arise in this appeal. The arguments in this court
fell under three separate headings:

(1)   Whether the amended writ was effectively served on the defendants on 12 August
       1991.

(2)   Whether, in the exercise of its discretion under RSC, O. 2, r. 1, the court could
       allow the service to be treated as good service notwithstanding the failure to effect
C   service in accordance with sec. 695 of the *Companies Act* 1985.

(3)   Whether, in the exercise of its discretion under RSC, O. 6, r. 8, the court could
       extend the validity of the amended writ.

I can turn at once to the first issue.

D   **(1) Whether the service of the amended writ on 12 August 1991 was in accordance with
the rules**

Hilton International Co is a corporation registered in Delaware in the USA. It is clear
from the affidavit sworn by Mr Crispin Kenyon on 3 February 1992 that the Hilton Hotel
in Dubai was at all material times managed by Hilton International. In addition Hilton
International has at all material times had a place of business in Great Britain. It is also
clear that in due compliance with sec. 691(1)(b)(ii) of the *Companies Act* 1985 (the 1985
E   Act) (or its predecessor) Hilton International has delivered to the registrar of companies
a return in the prescribed form containing a list of the name and address of a person
"resident in Great Britain authorised to accept on the company's behalf service of
process and any notices required to be served on it". The person so named was
Mr Geoffrey Chester whose address was given as International Court, 2–3 Rhodes Way,
Watford.

F   Section 695 of the 1985 Act contains provisions relating to the service of documents
on an oversea company. It is in these terms:

"(1) Any process or notice required to be served on an oversea company is
sufficiently served if addressed to any person whose name has been delivered to
the registrar under preceding sections in this Part and left at or sent by post to the
address which has been so delivered.

G   (2) However—

(a) where such a company makes default in delivering to the registrar the name
     and address of a person resident in Great Britain who is authorised to accept
     on behalf of the company service of process or notices, or

(b) if at any time all the persons whose names and addresses have been so
     delivered are dead or have ceased so to reside, or refuse to accept service
H   on the company's behalf, or for any reason cannot be served,

a document may be served on the company by leaving it at, or sending it by post
to, any place of business established by the company in Great Britain."

It is common ground that neither the letter to Hilton International Co dated 12
August 1991, which accompanied the copy of the amended writ and other documents,
nor the envelope in which these documents were enclosed was addressed to Mr Chester

personally. The letter was received by Hilton International in Watford on 14 August   A
1991 and was stamped by or on behalf of Mr Chambury. It is also common ground,
however, that either on that day or shortly afterwards the letter and the amended writ
were seen by Mr Geoffrey Chester himself.

It was argued on behalf of the defendants that sec. 695 prescribes the only manner in
which a writ can be served on an oversea company. In the present case the exceptions in
sec. 695(2) have no application and accordingly service should have been effected
strictly in accordance with sec. 695(1). It was argued on behalf of the plaintiff on the   B
other hand that sec. 695(1) should be construed in a practical and pragmatic manner.
The amended writ had been served at the correct address and had come into the hands
of the person nominated by the defendants to accept service. In any event sec. 695(1)
merely prescribed what should be "sufficient" service and did not exclude the possibility
of other forms of service in an appropriate case. The rules for service were laid down to
ensure that legal proceedings were brought to the attention of a defendant and in the   C
present case there could be no doubt that the defendants and their solicitors were fully
aware of the existence and terms of the amended writ from the middle of August 1991.

In these circumstances I propose to consider first whether sec. 695 contains a complete
code as to the manner in which process may be served on an oversea company.

The basic rule as to the service of originating process is contained in RSC, O. 10,
r. 1(1) which prescribes that: D

"A writ must be served personally on each defendant by the plaintiff or his agent."

By O. 10, r. 1(7) however it is provided:

"This rule shall have effect subject to the provision of any Act and these rules and
in particular to any enactment which provides for the manner in which documents
may be served on bodies corporate."

It is therefore necessary to turn first to O. 65 which is concerned with the service of   E
documents, and in particular to O. 65, r. 3 which is concerned with service of documents
on a body corporate. O. 65, r. 3 is in these terms:

"(1) Personal service of a document on a body corporate may, in cases for which
provision is not otherwise made by any enactment, be effected by serving it in
accordance with rule 2 on the mayor, chairman or president of the body, or the
town clerk, clerk, secretary, treasurer or other similar officer thereof.   F

(2) Where a writ is served on a body corporate in accordance with Order 10, rule
1(2), that rule shall have effect as if for the reference to the usual or last known
address of the defendant there were substituted a reference to the registered or
principal office of the body corporate and as if for the reference to the knowledge
of the defendant there were substituted a reference to the knowledge of a person
mentioned in paragraph (1)."   G

I do not think it is necessary to set out the terms of O. 10, r. 1(2) (though it may be
noted that this paragraph does not appear to contain the words "the knowledge of the
defendant"), or of O. 65, r. 2. It is sufficient to summarise the matter by saying that, in
the absence of any relevant enactment, service of originating process on a body
corporate can now be effected either by personal service on one of the persons named in
O. 65, r. 3(1), or (following the changes made in 1979 which allowed postal service) by
sending a copy of the writ to the registered office of the body corporate. In the present   H
case, however, the 1985 Act makes provision as to service and it seems to me that, in the
light of O. 10, r. 1(7), sec. 695(1) governs the matter despite the fact that there is no
reference to "any enactment" in O. 65, r. 3(2).

It is true that the words "sufficiently served" in sec. 695(1) are prima facie consistent
with the view that other forms of service may be permissible or sufficient. But the rules

A to which I have referred seem to exclude the possibility of any forms of service other than those prescribed by the relevant enactment. Furthermore, this view is in accordance with the conclusion reached by *Brandon* J in *The Theodohos* [1977] 2 Lloyd's Rep 428, where he said at p. 431:

"Both formally under the old O. 9, r. 8 and now under the present O. 65, r. 3 the method of serving a corporation by personal service on an appropriate officer has,
B by the express terms of the two rules, only been applicable in the absence of any statutory provision regulating such service."

It is true that at the time when *The Theodohos* was decided the provisions for postal service had not yet been introduced, but it is to be remembered that the provisions of O. 10, r. 1(2) as to postal service are subject to "any enactment": see O. 10, r. 1(7).

In *Singh v Atombrook Ltd* [1989] 1 WLR 810 the Court of Appeal considered the
C provision for service on a limited company set out in sec. 725 of the 1985 Act. Section 725(1) provides that a document may be served on a company by leaving it at, or sending it by post to, the company's registered office. At p. 819 *Kerr* LJ expressed doubts as to whether the word "may" had to be construed as "must" and appears to have left open the possibility that some other form of service would be adequate. It seems to me, however, that though the matter is not wholly free from doubt, the combined effect of O. 10, r. 1(7) and O. 65, r. 3(1) is to limit the methods of service of originating process to
D the methods prescribed in the 1985 Act. In the present case the writ was not addressed to Mr Chester and accordingly the service was not effected in accordance with sec. 695(1).

I turn therefore to the second and third issues which I can consider together.

**(2) Whether the court can in the circumstances exercise its discretion either under
E O. 2, r. 1 or under O. 6, r. 8**

It is necessary to set out the texts of these two rules. Order 2, r. 1, which is concerned with non-compliance with rules, is in these terms:

"(1) Where, in beginning or purporting to begin any proceedings or at any stage in the course of or in connection with any proceedings, there has, by reason of any thing done or left undone, been a failure to comply with the requirements of these
F rules, whether in respect of time, place, manner, form or content or in any other respect, the failure shall be treated as an irregularity and shall not nullify the proceedings, any step taken in the proceedings, or any document, judgment or order therein.

(2) Subject to paragraph (3) the Court may, on the ground that there has been such a failure as is mentioned in paragraph (1) and on such terms as to costs or
G otherwise as it thinks just, set aside either wholly or in part the proceedings in which the failure occurred, any step taken in those proceedings or any document, judgment or order therein or exercise its powers under these rules to allow such amendments (if any) to be made and to make such order (if any) dealing with the proceedings generally as it thinks fit."

It is unnecessary to refer further to para. (3).

H Order 6, r. 8, which is concerned with the duration and renewal of a writ, provides, so far as is material, as follows:

"(1) For the purposes of service, a writ (other than a concurrent writ) is valid in the first instance—

(a) where leave to serve the writ out of the jurisdiction is required under Order 11, for 6 months,

British Company Cases

(b)   in any other case, for 4 months   A

beginning with the date of its issue.

. . .

(2) Subject to paragraph (2A), where a writ has not been served on a defendant, the Court may by order extend the validity of the writ from time to time for such period, not exceeding 4 months at any one time, beginning with the day next following that on which it would otherwise expire, as may be specified in the order, if an application for extension is made to the Court before that day or such later day (if any) as the Court may allow."   B

It will be convenient to start by referring to the principles on which the discretion to extend the validity of a writ under O. 6, r. 8 are to be exercised. These principles were considered by the House of Lords in *Kleinwort Benson Ltd v Barbrak Ltd* [1987] AC 597 and in *Waddon v Whitecroft Scovell Ltd* [1988] 1 WLR 309. In *Waddon*, Lord   C
Brandon at pp. 313–314 summarised the principles laid down in the *Kleinwort Benson* case in the previous year which were applicable to the exercise of the court's discretion on an application for the extension of the validity of a writ in cases where questions of limitation of action were involved as follows:

"(1) On the true construction of Ord. 6, r. 8 the power to extend the validity of a writ should only be exercised for good reason. (2) The question whether such good reason exists in any particular case depends on all the circumstances of that   D
case. Difficulty in effecting service of the writ may well constitute good reason but it is not the only matter which is capable of doing so. (3) The balance of hardship between the parties can be a relevant matter to be taken into account in the exercise of the discretion. (4) The discretion is that of the judge and his exercise of it should not be interfered with by an appellate court except on special grounds the nature of which is well-established."   E

In the present case the judge was referred to the two decisions in the House of Lords as well as to other relevant authorities on O. 6, r. 8. He then applied the principles to the facts of the present case and set out in his judgment the chronology which had been put before him and the arguments of counsel. At p. 14F of the transcript of his judgment he concluded:

"I can say no more in this case than that on the basis of the authorities cited to me   F
and the principles which must guide me, the answer to the question must be that there is no good reason for me to extend the validity of the period and consequently the question of the exercise of my discretion, about which I shall say nothing, does not arise."

It seems to me that the judge treated the question of the establishment of "a good reason" and the exercise of his discretion as separate matters. On the facts of this case that may well have been a sensible approach. What seems to me to be quite clear,   G
however, is that no adequate grounds have been put forward for showing that the judge exercised his powers under O. 6, r. 8(2) by ignoring some relevant circumstance or taking into account something which was irrelevant, nor is it possible to say that the judge's decision was plainly wrong. Indeed I for my part consider that he was right.

One therefore turns to consider whether there is any room for the exercise of a separate discretion under O. 2, r. 1 in relation to the irregular service of the amended   H
writ in August 1991.

There is clear authority for the proposition that the court should not exercise its discretion under O. 2, r. 1 more favourably to a plaintiff than it would do under O. 6, r. 8. As *Slade* LJ put the matter in *Leal v Dunlop Bio-Processes International Ltd* [1984] 1 WLR 874 at p. 885D:

A   "If he [the plaintiff] cannot properly enter through the front door of Ord. 6, r. 8, he should not be allowed to enter through the back door of Ord. 2, r. 1."

The decision in *Leal* was followed by the Court of Appeal in *Camera Care Ltd v Victor Hasselblad* [1986] 1 FTLR 347. It is to be noted, however, that both in *Leal* and in the *Camera Care* case the irregularity had occurred in connection with proceedings which required leave to serve out of the jurisdiction. In addition both decisions were reached at a time when the courts applied the long established principle that the validity
B   of a writ would not be extended unless there were "exceptional circumstances sufficient to justify such extension" (see *Leal* at p. 885B per *Slade* LJ). In the *Kleinwort Benson* case however, Lord *Brandon* at p. 622G regarded the "exceptional circumstances" test as too high:

C   "I think on the whole that it has been unhelpful to put the condition for extension as high as 'exceptional circumstances', an expression which conveys to my mind at any rate a large degree of stringency. The old rule in force until 1962 referred to 'any other good reason', and I think that the new rule should be interpreted as requiring 'good reason' and no more."

Nevertheless I would not interfere with the judge's decision under O. 6, r. 8. For my part, however, I agree with the view of Sir *John Megaw* in *The Goldean Mariner* [1990] 2 Lloyd's Rep 215 at p. 225 where he referred to,
D

"the potent argument that special considerations apply to the exercise of the discretion under O. 2, r. 1 where the failure or irregularity has occurred in connection with proceedings which involve the requirement of leave to serve out of the jurisdiction . . ."

—though I see the force of *Slade* LJ's comment in *Leal* that the court should not exercise its discretion under O. 2, r. 1 where it is unwilling to do so by extending the writ under
E   O. 6, r. 8. It is always necessary to remember, however, that guidance which is given relating to the exercise of a general discretion has to be applied with caution. If a general discretion is circumscribed by binding rules it ceases to be a general discretion.

In the present case the judge was not invited to consider the case on the basis that the court had power under O. 2, r. 1 to allow the service of the amended writ in August 1991 to stand despite the fact that the mode of service did not comply with sec. 695 of the 1985
F   Act. This court can therefore view the matter afresh. The facts are very striking. Hilton International and their insurers knew of the claim from shortly after the accident in 1987. Detailed discussions followed. The chairman of Hilton International was clearly anxious that the claim should be settled. Liability has not been in dispute. There have been some interim payments of Mrs Boocock's expenses. Mr Chester knew about the claim and was aware almost immediately of the service of the amended writ at his office. It is true that Hilton International has what Lord *Brandon* in the *Kleinwort Benson* case
G   at p. 616C called "an accrued right of limitation", but the surest guideline for the exercise of any general discretion is to consider what the justice of the case demands.

In the present case I am satisfied, despite the cogent arguments put forward by counsel for Hilton International, that in the interests of justice the court's power under O. 2, r. 1 to cure an irregularity should be exercised. In the light of the particular facts of this case I would allow the appeal and order that the service of the writ in August 1991 was good
H   service.

Mann LJ: I have had the advantage of reading in draft the judgment of *Neill* LJ and for the reasons which he gives I would allow this appeal and order that the service on 14 August 1991 was a good service. The service was not in accord with sec. 695(1) of the *Companies Act* 1985 and there being no other relevant enactment, it follows that O. 10, r. 1(1) of the Rules of the Supreme Court was not satisfied. This was an irregularity.

A

However, if the irregularity could not be cured under O. 2, r. 1(2), then the discretion conferred by that paragraph must by binding decision have been constrained so as to require this court to impose injustice on Mrs Boocock in the circumstances of her case. I am happy to share *Neill* LJ's conclusion that there is no such constraint.

Hoffmann LJ: I agree with both judgments and have nothing to add.

(*Appeal allowed*)

B

C

D

E

F

G

H

A **Turner, Petitioner.**

Court of Session (Outer House).
Lord Kirkwood.
Judgment delivered 10 February 1993.

B *Receivership — Scotland — Preferential debts — Set-off — Whether Crown was entitled to choose to set off debt owed to company in receivership against non-preferential debt owed by company rather than preferential debt — Crown Proceedings Act 1947, sec. 35(2)(d); Companies Act 1985, sec. 471(1)(e) (repealed; see Insolvency Act 1986, sec. 63), sec. 614 (repealed; see Insolvency Act 1986, sec. 59).*

This was a petition by a receiver for directions in terms of sec. 471(1)(e) of the Companies Act 1985.

C The preferential debts due by the company in receivership to the Inland Revenue totalled £58,679 and the non-preferential debt amounted to £12,508. The company was entitled to a VAT repayment amounting to £11,338.10. The company had not raised proceedings with a view to recovering the VAT repayment, and, accordingly, the Inland Revenue had not sought leave, under sec. 35(2)(d) of the Crown Proceedings Act 1947, to avail itself of any set-off. The question before the court was how, on the assumption that

D the company sued for the VAT repayment and the Inland Revenue was granted leave by the court to avail itself of set-off, the right of set-off would fall to be applied. The Inland Revenue contended that it would be entitled to set off the VAT repayment against the non-preferential debt due by the company, leaving the whole of the preferential debt standing. The petitioner contended that there should be rateable allocation. He also submitted that in England the Inland Revenue accepted the principle of rateable allocation, whereas in Scotland it claimed to be entitled to select the debt to be used for the purposes of set-off: in

E the circumstances, companies in receivership in Scotland were being treated less favourably than companies in receivership in England.

Held, giving the direction sought by the Inland Revenue:

1. The Scottish law of compensation applied and if the Inland Revenue was granted leave under sec. 35(2)(d) of the 1947 Act to avail itself of set-off in relation to a claim by the company for the VAT repayment of £11,338.10, it would be entitled to set that off

F against the non-preferential debt of £12,508 with the result that the preferential claim would be unaffected.

2. The English law relating to balancing of accounts in bankruptcy was statutory and quite different from the law applicable in Scotland, and accordingly there was no useful purpose to be gained by detailed consideration of the English authorities.

3. The Inland Revenue formerly accepted the principle of rateable allocation in both

G countries. However, in 1981 they changed their policy and decided to adopt the basis which was most favourable to the Exchequer. The practical application of that policy was different in Scotland, as compared to England, by reason of the fact that the law relating to set-off in bankruptcy was different in each country.

The following cases were referred to in the opinion:

Atlantic Engine Co (1920) Ltd & Anor v Lord Advocate 1955 SLT 17.
H *Brown & Co v Wylie* (1809) Hume's Decisions 97.
Cushla Ltd, Re [1979] 3 All ER 415.
Devaynes v Noble. Clayton's Case (1816) 1 Mer 572; 35 ER 781.
Dickson v Moncrieff (1853) 16 D 24.
Hall (William) (Contractors) Ltd, Re [1967] 1 WLR 948.
HTV Ltd v Price Commission [1976] ICR 170.
Laing v Lord Advocate 1973 SLT (Notes) 81.

Maxwell v McCulloch's Creditors (1738) Mor 2550.

Morel (E J) (1934) Ltd [1962] Ch 21.

M S Fashions Ltd & Ors v Bank of Credit and Commerce International SA & Anor [1992] BCC 571.

National Westminster Bank Ltd v Halesowen Presswork & Assemblies Ltd [1972] AC 785.

Pollock and Co v Murray and Spence (1863) 2 M 14.

R v IR Commrs, ex parte Preston [1985] AC 835; [1985] BTC 208.

Smith v Lord Advocate 1980 SC 227.

Unit 2 Windows Ltd, Re (1985) 1 BCC 99,489; [1985] 1 WLR 1383.

N J Mackinnon (instructed by Dorman Jeffrey & Co) for the petitioner.

P S Hodge (instructed by T H Scott) for the Crown.

OPINION

Lord Kirkwood: This is a petition for directions in terms of sec. 471(1)(e) of the *Companies Act* 1985. The petition was presented by the receiver of McLean & Co (Civil Engineering and Building Contractors) Ltd ("the company") and answers had been lodged by the Lord Advocate on behalf of the Commissioners of Inland Revenue. The material facts relating to the petition are not in dispute.

On 27 October 1983 the petitioner was appointed receiver of the property and undertaking of the company. The petitioner was appointed by deed of appointment by the Clydesdale Bank plc, the holder of a bond and floating charge granted by the company in its favour dated 16 December 1971 and registered on 20 December 1971 as amended by instrument of alteration dated 19 and 29 October and registered on 2 November 1982. The obligations of the petitioner are governed by the provisions of the *Companies Act* 1985 (see sec. 29 of the *Companies Consolidation (Consequential Provisions) Act* 1985 and para. 3 of Sch. 11 to the *Insolvency Act* 1986). The company was subsequently wound up by interlocutor of the sheriff at Glasgow dated 6 February 1986 and Murdoch Lang Mckillop, chartered accountant, Glasgow, was appointed as official liquidator. Parties were agreed that when the petitioner was appointed receiver in October 1983 the company was insolvent.

Section 475 of the *Companies Act* 1985 provided inter alia as follows:

"(1) Where a receiver is appointed and the company is not at the time of the appointment in course of being wound up, the debts which fall under subsection (2) of this section shall be paid out of any assets coming to the hands of the receiver in priority to any claim for principal or interest by the holder of the floating charge by virtue of which the receiver was appointed.

(2) Debts falling under this subsection are debts which satisfy the conditions of this subsection, that is to say, they are debts—

    (a) which in every winding up are, under the provisions of Part XX relating to preferential payments, to be paid in priority to all other debts . . ."

Section 614 of the 1985 Act provided inter alia as follows:

"(1) In a winding up the preferential debts listed in Schedule 19 shall be paid in priority to all other debts . . ."

Paragraph 3 of Sch. 19 provided inter alia as follows:

"3. Any sums due at the relevant date from the company on account of tax deductions for the 12 months next before that date.

A   The sums here referred to—

(a) are those due by way of deduction of income tax from emoluments during the relevant period, which the company was liable to make under section 204 of the Income and Corporation Taxes Act 1970, less the amount of the repayments of income tax which the company was liable to make during the same period . . .''

B   By letter dated 28 October 1983 the petitioner requested the Commissioners of Inland Revenue to intimate to him the preferential debt which they claimed was owed to them by the company. After sundry correspondence the Inland Revenue intimated by letter dated 23 May 1986 that they claimed to rank as a preferential creditor in respect of the following debts, namely (1) the sum of £12,413.85 in respect of part of the arrears of income tax on the employees of the company for the tax year from 6 April 1982 to
C   5 April 1983 which should have been accounted for to the Inland Revenue in terms of the 1973 Pay As You Earn regulations (the *Income Tax (Employment) Regulations* 1973 (SI 1973/334)), (2) the sum of £41,498.45 in respect of part of the arrears of income tax due by the employees of the company for the taxation year from 6 April 1983 to 5 April 1984 and which should have been accounted for to the Inland Revenue in terms of the 1973 regulations, and (3) the sum of £5,936.70 in respect of corporation tax for the taxation year to 5 April 1982 due by the company. The total of these preferential debts
D   was £59,849. The Inland Revenue deducted from that figure the sum of £1,170 in respect of a liability of the company for income tax which had been accounted for to the Inland Revenue by an employer under a building contract in terms of sec. 69 of the *Finance (No. 2) Act* 1975. Accordingly, the total of the preferential debts due to the Inland Revenue was £58,679. The Inland Revenue also claimed to be entitled to be ranked as an ordinary creditor for the sum of £12,508 in respect of the balance of the arrears of
E   income tax due by the company's employees for the tax year 6 April 1982 to 5 April 1983 and in respect of which the company should have accounted to the Inland Revenue.

However, as at 27 October 1983 the Commissioners of HM Customs and Excise were liable to repay to the company the sum of £11,338.10 in respect of overpayments of VAT. Accordingly, it was agreed that the preferential debts due by the company to the Inland Revenue totalled £58,679 and that the non-preferential debt due by the company to the
F   Inland Revenue amounted to £12,508. At the same time the company was entitled to a repayment of VAT amounting to £11,338.10.

It was narrated in the petition that a dispute had arisen between the petitioner and the Inland Revenue as to the actual amount of the preferential debts payable to the Inland Revenue by reason of the VAT repayment which was due to the company. In particular, the parties were in dispute as to whether the law requires the Inland Revenue (1) to deduct the VAT repayment from the non-preferential debt, or (2) to deduct the VAT
G   repayment from the preferential debts and the non-preferential debt in the proportion which these debts bore to the total indebtedness of the company to the Inland Revenue, or (3) to deduct the VAT repayment from the 1982–83 PAYE preferential debt and the non-preferential debt in the proportions which these debts bore to the total indebtedness of the company in respect of arrears of income tax for the tax year 1982–83.

The petitioner averred that the Inland Revenue had contended that the first method
H   is the correct one although its previous practice was to apply the second method and that is still its practice in relation to receiverships of companies incorporated in England. The petitioner had been advised that either the second or third method is correct. The petitioner further averred that the present dispute raised issues which were of great practical importance to receivers and to the Inland Revenue and that there is no direct or modern authority on the matter in Scotland. Accordingly, the receiver required to

apply to the court for directions as to the correct method of calculating the total   A
preferential debt which is payable by the company to the Inland Revenue.

In their pleadings the Inland Revenue admitted that they have contended that they
are not obliged to accept that the VAT repayment should be credited other than against
the non-preferential debt. It was also admitted that on previous occasions when dealing
with receiverships the Inland Revenue have proceeded upon the basis that they would
abate their preferential claim by an amount equal to so much of any VAT repayment due   B
as might represent the ratio of the preferential debt to the entire tax debt owed by a
company to the Inland Revenue, i.e. the second method described by the petitioner.
This method continues to be adopted by the Inland Revenue in respect of receiverships
of companies incorporated in England. The Inland Revenue averred that when a VAT
repayment was due and outstanding it was the practice of the Inland Revenue to give
allowance to the company for the amount of the VAT repayment against the tax due. In
strict terms (1) the preferential debt due to the Inland Revenue is payable in full from   C
funds held by a receiver and no right of set-off exists (sec. 50 of the *Crown Proceedings
Act* 1947), and (2), were a receiver to attempt to recover the VAT repayment from the
Commissioners of Customs and Excise, it would be open to those Commissioners to
obtain leave that the claim be met by a defence of set-off of the tax due (sec. 35 and 50 of
the 1947 Act). Leave could have been sought and obtained for set-off of PAYE
indebtedness not included in the present preferential claims. In 1981 government policy   D
was changed to the effect that, in future, claims by government departments should be
made on the basis most favourable to the Exchequer. This change of policy had been
given effect to in the change of stance of the Inland Revenue in cases such as the present
and, in consequence, a difference in practical result had arisen between Scotland and
England.

In England the rules of set-off in bankruptcy are different from those in Scotland and,   E
because of those rules, the practice of rateable allocation continues to be accepted in
England. The practice in England rests on the English court's interpretation of sec. 31
of the *Bankruptcy Act* 1914 but this practice does not apply in Scotland. In Scotland, the
present approach of the Inland Revenue is sound in law. In terms of sec. 35(2)(d) of the
Crown Proceedings Act 1947 (as applied to Scotland by sec. 50 thereof) the petitioner
would not be entitled to avail himself of any set-off or counterclaim in any proceedings
by the Crown to recover its preferential debt. In terms of sec. 35(2)(d) of the 1947 Act   F
the Crown could seek leave of the court to avail itself of a set-off of its non-preferential
debt against the petitioner's claim for the VAT repayment and, as both claims arise out
of legislation of a fiscal character, it is probable that the court would grant leave.

In these circumstances the Inland Revenue contended that the court should direct the
petitioner that in considering the claim of the Commissioners of Inland Revenue, or in
adjudicating upon that claim, it is not required as a matter of Scots law that any sum due   G
to a company by way of repayment of VAT be deducted to any extent from sums due by
that company by way of preferential tax claims if or in so far as there are ordinary tax
debts of at least the same amount.

A joint minute was lodged and in terms thereof it is agreed inter alia (1) that before
1981 the practice of the Commissioners of Inland Revenue in Scotland, which was based
on a policy decision, was to adopt the second method of set-off averred by the petitioner,
and (2) that in 1981 government policy was changed to the effect that from then on   H
claims by government departments should be made on the basis most favourable to the
Exchequer. Parties were also agreed that the petition was competently presented under
sec. 471(1)(e) of the *Companies Act* 1985 (see sec. 31(2) of the *Companies Consolidation
(Consequential Provisions) Act* 1985).

A Counsel for the petitioner submitted that in terms of reg. 26(1) of the *Income Tax (Employment) Regulations* 1973 the company was under an obligation to account monthly for payments of income tax and that the preferential debt claimed by the Inland Revenue was an artificial statutory apportionment of a real debt. However, if the Inland Revenue was permitted to set off the VAT repayment, they were not entitled to set it off against the non-preferential debt due by the company. Instead, there should be rateable allocation which was the position in England (*Re Unit 2 Windows Ltd* (1985) 1 BCC

B 99,489). The circumstances in Scotland and England were sufficiently similar to enable the court to derive assistance from the decided cases in England.

The issue in this case is what should happen where there was a right to set off a debt against preferential and non-preferential debts. If the Inland Revenue took a plea of compensation, consideration had to be given to whether set-off would be allowed and, if it was allowed, in what manner the set-off was to be carried into effect. The latter

C question could not be answered simply by an assertion that the Inland Revenue is entitled to choose the debt against which the VAT repayment is to be applied. In *Smith v Lord Advocate* 1980 SC 227 Lord *Avonside* observed (at p. 235) that the clear policy of the common law was that there should be a balancing of accounts in bankruptcy. Counsel also referred to *Bell's Commentaries*, vol. II, pp. 118–124; *Green's Encyclopaedia*, vol. 4, pp. 157–158, and St Clair and Drummond Young, *The Law of Corporate Insolvency in Scotland*, pp. 266–269. In *McBryde on Bankruptcy*, pp. 202–203 the

D author posed the present problem and observed that the logic of the *Unit 2 Windows* case could be applied in Scotland.

Turning to the English law on the subject, counsel referred to the provisions of sec. 31 of the *Bankruptcy Act* 1914. That statutory provision was the equivalent of the Scottish common law rule relating to a balancing of accounts in bankruptcy. Section 31 is silent as to how the principle of set-off had to be applied in practice where there were

E preferential and non-preferential debts. Similarly, there is no authority in Scotland as to how set-off has to be applied in such circumstances. Counsel referred to Bertram on *Tax Consequences of Receivership and Liquidation*, pp. 30–32; *Paget's Law of Banking* (10th ed.) at p. 510; *Palmer's Company Law*, vol. 2, para. 15.417 and 15.675 and *Encyclopaedia of Banking Law*, E368 and E553. There was no material difference between the law of England and the law of Scotland on the issue of how the rules of set-off fell to be applied on bankruptcy. In *National Westminster Bank Ltd v Halesowen*

F *Presswork & Assemblies Ltd* [1972] AC 785 Lord *Kilbrandon* (at p. 822) had pointed to differences between the law of England and the law of Scotland but he had not referred to any matter which necessarily resulted in the English doctrine not being relevant in Scotland. The issue before the court had not previously been considered in Scotland. In *Stair Memorial Encyclopaedia*, vol. 4, para. 842, the question now before the court had been raised but the author stated that it was unclear whether the Scottish courts would

G apply the same principles as apply to secured claims or whether they would follow the *Unit 2 Windows* decision. The fact of the matter is that rateable allocation had been the practice in Scotland until the Inland Revenue's change of policy in 1981. In *E J Morel (1934) Ltd* [1962] Ch 21, *Buckley* J had held that the debt should be set off against the preferential debt. However, in the *Unit 2 Windows* case, *Walton* J did not follow the decision of *Buckley* J but applied the principle of rateable allocation. In that case

H *Walton* J observed (at p. 99,496) that:

> "equality, proportionate equality, is in the circumstances of the silence of the relative section, equity."

The present case did not relate to a banker's common law right to combine or consolidate accounts but banking textbooks had accepted the principle of rateable allocation (e.g. Penn and others, *The Law relating to Domestic Banking*, para. 13.34).

Re William Hall (Contractors) Ltd [1967] 1 WLR 948 turned on a speciality of the law   A
relating to appropriation of payments, which was equivalent to the Scottish law of
ascription. There was no such speciality in the present case.

There were six possible ways in which the court could approach the issue which was
before it for determination:

(1)   Given that the Inland Revenue now apply different policies north and south of the
border, the court could refuse to permit set-off so that there was no difference   B
between the rules which applied in each of the jurisdictions. The current practice
of the Inland Revenue of applying their policy unfairly and inconsistently in
England and Scotland amounted to an abuse of power and was unlawful (*HTV
Ltd v Price Commission* [1976] ICR 170 per Lord *Denning* at p. 185; *R v IR
Commrs, ex parte Preston* [1985] AC 835 per Lord *Scarman* at p. 851).

(2)   The court could adopt the preferred approach of the Inland Revenue and permit   C
them to set off the VAT repayment against the non-preferential debt. However,
there was no averment on record which would support the Inland Revenue's
contention that they were entitled to follow that course. All they said was that
such a course suited them. That may be a fact but it was not an argument (*Re Unit
2 Windows Ltd* per *Walton* J at p. 99,496).

(3)   The court could find that the VAT repayment had to be set off against the
preferential debt (on the basis of the decision in *Morel*) but counsel accepted that   D
there was no Scottish authority which supported this course and that it would be
unlikely to find favour in Scotland.

(4)   The court could find in favour of rateable allocation, which was the course urged
by the petitioner. The preferential debt in this case was an artificially statutory
apportioned single real debt and accordingly the court need not concern itself
with the law relating to security-holders and what a security-holder is entitled to
do, so far as set-off was concerned, with the proceeds of sale of the security. There   E
was no reason to distinguish between the preferential and non-preferential elements
of what was essentially the same debt.

The older authorities, such as *Maxwell v McCulloch's Creditors* (1738) Mor 2550,
were of no real assistance in this case. The court should follow the approach of
Walton J in the *Unit 2 Windows* case in which it was stated that equality was the   F
objective. In the circumstances the court could and should have regard to the
equities of the case. Counsel referred to Gloag and Irvine, *Law of Rights in
Security*, at pp. 852–853 where, in relation to cautionary obligations, there was a
reference to rateable distribution. Counsel also referred to *Dickson v Moncrieff*
(1853) 16 D 24 and *Brown & Co v Wylie* (1809) Hume's Decisions 97, and
submitted that the latter case was an example of rateable allocation being adopted
by a Scottish court as the only sensible means of dealing with a situation where   G
there was no prior authority. The principle of rateable allocation has a respectable
history in Scots law and it had been the practice of the Inland Revenue to apply
that principle in Scotland prior to their change of policy in 1981. If the principle of
rateable allocation was adopted in Scotland it would mean that companies which
were in receivership in Scotland and England would be treated in the same way.

(5)   The court could adopt option (3) set out in the petition and thus leave out of   H
account the later year and apply the principle of rateable allocation to the earlier
year only (the VAT repayment being referable to the earlier year).

(6)   The court could approach the matter by reference to the rule in *Clayton's Case*
(*Devaynes v Noble* (1816) 1 Mer 572) which would be the most simplistic
approach.

A   Counsel indicated that, as this was a petition for directions, he had thought it right to set out all the possible approaches which the court could adopt but he made it clear that the petitioner's contention was that in the circumstances of this case the principle of rateable allocation fell to be applied.

Counsel for the respondents submitted that the issue before the court could be focused by asking whether, if the company sued for the VAT repayment and the Crown sought leave of the court, in terms of sec. 35(2)(d) of the *Crown Proceedings Act* 1947, to set

B   off the repayment against the company's non-preferential debt in respect of income tax, there would be any good reason for refusing leave. Counsel submitted that the Crown, which was an indivisible *persona*, could plead compensation as a defence and set off the VAT repayment against the company's non-preferential debt, leaving the full amount of the company's preferential debt to the Inland Revenue standing. There was no good reason why the court should refuse the Inland Revenue leave to avail itself of set-off. If

C   the court refused to grant leave, it would be treating the Crown less favourably than a bank which had advanced money to the company. For example, if a bank which had both preferential and non-preferential claims against an insolvent company was sued for a debt due by the bank, the bank could choose which claim it wished to set off against the claim by the company. Thus, the bank could set off the debt due to the company against its non-preferential claim, thereby preserving the full amount of its preferential claim. It is only because of sec. 35(2)(d) of the 1947 Act, which requires the Crown to seek the

D   leave of the court in order to claim set-off, that the court comes into the matter at all. If, in Scotland, the Crown applied to the court for permission to set off the VAT repayment against their non-preferential debt, there was no reason why the court should penalise the Crown — compared to other creditors — by refusing leave.

However, counsel accepted that in this case there was no application before the court in terms of sec. 35(2)(d) and that the real issue for determination was how, if leave was

E   granted, the Crown's right of set-off would fall to be applied. In this connection counsel submitted that, if leave was granted, the Inland Revenue would be entitled to choose which debt or debts the company's claim for the VAT repayment should be set off against and, in particular, that the Inland Revenue could choose to set off the VAT repayment against their non-preferential debt, thereby preserving the whole of their preferential debt. The Inland Revenue follows the same policy in England and Scotland, namely,

F   the policy that claims by government departments should be made on the basis most favourable to the Exchequer. The differences in the practical application of that policy in the two jurisdictions were due to the fact that the English law of set-off in bankruptcy is different from the law of Scotland.

In England, sec. 31 of the *Bankruptcy Act* 1914 requires rateable allocation between preferential and non-preferential claims, whether the creditor is the Crown or a bank or a private individual. However, that statutory provision did not apply in Scotland.

G   Counsel put forward six principal submissions as follows:

(1)   In Scots law, a creditor has a right to plead the defence of compensation, and this has been extended, in cases of bankruptcy, into a right to retain sums due to the bankrupt where the creditor has a future or contingent debt or an illiquid claim. *Goudy on Bankruptcy* (4th ed.) at pp. 550–551 shows that compensation is extended into bankruptcy and operates as a right of retention. The purpose of the

H   extension is simply to allow retention to permit set-off of future or contingent or illiquid debts. In *Bell's Commentaries*, vol. II, at p. 119 it is stated that the purpose of balancing of accounts in bankruptcy is to avoid injustice, but under Scots law there is no requirement, as there is in England, to add up all the debits and credits and make payment only of the balance which is due. However, the present case deals with compensation of liquid debts and not with the extension which applied

to the balancing of accounts in bankruptcy. A creditor has a right, under Scots   A
law, to select which debt due to him should be set off against his liability to the
bankrupt, a rule which was approved by the whole court in *Maxwell v McCulloch's
Creditors*. A preferential debt is a separate debt created by statute. As Scots law
has its own rule, no assistance can be derived from English law which has different
origins and which leads to a different result in relation to the question which is
now before the court. Under Scots law, compensation or retention is a defence
although it does not operate *ipso iure* and must be pled, and it is radically different   B
from the English doctrine of balancing of accounts in bankruptcy.

In *More's Notes on Stair*, vol. 2, at p. 131 it is explained why the Scots law of
retention is historically different from the English law of retention by reference to
the different rules relating to diligence. In Scotland, (1) the origin of the law of
compensation and retention was in the civil law, (2) compensation is extended in
bankruptcy as a right of retention to allow the debtor of the bankrupt to establish   C
future, contingent or illiquid claims, and (3) while the Scottish rules operate
broadly to the same effect as the English rules they do so by means of a different
mechanism, namely, by retention rather than by a preparation of accounts by
totalling the respective debts of the parties and striking a balance, as is the case in
England. The Scottish method is the right of compensation in terms of which the
creditor can choose against which of the debts due to him he will set off the sum
which he is due to pay to the debtor.   D

Section 475 of the 1985 Act created a preferential debt which had to be paid
forthwith by the receiver in preference to the debt due to the holder of the floating
charge. A debt is a right to demand payment of money at a stipulated time (Wilson
on *The Scottish Law of Debt* (2nd ed.) p. 1). The preferential debt is separately
prestable and enforceable at a stipulated time (sec. 614(3) of, and para. 2 and 3 of
Sch. 19 to, the *Companies Act* 1985 (repealed)). The effect of the relevant   E
statutory provisions was to aggregate 12 monthly PAYE debts into a separate and
distinct preferential debt which was payable forthwith. Paragraph 3(a) of Sch. 19
provided for a form of set-off but there was no statutory provision for any wider
set-off against the preferential claim. There was no substance in the petitioner's
contention that there was, in effect, one fiscal debt due by the company to the
Crown which had been artificially apportioned into preferential and non-
preferential elements. The preferential debt is not a single real debt which has   F
been statutorily apportioned, but has to be treated as a separate debt (Penn, *Law
of Domestic Banking*, para. 27-07). Further, and in any event, PAYE is due and
payable on a monthly basis and accordingly, but for its aggregation into a single
statutory preferential debt, there would be a series of monthly debts each with a
stipulated time for payment (reg. 39 of the *Income Tax (Employment) Regulations*
1973). If it was the case, as the petitioner contends, that the preferential debt was   G
simply the statutory apportionment of a single real debt then this would result in
anomalies depending on whether a receivership occurred on 6 April or on some
other date.

(2)   In Scotland, compensation is a defence which a defender requires to plead and the
party pleading compensation, if owed several debts by the pursuer, has the right
to select which of the debts due to him he wishes to use in the set-off. This case
deals with compensation in relation to liquid debts. The right of the creditor to   H
choose which of the debts due to him he wishes to set off against the debt which he
is due to the debtor is vouched by the decision of the whole court in *Maxwell v
McCulloch's Creditors*, which was a case which involved insolvency. That case has
since been regarded as authoritative (*Bankton's Institute*, Book I, p. 494; *Green's
Encyclopaedia*, vol. 4, p. 152; Wilson on *Debt* (2nd ed.) para. 13.6; *Stair Memorial*

A   *Encyclopaedia*, vol. 4, para. 842). On a proper analysis, the application of Scots law leads to a different result from the English rule which is based on an interpretation of the provisions of sec. 31 of the *Bankruptcy Act* 1914.

(3)   Before 1947 the Crown which is in law a single entity (even though it consists of a number of departments) could plead set-off at common law, even if the debts were owed to and by different departments.

B   (4)   In deciding whether to allow the Crown to set off one department's claim against a debt due by another department, case law indicates that the Crown has a prima facie entitlement to set-off and it is necessary for there to be particular and cogent reasons to justify a refusal to permit set-off. In *Smith v Lord Advocate* 1980 SC 227 the Crown was permitted to set off debts due by the company to the Department of Industry, the DHSS and the Inland Revenue. The pursuer argued that leave to set off should be granted only if there existed a strong connection or

C   similarity between the nature of the respective claims. The court observed (at p. 235) that there was no point in comparing Scots common law and English statute law as the Scottish and English rules were different in origin and scope. Counsel also referred to *Atlantic Engine Co (1920) Ltd v Lord Advocate* 1955 SLT 17 and *Laing v Lord Advocate* 1973 SLT (Notes) 81 where leave to set off was granted. The present case is similar to the case of *Laing* in that both claim and

D   counterclaim arise out of legislation of a fiscal character.

(5)   In England, the law of insolvency has developed a doctrine of balancing accounts in bankruptcy which has a completely different history from the Scots law of compensation or retention. It is by virtue of the construction placed by the English courts on sec. 31 of the *Bankruptcy Act* 1914 that English law has reached the position that there should be a proportional allocation or set-off between preferential and non-preferential debts. As the Scottish rules relating to set-off

E   are quite different from the statutory provisions applicable in England, there was no reason why the Scottish courts should use their powers under sec. 35(2)(d) of the 1947 Act in order to assimilate the different English and Scottish rules, so far as the Crown was concerned, while leaving other creditors with preferential and non-preferential claims in a better position in Scotland than they are in England. In Scotland, at common law a creditor with preferential and non-preferential

F   claims is entitled to choose which claim he will set off against the demand for payment. In England, on a proper interpretation of sec. 31 of the *Bankruptcy Act* 1914, it has been held that the debts due to each party should be added together and the balance due should be payable and this amounts to a balancing of accounts in bankruptcy properly so called. In England, the practice of the Inland Revenue is based on the court's interpretation of a statute which does not apply in Scotland and is not based on any general principle of equity.

G   In the case of *Re William Hall (Contractors) Ltd* [1967] 1 WLR 948 a bank, which was a secured creditor, was held to be entitled to apply its security to its non-preferential debts and prove for its preferential debts in the liquidation of the company. In a case where sec. 31 did not apply, there was no general equity which required rateable allocation (cf. *Pollock and Co v Murray and Spence* (1863) 2 M 14). In the case of *E J Morel (1934) Ltd* the court had simply construed sec. 31 of

H   the 1914 Act. Similarly, *Re Cushla Ltd* [1979] 3 All ER 415 dealt with the application of sec. 31 and it was conceded that if sec. 31 applied it would have the effect of superseding the rule relating to set-off. In that case it was held that the provisions of sec. 31 were mandatory and required a balance to be struck of debts due to and by the Crown. However, it was observed by *Vinelott* J (at p. 422h) that in Scotland "rules of set-off in bankruptcy are different, both in their origin and

scope". It was of significance that sec. 31 made no distinction between liquid and   A
illiquid debts. Accordingly, in England sec. 31 of the *Bankruptcy Act* 1914 is
mandatory and supersedes the set-off rules in the *Crown Proceedings Act* 1947.
In Scotland, sec. 31 is not applicable and the 1947 Act applies to the Crown's
exercise of its common law right to avail itself of set-off.

The case of *Re Unit 2 Windows Ltd* had been founded on heavily by the petitioner.
However, this case simply involved an application of sec. 31 of the 1914 Act and   B
established that, in England, a creditor cannot appropriate a particular credit to a
particular debt. This, however, is not the position in Scotland. The English
exercise of balancing accounts in bankruptcy does not take place in Scotland. *M S
Fashions Ltd v BCCI* [1992] BCC 571 was a case which dealt with the new
insolvency rules which were the statutory successor to sec. 31. All the English
cases founded on by the petitioner were based on English statute law which was
not applicable in Scotland. In *National Westminster Bank v Halesowen Presswork*   C
& Assemblies Ltd [1972] AC 875 the majority of the House of Lords held that
sec. 31 was mandatory and that it was not possible to contract out of it. In that case
Lord *Kilbrandon* contrasted the laws of Scotland and England and warned against
the danger of looking at English law. There is nothing in that case which supports
the petitioner's view that there is any assistance to be gained from an examination
of the English authorities.
                                                                                     D
(6)   The present case involved an insolvent company which was in receivership.
        However, as all the debts involved were present and liquid, the principle of
        compensation applied and there was no need to invoke the right of retention in
        bankruptcy, nor did any question of balancing accounts in bankruptcy arise. This
        is a case which deals with compensation properly so called, namely, the setting-
        off of present and liquid claims, albeit against a background of insolvency.

Counsel then commented on the six options which counsel for the petitioner had   E
suggested were open to the court in this case.

In relation to the first option, the petitioners were wrong in saying that the Inland
Revenue were applying different policies in Scotland and England. The same policy was
being applied in both countries, namely, the policy which achieved the result most
favourable to the Exchequer but this policy was, of necessity, being applied against
different legal backgrounds. It creates no anomaly as the laws of Scotland and England F
are different. In this case the respective claims arose out of statutory liabilities of a fiscal
character which were liquid debts.

The second option was the correct one to adopt, subject to leave of the court being
granted in terms of sec. 35(2)(d) of the 1947 Act. In this case there was no good reason
for refusing to allow the Crown to set off its chosen debt in accordance with its common
law right.
                                                                                     G
The third and fourth options are available only as a result of the English courts'
construction of sec. 31 of the *Bankruptcy Act* 1914 which has no application in Scotland.
Accordingly, there is no need to consider the equitable rules for the application of
sec. 31. The petitioner argued that there was a precedent for the application of equitable
considerations in the law of cautionary (Gloag and Irvine, *Law of Rights in Security*, pp.
851–852) but this was only in relation to a particular context where the law imports
equity to protect the cautioner and to regulate the behaviour of the principal debtor and   H
creditor. However, the fact that in one particular area of Scots law appropriation by a
creditor is not allowed does not alter the general rule which is applicable elsewhere and
which was authoritatively established in *Maxwell v McCulloch's Creditors*.

The fifth and sixth options were not pressed by the petitioner and did not require any
comment.

A In conclusion, counsel submitted that in relation to the issue before the court, the laws of Scotland and England were materially different. In Scotland, where there are two or more liquid debts then the law of compensation applied and it applied when both parties were solvent and also when the debtor was insolvent. The creditor can choose against which debt he will apply set-off. In contrast, according to English law there is a statutory accounting procedure under sec. 31 of the *Bankruptcy Act* 1914 and the creditor is not entitled to appropriate. In these circumstances there is no inconsistency in the policy

B being applied by the Inland Revenue. The Inland Revenue adopts the basis which is most favourable to the Exchequer, according to the rules which apply in each jurisdiction.

Against the background of the Crown's common law right to set-off, the court, in the exercise of its discretion, should allow set-off as both debts are of a fiscal character. There are no strong or cogent reasons for refusing to permit the Crown to exercise its right of set-off and a refusal would prejudice the Crown compared to other creditors

C who would still be entitled to exercise their right of set-off, by selecting the debt to be set off, without having to seek the leave of the court.

On the whole matter the court should give the direction sought by the Inland Revenue on p. 17 of the closed record.

Having considered the contentions of the parties I have reached the conclusion that the submissions of counsel for the Inland Revenue are well-founded. As I have already

D observed, the facts of the case are not in dispute. The preferential debts due by the company to the Inland Revenue total £58,679 and the non-preferential debt amounts to £12,508. The company is entitled to a VAT repayment amounting to £11,338.10. The company has not raised proceedings with a view to recovering the VAT repayment, and, accordingly, the Inland Revenue has not sought leave, under sec. 35(2)(d) of the *Crown Proceedings Act* 1947, to avail itself of any set-off. However, the question before the

E court is how, on the assumption that the company sued for the VAT repayment and the Inland Revenue was granted leave by the court to avail itself of set-off, the right of set-off would fall to be applied. The Inland Revenue contended that they would be entitled to set off the VAT repayment against the non-preferential debt due by the company, leaving the whole of the preferential debt standing. The petitioner's principal contention was that there should be rateable allocation.

F At the outset it is, I think, important to note that all the debts with which this case is concerned are liquid debts which were due and payable and they were all debts which arose out of legislation of a fiscal nature. The law of compensation applies in the case of liquid debts which are due at the same time. There must be *concursus debiti et crediti*, the debts must be of the same nature and compensation must be pleaded. Further, in Scotland, I am satisfied that, where both parties are solvent and a debtor, who owes a number of liquid debts to a creditor, sues the creditor for a debt due by the creditor, then

G the creditor is entitled to choose which of the debts due to him is to be used for the purposes of set-off (*Bankton's Institute*, Book I, p. 494). Accordingly, when the creditor is entitled to a secured debt and an unsecured debt, I consider that he is entitled to set-off the debt which he is due to the debtor against the unsecured debt so that he retains the benefit of his security (*More's Notes on Stair*, p. 128).

In a case where the debtor is insolvent, the law of compensation is extended to the

H effect of entitling the creditor to set off an illiquid claim against a liquid debt. This extension has been referred to as a right of retention or the balancing of accounts in bankruptcy. The reason for the extension is that it is regarded as inequitable that the creditor should be obliged to pay his debt in full while he only receives a dividend for the debt due to him by the debtor (*Goudy on Bankruptcy* pp. 550–551; Gloag and Irvine, *Law of Rights in Security*, pp. 314–315).

However, in a case where the debtor is insolvent and all the debts in question are   A
liquid, being ascertained and due and payable, I am of the opinion that the normal rules
of compensation apply and that a creditor, who is owed several debts by the debtor, is
entitled to select which of the debts due to him he will use for the purposes of set-off.
Thus, in the case of a creditor who is entitled to a preferential debt and a non-preferential
debt, the creditor is entitled to set off the debt which is due by him against the non-
preferential debt with the result that, if the debt due by the creditor was less than the
amount of the non-preferential debt, the whole of the preferential debt will remain due   B
and payable. The right of a creditor in such circumstances to select the debt which should
be used for the purposes of set-off was decided in the case of *Maxwell v McCulloch's
Creditors*, a decision of the whole court which must still, in my opinion, be regarded as
authoritative (cf. *Stair Memorial Encyclopaedia*, vol. 4, para. 842; Wilson on *Debt* (2nd
ed.) pp. 161–162).

Counsel for the petitioner founded on a line of English authorities, particularly *Re*   C
Unit 2 Windows, in support of his contention that there should be rateable allocation in
this case and he also submitted that the Inland Revenue had, since 1981, been adopting
a different policy in Scotland, in relation to companies in receivership, compared with
the policy which they were pursuing in England. Thus, it was said that in England the
Inland Revenue accepted the principle of rateable allocation, in the case of an insolvent
company which was in receivership, whereas in Scotland they claimed to be entitled to
select the debt to be used for the purposes of set-off. In these circumstances, companies   D
in receivership in Scotland were being treated less favourably than companies in
receivership in England.

So far as the English authorities to which I was referred are concerned, I do not
consider that they are of any real assistance to me in determining the issue before the
Court. As Lord *Avonside* observed in *Smith v Lord Advocate* 1980 SC 227 (at p. 235):

> "There is no profitable purpose in attempting to compare the common law of   E
> Scotland with the statutory law of England."

In *Re Cushla Ltd* [1979] 3 All ER 415, *Vinelott* J observed as follows (at p. 422h):

> "It appears from the decision of Lord Keith in *Laing v Lord Advocate* that in
> Scotland the provisions of the 1947 Act do apply to set-off in bankruptcy. But in
> Scotland rules of set-off in bankruptcy are different, both in their origin and
> scope."   F

The English cases, including *Re Unit 2 Windows*, have been based on the courts'
interpretation of sec. 31 of the *Bankruptcy Act* 1914 in terms of which the respective
debts fell to be aggregated and a balance struck. The creditor had no right to appropriate
the debt due by him to a non-preferential debt due by the bankrupt, leaving the
preferential debt standing. In England, it was held that the provisions of sec. 31 were
mandatory (*National Westminster Bank Ltd v Halesowen Presswork & Assemblies Ltd*   G
[1972] AC 785). In that case Lord *Kilbrandon* observed as follows (at p. 822G):

> "So, if set off be mandatory in England, this seems to be one of the fields in which
> the law relating to British companies varies according as they are registered in
> England or in Scotland."

However, sec. 31 of the *Bankruptcy Act* 1914 has no application in Scotland. It is, in   H
my view, clear that the English law relating to balancing of accounts in bankruptcy is
statutory and quite different from the law applicable in Scotland, and accordingly I do
not consider that there is any useful purpose to be gained by detailed consideration of
the English authorities. I am satisfied that, according to the law of Scotland, the Inland
Revenue, if granted leave to apply set-off in terms of sec. 35(2)(d) of the 1947 Act,
would be entitled, on the basis of the normal rules of compensation applicable in the

A   case of liquid debts, to set off the VAT repayment against their non-preferential debt, leaving the preferential debt unaffected.

As I have said, it was pointed out by the petitioner that in England the Inland Revenue accept the principle of rateable allocation whereas in Scotland they are now claiming to be entitled to choose which debt due by the insolvent company in receivership is to be used for the purposes of set-off. It was submitted that this meant that an insolvent company in receivership in Scotland was being treated less favourably than a similar
B   company in England and that this amounted, in practice, to the adoption by the Inland Revenue of different policies in the two jurisdictions. It is true that the Inland Revenue formerly accepted the principle of rateable allocation in both countries. However, in 1981 they changed their policy and decided to adopt the basis which was most favourable to the Exchequer. One consequence of this change of policy has been that they are now claiming that in Scotland they are entitled to set off a debt due to the company against
C   their non-preferential debt. However, I am satisfied that the Inland Revenue is, in fact, adopting the same policy in both countries, namely, the basis which is most favourable to the Exchequer and that the practical application of that policy is different in Scotland, as compared to England, by reason only of the fact that the law relating to set-off in bankruptcy is different in each country. In Scotland, the law of compensation applies in the case of liquid debts, even if the company is insolvent, whereas in England the position has been regulated by sec. 31 of the *Bankruptcy Act* 1914 which provides for
D   the balancing of accounts in bankruptcy. In these circumstances the Inland Revenue are obliged, by statute, to accept the principle of rateable allocation in England whereas in Scotland they are entitled to take advantage of the law of compensation which is applicable in the case of liquid debts even if the company is insolvent and in receivership. In my opinion the Inland Revenue are perfectly justified, in law, in adopting this approach even though it has the practical effect that Scottish companies in receivership are treated less favourably than similar companies in England. However, this difference
E   in treatment is solely due to the fact that the laws of the two countries are different and not to any differences in the policy being adopted by the Inland Revenue.

On the whole matter I am satisfied, on the basis of the agreed facts in this case, that the Scottish law of compensation applies and that, if the Inland Revenue were granted leave under sec. 35(2)(d) of the 1947 Act to avail themselves of set-off in relation to a claim by the company for the VAT repayment of £11,338.10, they would be entitled to
F   set it off against their non-preferential debt of £12,508 with the result that their preferential claim would be unaffected.

While there was no application under sec. 35(2)(d) before the court, I can see no reason in principle, in the particular circumstances of this case, why the court should refuse to grant leave if it were sought. In my opinion, on the basis of the facts in this case, the principle of rateable allocation is not applicable nor are any of the other possible
G   options suggested by counsel for the petitioner. In these circumstances I shall give the direction sought by the Inland Revenue.

(Order accordingly)

H

Re Swift 736 Ltd.
Secretary of State for Trade and Industry v Ettinger.

Court of Appeal (Civil Division).

Nicholls V-C, Farquharson and Steyn L JJ.

Judgment delivered 16 February 1993.

Disqualifying unfit directors of insolvent companies — Whether disqualification period was too short — Company Directors Disqualification Act 1986, sec. 6.

This was an appeal by the Secretary of State for Trade and Industry against a director disqualification order (see [1992] BCC 93). The Secretary of State contended that the disqualification period was too short.

The respondent was the director or de facto director of some 16 companies which went into insolvent liquidation. There were six companies which had carried on the same business in succession before being wound up, but of which the respondent was not the principal director; the principal directors of those companies were disqualified for five years (in other proceedings). In relation to the other companies there were complaints of failure to comply with the requirements of the Companies Act in respect of keeping proper books and records, and filing accounts and returns.

The judge disqualified the respondent for three years on the grounds that the pattern of trading in the first six companies was a misuse of the privilege of limited liability and the respondent's involvement demonstrated that he was unfit to be concerned in the management of a company, and that in relation to compliance with the company administration requirements of the Companies Act, a failure of duty as a director amounting to showing unfitness had been made out. The judge also took account of the facts that the respondent had derived no financial gain from the six companies, that he had been made bankrupt and that the principal directors had been disqualified for five years.

Held, increasing the disqualification period to five years:

Leaving aside the length of the disqualification orders in respect of the other directors, the respondent's case fell comfortably within the intermediate bracket of six to ten years. The judge misdirected himself. He was over-influenced by the position regarding the other directors and seemed not to have taken into account the extent to which the respondent's misconduct included his serious misconduct in relation to the other 11 companies. His breaches of the statutory provisions regarding those other companies could not, taken cumulatively, be regarded as relatively not very serious. It was therefore for the court to exercise its own discretion. Were it not for the five-year period ordered regarding the other directors, a longer period of disqualification would have been called for, despite the hardship which the respondent had suffered by reason of his personal bankruptcy, consequential on the insolvency of the companies.

The following case was referred to in the judgment of Nicholls V-C:

Sevenoaks Stationers (Retail) Ltd, Re [1990] BCC 765; [1991] Ch 164.

Matthew Collings (instructed by the Treasury Solicitor) for the Secretary of State.

The respondent appeared in person.

JUDGMENT

Nicholls V-C: This is an appeal by the Secretary of State from an order made on 17 October 1991 by *Hoffmann* J in company director disqualification proceedings (see [1992] BCC 93). The respondent to this appeal, Mr Raymond Phillip Ettinger, and, in respect of five companies, his wife, were directors of companies which became insolvent.

A   The judge found that the conduct of each of them as directors made them unfit to be concerned in the management of a company. He made a disqualification order against Mr Ettinger for a period of three years. In the case of Mrs Ettinger he made an order for two years, which is the period prescribed by the *Company Directors Disqualification Act* 1986 as the minimum.

B   The Secretary of State contends that the period of disqualification in respect of Mr Ettinger is too short. He submits that an order for disqualification should be made for between six and ten years. We were told that this is the first time there has been an appeal by the Secretary of State regarding the length of disqualification imposed by a judge. The Act makes no express provision for such an appeal, but I can see no reason to question that the general right of appeal against decisions made by judges on matters arising under the Act applies as much in this case as any other, subject always to the consideration that the statute entrusts to the judge the decision on the period for which

C   a disqualification order is to be made. Under sec. 6 the judge is obliged to make a disqualification order if satisfied on the two matters mentioned in sec. 6(1). As to that, he has no discretion. But the judge has a discretion as to the period of disqualification. This court may only intervene and interfere with the judge's exercise of this discretion in accordance with the usual, well-established principles concerning the circumstances in which this court will intervene in a judge's exercise of a discretion vested in him.

D   As can happen in these cases, the factual background set out in the evidence is complicated, because several companies are involved. Mr Ettinger was a director or shadow director of 16 companies altogether. The judge set out his findings and reasoning in a judgment which was characteristically lucid and concise. It is reported in [1992] BCC 93, and accordingly I shall not burden this judgment with a repetition of the basic facts as found by the judge. These are publicly available in the report for those who wish

E   to read them. This judgment should therefore be understood and read in conjunction with that report of the judge's decision.

     The challenge before us is not to the judge's findings of fact, but to the seriousness, or lack of seriousness, which he attached to the shortcomings in the conduct of Mr Ettinger. It is said that the judge misdirected himself. This case, it is said, falls into the middle bracket of the three brackets accepted by *Dillon* LJ in *Re Sevenoaks Stationers (Retail)*

F   *Ltd* [1990] BCC 765, where, at p. 771H, he set out guidelines which assist in achieving broad fairness of treatment between one case of disqualification and the next. The top bracket of disqualification, for over 10 years and up to the statutory maximum of 15 years, should be reserved for particularly serious cases, which might include a case where a director has already been disqualified. The minimum bracket, of disqualification for between two years and five years, should be applied where, though disqualification is mandatory, the case is relatively not very serious. The intermediate bracket of

G   disqualification, for from six to ten years, should apply to serious cases which do not merit the top bracket.

     The Secretary of State submits that this is a serious case and merited disqualification, as I have said, for between six and ten years.

     I preface reference to the judge's conclusions by mentioning that the most serious misconduct related to the Jacobs group of companies. Mr and Mrs Jacobs were the

H   principal directors of this group, and in charge of the day-to-day operations. Here, there was a deplorable pattern of six companies succeeding one another, carrying on the same business of shirt manufacturing from the same premises, as each became insolvent, one after the other. Mr Ettinger was a customer of these companies and he became a director or shadow director of three of them. Regarding these companies, the judge said (at p. 94H):

"The pattern of trading of the Jacobs companies constituted, in my view, a misuse of the privilege of limited liability. By the time that Jake Unit took over the business, it had reached the state in which — partly on account of the nature of the business and partly on account of its uncreditworthiness — the only credit which the company could obtain was by the withholding of PAYE and VAT due to the Crown. When Jake Unit was eventually wound up, virtually the whole of its indebtedness was in respect of Crown debts. Similarly in the case of Lucky Trump, [of] a deficiency of about £87,000 all but £10,000 was owed to the Crown.

That form of trading, where one has a succession of companies which no doubt pay a salary to their principal directors and are then allowed to sink, having lived on involuntary credit provided by the Crown, is the very thing which the provisions for disqualification of directors is intended to prevent, and I have no doubt that the Jacobses were rightly disqualified by the Medway County court in an earlier application."

When Mr Ettinger took over his practical responsibilities within Jake Unit, he knew from his previous directorships of two Jacobs companies what had happened regarding the previous companies. "He must have known", found the judge, "that there had been other corporate embodiments in between", and it was not right, the judge concluded, "to absolve him from responsibility for participating in this series of insolvencies simply on the grounds that he was only doing it in order to assist the Jacobses in obtaining bank facilities" (p. 95B–D).

In relation to the Ettinger group of companies, the judge held it was a case where the books and records had not been kept in a way best calculated to enable those in charge of the liquidation to see what had happened. In addition, there were failures to comply with the statutory obligations regarding the filing of accounts and returns.

As to the third group of companies, in which Swift 736 Ltd was the principal company, and which carried on businesses under the name McKenzie, the principal matter of complaint upheld by the judge was the failure to make proper returns.

Finally, in relation to the companies carrying on businesses as manufacturers of extruded plastics, again the judge found no misconduct other than failure to comply with the statutory provisions.

In determining the period of disqualification, the judge took into account four factors. First, that the conduct of the Jacobs group of companies did constitute a breach of accepted commercial morality, and to that extent, would be a very serious case. But the involvement of Mr Ettinger was by no means comparable with that of the Jacobses themselves. In relation to the other companies, he said (at p. 97B) there were certainly:

"breaches which, by virtue of the mandatory provisions of sec. 6 of the Act, would impose upon me a duty to disqualify Mr Ettinger, but I would not regard them as constituting really serious breaches of his duties as a director."

Secondly, the judge took into account that Mr Ettinger personally derived no financial gain from the way the companies were conducted. His relationship was solely in his capacity as a purchaser and he was not a shareholder. He received no director's remuneration.

Thirdly, Mr Ettinger had put his own assets and mortgaged his house in support of personal guarantees and as a result his home had been repossessed and he had been made bankrupt. In this way, he had already suffered considerable misfortune.

Fourth, the judge had some regard to the fact that the penalty which Medway County Court saw fit to impose on the Jacobses was a period of five years. The judge said (at p. 97D):

A

"It is perfectly true that the fact that one director receives a disqualification of a particular length or indeed is not proceeded against at all is no reason why another director should not be disqualified for some different period. But I think that most people's notion of fairness requires me to have some regard to another penalty which has been imposed in a very closely related case."

B

The thrust of the Secretary of State's criticism is that the three-year disqualification might have been appropriate for Mr Ettinger in relation to the Jacobs group of companies alone, when one takes into account the fact that Mr Ettinger did not gain personally from the group and the fact that the Jacobses' period of disqualification was five years. However, it is submitted that the judge failed to attach appropriate weight to Mr Ettinger's misconduct in relation to the other companies. It was submitted, in particular, that the judge failed to take into account the repeated failures by Mr Ettinger to comply with the statutory provisions for preparing and filing accounts and providing explanations of deficiencies.

C

I have to say that I think there is some force in these criticisms. As I read his judgment, the judge was much concerned, and I believe rightly so, to maintain some sort of fairness between the order made against the Jacobses and the order being made against Mr Ettinger. Whether the Jacobses were fortunate in not being disqualified for a longer period is not a matter before us and not a matter on which I am therefore to be taken to express any view. But Mr Ettinger was involved in other companies as well. In respect of these other companies Mr Ettinger's default lay principally in failure to comply with Companies Act obligations.

D

These are themselves serious matters. Limited liability is a valuable tool in the promotion of trade and business, but it must not be misused. Those who make use of limited liability must do so with a proper sense of responsibility. The director disqualification procedure is an important sanction introduced by Parliament to raise standards in this regard. Those who take advantage of limited liability must conduct their companies with due regard to the ordinary standards of commercial morality. They must also be punctilious in observing the safeguards laid down by Parliament for the benefit of others who have dealings with their companies. They must maintain proper books of account and prepare annual accounts; they must file their accounts and returns promptly; they must fully and frankly disclose information about deficiencies in accordance with the statutory provisions. Isolated lapses in filing documents are one thing and may be excusable, but not so persistent lapses which show overall a blatant disregard for this important aspect of accountability. Such lapses are serious and cannot be condoned even though, and it is right to have this firmly in mind, they need not involve any dishonest intent.

E

F

G

The seriousness with which such conduct is to be viewed is shown by the provisions of the Disqualification Act itself. The extent to which a director is responsible for any failure to comply with the statutory provisions regarding accounting records and the preparation of annual accounts is one of the matters to which the court is required to have regard in determining unfitness to be concerned in the management of a company. Those who persistently fail to discharge their statutory obligations in this respect can expect to be disqualified, for an appropriate period of time, from using limited liability as one of the tools of their trade. The business community should be left in no doubt on this score. It may be that, despite the disqualification provisions having been in operation for some years, there is still a lingering feeling in some quarters that a failure to file annual accounts and so forth is a venial sin. If this is still so, the sooner the attitude is corrected the better it will be. Judicial observations to this effect have been made before, but they bear repetition.

H

Here the evidence showed there were repeated failures in respect of company after company, though not in every case, to keep proper accounting or other statutory records, to prepare and file annual accounts and, although this was to a lesser extent, to deliver annual returns. The affidavit evidence of the Secretary of State also showed that likewise, after the companies had gone into insolvent liquidation with very substantial deficiencies, in case after case there was a failure by Mr Ettinger at the time to account for the deficiencies or provide explanations of them.

As to this latter matter, I must mention one unsatisfactory feature which emerged before us. Mr Ettinger appeared before us in person as he did before the judge. At the trial he filed no affidavit evidence, nor did he go into the witness-box and give oral evidence. Instead, he made submissions in mitigation. We were told that inevitably, as he did so, he made statements to the judge that were inconsistent with the Secretary of State's affidavit evidence. He did this without objection from the Secretary of State, who was content to treat such statements as evidence.

This is not a satisfactory procedure. The distinction between evidence and submission is not an easy one for non-lawyers to grasp. If a litigant does not produce affidavit evidence, it behoves the judge to point out to him that unless he goes into the witness-box the evidence against him will stand unchallenged. If he wishes to dispute it, he must give evidence. Unless the judge takes this course there is a risk of misunderstanding, although it is not suggested that was so in this case. There is also the difficulty, which arises in the present case, that there is no way in which the Court of Appeal can satisfactorily decide what was the evidence before the judge on any particular point.

In the present case, Mr Ettinger told us that before the judge he did challenge the allegation that he had failed to account for the deficiencies. As to that, although the position is not wholly as clear as it ought to be, I think that, even if Mr Ettinger did so submit to the judge, it is tolerably plain from his judgment that the judge did not accept this. In particular, as I have indicated in relation to the Ettinger group of companies, the judge rejected the more serious charges and regarded this as an instance where those in charge of a liquidation were not best able, from the books and records kept, to see what had happened. I do not think the judge would have stopped there for one moment and expressed himself in that way if he had accepted that Mr Ettinger had none the less duly accounted for the deficiencies to the official receiver or others when the companies went into liquidation.

So where does the matter stand? In my view, leaving aside the length of the disqualification orders in respect of the Jacobses, Mr Ettinger's case is one falling comfortably within the intermediate bracket. I do not doubt the judge would have ordered disqualification for a longer period than he did, had it not been, as it seems to me, that he was over-influenced by the position regarding the Jacobses. I say "over-influenced", for two reasons: first, if one disregards altogether the disqualification orders made regarding Mr and Mrs Jacobs, three years (which is one year more than the statutory minimum) could not possibly be an appropriate period of disqualification in this case. Second, as to the impact of the Jacobses' period of disqualification, the judge described the Jacobs case as a very closely related case. In saying this, he seems not to have taken into account the extent to which Mr Ettinger's misconduct included his serious misconduct in relation to the other 11 companies in which the Jacobses were not involved. Mr Ettinger's breaches of the statutory provisions regarding those other companies cannot, taken cumulatively, be regarded as relatively not very serious.

Taking all these matters into account, I am in no doubt the judge misdirected himself. It is therefore for this court to exercise its own discretion. Doing so, in my view the appropriate period of disqualification is five years. I emphasise that in fixing this period

A   I have taken into account in favour of Mr Ettinger the position regarding the Jacobses. Were it not for the five-year period ordered regarding them, I would have concluded that a longer period of disqualification was called for, despite the hardship which Mr Ettinger has suffered by reason of his personal bankruptcy, consequential on the insolvency of the companies.

I would allow this appeal to that extent.

B   **Farquharson LJ:** I agree.

Steyn LJ: I agree.

(*Appeal allowed in part. No order as to costs*)

Re Noble Trees Ltd.

Chancery Division (Companies Court).
Vinelott J.
Judgment delivered 1 March 1993.

Disqualifying unfit directors of insolvent companies — Whether director disqualification application should be struck out for delay — Company Directors Disqualification Act 1986, sec. 6, 7.

The Companies Court, on the respondent's application, struck out director disqualification proceedings on the grounds that there had been inordinate and inexcusable delay by the Secretary of State in prosecuting the proceedings and that the respondent had suffered prejudice as a result of the delay.

The following cases were referred to in the judgment:

Birkett v James [1978] AC 297.
County & District Properties Ltd v Lyell [1991] 1 WLR 683.
Reynolds v British Leyland Ltd [1991] 1 WLR 675.
Roche v Church [1992] TLR 634.

Geoffrey Vos (instructed by Pickering Kenyon) for the applicant.

Matthew Collings (instructed by the Treasury Solicitor) for the Secretary of State.

JUDGMENT

Vinelott J: This is an application to set aside proceedings brought by the Secretary of State in which he seeks an order under the *Company Directors Disqualification Act* 1986 barring the respondent, John Arthur Francis Cassia, from being a director of or concerned in the management of a company for a period to be determined by the court. The proceedings have had a long and unfortunate history. It seems to me to do little credit to either party. I must deal with it in some detail.

Noble Trees Ltd was incorporated on 5 July 1983 with an issued share capital of £20,000. The business of the company was growing trees for sale. It occupied some 110 acres of land, the larger part of which was occupied under short-term licences from local farmers. Mr Cassia was one of the directors appointed on its incorporation. Joint receivers were appointed by a debenture holder, the National Westminster Bank, on 11 August 1988. The same persons were appointed joint receivers by a second debenture holder, 3i, on 12 August 1988.

Following a report made by the receivers pursuant to sec. 7(3) of the Act, the Secretary of State issued an application for a disqualification order against Mr Cassia. The application was issued on 2 August 1990, just nine days before the expiry of the period of two years from the appointment of the joint receivers prescribed by sec. 7(2) of the Act.

The grounds relied on as founding the claim that Mr Cassia is unfit to be a director are that he caused the company to trade knowing it to be insolvent, that he had misapplied company moneys for his own benefit, that he had issued cheques which he knew would be dishonoured and that he had failed to co-operate with the receivers.

As regards the second of these grounds, the joint receivers had previously started proceedings to recover directors' loans of some £7,000, which it was said had been improperly made by Mr Cassia, and had applied for summary judgment. Mr Cassia was given unconditional leave to defend and in addition he filed a counterclaim. As I understand it the receivers in effect abandoned the proceedings when they found that Mr Cassia was legally aided. They took the view that it would be uneconomic to pursue a claim against a legally aided defendant which would be unlikely to produce any money

A   for the company even if the claim succeeded. It is not clear what has happened to the counterclaim.

The application for the disqualification of Mr Cassia was supported by an affidavit by Mr Somerfield, one of the joint receivers. It was sworn shortly before the application was made. Mr Cassia deposed to his affidavit in answer on 28 September 1990. Then on 25 October 1990 Mr Registrar *Dewhurst* gave the Secretary of State leave to file evidence in reply within 56 days and made the usual direction that the evidence of any deponent should not be read unless he attended for cross-examination. So far, all was well.

B

However, the Secretary of State's evidence in reply was not filed within 56 days from the date of the order. On 14 February 1991, nearly two months after the expiry of the 56-day period, Mr Cassia's solicitors, Pickering Kenyon ("PK"), issued a summons seeking an order that the action be dismissed with costs on the grounds that the applicant had failed to comply with the order of Mr Registrar *Dewhurst*.

C

There was a telephone conversation between Mr Yeudell, the solicitor in the office of the Treasury Solicitor dealing with the matter, and Mr Oakley, a partner in PK, on 21 February, which was followed by a letter from Mr Yeudell in which he confirmed that:

> "the applicant consents to a final order extending time for the evidence in reply by 14 days, costs to be the respondent's in any event. Please produce this letter to the registrar."

D

There is considerable dispute as to what was said in the telephone conversation on 21 February. Mr Yeudell says that he agreed to consent to a final order that the evidence be filed on or before 8 March. Mr Oakley says that he understood that Mr Yeudell had consented to an order in the terms sought in the summons, that is an order striking out the application altogether unless the evidence was filed before 8 March.

E

Mr Yeudell did not attend at the hearing before the registrar. He was content to leave it to Mr Oakley to produce his letter of consent. As I understand it, the registrar was told by Mr Oakley that Mr Yeudell had consented to an order striking out the application altogether unless the evidence was filed before 8 March. It seems to me quite clear that the registrar must have understood Mr Oakley to have so represented the conversation he had had with Mr Yeudell. The registrar clearly would not otherwise have made an order which on its face was inconsistent with the letter of consent and which in my experience is quite unprecedented in the context of a failure to file evidence in reply promptly.

F

Mr Yeudell did not learn of the order until very many months later. The affidavit in reply was not in fact filed before 8 March. Mr Collings, the counsel nominated by the Attorney-General, had suffered periods of ill-health in the early months of 1991 and when he returned to work he was heavily engaged in court and behind-hand with his paperwork. He did not settle the draft affidavit until 15 March.

G

Mr Oakley says that in the meantime on 12 March, Miss Kular, an assistant solicitor with PK, delivered a letter by hand to the Companies Office seeking confirmation that the proceedings had been struck out. Mr Yeudell sent Mr Oakley what is described as a "copy" of Mr Somerfield's affidavit of reply, although in fact it was unsworn. Having explained Mr Collings' difficulties, he said that he would let Mr Oakley have details of the jurat later.

H

The letter is dated 22 March and was received by Mr Oakley on 25 March, which I understand was a Monday. No reply had then been received from the Companies Office and following receipt of the unsworn affidavit, Mr Oakley sent Miss Kular to the Companies Office where she saw Mr Adewala, a clerk in the office. She asked what had happened to the letter of 12 March. It transpired that it could not be traced. After some discussion and a delay while a search was made for it, she read Mr Adewala a copy of the letter of 12 March and Mr Adewala apparently confirmed that, as the affidavit had not been supplied in time, the proceedings were at an end.

Mr Oakley says that on the same day he replied to Mr Yeudell's letter of 22 March. In his reply he said that as the affidavit had not been received by 8 March, the court had been notified on 12 March of the non-compliance and that the action had automatically been struck out. He says that he obtained a sealed copy of the order of 22 February on the following day and wrote again to Mr Yeudell on 26 March enclosing a copy of it.

Mr Yeudell says that he did not see either of these letters and that in the five years in which he has been in the Treasury Solicitor's office he has never known a letter properly addressed to go astray. In the absence of a reply to his letter of 22 March, he assumed (reasonably I think) that the explanation he had given had been accepted and that an application to the court to extend the time for service of the evidence in reply, which would have been a mere formality, would not be necessary. He sent Mr Oakley details of the jurat on 26 April. He heard nothing more from PK for many months.

I should I think make three observations on the history of this matter up to 26 April. First, the correspondence between PK and with the Companies Office and with the DTI seems to have been almost singled out by providence for exceptional treatment. However, I must accept Mr Oakley's evidence that these letters were duly delivered or posted with the correct address and that they have gone astray.

Secondly, I must accept that Mr Oakley genuinely misunderstood Mr Yeudell or Mr Yeudell's agreement to consent to what he described in his letter as "a final order" and thought that Mr Yeudell was consenting to an order striking out the proceedings unless the affidavit was filed in time. I think I should say, however, that an order imposing the sanction of dismissal of proceedings for failure to file evidence in reply is in my experience and in the experience of counsel who have appeared wholly unprecedented. The appropriate penalty for failure to file evidence in reply promptly is the exclusion of that evidence. It may be appropriate in an extreme case to make an order that unless the evidence is filed before a given date, the evidence shall not be used, although even an order in those terms would of course yield to the discretion of a judge if an adequate explanation for delay were given later. In the circumstances of this case, given that there was an explanation of the failure to deliver the evidence in reply in good time and that Mr Yeudell honestly and reasonably believed that no objection was being taken to its late delivery, an extension of time, if sought, even at the trial, would have been granted as a matter of course, either when the misunderstanding came to light or, subject to giving Mr Cassia ample opportunity to file further evidence, if necessary at the trial. Mr Oakley, as appears from his evidence, seems to understand very imperfectly the difference between a final and an unless order, a difference which in later correspondence Mr Oakley described as "esoteric". I find that a surprising observation coming from a litigation partner in a firm of solicitors.

Thirdly and lastly, I must I think accept that Mr Oakley did not deliberately set out to take advantage of a misunderstanding on the part of Mr Yeudell. But having said that, I think I am also justified in saying that in my view Mr Oakley did not show the fair-mindedness and openness which the court is entitled to expect from its officers. Mr Oakley must have known when he received Mr Yeudell's letter of 22 March with the uncompleted affidavit that Mr Yeudell assumed that no objection would be raised to its late service, but although he then sent Mr Yeudell a copy of the order of 22 February, he did not tell Mr Yeudell that he had taken the trouble to send Miss Kular in person to the Companies Office to obtain confirmation that the proceedings were at an end.

More importantly, when he received details of the jurat in the letter of 26 April, he must have appreciated that Mr Yeudell thought that the proceedings were still alive. But he did nothing to disabuse Mr Yeudell. He could have telephoned him to make sure that there had been no misunderstanding as to the agreement he says was reached in the telephone conversation before the hearing before the registrar which, as I have said, Mr Yeudell did not attend because he relied on Mr Oakley to explain the position to the registrar. He took no step to confirm that Mr Yeudell had seen his letters of 25 and 26 March and the copy order. He had experienced no difficulty in reaching Mr Yeudell on the telephone earlier and his failure to take this step is in marked contrast with the prompt steps he took to obtain direct confirmation from the Companies Office that the application had been struck out.

After this series of misunderstandings, Mr Yeudell did nothing for many months. On 9 December he set the application down for hearing. However, he did not inform Mr Oakley that this step had been taken. Strictly he should have done so. Regulation 2 of the *Insolvent Companies (Disqualification of Unfit Directors) Proceedings Rules 1987* applies the Rules of the Supreme Court and under O. 34, r. 8, the party to an action setting it down for trial is required, within 24 hours after doing so, to notify the other party to the action that it has been set down.

Mr Yeudell admits that he was unaware that this rule applied and I think it may well be that its application in this field is not widely appreciated. However, having set the application down, Mr Yeudell again did nothing for several months. The application came to light again in July, when he asked Mr Collings' clerk to provide the certificate of length of hearing that would be needed before a hearing could be arranged. Nothing more happened until 4 November, when Mr Yeudell again wrote to PK to enquire the name of the counsel they proposed to instruct. I shall return in more detail to this part of the history a little later.

On 9 November the Treasury Solicitor issued a summons to set aside the order of 22 February 1991. On 23 November 1992 Mr Registrar *Buckley* duly set aside the order. PK gave notice of an appeal, although not until 5 January of this year. The appeal came before *Ferris* J on 25 January. It was stood over to be heard later in the week. It was heard and dismissed by His Honour Judge *Moseley* on 28 January. The application to set aside the proceedings which is now before me was then made, although not until 10 February. Again, I shall want to return to this part of the history in more detail later. That is all I need say about the history at this stage.

In my judgment in considering whether there was undue delay between 22 February 1991 and 9 November 1992, the right course is to leave out of account the unless order and the subsequent appeal, that is to say, to treat the unless order as if it had been a final order, which is what Mr Yeudell thought it was, and to ask whether, on that footing there has been such delay as to justify striking out the proceedings.

It is suggested in the evidence in support of the application to strike out the proceedings that the Secretary of State has been guilty of contumelious disobedience of the order of the court and of the rules governing procedure. That suggestion was, rightly I think, not pursued by Mr Vos, who appeared for Mr Cassia. The question is whether the Secretary of State has been guilty of inordinate or inexcusable delay resulting in prejudice to Mr Cassia.

In approaching this question, the question whether there has been inordinate or inexcusable delay, I must bear in mind that the application by the Secretary of State was made at the very end of the two-year period prescribed by sec. 7(2). Greater diligence in prosecuting proceedings is expected of a litigant who delays issuing proceedings until the end of a limitation period and I see no reason why a different approach should be adopted if the Secretary of State delays the institution of proceedings under the 1986 Act until the end of the permissible period.

It is, I think, immaterial that there may have been no undue delay by the Secretary of State in giving consideration to the report of the joint receivers and in instituting other necessary enquiries before deciding whether or not to institute proceedings. Whether the Secretary of State was or was not justified in leaving the institution of proceedings until the eleventh hour, it was his duty thereafter to ensure that every possible step was taken to bring the proceedings before the court without delay. Dispatch was required not only in the interests of the respondent, but in the public interest. It is wrong that a person whom the Secretary of State considers to be unfit to act as a director should be left free to do so any longer than is necessary.

Returning to the delay relied upon, Mr Yeudell cannot be accused of dilatoriness after the proceedings had been commenced and in obtaining directions from the registrar. However there was then delay in filing evidence in reply. The 56-day period fixed by Mr Registrar *Dewhurst* expired in early December and the order made by Mr Registrar *Buckley* which Mr Yeudell believed to be a final order was not complied with. When the evidence was supplied to the respondent, it was over three months late. And even then details of the jurat were not supplied for another month.

I do not think that this delay could be said by itself to be inordinate. However, it was the prelude to a period of over 15 months during which nothing was done, except first to set down the case for hearing on 9 December, a step of which Mr Yeudell mistakenly failed to inform PK, and secondly to ask Mr Collings' clerk to obtain a joint certificate of counsel of the estimated length of the hearing and then to attend on the Clerk of the List to arrange a convenient date. Nothing then happened for a further four months. No blame can be attached to Mr Collings' clerk. He was waiting to hear from the clerk to counsel instructed on behalf of Mr Cassia. It was not until 2 November that Mr Yeudell spoke again to Mr Collings' clerk when he was asked to arrange with PK for their counsel to attend the Clerk of the List on 4 November. By then nearly 20 months had passed without any communication at all between the Treasury Solicitor and PK.

Mr Yeudell in his affidavit evidence explains the great pressure of work that he was under during this period. I do not underestimate his difficulties. I think I am entitled to take notice of the fact that the Treasury Solicitor and the legal department of the DTI are seriously understaffed. But I cannot take these difficulties into account in considering whether there has been inordinate and inexcusable delay. If legislation to provide for the disqualification of persons who are shown to be unfit to be directors is required in the public interest, the government must find ways of providing adequate resources. It seems to me intolerable in the public interest that if the Secretary of State considers a person to be unfit to be a director of a company that he should be allowed to remain free so to act for as long as the period of five years which in this case elapsed after the insolvency which gave rise to the report and enquiries which in turn led the Secretary of State to take that view. It is also unfair to the individual concerned that the proceedings should remain in suspense for such a protracted period.

I have reached the clear conclusion that the delay in this case was inordinate and inexcusable. On the other hand, I do not think that the Secretary of State can be said to have been guilty of any contumelious failure to observe an order of the court and, as I said, Mr Vos did not suggest that that was so.

The further question that arises therefore is whether Mr Cassia has suffered prejudice as a result of this delay. For this purpose:

> "the additional prejudice need not be great compared with that which may already have been caused by the time elapsed before the writ was issued, but it must be more than minimal."

(See *Birkett v James* [1978] AC 297 per Lord *Diplock* at p. 323.)

Mr Cassia's evidence is that during the last 18 months he has been in negotiation with a US company, Pipelines Inc, for the creation of a UK company, Pipelines Central,

A   which is to be granted a licence to sell the product of Pipelines Inc throughout Eastern Europe and Africa. The negotiations have been conducted on the footing that he, Mr Cassia, will be a director of the new UK company. He has also been in negotiation with a UK company, LH Property & Leisure plc regarding a project in Spain. He hopes to be appointed marketing director at a salary with a commission on the sale of golf debentures. This evidence is supported by letters from these two companies. Mr Cassia says that he has invested considerable time and expense in pursuing these negotiations

B   and, in the one case, looking for purchasers for the debentures, and in the other pursuing and agreeing the terms of contracts between Pipelines Inc, itemised new subsidiaries and customers in Russia and Nigeria.

   Mr Collings submitted that Mr Cassia has not established that there is any causal nexus between the efforts and expense which he has incurred and the Secretary of State's delay. The prejudice to him was caused by his belief that the proceedings were at

C   an end, a mistaken belief for which his solicitors must accept primary responsibility. It arises because they informed Mr Registrar *Buckley* that Mr Yeudell had agreed to submit to an unless order and because after receipt of his letter of 26 April they failed to make sure that Yeudell was not under any misapprehension.

   Further, if this application to strike out had not been pursued, the Secretary of State's application would have been heard or at least commenced on 25 February last and if

D   Mr Cassia's opposition is well-founded, he would by now be free to act as a director and would not have suffered any prejudice. If the application had succeeded, it would still be open to him to apply for leave to take up the appointment that had been offered.

   I find this argument over-subtle. I think the answer to it is that if Mr Yeudell had proceeded promptly after 26 April to set the application down for hearing and had taken appropriate steps to fix the date of the hearing and to inform PK, the misunderstanding

E   would have come to light long before and application might have been made many months ago to set aside the order of 22 February. Mr Cassia might then not have incurred expense in pursuing negotiations with these two companies until the applications had been disposed of.

   Mr Collings' last ground of opposition to Mr Cassia's application was founded on the principle of estoppel by conduct, applied in *County & District Properties Ltd v Lyell* [1991] 1 WLR 683, *Reynolds v British Leyland Ltd* [1991] 1 WLR 675 and *Roche v*

F   *Church* [1992] TLR 634.

   When the application to set aside the order of 26 February 1991 was made and before the hearing before the registrar, Mr Oakley, in an affidavit sworn on 20 November 1992 pointed out that there had been no contact between him and Mr Yeudell for 20 months and contended that the Treasury Solicitor had, I cite,

G   "not acted expeditiously in relation to this matter and this appeal should be dismissed."

   The reference to an appeal is of course to the Treasury Solicitor's application to set aside the order.

   As I understand it, delay in making the application was not a ground relied on at the hearing before Mr Registrar *Buckley*. He set aside the order on the ground that the

H   order of 22 February 1991 purported to be made by consent and that the Treasury Solicitor had not in fact consented to it. Mr Collings did not contend that the assertion and apparent abandonment of the claim that the application to set aside the order was barred by delay gave rise to an issue estoppel precluding Mr Cassia from relying on delay as a ground for striking out the proceedings. However, Mr Collings did rely upon the failure of PK to raise the question of delay again until 25 January, when the appeal against the decision of Mr Registrar *Buckley* first came before *Ferris* J. He was sitting as the companies judge. As I understand it he was informed that Mr Cassia intended to apply to strike out the Secretary of State's application on the ground of delay and was invited to stand over the appeal so that the two matters could be heard together. Counsel for the Treasury Solicitor opposed that course and *Ferris* J directed that the appeal from the decision of the registrar should be heard later that week.

It was in fact heard and dismissed by His Honour Judge *Moseley*, sitting as a High Court judge, on 28 January. But then the application to set aside the Secretary of State's application on the ground of delay was not made until 9 February. The Secretary of State did not learn of it until 10 February, when he was supplied with an affidavit by Miss Kular, which refers to the intention to make such an application. In the meantime there was correspondence between the Treasury Solicitor and PK concerning an application to adjourn the hearing of the Secretary of State's application and the preparation of evidence and it is said the Secretary of State incurred expense in the preparation of bundles of documents for use at the hearing and in delivering a brief to counsel.

The case for the Secretary of State is that the apparent abandonment of delay as a ground for opposing the Secretary of State's application to set aside the order of 22 February and the failure after the hearing before *Ferris* J to make that application promptly, notwithstanding that expense was being incurred and was known to be being incurred by the Secretary of State in preparing for the substantial hearing, founds an implied representation that delay would not be relied on as a ground to found an application to set aside the proceedings and that the Treasury Solicitor acted to his detriment in reliance on this implied representation.

I think the answer to that submission is that after the appeal against the decision from Mr Registrar *Buckley* had been lodged, the Secretary of State's application was in effect in abeyance. On 25 January, PK made it clear that an application to set aside the proceedings would be made if the appeal failed and the application was in fact made some ten days after the appeal had been dismissed by His Honour Judge *Moseley*. If the Secretary of State had then been anxious not to incur further expense until it was clear that an application to set aside the proceedings of which he had been duly warned would not be pursued, he could and should have made further enquiry of PK.

I have therefore, after careful and anxious consideration, come to the conclusion that this application must succeed. I will invite counsel, on consideration of this judgment, to address me on a more convenient occasion as to whether any consequential orders are needed and on the question of costs.

(*Order accordingly*)

A
Re a Company No. 001126 of 1992.

Chancery Division (Companies Court).
Lindsay J.
Judgment delivered 4 March 1993.

B
Unfair prejudice petition — Whether and extent to which company's participation in unfair prejudice petition was proper — Whether court would sanction such participation in advance — Companies Act 1985, sec. 459.

This was an application by a company in relation to which a petition under sec. 459 of the Companies Act 1985 had been presented, seeking directions permitting it actively to participate in the sec. 459 petition, and as to the costs it would thus incur. The petitioner did not oppose the company's "passive" participation in the petition, consisting of discovery, attendance at judgment, and activities of that kind.

C
Held, making no order on the company's application:

1. Leaving aside a case where a company's active participation in the petition and payment of its costs were ultra vires (being beyond the powers conferred by its objects clause), there was no rule that active participation and expenditure by a company in a sec. 459 petition relating to its affairs was necessarily improper.

D
2. The test was whether such participation and expenditure was necessary or expedient in the interests of the company as a whole. There was a heavy onus on a company to satisfy the court with evidence of the necessity or expedience in the particular case. Advance approval by the court of such participation and expenditure was very unlikely in the absence of the most compelling circumstances proven by cogent evidence.

E
3. The company's evidence did not demonstrate that the board's decision to participate had been arrived at by an honest and reasonable board properly looking to what was necessary or expedient in the interests of the company as a whole. Conversely, there was no sufficient case on the evidence that the company, as a party to the petition, should be denied the ordinary liberty to engage in intra vires activities of such kinds as had been duly resolved upon by its board. But if the company did engage in those activities then it did so entirely at its own risk and at the risk of the directors who resolved that it should do so.

F
The following cases were referred to in the judgment:

Beddoe, Re. Downes v Cottam [1893] 1 Ch 547.
Company No. 004502 of 1988, Re a, ex parte Johnson [1991] BCC 234.
Crossmore Electrical and Civil Engineering Ltd, Re (1989) 5 BCC 37.
Hydrosan Ltd, Re [1991] BCC 19.
Kenyon Swansea Ltd, Re (1987) 3 BCC 259.
Land and Property Trust Co plc, Re (No. 2) [1993] BCC 462.
G
Milgate Developments Ltd, Re [1991] BCC 24.
Pickering v Stephenson (1872) LR 14 Eq 322.
Taylor & Anor v Pace Developments Ltd [1991] BCC 406.
Wallersteiner v Moir (No. 2) [1975] QB 373.

Robert Hildyard (instructed by Freshfields) for the applicant company.

Martin Moore (instructed by Mishcon de Reya) for the respondent petitioner.

H
JUDGMENT

Lindsay J: I have before me an application in which the company — the affairs of which are said in a petition under sec. 459 of the *Companies Act* 1985 to have been conducted in an unfairly prejudicial manner — seeks directions permitting it actively to participate in that sec. 459 petition, and as to the costs it would thus incur.

The sec. 459 petition which was presented in February 1992 has not been advertised.
I shall, accordingly, avoid detail which might identify the company and shall refer to the
parties concerned as "the company", "the petitioner" and "the respondents", of whom,
leaving aside the company, there are 11 principal ones and, if their subsidiaries are
included, many more.

It is very far from being a usual sec. 459 petition (if such a thing can be said to exist). It
is unusual as to the number of parties involved, the size of the parties involved, the
amounts previously brought in or procured to be brought in to the company by the
parties (which amount to literally hundreds of millions of pounds), as to the size of the
company's undertaking, the nature of the relief sought and the complexity of the
transactions which the court will need to study.

The petition is 49 pages long. Points of defence of the principal respondents are 83
pages long. The points of reply occupy 20 pages. The particulars of the petition already
delivered take up 34 pages. Even at an earlier stage when the pleadings were not
complete, as they are now, *Vinelott* J, when dealing with a question relating to the same
petition on 24 July 1992, had described the transactions involved as "very complex" — a
conclusion with which no one could disagree. I am indebted to him for his summary of
the matter, which itself took some 12 pages of transcript. Nothing would be gained by
my attempting a fresh summary of my own, so I shall proceed as if *Vinelott* J's summary
is to be taken as read into this judgment. Even so, I shall need briefly to refer to some of
the allegations in the petition and to some of the defences to them in order to make the
rest of the judgment intelligible.

The company was incorporated in the latter half of the 1980s. The petitioner, a
corporate investor, became interested in the company as the holder of a proportionately
small number of shares in it when its participation was invited by a consortium of the
company's principal investors, a group small in number but considerable in their
resources and which hold the majority of the company's shares.

The development of the company's business absorbed far greater outlay than had at
first been thought likely. Nor, for various reasons, was it profitable as greatly or as soon
as had first been thought likely. The company thus needed refinancing more than once
and elaborate arrangements were made by, inter alios, the company, by its board, under
which the business of the company be shifted to another company on certain terms,
including underwriting, substantial loans and the issue of various classes of shares —
which arrangements (the petitioner says) have worked, and indeed were intended to
work, unfairly to its prejudice and to the prejudice of other shareholders in the minority.
The outcome of the complex arrangements, says the petitioner, has been that the
company has become a holding company with its erstwhile business and its worth
effectively concentrated in the small consortium of shareholders and all this has been
procured, says the petitioner, by unfair means. Those unfair means, says the petitioner,
have included arrangements made by the company which have been bogus in the sense
of their not being truly commercially necessary or desirable and not being intended to
have taken effect according to their tenor, but which were devised to exclude, inter alios,
the petitioner from the participation to which it alleges it was entitled.

These arrangements entered into by the company were made by a board of directors
which has either been dominated by appointees of members of the consortium or, later,
which has consisted solely of persons appointed by such members.

The relief which the petitioner seeks, with one minor exception, does not require the
company itself to do anything or, indeed, to omit doing anything but does seek that
shares held by the controlling consortium ("the consortium") shall be offered amongst
the other shareholders in the company on specified terms intended, says the petitioner,
to redress the unfairness which the consortium has procured.

A   It is important to note that it is admitted that at present, and for some time past, the board of the company has been comprised *solely* of persons appointed by the members of the consortium, or their subsidiaries, or by persons who are alternates for such persons.

In their points of defence the consortium says that in negotiating the terms for the company's refinancing its directors acted honestly and reasonably and in the best interests of all the company's shareholders.

B   It will be in issue in the petition how far and to what extent the company consulted and acted upon the advice of its own independent solicitors, accountant and merchant bankers in the refinancing arrangements. It will be in issue whether there were true negotiations between the company and the consortium or whether the consortium laid down stringent terms for their involvement in the refinancing which the company's board, as consortium nominees, simply accepted without testing the real need therefor

C   and without considering, or sufficiently considering, the effects thereof on minority shareholders.

There is no doubt but that the directors of the company, who are, in general, persons holding senior posts in their respective appointors, members of the consortium, will be giving evidence at the hearing of the petition, which is not expected to be before 1995. If they are not giving evidence for the consortium respondents they will be giving evidence,

D   perhaps under subpoena, at the behest of the petitioner. The company's papers will be opened to both sides on discovery. The advisers to the company, subject perhaps to questions of legal privilege where appropriate, are also likely to be required to give evidence, either voluntarily or on subpoena.

One way or another the company will be closely involved in the litigation to which it is, in any event, a necessary party under the appropriate *Companies (Unfair Prejudice*

E   *Applications) Proceedings Rules* 1986. Indeed, it has already spent over £35,000 at its solicitors simply on preparing *part* of its list for discovery.

It is against that background that Mr Hildyard, for the company, seeks the following relief:

"1. An order that the company be at liberty, if so advised:

F   (i)   to serve points of defence to such of the allegations in the petition (including those in para. 73–77 thereof) as relate to the conduct and direction of the company's affairs by its directors in the discharge of their functions as such;

     (ii)   to adduce oral evidence at the trial of the petition provided that the statement of any witness to be adduced by the company is exchanged not later than six months before trial; and that, unless otherwise ordered, the statement do stand as the evidence in chief of the witness at trial;

G   (iii)   to be represented by counsel at the trial of the petition.

2. An order as to the costs of the company's participation in the proceedings, and also in relation to discovery and inspection, as follows:

     (a)   that the directors of the company be at liberty to pay out of the funds of the company such costs on the indemnity basis, as defined in RSC, O. 62, r. 15;

H   (b)   that such costs be costs in the petition, to be taxed (if not agreed) on the indemnity basis (as so defined) and (failing other agreement) paid by whichever party or parties to the petition shall be directed to pay such costs by the judge at trial."

The expression "such costs" in the last line of para. 2(b) of the notice of motion, it is accepted, means the costs of the petition.

British Company Cases

A

I do not understand Mr Moore, for the petitioner, to oppose the company's consulting its own solicitors and, if necessary, counsel as to its discovery or to oppose its incurring costs in that way, although he would wish later to be able to query the propriety of the amount spent. Nor, I think, does he oppose the relatively passive role which any company involved in sec. 459 proceedings is likely to play and which is likely to consist of attendance at judgment so as to ensure the company is able to contribute to the framing of an appropriate order. Activity of that kind, which, with discovery by the company, when appropriate, I will call "passive participation", is not for the moment in issue.

B

Mr Hildyard contemplates an active role for the company. Thus, broadly stated, two questions arise on the motion. Firstly, should the company be given liberty *actively* to participate in the petition? Secondly, should some, and if so what, advance provisions be made in connection with its costs of that active participation? Mr Moore opposes the company on both questions. All respondents other than the company have either indicated support for the company's application or neutrality or, having been given the opportunity to make representations, have not attended to do so.

C

I have been referred to a number of authorities which deal with the subject of a company's involvement in or expenditure upon contests between their shareholders. Because later cases tend to refer to rather than to examine it, I shall need to look in some detail at the first in the series of cases to which I was referred: *Pickering v Stephenson* (1872) LR 14 Eq 322. It was a minority shareholder's action brought by the holder of some shares in the Ottoman Railway, an anonymous partnership ("the company"). It was incorporated under the laws of Turkey. The defendants were the individuals who were members of its general council, in effect its board, and the company itself. Letters had been written to the British Secretary of State for Foreign Affairs by Mr Ellissen, the secretary of what might nowadays be called a shareholders' action group. The letters were strongly condemnatory of the company's board. The company resolved in general meeting, but merely as a matter of expression of opinion, to take strong measures to put a stop to the activities of the shareholders' action group and in consequence not the company itself but the individuals on its board instituted proceedings for criminal libel against Mr Ellissen.

D

E

The criminal libel proceedings had not succeeded, despite a number of hearings, and the libel case was still pending when the matter was heard before Vice-Chancellor *Wickens*. The company had, in general meeting, approved expenditure, including money spent to date on the criminal libel proceedings against Ellissen. Some of those costs had already been paid by the time the matter was before the Vice-Chancellor. Some were intended to be paid in the future.

F

The plaintiff shareholder, who engaged Mr Lindley QC, as he then was, claimed on behalf of himself and all shareholders, save the defendants, that the costs of the criminal libel proceedings were not chargeable to the company and that it was beyond the power of any general meeting to burden the company with such costs.

G

In the absence of evidence as to the laws of Turkey the matter proceeded as if regulated by English law. Mr Lindley argued that the payment of the costs of the individuals who made up the board (not the company's costs) in the libel proceedings was ultra vires the company and that no resolution could make it intra vires. The libel was, he said, against individuals, the directors, not on the company itself, and did not touch the company in its corporate capacity. The costs paid, and intended to be paid, were not the company's costs but the directors' costs. Whilst it would be regular for a company to defend itself if attacked in its commercial character it could not spend money on any litigation not strictly within the objects for which the company was created. The plaintiff thus sought repayment of what had already been paid and an

H

A   injunction to restrain further payment. The defence was that what Mr Ellissen had done was beneficial to the company and that it could not be bad or ultra vires to do something ending in such advantage to the company.

It happened that Mr Ellissen was a shareholder in the company but that was fortuitous and irrelevant to Mr Lindley's argument. The Vice-Chancellor held that the plaintiff was substantially right in its contention and that the payment was "ultra vires of the majority". The Vice-Chancellor did not disturb payments already made, either those

B   before or after Pickering had launched his proceedings, but restrained further payments. The plaintiff was denied his costs.

It is far from easy to know what to make of the holding that the payment was ultra vires because the distinction now generally observed between ultra vires in the strict sense and in the broad sense is not clearly visible in that case. The strict sense in common usage denotes corporate capacity. Ultra vires in the strict sense thus meaning beyond

C   both the powers conferred by the objects clause and any further powers necessarily incidental thereto. In the broad sense ultra vires means abusive exercise of power; the activity, whilst being within the letter of such powers, nonetheless is an abuse of them. Activity which is ultra vires in the broad sense can, in appropriate circumstances, be cured of its vice by the unanimous approval of all shareholders.

The Vice-Chancellor asked himself whether the payments in issue were so inconsistent

D   with the objects and spirit of the company that no majority could bind the minority. He refers, at the top of p. 341, to the question being independent of the size of the majority. At p. 340 he had made the point that the powers, however absolute in terms, are to be construed as subject to an inherent restraint that they are to be exercised in subjection to the special purposes of, in effect, the memorandum of association. Moreover, he did not require the directors to repay even the costs the company had paid after Pickering's suit had begun. Such a conclusion is more consistent with an examination of vires in the

E   broad sense. So also he was careful to point out at p. 338 that the resolution of the company in general meeting which might otherwise have been said to have authorised what the directors had done was not a true resolution. "This, it will be understood," he said, "was a mere expression of opinion and not a formal resolution" — a point that would have been irrelevant to an inquiry into vires in the strict sense.

However, in his reply Mr Lindley QC had emphasised that on a strict construction of

F   what was, in effect, the objects provision, the relevant article, art. 40, did not authorise the payments in question. When that is coupled with the Vice-Chancellor's response that Mr Lindley's argument had been substantially right I see *Pickering* as being a decision that in the light of the specified objects of that company the payments made and proposed were ultra vires the company in the strict sense.

That conclusion colours my approach to the passage at the foot of p. 340, which, if I am right in saying the case is relating to vires in the strict sense, becomes obiter. What

G   the learned Vice-Chancellor there said was:

> "It seems to me that where a *quasi* partnership of this sort is divided into a majority and minority who differ on the question of internal administration, and litigation results from the difference, it is contrary to the spirit of the partnership to pay the expense of the litigation out of the general fund."

The defamation proceedings to which, of course, the company had not been party,

H   had not, it seems to me, resulted from a difference between the views of the majority and a minority but rather from Ellissen having chosen to express those differences in a manner that was, at least arguably, a criminal libel and not a libel against the company but against individuals on its board. However, I take it from the reference to its being only "contrary to the spirit" that payments of the kind there in issue should be borne by the general fund that there was not seen by the Vice-Chancellor to be any overriding principle to that effect which could not be excluded by express provision or necessary implication or, I suggest, by appropriate surrounding circumstances.

I do not see it as possible to derive from *Pickering* as a matter of ratio that even where such activity or such a payment would be intra vires in the strict sense it could, nonetheless, *never* be proper for a company either to intervene or take part, on one side or another, in what was otherwise a dispute only between its shareholders, nor that it should *never* bear its own costs out of its own general funds were it to do so. The Vice-Chancellor had spoken of it being contrary to the spirit of *the* partnership, which points to his looking to the particular case in front of him.

However, the passage I have cited is powerful obiter which suggests that even where the vires in the strict sense would permit such intervention or outlay it would be against the spirit, though not then against the letter, to do so and that, accordingly, an onus would always be on those who sought to exercise the power to show that it was indeed being used bona fide for the purposes of the company. In effect, the exercise of the power in such a way will be taken to be abusive unless and until specifically justified.

There is a long gap in time till the next case cited, *Re Kenyon Swansea Ltd* (1987) 3 BCC 259. *Vinelott* J had before him an application to strike out a sec. 459 petition on the ground that it disclosed no cause of action. The application failed. However, the company had incurred considerable expense in retaining solicitors, filing evidence and instructing counsel to oppose the application. *Vinelott* J said at p. 265:

> "I can see no possible justification for this course. The directors concerned no doubt have very strong feelings as to the person they would like to see in control of the company and able to appoint and remove its directors including themselves. But they are not entitled at the expense of the company to take part in a dispute as to whether (one director's) shares should be compulsorily acquired by (another director) or by the company. I have not heard argument as to the order I should make in relation to the costs incurred by the company."

He reserved the costs to be dealt with later and no report tells what became of them.

Whilst *Pickering* was not cited to *Vinelott* J, I see his case as not inconsistent with my view, derived from *Pickering*, that even where a company's active participation is intra vires in the strict sense an exercise of the power will be taken to be abusive unless specifically justified.

Next comes *Re Crossmore Electrical and Civil Engineering Ltd* (1989) 5 BCC 37. There the question arose on an application by a company, which was the object of a winding-up petition, for relief under sec. 127. The question arose whether it would, under the sec. 127 order, be entitled to pay costs which it was incurring as the nominal party to a sec. 459 petition that was running at the same time. *Hoffmann* J held that expenditure in defending the sec. 459 petition would not be in the ordinary course of business and that the order authorising payments under sec. 127 should expressly state that to be the case. He said, at p. 38G:

> "It is a general principle of company law that the company's money should not be expended on disputes between the shareholders: see *Pickering v Stephenson* (1872) LR 14 Eq 322."

There is no indication that the board of that company, or independent members of the board, had sought to justify active participation in the sec. 459 petition or outlay in that behalf by filing evidence on the point. There is some indication, at p. 38G, where the judge says: "I am, however, asked to clarify in advance one question which may be a matter of potential dispute", that the sec. 459 costs question was seen only as a future difficulty rather than a present one.

A

It would have sufficed for *Hoffmann* J's purposes of concluding that sec. 459 outlay was not in the ordinary course of a company's business that it had not been sought to show by evidence that on the facts of that case it was expenditure bona fide for the purposes of the company. Indeed, on the facts of that case (which, it would seem, involved only two shareholders with the dispute being, in substance, between the two of them) it is likely to have been quite impossible to argue that the expenditure was indeed bona fide for the purposes of the company. *Hoffmann* J did not purport or need to extend *Pickering* and his decision is consistent with my reading of that case.

B

Next is *Re Hydrosan Ltd* [1991] BCC 19, a decision of *Harman* J. In the course of a subsequent sec. 459 petition the petitioner had sought discovery of the solicitors' narrative bills in relation to the company's own involvement in an earlier sec. 459 petition. The petitioner hoped to show, by reference, inter alia, to *Crossmore*, that in funding a shareholder's defence to the earlier sec. 459 petition there had been a misapplication of company funds by the respondents to the second 459 petition. Having had *Crossmore* put to him, *Harman* J went on, at p. 20F:

C

> "Thus one starts with the proposition that any material which will show that the company had been funding the defence of shareholders to a sec. 459 petition must show a wrongful application of the company's funds."

He was there speaking not of a company's funding of its own costs in a sec. 459 petition, as did *Crossmore*, but rather with a funding by a company of a shareholder's costs. A little later on, at pp. 21–22, *Harman* J cited the passage from *Kenyon Swansea* and said of *Vinelott* J's decision as follows:

D

> "the judge said — and I wholly agree with him — it could not properly be an action where the company's finances should be employed to influence the result of the claim."

E

Harman J was simply ruling on whether documents relating to the earlier sec. 459 petition were documents in an action brought by the company against a shareholder and hence were within a recognised class of documents excepted from discovery as between the company and that shareholder. He ruled that for the purposes of that exception the earlier sec. 459 papers were not to be regarded as being in proceedings brought by the company against the shareholder. I cannot think he was intending, nor did he need, to rule that in no case, even where such a course was intra vires in the strict sense, could it ever be proper for a company to participate in, or to bear its own costs of participation in, a sec. 459 petition directed to its own affairs.

F

Next among the authorities is *Re Milgate Developments Ltd* [1991] BCC 24. *Milgate* was, in some respects, close to the converse of the present case as there instead of, as here, the company asking for liberty to participate in a sec. 459 petition and for special provision for its costs of doing so, the petitioner under sec. 459 was there seeking to restrain the other shareholders from procuring that the two companies involved should actively participate. At p. 28E, Mr *Edward Nugee* QC, sitting as a deputy judge of the Chancery Division, said:

G

> "There is in my judgment nothing in the petition or in the evidence filed by the petitioner which suggests that there is any possibility of the companies being affected by the dispute between the shareholders to any greater extent than was the case in *Re Kenyon Swansea Ltd* or *Re Crossmore Electrical and Civil Engineering Ltd*. Notices of motion were given three weeks ago and if there had been any justification for the companies taking an independent part in the litigation, which is not apparent from the evidence filed by the petitioner, there was ample opportunity for the individual respondents or even the companies themselves to file evidence stating what that justification was. On the evidence

H

before me I can see no possible justification for the companies incurring further expense in taking part in this dispute . . ."

He thus granted the injunction sought. By his references to the evidence and to the extent to which the companies were possibly affected by the shareholders' dispute the deputy judge plainly had in mind not that there was any total prohibition but that on certain facts a proper case could be made for a company's intervention and expenditure.

The last of the authorities on this part of the case was *Re a Company No. 004502 of 1988, ex parte Johnson* [1991] BCC 234. So far as concerned an application before him by the petitioner under a sec. 459 petition to restrain other directors from procuring the company itself to be represented on the petition *Harman* J said, at p. 235H, that apart from its involvement in discovery, and in a case where a purchase by the company of its own shares was in issue, its involvement in that, a company itself had,

"no business whatever to be involved in the sec. 459 petition on the principle that, as was said in *Pickering v Stephenson*, the company's moneys should not be expended on disputes between shareholders."

After referring to the cases I have already dealt with *Harman* J said, at the foot of p. 236:

"Such expenditure is a misfeasance, there is no excuse for it law and it is not a question of an arguable case being raised showing that it may be right to permit misfeasances."

The evidence before him indicated that the directors' own report spoke of the company having spent money on the *defence* of the sec. 459 petition and that the company in that case had no interest in the outcome of the petition. Counsel indeed there conceded that part at least of the company's expenditure was wrongful. Reference is made to admitted misfeasances. *Harman* J was not saying, and had no need to say, that it could never be right for a company actively to participate, only that on the facts of that case it was not right.

He then turned to the application by the company, that it should "in blanket form" be given approval for its separate representation on the petition. Leaving aside the "blanket form" this and the next part of *ex parte Johnson* are the only reported cases truly close to the applications now before me. When *Harman* J said that the order sought was not one which he thought any court would be likely to make under sec. 459 he was referring, I think, to the excessive width of the "blanket form". As earlier, I do not read him as saying that active participation of a company under sec. 459 was necessarily and in all cases improper. He would not have referred, as he did at p. 239H, to a test of whether such representation would be necessary or expedient in the interests of the company as a whole had the test been redundant, as it would have been if, even if it were passed, the representation thus seen as necessary or expedient would nonetheless be improper. Indeed, when he turned to the company's application for liberty to pay its sec. 459 costs out of its assets, he indicated there could be company costs, beyond those of what I have called passive participation, which may be expedient or necessary in the interests of the company as a whole and hence which could be properly incurred and be properly payable out of a company's assets. He was, in effect, making the point Mr Lindley had made in argument in *Pickering*, that if a company was truly touched in its corporate capacity, if it was affected in its commercial character, it could be proper for the company to become involved in what was otherwise a mere dispute between its shareholders. *Harman* J said at p. 240C (with my emphasis):

"*In advance*, one cannot say whether any of the fees here referred to are such costs or not, and, in my judgment, this order is one which I would not consider could be made in a matter such as this, a sec. 459 petition."

A   Those, then, are the authorities to which I was referred. As a body they suggest to me the following.

Firstly, that there may be cases (although it is unlikely nowadays when wide objects clauses are the norm) where a company's active participation in or payment of its own costs in respect of active participation in a sec. 459 petition as to its own affairs is ultra vires in the strict sense.

B   Secondly, leaving aside that possible class, there is no rule that necessarily and in all cases such active participation and such expenditure is improper.

Thirdly, that the test of whether such participation and expenditure is proper is whether it is necessary or expedient in the interests of the company as a whole (to borrow from *Harman* J in *ex parte Johnson*).

Fourthly, that in considering that test the court's starting point is a sort of rebuttable
C distaste for such participation and expenditure, initial scepticism as to its necessity or expediency. The chorus of disapproval in the cases puts a heavy onus on a company which has actively participated or has so incurred costs to satisfy the court with evidence of the necessity or expedience in the particular case. What will be necessary to discharge that onus will obviously vary greatly from case to case.

Fifthly, if a company seeks approval by the court of such participation or expenditure *in advance* then, in the absence of the most compelling circumstances proven by cogent
D evidence, such advance approval is very unlikely.

Mr Moore would have me add that such participation and expenditure should never be approved in advance, or at all, unless there is a clear demonstrable and unchallenged independence between the company and the protagonists under sec. 459. Obviously, where that independence is present the task of satisfying the tests I have described is likely to be easier than in those cases where it is absent, but I am reluctant to specify that
E independence as either a sufficient or a necessary condition. It is not sufficient because even truly independent board members can be swayed by partisan or other considerations they should not have entertained. It is not necessary because even where that independence is lacking, directors, for all their lack of independence, could arrive at a true view of what was necessary or expedient in the interests of the company as a whole and might even arrive at that view for the right reasons.

F   Finally on the law, I comment that I do not see this analysis as opening floodgates such that the courts will be swamped with applications of the kind before me. In the vast majority of sec. 459 petitions there will, I think, be no real prospect of satisfying the tests I have mentioned and applications of the kind before me will be so hopeless as not even to be embarked upon.

I now turn to applying that law to this case.

G   First, whilst I have not seen the company's objects clause, it is expressly not argued that the company's active participation or expenditure in that behalf is ultra vires in the strict sense.

Next I ask whether the company satisfies the onus of proving by cogent evidence that its proposals are, to a compelling degree, necessary or expedient in the interests of the company as a whole. The company's evidence, at para. 12 of the first affidavit of the company secretary, is that it is the considered view of the board, having taken the advice
H of leading counsel, that it should participate in the petition. The directors' considered view, he says, is that the position and interests of the company should be stated independently and that it is inappropriate that justification of the company's conduct in the refinancing should be left to the consortium when in fact the company's affairs were conducted by its directors acting on independent legal and financial advice in what they considered to be the interests of the company as a separate legal entity and in the

interests of the members as a whole. In his second affidavit, the company secretary says the company's course of conduct generally was decided by the board acting on independent financial and legal advice. It will be remembered that the present board is comprised solely of persons appointed by the respondent consortium members or by their subsidiaries or alternates to those persons. In that circumstance I do not see the company's evidence as satisfying the onus I have described. I do not know what independent legal or financial advice was given to the board as to its participation in the petition, nor what facts were put to the advisers on the subject. I do not know the degree to which the board members studied that advice before concluding as they did. I do not know whether they acted exactly as it is suggested they should. Beyond the brief summary given I do not know what reasons emerged in the course of the board's deliberations for its decision that it should participate.

I can quite see that the company might not wish to disclose information of this kind to the petitioner but it is, after all, the company that has chosen to go by notice of motion with the petitioner as respondent rather than by a process analogous to a *Re Beddoe* application, as would have been more appropriate (at any rate in the first place) had it wished both to disclose the advice it received to the court and yet to have retained confidentiality of the subject. I do not know either how far, if at all, when considering the necessity or expedience of its participation, the company had in mind that its officers and advisers are all likely to be able to make any relevant evidence of theirs available to the court by way of evidence given voluntarily or under subpoena.

I am not ruling that the company's position here is so far from satisfying the onus that I have mentioned that an application of the present kind, even if renewed on further evidence, could never succeed. I am saying that, given the close relationship between the board and the respondent consortium members, it is not enough merely to assert that it is the board's view, having taken the advice of leading counsel, that it should participate in the petition. If the onus is to be discharged the court will need to be satisfied not merely that the board's decision to participate *could* have been, but that it *was*, arrived at by an honest and reasonable board properly looking to what was necessary or expedient in the interests of the company as a whole.

Mr Hildyard makes an attractive case for the need for the company to participate. However, in a case such as this where intervention by the company could so easily be motivated either by a wish to advance the consortium respondents or to hinder or increase the burden on the petitioner, what is relevant is not argument, however attractive, as to what the board *could* properly have had regard to in coming to its conclusion but rather what the board *did* have regard to in coming to its conclusion. As to that, in my judgment, the facts so far proved fall short.

If, then, I feel unable on the present evidence to approve the active participation of the company then I cannot give the company the relief it seeks under para. 2(a) of the notice of motion, which is, in effect, that expenditure on participation would be no misfeasance. On my view of the law, as I have said, such approval in advance is likely to be given only upon proof by cogent evidence of the most compelling circumstances. Mr Moore argues that there can never be any such approval in advance. I see that as too extreme. It could lead to directors who honestly and reasonably believe, for good reason, that active participation was necessary in the commercial interests of a company not sanctioning it for fear that at the end of a long and expensive petition they might be made personally liable for massive costs. I thus see a need for some mechanism, by analogy with *Re Beddoe* applications, under which, when the evidence aspires to the standard I have indicated, advance approval can be given. But the evidence so far adduced is, in my judgment, far short of the necessary standard. On that footing I need

A say nothing as to Mr Moore's argument and Mr Hildyard's counter-argument as to the indemnity basis mentioned in para. 2(a).

As for para. 2(b), even were the company actively to participate, the trial judge may have good reason to wish to order that some or all of its costs should be borne otherwise than by the party or parties who shall be directed to pay the costs of the petition, even supposing some one or more persons are directed to pay the costs of the petition and that they are indeed parties. I appreciate that in some cases, of which *Wallersteiner v*
B *Moir (No. 2)* [1975] QB 373 is an example, justice cannot be done unless some specific advance provision is made as to costs.

I thus shrink from using the word "never", but I cannot see the present case as one in which justice cannot be done without such an order and I see no reason to fetter the broad discretion as to costs which the trial judge should have.

C I thus do not grant relief in terms of para. 2(b) of the notice of motion.

Coming back to para. 1, it asks merely for "liberty". The company is a necessary party under the rules. Company law apart, it is no abuse of process that it should actively participate. Coming on to company law, so long as, as must be taken to be the case, its participation is intra vires there is no overriding principle such that its participation is necessarily and in all cases wrongful. No injunction has been sought to restrain its participation or to restrain its directors from causing or procuring its representation and
D even if there was the company or directors would then, if the injunction was granted, have the benefit of a cross-undertaking in damages. Whilst the evidence so far filed on the point has failed to satisfy me that the board's decision that the company should participate was a decision that participation was necessary or expedient in the interests of the company as a whole, neither have I yet the material to rule that it was not. I thus do not see that the company needs to be given liberty actively to participate. It already
E has it. I must emphasise that I am neither approving nor disapproving of the activities contemplated in subpara. (i)–(iii) of para. 1. I am merely ruling that no sufficient case has as yet been put on evidence such that the company, as a party to litigation, should be denied the ordinary liberty to engage in intra vires activities of such kinds as shall have been duly resolved upon by its board, to whom the conduct of its management has been given.

F If the company does engage in those activities then it does so entirely at its own risk and the directors who resolved that it should do so are equally unprotected by my decision. They may, I know not, be susceptible to misfeasance proceedings or under the broad jurisdiction, as it is now seen to be, under which non-parties, including directors, may be made liable to pay the costs of the company (see *Taylor v Pace Developments* [1991] BCC 406 (CA) and *Re Land and Property Trust Co plc (No. 2)* [1993] BCC 462
G (CA)). In neither of those cases, for differing reasons, was an order made that the directors should bear their company's costs but the jurisdiction to require them to do so was not doubted. As to that I say nothing further. The company has the liberty it seeks not by way of any order of mine but simply because no application is made on adequate evidence such as would entitle me to deprive the company of the liberty it ordinarily has.

I thus conclude my judgment by making no order on para. 1 of the notice of motion and hence no order on any substantive paragraph of the notice of motion at all.

H *(Ruling accordingly)*

Re Carecraft Construction Co Ltd.

A

Chancery Division (Companies Court).
Ferris J.
Judgment delivered 18 March 1993.

> *Disqualifying unfit directors of insolvent companies — Whether court could adopt summary procedure on disqualification applications — Whether court could be satisfied that directors were unfit and that particular period of disqualification was appropriate — Company Directors Disqualification Act 1986, sec. 6.*

B

These were applications under sec. 6 of the Company Directors Disqualification Act 1986 for the disqualification of two directors of five companies all of which had gone into insolvent liquidation.

The court was asked to follow a summary procedure having regard to the limited areas of dispute on factual matters, the procedural delay which had occurred (there was a period of some two years in which little or no progress was made towards the substantive hearing of the applications) and the attitude adopted by the respondent directors.

C

The proposed summary procedure comprised the following elements in outline. There was a schedule of agreed facts. The respondents accepted that the court would be likely to find that their conduct as directors of the companies made them unfit to be concerned in the management of a company, and that the court would be obliged to make disqualification orders for the minimum period of two years. On that footing the official receiver agreed that it was not necessary for the various issues about which there was no agreement to be determined, and accepted that findings in his favour on those issues would not raise the case against either respondent into a different bracket of seriousness. In all the circumstances, including the mitigation advanced on behalf of the respondents, the official receiver was content not to submit that the case was one in which more than the minimum period of disqualification ought to be imposed. On the same footing the respondents did not submit that no disqualification order should be made, but submitted that the period of disqualification should be no longer than two years, having regard to the seriousness of the conduct complained of and various features of mitigation.

D

E

There were three issues: (1) whether the court had jurisdiction to proceed in this way, (2) if so, whether these were appropriate cases, and (3) whether, in all the circumstances, the court could be satisfied both that a disqualification order had to be made and that it should be for no longer than two years.

F

***Held*, answering the questions in the affirmative and disqualifying the respondents each for two years:**

1. The court did have jurisdiction to deal with an application under the 1986 Act by a summary procedure of the kind which was proposed.

G

2. The court accepted the undisputed evidence which established unfitness within the lowest bracket. The disputed evidence did not have such a significant potential impact on the seriousness of the conduct as to require there to be a full hearing at which it could be evaluated. Therefore its existence did not make it inappropriate to deal with the cases on the summary basis proposed.

3. The finding of unfitness meant that disqualification orders had to be made. In the light of mitigating factors in each case, the periods of disqualification would each be two years.

H

The following cases were referred to in the judgment:

Cedac Ltd, Re. Secretary of State for Trade and Industry v Langridge [1990] BCC 555; [1991] BCC 148, [1991] Ch 402 (CA).

A   *Cutts v Head & Anor* [1984] Ch 290.
       Fullard, Re [1982] Fam 42.
       Net Book Agreement 1957, Re (1962) LR 3 RP 246.
       Net Book Agreement 1957, Re (No. 2) (1964) LR 4 RP 484.
       R v Newton (1982) 4 Cr App R (S) 388.
       Sevenoaks Stationers (Retail) Ltd, Re [1990] BCC 765; [1991] Ch 164.

B   William Charles and Matthew Collings (instructed by the Treasury Solicitor) for the
       official receiver.

       Marcia Shekerdemian (instructed by Shepherd Harris & Co) for the first respondent.

       Roger Kaye QC (instructed by Binks Stern) for the second respondent.

                                             JUDGMENT

C   **Ferris J:** These applications under sec. 6 of the *Company Directors Disqualification
       Act* 1986 for disqualification orders against the respondents Paul John Wilson and
       Andrew Jonathan Hayes came before me on 9 and 10 December 1992. At that hearing
       I was asked to deal with the applications in what may be described as a summary way.
       I will explain later what is meant by that. It was common ground between the parties
       that if I found that I had no jurisdiction to deal with the applications in this way, or if I
       found that these particular applications were not appropriate to be dealt with in such a
D   way, the applications would have to be adjourned for a full hearing at a later date. After
       hearing argument I concluded that I had the requisite jurisdiction and that these cases
       could properly be dealt with in exercise of it. I made a disqualification order in relation
       to each of the respondents for the period of two years, which is the minimum period of
       disqualification in a case where the court is satisfied of the matters referred to in sec. 6.
       I said that I would put my reasons for making these orders in writing and deliver them at
E   a later date, which I now do.

       So far as material sec. 6 of the 1986 Act provides as follows:

       "*Duty of court to disqualify unfit directors of insolvent companies*

       (1) The court shall make a disqualification order against a person in any case
       where, on an application under this section, it is satisfied—

F   (a)   that he is or has been a director of a company which has at any time become
             insolvent (whether while he was a director or subsequently), and

       (b)   that his conduct as a director of that company (either taken alone or taken
             together with his conduct as a director of any other company or companies)
             makes him unfit to be concerned in the management of a company.

       (2) For the purposes of this section and the next, a company becomes insolvent
       if—
G
       (a)   the company goes into liquidation at a time when its assets are insufficient
             for the payment of its debts and other liabilities and the expenses of the
             winding up,

       (b)   an administration order is made in relation to the company, or

       (c)   an administrative receiver of the company is appointed;

H   and references to a person's conduct as a director of any company or companies
       include, where that company or any of those companies has become insolvent,
       that person's conduct in relation to any matter connected with or arising out of the
       insolvency of that company."

       The applications are made in respect of the conduct of the respondents as directors of
       five companies, namely Carecraft Construction Co Ltd ("Carecraft"), Carecraft

Development Co Ltd ("CDC"), Carecraft Plumbing and Heating Supplies Ltd   A
("CPHS"), Carecraft Group Ltd ("CG"), and Carecraft Roofing Co Ltd ("CRC"). All
these companies are now in compulsory liquidation or in creditors' voluntary liquidation.
The dates of their incorporation and liquidation are set out in the following table:

Company	Incorporation date	Liquidation date
Carecraft	3 August 1984	14 November 1986
CDC	3 August 1984	25 May 1988
CPHS	9 April 1984	17 June 1986
CG	28 May 1985	14 November 1986
CRC	14 August 1984	18 November 1986

There is no doubt that the assets of each company were, at the date of its liquidation,
insufficient for the payment of its debts and other liabilities and the expenses of its
winding up. Accordingly each company became insolvent for the purposes of sec. 6 on   C
the date mentioned opposite its name in the third column of the table.

The respondent Paul John Wilson ("Mr Wilson") is a builder who traded as a sole
trader until the companies were incorporated in 1984. Upon incorporation Mr Wilson
became a director of each of the companies and he remained a director until the
commencement of the winding up of each company.

The respondent Andrew Jonathan Hayes ("Mr Hayes") is a chartered accountant.   D
He advised Mr Wilson in relation to the structure of the companies. He became a
director of each of them on 26 July 1985 (or 24 July 1985 in the case of CG) and remained
as a director until the commencement of the winding up of each company. Initially he
worked for each company only on a part-time basis, but he started to work full time for
the companies in April 1986. He was principally responsible for the accounting side of
each company's activities.

Apart from Mr Wilson and Mr Hayes there was at least one other director of each
company except CG. In the case of Carecraft there were three other directors at all
material times and in the case of CRC there were two other directors. The third director
of CPHS ceased to hold office on 14 March 1985, so that between that date and 26 July
1985 Mr Wilson was sole director and after 26 July 1985 Mr Wilson and Mr Hayes were
the only directors of CPHS.

The facts which I have stated so far were not in dispute. The further facts which I am   F
about to state in relation to each of the companies were either formally agreed or
constitute facts which the respondents were content for me to assume to be correct,
although some of them might have been disputed or qualified if I had not been willing to
proceed on the summary basis which I shall describe.

Carecraft

Carecraft carried on the business formerly carried on by Mr Wilson as sole trader. Its
statement of affairs discloses trade creditors amounting to £191,911.16, some of which
go back to March 1986. There are six other creditors whose debts amount to something
over £66,000. These include Mr Wilson and Mr Dawkins (one of the other directors of
Carecraft) who had together lent Carecraft about £50,000. All of these debts are
unsecured and there will be no dividend for unsecured creditors in the liquidation. In   H
addition Mr Wilson and Mr Hayes guaranteed the indebtedness of Carecraft to its bank,
National Westminster Bank. Mr Wilson has been required to pay more than £100,000 to
the bank in his capacity as guarantor and Mr Hayes has paid £30,000.

No annual returns or accounts in respect of Carecraft were ever filed at the Companies
Registry. Cash flow problems were being suffered in Carecraft from April 1986 at the

A latest, but trading was continued on the assumption that work in progress and trade debtors, when realised, would be sufficient to cover liabilities. Suppliers and wages were generally paid, but Crown debts accrued, some of which dated back to June 1984. No returns were made in respect of PAYE and National Insurance. On 23 July 1986 a creditor obtained judgment in the sum of £6,665 and this remained unsatisfied when Carecraft went into liquidation.

B When Mr Hayes began to work full time for Carecraft and the other companies in April 1986 the financial and other records of Carecraft were inadequate. Mr Hayes sought to bring them up to date, but he was unable to do so quickly because of the inadequacy of the books, records and accounts and because he had to deal with other pressing problems concerning Carecraft's trading and business. He also lacked input and assistance from others, including Mr Wilson who was primarily concerned with the day-to-day building business. Mr Hayes' difficulties were increased when many books

C and documents of Carecraft were destroyed or stolen as a result of a break-in at Carecraft's premises in October 1986.

Accounts were not prepared for Carecraft until October 1986. The true financial position of Carecraft was then realised. Mr Hayes promptly brought in a qualified insolvency practitioner who advised liquidation. The requisite resolution was passed on 14 November 1986.

D **CDC**

CDC traded only to a very limited extent. It operated rent-free from Carecraft's office. It was involved in only one transaction, namely the prospective purchase of a property at Enfield. A contract was entered into and a deposit of £4,500, all of which was borrowed from National Westminster Bank, was paid. When the time for completion came sufficient funds to enable CDC to complete could not be raised and the deposit was

E forfeited. The indebtedness of CDC to the bank in respect of the money lent for the deposit was covered by the directors' guarantee. It appears that at some stage CDC borrowed £28,000 from the bank on loan account, but in July 1986 this sum was, on the authority of Mr Wilson alone, transferred from CDC's account to Carecraft's account. The result appears to have been that CDC remained indebted to the bank for £28,000 but became a creditor of Carecraft for an equivalent sum. Apart from this CDC has one unsecured trade creditor in the sum of £2,627. This seems to have arisen from an

F invoicing error under which the creditor rendered its invoice to CDC instead of Carecraft, which was the party truly liable. Nevertheless the creditor successfully petitioned for the winding up of CDC on the basis of this debt.

CPHS

CPHS has unsecured trade creditors of £33,138 to whom no dividend will be paid. It

G also has preferential debts and unsecured crown debts. It lent £8,637 to Carecraft, none of which is recoverable. No annual returns or accounts were filed at the Companies Registry in respect of CPHS. The position regarding its books and records is similar to that regarding the books and records of Carecraft.

CG

CG has two unsecured trade creditors in the total sum of £2,542. No annual returns or

H accounts were filed at the Companies Registry in respect of it. The position regarding its books and records is similar to that regarding the books and records of Carecraft.

CRC

CRC has unsecured trade creditors of £5,683 to whom no dividend will be paid. It also has preferential debts and unsecured crown debts. No annual returns or accounts were filed at the Companies Registry in respect of CRC. The position regarding its books and records is similar to that regarding the books and records of Carecraft. The management of CRC seems to have been largely in the hands of a director other than Mr Wilson and Mr Hayes. This director had experience of roofing, but knew little about the management of a limited company. Mr Wilson was a director of CRC, but concentrated his efforts on Carecraft and left the management of CRC to this other director.

Some other facts have been alleged by the official receiver in relation to all the companies, but these are not agreed and would, if the application proceeded to fully contested hearings, be subject to dispute and cross-examination. I think it is neither necessary nor fair to set out these disputed facts in any detail for present purposes, but I will refer to them in general terms at a later stage.

Course of the proceedings

On 2 November 1988 the official receiver sent to Mr Wilson and Mr Hayes notice of his intention to apply for disqualification orders as required by sec. 16 of the 1986 Act. On 11 November 1988 a summons seeking such an order was issued against each respondent. These summonses were supported by reports made by the official receiver in each case on 9 November 1988. Evidence in answer was sworn by each respondent; the official receiver made a second report in reply to the affidavit of Mr Wilson; and Mr Wilson swore an affidavit in answer to certain evidence of Mr Hayes which made criticisms of him.

The two summonses which I have mentioned, although issued within the two-year period prescribed by sec. 7(2) of the 1986 Act, were issued on the tenth day after the date of the letters if the day on which the letters were sent and the day on which the summonses were issued are both included in the period, but there were only eight clear days between the letters and the issuing of the summonses.

In *Re Cedac Ltd* [1990] BCC 555, *Mummery* J held, in relation to a different application under the 1986 Act, that the ten-day period referred to in sec. 16(1) was a period of ten clear days, that the provision for a ten-day notice was mandatory, and that the summons in that case should be struck out. Nevertheless he gave leave for a new summons to be issued out of time pursuant to sec. 7(2). The judgment of *Mummery* J was given on 18 May 1990. There was an appeal and a cross-appeal. On 12 February 1991 the Court of Appeal allowed the appeal on the striking-out issue on the ground that the requirement of a ten-day notice was directory not mandatory. The question of leave to issue a new summons out of time did not therefore arise (see *Re Cedac Ltd. Secretary of State for Trade and Industry v Langridge* [1991] BCC 148).

These events had an important impact on the present cases. On 30 July 1990 the official receiver issued new summonses against Mr Wilson and Mr Hayes seeking leave, in case the existing summonses were struck out, to commence new proceedings under the 1986 Act. On 18 and 22 October 1990 respectively Mr Hayes and Mr Wilson made applications for the original summonses against them to be struck out, and on 25 October 1990 Mr Registrar *Dewhurst* made what were thought to be striking-out orders. The official receiver appealed against these orders. There was then some delay while the decision of the Court of Appeal in *Re Cedac Ltd* was awaited. There was also some confusion when doubt was cast upon precisely what the registrar had done and upon precisely what grounds he had acted. The procedural difficulties were not finally removed until orders were made by *Chadwick* J on 18 May 1992. These orders left the official receiver free to proceed with the applications made by the original summonses issued on 11 November 1988.

A   The relevance of this procedural history is that there was a period, which appears to have lasted from some time in or before May 1990 until May 1992, in which little or no progress was made towards the substantive hearing of these applications.

The summary procedure now proposed

B   Having regard to the areas of dispute on factual matters which remain in these cases, the procedural delay which has occurred and the attitude adopted by Mr Wilson and Mr Hayes, I was asked to follow a procedure which has not hitherto been adopted in cases of this kind. What was proposed can be summarised as follows.

(1)   There was presented to me a schedule of agreed facts. These were, in substance, the facts which I have already stated.

(2)   It was stated on behalf of Mr Wilson and Mr Hayes that, on the footing that I was prepared to deal with the matter as proposed, they accepted that I would be likely to find that their conduct as directors of Carecraft, taken in conjunction with their conduct as directors of CDC, CPHS, CG and CRC, made them unfit to be concerned in the management of a company. The result of my so finding would be that I would be obliged to make a disqualification order for the minimum period of two years in the case of each of them.

(3)   On this footing the official receiver stated through counsel that he did not think it necessary to press me to decide the various issues about which there was no agreement. Moreover he accepted that, even if I were to find in his favour on most or all of these issues, such findings would not raise the case against either Mr Wilson or Mr Hayes into a different bracket of seriousness. Although such findings, if made, might cause me to make a disqualification order for longer than the minimum period, the official receiver was content, in all the circumstances, including the mitigation advanced on behalf of Mr Wilson and Mr Hayes, not to submit that the case is one in which more than the minimum period of disqualification ought to be imposed.

(4)   On the same footing it was not submitted on behalf of Mr Wilson and Mr Hayes that no disqualification order at all should be made. Counsel for Mr Wilson and Mr Hayes did, however, make submissions to me to the effect that the period of disqualification should be no longer than two years. These submissions were both as to the seriousness of the conduct of Mr Wilson and Mr Hayes, as appearing from the agreed facts, and as to various features of mitigation based upon those facts and upon evidence not going directly to the conduct complained of.

(5)   It was common ground between the parties that if I were unwilling to proceed on the basis I have summarised at para. (1)–(4) and to make a disqualification order for two years only, I should make no further decision but should give procedural directions with a view to the applications coming before another judge for a full hearing.

   It appears to me that these proposals raised three issues, namely (1) whether the court has jurisdiction to proceed in this way, without requiring a full hearing; (2) if the court has such jurisdiction, whether the present cases are appropriate to be dealt with in accordance with it; and (3) whether, in all the circumstances, I can be satisfied both that a disqualification order has to be made and that it should be for no longer than two years. After hearing argument I came to the conclusion that each of these questions is to be answered in the affirmative.

Has the court jurisdiction to proceed in the way proposed?

   In order to answer this question reference must be made to the 1986 Act. Section 1 is a general provision which says that the court may, and under sec. 6 must, in certain

circumstances make a disqualification order, the scope of which is prescribed. I have   **A**
already cited the provisions of sec. 6, so far as material. By sec. 7(1) an application under
sec. 6 is to be made by the Secretary of State or, in certain cases, by the official receiver
at the direction of the Secretary of State:

> "If it appears to the Secretary of State that it is expedient in the public interest
> that a disqualification order under section 6 should be made . . ."

It is right to note also sec. 8 under which the court has power to make a disqualification   **B**
order in certain cases where a company has been investigated under specific statutory
provisions. An application for an order under sec. 8 may be made by the Secretary of
State if it appears to him from the results of the investigation,

> "that it is expedient in the public interest that a disqualification order should be
> made . . ."

-—against a person who falls within a particular description. It is clear that an application   **C**
under sec. 6 or sec. 8 is only to be made when the Secretary of State is satisfied of the
matters described in the passages which I have quoted.

Section 9 of the 1986 Act requires the court, in determining whether a person's
conduct as a director or shadow director makes him unfit to be concerned in the
management of a company, to have regard "in particular" to certain matters mentioned
in the schedule to the Act. Sections 13–15 prescribe the consequences of acting in   **D**
contravention of a disqualification order. To do so is an offence punishable by
imprisonment or a fine or both. It also gives rise to personal liability for certain debts of
any company in whose management the disqualified person became concerned. Under
the joint operation of sec. 1 and 17 the court has power to give leave to a disqualified
person to do certain things which would otherwise be prohibited by the disqualification
order made against him.

From these provisions the following conclusions emerge.   **E**

(1)   The purpose of sec. 6 of the Act is to protect the public, and in particular potential
creditors of companies, from losing money through companies becoming insolvent
when the directors of those companies are people unfit to be concerned in the
management of a company (see *Re Sevenoaks Stationers* [1990] BCC 765 at
p. 773B).

(2)   While a disqualification order is not in itself penal, it is clearly restrictive of the   **F**
liberty of the person against whom it is made, and its contravention can have
penal consequences under sec. 13 (see *Re Cedac Ltd* [1991] BCC 148 at p. 153G).

(3)   An important safeguard is provided for those against whom a disqualification
order is sought under sec. 6 by the requirement, arising from the wording of
sec. 7(1), that an application is only to be made where it appears to the Secretary
of State that it is expedient in the public interest that a disqualification order   **G**
should be made. The wording of sec. 8(1) provides an equivalent safeguard in
relation to sec. 8.

(4)   Nevertheless a disqualification order is to be made against a person under sec. 6
or sec. 8 only if (inter alia) the court is satisfied that the conduct of that person in
relation to a particular company or companies "makes him unfit to be concerned
in the management of a company". This requirement is, in effect, a condition   **H**
precedent to the making of a disqualification order (see *Re Sevenoaks Stationers*
at p. 770F; cf. in a different context *Re Fullard* [1982] Fam 42 at p. 46).

(5)   In determining whether a person's conduct makes him unfit to be concerned in the
management of a company the court is required to have regard in particular to
certain matters specified in the schedule to the Act.

A   (6)   If a disqualification order is made the period of disqualification has to be determined by the court and by no one else, subject to a maximum of 15 years in all cases and a minimum of two years under sec. 6. While guidelines have been stated in *Re Sevenoaks Stationers*, these are no more than guidelines.

B   Having regard to conclusion (3), the Secretary of State can and should cause an application for a disqualification order under sec. 6 or sec. 8 to be abandoned if it ceases to appear to him that the making of a disqualification order against the respondent to that application is "expedient in the public interest". I was told that the Secretary of State does in fact act upon this principle and I have no doubt that this is so. But the Secretary of State has no general power to compromise a claim for a disqualification order which he continues to regard as being expedient in the public interest. In particular he cannot accept an undertaking in lieu of a disqualification order, because that would not protect the public in the way that a disqualification order does by virtue of the consequences presented by sec. 13 and 15. He cannot decide that particular conduct does or does not amount to unfitness, for it is the court, not the Secretary of State, which has to be satisfied of the relevant matters. He cannot agree that matters to which regard must be had by virtue of sec. 9(1) shall be left out of account. And he cannot bargain with a respondent concerning the length of any period of disqualification, for it is the court which has to decide this, subject to the statutory limits.

C

D   In disqualification proceedings, therefore, there is no scope for the parties to reach an agreement and then ask the court to embody their agreement in a consent order. The court itself has to be satisfied, after having regard to the prescribed matters and other facts which appear to be material, that the respondent is unfit to be concerned in the management of a company; and the court itself must decide the period of disqualification if it decides to make a disqualification order.

E   Does it follow from this that the court ought to insist upon a fully contested hearing in every case under the 1986 Act? Pragmatically it would seem that the answer ought to be in the negative. It would be unrealistic for the court to disregard any admission which one party may make in respect of factual contentions advanced by the opposite party. Moreover in practical terms the court has no means to control the way in which either party conducts its case, whether in respect of the scope and definition of the charges made or disputed or in respect of the evidence which is presented in order to support or rebut the charges.

F   It was suggested in argument that a number of analogous situations exist in which a court, while needing to be satisfied of certain matters and to exercise its own discretion, has been able, in appropriate cases, to dispense with a full hearing.

    The most obvious of these, perhaps, is where an accused person pleads guilty in a criminal case. The whole purpose of the time-honoured and thoroughly entrenched practice of requiring an accused person to plead guilty or not guilty at the time of arraignment is to decide whether or not there is to be a trial. If there is a plea of guilty to a particular charge there is no need for a trial upon that charge and the court proceeds to deal with sentence. Presumably the rationale of this is that at the initial stage what the court needs to know is whether the accused person is guilty or not and an admission, in the form of an unequivocal plea of guilty, is unambiguous evidence of guilt. It may be said that unfitness to be concerned in the management of a company ought to be as susceptible to a guilty plea as the elements of a criminal charge. But unfitness has a qualitative aspect to it which is not, I think, usually present in criminal charges. Moreover difficulty arises in criminal cases where there is a plea of guilty and the court needs to know, in order to assess the seriousness of the offence for purposes of sentence, which of two or more positive versions of the facts of the offence is to be accepted. The problem is discussed in *Archbold* (1992 ed.) at para. 5-41 to 5-47. In some cases the court

G

H

will require evidence to be called to deal with the matter (see *R v Newton* (1982) 4 Cr App R (S) 388).

Another analogy is that of applications under the *Inheritance (Provision for Family and Dependants) Act* 1975 and its predecessors. It is not a perfect analogy because when the parties to such an application are of full age they can usually compromise the application in any way they think fit, including a manner which produces a result which the court could not itself have directed under the Act. When minor or unborn persons are concerned a similar compromise may be implemented with the approval of the court, and in deciding whether to give or withhold its approval to a compromise the court will not be limited by what it could itself order under the Act. There is, however, a further possibility, namely that the parties may wish the court to make an order under the Act of a kind which gives rise to little or no contention between them. In my experience this was not uncommon in the days when the Inland Revenue were not, or not always, willing to treat a variation of the terms of a will effected by agreement between the parties as being effective from the death of the deceased, but were usually bound by the terms of the legislation to treat a variation effected by order of the court within the jurisdiction conferred by legislation as being retrospective to the date of death. In such a case it would be usual for the plaintiff to open the case with moderation and to ask for provision which it was known that the defendant would not object to. The defendant would refrain from challenging the plaintiff's evidence and would indicate that if the court were minded to make the further provision asked for by the plaintiff the defendant would not resist this. In a proper case the court was, and if the procedure were resorted to nowadays still would be, willing to make the order proposed. It would need to be satisfied that the will did not make reasonable provision for the plaintiff and that the proposed provision was itself reasonable, but, given the attitude of the parties which I have assumed, there would ordinarily be no difficulty about this. The jurisdiction under the Inheritance Act and its predecessors is, however, one which has little or no element of public interest about it and it is exercisable for the benefit of deserving applicants rather than the protection of the public from mischief.

A third analogy comes from the field of competition law. Under sec. 21 of the *Restrictive Trade Practices Act* 1956 (now sec. 10 of the *Restrictive Trade Practices Act* 1976) a restriction accepted in pursuance of an agreement of a particular kind was deemed to be contrary to the public interest, and thus void and susceptible to injunctive relief, unless the court was satisfied of any one or more of specified sets of circumstances. In *Re Net Book Agreement 1957* (1962) LR 3 RP 246 certain restrictions in an agreement between members of the Publishers' Association were, after a hearing lasting more than 20 days, held not to be contrary to the public interest on the ground that the court was satisfied of various of the specified circumstances in relation to each restriction. In *Re Net Book Agreement 1957 (No. 2)* (1964) LR 4 RP 484, another agreement, containing virtually identical restrictions but made between different parties, came before the court. A procedure was followed under which (1) the Registrar of Restrictive Trading Agreements did not deliver an answer in response to the statement of case of those who were concerned to uphold the restrictions; (2) evidence in support of the restrictions was given by a short affidavit verifying the statement of case and deposing to a few other relevant matters, on which the deponent was not cross-examined; and (3) the matter was heard summarily, the registrar making no submissions against the making of the declaration which was asked for. In acceding to this procedure *Mocatta* J, giving the decision of the court, said (at p. 489):

> "Clearly the view of the registrar is important and we give much weight to it, but the court cannot rely exclusively on his view before it can be satisfied that the restrictions in the . . . . agreement are not contrary to the public interest."

A   After reading the affidavit the court made the declaration asked for, thus implicitly, if not expressly, indicating that it was satisfied of the relevant matters. A similar procedure was, to my knowledge, later followed in respect of substantially the same restrictions under the *Resale Prices Act* 1964 (see *Halsbury's Laws of England* (4th ed.), vol. 47, para. 240, note 10).

B   This, I think, is a fairly close analogy. The *Restrictive Trade Practices Act* 1956, like its successors, was passed to protect the public interest against anti-competitive agreements and it required the court to be satisfied of particular matters. The approach adopted by the Restrictive Practices Court shows how the court may be satisfied of those matters without requiring a full trial and without requiring the parties to contest every point. The fact that in *Re Net Book Agreement (No. 2)* the relevant matters had already been established in other proceedings does not, in my judgment, qualify the effect of the decision so far as jurisdiction is concerned. It merely resulted in it being easy for the

C   court to be satisfied of the relevant matters by evidence which was little more than formal.

No example was called to my attention of a jurisdiction in which any court has held that there must be a full trial of all potentially relevant issues, regardless of any agreement or admission of material facts. I myself can think of none. In my judgment the court does have jurisdiction to deal with an application under the 1986 Act by a

D   summary procedure of the kind which was proposed in this case.

I make four further observations. First, as the court has to be satisfied of the unfitness of the person against whom it is asked to make an order, there must be presented to the court some evidence which establishes unfitness. A mere assertion of no evidential value, or a mere admission which is unsupported by evidence, would not by itself suffice. But if there is evidence which, if accepted, will establish a particular fact, the court may,

E   in appropriate circumstances, be prepared to accept that evidence if it is not challenged by the party whose duty or interest it is to challenge it. I emphasise the word "may". Clearly the court is not bound to accept unchallenged or admitted facts about which it is not, in all the circumstances, satisfied.

Secondly, in deciding whether or not to accept a proposal that an application shall be dealt with in a summary way, the court needs to consider not only the unchallenged or admitted evidence but also the general scope of the disputed evidence. The reason for

F   this is that, although the unchallenged or admitted evidence may be enough to satisfy the court as to unfitness, the other evidence may be such that, if it were accepted, it would substantially affect the seriousness of the unfitness. This might take the case out of one of the lower brackets suggested by the Court of Appeal in *Re Sevenoaks Stationers* into a higher bracket, or it might move the case from one end of a particular bracket to the other. While the court cannot, of course, fully appraise the disputed evidence under the summary procedure, it will need to consider its potential impact. If

G   this will or may be substantial the court will, no doubt, decline to deal with the matter summarily and will direct a full hearing.

Thirdly, and by parity of reasoning, it is possible (although not perhaps all that likely, given the premise that the respondents will, in substance, be accepting their own unfitness) that the court will not be satisfied of such unfitness on the basis of the agreed or unchallenged evidence. If the court considers that the disputed evidence would not,

H   even if accepted, tip the scales in favour of a finding of unfitness it will, no doubt, dismiss the application under the summary procedure. When the position is less clear it will be necessary for directions to be given in order to lead to a full hearing.

Fourthly there is inherent in the procedure the possibility that a case which the parties hoped to have dealt with summarily will be adjourned for a full hearing. If this happens, each party may properly wish not only not to be bound by admissions or concessions made in anticipation of summary disposal but to conceal from the court which conducts the full hearing the fact that such admissions or concessions were made or proposed. It may be that there ought to be implied into any negotiations which take place a term that this is so, or that the conventional "without prejudice" rubric would cover the matter. But in order to make certain it seems to me that a party who desires that relevant statements shall only be referred to or relied upon in connection with a summary hearing and shall not be referred to or relied upon if there has to be a full hearing, would be wise to protect his position by express words. Having regard to the reasoning in *Cutts v Head* [1984] Ch 290, I do not see why this should not be effective if the chosen form of words is apt.

Are the present cases appropriate to be dealt with in accordance with the summary procedure?

I am satisfied that the evidence establishes all the facts which I have previously narrated as being undisputed, agreed or facts which the respondents are content for me to assume. This is so even in respect of facts which the respondents might have wished to challenge at a full hearing. I take the view that, in the absence of such a challenge, I am entitled to accept the evidence which supports these facts at its face value, and I do accept it.

I am satisfied also that, on the basis of these facts, the conduct of Mr Wilson and Mr Hayes as directors of the companies which I have mentioned makes them unfit to be concerned in the management of a company. I refer in particular to the failure to file annual returns and accounts; the failure to keep adequate financial and other records; the consequential failure to appreciate the true financial position of Carecraft until just before it went into liquidation; the failure to cause Carecraft to make returns in respect of PAYE and National Insurance; and the non-payment of crown debts in contrast to the payment of suppliers and wages, which is indicative of a tendency to pay creditors who were pressing for payment, or were in a position to exert pressure for payment, and to use the money due to other creditors as additional working capital. I have not attempted to arrange these factors in order of importance.

So far as the evidence which has been challenged is concerned, there is no need to rely on this in order to establish unfitness. The undisputed evidence, which I accept as I have said, establishes unfitness which comes within the lowest of the brackets referred to in *Re Sevenoaks Stationers* at p. 771H. In other words although disqualification is mandatory, the cases before me are, relatively, not very serious. In the absence of mitigation, which I shall come to, I would have thought that a three-year period of disqualification in each case would have been appropriate on the basis of this evidence.

Would the disputed evidence, if proved, cause a different view to be taken? This evidence relates mainly to the state of knowledge of Mr Wilson and Mr Hayes respectively and to matters raised by each of them in order to shift a greater degree of responsibility onto the other in partial exoneration of himself. There could be no question of this evidence, if proved, taking the case into the highest of the *Sevenoaks* brackets, namely periods over ten years which "should be reserved for particularly serious cases". Moreover I accept the view of Mr Charles, for the official receiver, that it would not take either case into the middle bracket of six to ten years which "should apply for serious cases which do not merit the top bracket". The disputed evidence, if accepted, would in my judgment at most raise the period of disqualification (subject to mitigation) to perhaps four years, or lead to a longer period of disqualification (of not more than four years) in one case and a shorter period in the other.

I take the view that the disputed evidence does not have such a significant potential impact on the seriousness of the conduct which I have to appraise as to require there to

A   be a full hearing at which it can be evaluated. Therefore its existence does not in my judgment make it inappropriate to deal with these cases on the summary basis proposed.

Am I satisfied both that a disqualification order must be made in each case and that it shall be for no longer than two years?

B   The finding of unfitness which I have made means that a disqualification order must be made for at least two years. As I have indicated, my starting point, subject to mitigation, was disqualification for three years in each case.

On behalf of Mr Wilson, Miss Shekerdemian asked me to take account of his youth and background. He left school at the age of 16. He is a builder, with no qualifications. He had no experience of running a limited company when he incorporated Carecraft at the age of 25. There is no suggestion that he acted dishonestly or for his own benefit. His remuneration from Carecraft was modest, beginning at £3,500 in 1984–85 and rising to

C   only a little over £10,000 in 1986–87. He received no remuneration from any of the other companies. He lent substantial sums to the companies all of which have been lost. He has also had to pay over £100,000 under his bank guarantee. He should be given credit for what is, in effect, a plea of guilty. The fact that this application has been hanging over his head for an unusually long time, largely due to the "ten-day notice point" which was attributable to an error or delay in the office of the Secretary of State, should also be

D   taken into account. Miss Shekerdemian also asked me to accept as an explanation of the want of financial records, although not an exoneration from responsibility for it, the fact that Mr Wilson had delegated responsibility for these to Mr Hayes.

I found that all these factors, except perhaps the last, carried some weight. In all the circumstances I took the view that the period of disqualification in respect of Mr Wilson should be two years.

E   On behalf of Mr Hayes, Mr Kaye pointed out that he too is young, having been born in 1956, and without any real experience as a company director or any experience at all as a builder. He became a director on a part-time basis and was faced with a situation in which inadequate records had been kept. In order to remedy this he became a full-time director after about nine months and, within the next ten months, brought the companies' books up to date, despite various difficulties, including a lack of input and assistance from Mr Wilson. When he realised the true position of the companies he called in expert

F   assistance and, since the liquidation, he has co-operated fully with the official receiver. He received little benefit from the companies while they were trading, and he has had to pay £30,000 under his guarantee. He will also have to pay at least some of the costs of these proceedings. He is a chartered accountant, so that the stigma of a finding of unfitness will be considerable, regardless of the period of disqualification. He may be further penalised in disciplinary proceedings brought by his professional body. Like Mr Wilson he should be given credit for a guilty plea and the fact that these proceedings

G   have been pending for a long time should be taken into account.

I found that all these points of mitigation carried some weight. In the case of Mr Hayes too I took the view that the period of disqualification should be two years.

(Order accordingly)

H

A

Re Looe Fish Ltd.

Chancery Division (Companies Court).
Jonathan Parker J.
Judgment delivered 25 March 1993.

*Director disqualification after investigation of company — Whether director
exercised power of allotment in breach of duty — Whether director was unfit
— Company Directors Disqualification Act 1986, sec. 8.*

B

This was an application by the Secretary of State for Trade and Industry under
sec. 8(1) of the Company Directors Disqualification Act 1986 for a disqualification order
against "S" on grounds of unfitness.

The application concerned the affairs of Looe Fish Ltd ("LFL"), and in particular
certain dealings with shares in LFL carried out by S while he was a director of LFL. The
Secretary of State contended that S breached his duty as a director of LFL by manipulating
the voting control of LFL so as to defeat attempts by a rival faction among the members of
LFL to gain control of the board; and that in the course of so doing he also contravened
the Companies Act 1985; and that S's conduct in this respect demonstrated that he was
unfit to be concerned in the management of a company.

C

In July 1991, a member of the Investigations Division of the Department of Trade and
Industry was authorised under sec. 447 of the Companies Act 1985 to require S to produce
documents and to give explanations. The DTI's evidence was that S was responsible
for two artificial and illegal transactions whereby he (in the second case through the
co-operation of his associate, "M") gained a temporary majority of the voting rights in
LFL to enable him to defend attempts by other shareholders, who would otherwise have
commanded a majority of votes, to wrest control of the company from him. The
transactions involved S (or M) subscribing for sufficient shares to enable them to outvote
the opposition, borrowing money to enable them to pay for such shares, procuring that
LFL deposited the money received for the shares with the original lender and subsequently
arranging for the money to be withdrawn and used by LFL to "repurchase" the shares
from S or M. (M had been disqualified by the registrar for a period of two years.)

D

E

Held, disqualifying S for a period of two years and six months from the date of the
order:

F

1. There was a clear breach of duty by S in relation to each allotment. As to unfitness,
in using the power to allot shares in the way he did, S displayed a clear lack of commercial
probity. It was not enough for him to say that he did what he did in the best interests of
LFL as he saw them. A director who chose deliberately to play fast and loose with his
powers, in order to remain in control of the company's affairs, was unfit to be concerned
in the management of a company.

G

2. As to the period of disqualification, the case was not among the most serious which
might arise under sec. 8 of the Act. Moreover, no question of insolvency arose in the case,
nor did S act out of motives of personal gain, nor did he receive any improper benefit. In
the circumstances, a period of two years and six months was appropriate. M had been
disqualified for a period of two years. M was only involved in one set of transactions,
whereas S was not only involved in both sets, he was a director who approved the
allotments in each case. Moreover, S had throughout played a far more prominent part in
the affairs of LFL than M.

H

The following cases were referred to in the judgment:

Lo-Line Electric Motors Ltd & Ors, Re (1988) 4 BCC 415; [1988] Ch 477.
Piercy v S Mills & Co Ltd [1920] 1 Ch 77.

A   Mark Cunningham (instructed by the Treasury Solicitor) for the Secretary of State.

Alexander Stewart (instructed by Murdoch Tromans, Truro) for the respondent.

JUDGMENT

Jonathan Parker J: This is an application by the Secretary of State for Trade and Industry under sec. 8(1) of the *Company Directors Disqualification Act* 1986 ("the
B   Act") for a disqualification order against the first respondent, Michael Hugh Soady ("Mr Soady"), on grounds of unfitness. I am not concerned on this application with the second respondent, Malcolm Frederick Moore, a disqualification order having been made against him under the section on 22 June 1992 by Mr Registrar *Buckley* disqualifying him for two years. Mr Moore was not represented, nor did he appear, on that occasion.

This application concerns the affairs of Looe Fish Ltd ("LFL"), and in particular certain dealings with shares in LFL carried out by Mr Soady while he was a director of
C   LFL. Put very shortly, the Secretary of State contends that Mr Soady breached his duty as a director of LFL by manipulating the voting control of LFL so as to defeat attempts by a rival faction among the members of LFL to gain control of the board; and that in the course of so doing he also contravened the *Companies Act* 1985. It is contended on behalf of the Secretary of State that Mr Soady's conduct in this respect demonstrates that he is unfit to be concerned in the management of a company.

D   Section 8 of the Act applies (inter alia) where, as here, information or documents have been obtained pursuant to a direction by the Secretary of State under sec. 447 of the *Companies Act* 1985. Section 8(1) of the Act provides that if it appears to the Secretary of State from such information or documents that:

"it is expedient in the public interest that a disqualification order should be made against any person who is or has been a director or shadow director of any
E   company, he may apply to the [High Court] for such an order to be made against that person."

Section 8(2) of the Act is in the following terms:

"The court may make a disqualification order against a person where, on an application under this section, it is satisfied that his conduct in relation to the company makes him unfit to be concerned in the management of a company."

F   The maximum period of disqualification under sec. 8 of the Act is 15 years. In contrast to sec. 6 of the Act (which specifies a minimum period of two years), no minimum period is specified in sec. 8.

Section 9(1) of the Act provides that in considering the question of unfitness the court shall have regard in particular to the matters set out in Pt. I of Sch. 1 to the Act. In this case the only relevant matter there set out is para. 1:

G   "Any misfeasance or breach of any fiduciary or other duty by the director in relation to the company."

The other items set out in Pt. I of the schedule are not material. In particular, it is not suggested that Mr Soady has received any improper benefit from LFL.

I turn next to the factual background to the present application.

LFL was incorporated on 22 March 1988 as a private company under the name Looe
H   Fish (88) Ltd (which name was changed to its present name on 12 February 1991), with an authorised capital of £100,000 divided into 100,000 shares of £1 each. Its main object (as set out in cl. 3 of its memorandum) was to carry on business as fishermen, preservers, packers, curers, processors and preparers for sale of and dealers in fish.

Article 1(a) of the articles of association of LFL incorporated Table A in the *Companies (Tables A to F) Regulations* 1985 ("Table A"), subject as thereinafter provided. In the

light of what happened later it is material to note at this stage that reg. 35 of Table A   A
(which was incorporated into the articles without variation) provides as follows:

> "Subject to the provisions of the Act, the company may purchase its own shares
> (including any redeemable shares) and, if it is a private company, make a payment
> in respect of the redemption or purchase of its own shares otherwise than out of
> distributable profits of the company or the proceeds of a fresh issue of shares."

It appears that LFL was formed following the collapse of a company called Brixham   B
& Torbay Fish Ltd, which had operated a fuel supply service to the Looe fishing fleet and
which had been the principal buyer of fresh fish on the Looe fish auction.

The first directors of LFL were Mr Hocking, Mr Newman, Mr Pengelly and
Mr Matthews. Mr Soady was appointed company secretary. Mr Soady told me that
although there was substantial support for his appointment as a director of LFL he did
not at that stage wish to accept a directorship. In April 1988, however, Mr Soady was   C
appointed "chief executive" of LFL for a period of 12 months at a salary of £20,000 for
the year (although at that stage he was not on the board) and at about the same time
Mr Cairns was appointed an additional director.

Mr Soady is now about 55 years of age. When LFL was formed Mr Soady was a full-
time fisherman and trawler owner operating from Looe. At that time he was a member
of the Looe Town Council, a member of the South West Fish Producer Organisations
management committee and a shareholder in Brixham & Torbay Fish Ltd. He had   D
also been chairman of Looe Harbour Commissioners for over 16 years. He was, and is,
a man of some standing and influence in the local fishing community.

LFL had two immediate objectives: first, to secure the port's diesel supply; and
secondly to stabilise and support fish prices for the benefit of local fishermen. The first
objective was achieved by the purchase of a diesel tank from the receiver of Brixham &
Torbay Fish Ltd. With a view to achieving the second objective in August 1988 a wholly   E
owned subsidiary of LFL, called Looe Fish (Wholesaling) Ltd ("LFW"), began trading
as a fish buyer on the Looe fish market.

In commercial terms there was an important link between the provision of fuel and
the wholesaling of fish in that the wholesale business carried on by LFW required to be
subsidised in its initial stages at least by LFL and LFL's only source of income was from
the sale of fuel. So the price of fuel supplied to the local fishermen was marked up   F
accordingly.

This resulted, over a period, in deep-seated disagreement between, on the one hand,
those members of LFL who wanted LFL to supply fuel as cheaply as possible and who in
consequence wished the wholesaling business to be restricted if not closed down and, on
the other hand, those members of LFL who considered that the wholesaling business
should be maintained at the cost of marking up the fuel price. Among tne leaders of the   G
former group of members were Mr Cairns, Mr Matthews and Mr Pengelly (and I will call
that group "the Cairns group"). Among the leaders of the latter group of members was
Mr Soady (and I will call that group "the Soady group"). The Cairns group included a
number of fishermen who sailed large fuel burning boats and it was at all material times
Mr Soady's belief that the Cairns group was acting out of self-interest in seeking a
reduction in the price of fuel at the expense of the wholesaling business. Whether or not
that was in fact the case (and whether, if it was the case, the Cairns group can be criticised   H
in any way for so acting) are not questions which I can address on this application. I am,
however, satisfied that at all material times Mr Soady held that belief.

The division between the Cairns group and the Soady group came to light in early
1989 and on 17 May 1989 an extraordinary general meeting was held at which it was
proposed by the board (as a special resolution) that LFW be offered for sale to its

A
employees. It seems that only two of the then directors (Mr Matthews and Mr Pengelly) were present. The question whether LFL should retain LFW turned into a question of confidence in the board. The resolution was lost, and Mr Matthews thereupon announced that the board would resign *en bloc*. Mr Hocking, Mr Cairns and Mr Pengelly resigned the following day. Mr Matthews resigned on 23 June 1989 and Mr Soady's brother, Mr Alan Soady, was appointed in his place.

B
Mr Alan Soady then proceeded to co-opt onto the board Mr Soady, together with Mr Dingle and Mr Sutton. Mr Sutton resigned shortly afterwards, due to a perceived conflict of interest. Mr Soady was appointed managing director with a five-year contract at £18,000 per year. In August 1989, Mr Faulkner was also co-opted onto the board. On 8 February 1990 Mr Alan Soady, Mr Dingle and Mr Faulkner resigned as directors, leaving Mr Soady as sole director. Mr Soady thereupon co-opted Mr Bussell onto the board.

C
During all this time, the disagreement between the Cairns group and the Soady group over the wholesaling business continued.

On Friday, 23 February 1990 an EGM of LFL was held, at which Cairns, Pengelly and Matthews offered to be co-opted as directors. Mr Soady, as chairman of the meeting, ruled that offer out of order. There followed what is described in the evidence, with (I suspect) considerable understatement, as a lively meeting. At one stage in the meeting

D
Mr Pengelly invited Mr Soady to resign, but Mr Soady responded that he would not break his contract with LFL no matter what pressures were brought to bear from ex-directors, who seemed to him to be out for personal gain. According to the minutes of the meeting, which were signed by Mr Soady, at the conclusion of the meeting Mr Soady asked whether any one at the meeting was in favour of selling LFW, but there was no support for such a sale.

E
On the following Wednesday, 28 February 1990, Mr Soady faxed Mr Daryl Hidson of Peter Riley & Co, LFL's accountants and auditors, asking for advice on a number of matters. It reads:

"Dear Daryl,

Reference our conversation this morning and your letter DLH/KF/L60 dated 27 February 1990.

F
(1) Can limited companies purchase shares in a company which operates under the Business Expansion Scheme, i.e. could a limited company buy shares in Looe Fish (88) Ltd.

(2) Page 3 of the Business Expansion Scheme booklet only states that one does not qualify for tax relief if one or one's relatives own more than 30 per cent of the shares, it does not say that one cannot legally own more than 30 per cent of the

G
shares in any Business Expansion Scheme company. Can one own more than 30 per cent of the shares in a Business Expansion Scheme company?

(3) Article 3 of the articles of association of Looe Fish (88) Ltd seems really subject to art. 4. The remaining shares in Looe Fish (88) Ltd were offered to shareholders pro rata to their initial issue on 7 March 1989. Very few options were taken and there still remains 48,000 of the original issue of 100,000 unissued;

H
although a few have been issued intermittently since 7 March 1989.

One would assume (subject to directors' agreement) that these intermittent issues can continue without recourse to another offer to the present shareholders.

(4) Finally, we have a request from a shareholder for a copy of the list of shareholders and their holding and also a request to view the minutes of meetings. I would appreciate a reply by fax."

On the same day Mr Hidson replied giving his answers to the various queries raised by   A
Mr Soady. In relation to the query about business expansion schemes, Mr Hidson said
that a shareholding in excess of 30 per cent in a company within such a scheme would
result in loss of tax relief. As to the allotment of further shares in LFL he said:

> "It would appear that as the remaining shares in [LFL] have been offered to
> shareholders pro rata, the directors are now able to offer shares to any person or
> company where they believe that in doing so it would be in the best of interests of   B
> [LFL]. I was unable to find any legislation regarding time statutes and the answer
> that I have given will need to be clarified by you taking the appropriate legal
> advice."

The solicitors to LFL were Caunters, the partner concerned being Mr Browning.
Mr Soady had regular dealings with Mr Browning, but on this occasion he chose not to
seek his advice in relation to the question of allotment of unissued shares in LFL.
Instead, at 9.50 am on the following day (Thursday, 1 March 1990) a special meeting of   C
the board of LFL was held, attended by Mr Soady and his co-director Mr Bussell, at
which an application by Mr Soady for the allotment to himself of 24,000 unissued shares
in LFL at par was approved. I must read the minutes of this meeting (which were signed by
Mr Soady) in full. They record that the directors present were Mr Soady, as chairman,
and Mr Bussell and that there was no agenda for the meeting. They then continue:

> "*Item 1.* To discuss a letter from Looe Fish Selling regarding the rebate system.   D
>
> It was agreed to meet with the directors of Looe Fish Selling on Wednesday,
> 7 March 1990 at an appropriate time.
>
> *Item 2. Financial situation of the company.*
>
> The financial position of the company was discussed. The weather conditions over
> the past three months having a marked effect on the wholesale operation and fuel   E
> sales reduced to a minimum level. Having laid off one of the staff and looking
> ahead to the finish of construction of the packing units, the chairman, as major
> shareholder, to protect the interests of the remainder of the shareholders would
> put a further capital injection into the company if needed by taking a further
> allotment of 24,000 £1 shares at par value. An application was submitted and
> agreed unanimously.
>   F
> *Item 3.* It was agreed that Mrs G Sammells could sell her 200 shares in the
> company to whomsoever she wished.
>
> *Item 4.* It was agreed that the register of shareholders could be inspected between
> 10 am and 12 noon any day the company was open for business. Subject to
> sec. 356(2) of the *Companies Act* 1985.
>
> There being no other business the meeting closed at 14.50 pm. (The meeting had   G
> been adjourned from 10.30 am to 2 pm.)"

The minutes were signed, as I have said, by Mr Soady.

On or about 5 March 1990 Mr Browning received from Mr Steinbach of Bond Pearce,
the solicitors acting for Cairns, Pengelly and Matthews, a request that an EGM be
convened, without the necessity for a formal requisition. Mr Soady's response to that
request, relayed through Mr Browning, was that he saw no reason to depart from the   H
procedure laid down in the Companies Act. In other words, Mr Soady refused the
request.

On 7 March 1990 Mr Browning wrote to Mr Soady informing him that Mr Steinbach
had searched the share register, but that the search had revealed only part of the
membership. Mr Browning's letter continued:

A
"I said that I did not know why this should be so as to the best of my knowledge and belief all the members' shareholdings had been duly registered in the Company's Registry, and that in any event I understood that you were arranging for Mr Cairns to be supplied with extracts from the company's share register. If you have a typed list of the present shareholdings I should be grateful if you would let me have this so that I may send on a copy to Bond Pearce as soon as possible.

B
I expect to receive a formal requisition for a meeting at this office, and when I do I will forward the same to you."

On 13 March 1990 the requisition duly arrived, delivered to Mr Browning by Mr Cairns. It was signed by 17 members (including Cairns, Pengelly and Matthews) holding between them 29,600 out of the 48,000 then issued shares in LFL — more than 61 per cent. It required the board to convene an EGM to consider a resolution that Cairns, Pengelly and Matthews be appointed directors of LFL with immediate effect.

C
On the following day, 14 March 1990, 24,000 shares in LFL were allotted to Mr Soady and a share certificate issued in respect of them. The effect of that was to reduce the proportion of the issued shares held by the requisitioners well below 50 per cent. At that stage, however, the requisitioners did not know of the allotment. Nor, for that matter, did Mr Browning. Thus, he wrote to Mr Soady on 19 March 1990, 23 March 1990 and 27 March 1990 seeking information about the issued share capital to pass on to Bond Pearce, who were seeking confirmation that the issued share capital was some £48,000.

D
On 2 April 1990 notice was sent to members of an EGM to be held on 27 April 1990.

On the same day Mr Soady wrote to Mr Browning about (among other things) the share capital, saying merely:

"The up to date position in the company is 77,900 issued and fully paid up shares as at today's date, 29 March 1990."

E
It is to be noted that he did not refer to the fact that 24,000 shares had been allotted to him.

On 20 March 1990 a sum of £24,000 had been credited to LFL's business premium account at Barclays Bank, Looe. Mr Soady's evidence is that this sum had been borrowed by him from a company called Jackson & Co Financial Services ("JFS"), of which a friend of his, Mr Dennison, was a director. On 2 April 1990 that sum was transferred to LFL's current account, and on the following day it was deposited with JFS. In the documentation before me is a letter from JFS to Mr Soady acknowledging receipt of £24,000 from LFL "for investment" at 14.5 per cent interest. I have seen no documentation relating to any loan from JFS to Mr Soady but Mr Soady told me that his recollection is that the loan was at interest at the rate of 1–2 per cent over Barclays' base rate, which at that time was 12.5 per cent. In the circumstances, it must be very unlikely that the rate of interest payable by Mr Soady to JFS was less than 14.5 per cent.

F

G
On 11 April 1990 Mr Bussell resigned as a director of LFL, leaving Mr Soady as sole director. Following Mr Bussell's resignation, Mr Soady resigned as secretary and was succeeded by Mrs Gould.

On 27 April 1990 the EGM was held. Mr Soady voted his total shareholding of 36,100 shares (including the 24,000 shares recently allotted to him) against the resolution and the resolution was duly defeated. Without the allotment of the 24,000 shares to Mr Soady, the resolution would have been passed and Cairns, Pengelly and Matthews appointed directors.

H
By this stage, as may well be imagined, feelings on all sides were running very high. Thus, it is evident from the strong language employed by Mr Soady in a letter to Mr Browning dated 21 May 1990 that he distrusted the motives of the Cairns group, who, he said, were trying to "besmirch" his name in relation to the allotment of the 24,000 shares.

On 18 July 1990 Mr Soady wrote to himself as chairman of LFL asking LFL to buy   A
back 24,000 shares out of his total holding. He concluded by asking himself to discuss
this proposal with himself (he being the sole director) at the next board meeting. Given
the terms of the minute of the special board meeting of 1 March 1990 (at which the board
agreed to allot the 24,000 shares) it is instructive to see the reasons which Mr Soady gave
in his letter of 18 July 1990 for wishing LFL to repurchase those shares. The letter is
addressed to Mr Soady as chairman of the company. It reads as follows:

"Dear Sir,   B

It seems evident in recent weeks that the political upheaval by ex-directors of this
company has subsided especially with the advent of the fuel rebate system and the
reduction in the rate of fishermen's commission to our members.

In the light of this and my matrimonial difficulties, I would like to sell 24,000
shares out of my total shareholding.
                                                                                  C
Would you please discuss this at your next directors' meeting.

Yours faithfully,

M H SOADY."

At a meeting on the next day (19 July 1990), attended by Mr Soady and Mrs Gould, it
is recorded that it was agreed that LFL would buy back the 24,000 shares at par "rather
than let them be floated on the open market".   D

The earlier dealings in relation to the 24,000 shares were then reversed. On 6 August
1990 LFL requested JFS to remit the monies invested, which JFS did on 10 August 1990,
together with £1,233 representing interest. The moneys were credited to LFL's current
account on 16 August 1990 and on 20 August 1990 LFL paid £24,000 to Mr Soady.
Thereupon, no doubt, Mr Soady repaid his indebtedness to JFS.

On about 10 October 1990 Mr Matthews once again raised with Mr Browning the   E
possibility of changes to the board of LFL and the possible requisitioning of an EGM for
that purpose (Mr Matthews having become aware by this time that Mr Soady no longer
held the 24,000 shares).

At the end of October 1990 Mr Soady set 23 November 1990 as the date for LFL's
annual general meeting. The notice stipulated that any one wishing to be elected a
director must give LFL notice in writing by close of business on 15 November 1990. F

On 9 November 1990, Mr Moore (an employee of LFW) submitted an application to
subscribe for 13,000 shares in LFL. That application was approved by Mr Soady on
12 November 1990, and a share certificate issued to Mr Moore on 14 November 1990.
Mr Moore was a supporter of the Soady group and he did not want the Cairns group to
gain control of LFL. Moreover, it is common ground that Mr Moore did not pay for the
13,000 shares out of his own resources. Rather, it appears that Mr Soady borrowed
£13,000 from JFS which he then lent on (interest-free) to Mr Moore. Mr Moore then   G
paid £13,000 to LFL as the price of the shares and LFL then deposited that sum with JFS
"for investment".

Minutes of a meeting of the board of LFL (consisting of Mr Soady as sole director)
held on 15 November 1990 record that it was agreed to recommend to shareholders at
the forthcoming AGM that Mrs Gould, Mr Moore and Mrs J Fletcher (all of them
employees of LFW) be appointed directors of LFL. The minutes also show that   H
nominations had been received from Cairns, Pengelly and Matthews and from
Mr D Fletcher.

The AGM was duly held on 23 November 1990 and in the event only two of the four
vacant places on the board of LFL were filled, the appointees being Mrs Gould and
Mr Moore. Had Mr Moore not had available to him the 13,000 shares recently allotted

A   to him and had the same voting pattern been repeated all four vacancies would have been filled, Cairns, Pengelly and Fletcher being elected together with Mrs Gould.

In early January 1991 LFL "repurchased" Mr Moore's shares and the transaction was reversed in the same way as the earlier dealings in relation to Mr Soady's 24,000 shares. JFS paid £13,000 plus £212 interest to LFL. LFL then paid £13,000 to Mr Moore, who repaid Mr Soady, who in turn repaid JFS.

B   On 19 July 1991, Mr Edwards of the Investigations Division of the Department of Trade and Industry was authorised under sec. 447 of the *Companies Act* 1985 to require Mr Soady to produce documents and to give explanations. On 27 March 1992 he swore his principal affidavit in support of the present application and on 7 April 1992 the originating summons was issued.

In his principal affidavit Mr Edwards sets out the factual background as I have
C   attempted to summarise it. Paragraphs 118 and 119 of that affidavit read as follows:

> "It is clear from the foregoing evidence that Mr Soady was responsible for two artificial and illegal transactions, one between 1 March 1990 and 20 August 1990 and the second between 9 November 1990 and 7 March 1991 whereby Mr Soady (in the second case through the co-operation of his associate, Mr Moore) gained a temporary majority of the voting rights in LFL to enable him to defend attempts
D   by other shareholders, who would otherwise have commanded a majority of votes, to wrest control of the company from him. The transactions involved Mr Soady (or Mr Moore) subscribing for sufficient shares to enable them to outvote the opposition, borrowing money to enable them to pay for such shares, procuring that LFL deposited the money received for the shares with the original lender and subsequently arranging for the money to be withdrawn and used by LFL to 'repurchase' the shares from Mr Soady or Mr Moore. Thus at little or no
E   cost to themselves, they acquired an artificial and temporary majority of votes and used such majority in order to defeat opponents who disagreed with their conduct of the company's affairs.

> 119. Mr Soady denied knowledge of the provisions of the *Companies Act* 1985 which forbid, subject to various exceptions, a company from acquiring its own shares whether by purchase, subscription or otherwise. Nevertheless, both the
F   series of transactions mentioned in the previous paragraph amounted to the acquisition by LFL of its own shares and none of the qualifications to sec. 143 of the *Companies Act* 1985 appear to apply. The transactions were therefore illegal and Mr Soady and Mr Moore are responsible for such illegality. With the assistance of Mr Moore, Mr Soady retained his control of LFL in an unscrupulous and illegal manner. I respectfully submit that neither of them are fit persons to have control of the management of any company."

G   Mr Soady swore an affidavit in opposition to the application on 18 September 1992. In relation to the allotment and repurchase of the 24,000 shares he says:

> "Firstly, I wish to make it clear that I have acted throughout in good faith. The company has legal advisors and auditors to whom the company has turned regularly for advice. The company has relied upon the advice which it has been given by professionals.

H
> (b) Full records have been kept of all the company's dealings of whatever nature. No attempt has ever been made to hide or cover up the nature of the dealings.

> (c) I purchased 24,000 shares in the company:

>> (i) because Mr Peter Riley had advised us to endeavour to sell the rest of the shares, initially by allotment offered pro rata;

(ii)   as I understood the position, following advice, I was entitled to take up that number of shares;

(iii)   at that time, I considered it beneficial for the company to have that amount of capital at its disposal; the company was having financial problems at the time;

(iv)   the sale was agreed by the board and was a legitimate further allotment.

(d)   The shares were repurchased by LFL at my request. I was involved in divorce proceedings and my ex-wife knew that I had purchased the shares. In pursuing her claims for ancillary relief, which remain unresolved, my ex-wife was seeking ownership of those shares. I therefore wrote to the company asking if the company could repurchase them. The shares were repurchased by the company for £24,000.

(e)   I would also point out that at the very first 'board meeting' in early 1988 it was agreed what the articles of association should incorporate. Those dealing with the formation of the company were given specific instructions as to the company's requirements including a requirement that the company should have power to buy back its own shares. The board has always considered that it had power to repurchase shares without consulting shareholders.

(f)   I deny, absolutely, that the purpose for which I purchased the additional 24,000 shares was to defeat any proposal put to a general meeting.

(g)   I should also make it clear that at the time that I purchased the 24,000 shares I did not have capital at my disposal. I therefore asked Mr Dennison if he would lend me £24,000 with a view to supporting the wholesale side of the business financially. He agreed to this. The £24,000 payable for the shares was paid into the business premium account initially rather than be swallowed up in another account. On the repurchase of the shares from me no financial difficulty was caused to the company. The company had not had cause to use the money but had earned interest. I repaid the £24,000 to Mr Dennison. I also paid him interest on the loan from my own account."

Mr Soady was cross-examined on his affidavit evidence and in cross-examination he maintained the statements in his affidavit to which I have referred.

Mr Soady revealed himself as a man of firm convictions and considerable ability, although he is not, of course, an expert in company law. Although certain suggestions were made to him in the course of his cross-examination that he was acting out of motives of personal gain (in that if the Cairns group obtained control of LFL he would lose his job), I am satisfied that his actions throughout were dictated not by thoughts of personal gain but rather by a deeply held belief that the good of LFL would best be served by keeping the Cairns group off the board.

However, I am unable to accept his denial (in para. 9(f) of his affidavit, repeated in cross-examination) that the purpose of his purchase of 24,000 shares was to defeat the requisitioners, that is to say the Cairns group. Equally, I am unable to accept his assertion (in para. 9(c)(iii) of his affidavit, also repeated in cross-examination) that his purpose in taking the 24,000 shares was to make more capital available to LFL; or his assertion (in para. 9(c)(ii) of his affidavit) that as he understood the position, "following advice", he was entitled to allot the further shares to himself. On the contrary, I find that Mr Soady's motives and purposes in relation to the allotment of the 24,000 shares were as set out in paras. 118 and 119 of Mr Edwards' affidavit, which I have read.

A number of factors lead me to this conclusion, in particular the following.

(1)   The fact that it was the inevitable effect of the allotment that the requisitioners' resolution would be lost. I have no doubt at all that one of the first things Mr Soady did

A   when he saw the requisition was to calculate whether the requisitioners could together command a majority, and if so by how much. He plainly studied the requisition with some care (as one would expect) for he told me in cross-examination that he had noticed that two of the named requisitioners had not in fact signed the requisition, and accordingly might not vote in favour of the resolution.

(2) The fact that Mr Soady was motivated by a strong desire to keep the Cairns group off the board, and accordingly to prevent the resolution being passed. It is plain that

B   since the disagreement between the Cairns group and the Soady group first surfaced in early 1989 it had become progressively more marked, and by March of 1990 attitudes generally had polarised. So far as Mr Soady was concerned, his opposition to the Cairns group appears to have become something of a crusade.

(3) The fact that Mr Soady was plainly coy (to put it at its lowest) about revealing to Mr Browning — and thus to the Cairns group — the fact that the allotment had been

C   made. It will be remembered that Mr Browning had to write to Mr Soady a number of times seeking confirmation as to the issued share capital in order to pass that information on to the Cairns group, and that when Mr Soady eventually told him of the increase, he said nothing at that stage about the allotment of 24,000 shares to him.

(4) The fact that the £24,000 (even assuming it to have been at the disposal of LFL) was never in fact used by LFL, but was simply placed on deposit. This despite the fact

D   that, as Mr Soady accepted in evidence, at the time LFL and LFW had substantial overdrafts. In evidence, Mr Soady said that the important thing was that funds should be available to LFL, even if not used. But that objective could have been achieved more simply and more speedily by JFS merely confirming that it would lend LFL, or LFW, £24,000 if required: there would have been no need for any shares to be allotted at all.

(5) The failure of Mr Soady to take Mr Browning's advice in relation to the allotment, as Mr Hidson had expressly recommended. I find that when he proceeded with the

E   allotment, Mr Soady was very much alive to the possibility that what he was doing was wrong in law, but that he decided to go ahead nevertheless. It is apparent from the documentation that in a number of respects and on a number of occasions Mr Soady was punctilious in ensuring that legal formalities and requirements were met. Yet in relation to the important question of the allotment of the 24,000 shares he failed to ask Mr Browning's advice when specifically recommended to do so. He accepted in cross-

F   examination that there was no obstacle to his simply picking up the telephone and speaking to Mr Browning.

(6) The timing of the allotment and the issue of the share certificate in relation to the receipt of the requisition from the Cairns group (the allotment being made on the day following receipt of the requisition). It is too much of a coincidence that the alleged need for the availability of funds arose just at the moment when an extra 24,000 votes in the

G   hands of Mr Soady would result in the defeat of the Cairns group.

(7) The artificial nature of the transaction, involving the circular transmission of £24,000. The nature of the transaction leads me seriously to doubt whether the £24,000 was ever available to LFL; if LFL had demanded the return of its "investment" from JFS, I strongly suspect that that demand would have been swiftly followed by a demand by JFS for repayment of its loan to Mr Soady.

(8) Finally, the clearest indication of the true position appears, in my judgment, in

H   Mr Soady's letter to himself of 18 July 1990. In contrast to the minutes of the special board meeting at which the allotment was agreed, there is no reference in the letter to the financial position of LFL: instead, one finds a reference to the "political upheaval" by the Cairns group having subsided. That being the situation as Mr Soady saw it at that stage, the allotment could safely be reversed. Mr Soady accepted in cross-examination that the contents of his letter represented the true position. In my judgment, that letter

establishes clearly that the minute of the special board meeting of 1 March 1990 (at A
which the 24,000 shares were agreed to be allotted) was no more than window dressing.

So far as the 13,000 shares issued to Mr Moore are concerned, this aspect of the matter
is not addressed at all in Mr Soady's affidavit. As in the case of the 24,000 shares,
however, I find that Mr Soady's purposes in relation to the allotment of the 13,000 shares
were as described by Mr Edwards in his affidavit. In the face of a renewed attempt by
the Cairns group to gain control of the board, Mr Soady was effectively repeating, via
Mr Moore, his (apparently successful) manoeuvre earlier in the year.   B

As to the repurchases of the 24,000 shares and the 13,000 shares, however, I accept
Mr Soady's evidence that at all material times he believed that shares issued by LFL
could be repurchased by LFL in the manner in which LFL purported to repurchase
them. It had been the original intention of the members when LFL was formed that
power should be included in the articles of association enabling LFL to repurchase its
shares, and such a provision was indeed included (reg. 35 of Table A); but the significance C
of the opening words of the regulation ("Subject to the provisions of the Act") was not
appreciated. Moreover it appears that on a number of earlier occasions LFL had
repurchased some of its issued shares without any consideration being given to compliance
with statutory requirements, and without any question being raised by LFL's accountants
or legal advisers.

I turn next to the submissions made to me by Mr Cunningham (for the Secretary of D
State) and Mr Stewart (for Mr Soady).

First, I must address a preliminary point raised by Mr Stewart. He submitted that in
the light of r. 3(3) of the *Insolvent Companies (Disqualification of Unfit Directors)
Proceedings Rules* 1987, which provides that the affidavit in support of an application
for disqualification must include "a statement of the matters by reference to which the
respondent is alleged to be unfit to be concerned in the management of a company", it is
incumbent on the applicant to include in the affidavit a list of the "charges" made against E
the respondent. He submits that since there is no express reference in para. 118 and 119
of Mr Edwards' affidavit to breach of fiduciary duty, that is not a "charge" which
Mr Soady has to answer on this application. In making that submission, however,
Mr Stewart accepted (as he was in my judgment bound to do) that Mr Soady was not
taken by surprise in this case, and that at all material times he knew what case he had to
meet.   F

I reject Mr Stewart's submission. Plainly it is necessary that a director faced with an
application for a disqualification order should know the substance of the charges which
he has to meet, but, as *Browne-Wilkinson* V-C made clear in *Re Lo-Line Electric
Motors* (1988) 4 BCC 415 at p. 420, that is not to say that this requirement should lead to
the technicalities associated with criminal charges. Mr Edwards' affidavit in this case
leaves no room for doubt as to the charges which Mr Soady has to answer. Once that G
situation is reached, so that natural justice is satisfied, there is in my judgment no
additional requirement to state, list or summarise the "charges" against him. To assert
the existence of some further requirement in such circumstances is, in my judgment, to
fall into precisely the trap against which the Vice-Chancellor was warning in *Lo-Line*.

Turning then to the substance of the application, Mr Cunningham submits first that
the repurchases of the shares (both the 24,000 shares allotted to Mr Soady and the
13,000 shares allotted to Mr Moore) were made in contravention of the provisions of H
sec. 143 of the *Companies Act* 1985 and it is accepted by Mr Stewart that they were.
Mr Cunningham submits that sec. 143 contains a penal sanction, and that a director is
under a duty to ensure that the company complies with its provisions. That may well be
so, but given my finding that Mr Soady at all material times believed that LFL had the
necessary power to repurchase its shares, coupled with the fact that earlier repurchases

A   had proceeded without any question being raised by LFL's advisers, I would not on that ground alone find Mr Soady to be unfit.

Turning to the allotment of the 24,000 shares, Mr Cunningham referred me to para. 8.511 of *Palmer's Company Law*, vol. 1, and to *Piercy v S Mills & Co Ltd* [1920] 1 Ch 77 and submitted that in exercising his power to allot shares in order to maintain his control of the company (as I have found that he did, both in relation to his own 24,000 shares and in relation to Mr Moore's 13,000 shares), Mr Soady acted in clear breach of

B   duty. On that footing, Mr Cunningham invited me to find that Mr Soady is unfit for the purposes of the Act.

In my judgment there was a clear breach of duty by Mr Soady in relation to each allotment.

As to unfitness, I find that in using the power to allot shares in the way he did, Mr Soady displayed a clear lack of commercial probity. He allowed his concern to keep

C   the Cairns group from obtaining control of the company to lead him to abuse his power as a director to allot shares in the company. It is not enough for him to say that he did what he did in the best interests of LFL as he saw them. A director who chooses deliberately to play fast and loose with his powers, as Mr Soady has done in this case, in order to remain in control of the company's affairs, is in my judgment unfit to be concerned in the management of a company, and it is expedient in the public interest

D   that a disqualification order be made against him.

I therefore conclude, on the material before me, that Mr Soady has been shown to be unfit to be concerned in the management of a company and I propose to make a disqualification order accordingly.

As to the period of disqualification, I do not place this case as among the most serious which may arise under sec. 8 of the Act. Moreover, I bear in mind that no question of insolvency arises in this case, and I also bear in mind that Mr Soady did not act out of

E   motives of personal gain, nor did he receive any improper benefit. In the circumstances, I take the view that a period of two years and six months is appropriate. I bear in mind in this connection that Mr Moore was disqualified for a period of two years. Mr Moore was only involved in one set of transactions (in relation to the 13,000 shares allotted to him), whereas Mr Soady was not only involved in both sets, he was a director who approved the allotments in each case. Moreover, Mr Soady has throughout played a far more prominent part in the affairs of LFL than Mr Moore. In the circumstances, in my

F   judgment a comparison between the two year disqualification imposed on Mr Moore and the two years and six months period which I propose to order in relation to Mr Soady leads to no unfairness.

Accordingly I make a disqualification order against Mr Soady limited to the period of two years and six months. (If it is necessary, and it may be because of the terms of r. 9 of the 1987 rules, I will make an otherwise order. My order is that the disqualification shall

G   take effect on the day on which the order is made and run for two years and six months thereafter.)

Costs

In the particular circumstances of this case I am not prepared to depart from what I take to be the usual approach in party and party litigation, which is that costs should be ordered on the standard basis. On that basis, therefore, I will make an order for costs in

H   favour of the Secretary of State but in relation to costs after the relevant date when Mr Soady obtained legal aid that order is not to be enforced without the further leave of the court, that date being 29 January 1993.

(*Order accordingly. Legal aid taxation of Mr Soady's costs*)

High Street Services Ltd & Ors v Bank of Credit and Commerce International SA.

Court of Appeal (Civil Division).
Dillon, Nolan and Steyn L JJ.
Judgment delivered 25 March 1993.

Liquidation — Set-off — Directors guaranteed companies' liabilities to bank as "principal debtor" — Directors had deposits with bank as security for companies' indebtedness — Bank went into liquidation — Whether deposits could be set off against companies' indebtedness — Whether nature of deposits as security destroyed mutuality of debts — Insolvency Rules 1986 (SI 1986/1925), r. 4.90.

These were two appeals by a bank in liquidation ("BCCI") against a High Court judgment (see [1993] BCC 70) that the plaintiffs were entitled in the bank's liquidation to set off deposits with the bank against their companies' indebtedness to the bank. BCCI's liquidators contended that in the circumstances it could require full repayment of the indebtedness without regard to the deposits leaving the depositors to prove as unsecured creditors in the liquidation of the bank.

In both the cases under appeal, directors had guaranteed the indebtedness of their companies to BCCI and had deposits with BCCI as security which were charged with the repayment of the companies' indebtedness. The director's liabilities under the security documents were expressed to be those of a "principal debtor".

BCCI further argued that the moneys placed on deposit by the directors were moneys paid to BCCI for a special purpose, viz. to be charged in favour of BCCI as security for the indebtedness to BCCI of the relevant companies, and that, on authority, moneys paid for a special purpose were, whether before or after that purpose had been achieved, outside the scope of the set-off and mutual dealings provisions of r. 4.90 of the Insolvency Rules 1986.

Held, dismissing the appeals:

1. The directors had agreed that the liabilities of their companies should be recoverable from them as principal debtor. There was therefore a tripartite situation in which all the rights were immediately enforceable so far as relevant to the question of set-off. There was a debt presently due from each of the companies to BCCI and equally due from the director as a principal debtor to BCCI and there was the liability from BCCI to the director for the deposits. That satisfied entirely the requirements for statutory set-off and r. 4.90 had automatic effect.

2. If there was set-off between the directors and BCCI, that automatically reduced or extinguished the indebtedness to BCCI of the companies. The statutory set-off operated to reduce or extinguish the liability of the guarantor and necessarily therefore operated as, in effect, a payment by him to be set against the liability of the principal debtor.

3. There was no authority which compelled the conclusion that set-off was not available to the respondents on the ground that a transaction in which property was made over for a special or specific purpose destroyed the mutuality required by r. 4.90.

The following cases were referred to in the judgment of Dillon LJ:

Barnett, Ex parte (1874) LR 9 Ch App 293.
Bradford Old Bank Ltd v Sutcliffe [1918] 2 KB 833.
Brown's Estate, Re [1893] 2 Ch 300.
Caldicott, Ex parte (1884) 25 ChD 716.
City Equitable Fire Insurance Co Ltd, Re (No. 2) [1930] 2 Ch 293.

A
Daintrey, Re. Ex parte Mant [1900] 1 QB 546.
Ellis & Co's Trustee v Dixon-Johnson [1924] 2 Ch 451 (CA); [1925] AC 489 (HL).
Hiley v Peoples Prudential Assurance Co Ltd & Ors (1938) 60 CLR 468.
Joachimson v Swiss Bank Corporation [1921] 3 KB 110.
Mid-Kent Fruit Factory, Re [1896] 1 Ch 567.
National Westminster Bank Ltd v Halesowen Presswork & Assemblies Ltd [1972] AC 785.

B
Palmer v Day & Sons [1895] 2 QB 618.
Pollitt, Re [1893] 1 QB 455.
Rowe v Young (1820) 2 Bligh 391; 4 ER 372.
Sovereign Life Assurance Co v Dodd [1892] 2 QB 573.
Young & Ors v Bank of Bengal (1836) 1 Moore Ind App 87; 18 ER 34.

Neville Thomas QC and Robin Dicker (instructed by Lovell White Durrant) for
C   BCCI.

Jonathan Sumption QC and Mark Hapgood (instructed by Glanvilles, Portsmouth) for the respondents in *High Street Services* and (instructed by Slaughter and May) for the respondents in *Impexbond*.

JUDGMENT

D
Dillon LJ: Preliminary

The court has before it appeals by the Bank of Credit and Commerce International SA ("BCCI"), a company in liquidation acting by its liquidators, against orders made by *Hoffmann* LJ sitting as an additional judge of the Chancery Division on 15 December 1992 (see [1993] BCC 70) in two cases which raise, on slightly different documents and facts, essentially the same questions.

E
Stated broadly, the problem is this. If a bank lends money to a company and takes a guarantee of the company's indebtedness from a director of the company, and also takes from the director a deposit of money with the bank which is charged in favour of the bank with the payment to the bank of the company's indebtedness to the bank or the director's liability to the bank as guarantor of the company's indebtedness, and if the bank later becomes insolvent and is put into liquidation, can the company or the director compel the bank to apply the director's deposit in reduction of the company's
F indebtedness, and also of the director's liability as guarantor, or can the bank require the company to pay the full amount of its indebtedness to the bank without regard to the director's deposit and, if so, does that leave the director to prove as an unsecured creditor in the liquidation of the bank for the amount of his deposit?

To answer this involves consideration of the law of set-off in companies liquidation and can also raise questions as to the principles of equity as to the enforcement of
G securities if set-off is not available.

The facts and documents

Impexbond

One of the appeals concerns two associated companies, Impexbond Ltd and Tucan Ltd. These both banked with BCCI and unlimited guarantees in BCCI's standard form of the companies' indebtedness to BCCI were given by Mr Nasir Abdul Amir on, in
H relation to Impexbond, 11 March 1985, and in relation to Tucan, 29 May 1986. In addition, on 11 March 1985 in respect of Impexbond and on 29 May 1986 in respect of Tucan, Mr Amir signed the bank's form designated "Letter of charge by an individual as security for the liabilities of a third party". By those letters of charge Mr Amir agreed that BCCI might hold any money standing to the credit of certain specified accounts of his as security, and he charged such moneys or deposits so standing with the repayment

of all the moneys due to the bank on any account from Impexbond and Tucan. He also   A
agreed in each letter of charge that his liabilities thereunder should be as that of a
principal debtor.

When BCCI was ordered to be wound up on 14 January 1992 the aggregate liability of
Impexbond and Tucan to BCCI was about £3.3m (with cross-guarantees in favour of
BCCI), while the amount to the credit of Mr Amir's specified accounts (renumbered on
transfer to a different branch of BCCI) was about £4.5m.
                                                                                      B
High Street Services

The other appeal concerns three associated companies, High Street Services Ltd, Cira
Ltd and Portman Fashions Ltd, which all banked with BCCI. On 24 April 1989 a
director, Mr Raees Ahmed, signed unlimited guarantees in BCCI's standard form of
each of the three companies' indebtedness to BCCI. He also on the same date, 24 April
1989, signed in respect of each of the three companies a document in the same printed   C
form headed "Cash deposit security terms — third party".

In these latter documents the term "deposited moneys" was defined as meaning any
moneys including accrued interest standing to the credit then or in the future of any
deposit account Mr Ahmed might have with BCCI. It was agreed that BCCI might at
any time, without further order or notice, appropriate whether by way of set-off or
otherwise the deposited moneys in or towards satisfaction of the indebtedness of
Mr Ahmed to BCCI. It was acknowledged by Mr Ahmed that repayment to him of the   D
deposited moneys was conditional upon BCCI having received payment in full of his
indebtedness to BCCI, and that otherwise he should not be entitled to withdraw the
deposited moneys except at the absolute discretion of BCCI.

In a further section of the "cash deposit security terms" Mr Ahmed agreed to
guarantee to pay and/or discharge to BCCI upon written demand all liabilities of the
company to BCCI. Mr Ahmed further declared "as a separate and independent obligation   E
hereunder" that the company's liabilities,

> "shall be recoverable by you from me as principal debtor and/or by way of
> indemnity and shall be repaid by me on demand made in writing by you or on your
> behalf whether or not demand has been made on the [company]."

At the time of the order for the compulsory winding up of BCCI Mr Ahmed had about
£426,000 on deposit with BCCI, and the three companies owed BCCI in the aggregate   F
over £1m. BCCI had the benefit of cross-guarantees in its favour by the three companies
and charges on other properties including a charge by Mr Ahmed on his home.

Before the judge there was also a third case, heard at the same time, which involved a
company, M S Fashions Ltd, and Mr Sarwar. But the facts were slightly different in that
a demand had actually been made by the liquidators of BCCI on M S Fashions and
Mr Sarwar, and BCCI has not appealed the decision of *Hoffmann* LJ in relation to   G
M S Fashions. That matter is resolved.

Set-off in companies liquidation

It has for long been established that in personal bankruptcy or insolvency and
companies liquidation there is to be set-off where there have been mutual credits,
mutual debts or other mutual dealings. The current provision applicable to companies
liquidation is r. 4.90 of the *Insolvency Rules* 1986, which provides so far as material as   H
follows:

> "(1) This Rule applies where, before the company goes into liquidation there
> have been mutual credits, mutual debts or other mutual dealings between the
> company and any creditor of the company proving or claiming to prove for a debt
> in the liquidation.

A
(2) An account shall be taken of what is due from each party to the other in respect of the mutual dealings, and the sums due from one party shall be set off against the sums due from the other.

. . .

(4) Only the balance (if any) of the account is provable in liquidation. Alternatively (as the case may be) the amount shall be paid to the liquidator as part of the assets."

B
It is common ground that where there are such mutual credits, mutual debts or other mutual dealings the set-off is mandatory and cannot be excluded by any contract between the parties: see *National Westminster Bank Ltd v Halesowen Presswork & Assemblies Ltd* [1972] AC 785.

If there are indeed mutual credits or mutual debts or mutual dealings between a
C
company, or a bankrupt, and a creditor, then the set-off applies notwithstanding that one or other of the debts or credits may be secured. See, for instance the judgment of Lord *Selborne* LC in *Ex parte Barnett* (1874) LR 9 Ch App 293 and the judgment of *Dixon* J in *Hiley v Peoples Prudential Assurance Co Ltd* (1938) 60 CLR 468 at p. 498. *Dixon* J added:

"To the extent that the secured debt is answered by set-off the security is freed."

D
In *Hiley* a life assurance company had issued a policy to a policy holder. Subsequently the policy holder charged the policy and other property to the company to secure an advance by the company to the policy holder. Later the company was ordered to be wound up and the liquidator repudiated the policy. It was held that the policy holder was entitled to set off his claim against the company for repudiating his policy against his liability to the company in respect of the advance. *Dixon* J said at pp. 496–497:

E
". . . in the first place, the general rule does not require that at the moment when the winding up commences there shall be two enforceable debts, a debt provable in the liquidation and a debt enforceable by the liquidator against the creditor claiming to prove. It is enough that at the commencement of the winding up mutual dealings exist which involve rights and obligations whether absolute or contingent of such a nature that afterwards in the events that happen they mature or develop into pecuniary demands capable of set off. If the end contemplated by
F
the transaction is a claim sounding in money so that, in the phrase employed in the cases, it is commensurable with the cross-demand, no more is required than that at the commencement of the winding up liabilities shall have been contracted by the company and the other party respectively from which cross money claims accrue during the course of the winding up."

That is in line with the judgment of *Romer* LJ in *Re Daintrey* [1900] 1 QB 546 at
G
pp. 573–574 and the judgment of Lord *Russell of Killowen* CJ in *Palmer v Day & Sons* [1895] 2 QB 618. It also covers the actual circumstances in *Sovereign Life Assurance Co v Dodd* [1892] 2 QB 573. In that case the policy, which had been charged by the holder to the issuing company as security for a loan, matured after a petition had been presented for the winding up of the company but before any winding-up order had been made; but it was then the general view, contrary to the present view, that the relevant date for the application of set-off was the date of the presentation of the petition rather than the date
H
of the order. Set-off was none the less held to be applicable.

It is said, however, for BCCI that, even accepting the foregoing, there is even now — let alone at the date of the winding-up order — no relevant personal liability on Mr Amir or Mr Ahmed to be set off against their deposits because the personal liability of each of them is merely that of a guarantor, a guarantor's liability is contingent on the demand being made, and no demand has even now been made on Mr Amir or Mr Ahmed.

It is accepted by BCCI that the liabilities of the principal debtors, the various   A
companies, to BCCI were at all times presently enforceable by BCCI without any need
for a demand before the issue of a writ, even if the indebtedness was described in the
relevant documents as "repayable on demand". That is in accordance with many
authorities and it is sufficient to take the statement by *Bayley* J in *Rowe v Young* (1820)
2 Bligh 391; 4 ER 372 at p. 465; 404 where he said:

> ". . . the rules which the law has laid down as to cases in which a demand is or is   B
> not necessary, must be considered. One of these rules I take to be this, that where
> a man engages to pay upon demand what is to be considered his own debt, he is
> liable to be sued upon that engagement, without any previous demand . . ."

But *Bayley* J went on to say:

> "but . . . if he engage to pay upon demand what was not his debt, what he is under
> no obligation to pay, what but for such engagement he would never be liable to   C
> pay any one, a demand is essential, and part of the plaintiff's title."

Consequently it has been held in various contexts that to enforce liability against a mere
surety there must be a demand before action brought: see the decision of *Chitty* J in *Re
Brown's Estate* [1893] 2 Ch 300 and the decision of this court in *Bradford Old Bank Ltd
v Sutcliffe* [1918] 2 KB 833.

Essentially, however, the question is one of the construction of the contract: see   D
Joachimson v Swiss Bank Corporation [1921] 3 KB 110 at p. 129 where *Atkin* LJ said:

> "The question appears to me to be in every case, did the parties in fact intend to
> make the demand a term of the contract? If they did, effect will be given to their
> contract, whether it be a direct promise to pay or a collateral promise, though in
> seeking to ascertain their intention the nature of the contract may be material."

In the present case in the letters of charge signed by Mr Amir in respect of Impexbond   E
and Tucan he has expressly agreed that his liabilities thereunder — namely the companies'
liabilities charged on his deposits — shall be as that of a principal debtor.

Similarly in the forms setting out the cash deposit security terms which Mr Ahmed
signed in respect of High Street Services Ltd and its associated companies he accepted
that the liabilities of those companies should be recoverable from him as principal
debtor and they were thus within the definition of his indebtedness; he also authorised   F
the appropriation of the deposited moneys in satisfaction of his indebtedness without
further notice to him.

The effect of that must be to dispense with any need for a demand in the case of Mr
Amir since he has made the companies' debts to BCCI his own debts and thus immediately
payable out of the deposit without demand. In the case of Mr Ahmed there must be
immediate liability even though the word "demand" was used, because he accepted
liability as a principal debtor and his deposit can be appropriated without further notice.   G

The banking relationship between BCCI and the various companies of course ceased
when BCCI went into liquidation. Therefore we have a situation in which, though the
situation is tripartite rather than bipartite as in the cases referred to earlier, all the rights
are immediately enforceable so far as relevant to the question of set-off. There is a debt
presently due from each of the companies to BCCI and equally due from Mr Amir or Mr
Ahmed as the case may be as a principal debtor to BCCI and there is the liability from   H
BCCI to Mr Amir or Mr Ahmed for the deposits. That satisfies entirely, in my judgment,
the requirements for statutory set-off as explained by *Dixon* J, and consequently r. 4.90
has automatic effect.

If there is set-off between Mr Amir and Mr Ahmed and BCCI, that must automatically
reduce or extinguish the indebtedness to BCCI of the companies. The statutory set-off

A   is not something which BCCI can, as it were, place in a suspense account. It operates to reduce or extinguish the liability of the guarantor and necessarily therefore operates as, in effect, a payment by him to be set against the liability of the principal debtor. A creditor cannot sue the principal debtor for an amount of the debt which the creditor has already received from a guarantor.

This is subject, however, to one point, which has been called "the charge point" to which I now turn.

B

The charge point

The basis of this is that it is said for BCCI that the moneys placed on deposit by Mr Amir and Mr Ahmed were moneys paid to BCCI for a special purpose, viz. to be charged in favour of BCCI as security for the indebtedness to BCCI of the relevant companies, and it is said also that, on authority, moneys paid for a special purpose are, C   whether before or after that purpose has been achieved, outside the scope of the set-off and mutual dealings provisions of insolvency law — for present purposes r. 4.90 of the 1986 rules.

The argument put forward depends in part on a decision of this court in *Ex parte Caldicott* (1884) 25 ChD 716 but even more on a decision of this court in *Re City Equitable Fire Insurance Co Ltd (No. 2)* [1930] 2 Ch 293 and an earlier case of *Young v* D   *Bank of Bengal* (1836) 1 Moore Ind App 87.

In *Ex parte Caldicott* a father and his son had entered into a partnership and had arranged banking facilities for the partnership with Lloyd's Banking Co. The father had charged certain land owned by himself to the bank, but the land had been sold, and had been replaced by the proceeds, placed on deposit with the bank. The firm later became bankrupt, which involved the administration in bankruptcy of their joint estate, and the separate administration in bankruptcy of the separate estate of the father. The issue E   before the court was whether the bank, in proving against the joint estate, had to give credit for the moneys it held on deposit from the father. The essence of the decision, as I understand it, is contained in the final paragraph in the brief judgment of Lord *Selborne* LC, with which *Cotton* and *Lindley* L JJ agreed, viz. that the money on deposit with the bank was a security, but not a security on the joint estate, and the rule in bankruptcy was that a valuation or giving up of a security was only necessary when, in the case of a proof F   by creditors of the joint estate it was a security on the joint estate. The judgment was only concerned with the joint estate.

Lord *Selborne* did, however, say in the penultimate paragraph of his judgment (at p. 722):

> "It appears to me a fallacy to say that the money so deposited was a debt due from the bank to the father, in the sense that an action could have been brought by him G   for it, so long as it remained in the hands of the bank, and there was a balance due from the firm to them which the mortgage of the real estate was intended to secure; and I cannot think that the conversion of the security into money, and the deposit with the bank of the money, which continued to be the subject of the security, can make any difference in principle."

What I understand him to have been meaning by that is that the money still in the hands of the bank was held by the bank as a security and therefore as it was not a security H   on the joint estate it did not have to be taken into account in determining the amount of the bank's proof against the joint estate. I do not understand him to have been saying that as the father could not have brought an action against the bank for the money so long as there was a balance due from the firm to the bank, there could not have been any statutory set-off in the father's separate estate to reduce the joint indebtedness to the bank.

If that is the correct interpretation, *Ex parte Caldicott* does not govern the present   A
case.

Re City Equitable Fire Insurance Co Ltd (No. 2) is the most important of the trio of
cases which, in the words of Lord *Simon of Glaisdale* in *National Westminster Bank v
Halesowen Presswork & Assemblies Ltd* [1972] AC 785 at p. 808B show that "mutual
dealings" in, as it is now, r. 4.90 do not cover a transaction in which property is made
over for a "special (or specific) purpose". Lord *Kilbrandon* said, at p. 821E–F in   B
National Westminster Bank v Halesowen Presswork & Assemblies Ltd:

> "In *In re City Equitable Fire Insurance Co. Ltd.* [1930] 2 Ch. 293 a fund held by
> way of guarantee against the carrying out of specific obligations was held to be
> 'special' in this sense. In all these cases the funds may be said to have been
> impressed with quasi-trust purposes, and that is sufficient to destroy the mutuality
> which is a prerequisite of the right to set off arising, since it is necessary that the
> debts were between the parties in the same right, a condition which the holding of   C
> a sum as trustee would destroy . . ."

The other two cases in the trio are *Re Pollitt* [1893] 1 QB 455 and *Re Mid-Kent Fruit
Factory* [1896] 1 Ch 567.

The essential facts of *Re City Equitable Fire Insurance Co Ltd (No. 2)* were that the
City Equitable, as reinsurer, entered into a treaty of reinsurance with an insurance
company. Under that treaty a certain percentage of the premiums payable to the City   D
Equitable as the reinsurer was to be retained and accumulated by the insurer "as security
for the due performance of the obligations of the reinsurer" under the treaty. The City
Equitable was put into compulsory liquidation and the treaty of reinsurance was
terminated in accordance with its terms. Then, after all claims of the insurer under the
treaty had been satisfied out of the accumulated fund, there was a surplus of £8,000 left
in the hands of the insurer. The insurer claimed to set off against that surplus sums due
from the City Equitable under other contracts, relying on sec. 31 of the *Bankruptcy Act*   E
1914, the then current predecessor of r. 4.90. It was only the set-off of the surplus that
was in issue, and it was held that the insurer was not entitled to that.

In giving the leading judgment in this court Lord *Hanworth* MR said, at p. 312:

> "Different considerations apply where money has been handed over for a specific
> purpose and not treated as a mere item in accounts kept between the bankrupt
> and his creditors . . . The effect of handing over money for a specific purpose   F
> appears from the cases to be that it is taken out of the course of accounts between
> the parties to be held, so to speak, in suspense between them, until that specific
> purpose for which it had been handed over has been completed; and even then it
> appears that the nature and quality of the specific purpose still attaches to the
> balance of the fund, if any, which remains in the hands of the depositee. The fund
> having been originally placed in the depositee's hands for the particular purpose,   G
> the nature and quality of that purpose still attaches to the balance of the fund
> unless and until there has been some subsequent agreement releasing it from the
> specific purpose. Indeed, it must in all cases be the balance of the fund which is in
> dispute in cases such as this."

Because the fund was accumulated by the depositee/insurer for a special purpose
under the particular treaty of reinsurance, there was no mutuality between the liquidator
of the City Equitable's claim for the balance of the accumulated fund and, on the other   H
hand, the claims of the insurer against the City Equitable under other contracts. Those
debts were not, in Lord *Kilbrandon*'s words "in the same right". Therefore, there was
no set-off.

But, as I see it, there had at the earlier stage, before the surplus was ascertained, been
ample mutuality between the liquidator's claim for the accumulated fund and the claims

A   of the insurer for the due performance of the obligations of the City Equitable under the
particular treaty of reinsurance under which the accumulated fund had been accumulated.
Therefore, at that earlier stage, there was no objection to set-off of the claims under the
particular treaty of reinsurance; the insurer was not required to hand over the accumulated
fund to the liquidator intact and without deductions even under the particular treaty of
reinsurance.

B   The two other cases in the trio, *Re Pollitt* and *Re Mid-Kent Fruit Factory*, were
likewise cases in which what was in issue was the surplus of a deposited fund remaining
after the specific purpose for which it had been deposited had been satisfied; it was held
that the surplus could not be set off under the statutory provisions against other debts
which had nothing to do with those specific purposes.

These three cases do not, in my judgment, bear at all on the problem with which we
C   are concerned in the present case, and do not prevent the set-off which the present
respondents assert.

Young v Bank of Bengal (1836) 1 Moore Ind App 87; 18 ER 34 is a very similar case to
Re City Equitable Fire Insurance Co Ltd (No. 2). A firm of merchants had deposited
paper with the bank to secure a particular loan. When the firm became bankrupt, the
bank sold the paper, and the proceeds produced a surplus after paying off the particular
D   loan and interest on it. The bank claimed to set the surplus off under the statute against
other debts due from the firm to the bank for which the bank held the firm's promissory
notes. It was held that the bank could not do so because the case did not come within the
clause of mutual credit in the Indian Insolvency Act. The reasoning of Lord *Brougham*
seems to me to be in line with that of Lord *Hanworth* in *Re City Equitable Fire Insurance
Co (No. 2)*.

E   Lord *Brougham* incidentally states, at p. 145; 55, that the introduction of the words
"mutual credit" extends the right of set-off to cases where the party receiving the credit
is not debtor *in presenti* to him who gives the credit:

> "Accordingly the relation contemplated by the Statute has been held to be
> established where the debt is immediately due from the one party, and only due at
> a future day from the other."

F   This anticipates *Dixon* J's statement in *Hiley*.

In the present case, therefore, there is nothing in the charge point to defeat the set-off
claimed.

Mr Amir is, of course, claiming to prove in the liquidation for his deposits, subject to
the set-off. Mr Ahmed technically has no claim to prove because the amount due from
G   him to BCCI exceeds the amount of his deposit; but the wording "balance (if any) of the
account" in para. 4 of r. 4.90 shows that the set-off applies even if its effect is to reduce
the claim in the liquidation to nil.

Principles of equity as to enforcement of securities

My conclusions on the foregoing points make it unnecessary to consider the implications
H   of the rule in equity, stated by Viscount *Cave* LC in *Ellis & Co's Trustee v Dixon-
Johnson* [1925] AC 489 at p. 491, and stated also by *Sargant* LJ in the court below ([1924]
2 Ch 451 at p. 473), that if a creditor holding security sues for his debt he is under an
obligation on payment of the debt to hand over the security, and if, having improperly
made away with the security he is unable to return it to his debtor, he cannot have
judgment for the debt.

A

Nolan LJ: I agree with the judgment of *Dillon* LJ.

Steyn LJ: I agree with the reasons given by *Dillon* LJ, and with the order which he has proposed. There is nothing which I can usefully add.

(*Appeals dismissed with costs. Leave to appeal to the House of Lords refused*)

———————————

B

C

D

E

F

G

H

Re Maxwell Communications Corporation plc (No. 3).

Chancery Division (Companies Court).
Vinelott J.
Judgment delivered 26 March 1993.

> *Administration — Scheme of arrangement — Whether subordinated creditors*
> *entitled to vote on scheme — Whether subordination agreement was invalid*
> *under insolvency law — Companies Act 1985, sec. 425; Insolvency Act 1986,*
> *sec. 14(3).*

This was an application for directions by the administrators of Maxwell Communications Corporation plc ("MCC"). The question on which directions were sought was whether MCC was entitled to exclude from a scheme of arrangement under sec. 425 of the Companies Act 1985, which the administrators proposed to submit to the creditors and, if approved, for the sanction of the court, the holders of convertible subordinated bonds of Maxwell Finance Jersey Ltd ("MFJ") which were guaranteed by MCC.

It was not in question that MFJ would be unable to meet its liabilities under the bonds and that the liabilities of MCC far exceeded its assets, so that if liability to the bondholders was subordinated to MCC's liabilities to other unsecured creditors the bondholders would receive nothing. The question was whether liabilities to the bondholders under the guarantee were effectively subordinated to MCC's liabilities to other unsecured creditors.

The guarantee was governed by Swiss law, and the expert evidence was that under that law it constituted an indemnity independent of the validity and enforceability of the bonds, and created a direct undertaking to pay on demand on confirmation that MFJ had not met its obligations under the bonds. The provision subordinating the liability of MCC was valid and effective: under Swiss law a creditor could waive his right to equal treatment with the other creditors in the insolvency of a debtor. However, no trust of any moneys received by Swiss Bank Corporation (to which payments under the guarantee were to be made on behalf of the bondholders) in the winding up of MCC could be implied. Swiss law did not recognise trusts and the agreement for subordination could not be given effect as an implied agreement by SBC to assign any moneys taken in the winding up of MCC to the other unsubordinated creditors.

SBC, appointed to represent the bondholders in the application, argued that the principle of pari passu distribution of unsecured non-preferential debts invalidated the subordination agreement.

Held, declaring that the subordination agreement was valid and effective:

1. After the commencement of a bankruptcy or winding up a creditor was entitled to waive his debt just as he was entitled to decline to submit a proof. If the creditor could waive his right altogether, he could waive his right to prove save to the extent of any assets remaining after the debts of other unsecured creditors had been paid in full; or if he was a preferential creditor, to agree that his debt would rank equally with unsecured non-preferential debts. So also, if the creditor could waive his right to prove or agree the postponement of his debt after the commencement of the bankruptcy or winding up, he could agree with the debtor that his debt would not be payable or would be postponed or subordinated in the event of a bankruptcy or winding up.

2. A contract between a company and a creditor, providing for the debt due to the creditor to be subordinated in the insolvent winding up of the company to other unsecured debt, was not rendered void by the insolvency legislation.

The following cases were referred to in the judgment:

British & Commonwealth Holdings plc, Re (No. 3) [1992] BCC 58; [1992] 1 WLR 672.

British Eagle International Air Lines Ltd v Compagnie Nationale Air France [1973]   A
1 Lloyd's Rep 414; [1974] 1 Lloyd's Rep 429 (CA); [1975] 1 WLR 758 (HL).
Deering & Ors v Hyndman (1886) 18 LR Ir 323.
De Villiers & Anor, Ex parte. Re Carbon Developments (Pty) Ltd [1992] 2 SA 95;
[1993] 1 SA 493(A).
First National Bank of Hollywood & Ors v American Foam Rubber Corp & Anor
(1976) 530 F(2d) 450.
Horne v Chester & Fein Property Developments Pty Ltd & Ors (1987) 5 ACLC 245.   B
Lind v Lefdal's Pianos Ltd & Ors [1929] TPD 241.
National Westminster Bank Ltd v Halesowen Presswork & Assemblies Ltd [1971]
1 QB 1 (CA); [1972] AC 785 (HL).
Rolls Razor Ltd v Cox [1967] 1 QB 552.

John Cone (instructed by Norton Rose) for the administrators.

Charles Purle QC and Mark Phillips (instructed by Gouldens) for Swiss Bank   C
Corporation.

JUDGMENT

Vinelott J: This is an application for directions by the administrators of Maxwell
Communications Corporation plc ("MCC"). The question on which directions are
sought is whether MCC is entitled to exclude from a scheme of arrangement under   D
sec. 425 of the *Companies Act* 1985, which the administrators propose to submit to the
creditors and, if approved, for the sanction of the court, the holders of convertible
subordinated bonds of Maxwell Finance Jersey Ltd ("MFJ") which were guaranteed by
MCC.

It is not in question that MFJ will be unable to meet its liabilities under the bonds and
that the liabilities of MCC far exceed its assets, so that if, as the title to the bonds   E
suggests, liability to the bondholders was subordinated to MCC's liabilities to other
unsecured creditors the bondholders will receive nothing. The question is whether
liabilities to the bondholders under the guarantee were effectively subordinated to
MCC's liabilities to other unsecured creditors.

A similar situation arose in *Re British & Commonwealth Holdings plc (No. 3)* [1992]
BCC 58. In that case the company had issued convertible subordinated loan stock and   F
the trust deed governing the loan stock provided that the claims of holders of the stock
were:

> "In the event of the winding up of the company . . . subordinated in right of
> payment to the claims of all other creditors of the company . . ."

The administrators estimated that the debts owing to other creditors who benefited
under the scheme ("the scheme creditors") amounted to £1.2 billion and that the   G
deficiency of the assets available to meet those debts was £800m. The question was
whether the administrators could convene a meeting of the scheme creditors and exclude
the trustee of the subordinated loan stock (who did not admit that in a winding up there
would inevitably be a deficiency) and whether the court could then sanction the scheme,
notwithstanding the opposition of the trustee of the loan stock. I took the view that to
the extent that the assets of the company were insufficient to meet the liabilities to
unsecured creditors, other than the holders of the loan stock, the holders of the loan   H
stock had no interest in the assets of the company and no right to vote at a meeting of
unsecured creditors; that, in the very unlikely, indeed, merely theoretical possibility,
that the realisation of the company's assets would suffice to meet the claims of the
scheme creditors, the rights of the holders of the unsecured creditors would be unaffected
by the scheme; and that in these circumstances the liquidator could properly call a

A   meeting of the scheme creditors alone, and if the scheme of arrangement was approved, apply to the court to sanction the scheme.

Mr Purle, who appeared for the Swiss Bank Corporation, did not challenge the correctness of my decision on the facts of that case. However, there is one vital distinction. In *British & Commonwealth Holdings plc (No. 3)* the subordination of the subordinated loan stock did not rest solely on the terms of a contract between the company and the trustee of the subordinated loan stock. The trust deed governing the
B   issue of the subordinated loan stock provided that any moneys payable to the trustee would be held in trust to apply the same in payment of its own expenses and remuneration and then towards payment of the claims of other creditors submitted to proof in the winding up. That machinery, which is a very common means of ensuring that debt is effectively subordinated, was not available in the instant case because the guarantee is governed by Swiss law which does not recognise trusts. Under Swiss law a provision for
C   the subordination of debt is recognised and effective, but to the extent that English assets of MCC fall to be dealt with in an insolvent winding up, the distribution of the assets will be governed by English law. In these circumstances I must now decide whether a contractual provision for the subordination of a debt unsupported by the trust mechanism used in *Re British & Commonwealth Holdings plc* is effective under English law.

D   Before turning to that question I should, I think, set out the relevant facts in greater detail. In June 1989 MFJ issued $5\frac{1}{2}$ per cent convertible bonds 1989–94 ("the MFJ bonds") in the nominal amount of SFr 125m. Clause 4 of the MFJ bonds provided that:

> "The due and punctual payment by [MFJ] of the nominal value (or, in the case of an event of default only, of the paid up value) of the bonds and interest on the paid up value of the bonds . . . is unconditionally and irrevocably guaranteed on a subordinated basis, in accordance with art. 111 of the Swiss Federal Code of
E   Obligations by Maxwell Communication Corporation."

Under the guarantee MCC undertook to pay on first demand by the Swiss Bank Corporation in summary, in the event of default, the paid-up value of the outstanding bonds with interest. It was provided that:

> "The guarantee of payment of the nominal value (or in the case of an event of default only of the paid up value) and interest with regard to the bonds and of paid
F   up value of the preference shares under this guarantee, constitutes an unsecured and subordinated obligation of the guarantor in that in case of any distribution of assets by the guarantor, whether in cash or otherwise, in liquidation or bankruptcy of the guarantor, during a period in which a suspension of payment is granted to the guarantor or in case the guarantor negotiates with all its creditors with a view to a general settlement, creditors of unsubordinated indebtedness of the guarantor should be entitled to be paid in full before any payment shall be made on account
G   of payments under the bonds or preference shares but that payments to bondholders, couponholders and preference shareholders shall be made before any payment shall be made in such cases to the holder of any class of stock in the guarantor."

The rights of MCC as guarantor to indemnity by MFJ were in turn subordinated to the rights of the bondholders to recovery in full against MFJ. Lastly, it was provided that
H   payments under the guarantee would be made to Swiss Bank Corporation on behalf of the bondholders and that the form and contents of the guarantee would be governed by Swiss law. The Swiss Bank Corporation has been appointed to represent the bondholders in this application.

There is no dispute between the experts in Swiss law instructed by the administrators and by the Swiss Bank Corporation respectively. The guarantee constitutes an indemnity

independent of the validity and enforceability of the bonds, and creates a direct   A
undertaking to pay on demand by Swiss Bank Corporation ("SBC") on confirmation
that MFJ has not met its obligations under the bonds. The provision subordinating the
liability of MCC is valid and effective. Under Swiss law a creditor can waive his right to
equal treatment of the other creditors in the insolvency of a debtor. However, no trust
of any moneys received by SBC in the winding up of MCC can be implied. Swiss law
does not recognise trusts and the agreement for subordination cannot be given effect as
an implied agreement by SBC to assign any moneys taken in the winding up of MCC to   B
the other unsubordinated creditors.

MCC, as is well known, is hopelessly insolvent and so is MFJ. Administrators have
been appointed in England, and in the USA the Ch. 11 procedure has been invoked.
The administrators and the examiner appointed in the Ch. 11 proceedings have agreed a
scheme of arrangement and a plan of reorganisation to put before the English and US
creditors which is designed to harmonise the US and English procedures for the   C
distribution of MCC's assets. In very broad outline, secured and preferential creditors
in England and creditors with priority claims in the US will be paid out of the English or
the US assets as may be appropriate. The net balance will be pooled; claims will be
notified to the administrators or the US court in accordance with the procedure
appropriate to the jurisdiction where the claim falls to be made, but these claims will be
paid pari passu out of the pool.

Contractual subordination is recognised and given effect under the US code. The   D
scheme of arrangement and the plan for reorganisation have been prepared on the
assumption that the contractual subordination of the rights of bondholders under the
guarantee (which is the only subordinated debt of MCC) is also recognised in English
law and would be applied in the winding up of MCC. There would be grave and possibly
insuperable difficulties in negotiating an overall distribution to English and US creditors
out of the pooled assets if this assumption were ill-founded.   E

The case for SBC is founded on the decision of the Court of Appeal and the House of
Lords in *National Westminster Bank Ltd v Halesowen Presswork and Assemblies Ltd*
[1972] AC 785. The majority of their Lordships (Lord *Cross* alone dissenting) agreed
with the view expressed by the Court of Appeal in that case and in the earlier decision of
the Court of Appeal in *Rolls Razor Ltd v Cox* [1967] 1 QB 552 that the provisions for
mutual set-off in sec. 31 of the *Bankruptcy Act* 1914 could not be excluded by agreement
between a debtor and the creditors. Accordingly, a creditor could not validly make it a   F
term of his contract with a debtor that he would not be entitled to set-off a debt due to
him against a debt due from him to the debtor, and could not waive his right to set-off
after the commencement of the bankruptcy or winding up.

Section 31 of the *Bankruptcy Act* 1914 was expressed in mandatory terms. It was
introduced into the winding up of an insolvent company by sec. 317 of the *Companies
Act* 1948 which provided that in the winding up of an insolvent company the same rules   G
should prevail with regard to the respective rights of secured and unsecured creditors
and to debts payable as were in force under the law of bankruptcy.

Section 33 of the 1914 Act set out the order of priority of payments out of the property
of a bankrupt. The several subsections of sec. 33 were all expressed in mandatory terms.
Subsection (7) provided that:

"Subject to the provisions of this Act, all debts proved in the bankruptcy shall be   H
paid pari passu."

The case for SBC is that the decision of the Court of Appeal in the *Halesowen* case
([1971] 1 QB 1) and in *Rolls Razor v Cox* and of the House of Lords in the *Halesowen*
case (if the point was decided by the House of Lords) that the provisions for set-off of
mutual debts in sec. 31 cannot be excluded by agreement between a debtor and the

A   creditor, rested upon the mandatory language used in sec. 31, and that the same principle must apply to the order of priority of debts and to the application pari passu of any balance after meeting debts ranking in priority to unsecured non-preferential debts.

Under the new legislation the administration of the property of an insolvent company is not dealt with by reference to the bankruptcy legislation, but is the subject of a separate code. However, there is no material distinction between the new code and the earlier legislation which it replaces. Section 107 of the 1986 Act (which is in substantially
B   the same terms as sec. 302 of the *Companies Act* 1948) provides that in a voluntary winding up, subject to the provisions of the Act as to preferential payments, the company's property shall:

> "be applied in satisfaction of the company's liabilities pari passu . . ."

The distribution of a company's property in a compulsory winding up is not dealt with
C   in the 1986 Act itself but in rules made under sec. 411 of the Act. Rule 4.181 of the *Insolvency Rules* 1986, which is headed "Debts of insolvent company to rank equally", provides that:

> "(1) Debts other than preferential debts rank equally between themselves in the winding up and, after preferential debts, shall be paid in full unless the assets are insufficient for meeting them, in which case they abate in equal proportions between themselves."

D
The provisions of set-off, which were formerly contained in sec. 31, so far as applicable to insolvent companies are now also to be found in the rules (see r. 4.90).

In *Rolls Razor Ltd v Cox* the defendant was a door-to-door salesman employed by the plaintiff company. He sold washing machines and was provided with a van. He was remunerated by a commission but was required to pay his receipts to the company at
E   stated intervals without retaining his commission. On repaying his commission the company was entitled to keep back a retention fund up to a stated limit which was to be available to meet claims against the salesman and to be paid to him only after the determination of the agreement. The company became insolvent and the question was whether the defendant could set-off moneys received by him on the sale of the company's goods and the value of goods remaining in his possession against the retention fund. It was held in the Court of Appeal that sec. 31 applied and permitted the set-off of the
F   sums received by the salesman and, by a majority, that it permitted the set-off also of the value of the retained goods.

It was, therefore, unnecessary for the Court of Appeal to decide whether sec. 31 could have been excluded by agreement; the agreement did not purport so to provide. However, Lord *Denning* (at p. 570A) rejected the claim that the agreement excluded the right of set-off:

G
> ". . . for the simple reason that the parties cannot contract out of the statute. Where there are mutual dealings, the statute says that 'the balance of the account and no more shall be claimed or paid on either side'. That is an absolute statutory rule which must be observed: see *Ex parte Barnett*, by Lord Selborne L.C."

Danckwerts LJ said (at p. 573A–B):

H
> "A question was raised whether the statutory set-off could be excluded by the terms of the agreement between the parties. The authorities are meagre on this point and not very clear, but in my opinion the statutory set-off being a matter of statute, cannot be excluded."

The Court of Appeal was not referred to the decision of the Irish Court of Appeal in *Deering v Hyndman* (1886) 18 LR Ir 323 — the only case in which this point fell to be decided and in which the Irish Court of Appeal had held unanimously that a creditor

could waive a right of set-off given by the Irish bankruptcy laws. The observation by
Lord *Selborne* relied on by Lord *Denning* was obiter.

In the *Halesowen* case the Halesowen company had a loan account which was
overdrawn at National Westminster Bank and a trading account in credit at Lloyds
Bank. On 4 April 1968 it was agreed that the trading account would be transferred to an
account at the same branch of the National Westminster Bank, where the loan account
was held. The loan account ("the No. 1 account") would be frozen and the current
account ("the No. 2 account") operated only when it was in credit. That agreement was
to continue, in the absence of a material change of circumstances, for four months. On
20 May the company gave notice convening a meeting of creditors at 2.30pm on 12 June
to consider a winding-up resolution. The bank took no steps to terminate the agreement.
On 12 June a cheque was paid into the No. 2 account. Later on the same day the
creditors' meeting confirmed a resolution for the winding up of the company. The case
for the bank, which succeeded at first instance, was that the bank was entitled
independently of sec. 31, which was not relied upon, to consolidate the two accounts. In
the Court of Appeal the bank also relied on sec. 31. It was held by the Court of Appeal
([1971] 1 QB 1) that the right of the bank to combine the accounts without notice to the
customer was excluded by the agreement and by a majority (*Buckley* LJ dissenting) that
the dealings on the two accounts were not mutual dealings within sec. 31. It was again
unnecessary for the Court of Appeal, in the light of its decision, to consider whether
sec. 31 could have been excluded by agreement. However, Lord *Denning* said at p. 36B:

> "I must mention finally the section as to mutual credit and set-off which is
> contained in section 31 of the Bankruptcy Act, 1914, and is applied to companies
> winding up by section 317 of the Companies Act, 1948. It has been held in this
> court that the parties cannot contract out of this section: see *Rolls Razor Ltd* v.
> *Cox.* . ."

Section 31 is not mentioned by *Winn* LJ. *Buckley* LJ, after referring to observations in
the Supreme Court of British Guiana and in the Privy Council as to whether a right of
set-off under similar provisions in the local law could be excluded, added (at p. 48F):

> "It has since been held in this country in *Rolls Razor Ltd* v. *Cox.* . . that the
> operation of section 31 of the Bankruptcy Act, 1914, cannot be excluded by
> agreement between the parties. The ground of the Privy Council decision in
> *British Guiana Bank* v. *Official Receiver* is accordingly not available in this court."

In the House of Lords the decision of the Court of Appeal that the dealings on the two
accounts were not mutual dealings within sec. 31 was reversed. It was also held that the
agreement did not in its terms purport to exclude sec. 31. Thus, it was again unnecessary
for the House of Lords to consider whether sec. 31 could have been excluded by more
apt words. However, the question was fully argued, and all the members of the judicial
committee who heard the appeal expressed their opinion on it. Lord *Cross*, after a very
full and lucid analysis of the earlier decisions, concluded ([1972] AC 785 at p. 818A):

> "I can see no reason in principle why the section should not be excluded by
> agreement; I do not think that Lord Selborne intended to indicate that he thought
> that it could not be excluded by agreement; and I prefer the decision in *Deering* v.
> *Hyndman* to that in the *Rolls Razor* case . . . Therefore if, contrary to my opinion,
> the agreement in this case did not determine on the winding up and was intended
> to exclude the operation of section 31 I would think that the respondents were
> entitled to succeed."

However, Viscount *Dilhorne*, after reviewing the authorities, concluded (at p. 805D)
that:

A

". . . the terms of section 31 and of the sections that follow it show that 'shall' was used in all those sections in its directory and mandatory sense, prescribing the course to be followed in the administration of the bankrupt's property."

Lord *Kilbrandon* agreed (at p. 824A):

B

"In my opinion, accordingly, the rule now is that the terms of section 31 are mandatory in the sense that not only do they lay down statutory directives for the administration of claims in bankruptcy but they also make it impossible for persons effectively to contract, either before or after an act of bankruptcy has occurred, with a view to the bankruptcy being administered otherwise in accordance with the statutory directives. In other words, as Lord Denning M.R. said in *Rolls Razor Ltd.* v. *Cox*. . . 'the parties cannot contract out of the statute'. I must admit to being impressed by the argument that such a rule — enunciated as it was for the first time in 1967 otherwise than by obiter dicta, albeit some of great weight —

C

may be expected to form a serious embarrassment to those wishing to adopt the beneficial course of agreeing to moratoria for the assistance of a business in financial difficulties. But, if that be so, it seems to call for the intervention of the legislature. It is, in any event, generally agreed that a restatement of law of bankruptcy, both for England and for Scotland, is overdue."

Lord *Simon* dealt with the position more fully (at p. 808E) and I should, I think, read that passage in his judgment in full:

D

"I turn finally, then, to the question whether section 31 can be excluded by agreement. On this matter I concur the reasoning and conclusions of my noble and learned friends, Viscount Dilhorne and Lord Kilbrandon. The maxim 'quilibet potest renunciare juri pro se introducto' (see *Broom, Legal Maxims*, 10th ed. (1939), p. 477) begs the question whether the statutory provision in section 31 was introduced for the benefit of any particular person or body of persons or was prescribing a course of procedure to be followed in the adminstration of a bankrupt's property. I appreciate that the imposition of a duty on a public officer does not necessarily preclude a private right arising therefrom: *Ashby* v. *White* (1703) 1 Smith L.C. . . But in *Broom* the maxim is, for good reason, translated: 'Anyone may at his pleasure, renounce the benefit of a stipulation or other right introduced *entirely in his own favour*' (my italics). It is also significant that, in the discussion of his maxim, section 31 of the Bankruptcy Act is nowhere mentioned. Having regard both to the terminology of section 31 and to its statutory context, it seems to me to be impossible so to construe the wording of the section as introducing a right entirely in favour of anyone. The change in terminology between the Bankruptcy Act 1849 . . and the Bankruptcy Act 1869 . . must have been, at the least, to avert doubts. This part of the Act is laying down a code of procedure whereby bankrupts' estates (and, by reference, insolvent companies)

E

F

G

are to be administered in a proper and orderly way; this is a matter in which the commercial community generally has an interest, and the maxim has no application in a matter where the public have an interest: see *Broom*, p. 481, citing *Ayr Harbour Trustees* v. *Oswald*. . . and *Spurling* v. *Bantoft*. . .

There is a clear preponderance of authority against there being a right to contract out of the section, and I agree with the analysis of the case law made by my noble and learned friend, Viscount Dilhorne.

H

It was argued for the respondents that, if there could be no contracting out of section 31, a very usual type of compromise between the creditors, in their common interest to keep an insolvent afloat, would be impossible. To this there are, I think, two answers: first, there would be nothing to prevent any such agreement after an act of bankruptcy had been committed, and, secondly, so far as companies are concerned, section 206 of the Companies Act 1948 gives power,

subject to the sanction of the court, for a compromise to be made in certain
circumstances with creditors which will be binding on all the creditors (or all
creditors of the class involved). But the mere fact that this argument could be
advanced at all in view of the conflict of dicta and what I cannot but regard as a
clear preponderance of authority emphasises the desirability that promised
legislation in this field should not be unduly delayed.''

As I see it, the decision of the majority in the House of Lords did not rest solely on the
mandatory language used in sec. 31 alone, but on the mandatory language used coupled
with the proposition that the liquidator and the general body of creditors might have an
interest in ensuring that debts due to and from a creditor arising from mutual dealings
are set off. This is quite explicit in the speech of Lord *Simon*, who considered and
rejected the claim that the section can be construed as "introducing a right entirely in
favour" of a creditor.

That proposition, it seems to me, must rest upon the inconvenience and potential
unfairness to the trustee or liquidator and so to other creditors that might arise if a
creditor was entitled either to exercise or, at his option, not to exercise the right of
set-off. For otherwise, the creditor might prove in the bankruptcy or winding up leaving
it to the trustee or liquidator to recover the debt due to the estate in proceedings which
might be protracted and expensive, and which might not result in the recovery of the full
amount due. In the meantime the distribution of the insolvent estate might be held up
and a question might arise whether a creditor who had waived his right of set-off would
be entitled to a dividend while proceedings to recover the debt due from him were still
on foot.

An agreement between the debtor and the creditor excluding the creditor's right of
set-off, or the waiver by the creditor of his right of set-off, even after the commencement
of the bankruptcy or winding up, might thus equally hinder the rapid, efficient and
economical process of bankruptcy. The question is whether this underlying consideration
of public policy should similarly invalidate an agreement between a debtor and a creditor
postponing or subordinating the claim of the creditor to the claims of other unsecured
creditors and preclude the waiver or subordination of the creditor's claim after the
commencement of a bankruptcy or winding up. I do not think that it does. It seems to
me plain that after the commencement of a bankruptcy or winding up a creditor must be
entitled to waive his debt just as he is entitled to decline to submit a proof.

There might, in any given case, be a question whether a waiver was binding on him
but that is irrelevant for this purpose. If the creditor can waive his right altogether I can
see no reason why he should not waive his right to prove, save to the extent of any assets
remaining after the debts of other unsecured creditors have been paid in full; or if he
is a preferential creditor, to agree that his debt will rank equally with unsecured
non-preferential debts.

So also, if the creditor can waive his right to prove or agree the postponement of his
debt after the commencement of the bankruptcy or winding up, I can see no reason why
he should not agree with the debtor that his debt will not be payable or will be postponed
or subordinated in the event of a bankruptcy or winding up. The reason for giving effect
to an agreement in these terms seems to me to be if anything stronger than that for
allowing the creditor to waive or postpone or subordinate his debt after the
commencement of a bankruptcy or winding up; for other creditors might have given
credit on the assumption that the agreement would be binding.

Mr Purle submitted that the reason for excluding such an agreement is that the
liquidator ought not to be required or entitled to look behind a proof to determine
whether a creditor submitting a proof was entitled to payment pari passu with other
unsecured creditors. I find this reason unconvincing. There are situations under the 1986

A   Act in which an unsecured debt is postponed to other unsecured debt. Under sec. 74(2)(f) (which re-enacts sec. 212(1)(g) of the 1948 Act) sums payable to a member are not to be deemed to be a debt payable to that member in a case of competition between himself and any other creditor not a member. Under sec. 215(4) where the court makes a declaration of fraudulent or wrongful trading under sec. 213 or 214 in relation to a creditor, the court may direct that the debt shall rank in priority after all

B   other debts owed by the company and after interest on those debts.

     In these cases the liquidator has to give effect to a subordination created by statute. However, I can see no reason why the liquidator should have any greater difficulty in giving effect to a contractual subordination. If it is plain that the assets will be insufficient to meet the claims of unsecured creditors whose claims are not subordinated, the proof of the subordinated creditor (which is no more than a document asserting a claim — see r. 4.73(3)) can be rejected; if admitted before it becomes plain that the assets will not

C   suffice to meet the claims of other creditors, then when the position is crystallised the proof can be expunged or varied (see r. 4.85 and 4.86).

     Mr Purle also relied on certain observations made by *Templeman* J ([1973] 1 Lloyd's Rep 414]) and by Lord *Simon* in the House of Lords in *British Eagle International Air Lines Ltd v Compagnie Nationale Air France* [1975] 1 WLR 758. That case concerned a very complex arrangement for the clearance of debt between airlines which were

D   members of the International Air Transport Association. These agreements and the issue between British Eagle and Air France are succinctly and, I think, sufficiently set out by *Russell* LJ who gave the judgment of the Court of Appeal in a passage which I will read in full. It is reported at [1974] 1 Lloyd's Rep 429 (at pp. 430–431).

     "Stated shortly, the position was this. Most major airlines are members of IATA.

E   For the general convenience of worldwide air passengers and consignors of cargo, it is the practice of airline 'A' to issue, for example, to an air passenger a ticket through to his destination, though airline 'A' does not supply flights the whole way. The passenger would need to change at some stage to airline 'B' for the rest of the journey. Airline 'A' would receive payment for the whole flight from the passenger in the currency of the country of departure. This system would involve a proportionate payment by airline 'A' to airline 'B' on the basis that the latter

F   had rendered services to the former. That is a very simple example of the rendering of services by one airline to another, and there were many different circumstances in which such services would be rendered between airlines, giving rise to a complicated network of debits and credits, with added complications in currency matters. It would obviously be a major convenience if a clearing house was set up by the major airlines and IATA whereby each airline could avoid settling with each of the 70 or more other airlines separately the balance in terms

G   of debit and credit in respect of services rendered between it and the other airline. This is what was done by agreement between IATA and all airline members of IATA wishing to participate in the clearing house. The clearing house was not itself a corporate or other body; it was an activity conducted by IATA — a Canadian corporate body, pursuant to the agreement to which all 'clearing house' members of IATA and IATA itself were parties.

H   Expressed in its simplest terms, the system was that in respect of every calendar month there was a clearance: sums for services inter se rendered to and by clearing house members based upon returns of the month to the clearing house were brought into calculation: in the result some airlines were in respect of the month in overall debit on clearance and others in overall credit on clearance: the former would pay the respective amounts of their overall debits to the clearance house

(IATA) and the clearing house would pay to the latter the respective amounts of   A
their overall credits on clearance.

On November 6, 1968, British Eagle (an English limited company) ceased to
operate, and on November 8 resolved upon a creditors' voluntary winding up. At
this time British Eagle had rendered services to the defendant Air France since
the end of August, 1968 (cross services in respect of which month had been fully
settled all round through the clearing house) to a value substantially in excess of   B
services rendered to British Eagle by Air France in respect of the same period.
But in respect of the same period other members had rendered net services to
British Eagle to a value greatly in excess of the last-mentioned value, and if all
inter-airline services for the period up to November 6, 1968, are processed
through the clearing house, British Eagle will be shown to be net debtors on
clearance in a substantial sum.

In this action the liquidator of British Eagle sues Air France in the name of British   C
Eagle for a sum of money on the footing of debt for net services rendered by
British Eagle to Air France after setting off contra services by Air France to
British Eagle. He contends that he is entitled to sue for that sum as a debt due
from Air France disregarding the clearing house agreement. The operation of the
clearing house agreement if carried through will, he asserts, result in the sum
claimed not being available to the general body of British Eagle's creditors, but
on the contrary being made available to a limited body of creditors for net services   D
rendered to British Eagle. This is correct.

It is be observed that it is a matter of indifference to Air France whether they pay
the sum to the liquidator or (so to speak) bring it into the clearing house pool in
reduction of Air France's debtor-on-clearance position: in fact it is held by IATA
on suspense: if the liquidator succeeds, the clearance will be adjusted so that Air
France does not pay twice, and all airlines which have a net credit against British   E
Eagle will prove for their respective net credits as unsecured creditors: if the
liquidator fails, IATA will prove for the net sum for which British Eagle is debtor
on clearance, any deficiency in a 100 per cent. dividend falling proportionately
upon those airlines whose services to British Eagle in the period exceeded in value
British Eagle's contra services to them respectively. Air France is therefore
fighting not so much its own battle as a battle on behalf of IATA and those airlines   F
who are in net services credit vis-à-vis British Eagle."

Russell LJ agreed with *Templeman* J that (at p.433):

". . . British Eagle having contracted with every other member of the clearing
house and with IATA not to enforce its net claim for services against, for example,
Air France otherwise than through the clearing house, it could not while a member
do so."   G

On that footing the clearing house arrangement clearly did not contravene any
principle of insolvency law. As *Russell* LJ observed (at p.434):

"Those laws require that the property of an insolvent company shall be distributed
pro rata among its unsecured creditors: but the question here is whether the claim
asserted against Air France is property of British Eagle."

In the House of Lords [1975] 1 WLR 758, Lord *Morris* and Lord *Simon* both agreed   H
with this analysis of the arrangements. Lord *Cross*, with whom Lord *Diplock* and Lord
Edmund Davies agreed, having set out the relevant terms of the clearing house
arrangement and having analysed the balance of debt as between British Eagle and Air
France, said (at p. 778E):

A

"On this aspect of the case we heard much argument as to whether the right of British Eagle to have any claim against Air France settled through the clearing house system could properly be called a debt due by Air France to British Eagle notwithstanding that British Eagle could not bring legal proceedings against Air France to enforce payment of the sums due from it. I have no doubt that in common parlance the right would be called a debt and the framers of the regulations — some of whom were presumably lawyers — had no hesitation in

B

describing the rights in question as 'debts' in regulation 18(c). It is to my mind undesirable that the law should give a more limited meaning to a word than the ordinary man would do unless there is good ground for doing so; and personally I can see no reason why the law should refuse to describe the legal right of British Eagle to be paid the sums in question by Air France as 'debts' because the contract under which the right to be paid arose did not permit British Eagle to sue Air

C

France for payment but provided for payment exclusively through the medium of the clearing house. But this question — as I see it — is simply a dispute as to the proper use of words which has no bearing on the decision of the case, and for my part I am prepared to assume in favour of Air France that the legal rights against Air France which British Eagle acquired when it rendered the services in question were not strictly 'debts' owing by Air France but were innominate choses in action having some, but not all, the characteristics of 'debts'."

D

On that analysis the claim by the clearing house creditors was clearly a claim to be entitled to be preferred to other unsecured creditors (p. 780E):

"that they have achieved by the medium of the 'clearing house' agreement a position analogous to that of secured creditors without the need for the creation or registration of charges on the book debts in question."

That claim was clearly "repugnant to our insolvency legislation".

E

It seems to me, therefore, that the only real issues in the *British Eagle* case related to the construction and the proper analysis of the rights and obligations conferred and imposed by clearance agreement. There was no issue as to the principle of insolvency law to be applied.

Section 31 and the decision in the *Halesowen* case were not referred to in the Court of Appeal. They are not referred to in the speech of Lord *Morris*. In the House of Lords,

F

Lord *Cross*, having observed that the liquidator rightly applied sec. 31 in relation to his claim against Air France, added (at p. 781C):

"But so far as I can see the section has no bearing on anything that we have to decide in this appeal. It is therefore unnecessary for us to say anything about the recent case in this House of *Halesowen Presswork & Assemblies Ltd.* v. *Westminster Bank Ltd.* [1972] A.C. 785."

G

Lord *Simon* having stated at (p. 771G) his conclusion that:

". . . no party to the interline agreement had any right to claim direct payment for interline service: its right thereafter was to have the value of the such service respectively credited and debited in the monthly IATA clearing house settlement account."

—added:

H

"I agree that *Halesowen* . . . applies by analogy to section 302 of the Companies Act 1948, so that one cannot contract out of its terms. But, in view of paragraph (2) of Article VI of the interline agreement (and the consequent provisions of the IATA regulations and manual of procedure), the 'property' of British Eagle (for the purpose of section 302) did not include any direct claim against Air France for the value of interline services performed by British Eagle for Air France but

merely the right to have the value of such services brought into the monthly   A
settlement account."

This observation reflects an observation of *Templeman* J at first instance [1973]
1 Lloyd's Rep 414. Having stated the submission of counsel for the liquidators of British
Eagle, Mr Heyman, as regards sec. 302 to be that (at p. 434):

> ". . . you cannot contract out of the requirement that the property of a company
> must be used to pay its creditors *pari passu* any more than you can contract out of   B
> sect. 31, which says you must have a set-off when there are mutual dealings"

—he added:

> ". . . in my judgment, Mr. Heyman is quite right. If there was a debt, that is to
> say a debt owed by Air France to British Eagle, which at the date of liquidation
> was vested in British Eagle, or was vested in IATA as an agent for British Eagle,
> with instructions to pay off the creditors in the clearing house, but no other   C
> creditors, or if that debt had been assigned to IATA, which had exactly the same
> instructions, namely to pay off the creditors of the clearing house but no other
> creditors, then in my judgment that debt would be the property of the company
> British Eagle. The result of it being vested in the company, say what you will
> about the rights of agents and the rights of assignees, would be to infringe sect.
> 302 of the Companies Act, 1948, and that cannot be allowed."
>   D

He continued:

> "In my judgment, Mr. Heyman is right when he says that if you look closely at the
> *Halesowen* case the parallel is exact. But, of course, that all turns on whether
> there was a debt vested in British Eagle on the date of liquidation. . ."

These observations were clearly obiter and were made in the context of a case in
which if the clearance arrangements had had the effect contended for by Air France they   E
would clearly have put a member of the clearance arrangements in a position which
would have been better than the position of other unsecured creditors. The arrangements
would therefore unquestionably have infringed a fundamental principle of bankruptcy
law, which is reflected in but not derived from sec. 302 or its predecessor, that a creditor
cannot validly contract with his debtor that he will enjoy some advantage in a bankruptcy
or winding-up which is denied to other creditors.

In my judgment I am not compelled by the decision of the House of Lords in the   F
Halesowen and the *British Eagle* cases or by the decisions of the Court of Appeal in
those cases, or in *Rolls Razor Ltd v Cox* to conclude that a contract between a company
and a creditor, providing for the debt due to the creditor to be subordinated in the
insolvent winding up of the company to other unsecured debt, is rendered void by the
insolvency legislation. A contrary decision would have wide-reaching repercussions. It
is not infrequently the case that a company can only continue to trade and incur credit   G
with the financial support of a parent or associated company, or a bank which is willing
to subordinate its debt to the debts owed to the other unsecured creditor. Subordinated
debt is in many contexts treated for accountancy purposes as if it were part of the
company's capital. So in this case the group balance sheet of MCC included the liability
under MCC's guarantee of the bonds under the heading "Minority shareholders interest".
Under the rules of the Securities and Futures Authority subordinated loans may be   H
included amongst a company's financial resources as "eligible capital substitutes". Of
course, a loan can be effectively subordinated if the creditor constitutes himself a trustee
for other unsecured creditors as in *Re British & Commonwealth (No. 3)*; or he may
contract to assign the benefit of his debt to other unsecured creditors without in either
case affecting the ordinary process of proof in the liquidation or the application of the
company's assets pari passu amongst creditors whose proofs have been submitted.

A   However, I think Mr Cone was right when he submitted that to recognise subordination by these means and not by a direct contract between the company and the creditor would represent a triumph of form over substance.

I was referred by Mr Cone to a number of cases in other jurisdictions in which the insolvency laws are derived from, or similar to, English law in which a contractual subordination has been held to be valid. In *Ex parte De Villiers. Re Carbon Developments (Pty) Ltd* [1992] 2 SA 95, Stegmann J refused the liquidator of the company leave to

B   convene meetings of creditors and members to consider an offer of compromise (in effect a scheme of arrangement) on the ground that the company had been trading while it was insolvent and that the liquidator had failed to furnish the creditors with sufficient information as to the potential liability of the directors for fraudulent trading. His conclusion, that there was a possible claim against the directors which would be precluded if the compromise were sanctioned, and which ought to have been investigated,

C   was founded on the view that on deciding whether directors were liable for allowing the company to trade while insolvent, the liquidator would not be entitled to have any regard to the terms of a subordination agreement because to do so would entail a rearrangement of the statutory ranking of claims. That view was rejected by the Court of Appeal of South Africa (*Corbett* CJ, *Van Heerden* and *Goldstone* JJA and *Nicholas* and *Harms* AJJA) ([1993] 1 SA 493). *Goldstone* JA, giving the judgment of the Court of

D   Appeal, described a subordination agreement in these terms (at p. 504F):

> "The essence of a subordination agreement, generally speaking, is that the enforceability of a debt, by agreement with the creditor to whom it is owed, is made dependent upon the solvency of the debtor and the prior payment of its debts to other creditors.

> Subordination agreements may take many forms. They may be bilateral, i.e. between the debtor and the creditor. They may be multilateral and include other

E   > creditors as parties. They may be in a form of a *stipulatio alteri*, i.e. for the benefit of other and future creditors and open to acceptance by them. The subordination agreement may be a term of the loan or it may be a collateral agreement entered into some time after the making of the loan.

> Save possibly in exceptional cases, the terms of the subordination agreement will have the following legal effect: the debt comes into existence or continues to exist (as the case may be), but its enforceability is made subject to the fulfilment of a

F   > condition. Usually the condition is that the debt may be enforced by the creditor only if and when the value of the debtor's assets exceeds his liabilities, excluding the subordinated debt. The practical effect of such a condition, particularly where, for example, the excess is less than the full amount of the subordinated debt, would depend upon the terms of the specific agreement under consideration and need not now be considered.

G   > In the event of the insolvency of the debtor, [that is the equivalent I think of vesting in the trustee] sequestration would normally mean that the condition upon which the enforceability of the debt depends will have become incapable of fulfilment. The legal result of this would be that the debt dies a natural death. . ."

Having referred to some authorities he continues:

> "The result would be that the erstwhile creditor would have no claim which could

H   > be proved in insolvency. To the extent that it may have been suggested in *Cooper v A & G Fashions (Pty) Ltd. Ex parte Millman* [1991] 4 SA 204 at pp. 207G–208D that on insolvency a value should be placed upon such a debt, this is not correct. The debt would not normally survive sequestration. A contingent liability can only be valued and proved in insolvency where at the time the condition upon which the liability depends is still capable of fulfilment."

Then having observed that in deciding whether the conduct of the directors in allowing   A
the company to incur debt was fraudulent or reckless he added (p. 505D):

> "In that context, the existence and terms of a subordination agreement would be
> material and relevant in deciding whether the persons conducting such business
> incurred the debts with the reasonable expectation of their being paid in the
> ordinary course. The fact that a major creditor has subordinated its claim and to
> that extent created a moratorium for the benefit of the other creditors is obviously
> relevant in determining the subjective state of mind of the debtor or those
> conducting its business."

He distinguished an earlier decision in *Lind v Lefdal's Pianos Ltd* [1929] TPD 241
(which had been relied upon by *Stegmann* J) on the ground that:

> "There certain creditors attempted to rearrange the order in which they would be
> paid by the liquidator. In the case of debt subordination, the creditor has no claim
> unless other creditors receive payment in full. There is no question of a
> rearrangement of the claims of the creditors who are to be paid out of the
> unencumbered assets of a company. The position would be no different in
> principle from the case of a debtor who, for whatever reason, decided not to prove
> a claim with the liquidator. Indeed, where there is a probability of a contribution
> being levied upon creditors, it is a common occurrence for creditors to refrain
> from proving a claim."

He then referred to the *British Eagle* case as being similarly distinguishable. I have
some doubt whether in English law a subordinated debt is accurately described as a
contingent liability and the analysis of the Justice of Appeal of the nature of subordinated
debt indicates that there may be some differences between the law of England and the
law of South Africa. In English law subordinated debt would not, I think, be accurately
described as a "contingent liability" even if the debt is expressed to be payable only in
the event of a winding up and is to be subordinated to other unsecured debts in a winding
up. It may still be paid in full or in part. The position is a fortiori if, as is more usually
the case, the debt may become payable while the company is a going concern but
is subordinated to other unsecured debts in a winding up. A debt cannot be said to be a
contingent debt merely because in a winding up it may rank behind other debts and
because the assets of the company may not suffice to pay the other debts in full.
However, nothing turns on the question whether a subordinated debt is aptly described
as a contingent claim. The essential feature pointed to by *Goldstone* JA is that it is a debt
payable only to the extent that there is a surplus after meeting the claims of other
unsubordinated creditors.

This question has also been considered in a number of cases in New Zealand and in
the states of Australia. It is only necessary to refer to the most recent of them, *Horne v
Chester & Fein Property Developments Pty Ltd & Ors* (1987) 5 ACLC 245 in which
Southwell J reviewed the earlier cases. In that case C and S, who had contracted to
purchase restaurant premises, entered into an agreement with F under which a unit trust
was established for the purpose of conducting the restaurant business. G was incorporated
on 8 July 1982 for the purpose of becoming the trustee of the unit trust. Each of C, S and
F held 25 units. It was provided by cl. 4 of the unit holders agreement that all moneys
advanced by C, S and F to G should be accepted by it as loans and should rank equally in
priority as to the payment by G, but this was qualified by a proviso that if any of C, S and
F made an additional loan to G exceeding his due proportion of the loans made by all of
them the additional loan would be repaid before any other repayment to other unit
holders.

It was common ground that C and S had made additional loans to G within the
proviso. At p. 248, after summarising the facts in the *Halesowen* case, *Southwell* J said:

A

"In the speech of Viscount *Dilhorne*, there is a discussion of a number of authorities, of which 'the weight of opinion expressed . . . appears to me to be in favour of the conclusion that it is not possible to contract out of sec. 31'. However, there, and, so far as I have seen in most other relevant cases, the term 'contract out' is used in circumstances where the contract relied upon is one the performance of which upon later insolvency, would adversely affect other creditors who were not parties to the contract. Viscount *Dilhorne* referred with approval (p. 805) to dicta of *Hallett* J. in *Victoria Products Ltd. v. Tosh & Co. Ltd.* (1940) 165 L.T. 78 where his Honour said that:

B

'an attempt to leave outside that process some particular item is one which should be regarded as against the policy of the insolvency laws.'

Repeatedly, over the years, 'the policy of the insolvency laws' has formed the basis of decision. That policy, as it appears to me, was never intended to alter the rights and obligations of parties freely entering into a contract, unless the performance of a contract would upon insolvency adversely affect the right of strangers to the contract. Authority for that proposition is to be found in *Ex parte Holthauren, Re Scheibler* (1874) 9 Ch. App. 722 at pp. 726–727 (referred to by Lord *Morris* in his dissenting speech in *British Eagle* at pp. 770–771)."

C

He then summarised the facts in the *British Eagle* case and cited the observations by Lord *Simon*, which I have already cited. He cited also the passage from the speech of Lord *Cross* to which I have referred. His conclusion (at p. 252) was that sec. 440 of the Companies (Victoria) Code (which is in substantially the same terms as sec. 33(7) of the 1914 Act: see p. 247 of the report):

D

". . . does not require that in all cases a liquidator must distribute pari passu. He may distribute in accordance with an agreement between the parties where to do so could not adversely affect any creditor not a party to the agreement."

E

In stating that the expression "contract out" was used by Viscount *Dilhorne* in *Halesowen* "in circumstances where the contract relied upon is one the performance of which upon later insolvency, would adversely affect other creditors who were not parties to the contract", *Southwell* J clearly had in mind the point more explicitly made by Lord *Simon* that there might be circumstances in which where there had been mutual credits mutual debits or other mutual dealings, the trustee or liquidator might take the view that it would facilitate the realisation and distribution of the estate for the benefit of the creditors as a whole that the mutual credits and debits should be set off.

F

Horne v Chester & Fein concerned an agreement between unit holders which was entered into before loans were made and indeed before the company to which they were made was incorporated. It would no doubt be easier in that context to give effect to the agreement by the implication of a term for the assignment of the benefit of the interest of F in the winding up to C and S to the extent necessary to meet the additional loans. However, that was not the ground on which *Southwell* J decided the case.

G

The Federal Bankruptcy Code

Section 501(a) of the US Federal Code of 1978 provides that:

H

"A subordination agreement is enforceable in a case under this title to the same extent that such an agreement is enforceable under applicable and non-bankruptcy law."

That provision gave effect to the law developed by the courts. In the earlier cases subordination agreements were given effect on a variety of grounds. However, in recent cases a subordination agreement has been recognised as having direct contractual effect. In *First National Bank of Hollywood v American Foam Rubber Corp* (1976) 530 F(2d)

450 at p. 454, *Van Graafeiland* J, giving the judgment of the court (US Court of Appeals,   A
Second Circuit), said:

> "Various theories have been advanced to support the enforcement of subordination
> agreements in bankruptcy: equitable lien, equitable assignment, constructive
> trust and enforcement of contractual rights."

Then, having referred to a number of cases, he continues:

> "This Circuit has favoured the recognition of priorities based upon the 'lawful   B
> contractual arrangement between the parties.' *In re Aktiebolaget Kreuger & Toll*,
> 96 F.2d 768, 770 (2d Cir. 1938). As we stated in *In re Credit Industrial Corporation*,
> *supra*, 366 F.2d at 407, if the terms of the contract are unambiguous, there is no
> need to resort to 'strained theories of third-party beneficiary, estoppel or general
> principles of equity' to determine the rights of the parties."

I have not been referred to the law of any continental jurisdiction except Switzerland.   C
It seems to me unlikely that in any system derived from the civil code the law will differ
in this respect from the position under Swiss law. It seems from the speech of Lord
Kilbrandon that under Scottish law a creditor can contract out of or waive his right to
set-off and if so he can presumably validly agree that his debt will be subordinated.
I have set out the leading authorities in South Africa, the US and Australia. It would,
I think, be a matter of grave concern if, at a time when insolvency increasingly has
international ramifications, it were to be found that English law alone refused to give   D
effect to a contractual subordination. I have reached the clear conclusion that such a
clause is valid and effective and is not avoided by any consideration of public policy and
I shall so declare.

(Order accordingly)

———————————

   E

   F

   G

   H

A   # Lipe Ltd v Leyland DAF Ltd & Ors.

Court of Appeal (Civil Division).
Lloyd, Kennedy and Hoffmann L JJ.
Judgment delivered 30 March 1993.

B
> *Administrative receivership — Retention of title — Unpaid supplier with*
> *retention of title claim obtained injunction restraining selling or dealing with*
> *goods — Administrative receivers gave undertaking to return or pay for goods*
> *— Whether injunction should be discharged.*

**Where administrative receivers had given an undertaking to an unpaid supplier with a
retention of title claim, to return the goods or pay the value of any goods used or sold
during the receivership in respect of which a claim for retention of title was subsequently
established, the supplier was not entitled to an injunction restraining selling or dealing**
C   **with the goods.**

The following case was referred to in the judgment of Hoffmann LJ:

American Cyanamid Co v Ethicon Ltd [1975] AC 396.

Gabriel Moss QC, Miss Linden Ife and Peter Arden (instructed by Wilde Sapte) for
the administrative receivers.

D   Brendan Hegarty QC and Gerard McDermott (instructed by Boote Edgar Esterkin,
Manchester) for the plaintiff.

JUDGMENT

Hoffmann LJ: The plaintiff ("Lipe") is a manufacturer of clutch assembly parts for
motor vehicles. The first defendant ("Leyland") is a motor vehicle manufacturer and
distributor. Lipe has supplied Leyland with parts under contracts which it says incorporate
E   standard terms and conditions which include a reservation of title clause. Whether Lipe
is right depends upon the resolution of a battle of forms on which it is accepted that there
is a triable issue.

On 3 February 1993 the second defendants ("the receivers") were appointed
administrative receivers of Leyland. On that date the Leyland spares division in
Chorley, Lancashire held stocks of clutch parts supplied by Lipe which are said to be the
F   subject of outstanding invoices to the value of about £93,000. Lipe claims that these
parts remain its property and has asked to be allowed to take them away. The receivers,
on the other hand, are carrying on Leyland's business, which has an annual turnover of
about £270m. They want to be able to preserve as much of the business as can be made
commercially viable and sell it as a going concern. For this purpose they need these and
the other 110,000 varieties of spare parts which Leyland holds in its Chorley depot.
Unless the receivers can continue to supply these parts to dealers and garages, the whole
G   business will be damaged. Furthermore, the spare parts inventory represents at cost
some £36m and sales are running at £300,000 to £400,000 a day. This represents a useful
source of cash to fund the rest of the business.

There have been about 400 retention of title claims made against the receivers, of
which 190 relate to the spare parts operation. In the case of each claim the receivers have
asked for information to enable them to investigate its validity. They have undertaken
H   that if the claim is found to be valid, the supplier will be paid the value of any goods used
or sold after their appointment.

Lipe was not satisfied with this undertaking. It said that unless its claim was immediately
accepted and satisfied in full, it would come and take its goods away. The receivers
refused to allow this and on 9 March Lipe issued proceedings for delivery of its parts and
an injunction restraining Leyland and the receivers from dealing with them. On the

A

same day *Colman* J granted ex parte an injunction until trial or further order restraining Leyland from selling or otherwise dealing in the goods. On 24 March he refused Leyland's application to discharge this order. From that refusal Leyland and the receivers now appeal.

The judge decided the question according to the guidelines laid down by the House of Lords in *American Cyanamid Co v Ethicon Ltd* [1975] AC 396. Mr Hegarty for Lipe had contended that this was an exceptional case which fell outside the guidelines, but that argument has not been pursued before us. The first question is therefore whether damages would be an adequate remedy. If so, no interlocutory intervention by injunction was needed to protect the position of Lipe pending trial.

B

The purpose of a retention of title clause is to give the supplier the security of being able to repossess the goods rather than prove in the liquidation of the company and receive a dividend. If Lipe proves at trial that its retention of title clause was incorporated into the relevant contacts, it will have a claim against Leyland for damages for conversion of those clutches which have meanwhile been sold. This would be an unsecured claim and therefore not in itself adequate. It has therefore become customary for receivers to supplement this remedy with a personal undertaking to pay the value of any goods used or sold during the receivership in respect of which a claim for retention of title has subsequently been established. By a letter dated 9 March 1993 these receivers offered the undertaking in the following terms:

C

D

> "We write to confirm that our clients are prepared to undertake to your clients that in the event that your clients are able to prove their retention of title claim in respect of the goods in their possession as at the date of their appointment, either to the satisfaction of our client or to the satisfaction of the court, our clients will return the goods, the subject matter of the claim, to your clients or, in the event of the goods having been sold or otherwise disposed of by our clients, they will pay to your clients the value of those goods."

E

Subject to two points which have been argued by Mr Hegarty and to which I shall return, the effect of that undertaking is as follows. If Leyland by its receivers sells goods which turn out to have belonged to Lipe, Lipe will of course no longer be able to recover them in specie. But it will become entitled as against the receivers to their value. Strictly speaking, the damages for conversion would be the market value, but Lipe says that in order to avoid arguments it would prefer to settle on an invoice value, and Mr Moss for Leyland and the receivers said he foresaw no difficulty about obtaining instructions to agree. Thus the purpose of the retention clause will have been fully achieved because Lipe will have recovered the goods or their value instead of having to be satisfied with a dividend. Lipe has no further interest which needs to be protected. This is not a case in which it has any interest in recovering the clutches in specie rather than their value. Accordingly, subject to the two points I have mentioned, damages against the receivers for any breach of their contractual undertaking would be an adequate remedy.

F

G

The first objection raised by Mr Hegarty is that the undertaking does not necessarily cover all cases in which Leyland might dispose of its clutches. It says that it applies to clutches "disposed of by our clients" and, taking the clients to be the receivers, this means that the receivers personally must have been sufficiently involved in the disposal to render themselves liable in damages for conversion. Mere overall control of the business would not necessarily be enough.

H

This was not a point which occurred to the solicitor who replied on Lipe's behalf to the letter of 9 March, and I am not surprised. It seems to me an impossible construction. "Our clients", in my judgment, means both Leyland and the receivers through whom it is now acting and the undertaking covers all goods of Lipe which the company may sell

A   or otherwise dispose of. Mr Hegarty accepts that if this is the true construction of the letter, the first objection falls away.

The second point is that upon which the judge refused to discharge his injunction. He said that although in principle damages were an adequate remedy, he was not satisfied that the receivers would be able to pay them. He had no evidence about the personal resources of the receivers in relation, not merely to the plaintiff's claim, but also to the B   400 other suppliers to whom they had given personal undertakings. He suggested that the difficulty might be avoided by an undertaking from the banks which had appointed the receivers or an agreement to pay the proceeds of sale into a joint account. But in the absence of such arrangements, he declined to discharge the injunction.

It seems to me that by concentrating on the personal resources of the receivers the judge ignored the realities of the way receiverships are conducted. Administrative C   receivers who carry on the business of an insolvent company will almost invariably incur personal liability under the contracts they make, sometimes in very large amounts: see sec. 44 of the *Insolvency Act* 1986. The counterparties who deal with them are not concerned with their personal resources and do not rely upon such resources in giving them credit. They rely instead upon the fact that a receiver, acting as an agent for the company, is entitled to be indemnified out of the company's assets under his control for all liabilities which he personally has incurred in exercising his powers as receiver. D   Furthermore, they rely upon the fact that receivers, as sensible professional men, will not lightly risk personal bankruptcy and will therefore not incur liabilities unless they are satisfied that there are sufficient assets to enable those liabilities, to say nothing of the receiver's personal expenses and remuneration, to be paid in full.

Mr Hegarty said that it was not certain that the right to be indemnified would apply to an undertaking to be answerable for damages for conversion, which would be a tortious E   act. It may turn out to have been technically a wrongful act against Lipe, but, in my judgment, the question of whether the receivers will be entitled to their indemnity depends upon whether it would be wrongful as against the debenture holder, to whom the assets are equitably charged, and so far as there may be a surplus, as against the company. For my part, I do not see how it could be wrongful against either of these parties. It would appear to me to be a prudent way of dealing to best advantage with assets which may or may not belong to the company and for which the company is in any F   event liable to either a contractual or a proprietary claim.

The judge made no mention of the receiver's right to pay liabilities out of the assets of the company and in my judgment the exercise of his discretion was vitiated by his failure to take this important factor into account. Of course it is possible that the receivers may conduct this receivership so imprudently as to leave themselves with inadequate assets to pay their personal liabilities, but I do not regard this as a sufficiently serious possibility G   as to prevent the undertaking from providing an adequate remedy. It is always possible that even the most prosperous-looking defendant may plunge into insolvency before trial, but this theoretical possibility is not enough to prevent damages from being regarded as a sufficient remedy within the *Cyanamid* guidelines. The risk in this case is, in my view, of the same order.

Even if one treats the risk as sufficient to require one to move to the next stage of the H   *Cyanamid* guidelines and examine the balance of convenience, Lipe in my judgment fares no better. If no injunction is granted, there is a remote risk that its claim against the receivers for goods sold pending trial will turn out to be worthless. If an injunction is granted, and in particular if others asserting an arguable claim to retention of title are encouraged to adopt similar tactics, the goods in question will be frozen and there will be a substantial risk of damaging the business which the receivers are trying to sell. The practical consequence is likely to be that the receivers will be forced to abandon their

challenge to the retention of title clauses and pay the suppliers immediately on the sale   A
of the goods in dispute. To force a party to abandon a bona fide defence by this kind of
commercial pressure seems to me an injustice which outweighs any risk which will have
to be borne by Lipe.

So both on the balance of convenience and because damages would be an adequate
remedy, I think that the judge should have discharged this injunction and I would allow
the appeal.   B

Kennedy LJ: I agree.

Lloyd LJ: I also agree, and although we are differing from the judge I do not think it
necessary to add anything.

(*Appeal allowed with costs in the Court of Appeal and below*)

C

D

E

F

G

H

A
Leyland DAF Ltd v Automotive Products plc.

Chancery Division and Court of Appeal.
Nicholls V-C; Dillon, Steyn and Rose L JJ.
Judgment delivered 2 April and 6 April 1993.

B
*Administrative receivership — Supplier refused to continue to supply insolvent
company unless pre-receivership debts paid — Receivers applied for injunction
to compel supply — Whether refusal to supply was abuse of dominant position
within Common Market — EEC Treaty, art. 86.*

**An unpaid supplier of goods withholding further supplies from an insolvent company
until goods already supplied had been paid for, was not abuse of a dominant position
within art. 86 of the EEC Treaty.**

C
The following cases were referred to in the judgments:

Belgische Radio en Televisie & Anor v SV SABAM & Anor (Case 127/73) [1974]
ECR 51.
Brass Band Instruments Ltd & Ors v Boosey & Hawkes plc (Commission Decision
87/500, OJ 1987 L286/36) [1988] 4 CMLR 67.
Chalmers, Ex parte. Re Edwards (1873) LR 8 Ch App 289.
Garden Cottage Foods Ltd v Milk Marketing Board [1984] 1 AC 130.

D
Hoffmann-La Roche & Co AG v EC Commission (Case 85/76) [1979] ECR 461.
Hugin Kassaregister AB & Anor v EC Commission (Case 22/78) [1979] ECR 1869.
*Istituto Chemioterapico Italiano SpA & Commercial Solvents Corporation v EC
Commission* (Joined cases 6 & 7/73) [1974] ECR 223.
Nederlandsche Banden-Industrie Michelin (NV) v EC Commission (Case 322/71)
[1983] ECR 3461.

E
*R v Secretary of State for Transport, ex parte Factortame Ltd & Ors ("Factortame
No. 2")* (Case C-221/89) [1991] 2 CEC 200; [1992] QB 680.
Rother Iron Works Ltd v Canterbury Precision Engineers Ltd [1974] QB 1.
United Brands Co & Anor v EC Commission (Case 27/76) [1978] ECR 207.

Michael Crystal QC and Martin Pascoe (and Paul Lasok in the Court of Appeal)
(instructed by Wilde Sapte) for Leyland DAF Ltd.

F
John Higham QC and David Alexander in the High Court, David Donaldson QC and
Adam Lewis in the Court of Appeal (instructed by Dibb Lupton Broomhead) for
Automotive Products plc.

HIGH COURT JUDGMENT
(2 April 1993)

G
Nicholls V-C: Leyland is a household name as a manufacturer of commercial vehicles.
Leyland trucks are manufactured at Leyland in Lancashire and Leyland vans at
Birmingham. Axles for the vehicles are manufactured at Albion in Glasgow, and the
company also has trading units at Chorley in Lancashire, concerned with the distribution
of spare parts, and at Thame in Oxfordshire, concerned with marketing and sales.

Leyland is part of the DAF group of companies which operate principally in the
Netherlands and Belgium. The main manufacturing company in the UK is Leyland DAF
H
Ltd. In recent years Leyland DAF's annual turnover was £270m and the company had
5,500 employees. In 1992 Leyland DAF trucks were the market leader in the UK truck
market, with a share of 25 per cent. Leyland DAF vans had a 15 per cent share of the UK
van market.

Unhappily Leyland DAF is now insolvent. Banking facilities were provided by a
syndicate of banks. About eight weeks ago, on 3 February 1993, in exercise of their

powers under a mortgage debenture the banks appointed two partners in Arthur Andersen to be administrative receivers of Leyland DAF. At the same time the Dutch court appointed administrators of DAF NV and other Dutch companies in the group.

The outlook for creditors of Leyland DAF is bleak. It is unlikely that unsecured creditors will receive any payment in the winding up of the company. The receivers have been doing all they can to keep the vehicle production lines going. They believe there is a real prospect of selling all or part of the UK business, either to a management buy-out team or to another buyer, provided production can be maintained meanwhile. The proviso is of crucial importance. There is fierce competition between rival manufacturers of light trucks and vans. If production at Leyland DAF were brought to a standstill, the demand for its vehicles would erode quickly. Leyland DAF's attraction as a market leader would be lost. Possible buyers and those financing them would lose interest. The business would have to be closed down, with the loss of the jobs of all the workforce and further adverse consequences to Leyland DAF's suppliers.

Leyland DAF's suppliers run into hundreds. There are about 400 suppliers to the plant at Leyland and a similar number for the Birmingham plant. The receivers have had to co-ordinate the resumption of supplies by each of the suppliers, many of whom are owed substantial sums for components supplied before Leyland DAF went into receivership. The absence of one part, however small or trivial, from any one supplier can bring the production line to a halt and frustrate the entire exercise.

Automotive Products plc ("AP") of Leamington Spa in Warwickshire is one of Leyland DAF's suppliers. AP's Lockheed division manufactures brake systems, and its Borg & Beck division manufactures clutch systems. Leyland DAF has been a substantial customer for many years. Last year the company ordered goods to the value of about £6m from AP. When the receivers were appointed Leyland DAF owed AP £758,955.

After the appointment of the receivers AP continued to supply brakes and clutches to the receivers. As with the other suppliers, the receivers accept liability for payment for the goods supplied to them. The receivers are not liable for payment for the goods supplied to the company before their appointment, although they have power to pay pre-receivership debts if this is necessary for carrying out their receivership functions: see sec. 42 of the *Insolvency Act* 1986 and para. 13 of Sch. 1.

The orders placed by the receivers with AP have been for substantially reduced quantities. Initially the orders were on a one-off or week-by-week basis, as the receivers were unable to look far ahead. More recently the orders enabled AP to plan its production a month or so ahead. Despite this, the transition has inevitably caused considerable disruption, and hence some additional expense, to AP. To reflect this AP has been charging the receivers an increased price for the brakes and clutches.

AP is understandably anxious about its unpaid bill. It has its own suppliers who have to be paid, and it has to pay its own workforce. AP's invoices and delivery notes and other documents used in its dealings with Leyland DAF were endorsed with printed conditions of sale. One of these was a retention of title condition. AP claims that the retention of title condition was incorporated into the contracts under which the components were sold and delivered to Leyland DAF. It has asserted its rights over goods having an invoice value of £1.2m. AP asserted this claim as soon as the receivers were appointed. The receivers, for their part, dispute the claim. This has given rise to a not unfamiliar type of dispute. The receivers contend the conditions of sale were printed on post-contractual documents, and even then only on the reverse side. AP points to a long-continuing course of dealing. AP has now started an action seeking the resolution of this issue. I need not go further into this. The receivers have undertaken that if and to the extent that AP's claim is upheld by the court, they will return the goods in question or if they have been used or sold meanwhile, they will pay for them. So AP's proprietary

A　rights have been adequately secured. AP is not at risk in this respect. If its retention of title claim is well founded, it will recover its unpaid £750,000.

What, however, if AP's claim fails? It is this possibility which has given rise to this litigation. By the middle of March the receivers had made plain they did not accept AP's retention of title claim. This brought matters to a head. On 18 March AP told the receivers it was intending to cease supplying brakes and clutches forthwith unless they acknowledged the validity of AP's retention of title claim in full. In other words, unless

B　the receivers agreed in effect to pay the whole of the pre-receivership debt, no further components would be supplied. The receivers protested, but AP remained adamant. It has relented only to the extent of agreeing to carry out existing orders already placed by the receivers with AP. On 19 March its solicitors wrote:

C　　"Our client objects to the allegation that it is holding your clients to ransom. Our client reiterates its willingness to support the receivership providing proper commercial terms can be agreed. However our client cannot be forced to trade with your clients and is reluctant to do so whilst your clients continue to prevaricate over our client's perfectly valid retention of title claim."

The difficulty now confronting the receivers is that in practice there is no alternative source of supply for the brakes and clutches they need to keep the production line moving. The parts are designed and produced to Leyland DAF's specification and

D　cannot be bought elsewhere in the market. Stringent product liability legislation relating to the manufacture and distribution of motor vehicles requires Leyland DAF to test all components exhaustively before commencing a product run. Test procedures alone can take several months. Finding a potential new supplier and repeating with him the necessary process of design, engineering, costing, tooling and testing would take many months. It would be at least six to eight months before production could be resumed with a new supplier.

E　Further, the receivers cannot attempt to struggle on for the time being without further supplies of brakes and clutches. The factories at Leyland and Birmingham operate on a "just in time" delivery basis, under which minimum stocks are held and deliveries are called for from standing orders shortly before required for the assembly lines. Trucks and vans have to be assembled in a predetermined sequence and it is not feasible to finish a vehicle except for the brake and clutch assemblies to be provided by AP.

F　The upshot, therefore, is that unless the receivers comply with AP's demand, manufacturing at Leyland and Birmingham will cease, perhaps for good. Over a six month shut-down Leyland DAF's business would be lost completely. Unless supplies continue, production will stop at Birmingham today and at Leyland next Tuesday.

The receivers, therefore, commenced this action against AP earlier this week, on 30 March. They now seek, by way of urgent interlocutory relief, a mandatory order that

G　AP do supply specified brake and clutch assemblies and other components to Leyland DAF in specified quantities and at specified prices and times on AP's standard conditions of sale over the next three months. They say these arrangements meet all AP's commercial terms. All that stands between them is AP's demand that, regardless of whether or not its retention of title claim is sound, the receivers must pay the £750,000 pre-receivership debt in full before supplies will be continued. The receivers contend that that demand is unlawful.

H
The common law position

The relief claimed is most unusual. In general, in the absence of a contractual or statutory obligation, one person is not compelled to trade with another. He cannot be forced to supply goods to someone else if he does not wish to do so. Further, even if a long-term supply contract is in existence, and subject always to the terms of the

particular contract, the seller is not bound to continue to supply once the buyer has   A
defaulted in making payment due for goods already supplied. In *Re Edwards. Ex parte
Chalmers* (1873) LR 8 Ch App 289 at p. 291, *Mellish* LJ summarised the position where
a buyer through insolvency has failed to make due payments for goods supplied in these
terms:

> "The first question that arises is, what are the rights of a seller of goods when the
> purchaser becomes insolvent before the contract for sale has been completely   B
> performed? I am of opinion that the result of the authorities is this — that in such
> a case the seller, notwithstanding he may have agreed to allow credit for the
> goods, is not bound to deliver any more goods under the contract until the price of
> the goods not yet delivered is tendered to him; and that, if a debt is due to him for
> goods already delivered, he is entitled to refuse to deliver any more till he is paid
> the debt due for those already delivered, as well as the price of those still to be
> delivered."   C

In the present case when the receivers were appointed the floating charge, which
presumably the banks had over Leyland DAF's business, crystallised. I say presumably,
because the mortgage debenture is not in evidence. All the company's assets and rights
became subject to a fixed charge in favour of the banks. This does not displace the
application of the principle I have just mentioned. As against the unpaid suppliers of
goods to Leyland DAF pre-receivership, the banks as chargees, or the receivers appointed
by them, are in no better position under a contract of supply than Leyland DAF itself: D
see *Rother Iron Works Ltd v Canterbury Precision Engineers Ltd* [1974] QB 1 per
Russell LJ at p. 6. Thus, even if a contract of supply had been in existence pre-
receivership, the receivers could not have insisted on AP continuing to supply Leyland
DAF without first paying what was owed by the company for components already
delivered.

These principles may place public utilities and other monopoly suppliers of goods or   E
services in a strong position when insolvency comes about. The Review Committee on
Insolvency Law and Practice under the chairmanship of Sir Kenneth Cork commented
on this in its report published in 1982 (Cmnd 8558) at para. 1451ff. The committee
observed that it was the common practice for public utilities, on the insolvency of a
customer, to threaten to cut off supplies of electricity or gas or water unless the
outstanding account was paid in full. When supply is essential to maintain a continuous
production unit the liquidator or receiver has no choice; he must pay in full. In   F
para. 1453 the committee continued:

> "To a lesser extent, the situation is not confined to public utilities. It may arise
> whenever there is an outstanding account with a private supplier, and there is no
> practicable alternative supplier. In such a case, the creditor is doing no more than
> exploit the commercial advantages of his position."
G
The committee recommended, in para. 1462, that the law should be changed in
respect of statutory undertakings. That was done. Section 233 of the Insolvency Act
prohibits such undertakings from making it a condition of further supply, when a
company has gone into liquidation or administrative receivers are appointed, that the
outstanding charges should first be paid. That section does not apply to trade suppliers
such as AP.

This distinction is not altogether without rationale. Public utilities enjoy a monopoly   H
granted by Parliament, in return for which they are under a statutory obligation to
provide a service. They have statutory powers enabling them to discontinue service to a
customer unless the outstanding account is paid in full. Trade creditors do not enjoy this
special status. When an administrative receiver is appointed by a debenture holder, and
he seeks to carry on the customer's business with a view to selling it as a going concern,

A   the person who primarily stands to benefit is the debenture holder. There is no obvious reason why a supplier of goods should be expected to bear, for the benefit of the debenture holder, the burden of an unpaid pre-receivership debt.

Article 86

Mr Crystal did not dispute that this is the position under English common law. In
B   support of this present application he relied primarily on art. 86 of the Treaty of Rome. The UK is now part of a wider market regulated by the EEC Treaty. Practices established as acceptable and lawful under domestic English law before the enactment of the *European Communities Act* 1972 may not be lawful any longer. In particular, art. 86 regulates misuse of monopoly power which flows from having a dominant position in the Common Market. Unlike sec. 233 of the Insolvency Act, art. 86 applies to trade suppliers as much as to public utilities. Article 86 provides:

C   "Any abuse by one or more undertakings of a dominant position within the common market or in a substantial part of it shall be prohibited as incompatible with the common market in so far as it may affect trade between Member States.

        Such abuse may, in particular, consist in:

        (a) directly or indirectly imposing unfair purchase or selling prices or other
D   unfair trading conditions;

        (b) limiting production, markets or technical development to the prejudice of
             consumers;

        (c) applying dissimilar conditions to equivalent transactions with other trading
             parties, thereby placing them at a competitive disadvantage;

        (d) making the conclusion of contracts subject to acceptance by the other
E   parties of supplementary obligations which, by their nature or according to
             commercial usage, have no connection with the subject of such contracts."

This article has direct effect. It creates direct rights in favour of individuals which national courts must safeguard: see the decision of the European Court of Justice in *Belgische Radio en Televisie v SV SABAM* [1974] ECR 51 at p. 62. In *Garden Cottage Foods Ltd v Milk Marketing Board* [1984] 1 AC 130 at p. 141E Lord *Diplock* observed:

F   "A breach of the duty imposed by article 86 not to abuse a dominant position in the common market or in a substantial part of it, can thus be categorised in English law as a breach of statutory duty that is imposed not only for the purpose of promoting the general economic prosperity of the common market but also for the benefit of private individuals to whom loss or damage is caused by a breach of that duty."

G   Leyland DAF's case is that AP has committed, and is intent on continuing to commit, a breach of that new statutory duty which now forms part of English law. Mr Crystal submitted that Leyland DAF has a seriously arguable case, and that the balance of convenience favours the grant of interlocutory relief. Otherwise production will stop and that will be that.

The essential ingredients of art. 86 are (1) an abuse of (2) a dominant position in the Common Market or a substantial part of it which (3) may affect trade between member
H   states. I am prepared to assume in favour of Leyland DAF, although without deciding this, that Leyland DAF has a seriously arguable case on the second and third ingredients. Leyland DAF needs brakes and clutches for its vehicles, and in practice it cannot obtain them from any source other than AP. I have already referred to Leyland DAF's share of the UK truck and van market. In 1991 Leyland DAF's share of the European Common Market (excluding the UK) was 3.3 per cent in the case of trucks and one per cent for

vans. Over half (56 per cent) of the trucks produced at Leyland comprise the 45 Series, all of which use brakes and clutches supplied by AP. All vans produced at Birmingham use brakes supplied by AP.

Abuse of a dominant position

I turn to the other ingredient: abuse. Abuse is not defined in art. 86, although the article contains some examples of it. In *Hoffmann-La Roche & Co AG v EC Commission* [1979] ECR 461 at p. 541 the European Court of Justice observed, at para. 91 of its judgment:

> "The concept of abuse is an objective concept relating to the behaviour of an undertaking in a dominant position which is such as to influence the structure of a market where, as a result of the very presence of the undertaking in question, the degree of competition is weakened and which, through recourse to methods different from those which condition normal competition in products or services on the basis of the transactions of commercial operators, has the effect of hindering the maintenance of the degree of competition still existing in the market or the growth of that competition."

This passage therefore directs attention at the use by the dominant undertaking of:

> "methods different from those which condition normal competition in products . . . on the basis of the transactions of commercial operators."

In my view, when payment is overdue for goods supplied and the supplier is under no contractual obligation to continue supplies, the refusal by the supplier to deliver further goods until paid what he is already owed cannot be regarded as an abuse within art. 86. I accept that in some circumstances a refusal to supply goods may constitute abuse. *Commercial Solvents Corporation v EC Commission* [1974] ECR 223 is an example of this. But where the reason for the refusal is the buyer's failure to pay for goods already delivered to him, and the sole purpose of the refusal is to exert commercial pressure to obtain payment, I can see nothing in the supplier's conduct which departs from normal and reasonable commercial behaviour in a competitive market. There might, I suppose, be a very exceptional case where, although that is the reason and purpose, the failure to supply might still be regarded as an abuse, but I confess no example of such a case springs to mind.

I appreciate that, because of his dominant position, such a supplier is able to exercise over the buyer a degree of commercial pressure he would otherwise lack. This does not turn into an abuse conduct which would otherwise not be such. It is important to keep in mind that holding a dominant position is not itself contrary to the EEC Treaty. Article 86 is concerned to prevent the misuse of the economic power possessed by those who are in a dominant position. They must not impose unfair prices, or limit production to the prejudice of consumers, or trade on discriminatory terms, or impose conditions having no connection with the subject of the contract. In short, they must not use their power to "impair genuine, undistorted competition in the common market": see *Michelin v EC Commission* [1983] ECR 3461. But the obligation to pay for goods supplied is a fundamental feature of a normal market. Likewise, a refusal to sell any more goods to a particular buyer until he pays what he owes for goods already sold to him by that seller is an altogether normal and unexceptional feature of a competitive market. Indeed, in the present case one of AP's normal trading terms, set out in its standard conditions of sale, is that if the buyer fails to pay as agreed for goods delivered to him, AP is entitled to refuse to deliver any further goods, whether under the same or any other contract. Article 86 cannot have been intended to deprive a supplier of the freedom to impose and implement such terms, or to behave in this sort of way, just because he is in a dominant position. To compel an unpaid seller to supply further goods

A   to the defaulting buyer would not be to promote normal competition. On the contrary, it would distort the normal functioning of the market, because normal competition in the market is between those who pay for their goods.

On this analysis Leyland DAF's difficulty stems not from any unusual or unreasonable conduct on the part of AP as a supplier in the market but from Leyland DAF's insolvency. That feature does not assist Leyland DAF in this case. Leyland DAF's

B   insolvency cannot be a sufficient reason for compelling AP to depart from normal trading behaviour. That would be to place an insolvent undertaking at an advantage over a solvent one. I think I can assert with confidence that that was not one of the objects of the Treaty.

The matter can be taken a step further. The receivers are seeking to preserve Leyland DAF's business and sell it, or parts of it, as a going concern. That is why the order is

C   sought against AP. If the order is made, the persons who stand to benefit financially from the proceeds of sale of the business as a going concern are the debenture holders who appointed the receivers, namely the banks. Again, I do not believe art. 86 was aimed at producing that result. I can see no reason why an unpaid seller of goods should be regarded as any less deserving than a lender of money.

Mr Crystal submitted that the purpose of AP's refusal to supply save on terms that the

D   pre-receivership debt is paid, is to enable AP to obtain an advantage over other creditors. Suppliers who are not in a dominant position cannot dictate such terms. It is not fair or reasonable that AP should use its dominant position to that end. I cannot accept this appraisal. As I have noted, if AP were forced to supply brakes and clutches to the receivers without first being paid the pre-receivership debt, the benefit would accrue wholly to the debenture holders who appointed the receivers. So payment to AP would not be at the expense of the other creditors generally. But even if it were at the

E   expense of the other creditors, because there was likely to be a surplus for unsecured creditors after paying off the banks, I do not think AP's conduct could be regarded as unfair or unreasonable so far as the other creditors were concerned. The pre-receivership debts of the unsecured trade creditors all rank equally. If the receivers must have further goods from one existing supplier, A, but can look elsewhere for goods formerly bought from another supplier, B, then A enjoys a stronger bargaining position than B. That is

F   his good fortune. That is a normal incident of trading. For A to exercise his rights is not unfair or unreasonable so far as B is concerned.

I mention one further point. The overall picture sought to be presented by the receivers is that here is an industrial calamity which can be averted or mitigated if, but only if, all creditors pull together and behave reasonably. AP is seeking to hold everyone else to ransom by selfishly looking after its own interests, regardless of the consequences this will have for the employees and other suppliers whose future is dependent on the

G   business surviving and being sold as a going concern. I fully recognise the hardship many people involved with Leyland DAF have already suffered and will suffer if the business closes: employees have been dismissed, many more will lose their jobs if the business closes, suppliers are unpaid. AP itself is owed a very substantial sum. But, beyond this, I know very little. I know nothing of the financial arrangements made by the syndicate banks or the circumstances in which trading took place in the months leading up to the

H   appointment of the receivers. I know nothing of the banks' indebtedness or the financial state of the receivership. In short, I know very little indeed about the financial affairs of Leyland DAF. In these circumstances it would be quite improper for me, even if it were relevant, to express any view either way on this sort of criticism of AP's conduct. Suffice to say, in my view Leyland DAF does not have a seriously arguable case that AP's conduct infringes art. 86.

Estoppel   A

Leyland DAF has a second string to its bow: estoppel. Mr Crystal contended that by
the post-receivership correspondence AP led the receivers to believe it would continue
to supply long term without insisting on payment of the pre-receivership debt. The
receivers entered into commitments with other suppliers on the faith of that
understanding. It would be unconscionable for AP to seek to resile from that position
now. I cannot accept this. There is nothing in the correspondence which can fairly be
read as a supply commitment by AP from which it is now seeking to resile. The   B
commitments were limited to supplying in response to particular orders or for very
limited periods of time. Nor is there anything to show the receivers thought otherwise,
or that they have done anything in reliance on such a belief. In my view, on this point
also Leyland DAF's case cannot succeed. Accordingly, I shall not make the order as
asked.

(*AP's costs of the application to be taxed and paid as an expense of the receivership*   C
in any event)

COURT OF APPEAL JUDGMENT
(6 April 1993)

Dillon LJ: This matter comes before the court by way of an appeal by the plaintiff,
Leyland DAF Ltd, against a decision of *Nicholls* V-C given last Friday, 2 April.   D

As is well-known, Leyland DAF Ltd, the manufacturing company which, by virtue of
a merger with interests in Holland, carried on the former business of Leyland,
manufactured Leyland DAF trucks, which were a market leader in the UK truck market
with a 25 per cent share, and Leyland DAF vans, which had a 15 per cent share in the
UK van market.

On 3 February 1993, administrative receivers were appointed of Leyland DAF, by the   E
banks with whom it had dealt, under the powers in a mortgage debenture. At the same
time the Dutch court appointed administrators of DAF Netherlands and other Dutch
companies in the group. The Vice-Chancellor summed the position up in his judgment,
saying that the outlook for creditors of Leyland DAF is bleak, and it is unlikely that
unsecured creditors will receive any payment in a winding up of the company.

The receivers have been doing all they can to keep the vehicle production lines going.   F
The receivers desire to continue to do that in the hope that it will be possible to find
a purchaser for the truck and van businesses (either an outside purchaser or through
a management buy-out). So far the businesses have been continued on a somewhat
short-term, or even hand-to-mouth basis, but the receivers want to establish a continuous
trading period for at least 12 weeks or three months. That however needs the co-
operation of many suppliers of parts and materials since, like many other vehicle
builders, Leyland DAF did not make all its own parts.   G

The defendant in the action, Automotive Products plc, which is conveniently referred
to as "AP", has supplied Leyland DAF with brake systems and clutch systems. It is said
that the brake systems are supplied for over half of the trucks, namely, all the 45 Series
of trucks. They have brakes and clutches supplied by AP. All the vans use brakes
supplied by AP. AP are very conscious of the large amount — £758,955 — they were
owed when the receivers were appointed. It is said that at that time there were stocks of   H
AP parts then held to a value in excess of the £758,955 then owed, and AP claim that in
its contracts for the supply of brake and clutch systems before the receivership there
were clauses providing for retention of title.

Before the hearing of this appeal began, it was accepted by the receivers, first of all,
that they were personally liable to pay in full for parts supplied to them after the

A   commencement of the receivership. It was accepted, secondly, that AP was not unreasonably putting its prices some 20 per cent higher than they had been before the receivership because there was no longer as big a demand by Leyland DAF, through the receivers, for the parts and there was no longer the guaranteed continuous flow of orders and that led to disruption in the production procedures of AP. Thirdly it was accepted that, if it established that the pre-receivership supplies were subject to reservation of title clauses, AP would be paid in full for stocks in-hand at the commencement of the receivership and since used by the receivers in completing vehicles to keep the production lines going.

B

AP have, however, stipulated that, if they are to supply for a further three months, as proposed, then, in addition to the terms otherwise agreed, they must be paid in full the £750,000 pre-receivership debt, whether or not their claim to a retention of title clause is valid. There is, in the correspondence, a letter from AP's solicitors, dated 19 March, in

C   which the solicitors said:

"Our client objects to the allegation that it is holding your clients to ransom. Our client reiterates its willingness to support the receivership providing proper commercial terms can be agreed."

It is not surprising, given the widespread concern at the collapse of Leyland DAF, and the numbers of employees of Leyland DAF and its suppliers who may lose their jobs if

D   no salvage of the business is possible, that AP should be regarded as holding the receivers to ransom. The other side of the coin, if the present claim by the receivers fails, is that the banks who appointed them will have the responsibility of deciding whether to put up the money for the £750,000 to salve the businesses for realisation. If neither AP, nor the banks yield, then the businesses will no doubt be closed and people will lose their jobs.

E   The Court does not provide the money. It merely has to answer the specific legal question put to it, which is founded only on European Community law and art. 86 of the Treaty of Rome. That is the question which, it is suggested, enables the courts to order AP to continue supplying parts for 12 weeks without payment of the £750,000.

Now, the normal approach to any question of interlocutory relief, and what is proposed here is merely interlocutory and not permanent, is that the court considers whether there is a serious question to be tried, and then considers the balance of

F   convenience.

At the opening of the hearing of this appeal I suggested to Mr Crystal, appearing for Leyland DAF, that if we got to the question of balance of convenience then I took the view that if there were to be an interlocutory injunction requiring AP to continue supplying parts to Leyland DAF, there would have to be a reference to the European Court to consider whether European law required the grant of such an injunction and, indeed, overrode AP's reluctance to continue supplies without receiving the £750,000.

G   It appeared to me also, in those circumstances, that the balance strongly required, if an injunction were granted, that the receivers would have to bring into court the whole of the £750,000 so that, if their contentions on European law failed and they had nonetheless in the interim had the benefit of the continued supply, then AP would get the £750,000 — because it would have been established that European law did not require it to continue the supply without receiving that sum. As the course of argument has gone,

H   Mr Crystal did not receive instructions authorising him to consent to bringing that money into court, pending a reference, until after we had intimated that we did not think that he overcame the first hurdle of showing that there was a serious question to be tried.

That being so I leave aside, for the moment, the question of whether there is any other basis on which the money would fall to be brought into court and I deal strictly with the question which has been argued.

A

First of all, it is common ground, as set out in the judgment of the Vice-Chancellor that, apart from EC law, the stance that AP is taking is as a matter of law legitimate. As the Vice-Chancellor said, in general, in the absence of a contractual or statutory obligation, one person is not compelled to trade with another. He cannot be forced to supply goods to someone else if he does not wish to do so. That was clearly summarised in the decision to which the Vice-Chancellor refers, *Re Edwards. Ex parte Chalmers* (1873) LR 8 Ch App 289.

B

It followed that if a liquidator or a receiver wanted a continued supply of goods or services from someone who was an unsecured creditor of the company in question at the commencement of the liquidation or receivership, the creditor was entitled to stipulate that he would not make a further supply available unless paid in full for his pre-liquidation or pre-receivership debt.

C

What happened then was a question of strength of bargaining power. So far as I can recall, there were decisions under the *Companies Act* 1929 in relation to the topic. It seems that the public utilities — the suppliers of gas, electricity, water and telephone services — found themselves in a strong position to insist on payment in full of their pre-liquidation or receivership debts if they were to continue to provide services.

There were recommendations, as the Vice-Chancellor points out, in the Report of the Cork Committee, that the law should be changed in that respect so far as public utilities are concerned. That has been done by sec. 233 of the *Insolvency Act* 1986.

D

That does not deal with the position of AP. AP's position, vis-à-vis Leyland DAF, depends solely, EC law apart, on strength of will and strength of bargaining power.

I should add this in relation to pre-European law. Where it was desired to produce a state of affairs which would enable a company to continue trading free from the pressures of creditors whom it currently was unable to satisfy, the course adopted used to be a scheme for a moratorium, or a scheme of arrangement affecting all creditors. That emphasises perhaps that, under English law, there was no objection to the individual creditor using his bargaining strength, so long as the company was not in receivership or liquidation, to enforce payment.

E

Article 86 of the Treaty of Rome provides that any abuse by one or more undertakings of a dominant position within the Common Market, or in a substantial part of it, shall be prohibited as incompatible with the Common Market in so far as it may affect trade between member states. It goes on to state that such abuse may in particular consist of: (a) directly or indirectly imposing unfair purchase or selling prices, or other unfair trading conditions; (b) limiting production, markets or technical development to the prejudice of consumers; (c) applying dissimilar conditions to equivalent transactions with other trading parties, thereby placing them at a competitive disadvantage, and (d) making the conclusion of contracts subject to acceptance by the other parties of supplementary obligations which, by their nature or according to commercial usage, have no connection with the subject of such contracts.

F

G

It appears to me, from that wording, which has of course been considered in the course of extensive European Community jurisprudence, that there is a considerable emphasis on abuse and unfairness.

H

The Vice-Chancellor correctly pointed out that the essential ingredients of art. 86 are (1) an abuse of (2) a dominant position in the Common Market, or a substantial part of it which (3) may affect trade between member states. The Vice-Chancellor decided the case particularly on the ground that there was no abuse. AP was only exercising the normal rights of a trader who has not been paid to refuse to continue supplies unless he is paid in full.

A   For my part I find it convenient to look, first, at the requirement that there is a dominant position in the Common Market, or a substantial part of it. That is an essential for there to have been any infringement of art. 86. It is not suggested that Leyland DAF has, or ever had, a dominant position. I have already mentioned the percentages that it had in the UK market. It is clear that it has many competitors, even in the UK market, including Iveco. Beyond that, in so far as it has to be suggested that the person in a dominant position is AP, AP is not the designer of the parts it makes. They are made to

B   Leyland DAF's designs and specifications and supplied to Leyland DAF's orders. They could be made by any other competent engineers or suppliers in the trade. Leyland DAF's difficulty is merely that time would be needed for an alternative supplier to be given the designs and specifications and to tool-up for production, and to prove that the parts it produced satisfied all requirements for safety on the road and efficient running of the vehicles. In those circumstances, in my judgment, it would be going far beyond

C   any previous decision of the European Court to hold that AP has a dominant position in the Common Market.

    We were referred, in relation to that aspect, to the case of *Hugin Kassaregister v EC Commission* [1979] ECR 1869 a decision of the European Court of Justice. That indicates that the market may be a very restrictive market. That was a case in which the Hugin company was a manufacturer of cash registers. It also manufactured spare parts

D   for its cash registers. It was held that where the manufacturer had a monopoly in the production of spare parts, the only alternative source being the cannibalising of old machines, it occupied a dominant position in the market for those spare parts for its own machines. The position was that another company had established a business of repairing cash registers, and it needed Hugin's spare parts for that purpose, and Hugin had refused to supply. It was held that that was an abuse within art. 86. It seems to me to be a very long distance away from the present case where AP is, as I have indicated, not the

E   source of the design of the brake or clutch parts. They are only supplied to Leyland DAF for incorporation in Leyland DAF's machines. Leyland DAF itself is not in a dominant position in any relevant market; so I do not see how AP can be.

    I come back then to the question of abuse, which the Vice-Chancellor decided. He directed himself, in particular, by reference to the decision of the European Court in *Hoffmann-La Roche & Co AG v EC Commission* [1979] ECR 461, where at para. 91 of

F   the judgment of the European Court (p. 541) it is said:

> "The concept of abuse is an objective concept relating to the behaviour of an undertaking in a dominant position which is such as to influence the structure of a market where, as a result of the very presence of the undertaking in question, the degree of competition is weakened and which, through recourse to methods different from those which condition normal competition in products or services

G   > on the basis of the transactions of commercial operators, has the effect of hindering the maintenance of the degree of competition still existing in the market or the growth of that competition."

That is a definition which has been frequently applied by the European Court and is thus of high authority.

H   Mr Crystal points out that the variety of abuse which was in question there was the variety of abuse which is referred to as "exclusionary"; that is to say, excluding particular people from being in competition. He says that there is an alternative well-recognised form of abuse, which is called "exploitative", which is concerned with deriving excess advantage from exploiting the dominant position. That would be particularly by imposing unfair conditions. He says that the cases can be divided into two strands, and the present case falls into the "exploitative" strand.

I doubt whether the division into two strands is by any means a universal or hard and fast guideline, but certainly there may be cases which are to be regarded as exploitative rather than exclusionary. It appears that there is another variety of abuse which is not relevant in the present case which is designated "structural".

We were referred in particular, as an instance of exploitative abuse, to the case of *United Brands Co v EC Commission* [1978] ECR 207. This was an appeal against a decision of the Commission, whose decision was upheld. There it is said, at para. 130 (p. 285):

"The Commission takes the view that the applicant has abused its dominant position *vis-à-vis* ripener/distributors in the first place by using a clause incorporated in its general conditions of sale forbidding its distributor/ripeners to resell its bananas while still green, to sell bananas other than those supplied by (United Brands Co) while they were distributors of UBC's bananas and to resell UBC's bananas to competing ripeners."

That was the form of abuse that was considered there. Also there was a question of refusing to supply a Danish company because it had at one stage, when it was supplying the goods of a rival, advertised that rival's goods. The conclusion of the European Court asserted positively that an undertaking in a dominant position for the purpose of marketing a product, which cashes in on the reputation of a brand name known and valued by the consumers, cannot stop supplying a long-standing customer who abides by regular commercial practice if the orders placed by the customer are in no way out of the ordinary. Then there is reference to art. 3(f) of the Treaty, and art. 86.

In the present case, I do not find any disharmony between the passage in *Hoffmann-La Roche*, which the Vice-Chancellor applied, and the passages to which we were referred in the *United Brands* case — they are all concerned with abuse of position. In my judgment, that does not prevent different considerations applying when the customer fails to pay for the goods supplied. Indeed, the passage I have just referred to emphasises the customer who abides by regular commercial practice.

It is one of the regular commercial practices that buyers of goods are expected to pay for them. I can find nothing which warrants the conclusion that the importance of preserving competition under the Treaty entirely overrides the conventional obligation to pay for goods purchased.

We were referred to a decision of the Commission in a case involving brass band instruments — *Brass Band Instruments Ltd v Boosey & Hawkes plc* [1988] 4 CMLR 67. That was a case in which interim relief was being granted by the EC Commission. Boosey & Hawkes were manufacturers of brass band instruments and were declining to supply them to Brass Band Instruments Ltd, and certain associated companies. There was a suggestion that the reason for not supplying them was that they had not paid for previous supplies. There were also suggestions, on the other side, that Boosey & Hawkes were taking reprisals against the companies that sought supply because they were setting up a new manufacturing venture. It was suggested that the actions taken by Boosey & Hawkes were to ensure that the new manufacturing venture was eliminated before it could become established.

The Commission, granting interim relief, did not seek to resolve those issues. It seems that, as is borne out by the case of *Factortame No. 2*, to which we were also referred, they adopted conventional procedures for preserving the balance in the meanwhile. What they did was to say: yes, let supplies continue, provided that they are supplied on the basis of cash with order, or cash against delivery of the goods — not on credit. That simple application of the solution does not apply to the facts of the present case.

The significant point is, however, that it was not suggested that it would be an abuse of position for the manufacturer to insist that his customers paid cash when, it was said,

A   they had fallen into arrears with their payments. Does it then become an abuse of process that the supplier in the present case is insisting, by use of his commercial bargaining power, on the customer paying in full for earlier supplies which, despite the retention of title clause, if there was one, have not been paid for?

I do not think it does. It is a normal commercial situation which, as I have mentioned, was very common in this country up to the *Insolvency Act* 1986, with the public utilities.

B   I would agree, therefore, with the Vice-Chancellor that no arguable case of abuse is made out even if, contrary to my view, AP occupied a dominant position.

It follows that the threshold is not passed.

I would dismiss this appeal.

Steyn LJ: Automotive are unpaid sellers of components manufacturing to Leyland's specifications. A sum of the order of £750,000 is owing to Automotive in respect of past
C   deliveries. Automotive are not obliged, as a matter of English law, to supply further components to Leyland. Faced with the insolvency of Leyland, Automotive are refusing to make any future deliveries unless the arrears are cleared. The question is whether art. 86 affords Leyland a remedy.

Like the Vice-Chancellor I will assume that, within the meaning of art. 86, Automotive are in a dominant position and their conduct will affect trade between member states.
D   The question is whether the conduct of Automotive in this case, circumstanced as it was vis-à-vis Leyland, can arguably amount to abuse within the meaning of art. 86.

The Vice-Chancellor observed:

> "To compel an unpaid seller to supply further goods to the defaulting buyer would not be to promote normal competition. On the contrary, it would distort the normal functioning of the market, because normal competition in the market is
E   between those who pay for their goods."

In making that observation the Vice-Chancellor approached the matter on the assumption that Automotive was in a dominant position. That is how I will approach the matter too. In agreement with the Vice-Chancellor it seems to me that the conduct of Automotive, circumstanced exactly as they were vis-à-vis Leyland, was reasonable and normal.

F   Moreover, the Vice-Chancellor observed that the order that (he) is seeking is simply designed to benefit the debenture holders. That observation seems inescapable. We are in effect being asked to accord a primacy to the interests of the debenture holders over the interests of unpaid sellers.

I regard the Vice-Chancellor's analysis of this matter, and his reasoning, as entirely convincing. There is very little that I would wish to add.

G   Mr Crystal QC has emphasised three points to us. First, he emphasised the exploitative category of cases that can fall within the scope of art. 86. He says that exploitative abuse consists of behaviour which is unfair or unreasonable towards those persons who depend upon the dominant firm for the supply of the relevant goods. The adjectives "unfair" and "unreasonable" must be noted. Those qualifications of the submission were really inevitable and followed from the fact that the mere existence of a dominant position is not prohibited. Inevitably, those criteria of "unfairness" and "unreasonableness" must
H   be taken into account in considering the position of Automotive in this case. In my judgment it cannot be said, for the reasons given by the Vice-Chancellor, that the conduct of Automotive amounted to unfair exploitation.

Mr Crystal then made submissions under another heading. He dealt with the question of justification. I believe he accepted, after some discussion, that if one accepts the relevance of the criteria of "unfairness" and "unreasonableness" under art. 86, the

question of justification does not really arise in this case. If I have misunderstood   A
Mr Crystal on this aspect, I would so rule in this case. Therefore, in view of my
conclusion that there is no unfair exploitation on the part of Automotive, it is unnecessary
to consider the question of justification separately.

Thirdly, Mr Crystal relies on the doctrine of proportionality. No doubt it has a useful
role to play in European jurisprudence. Mr Crystal says that the purpose of the
prohibition of exploitative abuses under art. 86 is to prevent the dominant undertaking   B
from acting in an excessive or disproportionate manner, even if its conduct could
otherwise be described as normal. In support of his submission under that heading, he
attached considerable importance to the case of *Boosey & Hawkes*, to which *Dillon* LJ
has already referred. As I understand that case, the fact that the buyers had a bad record
as payers was completely overshadowed by the dominant suppliers concerted attempt
to eliminate their competition. The dominant suppliers were not willing to resume
deliveries on the clearing of a small amount of the overdue account. It was, therefore, a   C
straightforward case of action to eliminate competition. It is to be contrasted with the
present case in which Automotive are quite willing to resume supplies if the arrears are
cleared. In my judgment the conduct of Automotive is not in any way disproportionate
to the commercial interests which they are seeking to protect. It is exactly tailored to
achieve the payment of an overdue bill which is, in my judgment, a reasonable and
normal response in such a case, even if Automotive are in a dominant position within   D
the meaning of art. 86.

In my view, it is not an abnormal practice for an unpaid seller to refuse to deliver
future goods to a solvent buyer who is in arrears. If that is so, it does not seem to me that
the buyer who is in arrears because he is insolvent can be in any better position. Nothing
in European jurisprudence has been drawn to our attention which compels, in my
judgment, this court to categorise Automotive's conduct as an abuse within the meaning
of art. 86.   E

Despite Mr Crystal's interesting arguments, my conclusion is that Leyland have no
arguable prospect of demonstrating that Automotive's conduct amounts to an abuse
within the meaning of art. 86.

In my view there is nothing in this case worth referring to the European Court.

I would dismiss the appeal.   F

Rose LJ: I agree that, for the reasons given by my Lords, the Vice-Chancellor's
decision to refuse the interlocutory relief sought is unassailable.

Even if the Vice-Chancellor had applied the test in *United Brands Co v EC Commission*
[1978] ECR 207 at para. 248 and 249 (p. 301) on which Mr Crystal relied, he could not,
in my judgment, have reached any different conclusion as to the absence of an arguable
case of exploitative abuse.   G

Furthermore, the assumption on which the Vice-Chancellor proceeded, that the
defendants are in a dominant position within art. 86, was, as it seems to me, unduly
favourable to them. It is to be noted that in all the European authorities which have
been cited to this court, the party in a dominant position had a monopoly, or near
monopoly, in a particular commercial field — however narrow that field. See, for
example, *Hugin*, to which *Dillon* LJ has referred. Albeit that it is not a necessary   H
prerequisite to a dominant position that a monopoly or near-monopoly exists, I am
wholly unpersuaded that, in the present case, the defendants can, even arguably, be said
to be in a dominant position. It is true that they are the sole supplier of brakes and
clutches to the plaintiffs, and that no other supplier can presently be readily obtained by
the plaintiffs. To that extent the defendants are in a dominant position vis-à-vis the
plaintiffs. But that is not the question. The defendants supply goods to the plaintiffs as

A   a consequence of the plaintiff's choice, and in accordance with the plaintiff's specification and design, not as a consequence of the defendants' position in the market. The defendants were not "an unavoidable trading partner" of the plaintiffs. There are many other manufacturers of brakes and clutches within the UK and elsewhere within the European Common Market.

     Accordingly the defendants do not, as it seems to me, even arguably have a dominant position within the Common Market or in a substantial part of it, in the terms of art. 86.

B

     I share the regret expressed by the Vice-Chancellor and by *Dillon* LJ as to the consequences — to the plaintiffs and their workforce — of the decision which I feel compelled to reach.

     In my judgment, this appeal must be dismissed.

C   *(Appeal dismissed with costs to be taxed forthwith and paid by the receivers as a receivership expense. Leave to appeal to the House of Lords refused)*

D

E

F

G

H

Re Telomatic Ltd.
Barclays Bank plc v Cyprus Popular Bank Ltd.

Chancery Division (Companies Court).
His Honour Judge Micklem (sitting as a High Court judge).
Judgment delivered 31 March 1993.

A

B

Registration of company charges — Extension of time for registration — Company's solicitors failed to register charge given to bank — Bank attempted to procure valid charge before applying to register out of time — Whether bank should have leave to register out of time — Whether there was sufficient evidence of circumstances of omission to register — Whether any order extending time should preserve rights of secured creditors acquired before actual registration — Companies Act 1985, sec. 404.

This was an appeal from an order made by the registrar on the application of Barclays Bank plc under sec. 404 of the Companies Act 1985 for a legal charge made by Telomatic Ltd ("the company") in favour of Barclays to be registered out of time, subject to a proviso that it be without prejudice to the rights of any person acquired between the date of creation of the charge and the date of its actual registration.

C

Barclays sought an order removing the proviso or modifying it so as to exclude the respondent, Cyprus Popular Bank Ltd, from its protection. Cyprus Bank was a subsequent chargee.

D

Barclays' charge was made on 4 January 1989 and registered at HM Land Registry on 19 July 1989, but it was not registered at the Companies Registry. Barclays became aware on 4 October 1989 that the charge was not registered at the Companies Registry. Barclays then made three separate unsuccessful attempts to procure a valid charge to secure its loan to the company. Cyprus Bank took a second charge over the property concerned in October 1990. In September 1991 the property was valued at £265,000; as at 17 July 1992 the company owed Barclays some £370,000 secured on it. The company appeared not to have any other assets. It had been struck off the register and dissolved.

E

Cyprus Bank submitted that it was inappropriate that any order at all giving leave should be made in the circumstances of the case, as well as submitting that if that submission did not succeed, the proviso to the order preserving its priority was appropriate.

Held, refusing registration out of time:

F

1. There was no evidence from the company's solicitors as to the circumstances in which Barclays' charge was omitted to be registered. There was no evidence that the company's solicitors omitted to register the charge accidentally or inadvertently. If there was some other significant cause for the omission to register, the court was not told what it was, nor were there any other grounds stated or relied on as showing that, in the circumstances surrounding the omission, relief was just and equitable. The omission to register might have prejudiced other creditors, and no case was made on the evidence that it had not done so. Therefore the court's discretion to extend time under sec. 404 did not arise.

G

2. Had any discretion arisen, this was not a case in which the court ought to have exercised its discretion under the section, in view of the long delay in making the application. Instead of quickly applying for leave to register the charge out of time, as it should have done if the remedy under sec. 404 was the remedy it sought, Barclays chose to attempt to remedy the situation without applying to the court by taking another charge, and then another, and then another. Barclays only issued the application for leave when it became apparent to it that its other remedies had failed and at a time when the company had been dissolved and would, if restored to the register, in all probability (so far as it was aware) be insolvent. (Re Ashpurton Estates Ltd [1983] Ch 110 applied.)

H

A   **3. Had it been proper to give leave for registration of the charge, the order would have been made, as was the registrar's order, subject to the usual proviso protecting the rights of secured creditors acquired before actual registration.**

The following cases were referred to in the judgment:

Abrahams (S) & Sons Ltd, Re [1902] 1 Ch 695.

Ashpurton Estates Ltd, Re [1983] Ch 110.

B   *Braemar Investments Ltd, Re* (1988) 4 BCC 366; [1989] Ch 54.

Charles (L H) & Co Ltd, Re [1935] WN 15.

Ehrmann Bros Ltd, Re [1906] 2 Ch 697.

Fablehill Ltd, Re [1991] BCC 590.

Johnson (I C) & Co Ltd, Re [1902] 2 Ch 101.

Joplin Brewery Co Ltd, Re [1902] 1 Ch 79.

Monolithic Building Co, Re [1915] 1 Ch 643.

C   *Probe Data Systems Ltd, Re (No. 3)* [1992] BCC 110.

Watson v Duff, Morgan & Vermont (Holdings) Ltd & Anor [1974] 1 WLR 450.

Clare Hoffmann (instructed by Fladgate Fielder) for the plaintiff.

Anthony Radevsky (instructed by Judge Sykes & Harrison) for the defendant.

JUDGMENT

D   **His Honour Judge Micklem:** This is an appeal from an order made by Mr Registrar *Pimm* on 23 December 1992 on an application made by Barclays Bank plc under sec. 404 of the *Companies Act* 1985, whereby he ordered that a legal charge dated 4 January 1989 and made by Telomatic Ltd ("the company") in favour of Barclays over land known as 6/7 Empire Yard, Holloway, be registered out of time at the Companies Registry, subject to a proviso that it be without prejudice to the rights of any person acquired between the date of creation of the charge and the date of its actual registration,

E   "the *Joplin* proviso" (*Re Joplin Brewery Co Ltd* [1902] 1 Ch 79). Barclays seeks an order that the proviso be removed or, as appeared at the hearing of the appeal, that the proviso be modified so as to exclude the respondent, Cyprus Popular Bank Ltd, from its protection.

I am satisfied that on this appeal I must look at the matter de novo and exercise my own discretion, as was the position prior to the passing of the *Insolvency Act* 1986 (see

F   *Re Ashpurton Estates Ltd* [1983] Ch 110 at p. 131H. It cannot be suggested that the Insolvency Rules apply to proceedings under the Companies Act (see per *Scott* LJ in *Re Probe Data Systems Ltd (No. 3)* [1992] BCC 110 at p. 118E–F).

The main subject of debate before the registrar was whether or not a *Joplin* proviso should be inserted in the order made. Mr Registrar *Pimm* appears to have been under the impression that before him it was conceded that an order giving leave to register the

G   charge out of time in one form or another should be made. Counsel for Cyprus Bank tells me that Mr Registrar *Pimm* misunderstood his position on this point and that no such concession was intended to be made. That is now water under the bridge. Before this court counsel for Cyprus Bank submitted that it was inappropriate that any order at all giving leave should be made in the circumstances of this case, as well as submitting that if that submission did not succeed, the usual Joplin proviso was appropriate without modification.

H   The bare facts of the matter are these. Barclays' charge was made on 4 January 1989 and registered at HM Land Registry on 19 July 1989, but it was not registered at the Companies Registry. Barclays became aware that the charge was not registered at Companies House on 4 October 1989. Barclays then made three separate unsuccessful attempts to procure a valid charge to secure its loan to the company. What happened is set out in an affidavit of Jeremy Andrew Dalton, a corporate manager at Barclays Bank

at their branch at 27 Regent Street, London SW1, sworn on 22 July 1992. He deposes   A
that:

> "Barclays received the charge certificate on 4 October 1989 and I noted that there
> was not a certificate of registration on the Companies Register as there should
> have been. The 21-day period had already elapsed by a considerable period.
> There were no further charges registered against the land, and the company
> agreed to execute a further charge. I mistakenly advised the solicitors" — and in   B
> this affidavit a reference to "the solicitors" is a reference to the company's
> solicitors — "that it could be dated as at the original completion date, i.e.
> 4 January 1989. I later advised the solicitors of my error, but by that time the
> charge form had already been rejected by the registrar at Companies House."

In para. 6, Mr Dalton deposes:

> "I then arranged for a further charge to be executed and registered, but the
> solicitors delayed in sending the form to Companies House and it was again out of   C
> time. I do not know the precise date of that further charge and I have been unable
> to obtain a copy from the company's solicitors."

Then in para. 7 he deposes:

> "I personally delivered a further charge form to the company and arranged for its
> completion. It was completed on 8 June 1990 ('the second charge') together with
> a floating charge debenture in favour of Barclays at the same date ('the floating   D
> charge'). The floating charge was registered on the Companies Register on
> 19 June 1990 and the second charge was registered on 20 June 1990. Unfortunately,
> the second charge was not registered at the Land Registry. The securities clerk at
> Barclays who was responsible has told me that he mistakenly relied upon a file
> note which stated that the registration had been made in June 1990. I assume that
> he had seen a note referring to the first charge. The floating charge contains the   E
> usual restriction on dealing at cl. 3."

At this point, Cyprus Bank came on the scene. Mr Dalton describes what happened
in para. 9 and 10 of his affidavit. On 4 October 1990, Barclays received by fax a letter of
the same date from Cyprus Bank informing Barclays that Cyprus Bank was considering
taking a second charge over the land and enclosing a questionnaire for the mortgagee.
A further copy of the questionnaire was received in the post on 5 October 1990. The   F
questionnaire asked whether Cyprus Bank needed permission from Barclays to take a
subsequent mortgage and, if so, whether or not Barclays consented.

Barclays replied on a copy of the fax that permission was needed, and that it did not
consent to Cyprus Bank taking a further charge and, to the best of Mr Dalton's
knowledge, that reply was sent by post to Cyprus Bank on about 5 October 1990. In fact,
Cyprus Bank took a second charge over the land on 5 October to secure all moneys due
or to become due from a company known as Celeste Ltd. That charge was registered on   G
the Companies Register on 19 October 1990 and the Cyprus Bank charge was registered
at the Land Registry on 30 October 1990.

The current value of the property is not known, but on 24 September 1991 valuers
appointed by Barclays put a value of some £265,000 on the property. As at 17 July 1992,
the company owed Barclays some £370,000 secured on it.

Matters came to a head when Cyprus Bank wrote to Barclays on 12 February 1992.   H
They wrote in these terms:

> "We understand that you hold the first charge over the above property, i.e.
> 6/7 Empire Yard, Holloway Road, and that we hold a subsequent charge. Please
> advise us of the current amount outstanding under your charge, whether there are
> any arrears and if you are contemplating further action at this time."

A   That letter was apparently received by Barclays on 17 February 1992. The company had, in fact, been struck off the register on 11 February 1992 and was dissolved on 18 February 1992.

     On 22 April 1992, Mr Dalton wrote to Mr Karis of Cyprus Bank, as he put, to advise him of "the defect in our security and to seek your agreement to give us priority". On or about 28 May 1992, Mr Karis told Mr Dalton that Cyprus Bank would not give Barclays priority. The evidence is that the sum secured by the Cyprus Bank charge is of the order

B   of £200,000. Assuming that the property remains worth £265,000, if Barclays' charge as registered takes priority over Cyprus Bank's charge, there will be no surplus. If Barclays' charge is not registered, there is likely to be a surplus for unsecured creditors after discharge of the Cyprus Bank charge. Mr Dalton deposes that he is not aware of any further assets of the company, and I must proceed on the basis that the company is in all probability insolvent.

C   At this point in the story, Barclays then issued an originating summons seeking both that the company be restored to the register and that Barclays' charge be registered out of time. The registrar expressed the view that it was not proper to join these two claims for relief in one summons and, accordingly, Barclays issued two further summonses, seeking by the first that the company be restored to the register and by the second, which is dated 20 July 1992 and is the one before me, leave to register out of time.

D   At the time when Mr Dalton swore his affidavit, on 22 July 1992, the company had not been restored to the register, yet Mr Dalton makes no mention of the fact that at the time of his application the company had been struck off the register and dissolved. Paragraph 16 of his affidavit, in which he says no more than "so far as I am aware, there is no winding-up petition pending against the company", is not simply grossly inadequate to inform the court as to the true facts but in its context positively misleading. It is deplorable that Barclays saw fit to come to the court on this application on that evidence,

E   and it is no answer to say that it was not thought to be relevant, as by the time the present application came on for hearing, if it came on at all, the company would have been restored to the register.

     As to the law, as Barclays failed to register its charge on the Companies Register within time, it was and remained at the time of Barclays' application to the court void against the liquidator and any creditor of the company by virtue of sec. 395 of the

F   *Companies Act* 1985. In the context of that section, "creditor" means only a creditor who has acquired a property right to or an interest in the subject-matter of the unregistered charge (see *Re Ehrmann Bros Ltd* [1906] 2 Ch 697).

     Section 404 of the Companies Act 1985 gives the court a discretionary power to extend the time for registration if:

> "the court is satisfied that the omission to register . . . within the time required by this Chapter . . . was accidental, or due to inadvertence or to some other sufficient

G   > cause, or is not of a nature to prejudice the position of creditors or shareholders of the company, or that on other grounds it is just and equitable to grant relief."

Under that section the court's discretion arises in five separate cases.

     The evidence directed to founding the jurisdiction is minimal. All that Mr Dalton says is this, in para. 4:

H   > "The company executed a legal charge of the land in favour of Barclays dated 4 January 1989. At the request of Barclays, the company's solicitors ['the solicitors'] agreed to register the charge. Barclays did not specifically request that they register the charge pursuant to sec. 395 on the *Companies Act* 1985 on the Companies Register. By a letter which was in the form of Barclays' standard solicitor's undertaking dated 23 February 1988 . . . the company's solicitor confirmed that he would register the charge"— and he exhibits the letter. "I on

A

behalf of the bank assumed the solicitors would register the charge on both the
Land Register and on the Companies Register. The first charge was registered at
the Land Registry on 9 July 1989 but it was not registered on the Companies
Register."

Then by para. 5:

"Barclays received the charge certificate on 4 October 1989 and I noted there was
not a certificate of registration."

B

There was no other evidence and, in the absence of any evidence from the company's
solicitors, no evidence at all as to the circumstances in which Barclays' charge was
omitted to be registered. I am not satisfied that the company's solicitors omitted to
register the charge accidentally or inadvertently in the absence of any evidence from
them. If there was some other significant cause for the omission to register, the court is
not told what it was, nor are there any other grounds stated or relied on in Mr Dalton's
affidavit as showing that, in the circumstances surrounding the omission, relief is just
and equitable. The omission to register may have prejudiced other creditors, and no
case is made on the evidence that it has not done so.

C

I am not satisfied that any of the five grounds set out in the section are made out, and
in my judgment the court's discretion to extend time in this case has not arisen.

In case I am wrong as to this, I go on to consider whether, had the discretion arisen, it
would have been proper to exercise it in this case. The Court of Appeal considered the
jurisdiction under the former section enabling the grant of leave to register charges out
of time in *Re Ashpurton Estates Ltd* [1983] Ch 110. In that case, the company was free
of liquidation at the date of the application to extend time, but a liquidation was
imminent when the application came before the registrar, and the company was actually
in liquidation when the matter came before the judge. It was held that:

D

"it was the established practice of the court, in the exercise of its discretion to
grant an extension of time for registration of a charge under section 101 of the
Companies Act 1948, to make the order with a proviso that it was made without
prejudice to the rights of parties acquired prior to the time when the charge
became registered and it was also firmly established practice that the order would
not be made once a company went into liquidation . . ."

E

Brightman LJ giving the judgment of the court summed up their conclusion at
p. 131G:

F

"To sum the matter up, in our judgment, the registrar was entitled to exercise his
discretion against Victoria on June 11 on the ground of the inadequacy of the
evidence and the imminence of liquidation. As we have already said, the majority
of this court in the *Resinoid* case decided that the imminence of liquidation is a
relevant factor. When the matter came before the deputy High Court judge upon
further evidence, he was entitled to exercise his own discretion, and (i) to take
into account as decisive against Victoria the then fact of the liquidation, (ii) to
reject the submission that exceptional circumstances existed which entitled him
to give Victoria priority notwithstanding the liquidation, and (iii) to take into
account, as equally decisive against Victoria, the fact that Victoria deliberately
chose not to apply for an extension of time when the mistake of non-registration
was first discovered.

G

On this last point, we think that, when an unregistered chargee discovers his
mistake, he should apply without delay for an extension of time if he desires to
register; and the court, when asked to exercise its discretion, should look askance
at a chargee who deliberately defers his application in order to see which way the
wind is going to blow."

H

A In the present case, Barclays became aware that the charge was not registered on 4 October 1989, but delayed to make an application for leave to register out of time until, at earliest, June of 1992. Instead of applying to register the charge quickly as it should have done, if the remedy under sec. 404 was the remedy it sought, Barclays chose to attempt to remedy the situation without applying to the court by taking another charge, and then another, and then another. Barclays only issued the application for leave when it became apparent to it that its other remedies had failed and at a time when

B the company had been dissolved and would, if restored to the register, in all probability (so far as it was aware) be insolvent.

Had I been satisfied that any discretion had arisen, I would not have regarded this as a case in which the court ought to exercise its discretion under the section, in view of the long delay in making the application. The fact is that decisions were repeatedly taken to seek to remedy the situation in other ways and that the application, when it was at last

C made, was only made when the company had been dissolved and was believed to be insolvent.

Had I thought it proper to give leave for registration of the charge, the order would have been made, as was the order of Mr Registrar *Pimm*, subject both to the *Joplin* proviso in its usual form and to the proviso in *Re L H Charles & Co Ltd* [1935] WN 15. In the circumstances, I will state my reasons shortly. Despite the full and careful

D argument of Miss Hoffmann, I am not persuaded that it would have been right to modify, much less to omit altogether, the *Joplin* proviso in this case, on the ground that Cyprus Bank had notice of the Barclays charge. I need not restate here the history of the proviso, recorded by the Court of Appeal in *Re Ashpurton Estates Ltd* at p. 122F and the following pages. The only modification sanctioned by authority appear to me to be a modification designed to give effect to pre-existing contractual rights, as in *Re I C Johnson & Co Ltd* [1902] 2 Ch 101, or a modification designed to prevent what is, in

E effect, an equitable fraud, as in *Re Fablehill Ltd* [1991] BCC 590.

As to the other cases relied upon, I accept that *Re Monolithic Building Co* [1915] 1 Ch 643, was a case in which the *Joplin* proviso was contained in an order which had already been made and was not a case in which the court was deciding whether or not it was appropriate that a *Joplin* proviso should be included in an order giving leave to register out of time. Nonetheless, the Court of Appeal made it clear in *Re Ashpurton Estates Ltd* at pp. 130E and 131D, that their view was that in considering whether or not to make

F an order permitting registration out of time, knowledge by a subsequent chargee, such as Cyprus Bank, was not a special circumstance such as had been envisaged by *Buckley* J in *Re S Abrahams & Sons Ltd* [1902] 1 Ch 695 and was, indeed, irrelevant. The statutory scheme is one based on registration on the Companies Register, not one based on actual notice apart from that register.

In *Re Braemar Investments Ltd* (1988) 4 BCC 366, to which Miss Hoffmann also

G referred me, *Hoffmann* J was not dealing directly with the *Joplin* proviso, and in *Watson v Duff, Morgan & Vermont (Holdings) Ltd* [1974] 1 WLR 450, *Templeman* J was considering the effect of an existing *Joplin* proviso, not whether or not one should be included. In the light of the observations of the Court of Appeal in *Re Ashpurton Estates Ltd* to which I have referred, and bearing in mind the comments made on those observations by *Vinelott* J in *Re Fablehill Ltd* at p. 598B, those cases do not to my mind lead to the conclusion that the *Joplin* proviso should be modified to exclude Cyprus

H Bank had that point arisen for a decision, much less to the conclusion that the *Joplin* proviso should be omitted altogether.

For the reasons I have given, I modify Mr Registrar *Pimm*'s order and dismiss Barclays' application.

(*Order accordingly*)

Re Devon and Somerset Farmers Ltd.   A

Chancery Division.

His Honour Judge Hague QC (sitting as a deputy judge of the Chancery Division).

Judgment delivered 4 May 1993.

> *Receivership — Preferential debts — Bank appointed receivers to society*   B
> *registered under Industrial and Provident Societies Act — Society subsequently*
> *went into creditors' voluntary liquidation — Whether society was "company"*
> *for purposes of payment of preferential debts out of assets subject to floating*
> *charge — Companies Act 1985, sec. 735; Insolvency Act 1986, sec. 40, 251.*

This was an application by the receivers of Devon and Somerset Farmers Ltd, a society registered under the Industrial and Provident Societies Act, to determine whether the society was a company for the purposes of sec. 40 of the Insolvency Act 1986.   C

Receivers of the society were appointed on 17 July 1990. On 4 April 1991 the society went into creditors' voluntary liquidation. The receivers had realised the society's assets and had in their hands a substantial surplus after discharging the debt owed to the bank which appointed them under a floating charge debenture. There were insufficient funds to satisfy all the creditors of the society in full. The receivers sought the determination of the court as to whether they were under a duty by reason of sec. 40 of the Insolvency Act   D
1986 to pay preferential creditors of the society ascertained as at the date of their appointment (17 July 1990) as the "relevant date" under sec. 387(4) of the 1986 Act, before handing over the balance to the liquidator. (The preferential debts would be different if the relevant date for ascertaining them was, under sec. 387(3)(c), the date of the resolution to wind up the society, 4 April 1991.) The question whether sec. 40 applied depended upon whether the society was a "company" for the purposes of the section.

The receivers argued that the section did apply. They relied among other things on the   E
decision of Mummery J in Re International Bulk Commodities Ltd [1992] BCC 463. That was a decision that receivers appointed to a foreign company were administrative receivers within the meaning of sec. 29(2) of the 1986 Act because "company" in Pt. III of the 1986 Act for those purposes did not mean only a Companies Act company (by virtue of sec. 251 of the 1986 Act and 735(1) of the Companies Act 1985) but extended to a foreign (unregistered) company, because the "contrary intention" required by sec. 735(4) of the   F
1985 Act did appear in the legislation.

The liquidator argued that International Bulk Commodities should not be followed because Mummery J had gone too far in a purposive approach to construing the legislation and because Mummery J was not referred to certain provisions of the Insolvency Act 1985 which was consolidated by the 1986 Act.

Held, declaring (1) that the society was not a "company" for the purposes of sec. 40 of   G
the Insolvency Act 1986, and (2) that the receivers were entitled to distribute the assets of the society in their hands to the liquidator of the society without regard to the provisions of that section:

1. It was doubtful whether the subject and purpose of the provisions could be sufficient to amount to a contrary purpose appearing. If Parliament had intended that any of the sections in Pt. II or III of the 1986 Act should extend to unregistered companies it was   H
hard to understand why it had not so provided.

2. Although he referred in general terms to "unregistered companies", Mummery J in International Bulk Commodities was only concerned with overseas companies. He did not hear argument on the rather different position of industrial and provident societies and their own special legislation, including specific provisions as to receivers and floating

A   charges. His general references to "unregistered companies" were not necessary for his decision and were obiter. Moreover, he was only concerned with the powers of a receiver, and not with any question of preferential debts. It was not necessary to come to any conclusive view as to the correctness of International Bulk Commodities, which was distinguishable and should be confined to the powers of receivers of overseas companies appointed under debentures. (**Re International Bulk Commodities Ltd [1992] BCC 463 distinguished.**)

B

    3. Section 40 was derived from sec. 196 of the Companies Act 1985 which was limited to Companies Act companies and continued to be so after amendments made by the Insolvency Act 1985. By the 1986 Act, the part of sec. 196 which related to the appointment of a receiver was removed from the section and became sec. 40(1). But the rest of the section dealing with possession being taken by the debenture holders remained unaltered and continued to apply only to Companies Act companies. More importantly, the transfer

C   of part of sec. 196 to Pt. III of the consolidating 1986 Act could not have had the consequences for which the receivers contended of extending the application of the section to unregistered companies or, in particular, to industrial and provident societies.

    4. The word "company" could not be interpreted for the purposes of sec. 40 as including industrial and provident societies. As such societies had their own legislation, including provisions regarding receivers, it was impossible to find that they were included

D   within the definition of "company" by reason of sec. 735 of the Companies Act 1985.

    The following cases were referred to in the judgment:

Bishopsgate Investment Management Ltd, Re [1992] BCC 222; [1993] Ch 1.
Dallhold Estates (UK) Pty Ltd, Re [1992] BCC 394.
Farrell & Anor v Alexander [1977] AC 59.
Felixstowe Dock & Railway Co v United States Lines Inc [1989] QB 360.

E   *International Bulk Commodities Ltd, Re* [1992] BCC 463; [1993] Ch 77.
National Employers' Mutual General Insurance Association Ltd v Jones [1990] AC 24.
Norse Self Build Association Ltd, Re (1985) 1 BCC 99,436.

John Nicholls (instructed by Cameron Markby Hewitt) for the receivers.

Stephen Davies (instructed by Anstey Sargent & Probert, Exeter) for the liquidator.

F

JUDGMENT

    His Honour Judge Hague QC: This application raises a difficult point of construction which arises under certain sections of the *Insolvency Act* 1986 and the *Companies Act* 1985. The application is made by the receivers of Devon and Somerset Farmers Ltd (which I will refer to as "the society"), a society originally formed and registered under the *Industrial and Provident Societies Act* 1893 and so deemed to be registered under

G   sec. 4 of the *Industrial and Provident Societies Act* 1965 ("the 1965 Act") which replaced it. The receivers were appointed under a debenture creating a floating charge granted by the society. The question for my determination is whether they are under a statutory duty imposed by sec. 40 of the *Insolvency Act* 1986 to pay the preferential debts of the society.

H   **The Industrial and Provident Societies Acts**

    It is convenient at the outset to consider some of the main provisions of the 1965 Act and related acts in a little detail. The 1965 Act, which consolidated the 1893 Act and other previous acts, permits a society to be registered under the Act if certain conditions are fulfilled, in particular (under sec. 1(2) as amended):

"(a)　that the society is a bona fide co-operative society; or　　　　　　A

(b)　that, in view of the fact that the business of the society is being, or is intended to be, conducted for the benefit of the community, there are special reasons why the society should be registered under this Act rather than as a company under the Companies Act 1985."

A registered society has members, but sec. 3 provides:

"A registered society shall by virtue of its registration be a body corporate by its　　B registered name, by which it may sue and be sued, with perpetual succession and a common seal and with limited liability . . ."

A registered society must have registered rules, which must make provision for the various matters listed in Sch. 1, and such rules bind its members: see sec. 14. "Any body corporate" may hold shares in a registered society: see sec. 19(1). Section 39 provides for an annual return, including an auditor's report to be made to the "appropriate　C registrar", i.e. (in England and Wales) the registrar of friendly societies. Under sec. 43, any receiver or manager of a registered society appointed under the powers contained in any instrument must give notice of his appointment and deliver periodic returns to the registrar. By sec. 52 and 53, provision is made for a registered society to convert to a company under the Companies Acts and vice versa.

Section 55 of the 1965 Act, which replaced a similar provision in the 1893 Act,　　D provides (as amended) that a registered society may be dissolved—

"(a)　on its being wound up in pursuance of an order or resolution made as directed in regard to companies by the Insolvency Act 1986, the provisions whereof shall apply to that order or resolution as if the society were a company, but subject to the following modifications, that is to say—

(i)　any reference in those provisions to the registrar within the meaning of that　E Act shall for the purposes of the society's winding up be construed as a reference to the appropriate registrar within the meaning of this Act . . ."

It was confirmed in *Re Norse Self Build Association Ltd* (1985) 1 BCC 99,436 that this section enables the court to wind up a registered society exactly as if it were a company under the Companies Acts, i.e. under what is now Pt. IV of the *Insolvency Act* 1986, and it is unnecessary to have resort to the power to wind up unregistered companies in Pt. V of that Act.　　　　　　F

Under the *Industrial and Provident Societies Act* 1967, a registered society has power to create a fixed or floating charge over its assets, which does not have to be registered as a bill of sale (as was the position prior to the passing of the Act). The instrument creating the charge must be recorded with "the appropriate registrar". By the *Friendly and Industrial and Provident Societies Act* 1968, further detailed requirements were made concerning a registered society's accounts, including group accounts, and the auditing　G of those accounts.

A registered society is thus in many ways similar to a company registered under the Companies Acts. It is a body corporate, its members have limited liability, the word "limited" is the last word in the title of every society, there are comparable provisions as regards rules, accounts and the registration of charges, and so on. But the 1965 Act and the subsequent acts nevertheless provide a quite separate and distinct statutory　H framework. Importantly for present purposes, there are separate and different provisions regarding floating charges and the appointment of receivers.

Devon and Somerset Farmers Ltd

This society, which formerly had other names, was originally registered in 1919. Under the powers conferred by the 1967 Act referred to above, it created fixed and

A   floating charges over its assets in favour of Lloyds Bank by a debenture dated 27 April 1981. The debenture was duly recorded with the registrar of friendly societies. It contained (in cl. 7 thereof) the usual wide power for the bank to appoint receivers, with power to manage the society's business. That power was exercised by the bank on 17 July 1990 when it appointed DHA Peacock and CM Clapp, of Ernst and Young, as joint receivers and managers.

B   Subsequently, on 4 April 1991, the society was put into a creditors' voluntary liquidation, and RP Neville, of KPMG Peat Marwick, was appointed liquidator.

The receivers have realised the society's assets and now have in their hands a substantial surplus after discharging the debt owed to the bank. There will however be insufficient funds to satisfy all the creditors of the society in full.

The question

C   The question which has arisen is whether the receivers are under a duty by reason of sec. 40 of the *Insolvency Act* 1986 to pay preferential creditors of the society, ascertained as at the date of their appointment (17 July 1990) as the "relevant date" under sec. 387(4), to which I shall refer, before handing over the balance to the liquidator. It was originally considered by the receivers and those advising them that they were under no such duty, and indeed the major preferred creditors as at that date concurred in that.

D   (On this basis, the consequence would be that "the relevant date" for the ascertainment of the preferential debts would, under sec. 387(3)(c), be the date of the resolution to wind up the society, 4 April 1991. If on the other hand "the relevant date" is the date of appointment of the receivers, the preferential debts would be quite different.) However, the matter has now been reconsidered by the receivers, particularly in the light of the recent decision of *Mummery* J in *Re International Bulk Commodities Ltd* [1992] BCC 463 and they have sensibly sought the determination of the court on the matter.

E   The respondent to the application is the liquidator. Mr Stephen Rees Davies has appeared for him, and argued that sec. 40 of the *Insolvency Act* 1986 does not apply. Mr John Nicholls appeared for the receivers and argued that it does. I am grateful to both counsel for their careful and cogent arguments which I found most helpful.

Insolvency Act 1986

F   Mr Nicholls referred me to several provisions of the 1986 Act, and it is necessary to discuss some of them in a little detail. The Act is divided into three "Groups of Parts". The first group concerns company insolvency and winding up, and consists of the following parts: Pt. I, company voluntary arrangements; Pt. II, administration orders, a new concept first introduced by the *Insolvency Act* 1985 which was replaced by the 1986 Act; Pt. III, receivership, which has separate chapters dealing with England and Wales and with Scotland; Pt. IV, winding up of companies registered under the Companies Acts; Pt. V, winding up of unregistered companies; Pt. VI, miscellaneous provisions; and Pt. VII, definitions. The second group of parts relates to the insolvency of individuals. The third group contains matters relating to both company and individual insolvency, including (in Pt. XII) provisions as to preferential debts.

G

It is convenient to start with Part XII. Preferential debts are listed in Sch. 6, nearly all of them being defined by reference to periods prior to "the relevant date". That expression is defined by sec. 387, subsec. (4) of which provides:

H

"In relation to a company in receivership (where section 40 or, as the case may be, section 59 applies), the relevant date is—

    (a) in England and Wales, the date of the appointment of the receiver by debenture-holders . . ."

Subsection (3) of sec. 387 deals with companies being wound up and, on the facts of this   A
case, under para. (c) "the relevant date" is "the date of the passing of the resolution for
the winding up of the company".

I turn to the critical provisions on which this case turns. Section 40, in Pt. III, reads as
follows:

> "(1) The following applies, in the case of a company, where a receiver is appointed
> on behalf of the holders of any debentures of the company secured by a charge   B
> which, as created, was a floating charge.
>
> (2) If the company is not at the time in course of being wound up, its preferential
> debts (within the meaning given to that expression by section 386 in Part XII) shall
> be paid out of the assets coming to the hands of the receiver in priority to any
> claims for principal or interest in respect of the debentures.
>
> (3) Payments made under this section shall be recouped, as far as may be, out of   C
> the assets of the company available for payment of general creditors."

The crucial word in the above, in relation to this case, is "company". If, but only if, the
society is a "company" for the purposes of sec. 40, the section will apply.

I must also mention sec. 29(2), likewise in Pt. III, which reads, so far as material, as
follows:

> "In this Chapter, 'administrative receiver' means—   D
>
> > (a) a receiver or manager of the whole (or substantially the whole) of a
> > company's property appointed by or on behalf of the holders of any
> > debentures of the company secured by a charge which, as created, was a
> > floating charge, or by such a charge and one or more other securities . . .."

The receivers in this case were appointed in respect of the whole of the society's
property. It is thus similarly clear that if, but only if, the society is a "company" for the   E
purposes of sec. 29(2), they are "administrative receivers".

There is no express definition of the word "company" for the purposes of sec. 40 or
sec. 29(2), or Pt. III as such. Section 251 is the definition section which is applicable to
the whole of the first group of parts. It provides:

> "In this Group of Parts, except in so far as the context otherwise requires—"

— there follow a number of definitions (including "administrative receiver" which   F
merely refers to sec. 29(2)), but no definition of "company"—

> "and any expression for whose interpretation provision is made by Part XXVI of
> the Companies Act, other than an expression defined above in this section, is to
> be construed in accordance with that provision."

That takes one to Pt. XXVI of the *Companies Act* 1985. The relevant section is sec. 735   G
which provides, so far as material, as follows:

> "(1) In this Act—
>
> > (a) 'company' means a company formed and registered under this Act, or an
> > existing company;
>
> . . .
>
> (4) The definitions in this section apply unless the contrary intention appears."   H

Apart from authority, I would not myself have considered that there was anything in the
context of either Pt. II of the 1986 Act (which includes in sec. 8 the power to make
administration orders) or in Pt. III amounting to a "contrary intention" (under
sec. 735(4) above) or to "otherwise require" (under sec. 251 of the *Insolvency Act*
1986), so as to extend the meaning of "company" beyond the prima facie meaning of

A
what can conveniently be called a Companies Act company. A similar view was taken, in relation to the power to make an administration order contained in sec. 8 of the *Insolvency Act* 1986, by *Hirst* J in *Felixstowe Dock & Railway Co v US Lines Inc* [1989] QB 360 where he said at p. 376B:

> "It is not in dispute . . . (ii) that Part II of the Insolvency Act 1986 does not give
> the English court jurisdiction to make an administration order in respect of a
B
> foreign company."

Likewise in *Re Dallhold Estates (UK) Pty Ltd* [1992] BCC 394, *Chadwick* J said at p. 396G:

> "A company is defined for those purposes by sec. 735 of the *Companies Act* 1985,
> which is incorporated into the *Insolvency Act* 1986 by the provisions of sec. 251 of
> that Act. The definition in sec. 735 of the *Companies Act* 1985 makes it clear that
C
> a company, for the purposes of those Acts, and except where otherwise expressly
> defined, means a company formed and registered under the 1985 Act or former
> UK Acts; and does not include a company incorporated overseas."

However, it is clear that the contrary was not argued in the Felixstowe case and it seems probable that the same applies to the *Dallhold* case. But in *Re International Bulk Commodities Ltd*, *Mummery* J held that in Pt. III of the 1986 Act at any rate, and in
D
particular in sec. 29(2), "company" does include an unregistered company. Mr Nicholls naturally placed great reliance on the reasoning of *Mummery* J in that case, and I must consider it in a some detail.

Re International Bulk Commodities Ltd

E
This case concerned an overseas company which traded in the UK and which had granted a debenture in English form to a bank creating fixed and floating charges over its assets. It was accepted that English law applied as regards the debenture. In due course the bank appointed joint receivers under its power in the debenture, and the question arose whether they were "administrative receivers" under sec. 29(2) of the 1986 Act with the powers of administrative receivers set out in Sch. 1, or whether their
F
powers were limited to those conferred by the debenture.

Mummery J discussed the background to the innovation of the concept of an administrative receiver and the beneficial consequences of that concept. He said at p. 466A:

> "Administrative receivership has to be viewed in the context of the whole range
> of remedies now available in situations where a company is, or is likely to become,
G
> unable to pay its debts. The changes made by the 1986 Act provide both greater
> flexibility and increased protection for those affected by actual or potential
> insolvency situations."

Mummery J then considered sec. 29(2) and 251 of the 1986 Act and sec. 735 of the *Companies Act* 1985, set out above, and continued at p. 467A:

> "The relevant question is therefore: is there any indication in the subject-matter
H
> and statutory purpose of the provisions concerning administrative receivers
> generally, or in the 1986 Act considered as a whole, from which it appears that
> Parliament intended that the word 'company' in the context of sec. 29(2)(a)
> should not be confined to its prima facie meaning of a company formed and
> registered under the Companies Acts, but should also embrace unregistered
> companies liable to be wound up under Pt. V of the Act.

In my judgment, there are indications that the provisions relating to administrative   A
receivers generally apply both to companies formed and registered under the
Companies Acts and to unregistered companies liable to be wound up under
Pt. V. The starting point is that the legislative concept of administrative receiver,
and the statutory scheme of the provisions relating to his qualifications, functions,
powers and duties, all rest on a contractual base, namely, a receiver appointed by
or on behalf of debenture holders under a debenture secured by a floating charge.
Every administrative receiver is born this way. As already noted, the underlying   B
contractual regime is applicable both in the case of a debenture granted by a
company formed and registered under the Companies Acts, and in the case of a
debenture granted by an unregistered company. The general purpose and scheme
of the statutory superstructure is to strengthen and build on the continuing
contractual foundation for the greater benefit of all affected — the company, the
contributories, the creditors, both secured and unsecured, and the preferential   C
creditors, as well as the public generally. The attainment of that general purpose
and the nature of the scheme are prima facie as appropriate to the case of an
unregistered company as they are to the case of a registered company.

Why should the range of companies affected by the statutory scheme of
administrative receivers not be co-extensive with the range of companies affected
by the underlying contractual receivership regime? Why should a receiver   D
appointed over the property of a registered company and a receiver appointed
over the property of an unregistered company under the same form of debenture
and by the same debenture holder not both fall within the definition of an
administrative receiver? It makes no sense to confine the purpose and scheme of
administrative receivership to appointments of receivers made over the property
of registered companies."

A little later, after mentioning sec. 230(2) of the 1986 Act, which relates to the   E
qualifications required by a person appointed as administrative receiver, and sec. 388(4)
(set out below), *Mummery* J continued at p. 468B:

"In my judgment, the court should construe the relevant provisions, where the
wording so permits, to promote and not to frustrate the evident legislative
purpose, in this case reinforcing the position of contractual receivers. The express
statutory definition of 'company' is only its prima facie meaning, since it is   F
expressly provided in sec. 735(4) of the Companies Act that the defined meaning
may be displaced where a contrary intention appears. For the reasons I have
stated above, a contrary intention does appear from the subject and the purpose
of the provisions. The court should favour a construction which is consistent with
and contributes to the smooth and efficient working of the contractual machinery
recognised and reinforced by the legislation."

Mr Davies submitted that *Re International Bulk Commodities Ltd* was wrongly   G
decided, and that I should not follow it. He said that the reasoning of *Mummery* J was
based on a "why not" approach which was not sufficient, and that the decision took the
modern "purposive" approach too far. He also pointed out that *Mummery* J was not
referred to certain provisions of the *Insolvency Act* 1985 which was consolidated by the
1986 Act and to which I will refer. I have felt the force of these submissions. For my part,
I doubt if the subject and purpose of the provisions can be sufficient to amount to a   H
"contrary intention" appearing; it seems to me that something more is required for that
purpose. Parliament may have had reasons for confining the new concept of administrative
receivers to Companies Act companies (e.g. to see how it worked in practice before
extending it to unregistered companies). Moreover, in sec. 388(4) of the 1986 Act, which
is concerned with the qualifications required for an insolvency practitioner, "company"
is defined for the purposes of the section as follows:

A
"'company' means a company within the meaning given by section 735(1) of the Companies Act or a company which may be wound up under Part V of this Act (unregistered companies). . ."

If Parliament had intended that any of the sections in Pt. II or Pt. III of the Act should extend to unregistered companies, it is hard to understand why a similar definition was not included. The contrast with sec. 251 of the 1986 Act and sec. 735 of the *Companies Act* 1985 is striking, and in my view significant.

B
Mr Nicholls submitted that, although not technically binding on me, *Mummery* J's decision was a fully reasoned decision which ought to follow. I respectfully decline to do so. Although he referred in general terms to "unregistered companies", *Mummery* J in that case was of course only concerned with overseas companies. He did not hear argument on the rather different position as to industrial and provident societies and their own special legislation, including the specific provisions which I have mentioned as

C
to receivers and floating charges. His general references to "unregistered companies" were not necessary for his decision and were obiter. Moreover, he was only concerned with the powers of a receiver, and not with any question of preferential debts. That being so, I do not consider it is necessary for me to come to any conclusive view as to the correctness of *Re International Bulk Commodities Ltd*, which in my judgment is distinguishable and should be confined to the powers of receivers of overseas companies

D
appointed under debentures.

Legislative history

It is convenient at this point to refer to the legislative history of sec. 29(2) and 40 of the 1986 Act which Mr Davies drew to my attention. Section 29(2) first appeared, in identical terms, in sec. 45(2) of the *Insolvency Act* 1985. Section 108 of that Act, which was headed "Construction of Part II" (which included sec. 45) provided, so far as

E
material, as follows:

"(1) The provisions of this Part shall be construed as one with the 1985 Act [i.e. the Companies Act 1985, see sec. 232] and–

. . .

(b) so far as relating to receivers or managers, with Part XIX of that Act;

. . .

F
and references in that Act to itself and to any of those Parts of that Act shall be construed accordingly."

Part XIX of the *Companies Act* 1985, comprising sec. 488–500 (relating to receivers and managers), clearly did not apply to unregistered companies in general and industrial and provident societies in particular.

G
Of more direct importance for present purposes is the history of sec. 40 of the 1986 Act. This is derived from sec. 196(1) of the *Companies Act* 1985, which replaced sec. 94(1) *Companies Act* 1948. Prior to its amendment by the *Insolvency Act* 1985, this read so far as material as follows:

"(1) The following applies, in the case of a company registered in England or Wales, where either a receiver is appointed on behalf of the holders of any debentures of the company secured by a floating charge, or possession is taken by

H
or on behalf of those debenture-holders of any property comprised in or subject to the charge.

(2) If the company is not at the time in the course of being wound up"

—the preferential creditors shall be paid in priority to other creditors and the debenture holders, etc. It is clear from its wording that this section was limited to Companies Act companies. The amendments made by the *Insolvency Act* 1985 to sec. 196 of the

Companies Act 1985 related only to the nature and extent of preferential debts. They A
did not alter the companies to which that section applied. The section continued to apply
only to Companies Act companies, and to cover the case of possession being taken by
debenture holders as well as a receiver being appointed.

It follows from the foregoing that, immediately before the 1986 Act came into force,
neither the forerunner of sec. 29(2) nor sec. 196 of the *Companies Act* 1985 applied to
either unregistered companies or (in particular) to industrial and provident societies.   B

The *Insolvency Act* 1986 was a consolidating Act. In *Re Bishopsgate Investment
Management Ltd* [1992] BCC 222, *Dillon* LJ described its effect as follows at p. 229F:

> "This Act is a major Act of Parliament which consolidated, with amendments, the
> law of personal and corporate insolvency. The amendments are contained in the
> *Insolvency Act* 1985, whose legislative purpose was to enact the amendments so
> that they could be consolidated by the 1986 Act with what remained of the   C
> previous insolvency law."

The *Insolvency Act* 1985 followed the "Cork Report", i.e. the *Report of the Review
Committee on Insolvency Law and Practice* (Cmnd 8558, 1982) and a government White
Paper on the subject (Cmnd 9175, 1984). I was told that neither the Cork Report nor the
White Paper contains any reference to industrial and provident societies or indeed to
any other kind of unregistered company. I was also told that nothing of assistance can be
derived from *Hansard*.   D

By the 1986 Act, the part of sec. 196 of the *Companies Act* 1985 which related to the
appointment of a receiver was removed from the section and became sec. 40(1). But the
rest of the section dealing with possession being taken by the debenture holders
remained unaltered and continues to apply only to Companies Act companies. Thus
there will be an anomaly if sec. 40 extends to unregistered companies. For a different
regime as to preferential debts will apply if a debenture holder decides to go into   E
possession rather than appoint a receiver.

More importantly, the transfer of part of sec. 196 to Pt. III of the consolidating 1986
Act cannot in my view have had the important amending consequences for which
Mr Nicholls contends. The only relevant new provisions are those contained in the
definition section, sec. 251 of the 1986 Act discussed above. In my judgment, these fall a
long way short of being sufficient to effect such an amendment. I do not overlook the   F
fact that the primary task of the court is to construe the 1986 Act as it stands,
notwithstanding that it is a consolidating act: see *Farrell & Anor v Alexander* [1977] AC
59. But where the construction is in doubt, in my view regard should be had to the
legislative history: cf. per *Dillon* LJ in *Bishopsgate Investment Management* at p. 229G,
and the approach of the House of Lords (admittedly in a different context, but in relation
to a consolidating act) in *National Employers' Mutual General Insurance Association
Ltd v Jones* [1990] AC 24. I respectfully think that the legislative history of sec. 29(2)   G
outlined above (to which *Mummery* J was not referred) casts doubt on the correctness
of his decision in *Re International Bulk Commodities Ltd*.

Mr Nicholls' alternative submission

Mr Nicholls submitted that, even if the ratio decidendi of *Re International Bulk
Commodities Ltd* is properly confined to overseas companies (as I have held to be the   H
case), it is still proper to include industrial and provident societies within the meaning of
"company" in sec. 40 of the 1986 Act. He drew attention to three matters in support of
this submission.

First, he said that the same important policy considerations as those discussed by
Mummery J in that case at pp. 467B and 468B (set out above) apply equally to industrial

A
and provident societies. I have already indicated that I do not consider that these are sufficient to lead to the conclusion that there is "contrary intention" appearing in the prima facie limitation of the word "company" to Companies Act companies.

Second, Mr Nicholls stressed that an industrial and provident society is an "unregistered company" capable of being wound up under Pt. V of the 1986 Act and also (under sec. 55 of the 1965 Act) can be wound up directly under Part IV. The preferential debt provisions of sec. 175 apply to a winding up under either Part (as to Pt. V, see sec. 221).

B
However, in my view that is of no assistance in determining what is "the relevant date" under sec. 387(4) and sec. 40 of the 1986 Act.

Third, Mr Nicholls said that unless sec. 40 applies, the interests of the persons who would be preferential creditors will be unprotected and there will therefore be a positive inducement to them to wind up a society rather than put it into receivership. He also pointed to other anomalies, in that until there is a crystallisation on a society being

C
wound up, the debts secured by a floating charge can be paid in priority to the preferential debts. These anomalies, which in any event existed prior to the 1986 Act, are in my view insufficient to lead to the conclusion that there is a "contrary intention" appearing. Moreover, they are in my view more than balanced by the anomalies mentioned below which will arise if sec. 40 does apply.

D
Conclusion

For the reasons which I have outlined above, in my judgment the word "company" cannot be interpreted for the purposes of sec. 40 as including industrial and provident societies. As such societies have their own legislation, including provisions regarding receivers, I find it impossible to find that they are included within the definition of "company" by reason of sec. 735 of the *Companies Act* 1985. I would have reached this conclusion independently of the previous legislative history, but I think it is confirmed

E
by that history. I agree with Mr Davies that Parliament cannot have intended by the relatively minor alterations in the definition sections of the 1986 Act to effect a substantial extension of the law relating to receivers so as to cover industrial and provident societies. I also agree with Mr Davies that Parliament cannot have intended to apply different schemes for the payment of preferential creditors depending whether the debenture holders appoint a receiver or take possession themselves. In the latter

F
case, there is no question of sec. 196 of the *Companies Act* 1985 applying.

Mr Davies also drew attention to certain further anomalies which would arise if "company" in Pt. III includes industrial and provident societies. It would mean that the receivers of such a society would have dual reporting and other obligations to the registrar of friendly societies and to the registrar of companies. It would also mean that the provisions of that Part would apply without (apparently) the charge having to be

G
registered under sec. 395 of the *Companies Act* 1985.

I should mention that Mr Davies also addressed an argument to me based on the legislation relating to floating charges created by Scottish industrial and provident societies. In view of my conclusion set out above, I do not find it necessary to deal with that argument.

Order

H
I will therefore make declarations (1) that the society is not a "company" for the purposes of sec. 40 of the *Insolvency Act* 1986, and (2) that the applicants are entitled to distribute the assets of the society in their hands to the respondent liquidator of the society without regard to the provisions of that section. I also consider it expedient to make representation orders that the applicants do represent the persons who would be preferential creditors of the society on the footing that sec. 40 of the *Insolvency Act* 1986

A

applied and that the respondent do represent all other creditors (including preferential creditors) in the liquidation of the society. The order for costs will be the same as that made by the registrar.

(Order accordingly)

B

C

D

E

F

G

H

A   **Marleasing SA v La Comercial Internacional de Alimentación SA (Case C-106/89).**

Court of Justice of the European Communities (Sixth Chamber).

G F Mancini, President of the Chamber, T F O'Higgins, M Díez de Velasco, C N Kakouris and P J G Kapteyn JJ, W van Gerven, Advocate General.

B   Judgment delivered 13 November 1990.

> *Community rules on nullity of companies — Directive providing for cases in which nullity may be ordered — Directive not implemented in national law — Whether national court obliged not to allow nullity in other cases — Clarification of concept of objects of the company — EC Directive 68/151 (first company law directive), preamble, art. 11 (OJ 1968 (I) Eng Spec Ed 41).*

C   This was a reference by the court of first instance and examining magistrates' court No. 1, Oviedo, for a preliminary ruling under art. 177 of the EEC Treaty on the interpretation of art. 11 of Directive 68/151 on co-ordination of safeguards which, for the protection of the interests of members and others, are required by member states of companies within the meaning of the second paragraph of art. 58 of the treaty, with a view to making such safeguards equivalent throughout the Community (the first company law directive).

D   The question referred arose in proceedings between two companies in which the plaintiff company claimed principally, on the basis of certain provisions of the Spanish Civil Code which rendered ineffective contracts lacking consideration or lacking lawful consideration, a declaration as to the nullity of the founders' contract establishing the defendant company on the ground that it was based on no consideration, was vitiated by misrepresentation and was entered into solely for the purpose of putting the assets of a third company, a co-founder of the defendant company, beyond the reach of its creditors, E   including the plaintiff company. The defendant company contended that the claim should be rejected, relying on the fact that art. 11 of Directive 68/151, which listed the cases in which the nullity of a company could be declared, did not include lack of consideration among those cases.

The national court noted that, at the date of the reference, Spain had not, as it was required to do, implemented Directive 68/151 into its national law. Considering, therefore, F   that the dispute raised a problem concerning the interpretation of Community law, the court stayed the proceedings and made a reference to the Court of Justice asking whether art. 11 of the directive was directly applicable so as to preclude a declaration of nullity of a public limited company on a ground other than those set out in that article.

Held, ruling accordingly:

1. It was well established that a directive could not by itself create obligations for an G   individual and, accordingly, its provisions could not be relied upon against such a person. However, it was also well established that it followed from the obligation on member states to take all measures appropriate to ensure the performance of their obligation to achieve the result provided for in directives, that in applying national law, whether it was a case of provisions prior to or subsequent to the directive, the national court called on to interpret the national law was required to do so as far as possible in the light of the wording and purpose of the directive, in order to achieve the result sought by the directive, H   and thus to comply with the third paragraph of art. 189 of the treaty.

2. With regard to the interpretation to be given to art. 11 of the directive, in particular art. 11(2)(b) which provided that nullity could be ordered if the "objects of the company" were unlawful or contrary to public policy, it was clear from the preamble that the purpose of the directive was to limit the cases in which nullity could arise and the retroactive effect of a declaration of nullity. Consequently, each ground of nullity

provided for in art. 11 had to be interpreted strictly. In those circumstances the words
"objects of the company" had to be understood as referring to the objects of the company
as described in the instrument of incorporation or the articles of association. The nullity
of a company, therefore, could not be declared on the basis of the activities which it
actually carried on, such as, for example, defrauding the founders' creditors.

3. Accordingly, a national court hearing a case which fell within the scope of Directive
68/151 was required to interpret its national law in the light of the wording and the
purpose of that directive in order to preclude a declaration of nullity of a public limited
company on grounds other than those listed in art. 11 of the directive.

The following cases were referred to in the judgment:

*Marshall v Southampton and South-West Hampshire Area Health Authority
(Teaching)* (Case 152/84) [1986] QB 401; [1986] ECR 723.
Von Colson & Anor v Land Nordrhein-Westfalen (Case 14/83) [1984] ECR 1891.

José Ramón Buzón Ferrero, of the Oviedo Bar, for the plaintiff in the main proceedings.

Antonio Caeiro, its legal adviser, and Daniel Calleja, a member of its legal department,
acting as agents, for the Commission.

REPORT FOR THE HEARING

I — Legal background

1. Article 395 of the Act concerning the conditions of accession of the Kingdom of
Spain and the Portuguese Republic and the adjustments to the Treaties (OJ 1985 L302/
23) provides that the two new member states are to put into effect the measures
necessary for them to comply, from the date of accession, with the provisions of
Community directives.

2. The object of the First Council Directive 68/151 (OJ 1968 (I), Eng Spec Ed,
p. 41), based in particular upon art. 54(3)(g) of the EEC Treaty, is to ensure certainty in
the law as regards relations between certain forms of companies, including public limited
companies and third parties and between members.

To that end art. 11 limits the instances of nullity of companies. It provides:

"The laws of the Member States may not provide for the nullity of companies
otherwise than in accordance with the following provisions:

(1) Nullity must be ordered by decision of a court of law;

(2) Nullity may be ordered only on the following grounds:

(a) that no instrument of constitution was executed or that the rules of
preventive control or the requisite legal formalities were not complied
with;

(b) that the objects of the company are unlawful or contrary to public
policy;

(c) that the instrument of constitution or the statutes do not state the
name of the company, the amount of the individual subscriptions of
capital, the total amount of the capital subscribed or the objects of
the company;

(d) failure to comply with the provisions of the national law concerning
the minimum amount of capital to be paid up;

(e) the incapacity of all the founder members;

(f) that, contrary to the national law governing the company, the number
of founder members is less than two.

A   Apart from the foregoing grounds of nullity a company shall not be subject to any cause of non-existence, nullity absolute, nullity relative or declaration of nullity."

3. The Spanish Law of 17 July 1951 (*Boletin Oficial* No. 199 of 18 July 1951; corrigendum in BOE No. 218 of 6 August 1951) on the law governing public limited companies does not specifically set out the cases of nullity of such companies. Legal literature considers that the matter is governed by the rules of ordinary law but stresses

B   the difficulties posed by the application by analogy of those rules (see J Garrigues: *Curso de Derecho Mercantil*, vol. I, Madrid, 1982, p. 435 et seq.).

Articles 1261 and 1275 of the Spanish Civil Code, on the fundamental conditions for the validity of contracts under Spanish law, provide:

Article 1261:

C   "A contract arises only when the following requirements are met:

(1) the parties are agreed,

(2) the subject matter of the contract is certain,

(3) there is a cause for the obligation which is created";

D   Article 1275:

"Contracts with no cause or whose cause is unlawful are of no effect. A cause is unlawful when it is contrary to law or morality."

4. The Kingdom of Spain notified the Commission of the text of a draft law on the partial reform and adjustment of the Spanish commercial legislation to comply with the EEC directives on company law (Ministry of Justice: *Supplement to Bulletin* No. 1469

E   of 5 October 1987, Year XLI, Madrid, 1987), the preamble to which states as follows:

"An important new feature is the inclusion of two provisions on the nullity of companies, which although they are included in order to comply with Community directives fill a serious lacuna in our company law. First, they expressly restrict the causes of nullity to cases provided for by the law to the exclusion of all others whatsoever, in view of the serious effects of nullity, on which the courts alone

F   have jurisdiction to give a ruling. Secondly, nullity entailing the liquidation of the company may not adversely affect creditors since the declaration of nullity does not affect the company's obligations or debts with third parties."

Article 32(f) (grounds of nullity) of the preliminary draft provides:

"...

G   8. Nullity of the company must be declared by a judgment of the court and only on the following grounds:

(1) if the notarial act of the instrument of incorporation is not drawn up or filed at the commercial registry,

(2) if the company's object is unlawful or contrary to public policy,

H   (3) if the name of the company, the members' contributions, the amount of capital subscribed, or the company's object are not contained in the notarial act or statutes or if the minimum amount of capital provided for in art. 10 is not paid up,

(4) incapacity of all the founder members,

(5) if the instrument of incorporation does not express the effective intention of at least two founder members where there must be more than one pursuant to art. 12(l) of the present law.

9. Apart from cases referred to in the previous paragraph there may be no declaration of non existence, absolute nullity or relative nullity of the company."

5. That preliminary draft law has since become Law 19/1989 of 25 July 1989 (Law on the partial reforming and adjustment of commercial legislation in order to comply with the directives of the EEC on companies). Article 31, in the fourth section (nullity of companies), includes the last four cases of nullity contained in the preliminary draft.

According to its final provisions the law entered into force on 1 January 1990.

II — Facts and procedure

Marleasing SA brought an action on 29 September 1987 before the Juzgado de Primera Instancia e Instrucción No. 1, Oviedo, for annulment of the contract of association of La Comercial Internacional de Alimentación SA on the ground of misrepresentation and annulment of its instrument of incorporation for lack of cause; or in the alternative, an order that the contract of association and instrument of incorporation be set aside as frauds on creditors' rights; and in the further alternative annulment of the contribution in kind by Barviesa SA in favour of La Comercial Internacional de Alimentación SA, as a fraud on creditors' rights.

The application was based on the view that the defendant company, formed on 7 April 1987, had been created by Barviesa SA and two men of straw for the sole purpose of removing the assets of the latter company from the reach of its creditors, including Marleasing SA. The application was based on the general principles contained in the Civil Code, namely art. 1261 concerning the requirements necessary for the existence of contracts and art. 1275 concerning the ineffectiveness of contracts with no cause.

The defendant contended that the application should be rejected in its entirety, inter alia, on the ground that the first directive, art. 11 of which sets out the exhaustive list of cases in which a public limited company may be declared void, does not include lack of cause.

The national court stated that the first directive has not been implemented in the Kingdom of Spain in spite of the obligation to do so which it has had since 1 January 1986 under art. 395 of the Act of Accession. The national court thus considered that the case raised the question of the direct effect in relations between private persons of Community directives which have not been implemented within the requisite period by the member states. In listing the grounds of nullity exhaustively, art. 11 of the first directive leaves no discretion to extend them in national law. Moreover, if the directive has direct effect in relation to private persons the nullity of a public limited company has repercussions going beyond the strict sphere of relations between private individuals, in as much as it affects the interests of members and third parties, who are protected under art. 54(3)(g) of the EEC Treaty.

By order of 13 March 1989 the national court therefore decided, pursuant to art. 177 of the EEC Treaty, to stay the proceedings until the Court of Justice had given a preliminary ruling on the following question of interpretation:

"Is art. 11 of Council Directive 68/151 of 9 March 1968, which has not been implemented in national law, directly applicable so as to preclude a declaration of nullity of a public limited company ('*sociedad anónima*') on a ground other than those set out in the said article?"

The order for reference was received at the Court Registry on 3 April 1989.

A　　Pursuant to art. 20 of the protocol on the statute of the Court of Justice of the European Communities, written observations were submitted by the Commission of the European Communities, represented by its legal adviser A Caeiro, and D Calleja, a member of its Legal Department, acting as agents, and by the plaintiff in the main proceedings, represented by J R Buzón Ferrero, of the Oviedo Bar.

Upon hearing the report of the Judge-Rapporteur and the views of the Advocate General, the court decided to open the oral procedure without any preparatory inquiry.
B　　Pursuant to art. 95(1) and (2) of the rules of procedure the court assigned the case to the sixth chamber by decision of 17 January 1990.

III — Written observations submitted to the court

The *Commission of the European Communities* states that the court has consistently held that provisions which are clear, unconditional and sufficiently precise may be relied
C　　upon before a national court by an individual vis-à-vis any public authority of a member state which has failed to fulfil its obligation to implement the directive in its national legal system within the time-limit laid down (see, in particular, the judgment of 19 January 1982 in Case 8/81 *Becker v Finanzamt Münster-Innenstadt* [1982] ECR 53; Common Market Reporter ¶8789).

The Commission goes on to raise the question whether, under Community law, the
D　　provisions of a directive may be relied upon by an individual in legal relations with another individual where the directive has not been implemented in the law of the member state to which it was addressed after the expiry of the time-limit laid down for its implementation.

The answer to that question would seem to be in the negative. The Commission points out in that respect that in its judgment of 26 February 1986 in Case 152/84 *Marshall v*
E　　*Southampton and South-West Hampshire Area Health Authority (Teaching)* [1986] ECR 723 at para. 48; Common Market Reporter ¶14,295, the court clearly stated that:

"... according to Article 189 of the EEC Treaty the binding nature of a directive, which constitutes the basis for the possibility of relying on the directive before a national court, exists only in relation to 'each Member State to which it is addressed'. It follows that a directive may not of itself impose obligations on an individual and that a provision of a directive may not be relied upon as such
F　　against such a person."

It follows from the foregoing and the prevailing academic view that Community directives have no "horizontal" legal effect and that their provisions cannot be relied upon in legal relations between individuals. The fundamental objection is no doubt the legal uncertainty which the opposite view would cause in legal relations between individuals.
G　　The Commission considers that art. 11 of the first directive, whose ultimate object is to ensure legal certainty as far as possible by restricting the possible cases of nullity of companies having legal personality, imposes on the member state to which it is addressed a clear, unconditional and sufficiently precise obligation to achieve a result.

The court's case law does not however allow such a provision of a directive which has not been implemented in national law within the time-limit laid down, as in the present
H　　case, to be relied upon by an individual against another individual to whom, under art. 189 of the EEC Treaty, the directive has not been addressed. That must be so particularly in a matter as delicate as company law, in which the Community system must be interpreted uniformly, in view of the balance required in the protection of the interests of shareholders, creditors and third parties in general. It is obvious that there would be legal uncertainty if there were a right to rely on a provision of a Community

directive against another individual who had relied on the validity of the national law in force. It does not seem permissible to rely against an individual on a provision of a Community measure whose publication is not compulsory and which is not addressed to that individual.

It would seem therefore that the answer to be given to the question put by the Spanish court must be in the negative.

The Commission nevertheless considers that the previous Spanish legislation largely, even if not completely, incorporated the fundamental principles set out in the first directive. The main difference between the directive and the previous Spanish law on public limited companies or, more precisely, between the directive and the interpretation of that legislation by legal literature, is the fact that the directive allows as grounds of nullity only those it expressly mentions (art. 11(2)), whereas the previous law was silent on that issue.

That lacuna, which the Spanish legislature expressly recognises in the preamble to the above-mentioned preliminary draft law, is covered according to legal writers, by recourse to the general rules which apply to contracts in civil matters, to which may be added grounds based on failure to observe the commercial rules applicable to the establishment of public limited companies (absence or nullity of an essential reference in the document, incomplete subscription of the authorised capital and so forth).

In view of the foregoing the Commission considers that the question asks whether the legal lacuna which existed in relation to the nullity of public limited companies could be covered not by reliance on the general rules applicable to civil contracts but by recourse to the principles and rules of Community law contained in the first directive.

It is true the Kingdom of Spain ought to have adopted the measures needed to bring its national law into conformity with Community law by 1 January 1986.

However, the previous Spanish legislation had already taken the same direction in seeking to achieve the same objectives as the first directive on company law.

In those circumstances it does not seem that, in the absence of express provision in the previous Spanish provisions relating to grounds of nullity of companies, the national court is unable to cover that lacuna in its national system by interpreting the national law in a way consistent with art. 11(2) of the directive, which sets out the only cases in which nullity of a company may be ordered.

In so far as the national court may choose between various interpretations of its national law the Commission considers that it is not possible to prevent it from choosing the interpretation consistent with the Community directive. There is thus no question of replacing national law with a directive which had not yet been implemented in Spanish law and which could not be relied upon against an individual or of requiring the national court to choose an interpretation *contra legem* by directly applying the Community directive, since there was no expressly applicable national provision.

It may simply be considered that in the absence of conditions enabling the directive to have full effect in national law the interpretation of the provisions of national law in accordance with Community law may safeguard the principles of Community law. As a result of such an approach the interpretation of national law in accordance with Community law may prevail over the rules of interpretation commonly recognised in the national law, but precisely because of the principle of the primacy of Community law any rule of interpretation which might frustrate the result intended by the authors of a directive must be regarded as precluded.

As a result of the accession of Spain to the European Communities the national court has a new legal system on which it may base its interpretation of national law in certain cases. That legal system is an integral part of national law since the national court is also

A a Community court. The national court cannot be denied the possibility of having regard to the solution desired by the Community legislature in interpreting national law in the event of a lacuna in the latter. It is not possible to preclude that court from interpreting the previous Spanish law in accordance with the solution applied in the other member states of the Community.

The *plaintiff in the main proceedings* considers that the directive is not applicable in the present case.

B Pursuant to the third paragraph of art. 189 of the EEC Treaty directives are binding only on member states and effect only the member states to which they are addressed; they cannot directly bind individuals.

By definition, a directive is an incomplete rule which can therefore produce no horizontal effect between individuals. The latter can be directly affected only by the national provision implementing the directive.

C The Court of Justice itself does not give directives which have not been implemented within the time-limits any direct effect in relations between individuals, for that would cause uncertainty since it would require individuals, in order to defend themselves in proceedings under national law, to acquire exhaustive knowledge of directives, especially if it is borne in mind that publication is not a condition for their entry into force.

D Directives cannot as a general rule give rise to rights which can be relied upon in a court of law by individuals. Similarly, an individual cannot be considered to have failed to comply with an obligation which does not directly affect him since it has another addressee, namely the member state.

In the present case the proceedings are between two Spanish trading companies, which are established and have their registered office in Spanish territory, in relation to a question of civil and commercial law; consequently, there is no ground for an extensive interpretation of the application of the first directive, since it contains no provision which might indicate that by way of exception, although addressed only to the member states, it also affects individuals. Nor does the directive directly relate to any article of the Treaty or regulation which might bring it within the scope of provisions applicable by way of exception.

E The directive states in its title, its preamble and its main text that it is adopted "for the protection of the interests of members and others". The best way to protect the interests of others is obviously to preclude the donation, sheltered by a broad interpretation of a directive which is not fundamental, of phantom companies which, by absorbing the capital of other companies preceding them, make it impossible to satisfy the rights of their creditors and in consequence prevents obligations and contracts from being honoured.

F

G   OPINION OF MR ADVOCATE GENERAL VAN GERVEN
                              (12 July 1990)

1. The Juzgado de Primera Instancia e Instrucción, Oviedo, has asked the court to give a preliminary ruling on the interpretation of art. 11 of the First Council Directive 68/151 of 9 March 1968, hereinafter referred to as "the first directive" (Council directive on co-ordination of safeguards which, for the protection of the interests of members and others, are required by member states of companies within the meaning of the second paragraph of art. 58 of the treaty, with a view to making such safeguards equivalent throughout the Community (OJ 1968 (I), Eng Spec Ed, p. 41)).

H

Background

2. This reference has been made in the context of a dispute between Marleasing SA, the plaintiff, and a number of defendants including La Comercial Internacional de

Alimentación SA (hereinafter referred to as "La Comercial"). The latter was incorporated   A
in the form of a public limited company by three persons, including the company
Barviesa SA, which contributed its own assets. Marleasing, which is an important
creditor of Barviesa, contends that La Comercial was in fact set up by Barviesa alone
and that the two other founders were men of straw. In its view, La Comercial was created
for the sole purpose of putting Barviesa's assets beyond the reach of its creditors.
Relying on the provisions of the Spanish Civil Code on the validity of contracts,   B
art. 1261 and 1275, according to which contracts lacking cause or whose cause is unlawful
have no legal effect, Marleasing sought primarily a declaration as to the nullity of the
founders' contract on the ground that it was a sham transaction and of the instrument
incorporating La Comercial on the ground that it was vitiated by the lack of (lawful)
cause. In the alternative, Marleasing sought an order setting aside the founders' contract
and instrument of incorporation on the ground that their purpose was to defraud the
creditors, and, in the further alternative, a declaration cancelling Barviesa's contribution   C
to the company's assets for the same reason.

In its defence, La Comercial relied, inter alia, on art. 11 of the first directive, which
lists exhaustively the cases in which the nullity of a company may be declared. The lack
of (lawful) cause, which is the primary ground relied upon by Marleasing, is not included
amongst those cases. Accordingly, in La Comercial's view, there can be no declaration
of nullity of the company.   D

3. The court making the reference considers that this case raises the problem of the
direct effect of a directive which has not yet been transposed into national law by a
member state. It points out in that connection that, pursuant to art. 395 of the Act of
Accession (Act concerning the conditions of accession of the Kingdom of Spain and the
Portuguese Republic and the adjustments to the Treaties, OJ 1985 L302/23), the
Kingdom of Spain was under an obligation to implement the first directive as from the   E
date of its accession, but this had not yet been done at the date of the order for reference.
(In the meantime the Spanish legislature has approved Law No. 19/1989 of 25 July 1989
on the adjustment of commercial legislation to comply with the Community directives
(BOE No. 178 of 27 July 1989). The provisions concerning public limited companies
were subsequently co-ordinated by Royal Decree No. 1564/1989 of 22 December 1989
(BOE No. 310 of 27 December 1989). Articles 34 and 35 of that decree regulate the
nullity of public limited companies in accordance with the rules as to nullity established   F
by the first directive. Whether those later provisions are relevant to the dispute in the
main proceedings is a matter for the national court, and need not be investigated here.)
The national court therefore submitted the following question to the Court of Justice for
a ruling on interpretation:

> "Is art. 11 of Council Directive 68/151 of 9 March 1968, which has not been
> implemented in national law, directly applicable so as to preclude a declaration of   G
> nullity of a public limited company on a ground other than those set out in the said
> article?"

4. The national court correctly proceeds on the assumption that the legal form in
which La Comercial was constituted, namely that of a public limited company, falls
within the scope of the first directive (see art. 1 of the first directive, as amended by the
Act of Accession, according to which the following types of company fall within the   H
scope of the directive: la sociedad anónima, la sociedad comanditaria por acciones, la
sociedad de responsabilidad limitada). The national court is also correct in assuming
that this directive permits a declaration of nullity of such a company only on the grounds
listed in art. 11(2). It is quite apparent from the final subparagraph of art. 11 that the
grounds of nullity listed in that provision are exhaustive:

A   "Apart from the foregoing grounds of nullity, a company shall not be subject to any cause of non-existence, nullity absolute, nullity relative or declaration of nullity."

The question whether the first directive has direct effect may therefore be relevant for the solution of the dispute in the main proceedings. I shall begin by briefly considering that question and answering it in the negative. Notwithstanding my negative answer, the directive must still serve as a frame of reference for the interpretation of national
B   law (see para. 7 et seq. below), but only, of course, within its own field of application (see para. 12 below).

A provision of a directive may not be relied upon as such against an individual

5. In its judgment of 19 January 1982 in Case 8/81 *Becker v Finanzamt Münster-*
C   *Innenstadt* [1982] ECR 53 at para. 23–25; Common Market Reporter ¶8789, the court stated that where a provision of a directive is unconditional and sufficiently precise, it may be relied upon by an individual against a member state which has failed to transpose the directive into national law within the prescribed period. In its judgment of 26 February 1986 in Case 152/84 *Marshall v Southampton and South-West Hampshire Area Health Authority (Teaching)* [1986] ECR 723; Common Market Reporter ¶14,295,
D   the court added that that possibility exists only in relation to the member state concerned and state bodies. It follows from that finding:

       ". . . that a directive may not of itself impose obligations on *an individual* and that a provision of a directive may not be relied upon as such against *such a person*" (*Marshall* para. 48, emphasis added).

That position has since been repeatedly reaffirmed, most recently in the judgment of 22 February 1990 in Case 221/88 *ECSC v Acciaierie e Ferriere Busseni SpA (in liq.)*
E   [1990] ECR I-495.

6. In this case La Comercial relies, in its defence against Marleasing's main contention, on a provision of a directive, namely art. 11 of the first directive, which had not yet been transposed into Spanish law at the date of the order for reference. The prohibition laid down in that article on a declaration of nullity of a company on grounds other than those listed therein is without the slightest doubt unconditional and sufficiently precise to be
F   regarded on principle as directly applicable. In the light of the established case law of the court, however, that provision cannot be relied upon by La Comercial against Marleasing in the main proceedings. There is no evidence whatsoever that Marleasing is acting as a state body or public authority, not even in the broad sense in which the court has interpreted those terms again today (see in that regard my opinion of 8 May 1990 in Case C-188/89 *Foster & Ors v British Gas plc* [1990] ECR I-3313; [1990] 2 CEC 598 at p. 608, and, more generally, my opinion of 30 January 1990 in Case 262/88 *Barber*
G   *v Guardian Royal Exchange Assurance Group* [1990] ECR I-1889; [1990] 1 CEC 653 at p. 669).

The obligation to interpret national law in conformity with the directive

7. Although a provision of a directive may not be relied upon against an individual, national courts are still required, as the Court of Justice stated in its judgment of
H   10 April 1984 in Case 14/83 *Von Colson & Anor v Land Nordrhein-Westfalen* [1984] ECR 1891 at para. 26; Common Market Reporter ¶14,092 (see also the judgment of 10 April 1984 in Case 79/83 *Harz v Deutsche Tradax GmbH* [1984] ECR 1921 at para. 26; Common Market Reporter ¶14,093):

       ". . . in applying the national law and in particular the provisions of a national law specifically introduced in order to implement [the] Directive . . . to interpret [their] national law in the light of the wording and the purpose of the directive in order to achieve the result referred to in the third paragraph of Article 189."   A

That obligation on the part of the national courts to interpret their national law in conformity with a directive, which has been reaffirmed on several occasions (judgment of 15 May 1986 in Case 222/84 *Johnston v Chief Constable of the Royal Ulster Constabulary* [1986] ECR 1651 at para. 53; Common Market Reporter ¶14,304, judgment of 8 October 1987 in Case 80/86 *Re Kolpinghuis Nijmegen BV* [1987] ECR 3969; [1989] 1 CEC 118 at para. 12, judgment of 20 September 1988 in Case 31/87 *Gebroeders Beentjes BV v Netherlands State* [1988] ECR 4635 at para. 39, and judgment of 7 November 1989 in Case 125/88 *Re Nijman* [1989] ECR 3533 at para. 6), does not mean that a provision in a directive has direct effect in any way as between individuals (that is why, moreover, the relevant provision of the directive need not be "unconditional and sufficiently precise" in order to serve as an interpretative criterion; see also, for the same view, para. 15 of the joined opinion of Mr Advocate General Darmon of 14 November 1989 in Case 177/88 *Dekker v Stichting Vormingscentrum voor Jong Volwassenen (VJV-Centrum) Plus* [1990] ECR I-3941 and Case 179/88 *Handels- og Kontorfunktionærernes Forbund i Danmark v Dansk Arbejdsgiverforening* ("*Hertz*") [1990] ECR I-3979). On the contrary, it is the national provisions themselves which, interpreted in a manner consistent with the directive, have direct effect.   B

C

8. The obligation to interpret a provision of national law in conformity with a directive arises whenever the provision in question is to any extent open to interpretation (with regard to that obligation see, amongst others, Y Galmot and J C Bonichot: "La cour de justice des Communautés européennes et la transposition des directives en droit national", *Revue Française de Droit Administratif*, 1988, p. 1 et seq., especially at p. 20 et seq.). In those circumstances the national court must, having regard to the usual methods of interpretation in its legal system, give precedence to the method which enables it to construe the national provision concerned in a manner consistent with the directive (for a recent example, see the judgment of the House of Lords of 16 March 1989 in *Litster & Ors v Forth Dry Dock and Engineering Co Ltd & Anor* [1989] All ER 1134).   D   E

The obligation to give an interpretation in conformity with a directive is, it is true, restricted by Community law itself, of which the directive forms part, and in particular by the principles of legal certainty and non-retroactivity which also form part of Community law. In cases involving criminal proceedings, for example, such an interpretation cannot result in criminal liability unless such liability has been introduced by the national legislation implementing the directive (judgment in Case 80/86 *Re Kolpinghuis Nijmegen BV*, cited above, para. 13). Nor, similarly, can a directive of itself — that is to say in the absence of national implementing legislation — introduce a civil penalty, such as nullity, in national law. However, that is not the issue here: this case is concerned with a provision of a directive which *excludes* certain grounds of nullity.   F   G

9. The question whether an interpretation is in conformity with a directive usually arises in relation to provisions of national law which are specifically intended to implement the directive concerned. That was the case in *Von Colson* (cited above) and in the cases referred to in para. 7 above [namely, Case 222/84 *Johnston v Chief Constable of the Royal Ulster Constabulary*, Case 80/86 *Re Kolpinghuis Nijmegen BV*, Case 31/87 *Gebroeders Beentjes BV v Netherlands State*, and Case 125/88 *Re Nijman*].   H

However, there is no reason to restrict the requirement that an interpretation must be in conformity with a directive to that situation (see also, for the same view, my opinion of 30 January 1990 in Case 262/88 *Barber v Guardian Royal Exchange Assurance Group*, cited above, para. 50). That follows, in my view, from the reasoning used by the

A court to underpin that requirement. It is based on the consideration that judicial authorities, like the other public authorities of the member states, are required, in the light of art. 5 of the EEC Treaty, to seek to achieve the result pursued by the directive by *all* appropriate measures within their power. Furthermore, as part of Community law, the directive concerned in principle takes precedence over *all* provisions of national law. That is true in particular in the case of national provisions which, as in this case, relate to the branch of the law covered by the directive, even though they predate the

B directive and were thus not enacted for its implementation. That ought to be clear now that the court has held in its judgment of 13 December 1989 in Case 322/88 *Grimaldi v Fonds des Maladies Professionelles* [1989] ECR 4407, that national courts are required to take a non-binding recommendation into consideration in connection with the interpretation of provisions of national law, even though those provisions do not give effect to the recommendation. (In the case of national provisions adopted previously,

C an interpretation in conformity with the directive is normally applicable only as from the expiry of the time-limit for implementation prescribed by the directive (or even as from the entry into force of the directive: see the judgment in *Re Kolpinghuis Nijmegen BV*, cited above, para. 15 and 16). Events occurring prior to that date continue of course to be governed by the national provisions construed without regard to the directive. In this case, however, the company in question, La Comercial, was incorporated on 7 April 1987, that is to say at a time when the time-limit for the implementation of the first

D directive by Spain had already expired (namely on 1 January 1986).)

10. Let us apply the foregoing principles to the question under consideration. Since the first directive had not been transposed into Spanish law at the material time, and the Spanish Law of 17 July 1951 concerning public limited companies lacked a specific rule as to nullity applicable to those companies, the prevailing view in legal literature (on that point, the Commission refers to J Garrigues: *Curso de Derecho Mercantil*, I,

E Madrid, 1982, p. 435 et seq.: see for that matter, art. 50 of the Spanish Commercial Code, which provides that commercial agreements — according to art. 116 of that code, a (trading) company constitutes a commercial agreement — are governed by the rules of ordinary law, except where otherwise provided by special rules) is that the provisions relating to the nullity of contracts are to be applied by analogy. In accordance with that view, Marleasing based its primary claim for a declaration of nullity of the instrument of

F incorporation of La Comercial on the provisions of the Spanish Civil Code to the effect that contracts lacking cause or whose cause is unlawful have no legal effect.

The national court is thus faced — as I understand it — with a problem concerning the interpretation of company law. The question which arises is to what extent the grounds of nullity under ordinary law can be applied by analogy to public limited companies. It follows, in my view, from the reasoning set out in the preceding paragraphs that the

G requirement that an interpretation must be consistent with a directive precludes the application to public limited companies of the provisions on nullity under ordinary law in such a way as to permit a declaration of nullity of such a company on grounds other than those exhaustively listed in art. 11 of the first directive.

The scope of the rules on nullity in the first directive

H 11. The question submitted by the national court for a preliminary ruling concerns the grounds of nullity listed in art. 11 of the first directive. That article must in consequence also be the focus of attention with regard to the interpretation of national legislation in conformity with the directive. From that article, which is set out in full in the Report for the Hearing (in para. 2), I shall quote only the two grounds of nullity to be discussed here. The laws of the member states may provide for nullity to be ordered by decision of a court of law on the following grounds:

"(a) . . .

(b) that the objects of the company are unlawful or contrary to public policy;

. . .

(f) that, contrary to the national law governing the company, the number of founder members is less than two."

In addition to art. 11 of the first directive, art. 12 must also be borne in mind. That article governs the effects of nullity. Once again, I shall quote only the provisions which are relevant to this case:

"1. . . .

2. Nullity shall entail the winding up of the company, as may dissolution.

3. Nullity shall not of itself affect the validity of any commitments entered into by or with the company, without prejudice to the consequences of the company's being wound up.

4. The laws of each Member State may make provision for the consequences of nullity as between members of the company.

5. . . ."

12. Article 11 of the first directive can of course be of assistance to the national court in interpreting its own national legislation only in so far as the dispute before it relates to the nullity of a (limited) company. None of the other matters raised in Marleasing's primary or alternative claims before the national court is affected by the directive.

That is true particularly as regards Marleasing's action to set aside Barviesa's contribution to La Comercial's capital in so far as that contribution was allegedly made in order to defraud Barviesa's creditors. Such a claim is not affected by the rules on nullity laid down by the first directive.

Nor, it seems to me, does a (preliminary) contract between shareholders — in so far as it is to be distinguished from the actual instrument of incorporation — of itself fall within the ambit of the rules on nullity established by the directive, at least in so far as the cancellation of the contract does not automatically lead to the nullity of the company.

Finally, the first directive does not contain any rules governing the dissolution of companies, since I assume that the dissolution of a company normally has no retroactive effect and the commitments entered into by the company prior to its dissolution therefore remain valid.

13. On the other hand, in so far as Marleasing's claim seeks a declaration of nullity of La Comercial as such, it does fall within the scope of art. 11 and 12 of the first directive. In so far as the national court is under an obligation to take those provisions into consideration when interpreting its own national law (see above, para. 7 et seq.), it must deal with the question whether the ground of nullity referred to in art. 11(2)(b) of the directive covers the case of a company purportedly set up with the aim of placing the founders' creditors at a disadvantage. This, therefore, is a question involving the interpretation of the directive itself (an interpretation which, in turn, must be taken into consideration in the interpretation of national law).

Before considering that question of interpretation, which is a controversial one in some member states, I should point out that in interpreting national company law the national court could perhaps also have had recourse to some of the other grounds of nullity set out in art. 11. The most obvious ground is the one referred to in art. 11(2)(f), according to which a member state *may* provide for the nullity of a company where, contrary to its national law, the number of founder members is less than two (which means that the state rules out the possibility of a one-man company, either altogether or in the case of certain types of companies (in the meantime, the Council has adopted the Twelfth Company Law Directive 89/667 of 21 December 1989 on single-member private

A   limited liability companies, OJ 1989 L395/40)). Marleasing contended in the main proceedings that La Comercial was set up exclusively by Barviesa and that the other signatories of the instrument of incorporation were men of straw.

Notwithstanding that contention, the ground of nullity in art. 11(2)(f) has not been raised before the court either in the written observations or at the hearing. Nor is it clear from the order for reference whether at the material time Spanish civil or commercial law contained any rules in that regard and if so what rules, and whether nullity was the

B   penalty for contravening them. I do not therefore propose to consider this ground further and shall confine myself to the observation that it depends on national law, to which art. 11(2)(f) expressly refers — if it provides that there must be (at least) two shareholders to set up a company — whether and to what extent the presence of founder members not acting on their own account may entail the nullity of the company (frequently a distinction is drawn in that connection between persons who, without

C   seeking to evade a mandatory rule, properly act in their own name but on account of another as trustees, nominees or under a borrowed name, and persons who act as men of straw with a view to evading a mandatory rule such as the rule that a natural or legal person may have only one set of assets). The national legislature may refrain from adopting, or adopt only in part, the grounds of nullity set out in art. 11, and consequently restrict its field of application. However, it may not extend either the number or the scope of those grounds.

D   14. Hence the question raised by way of a reference for a preliminary ruling is, essentially, how art. 11(2)(b) is to be interpreted. In the light of the facts central to the dispute in the main proceedings, this case turns on the meaning of the phrase "the objects of the company". The phrase, "unlawful or contrary to public policy", also in art. 11(2)(b), is not at issue. Nevertheless, let me point out that the concept of "public policy" has frequently been raised in the court's judgments in another connection,

E   namely in connection with art. 48(3) of the EEC Treaty. In that context the court has stated that although the scope of that concept cannot be terminated unilaterally without being subject to control by the Community institutions, nevertheless it may vary from one country to another and from one period to another and it is therefore necessary to leave the national authorities an area of discretion "within the limits imposed by the Treaty and the provisions adopted for its implementation". In any event, says the court, that concept presupposes:

F

> ". . . the existence, in addition to the perturbation of the social order which any infringement of the law involves, of a genuine and sufficiently serious threat . . . affecting one of the fundamental interests of society" (judgment of 27 October 1977 in Case 30/77 *R v Bouchereau* [1977] ECR 1999 at para. 33–35; Common Market Reporter ¶8441).

G   As for the term "unlawful", it refers, in my view, to a conflict with a mandatory or unconditional statutory prohibition or with public morality (to the extent that it does not fall within "public policy"). The concept of "public morality" has also been discussed in the court's case law, particularly in connection with art. 36 of the EEC Treaty, where reference has also been made to the existence of a discretion on the part of the national authorities within the limits of Community law (judgment of 11 March 1986 in Case 121/85 *Conegate Ltd v HM Customs & Excise* [1986] ECR 1007 at para. 14–16; Common

H   Market Reporter ¶14,275). The limits set by Community law with regard to all of those concepts are essentially those contained in the first directive.

15. This case is therefore concerned with the interpretation of the phrase "the objects of the company". That task is all the more delicate in view of the divergences on that point between the different language versions of art. 11(2)(b). (In the Dutch version, reference is made to "het werkelijk(e) doel van de vennootschap". In the German

version, the words used are "(der) tatsächlich(er) Gegenstand des Unternehmens". In   A
the French version ("l'objet de la société") and in the Italian version ("(il) oggetto della
società") the company's objects are not qualified in any way. That is also true of the
other language versions drawn up by the Council following the adoption of the directive,
including the Spanish version ("(el) objeto de la sociedad"), which are equally authentic.)
According to the Dutch version of that provision, a declaration of nullity of a company
may be made where its "werkelijke doel" (actual objects) are unlawful or contrary to
public policy. Must the phrase "doel van de vennootschap" (in the French version: B
"objet de la société") be understood as meaning exclusively the company's objects
described in its instrument of incorporation or its statutes, or must it be understood as
referring also to the activity actually carried on by the company or even the aim actually
pursued by means of the company (in the sense of "le but de la société")? (These three
concepts are used side by side in the 1968 convention on the mutual recognition of
companies and legal persons: see para. 18 below.) Only in the latter case can the national
court take the view, without interpreting its national law in a manner inconsistent with   C
the directive, that a declaration of nullity of a company can be made if it was incorporated
for the (sole) purpose of placing the founders' creditors at a disadvantage, as Marleasing
contends in the main proceedings.

In some member states the ground of nullity set out in art. 11(2)(b) has given rise to
divergent interpretations on this very point. (For instance in Belgium and France (but
also in Germany and Italy — see the references in para. 17 below): see, in particular,   D
L Simont: "Les règles relatives à la publicité, aux nullités et aux actes accomplies au
nom d'une société en formation", in *Les Sociétés Commerciales*, Jeune Barreau,
Bruxelles, 1985, p. 102 et seq.; R Houin: "Chroniques de législations et de jurisprudence
françaises — sociétés commerciales", *Revue Trimestrielle de Droit Commercial*, 1970,
p. 736 et seq. In France the prevailing view seems to be that the French Law on
companies, which was brought into line with the directive by Ordonnance No. 1176 of
20 December 1969, leaves intact the grounds of nullity under ordinary law (amongst   E
others "la cause illicite") which are not expressly excluded by art. 360. Some authors
(see amongst others, Y Serra: *Chronique*, Dalloz, 1973, p. 17 et seq.) have raised the
question whether those French rules are contrary to the first directive. In Belgium's
Dutch-language legal literature and case law, in particular, the broad meaning is
advocated, having regard to the Dutch version of art. 11(2)(b) of the directive (see the
first subparagraph of this paragraph above): see, in particular, J Ronse et al: *Overzicht
van Rechtspraak (1975–78) Vennootschappen, Tijdschrift voor Privaatrecht*, 1986, p.   F
885 et seq. and the very recent judgment of the Rechtbank van Koophandel, Hasselt, of
28 May 1990, not yet reported.) That is not surprising in the light of the discussions and
compromises between the Commission and the experts of the member states in connection
with the adoption of art. 11 (discussed in E Stein: *Harmonisation of European Company
Laws*, 1971, p. 299 et seq.). In other member states, however, scarcely any attention has
been paid to that ground of nullity or, for that matter, to the entire system of nullity   G
established by the directive.

The reason for that very uneven level of interest is not easy to determine. The
existence in some countries of a preliminary (judicial or administrative) review in
connection with the incorporation of joint-stock companies (see art. 10 of the directive)
may undoubtedly preclude the application of the rules on nullity. The more formal
nature of the instrument of incorporation, which has the effect of "detaching" it from   H
the underlying contractual relationship to a greater extent in some member states than
in others is another possible reason which is especially relevant in this case.

16. In any event, it is clear from the rules on nullity in the first directive and also from
the other rules set out therein concerning the disclosure and validity of commitments
entered into by a company that the objective of "protecting the interests of third parties"

A   (second recital in the preamble to the directive) must be reinforced in an expanded market as regards companies which have no safeguards they can offer to third parties other than their assets (first and third recitals in the preamble). The rules on nullity themselves reflecting the need "to limit the cases in which nullity can arise and the retroactive effect of a declaration of nullity", are designed "in order to ensure certainty in the law as regards relations between the company and third parties, and also between members" (sixth recital in the preamble). (As regards the effects of nullity vis-à-vis third

B   parties, they are regulated in a mandatory manner by the directive (see, in particular, art. 12(2) and (3), quoted in para. 11 above). The effects as between the members themselves may be determined by the laws of each member state (art. 12(4), also quoted above).)

    In those circumstances, it seems clear to me that each ground of nullity, even taken on its own, must be given a narrow interpretation with a view to protecting the interests of

C   third parties — that is to say the company's creditors — and that a declaration of nullity as a result of infringements arising from the contractual relationship between the members of the company or between the members and the company is a penalty which must be avoided as far as possible. That does not rule out either the possibility or desirability of penalising such infringements in a different manner which does not jeopardise the existence of the company and is less detrimental to its creditors.

D   Accordingly, I consider that the phrase "the objects of the company" in art. 11(2)(b) of the directive must be understood as meaning the company's objects as described and disclosed in the instrument of incorporation or the statutes (see art. 2(1)(a) and also art. 3 of the directive) (the phrase "objects of the company" is also used in art. 9(1) of the first directive; see, on that point, E Stein, cited above, p. 282 et seq.: in that provision as well, the phrase must be understood as referring to the company's objects as described in the instrument of incorporation or the statutes, having regard to the special status of

E   legal persons under the law). Only where the objects, in that sense, "are unlawful or contrary to public policy" can a declaration of nullity of the company be made. An aim for which the company was incorporated but which is not stated in the instrument of incorporation or the statutes, for example to defraud the members' creditors, cannot have that consequence: such illegality or conflict with public policy (for instance, with the rule concerning the unity of the founders' assets) must be dealt with otherwise than by a declaration of nullity (see para. 19 below). (The protection offered to third parties

F   by the first directive is restricted to specified third parties, namely the company's creditors, and does not extend to third-party creditors of the members. The reason for the special protection afforded to the company's creditors lies in the fact that, in the case of joint-stock companies, they have no safeguard other than the company's assets: see the third recital in the preamble to the directive.)

    17. The foregoing observations must be qualified by an important consideration.

G   Both the German and Dutch versions of art. 11(2)(b) specify that a company's objects are to be understood as the actual (in Dutch "werkelijke" and in German "tatsächlich") objects of the company. In my view that is a useful clarification which is not contradicted by the other language versions. It demonstrates that if the company's real activity, as carried on from the outset, is unlawful or contrary to public policy, the ground of nullity provided for in art. 11(2)(b) can be relied upon, even though that activity is not in accordance with the company's presumably lawful objects as described in the instrument

H   of incorporation or the statutes. (See, for that view, amongst others J Van Ryn en P Van Ommeslaghe: "Examen de jurisprudence (1972–78), les sociétés commerciales", *Revue Critique de Jurisprudence Belge*, 1981, who on p. 241 suggest that a heated controversy in that regard — to which the French legislation also gives rise (R Houin, cited above, p. 736 et seq.) — should be resolved as follows: "regard should be had not only to the company's objects as set out in the statutes but also to the activities actually carried on

under that veil". See also L Simont, cited above, No. 28, who adds that the possibility of　A
nullity as a result of unlawful activities in practice is all the more appropriate since in
accordance with art. 9(1) of the first directive the company is also bound by acts which
are ultra vires. The same view would appear to be taken in German legal literature: see
Gessler, Hefermehl, Eckardt and Kropff: *Aktiengesetz*, 1986, pp. 275 and 276. In
Italian legal literature, on the other hand, views are divided: see A Borgioli: *La Nullità
della Società per Azioni*, 1977, p. 414 et seq., and the references for and against in
footnote 126 on p. 414.) Here are some examples:　　　　　　　　　　　　　　　　　B

(a)　　the company's objects as specified in the instrument of incorporation or the
　　　　statutes are the operation of a hotel, whilst it is apparent in practice that this
　　　　means operating an (illegal) gaming room or allowing (the criminal offence of)
　　　　prostitution;

(b)　　the company objects, as set out in the instrument of incorporation, are the
　　　　production and exportation of steel tubes, whilst under that veil the company　C
　　　　(unlawfully) produces and supplies weapons.

The activity must be one which was carried on from the outset (see, for that view, in
particular, F Galgano: "La società per azioni", *Trattato di Diritto Commerciale e di
Diritto Pubblico dell'Economia*, VII, 1984, p. 101; J Ronse: *De Vennootschapswetgeving*,
1973, p. 76, and L Simont, cited above, No. 28). If a company whose objects are lawful
only subsequently carries on unlawful activities, contrary to its objects, that cannot give　D
rise to the nullity of the company but may lead to its dissolution if national law so
provides.

18. The qualification set out in the previous paragraph, which I think is a useful one
and finds support in the German and Dutch versions of art. 11(2)(b), does not strike me
as being incompatible with the protection of the interests of third parties. It helps to
prevent third parties from being misled by an activity which is falsely stated as an object　E
in the instrument of incorporation or in the statutes but which from the outset does not
correspond to reality. Furthermore, the activity actually carried on, unlike the intentions
by which the members were guided in setting up the company, can normally be
ascertained by third parties who enter into transactions with the company. Finally, if
such a qualification is not made the ground of nullity in art. 11(2)(b) is emptied of a
considerable part of its substantive content since the prohibition, so restricted, of objects
which are unlawful or contrary to public policy is then easily circumvented by stating　F
objects in the instrument of incorporation or the statutes of the company which are
lawful but spurious. (It is noteworthy that art. 9 of the convention of 29 February 1968
on the mutual recognition of companies and legal persons (*Bull. Supp. EC* 2-1969),
which was signed shortly before the adoption of the first directive, refers to a broader
concept of the (company's) objects. It encompasses not only the "company's objects"
and the "activity actually carried on" but also "the purpose" (rendered in the French　G
version as "objet", "activité effectivement exercée" and "but" respectively). When one
of those three is contrary "to the principles or rules which the state concerned regards as
matters of public policy as defined in private international law", that state may refuse to
recognise a foreign company. That difference between art. 9 of the convention and
art. 11(2)(b) of the first directive is no doubt connected with the specific purpose of the
directive, which is to restrict the nullity of companies in order to protect the interests of
third parties. For the reasons given above, however, that restriction may not go so far as　H
to exclude from the company's objects the "activity actually carried on (from the
outset)" as well, although it may exclude the "purpose" of the founders of the company,
which is unknown to third parties.

19. The practical significance of the suggested definition of the ground of nullity
referred to in art. 11(2)(b), which, though restrictive, is not excessively so, should not

A   be overestimated. For the creditors of a debtor who has contributed his assets to a
company with a view to removing those assets from their grasp — a possibility that does
not come within that definition — a declaration of nullity of the company would offer
only limited protection. The legal effects of a declaration of nullity must, after all, be
consistent with the provisions of art. 12 of the first directive, cited above (para. 11). This
means that nullity entails winding-up of the company, in the same manner as dissolution.
It also means that nullity does not of itself affect the validity of the company's
B   commitments. The rules in the directive thus leave intact the separate assets of a
company which has been declared void, with the result that in principle the members'
creditors cannot recoup themselves out of the goods contributed to the company by the
members.

As stated earlier (para. 12), the first directive does not affect other penalties provided
for by national law in those circumstances, and the creditors retain, for instance, the
C   possibility of bringing an action to set aside in their interests any *capital contribution*
made in disregard of their rights. (This point would appear to be undisputed. Only one
reference: P Van Ommeslaghe: "La première directive du Conseil du 9 Mars 1968 en
matière de sociétés", *Cahiers de Droit Européen*, 1969, at p. 657.) Such an action will
usually be more effective in protecting their interests than a declaration of nullity of the
company itself.

D   **Summary**

20. To recapitulate, I have come to the following conclusions. Article 11 of the first
directive does not have direct effect as between individuals, with the result that La
Comercial cannot rely directly on the exhaustive list of grounds of nullity set out in the
directive against Marleasing's claim. However, the national court is under an obligation
to interpret its national company legislation in conformity with the directive whenever
such legislation is open to divergent interpretations. This would appear to be the case
E   where, with regard to the nullity of (public limited) companies, general concepts of the
law of contract are applied by analogy, first because such concepts are open to
interpretation, and secondly because application by analogy is only one possible method
of interpretation. In such a case, it seems to me, the national court can easily, when
applying national law, apply the exhaustive list of grounds in art. 11 and possibly —
should a declaration of nullity of the company nevertheless be made — the restriction
F   on the retroactive effect of nullity pursuant to art. 12 of the first directive.

The ground of nullity in art. 11(2)(b) must be understood as encompassing only
unlawful objects or objects contrary to public policy which are set out in the instrument
of incorporation or the statutes or are shown by the activity actually carried on by the
company from its inception. The aim, pursued by the founder members in setting up the
company, where it is not expressed in the manner indicated above, does not come within
G   the company's objects in that sense. However, that does not prevent national law from
enabling creditors of founder members whose interests have been detrimentally affected
from availing themselves of other remedies (such as the action to set aside transfers
made in order to defraud creditors) which — in the light of the limited effect of a
declaration of nullity — are usually just as effective and which the directive leaves intact.

H   **Conclusion**

21. In the light of the foregoing considerations, I propose that the question submitted
for a preliminary ruling should be answered as follows:

1. Article 11 of Council Directive 68/151 of 9 March 1968 cannot be relied
upon as such against an individual. However, the national court must interpret
its national legislation in the light of the wording and the purpose of that

provision of the directive and, where a declaration of nullity is made, in the
light of art. 12 of that directive.

2. The phrase "the objects of the company", in art. 11(2)(b) of Directive
68/151 must be interpreted as meaning the objects as described in the published
instrument of incorporation or statutes of the company, or as shown by the
activity actually carried on by the company from its inception.

JUDGMENT
(13 November 1990)

1. By order of 13 March 1989, which was received at the court on 3 April 1989, the
Juzgado de Primera Instancia e Instrucción No. 1, Oviedo, referred a question to the
court pursuant to art. 177 of the EEC Treaty for a preliminary ruling on the interpretation
of art. 11 of Council Directive 68/151 of 9 March 1968 on co-ordination of safeguards
which, for the protection of the interests of members and others, are required by
member states of companies within the meaning of the second paragraph of art. 58 of
the treaty, with a view to making such safeguards equivalent throughout the Community
(OJ 1968 (I), Eng Spec Ed, p. 41).

2. Those questions arose in a dispute between Marleasing SA, the plaintiff in the
main proceedings, and a number of defendants including La Comercial Internacional de
Alimentación SA (hereinafter referred to as "La Comercial"). The latter was established
in the form of a public limited company by three persons, including Barviesa SA, which
contributed its own assets.

3. It is apparent from the grounds set out in the order for reference that Marleasing's
primary claim, based on art. 1261 and 1275 of the Spanish Civil Code, according to
which contracts without cause or whose cause is unlawful have no legal effect, is for a
declaration that the founders' contract establishing La Comercial is void on the ground
that the establishment of the company lacked cause, was a sham transaction and was
carried out in order to defraud the creditors of Barviesa SA, a co-founder of the
defendant company. La Comercial contended that the action should be dismissed in its
entirety on the ground, in particular, that art. 11 of Directive 68/151, which lists
exhaustively the cases in which the nullity of a company may be ordered, does not
include lack of cause amongst them.

4. The national court observed that in accordance with art. 395 of the Act concerning
the conditions of accession of Spain and the Portuguese Republic to the European
Communities (OJ 1985 L302/23) the Kingdom of Spain was under an obligation to bring
the directive into effect as from the date of accession, but that that had still not been
done at the date of the order for reference. Taking the view, therefore, that the dispute
raised a problem concerning the interpretation of Community law, the national court
referred the following question to the court:

"Is art. 11 of Council Directive 68/151 of 9 March 1968, which has not been
implemented in national law, directly applicable so as to preclude a declaration of
nullity of a public limited company on a ground other than those set out in the said
article?"

5. Reference is made to the Report for the Hearing for a fuller account of the facts of
the case, the course of the procedure and the observations submitted to the court, which
are mentioned or discussed hereinafter only in so far as is necessary for the reasoning of
the court.

6. With regard to the question whether an individual may rely on the directive against
a national law, it should be observed that, as the court has consistently held, a directive
may not of itself impose obligations on an individual and, consequently, a provision of a

A directive may not be relied upon as such against such a person (judgment of 26 February 1986 in Case 152/84 *Marshall v Southampton and South-West Hampshire Area Health Authority (Teaching)* [1986] ECR 723; Common Market Reporter ¶14,295).

7. However, it is apparent from the documents before the court that the national court seeks in substance to ascertain whether a national court hearing a case which falls within the scope of Directive 68/151 is required to interpret its national law in the light
B of the wording and the purpose of that directive in order to preclude a declaration of nullity of a public limited company on a ground other than those listed in art. 11 of the directive.

8. In order to reply to that question, it should be observed that, as the court pointed out in its judgment of 10 April 1984 in Case 14/83 *Von Colson & Anor v Land Nordrhein-Westfalen* [1984] ECR 1891 at para. 26; Common Market Reporter ¶14,092, the member states' obligation arising from a directive to achieve the result envisaged by the
C directive and their duty under art. 5 of the treaty to take all appropriate measures, whether general or particular, to ensure the fulfilment of that obligation, is binding on all the authorities of member states including, for matters within their jurisdiction, the courts. It follows that, in applying national law, whether the provisions in question were adopted before or after the directive, the national court called upon to interpret it is required to do so, as far as possible, in the light of the wording and the purpose of the
D directive in order to achieve the result pursued by the latter and thereby comply with the third paragraph of art. 189 of the treaty.

9. It follows that the requirement that national law must be interpreted in conformity with art. 11 of Directive 68/151 precludes the interpretation of provisions of national law relating to public limited companies in such a manner that the nullity of a public limited company may be ordered on grounds other than those exhaustively listed in art. 11 of
E the directive in question.

10. With regard to the interpretation to be given to art. 11 of the directive, in particular art. 11(2)(b), it should be observed that that provision prohibits the laws of the member states from providing for a judicial declaration of nullity on grounds other than those exhaustively listed in the directive, amongst which is the ground that the objects of the company are unlawful or contrary to public policy.

F 11. According to the Commission, the expression "objects of the company" must be interpreted as referring exclusively to the objects of the company as described in the instrument of incorporation or the articles of association. It follows, in the Commission's view, that a declaration of nullity of a company cannot be made on the basis of the activity actually pursued by it, for instance defrauding the founders' creditors.

12. That argument must be upheld. As is clear from the preamble to Directive
G 68/151, its purpose was to limit the cases in which nullity can arise and the retroactive effect of a declaration of nullity in order to ensure "certainty in the law as regards relations between the company and third parties, and also between members" (sixth recital). Furthermore, the protection of third parties "must be ensured by provisions which restrict to the greatest possible extent the grounds on which obligations entered into in the name of the company are not valid". It follows, therefore, that each ground of nullity provided for in art. 11 of the directive must be interpreted strictly. In those
H circumstances the words "objects of the company" must be understood as referring to the objects of the company as described in the instrument of incorporation or the articles of association.

13. The answer to the question submitted must therefore be that a national court hearing a case which falls within the scope of Directive 68/151 is required to interpret its national law in the light of the wording and the purpose of that directive in order to

preclude a declaration of nullity of a public limited company on a ground other than   A
those listed in art. 11 of the directive.

Costs

14. The costs incurred by the Commission of the European Communities, which has
submitted observations to the court, are not recoverable. As these proceedings are, in
so far as the parties to the main proceedings are concerned, in the nature of a step in the
action pending before the national court, the decision on costs is a matter for that court.   B

Ruling

On those grounds, the court (sixth chamber), in answer to the question referred to it
by the Juzgado de Primera Instancia e Instrucción No. 1, Oviedo, by order of 13 March
1989, hereby rules:

> **A national court hearing a case which falls within the scope of Council Directive**   C
> **68/151 of 9 March 1968 on co-ordination of safeguards which, for the protection**
> **of the interests of members and others, are required by member states of**
> **companies within the meaning of the second paragraph of art. 58 of the treaty,**
> **with a view to making such safeguards equivalent throughout the Community,**
> **is required to interpret its national law in the light of the wording and the**
> **purpose of that directive in order to preclude a declaration of nullity of a public**   D
> **limited company on a ground other than those listed in art. 11 of the directive.**

E

F

G

H

A # Thrells Ltd v Lomas & Anor.

Chancery Division.
Sir Donald Nicholls V-C.
Judgment delivered 2 and 7 April and 31 July 1992.

B *Liquidation — Pension scheme surplus — Company and company's pension scheme being wound up — Whether company could alter pension scheme rules when scheme being wound up — Whether statute required "limited price indexing" of pensions before surplus paid to employer — Whether and how discretion under rules for winding up scheme should be exercised to increase pensions of prospective pensioners — Social Security Act 1990, sec. 11(3).*

This was an application concerning the distribution of the surplus in a pension scheme, which was being wound up after the company which had operated the scheme, and was
C the sole trustee, went into liquidation. The application was brought by the company acting by its liquidator. The liquidator was also the first defendant, representing the company's unsecured creditors. The second defendant was a representative pensioner.

Because the liquidator was confronted with a conflict of duties, acting as the representative of the unsecured creditors and for the sole trustee of the scheme, he surrendered to the court the exercise of any discretion vested in the company as trustee of
D the scheme.

A number of questions arose on the application: first, whether a power of alteration contained in the declaration of trust and the scheme rules could still be exercised even though under the rules the scheme was being wound up.

Secondly, how sec. 11(3) of the Social Security Act 1990, providing that no payment could be made out of the resources of a scheme to the employer until provision had been
E made for "limited price indexing" ("LPI") of pensions under the scheme, operated regarding the payment of the surplus to the company under the rules for winding up the scheme.

Thirdly, how the court should exercise the discretion conferred on the trustee under the rules for winding up the scheme to increase the pensions of prospective pensioners.

Held, giving directions to the trustee to administer and wind up the scheme accordingly:

F 1. The rules providing for the consequences of a winding up were inconsistent with the company retaining any right thereafter to change the rules so far as those consequences were concerned. The winding-up provisions in the rules were excluded from the power of alteration.

2. Parliament could not have intended that sec. 11(3) could be side-stepped, and a payment made to an employer without complying with the payment condition, by the
G simple expedient of the employer winding up the scheme and making provision only for non-indexed benefits. When a scheme was being wound up, and a payment fell to be made to a former employer pursuant to the rules applicable in the winding up of a scheme, the pensions to which the payment condition in sec. 11(3) applied were to be understood as being those for which provision was being made in the course of that self-same winding up. When the payment to the former employer was triggered by a winding up of a scheme, the pensions which were to have the benefit of LPI before the payment could be made
H were those which were payable under the scheme, either actually or prospectively, when the scheme went into liquidation. Otherwise the winding up process would itself operate to defeat the application of the subsection.

3. The date of the liquidation preceded the date on which sec. 11(3) came into force. But that did not mean that the legislation was being given retrospective effect. The payment to the company had not been made by 17 August 1990. If it had, the subsection

would not have applied to the payment. Since it had not, the subsection applied. The   A
earlier date was material merely for crystallising the pensions to which the payment
condition applied. The LPI increases would be payable in respect of those pensions, but
only for the future. They would not date back to 28 November 1984. LPI must be provided
for the future, and pensions secured on that footing, before any payment to the company
could be made.

4. The cost of satisfying the payment condition under sec. 11(3) would have to be met
before any surplus could be paid to the company. However, the discretion under the rules   B
for winding up the scheme to increase the pensions of prospective pensioners ranked
ahead of the satisfaction of the sec. 11(3) payment condition.

5. The power to increase the pensions of prospective pensioners was an integral part of
the scheme. It assumed the existence of a surplus. A trustee should not decline to exercise
it solely on the ground that the employer was under no legal obligation to provide the
surplus. (Mettoy Pension Trustees Ltd v Evans & Ors [1990] 1 WLR 1587 at pp. 1618–   C
1620 followed.)

6. First, the discretion should be exercised in a manner which would let sec. 11(3)
operate fully. This would benefit both pensions in payment and also deferred pensions. It
was equitable that that should be so. Secondly, having regard to the purpose for which
the power was created, it was right that, within reason, deferred pensions should be
increased by LPI. The balance should go to the creditors. The cost of providing the   D
revised benefit for the prospective pensioners would be £192,000. That meant that the
balance available to the liquidator would be £191,000. It also meant that the liquidator
and the pensioners would share more or less equally the amount of the surplus that would
be available if the discretion were not exercised at all and the liquidator were to receive
the whole balance (viz. £383,000) remaining after the payment condition under sec. 11(3)
had been met.

The following cases were referred to in the judgment: E

Barber v Guardian Royal Exchange Assurance Group (Case 262/88) [1990] 1 CEC
653; [1991] 1 QB 344.
Mettoy Pension Trustees Ltd v Evans & Ors [1990] 1 WLR 1587.

John Stephens (instructed by Allen & Overy) for the applicant.

Nicholas Warren (instructed by Allen & Overy) for the first defendant.

Terence Cullen QC and James Clifford (instructed by Alexander Tatham, Manchester)   F
for the second defendant.

JUDGMENT

2 April 1992

Nicholls V-C: Thrells Ltd ("the company") carried on business as a textile merchant.
On 28 November 1984 it went into insolvent liquidation. There was a deficiency so far as   G
creditors were concerned of the order of £2m. For some ten years the company had
operated a pension scheme, known as the "Thrells Ltd (1974) Pension Scheme" ("the
scheme"). When the company went into liquidation the scheme also fell to be wound
up. The scheme was substantially overfunded. According to the most recent valuation,
there is a surplus of about £505,000 after providing for the discharge of the fund's
liabilities applicable on a winding up of the fund.

Before me is an application concerning the distribution of this surplus. The application   H
is brought by the company acting by its liquidator, Mr Peter Lomas. The company was
the sole trustee of the scheme. That is still the position. It has not been possible to find
anyone willing to accept appointment as trustee in place of the company. Mr Lomas is
also the first defendant. He has been joined to represent the unsecured creditors because
of difficulties experienced in practice in finding an unsecured creditor, most of whom are

A   resident overseas, willing to participate in the proceedings. The second defendant, Mr Morris, is a pensioner. He has been joined to represent the interests of pensioners and other beneficiaries interested in the scheme.

In those circumstances, the liquidator is confronted with an impossible conflict of duties. He is acting as the representative of the unsecured creditors. He also acts for the sole trustee of the scheme. Accordingly and properly, he has surrendered to the court

B   the exercise of any discretion vested in the company as trustee of the scheme.

Several questions arise on this application. One of them concerns the way in which the court should exercise that discretion. There is also a question concerning the interpretation and application of a provision in the *Social Security Act* 1990. The questions are being argued before me in a different order from that set out in the originating summons. The first question, which has now been argued before me,

C   concerns whether a power of alteration contained in the declaration of trust and the scheme rules can still be exercised even though under the rules the scheme is now required to be wound up. That is a question of construction or interpretation of, in particular, the rules.

The scheme was established by a declaration of trust dated 7 October 1974. That was made by the company, which was referred to in that deed and in the rules as the "founder". The object of the scheme was stated in cl. 1 as:

D

> "to provide relevant benefits"—as defined in certain provisions in the *Finance Act* 1970—"for such of the directors and employees of the founder as are admitted to membership thereof secured by contributions of the founder and where the founder has so determined by contributions of such directors and employees."

Clause 3 provided that any policy of assurance providing relevant benefits should be effected with the Norwich Union Life Insurance Society, and vested in and held by the

E   founder as trustee upon trust to hold, apply and dispose of the proceeds in accordance with the provisions of the rules. The founder as trustee undertook to adopt rules not later than two years from the execution of the deed, in a form which would enable the scheme to be treated as an exempt approved scheme. Clause 5 provided that:

> "Subject to adequate prior notice being given to all members the founder may at any time alter or modify by resolution or deed any of the provisions of this declaration but not so as to reduce the benefits already accrued without the prior

F   > consent of the majority of members affected by such alteration or modification."

I do not need to refer to any of the other clauses of the declaration of trust.

The rules before me are the rules revised with effect from 1 September 1977. They provide for a conventional final salary pension scheme offering one-sixtieth of retiring salary for each year of service. The scheme was contracted out of the state earnings related pension scheme, SERPS. Most of the members paid four per cent of their

G   salaries towards the cost of providing the benefits. Directors and consultants were not required to contribute. The employer was required to pay the balance. The scheme contributions were invested in an insurance policy effected with Norwich Union.

For the purposes of the question I am now considering, I need refer only to a few of the rules. In the events which happened the employer, as defined in the rules, meant the founder, that is to say, the company. Rule 14(2) provided for what should happen if the

H   employer were wound up otherwise than for the purposes of reconstruction. Rule 14(2) provided that:

> "the founder shall proceed to wind up such part of the scheme as relates to that employer. In this event the benefits secured to the date of discontinuance shall be dealt with in accordance with r. 12 or that part of the scheme shall be wound up under r. 15."

In fact the whole of the scheme related to the company. Rule 14(3) provided that when A
the employer was so wound up its liability to make contributions should cease. Rule 12
provided, amongst other things, for the transfer of benefits to another retirement
scheme at the request of a member.

Rule 15 was concerned with winding up, and r. 15(1) provided as follows:

"On the winding up of the scheme"—and I omit immaterial words—"the
entitlement to benefits of existing pensioners and members who had previously B
left the service shall remain unaltered, and all other members shall be entitled to
benefits calculated in accordance with r. 11(1) as if the members had left service
on the date of winding up. The liability of the trustees shall, however, be limited
to the policies, or the proceeds thereof, which shall be applied as follows.

(a) First, in securing non-assignable and non-commutable pensions for existing
pensioners equal in amount to their existing pensions under these rules, and
any other benefits to which such pensioners' widows or dependents will be C
entitled on the death of such pensioners.

(b) Second, in securing pensions with associated death benefits, if applicable,
payable to members or other beneficiaries to which entitlement to payment
has already arisen, including the pension and other benefits in respect of
members who have attained normal pension age but who have deferred
retirement. D

(c) Third, in securing for prospective pensioners pensions with associated
death benefits, if applicable, commencing on the normal pension age of the
amounts secured by members' voluntary contributions (if any) which have
not been secured under para. (b) of this rule.

(d) Fourth, in securing for prospective pensioners non-assignable pensions with
associated death benefits, if applicable, commencing at the normal pension E
age of the amounts (having taken into consideration amounts of benefit, if
any, secured under para. (c) of this rule) which would have been secured by
the policies or proceeds thereof if the scheme had been wound up as at the
day before the scheme was contracted out.

(e) Fifth, in securing for prospective pensioners guaranteed minimum pensions
and accrued rights to such guaranteed minimum pensions which have not
been secured under para. (b) and (d) of this rule and in payment of any state F
scheme premiums for which the scheme is liable.

(f) Sixth, in securing so far as the policies permit non-assignable pensions (with
associated death benefits if applicable) for prospective pensioners
commencing at the normal pension age of the balance of the amounts to
which they are entitled provided that the pension and associated death
benefits may be increased if the value of the policies will permit and the G
trustees so decide except that no pensions shall exceed the maximum
approvable pension for the period of service up to the date of winding up of
the scheme nor shall the associated death benefits exceed the limits set out
in r. 10.

(g) Seventh, if any balance remains after the policies or the proceeds thereof
have been applied as above it shall be paid to the employer . . ." H

Rule 18 is headed "Alterations" and reads:

"The founder may from time to time alter or modify all or any of the provisions of
these rules provided that no such alteration or modification shall be made which
reduces the benefits of a member already accrued at the date of such alteration or
modification."

A   In the interests of the creditors of the company, the first defendant argued that this power of alteration is still exercisable. The rule is expressed in open-ended terms. There is no justification for implying a limitation to the effect that the power ceases to be exercisable at any particular point of time.

   I am unable to accept this. Rule 14(2) provides for the consequences of a winding up in terms which seem to me to be inconsistent with the founder retaining any right thereafter to change the rules so far as those consequences are concerned. Rule 14(2)

B   provides that the benefits secured should be dealt with in accordance with r. 12, or that the scheme should be wound up under r. 15. I cannot think that the r. 18 power to make alterations was intended to enable the founder to detract from that provision in r. 14(2) once it had come into operation.

   The first defendant submitted that continuance of the power of alteration was not inconsistent with these winding up provisions having already come into operation,

C   because the power of alteration in its terms cannot impinge on benefits already accrued. Accrued benefits are expressly excluded from the scope of the alterations which may be made. It was submitted that would leave untouched the discretionary power conferred by r. 15(1)(f). Again, I cannot accept this. That discretionary power nestles within the fold of para. (a)–(g) of r. 15(1). In my view, the effect of r. 14(2) when it came into operation on the company being wound up, was to exclude the entirety of the winding

D   up provisions in r. 15(1) from the founder's power of alteration.

(Ruling accordingly)

7 April 1992

   Nicholls V-C: The next question which arises on this summons concerns the application of sec. 11(3) of the *Social Security Act* 1990. This raises a point of statutory construction

E   of some difficulty.

   Before turning to the Act, I must mention some further facts concerning the scheme.

   Rule 15(1), which I have already set out fully, provides that on a winding up the entitlement to benefits of existing pensioners and of members who had previously left service should remain unaltered. That covers most of the members of this scheme. The company went into creditors' voluntary liquidation on 28 November 1984, having been

F   in receivership since the previous June. Most of the remaining employees were dismissed during the receivership. As to the employees who were still in service when the scheme fell to be wound up because of the liquidation of the company, their position is that under r. 15(1) they became entitled to benefits in accordance with the rules as if they had left the service at the date of the winding up. The last employee left on 7 December 1984.

G   Rule 15(1) then makes provision for the policy effected by the trustee with the Norwich Union and the proceeds of that policy to be applied in securing pensions and associated benefits for existing pensioners and others in the manner and in the sequence prescribed in para. (a)–(f). That has yet to be done in the present case. At present, the pensions in payment when the scheme went into liquidation are still being paid under the master policy or policies effected by the trustee with the Norwich Union. However,

H   it is anticipated that in due course, pursuant to para. (a), scheme funds will be applied in securing these pension rights and other benefits by means of insurance policies in the names of the individuals. There are 13 persons in this category, plus a further three whose pensions came into payment since the commencement of the winding up. Provision has also to be made in like fashion for the pension and other benefits of some 22 employees who left service before attaining normal pension age. That is the "early leavers" category. In addition, since the winding up two early leavers have taken a

transfer of their benefits to another pension scheme. That was pursuant to r. 12. Finally,　　A
although this has not affected the winding up, in 40 instances employees left the service
of the company before the winding up and thereupon took their benefits by way of
transfers to another scheme.

In all these instances, therefore, there will come a time in the course of the winding up
when none of those now entitled to pensions, prospectively or immediately, will
continue to look to the scheme for payment thereof. They will have ceased to be
members, pursuant to r. 12, and taken a transfer of their benefits to another scheme, or　　B
they will have had their benefits fully secured by the provision of policies in their own
names: r. 15.(3) provides for the latter means of satisfying pensioners' rights. Either
way, their rights against the scheme will have been discharged. The scheme fund will
become devoid of liabilities. The money in hand will then be an actual surplus which, in
accordance with the rules, is not and will not be needed. This applies as much to any
increased amounts of pensions payable pursuant to an exercise of the discretionary　　C
power to increase pension and associated death benefits pursuant to para. (f) as to other
amounts payable under the rules.

Against that background I turn to sec. 11 of the 1990 Act. Subsection (1) provides for
the insertion of a new section, (sec. 58A) into the *Social Security Pensions Act* 1975.
Section 58A applies in relation to specified occupational pension schemes in terms which
embrace the scheme with which I am concerned. All I need mention is that under　　D
sec. 58A(1)(b) the scheme must be one,

> "whose rules do not require the annual rate of every pension which commences
> or has commenced under the scheme to be increased each year by at least an
> amount equal to the appropriate percentage of that rate."

"The appropriate percentage" means, in short, the percentage specified in the last
revaluation order made before the increase is to take effect. Revaluation orders are
made by the Secretary of State under sec. 52A of the Act of 1975, and they reflect the　　E
percentage increase in prices in Great Britain over the relevant period, limited to five
per cent compound per annum. Such increases are usually referred to as "limited price
indexing" or "LPI" for short. In sec. 58A "pension" does not include a guaranteed
minimum pension ("GMP") or any increase in such a pension under sec. 37A of the Act
of 1975. Section 58A(2) provides that from the appointed day a new schedule, Sch. 3A
to that Act, is to have effect for the purpose of requiring the provision by schemes to　　F
which the section applies of annual increases in the annual rates of pensions under those
schemes.

Section 11(3) of the *Social Security Act* 1990 reads as follows:

> "In the case of an occupational pension scheme—
>
> (a)　such as is mentioned in subsection (1) of section 58A of the Pensions Act,
> and　　　　　　　　　　　　　　　　　　　　　　　　　　　　　　　　　　　　　G
>
> (b)　which is constituted by trust deed,
>
> no payment shall be made out of the resources of the scheme to or for a person
> who is or has been the employer of persons in the description or category of
> employment to which the scheme relates until such time as provision has been
> made by the scheme for every pension which commences or has commenced
> under it to be increased as mentioned in paragraph (b) of that subsection."　　　　H

Subsection (6) enacts that the provisions of subsec. (3) override any conflicting provisions
of a scheme. Section 11(3) came into operation on 17 August 1990. A day has yet to be
appointed for the coming into operation of sec. 58A.

The question which has arisen is how sec. 11(3) operates in the present case regarding
payment of the surplus to the company pursuant to r. 15(1)(g). Several features of

A　　sec. 11(3) are to be noted. First, the subsection does not itself operate to increase the benefits payable to pensioners. It is a negative provision, imposing a restriction. Loosely stated, what the subsection does, but all it does, is to stop money being paid from the scheme funds to the employer until a condition has been satisfied. I shall refer to that as "the payment condition". If a fund is in surplus, an employer is precluded from taking or receiving that surplus out of the pension scheme unless the payment condition has been satisfied. But the subsection does not prevent the employer, in a "balance of costs"

B　　scheme such as the present scheme, from taking a prolonged "contribution holiday" and making no further contributions while the fund is in surplus. If he does that, and I am now referring to a continuing scheme which is not in course of being wound up, the employer may by this means ultimately achieve the same end result, albeit over a period of time, as if he had withdrawn the surplus from the fund. He will achieve that result without having to satisfy the payment condition. Thus, this statutory provision is a fairly

C　　blunt instrument. It is not a sophisticated tool. It stops cash withdrawals unless the payment condition is satisfied. It achieves an improvement in the non-GMP benefits to the extent only that an immediate payment out of surplus cash to the employer is sought to be made even at the price of satisfying the payment condition.

　　　　Second, the payment condition provides for LPI in "every pension . . . under [the scheme]". Thus, the condition relates only to pensions which at the relevant time fall within the description of pensions under the scheme. As one might expect, the pensions

D　　to which the subsection relates are those payable under the scheme whose resources are proposed to be used for making the payment to the employer or former employer.

　　　　Third, the relevant time for this purpose must be the date when the payment condition falls to be fulfilled. That, in turn, must be the date when the payment out of the resources of the scheme to the employer or former employer is being made. No other date is stated. The sense of the subsection points to that date. If at that date the payment

E　　condition is satisfied, the payment can be made; if not, not.

　　　　Fourth, the payment condition embraces prospective pensions as well as present pensions ("pensions in payment"). The words "which commences", when used in conjunction with "or has commenced", are apt to encompass a pension which will or may commence in the future. The subsection applies to such a pension as much as one already being paid under the scheme.

F　　　　Fifth, the payment condition envisages provision being made by the scheme for the pensions to be increased for the future. That sufficiently appears from the words "to be increased". The payment condition does not require LPI to be backdated.

　　　　Sixth, and this follows from what I have already said, if at the relevant time a person no longer has any right to look to the pension scheme for payment of a pension as defined in sec. 58A(3), either currently or from some future date, his pension is no

G　　longer within the payment condition. For instance, if an employee leaves employment and accepts a transfer of all his rights under a scheme to another pension scheme, thenceforward his rights exist under and against his new pension scheme. He no longer has any claim to a pension under his old scheme. His pension rights under the old scheme have been wholly superseded and replaced by his rights, whatever they may be, under the new scheme. In his case the payment condition will apply, if at all, to his new scheme. It will not apply to the pension to which at one time he was prospectively entitled under

H　　the old scheme but which ceased to be a liability of that scheme before the relevant time.

　　　　Likewise, in respect of any other pension which, before the relevant time, has by some other means ceased altogether to be a liability of the scheme. An instance of this would be if, pursuant to a provision in the scheme, trustees purchased for the member his own insurance policy in his own name, and that purchase wholly satisfied the member's rights and discharged the trustee and the scheme from any further liability to

the member. For the future the former member's rights would comprise rights against   A
the insurance company under the policy. The scheme would drop out of the picture.
Such a purchase might be made in respect of a pension payable from a future date. Or,
equally, it might be made in respect of a pension already in payment.

Thus far I have been addressing myself to an ongoing pension scheme. Thus far there
is no particular difficulty. But when one turns to apply these principles in the present
case, where the scheme is being wound up, the result is surprising. In the present case,   B
as already noted, there will come a time in the course of the winding up when the rights
of all those with payments in pension, and the rights of all those who left service with the
company before or after the winding up began, will have been secured and satisfied
either by the purchase of their own insurance policies or by transfers to other pension
schemes or otherwise. Then there will be no pensions which fall within the payment
condition, if what I have set out so far applies without modification to a payment made
to a company when a scheme is being wound up. There will be no such pensions because   C
all the liabilities of the scheme will have been discharged. Such a discharge is to be
expected in the ordinary course of events in the winding up of a scheme. That is part of
the winding up process. But it would be quite extraordinary, and to my mind absurd, if
the consequence of that ordinary course of events in a winding up were that sec. 11(3)
would never apply, either in this case or presumably in any other case when a scheme is
being wound up. On that footing sec. 11(3) would seldom, if ever, operate as a brake on
repayments to a former employer once the scheme were being wound up.   D

I am unable to accept that as the proper interpretation of sec. 11(3). When a scheme
is being wound up, and a payment falls to be made to a former employer pursuant to the
rules applicable in the winding up of a scheme, the pensions to which the payment
condition applies are to be understood as being those for which provision is being made
in the course of that self-same winding up. When the payment to the former employer is
triggered by a winding up of a scheme, the pensions which are to have the benefit of LPI   E
before the payment can be made are those which were payable under the scheme, either
actually or prospectively, at the time the trigger was pulled, namely when the scheme
went into liquidation. In my view, that is necessarily implicit. That is the only sensible
way in which sec. 11(3) can work in the case of a winding up. Otherwise the winding up
process would itself operate to defeat the application of the subsection.

The alternative, that sec. 11(3) does not apply in a winding up, cannot have been the   F
intention of Parliament. To construe the legislation as having that effect would be
exceedingly pusillanimous. After all, when interpreting legislation courts are striving to
identify the intention of Parliament expressed in the language used. Parliament intended
a workable result, not an absurdity. Take this very case. Under r. 3(2) the company had
power to wind up the scheme at any time. Section 11(3) may be a fairly blunt instrument,
but Parliament cannot have intended that it could be side-stepped, and a payment made
to an employer without complying with the payment condition, by the simple expedient   G
of the employer winding up the scheme and making provision only for non-indexed
benefits.

That this was not the intention of Parliament gains support from the purpose of the
legislation as foreshadowed in the report of the Occupational Pensions Board which
preceded the enactment of sec. 11 and to which Mr Clifford drew my attention. On
22 October 1988 the board made a report in accordance with sec. 66 of the *Social*   H
Security Act 1973 to the Secretary of State. This was presented to Parliament in February
1989, entitled "Protecting Pensions, Safeguarding Benefits in a Changing Environment"
(Cm 573). Chapter 10 was concerned, among other matters, with winding up and
insolvencies. In para. 10.7 the board expressed the view that even in a scheme which had
not provided for pension increases while the scheme was in full force, such increases

A
should be provided on winding up due to the insolvency of the employer before any surplus remaining in the fund could be paid to the company. In para. 10.9 and 10.11 the board recommended that there should be a requirement for those parts of present and future pensions in course of payment which did not represent GMPs to be provided with annual increases in line with price increases but limited to five per cent or such lower figure as scheme assets permitted, and that this should be achieved by overriding legislation.

B
Accordingly, I hold that, properly construed, sec. 11(3) applies in this case to every pension which on 28 November 1984 was prospectively payable or was already being paid under the scheme.

I have not overlooked that this date precedes the date on which sec. 11(3) came into force. But that does not mean that the legislation is being given retrospective effect. The payment to the company had not been made by 17 August 1990. If it had, the subsection

C
would not have applied to the payment. Since it had not, the subsection applies. The earlier date is material merely for crystallising the pensions to which the payment condition applies in this case. The LPI increases will be payable in respect of those pensions, but only for the future. They will not date back to 28 November 1984. LPI must be provided for the future, and pensions secured on that footing, before any payment to the company can be made.

D
Discretion

I turn next to the question of how I should exercise the discretion, conferred on the trustee by r. 15(1)(f), which the trustee has now surrendered to the court. I am told that this is the first occasion a trustee has surrendered such a discretion in the winding up of a pension scheme in this way. In exercising this discretion I must act in the manner a reasonable trustee could be expected to act having regard to all the material circumstances.

E
I must do what is just and equitable. The following are the principal factors material in this case:

(1) *The scope of the power*

For convenience, I repeat the terms of para. (f):

"Sixth, in securing so far as the policies permit non-assignable pensions (with

F
associated death benefits if applicable) for prospective pensioners commencing at the normal pension age of the balance of the amounts to which they are entitled provided that the pension and associated death benefits may be increased if the value of the policies will permit and the trustees so decide except that no pension shall exceed the maximum approvable pension for the period of service up to the date of the winding up of the scheme nor shall the associated death benefits exceed the limits set out in r. 10."

G
Not without some encouragement from the bench, Mr Clifford contended that the power conferred by the proviso applied to all the paragraphs (a)–(f), and that the power was not confined to para. (f). Certainly the terms in which it is expressed are such that it could be applied, without modification of language, to existing pensioners as well as prospective pensioners. Further, there is no immediately obvious reason why the trustees should have been given a wide power to increase benefits for prospective pensioners and at the same time given no power at all in any circumstances to increase

H
benefits for existing pensioners. So I am sympathetic to Mr Clifford's submission. In the end, however, I am unable to read the proviso as having a wider application than para. (f). One is familiar with mistakes being made in the layout of documents whereby a proviso intended to qualify more than one precedent provision is typed or printed in such a way that it reads as a qualification of only the last of those provisions. It is, I suppose, possible that that has occurred here. But, as printed, the proviso runs directly

on, in mid-line and with a small "p" for the introductory word "provided", from the preceding words. I can see no sufficient justification for ignoring that textual arrangement.

(2) *The purpose of the power*

Since the power is given in relation to prospective pensioners but not existing pensioners, the principal purpose of the power seems to be to enable the trustee in its discretion to increase prospective pensioners' pensions to compensate for the fact that early-leavers' pensions are geared to the amount of salaries at a date which is earlier, and often many years earlier, than the date from which the pensions will actually be paid. The value of early-leavers' pensions is thus subject to erosion by inflation. That purpose is particularly in point in the present case with regard to employees who became early-leavers, with adverse consequences for their pensions, by being dismissed because of the company's insolvency.

(3) *The source of the surplus*

As already noted, the scheme was a balance of costs scheme. The scheme was non-contributory for directors and consultants. Other employees were required to contribute an amount equal to four per cent of their actual salary or wages. The company was required to contribute each year an amount which should be applied "together with the members' contributions to secure benefits under these rules". The precise rate at which the company's contributions were made is not now clear. Between 1980 and 1982 the contribution rate was 16.6 per cent, which was a substantially higher rate than recommended by the Norwich Union's actuary. Why the company continued to fund the scheme at the higher rate is not now known.

Doing the best he could with inadequate material, the actuary, Mr Nicholas Salter, instructed by the liquidator, gave evidence to the effect that the estimated surplus of £238,000 in 1984, which has subsequently increased because of accumulated interest and investment appreciation, was derived from several sources: from unnecessary contributions by the company between 1980 and 1982 (£55,000), from investment returns being at a higher rate than that assumed in the actuarial calculations made at the time (£50,000), from the release of reserves held in respect of the long-term pension expectations of members who left before normal retirement age (£35,000), and from the release of reserves kept for winding-up benefits (£15,000). He was not able to identify a particular source for the balance of £83,000.

So far as now can be judged, and that is quite a severe limitation in this case, the members' contributions alone would not have sufficed to buy all the benefits which have now been provided for the existing and prospective pensioners under the rules. I am unable, however, to proceed from there to a conclusion that all the surplus should be regarded as an unintended surplus arising from the company's contributions in which the members can have no reasonable expectation to share. It is necessary to disentangle several points. First, to the extent that an employer is under an obligation to make contributions, it is fair for some purposes to regard those as part of the employees' overall remuneration package, just as much as contributions made by the employees by deduction from their salaries and wages. Second, it is true that in a balance of costs scheme the employer's obligation is to provide the necessary balance of contributions and no more. It may be that if actuaries were gifted with perfect foresight of the outcome of future uncertainties such as the rate of return on investment contributions, the rates at which salaries are assumed to rise, the dates on which and the circumstances in which employees will leave, and the cost of buying annuities at retirement, unintended surpluses would not usually arise from employer's contributions. It is necessary to have this in mind when exercising a discretion such as that conferred by r. 15(1)(f). But, thirdly, it is necessary also to have in mind that this scheme itself provided for the trustee

A   to have power to increase benefits. That power ranks ahead of the provision that any remaining balance of the scheme funds should be paid to the company. When a scheme so provides, members have a reasonable expectation that if the scheme funds permit, namely, if there is a surplus after providing for the estimated liabilities, or in a winding up, for the actual liabilities, the trustee will exercise that power to the extent that is fair and equitable in all the circumstances, having particular regard to the purpose for which the power was conferred. The power is an integral part of the scheme. It assumes the

B   existence of a surplus. A trustee should not decline to exercise it solely on the ground that the employer was under no legal obligation to provide the surplus. That accords with the approach adopted by *Warner* J with regard to the comparable provision in the winding-up rules in *Mettoy Pension Trustees Ltd v Evans* [1990] 1 WLR 1587 at pp. 1618–1620.

C   (4) *The size of the surplus and the impact of sec. 11(3)*

I have already mentioned that at the most recent valuation the surplus here is about £505,000. To set this in perspective, I add that discharge of the scheme liabilities in the winding up in accordance with the rules, by buying annuity policies etc., is estimated at the moment to cost about £73,000. From the sum of £505,000 there will have to be deducted the costs of all parties of this application, which are estimated to be of the order of £50,000 or possibly more. In addition, I must have in mind the cost of satisfying

D   the payment condition under sec. 11(3). That will have to be met before any surplus can be paid to the company. On this, the figures available are that, as matters now stand, the cost of providing LPI increases for pensions in payment is about £100,000, and for prospective pensions about £10,000. So, in very approximate terms, the surplus available for the company and, hence, for unsecured creditors, would on these figures be about £345,000. On these figures, the sum available to be applied pursuant to the para. (f) discretion, however, is £455,000, because that discretion ranks ahead of the satisfaction

E   of the sec. 11(3) payment condition.

The sum of £345,000 may, perhaps, fall to be reduced even further, regardless of any exercise of the discretion under para. (f), by reason of the decision of the European Court of Justice in *Barber v Guardian Royal Exchange Assurance Group* [1990] 1 CEC 653; [1991] 1 QB 344. The implications of that decision are still being worked out. The amendments to the EEC Treaty negotiated to form the Maastricht protocol, although

F   not yet ratified, may be regarded as showing the way ahead. However, I am told that in some quarters a challenge is being mounted to the constitutional propriety of that protocol. The liquidator, therefore, acting on advice wishes to retain such sum as on advice he considers appropriate to meet any obligations under this head. The very approximate figures available suggest that, as matters now stand, the cost of providing pensions for men at the age of 60 would be about £16,000. The cost of providing pensions

G   for men at this age would rise if, pursuant to an exercise of the discretion under para. (f), LPI increases were ordered for pensions while deferred or when in payment or if "franking" were removed. If all three of these improvements were directed, the total cost under this head would rise to a sum of the order of £86,000.

(5) *The financial position of the employer*

The deficiency in respect of the company's unsecured creditors is approximately

H   £2.4m. The dividend paid so far is negligible. Overfunding of the scheme can be said in one sense to have been at the expense of these creditors. As matters stand, they will suffer severe loss by the failure of the company to meet its obligations to them.

(6) *The needs of the members of the scheme*

I have before me no evidence regarding the financial situation of any particular prospective pensioner.

Taking all these factors into account, I consider, first, that the para. (f) discretion   A
should be exercised in a manner which will let sec. 11(3) operate fully. This will benefit
both pensions in payment and also deferred pensions. It is equitable that this should be
so. That would mean that the maximum sum available to be applied under the discretion
is about £345,000. Second, having regard to the purpose for which the para. (f) power
was created, it is right that, within reason, deferred pensions should be increased by
LPI. But this would be no more than a hollow gesture so long as "franking" remains in
operation. This is shown by the cost of such increases in the absence of franking, namely   B
£10,000. If franking is removed for the future but not the past, the additional sum
required is of the order of £154,000. In my view, that would be a fair and equitable
exercise of the discretion. The balance should go to the creditors, subject only to any
payments which the trustee may be compelled to make pursuant to art. 119 of the EEC
Treaty. In that regard, the liquidator should set aside a reserve as he seeks, but I confess
I do not expect that that reserve will be called upon.
                                                                                              C
I shall so direct. The trustee should administer and wind up the scheme accordingly.

                            (*Direction accordingly*)

31 July 1992

Nicholls V-C: I gave judgment in these proceedings on 7 April. One of the issues was
the exercise by the court of the discretionary power, given to the trustees by r. 15(1)(f),   D
to increase benefits for prospective pensioners. Subsequently it transpired that, due to a
misunderstanding by me of the figures, the cost of the additional benefits I decided
should be provided out of the surplus was substantially less than I had understood. I had
thought that the cost of satisfying the payment condition under sec. 11(3) was £110,000
and the cost of providing LPI increases for the period of deferment with franking
removed from the date of my judgment was £154,000. These two items totalled £264,000,
out of a distributable surplus of £455,000. Counsel very properly drew to my attention   E
that the correct figures were £72,000 and £96,000 respectively.

The cost of the benefits was a matter I took into account when deciding on the extent
to which it was reasonable for LPI increases to be provided. Having heard further
submissions and been provided with further figures I consider that the LPI increases for
deferred pensioners, and the removal of franking, should take effect from the date of
the winding up of the scheme, and not the date of my judgment. The cost of providing   F
this revised benefit for the prospective pensioners will be £192,000.

By a happy coincidence this means that the balance available to the liquidator will be
£191,000, exactly the same figure (£345,000 minus £154,000) envisaged in my judgment
of 4 April 1992. It also means that the liquidator and the pensioners will share more or
less equally the amount of the surplus that would be available if the discretion were not
exercised at all and the liquidator were to receive the whole balance (viz. £383,000)   G
remaining after the payment condition under sec. 11(3) had been met.

                            (*Order accordingly*)

                        ─────────────────

                                                                                              H

A

Re William Makin & Sons Ltd.

Chancery Division (Companies Court).
Vinelott J.
Judgment delivered 19 June 1992.

> *Liquidation — Pension scheme surplus — Whether and how discretion under
> scheme rules to increase benefits or pay surplus to company should be exercised.*

**This was an application by the liquidator of a company, William Makin & Sons Ltd,
for the determination of questions which arose in relation to the devolution of moneys
held by the company as trustee of a pension scheme which were not required to meet the
benefits payable under the scheme.**

**The company went into receivership and then liquidation. It was heavily insolvent, but
there was a substantial surplus in the pension fund. After making provision for increases
required by sec. 58A(1)(b) of the Social Security Pensions Act 1975 there would be a
surplus of over £200,000. It was conceded by the beneficiaries under the pension scheme
that the surplus was derived wholly from overfunding by the company.**

**The first question for the court was whether the liquidator was entitled to and ought to
exercise the discretion under the scheme rules in relation to the surplus so as not to cause
an increase in the benefits payable under the scheme, with the result that the surplus
would be paid to the company in liquidation. If it held that the liquidator was not so
entitled, the court was asked to exercise the discretion.**

Held, directing the representative beneficiaries joined as respondents (who were both
former directors) to prepare a scheme with the assistance of such actuarial and other
advice as they might think necessary; the matter to be restored for further argument as to
the correctness of the principles applied in formulating the scheme:

**1. The power to increase members' benefits if there was a surplus was a fiduciary
power.**

**2. The power could not be exercised by the liquidator. His duty to the unsecured
creditors conflicted with the duty owed to the objects of the power, or, if there were no
assets not caught by the floating charge, it would not be necessary either for distributing
the assets of the company or for winding up its affairs to determine what part of the
surplus should be applied for the benefit of the beneficiaries under the scheme. The power
could not be exercised by the receivers because it was not an asset caught by the floating
charge.**

The following cases were referred to in the judgment:

Baden's Deed Trusts, Re [1971] AC 424.
Icarus (Hertford) Ltd v Driscoll [1990] PLR 1.
Mettoy Pension Trustees Ltd v Evans & Ors [1990] 1 WLR 1587.

Gabriel Moss QC and Stephen Atherton (instructed by Benson Burdekin, Sheffield)
for the liquidator.

Keith Rowley (instructed by Dibb Lupton Broomhead, Leeds) for the debenture
holder.

Rodney Stewart-Smith (instructed by R C Moorhouse & Co, Leeds) for the
representative beneficiaries.

JUDGMENT

Vinelott J: This is an application by the liquidator of a company, William Makin &
Sons Ltd, for the determination of questions which arise in relation to the devolution of

moneys held by the company as trustee of a pension scheme which are not required to   A
meet the benefits payable under the scheme.

The scheme was established by means of an interim deed dated 1 July 1974 and a
definitive deed and rules annexed thereto which was executed on 31 October 1980. The
benefits under the scheme were provided by means of a group policy taken out with
Scottish Provident Institution. It was a contributory scheme of the kind commonly
referred to as a "balance of cost" scheme — that is, one under which the employer   B
undertakes to make good all moneys necessary to provide the benefits under the scheme
so far as not met by contributions by the members. It is unnecessary to say anything
about the interim deed except that it contains a definition of the company as "the
principal employer" and a declaration by the company that the trust thereby created is
to be irrecoverable and that the principal employer will hold all moneys becoming
payable in respect of every member upon trust to give effect to the rights and options of
the members and to provide the benefits to which a member is entitled under the   C
scheme. By the definitive deed the company is again defined as "the principal employer".
It confirmed the establishment of the scheme and that the company held the assets upon
the trusts and with and subject to the powers and provisions declared and contained in
the interim deed, the definitive deed and the rules.

The scheme is embodied in the rules. Rule 1 contains a number of definitions including
a definition of "associated employers" as employers other than the principal employer   D
participating in the scheme and of "trustees" as meaning "the person or persons who is
or are for the time being acting as trustee or trustees in accordance with the trust deed".
Subparagraphs (a)–(e) in r. 3 provide for contributions by members; subpara. (f)
provides that the participating employers will pay to the trustees the amounts required,
in addition to members contributions and other assets coming into the hands of the
trustees, to provide the benefits of the scheme and to meet any expenses incurred by the
trustees in such proportion as may be agreed between the trustees and the principal   E
employer. The rules provide for the payment of a pension calculated by reference to
final salary and years of service and other benefits including a lump sum, retirement and
death benefit, and a widow's pension.

Rule 20 contains power for the trustees with the consent of the principal employer
(1) to increase the amount of any pension or other benefit payable or prospectively
payable, (2) to provide an immediate or prospective pension or other benefit in respect   F
of a member which is not otherwise provided for by the rules, or (3) to provide a pension
or other benefit for or on the death of a former employee who is not a member or to
provide for any dependant of a former employee. It is provided that any increased or
additional retirement benefit is to be in pension form (save so far as the rules permit the
exchange of a pension for a lump sum) and that the amount of any benefit or increase in
benefit is not to be such as to prejudice the approval of the scheme under the relevant
provisions of the *Income and Corporation Taxes Act* 1970. Rule 21 which is headed   G
"Revenue limits" provides that no benefit for or in respect of a member is to be so great
as to exceed certain limitations there set out which formed the basis of the approval of
the scheme under the relevant provisions of the 1970 Act.

Paragraphs (a) and (b) of r. 27 provide for the cessation of participation of the
principal employer; participation is to cease if (amongst other things) the principal
employer ceases to carry on business. Paragraph (c) of r. 2 provides that on the principal   H
employer ceasing to participate in the scheme and (subject to an immaterial exception)
if no other employer takes the place of the principal employer all associated employers
are to cease to participate in the scheme and r. 29 is to apply. Paragraph (a) of r. 29
provides that on cessation members are to cease to be in pensionable employment but
are to remain liable to pay accrued contributions; para. (b) provides for the application

A   of the funds in the hands of the trustees after payment of all costs charges and expenses in providing accrued and prospective benefits subject to certain provisions to which I need not refer in detail. Subparagraph (i) of para. (c) provides for the abatement of benefit in the event of a deficiency; subpara. (ii) of para. (c) I must read in full:

> "If the trustees consider that there is a surplus in the assets of the scheme, they may in their discretion use that surplus, or any part of it, to increase the benefits
>
B   to be provided in respect of any one or more members under para. (b) of this rule in any manner approvable by the Commissioners of Inland Revenue. Any part of that surplus not so used shall be paid to the participating employers in such proportions as the trustees shall determine."

On 21 September 1984 receivers of the company were appointed by Barclays Bank plc pursuant to powers conferred by a guarantee and debenture dated 19 December 1979 and made between the company and certain subsidiaries of the company of the one
C   part and Barclays Bank plc of the other part. On 16 January 1985 an order for the compulsory winding up of the company was made in the Sheffield County Court. As I understand it none of the subsidiary companies was at the material time an associated employer; the only members were employees or former employees of the company. The company was heavily insolvent. The statement of affairs as at the appointment of receivers shows a surplus after paying debts secured by fixed charges and preferred creditors with claims ranking ahead of a floating charge of approximately £49,000 and
D   the debt due to debenture holders secured by a floating charge as £333,000 leaving a deficiency of just under £285,000. There were unsecured creditors ranking after the floating charge with debts amounting in the aggregate to just under £325,500. The overall deficiency is thus approximately £610,000. The debenture holder is Barclays Bank and the debt owed to Barclays Bank as at 7 November 1989 with accrued interest stood at just under £403,000.

E   There is, however, a substantial surplus in the pension fund. The Scottish Provident Institution calculates that on the footing that sec. 58A(1)(b) and (2) of the *Social Security Pensions Act* 1975 as modified by sec. 11(3) of the *Social Security Act* 1990 apply to pensions in payment when the relevant part of the 1990 Act came into force and after making provision for increases required by sec. 58A(1)(b), there will be a surplus of over £200,000, a sum which represents more than half the surrender value of the
F   pension reserve under the group policy. It was conceded by Mr Stewart-Smith who appeared for the representative beneficiaries under the pension scheme that the surplus is derived wholly from overfunding by the company.

The first question asked by the summons is:

> ". . . whether the liquidator is entitled to and ought to cause the company as trustee of the pension scheme to exercise his discretion in relation to the surplus
G   so as not to cause an increase in the benefits payable under that scheme with the result that the surplus in respect of the said scheme becomes payable to the estate of the company in liquidation."

This question gives rise to two subsidiary questions. The first is whether the power in para. (c)(ii) of r. 29 is a fiduciary power; the second is whether if it is a fiduciary power it is capable of being exercised by the liquidator.

H   These questions also arose in two recent cases. The first is the decision of *Aldous* J in *Icarus (Hertford) Ltd v Driscoll* [1990] PLR 1; the second is the decision of *Warner* J in *Mettoy Pension Trustees Ltd v Evans* [1990] 1 WLR 1587. *Aldous* J gave judgment on 4 December 1979. *Warner* J reserved judgment on 27 November and gave judgment on 12 December 1989. Neither was aware that these two points were being considered by the other.

Icarus was an insurance-based balance of cost scheme. The benefits under the scheme   A
were provided by a contract with an insurance company. The rules provided that on
termination after all benefits and entitlements had been secured,

> "the principal employer may, subject to revenue limitations at their discretion,
> apply the whole or part of such balances as they may determine to augment
> entitlements of members or any of them . . ."

—and that: B

> "any credit balance remaining under the contract shall be paid to the principal
> employer and then distributed amongst the employers in such proportions as the
> principal employer shall determine."

Aldous J decided (at p. 6) that:

> ". . . when the words 'principal employer' are used in the rules, they denote the
> principal employer in the stated capacity as trustee and administrator unless the   C
> context is such as to make plain to the contrary . . ."

—and that in the context of the rule that I have cited there was no such contrary
meaning. He therefore declared that the discretion was exercisable by the company in a
fiduciary capacity. He went on to hold that the power was exercisable by the liquidator
and that provided that his discretion as to the proportion of the surplus to be used to
augment entitlements was exercised in good faith "in the sense that he does not act for   D
reasons that are irrational or perverse" his decision would not be capable of being
challenged and that any surplus would go to the principal employer. He held that:

> "in particular it would not be improper to take into account that the principal
> employer is in liquidation and that there are other creditors."

In *Mettoy* one question was whether a rule providing for the distribution of a surplus
on the winding up of the scheme (which started as an insurance-based scheme but which   E
later became a self-administered scheme) had been validly introduced by an amending
deed. The rule purportedly introduced provided that:

> "Any surplus of the trust fund remaining after securing all the aforesaid liabilities
> . . . in full may at the absolute discretion of the employer be applied to secure
> further benefits within the limits stated in the rules, and any further balance
> thereafter remaining shall be properly apportioned amongst the principal employer   F
> and each participating employer and shall be paid to them in cash."

Warner J held that this new rule had been validly incorporated as one of the rules of
the scheme. He then had to consider whether the power conferred fiduciary obligations
on the "employer" and whether it was capable of being exercised by the liquidator of
the company which had gone into compulsory winding up. He accepted a classification
proposed by Mr Walker QC of fiduciary discretions into four categories. I think I should   G
read this part of his judgment (at p. 1613G) in full.

> "In this classification, category 1 comprises any power given to a person to
> determine the destination of trust property without that person being under any
> obligation to exercise the power or to preserve it. Typical of powers in this
> category is a special power of appointment given to an individual where there is a
> trust in default of appointment. In such a case the donee of the power owes a duty
> to the beneficiaries under that trust not to misuse the power, but he owes no duty   H
> to the objects of the power. He may therefore release the power but he may not
> enter into any transaction that would amount to a fraud on the power, a fraud on
> the power being a wrong committed against the beneficiaries under the trust in
> default of appointment: see *In re Mills* [1930] 1 Ch. 654 and *In re Greaves* [1954]
> Ch. 434. It seems to me to follow that, where the donee of the power is the only

A

person entitled under the trust in default of appointment, the power is not a fiduciary power at all, because then the donee owes no duty to anyone. That was the position in *In re Mills* [1930] 1 Ch. 654 and will be the position here if the discretion in the last paragraph of rule 13(5) of the 1983 rules is in category 1. Category 2 comprises any power conferred on the trustees of the property or on any other person as a trustee of the power itself: *per* Romer L.J., at p. 669. I will,

B

as Chitty J. did in *In re Somes* [1896] 1 Ch. 250, 255, call a power in this category 'a fiduciary power in the full sense.' Mr. Walker suggested as an example of such powers vested in persons other than the trustees of the property the powers of the managers of a unit trust. A power in this category cannot be released; the donee of it owes a duty to the objects of the power to consider, as and when may be appropriate, whether and if so how he ought to exercise it; and he is to some extent subject to the control of the courts in relation to its exercise: see, for

C

instance, *In re Abrahams' Will Trusts* [1969] 1 Ch. 463, 474, *per* Cross J.; *In re Manisty's Settlement* [1974] Ch. 17, 24 *per* Templeman J.; and *In re Hay's Settlement Trusts* [1982] 1 W.L.R. 202, 210, *per* Sir Robert Megarry V.-C. Category 3 comprises any discretion which is really a duty to form a judgment as to the existence or otherwise of particular circumstances giving rise to particular consequences. Into this category fall the discretions that were in question in such cases as *Weller v. Ker* (1886) L.R. 1 Sc. & Div. 11; *Dundee General Hospitals*

D

Board of Management v. Walker [1952] 1 All E.R. 896 and the two cases reported by Lexis that I have already mentioned, namely *Kerr v. British Leyland (Staff) Trustees Ltd.*, Court of Appeal (Civil Division) Transcript No. 286 of 1986 and *Mihlenstedt v. Barclays Bank International Ltd.*, The Times, 18 August 1989; Court of Appeal (Civil Division) Transcript No. 817 of 1989. Category 4 comprises discretionary trusts, that is to say cases where someone, usually but not necessarily the trustees, is under a duty to select from among a class of beneficiaries those

E

who are to receive, and the proportions in which they are to receive, income or capital of the trust property. Mr. Walker urged me to eschew the phrases 'trust power,' 'power coupled with a duty,' 'power coupled with a trust' and 'power in the nature of a trust,' which, as he demonstrated by means of an impressive survey of reported cases, have been variously used to describe discretions in categories 2, 3 and 4.''

F

He then stated the first question as whether the discretion given to the employer by the rule which I have cited means in effect no more than that the employer is free to make gifts out of property of which it is the absolute beneficial owner or whether these words import that the employer is under a duty to the objects of the discretion to consider whether and if so how the discretion ought to be exercised. He came to the conclusion that the power was one which imposed on the employer a duty to the objects of the

G

discretion. Then, having pointed out that the power being a fiduciary power was not an asset of the company and could not be the subject of a charge created by a debenture, he went on to hold that it was not capable of being exercised by the liquidator. I should again read this passage in his judgment (at p. 1616F) in full:

"Leaving aside section 74 of the Companies Act 1980, the powers of a liquidator in a winding up by the court were defined, in 1983, by section 245 of the Companies Act 1948. (That section was re-enacted without material change first by section

H

539 of the Companies Act 1985, and then by Schedule 4 to the Insolvency Act 1986.) The widest powers of the liquidator are those contained in what was paragraph (*h*) of section 245(2) of the Act of 1948, i.e. 'to do all such other things as may be necessary for winding up the affairs of the company and distributing its assets.' The exercise of a fiduciary power in the full sense vested in the company cannot be necessary for distributing its assets. Whether it may be necessary for

winding up the affairs of the company is less clear. However the liquidator in this case would, as Mr. Inglis-Jones submitted, be precluded from exercising the power because, if he did so, he would be in a position where his duties conflicted. As trustee of the power he would be under a duty to hold the balance between the interests of the beneficiaries under the pension scheme and the interests of the persons entitled to share in the assets of the company, namely its creditors and possibly its contributories. As liquidator his duty would be to have regard primarily, if not exclusively, to the interests of the creditors and contributories. His position in that respect would differ from that of the directors of the company while it was a going concern, for they would be able to pay proper regard to the interests of the beneficiaries under the pension scheme and would be concerned to do so if only for the sake of the company's reputation as an employer."

The decision of *Aldous* J in *Icarus* that the power conferred on "the principal employer" and the decision of *Warner* J that the power conferred on "the employer" was in each case a fiduciary power apply a fortiori to the instant case where the power is in terms conferred on "the trustees".

Mr Moss QC, who appeared for the liquidator, and Mr Rowley who appeared for the debenture holder, accepted that in these circumstances I ought to follow these decisions without expressing any opinion of my own though, Mr Rowley reserved for consideration by a higher court the question whether in the context of the rules as a whole the power in r. 29(c)(ii) should be construed as a power conferred on the company which it was free either to exercise or to refrain from exercising.

On the second question whether the power is capable of being exercised by the liquidator the two decisions are irreconcilable and I must decide which I should follow. I have no hesitation in preferring the decision of *Warner* J. The difficulty clearly explained by *Warner* J in the second of the two passages which I have cited, that the duty owed by the liquidator to the unsecured creditors conflicts with the duty owed to the objects of the power, was not drawn to the attention of *Aldous* J. Indeed so far as can be judged from the report the question whether if the power was a fiduciary power the liquidator could decide to what extent and for whose benefit it could be exercised was not argued. Mr Rowley submitted that if that is the right analysis the power in r. 29(c)(ii) is one that never could have been exercised so long as the company remained a trustee and that the appointment of the company as sole trustee at the inception of the scheme is an indication that the intention of the company as the settlor and of the members who contributed to the scheme was that the principle that a trustee cannot act if he finds himself in a position where he owes conflicting duties or where his duty conflicts with his own interest should not apply.

I do not find it necessary to consider the doubtful and difficult question whether the application of this principle can in fact be excluded by an express provision in a trust instrument. The answer to Mr Rowley's submission is that if the power had become exercisable whilst the company was a going concern there would have been no reason why the company should not have exercised the power. What the company could not do would have been to have decided not to exercise or to refrain from exercising the power with the consequence that the surplus or part of it would become payable to the company. As *Warner* J pointed out there might be good commercial reasons why the company should exercise the power. If the company failed to do so it would be open to any beneficiary under the scheme to apply to the court either to appoint new trustees who could bring an unprejudiced mind to the question to what extent the power could be exercised, or to direct that a scheme for distribution be prepared and to give directions as to the distribution of the surplus. In *Mettoy* the insolvency of the company and the appointment of a liquidator created a new situation because the duty owed by the

A   liquidator to the creditors precluded the exercise of the power in favour of the beneficiaries under the scheme. A fortiori the power could not be exercised by the receiver. Any part of the surplus which was not distributed pursuant to the power would vest in the receiver but the power itself was not an asset of the company which is vested in the receiver.

    It is not clear from the facts stated in *Mettoy* whether there were any assets of the company which were not caught by the floating charge and whether the surplus in the pension fund was more than sufficient to discharge the balance of the debt due to the

B   debenture holder, but it seems probable that the surplus which was very large, some £9m, was more than sufficient to discharge the balance of the debt due to the debenture holder. *Warner* J referred to the duty of the liquidator if the power was exercisable by him, as a duty to hold the balance between the interests of the beneficiaries under the pension scheme and the interests of the persons entitled to share in the assets of the company, namely, its creditors and possibly its contributories.

C   As I understand the position in the instant case the preferential creditors with claims ranking ahead of the bank's floating charge have been paid in full, there are no assets which are not caught by the floating charge, and there is clearly no real possibility that the surplus in the pension fund even if no part were paid to the beneficiaries under the pension scheme would suffice to meet the balance due to the bank. In these circumstances there may be a question whether the liquidator owes any duty which conflicts with the power in r. 29(c)(ii), that is whether he owes a duty to the debenture holder to ensure so

D   far as he can that the surplus is not applied for the benefit of the objects of this power, or whether his only object is to account for what is left after the power has been exercised if it is exercised. I have not heard any argument on this point. I think it is unnecessary for me to explore this. It could only arise if apart from any conflict of duty the power in r. 29 (c)(ii) would have been exercisable by the liquidator. The only relevant powers of the liquidator are those conferred by sec. 245(2) of the *Companies Act* 1948 and the only relevant power there listed is that in para. (h) which confers power on the liquidator to

E   do all such things as may be necessary for winding up the affairs of the company and distributing its assets.

    Mr Moss QC submitted that the observation of *Warner* J in *Mettoy* that the exercise of a fiduciary power vested in the company cannot be necessary for distribution of its assets is too widely stated and that the doubts he expressed "whether it may be necessary for winding up the affairs of the company" are not well founded. It may be that in a case

F   where the surplus not applied to the benefit of the beneficiaries of a pension scheme is not caught by or needed to satisfy a floating charge which has already crystallised, the exercise of the power to the extent of determining the proportion that should be so applied is a step that is necessary in order to determine what are the assets of the company available for distribution by the liquidator and the claims provable in the liquidation (including any claim by the debenture holder if and in so far as not satisfied by assets caught by the floating charge). But, of course, in such circumstances the power

G   cannot be exercised because of the liquidator's conflicting duties. It may also be that in the circumstances I have envisaged (that the whole surplus is caught by the floating charge and that there are no other assets not so caught in respect of which the debenture holders would be entitled to prove for any deficiency) the liquidator owes no conflicting duty. But then if that were the case it would not be necessary either for distributing the assets of the company or for winding up its affairs to determine what part of the surplus should be applied for the benefit of the beneficiaries under the scheme. In this case there

H   is the further difficulty that the liquidator has already expressed his clear intention, if and so far as the power is vested in him, not to exercise it in favour of any beneficiary under the pension scheme.

    In my judgment therefore the power cannot be exercised by the liquidator. It clearly cannot be exercised by the receivers. The power is not itself an asset that was caught by the floating charge.

British Company Cases

The second question raised by the originating summons is in these terms: A

> "that if and in so far as it may be held that the liquidator is not so entitled, the
> exercise by the court of such discretion so as not to cause an increase, alternatively
> so as to cause such an increase if any as the court may deem fit and proper, and the
> payment of the surplus to the receivers of the company and/or liquidator in such
> proportions as they may be entitled."

In *Mettoy*, *Warner* J cited (at p. 1617E) the following passage in the speech of Lord   B
Wilberforce in *Re Baden's Deed Trusts* [1971] AC 424 at p. 456G:

> "As to powers, I agree with my noble and learned friend Lord Upjohn in *In re
> Gulbenkian's Settlements* [1970] A.C. 508 that although the trustees may, and
> normally will, be under a fiduciary duty to consider whether or in what way they
> should exercise their power, the court will not normally compel its exercise. It will
> intervene if the trustees exceed their powers, and possibly if they are proved to
> have exercised it capriciously. But in the case of a trust power, if the trustees do   C
> not exercise it, the court will: I respectfully adopt as to this the statement in Lord
> Upjohn's opinion (p. 525). I would venture to amplify this by saying that the
> court, if called upon to execute the trust power, will do so in the manner best
> calculated to give effect to the settlor's or testator's intentions. It may do so by
> appointing new trustees, or by authorising or directing representative persons of
> the classes of beneficiaries to prepare a scheme of distribution, or even, should   D
> the proper basis for distribution appear by itself directing the trustees so to
> distribute. The books give many instances where this has been done, and I see no
> reason in principle why they should not do so in the modern field of discretionary
> trusts."

Warner J then observed (at p. 1617H):

> "Clearly in the first two sentences of that passage Lord Wilberforce was referring   E
> to a discretion in category 2 and in the following part of it to a discretion in
> category 4. In that latter part he was indicating how the court might give effect to
> a discretionary trust when called on to execute it. It seems to me however that the
> methods he indicated could be equally appropriate in a case where the court was
> called on to intervene in the exercise of a discretion in category 2."

Later in his judgment at p. 1632D he said: F

> "No one suggests that I should, in this case, appoint new trustees. So the question
> is what directions I should give under paragraph (3) of the originating summons."

Paragraph 3 sought directions as to the exercise of the power if, as *Warner* J decided, it
was not exercisable by the liquidator or the receivers.

I have felt considerable doubt whether in the instant case I should take the same
course. The question over what part of the surplus the power should be exercised and   G
what part should be free from the power gives rise to problems which do not arise in the
usual case where trustees of a private trust have to decide how much of, for instance, the
income of a trust fund should be applied for the benefit of a wide class and how much
should devolve on a narrow class in default of the exercise of the power. The claims of,
for instance, impoverished pensioners on the one hand and of Barclays Bank on the
other are incommensurable. Further, in evaluating the claims as between different
groups of beneficiaries, for instance, as between pensioners who have retired with a   H
pension earned by their own and the company's contributions and which has been
increased to the extent required by sec. 58A(1)(b) on the one hand, and members whose
employment was terminated by the insolvency of the company, some of whom may not
have found alternative employment, difficult questions may again arise. I would have
preferred to appoint new trustees who could prepare a scheme for distribution setting

A   out and explaining the principles on which it has been prepared and who would either surrender their discretion to the court or alternatively and preferably seek a declaration by the court that the scheme was one which they could properly carry into effect. The representatives of members of the classes of beneficiaries and either the liquidator or the receiver would then be in a position to advance any argument whether the scheme should be accepted or modified. However, all the parties are anxious to avoid any delay which might result from appointing new trustees and I have after some hesitation come

B   to the conclusion that this is a case where the court can assume the duty of directing how the surplus should be applied. The representative beneficiaries who have been joined as respondents are both former directors. They will have to prepare a scheme with the assistance of such actuarial and other advice as they may think necessary. The matter can then be restored for further argument as to the correctness of the principles applied in formulating the scheme.

C   I should add for completeness that they will be entitled to full indemnity against any costs incurred in preparing the scheme in just the same way as if they were trustees; they must of course accept that they themselves will have to be excluded from any benefit under the scheme.

     There is one other matter I should mention. This application is made in the Companies Court for the determination of questions arising in the winding up of the company. On

D   the view I take, the remaining question of the extent to which the manner of applying r. 29(c)(2) should be exercised arises in consequence of but not in the winding up of the company. The originating summons will have to be amended and entitled in the matter of the trusts of the definitive deed and the rules and to seek relief under the inherent jurisdiction of the court. I will extend the order made by Registrar *Dewhurst* for the payment of the costs of all parties on an indemnity basis out of the surplus of the pension fund to include the costs of the hearing before me.

E

(Order accordingly. Leave to appeal granted)

F

G

H

Re Land and Property Trust Co plc (No. 2).

A

Court of Appeal (Civil Division).
Nourse and Beldam LJJ and Sir John Megaw.
Judgment delivered 11 February 1993.

*Directors — Administration order petition dismissed — Winding-up order
made on creditor's petition — Directors ordered to pay petitioning creditor's
costs of administration order petition personally — Appeal — Whether directors
entitled to adjournment to put in evidence — Whether personal costs order
properly made.*

B

This was an appeal by directors from an order for costs against them personally.

A creditor presented a winding-up petition against the company of which the appellants
were directors. The company presented an administration order petition which was
heard immediately before the winding-up petition. The administration order petition was
dismissed, and a compulsory winding-up order made. The directors were ordered to pay
the petitioning creditor's costs of the administration order petition personally (see [1991]
BCC 446). An adjournment to enable the directors to put in evidence was refused.

C

Held, allowing the directors' appeal:

1. The judge erred in principle in refusing the directors an adjournment and making
the order only on the evidence which was already before him because that evidence was
clearly inadequate for the purpose of making a decision on the application against the
directors. A quite separate issue having been raised against them, the directors were
entitled to a proper opportunity to put in evidence of their own.

D

2. The consequence of the judge's erroneous refusal of an adjournment was that he did
not take into account matters which he ought to have taken into account, which led to the
conclusion that the personal costs order should be discharged.

E

3. The directors had observed all the requirements of the Insolvency Rules 1986. At all
material times they had the support of experienced insolvency practitioners who produced
r. 2.2 reports. They acted under the advice of solicitors experienced in insolvency matters
and under that of leading and junior counsel with similar experience. It was true that the
directors may all along have been deceiving their advisers. But directors of insolvent
companies were notoriously optimistic and optimism was not necessarily inconsistent
with good faith. Without cross-examination the court could not proceed as if a deception
had been proved.

F

The following cases were referred to in the judgment of Nourse LJ:

Aiden Shipping Co Ltd v Interbulk Ltd [1986] AC 965.
Beddoe, Re [1893] 1 Ch 547.
Gosscott (Groundworks) Ltd, Re (1988) 4 BCC 372.
Land and Property Trust Co plc & Ors, Re [1991] BCC 459; [1991] 1 WLR 601.
Scherer & Anor v Counting Instruments Ltd & Anor [1986] 1 WLR 615n.
Taylor & Anor v Pace Developments Ltd [1991] BCC 406.

G

Nicholas Stewart QC and Jennifer Lemkey (instructed by Kanter Jules Grangewoods)
for the directors.

Richard Ritchie (instructed by Masons) for the petitioning creditor.

H

JUDGMENT

Nourse LJ: On 8 February 1991 *Harman* J, sitting in the Companies Court, made an
order for the compulsory winding up of the Land and Property Trust Co plc ("LPT") on
the petition of one of its creditors, John Lelliott Management Ltd ("Lelliott"): see

A [1991] BCC 446. Before making that order the judge had considered and adjudicated on LPT's own petition for an administration order, to which Lelliott, as the person who had presented the winding-up petition, was duly made a respondent. The administration petition was dismissed, with an order that the directors of LPT should pay Lelliott's costs personally. Against that order the directors now appeal to this court.

B Although the directors were not parties to the administration petition, they do not dispute that there was jurisdiction to make an order against them under sec. 51(1) of the *Supreme Court Act* 1981; see *Aiden Shipping Co Ltd v Interbulk Ltd* [1986] AC 965. Their case is that they did not have a proper opportunity of putting in evidence; that in refusing them an adjournment and making the order only on the evidence which was already before him the judge erred in principle; and that on the fresh evidence now before this court the order ought not to have been made and ought now to be discharged.

C *Harman* J having refused leave to appeal, it may have been feared that, unless they were able to bring themselves within the principle of *Scherer v Counting Instruments Ltd* [1986] 1 WLR 615, the directors would have been barred access to this court by sec. 18(1)(f) of the *Supreme Court Act* 1981. However, on 2 May 1991 Lord *Donaldson of Lymington* MR and *Nicholls* LJ held that they were entitled to appeal as of right and without the leave of the judge: see *Re Land and Property Trust Co plc* [1991] BCC 459.

D I will start by stating the background facts and the history of the proceedings up to the making of the judge's order, ignoring at this stage the fresh evidence now before this court.

LPT was the holding company of a group of land investment and development companies which included 29 wholly-owned subsidiaries of LPT ("the core subsidiaries") holding long-term investment properties. Ten of the core subsidiaries held properties charged to the Norwich Union Life Insurance Society ("Norwich Union"). LPT's principal banker, a New York bank called Manufacturers Hanover Trust Co ("MHT"),
E had charges over properties held by each of the core subsidiaries, some of them already charged to Norwich Union.

On 13 October 1989 another company within the group, Pointwest Developments Ltd ("Pointwest"), entered into a management contract with Lelliott for the redevelopment of the former British Airways terminal in Cromwell Road, London SW7. Pointwest's obligations under that contract were guaranteed by LPT. On 21 August 1990 Lelliott
F served a statutory demand on LPT for £6.927m owing under the guarantee. That demand not having been met, on 9 November Lelliott presented its petition for the compulsory winding up of LPT. The petition was not advertised pending negotiations for the further financing of the Pointwest development.

On 7 December 1990 administrative receivers were appointed over Pointwest by Banque Bruxelles Lambert SA, the main financier of the Pointwest development.
G On 20 December Norwich Union made a demand on LPT for just under £50m. On 21 December there was an agreement between LPT and Lelliott for the payment to Lelliott of the £6.927m by instalments with security. On the same day Norwich Union appointed a receiver over the properties held by the ten core subsidiaries which were subject to its charges.

On 3 January 1991 there was a meeting of the directors of LPT, at which it was noted, so the minutes record, that the company was now wholly dependent upon the continued
H support of its bankers and lenders and that the directors were therefore concerned as to its solvency. The chairman, Mr Berish Berger, having reported that in the event of an insolvency it was likely that the company's assets would best be realised by the making of an administration order, it was resolved that the company should set in train the necessary steps to lead to an application to the court for such an order. To that end it was further resolved that:

British Company Cases

"(1) Malcolm Cohen and Peter Richard Copp of Messrs Stoy Hayward . . . should be requested to advise upon the appropriateness of the administration procedure and if appropriate to act as administrators of the company upon the granting by the court of an order.

(2) Messrs Stoy Hayward should be instructed to prepare an independent report of the company's affairs for use in connection with the proposed application to the court.

(3) Such firm of solicitors as Messrs Stoy Hayward shall advise us should be instructed to prepare an application to the court for an administration order."

On 4 January there was an extraordinary general meeting of LPT, at which it was resolved:

"That in view of the company's financial position the company should present a petition to the court for an administration order."

On 7 January the directors of each of the core subsidiaries passed resolutions in similar terms to those passed by the directors of LPT on 3 January. On 8 January there were extraordinary general meetings of the core subsidiaries, at which resolutions were passed in terms similar to those passed at the extraordinary general meeting of LPT on 4 January.

As at 4 January the directors of LPT were Mr Berger, who was also a beneficiary under a discretionary trust of shares in LPT's ultimate holding company; Mr Michael Fielding, a partner in Brechers, the solicitors to LPT and the core subsidiaries (though not in relation to the administration petitions); Mr Mark Gurney, the managing director; Mr Daniel Lewis, the finance director and company secretary; and Mr Sylvain Reinhold, the director responsible for building. Mr Gurney, Mr Lewis and Mr Reinhold worked full time in the group. Mr Fielding was a part-time director. None of those four had any direct or indirect interest in the shares of LPT. Mr Fielding resigned as a director on 4 January. At all material times the directors of the core subsidiaries were Mr Berger, Mr Gurney and Mr Lewis.

On 11 January MHT appointed receivers over the properties of the core subsidiaries charged to them, some of which were already subject to Norwich Union's receiver. On 15 January Lelliott's winding-up petition was advertised and on the following day the hearing of it was adjourned until 30 January. On 25 January, on Lelliott's application, *Harman* J appointed a provisional liquidator of LPT. On 28 January Mr Cohen and Mr Copp produced an independent report pursuant to r. 2.2 of the *Insolvency Rules* 1986, in which they expressed the opinion, based on the information presently available, that it was likely that administration orders would achieve one or more of the purposes mentioned in sec. 8(3) of the *Insolvency Act* 1986. On the same day petitions for administration orders were presented by LPT and the core subsidiaries, affirmations in support exhibiting the independent report and other documents being made by Mr Berger in each case. Also on the same day *Harman* J abridged the time for service of the petitions and fixed the hearing of them for 30 January, to come on before the hearing of the winding-up petition. He suspended certain powers of the provisional liquidator of LPT in the meantime.

On 30 January the hearing of all the petitions was stood over until 6 February. Pursuant to r. 2.9(1)(e) of the *Insolvency Rules* 1986 LPT's administration petition had already been served on Lelliott. The judge gave leave for Norwich Union and MHT to be joined as respondents to all the petitions under para. (g) of that subrule. Further evidence was filed on the administration petitions, including affidavits in opposition sworn on behalf of Lelliott, Norwich Union and MHT. On 4 February Mr Cohen and Mr Copp produced an addendum to their independent report.

A On Wednesday, 6 February the administration petitions came on for an effective hearing before *Harman* J. Lelliott, Norwich Union and MHT were separately represented by counsel. At the start of the hearing the core subsidiaries abandoned their petitions, which were dismissed accordingly. Norwich Union applied for its costs of the ten petitions relating to the core subsidiaries which had charged properties to it to be paid by the directors of those subsidiaries personally. Lelliott gave notice that, if successful in its opposition, it would ask for a similar order in relation to its costs of LPT's petition.

B Directions were given for the directors to be made aware of those applications. Argument proceeded in relation to the substance of LPT's petition. At the end of the day the judge adjourned the hearing until 8 February.

On 7 February Mr Cohen made an affirmation stating his opinion, based on the information presently available, that one or more of the statutory purposes was still likely to be achieved by an administration order in respect of LPT alone. On the same

C day a further affidavit opposing such an order was sworn by a partner in Peat Marwick on behalf of Lelliott. Mr Berger also made a second affirmation in support of LPT's petition, effectively an updated version of his first affirmation.

On Friday, 8 February the directors of LPT and the ten subsidiaries were represented by separate counsel and solicitors. Counsel applied for a further adjournment to enable the directors to put in evidence. The application was opposed by Lelliott and Norwich

D Union and refused by the judge. During the course of the day the judge gave judgment on four different questions. The judgments are reported at [1991] BCC 446. First, he held that LPT had locus standi to present its petition for an administration order. Secondly, having concluded that it was extremely unlikely that any of the statutory purposes for making such an order could possibly be achieved, he held that he had no jurisdiction to make an administration order and dismissed the petition accordingly. Thirdly, he made the order under appeal against those who had been directors of LPT

E on 4 January 1991. They included Mr Fielding, who was thus put under a joint and several liability for all of the costs, notwithstanding that he had resigned on that date. Fourthly, the judge made a similar order in favour of Norwich Union against the directors of the ten subsidiaries. Those directors also appealed against that order, but it was dismissed by consent before the registrar on 16 June 1992. Nothing more need be said about that appeal.

F The report of the judgment which led to the order appealed against begins at [1991] BCC 453. No order was made or, as it seems, sought in respect of the costs of Norwich Union or MHT, each of whom had applied to be joined in its own interest. As to Lelliott's costs, it seemed to the judge that that company was in a quite different position. At p. 454D, he recorded a submission for the directors that an order for costs of the kind sought should only be made in an exceptional case, counsel having referred to *Re Gosscott (Groundworks) Ltd* (1988) 4 BCC 372, where *Mervyn Davies* J, in

G refusing to make an order against directors personally, had said that they had made desperate efforts in all good faith to save the company and that they had not acted irresponsibly. At p. 454G, *Harman* J pointed out that the application was in respect of the persons who were directors on 4 January and that the report of Mr Copp and Mr Cohen was not prepared until 28 January. At p. 454H, he said:

H "Nonetheless, there is no hint in the evidence that by 4 January there had been even tentative and provisional advice from Mr Copp and Mr Cohen that an administration order was suitable."

Having then referred to clear indications that an administration order would be opposed by LPT's principal creditors, the judge continued, at p. 455B:

"In those circumstances, to have resolved on 4 January to present an administration petition seems to me to have had no independent support at all, and not to have

A

been the act of persons making desperate efforts in all good faith to save the company. On the material before me I could not apply that description to the efforts of these directors.

Further, these directors have not abandoned their petition for administration the moment they saw the opposing evidence and heard, as they did at a very early stage, the applications to be added by Norwich Union and Manufacturers Hanover to oppose, and knew that John Lelliott, served with the petition, were opposing. No question of saving of costs and time seems to have occurred to the directors. They pressed on to the bitter end, which occurred when I concluded, as I just have, not only that I could not consider that it was likely that the object of the petition would be achieved, but that I positively considered that it was unlikely that any such objective could be achieved. That is a very strong conclusion which I have very rarely come to on an administration petition, but of which I was convinced in this case.

B

C

It seems to me that this is a wholly exceptional case where the petition was resolved upon without proper consideration of its purposes and was persisted in in the face of overwhelming opposition and without reason."

The judge did not refer to his refusal of the directors' application for an adjournment.

The only material on which we can act is an affirmation of Mr M J Pottesman, the directors' solicitor, made in support of their application for leave to adduce fresh evidence in this court. Mr Pottesman says:

D

"They were not afforded a fair opportunity to put in evidence below, which is already one of their grounds of appeal in para. 5(b)(iv) of the notice of appeal. The judge having indicated on 6 February 1991 that he was minded to make orders for costs against the directors personally and having stood over the petitions until Friday, 8 February for that purpose, my firm were instructed on behalf of the directors on Thursday, 7 February and we instructed junior counsel on that day who appeared for them on Friday, 8 February. On both of those days public transport and the business of the court was disrupted by heavy snowfalls and it was impossible to assemble proper instructions for counsel or to bring the appellants together to consider how to meet the applications made against them. Counsel applied for an adjournment on Friday, 8 February in order to obtain full instructions and if necessary prepare evidence on behalf of the appellants; but this was refused."

E

F

Although the directors' application to adduce fresh evidence on the appeal was initially opposed, the opposition was very properly abandoned by Mr Ritchie, for Lelliott, at the start of the hearing in this court. It may be assumed that that evidence is broadly the same as that which the directors would have put in before the judge, had they been able to do so. I will have to consider it more closely in due course. At this stage it is enough to say that if it had been before the judge, he would at the least have regarded it as making out a good arguable defence to the claim against the directors.

G

With the benefit of the fresh evidence before us, the first question we have to decide is whether the judge erred in principle in refusing the directors an adjournment and making the order only on the evidence which was already before him. That question must be answered in the affirmative. While allowing for the possibility that there was not an opportunity for a justification of the adjournment to be urged on him as fully as it has been urged on us, I am quite satisfied that the judge was wrong not to grant one. Moreover, the evidence already before him was clearly inadequate for the purpose of making a decision on the application against the directors.

H

The issue for decision on the petition was whether the making of an administration order would be likely to achieve one or more of the purposes mentioned in sec. 8(3) of

A   the *Insolvency Act* 1986. The issue for decision on the application against the directors was whether they had acted properly in causing LPT to present the petition. The latter was not an issue to which the existing evidence could have been expected to be directed. Nor was it. The only evidence of the circumstances in which the decisions to present and pursue the petition were taken was contained in para. 1 of Mr Berger's first affirmation:

B
> "Pursuant to a members' resolution passed at an extraordinary general meeting on 4 January 1991, the members of the company resolved that the company should petition for the making of an administration order. The directors of the company have also passed a board resolution to that effect."

Copies of the resolutions were exhibited. That evidence proved due compliance with the general requirements of company law in the presentation of the petition. The particular requirements of r. 2.2 of the *Insolvency Rules* 1986 were satisfied by the due preparation of the reports of Mr Cohen and Mr Copp, which were also put in evidence.

C   The evidence on the petition did not have to go further than that.

So, with respect to the judge, it was hardly surprising that there was no hint in the existing evidence of advice from Mr Copp and Mr Cohen on or before 4 January, or indeed of any other advice received by the directors between the beginning of January and 8 February. A quite separate issue having been raised against them, the directors were entitled to a proper opportunity to put in evidence of their own. Even without the

D   effects of the severe winter weather to which their solicitor has appealed, it could not reasonably have been thought that they had had that opportunity by the afternoon of 8 February when the application was heard and determined. The claim, if successful, could have had serious consequences for the directors, not only to their pockets — Lelliott's costs of the petition have now been estimated at £40,000 — but also to their reputations, especially perhaps to Mr Fielding's. On every score it deserved to be fully investigated. Nor could there have been any urgency about it. Certainly there was

E   urgency in the disposal of the petition because, if it was to be dismissed, it was important that a winding-up order should be made at the earliest possible moment. But the question of costs could easily have been put on one side and dealt with later.

The consequence of the judge's erroneous refusal of an adjournment was that he did not take into account matters which he ought to have taken into account, namely those deposed to in the fresh evidence now before this court. He therefore erred in principle

F   and his decision may be interfered with by this court. In deciding whether an order for costs ought to be made against the directors personally we must exercise an original discretion of our own. For this purpose the fresh evidence must be fully referred to and carefully considered.

It consists of affidavits or affirmations made by Mr Cohen; Mr M B Andrews, a partner in Wilde Sapte, the independent solicitors with a specialised insolvency

G   department who, on Stoy Hayward's advice, were instructed to act for LPT on the administration petitions; Mr Fielding; and Mr Lewis. No evidence was put in by Lelliott in answer, nor was application made for an adjournment to enable such evidence to be put in. No application was made for the cross-examination of the deponents.

The story can be told mainly in the words of Mr Cohen and Mr Andrews. On 31 December 1990 Mr Cohen attended a meeting with Mr Berger and others at which the financial circumstances of LPT were outlined to him. He said that he thought that

H   some form of refinancing might well be feasible and that the directors should consider the possibility of exploring the administration route. He added that a formal resolution of the board would be necessary before he could take the possibility of administration further. On 2 and 3 January Mr Cohen had various discussions on the telephone with Mr Berger and others in LPT and he was given further details of a suggested refinancing scheme with the assistance of a German bank. He also spoke on both days to

Mr Andrews and invited him to attend a meeting on the evening of 3 January. On the
morning of that day he spent a number of hours at LPT's office looking at the financial
situation of the LPT companies with the help of Mr Lewis and another.

     Late in the afternoon of 3 January Mr Andrews called at the offices of Stoy Hayward,
when Mr Cohen gave him a background briefing preparatory to the evening meeting.
That meeting was attended by Mr Cohen, Mr Andrews, Mr Berger and two others from
LPT and a partner in the firm of solicitors now acting for the directors. It lasted from
about 6.30 pm to about 11 pm. In the words of Mr Andrews:

> "We discussed at length the affairs of the LPT companies and the possibility of
> applying for administration. Mr Cohen expressed the preliminary view that
> administration would appear to be beneficial to all the companies' creditors and
> that he thought that administration applications would be appropriate and would
> stand a good chance of success. I agreed that there appeared to be a coherent case
> for administration. It was agreed that Mr Cohen would prepare a report for the
> purposes of r. 2.2 of the *Insolvency Rules* 1986."

So, contrary to the judge's understanding, by 4 January provisional advice as to the
suitability of administration had been given not only by Mr Cohen but by Mr Andrews
as well.

     After the meeting on 3 January Mr Cohen continued with his investigations into the
LPT companies. On 4 January he spoke on the telephone to someone in the German
bank, who indicated that it might be interested in helping LPT. At about the same time
MHT said that it would be willing to support administration for LPT, provided that it
would not interfere with the appointment by them of receivers over the properties
charged to them by the core subsidiaries. However, on 8 January Mr Cohen expressed
the view that the core subsidiaries were integral to the proposed refinancing, which
would be rendered difficult, if not impossible, if administration were to be limited to
LPT alone. The immediate result of that was MHT's appointment of receivers on
11 January. Meanwhile, on 7 January, Mr Cohen had instructed Mr Andrews to proceed
with the preparation of applications to the court in respect of all 30 companies. The
whole of that week was taken up in drafting the necessary documents, with a view to
presenting the petitions on 15 January, the day before Lelliott's winding-up petition was
fixed to come on for its first hearing.

     On 9 January Mr Andrews retained leading and junior counsel to act on behalf of the
30 companies. On 11 January he, Mr Copp and four others attended a consultation with
counsel when the viability of the proposed administration applications was discussed in
detail. Counsel agreed that the administration petitions appeared to be appropriate and
stood, on the information then available, at least a reasonable chance of success.

     However, on 15 January the directors informed Mr Cohen of their belief that they had
refinancing facilities available and that administration was unnecessary. Although he
advised them that they should nevertheless proceed with the administration applications,
they considered it better to wait. Mr Andrews was instructed not to present the
administration petitions; merely to complete the documentation so that they could, if
necessary, be presented quickly at a later stage. Mr Andrews has said that it has always
seemed to him that the decision to delay presentation of the administration petitions
was a serious error of judgment.

     By 23 January it had become clear that the refinancing scheme with the assistance of
the German bank was by no means assured of success. Between then and 28 January the
r. 2.2 report was revised and updated, the final version being signed on the latter date.
It remained Mr Cohen's view that a good coherent case had been made and that an
administration had a reasonable chance of being successful. As stated in their report,

A   Mr Cohen and Mr Copp considered that administration orders were likely to achieve one or more of the purposes listed in sec. 8(3) of the 1986 Act.

In the period after 23 January Wilde Sapte discussed the case several times with counsel on the telephone and there were consultations with leading and junior counsel on 28, 29 and 30 January. Mr Andrews has said that by 30 January it had become clear that MHT and Norwich Union, as well as Lelliott, intended to resist the petitions. He

B   continues:

> "Although the position had changed dramatically, it was not suggested by counsel during the course of the various discussions and consultations that it was inappropriate for the companies to apply for administration. I understood [leading counsel] to believe (as I still did) that the petitions had a certain attraction and stood a reasonable prospect of success."

C   By 1 February Lelliott, Norwich Union and MHT had all put in evidence opposing the administration petitions and Mr Andrews had attempted, without success, to agree terms with MHT which would have enabled it to support the application for administration, at least in relation to LPT. Mr Andrews continues:

> "In the light of these developments, [leading counsel] told me on the telephone on Friday, 1 February that he was becoming increasingly pessimistic about the

D   > chance of the petitions succeeding. This was, however, the first occasion upon which [he] had expressed such a pessimistic view. Hitherto, he had always accepted the coherence of the case for administration and appeared to agree that the petitions had a reasonable prospect of success."

On 5 February there was a further consultation with leading and junior counsel attended by Mr Cohen and another from Stoy Hayward, two representatives of Wilde

E   Sapte and five from LPT, including Mr Berger and Mr Lewis. Again I refer to the affidavit of Mr Andrews:

> "In the course of the consultation, [leading counsel] advised that, in view of the unremitting opposition of the major secured creditors, the petitions in respect of the subsidiaries were now hopeless and, accordingly, it was agreed that these should be abandoned. As to LPT itself, however, Mr Cohen indicated that he still

F   > felt administration would be of advantage to LPT's creditors and that it was appropriate to proceed with this one petition. [Leading counsel] agreed that a coherent (albeit much less wide-ranging) case could be made for administration of LPT alone and that the LPT petition still had some chance of success. He felt that the court could still exercise its discretion to make an administration order notwithstanding the opposition of the creditors. It was, therefore, decided that

G   > this petition alone should be pursued."

Mr Cohen has said that, having read the opposing evidence, he concluded that the applications in respect of the subsidiaries no longer had any real prospect of success. It seemed to him, however, that administration would still be of benefit to LPT's unsecured creditors and that the petition relating to that company continued to have a reasonable chance of success.

H   On the strength of that evidence the directors, through Mr Stewart QC, say that they acted throughout in good faith in the interests of LPT, with the support of independent r. 2.2 reports and in accordance with the advice of solicitors and leading and junior counsel experienced in the field. At worst they were guilty of no more than an error of judgment. In the circumstances, they say that there is no ground on which they can properly be ordered to pay Lelliott's costs personally.

Mr Ritchie's argument to the contrary can be summarised as follows. He submitted,   A
correctly, that in the case of an insolvent company the question whether directors have
acted in good faith in its interests becomes in practice a question whether they have
acted in good faith in the interests of the creditors. He accepted that their duty is to act
in good faith in what they, and not the court, consider to be in those interests. Then,
relying on *Re Beddoe* [1893] 1 Ch 547, he sought to draw an analogy between the
directors here and a trustee who, having prosecuted or defended an action without
reasonable cause, is not entitled to retain his costs of it out of the trust estate.   B

Such an analogy has never been drawn before and is without doubt misconceived.
The position of a director of a going company is not for this purpose to be equated to
that of a trustee. The difference in their positions is demonstrated by the absence of any
machinery for a director, as opposed to a trustee or a liquidator, to apply to the court for
directions as to the prosecution or defence of the action. A director, having sought such   C
professional advice as is appropriate, must make his own judgment as to what is in the
interests of the company.

Mr Ritchie also submitted that the recent decision of this court in *Taylor v Pace
Developments Ltd* [1991] BCC 406, on which Mr Stewart had relied, was not of
assistance where the contest was not between a director and a third party who had
successfully sued the company and had been unable to recover his costs from it, but   D
between a director and the company itself. With that submission I agree. In the former
case an order against the director personally pierces the corporate veil. In the latter it
does not.

Turning to the facts, Mr Ritchie conducted a conscientious review of the material
events as they now appear from all the evidence before the court. He submitted that
there were only three major creditors, each of whom, at any rate after 8 January when   E
the basis for MHT's assent to an administration order fell away, must have been known
by the directors to be opposed to such an order. While accepting that as late as
5 February LPT's legal advisers still thought that the LPT petition had some chance of
success, Mr Ritchie said that it was only the directors themselves who knew the strength
of the opposition and that they did not adequately communicate that knowledge to their
advisers. Addressing the question of good faith more closely, he said that Mr Berger had   F
sought to prefer himself and his family by taking charges over various properties and
that it was clear that he and they would have done everything they could to avoid the
stigma of liquidation.

Powerful though these arguments and others in the same vein may be, they have
failed to satisfy me that we ought, in the exercise of our discretion, to order the directors
to pay Lelliott's costs of the administration petition personally. The directors observed
all the requirements of the *Insolvency Rules* 1986, in particular those of r. 2.1, 2.2 and   G
2.3. At all material times they had the support of the experienced insolvency practitioners
who produced the r. 2.2 reports. From 3 January onwards they acted under the advice of
solicitors experienced in insolvency matters and from 11 January under that of leading
and junior counsel with similar experience. On 5 February, when leading counsel
advised that the unremitting opposition of the major secured creditors had rendered the
petitions in respect of the core subsidiaries hopeless, it was immediately agreed that they   H
should be abandoned. In spite of that unremitting opposition leading counsel thought
that a coherent (albeit much less wide-ranging) case could still be made for an
administration order in the case of LPT alone and that that petition still had some chance
of success. Even if, which without cross-examination of the deponents cannot be
assumed, the directors were less than forthcoming in their communications with their

A   advisers, how can that be held against them when, with full knowledge of the unremitting opposition of the major secured creditors, the advisers still thought that the LPT petition had some chance of success?

On the matter of good faith it is worth recording the final words of Mr Andrews' affidavit:

B   "Moreover, the directors appeared at all times to be in close contact with Lelliotts and the major secured creditors. They were extremely confident until very late in the day that, when the merits of administration were demonstrated to them, they would adopt a much less hostile approach to the initiative. Regrettably, their confidence upon this point proved to be misplaced."

It is true that the directors may all along have been deceiving their advisers. But directors of insolvent companies are notoriously optimistic and optimism is not necessarily

C   inconsistent with good faith. Without cross-examination we cannot proceed as if a deception had been proved.

It may be a matter for comment that the fresh evidence does not include an affirmation from Mr Berger, although I did not understand that comment to be made by Mr Ritchie himself. The only deponent amongst the four who were directors during the whole of the material period is Mr Lewis. In para. 6 and 7 of his affirmation he says:

D   "6. Following the resolutions of 3 and 4 January in the case of LPT and 7 and 8 January in the case of the core subsidiaries, I and my co-directors acted entirely in accordance with the advice of Messrs Stoy Hayward and Wilde Sapte both when the petitions were presented to the court on 29 January and at each of the stages in the proceedings which followed down to 8 February when they were finally disposed of. I considered it my duty as a director to authorise the petitions

E   for administration of LPT and the core subsidiaries as an alternative to compulsory winding up of LPT in the light of the opinion expressed in Stoy Hayward's independent report dated 28 January 1991 under r. 2.2 that such administrations were expedient for the statutory purpose. I subsequently concurred in the decision to abandon the petitions in respect of the core subsidiaries because that was the advice which we were given by our leading counsel in a consultation which I attended. I also concurred, however, in the decision to continue with the petition

F   in respect of LPT alone on the advice of leading counsel since Stoy Hayward continued to advise that that was expedient for the statutory purpose as confirmed in Mr Cohen's affirmation of 7 February 1991 . . .

7. In my respectful submission the criticisms levelled against me and my fellow directors by the judge in respect of the presentation and conduct of the petitions were unfair. We felt at the time and still feel that we would have been open to

G   criticism had we not proposed to the court administration as an alternative to winding up in the light of a report by independent insolvency practitioners (of whom the judge made no criticism at all) to the effect that administration would be expedient for one of the statutory purposes."

Mr Lewis not having been cross-examined, we must accept that evidence at its face value. Having thus accepted it, we cannot in my view be satisfied that the directors did

H   not act in good faith in what they considered to be in the interests of LPT. We cannot, in the exercise of our discretion, order the directors to pay Lelliott's costs of the petition personally.

This case provides a good illustration of the dangers inherent in treating an application for costs against a third party in the same manner as one against a party to the proceedings. It demonstrates that such an application will often raise entirely different issues from those which the court has so far considered and to which the evidence has so far been directed. Every judge of first instance will wish to ensure that the procedures of his court allow such applications to be justly determined.

I would allow the directors' appeal and discharge the order for costs against them.

Beldam LJ: I agree.

Sir John Megaw: I also agree.

(*Appeal allowed with costs*)

_____

Re Arrows Ltd (No. 4).

Court of Appeal (Civil Division).
Dillon, Steyn and Rose L JJ.
Judgment delivered 7 April 1993.

Insolvency — Private examination — Whether liquidators should supply transcripts of private examination to Serious Fraud Office — Judge ordered disclosure subject to restrictions on use of transcripts as evidence — Appeal — Insolvency Act 1986, sec. 236, 433; Criminal Justice Act 1987, sec. 2(3), (8); Insolvency Rules 1986 (SI 1986/1925), r. 9.5.

This was an appeal by the Director of the Serious Fraud Office against an order of Vinelott J ([1992] BCC 987) made on an application by the liquidators of Arrows Ltd seeking directions and a determination whether, and if so how, the liquidators should deal with the transcripts of the examination of the respondent, Mr Naviede, under sec. 236 of the Insolvency Act 1986, in consequence of the receipt by the liquidators of a letter from the Director of the Serious Fraud Office requesting copies of the transcripts under sec. 2(3) of the Criminal Justice Act 1987.

The order of the judge directed that the liquidators release and disclose the transcripts and certain affirmations made by Mr Naviede in the course of his examination under sec. 236 to the Director of the Serious Fraud Office upon the director undertaking (1) that he would not use the transcripts or affirmations or any copies thereof in evidence against Mr Naviede save in the circumstances specified in sec. 2(8) of the 1987 Act, and (2) that he would procure an undertaking in the same terms as (1) from any party to whom he supplied such transcripts or affirmations. The director appealed against the exaction by the judge of the undertakings.

Held, allowing the appeal and releasing the Director of the Serious Fraud Office from the undertakings:

1. The liquidators were persons within sec. 2(3) and the transcripts and affirmations were documents within that subsection which the liquidators could be required to produce. The judge had no power to impose the restrictions in sec. 2(8) on the use by the Serious Fraud Office of the transcripts of Mr Naviede's examination under sec. 236 and affirmations supplied by the liquidators. Moreover the judge did not have power to exact undertakings from the Director of the Serious Fraud Office in order to achieve a condition which he had no power to impose.

2. The transcripts were not privileged because it could not be said that the dominant purpose for which they came into existence was that of obtaining legal advice or aiding in the conduct of litigation. (Waugh v British Railways Board [1980] AC 521 applied.)

3. Information given to office-holders in the course of an examination under sec. 236 was, in certain respects, confidential, but such confidentiality was overridden by sec. 433 which made the statements admissible in evidence against the maker.

4. There was no public interest immunity to prevent the disclosure of transcripts or other documents by office-holders to prosecution or regulatory authorities under the statutory duties or powers of the office-holders including their duties under sec. 2 of the 1987 Act.

5. The Chancery Division did not have any discretion over the use of the transcripts of the examinations in criminal proceedings. Rule 9.5 of the Insolvency Rules was mere machinery as to how the transcripts in possession of the court were to be kept. It did not enable the court to deny the Serious Fraud Office, or other prosecuting authority, anything that the Serious Fraud Office or other prosecuting authority was entitled to by statute for the investigation or prosecution of crime. If the Serious Fraud Office wanted

to inspect the actual transcripts held by the court (instead of asking the liquidators to
supply the documents the liquidators held) there would have to be an application to the
court (under r. 9.5) but that should be granted automatically.

The following cases were referred to in the judgments:

AT & T Istel Ltd & Anor v Tully & Anor [1992] QB 315 (CA); [1993] AC 45 (HL).
Bank of England v Riley & Anor [1992] Ch 475.
Barlow Clowes (Gilt Managers) Ltd, Re [1991] BCC 608; [1992] Ch 208.
Bishopsgate Investment Management Ltd, Re [1992] BCC 222; [1993] Ch 1.
British & Commonwealth Holdings plc, Re (No. 2) [1992] BCC 977; [1993] AC 426.
Esal (Commodities) Ltd, Re (No. 2) [1990] BCC 708.
FMS Financial Management Services v FMS Nominees Ltd (unreported, 5 June 1987,
Harman J).
London & County Securities Ltd & Ors v Nicholson & Ors [1980] 1 WLR 948.
London United Investments plc, Re [1992] BCC 202; [1992] Ch 578.
Lonrho Ltd & Anor v Shell Petroleum Co Ltd & Anor [1980] 1 WLR 627.
Padfield & Ors v Minister of Agriculture, Fisheries and Food & Ors [1968] AC 997.
Poulson, Re [1976] 1 WLR 1023.
R v Director of the Serious Fraud Office, ex parte Smith [1993] AC 1.
R v Governor of Brixton Prison, ex parte Osman [1991] 1 WLR 281.
R v Harris & Anor [1970] 1 WLR 1252.
R v Hennessey & Ors (1978) 68 Cr App R 419.
R v Rankine [1986] QB 861.
R v Taylor (The Times, 21 October 1986).
Rank Film Distributors Ltd & Ors v Video Information Centre & Ors [1982] AC 380.
Sociedade Nacional de Combustiveis de Angola UEE & Ors v Lundqvist & Ors
[1991] 2 QB 310.
Tate Access Floors Inc & Anor v Boswell & Ors [1991] Ch 512.
Waugh v British Railways Board [1980] AC 521.

Matthew Collings (instructed by Burton Copeland, Manchester) for Mr Naviede.

John Jarvis QC, Ewan McQuater and Richard De Lacy (instructed by Lovell White
Durrant) for the liquidators.

Roger Kaye QC and Richard Ritchie (instructed by the Treasury Solicitor) for the
Director of the Serious Fraud Office.

AWH Charles (instructed by the Treasury Solicitor) for the Secretary of State for
Trade and Industry.

JUDGMENT

Dillon LJ: The court has before it an appeal, by leave of the judge, by the Director of
the Serious Fraud Office against an order of *Vinelott* J made on 10 November 1992 (see
[1992] BCC 987). That was an order made by the judge on an application by the
liquidators of Arrows Ltd (which is in compulsory liquidation) under sec. 168(3) of the
Insolvency Act 1986 seeking directions and a determination whether, and if so how, the
liquidators should deal with the transcripts of the examination of the respondent,
Mr Naviede, under sec. 236 of that Act, in consequence of the receipt by the liquidators
of a letter from the Director of the Serious Fraud Office requesting copies of the
transcripts. The liquidators had been directed by an earlier order of *Millett* J to make
such an application under sec. 168(3) on receipt of any request or demand by the Serious
Fraud Office for copies of the transcripts.

The order of the judge directed that the liquidators release and disclose the transcripts
and certain affirmations made by Mr Naviede in the course of his examination under

A sec. 236 to the Director of the Serious Fraud Office upon the director undertaking (1) that he will not use the transcripts or affirmations or any copies thereof in evidence against Mr Naviede save in the circumstances specified in subsec. 2(8) of the *Criminal Justice Act* 1987, and (2) that he will procure an undertaking in the same terms as (1) from any party to whom he supplies such transcripts or affirmations. But the order further provided that the undertakings of the director should cease to have effect in the event of a successful appeal by the director against the judge's order. The present appeal

B is therefore an appeal against the exaction by the judge of the undertakings.

To understand the undertakings it is necessary to look at provisions in the *Criminal Justice Act* 1987.

Section 1 of that Act constituted the Serious Fraud Office, provided for the appointment of the director and prescribed his functions.

C Section 2 provides for investigations by the director. In particular, subsec. (2) provides that the director may by notice in writing require the person whose affairs are to be investigated ("the person under investigation") or any other person whom he has reason to believe has relevant information to answer questions or otherwise furnish information with respect to any matter relevant to the investigation.

Subsection (3) provides that the director may by notice in writing require the person under investigation or any other person to produce any specified documents which

D appear to the director to relate to any matter relevant to the investigation or any documents of a specified description which appear to him so to relate.

Subsection 2(8) then provides:

"A statement by a person in response to a requirement imposed by virtue of this section may only be used in evidence against him—

E   (a)   on a prosecution for an offence under subsection (14) below; or

     (b)   on a prosecution for some other offence where in giving evidence he makes a statement inconsistent with it."

Subsection (14) there mentioned is not relevant to the present case.

Subsection 2(9) preserves legal professional privilege and subsec. (10) contains special

F provisions as to bankers' obligations of confidence.

Subsection 3(3) of the *Criminal Justice Act* 1987 provides:

"Where any information is subject to an obligation of secrecy imposed by or under any enactment other than an enactment contained in the Taxes Management Act 1970, the obligation shall not have effect to prohibit the disclosure of that information to any person in his capacity as a member of the Serious Fraud Office

G . . ."

Section 236 of the *Insolvency Act* 1986 provides by subsec. (2) that the court may on the application of the office-holder — which includes the liquidators in the present case — summon to appear before it (a) any officer of the company in question, (b) any person known or suspected to have in his possession any property of the company or supposed to be indebted to the company, or (c) any person whom the court thinks capable of

H giving information concerning the promotion, formation, business, dealings, affairs or property of the company. Subsection 237(4) provides that any person who appears or is brought before the court under sec. 236 or 237 may be examined on oath, either orally or (except in Scotland) by interrogatories, concerning the company or the matters mentioned in sec. 236(2)(c). By subsec. 236(3) the person summoned under 236(2) may be required to submit an affidavit (or an affirmation) to the court or to produce documents.

In *Re Bishopsgate Investment Management Ltd* [1992] BCC 222 this court held that a person summoned to appear before the court under sec. 236 could not rely on the privilege against self-incrimination as an excuse for refusing to answer questions put to him in the course of his examination. Beyond that any statement made by a person during his examination under sec. 236 (or other provisions of the Insolvency Act) is admissible in evidence against him in any proceedings whether criminal or civil. See sec. 433.

I should refer next to the *Insolvency Rules* 1986. Rule 9 deals with examination under sec. 236. Rule 9.5 is concerned with the record of any such examination, and provides as follows:

"(1) Unless the court otherwise directs, the written record of the respondent's examination, and any answer given by him to interrogatories, and any affidavits submitted by him in compliance with an order of the court under the applicable section, shall not be filed in court.

(2) The written record, answers and affidavits shall not be open to inspection, without an order of the court, by any person other than—

(a) the applicant for an order under the applicable section, or

(b) any person who could have applied for such an order in respect of the affairs of the same insolvent.

(3) Paragraph (2) applies also to so much of the court file as shows the grounds of the application for an order under the applicable section and to any copy of proposed interrogatories.

(4) The court may from time to time give directions as to the custody and inspection of any documents to which this Rule applies, and as to the furnishing of copies of, or extracts from, such documents."

I should record for completeness that sec. 235 of the Insolvency Act imposes an obligation on various classes of persons, including those who are or have at any time been officers of the company and those who are in the employment of the company to give to the office-holder such information concerning the company and its promotion, formation, business, dealings, affairs or property as the office-holder may reasonably require and to attend on the office-holder at such times as the latter may reasonably require. Under r. 7.20(1)(c) of the Insolvency Rules the court may make such orders as it thinks necessary for the enforcement of obligations falling on any person in accordance with sec. 235. So far as I am aware there was no express statutory antecedent of sec. 235. But for obvious reasons, it has for a very long time been the practice of the court not to order the private examination of a person under sec. 236 if it appears that that person is willing to co-operate and supply whatever information is sought informally, i.e. now under sec. 235. In fact in Mr Naviede's case we are not concerned with any questioning under sec. 235; the only questioning of him was under sec. 236.

There have been suggestions, for instance in the skeleton arguments of the liquidators, that a distinction ought to be drawn, in relation to public interest immunity, between a formal private examination under sec. 236 and informal questioning under sec. 235. For my part, I see no such distinction. The informal questioning, under sec. 235, is backed by the sanction in r. 7.20(1)(c), and informal questioning is and always has been subject to the threat, express or implicit, that if the person being questioned does not co-operate there will be an application to the court by the office-holder for the formal examination of that person under sec. 236.

Given therefore that the transcripts of Mr Naviede's examination under sec. 236 and the affirmations he made are admissible evidence against him in the criminal proceedings now pending against him, I find it surprising that the chancery court should be invited to

A   restrict the use of that evidence in the criminal court. The starting point, in my judgment, is the statement by Lord *Wilberforce* in *Rank Film Distributors Ltd v Video Information Centre* [1982] AC 380 at p. 442F–G:

> "But I cannot accept that a civil court has any power to decide in a manner which would bind a criminal court that evidence of any kind is admissible or inadmissible in that court."

B   A fortiori the civil court has no power to decide to what extent evidence which would be by statute admissible in criminal proceedings should be allowed to be used.

In reliance on that principle this court in *AT & T Istel Ltd v Tully* [1992] QB 315 refused to include in a Mareva injunction against the defendants which provided for disclosure a condition that no disclosure made in compliance with the order should be used as evidence in the prosecution of any offence alleged to have been committed by the person required to make the disclosure. The actual decision of this court in *AT & T*
C   *Istel Ltd v Tully* was overruled by the House of Lords [1993] AC 45, but that was only on the very special ground that the Crown Prosecution Service had, by a letter before the hearing in this court, intimated that they had no objection to the proposed condition in the circumstances of that particular case. Lord *Templeman* said on this topic at p. 56E in the report of the decision of the House of Lords:

> "I agree that the Crown Prosecution Service cannot be bound against their
D   wishes."

Section 31 of the *Theft Act* 1968 contains a provision that a person shall not be excused, by reason that to do so might incriminate him, from answering any question put to that person in certain forms of civil proceeding, but it is also provided that no statement or admission made by a person in answering such a question shall be admissible in evidence against that person in proceedings for an offence under the Theft
E   Act. Many judges have expressed the wish that sec. 31 could be extended to other proceedings relating to property so that, as Lord *Russell of Killowen* put it in *Rank Film Distributors Ltd v Video Information Centre*, the privilege against self-incrimination would be removed while at the same time preventing the use in criminal proceedings of statements which otherwise have been privileged. See also per Sir *Nicolas Browne-Wilkinson* V-C in *Sociedade Nacional de Combustiveis de Angola UEE v Lundqvist* [1991] 2 QB 310 at p. 338G–H, and in *Tate Access Floors Inc v Boswell* [1991] Ch 512 at
F   p. 532C–G, and per Lord *Donaldson of Lymington* MR in *AT & T Istel Ltd v Tully* at p. 325H. But no such general provision has yet been enacted by Parliament, and no one has suggested that there is power in the civil courts to imply or impose a provision such as that in sec. 31 of the Theft Act so as to fetter the use in the criminal courts of evidence given in civil proceedings where sec. 31 or a comparable limited statutory provision does not apply.

G   I cannot see, therefore, any basis on which the judge could have imposed the restrictions in sec. 2(8) on the use by the Serious Fraud Office of the transcripts of Mr Naviede's examination and affirmations supplied to them by the liquidators. Moreover I do not see how the judge could have had power to exact undertakings from the Director of the Serious Fraud Office, in order to achieve a condition which he had no power to impose. On the plain wording of sec. 2 of the Criminal Justice Act the liquidators are "persons" within the meaning of subsec. (3) and the transcripts and affirmations are
H   "documents" within that subsection which the liquidators, as such "persons" can be required to produce.

I would add, that in the course of the argument on the application in relation to sec. 2 of the Criminal Justice Act, which immediately followed the argument in the present case, we were referred to passages in *Hansard* recording statements by ministers in the course of the parliamentary debates on the Criminal Justice Bill. It is there made clear

in a speech of the Earl of Caithness, the minister who had charge of the bill in the House
of Lords, that in introducing the inhibitions in cl. 2(8) of the bill on using compulsorily
obtained information in court against the provider of that information the government
had deliberately not followed the precedent in companies legislation and the Financial
Services Act under which statements made to DTI inspectors in the exercise of their
powers are admissible as evidence of those making them. See *Hansard* for 12 May 1987,
columns 577–578.

It is urged for Mr Naviede that the justification for the undertakings required by the
judge can be found in the confidentiality of information obtained under sec. 235 or 236,
in a public interest immunity referable to the importance of promoting the smooth
operation and efficiency of the process of company liquidation, or in legal professional
privilege, coupled in each case with the need for the liquidators to obtain an order of the
court, either under r. 9.5 of the Insolvency Rules or as a result of the earlier order of
Millett J. It is said that the need for the liquidator to apply to the court gives the court a
discretion from which all else may flow.

I propose to deal first with the suggestion that legal professional privilege is relevant.

Documents protected by legal professional privilege do not, of course, have to be
produced under sec. 2 of the Criminal Justice Act. It is said that the transcripts of
Mr Naviede's examination under sec. 236 have that privilege because the object of the
examination was to enable the liquidators to get evidence to use against Mr Naviede in
civil proceedings to recover money from him for Arrows Ltd.

But if that is so, the privilege is a privilege of the liquidators and not of Mr Naviede.
But the liquidators do not claim to invoke any such privilege. On the contrary they agree
with *Vinelott* J that it cannot be said that the dominant purpose for which the transcripts
came into existence was that of obtaining legal advice or aiding in the conduct of
litigation as required by the test in *Waugh v British Railways Board* [1980] AC 521.
Therefore there is no such privilege. I see no reason to differ from that assessment that
the transcripts are not privileged, and no reason anyhow to compel the liquidators to
invoke any privilege for the by-purpose of protecting Mr Naviede who has no such
privilege. The liquidators further state, in the skeleton argument of their counsel,
Mr John Jarvis QC and Mr McQuater, that "the liquidators have difficulty in seeing how
an assertion of privilege by them would assist this liquidation". I agree.

I pass therefore to the questions of confidentiality and the suggested public interest
immunity.

There is no doubt that information given to office-holders in the course of an
examination under sec. 236 is, in certain respects, confidential. This is underlined by the
fact that under r. 9.5 the transcript is, unless the court otherwise orders, not to be placed
on the court file which is open to public inspection. There must be the same degree of
confidentiality in relation to statements given to office-holders informally under
sec. 235. But since statements made to office-holders under either of those sections are
admissible in evidence against the maker of the statement in any proceedings, that
degree of confidentiality cannot override the right of the office-holders or prosecuting
authorities to use the statements in that way. On the contrary such confidentiality as
there is is overridden by the section which makes the statements admissible in evidence
against the maker of the statements. See *London & County Securities Ltd v Nicholson*
[1980] 1 WLR 948 per *Browne-Wilkinson* J. (That case was actually concerned with
statements made to inspectors appointed by the Department of Trade and Industry, but
sec. 434(5) of the *Companies Act* 1985 in respect of answers to inspectors is closely
analogous to sec. 433 of the Insolvency Act, and the original decision in *R v Harris*
[1970] 1 WLR 1252, that answers to inspectors are admissible in criminal proceedings as
evidence against the person who gave the answers, was founded on statutory provisions

A   in the *Companies Act* 1948 which are very similar to sec. 237(4) of the *Insolvency Act* 1986.)

Mere confidentiality thus not being enough it is suggested that there is a public interest immunity, founded on the public interest that liquidations should be conducted speedily and efficiently, which warrants excluding statements under sec. 236 from evidence in subsequent proceedings, or at any rate excluding them except under safeguards comparable to those in sec. 2(8) of the Criminal Justice Act even though sec. 433 of the

B   *Insolvency Act* 1986 and sec. 434 of the *Companies Act* 1985 provide no such safeguards.

The reasoning is that persons examined under sec. 236 are more likely to be co-operative and to give full and truthful answers to the office-holders if they believe that their answers will be treated as confidential and will thus not be used against them in any prosecution. Consequently it appears that some office-holders make a practice of giving, or giving if asked, assurances of confidentiality to persons who are being examined

C   under sec. 236.

The opinions of insolvency practitioners appear to differ on this question.

The liquidators of Arrows Ltd state that they do not consider that the efficient conduct of liquidations will be adversely affected if there is perceived to be a risk that transcripts of interviews conducted under the compulsory powers in sec. 236 may come into the hands of the Serious Fraud Office and they further state that the court may allow

D   disclosure of the transcripts and affirmations in the present case (procured under sec. 236) to the Serious Fraud Office without prejudicing the liquidators' position. They do suggest that a distinction might be drawn between examination under sec. 236 and questioning under sec. 235, but with that, for the reasons indicated briefly earlier, I disagree. The liquidators of Arrows also say that they are neutral on the question whether the undertakings required by the judge should or should not be imposed.

E   By contrast, the office-holders in various of the companies associated with the late Robert Maxwell assert in the joint statement of submissions put forward by their counsel for the purposes of applications heard immediately after the argument on this appeal, that there is an important public interest in the administration of insolvencies generally, and that material obtained by the use of or under the threat of sec. 236 proceedings ought not to be authorised to be used by persons other than the office-holders unless the use proposed to be made of the material is within the purposes of the statutory scheme

F   applicable to the insolvency, i.e. it must assist the beneficial management of the insolvent estate.

The Maxwell office-holders refer to a passage in the speech of Lord *Diplock* in *Lonrho Ltd v Shell Petroleum* [1980] 1 WLR 627 where he said at p. 637G:

> "Even without the Minister's certificate, I should not have needed evidence to satisfy me that the likelihood of success of an inquiry of this kind in discovering
G   the truth as to what happened is greatly facilitated if those persons who know what happened come forward to volunteer information rather than waiting to be identified by the inquiry itself as likely to possess relevant information and having it extracted from them by question and answer. Nor would I need any evidence to satisfy me that without an assurance of complete confidentiality information is less likely to be volunteered."

H   That was said in the context of a claim by a public company to inspect documents in respect of which public interest immunity was claimed by the Lord Privy Seal on the ground that they had been prepared for the purposes of an inquiry by Mr Bingham QC as he then was and another, who had been appointed to conduct the inquiry by the Secretary of State for Foreign and Commonwealth Affairs pursuant to the *Southern Rhodesia (United Nations Sanctions) (No. 2) Order* 1968 — obviously a different field of law.

The Maxwell office-holders also asserted that by imposing the undertakings — and similar undertakings were required by the judge as a condition of the disclosure to the Serious Fraud Office of the transcripts of sec. 236 examinations in relation to Maxwell companies — the judge has struck a reasonable balance between the public interest that fraud should be prosecuted and the public interest in the speedy and efficient conduct of liquidations, in that the readiness of persons questioned to talk openly to office-holders under sec. 236 or otherwise will not be impaired if they know that their answers can only be used against them in a prosecution in the circumstances specified in sec. 2(8) of the Criminal Justice Act.

By way of further contrast, counsel for the Secretary of State for Trade and Industry, who was given leave to intervene on the hearing of this appeal, has provided us with a very helpful skeleton argument which draws attention to the wide scope of the office-holders' powers and duties, and stresses the importance of ensuring the efficient, thorough and fair investigation and prosecution of crime.

Obviously the immediate purpose of a sec. 236 examination is to enable the office-holders to get information, and where appropriate documents, in relation to the company's affairs, sc. the promotion, formation, business, dealings, affairs and property of the company as set out in sec. 236(2). It was held by the House of Lords in *Re British & Commonwealth Holdings plc (No. 2)* [1992] BCC 977 that the scope of the office-holder's powers extends to anything reasonably required by the office-holder to carry out his functions, and is not limited to reconstituting the state of knowledge the company should have possessed before the office-holder was appointed.

The main objects of the office-holder in conducting a sec. 236 examination are likely to be to see if it is possible to trace and get in further assets of the company and to see if it is possible to establish money claims for the benefit of the company against the person currently being examined or against someone else. Such money claims may have no criminal implications, e.g. a claim for damages for professional negligence against a company's auditors. But other claims, particularly against directors, may have serious criminal implications, e.g. claims against directors for fraudulent trading, theft of the company's moneys or for damages for conspiracy to defraud the company. Any director or other person being examined will know that his answers may be used in evidence against him in any civil proceedings brought against him by the office-holder on behalf of the company. Nobody would expect such confidentiality as there is in a sec. 236 examination to extend to prevent that. Indeed the confidentiality is not for the protection of the person being examined but for the protection of the office-holder. The particular purpose of the provision in r. 9.5 that the transcripts of sec. 236 examinations are not to be placed on the court file is, I apprehend, to ensure that a person who the office-holder suspects the company may have a claim against, e.g. for fraud on the company or theft, is not to be able by searching the court file and reading the transcripts of the examinations of other persons to see how strong the office-holder's case may be. Each person examined will of course have a copy of the transcripts, which he will have signed, of his own examination. But any further disclosure by the office-holder, e.g. to a director who has been examined under sec. 236, will follow the ordinary course in civil proceedings, by discovery, exchange of witness statements and so forth, if the office-holder brings civil proceedings against him.

Since that is the practical object of a sec. 236 examination from the office-holder's point of view, *Millett* J deduced a principle which he formulated in *Re Esal (Commodities) Ltd (No.2)* [1990] BCC 708 at p. 723H and restated and elaborated in *Re Barlow Clowes (Gilt Managers) Ltd* [1991] BCC 608 at p. 614C, that:

"... where leave is sought to make use of material obtained by the use or under the threat of sec. 268 [of the *Companies Act* 1948, now sec. 236 of the Insolvency

A   Act] proceedings, then, save in exceptional circumstances, leave should be granted only if the use proposed to be made is within the purpose of the statutory procedure, that is to say, that the use proposed to be made of the material is to assist the beneficial winding up of the company."

Millett J regarded that as the overriding principle against which any allegedly countervailing public interest had to be weighed. In reliance on the decisions of *Millett* J

B   the same view has been taken by other judges of the Chancery Division sitting at first instance including *Vinelott* J in the present case, and it is the view which, as indicated above, the Maxwell office-holders support and seek to uphold, as does Mr Collings on behalf of Mr Naviede.

In my judgment, however, the approach of *Millett* J cannot be a valid universal test because it wholly overlooks the fact that office-holders are by statute subject to obligations which are part of the statutory regulatory process over companies and company directors.

C   These are obligations imposed in the public interest and are not ancillary to the supposedly overriding purpose of assisting the beneficial winding up of the individual company. I refer to instances below. These obligations cannot be subject to any balancing jurisdiction or dispensing power in the judges of the Chancery Division.

In addition, the approach of *Millett* J, in my judgment, overlooks the fact that by sec. 433 of the Insolvency Act, Parliament has made statements made by a person during

D   his examination under sec. 236 admissible in evidence against him in criminal as well as civil proceedings. With all respect to *Vinelott* J, I cannot accept the reconciliation suggested by him between sec. 433 and the approach of *Millett* J, viz. (in effect) that sec. 433 makes the statements made in sec. 236 examinations admissible in evidence in criminal proceedings if and in so far as the Chancery Division in its discretion allows the prosecution to use such evidence in the criminal proceedings and subject to such conditions as the Chancery Division may impose. I find it inconceivable that Parliament,

E   which has by the Insolvency Act, as was held in *Re Bishopsgate Investment Management Ltd*, impliedly abrogated the privilege against self-incrimination where a person is examined under sec. 236, and which has similarly by sec. 434(5) of the *Companies Act* 1985 impliedly abrogated that privilege where a person is examined by inspectors appointed by the Department of Trade and Industry, should in the former case, though not apparently in the latter, have impliedly given the Chancery Division, and not merely

F   the criminal court, a discretion over the use of the transcripts of the examinations in criminal proceedings.

I turn to the obligations of the office-holders under the regulatory procedures.

One of the most important is imposed by sec. 218 of the Insolvency Act, which provides so far as material as follows:

"*Prosecution of delinquent officers and members of company*

G   (1) If it appears to the court in the course of a winding up by the court that any past or present officer, or any member, of the company has been guilty of any offence in relation to the company for which he is criminally liable, the court may (either on the application of a person interested in the winding up or of its own motion) direct the liquidator to refer the matter to the prosecuting authority.

(2) 'The prosecuting authority' means—

H   (a) in the case of a winding up in England and Wales, the Director of Public Prosecutions, and

(b) in the case of a winding up in Scotland, the Lord Advocate.

(3) If in the case of a winding up by the court in England and Wales it appears to the liquidator, not being the official receiver, that any past or present officer of the

company, or any member of it, has been guilty of an offence in relation to the   A
company for which he is criminally liable, the liquidator shall report the matter to
the official receiver.

(4) If it appears to the liquidator in the course of a voluntary winding up that any
past or present officer of the company, or any member of it, has been guilty of an
offence in relation to the company for which he is criminally liable, he shall—

     (a)   forthwith report the matter to the prosecuting authority, and   B

     (b)   furnish to that authority such information and give to him such access to
         and facilities for inspecting and taking copies of documents (being
         information and documents in the possession or under the control of the
         liquidator and relating to the matter in question) as the authority requires."

This is supported by subsec. 219(3) and that is backed by a power for the prosecuting
authority to apply to the court for an order under subsec. 219(4) to enforce compliance.   C

Section 218 is widely drawn and the expression "offence in relation to the company"
would include not only offences under the Insolvency Act itself, but also offences such
as theft of the company's moneys contrary to the Theft Act, and conspiracy to defraud
the company.

I have no doubt that if a liquidator in a compulsory liquidation reports a matter to the
official receiver under subsec. (3) of sec. 218, the official receiver would be entitled to   D
refer that matter to the relevant prosecuting authority although that is not spelt out in
the section. It would be nonsense to hold that the prosecuting authority can get the
relevant material if the company is in voluntary liquidation, because subsec. 218(4)
expressly says so, but could not get it if the company is in compulsory liquidation because
it is to go to the official receiver who is not expressly authorised to pass it on.

It was also drawn to our attention that when the Serious Fraud Office was created by   E
the *Criminal Justice Act* 1987, the opportunity was not taken to amend subsec. (4) of
sec. 218 by adding a reference to the Director of the Serious Fraud Office as an
alternative to the Director of Public Prosecutions. But there is no significance in that,
since in an appropriate case the Director of Public Prosecutions can pass on any material
he may receive under the subsection to the Serious Fraud Office. If that were not so,
there would be a strange anomaly between the law of England and the law of Scotland,
in that the Lord Advocate, who is designated in sec. 218 as originally drawn as the   F
prosecuting authority in Scotland for the purposes of the section, happens also to be the
person charged with giving directions in relation to serious fraud in Scotland under
sec. 51 of the *Criminal Justice (Scotland) Act* 1987.

Apart from sec. 218 there are other obligations on office-holders to provide information
to the official receiver or to the Secretary of State. In particular there are obligations on
office-holders under the *Company Directors Disqualification Act* 1986 and the *Insolvent*   G
Companies (Reports on Conduct of Directors) No. 2 Rules 1986 (SI 1986/2134) to make
reports and supply information and produce documents to the Secretary of State for
Trade and Industry where it appears that a disqualification order ought to be made, or
the Secretary of State is considering exercising his functions under the Disqualification
Act. The Disqualification Act provides a much needed protection for the public against
persons continuing to act as directors when their past conduct has shown them to be
unfit. I cannot conceive that the Chancery Division has any power to order office-   H
holders not to supply information or make reports under the Disqualification Act, or
only to supply it on undertakings by the department limiting the use of the information,
on the ground that directors would be more forthcoming in their answers to liquidators
if they knew that their answers were given in confidence and could not be used to found
an application for their disqualification under the Disqualification Act.

A   All these various obligations of liquidators or other office-holders to supply information
or documents for regulatory purposes cannot, in my judgment, be curtailed by the court
under the heading of public interest immunity. They are obligations imposed by the
relevant statutes according to their terms, and the court has, in my judgment, in such
cases no relevant discretion.

The liquidators' clear obligations under sec. 2(2) and (3) of the Criminal Justice Act
are, like their obligations under the Insolvency Act and the Disqualification Act,
B   obligations in respect of which the court has no relevant discretion. I can see no
distinction.

I regard r. 9.5 as mere machinery as to how the transcripts in the possession of the
court are to be kept. It is not "an obligation of secrecy imposed by or under any
enactment" for the purposes of sec. 3(3) of the Criminal Justice Act and is thus not
overridden by that subsection. But equally it does not enable the court to deny the
C   Serious Fraud Office, or other prosecuting authority, anything that the Serious Fraud
Office or other prosecuting authority is entitled to by statute for the investigation or
prosecution of crime. If indeed the Serious Fraud Office was wanting to inspect the
actual transcripts held by the court (instead of asking the liquidators to supply the
documents the liquidators hold) there would as a matter of mechanics have to be an
application to the court. But that should be granted automatically as in *Re Poulson*
D   [1976] 1 WLR 1023; there is a distinction, as pointed out there, between making the
documents in the possession of the court available to the Crown for the investigation or
prosecution of crime, and making them available to an individual or company for private
ends of that individual or company.

For my part, I consider that because of the powers of enforcement that back up
sec. 236 there should be no practical difficulty in securing the co-operation of the person
being questioned on examination under sec. 236. There will be the less difficulty for
E   office-holders as the scope and force of the legislation comes to be more widely
appreciated in the light of the present decision and other recent decisions of this court
and recent decisions of the House of Lords. Plainly office-holders should not give
assurances of confidentiality to persons they are about to question which are inconsistent
with the other statutory obligations of the office-holders, including those which would
arise under sec. 2 of the Criminal Justice Act on demand by the Serious Fraud Office.
F   As I see it, any assurance given by an office-holder to, for example, a director of
a company which, if observed, would prevent the office-holder from complying with
a statutory obligation must to that extent be invalid.

Finally, it was urged on us that though the privilege against self-incrimination had
been abrogated in relation to examinations under sec. 236, the accused person's right to
silence had not been abrogated in so far as it was represented by the fourth and sixth
G   immunities listed by Lord *Mustill* in *R v Director of Serious Fraud Office, ex parte Smith*
[1993] AC 1 at pp. 30–31:

"(4) A specific immunity, possessed by accused persons undergoing trial, from
being compelled to give evidence, and from being compelled to answer questions
put to them in the dock.

. . .

H   (6) A specific immunity . . . possessed by accused persons undergoing trial, from
having adverse comment made on any failure (a) to answer questions before the
trial, or (b) to give evidence at the trial."

But there is nothing, in an order making the transcripts of his examination, and his
affirmations, available to the Serious Fraud Office, which interferes at all with these
immunities of Mr Naviede's. He can still elect, if he wishes, not to give evidence or

answer questions at his trial, leaving it to the prosecution to prove their case if they can.   A
The prosecution do not deprive an accused person — and I do not here particularly refer
to Mr Naviede — of those immunities by putting forward cogent evidence against him
such as might make it foolhardy for him to rely on the immunity.

For these reasons, I would allow this appeal and release the Director of the Serious
Fraud Office from the undertakings which the judge required him to give.

Steyn LJ: The issue   B

Vinelott J defined the critical question to be decided as follows, [1992] BCC 987 at
p. 994E:

> ". . . whether the director [of the Serious Fraud Office] should be entitled to
> adduce them [the answers given by Mr Naviede in an examination under sec. 236
> of the *Insolvency Act* 1986] in evidence otherwise than in the circumstances
> envisaged in sec. 2(8) of the 1987 Act."   C

The judge answered that question by ruling that the liquidators would only be allowed
to produce the transcripts of Mr Naviede's examination, conducted under sec. 236 of the
Insolvency Act 1986 to the Director of the Serious Fraud Office if the director undertook
to treat those transcripts as if they were in fact governed by the provisions of sec. 2(8) of
the *Criminal Justice Act* 1987. On this appeal, the question of law arises as to whether
the judge was entitled to exact such an undertaking.   D

A lawful notice under sec. 2(3)

On 15 September 1992 the Director of the Serious Fraud Office gave notice to the
liquidators to produce transcripts of the oral examination of Mr Naviede under sec. 236
of the *Insolvency Act* 1986. That notice was given pursuant to sec. 2(3) of the *Criminal
Justice Act* 1987. Section 2(3), so far as relevant, reads as follows:

> "The Director may by notice in writing require the person under investigation or   E
> any other person to produce at such place as may be specified in the notice and
> either forthwith or at such time as may be so specified, any specified documents
> which appear to the Director to relate to any matter relevant to the investigation
> or any documents of a specified description which appear to him so to relate . . ."

It is rightly conceded on behalf of Mr Naviede that the transcripts are "documents"
within the meaning of sec. 2(3): see *Re British & Commonwealth Holdings plc (No. 2)*   F
[1992] BCC 977 at p. 984G–H. It is also accepted that the director could reasonably have
taken the view that the transcripts relate to matters relevant to his investigation of the
affairs of Mr Naviede. Prima facie the notice given by the director to the liquidators
under sec. 2(3) was lawful.

Section 2(8): the context   G

The judge founded his decision on sec. 2(8) of the *Criminal Justice Act* 1987. This
provision refers to an examination by the director under sec. 2(2). It plainly does not
relate to a notice to produce documents under sec. 2(3). Section 2(8) reads as follows:

> "A statement by a person in response to a requirement imposed by virtue of this
> section may only be used in evidence against him—
>
> (a)   on a prosecution for an offence under subsection (14) below; or   H
>
> (b)   on a prosecution for some other offence where in giving evidence he makes
>   a statement inconsistent with it."

Section 2(14) makes it an offence for a person interviewed under sec. 2(2) knowingly
or recklessly to make a false statement. In the present case the judge exacted an
undertaking in the terms of sec. 2(8) as a precondition to allowing the release of

A   transcripts of an examination under sec. 236 of the *Insolvency Act* 1986, to which sec. 2(8) does not by its terms apply.

Mr Collings submits, on behalf of Mr Naviede, that the director is seeking to achieve indirectly a result which he cannot achieve directly if he exercised his power of questioning Mr Naviede under sec. 2(2) of the *Criminal Justice Act* 1987. Section 2(8) restricts the use of answers given in an examination under sec. 2(2) to two narrowly defined purposes,

B   namely (a) in a prosecution for knowingly or recklessly giving false evidence and (b) by way of rebuttal of inconsistent evidence under oath. Subject to these two exceptions answers given by a person in an examination under sec. 2(2) may not be used by the prosecution at a criminal trial. That is what sec. 2(8) says and it says no more. Mr Collings submits that the director is seeking to avoid the limitation of sec. 2(8) by calling for the production of the transcripts of Mr Naviede's examination under sec. 236 of the 1986 Act instead of conducting his own examination under sec. 2(2) of the 1987

C   Act. Mr Collings says that the director is using a "back door" method.

It is necessary to assess what this argument seeks to prove. It is always possible that a statutory power might be abused. If an abuse of power is established the exercise of the power is invalid: *Padfield v Minister of Agriculture, Fisheries and Food* [1968] AC 997. It may well be that restraint must be shown by the courts in reviewing the conduct of prosecuting authorities since the criminal justice system ought to provide its own protections. Nevertheless, if in the present case the power under sec. 2(3) had in truth

D   been abused by the director, the notice under sec. 2(3) would be invalid. There is, however, no suggestion of an abuse of power in this case. Mr Collings concedes that. My provisional conclusion is therefore confirmed: the notice served under sec. 2(3) was lawful.

What then is the relevance of the argument that the director is trying to achieve indirectly what, in law, is forbidden under sec. 2(8)? The argument appears to be that it

E   is a strange and unfair result that the director should be able, by the use of his powers under sec. 2(3) to call for transcripts of Mr Naviede's interviews to achieve what the director cannot achieve by his own examination under sec. 2(2), viz. the right to adduce in evidence Mr Naviede's admissions as part of the prosecution case. The argument suggests that the court ought not to countenance such a result unless it is unavoidable. In my view there is nothing strange or unfair about the result. A common feature of examinations under sec. 2(2) of the 1987 Act and under sec. 236 of the 1986 Act is that

F   the common law privilege against self-incrimination is excluded: see *Re Bishopsgate Investment Management Ltd* [1992] BCC 222 and *R v Director of Serious Fraud Office, ex parte Smith* [1993] AC 1. Procedurally, however, there is a material distinction. The power entrusted to the director, or his duly authorised subordinate, to question a person suspected of committing serious or complex fraud under sec. 2(2) is in truth akin to the general power of the police to question suspects. In modern times our law has been

G   vigilant to protect subjects from abuses of police power. The procedural safeguards of the *Police and Criminal Evidence Act* 1984, and its codes, which generally serve to protect the interests of a suspect, do not extend to a person questioned under sec. 2(2). Moreover, a suspect questioned under sec. 2(2) does not have the privilege against self-incrimination. In the light of these curtailments of a suspect's ordinary rights, it is not altogether surprising that Parliament considered that the statement of a person questioned under sec. 2(2) ought not be led in evidence against him. The explanation of the restraint

H   under sec. 2(8) lies in the fact that Parliament considered that in view of the differential treatment of persons suspected of committing serious or complex fraud, there must be a compensating safeguard, viz. that the evidence of the interview under sec. 2(2) may not be led by the prosecution. It is a curb on a police power. On the other hand, an examination under sec. 236 takes place by an examiner appointed by the court and responsible to the High Court. In the present case, the examiner was a judge. In all cases

the examiner is a permanent or part-time judge who functions subject to the control of
the High Court. The reason for the safeguard contained in sec. 2(8) is absent. This
distinction does not by itself provide the answers to the critical questions in this case, but
it does go some way towards explaining why there would be nothing inherently
incongruous if the restriction under sec. 2(8) only applies in the circumstances defined
in sec. 2 of the *Criminal Justice Act* 1987, and not to admissions made in examinations
under other statutory regimes.

When Parliament created the Serious Fraud Office system in 1987, it did so against
the background that parallel examinations may take place under a number of statutes.
The following may be mentioned: sec. 431–437 and 447 of the *Companies Act* 1985;
sec. 41–44 of the *Banking Act* 1987; sec. 44 of the *Insurance Companies Act* 1982, and
sec. 94, 105 and 177–178 of the *Financial Services Act* 1986. The scheme of these
statutory provisions excludes the common law privilege against self-incrimination. See
Re London United Investments plc [1992] BCC 202 and *Bank of England v Riley* [1992]
Ch 475. It was self-evident that transcripts of all such examinations were potentially
within the scope of sec. 2(3). That important fact could not have been overlooked in the
drafting of sec. 2. Yet the procedural safeguard of section 2(8) was not made applicable
to such examinations. This seems a cogent indication that Parliament considered that it
was not necessary to extend the safeguard enshrined in sec. 2(8) beyond the limits of sec.
2(2). And this reasoning applies equally to examinations under the *Insolvency Act* 1986,
namely examinations under sec. 235 (duty to co-operate with office holder), sec. 236
(inquiry into company's dealings), sec. 290 (public examination of bankrupt) and
sec. 366 (inquiry into bankrupt's dealings). Section 2(3) plainly covers answers given in
such examinations. Section 2(8) was not extended to such examinations. The matter
could again not have been overlooked. It seems to me that the omission to extend the
protection of sec. 2(8) to such cases is significant. The conclusion is inescapable; that the
safeguard of sec. 2(8) was not intended to apply beyond the territory expressly assigned
to it by Parliament.

Legal professional privilege

Given the fact that the notice under sec. 2(3) is lawful, it prima facie imposes a duty
on the liquidators to produce the transcripts to the director. There are two circumstances
in which a person will be excused from complying with lawful notices under sec. 2(2) and
(3) of the 1987 Act. The first is the case of legal professional privilege, which is expressly
preserved in sec. 2(9). Applying the principles laid down in *Waugh v British Railways
Board* [1980] AC 521 the judge ruled that it had not been shown that the dominant
purpose of the examination was for the purpose of preparing for litigation. The judge
observed that the privilege was that of the liquidators, who did not wish to raise it. The
judge added that he could not see any reason why he should direct the liquidators to
claim privilege. Mr Collings recognised his difficulties but formally challenged the
judge's ruling. I will try to match his economy of words on this particular point. The
judge is so obviously right on this point that it would serve no purpose to dignify what
was said on behalf of Mr Naviede with further analysis.

Public interest immunity

The second case, which might excuse a failure to comply with a valid notice under
sec. 2(2) and (3) is public interest immunity. It is not mentioned in the 1987 Act. But
there is no doubt about its potential applicability in criminal proceedings: see *R v
Governor of Brixton Prison, ex parte Osman* [1991] 1 WLR 281 at pp. 288-289. On
behalf of Mr Naviede reliance was placed on public interest immunity before the judge.
The judge ruled against Mr Naviede on this point. By way of a respondent's notice
Mr Collings now seeks to resurrect the point before us. It is important to identify

A precisely the aspect of public interest on which Mr Collings relies. He puts forward a "class" claim as opposed to a "contents" claim. Mr Collings relies on observations of *Millett* J in *Re Barlow Clowes (Gilt Managers) Ltd* [1991] BCC 608. *Millett* J explained why he took the view that there was an important public interest against disclosure of transcripts of voluntary interviews. In his view such disclosure would undermine the effectiveness of the liquidation. Mr Collings submits that if the transcripts are unconditionally released to the director, and used against Mr Naviede at the criminal

B trial, the public interest in a free flow of information between officers of a company in liquidation and the liquidators will be eroded. He argues that the effectiveness of sec. 235 and 236 of the *Insolvency Act* 1986 will be undermined.

In my judgment there are two clear answers to the submissions made on behalf of Mr Naviede. The first is a procedural point but, nevertheless, a matter of the first importance. It is well-established that a civil court has no power to decide what evidence

C will be admissible at a criminal trial: see *Rank Film Distributors Ltd v Video Information Centre* [1982] AC 380 at p. 442G per Lord *Wilberforce* and p. 446E per Lord *Fraser of Tullybelton*. A civil court should not directly or indirectly impose restrictions on the use of evidence by prosecuting authorities without their consent: see *AT & T Istel v Tully* [1993] AC 45. Similarly, the question whether public interest immunity would attach to the transcripts of Mr Naviede's examinations under sec. 236, if the director wishes to tender them in evidence at the criminal trial, is a matter exclusively for the judgment of

D the trial judge. On this simple basis I would rule that, as a matter of legal principle, we ought not to entertain the submission based on public interest immunity at all.

Secondly, and on substantive grounds, it is in my judgment clear that there is no public interest immunity which could preclude the prosecution from putting in evidence, subject to the trial judge's discretion under sec. 76 and 78 of the *Police and Criminal Evidence Act* 1984, admissions made by Mr Naviede during the course of his examination

E under sec. 236 of the *Insolvency Act* 1986. In my judgment the approach of *Millett* J in *Barlow Clowes* was too narrow. It is necessary to place the matter in context. There are a number of established categories of public interest immunity. The type of public interest invoked in the present case is based on an asserted public interest in protecting the free flow of information from officers of a company in liquidation to the liquidators. In criminal cases the closest analogy seems to be the immunity generally allowed in respect of informers (see *R v Hennessey* (1978) 68 Cr App R 419), information upon

F which a search warrant is based (see *R v Taylor*, The Times, 21 October 1986) and information about police surveillance sites (see *R v Rankine* [1986] QB 861). These are, however, cases where the law allows an immunity from disclosure of police sources, in the fight against crime, in respect of information or assistance voluntarily provided to the police. The present case is different. Under sec. 235 (which must be read with r. 7.20) and sec. 236 the officers of the company are obliged to answer questions. If they fail to do so, the sanctions of the law can be applied to them. The encouragement to co-

G operate is supplied not by an expectation of confidentiality, but by the compulsion of the law. In these circumstances an immunity is not needed to promote the effectiveness of examinations under sec. 235 and 236.

There is, however, another insurmountable obstacle in the way of introducing a public interest immunity in this corner of the law. The law does not act in vain. There can be no public interest in preserving confidentiality in information which can routinely and

H legitimately become available to law enforcement agencies. Official receivers and liquidators are obliged to report information about the commission of offences to prosecuting authorities: see sec. 218 and 219 of the *Insolvency Act* 1986. There is a corresponding duty under sec. 7 of the *Company Directors Disqualification Act* 1986. These statutory duties extend to information coming to the notice of official receivers and liquidators as a result of examinations under sec. 235 and 236. Section 433 of the

Insolvency Act 1986 renders transcripts of examinations under sec. 235 and 236 admissible in criminal and civil proceedings against the examinee. Moreover, sec. 3(3) of the 1987 Act overrides, subject to one immaterial exception, all obligations of secrecy imposed by statute. On examination the particular public interest, put forward on behalf of Mr Naviede, evaporates. Indeed, the *Insolvency Act* 1986 and the *Criminal Justice Act* 1987 reflect an overriding public interest in the free flow of information from official receivers and liquidators to prosecuting authorities about the commission of offences.

In my judgment the claim to public interest immunity fails.

Reasonable excuse

Given the fact that neither legal professional privilege, nor public interest immunity, can avail Mr Naviede, it follows that the liquidators were under a duty under the provisions of sec. 2(3) to produce the transcripts to the director. Section 2(13) provides a person with a defence to a criminal charge that he failed to comply with a notice under sec. 2(2) or (3) if he had a "reasonable excuse" for his failure. That means that an excusable inability to produce the transcripts (e.g. due to the physical inability or accidental loss or destruction of the transcripts) provides an answer to the criminal charge: see *Bank of England v Riley* [1992] Ch 475 at p. 482B. But sec. 2(13) is plainly not a peg on which one can hang a general discretionary power in a judge to relieve a person from criminal liability under sec. 2. It follows that under the provisions of the *Criminal Justice Act* 1987 the liquidators are in this case under an absolute duty to comply with the duty imposed upon them by sec. 2(3).

The discretion under the Insolvency Act 1986

The question is, what is the foundation of the discretion which the judge purported to exercise? On behalf of Mr Naviede, Mr Collings relies on the power of the High Court to give directions to liquidators. He relies on the express powers contained in sec. 168(3) of the *Insolvency Act* 1986, and on r. 9.5(4). He also relies on the inherent jurisdiction of the court to give directions to liquidators in their capacity as officers of the court. For my part I am willing to accept that the High Court has an extensive discretionary power to give directions to liquidators about the discharge of their statutory duties and functions.

Let me further assume that the order which the judge made was within his jurisdiction. On this supposition I would hold that if the judge was entitled to exact the relevant undertaking from the director, he must have had a discretionary power to impose a corresponding condition. Moreover, if he had a power to impose such a condition, it seems to follow that he had a discretion to refuse to release the transcripts to the director even if they contained most material information regarding the commission of offences by Mr Naviede. Mr Collings asserts that to be the position. The experienced counsel who appeared before us only knew of one case where a judge directed liquidators not to disclose information to prosecuting authorities. The case was apparently decided on rather special facts and cannot be regarded as enunciating any principle of law (see *FMS Financial Management Services v FMS Nominees Ltd*, unreported, 5 June 1987, per *Harman* J). This relative absence of authority is not surprising. Moreover, in practice official receivers and liquidators apparently do not seek the directions of the court when considering whether they should report to prosecuting authorities. That position also seems unremarkable.

If it is assumed that the judge's order was technically within his jurisdiction, it seems to me that there are a number of factors which militated against the order which the judge made. Official receivers and liquidators are obliged to report the commission of criminal offences by officers of the company to the prosecuting authorities: see sec. 218

A   and 219. In other words, apart from their primary function of getting in the company's property, liquidators are under a statutory duty to co-operate with prosecuting authorities. That duty entails providing the prosecuting authorities with evidence of the commission of offences, including offences disclosed by examinations under sec. 235 and 236. Section 433 expressly renders admissible in civil and criminal proceedings answers given in examinations under sec. 235 and 236. Having thus come into the public domain it would be idle to contend that the director must ignore the existence of such evidence.

B   Moreover, there are a number of other routes by which the transcripts might reach the Director of the Serious Fraud Office. Thus, the Secretary of State may require the liquidators, under sec. 7(4) of the *Company Directors Disqualification Act* 1986, to furnish him with copies of transcripts of examinations in order to enable him to decide whether to exercise his powers under sec. 7. In that way the transcripts could come into the public domain. But even before that happens, the Secretary of State would be fully entitled to send the transcripts to the Director of the Serious Fraud Office. Another

C   route is for the official receiver to call for the transcripts and then to pass them on to the Director of the Serious Fraud Office. Cumulatively, these factors made it inappropriate for the judge to exact the undertaking modelled on sec. 2(8).

The critical factor in the judge's reasoning was his desire to ensure that a potential defendant should receive a fair criminal trial. The judge relied on his discretionary power to give directions to liquidators. But it is important to bear in mind that the

D   undertaking, which the judge required from the director, is not referable to any legal duty of the director or legal right of Mr Naviede. The judge used his power to give directions to liquidators in order to supplement the protections given to the subject by the criminal justice system by extending sec. 2(8) beyond its field of operation as defined by Parliament. The judge's decision is in disharmony with the settled rule that a civil court ought not to place restrictions on the use by prosecuting authorities of evidence without their consent (see *Rank Film Distribution Ltd v Video Information Centre* and

E   *AT & T Istel v Tully*). And Mr Collings accepts that the judge would not have been entitled to impose a condition providing that evidence of the transcripts would be inadmissible at a criminal trial: sec. 433 of the *Insolvency Act* 1986. But the judge achieved that end obliquely by exacting an undertaking along the lines of the inapplicable sec. 2(8). The judge's decision wrongly intruded into an area which is best left to the existing protections offered by the criminal justice system. He exercised his discretion

F   for an impermissible purpose: pro tanto he restored the privilege against self-incrimination which the legislature took away by the terms of the *Insolvency Act* 1986. The judge did not have the benefit of the full argument which was placed before us on this appeal. In the result the judge misdirected himself in material respects. In my view the judge ought to have allowed the transcripts to be released to the director without requiring any undertaking.

G   **Jurisdiction**

That brings me to the question of whether the judge had any jurisdiction to exact the relevant undertaking. For this purpose I will assume that under sec. 168(3) of the *Insolvency Act* 1986, under r. 9.5(4), or by virtue of the court's inherent jurisdiction, the court had a discretion to exact the undertaking in question. The *Criminal Justice Act* 1987 was a response to widespread public perception that the existing criminal justice system was inadequate to deal with the problem of rampant serious and complex fraud.

H   It was a special statute designed to deal with special problems affecting one particular class of crime. It did so by entrusting to the Director of the Serious Fraud Office extensive new inquisitorial powers. In *R v Director of the Serious Fraud Office, ex parte Smith* [1993] AC 1, Lord *Mustill* said (at pp. 43–44):

"... I conclude that as a matter of interpretation the powers of the Director do not cease, as regards the questioning of the person under investigation, when he is charged; that the principle of common sense, expressed in the maxim generalia specialibus non derogant, entails that the general provisions of the Code yield to the particular provisions of the Act of 1987 in cases to which that Act applies; and that neither history nor logic demands that any qualification of what Parliament has so clearly enacted ought to be implied."

In the same way as the special provisions of the 1987 Act override the general provisions of the *Police and Criminal Evidence Act* 1984 and the codes, they also override the general provisions of another earlier general statute — the *Insolvency Act* 1986. If the court has a discretion over transcripts of examinations under any of the sections of the *Insolvency Act* 1986, which is wide enough to prevent the release of transcripts to the Serious Fraud Office, or to allow release of transcript only subject to conditions and undertakings, then in my judgment that discretion is to that extent overridden by the clear terms and manifest intent of the 1987 Act. For these further reasons I would hold that the judge was bound to allow the unconditional release of the transcripts to the Serious Fraud Office in response to the lawful notice under sec. 2(3).

Conclusion

The consequence of this decision seems to me entirely satisfactory. The director will be able to produce, subject to the trial judge's ruling under sec. 78 of the *Police and Criminal Evidence Act* 1984, the transcripts of interviews of a defendant under sec. 235 and 236 of the Insolvency Act. That will enable the contextual scene — such as the hierarchy of companies, the role of individuals, the flow of funds, and like matters — to be placed before the jury far more efficiently than has hitherto been regarded as possible. It should help to narrow the issue. It should mean that the prosecution will not be faced at the trial with a constantly moving target. It should significantly improve the chances of the Serious Fraud Office functioning more efficiently. And it should assist in reducing the extravagant length of some serious fraud trials.

I would also allow the appeal.

Rose LJ: I agree with both previous judgments. I add a few words solely because we are differing from the judge below.

In my judgment the power conferred on the Director of the Serious Fraud Office by sec. 2(3) of the *Criminal Justice Act* 1987 is clear. The subsection states in terms that he can require any person to produce any specified documents which appear to be relevant to his investigation under sec. 1(3) of any suspected offence involving serious or complex fraud. Failure, without reasonable excuse, to comply with such a requirement is a summary offence (sec. 2(13)).

It seems to me that Parliament plainly intended, when conferring this power on the Director of the Serious Fraud Office which the Act created, that it would be a power in addition to those already vested in prosecuting authorities by virtue of the *Insolvency Act* 1986, or otherwise.

The limitation imposed by sec. 2(8) on the evidential use of statements made to the director in response to questions under sec. 2(2) is in my judgment not in point.

Such questioning is akin to that by police officers and it is therefore not surprising that Parliament, having granted wide powers of questioning under sec. 2(2), should to some extent limit the use of answers given. But there is, as it seems to me, no warrant for construing sec. 2(8) as imposing a similar limitation on the use of documents obtained under sec. 2(3). If this had been Parliament's intention, sec. 2(8) could have been readily so drafted by inserting after the words "a statement", the words "or document produced".

So far as the Insolvency Act is concerned, sec. 433 provides that any statement made in pursuance of a requirement imposed by the Act or, rules made under it, may be used

A   in evidence against the maker in any proceedings. Rule 9.4(7) of the Insolvency Rules contains a like provision in relation to the written record of an examination under sec. 236. By sec. 218 material appearing in the course of winding up can be passed by office-holders to the Crown Prosecution Service and by sec. 219(2) answers given in a winding up may be used in evidence.

B   Accordingly, it seems to me to be impossible to contend that that Act can be read either as limiting the terms of the subsequently passed Criminal Justice Act, or as providing any basis for the existence of a discretion in applying that later Act. The court of course has a discretion as to the directions which it gives to office-holders on their application. But that discretion does not extend to giving a direction that a criminal offence shall be committed. Nor should a direction be capable of amounting to a reasonable excuse for failing to comply with a sec. 2(3) notice.

C   It follows that the judge had no jurisdiction to require the undertakings given in the present case.

This conclusion is in accordance with the principle, well-established by authority, that it is inappropriate for a civil court to seek to interfere with the admissibility of evidence in a criminal trial (see *Rank Film Distributors Ltd v Video Information Centre* [1982] AC 380 at p. 442F per Lord *Wilberforce*, and at p. 446E per Lord *Fraser of Tullybelton*).

D   Such admissibility, subject to appeal to the Court of Appeal Criminal Division, is, first and last, the responsibility of the trial judge acting, in particular, in the light of sec. 78 of the *Police and Criminal Evidence Act* 1984.

I, too, would allow this appeal.

(*Appeal allowed. Director of SFO released from undertakings. Leave to appeal to House of Lords refused*)

E   ———————————

F

G

H

Re Adviser (188) Ltd & Bishopsgate Investment Management Ltd, ex parte Trachtenberg.

Court of Appeal (Civil Division).
Dillon, Steyn and Rose L JJ.
Judgment delivered 7 April 1993.

Insolvency — Private examination — Whether Serious Fraud Office entitled to transcripts of private examination after examinee had been charged with criminal offence — Insolvency Act 1986, sec. 236; Criminal Justice Act 1987, sec. 2.

This was an application by "T" for leave to appeal against an order of Vinelott J relating to the right of the Serious Fraud Office to require the production under sec. 2 of the Criminal Justice Act 1987 by office-holders of the transcripts of private examinations conducted under sec. 236 of the Insolvency Act 1986.

T was a director of two companies with which the late Robert Maxwell was concerned. After the death of Robert Maxwell one of the companies went into administrative receivership, the other went into compulsory liquidation. The office-holders — the receivers and liquidators — examined T under sec. 236 in relation to the respective affairs of the two companies. Later T was arrested and charged with four charges of theft and two of conspiracy to defraud. T was then served by the Serious Fraud Office with a notice under sec. 2 of the 1987 Act requiring him to answer questions and supply information. T refused to comply with that notice, claiming that he had a "reasonable excuse" under sec. 2(13) for his refusal in that he had been charged with criminal offences and had the right not to disclose his defence. T was prosecuted in the magistrates' court under sec. 2(13); his plea of "reasonable excuse" was upheld and the charge dismissed.

In the meantime, the Serious Fraud Office served notices under sec. 2(3) on the office-holders of the two companies requiring them to produce the transcripts of T's examinations under sec. 236. T argued that he had a "reasonable excuse" for not answering the questions of the Serious Fraud Office because he had already been charged, and that because of that the Serious Fraud Office had no right to get, or if it was a matter of discretion should not be allowed by the court to get, the information they wanted from him by a side-wind by getting the transcripts of his examinations from the office-holders.

Held, dismissing T's application for leave to appeal:

1. The investigative powers of the Director of the Serious Fraud Office under sec. 2 did not cease after a charge was laid. (R v Director of the Serious Fraud Office, ex parte Smith [1993] AC 1 applied.)

2. Likewise, the fact that a charge had been laid did not create a defence of reasonable excuse under sec. 2(13).

3. In any event the examinations of T took place before he was charged. The office-holders were not prevented from handing over material which came into their hands before charges were preferred and accordingly at a time when no excuse would have been available to T under sec. 2(13).

The following cases were referred to in the judgments:

Arrows Ltd, Re (No. 4) [1993] BCC 473; [1993] Ch 452.
Bank of England v Riley & Anor [1992] Ch 475.
Bishopsgate Investment Management Ltd, Re [1992] BCC 222; [1993] Ch 1.
London United Investments plc, Re [1992] BCC 202; [1992] Ch 578.
Pepper (HMIT) v Hart and related appeals [1992] BTC 591; [1993] AC 593.
R v Director of the Serious Fraud Office, ex parte Smith [1993] AC 1.
Rank Film Distributors Ltd & Ors v Video Information Centre & Ors [1982] AC 380.

A   Michael Hill QC, Peter James Richardson and Stephen Moverley Smith (instructed by Russell Jones & Walker) for Mr Trachtenberg.

Mary Arden QC and Kate Thirlwall (instructed by the Serious Fraud Office) for the Serious Fraud Office.

AWH Charles (instructed by the Treasury Solicitor) for the Secretary of State for Trade and Industry.

B

JUDGMENT

Dillon LJ: On 26 March 1993 the court dismissed, for reasons to be given later, an application by Mr Trachtenberg for leave to appeal against an order of *Vinelott* J of 10 February 1993, leave having been refused by the judge. We now give our reasons for refusing the application.

C   Mr Trachtenberg's application raised issues as to the right of the Serious Fraud Office to require the production under sec. 2 of the *Criminal Justice Act* 1987 ("the 1987 Act") by office-holders of the transcripts of private examinations conducted under sec. 236 of the *Insolvency Act* 1986. For that reason the application was adjourned to be heard by the full court immediately after the hearing of the appeal of the Director of the Serious Fraud Office in *Re Arrows Ltd (No. 4)* [1993] BCC 473, which raised other issues on the interplay of sec. 2 and sec. 236 and with a direction that Mr Trachtenberg's appeal be

D   heard immediately after the hearing of the application if leave to appeal were granted.

In the event we took time to put our judgments on the *Arrows (No. 4)* appeal into writing and they have just been handed down. For practical purposes my present judgment on Mr Trachtenberg's application is a footnote to the *Arrows (No. 4)* judgments, and so I do not intend to set out again in full in this judgment the statutory provisions which I set out in the *Arrows (No. 4)* judgment.

E   Mr Trachtenberg had nothing to do with Arrows Ltd, but he was a director of two companies with which the late Robert Maxwell had been concerned. After the death of Robert Maxwell joint administrative receivers were appointed of one of these two companies, and the other went into compulsory liquidation.

The office-holders — the receivers and liquidators — obtained orders for the private examination of Mr Trachtenberg under sec. 236 in relation to the respective affairs of

F   the two companies, and the examinations duly took place over a number of days in February and March 1992.

On 18 June 1992 Mr Trachtenberg was arrested and charged with four charges of theft and two of conspiracy to defraud. No notice of transfer to the Crown Court has yet been given in relation to those charges.

Before his arrest he had not been questioned at all by the Serious Fraud Office, which

G   had from November 1991 been conducting an investigation into the affairs of Robert Maxwell and of many of the companies with which he had been concerned. On 29 June 1992, however, Mr Trachtenberg was served by the Serious Fraud Office with a notice under sec. 2 of the 1987 Act requiring him to answer questions and supply information.

Mr Trachtenberg refused to comply with that notice (save for giving bare personal details), claiming that he had a "reasonable excuse" within the meaning of subsec. (13)

H   of sec. 2 for his refusal in that he had been charged with criminal offences and had the right not to disclose his defence, at any rate until a very much later stage after he has received the full prosecution case statement under sec. 9 of the 1987 Act.

The consequence of that refusal was that Mr Trachtenberg was prosecuted by the Serious Fraud Office in the Clerkenwell Magistrates' Court under subsec. 2(13) of the 1987 Act. But the outcome of that — so far — has been that after a prolonged hearing

the magistrate, by a reserved judgment on 9 February 1992, upheld Mr Trachtenberg's   A
plea of "reasonable excuse" and dismissed the charge. We are told that the Serious
Fraud Office proposes to take steps, by appeal or judicial review, to quash the magistrate's
decision, but that has not yet happened.

In the meantime, in December 1992 and January 1993 the Serious Fraud Office served
notices under sec. 2(3) on the office-holders of the two companies requiring them to
produce the transcripts of Mr Trachtenberg's examinations under sec. 236.
   B

The essence of Mr Trachtenberg's point is that he claims to have a "reasonable
excuse" for not answering the questions of the Serious Fraud Office, because he has
already been charged and he says, by his counsel Mr Michael Hill QC, that because of
that the Serious Fraud Office has no right to get, or if it is a matter of discretion should
not be allowed by the court to get the information they want from him by a side-wind by
getting the transcripts of his examinations from the office-holders. The essence of the   C
case is that, as he has been charged, and he cannot be compelled to disclose his defence
at this stage, he cannot be compelled to answer questions or supply information if he
does not want to.

That faces, as Mr Hill recognises, the rather formidable obstacle that in *R v Director
of the Serious Fraud Office, ex parte Smith* [1993] AC 1 the House of Lords has held the
precise opposite, viz. that the powers of the Director of the Serious Fraud Office do not
come to an end when the person under investigation has been charged and the director   D
is accordingly entitled to compel that person to answer questions even after he has been
charged. But Mr Hill submits that the decision of the House of Lords is wrong, and
should be reconsidered and not followed, for either or both of two reasons:

(1)   the decision was given per incuriam without a proper analysis of the 1987 Act and
        therefore without appreciating that the scheme of the Act provides for two stages,
        an investigation stage, including sec. 2, which applies until the person under   E
        investigation has been charged, and a prosecution stage which takes over when
        the person has been charged; and

(2)   alternatively, on the basis of *Pepper v Hart* [1992] BTC 591, the intention of
        Parliament as shown by the speech of the minister in charge of the bill in the
        House of Lords, the Earl of Caithness, was that the person being examined under
        sec. 2 would be at most "a suspect" — meaning, it is said, a person who has not
        been charged — and might of course be a mere witness who was under no suspicion   F
        at all.

Mr Hill recognises that the decision of the House of Lords in *ex parte Smith* is binding
on the civil Court of Appeal and reconsideration of *ex parte Smith* on either of his
suggested grounds is a matter for the House of Lords. He therefore submits that justice
requires that Mr Trachtenberg be given leave to appeal against the decision of *Vinelott*
J, in order that he may have the opportunity of applying for leave to appeal to the House   G
of Lords so as to be able to persuade the House to reconsider its own decision in *ex parte
Smith*.

I do not for my part see much force in these submissions of Mr Hill, but I find it wholly
unnecessary to express a view because the real point in this case is different. The
examinations of Mr Trachtenberg took place before he was charged. It is one thing to
say that a person cannot be compelled to answer further questions after he has been   H
charged; it is quite a different thing to say that further evidence against him cannot be
obtained from third parties after he has been charged in respect of matters which
happened before he was charged.

It has never been the law that in a criminal case the prosecution have to go to trial on
such evidence only as they had when the defendant was arrested and charges were first

A
preferred against him. Under the *Criminal Justice Act 1987 (Notice of Transfer) Regulations* 1988 (SI 1988/1691) a notice of transfer to the Crown Court has to be accompanied by a statement of the evidence on which any charge to which the notice of transfer relates is based, but there is nothing to limit that evidence to evidence obtained by the prosecution before the person concerned was arrested. It could be evidence, for instance, of admissions by the accused contained in a letter of the accused to a third party, and obtained by the Serious Fraud Office from the third party, after the accused

B
had been charged, either because the third party voluntarily handed it over or as a result of an examination of the third party under sec. 236. It matters not that the examinations in the present case under sec. 236 were examinations of Mr Trachtenberg himself, since there is clear statutory provision in sec. 433 of the *Insolvency Act* 1986 making his answers under examination admissible as evidence against him in criminal proceedings.

C
Mr Hill accepts that if the Serious Fraud Office had applied to the office-holders for the transcripts before Mr Trachtenberg was arrested and charged, the points he now takes would have provided no answer to the Serious Fraud Office claim to have the documents. There is nothing, in my judgment, to make the position different now that Mr Trachtenberg has been charged.

Vinelott J set out in his judgment all the arguments which Mr Richardson had put forward for saying that Mr Trachtenberg had a "reasonable excuse" for not answering

D
questions put to him by the Serious Fraud Office after he had been charged; these are substantially the same as Mr Hill has put to us. *Vinelott* J then concluded that even if those arguments proved right:

> "it does not, as I see it, follow that the liquidator should be prevented from handing over material which came into his hands before charges were preferred and, accordingly, at a time when admittedly no excuse would have been available to Mr Trachtenberg under subsec. (13)."

E
I respectfully agree. I see no arguable case for reversing that conclusion of the learned judge, and therefore there is no basis for granting leave to appeal.

Steyn LJ: I agree. In my judgment none of the arguments advanced on behalf of Mr Trachtenberg on this application for leave to appeal passes the threshold test of arguability. I can deal relatively briefly with the main submissions advanced by Mr Hill QC on behalf of Mr Trachtenberg.

F
(1) Invalidity of sec. 2(3) notice

In June 1992 Mr Trachtenberg was charged with four offences of theft. By a subsequent notice given under sec. 2(3) of the *Criminal Justice Act* 1987, the Director of the Serious Fraud Office sought production by the liquidators of inter alia transcripts of the examination of Mr Trachtenberg under sec. 236 of the *Insolvency Act* 1986. Subject to

G
certain undertakings, the judge ordered the liquidators to deliver the transcripts to the Director of the Serious Fraud Office. On this application Mr Hill submits that after Mr Trachtenberg was charged the director was no longer in law entitled to serve a notice on the liquidators to produce transcripts of Mr Trachtenberg's interviews. Mr Hill argues that this follows from the structure of the *Criminal Justice Act* 1987, and he relies in particular on sec. 9, which makes clear that at the preparatory hearing the judge may order a defence statement to be produced, but only after the prosecution has produced

H
a prosecution case statement. He argues that a study of the Act reveals a distinction between investigative powers, such as those contained in sec. 2, and accusatorial powers, which commence after the charge is laid. And he says that under the Act the investigative powers cease upon the laying of a charge. The contrary is established by binding authority: *R v Director of Serious Fraud Office, ex parte Smith* [1993] AC 1. Lord *Mustill* carefully explained why the director's compulsory powers under sec. 2(2) and

2(3) continue after a charge is laid at pp. 39–40. Mr Hill argues that the House of Lords,   A
assisted by the able counsel who argued the appeal in *Smith*, overlooked a fundamental
distinction between investigative and accusatorial powers under the Act. In my respectful
view, the House of Lords overlooked nothing of the kind. Under the 1987 Act,
investigative and accusatorial powers can be exercised at the same time. This is clear
from the language of the Act, and the nature and width of the inquisitorial powers
conferred on the director. It was so held by the House of Lords in *Smith*. None of the
passages in the literature, or in the *Fraud Trials Committee Report* to which we have   B
been referred, have any direct bearing on the scheme of the *Criminal Justice Act* 1987,
as it subsequently evolved. Relying on *Pepper v Hart* [1992] BTC 591, Mr Hill referred
us to a number of passages in *Hansard*. The truth is that there is no ambiguity, obscurity
or absurdity warranting a resort to *Hansard*. In any event, the deployment of
parliamentary materials proved to be a damp squib. There is nothing in any of the
passages which supported the submission that any assurance was given on behalf of the
Government that after a charge was laid the director's powers under sec. 2 would cease.   C
In deference to submissions of most experienced leading counsel, I have said more than
is necessary. The point is hopeless.

(2) Section 2(13): reasonable excuse

Mr Hill also submits that even if a valid notice under sec. 2(3) may be served after a
charge is laid, it does not mean that the person to whom the notice is addressed must
respond. Mr Hill points to sec. 2(13), which provides that any person who, without   D
reasonable excuse, fails to comply with a requirement imposed upon him under sec. 2(2)
and (3) is guilty of an offence. He submits that after a charge has been laid the person to
whom a notice is addressed will always have a reasonable excuse if he fails to respond.
This submission applies equally to a notice directed to a defendant under sec. 2(2) and a
notice addressed to third parties under sec. 2(3) to produce documents, e.g. the books
of account of the company. The same issue recently arose in criminal proceedings which
followed after Mr Trachtenberg was charged with a failure to respond to a sec. 2(2)   E
notice. The hearing lasted an astonishing eight days. In a judgment dated 9 February
1993, Mr Christopher Bourke, a stipendiary magistrate, adopted the interpretation
urged on us by Mr Hill. That decision is now subject to judicial review proceedings.
Obviously it would be better if we could avoid expressing a view on the matter in advance
of the judicial review proceedings. Mr Hill tries to have it both ways. He asks us to adopt
his interpretation. But, if we are minded to disagree, he asks us not to say anything   F
contrary to what had been held by Mr Bourke in a court of competent jurisdiction. I fear
that will not do. The issues canvassed before us compel us to deal with the point. Mr Hill
acknowledges that his submission is in conflict with passages in the speech of Lord
Mustill. He submits that the House of Lords overlooked the true scope of the defence of
reasonable excuse. Here he cannot pray in aid literature or *Hansard*. The intent of
Parliament must be found in the words of the Act. The scheme of the Act, as interpreted
in *Smith* destroys Mr Hill's submission. The suggested interpretation emasculates the   G
extensive inquisitorial powers entrusted to the director by Parliament. By a side-wind it
reverses the manifest intent of the legislature to abolish the privilege against self-
incrimination and to permit the extensive compulsory powers of investigation to continue
after a charge is laid. In the context of sec. 2(3) reasonable excuse is plainly a defence
intended to cover particular circumstances such as physical inability to comply with the
notice or accidental loss or destruction of the transcripts and the like. The fact that a   H
charge has been laid does not create a defence under sec. 2(13). In my view the contrary
is unarguable.

(3) Public interest immunity

Mr Hill submits that the transcripts of Mr Trachtenberg's interviews are protected
from disclosure by public interest immunity. He relies on arguments which I have

A   already discussed in my judgment in the *Arrows (No. 4)* appeal, which was handed down today. For the reasons given in that judgment, I am of the opinion that there is no public interest immunity which can assist Mr Trachtenberg in this case.

But Mr Hill submits that after a charge has been laid the public interest in a fair criminal justice system requires that "nothing sourced from Mr Trachtenberg" — by which I understand Mr Hill to mean transcripts of interviews with Mr Trachtenberg and documents produced by him under sec. 236 — ought to be produced to the Director of

B   the Serious Fraud Office. This is the argument which I have already discussed under another guise, viz. that upon the laying of a charge a shutter comes down which prevents further investigation under sec. 2(2) and (3) in order to obtain materials emanating from the defendant. In neither form can the argument be squared with the extensive inquisitorial powers which the Act created. In my judgment there is no substance in this argument.

C

(4) Miscellaneous points

In oral argument a number of other arguments were deployed. Mr Hill submits that the director is setting out to achieve, by the use of a sec. 2(3) notice, what he cannot achieve by his own examination under sec. 2(2). He calls it a "back door" method. This is a point which I dealt with in my judgment in *Arrows (No. 4)* and I will not repeat what

D   I said there. Mr Hill says that the director has taken a tactical decision to delay the transfer of the case to the Crown Court thereby depriving the defence of the benefit of rights under the Act. He says it is an abuse of power. Mr Hill is not using the phrase in its administrative law sense. He is not submitting that the director has acted unlawfully. In any event, on the materials before the court, an arguable case of unlawfulness has not been made out.

E   I would also dismiss this application.

Rose LJ: I agree. Counsel for the applicant submits that as Mr Bourke, Metropolitan Stipendiary Magistrate, has held that Mr Trachtenberg has a reasonable excuse under sec. 2(13) for not answering questions put in an interview under sec. 2(2) of the *Criminal Justice Act* 1987, he would have a reasonable excuse for not producing transcripts of interviews under sec. 236 of the *Insolvency Act* 1986. Accordingly, it is said to be arguable that the Director of the Serious Fraud Office should not, by means of a

F   sec. 2(3) notice, be able to obtain from office-holders material which he could not obtain directly from Mr Trachtenberg. It seems to me that this submission is flawed both in its reliance on the stipendiary's decision, and in its analysis of Mr Trachtenberg's position.

Section 433 of the Insolvency Act has the effect that statements made in a sec. 236 inquiry may be used in evidence against the maker in any proceedings. It follows that, at the time of the inquiry, Mr Trachtenberg was at risk, under that Act, of his answers

G   being used in evidence against him, despite the involuntary nature of the inquiry. This, as it seems to me, and as this court held in *Re Bishopsgate Investment Management Ltd* [1992] BCC 222, is a statutory breach of the common law privilege against self-incrimination. Furthermore, by sec. 218 of the Insolvency Act, material can be passed to the Crown Prosecution Service by office-holders. It is accepted by counsel for Mr Trachtenberg that material is and can properly be passed between the Crown Prosecution Service and the Serious Fraud Office.

H   In *R v Director of Serious Fraud Office, ex parte Smith* [1993] AC 1, the House of Lords held that, after a defendant had been charged, a sec. 2(2) notice compelling him to answer questions on pain of committing a criminal offence under sec. 2(13) can properly be served. The subsection abrogates the common law privilege against self-incrimination even after charging: a fortiori it does so when, as in Mr Trachtenberg's case, he was questioned under sec. 236 before he was charged.

In my judgment the inescapable conclusion is that, under both statutes, there is power to compel a person to answer questions whether or not he has been charged with a criminal offence. Although the 1987 Act deals separately with the director's investigative and prosecuting roles, I am wholly unpersuaded that this in any way limits the wide investigative powers conferred by sec. 2(2) and sec. 2(3) or renders material, for present purposes, either the timing of a sec. 2(3) notice or the director's reason for issuing it. The provisions of sec. 9, which empower a Crown Court judge after the special transfer procedure has taken place, to require case statements, albeit in different detail, from prosecution and defence, do not, as it seems to me, inhibit the director's very wide investigative powers.

Furthermore, the fact that, for the purposes of trial, a defence statement of case cannot be required prior to the prosecution statement of case, does not prevent questions being asked at an earlier stage under sec. 2(2), the answers to which may reveal the nature of the defence. I do not share the stipendiary's view as to the limited effect of the House of Lords decision in *ex parte Smith*. He concluded that it shed no light on "reasonable excuse" under sec. 2(13). But Lord *Mustill* not only concluded that the director's powers of investigation survive the moment of charge, he also said that "the whole purpose of sec. 2 is to ensure that" answers given are not voluntary (see p. 43C). This, as it seems to me, not only disposes of any requirement for a caution in relation to sec. 2(2) questioning, but also negates any possibility that a refusal to answer on the grounds of self-incrimination can be regarded as a reasonable excuse in the terms of sec. 2(13). If it were a reasonable excuse, it would defeat the whole purpose of sec. 2(2). (See also *Bank of England v Riley* [1992] Ch 475, *Arrows (No. 4)*, and *Re London United Investments plc* [1992] BCC 202). The suggestion that such an interpretation reverses the burden of proof is, in my view, misconceived. Whether a suspected person chooses (1) to answer questions and, thereby, either to incriminate or exculpate himself, or (2) not to answer, thereby falling foul of sec. 2(13), the burden of proof at any subsequent trial remains in each case on the prosecution. But sec. 2(2) is, as it seems to me, clearly designed to assist the director in discharging that burden. The question of what use can thereafter at a criminal trial be made of such answers as are given is, as it seems to me, a matter not for a judge of the Chancery Division by way of anticipatory strike (see *Rank Film Distributors Ltd v Video Information Centre* [1982] AC 380 at pp. 442F and 446E), but for the judge at trial, having regard to sec. 2(8) of the Criminal Justice Act, sec. 76 and 78 of the *Police and Criminal Evidence Act* 1984, and such other considerations as are then pertinent.

In any event, even if the stipendiary magistrate's construction of sec. 2(13) is correct, that subsection is relevant only to questioning under sec. 2(2). It does not bear on sec. 2(3). (See the reasons given in *Arrows (No. 4)*). Indeed, counsel for Mr Trachtenberg accepted that the section draws a distinction between questioning and documents, and that if the sec. 236 transcripts had been obtained by the Serious Fraud Office before Mr Trachtenberg was charged, they would be admissible.

I am equally unpersuaded that resort to *Hansard* to construe sec. 2 is justified under *Pepper v Hart* [1992] BTC 591. I see no ambiguity, obscurity or absurdity to justify that course. In any event, this court having been referred to *Hansard* de bene esse it is, to my mind, clear that nothing there appears which could conceivably persuade the House of Lords to construe the section differently from the way in which it was construed by Lord *Mustill* in *ex parte Smith*.

For the reasons already given in *Arrows (No. 4)*, the office-holders must comply with a sec. 2(3) notice, without the imposition of any undertakings by the Serious Fraud

A   Office. As it is not, for the reasons given, arguable that Mr Trachtenberg is in any better position than the office-holders, the argument set out at the beginning of the judgment in my view fails.

I, too, would dismiss this application for leave to appeal.

(*Application for leave to appeal dismissed*)

B

C

D

E

F

G

H

Re Headington Investments Ltd & Ors, ex parte Maxwell.

A

Court of Appeal (Civil Division).
Dillon, Steyn and Rose L JJ.
Judgment delivered 7 April 1993.

Insolvency — Private examination — Whether office-holders should disclose transcripts of private examinations to defendant as well as to Serious Fraud Office — Insolvency Act 1986, sec. 236; Criminal Justice Act 1987, sec. 2.

B

This was an application by Kevin Maxwell ("KM") for leave to appeal against an order of Vinelott J relating to the disclosure by office-holders of the transcripts of private examinations conducted under sec. 236 of the Insolvency Act 1986, to the Serious Fraud Office pursuant to a request under sec. 2 of the Criminal Justice Act 1987.

KM was a director of various companies which had, since the death of Robert Maxwell, gone into liquidation or receivership. He had been examined by the various office-holders under sec. 235 or 236 of the Insolvency Act. He was later charged with theft and fraudulent conspiracy in relation to the companies. Thereafter he had several further interviews with office-holders and he was also examined on several occasions by the Serious Fraud Office under sec. 2 of the 1987 Act.

C

The Director of the Serious Fraud Office had subsequently called on the office-holders to produce to the Serious Fraud Office all transcripts of interviews conducted by them or on their behalf under either sec. 235 or sec. 236 of the Insolvency Act or on a voluntary basis or equivalent principles, with KM and a large number of other people (not limited to those who faced charges) together with copies of all documents or other material supplied to the office-holders by those persons including affidavits and witness statements.

D

KM asked that the office-holders should be ordered to disclose simultaneously to him and his advisers copies of all the transcripts and other documents which they disclosed to the Serious Fraud Office. He accepted that there was no statutory basis for such simultaneous disclosure but submitted that if it was not ordered he would suffer prejudice in the conduct of his defence.

E

Held, dismissing KM's application:

1. Such, if any, material in the interviews as the prosecution wished to rely on in criminal proceedings, together with other unused material which came into the prosecution's possession from that source, would have to be disclosed to KM in due course.

F

2. If there was any unfairness to KM resulting from non-concurrent disclosure to him, that was a matter for the judge at trial and not for the Companies Court (or Court of Appeal).

The following cases were referred to in the judgments:

G

Arrows Ltd, Re (No. 4) [1993] BCC 473; [1993] Ch 452.
Barlow Clowes (Gilt Managers) Ltd, Re [1991] BCC 608; [1992] Ch 208.
Bishopsgate Investment Management Ltd, Re [1992] BCC 222; [1993] Ch 1.
Makanjuola v Commissioner of Police of the Metropolis [1992] 3 All ER 617.
Poulson, Re [1976] 1 WLR 1023.
R v Director of Serious Fraud Office, ex parte Smith [1993] AC 1.
R v Ward (1992) 96 Cr App R 1; [1993] 1 WLR 619.
Rank Film Distributors Ltd & Ors v Video Information Centre & Ors [1982] AC 380.

H

Alun Jones QC and Clare Montgomery (instructed by Peters & Peters) for Kevin Maxwell.

Mary Arden QC and Kate Thirlwall (instructed by the Serious Fraud Office) for the Serious Fraud Office.

A   AWH Charles (instructed by the Treasury Solicitor) for the Secretary of State for
Trade and Industry.

JUDGMENT

Dillon LJ: On 26 March 1993 the court dismissed, for reasons to be given later, an
application by Mr Kevin Maxwell for leave to appeal against an order of *Vinelott* J of
10 February 1993, leave having been refused by the judge. We now give our reasons for
B   refusing the application.

The application had been adjourned to be heard by the full court immediately after
the hearing of an application for leave to appeal by Mr Trachtenberg, and that in turn
was to be heard immediately after the hearing of the appeal of the Director of the
Serious Fraud Office in *Re Arrows Ltd (No. 4)* [1993] BCC 473. As with
Mr Trachtenberg's application it was directed that Mr Kevin Maxwell's appeal be heard
C   immediately after the hearing of the application if leave to appeal were granted.

The reason why these three proceedings were directed to be heard in succession was
that all raised points, albeit different points, affecting the interplay of sec. 2 of the
Criminal Justice Act 1987 and sec. 236 of the *Insolvency Act* 1986. In particular, all
raised different aspects of the question whether the transcripts of private examinations
under sec. 236 should or must be made available, and if so on what terms, to the Serious
D   Fraud Office or other prosecuting authority for the purpose of investigating crime or
prosecuting persons charged with crime. Mr Kevin Maxwell's application also raises
further questions as to whether such transcripts should be supplied not merely to the
prosecution but also to defendants in criminal proceedings.

As is well known, Mr Kevin Maxwell is a son of the late Robert Maxwell who died on
5 November 1991. From November 1991 the Serious Fraud Office has been conducting
an investigation into the affairs of Robert Maxwell and of many of the companies with
E   which he had been concerned. Mr Kevin Maxwell was at one time a director of various
of those companies which have, since the death of Robert Maxwell, gone into liquidation
or administrative receivership. The office-holders in those companies desired to examine
Mr Kevin Maxwell under sec. 236 in relation to the affairs of the respective companies,
and in a case to which Mr Kevin Maxwell was a party, *Re Bishopsgate Investment
Management Ltd* [1992] BCC 222, it was held that the privilege against self-incrimination
F   was impliedly abrogated by the Insolvency Act in respect of persons being examined
under sec. 236 and various other sections of that Act. Thereafter Mr Kevin Maxwell was
examined or interviewed by the various office-holders under sec. 235 or 236 of the
Insolvency Act as were many other people, including people who could supply information
to the office-holders and were not under suspicion of any criminal offence.

On 18 June 1992 Mr Kevin Maxwell was charged with offences of theft and fraudulent
G   conspiracy in relation to the companies. Thereafter he had several further interviews
with office-holders and he was also, legitimately and without any objection on his part,
examined on several occasions by the Serious Fraud Office under sec. 2 of the 1987 Act.

The Director of the Serious Fraud Office has now called on the office-holders to
produce to the Serious Fraud Office all transcripts of interviews conducted by them or
on their behalf under either sec. 235 or sec. 236 of the Insolvency Act or on a voluntary
basis or equivalent principles, with Mr Kevin Maxwell and a large number of other
H   people (not limited to those who face charges) together with copies of all documents or
other material supplied to the office-holders by those persons including affidavits and
witness statements.

Mr Kevin Maxwell supported the submissions against the Serious Fraud Office
made in *Arrows (No. 4)*; I have expressed my views on those in my judgment in *Arrows
(No. 4)*. In one respect, as I understand his counsel's submissions, his counsel went

further than counsel for Mr Naviede in *Arrows (No. 4)* in that it was submitted that the   A
alleged public interest immunity founded on the public interest that liquidations should
be conducted speedily and efficiently was a general immunity which imposed a duty on
the office-holders not to disclose e.g. transcripts which could not in any normal sense be
waived, even by the consent of the person examined, though it might in some
circumstances be overridden by some other public interest: see the observations of
Bingham LJ at p. 623f–h and Lord *Donaldson* MR at p. 621b–c in *Makanjuola v*   B
Commissioner of Police of the Metropolis [1992] 3 All ER 617. In my judgment,
however, as indicated in *Arrows (No. 4)*, there is no public interest immunity to prevent
the disclosure of transcripts or other documents by office-holders to prosecution or
regulatory authorities under the statutory duties or powers of the office-holders including
their duties under sec. 2 of the 1987 Act.

Further points are however taken on behalf of Mr Kevin Maxwell by his counsel which
are founded on the course of the prosecution against him. Put crudely, the submissions   C
of his counsel come down to a plea that the Serious Fraud Office is playing tactics in the
handling of the prosecution and this Court should reciprocate to ensure fairness to
Mr Kevin Maxwell.

On the facts the fundamental objection is that, though Mr Kevin Maxwell was charged
on 18 June 1992, no notice of transfer to the Crown Court under sec. 4 of the 1987 Act
has yet been given in relation to these charges. It appears that at a hearing before the   D
City of London Magistrates on 1 December 1992 the Serious Fraud Office gave an
undertaking by counsel that a substantial part of the case would be the subject of a notice
of transfer to the Crown Court by 1 April 1993 at the latest, and it was said by counsel
that it was hoped that the rest of the case would be ready for transfer within a month or
two thereafter. However on 11 February 1993 a further application was made by the
Serious Fraud Office to the City of London magistrates, as a result of which, despite   E
opposition by the defendants, the Serious Fraud Office was released from the earlier
undertaking on giving a fresh undertaking to transfer the whole of the case not later than
19 July 1993.

It is said that the vice of that, from the point of view of Mr Kevin Maxwell, is that,
though when a notice of transfer has been given there will be a judge appointed to try
the case to whom interlocutory applications can be made, until a notice of transfer is   F
given there is no effective machinery for preliminary directions to be obtained. It is said
that this has the general consequence that Mr Kevin Maxwell is, at this stage, hampered
in preparing his defence because he does not know what, precisely, the evidence against
him is. It is further said that he is also thereby hampered in particular matters. One such
particular matter which was mentioned to us is that the Serious Fraud Office has applied
by letters rogatory for the evidence of Dr Rechsteiner to be taken in a Swiss court, and
under Swiss law Mr Kevin Maxwell has the right to be represented and to ask questions   G
in the Swiss court when the evidence of Dr Rechsteiner is taken; but he cannot usefully
avail himself of his rights under Swiss law while he does not know what material the
Serious Fraud Office has which may relate to Dr Rechsteiner, or to matters on which
Dr Rechsteiner might be able to assist Mr Kevin Maxwell's defence.

For my part, I see no basis on which this court could or should refuse disclosure to the
Serious Fraud Office by the office-holders of the various transcripts or other documents   H
which the Serious Fraud Office has applied for under sec. 2 of the 1987 Act — or could
or should defer disclosure of those documents until after notice of transfer to the Crown
Court has been given in relation to the charges against Mr Kevin Maxwell, accompanied
as it has to be by a statement of the evidence on which the charges are based: see reg. 4
of the *Criminal Justice Act 1987 (Notice of Transfer) Regulations* 1988 (SI 1988/1691).

A   It is therefore asked by counsel for Mr Kevin Maxwell that the office-holders should be ordered to disclose simultaneously to Mr Kevin Maxwell and his advisers copies of all the transcripts and other documents which they disclose to the Serious Fraud Office.

As to this application, there is, in my judgment, help to be derived from the judgment of the Divisional Court in Bankruptcy in *Re Poulson* [1976] 1 WLR 1023. In that case a third party to the bankruptcy which was a defendant to a civil action for defamation
B   brought against it by an individual — not the bankrupt himself — who had been privately examined in what was then a fairly notorious bankruptcy, applied for production, for the purposes of the civil proceedings, of the transcripts of that individual's private examination, and it was pointed out that the transcripts had been disclosed to Scotland Yard. But the Divisional Court ruled, in my judgment rightly, that different considerations applied where Scotland Yard applied for transcripts.

C   Cases where persons other than prosecution or regulatory authorities seek disclosure or inspection of transcripts may raise a variety of different considerations. In some cases, disclosure will clearly be justified because, to adopt the words of *Millett* J (in *Re Barlow Clowes (Gilt Managers) Ltd* [1991] BCC 608 at p. 614C):

> "the use proposed to be made of the material is to assist the beneficial winding up of the company."

D
An instance would be where a parent company in compulsory liquidation has solvent subsidiaries which are not in liquidation at all but are under the control of directors nominated by the liquidators of the parent company, and it is desired to disclose transcripts to the directors of the subsidiary so that the subsidiary can bring proceedings for the ultimate benefit, indirectly, of the winding up of the parent company.

E   But the mere fact that the transcript is wanted for use in proceedings, whether civil or criminal, is not enough. The process of private examination does not leave the court with a pool of information to be made available to any third party who may want to go fishing to see what he can find that might be helpful in civil or criminal proceedings, e.g. as material for cross-examination if a witness gives evidence in such proceedings which might be thought inconsistent with what he had said on examination under sec. 236 or as material to anticipate discovery.

F
In the present case, it is likely that the transcripts and other documents which the Serious Fraud Office has obtained or will be obtaining from the office-holders will be obtained by Mr Kevin Maxwell in due course of the criminal proceedings, at some stage after a notice of transfer has been given if not before. That will be a matter for the court in the criminal proceedings — be it the magistrates' court or the judge after notice of transfer — to deal with without further reference to the Chancery court since disclosure
G   to defendants in the criminal proceedings, as appropriate under the practice of the criminal court, will be a corollary of the documents having come into the possession of the Serious Fraud Office for the purposes of the prosecution.

It is not, however, for this court or the Chancery Division to anticipate or interfere with the procedure of the criminal court. Still less is it for this court, as the civil division of the Court of Appeal, or the Chancery Division to mark its disapproval of the
H   magistrates' decision to allow the Serious Fraud Office more time before giving notice of transfer.

I agree therefore with the decision of *Vinelott* J that there should be no simultaneous disclosure.

I see no basis, therefore, for granting Mr Kevin Maxwell leave to appeal.

Steyn LJ: I agree. For the reasons given in my judgments in *Re Arrows Ltd (No. 4)*   A
and in Mr Trachtenberg's application, I am of the opinion that the following submissions
made on behalf of Mr Kevin Maxwell, by Mr Alun Jones QC must be rejected:

(1)   the submission based on public interest immunity;

(2)   the submission that the director's power to serve a notice under sec. 2(2) and (3)
        of the *Criminal Justice Act* 1987 lapses when a charge is laid;
                                                                                        B
(3)   the submission that when a charge is laid that affords reasonable excuse for a
        failure to comply with notices under sec. 2(2) and (3) of the Act; and

(4)   the submission that the judge was in law empowered to order that the liquidators
        need not produce the transcripts to the Director of the Serious Fraud Office.

Mr Jones submitted that the Director of the Serious Fraud Office is abusing his powers
by delaying the transfer of Mr Kevin Maxwell's case to the Crown Court. He contended   C
that the director was acting unlawfully. It is sufficient to say that on the materials before
the court an arguable case of unlawfulness has not been made out.

By way of alternative, Mr Jones submitted that the office-holders should be ordered
to disclose the sec. 236 transcripts simultaneously to the director and to him. In my view
Mr Kevin Maxwell has no legal right to such an order for disclosure in these proceedings
and at this stage. In due course he will, in the usual way, become entitled to disclosure,   D
and, if he has been unfairly treated, he will be able to raise the matter with the trial judge
under sec. 78 of the *Police and Criminal Evidence Act* 1984.

I would also dismiss the application.

Rose LJ: I agree with the judgments of *Dillon* LJ and *Steyn* LJ.

For the reasons given in *Re Arrows Ltd (No. 4)* sec. 2(3) of the *Criminal Justice Act*
1987 in my view confers on the Director of the Serious Fraud Office power to obtain   E
documents which it is not open to a judge of the Chancery Division to fetter.

For the reasons given in Mr Trachtenberg's application, in the light of *R v Director of
Serious Fraud Office, ex parte Smith* [1993] AC 1, that power extends to obtaining from
office-holders transcripts of interviews under sec. 236 of the *Insolvency Act* 1986,
whether or not the interviewee has, at the time of the interview, been charged with a
criminal offence.   F

Mr Kevin Maxwell's application raises only one additional question; namely, should
the office-holders be ordered to give disclosure of sec. 236 transcripts to him at the same
time as to the Serious Fraud Office?

Mr Maxwell's counsel accepts that there is no statutory basis for such simultaneous
disclosure. But he submits that, if it is not ordered, Mr Maxwell will suffer prejudice in
the conduct of his defence to criminal charges, in particular because the passage of time   G
will dim the recollection of witnesses on whom he may wish to rely.

In my judgment, there are a number of reasons why this submission fails. First, having
been repeatedly interviewed, both under sec. 236 of the *Insolvency Act* 1986, and
sec. 2(2) of the *Criminal Justice Act* 1987, Mr Maxwell must be well aware of the lines of
enquiry which are being pursued, both in relation to company assets and possible
criminal offences. He has copies of his own interviews. In consequence he no doubt   H
knows which potential witnesses are capable of assisting him and they can be interviewed
on his behalf, if this has not already been done, without delay.

Secondly, such, if any, material in those interviews as the prosecution may wish to
rely on in criminal proceedings, together with other unused material which comes into
the prosecution's possession from this source, will have to be disclosed to Mr Maxwell in

A   due course either in the form of a prosecution statement under sec. 9(4) of the *Criminal Justice Act* 1987, or in accordance with *R v Ward* (1992) 96 Cr App R 1.

Thirdly, if there is any unfairness to Mr Maxwell resulting from non-concurrent disclosure to him, that is a matter for the judge at trial and not for this court on appeal from the Companies Court (see *Rank Film Distributors Ltd v Video Information Centre* [1982] AC 380 at pp. 442F and 446E).

B   I, too, would dismiss this application for leave to appeal.

(*Application for leave to appeal dismissed*)

S N Group plc v Barclays Bank plc.

Chancery Division (Companies Court).
Jonathan Parker J.
Judgment delivered 7 May 1993.

> *Winding-up petition — Advertisement of petition — Company's bank allegedly notified of petition — Whether notification was breach of rules — Meaning of "advertisement" — Whether notification was abuse of process — Whether petition should be dismissed — Insolvency Rules 1986 (SI 1986/1925), r. 4.11.*

This was an application by S N Group plc to dismiss a winding-up petition presented against it by Barclays Bank plc on the ground that the petition was an abuse of the process of the court.

The petition was based on a statutory demand for arrears of rent under a lease of premises of which Barclays was the landlord and the company was the tenant.

According to the company's evidence the company's bank was notified of the petition by Barclays some four days after presentation, and the company's bank account was accordingly frozen. The company argued that such notification was a breach of the relevant rule as to advertisement, r. 4.11 of the Insolvency Rules 1986, which required seven business days between service and advertisement; further or alternatively, that it amounted to improper pressure on the company. The company asked for the petition to be dismissed either pursuant to the provisions of r. 4.11 or under the inherent jurisdiction of the court.

Barclays submitted that the company had failed to establish a prima facie case, applying the test in Coulon Sanderson & Ward Ltd v Ward (1986) 2 BCC 99,207. The company submitted that that test was only applicable to restraining presentation and not to restraining advertisement.

Held, dismissing the company's application:

1. The test set out in Coulon Sanderson & Ward Ltd v Ward was equally applicable whether the court was being asked to restrain presentation of a petition or to restrain advertisement of a petition which had already been presented.

2. "Advertisement" in r. 4.11 referred to the advertisement in the Gazette. If that were not the case it would follow that notification of the company's bank, not being advertisement in the Gazette, would be a breach of the rule whenever it took place, which could not be right. (Re a Company No. 00687 of 1991 [1991] BCC 210 considered.)

3. On the footing that the petitioner's debt was undisputed and that on the material before the court, far from any indication of solvency, the strong inference was that the company was insolvent, no prima facie case had been established that the notification given, or assumed to be given, to the company's bank amounted to an improper purpose. (Re Bill Hennessey Associates Ltd (Company No. 0013925 of 1991, ex parte Rousell) [1992] BCC 386 distinguished.)

The following cases were referred to in the judgment:

American Cyanamid Co v Ethicon Ltd [1975] AC 396.
Company No. 00687 of 1991, Re a [1991] BCC 210.
Company No. 006273 of 1992, Re a [1992] BCC 794.
Coulon Sanderson & Ward Ltd v Ward (1986) 2 BCC 99,207.
Hennessey (Bill) Associates Ltd, Re (Company No. 0013925 of 1991, ex parte Rousell) [1992] BCC 386.
Signland Ltd, Re [1982] 2 All ER 609n.

A   A Thompson (instructed by Rippon Patel & French) for the applicant.

Christopher R Parker (instructed by Denton Hall Burgin & Warrens, Milton Keynes) for the respondent.

JUDGMENT

Jonathan Parker J: Before me is an application by S N Group plc, which is represented by Mr Thompson, to dismiss a winding-up petition presented against it by
B   Barclays Bank plc, the respondents to the application, who are represented by Mr Parker, on the ground that the petition is an abuse of the process of the court. The application is technically made ex parte, but it has been made on notice to the bank and I have heard full submissions from Mr Thompson in support of the application and from Mr Parker in opposition to it.

The factual and procedural background to the application, so far as I need to state it
C   for present purposes, is as follows.

On 28 April 1992, Barclays issued a writ against the company in the Queen's Bench Division, claiming arrears of rent and service charge under a lease on premises of which Barclays was a landlord and the company was the tenant, having taken an assignment from the original tenant. Barclays applied for summary judgment, and on 15 October 1992 District Judge *Groves* gave the company unconditional leave to defend.

D   Barclays then appealed against that order, and on 9 March 1993, Lord *Williams* QC, sitting as a deputy judge of the High Court, allowed Barclays' appeal and gave judgment in favour of Barclays in the sum of £44,501.83. He refused any stay of execution pending an appeal. Subsequently the company served notice of appeal against the judgment, and it appears on the evidence that the appeal had been in the warned list for hearing since 27 April.

E   In the meantime, on 19 April, Barclays presented the winding-up petition which is sought to be dismissed on the application before me. That petition is based on two statutory demands, alleged to have been served on the company on 29 March, although there is, it seems, a dispute as to proper service of these statutory demands.

One such demand was for the sum in respect of which judgment was given, that is to say £44,501.83. The second was for a further sum of £12,382.36 in respect of further arrears of rent arising under the lease, together with interest thereon, so that the total
F   debt upon which the petition is based amounts to £56,884.19.

According to affidavit evidence lodged on behalf of the company — at this stage, no evidence has been lodged on behalf of Barclays Bank — on 23 April, some four days after the presentation of the petition, the company's accountant attended at the company's bankers, National Westminster, King's Cross branch, to be told by the Natwest that it had received notice of the presentation of the petition from Barclays, and that the
G   company's bank account was accordingly frozen. The company's evidence indicates that Barclays may have notified the Natwest of the presentation of the petition the previous day, 22 April 1993.

On 28 April the company applied ex parte to *Morritt* J to restrain Barclays from advertising the petition. The company was represented at that hearing by Mr Thompson. Nobody at that stage appeared on behalf of Barclays. The company's evidence before
H   *Morritt* J dealt with the alleged notification to the Natwest, and it also referred to an alleged cross-claim by the company against Barclays. I am told by Mr Thompson, and of course I accept, that before *Morritt* J the only ground relied upon in support of the company's application was that the notification to the Natwest was a breach of the Insolvency Rules, and amounted to improper pressure. Mr Thompson told me that he did not rely at all, on that occasion, on the evidence as to the existence of an alleged cross-claim.

I should say that initially in his submissions before me Mr Thompson did seek to rely
on the alleged cross-claim as an additional ground for granting the relief which he seeks,
but in the course of his submissions he elected to abandon all further reliance on that
aspect of the evidence for present purposes. It follows that, as the matter stands before
me, the debts on which the petition is based are undisputed debts.

Returning to the procedural history: *Morritt* J made an order, on Mr Thompson's
application, restraining advertisement of the petition until after Tuesday, 4 May, which
was the first Companies Court sitting of these sittings, and he gave the company liberty
to serve an inter partes application for 4 May by noon the following day, 29 April. On
the following day, as I understand it, an inter partes application was served.

On 4 May, both counsel appeared before me, but the company's application could not
be effective due to confusion as to the whereabouts of certain of the affidavits lodged by
the company, and also to lack of availability of any copies of those sworn affidavits. The
application was, however, renewed on 6 May, and it has continued over today.

As I have said, Mr Thompson, in seeking the dismissal of the winding-up petition,
now relies only on the alleged notification of the Natwest by Barclays, and he asserts
that such notification amounts to an abuse of the process. He submits that it amounts to
a breach of the relevant rules as to advertisement, which are to be found in r. 4.11 of the
Insolvency Rules 1986. Further or alternatively, he submits that it amounted to improper
pressure on the company. On that basis he invites me to dismiss the petition today,
either pursuant to the specific provisions of r. 4.11, to which I shall refer in a moment,
alternatively under the inherent jurisdiction of the court.

In support of this submission Mr Thompson relies upon a number of authorities,
principally the decision of His Honour Judge *Bromley* QC, sitting as a High Court
judge, in *Re Bill Hennessey Associates Ltd (Company No. 0013925 of 1991, ex parte
Rousell)* [1992] BCC 386. I shall return to that in a moment.

Mr Parker, for Barclays, has not as yet been able to take full instructions as to whether
a notification was in fact given by his clients to the Natwest, and if so, in what
circumstances, and accordingly if the application proceeds he seeks time to put in such
evidence.

However, Mr Parker submits that the application ought to go no further, since, as he
submits, the company has failed to establish a prima facie case for the dismissal of the
petition on the grounds put forward. He submits first of all that such a test is appropriate,
by reference to the decision of the Court of Appeal in *Coulon Sanderson & Ward Ltd v
Ward* (1986) 2 BCC 99,207. Mr Thompson, however, submits that that test is only
applicable where, as in that case, the relevant incident is the presentation of a petition,
whereas in the present case the petition has already been presented and effectively what
is sought is restraint on advertisement.

In my judgment the test set out in *Coulon Sanderson & Ward Ltd v Ward* is equally
applicable whether the court is being asked to restrain presentation of a petition or to
restrain advertisement of a petition which has already been presented. In many cases a
company may be too late to seek an injunction preventing the presentation of a petition,
and may be forced to seek an injunction instead restraining advertisement. I can see no
good reason why different tests should apply, depending upon whether the company is
in time to seek relief preventing the presentation of a petition. Accordingly, it seems to
me that the test set out in the *Coulon Sanderson & Ward Ltd* case will apply in this case.

Applying that test, Mr Parker then goes on to say that there is here in the first place no
established prima facie case for a breach of r. 4.11 of the *Insolvency Rules* 1986.
Mr Thompson's submission in that respect is that notification of the Natwest by Barclays
which, for present purposes, I shall assume took place, amounted to an advertisement

A   of the petition for the purposes of that rule, and he submits that that advertisement was not made in accordance with the rule and is accordingly in breach of it. He refers me in that respect to r. 4.11(5), which reads:

> "If the petition is not duly advertised in accordance with this Rule, the court may dismiss it."

B   Mr Parker, however, submits that notification to the Natwest is not, on a true construction of this rule, an advertisement within the terms of the rule, and he submits that "advertisement" in the context of r. 4.11(2) means advertisement in the *Gazette*.

I should make it clear that the burden of Mr Thompson's argument under this rule is that r. 4.11(2)(b) provides that the advertisement must be made to appear not less than seven business days after service of the petition on the company, nor less than seven business days before the day appointed for the hearing of the petition, and Mr Thompson C   asserts that the breach of the rule in this case occurred because notification was given to the Natwest, assuming it was given, within seven days after presentation of the petition.

Returning then to the submissions as to the meaning of "advertisement" for the purposes of r. 4.11: Mr Parker submits that notification of the Natwest cannot amount to an advertisement for the purposes of r. 4.11(2)(b).

In my judgment that is a correct construction of the rule. It is necessary, I think, that I should read subr. (1) and (2) in full, in order to set the particular provision in context. D   Subrule (1) reads:

> "Unless the court otherwise directs, the petition shall be advertised once in the *Gazette*."

Subrule (2):

> "The advertisement must be made to appear—
>
> E   (a)   if the petitioner is the company itself, not less than 7 business days before the day appointed for the hearing, and
>
>   (b)   otherwise, not less than 7 business days after service of the petition on the company, nor less than 7 business days before the day so appointed."

In my judgment, reading the expression "The advertisement" at the beginning of subr. (2) in the context of r. 4.11 as a whole, and in particular in the context of subr. (1), it refers to the advertisement in the *Gazette*. Moreover, if that were not the case it would F   (as it seems to me) follow that notification of the Natwest, not being advertisement in the *London Gazette*, would be a breach of the rule whenever it took place, that is to say, whether it took place within seven days after the presentation of the petition or thereafter. That, in my judgment, cannot be right.

I have been referred in this connection to the decision of *Harman* J in *Re a Company No. 00687 of 1991* [1991] BCC 210, where a similar, although by no means identical G   question, arose in the context of a contributory's petition, to which different rules apply, and in the context not of the Insolvency Rules but of an order made by the court restraining advertisement of a petition without further order.

Harman J held in that case that the word "advertised", in r. 4.23(1)(c), meant "advertised" in its ordinary English sense — that is, primarily a paid announcement in a general publication, but also notifying the existence of the matter. On that basis he held H   that notification to the bank did constitute a breach of the order made in that case. That, however, is a different case, and I am concerned, as I see it, to construe the relevant provisions of r. 4.11, which applies to creditors' winding-up petitions.

Construing r. 4.11 in that context, I reach the conclusion that "advertisement" means, as I have said, advertisement in the *London Gazette*. Accordingly, in my judgment, Mr Thompson has not made out on behalf of the company any prima facie case for breach of r. 4.11.

He goes on however to assert that the petition ought to be dismissed, further or   A
alternatively advertisement of it restrained, on the basis that there has been here an
abuse of the process of the Companies Court in that its procedures have been employed
for an improper purpose, and he submits that the evidence before me discloses a prima
facie case to that effect (although, as I have said, he does not accept so high a burden,
but submits rather that on *Cyanamid* principles there is here a serious issue to be argued
on the hearing of the inter partes application, which he proposes to make).

I turn then to the question of the inherent jurisdiction. The authorities establish   B
clearly, as I read them, that the court will dismiss a petition if it concludes that the
procedures of the Companies Court have been used for the purpose of applying
improper pressure. Examples of that are to be found both in Judge *Bromley's* case of
Bill Hennessey Associates Ltd (Company No. 0013925 of 1991, ex parte Rousell), to
which I have already referred, and in a decision of *Slade* J in *Re Signland Ltd* [1982]
2 All ER 609 — and there are other authorities to similar effect.   C

Mr Thompson submits here that there is on the evidence a sufficient inference,
whether the test be a prima facie case or simply a *Cyanamid* test, of improper purpose
on the part of Barclays Bank in notifying the National Westminster — assuming that
notification took place — to justify my granting ex parte relief today over the hearing of
the proposed inter partes application.

Mr Parker however submits that although a petition will be dismissed where it is found   D
to have been presented for an improper purpose, nevertheless it is not an improper
purpose to present a petition with a view to the recovery of a debt which is not disputed.
He refers me, as authority for that proposition, to the decision of *Millett* J in *Re a
Company No. 006273 of 1992* [1992] BCC 794. He draws attention to the fact that here
the debt is, as I have already explained, not disputed — at least, in this court; and on that
basis, he submits that there can be no improper purpose involved where, as is effectively   E
the case, his clients have an undisputed debt in respect of which they are invoking the
procedures of the Companies Court.

He also reminds me that when Lord *Williams* gave judgment in favour of the bank he
refused any stay, and he reminded me of the provisions of O. 59, r. 13 of the Rules of the
Supreme Court, to the effect that an appeal per se does not operate as a stay.

Mr Parker goes on to say that if it be necessary to go further and look more generally   F
at the facts, the position becomes from his clients' point of view even stronger, in that on
the material before the court the company is insolvent. He draws attention to the fact
that the company has not paid the judgment, or any amount in respect of it,
notwithstanding that no stay was granted, and he also refers to such evidence as there is
as to the company's financial position, and submits that on that evidence the position is
clearly that the company is insolvent.   G

The evidence in question consists of accounts to the year ended 31 July 1992, which
have been placed in evidence, and which show net assets of some £18,000 — the figure,
I think, is £18,122 — but it is clear from the accounts that no account is taken of the debt
owed by the company to Barclays Bank. If that debt is taken into account then, according
to those accounts — which, as I say, relate only to the year ended 31 July 1992 — the
position is that the company is insolvent. It is accepted by Mr Thompson that the   H
accounts do not bring into account any sum on account of the indebtedness of the
company to Barclays Bank.

So, submits Mr Parker, the position here is that a petition has been presented by his
clients in respect of an undisputed debt against an insolvent company, and in those
circumstances, prima facie, when the petition comes to be heard, the company will be

A   wound up. In those circumstances, he submits that if his clients informed the Natwest of the presentation of the petition — as I assume, for present purposes, that they did — then the proper inference is that they did so for the proper purpose of preserving the assets of the company pending the making of a winding-up order on their petition. He submits that that is not merely a proper purpose, but is the specific purpose which sec. 127 of the *Insolvency Act* 1986 was designed to achieve.

For those reasons, submits Mr Parker, no prima facie case has been established.

B   I accept those submissions made by Mr Parker. As I have already explained, I have to proceed today on the footing that the petitioner's debt is undisputed, and I accept Mr Parker's submission that, on the material before the court, far from any indication of solvency the strong inference is that the company as of today is insolvent. On that basis it seems to me that it follows that no prima facie case has been established that the notification given, or assumed to be given, to the Natwest amounted to an improper purpose.

C   In that connection it is, I think, relevant to refer once again to the decision of Judge *Bromley* in the *Rousell* case, where it is in my judgment plain that the ratio of the judge's decision was the existence of improper pressure. I refer in particular to the final paragraph of the judgment, where the judge said this:

> "However I have no doubt that the interference with the company's bank account, on the evidence before me, was a principal purpose of giving virtually simultaneous notice of the petition to the company's bank. That is the first point. There is no evidence pointing any other way. Secondly it has had a serious consequence on the conduct of the company's business. In my judgment the right inference is that the sequence of events was designed to put pressure on the company, and that appears to me to be a wrong use of the Companies Court jurisdiction and procedures. It would, I think, be deplorable if creditors could select for the purpose of maximising pressure on a company whom they would inform, and how, and how quickly. I am reinforced in my view by the approach of *Slade* J in the *Signland* case. I think the right course is to dismiss the petition, and that I do."

Its to be noted that in the *Rousell* case, the petitioner's debt appears to have been substantially disputed. That appears, as I read it, from the recital of the facts made by the judge at p. 386 of the report. On those facts the judge drew the inference of improper pressure in the notification which had been given.

F   The facts of this case as they appear before me are, however, in the respects which I have mentioned, very different. There is no dispute as to the petitioner's debt, and there is, for reasons which I have indicated, a plain inference that the company is insolvent as of today.

In those circumstances, I come to the conclusion that the company has not shown what I regard as the requisite prima facie case to support its application to dismiss the winding-up petition, and for that reason it seems to me that the matter must go no further. If I am wrong in concluding that the appropriate test is the establishing of a prima facie case, and if it be the case, as Mr Thompson submits, that *Cyanamid* principles apply, then I am not satisfied that there is, on the material before me, a serious issue to be argued on the hearing of the inter partes application.

Accordingly, for those reasons, it seems to me that the matter should go no further, in that no relief should be granted on the application made before me today, and accordingly I reject the application.

(*Order accordingly*)

Re Walter L Jacob & Co Ltd.
Official Receiver v Jacob.

A

Chancery Division (Companies Court).
Hoffmann J.
Judgment delivered 7 October 1991.

Disqualifying unfit directors of insolvent companies — Whether company "became insolvent" when winding-up petition presented or winding-up order made — Company Directors Disqualification Act 1986, sec. 7(2).

B

A company which was ordered to be wound up "became insolvent" for the purposes of sec. 7(2) of the Company Directors Disqualification Act 1986 when the winding-up order was made and not when the winding-up petition was presented.

Philip Jones (instructed by the Treasury Solicitor) for the official receiver.

C

The respondent appeared in person.

JUDGMENT

Hoffmann J: This is an appeal by Mr Walter Jacob in person from a decision of Mr Registrar *Scott* by which the registrar refused to strike out an originating summons which had been issued by the official receiver under the *Company Directors Disqualification Act* 1986 seeking Mr Jacob's disqualification. The ground for the application was that the originating summons had not been issued within the two-year period prescribed by sec. 7(2) of the Act. That section provides that:

D

"Except with the leave of the court, an application for the making under [sec. 6] of a disqualification order against any person shall not be made after the end of the period of 2 years beginning with the day on which the company of which that person is or has been a director became insolvent."

E

In this case the company in question was wound up compulsorily by an order of the Court of Appeal on 21 December 1988. The originating summons was issued on 20 December 1990. Consequently, if the date upon which the company became insolvent within the meaning of sec. 7(2) was the date upon which the winding-up order was made then the summons was in time. The order was, however, made on a petition which had been presented as long before as 15 April 1987 and Mr Jacob's submission, which he has presented clearly and succinctly to this court, is that, for the purposes of sec. 7(2) the company must be taken to have become insolvent on the date of the presentation of the petition because that is the date on which, by virtue of sec. 129(2) of the *Insolvency Act* 1986, the winding up is deemed to have commenced.

F

The *Company Directors Disqualification Act* 1986 contains an interpretation section, sec. 22, which provides, in subsec. (3), that sec. 247 of the Insolvency Act applies as regards "references to a company's insolvency and to its going into liquidation". If one then turns to sec. 247(2), it provides that:

G

"For the purposes of any provision in this Group of Parts, a company goes into liquidation if it passes a resolution for voluntary winding up or an order for its winding up is made by the court at a time when it has not already gone into liquidation by passing such a resolution."

Mr Jacob submits that sec. 247(2) merely prescribes the condition which has to be satisfied for the company going into liquidation, namely, in this case, the making of the order. It uses the word "if". It does not follow that the company must be taken to have become insolvent on that date. It is logical for the date upon which the company is taken to have gone into liquidation for the purposes of the provisions of the Act to be deemed to be some earlier date and, in his submission, sec. 129(2) has that effect.

H

The purpose of sec. 129(2) in the context of winding up is clear. It deals with the validity of certain transactions entered into with the company and has the effect of retrospectively invalidating, by virtue of sec. 127, dispositions which were made before the winding-up order but after the presentation of the petition. The reason why the date of the presentation of the petition is taken as the date from which such dispositions are invalidated is perfectly clear as a part of the policy of the Act. It is, on the other hand, not at all easy to see why the date of the presentation of the petition should have any relevance to the period within which the official receiver is obliged to issue a summons for disqualification under the 1986 Act. It is only once the winding-up order has been made that the official receiver knows that he is under a duty to investigate the conduct of the directors and, if necessary, to apply for their disqualification. It seems to me that it would be quite illogical for the period within which the official receiver can take such steps to be abridged by the fact that the petition has taken a long time to come on for hearing or, as in this case, has been delayed by the necessity of an appeal to the Court of Appeal.

It is noticeable that sec. 7(2) uses the expression "the day on which the company became insolvent". It would, I think, have been perfectly easy, if Parliament had so intended, for the section to use the well-known expression "the date upon which the winding up commenced". That would have brought into play sec. 129(2). But Parliament has not done so and, in my view, the context of sec. 7(2) requires one to construe the words "became insolvent" with reference to sec. 247 of the Insolvency Act as meaning the date upon which the winding-up order was made.

In my judgment, therefore, the learned registrar was quite right and the appeal must, therefore, be dismissed.

(*Appeal dismissed with costs*)

Dempsey v Celtic Football and Athletic Co Ltd.

A

Court of Session (Outer House).
Lord Prosser.
Judgment delivered 15 May 1992.

Rectification of register of members — Shares transferred in breach of articles — Whether interim interdict restraining exercise of voting rights was properly granted — Companies Act 1985, sec. 359.

B

This was a petition by the holder of a number of fully-paid shares of the Celtic Football and Athletic Co Ltd ("the company") seeking an order that the register of members of the company be rectified under sec. 359 of the Companies Act 1985 by deleting the entries indicating that 31 persons called as respondents were the holders of the shares entered against their names. Interim interdict was granted against certain of the respondents in relation to the exercise of the votes attaching to their shares. They sought recall of the interim interdict.

C

The entries in the register which the petitioner sought to have deleted followed from transfers of partly-paid shares, and it was admitted that the share transfer forms used in respect of the transfers did not contain any acceptance or signature by the transferee as required by the company's articles of association.

Held, recalling the interim interdict:

D

1. There was an evident breach of the requirement of the articles in regard to the form of transfer which was used. Moreover, in relation to partly-paid shares, the absence of the transferee's signature was not a mere irregularity, as it might be in relation to fully-paid shares. There was a prima facie case for rectification, but the court was concerned only with the interim regulation of matters, pending resolution of that issue.

2. Beneficial ownership had passed to the transferees as a matter of contract. Once it was accepted that the transferees were entitled, in a question with the transferors, to insist that the vote be used as the transferees wished, the possibility of rectification, bringing the transferors back on to the register, became much less significant. That being so, it was questionable whether there was even a prima facie case for interim interdict against their using their votes.

E

3. On the question of balance of convenience, it was more appropriate to allow acquired beneficial rights to be exercised through voting, rather than exclude the holders of the shares from the voting process, pending resolution of an issue which related primarily to methods of transfer rather than its intended effects.

F

The following cases were referred to in the opinion:

Paradise Motor Co Ltd, Re [1968] 1 WLR 1125.
Piccadilly Radio plc, Re (1989) 5 BCC 692.

J L Mitchell QC and J A Baird (instructed by Drummond Miller WS) for the petitioner.

G

Neil Davidson (McGrigor Donald) for the respondents.

OPINION

Lord Prosser: The petitioner is the holder of a number of fully-paid shares of the Celtic Football and Athletic Co Ltd ("the company"). In this petition, he seeks an order that the register of members of the company be rectified by deletion of the entries indicating that 31 persons called as respondents are the holders of the shares entered against their names. He also seeks interdict against certain of these respondents in relation to the exercise of the votes attaching to the shares at present registered in their names.

H

A   On 29 March 1992, interim interdict was granted against such of these respondents as had lodged no caveat. They were thereby interdicted from:

> "exercising the votes attaching to the shares of the . . . company . . . which are at present registered in their names unlawfully and without sufficient cause, and in respect of which the petitioner seeks rectification of the register of members . . . and in particular from exercising those votes at the extraordinary general meeting of the said company to be held on 30 March 1992 or at any adjournment thereof or from granting a proxy to any other person to exercise on their behalf any such votes."

B

In so far as it relates to the particular meeting of 30 March 1992, or any adjournment thereof, the interlocutor granting interim interdict is spent. However, the more general interdict against exercising the votes unlawfully and without sufficient cause, or from granting a proxy to exercise such votes, remains in force. Since the interlocutor was C pronounced, answers have been lodged both on behalf of the company, and on behalf of 12 of the individuals affected by the interim interdict. These individuals now seek recall of that interim interdict.

The immediate background to the petition is to be found in a notice issued on 27 February 1992, giving notice of the holding of an extraordinary general meeting on 30 March 1992, for the purpose of considering certain resolutions relating to the appointment and removal of directors. Put more generally, it appears that there was a D potential battle for control of the board.

The problem in relation to the register of members is that the *Stock Transfer Act* 1963 provides for the transfer of registered securities by means of an instrument in a simple form set out in a schedule to the Act. That form is, however, only appropriate in the case of fully-paid shares. Article 14 of the company's articles provides that shares in the company shall be transferred in the form therein provided. That form, unlike the E statutory one, provides for acceptance by the transferee of the conditions under which the shares were held by the transferor, and a signature by the transferee to that effect. The entries in the register which the petitioner seeks to have deleted are averred to have followed from transfers of partly-paid shares, but it is said that none of the forms used in respect of these transfers contained any acceptance or signature by the transferee. The 12 individual respondents on whose behalf answers have been lodged admit that the F form of transfer employed in respect of their acquisition of shares did not conform to the company's articles, and a similar admission is made on behalf of the company in respect of the transfers more generally. The petitioner avers, and the company admits, that since February 1992, transfers of partly-paid shares have been effected in accordance with the provisions of the articles.

In seeking deletion of the relevant entries, the petitioner in his pleadings founds not merely upon the fact that the statutory form was inappropriate, and that the form G provided in the articles should have been used. He founds also upon sec. 183(1) of the *Companies Act* 1985, which provides that:

> "It is not lawful for a company to register a transfer of shares . . . unless a proper instrument of transfer has been delivered to it, or the transfer is an exempt transfer . . .
>
> This applies notwithstanding anything in the company's articles."

H   The transfers in question were not exempt, and the petitioner avers that it was not lawful for the company to have registered the transfers.

In moving me to recall the interim interdict, counsel for the respondents referred to a number of matters which were apparently seen as reflecting ill upon the petitioner. The interdict had only been obtained and intimated very shortly before the crucial meeting. The petitioner had selected those against whom interdict was sought, not merely because

they had lodged no caveat, but because these persons were thought to be on one side of
the dispute, while the petitioner and those against whom he did not seek interdict were
on the other. The petitioner was thus said to be using "illegitimate" means in pursuit of
his aims, and his "motive" in seeking rectification and interdict was said to be improper.
His grievance was not that the register was wrong, but that some of those whose names
appeared on it would vote in a way that he did not like, unless they were disenfranchised.

In the context of what is now an admitted and quite widespread breach of the
company's articles, I see nothing surprising in one party to a dispute of this kind
questioning the consequences of that breach, and while other votes might also have
been invalidated, it does not strike me as odd that such a party should restrict his
practical recourse to the law to those situations where he has an interest in doing so. I
have not found this line of argument useful.

As I have indicated, the petitioner's criticism of these entries in the register is based
not only upon the breach of the articles, but also upon an alleged breach of sec. 183(1)
of the *Companies Act* 1985. On the basis of the petitioner's pleadings, the contention
appears to be that since the wrong form of instrument had been used for these transfers,
there was no "proper instrument of transfer" within the meaning of sec. 183(1), and the
registration of the transfers was thereby rendered unlawful. However, counsel for the
respondents, under reference to *Re Paradise Motor Co Ltd* [1968] 1 WLR 1125,
submitted that this section did not render registration of these transfers unlawful, even
if the wrong form had been used. A "proper" instrument, for the purposes of this
section, meant merely an instrument which would attract stamp duty. The section was
not designed to ensure regularity between transferor and transferee, nor between them
and the company or other members. Having regard to what was said by the court in that
case, counsel for the petitioner did not seek to rely further upon this aspect of his case,
and I am satisfied that it was indeed ill-founded.

There is nonetheless an evident breach of the requirement of the articles in regard to
the form of transfer which was used. Moreover, in relation to partly-paid shares, I am
not prepared to see the absence of the transferee's signature as a mere irregularity, as it
might be in relation to fully-paid shares. One way of ensuring that this provision in the
articles is obeyed would be to refuse to register the name of any transferee, unless the
correct form, with his signature, had been used. That being so, there is in my view a
prima facie case for rectification if registration has in fact been granted on the basis of a
transfer form which is defective in terms of the articles. It was accepted by counsel for
the petitioner that if rectification were to be ordered in such circumstances, restoration
of the transferor's name to the register would be a necessary concomitant of deletion of
the transferee's name. I would observe that in my opinion it would always be a question
of circumstances whether the court should indeed order the clock to be put back in this
way. But I am not concerned at this stage with any eventual decision as to rectification,
in terms of sec. 359 of the *Companies Act* 1985. I am concerned only with the interim
regulation of matters, pending resolution of that issue.

Counsel for the respondents pointed out that the transferors of their shares had been
disenfranchised by the alteration of the register, and that they as transferees had been
disenfranchised, for all purposes, by the interim interdict. The respondents aver that the
transfer to them was made pursuant to a binding agreement between them and the
transferor, and that the transferor had at no time notified any challenge in respect of the
transfer or the binding nature of the agreement to transfer. The real question of principle
did not relate to the form which had been used, but to the issue of beneficial ownership.
That had indeed been transferred, and that being so, those who had acquired the
beneficial right ought not to be deprived of the title which they had obtained by
registration, even if they had obtained it in a defective manner. Counsel referred to *Re
Piccadilly Radio plc* (1989) 5 BCC 692. Rectification would serve no purpose in

A situations where the beneficial transfer was valid and unquestioned. Moreover, where that was the situation, there was no prima facie case for disenfranchising the transferees *ad interim*, and more particularly, the balance of convenience was against disenfranchising a beneficial owner *ad interim*, when no one else could exercise the voting rights attaching to these shares.

B Counsel for the petitioner emphasised that a breach of the articles was a wrong. The absence of the transferee's signature was not a technicality. The transfer of partly-paid shares had been recognised as unsuitable for the simplified statutory form, and it was left to individual companies to decide what was necessary when such a transfer occurred. This company had made specific requirements as to what the transferee must do. These positive requirements had been ignored, and the transferees' names had been entered in the register "without sufficient cause" for the purposes of sec. 359. A defective transfer had produced a defective register, and at least prima facie, that register should be rectified, and pending rectification the defective entry should not be given effect.

C This was the more true when those with this defect in their title to membership might by their votes have a determinative effect on important issues. As a member of the company, the petitioner was entitled to demand compliance with the articles, and upon the consequences of non-compliance being deprived of effect. In the circumstances, he also had an interest in ensuring that non-compliance should be ineffective. While he acknowledged that there were similarities with the case of *Re Piccadilly Radio plc*, it

D remained true that there was a prima facie case for eventual rectification, and pending such rectification, those who had arrived upon the register in breach of the articles, and who might in due course be removed from it, should not be allowed to exercise power in the affairs of the company.

I see genuine force in these submissions. Even if registration is not unlawful in terms of sec. 183 of the *Companies Act* 1985, I see the breach of the articles, and the absence of the transferee's signature, as a substantive matter, and not merely one of "form". It is

E perhaps the company itself, rather than other individual members, which is primarily affected by the breach. Nonetheless, other individual members are at least prima facie entitled to complain of the breach, if their interests are, even indirectly, affected.

I have, however, come to the view that as counsel for the respondents contended, the fundamental issue is that of beneficial ownership. Beneficial ownership having passed to the transferees as a matter of contract, it was accepted that they would be entitled to

F control and direct the use of the relevant votes by the transferor, pending alteration of the register. Being less direct, that position might be less effectual than having the actual right of voting as a member on the register. But once it is accepted, as it is, that the transferees are entitled, in a question with the transferors, to insist that the vote be used as the transferees wish, the possibility of a rectification, bringing the transferors back on to the register, becomes much less significant. The transferees would then still have control of these votes, despite the removal of their names from the register, by virtue of

G their beneficial right in the shares. That being so, the "wrongness" of their names being on the register might be seen as one of form rather than substance. Upon such a view, it is questionable whether there is even a prima facie case for interim interdict against their using their votes. Be that as it may, if one turns to the question of balance of convenience, I am satisfied that it is more appropriate to allow acquired beneficial rights to be exercised through voting, rather than exclude the holders of these shares (i.e. both the

H willing transferors and the willing transferees) from the voting process, pending resolution of an issue which relates primarily to methods of transfer rather than its intended effects.

In these circumstances I recall the interim interdict granted on 29 March 1992.

(*Order accordingly*)

Re Burnham Marketing Services Ltd & Anor.
Secretary of State for Trade and Industry v Harper.

Slough County Court.
District Judge Sonnex.
Judgment delivered 28 August 1992.

> *Disqualifying unfit directors of insolvent companies — Respondent was
> controlling shareholder and director of insolvent company — Materiality of
> respondent's purported delegation of responsibilities to managing directors —
> Company Directors Disqualification Act 1986, sec. 6.*

This was an application by the Secretary of State under sec. 6 of the Company Directors
Disqualification Act 1986.

The application related to the respondent's involvement with two companies: BMS and
FTP. He was the controlling shareholder and a director of BMS. He was the sole director
from May 1985 to August 1986. There was a managing director from 1983 (when the
company started trading) to 1985 and from August 1986 until about November 1987,
when the respondent resumed control. The company went into voluntary liquidation in
August 1988. The deficit appeared to be £244,000. FTP was incorporated in 1984, ceased
trading in January 1989, and went into voluntary liquidation in February 1989 with a
deficit of £219,000.

Three allegations made by the Secretary of State were proved against the respondent
involving failure to remit Crown moneys, to keep proper accounting records and to keep
clients' money separate from the company's own moneys. Two other allegations involving
failure to lodge accounts and to keep statutory records were also proved.

The respondent's defence raised the question of delegation. He argued that he had
appointed a managing director whom he believed to be competent and had placed reliance
on his judgment. He was let down badly. The Secretary of State argued that it was the
respondent's duty to maintain control and to verify regularly and thoroughly that the
company was being run in a proper fashion, and that his failure to do so and the
consequences of that failure amounted to conduct which rendered him unfit.

Held, disqualifying the respondent for three years:

1. There was no general rule that a director who entrusted the running of a company
to others who ran it into insolvency was necessarily guilty of conduct which rendered him
unfit.

2. The respondent was the owner of the company; he alone had the ultimate power to
dictate company policy and it was his decision whether to exercise that heavy responsibility.
He elected to place reliance in two managing directors. In the interim period he was sole
director but in that period the affairs of the company were never in a completely regular
state. Also the company was never very profitable. It was thus essential that the respondent
as proprietor kept a close eye and tight rein on those whom he had appointed.

3. The respondent was honest but had been shown to have a fundamental disregard
for his duties as a director by walking away from them. That was not a commercial
misjudgment and was conduct which made him unfit. In determining the period of
disqualification the court took account of the fact that there was no dishonesty and that
the respondent did make efforts to retrieve the situation in late 1987 and early 1988.

The following cases were referred to in the judgment:

Bath Glass Ltd, Re (1988) 4 BCC 130.
City Equitable Fire Insurance Co Ltd, Re [1925] Ch 407.
Cladrose Ltd, Re [1990] BCC 11.

A
C U Fittings Ltd & Anor, Re (1989) 5 BCC 210.
Dawson Print Group Ltd & Anor, Re (1987) 3 BCC 322.
Lo-Line Electric Motors Ltd & Ors, Re (1988) 4 BCC 415; [1988] Ch 477.
McNulty's Interchange Ltd & Anor, Re (1988) 4 BCC 533.
Majestic Recording Studios Ltd & Ors, Re (1988) 4 BCC 519.
Matthews (D J) (Joinery Design) Ltd & Anor, Re (1988) 4 BCC 513.
Melcast (Wolverhampton) Ltd, Re [1991] BCLC 288.
B
Rose Properties Ltd, Re (unreported).
Sevenoaks Stationers (Retail) Ltd, Re [1990] BCC 765; [1991] Ch 164.
Tansoft Ltd, Re [1991] BCLC 339.
Young, Re [1900] 2 Ch 753.

Richard Ritchie (instructed by the Treasury Solicitor) for the Secretary of State for Trade and Industry.

C
Ajmalul Hossain (instructed by Stewart-Wallace & Co, Gerrards Cross) for the respondent director.

JUDGMENT

District Judge Sonnex: This is an application by the Secretary of State under sec. 6 of the *Company Directors Disqualification Act* 1986. I have been referred during the
D
course of the hearing to the following cases:

Re Sevenoaks Stationers (Retail) Ltd [1990] BCC 765,
Re Bath Glass Ltd (1988) 4 BCC 130,
Re Tansoft Ltd [1991] BCLC 339,
Re Cladrose Ltd [1990] BCC 11,
Re C U Fittings Ltd (1989) 5 BCC 210,
E
Re Majestic Recording Studios Ltd (1988) 4 BCC 519,
Re Lo-Line Electric Motors Ltd (1988) 4 BCC 415,
Re Young [1900] 2 Ch 753,
Re City Equitable Fire Insurance Co Ltd [1925] Ch 407,
Re Rose Properties Ltd (unreported),
Re Dawson Print Group Ltd (1987) 3 BCC 322,
Re McNulty's Interchange Ltd (1988) 4 BCC 533,
F
Re D J Matthews (Joinery Design) Ltd (1988) 4 BCC 513, and
Re Melcast (Wolverhampton) Ltd [1991] BCLC 288.

It is for the applicant to prove first, that the respondent was a director; secondly, that the company became insolvent and thirdly, that his conduct makes him unfit to be concerned in the management of a company. There is no issue as to the first two requirements. The allegation of unfitness relies on the matters alleged in the affidavit of
G
Mr J M Iredale, the liquidator of Burnham Marketing Services Ltd ("BMS"), dated 6 July 1990 and of Mr Eliades, the liquidator of FTP Marketing Ltd ("FTP"), dated 26 February 1990. The response is contained in the affidavit by Mr Harper dated 28 May 1991.

The respondent, through counsel, sought to put in a further affidavit exhibiting substantial documentation. I refused that application for the reasons which I gave during the course of the hearing, but I permitted the admission of documents which were not in
H
conflict with matters raised in the principal affidavit and which explained or mitigated the respondent's conduct. The allegations in the case are not in the more serious category of matters that come before this court. There is no allegation of dishonesty on the part of the respondent, nor of milking the company for his own benefit, for example. But it does raise the important issue of the extent to which a director should involve himself in the control of the company's affairs. I shall deal first briefly with the

background and then with the allegations, in the order in which they appear in the affidavit, and then with the conclusions to be drawn.

A

The respondent is a man of 43; he has two degrees, one in psychology and the other in marketing. He started trading as Burnham Marketing Services some 11 years ago. That business was concerned with mail order sales promotion and from it two companies evolved: BMS commenced trading on 1 November 1983; FTP was incorporated on 12 June 1984 and traded from 1985 as Harper Harris Associates.

B

BMS's main function was handling and this is dealt with in a little detail in the respondent's affidavit. The respondent continued his own unlimited business which was mainly concerned with editorial promotions. He remained throughout the controlling shareholder and a director of BMS. He was not the managing director throughout; from 1983 to 1985 that position was filled by Mr Cummins. The respondent's oral evidence shows that Miss Butterworth, his cohabitee, was running the company thereafter, although there is no mention of her in the affidavit; the impression given by para. 8 being

C

that the respondent was running the company with Mr P Harris, his general manager. In due course Miss Butterworth became pregnant which effectively terminated her involvement in the management of the company and in August 1986 Ted Cox joined initially as general manager, but almost immediately he became managing director. The respondent had been sole director from May 1985 until August 1986. Cox continued as managing director until about November 1987 — there is an absence of notice about his cessation — whereupon the respondent resumed control. In early 1988 he brought in

D

Mr Zafar Alam, an accountant, at a stage at which the company's accounting was in some disarray.

The financial history is set out in the affidavits. Broadly, there was a small profit in 1984; a loss of £25,000 in 1985; the accounts for the year ended 31 December 1986 show a profit of £5,400, but the respondent never accepted those accounts as reflecting the true position.

E

So far as FTP is concerned its year ends on 30 September and in 1986 there was a profit of £6,000; in 1987 of £28,000; but a loss of £33,000 in 1988.

During early 1988 financial pressures continued to grow and this culminated for BMS in a flurry of demands and, in particular, distress for VAT of just over £20,000 in May 1988. In early July 1988 the respondent consulted Cork Gully. A voluntary arrangement was devised offering ten per cent to creditors. This was rejected by a creditors' meeting

F

and the company went into voluntary liquidation on 30 August 1988. The deficit appears to be £244,000.

FTP ceased trading in January 1989, went into voluntary liquidation in February 1989, and has a deficit of £219,000.

So much for the brief background history. I turn now to the unfitness allegations. The first, which is contained in para. 15 of Mr Iredale's affidavit, is that the company carried

G

on trading whilst insolvent:

> "The respondent allowed Burnham to carry on trading to the detriment of creditors at a time when he knew or should have known that Burnham was insolvent. Burnham could not pay its debts as they fell due for sometime prior to its liquidation and the respondent should have been aware of this from at least May 1988."

H

Now I agree with Mr Hussain that the Secretary of State is effectively stuck with that date, May 1988.

So far as the VAT debt is concerned, I am satisfied that the demand was not anticipated by the respondent. It arose by virtue of the company's inability to provide certain documentary evidence in support of input claims. There is no reason to believe either

A that the transactions themselves were not genuine or that the company did not have the reasonable expectation that its VAT returns would be accepted. Indeed, given time, one may conjecture those inputs might well have been allowed.

National Insurance contributions had been unpaid from 1982–83 onwards and so far as PAYE is concerned it is clear that the problem was known at least in March 1987. But I bear in mind, in the context of this allegation, that an offer was made by Mr Zafar Alam coupled with a payment of £5,000 on 23 March 1988 and that was accepted by the Collector of Taxes, and that the company may very well have had a reasonable belief at that time in its ability to pay in accordance with that offer. In fact, it can now be seen that the company was insolvent by November or December of 1987. Following that offer came the April 1988 management accounts and very soon thereafter the Customs & Excise distress levy on 10 May 1988. The writing then was clearly on the wall. The respondent spent some two to three weeks seeing his bank and taking advice and by early July had consulted Cork Gully. The writs and statutory demands referred to in para. 15(d) of Mr Iredale's affidavit were not in fact received until July. It is not without significance in my view that Cork Gully did not advise immediate liquidation but endorsed a scheme of voluntary arrangement.

In my judgment the period from May to July is far too short for the court to conclude that there was any lack of good faith. It may be that if the respondent had kept himself better informed he would have known the true position a lot earlier but that goes to other allegations. So far as this allegation is concerned actual knowledge is required and the Secretary of State cannot, by virtue of the specific allegation contained in the affidavit, go beyond May 1988 and I therefore reject that allegation as being unproved.

The second allegation is that there was a failure to comply with sec. 210 of the *Insolvency Act* 1986 as regards information contained in the statement of affairs; that is dealt with in para. 14 and relates to a foreign currency account. I cannot be satisfied on the evidence that the respondent, knowing of the existence of this specific account, consciously omitted to disclose it. The company made foreign currency transactions routinely. This was a dormant account, the balance was quite small and could easily have been forgotten so far as the respondent is concerned. Moreover the format of the statement of affairs is such that the respondent might well have assumed that the bank balance entry included several accounts and was entitled to assume that the liquidator would have asked the bank to provide details of the balances on all accounts. I therefore reject that allegation as unproved.

The third allegation is failure to remit Crown moneys. The allegation is that the respondent caused BMS to operate a policy of non-payment. In the liquidation both preferential and non-preferential Crown debts appear. Clearly the more serious in this context are the non-preferential debts which occurred during an earlier period. I take no account of liabilities which occurred on or immediately before the liquidation, and those non-preferential payments are £12,000 in respect of VAT, £15,000 for PAYE and £24,400 of NICs. As to VAT the problem was identified during a visit in May 1987. Imported goods had documentation missing, VAT having been paid. There is no evidence of false claims; it is a question of claims for which there was a shortage of requisite documents. Following the VAT visit there was correspondence, the accounts department being in touch with the importers and some documents were produced. Eventually the Customs & Excise got fed up and issued a demand in March 1988. That is indicative of problems in the accounts department but it cannot be said, in my judgment, in that context that the respondent caused the company to operate a policy. It seems, on the balance of probabilities, that these moneys would not have been due to the Crown if the accounts department had done its job properly.

British Company Cases

The PAYE and NICs fall into a quite different category. There were no payments of   A
PAYE between November 1985 and March 1987. For half of that period the respondent
was in control and from August 1986 Ted Cox was in control. It is not good enough to
say that it was Harris's fault, because a director who keeps proper control and insists on
proper accounts and management information will be aware of outstanding Crown
moneys and see that the situation is remedied. The same is true of NICs which date from
the year 1982–83. When Harris left in March 1987 there was a total of £52,000 in tax and
NICs outstanding and it is quite clear that the problems over payment were well known.   B

The respondent's attitude appears to have been: "Ted Cox is the managing director,
it's his job to sort it out". I must take issue with that. It is the job of every director to see
that the company is complying with its statutory obligations, not in the sense of
physically overseeing payments necessarily, but certainly reviewing the management
accounts to see that the job is being done. The respondent should have taken a far more
active role in ensuring that the default was remedied. By being in a position in which he   C
knew, or ought to have known, that Crown moneys were withheld and effectively used
by BMS as working capital and failing to take sufficient steps to correct the situation at
least until March 1988 (by which time it had proved too late) the respondent caused
BMS to operate a policy of non-payment of Crown moneys. I shall cite a passage from
Re Lo-Line Electric Motors Ltd (1988) 4 BCC 415 at p. 423:

> "Mr Browning says that so far as Lo-Line and Maldon were concerned he was not
> primarily responsible for the financial management of the companies. Even   D
> allowing for that, he must have been aware of the substantial Crown debts
> remaining unpaid and he could not consistently with his duties as a director
> abdicate all responsibility for financial management. In the case of Maldon he
> continued to trade even though these huge amounts of Crown debts were unpaid.
> So far as SEM is concerned, he was undoubtedly the financial manager throughout.
> In my judgment the history of his conduct in relation to all these companies shows   E
> a cynical willingness to use the unpaid Crown debts for the purpose of seeking to
> prop up the failing companies."

Now *Lo-Line* is no longer authority for the proposition that Crown debts should be
placed in a more serious category than debts due to other creditors, but the matter is put
in context by the leading case of *Re Sevenoaks Stationers (Retail) Ltd* [1990] BCC 765
at p. 779G–H as follows: F

> "But what is relevant in the Crown's position is not that the debt was a debt which
> arose from a compulsory deduction from employees' wages or a compulsory
> payment of VAT, but that the Crown was not pressing for payment, and the
> director was taking unfair advantage of that forbearance on the part of the Crown,
> and instead of providing adequate working capital, was trading at the Crown's
> expense while the companies were in jeopardy. It would be equally unfair to trade
> in that way and in such circumstances at the expense of creditors other than the   G
> Crown. The Crown is the more exposed not from the nature of the debts but from
> the administrative problem it has in pressing for prompt payment as companies
> get into difficulties."

Then the judge cites a passage from *Peter Gibson* J in *Re Bath Glass Ltd* (1988) 4
BCC 130 at pp. 133–134 in which he said:

> "Even if such conduct does not amount to wrongful trading within sec. 214 (of the   H
> *Insolvency Act* 1986), in my judgment it would still be conduct amounting to
> misconduct and so relevant to sec. 6. Whether in any particular case that
> misconduct, or the various matters of misconduct, proved to the satisfaction of
> the court, will justify a finding of unfitness will depend on all the circumstances of
> the case."

A
That allegation, therefore, is proven.

The next allegation is breach of fiduciary duty. It is contained in para. 13 and I confess to finding it the most confusing. So far as I can see the position in a nutshell is this. There were two lots of racking; some belonged to BMS, some was on lease from a company called Macepol. That is a company which was run by one Fitzpatrick, in which the respondent had no interest. The respondent wanted to use the leased racking for the benefit of Property Portfolio Ltd, a continuing company controlled by him, and agreed

B
to pay the liquidator £2,000 subject to making title and that sum was deposited. The liquidator contacted Fitzpatrick and endeavoured to buy the racking for less than £2,000 thereby realising a profit for the benefit of the creditors. Fitzpatrick it seems then contacted the respondent who wrote what I judge to be a somewhat ill-advised letter to the liquidator. He should simply have said to Fitzpatrick: "You deal with the liquidator, I'm having nothing to do with it." But that was explained in evidence by his anxiety that the racking should not be removed, which would have caused serious disruption to

C
Property Portfolio Ltd. The liquidator claims that the respondent spiked his guns, but I cannot be satisfied on the evidence that the respondent took the initiative in approaching Macepol or that his passive actions amounted to a breach of fiduciary duty. In any event I am not satisfied on the evidence that any loss to the liquidator accrued. Finally, I am not persuaded that there is a fiduciary duty as such after the liquidation, when the respondent's function as director has effectively ceased in so far as this particular

D
situation is concerned. I therefore reject that allegation.

I turn now to the accounting records dealt with at para. 12 and the respondent's reply to that allegation which is contained in para. 33 and 35. It is not denied by the respondent, and this is his affidavit evidence on which he primarily relies, that the books were inadequate. Indeed, para. 33 is clear admission that they were. The defence is an assertion of responsibility by others when in charge. Now a great deal of time was

E
occupied during the hearing in looking at accounting records and I do not propose to review that evidence in detail. The court is entitled to look at the overall picture and assess the extent of the failure and consequences of it. In the respondent's favour are that first, there was no fundamental criticism of his accounting system; no suggestion, for example, of a failure to keep essential books of account. Secondly, the company did take advice from accountants when the system was set up and it did employ bookkeepers and others whose job it was to look after the accounts. Thirdly, the assertion by

F
Mr Iredale in his affidavit, that at no time did the accounts display BMS's financial position correctly, was somewhat modified in evidence to the effect that his comments relate mainly to the position in 1988. Mr Iredale also conceded during cross-examination that it looked as though efforts had been made to keep the books properly. Conversely, the respondent does admit in para. 44 that the VAT arrears arose as there were no accurate accounts during Cox's time. If that is true it must be equally true of those Crown moneys which were outstanding in March 1987 and which the respondent should

G
have monitored.

Before the entry of Ted Cox the books appear to have been kept reasonably satisfactorily although there is some evidence that float moneys were not always recorded in precisely the correct way but thereafter, that is to say after Mr Cox's appointment, matters were allowed to slide. It is clear that by the time of the liquidation the books were in an unsatisfactory state, although I accept that from early 1988 on the respondent did make

H
efforts by employing Zafar Alam to disentangle the float moneys and to computerise the accounts. The fact remains that by virtue of the failure to maintain proper books of account the directors were unaware that the company was trading whilst insolvent. The allegation, it seems to me, is both admitted and proved.

The next allegation is that the debt of Property Portfolio Ltd was understated. It is quite clear on the evidence that this was a disputed amount. There was a counterclaim.

It became the subject of threats of litigation which was ultimately settled at a much lower figure. I am not satisfied that that allegation is made out and I reject it.

There is a further allegation of misapplication of company moneys contained in para. 16. I can deal with that very shortly. There is no evidence that the respondent caused the misapplication. The debtor was Time Life books. They paid moneys due to BMS into the Property Portfolio account of their own volition. Only one payment was made before the liquidation and Mr Iredale in his cross-examination agreed that it could be forgotten. I reject it.

The next allegation concerns trade advances. These were of two types. There were postal floats designed to fund the postage on product promotions, and redemption floats which were, in effect, advance payments against promotions which involved money back against vouchers and so forth. The specific allegation is that no separate accounts were maintained for float moneys and at the time of liquidation these were mixed in general funds resulting in a credit of £5,500 on the Unican account but a debit of £34,500 on the Bass Tennant account. This is potentially a serious matter. Clients' money should clearly be kept separate; that is a fundamental accounting principle. It is not perhaps comparable with a solicitor using his client's funds to run his own office, but it is nevertheless a serious breach if proven.

I would distinguish between postal and redemption floats. I am satisfied having heard the evidence that it would have been impractical to open separate accounts for each postal float. The post office records and the cash book, provided they were properly kept, should suffice. I am bound to say that it is not clear on the evidence that the system was always properly kept. Nevertheless, in my judgment, no criticism attaches to the respondent for the mere fact that separate bank accounts were not kept in respect of postal floats.

So far as the redemption floats are concerned the respondent acknowledges that separate accounts ought to have been kept, and I am satisfied that such accounts were in fact kept prior to August 1986 when Mr Cox was appointed, although there is some evidence that not all of the float moneys were initially paid into those accounts. Sometimes, it seems, they were paid into other accounts and then transferred out. But during the Cox period a different accounting system was adopted. The respondent was certainly aware of that by March 1987 by virtue of the accountant's report. It seems that he did nothing positive to ensure that the recommendations were implemented. It is true that when Cox was sacked one of the priorities given to Zafar Alam was to sort out the redemption floats and he was in the process of doing so — that is evidenced by documents produced — at the time of liquidation, but it was too late by then, and the matter was not corrected. I am satisfied that the person mainly responsible for the initial mixing of these funds was Ted Cox, but the respondent is culpable for his failure to exert proper control when he first became aware of the problem. I find that allegation proved.

The next matter is the failure to file company accounts. None were lodged for the year ending 31 December 1986 or 31 December 1987. 1986 accounts were produced; they were not approved by the respondent although given his lack of involvement in the running of the company it is not clear to me why he was able to withhold his approval. It is clear that a dispute with the accountants is not a good enough reason for failure to lodge accounts. If necessary another accountant should have been employed. The duty is to lodge audited accounts, and that the respondent failed to do, and the allegation is thus proved. It is not serious enough in itself to warrant disqualification. A greater importance must be attached, it seems to me, to the duty to lodge accounts when a company is struggling than when it is doing well because persons dealing with the company may take a view based on the accounts. There is some significance in the fact

A   that the 1986 accounts, although they show a small profit, still showed a net asset deficit of £19,000 which would have been of some interest to persons dealing with the company.

The next allegation is of failure to keep statutory records and make annual returns. The annual returns for the years 1984–86 were all late, in September 1987 and no return for 1987 was filed. The change of directors, the resignation of Cummins, the appointment and resignation of Cox were not notified to the registry. The respondent says he left that to the accountants and certainly for previous years there was a charge for annual returns.

B   That is not a complete excuse but I accept that these matters are things which small private companies frequently do rely upon their accountants for and, although I find the allegation proved, I do not regard it as serious, and it would weigh very lightly in the balance in deciding whether the court should accede to this application by the Secretary of State. I take account of Mr Eliades' comment that 95 per cent of companies default with these records.

C   The separate matters raised in Mr Eliades' affidavit add little weight, in my judgment, to this application. The annual returns and accounts were outstanding for a relatively short period and the use of Crown moneys relates to a period only shortly before the company ceased trading. So although those are formally proved they are, in my view, allegations of little consequence in the overall context.

In summary, therefore, the Secretary of State has proved three important allegations,

D   the failure to remit Crown moneys, the failure to keep proper accounting records and the failure to separate the redemption floats from the company's own moneys. It has proved two less important allegations: the failure to lodge accounts and the failure to keep statutory records. The three major allegations are linked by the fundamental question of delegation. Was the respondent entitled to delegate his responsibility to others or must he take responsibility for the fact that the company allowed these failures to occur? The tenor of the respondent's defence is that he appointed Ted Cox, a man

E   who was known to him in business, whom he believed to be competent, as the managing director of BMS in August 1986 and he placed reliance on Cox's judgment. He was let down badly. Cox changed the accounting system and, in particular, the way the floats were dealt with; he failed to ensure that the books were kept properly; his credit control was poor; he allowed Harris, the accountant, to fall into arrears with tax payments. He changed the system of work, employing subcontractors to write cheques; he made

F   unwise decisions in the choice of staff; he overstaffed increasing the overheads. All of this came to a head in late 1987 when Cox went and the respondent made strenuous efforts to pick up the pieces. He got in a new accountant who started to disentangle the floats mess and introduced a computerised accounting system, or had begun to do so.

The applicant's case is that whilst Mr Cox may have played a part in the growth of the company's problems, those problems existed before he was appointed, and it was the

G   respondent's duty to maintain control and to verify regularly and thoroughly that the company was being run in a proper fashion, that his failure to do so and the consequences of that failure amount to conduct which renders him unfit. In the words of Mr Iredale, who I think probably borrowed them from one of the reported cases: "He abdicated his responsibilities as director."

It is striking that the respondent does not essentially admit to any fault whatever. He

H   lays the entire blame squarely on the shoulders of others. Mr Hussain referred to a passage in which the court waxed biblical over a sinner who repenteth, but repentance is not Mr Harper's theme. He blames Mr A Harris, Mr P Harris, Mr Milne, the bank for making unauthorised transfers and above all Mr Cox. He went so far in his oral evidence as to allege a fraudulent conspiracy between Mr Cox and Mr Milne resulting in a loss of £130,000. Neither of those gentlemen was present or had the opportunity to refute the allegation and in any event one would certainly have expected so serious and fundamental a matter to be raised in the respondent's affidavit, but it appeared only in the oral evidence.

The starting point, it seems to me, is that a director by definition is one who takes part with others in the governing of a company's affairs. It may or may not be an executive role but it involves the duty of controlling the overall manner in which the company conducts its business. Mr Hussain referred me to *Re City Equitable Fire Insurance Co Ltd* [1925] Ch 407 in which the court examined the degree of care required of directors, dealing with the reasonable care expected of an ordinary man and so forth and it was pointed out in that case that the duties of a director varied substantially according to the size and type of the company. Logically the larger the company the greater degree of delegation which is necessary.

It is equally true that as between working directors a particular function may become the primary responsibility of one. In *Re Cladrose Ltd* [1990] BCC 11 there were two directors of three companies and the court was concerned with the total failure (which was far worse than this case in that particular respect) to file accounts and annual returns. One director was a chartered accountant who acknowledged that that was his responsibility. He was disqualified, the other director was not. The court did not exonerate the other director but decided that his conduct was not sufficient to render him unfit. What was said was this (at p. 13H):

> "As it seems to me, the directors are all responsible for the preparation of formal documents in any company. They cannot excuse the failure to produce documents by simply saying, 'Oh, I relied upon somebody else'; but they may be very much less blameworthy in some instances than in others if it can be said that they relied on somebody whom they had good and sufficient cause to believe was a proper person to rely upon, and who was equally with themselves responsible."

Re Majestic Recording Studios Ltd (1988) 4 BCC 519, which was a case under sec. 300 of the *Companies Act* 1985 (repealed), is another example. There one director dealt with technical matters and left financial affairs to his co-director, and at p. 522 the court says:

> "Mr Heath-Hadfield filed two affidavits . . . He accepted that he was an executive director of Majestic and Hadmor, but said that he was not involved in the running of Enterprises. He said he had no shares save 26 of the 100 issued shares of Hadmor. His line was that he had no concern in or control over any financial affairs, those matters being left to Mr Collier. He did not know why returns and accounts were not filed. [Counsel for Mr Heath-Hadfield] submitted that, in respect of all three companies, Mr Heath-Hadfield's conduct was 'peripheral' to financial matters, but he was not in breach of commercial morality and had not shown such a lack of care as to bring himself within sec. 300. It was rather, said [counsel], a case for admonition rather than disqualification. I do not agree. Having considered the facts I have outlined and the other matters contained in the affidavit evidence and seen Mr Heath-Hadfield in the witness-box, I am quite satisfied that Mr Heath-Hadfield is at present not a person who should be entitled to trade with the benefit of limited liability. Two references in the authorities seem to me to be appropriate. In *Drincqbier v Wood* [1899] 1 Ch 393, *Byrne* J said at p. 406:

> > 'It should be understood that a director, consenting to be a director, has assumed a position involving duties which cannot be shirked by leaving everything to others.'

and in *Re Stanford Services Ltd* (1987) 3 BCC 326, *Vinelott* J said at p. 336:

> > 'the public is entitled to be protected, not only against the activities of those guilty of the more obvious breaches of commercial morality, but also against

A   someone who has shown in his conduct of more than one company — or, since
the passing of the *Company Directors Disqualification Act* 1986, in the conduct
of any company — a failure to appreciate or observe the duties attendant on
the privilege of conducting business with the protection of limited liability.' "

Mr Ritchie also referred me to *Re Melcast (Wolverhampton) Ltd* [1991] BCLC 288.
There is a passage at p. 296h:

B   "Mr Evans seems to me to have treated himself, as Mr Chivers submitted, as
merely an employee of the company, as his former co-director Mr Paxton was,
responsible for running the workforce, working I fully believe extremely hard
trying to increase the orders and reduce the costs and expenses of operation, but
in no way at any point taking any of the duties of a director, that is the wider duties
to ensure that the company is trading properly, to ensure that it is paying its debts
properly, and to ensure that it has a future at all. He seems to have totally shut his

C   mind to all such things or to have never realised, although he had been advised by
accountants twice, that there were such duties and that he personally had a
responsibility to carry them out."

Mr Ritchie put the proposition as to directors' responsibility in very wide terms.
I cannot accept, without qualification, the general proposition that a director who
entrusts the running of a company to others who run it into insolvency is necessarily
guilty of conduct rendering him unfit. The non-executive director of a large public

D   company who attended board meetings and received regular management information
from colleagues which was apparently satisfactory might well be free from any substantial
criticism.

In small companies it is generally incumbent on all directors to play a much more
active part in governing. Even so, one can envisage this sort of scenario, that a father
has built up a business and then retires and hands over the shares and control to his son

E   and at the time of handover the books and everything else are in impeccable order; the
father remains a director because his name is useful and there are family considerations
involved. The son gives him regular information, produces management accounts which
show a healthy picture; in fact it is false and it turns out that the company is trading on
creditors' money. That father might be subject to criticism for trusting too well but it
would be a harsh judgment to deem him unfit to be concerned in the directorship of a

F   company.

In the respondent's case the situation is this. He has been at all material times the
owner of the company; he alone had the ultimate power to dictate company policy and
it was his decision whether to exercise that heavy responsibility. He elected to place
reliance first, in Cummins, and latterly in Cox. In the interim period he was sole director.
And yet on his evidence even then Miss Butterworth, who was not a director, was left in

G   charge and during that period board meetings consisted of an occasional chat over
supper in the evening.

This is a critical factor. At no stage after Cummins resigned and the respondent
delegated control were the affairs of the company in a completely regular state. During
the Butterworth/Harris period there accrued arrears of NICs from 1983 and PAYE
ceased to be paid from November 1985. So that when Cox took over there were
significant Crown debts. On the evidence, as I have indicated, I am not satisfied that

H   there were serious defaults in accounting procedures prior to the Cox period but the
liquidity position was such that very tight control in keeping floats up to date was needed
and such control was not exercised.

It is also the case that this company was never very profitable. It made a loss in 1985
and it had a net capital deficit. It was thus essential that the respondent as proprietor of
the company kept a close eye and tight rein on those whom he had appointed. If that was

so in August 1986 it was doubly so after March 1987 when the respondent became aware   A
that Cox and Harris between them had allowed the Crown debts to mount up to £50,000,
that the accounts were in a state of disarray, and that the float moneys were mixed with
company moneys.

The respondent had commissioned a report from Mr Milne but he took no steps to
ensure that the recommendations were complied with, or no effective steps. Milne's
firm had even provided a do-it-yourself trial balance kit but that seems not to have been
used. There were no regular directors' meetings; there is no evidence of board minutes;   B
there are no procedural instructions emanating from the respondent and frankly his
method of discharging his duties as controlling director seems to have been to breeze
into the office from time to time, look round at people working and ask Mr Cox, "How's
it going, Ted?", and on getting a reassuring reply depart contentedly. One has to ask
what documents, what solid evidence did the respondent see which gave him cause for
complacency? If he truly believed that the company was doing well surely he should   C
have said to Mr Cox: "Why aren't we paying off our creditors?"

All of this, in my judgment, adds up to a situation in which the respondent effectively
stepped aside and said: "Let Ted get on with it." By the time the rot finally stopped and
the respondent for the first time took actual control it was too late. I accept that from
then on he did his best to retrieve the situation but it was, in fact, irretrievable. He
should, certainly from the date of Cox's appointment, have held regular formal meetings,
reviewed management information, checked ledgers — certainly the nominal ledger —   D
on a regular basis, monitored the control system for clients' money, seen to it personally
that the accountant's recommendations were being implemented and seen to it, in
particular, that inroads were made in the long-term debts. I am satisfied that if he had
properly discharged those duties the company's insolvency would have been known to
him much earlier than it was.

Mr Hussain relies on *Re Bath Glass Ltd* in which despite a substantial accumulation
of Crown debts over a period similar to this case and despite a finding of trading whilst   E
insolvent over a considerable period, the court held that it was not appropriate to
disqualify. I accept that there are some similarities, but there is an important distinction
in the facts and it is this in my view: that was a case in which the directors had been
concerned actively throughout. There were mitigating factors, particularly strong
elements of misfortune; and the fact that they had acted on professional advice in the
belief of their ability to trade out of their difficulties and that belief was based on rational
if mistaken assumptions. The court found that the directors were honest but they had   F
made a commercial misjudgment in the way in which they ran the company.

The respondent is also honest but has been shown to have a fundamental disregard
for his duties as a director by walking away from them. That is not a commercial
misjudgment and it must be, in my view, conduct which makes him unfit to be concerned
in the management of a company. The *Sevenoaks* case has shown that that is the
statutory test and the only test that the court should apply. This being a sec. 6 application   G
the court must disqualify and cannot take into account any current conduct of the
respondent.

In determining the period of disqualification I take account of the fact that there is no
dishonesty element in the case. It is not a case in which the respondent took for himself
a substantial personal benefit at the expense of creditors (as is often the case in these
applications) and that he did make efforts to retrieve the situation in late 1987 and early
1988. Taking an overall view and taking those latter factors into account in my view that   H
places this case in the lower bracket, and having made a finding of unfitness, as I have
already indicated, I shall impose a period of disqualification of three years.

(Order accordingly)

A
Scottish Exhibition Centre Ltd, Noters.
Court of Session (Outer House).
Lord Morton of Shuna.
Judgment delivered 22 January 1993.

Effect of administration order — Whether landlord should have leave to bring action against tenant in administration — Insolvency Act 1986, sec. 11(3).

B
This was a note by lessors seeking leave to bring an action against a company in administration.

The noters leased to the company premises containing three restaurants which were the business the company carried on. After administrators of the company were appointed, the noters intimated that they were intending to exercise a right under the lease to terminate it. The holders of security over the company's interest in the lease had intimated C an intention to contest any attempt to remove the company from the premises.

It was accepted that the question on the note was governed by the guidelines set out in the Court of Appeal judgment in Re Atlantic Computer Systems plc [1990] BCC 859. It was also agreed that if the noters obtained possession of the property leased to the company, it would be impossible to sell the undertaking as a going concern, and therefore impossible to achieve the purpose for which the administration order was made.

D
The noters argued that since the lease was the company's only significant asset and the secured creditor was owed far more than the value of the lease, the secured creditor was the only creditor with any real interest; that if leave were refused, the noters would be denied any opportunity to exercise proprietorial rights; that a refusal of leave would result in significant loss to the noters because the company was only operating two of the three restaurants in the premises and under the terms of the lease the rent payable was E based on a percentage of gross sales; and that the administrators had been trying for more than 18 months to dispose of the undertaking as a going concern.

The administrators submitted that the balance was against leave being granted or, in any event, that the noters had failed to make out a case that it should be granted. The principal obligation under a lease was to pay the rent, and it was not averred that the tenant was unable to pay the rent. There was no obligation in the lease to keep the three F restaurants open, and the rent was based on turnover and not on profit. The administrators had not been idle and had endeavoured to dispose of the business as a going concern, and were still endeavouring to do so. Further time should be allowed for the administrators to try to dispose of the business.

Held, granting leave to bring proceedings against the company:

1. Points relating to termination of the lease would arise for decision only in the G subsequent action if leave to raise it were given. It was inappropriate to express any opinion on such points in deciding whether leave should be granted. The court needed to be satisfied only that the applicant had a seriously arguable case.

2. The noters did have a seriously arguable case, and as over 18 months had passed, during which time the administrators had endeavoured to dispose of the business, to grant a further period of time was unlikely to achieve anything, especially as administration H was intended to be only an interim and temporary regime.

The following case was referred to in the opinion:

Re Atlantic Computer Systems plc [1990] BCC 859; [1992] Ch 505.

J R Doherty (instructed by Dundas & Wilson, CS) for Scottish Exhibition Centre Ltd.

Neil Davidson (instructed by Bishop & Robertson Chalmers) for the administrators.

OPINION

Lord Morton of Shuna: Scottish Exhibition Centre Ltd has lodged a note seeking leave to bring proceedings against Mirestop Ltd, a company which is in administration. The respondents are the joint administrators of the company. They were appointed by the court on the petition of the company on the basis that the company was unable to pay its debts and that an administration order should be made. The company had obtained a valuation of its assets which showed that a valuation on a "going concern" basis was much greater than a valuation on a "for sale" basis. The respondents were appointed joint administrators *ad interim* on 4 June 1991 and were appointed joint administrators on 16 July 1991.

The noters leased to the company the premises known as "The Pumphouse" at the Scottish Exhibition and Conference Centre in Glasgow. The premises contain three restaurants which are the business the company carried on. By cl. 5 of the lease, it is provided:

"if the tenant shall become notour bankrupt or shall make any arrangement with creditors or shall suffer any diligence to be levied on the subjects, or being a company, shall go into liquidation, whether voluntary or compulsory (otherwise than a voluntary liquidation of a solvent company for the purpose of amalgamation or reconstruction on terms approved by the landlord in writing), or suffer a receiver or other administrator or manager for creditors to be appointed, then in any such case it shall be lawful for the landlord at any time thereafter, by notice in writing, to bring this lease to an end forthwith and to enter the subjects and repossess and enjoy the same."

By letter of 18 June 1991 to the respondents and of 19 June 1991 to the company, the noters intimated that they were exercising their right to irritate and terminate the lease. The respondents do not accept that the noters were entitled to irritate the lease and it is said that the holders of a standard security and floating charge over the company's interests in the lease, have intimated an intention to contest any attempt to remove the company from the premises. In these circumstances the noters have presented the note seeking leave to bring an action to resolve the question.

At the hearing before me, counsel for the noter and counsel for the respondents each accepted the guidelines set out in the Court of Appeal judgment in *Re Atlantic Computer Systems plc* [1990] BCC 859. It was agreed that if the noters obtained possession of the property leased to the company, it would be impossible to sell the undertaking as a going concern, and therefore impossible to achieve the purpose for which the administration order was made. Applying the guidelines suggested by the Court of Appeal, the court then had to carry out a balancing exercise.

For the noters, Mr Doherty submitted that various factors tipped the balance in favour of his clients and he accepted that it was for the noter to make out a case for leave to be given. The factors founded on were (1) that the lease was the company's only significant asset, and from the company's petition it was clear that the secured creditor was owed far more than the value of the lease. The result of this was that the secured creditor was the only creditor with any real interest; (2) if leave were refused, the noters would be denied any opportunity to exercise proprietorial rights; (3) a refusal of leave would result in significant loss to the noters. The primary loss was that they were prevented from regaining their property. A secondary loss occurred because of the parlous financial position of the tenants, who were only operating two of the three restaurants in the premises. Under the terms of the lease the rent payable after 11 November 1992 was based on a percentage of the gross annual sales for each year to the preceding August. As the company was only operating two restaurants, the turnover must be less than if they were operating three, and therefore the rent payable was less. A refusal to grant

A leave would result in the noters being tied in with a tenant in a poor financial situation, not operating the premises, which were part of the Exhibition Centre, and important for the noters' whole enterprise. Finally, Mr Doherty submitted that the respondents had had more than sufficient time to attempt to dispose of the undertaking as a going concern. The respondents had carried out a wide advertising campaign but this had produced no result. A hearing had been fixed to take place in September 1992, but this had been discharged on the motion of the noters because the respondents had entered

B on the second advertising campaign. This was understood to have produced no significant result. In these circumstances leave should be granted. Mr Doherty founded on the passage in the judgment in *Atlantic Computers* at p. 868G:

> ". . . an administration is intended to be only an interim and temporary regime.
> There is to be a breathing-space while the company, under new management in
> the person of the administrator, seeks to achieve one or more of the purposes set

C
> out in sec. 8(3). There is a moratorium on the enforcement of debts and rights,
> proprietary and otherwise, against the company, so as to give the administrator
> time to formulate proposals and lay them before the creditors, and then implement
> any proposals approved by the creditors. In some cases winding up will follow, in
> others it will not."

D For the respondents, Mr Davidson accepted that there was a conflict within the rights of the noters as landlords, and the rights of the secured creditor, and accepted the guidelines as in *Atlantic Computer Systems*. He submitted that the balance was against leave being granted or, in any event, that the noters had failed to make out a case that it should be granted. The principal obligation under a lease was to pay the rent, and it was not averred that the tenant was unable to pay the rent. There was no obligation in the lease to keep the three restaurants open, and the rent was based on turnover and not on

E profit. The administrators had not been idle and had endeavoured to dispose of the business as a going concern, and were still endeavouring to do so. Correspondence was produced showing that a company had expressed an interest in December 1992 in acquiring the business, but as I understand it, this interest was expressed on the basis of purchasing the premises as well as the business and it would not appear to meet the particular situation. Mr Davidson submitted that further time should be allowed for the

F administrators to try to dispose of the business.

Mr Davidson also made submissions regarding the validity of the notice of irritancy, and both counsel made reference to the averments by the respondents that it was not fair and reasonable for the noters to rely on their purported right to irritate the lease under reference to sec. 5 of the *Law Reform (Miscellaneous Provisions) (Scotland) Act* 1985. In my opinion, these points would arise for decision only in the subsequent action if leave to raise it were given. It is, in my opinion, inappropriate at this stage, to express

G any opinion on such points in deciding whether leave should be granted. As was said in *Atlantic Computer Systems* at p. 882B:

> "In some cases there will be a dispute over the existence, validity or nature of the
> security which the applicant is seeking leave to enforce. It is not for the court on
> the leave application to seek to adjudicate upon that issue, unless . . . the issue

H
> raises a short point of law which it is convenient to determine without further ado.
> Otherwise the court needs to be satisfied only that the applicant has a seriously
> arguable case."

I consider that the noters do have a seriously arguable case, and I do not consider that, as over 18 months have already passed, during which time the administrators have endeavoured to dispose of the business, to grant a further period of time would achieve anything, especially as the administration is intended to be only an interim and temporary regime.

In these circumstances I consider it appropriate to grant leave to bring proceedings against the company.

(*Order accordingly*)

A **First Energy (UK) Ltd v Hungarian International Bank Ltd.**

Court of Appeal (Civil Division).

Nourse, Steyn and Evans L JJ.

Judgment delivered 24 February 1993.

Contract — Agency — Whether employee who had no apparent authority to make offer could have apparent authority to communicate approval of offer.

B
This was an appeal from a judgment in a contract action in which two principal questions arose for decision. The first was whether a letter from the defendant bank's senior manager in Manchester, "J", contained an offer capable of acceptance. The judge decided this issue in favour of the plaintiffs. Secondly, the question arose whether the prima facie agreement was defeasible on the ground that J had no authority to make the offer. He did not have actual authority to do so. The question was whether the defendants

C
had conferred ostensible authority on him (1) to make the offer or (2) to communicate that the necessary authority had been obtained from the defendants to make the offer. The judge decided this issue in favour of the plaintiffs on the basis set out in (2). The defendants appealed arguing that the letter did not amount to an offer and that there was an irreconcilable inconsistency between a finding that J had no actual or ostensible authority to sanction the transaction and the finding that he had ostensible authority to communicate the information that head office had approved the transaction.

D
Held, dismissing the appeal:

1. In the circumstances the letter communicated an unconditional and firm offer, and that offer was accepted.

2. On the particular facts of the case, even though the plaintiffs knew that J's actual authority to enter into transactions on the defendants' behalf was limited, his position as

E
senior manager in Manchester was such that he was clothed with ostensible authority to communicate that head office approval had been given for the transaction in issue. (*Armagas Ltd v Mundogas SA* (1986) 2 BCC 99,197 distinguished.)

The following cases were referred to in the judgment:

Armagas Ltd v Mundogas SA (1986) 2 BCC 99,197; [1986] AC 717.

Berryere v Fireman's Fund Insurance Co (1965) 51 DLR (2d) 603.

F
British Thomson-Houston Co Ltd v Federated European Bank Ltd [1932] 2 KB 176.

Egyptian International Foreign Trade Co v Soplex Wholesale Supplies Ltd & Anor ("The Raffaella") [1985] 2 Lloyd's Rep 36.

Panorama Developments (Guildford) Ltd v Fidelis Furnishing Fabrics Ltd [1971] 2 QB 711.

Royal British Bank v Turquand (1855) 5 E & B 248, (1856) 6 E & B 327; 119 ER 474, 886.

G
Giles Wingate-Saul QC and Andrew Sander (instructed by Davies Arnold Cooper, Manchester) for the plaintiffs.

Mary Arden QC and Michael Todd (instructed by Chaffe Street, Manchester) for the defendants.

JUDGMENT

H
Steyn LJ: A theme that runs through our law of contract is that the reasonable expectations of honest men must be protected. It is not a rule or a principle of law. It is the objective which has been and still is the principal moulding force of our law of contract. It affords no licence to a judge to depart from binding precedent. On the other hand, if the prima facie solution to a problem runs counter to the reasonable expectations of honest men, this criterion sometimes requires a rigorous re-examination of the

problem to ascertain whether the law does indeed compel demonstrable unfairness. These general considerations are of some relevance to a question of ostensible authority which is the principal matter to be considered on this appeal. If we were to accept the implications which the appellants have placed on observations in the House of Lords in *Armagas Ltd v Mundogas SA* (1986) 2 BCC 99,197 our decision would in my view frustrate the reasonable expectations of the parties. Moreover, our decision would have to be based on an unreal premise as to the way in which commercial men transact business of the particular kind involved in this case. I shall attempt to show that the application of orthodox principles does not compel such a result.

During the course of a trial on liability His Honour Judge *Michael Kershaw* QC had to decide whether the plaintiffs had established a breach of contract. Two principal questions arose for decision. The first was whether the plaintiffs had prima facie established the conclusion of a binding agreement. This question resolved itself into an issue as to whether the defendants had made an offer capable of acceptance. The judge decided this issue in favour of the plaintiffs. Secondly, the question arose whether the prima facie agreement was defeasible on the ground that the defendants' agent had no authority to make the offer. The agent did not have actual authority to do so. The question was whether the defendants had conferred ostensible authority on the agent (1) to make the offer or (2) to communicate that the necessary authority had been obtained from the defendants to make the offer. The judge decided this issue in favour of the plaintiffs on the basis set out in (2). On this appeal the defendants challenge the judge's conclusions on the first issue and on the second issue so far as the judge ruled against the defendants. If the defendants succeed on either point, the judgment for the plaintiffs must be set aside.

The commercial story

It will be convenient to start with a brief account of the commercial dealings between the parties. Occam's razor requires elimination of all facts which are not essential to the subject to be examined. It is not always easy to follow this advice, but I will do my best. First Energy (UK) Ltd, the plaintiffs, specialised in the replacement of old-fashioned heating systems by a more economical form of space heating. In order to make such new systems financially attractive to customers First Energy devised a system whereby it would install a new heating system on the basis that a building owner would pay an annual sum over a number of years. At the end of the period the building owner would have paid in full for his new system. First Energy used subcontractors to perform most of the work. The idea seemed a good one. In November 1989 First Energy secured the first such order: it was an order for a heating system to be installed in a factory in Wisbech.

In order to make a success of the scheme First Energy needed credit facilities. First Energy entered into discussions with a number of lending institutions. One of those institutions was the Hungarian International Bank Ltd, the defendants in the action ("HIB").

HIB is a subsidiary of the National Bank of Hungary. HIB is not a clearing bank with high street branches. In evidence tendered on behalf of the defendants at the trial HIB was described as a merchant bank. On appeal counsel for HIB described HIB as a trading bank. It does not matter which description is correct. Unquestionably it specialised in commercial lending to trading companies. The head office of HIB was in London. Counsel for First Energy rightly reminded us that Manchester is a great European and international financial centre, which yields in this country in the range and extent of its financial services only to London. And HIB's only other office in this country was in Manchester. First Energy dealt with HIB's Manchester office.

A The negotiations between First Energy and HIB started in 1989. Mr Croft initiated the negotiations and acted on behalf of First Energy in subsequent discussions. He negotiated directly with Mr Jamison, who held the title of senior manager and was in charge of the Manchester office of HIB. Mr Jamison had greater actual authority than the manager of the commercial department of HIB in London. He had authority to sanction large credit transactions together with another senior employee. Like many merchant banks and trading banks HIB drew a distinction between internal authority to

B sanction a credit transaction and authority to sign a facility letter. Employees of substantially less seniority than Mr Jamison could sign such a facility letter, but two signatures were required. Mr Croft would not have been aware of the details of the internal hierarchy of HIB. But I mention these facts simply as a general indication of Mr Jamison's seniority in the hierarchy of HIB. Mr Croft would only have been aware of the outward trappings of the office conferred on Mr Jamison by HIB.

C In early 1990 discussions between Mr Croft and Mr Jamison about a facility to be granted by HIB to First Energy had reached an advanced stage. Mr Jamison had expressly told Mr Croft that he had no authority to sanction a facility. Nobody on behalf of HIB thereafter held Mr Jamison out as having authority alone or with another to sanction any particular size of facility.

On 9 February 1990 HIB sent a facility letter to First Energy. The letter was signed by

D Mr Newling, the managing director of HIB, and Mr Porter, an assistant director. The first page of the letter read as follows:

"Following your discussions with various members of our staff, we confirm that we are prepared to provide the following facilities:

Amount:	The maximum amount available shall not exceed £2m outstanding at any time.

E | | |
|---|---|
| | We understand that the immediate requirement will be less than this but once transactions begin to flow, you will rapidly build up to this level. |

Drawdown and repayment:	The facility may be drawn in the form of either loan, hire purchase, lease or a combination of all three. Drawings will be in respect of specific contracts so that the amount and type of drawing will be

F | | tailored to the contractual requirement. We will need to approve each contract prior to drawdown. |

| | Repayments will be structured in line with contractual receivables but typically would be by way of quarterly instalments over five years. We understand that an average drawdown will be in the region of £250,000. Hence we can discount the minimum committed |

G | | payments from your customer, to provide First Energy with an up-front cash sum, on a contract by contract basis. |

Period:	Whilst in accordance with normal banking practice the facility will be repayable on demand, it is intended, subject to our overriding discretion, that drawdowns will be available for the period required to fund the contract. It is not anticipated that this will exceed five years.

H | | |
|---|---|
| Security: | We will require a first fixed and floating charge over all assets of First Energy UK Ltd, to include contract receivables." |

The facility letter stipulated that HIB was to receive a 25 per cent interest in the equity share capital of First Energy. Under the heading "Documentation" the facility letter provided:

A
"To be agreed. This will include the above mentioned shareholders' agreement together with a loan agreement which will incorporate all the terms and security arrangements required to make a facility available."

The final paragraph of the facility letter read as follows:

B
"This letter does not constitute an offer made by the bank but does detail the terms and conditions upon which we are prepared to consider making facilities available to you. Should you find the terms acceptable you should return to us both of the enclosed copies of this letter duly countersigned together with your cheque for £2,500. The signing by us and the return to you of one of these copies shall only then create a binding contract between us. This letter is only available for acceptance within 14 days from the above date after which it will lapse."

C
First Energy duly signed the facility letter and returned it to HIB with a cheque for £2,500. HIB deposited the cheque in its bank account. HIB never returned a signed copy to First Energy. It is common ground that a binding contract on the terms of the facility letter never came into existence. Moreover, the documentation relating to the loan agreement, the first and fixed floating charge and the 25 per cent equity participation was never completed. Undoubtedly, those would be matters of importance to HIB. Nevertheless by February 1990 the parties had in a commercial sense achieved a solid and concrete basis for their future co-operation.

D
Despite the fact that the facility letter had not yet come into force the parties entered into an ad hoc binding agreement in respect of the equipment to be installed at Wisbech. That meant that HIB was involved in First Energy's first contract under the new scheme. On 28 March 1990 HIB wrote to First Energy saying that it was willing to enter into a hire-purchase agreement in respect of the equipment to be installed at Wisbech. The transaction involved a sale of the equipment by First Energy to HIB, and a hire-purchase agreement between HIB and First Energy in respect of the same equipment. HIB's letter of 28 March 1990 stated:

E
"We must however stress that such a hire-purchase contract would be governed by the terms and conditions set out in our facility letter dated 9 February 1990 and since a number of these terms and conditions have not yet been fully met we reserve the right to cancel the enclosed agreement and recall all funds outstanding in the event that all of our terms and conditions have not been satisfied within four months from today's date.

F
Please indicate your acceptance of the above by signing and returning a copy of this letter along with the completed hire-purchase documentation."

First Energy accepted this offer. In an evolving commercial relationship this was a pragmatic solution. The transaction was performed. While the facility letter was not yet in force, the Wisbech transaction marked progress in the sense that it was the first tranche of the credit envisaged in the earlier dealings between the parties.

G
Following the Wisbech transaction discussions took place between First Energy and HIB on two levels. First, there was the reality that First Energy had secured three more orders for the supply and installation of the new system of heating. The details of the three orders were as follows:

Customer's name	Invoice price (excluding VAT)
(1) Carnaud Metal Box, Neath	£366,826.99
(2) Kvaerner Govan Ltd, Glasgow	£195,169.45
(3) Sefton Metropolitan Borough Council, Southport	£54,154.99
	£616,151.43

H

A From HIB's point of view participation in these transactions seemed an attractive proposition.

The discussions also attempted to take forward the inchoate arrangements under the facility letter. On 17 July a meeting took place between Mr Croft, accompanied by his solicitor, Mr Cook, and Mr Jamison, accompanied by Mr Ponting, HIB's company secretary. The discussions were principally concerned with the charge contemplated by

B the facility letter. It was agreed that Mr Cook should draft wording for a priority which could be used on a transaction by transaction basis. It was contemplated that HIB's first fixed and floating charge over all First Energy's assets would be subordinated to a charge in favour of another lender if the particular contract was financed by a lender other than HIB. There was also a discussion of a prospective management buy-out.

By the end of July Mr Jamison was still enthusiastic about HIB's participation in First

C Energy's ventures. The Neath, Glasgow and Southport projects required financing. Mr Jamison was in contact with Mr Porter, an associate director based in London who raised no objection in principle. On the other hand, Mr Porter did not (even if he was able to do so) purport to sanction any commitment. The successful completion of negotiations about outstanding matters affecting a long-term relationship under the facility letter was still going to take some time. On the other hand, decisions about the three new projects could not wait.

D On 2 August Mr Croft and Mr Jamison discussed the possibility of another *interim* solution. On the same day Mr Jamison wrote to Mr Croft in the following terms:

"Further to our telephone conversation earlier today, I am pleased to attach herewith three hire-purchase agreements, one for each of the contracts recently concluded by First Energy.

E You will see that I have indicated in pencil how the documents should be completed and I would be obliged if you would arrange for the directors of First Energy to sign and have witnessed as appropriate.

In order to complete our transaction we shall require an invoice similar to that which was provided in respect of CMB Wisbech (copy attached). In each case the amount invoiced should be the cash price as shown on the HP agreement, plus

F VAT again as shown on the HP agreement, less deposit equal to the amount of VAT leaving the net amount due the same as the cash price. Our invoice should be accompanied by the appropriate supporting invoices from First Energy suppliers.

On receipt of the above we will be in a position to release funds of £616,151.43 which is approximately £30,000 in excess of the total installation costs.

I trust you will find the documentation self-explanatory and look forward to being

G of further assistance."

On 2 September First Energy sent the duly completed hire-purchase agreement and invoice in respect of the Neath project. On 2 October First Energy sent similar documentation to HIB in respect of the Glasgow and Southport projects.

In the meantime, and in the second half of September, the senior management of HIB in London decided that they were no longer interested in First Energy's business. That

H negative decision also covered the three specific projects. The reason for this sudden change of attitude is to be found in the fact that HIB had recently had some bad experiences of other commercial loans not being repaid. HIB's negative decision left First Energy without financing for the three new projects. On 2 October 1990 First Energy issued a writ against HIB in the Manchester commercial list. This action in due course came before Judge *Kershaw* for hearing of the issue of liability only.

A

The trial

It is not necessary, or helpful, to analyse the pleadings. Two of the issues, which were canvassed at the trial, are still in issue on this appeal. The first issue was whether prima facie First Energy and HIB concluded a contract on the terms of the letter of 2 August. If the conclusion of such a contract was prima facie established, the question arose whether Mr Jamison had ostensible authority to sanction the transaction or to inform First Energy by the letter of 2 August that head office approval of the transaction had been obtained.

B

At the trial three witnesses were called: Mr Croft, Mr Jamison and Mr Ponting. The evidence and speeches took three working days. The judge reserved judgment. He gave judgment on 23 October 1991.

The judgment

C

The judge concluded that the letter of 2 August 1990, read with its enclosures, amounted to an offer which was capable of acceptance by First Energy. He found that First Energy accepted the offer. The appellants challenge the judge's finding that the letter amounted to an offer. I will call this the construction point. The judge also had to deal with a question whether the transaction was one for sale of goods and the re-letting of them on hire purchase, as First Energy contended, or in reality a loan, as HIB contended. The judge ruled in favour of First Energy on this point, and in this respect his ruling is accepted.

D

The judge then considered the issue of ostensible authority. The judge found that Mr Jamison had no ostensible authority to enter into the transaction. He said that there was a distinction between sanctioning a facility and signing a letter which conveys information. The judge stated:

> "The letter of 2 August 1990 was a letter from the defendant bank. In my judgment Mr Jamison, as a senior manager and the man in charge of the defendant's Manchester office, had ostensible authority to sign letters on behalf of the defendant. He had, by virtue of his position, the usual authority to sign and send letters on behalf of the defendant and nothing was ever said or done to convey to the plaintiff that he did not have actual authority to sign any particular type of letter.

E

> As Mr Sander said, it would be a commercial nonsense if every bank customer had to enquire whether the senior manager had authority to sign a letter and then, if the answer was yes, perhaps to enquire higher still whether the person who had said 'yes' had authority to give such confirmation.

F

> I find as a fact that the defendant company had not, whether through Mr Jamison or in any other way, told the plaintiff that Mr Jamison did not have authority by himself to sign such letters on the defendant's behalf, and in particular I reject the suggestion that the lack of authority on the part of Mr Jamison to sign by himself letters on behalf of the defendant which committed the defendant was communicated to the plaintiff by the fact that certain earlier letters had two signatures.

G

> That being so, in my judgment the letter of 2 August constituted an offer communicated by someone who had ostensible authority to communicate such an offer on behalf of the defendant, and it was, as I have said, accepted in accordance with its terms. In my judgment, in those circumstances, the defendant is bound."

H

At one stage I was troubled that the judge might have decided the case on a basis which was not open to him. That was not a contention advanced in the grounds of appeal. While Miss Arden QC submitted that the judge's conclusion was not open to

A   him on the evidence and in law, she accepted that the basis on which he decided the issue had been fully canvassed. We were referred to exchanges between counsel and the judge which made that clear. Miss Arden accepted that HIB had not been prejudiced by the failure to plead the point in the way that the judge eventually decided it. Realistically, Miss Arden concentrated on the question whether in fact and in law the judge's conclusion was justified.

B   **The construction point**

In my view the judge's decision is correct. I entirely agree with Miss Arden QC that we must construe the letter against the contextual scene as it existed at the end of July. The court must take into account surrounding circumstances which reasonable persons in the position of the parties would have had in mind. That is hornbook law. What surrounding circumstances ought to be taken into account? Miss Arden attempted to
C   show that as at the end of July 1990 the financial position of First Energy was precarious. On the supposition that no medium-term financing was available that may be so. But at that time Mr Croft and Mr Jamison were enthusiastic about the success of the scheme. And both were apparently confident that it would be possible to reach agreement on the outstanding matters under the facility letter. The actual financial position of First Energy therefore throws no light on the meaning of the letter of 2 August.

D   A matter that would have been present in the minds of Mr Croft and Mr Jamison was the fact that there were three specific accounts which required financing. At the end of July there was no realistic prospect of immediately resolving all outstanding matters affecting the facility letter. The structure of the long-term relationship of the parties was still inchoate. HIB could have stepped aside and taken the risk of another lending institution financing the three projects. That was not what Mr Jamison wanted. There
E   was the precedent of the apparently successful *interim* solution in regard to Wisbech early in the year. In my view these are matters which would have been likely to be present in the minds of the parties when they discussed the matter early on 2 August.

The tenor of the letter is that of an unconditional offer of ad hoc financing of the three specific projects. The structure of the proposed arrangements was the sale of the equipment by First Energy to HIB, and the letting of the equipment on hire-purchase
F   terms to First Energy. The letter plainly was more than a mere step in continuing negotiations. That is clear from the opening paragraph which records: "I am pleased to attach herewith three hire-purchase agreements . . . ." It then stipulates that all that First Energy need do is return the hire-purchase agreements, which were on HIB's standard terms, together with three invoices. And, most importantly, it states that on receipt of the documents HIB "will be in a position to release funds of £616,151.43". Like the judge I read this sentence as saying that, "if you accept our offer we will release the
G   funds".

Miss Arden pointed to the fact that Mr Croft agreed in cross-examination that the facilities referred to in the letter must be seen in the context of the facility letter. In a commercial sense that was indeed the case. But the facilities mentioned in the letter were not granted conditionally on the finalisation of the facility letter or of any of the outstanding matters under it.
H   Miss Arden said that the judge failed to read the letter and the hire-purchase agreement together. She relied on the provision in the hire-purchase agreements to the following effect:

> "The agreement will become binding on the owner only after acceptance on its behalf by an authorised signature."

In my view the judge rightly held that the letter itself specified the mode of acceptance of the offer in it, and that those provisions in the letter overrode the terms of the hire-purchase agreements.

In my judgment a reasonable businessman, placed in the same objective setting as Mr Croft, would have read the letter as communicating an unconditional and firm offer. It was not argued, and could not be argued, that if the letter contained an offer its terms were too uncertain to be converted by acceptance into a binding contract. On the contrary it contained all the essentials for the conclusion of a binding contract. And that offer was accepted.

I would reject HIB's first argument.

Ostensible authority

In order for a plea of apparent authority to succeed it is necessary for First Energy to establish not only that HIB through its appropriate organs held out Mr Jamison as having such authority but also that First Energy relied on that fact in entering into the transaction. In context the letter was calculated to convey to First Energy that Mr Jamison had obtained the approval of the transaction at the appropriate level at head office. The evidence of Mr Croft was that he relied on that fact. That evidence was supported by the inherent probabilities. The judge found that the element of reliance was established. And the appellants do not challenge the judge's finding that the element of reliance was established.

The appellants' challenge was to the judge's finding that HIB had held out Mr Jamison to be HIB's agent for the purpose of conveying to First Energy approval of the offer contained in the letter of 2 August. It is common ground that a plea of apparent authority can only be based on a holding out, or representation, as to authority of the agent by the principal sought to be held bound by the particular act. Our law does not recognise, in the context of apparent authority, the idea of a self-authorising agent: see *Armagas Ltd v Mundogas SA* (1986) 2 BCC 99,197.

It is possible to narrow down the issue of ostensible authority, which arises in the present case. A principal may clothe an agent with apparent authority in more than one way. The present case falls into a category, which, in *Armagas Ltd v Mundogas SA*, was described by Lord *Keith* as follows (at pp. 99,201–99,202):

> "In the commonly encountered case, the ostensible authority is general in character, arising when the principal has placed the agent in a position which in the outside world is generally regarded as carrying authority to enter into transactions of the kind in question."

This type of apparent authority is often described as the usual authority of an agent. But it is important to remember that the idea of usual authority is used in two senses. First, it sometimes means that the agent had implied actual authority to perform acts necessarily incidental to the performance of the agency. Secondly, it sometimes means that the principal's conduct in clothing the agent with the trappings of authority was such as to induce a third party to rely on the existence of the agency. The issue in the present case is one of usual authority in the second sense.

In a lucid and helpful speech Miss Arden submitted that the judge in effect found that, although to First Energy's knowledge Mr Jamison had no actual or apparent authority to approve even an interim facility on behalf of HIB, Mr Jamison had ostensible authority to write the letter of 2 August to First Energy, the effect of which was to bind HIB to make available to First Energy the *interim* facility when First Energy accepted the offer made in the letter. She submitted that there was an irreconcilable inconsistency between a finding that Mr Jamison had no actual or ostensible authority to sanction the

A   transaction and the finding that he had ostensible authority to communicate the information that head office had approved the transaction. She submitted that as a matter of law this finding was not open to the judge.

Miss Arden took her stand squarely on observations by Lord *Keith* in the House of Lords in *Armagas Ltd v Mundogas SA*. In that case one of the issues was whether the vice-president and chartering manager of the defendant company had ostensible authority to enter into a time charter of a ship. The chartering manager had been bribed to enter
B   into the transaction. The chartering manager did not have actual authority to enter into the transaction. The judge found that the defendants were liable to the plaintiffs in contract on the basis that the chartering manager had ostensible authority to communicate that the defendants had given him express authority to enter into the agreement. The judge also upheld a claim against the defendants in deceit. On appeal by the defendants the Court of Appeal held that the defendants had not clothed the chartering manager
C   with apparent authority to communicate that he had obtained the defendants' authority to enter into the agreement. The Court of Appeal also held that the defendants were not vicariously liable in deceit. The House of Lords dismissed the appeal on both aspects. Lord *Keith* gave the unanimous reasons of the House of Lords. For present purposes it is only necessary to refer to that part of Lord *Keith*'s speech which deals with the issue of ostensible authority. He stated (at p. 99,202):

D   "The way he put it was that although Mr Magelssen did not have ostensible authority to conclude the three-year charterparty, yet he did have ostensible authority to notify to Mr Jensen and Mr Dannesboe approval by Mundogas of the transaction. He took the view that by appointing Mr Magelssen to be vice-president (transportation) and chartering manager Mundogas represented that he had authority to convey such approval. This conclusion appears to have originated in an idea which the judge himself had in the course of the trial.
E   Armagas had not pleaded any such representation nor reliance on it by Mr Jensen and Mr Dannesboe, and naturally there had been no evidence by the latter that they did rely on it."

Given that there was no evidence of reliance, the plea of apparent authority could never get off the ground. Lord *Keith* did, however, go on to consider whether there had been any holding out by the principal. In this context it is relevant to bear in mind that the
F   transaction had a number of unusual features, namely a secrecy provision, a minimum charter rate and the plaintiffs' option to cancel the charter. In the Court of Appeal *Goff* LJ described these features as "extraordinary" and he had held that, in any event, the plaintiffs were put on enquiry as to the authority of the agent: see [1986] AC at p. 734H. The judgment of *Goff* LJ was referred to with approval by Lord *Keith*. Against this background Lord *Keith* dealt with the appellants' arguments as follows (at p. 99,202):

G   "But no representation by Mr Magelssen can help Armagas. They must be in a position to found upon some relevant representation by the responsible management of Mundogas as to Mr Magelssen's authority: *Freeman & Lockyer v Buckhurst Park Properties (Mangal) Ltd* [1964] 2 QB 480 at p. 505, per *Diplock* LJ. Counsel for Armagas sought to find such a representation in the appointment of Mr Magelssen as vice-president (transportation) and chartering manager, the circumstance that he had some general authority to enter into charterparties and
H   that on two previous occasions he had entered into charterparties, with the specific approval of Mundogas conveyed by him, which were beyond his ostensible general authority, and the fact that it would have been unreasonable to expect Armagas to obtain direct confirmation from Mundogas of its approval, particularly in view of the shortness of time. But the nature of Mr Magelssen's appointment was known not to carry general authority to conclude a charterparty such as this

one, the two previous transactions referred to, though known to Mr Johannesen
the fellow conspirator, were not known to Mr Jensen or Mr Dannesboe, and the
difficulty of obtaining confirmation from Mundogas is irrelevant."

Lord *Keith* then discussed *Berryere v Fireman's Fund Insurance Co* (1965) 51 DLR (2d)
603, a decision of the Manitoba Court of Appeal. Lord *Keith* said (at p. 99,203):

> ". . . I do not regard [that] case as authority for the general proposition that
> ostensible authority of an agent to communicate agreement by his principal to a
> particular transaction is conceptually different from ostensible authority to enter
> into that particular transaction. *Robert Goff* LJ said of the trial judge's view in
> this case [at p. 730H]:
>
>> '. . . the effect of the judge's conclusion was that, although Mr Magelssen did
>> not have ostensible authority to enter into the contract, he did have ostensible
>> authority to tell Mr Jensen and Mr Dannesboe that he had obtained actual
>> authority to do so. This is, on its face, a most surprising conclusion. It results in
>> an extraordinary distinction between (1) a case where an agent, having no
>> ostensible authority to enter into the relevant contract, wrongly asserts that he
>> is invested with actual authority to do so, in which event the principal is not
>> bound; and (2) a case where an agent, having no ostensible authority, wrongly
>> asserts after negotiations that he has gone back to his principal and obtained
>> actual authority, in which event the principal is bound. As a matter of common
>> sense, this is most unlikely to be the law.'
>
> I respectfully agree. It must be a most unusual and peculiar case where an agent
> who is known to have no general authority to enter into transactions of a certain
> type can by reason of circumstances created by the principal reasonably be
> believed to have specific authority to enter into a particular transaction of that
> type. The facts of the present case fall far short of establishing such a situation. I
> conclude that the Court of Appeal rightly rejected the claim based on ostensible
> authority."

The overloading of judgments with massive quotations is the bane of modern
jurisprudence. I have already sinned in that respect. My lame excuse is that the precise
context of Lord *Keith*'s observations is central to an assessment of Miss Arden's
submissions.

    Two points seem to me clear. First, Lord *Keith*'s observations about specific as
opposed to general authority are not relevant to the case before us. The issue in the
present case relates to the existence of a general apparent authority arising from the
position in which HIB had placed Mr Jamison. Secondly, it is relevant to note that Lord
Keith was careful not to say that as a matter of law an apparent authority to communicate
approval can never arise where there is no authority in the agent on his own to enter into
the transaction. Lord *Keith*'s observation was a prediction that it will necessarily be
somewhat rare for a principal to be regarded as having authorised his agent to
communicate whether or not he has authority. That is valuable guidance, which judges
at every level will want to consider carefully when the occasion arises, but it does not
amount to a rule or a principle of law.

    Between the date of the judgment in the Court of Appeal in *Armagas Ltd v Mundogas
SA* and the date of Lord *Keith*'s speech in the House of Lords there were some relevant
observations in the Court of Appeal in *Egyptian International Foreign Trade Co v
Soplex Wholesale Supplies Ltd & Anor ("The Raffaella")* [1985] 2 Lloyd's Rep 36. In
that case the question was whether Mr Booth, the documentary credit manager of a
bank, had ostensible authority to give a certain undertaking. *Kerr* LJ referred to
Armagas Ltd v Mundogas SA. *Kerr* LJ's very general observations went further on the

A   point in issue than Lord *Keith* was subsequently to go. But *Browne-Wilkinson* LJ
analysed the matter in some detail. He said (at pp. 42–43):

"I have so far ignored the representation made by Mr Booth that 'in London one
signature is sufficient'. Mr Stamler submitted that a principal cannot be held liable
as a result of the agent holding himself out as possessing an authority he does not
in fact possess: he relied on remarks to that effect in the *Freeman & Lockyer* case
at p. 505, *Attorney General for Ceylon v Silva*, [1953] 1 Lloyd's Rep 563; [1953]
B   AC 461 at pp. 571 and 479, *The British Bank of The Middle East* case (sup.) and
Armagas Ltd v Mundogas SA, [1985] 1 Lloyd's Rep 1. As at present advised, I am
not satisfied that the principle to be derived from those cases is as wide as Mr
Stamler suggests: they were all cases or dicta dealing with the position where the
agent had neither authority to enter into the transaction nor authority to make
representations on behalf of the principal. It is obviously correct that an agent
C   who has no actual or apparent authority either (a) to enter into a transaction or
(b) to make representations as to the transaction cannot hold himself out as having
authority to enter into the transaction so as to affect the principal's position. But,
suppose a company confers actual or apparent authority on X to make
representations and X erroneously represents to a third party that Y has authority
to enter into a transaction; why should not such a representation be relied upon as
part of the holding out of Y by the company? By parity of reasoning, if a company
D   confers actual or apparent authority on A to make representations on the company's
behalf but no actual authority on A to enter into the specific transaction, why
should a representation made by A as to his authority not be capable of being
relied on as one of the acts of holding out? There is substantial authority that it
can be: see *British Thomson-Houston Co Ltd v Federated European Bank Ltd*,
[1932] 2 KB 176, especially at p. 182 (where the only holding out was an erroneous
E   representation by the agent that he was managing director); and the *Freeman &
Lockyer* case per Lord Justice Pearson at p. 499; *Hely-Hutchinson v Brayhead
Ltd.*, [1968] 1 QB 549 per Lord *Denning*, MR at p. 593A–D. If, as I am inclined to
think, an agent with authority to make representations can make a representation
that he has authority to enter into a transaction, then the judge was entitled to
hold, as he did, that Mr Booth, as the representative of Refson in charge of the
transaction, had implied or apparent authority to make the representation that
F   only one signature was required and that this representation was a relevant
consideration in deciding whether Refson had held out Mr Booth as having
authority to sign the undertaking. However, since it is not necessary to decide this
point for the purposes of this appeal, I express no concluded view on it."

Miss Arden said that the authorities referred to by *Browne-Wilkinson* LJ are in the
line of company law cases of which the decision in *Royal British Bank v Turquand* (1855)
G   5 E & B 248 is the classic illustration. That may be right. But in my view those authorities
are not irrelevant to the question before us. This line of authority reveals a tension
between two conflicting principles. The first is that the shareholders of a company should
be protected against hasty and ill-considered transactions entered into by the company.
The second is that third parties who deal with companies in good faith ought to be
protected. The *Royal British Bank v Turquand* line of cases represents an intensely
pragmatic and serviceable resolution of the competing considerations in particular
H   situations. Leaving aside cases which focused specifically on the impact of the public
document of a company, I regard this line of authority as throwing light on the approach
we ought to adopt.

It seems to me that the law recognises that in modern commerce an agent who has no
apparent authority to conclude a particular transaction may sometimes be clothed with
apparent authority to make representations of fact. The level at which such apparent

authority could be found to exist may vary and generalisation will be unhelpful. But let me take the concrete example of a company secretary. In *Panorama Developments (Guildford) Ltd v Fidelis Furnishing Fabrics Ltd* [1971] 2 QB 711 it was recognised that the managerial functions of a company secretary are today far greater than they once were. Mr Ponting was HIB's company secretary. He attended negotiations in July. If he had been asked for a resolution of the board of directors of HIB approving the transaction, and if he had in error sent a document purporting to be such a resolution, it is surely possible, depending on the evidence, that he might have acted within his apparent authority by virtue of his position as company secretary. That would be so despite the fact that he plainly had no apparent authority to sanction the transaction. My reason for this tentative view is that a company secretary is known to be the employee specifically charged with keeping the minutes of board meetings.

Miss Arden accepted that if the managing director of HIB had confirmed that the transaction had been approved by HIB a case of ostensible authority could be made out. While HIB did not in fact have a general manager, Miss Arden was prepared to accept that the same would generally be true of a general manager. Confining myself strictly to a situation of a merchant bank or a trading bank, such as HIB, I take the view that it would be unrealistic to assert the contrary. And the reason is that in accordance with the general understanding in commerce the managing director and general manager of such a bank is clothed with a general actual or apparent authority to convey such information. It would be absurd to suggest that the third party should seek information from the board of directors as a whole. But Miss Arden submitted that as senior manager in Manchester Mr Jamison was in a different position.

In agreement with the judge I have come to the conclusion, on the particular facts of this case, that Mr Jamison's position as senior manager in Manchester was such that he was clothed with ostensible authority to communicate that head office approval had been given for the facility set out in the 2 August letter. Although his status was below that of a managing director or general manager, it was nevertheless considerable. And, in the circumstances of this case, the idea that First Energy should have checked with the managing director in London whether HIB had approved the transaction seems unreal. This factor is, of course, not decisive, but it is relevant to the ultimate decision.

Having come to a conclusion, on the application of what I regard as orthodox principles of law, that the judge was entitled and indeed right to find as a matter of fact that ostensible authority to communicate head office approval of the transaction had been established, I return to the place where I started. In my judgment a decision that Mr Jamison did not have apparent authority to communicate head office approval would defeat the reasonable expectations of the parties. And it would fly in the face of the way in which in practice negotiations are conducted between trading banks and trading customers who seek commercial loans. I would reject this ground of appeal.

For these reasons, and for the reasons given by the judge in his careful judgment, I would dismiss the appeal.

Evans LJ: I agree that this appeal should be dismissed and with the judgments of my Lords. They refer to the commercial realities of the situation where the plaintiffs' directors were dealing with the person designated as the "senior manager" in charge of the defendants' office in Manchester. To describe this as a branch office is literally correct, but it should not be regarded as equivalent to one of the branch offices of a major clearing bank. The defendants carry on business as a merchant or trading bank in London and the Manchester office is their only other presence in the UK. That no doubt is a reflection of the importance to them of their existing or potential business in Manchester and the north of England. These facts underlie the judge's conclusions that Mr Jamison had apparent ostensible authority to write the letter dated 2 August 1990 on

A   behalf of the defendants, and that the letter had contractual effect. In my judgment, his decision was correct.

Both issues which arise on this appeal have to be considered against the background of dealings which went back as far as 1989. The plaintiffs' directors negotiated with Mr Jamison but they were aware, because he told them, that he had no authority to sanction any facility, certainly not one in the region of £2m, which was the kind of sum which was under discussion.

B

Consistently with this, the facility letter dated 9 February 1990 was signed by two persons, one described as a director and the other as assistant director. The plaintiffs duly countersigned the letter and returned it to the defendants together with the fee of £2,500 payable upon confirmation that the terms of the letter were acceptable to them. But no contract came into existence then, because the letter expressly provided that this should not occur until the defendants signed and returned one of the copies which the plaintiffs countersigned, and this they never did.

C

However, the plaintiffs' urgent need for finance for the Wisbech project resulted in what *Steyn* LJ has called the ad hoc arrangement recorded in the defendants' letter dated 28 March 1990 and the hire-purchase agreement dated 18 April 1990. There were two signatories of that letter on behalf of the defendants.

D

The security arrangements and the documentation called for by the facility letter were never formally agreed. They were discussed and what may have been an agreement in principle was reached on 17 July in Manchester. The defendants were represented at that meeting by Mr Jamison and their company secretary from London. The subsequent breakdown in these negotiations, and in the whole relationship between the parties, did not take place until after 2 August when Mr Jamison's letter was sent.

E

This followed further discussions between the plaintiffs and him regarding their need for further finance for three specific projects. The letter clearly constitutes an offer of finance on terms which include no reference to the facility letter dated 9 February or to the security arrangements and documentation required thereunder. Miss Arden QC does not contend that the terms were incapable of constituting a binding contract on grounds of uncertainty, but she does submit that, because those matters were still outstanding, the letter could not be regarded as an offer capable of giving rise to a contract according to its terms. In my judgment, that argument fails.

F

So the question becomes one of authority; did Mr Jamison have authority to sign that letter on behalf of the defendants as he purported to do? It is accepted that he had no actual authority and so the plaintiffs must rely upon his apparent or ostensible authority. This arose solely from the position that he held. It is not suggested that the defendants made or are bound by any other representation as to his authority. But they cannot deny that he enjoyed the usual authority of a person described as a "senior manager" in charge of a branch office such as theirs in Manchester, subject only to the express limitation with regard to signing facility letters which he himself communicated to the plaintiffs.

G

It is puzzling that this central issue of usual authority appears not to have been focused upon either in the pleadings or the evidence. The reason, I think, is as follows. The defendants were concerned to establish the limitation on Mr Jamison's apparent authority which they pleaded in para. 7(4) of the defence. This they succeeded in doing. But this did not foreclose the issue whether he had apparent authority to sign the letter dated 2 August on behalf of the bank, because the scope of his apparent authority depended upon the usual authority of a person in his position, and the judgment addressed the question whether such authority included signing the letter on behalf of the bank.

H

Authority

A

The judge's findings of fact were that Mr Jamison told Mr Croft that he had no authority to sanction any facility and that the defendants did not say or do anything which held Mr Jamison out as having authority alone or with another to sanction any particular size of facility. These findings were fatal to the plaintiffs' submission set out in four propositions in the judgment, the fourth being that the defendants were bound:

> "if . . . Mr Jamison made it appear that someone else with authority to do so had
> joined with him to sanction the advance."

B

This conclusion is clearly consistent with the House of Lords decision in *Armagas Ltd v Mundogas SA* (1986) 2 BCC 99,197 that an agent who has no authority to enter into a transaction on behalf of his principal cannot create the appearance of such authority by making a representation to that effect.

The plaintiffs succeeded, however, on the basis of the judge's further findings that Mr Jamison had "by virtue of his position, the usual authority to sign and send letters on behalf of the defendant", and therefore had "ostensible authority to communicate such an offer on behalf of the defendant". He commented that it would be "commercial nonsense if every bank customer had to ensure whether the senior manager had authority to sign a letter" — and perhaps to enquire higher still — and my Lords have based their judgments upholding the judge's conclusion on the commercial realities of the situation. I respectfully and entirely agree. Moreover, in my judgment the conclusion is consistent with the law as stated in the Court of Appeal and in the House of Lords in *Armagas* (per *Robert Goff* LJ at p. 731 and Lord *Keith* at pp. 99,201–99,203, in passages already quoted by *Steyn* LJ) which was not cited to the judge.

C

D

In *Armagas*, the trial judge, *Staughton* J, held that by appointing Mr Magelssen as their vice-president (transportation) and chartering manager the defendants represented that he was authorised to notify approval by the top management of chartering transactions ([1985] 1 Ll Rep 1 at p. 14). *Staughton* J assumed that the appointment did not involve any representation that Mr Magelssen had general authority to conclude charterparties for the relevant three-year period. The Court of Appeal reversed two significant findings of fact which although not directly relevant to the authority issue nevertheless had "a profound impact upon what are commonly called the merits of the case" (per *Robert Goff* LJ [1986] AC 717 at p. 728: see also [1985] 1 Ll Rep 1 at pp. 48–64). The Court of Appeal and the House of Lords therefore considered the issue against this changed background and on the basis, which *Staughton* J had assumed, that Mr Magelssen had no authority by virtue of his position to commit the company to a long-term time charter without the approval of his seniors. The plaintiffs knew and appreciated this, hence the importance for them of Mr Magelssen's assurances, express or otherwise, that he had received the necessary authority.

E

F

The issue decided by the Court of Appeal and the House of Lords was whether an agent whose apparent authority to conclude transactions is limited can enlarge the appearance of authority by a representation which he himself makes. He cannot do this, for the reasons given by *Robert Goff* LJ and Lord *Keith*, and the contrary answer would not be supported by common sense ([1986] AC at p. 731B). In this context, there is no conceptual difference between ostensible authority to enter into a transaction or to communicate agreement by the principal to a particular transaction (per Lord *Keith* at p. 99,203).

G

H

Neither of the two judgments in *Armagas* deals expressly with a situation where the agent does have apparent authority by virtue of his position to communicate decisions made by his seniors. (The reference to "ostensible authority" by *Robert Goff* LJ at p. 731B under (2) must be read, in my respectful view, as authority "to enter into the relevant contract", as stated in (1).) That such cases must exist, even though not

A
established on the facts in *Armagas*, is sufficiently demonstrated by the practical consideration that any board of directors or other senior management cannot always communicate directly with third parties. There must be someone authorised to communicate on its behalf. From the third party's point of view, there must be someone with whom to deal. It is not the practice, so far as I am aware, in normal commercial transactions for written proof, e.g. of board decisions to be demanded by contracting parties, and even where this may occur, e.g. in large-scale financing transactions, the

B
third party must always rely ultimately on some individual who has been held out as having, or who appears to have, the necessary authority to communicate with him. The third party cannot always insist, if ever, on attending the board or management meeting, or on speaking to the senior manager himself.

Moreover, there is clearly no requirement that the authority to communicate decisions should be commensurate with the authority to enter into a transaction of the kind in question on behalf of the principal. This is demonstrated by the possible example of a

C
company secretary referred to by *Steyn* LJ. Judicial authority for this view can be found in *British Thomson-Houston Co Ltd v Federated European Bank Ltd* [1932] 2 KB 176 and the observations (obiter) of *Browne-Wilkinson* LJ in *The Raffaella* [1985] 2 Lloyd's Rep 36 at p. 43.

Unlike *Armagas*, therefore, where the alleged authority to communicate was found not to exist, the present case is one where Mr Jamison by virtue of his position necessarily

D
had some authority to communicate with third parties dealing with the bank. The judge found that this included communications such as the letter of 2 August, and the plaintiffs were not aware that his usual and therefore apparent authority was limited so as to exclude such authority in the present case. The fact that they knew that his actual authority to enter into transactions on behalf of the defendants was limited does not necessarily mean that his authority to communicate decisions on their behalf was limited

E
also. These findings in my view were justified by the evidence and by common sense assumptions which the judge was entitled to make. As *Staughton* J said in *Armagas*, any other conclusion would be "a triumph of logic over common sense" ([1985] 1 Ll Rep 1 at p. 15). If the defendants were correct, it would mean that the plaintiffs were bound to seek confirmation from the defendants' head office in London of what Mr Jamison said on their behalf, which would defeat the apparent object of appointing a senior manager in charge of office in Manchester so that local businessmen could deal with him there.

F
Nourse LJ: I agree that this appeal must be dismissed for the reasons given by *Steyn* and *Evans* L JJ. I add some observations of my own on the question of ostensible authority.

A question of ostensible authority is primarily one of fact. Did the principal hold out the agent as having his authority to make the representation or to do the act on which the other party relies? Here First Energy claims that HIB held out Mr Jamison as having

G
its authority to inform First Energy that HIB had approved the facility offered in the letter of 2 August 1990 and to convey the offer accordingly.

The material facts are few in number. HIB is a merchant bank which, in an affidavit sworn in October 1990, Mr Jamison claimed to be of repute and of the most substantial assets. At the material time he was a senior manager and the person in charge of its Manchester office. During the material period First Energy's negotiations with HIB

H
were conducted by Mr Croft. Mr Jamison was the only person in HIB with whom Mr Croft ever dealt in face to face negotiations, except for a luncheon meeting with Mr Porter and Mr Ponting's visit to Manchester on 17 July 1990.

Judge *Kershaw* found, first, that in about February 1989 Mr Jamison told Mr Croft that he had no authority to sanction any facility and, secondly, that thereafter HIB did not say or do anything which held Mr Jamison out as having authority alone or with another to sanction any particular size of facility. In his evidence-in-chief Mr Jamison said that during the many discussions that he and Mr Croft had had, both face-to-face and by telephone, he was quite sure that he had made many references to having to revert to London for various decisions on various subjects. In the passage from his judgment which *Steyn* LJ has read, the judge found that Mr Jamison, by virtue of his position, had ostensible authority to sign and send letters on behalf of HIB generally and that nothing was ever said or done to convey to First Energy that he did not have actual authority to sign any particular type of letter. He concluded that Mr Jamison's letter of 2 August constituted an offer communicated by someone who had ostensible authority to communicate such an offer on behalf of HIB.

In my view the judge's conclusion was the only one to which he could have come on the evidence before him and on the findings he had made. I agree with Mr Wingate-Saul QC, for First Energy, that the argument of Miss Arden QC, for HIB, was reduced to the proposition that Mr Croft's knowledge of Mr Jamison's inability to sanction any facility was just as much knowledge of his inability to communicate head office's approval of a facility. That proposition involves a non sequitur which offends both commercial reality and common sense.

A reasonable person having Mr Croft's knowledge that Mr Jamison had no authority to sanction any facility himself and, further, that he had to revert to London for various decisions on various subjects would, on reading the letter of 2 August, have understood that HIB's head office had approved the facility offered in the letter. Moreover, such a person, knowing that Mr Jamison was the senior manager in charge of HIB's Manchester office with whom he had dealt in the great majority of the face-to-face negotiations would have assumed that he had been given authority by head office to communicate their approval and to convey the offer accordingly. While fully accepting Miss Arden's submission that the position of a senior manager in a branch office of a merchant bank is not for this purpose to be equated with that of a branch manager of a high street clearing bank, I am quite unable to see on what basis, either in commercial reality or in common sense, it can be suggested that a reasonable person in Mr Croft's position would have made some other assumption. It would have been most unreasonable to assume, or even to suspect, that Mr Jamison did not have HIB's authority to act as a mere channel of communication.

It should be recorded that Judge *Kershaw* was not referred to *Armagas Ltd v Mundogas SA* (1986) 2 BCC 99,197. His reasoning demonstrates that, like *Steyn* and *Evans* L JJ, he too would have distinguished it. I think that his decision of both questions was entirely satisfactory and I too would affirm it accordingly.

(*Appeal dismissed with costs. Leave to appeal to House of Lords refused*)

A
Re Synthetic Technology Ltd.
Secretary of State for Trade and Industry v Joiner.
Chancery Division (Companies Court).
Edward Evans-Lombe QC (sitting as a deputy High Court judge).
Judgment delivered 23 March 1993.

B
Disqualifying unfit directors of insolvent companies — Whether director should be disqualified — Whether Secretary of State should have costs on indemnity basis — Company Directors Disqualification Act 1986, sec. 6.

This was an application by the Secretary of State for Trade and Industry for a director disqualification order under sec. 6 of the Company Directors Disqualification Act 1986, and, if the application was successful, for costs on the indemnity basis.

C
Held, disqualifying the respondent director for seven years and ordering him to pay the costs on the standard basis only:

1. The director had procured the company to pay debts for which he was personally liable, had wrongly asserted ownership of an asset of the company in the administration, and had drawn remuneration out of proportion to the company's trading success and financial health; the company had failed to file accounts in time or at all and had traded while insolvent, taking unwarranted risks with its creditors' money and trading at the expense of moneys due to the Crown.

D
2. The case was a serious one of its kind. The company never traded profitably and for long periods traded at a substantial loss. Having regard to the company's size and capitalisation the deficiency revealed by the statement of affairs could only be described as substantial. Throughout its history the director appeared to have behaved in a markedly cavalier fashion with the company's creditors both actual and potential.

E
3. Where it could be shown that a director had by defending disqualification proceedings, albeit in the end unsuccessfully, substantially reduced the charges made good against him, so that in the result the case with which the court was confronted, albeit one justifying disqualification, was not as serious as that which was opened by the Secretary of State at the beginning of the case, so that the court could take the view that the delinquent director's defence was to that extent justified, then the order for costs should
F
not be on an indemnity basis. The director's defence was justified in that sense.

The following cases were referred to in the judgment:

Astor Chemical Ltd v Synthetic Technology Ltd [1990] BCC 97.
Bath Glass Ltd, Re (1988) 4 BCC 130.
Cargo Agency Ltd, Re [1992] BCC 388.
Euromove Ltd, Re (unreported, 30 July 1992, Evans-Lombe QC).
G
Godwin Warren Control Systems plc, Re [1992] BCC 557.
Keypak Homecare Ltd, Re (No. 2) [1990] BCC 117.
Sevenoaks Stationers (Retail) Ltd, Re [1990] BCC 765; [1991] Ch 164.

Guy Newey (instructed by the Treasury Solicitor) for the Secretary of State for Trade and Industry.

The respondent appeared in person.

H
JUDGMENT

Edward Evans-Lombe QC: This is an application by the Secretary of State for Trade and Industry pursuant to sec. 6 of the *Company Directors Disqualification Act* 1986 that the respondent, Dudley Arnold Joiner, shall be disqualified from acting as a director of a company.

The relevant facts in this case may be said to start on 28 May 1976 when a company, Yeltaway Ltd, was incorporated. On 11 June, Mr Joiner became a director of Yeltaway and the holder of half its issued shares. Mr Joiner is a businessman specialising in the manufacture and sale of oil-based lubricants and gels. Through the medium of Yeltaway he started trading in this field in 1978. It seems that in 1979 Mr Joiner formed an association with the two brothers Randisi, who were businessmen specialising in the same field as himself in America. From early 1980 their business was conducted through the medium of a company, Synco Chemical Corporation, incorporated in the state of New York in February 1980. On 17 September 1980 Yeltaway registered a change of name to Synco (UK) Ltd. It appears that at about this time it was contemplated by the Randisis and Mr Joiner that Synco (UK) Ltd would become a subsidiary of Synco Chemical Corporation to act as a manufacturing and possibly distributing agent for the American corporation in Europe. However, the relationship between Mr Joiner and the Randisis appears to have broken down resulting in lengthy litigation in the USA which litigation was ultimately settled on terms which have not been disclosed.

On 28 April 1982 Synco (UK) acquired a subsidiary, Syntec Ltd, which had been incorporated on 12 March 1982 as Edon Ltd. I will refer to this company as "Syntec I". Syntec I became the trading arm of Synco (UK) and took over part of Synco (UK)'s accrued indebtedness. Its business was the packaging and sale of lubricants for the motor industry which it purchased from third sources. Mr Joiner accepts that one of its products was a lubricant of which a constituent part was a chemical gel. Syntec I traded under the name of "Syntec". As in the case of Synco (UK), Syntec I's trading does not appear to have been profitable for any significant period of time. On 2 May 1984 a petition was presented for the winding up of Syntec I by a creditor which resulted in a winding-up order on 25 June 1984. The statement of affairs of Syntec I in its winding up reveals a deficiency of £197,000. On 15 June 1984 the Midland Bank, under debentures held by the bank, appointed receivers of Synco (UK) and Syntec I.

Meanwhile, on 8 December 1983 Arotel Ltd was incorporated. It was acquired off the shelf by Mr Joiner. On 6 March 1984 Mr Joiner became its director and chairman with four other directors. At about this time it started trading in collaboration with a substantial public company, Standard Telephones and Cables plc, to which I will refer as "STC", for the development, manufacture and sale of an insulating gel designed to be inserted in fibre-optic cables. It is suggested that Mr Joiner acquired the know-how to produce and market this insulating gel as a result of his association with the Randisi brothers whose company has become an important worldwide producer of such gels. I will refer to the company as "Syntec". The gels manufactured by Syntec came to be sold under the name "Rheogel".

On 16 May 1984, a fortnight after the petition had been presented for the winding up of Syntec I, Syntec was procured to pass a resolution changing its name to Synthetic Technology Ltd, of which name it is to be observed, "Syntec", the trading name of Syntec I, was a natural abbreviation. This new name was registered on 13 June 1984.

Meanwhile, also, Mr Joiner and two associates and a limited company had acquired, off the shelf, a further company, Amalgamated Industries Ltd, to which I will refer as "Amalgamated", which had been incorporated on 21 May 1984. Mr Joiner became a director of that company and held a quarter of its issued shares. On the same day that the receivers of Synco (UK) and Syntec I were appointed Amalgamated purchased from those receivers the goodwill, trading names, patents etc. of Synco (UK) and Syntec I in consideration of a payment of £28,000 to Synco (UK) and £10,000 to Syntec I.

The speed with which this transaction was put into effect by the Midland Bank's receivers appears startling. Mr Joiner, in his evidence, described the circumstances in this way: Mr Joiner and his associates had confidence in the prospects of the business of

A   Syntec I, which company, together with its parent, Synco (UK) Ltd, had become overburdened with debt as a result of its litigation with the Randisi brothers in America. It was intended in early 1984 that Mr Joiner's associates would introduce more capital into Syntec I so that it could continue to trade. It seems that the Midland Bank were becoming concerned about the company's borrowings from that bank and were threatening to appoint receivers. Notwithstanding discussions with the bank with a view to the introduction of further capital the bank nevertheless took the decision to appoint

B   receivers which it communicated to Mr Joiner a few days prior to their appointment on 15 June 1984. Mr Joiner said that he and his associates' reaction was to produce a company to purchase the goodwill and assets of Synco (UK) and Syntec I from its receivers. This was done in a great hurry by the acquisition of a shelf company, Amalgamated, the price being agreed in negotiation with the receivers on the day of their appointment. Not long after this acquisition Amalgamated assigned to Syntec the

C   right to use "Syntec" as a trade name together with the right to use Syntec I's packaging style and publicity material.

  In evidence, Mr Joiner said that once it became clear that the bank intended to appoint receivers of Synco (UK) and Syntec I, he and his associates, who were preparing to put new money into those companies to keep them going, deliberately acquired Amalgamated to purchase from the receivers their assets and goodwill. Mr Joiner did not accept that as a result of these transactions Syntec continued the business of Synco

D   (UK) and Syntec I using the same name and premises but leaving the creditors of those companies out in the cold. His evidence was that the trading premises of Syntec I were repossessed by the landlords and for a period Syntec had to trade from his house. He said that two of his associates, Mr Young and Mr Brewster, who became shareholders and directors with him in Amalgamated, were experts in the lubricant business. The business of Syntec I, he said, was the packaging and sale of lubricants with only limited

E   manufacturing capacity and this was intended to be, and was, passed to and continued by Amalgamated. The business of Syntec was entirely one of manufacture and selling insulating gels.

  On 27 February 1985 Syntec's relationship with STC matured into an agreement of that date whereby Syntec assigned to STC its manufacturing patents and rights for its insulating gels in consideration of a payment of £50,000 and received back a licence to manufacture. STC undertook certain marketing duties and obligations to assist in

F   research and development of the product. There was a provision of the agreement whereby STC's licence to Syntec would terminate on the liquidation of Syntec. Prior to entering into this agreement Mr Ridler of STC had written a letter to Syntec giving forecasts of likely production figures for the special gels for the next two years.

  Accounts of Syntec for a period of 16 months to 31 March 1985, after taking into account STC's payment of £50,000, showed a loss of £4,720.

G
  In June 1985, in order to meet these increased production figures, Syntec took a new factory in Tunbridge Wells. Mr Joiner said the equipment for this factory took the next 12 months until June 1986 to install.

  Meanwhile, the financial state of Syntec was declining. On 13 December 1985 the company's bankers, Barclays, appear to have stipulated a "debtor formula" whereby the company was required to repay by stages its overdraft facility of £50,000. In that

H   month also Syntec fell into arrears in payment of its rent. Mr Joiner's evidence was that the company's difficult financial position was discussed both with its bankers and its landlords continually. The landlords, Haslemere Estates, were sympathetic since Syntec had moved into its new premises when those premises were empty and the landlords would prefer to have the premises occupied even though they were having to give credit for the rent as it became due.

However, notwithstanding these apparent financial difficulties it seems that Investors   **A**
in Industry, to whom I will refer as 3i, were prepared at this time to introduce capital
into the company amounting to £125,000 by means of subscribing for 115,000 £1
preference shares and 15 per cent of the issued ordinary shares.

Accounts of Synco for the year to 31 March 1986 showed a loss of £128,000 and an
overall deficiency of £132,000. These accounts were not signed until 22 September 1987.

In June 1986 Syntec's bankers started returning cheques unpaid. By the date of the   **B**
administration order, three years later, this treatment had been given to 96 cheques
totalling at face value approximately £120,000. On 11 June the bank wrote pointing out
that the "debtor formula" had not been complied with and warning of the dangers of the
directors permitting Syntec to trade "wrongfully". Nonetheless, they appear to have
been prepared to continue Syntec's overdraft facility of £50,000 in the short term.

On 14 July 1986, a petition was presented by a creditor with a debt of approximately   **C**
£4,000 for the winding up of Syntec. It appears that that petition was compromised. On
25 July three of Mr Joiner's four co-directors of Syntec resigned.

It seems that in mid-1986 the trading of STC suffered a marked downturn and this was
reflected in the orders placed with Syntec for gel. On 29 August 1986 Syntec entered into
a distribution agreement with a company, Astor Chemical plc. By this agreement Astor
became the sole distributors of Rheogel outside North America and for that purpose   **D**
financed the supply of raw materials to Syntec charging slightly more than 22 per cent
commission on all sales within the area. Mr Spalton, Astor's managing director at the
material time, gave evidence. He said that Astor were concerned at the financial state of
Syntec. In order to protect their supply of Rheogel for their customers against Syntec
going into liquidation there was inserted into the agreement at cl. 12(a) a provision that,
in that event, Syntec would sub-licence Astor to continue manufacture of the product.
Meanwhile Astor had made a side arrangement with STC that, in the event of Syntec's   **E**
liquidation, STC would not exercise their right to terminate Syntec's licence from STC.
As consideration for the agreement Astor paid £75,000 to Syntec in two tranches of
£50,000 and £25,000, the latter payment being made in February 1987.

Disputes arose between Astor and Syntec as to the conduct of the agreement and on
13 January 1987 Mr Joiner wrote to Astor purporting to terminate the agreement by
reason of Astor's breaches of it. Astor's reaction was to launch proceedings against   **F**
Syntec in which proceedings, on 6 February, they obtained an injunction restraining
Syntec from selling their product elsewhere. The proceedings never came to a substantive
hearing because the parties compromised, as a result of which there were amendments
to the provisions of the distribution agreement.

On 19 February 1987 Syntec's landlords, Haslemere Estates, which company it
appears had been taken over by Dutch purchasers who were much less sympathetic to   **G**
the position of Syntec, issued a writ for the recovery of arrears of rent by then amounting
to some £102,000.

Accounts of the company for the year to 31 March 1987 show a loss of £324,000 and a
deficit on profit and loss account carried forward of £457,000. The balance sheet shows
an overall deficiency of £312,000. The third paragraph of the report of the auditors reads
as follows: **H**

> "As stated in note 13 the company is currently negotiating further loan facilities
> of £100,000; continuation of the company's activities is dependent on a successful
> outcome to these negotiations and on the continued financial support of the
> directors, loan creditor and bankers. The financial statements have been drawn
> up on a going-concern basis which assumes that adequate facilities will be obtained."

A   Note 13 to the accounts provides:

> "*Post-balance sheet events*
>
> Since the balance sheet date a further 69,000 ordinary shares of £1 each were issued at par for cash on 24 July 1987 to provide working capital. A further sum of £45,500 has been provided by one of the shareholders at the same date in the form of a loan which is also to provide working capital. Additionally and subject to
>
B   agreement between the shareholder and the company, a further £100,000 will be made available to the company."

Note 13 to the 1987 accounts describes an agreement dated 24 July 1987 under which a company, Monteagle Chemicals International Ltd, to which I shall refer as "Monteagle", one of a group of companies to which I shall refer as the "Monteagle group", agreed in terms summarised in the note. Mr Tipton was a director of Monteagle who came to play a substantial part in the subsequent conduct of the business of Syntec.

C   Prior to this agreement, Syntec had been attempting to raise capital to finance its increasing deficit. In early 1987 negotiations had taken place with Astor with a view to that company increasing its stake in Syntec and making further capital available. Those negotiations had not reached finality when Syntec was first approached by Monteagle.

Mr Spalton produced in evidence a prospectus by Syntec which appears to have been circulated in early March 1987 designed to attract an investor for that company who

D   would produce £350,000. Mr Joiner accepted that the first ten pages of this document indeed emanated from Syntec. He was at pains, however, to point out that the last three pages, which contain a projected profit and loss account for the years to March 1987 and March 1988 and a projected balance sheet as at 31 March 1987, were typed using a different typeface from the remainder of the document. Even disregarding the last three pages this document projects total sales for 1988 of £1.6m with a net pre-tax profit of £132,000, when accounts drawn to 31 March 1987, the time when this document was

E   being circulated, show a turnover figure of £245,000 and a loss of £324,000. When cross-examined about this document Mr Joiner indicated that in his view it was quite reasonable when seeking to raise capital to present forecasts known to be optimistic. Whereas the company's accounts for the year to 31 March 1987 were not signed until 22 September of that year, I am not prepared to accept that the management of Syntec and, in particular, Mr Joiner did not have a very good idea how the company was actually performing as at March 1987. A turn round in performance from that being achieved at

F   that time to that projected for the next year of trading, let alone the figures projected for subsequent years, cannot, in my judgment, have been realistically contemplated at this time by Mr Joiner.

In April 1987 the company received a statutory demand for £12,000 outstanding VAT. On 22 May 1987, Robson Rhodes wrote to the company warning the directors of the risks they ran by trading whilst the company was insolvent. By about this time the

G   company owed approximately £100,000 to its landlords. Documentary evidence was put in which shows that by September 1987 significant numbers of creditors of Syntec were threatening legal proceedings for payment of their debts, some of which had taken their claims to judgment before being paid. On 12 October 1987 a creditors' petition was presented for the winding up of Syntec for a debt of £2,500. Also in evidence were minutes of board meetings held on 12 November 1987 and 7 January 1988 which indicate that Mr Joiner was engaged in negotiations with the Revenue and the Commissioners of

H   Customs and Excise for the payment of arrears of tax and VAT by instalments. On 2 February 1988 the landlords of Syntec levied distress for rent.

Mr Joiner was cross-examined about his conduct of the company's business at this period. He naturally laid great stress on the fact that in the middle of it Monteagle were prepared to enter into the agreement of 24 July 1987 subscribing for shares and converting part of their trading debt into a loan and indicating a willingness to advance a further £100,000. He was, however, compelled to admit that in order to preserve Syntec from liquidation, in addition to Monteagle's actual and promised support, the company was compelled to obtain credit by leaving the payment of its ordinary trading debts to the last possible moment, in some cases paying those debts only after judgment had been obtained in proceedings.

I continue with the outline of the history of Syntec. On 17 February 1988 a further statutory demand was served on the company for outstanding VAT in the sum of £878. That was followed by a further statutory demand on 20 October 1988 by a creditor for £2,500-odd in respect of a debt which had become due in November 1986. Meanwhile, on 5 April 1988 the company's accounts for 1986 and 1987 were filed substantially late and notwithstanding that the directors had signed them on 22 September of the previous year.

There were produced in evidence, from Syntec's records, various management accounts for the company's trading for periods in the years 1985 to 1989. These present a confusing picture. In some instances there appear to be three sets of management accounts for the same period, each showing widely different trading performances by Syntec. The only management account to show a profit was that for the year to March 1988 where a profit of rather more than £6,000 was shown on a total turnover of £818,000. The draft balance sheet drawn at 31 March 1988 showed net current liabilities of £164,000 and an accumulated loss on profit and loss account of £457,000 and an overall deficiency of £167,000 after the introduction of capital by Monteagle in July 1987. Thereafter, the management accounts show a sharp decline in performance caused, according to Mr Joiner, by loss of sales due to strikes at two major customers, which sales could not be replaced. Draft profit and loss accounts for the period March 1988 to February 1989 show a loss of £215,000 on a turnover of £427,000. A draft balance sheet drawn to 28 February 1989 shows net current liabilities of £285,000 and an overall deficiency of £382,000. These figures appear to have been substantially optimistic. The company's statement of affairs drawn to a date approximately one month later revealed current liabilities of £552,000 and an overall deficiency of £740,000.

It seems that in early 1989 Mr Tipton of Monteagle lost his nerve and indicated that he was not prepared to continue with the support which he had been giving to Syntec. It was Mr Joiner's evidence that until that point Monteagle's support had been without limit in the sense that they were committed to providing sufficient finance to ensure that Syntec's pressing creditors were always paid. It is wholly unclear to me to what extent Monteagle was committed to the support of Syntec and to what extent Mr Joiner was entitled from July 1987 onward to place reliance on that support. Mr Tipton appears to have played an active part in the management of Syntec. He is recorded as attending many board meetings. In the end the Monteagle group are substantial creditors of Syntec. Mr Joiner produced in evidence an undated Monteagle document which he said was produced shortly before Syntec went into administration. This document appears to be an assessment by Monteagle of Syntec's future, and finishes by asking the question whether Syntec is rescuable or not. Its conclusion is that such a rescue was possible because Syntec was well placed to exploit what this document presents as a growing market for its products. Mr Tipton did not give evidence.

On 31 March 1989 the directors of Syntec, by this time only Mr Joiner and Mr Bury, procured Syntec to present a petition for its administration. That petition was precipitated by yet a further creditors' winding-up petition presented on 13 February 1989 and by Monteagle's refusal to pay off that petition. Three purposes of the administration are set out in the petition, first, the survival of the company or some part of it as a going concern, secondly, the approval of a voluntary arrangement and, thirdly, a more

A
advantageous realisation of assets than would result from a winding up. The petition was supported by a report from Robson Rhodes dated 31 March 1989. I quote from para. 3 and 4 of that report:

> "We have advised that Syntec should petition for an administration order in order to secure its survival as a going concern . . . we believe there is a real prospect that Syntec will be able to survive as a going concern . . ."

B
On 7 April 1989 Robson Rhodes made a further report on the prospects of Syntec if it entered administration. This report is in generally optimistic terms. At para. 3.6 that report reads as follows:

> "An independent market research report commissioned by Syntec estimates the size of the fibre-optic cable market. Using a simple formula it is possible to determine the volume of gel that would be needed to satisfy this market. The requirement for the year ending 31 March 1990 is some 3,326 metric tonnes and
C
> this is anticipated to increase at a compound rate of ten per cent per annum over the next five years. With increasing specification requirements resulting in the decline in use of the hot melt gels and the fact that there are only three major manufacturers of cold pump gels, Syntec is in a very good position to obtain a sizeable share of the world market. On the assumption of a selling price of approximately £2,800 per metric tonne the world market is worth £9.3m and will
D
> increase by 1994 to £14.6m assuming no selling price change. Syntec is forecasting sales of £2m in the year ending 31 March 1990 which represents a market share of 21.5 per cent."

Paragraph 5 of the report refers to Appendix VI where there is set out what is described as the "Directors' trading forecasts for the year ending 31 March 1990". This schedule forecasts total sales for the first three quarters of £1.35m and for the year of
E
just more than £2m. The forecast profit for the first three quarters was £69,000, £66,000 and £114,000, the total forecast profit for the year to 31 March 1990 being £387,000. Within these figures the directors forecast sales of £242,000 in the first quarter, £304,000 in the second quarter and £411,000 in the third quarter, of worldwide sales, excluding North America, for which Astor had sole distribution rights. Astor's revised budgets were £89,000, £88,000 and £94,000 respectively for approximately the same periods. Their actual sales for those periods were £65,000, £194,000 and £130,000 making a total
F
of £390,000 for the three quarters. The report states at para. 6.6(a):

> "The sales forecast has been constructed by reference to specific orders or known potential orders as indicated by Syntec's customers. The sales forecasts for April alone would generate £62,000 gross profit. Furthermore, as is stated in section 5 above, there is an even greater potential for future orders."

G
At para. 1.6 the report states:

> "We have not carried out an audit and our work should not be relied upon as such. We have not sought to verify the information supplied to us."

Nonetheless, Mr Jacob, in his evidence, did say that the joint administrators had checked the information being given to them by the directors in such ways as were possible and in particular they had spent some time checking the basis of the directors'
H
sales forecasts. At para. 1.4 of the report the future joint administrators state:

> "Our preliminary investigation showed that Syntec is presently unable to pay its debts. Of the options available to Syntec . . . the most favourable in our opinion is the appointment of administrators. It is our view that administration is likely to allow Syntec to continue trading and survive as a going concern and/or a voluntary arrangement with Syntec's creditors. Should this not be possible an administration

is likely to provide a better realisation of Syntec's assets than would be effected in A
a winding up.''

On 10 April 1989 an administration order was made against Syntec. It appears that
soon after the order the joint administrators were persuaded that the interests of Syntec
would be best served by terminating Astor's distributorship agreement notwithstanding
that they had described it in their report at para. 3.4 as ''a beneficial arrangement''. It
seems that the joint administrators were advised that they had, by reason of the
administration order and their appointment, a right at law to terminate the distributorship B
agreement and, if that were wrong, they also had a right to terminate it by reason of
breaches by Astor of the agreement. On 28 April 1989 the joint administrators wrote to
Astor pointing out the breaches and on 5 June wrote terminating the agreement. Astor's
reaction again was to launch proceedings and on 12 June 1989 *Peter Gibson* J made an
ex parte injunction restraining Syntec, through its joint administrators, from selling
Rheogel inconsistently with the provisions of the distribution agreement. C

In these proceedings brought by Astor one of the joint administrators, Mr Montgomery,
swore an affidavit. At para. 11 of that affidavit he said this:

> ''We formed the view that there was evidence of a probable significant upturn in
> demand for Rheogel, that Syntec had the capacity to manufacture sufficient
> Rheogel to meet the increased demand and that it was possible to finance trading
> in administration while setting about the achievement of the objectives for which D
> it was to be sought. We assumed at that stage that the distribution agreement
> would form an effective conduit between Syntec's productive capacity and the
> increasing market for its products.''

The affidavit then goes on to describe how the joint administrators discovered
breaches of the agreement by Astor and their conclusion that the distribution agreement
was terminable. The affidavit continues at para. 19: E

> ''Our projections show that, following termination, Syntec should trade profitably
> in administration by selling directly to customers in the UK and directly or through
> intermediaries in overseas territories.
>
> 20. The trading can be funded by Monteagle to the extent that income is insufficient
> to meet expenses.''

The affidavit continues at para. 24: F

> ''I should explain to this honourable court that the trading projections which
> accompanied my first affidavit reflected a great deal of further work which was
> carried out by my firm following our appointment. The fact that they are similar
> to the projections suggested by the directors prior to the administration order
> does indeed confirm that the directors had formed a reasonable view of the market
> at that date. Similarity does not, however, in any way invalidate our projections
> nor does it suggest and it is not the case that Robson Rhodes prepared the G
> forecasts merely by reliance on the directors' assertions.''

Mr Joiner produced in evidence various reports on the prospects for the market in
fibre-optic cable both in North America and in other parts of the world. Those reports
were commented on by Mr Spalton. Those reports would seem to justify the joint
administrators' optimistic view as to the future development of the market for Rheogel
which they expressed in their reports and in the evidence of Mr Montgomery. H

When Astor's motion for an injunction came to be heard inter partes the joint
administrators' contention that they were entitled, by force of their appointment, to
terminate the distribution agreement failed as did their alternative contention that they
were entitled so to terminate it as a result of breaches by Astor (see [1990] BCC 97).
Vinelott J who tried the case concluded his judgment by saying (at p. 111G):

"I have come to the conclusion after some hesitation that I ought to grant an injunction and that I should not leave Astor only with the protection of these undertakings. If Astor is left only as a non-exclusive distributor, its business is likely to suffer disruption and its reputation may well be injured. It has appointed sub-agents on the footing that it has exclusive rights of distribution. They may well be dissatisfied if they find that they are distributing the product against competition from Syntec direct or from Monteagle. The precarious financial situation of Syntec, if known, is also likely to affect the confidence of customers. There is evidence that one large cable manufacturer in Germany declined to place an order after making enquiries into the status and financial health of Syntec. This damage will be far more elusive and difficult to quantify than the potential damage to Syntec if the injunction is continued even if it is forced into an insolvent liquidation.

There are, moreover, other considerations which I think the court is entitled to take into account. It would, I think, be wrong that Syntec should be allowed to continue to trade with what must be on any view a very speculative expectation of profit at a time when it is hopelessly insolvent and has for some time continued to trade in part with the assistance of moneys for which it was liable to account to the Inland Revenue and under the day-to-day management of a former director who has recently been associated with two other insolvent companies. Moreover there must at the very least be considerable doubt whether full disclosure was made when the administration order was made and whether *Peter Gibson* J would have made that order if all the circumstances had been disclosed."

The judge went on to order Syntec to pay the costs of the proceedings. In the result I was informed that these proceedings placed an extra burden of some £200,000 on the assets of Syntec.

On 13 December 1989 the joint administrators entered into an agreement with Astor whereby Astor purchased Syntec's business and assets.

Finally, it seems that on 27 March 1990 Mr Joiner and his wife acquired all the issued shares and became directors of a company, Gel Technology Ltd, which had been incorporated under the name of Reliable Engineering Ltd on 13 March 1990. That company went into insolvent liquidation in 1992.

Section 6 of the *Company Directors Disqualification Act* 1986 provides as follows:

"(1) The court shall make a disqualification order against a person in any case where, on an application under this section, it is satisfied—

(a) that he is or has been a director of a company which has at any time become insolvent (whether while he was a director or subsequently), and

(b) that his conduct as a director of that company (either taken alone or taken together with his conduct as a director of any other company or companies) makes him unfit to be concerned in the management of a company.

(2) For the purposes of this section . . . a company becomes insolvent if—
. . .

(b) an administration order is made in relation to the company . . ."

Mr Joiner was a director of Syntec at all material times, which company has "become insolvent" within the meaning of sec. 6(1)(a).

Section 9 of the Act provides that the court in determining whether the conduct of the director was such as to make him unfit to be concerned in the management of a company shall take into account, in the case of a company which has become insolvent, the matters set out in Pt. I and II of Sch. 1 to the Act.

Mr Newey, who appeared for the Secretary of State, listed under ten heads the actions and defaults of Mr Joiner which he set out to prove and which he submitted justified the court in coming to the conclusion that his conduct as a director of Synthetic Technology Ltd taken with his conduct as a director of other companies made him unfit to be concerned in the management of a company within the meaning of sec. 6(1)(b) of the 1986 Act.

I will deal with these each in turn but not necessarily in the order in which they were presented by Mr Newey. It is convenient if I start with the ground which he presented as the second ground on his list.

This ground charged that Mr Joiner sought to make Syntec pay for debts for which he was personally liable.

The relevant events occurred in late 1985 and concerned Mr R D Culmer, an electrician trading as Tunbridge Wells Electrical. Mr Culmer gave evidence. His account was that at the request of Mr Joiner he undertook certain electrical works at Mr Joiner's house, Ashdown Cottage, near Uckfield. The cost of the work was £4,977 including VAT for which sum an invoice was submitted on 16 December 1985 addressed to Mr Joiner personally. A copy of this invoice is in evidence. It was not paid but rather Mr Joiner contacted Mr Culmer and asked him to charge Syntec instead by concealing the amount in invoices which Mr Culmer was submitting to the company for electrical work done to computer installations on the company's premises.

Accordingly, a series of false invoices were brought into existence in which the company was charged for the total of £4,977 for work done at Mr Joiner's house. One of the invoices was paid by the company as a result of which £1,495 was paid actually in respect of that work. The company failed to pay the remaining invoices as a result of which Mr Culmer was compelled to take proceedings in the Tunbridge Wells County Court and in the result he obtained judgment against the company dated 19 August 1986. Mr Culmer said that this judgment proved impossible to enforce against the company because of the existence of floating charges over the company's assets in favour of Barclays Bank. He said that as a result of further advice he then applied to have the judgment set aside which application was successful. He then commenced proceedings against Mr Joiner personally for the balance of the claim. Mr Joiner unsuccessfully defended the proceedings in the course of which he paid £2,000 into court. As a result, judgment was entered against him for £2,750 with costs. Subsequently, Mr Joiner offered a scheme of arrangement to his creditors in which Mr Culmer joined and received some 21p in the pound. Mr Culmer estimates that he has lost rather more than £4,000 together with a considerable expenditure of time and effort.

Mr Joiner's account of these events was that he accepted that the work was done for him personally but asked that the invoice of 16 December be sent to the company so that the company could pay, reducing the credit on his director's loan account. He denied that he had asked Mr Culmer to conceal the amount due in invoices to the company for work that Mr Culmer had done for the company. The difficulty facing Mr Joiner in his account was that at the relevant time his director's loan account was not in credit because it had been capitalised as part of the agreement with 3i in December 1985.

I unhesitatingly accept the evidence of Mr Culmer and reject the account of Mr Joiner. I therefore find this charge proved. This incident, although involving a relatively small sum of money, reflects no credit on Mr Joiner at all.

I turn to the third ground which is that Mr Joiner misled the court in the course of the administration proceedings.

It is submitted that he did so in three separate ways. In the first place he did so by representing in his affidavit evidence that the distribution agreement with Astor was

A   beneficial to the company and one which it was important that the company should not permit Astor to terminate by the company going into liquidation. It is then said that shortly after the administration order Mr Joiner changed his tune and sought to persuade the joint administrators that the distribution agreement was in reality a millstone and one which they should terminate if possible.

B   Mr Joiner's account was that he never faltered in his view that the Astor agreement was beneficial to the company because of its provisions that Astor would finance the purchase of stocks of raw materials in the manufacture of Rheogel, would finance Syntec's debtors and make available its sales and distribution network. He drew attention to a letter of 19 May 1989 which he and Mr Bury, his fellow director, sent to the joint administrators and in particular to para. 3 of that letter. In evidence Mr Jacob conceded that the joint administrators' sales forecasts were drawn on the basis that the Astor agreement should continue. He accepted that the joint administrators' view was that Syntec would trade profitably by continuing to use Astor but would do better if freed from the distribution agreement. It was, he accepted, the decision of the joint administrators to seek to avoid that agreement. In the light of this evidence it seems to me to be impossible to say that this charge is made out.

C   The second ground upon which it was said that the court was misled is that Mr Joiner failed to disclose that he had been associated previously with two companies which had failed due to insolvency. Mr Joiner's answer was that he was never asked by anybody and if he had been he would have disclosed the failure of Synco (UK) and Syntec I. It is not suggested that anyone did ask Mr Joiner about previous failed companies with which he was associated or that he ever gave anyone the impression that he had never been associated previously with failed companies. I am unable to find proof that Mr Joiner on this ground deliberately misled the court.

E   Finally under this head it is said that Mr Joiner misled the court by representing that the principal asset of Syntec was its licence to manufacture Rheogel and to use that trademark which right would be lost if it went into liquidation. By contrast on 20 June 1989 Mr Joiner seems to have written a letter to the joint administrators in which he represented that the rights were in some way personal to him. Mr Joiner's account of the letter was that it was written at a time when he understood the administrators were considering selling Syntec's business to Astor for a consideration which Mr Joiner did not think properly reflected the future prospects of that business. He said he wrote the letter of 20 June in an attempt to make the joint administrators stop short. He was compelled to accept that by the terms of the letter he sought to obtain a personal benefit as consideration for allowing a transfer of the Rheogel trademark.

   I will deal with this matter at the same time as the charge that Mr Newey made under his fourth head, namely, that Mr Joiner has wrongly laid claim to an asset of Syntec, that charge arising from the same facts.

G   It seems to me that Mr Joiner's letter of 20 June can only be read as an attempt wrongfully to assert Mr Joiner's ownership of the Rheogel trademark and accordingly the fourth charge is made out. It was not, however, to mislead the court for Mr Joiner to represent that the right to manufacture Rheogel and its trademark was a valuable asset of the company. At the time that representation was made, such was and now remains the case. I should state, however, that I do not regard the writing of the letter of 20 June in the circumstance in which it was written, and in the light of what the joint administrators must have known from the company's own records, as being a matter of great seriousness.

   Mr Newey's fifth charge was failure to pay Crown debts. My attention was drawn to the fact that in the receivership it was found that the company had not accounted for £89,000 of PAYE of which some £64,000 was non-preferential and that the company had failed to account for some £28,000 of VAT going back to March 1987. While accepting

these figures Mr Joiner drew my attention to the board minutes included in his exhibit in
respect of meetings of the board on 12 November 1987 and 7 January 1988. He said that
those minutes established that he was at that time seeking to make an agreement with
the Revenue and the Customs and Excise for payment of the company's arrears of PAYE
and VAT. He was, however, compelled to accept that any agreement which was made by
the company at that time was not honoured. Having set out the basic facts, which are
not in issue, I propose to delay dealing with this charge until I deal with Mr Newey's
charges under his first heading.

I therefore turn to Mr Newey's sixth heading, namely, a failure by the company,
under the management of Mr Joiner, to file accounts with the registrar of companies
within the time prescribed. Mr Joiner did not contest that the accounts to March 1986
due at the end of January 1987 and those for March 1987 and due at the end of January
1988 were not filed until 5 April 1988. Nor did he contest that the accounts to March
1988, due at the end of January 1989, were never filed at all. It follows that this charge is
made out.

The seventh charge is that Mr Joiner permitted the company to pay him excessive
remuneration, having regard to its financial position in the years 1986 and 1987 and
leading up to the making of the administration order. The relevant figures were
remuneration of £30,275 in the year to March 1986, when the company made a loss of
£128,000-odd, remuneration of nearly £32,000 in the year to March 1987, when the
company made a loss of £324,995, and remuneration at the rate of £34,000 in the period
up to the administration order when the company can also be shown to have been
making a substantial trading loss. Throughout these periods the company was providing
Mr Joiner with a motor car, for most of the time a very expensive motor car. Mr Joiner's
answer to these charges was that the joint administrators continued to employ his
services and those of Mr Bury after the making of the administration order and in doing
so paid them at the same rate (in the case of Mr Bury at a slightly increased rate) as that
which they had previously been enjoying.

In this regard my attention was drawn to two decisions of *Harman* J, *Re Keypak
Homecare Ltd (No. 2)* [1990] BCC 117, in particular the passage in the judgment at
p. 120B, and *Re Cargo Agency Ltd* [1992] BCC 388 at p. 391E. In those two judgments
Harman J concluded that it was not enough for a director, who had an equity stake in the
company concerned, to say that he was being paid no more than the job that he was
doing was worth, where nonetheless it was apparent that the total remuneration package
of the director, including any benefits of kind, was out of proportion to the company's
then trading success and financial health. Syntec's turnover for the year to March 1986
was some £435,000 and for the year to March 1987, £245,000. Management accounts for
the year to March 1988 show a turnover of £818,000 and a small profit but thereafter a
rapid decline so that its turnover in the year to March 1989 was some £428,000.

Applying *Harman* J's criteria it seems to me that, whereas it might be said that
Mr Joiner was not excessive in taking some £30,000-odd and the running costs of an
expensive car out of the company in the year to March 1986, a continuation of that level
of remuneration in the year to March 1987 was plainly not justified. It may be said that
he would have been justified in restoring his remuneration package because of the
company's increased turnover and apparent profitability in the year to March 1988
(although the figures contained in the relevant management accounts now seem suspect).
He was not however justified in continuing that remuneration level through the final
year of the company's trading. The fact that the joint administrators continued the cash
remuneration to Mr Joiner after the administration order is no answer, because by then
it had been demonstrated that the company was substantially insolvent and could only
survive upon the introduction of fresh capital which would have substantially diluted the

A directors' share stakes in the company. For these reasons it seems to me that this charge is partially made out.

I now turn to consider the eighth charge, namely, that Mr Joiner caused Syntec to be brought into existence with the intention of taking over the goodwill of the business of Synco (UK) and Syntec I, while leaving unpaid the creditors of those companies.

B In my description of the background facts of this case I set out the circumstances of Mr Joiner's acquisition of Syntec and the failures of Synco (UK) and Syntec I. It seems to me that this charge cannot be made out. There is no evidence that Syntec in truth took over the business of Syntec I, itself the trading arm of Synco (UK). To the extent that Syntec I acquired through Amalgamated the benefit of the trademarks, goodwill and advertising material of Syntec I and Synco (UK), the evidence before me is that those were acquired by Amalgamated by purchase from the receivers of those companies. It seems to me that I cannot treat the circumstances of the acquisition of Syntec by Mr Joiner and its commencement in trade as another example of a "phoenix" company which the public justifiably regards as objectionable. To this extent I feel myself bound

C to depart from the views expressed by *Vinelott* J in his judgment in Astor's case against the company.

The ninth and tenth charges were admitted by Mr Joiner, namely, that while a director of Lubricants, a subsidiary of Amalgamated, which actually never traded, that company failed to make any returns and that he failed to notify the companies registrar of his

D appointment as a director of Gel Technology Ltd, which company has also failed to make any returns.

I now turn to deal with the first charge which has caused me the greatest difficulty and, at the same time, to deal with the fifth charge. The first charge was that Mr Joiner had permitted the company to continue to trade whilst it was insolvent. Although this is not expressly made clear in the affidavit of Mr Jacob, Mr Newey, at the outset of this case,

E made plain that the period in respect of which the allegation is made is from early 1987 until the administration order.

In his judgment in *Re Sevenoaks Stationers (Retail) Ltd* [1990] BCC 765 at p. 779F, *Dillon* LJ said:

> "Mr Cruddas made a deliberate decision to pay only those creditors who pressed for payment. The obvious result was that the two companies traded, when in fact insolvent and known to be in difficulties, at the expense of those creditors who,
F like the Crown, happened not to be pressing for payment. Such conduct on the part of a director can well, in my judgment, be relied on as a ground for saying that he is unfit to be concerned in the management of a company. But what is relevant in the Crown's position is not that the debt was a debt which arose from a compulsory deduction from employees' wages or a compulsory payment of VAT,
G but that the Crown was not pressing for payment, and the director was taking unfair advantage of that forbearance on the part of the Crown, and, instead of providing adequate working capital, was trading at the Crown's expense while the companies were in jeopardy. It would be equally unfair to trade in that way and in such circumstances at the expense of creditors other than the Crown. The Crown is the more exposed not from the nature of the debts but from the administrative problem it has in pressing for prompt payment as companies get into difficulties.
H As *Peter Gibson* J observed in *Re Bath Glass Ltd* (1988) 4 BCC 130 at pp. 133–134 at the end of a paragraph which I would generally approve without limiting it to Crown debts:
>> 'Even if such conduct does not amount to wrongful trading within sec. 214 (of the *Insolvency Act* 1986), in my judgment it would still be conduct amounting to misconduct and so relevant to sec. 6. Whether in any particular case that

A

misconduct, or the various matters of misconduct proved to the satisfaction of the court, will justify a finding of unfitness will depend on all the circumstances of the case.'

Taking that view of the Crown debts in Rochester and Retail and adding to it (1) that there were never any audited accounts of any of the five companies let alone registered accounts, (2) the inadequacy of the accounting records of Retail, (3) the loan by Retail to Rochester, (4) the payment of debts of Hoo Paper by Hoo Waste Paper, (5) the guarantee given by Sevenoaks Stationers for the liabilities of Hoo Paper, (6) the continued trading while insolvent and known to be in difficulties of Rochester and Retail and, (7) the extent of the deficiency in each company after a relatively short period of trading, I have no doubt at all that it is amply proved that Mr Cruddas is unfitted to be concerned in the management of a company. His trouble is not dishonesty, but incompetence or negligence in a very marked degree and that is enough to render him unfit; I do not think it necessary for incompetence to be "total", as suggested by the Vice-Chancellor in *Lo-Line* [*Electric Motors Ltd* (1988) 4 BCC 415 at p. 419] to render a director unfit to take part in the management of a company."

B

C

From the combined judgments of *Dillon* LJ in the *Sevenoaks* case and *Peter Gibson* J in the *Bath Glass* case it is apparent that a director can permit his company to continue to trade whilst insolvent, while not exposing himself to a charge of wrongful trading under sec. 214 of the 1986 Act, but still be guilty of conduct amounting to misconduct under sec. 6. In the course of his submissions I was flattered by Mr Newey commending to me words which I used in my judgment in the case of *Re Euromove Ltd* where I sought to define such conduct as the taking of unwarranted risks with creditors' money by continuing to trade.

D

I have set out in the first part of this judgment a reasonably detailed history of the company's trading. But for two matters, that trading portrayed all the hallmarks of a company trading whilst it was insolvent and in so doing taking unwarranted risks with its creditors' money. I need only draw attention to Mr Joiner's admissions that by mid-1987 he was keeping the company alive by only paying creditors that were pressing and by leaving payment even of these until the last possible minute, in some cases after those creditors had obtained judgment against the company.

E

The principal countervailing circumstance is Mr Joiner's assertion of his continued belief in the company's ultimately successful future which appears to have been backed by others. In particular, it seems that the Monteagle group were prepared in July 1987 to make available some £200,000 worth of fresh capital to the company by way of subscription for shares and the taking over and postponement of the company's trading debts. In addition, I cannot overlook the fact that the joint administrators were prepared to depose to, in the proceedings against the company by Astor, and set out in their reports about the company, their confidence in the company's trading future in the manner which I have already described.

F

G

Nonetheless, I have come to the clear conclusion that Mr Newey's first charge is at least partially made out and that his fifth charge is also made out in the sense that the company, under the management of Mr Joiner, exploited the Crown, together with the company's other creditors, by deliberately pursuing a policy of only paying at the last minute those creditors which were pressing, which the Crown, together with the bulk of the company's other creditors, were not at the material time doing or not with sufficient persistence. It seems to me that Mr Joiner's continuation of the company's trading became culpable by at least September 1987 when it should have become apparent to Mr Joiner that the infusion of capital by the Monteagle group in July was insufficient. I am unable to accept that Mr Joiner was justified in regarding Monteagle's support as

H

A   unconditional. As events proved they were not prepared to bail the company out in all circumstances.

In my judgment, the apparently rosy prospects for the growth in the world market for fibre-optic cable, and so for the gels required to make that cable, did not justify Mr Joiner in continuing the company's trading from that time. It now seems to be clear that the company's management accounts for the year to March 1988 were optimistic,

B   but even if they adequately reflected the company's trading success, it must have been apparent that a profit of somewhat more than £6,000 on a turnover of £800,000 (much more than the company had been achieving previously and which it was to achieve in the future) was quite insufficient to service the company's accumulated debts. In the light of the company's past trading history I can only express my surprise that the joint administrators were prepared to make the forecasts of the company's future trading which they seem to have been prepared to make for the purposes of the administration

C   proceedings. In my view, they must have permitted themselves to be over-influenced by the directors' view of the imminent expansion in the worldwide market for insulating gels and in Syntec's ability to obtain an increased share of that market.

In my judgment, the conduct of Mr Joiner in procuring the company to continue to trade after September 1987, when taken with the other matters which I have found proved, is such as to render him unfit to be concerned in the management of a company.

D   It follows that I am required by the words of sec. 6 to make a disqualification order and it remains for me to assess the seriousness of the case and in consequence the length of the disqualification which I must impose.

In my judgment, I am justified in viewing this case as a serious one of its kind. This company never traded profitably and for long periods during its trading history traded at a substantial loss. Having regard to the company's size and capitalisation the deficiency revealed by its statement of affairs can only be also described as substantial. Throughout

E   its history Mr Joiner appears to have behaved in a markedly cavalier fashion with the company's creditors both actual and potential. I have already drawn attention to the irresponsible nature of the company's prospectus apparently being circulated to potential lenders or investors in March 1987. Having regard to the criteria established in the judgment of *Dillon* LJ in the *Sevenoaks* case, it seems to me that a period of disqualification of seven years should be imposed on Mr Joiner in this case.

F

Costs

It has, as I know from my own experience, been the practice in this court until recently that where the Secretary of State succeeds in an application to disqualify a director he obtains, save where exceptional facts occur, an order for costs against that director on an indemnity basis.

G   I have, however, had drawn to my attention the judgment of *Chadwick* J in the case of *Re Godwin Warren Control Systems plc* [1992] BCC 557 at p. 569H, where that judge comes to the view that there can be no reason why the Secretary of State in these cases should receive particular treatment and, as a matter of course, obtain an order for indemnity costs. I am told that that judgment was followed in a recent case by *Mervyn Davies* J. By contrast, it was not followed by the Vice-Chancellor, *Vinelott* J and a deputy judge in other cases of this kind. I am told, however, that the Vice-Chancellor, in

H   particular, did not give a reasoned judgment for why he did not follow what *Chadwick* J said in the case of *Re Godwin Warren*. It follows that I am confronted with two, perhaps, conflicting lines of authority, for one of which reasons are given and for the other of which no reason has apparently been given.

It seems to me that the differentiation should be this. That where it can be shown that a director has by defending the proceedings, albeit in the end unsuccessfully, substantially

A

reduced the charges made good against him, so that in the result the case with which the court is confronted, albeit one justifying disqualification, is not as serious as that which was opened by the Secretary of State at the beginning of the case, so that the court can take the view that the delinquent director's defence was to that extent justified, then the order for costs should not be on an indemnity basis. In each case, it seems to me it will be a matter of degree as to whether the successful defence was justified in the sense which I have sought to define.

B

I am satisfied that in this case Mr Joiner's defence was justified in that sense and that, in this case, I should follow the course which *Chadwick* J laid down in the *Godwin Warren* case and make an order for costs but on the standard basis only.

(*Order accordingly*)

C

D

E

F

G

H

A   # Re Mountforest Ltd.

Chancery Division (Companies Court).
Harman J.
Judgment delivered 29 March 1993.

B
*Unfair prejudice petition — Company subject of unfair prejudice petition
proposed sale of business and voluntary winding up — Whether sale should be
restrained — Whether receiver should be appointed pending trial of petition
— Respondents sought validation of sale in case of winding-up order —
Companies Act 1985, sec. 459; Insolvency Act 1986, sec. 127.*

**These were applications by the petitioner in a petition under sec. 459 of the Companies
Act 1985 and an application by the company.**

C   **The petitioner sought orders restraining the respondent shareholders from acting on
resolutions for the sale of the company's business and for a subsequent winding up, and
an order for the appointment of a receiver of the respondent company until trial of the
petition. The company's application was for an order that in the event of an order to wind
up the company the sale of the business should not be avoided under sec. 127 of the
Insolvency Act 1986.**

D   **The petition was based on allegations of expectation of participation in and subsequent
exclusion from management. The applications by the petitioner followed receipt by him
of notices convening extraordinary general meetings of the company on successive days to
pass resolutions for the sale of the company's assets to Unicare plc and for winding up.**

**The shareholders of Unicare were the first and second respondents, who were between
them majority shareholders in the company. The three directors of Unicare were the
three directors of the company.**

E   ***Held*, granting the two injunctions sought, refusing the sec. 127 application and
refusing to appoint a receiver:**

**1. Although the reason for the sale was a genuine reason, the transaction was a self-
dealing transaction. It was not that the transaction could never be justified, but on the
evidence it could not be said that the transaction was proper because so little was known
about it; there was a total lack of particularity. It was clear that the resolution as proposed
F   did not meet with the transaction and it would not be right to allow the company to pass a
resolution purporting to validate a transaction which did not comply with the resolution.**

2. If there was to be no sale there should be no resolution for liquidation.

**3. No sec. 127 order should be made because, although there was need for some
transaction, the transaction as proposed was entirely unsatisfactorily spelt out.**

G   **4. The slur which receivership would cast upon the assets of the company and its
business, the ousting of the respondents who were plainly competent directors, and the
expense of any receivership, were all matters which weighed against appointing receivers.**

The following cases were referred to in the judgment:

Boardman & Anor v Phipps [1967] 2 AC 46.
Burton & Deakin Ltd, Re [1977] 1 WLR 390.
H   *Jaber & Ors v Science & Information Technology Ltd & Ors* [1992] BCLC 764.
Keech v Sandford (1726) Sel Cas temp King 61; 25 ER 223.
Posgate and Denby (Agencies) Ltd, Re (1986) 2 BCC 99,352.
Regal (Hastings) Ltd v Gulliver & Ors [1967] 2 AC 134; [1942] 1 All ER 378.

Geoffrey Zelin (instructed by Kingsford Stacey, agents for Geoffrey Tew & Co,
Leicester) for the petitioner.

Kevin Garnett QC and Gregory Banner (instructed by Denham Foxon & Watchorn, Leicester) for the first and second respondents.

JUDGMENT

Harman J: I have before me two ordinary applications. The first is by the petitioner on this petition under sec. 459 of the *Companies Act* 1985 by ordinary application dated 24 February 1993. That seeks an order restraining the respondents from acting upon resolutions which must be intended to be passed at two extraordinary general meetings called for 11 and 12 March 1993, an order for discovery, orders for adjournments of the extraordinary general meetings and finally an order for the appointment of Mr Denney, a partner in Touche Ross in Nottingham, to be the receiver of the respondent company until the petition herein be tried.

I also have before me an application by the company, which is the seventh respondent to the petition although not listed as such on the document, for an order that in the event of an order to wind up the company the following dispositions and payments shall not be avoided pursuant to sec. 127 of the *Insolvency Act* 1986. The dispositions and payments referred to are:

"(1) All dispositions of the company's assets pursuant to an ordinary resolution of the company to sell the entire undertaking of the company to Unicare plc at current market value, such current market value being that set out in the second affidavit of Peter Van Herrewege [who is the first respondent to the petition on 12 March 1993] . . .

(2) All dispositions of the company's money in satisfaction of the company's debtors pursuant to the said resolution."

The petition was presented on Wednesday, 22 July 1992. It was based upon the normal sec. 459 allegations of expectation of participation of management, ousting from management and unfair prejudice to the petitioner, Mr Ingram. Mr Ingram holds 243 shares in the issued capital of the company, which constitutes 23.8 per cent of the issued share capital; thus a very substantial minority but not enough for negative control, that is the ability to prevent the passing of a special resolution.

The petition was met by points of defence which were served pursuant to the normal order of the registrar on 21 August 1992. One would have expected the matter to have proceeded to discovery by now; regrettably that does not seem to have happened.

The application by the petitioner of 24 February was caused by receipt by him of a notice of an extraordinary general meeting of the company, which notice was given on 11 February. That was a notice convening an extraordinary general meeting to be held on Thursday, 11 March at the company's registered office,

"for the purpose of considering and if thought fit passing the following ordinary resolution:

'THAT the company sells its assets at current market value to Unicare plc.' "

That notice of extraordinary general meeting was not accompanied by any form of circular or other letter giving any information to the shareholders of what was proposed.

I should observe that in addition to the petitioner there are six shareholders in this company. The first respondent I have already mentioned, Mr Van Herrewege, owns 405 shares (39.5 per cent). The second respondent, Mr Warner, who is also with Mr Van Herrewege a director of the company, holds 161 shares (15.9 per cent). The third respondent, Mr Bent, holds 161 shares (15.9 per cent). He has taken no part whatever in these proceedings although he has a very substantial equity interest in the company. I should add that the petitioner, the first, second and third respondents are joint and

A several guarantors of the company's liability to Allied Irish Banks, which is in debit to an extent exceeding £1m. There is therefore a very real commercial interest in all these four persons in the successful conduct of the company's business. The remaining shareholders are the fourth respondent holding 30 shares, the fifth respondent holding ten shares and the sixth respondent holding three shares. Thus the interest of Mr Van Herrewege is the largest interest in the company but that is only approximately a 40 per cent interest and there are very substantial interests to be protected other than the

B interests of the first and second respondents who were jointly represented before me. It is of course true that together they have control of the company in the sense of being able in combination to pass an ordinary resolution at any general meeting.

The notice of extraordinary general meeting given on 11 February was followed by a further notice given on 19 February 1993 convening a further extraordinary general meeting to be held on Friday, 12 March, the day following the meeting of 11 March, for

C the purpose of considering a special resolution that the company be wound up voluntarily with provisions for the appointment of a licensed insolvency practitioner and for his costs.

The notice of application by the petitioner is somewhat inadequate in its form. At the opening of his application Mr Zelin for the petitioner put before me the orders which in substance he truly sought, offering cross-undertakings in damages to the respondents,

D that is the individual respondents, paying costs of third parties, and to be answerable for the receiver sought to be appointed. Mr Zelin sought restraint upon the respondents from acting upon either of the resolutions (the ordinary resolution for sale or the special resolution for winding up), the appointment of the receiver and for a substantial number of consequential orders making the receivership operable.

The solicitors for the petitioner, upon receipt of the first notice for an extraordinary

E general meeting, asked for information about the proposed sale. In particular they asked for information about the proposed purchaser. They received the remarkable answer from the solicitors for the first and second respondents, Mr Van Herrewege and Mr Warner, that the affairs of Unicare plc were a matter for that company and the respondents would say nothing about it.

It has now emerged, by a search of the register at Companies House that the first and

F second respondents are the only shareholders in Unicare plc, each holding one share in that company at the moment. It is thus on the evidence a company wholly controlled by them. They are directors of it and, as I understand it, a third director of the company in this case (Mountforest Ltd), Mr Shacklock, who is not an equity shareholder in Mountforest at all, is also a director of Unicare plc. Thus, as I understand it on the evidence, there is a complete identity of the board of the company and the board of

G Unicare plc and there is a complete equity ownership in the hands of the first and second respondents. On these facts one has at once therefore a clear case where the intended transaction is a case of self-dealing. Nothing could be more obvious, and counsel for the respondents never suggested to the contrary, than that the court habitually, whatever the powers given by the articles to make dealings in the nature of self-dealings between directors and themselves, investigates with a very careful eye any case of self-dealing and requires to be satisfied that there is no advantage being taken of the position of self-

H interest where interest and duty may so obviously be in conflict. The authorities run from the old trustee case of *Keech v Sandford* (1726) 25 ER 223, through such cases as *Regal (Hastings) Ltd v Gulliver* [1967] 2 AC 134 down to the fairly recent instance of *Boardman v Phipps* [1967] 2 AC 46, the last two both of them in the House of Lords, where the vital importance of the principle was stressed. The principle is that the court must protect against the temptation which will so obviously exist to favour oneself and therefore the courts have always applied the extremely stringent test to self-dealing transactions.

Notwithstanding that fact, which is obvious to any competent lawyer practising in this field, no information about the details of Unicare plc's constitution, its share capital, its loan facilities or anything else about it were produced in evidence. No details of the proposed sale contract were produced in evidence. No example of the documents intended to be used in the proposed sale transaction were produced in evidence. No account of the consequences to the company, Mountforest Ltd, of the proposed transaction were produced. It is plain to anyone having the slightest knowledge that the transaction may well raise serious questions as to corporation tax upon capital gains arising in the books of Mountforest. It may be that those questions can be dealt with and no substantial liability would exist. It may not. The court and the petitioner are left in total ignorance.

There was an assertion in the evidence, which I was pressed by leading counsel for the respondents I should bear in mind, which said that explanations of the transaction would have been given to the shareholders either before or at the extraordinary general meeting convened for 11 March. In fact, as I say, even at this time no adequate explanations of a great many features of the transaction have yet been given.

The transaction is said to be based upon valuations which have been prepared on the instructions of the first and second respondents as directors, it may be also on the instructions of Mr Shacklock, as the third director, from a firm called Christie & Co. That valuation, as Christie & Co make absolutely plain, is not a valuation upon an open-market basis as defined in the guidelines laid down by the Royal Institution of Chartered Surveyors to persons conducting valuations within the special sphere of valuations of real estate which this valuation primarily was. It is expressly stated not to be an open-market valuation. How therefore such a valuation accords with the resolution proposed and the order under sec. 127 sought from the court to validate a sale on an open-market basis, is not in any way clear to me.

A sale on an open-market basis cannot be validated by a sale proposed to be on a non-open market or forced sale basis. Thus there is at once a major difficulty in the way of the respondents' application for this sale to be allowed to go through and there would have been a major difficulty in the way of acting upon the ordinary resolution which they proposed at the meeting intended to be held on 11 March.

The reason for the transaction, however, is undoubtedly a real and genuine reason in this sense. The company unfortunately had a conviction in 1987 under the *Registered Homes Act* 1984. On 23 November 1987 the company was convicted and fined £300 with £150 costs for breaches of that Act. The breaches appear to have been properly described as technical and not in any sense impinging upon the actual management of nursing homes. The evidence before me is quite clear that at present these nursing homes are well run and are accepted by the local authority and the Leicestershire County Council (as the health authority) as being proper and desirable homes, and there is no suggestion that the conviction in fact carries any slur upon the homes as properly run homes. It is however a conviction upon the record.

However, by the *National Health Service and Community Care Act* 1990 Parliament has passed certain legislation. That Act provided by sec. 42 a whole new series of subsections to be inserted into the *National Assistance Act* 1948. By the new subsec. (1D) to be inserted into sec. 26 of that Act by the 1990 Act it is provided that:

> "No arrangements may be made by virtue of this section with a person who has been convicted of an offence under any provision of the Registered Homes Act 1984 . . ."

A   The result of that provision which is to come into force on 1 April next is that the County Council is prohibited by statute from making new contracts with the company in respect of persons for whom the health authority is providing nursing home care for aged or mentally disordered persons. Why Parliament has thought it necessary to prohibit in that absolute and total form contracts with persons against whom, so far as I can see, there is no actual objection whatever, is a matter which is not for me. That is the effect, happy or unhappy, of the legislation.

B   Thus the company after 1 April next will be unable to take new patients from the Leicestershire County Council, which is the provider of something like 60 per cent of the company's total business. The patients are mostly aged and there is a turnover of something like a third of them a year by reason of the happy issue of death which terminates their suffering and therefore these beds are made vacant for a new contract with the health authority. Such contracts will be impossible and therefore the company

C faces from 1 April an inevitable run-down over the next three years, as I find on a one-third basis, which would at the end of three years leave them with 60 per cent of their beds unoccupied unless they have been able to find private customers who could take up the beds. That is, on the face of it, extremely unlikely. Thus the company faces an immediate need to do something to avoid the impact of the terms of subsec. (1D) as inserted by the 1990 Act. Plainly therefore steps had to be taken and nobody doubts that it was right and necessary to take some steps.

D   However, the difficulty is that the steps which have been taken are not steps which seem to be directed solely to dealing with that objective but seem to be steps taken with a view to cutting out the petitioner, Mr Ingram, from the company. The petitioner is, I do not doubt, a thorn in the flesh of management, because he requires a whole series of matters to be dealt with on this petition which they would much rather not have to investigate. The proposal thus is that this company's undertaking and assets be transferred

E to Unicare plc of which the first and second respondents are directors and in which, it may be but it is unclear, the individual respondents, that is the shareholders in the company other than Mr Ingram, will all be offered shares. Whether they will all be offered shares, whether they will all wish to subscribe for shares, and the terms of subscription which will be offered to them are all matters left entirely unexplained.

    As it seems to me there is therefore a real difficulty here. I have been referred first to

F the decision of *Slade* J in *Re Burton & Deakin Ltd* [1977] 1 WLR 390, and in particular his judgment at p. 397F–G where he reaches conclusions of principle on dealing with what were then applications under sec. 227 of the *Companies Act* 1948, now the equivalent sec. 127 of the *Insolvency Act* 1986, relating to a solvent company, and he holds that:

> "If on (such) an application . . . evidence is placed before the court showing that
G > the directors consider that a particular disposition, falling within their powers under the company's constitution, is necessary or expedient in the interests of the company, and . . . the reasons given for this opinion are reasons which the court considers that an intelligent and honest man could reasonably hold, it will in the exercise of its discretion normally sanction the disposition, notwithstanding the opposition of a contributory . . ."

H   I entirely follow and agree with *Slade* J. But in my judgment that principle does not carry one anywhere in this case because he refers specifically to a particular disposition. In this case the particular disposition must be the disposition to Unicare plc. *Slade* J refers to reasons supporting that disposition which "an intelligent and honest man could reasonably hold". Here I have no such evidence as would show that an ordinary, reasonable and honest man could reasonably conclude that this self-dealing transaction was the correct and proper transaction because so little is known about the proposed transaction. I do

not say that the transaction could never be properly justified. I say that upon the
evidence before me there is no proper justification advanced by reason of a total lack of
particularity and due to a regrettable and undesirable attitude on the part of the
respondents' solicitors in correspondence in refusing to give information which plainly
was needed.

I can refer to *Slade* J's observation at p. 397A where he refers to the principle that:

> "the court will not generally, save in the case of proven bad faith or other
> exceptional circumstances, interfere with the exercise of the discretion conferred
> on the directors by a company's articles of association at the instance of a
> shareholder."

In my judgment the words "other exceptional circumstances" plainly apply to cases of
self-dealing, unexplained and unjustified by detailed evidence, by directors of the
company with themselves. Such a transaction is plainly an exceptional, that is an
unusual, circumstance and one which the law requires it to be justified in detail. Thus
the decision in *Re Burton & Deakin Ltd* gives no useful guidance in this case.

I was referred further to the decision of *Hoffmann* J in *Re Posgate and Denby
(Agencies) Ltd* (1986) 2 BCC 99,352 and in particular to his observations at p. 99,359
where he refers to the question whether it would be just and convenient to grant an
injunction against directors exercising a power of sale in favour of a company in which
they undoubtedly had an interest so that it was in some degree a self-dealing case. He
holds that there was a clear power under sec. 461 of the *Companies Act* 1985 to enable
the court to make proper monetary recompense to a petitioner if it turned out that the
self-dealing sale by the directors was at an undervalue.

In this case a curious extra difficulty is interposed by the resolution for the winding up
of the company which, as it seems to me, prevents the normal order which would be
made under sec. 461 for the purchase of the petitioner's shares by one or more of the
respondent shareholders. But I was pressed, and I believe correctly, with the view that
sec. 461 is so wide that one could none the less discover a means of providing proper
monetary compensation if there were a sale at an undervalue.

None the less the facts in *Re Posgate and Denby (Agencies) Ltd* were a long way from
this in that it was demonstrated in evidence that the directors had done their best to sell
the assets of the company, which was in that case a Lloyd's managing agency, in the
open market, so far as such a thing exists within Lloyd's, and they had obtained careful
advice and revealed to the members all the details of the intended sale before it went
ahead. On the facts that is a very long way from this case. One of the major difficulties in
this case is the total lack of knowledge of what is in fact proposed here. Thus, as it seems
to me, there is a major difference on the basic underlying facts between this case and *Re
Posgate and Denby (Agencies) Ltd* and, although I entirely follow and accept *Hoffmann*
J's observations in that case, they do not apply in this case in that the transactions are
not properly explained.

It was a case which had this further similarity with the present in that the need to sell
the undertaking and assets derived from outside circumstances, not the fault of the
directors in that case, just as in this case the need to sell the undertaking and assets of the
company derives from outside circumstances not in any moral sense the fault of the
directors (although I suppose in a sense the conviction can be said to have been the fault
of the directors), merely an unhappy consequence of an event back in 1987 which was in
itself only a technical default. Thus there are similarities in that sense between this case
and *Re Posgate and Denby (Agencies) Ltd* but there are such gross dissimilarities in the
amount of information supplied and in the attempts made to make sure that the directors
demonstrate that a proper sale price was reached that I cannot find the decision,
although I find the principles helpful, of any guidance in this case.

I then have to consider the proposals by the petitioner. He seeks injunctions restraining any action upon the ordinary resolution proposed to be passed at the meeting now standing adjourned. In my judgment on the facts of this case it is quite clear that the resolution as proposed does not in any way meet with the transaction as presently outlined. The resolution refers to a sale of the assets at current market value. The actual sale proposed is, as I understand it, of the undertaking, that is of the whole of the business including such goodwill as is attached to the business, as opposed to goodwill attached to the name of the company, and it refers to a sale at current market value when there is no suggestion that the sale proposed is to be at current market value. It seems to me that in those circumstances it cannot be right to allow the company to pass a resolution which will have the effect of purporting to validate a transaction which does not in fact comply with the resolution. It is far better to restrain any action upon that resolution.

The resolution for liquidation seems to me to give rise to major difficulties in the way of this case and it seems to me that if there is to be no sale there plainly should be no resolution for liquidation. In my view it is not desirable that this company be faced with liquidation at this time. I have no idea, because there is no proper evidence before me, of the many consequences that can be foreseen as to the results of placing the company in liquidation and it seems to me that the petitioner would be likely to be prejudiced thereby. I therefore propose to restrain the company from acting upon any such resolution.

I have considered the sec. 127 application for an order validating a sale. In my judgment no such order should be made because the transaction, the actual detailed transaction as proposed, is entirely unsatisfactorily spelt out. Although there is need for some transaction there is no evidence that only this transaction can be done and there were suggestions in court this morning that a different transaction might be capable of structure although that was in no way adequately thought out.

I am left with the final question, which is whether the petitioner's application for the appointment of a receiver should be justified. In connection with that I would refer to the decision of *Ferris* J in *Jaber & Ors v Science & Information Technology Ltd & Ors* [1992] BCLC 764 and in particular his observations at p. 789e–f that he had been impressed at one point with the apparent fairness of appointing a receiver. He came to the conclusion in that case that it would be wrong to appoint a receiver upon the ground that receivership carries a slur and a damage in the market place to anybody seeking to sell assets, and that he had concluded that a receivership would be expensive. *Ferris* J therefore resolved that there would be no receivership.

In the present case Mr Banner for the respondents adds that the directors here in charge have legitimate expectations of running the business and it is not suggested by anybody that they have not run the business successfully and, upon the evidence before me, highly profitably on a rapidly increasing graph of profits. Indeed the demonstration of their competence and on the rapidly increasing graph of profits go, in my view, to affect the valuation evidence put forward which I have considered on the sec. 127 application. But it is also, in my view, relevant to the suggestion of the appointment of a receiver.

Mr Zelin has pressed me with one wholly unexplained item in the management accounts of an apparent payment from the company to Unicare plc. What justification there could be for that payment is entirely unclear; nobody has gone into it. It is plainly uncomfortable to have a payment from the company to Unicare plc which is in the exclusive control of two persons who are the controlling shareholders in and the directors of this company owing in their capacity as directors fiduciary obligations to all

shareholders. None the less it is a comparatively small sum, £5,600 I think or of that
order, and it is, as the file presently appears, an isolated payment.

In my view the undoubted slur which receivership, wrongly in this case, but in fact
would cast upon the assets of the company and its business, the ousting of the respondents
who have conducted this business extremely well so far as practical trading is concerned,
and the expense of the receivership are all matters which ought to weigh with me.

I conclude that I ought not to appoint receivers in this case but leave the company in
the hands of its directors who plainly are competent and, I hope, will now be advised to
produce a sensible scheme for dealing with the undoubted problem they have which will
enable these difficulties to be got over. I am, as I say, wholly unsatisfied that the present
proposed scheme is a proper and adequate one and I shall injunct that. I am therefore
wholly unsatisfied that they should have sec. 127 relief for this particular scheme. I do
not say that they may not be able to mount a perfectly sensible scheme with proper
circulated papers which justify it and I do not think it right to appoint receivers over the
assets of the company.

I shall therefore make the orders I have indicated, refusing the sec. 127 application,
granting the two injunctions sought and refusing the appointment of a receiver.

(*Order accordingly*)

A   # Re Homes Assured Corporation plc.

Chancery Division (Companies Court).
Lindsay J.
Judgment delivered 28 April 1993.

B
Disqualifying unfit directors of insolvent companies — Evidence in support of disqualification application was report by deputy official receiver — Whether deputy's report was "written report" within meaning of rules — Insolvent Companies (Disqualification of Unfit Directors) Proceedings Rules 1987 (SI 1987/2023), r. 3(2).

A "written report" in r. 3(2) of the Insolvent Companies (Disqualification of Unfit Directors) Proceedings Rules 1987 (SI 1987/2023), constituting the applicant official receiver's evidence in director disqualification proceedings, could be made by the official
C   **receiver's deputy.**

The following case was referred to in the judgment:

Gregg v Richards [1926] Ch 521.

David Richards QC and Philip Gillyon (instructed by the Treasury Solicitor) for the official receiver.

D   Franklin Evans (instructed by McBride Wilson) for the director.

JUDGMENT

Lindsay J: This matter first came before me on 18 and 19 March 1993. At that stage a good number of possible interlocutory directions and matters were in issue and were left over for further argument which involved not only the parties now before me but other parties as well. I had to break off from hearing the matter because from and after 22
E   March I was to be motions judge.

The matter was restored to me on 2 April by which time the parties had agreed all but one of the issues. On that day I therefore made a speaking order containing agreed directions and the formal drawing up of that order is either complete or in hand. The one remaining issue was principally a matter of construction but one material point of fact, as I shall mention, remained for the time being unknown. On 2 April I indicated
F   that if the fact could be confirmed to me informally, having been agreed as verified between Mr Richards QC, Mr Gillyon, for the official receiver, and Mr Evans for Mr Dobson, then I would give judgment on the one remaining issue without any further hearing. Only if, contrary to expectations, the fact could not be agreed was the matter to be restored for further argument. The fact has now been verified and Mr Dobson's solicitors treat the fact as sufficiently proved. I am thus now in a position to give
G   judgment and I now turn to the judgment proper.

On 29 August 1989 three related companies went into voluntary liquidation. They were Homes Assured Corporation plc, Homes Assured Essex Ltd and Homes Assured Midlands Ltd. On 25 October 1989 each of them was put into compulsory liquidation and the official receiver became, as he remains, the liquidator in each of those windings up. On 28 August 1991, one day short of the prescribed maximum of two years, originating applications were issued under the *Company Directors Disqualification Act*
H   1986 ("the Disqualification Act") and the *Insolvent Companies (Disqualification of Unfit Directors) Proceedings Rules* 1987 (SI 1987/2023) ("the Disqualification Rules").

On or about 2 September 1991 one such originating application was served on Mr Anthony Dobson, a one time director of Homes Assured Corporation plc ("PLC"), for whom Mr Evans, as I mentioned, appears. The applicant in that originating application is the official receiver who appears before me by Mr Richards QC and Mr Gillyon. By it

he seeks against Mr Dobson that a disqualification order should be made under sec. 6 of
the Disqualification Act on the ground that Mr Dobson had been a director of an
insolvent company and that he was guilty of conduct as a director of such company such
as to make him unfit to be concerned in the management of a company.

Under sec. 6 the minimum period of disqualification is two years and the maximum
15 years. The consequences of the imposition of a disqualification order are spelled out
in sec. 1 of the Disqualification Act. They amount to a very substantial impairment of a
man's potential for commercial and business activity during the currency of the order.

When the originating application was served, copies of the applicant's (that is to say
the official receiver's evidence) were served on Mr Dobson as is required under r. 3(1)
of the Disqualification Rules. The evidence consisted not of one or more affidavits but
of a body of papers divisible into two main kinds. Firstly, there was a spiral bound
volume of some 147 pages in length dated 28 August 1991 and entitled on its cover
"Official Receiver's Report". I shall call that "the main body". Secondly, served with
the main body and referred to in it, were a number of exhibits (which I shall together call
"the exhibits") varying in size, the most important of which, for present purposes, is
that called "ESB4", which itself consists of 37 separate statements from individuals,
although because some individuals have more than one of their statements within ESB4
it represents evidence from fewer than 37 people. ESB4 amounts to some 440 pages of
rather dense typescript. References to the exhibits are made in the main body very much
in the same style as ordinary affidavits make reference to their exhibits.

The official receiver, as the applicant in the disqualification proceedings, will, at the
hearing of the application, claim that the main body and the exhibits together comprise
"a written report" for the purposes of r. 3(2) of the Disqualification Rules. He will
claim, in turn, that the main body and the exhibits are thus to be treated as if they had
been verified by affidavit and that they are to be prima facie evidence of any matter
contained therein.

Rule 3(2) and (3) are as follows:

"(2) The evidence shall be by one or more affidavits, except where the applicant
is the official receiver, in which case it may be in the form of a written report (with
or without affidavits by other persons) which shall be treated as if it had been
verified by affidavit by him and shall be prima facie evidence of any matter
contained in it.

(3) There shall in the affidavit or affidavits or (as the case may be) the official
receiver's report be included a statement of the matters by reference to which the
respondent is alleged to be unfit to be concerned in the management of a
company."

I am not now concerned with those claims of the official receiver, nor with the
construction of the Disqualification Rules generally, nor with related questions such as
whether it would have been intra vires the rule-making provisions to arrive at any of the
consequences which the official receiver will contend for. In view of arrangements made
between the parties I am now left with only one principal and one subsidiary question
and I must emphasise that it is to those questions only that this judgment is addressed.
That sole principal question is this: can a report be a "written report" for the purposes
of r. 3 of the Disqualification Rules if it is made not by the applicant official receiver but
by a deputy official receiver? This question, the principal question, is inescapable here
because the main body begins:

"I, Elliott Simon Burns, deputy official receiver of 21 Bloomsbury Street, London,
WC1 hereby report to the court as follows . . ."

A   Mr Burns goes on in para. 1 as follows:

> "I am a deputy official receiver attached to the High Court of Justice. On 25 October 1989 Leslie Thomas Cramp was appointed by the court to be the official receiver of Homes Assured Corporation plc . . . and certain of its subsidiaries . . . for all purposes under the *Insolvency Act* 1986."

B   The main body does not include any references showing that Mr Burns had been authorised by Mr Cramp to make such a written report on Mr Cramp's behalf. It is plain from the text of the main body that it is Mr Burns himself who has investigated the matters there deposed to. Speaking of Mr Cramp as liquidator of the companies in the Homes Assured group, Mr Burns says, "I have the conduct of the liquidations on his behalf", and earlier he writes as follows:

> "The information contained in this report has come to my knowledge in the course of my supervision of the investigation of the company's affairs, the day-to-day enquiries being conducted by members of the official receiver's staff."

C

The principal question is to be answered by reference chiefly to a number of statutory provisions and to some subordinate legislation.

The office of official receiver is not at large but is to be spoken of in relation to some particular court or some particular bankruptcy or winding up. Thus, a person who is authorised by sec. 399 of the *Insolvency Act* 1986 to act as the official receiver in relation

D   to, say, PLC, is in relation to that liquidation to be described as "*the* official receiver": sec. 399 of the *Insolvency Act* 1986.

As for deputies, sec. 401 of that Act, so far as material, reads as follows:

> "*Deputy official receivers and staff*
>
> (1) The Secretary of State may, if he thinks it expedient to do so in order to facilitate the disposal of the business of the official receiver attached to any court, appoint an officer of his department to act as deputy to that official receiver.

E

> (2) Subject to any directions given by the Secretary of State under section 399 or 400, a person appointed to act as deputy to an official receiver has, on such conditions and for such period as may be specified in the terms of his appointment, the same status and functions as the official receiver to whom he is appointed deputy.

F

> Accordingly, references in this Act (except section 399(1) to (5)) to an official receiver include a person appointed to act as his deputy."

I have not understood it to be challenged that Mr Cramp is, in relation to PLC's compulsory liquidation, *the* official receiver under sec. 399.

The material points of fact, which remained still unknown when I rose on 2 April 1993, were the directions, if any, conditions and period specified in any terms of the appointment of Mr Burns as Mr Cramp's deputy. It has now been confirmed to me this

G   morning, without the matter needing to be restored for hearing and is accepted by Mr Dobson's advisers, that on 23 December 1986 Mr Carney, describing himself as "an authorised officer of the Department of Trade and Industry", signed a document which begins, under the heading of the "*Insolvency Act* 1986 and the Disqualification Act", as follows:

> "(1) The Secretary of State hereby under sec. 401 of the *Insolvency Act* 1986

H   appoints Elliot Simon Burns as a deputy official receiver to the official receiver attached under sec. 399(3) of that Act to the High Court.

> (2) The said Deputy Official Receiver shall have all the status and functions of the Official Receiver to whom he is Deputy . . ."

There then follows an exception I need not read. Paragraph 5 showed the appointment to take effect on 29 December 1986 and that it was to remain in force until revoked.

Mr Carney was, I understand (and the contrary has not been urged), as at 23 December 1986 authorised to sign such a document so as to make it an appointment by the Secretary of State within sec. 401(1). I am thus able to proceed on the basis that Mr Burns was duly appointed Mr Cramp's deputy. On that basis, in relation to the compulsory winding up of PLC, references in the *Insolvency Act* 1986 to an official receiver are to include Mr Burns as Mr Cramp's deputy and he, Mr Burns, has generally, in relation to that winding up the same status and functions as the official receiver — sec. 401(2) and sec. 399(1).

Turning to the Disqualification Act, I shall first read sec. 7(1):

"*Applications to court under section 6; reporting provisions*

(1) If it appears to the Secretary of State that it is expedient in the public interest that a disqualification order under section 6 should be made against any person, an application for the making of such an order against that person may be made—

    (a)   by the Secretary of State, or

    (b)   if the Secretary of State so directs in the case of a person who is or has been a director of a company which is being wound up by the court in England and Wales, by the official receiver."

I shall return to sec. 7(1) later. Going on to sec. 21(1) it reads as follows:

"*Interaction with Insolvency Act*

(1) References in this Act to the official receiver, in relation to the winding up of a company or the bankruptcy of an individual, are to any person who, by virtue of section 399 of the Insolvency Act, is authorised to act as the official receiver in relation to that winding up or bankruptcy; and, in accordance with section 401(2) of that Act, references in this Act to an official receiver includes a person appointed as his deputy."

Thus references in the Disqualification Act itself to the official receiver in relation to the compulsory liquidation of PLC include Mr Burns as Mr Cramp's deputy.

The Disqualification Act at sec. 21(2) confers on the Lord Chancellor with the concurrence of the Secretary of State a rule-making power and the Disqualification Rules thus came to be made on 25 November 1987. In the Disqualification Rules the terms "official receiver" or "the official receiver" are not defined, nor is the term "deputy official receiver". Mr Richards, for the Treasury Solicitor, says that there is no need for definition of those terms. He refers me to sec. 11 of the *Interpretation Act* 1978 which is as follows:

"*Construction of subordinate legislation*

Where an Act confers power to make subordinate legislation, expressions used in that legislation have, unless the contrary intention appears, the meaning which they bear in the Act."

Mr Richards thus argues that the Disqualification Act, having conferred power to make subordinate legislation, namely the Disqualification Rules, the expressions used in the Disqualification Rules are "unless the contrary intention appears" to have the same respective meanings that they have in the Disqualification Act. In relation to the present case, as "the official receiver" in the Act includes Mr Burns so must it also in the rules, he says, "unless the contrary intention appears".

I do not think Mr Evans for Mr Dobson argues with that, but he says that a contrary intention does here appear. He relies for that appearance of the contrary intention on three main points. First, he relies on r. 10 of the Disqualification Rules which is in the following terms:

A
"*Right of audience*

Official receivers and deputy official receivers have right of audience in any proceedings to which these Rules apply, whether the application is made by the Secretary of State or by the official receiver at his direction, and whether made in the High Court or a county court."

B
If the term "official receiver", without more, was in the rules intended to include a deputy, why, asks Mr Evans, should r. 10 provide expressly for both? It can only be, he says, because "official receiver" is not intended in the rules to comprehend a deputy.

Secondly, if, without more, any term defined in the Disqualification Act is to have in the Disqualification Rules the meaning ascribed to it in the Act why, asks Mr Evans, is the term "the Companies Act" defined in r. 1(2)(a) despite its having been defined in sec. 22(7) of the Disqualification Act? It can only be, says Mr Evans, because it is not intended that the meanings given in the Act should be taken to be the meanings contemplated in the rules.

C

Thirdly, Mr Evans draws attention to r. 7.9 of the *Insolvency Rules* 1986 which reads as follows:

"*Use of reports*
(1) A report may be filed in court instead of an affidavit—

D
    (a) in any case, by the official receiver (whether or not he is acting in any capacity mentioned in sub-paragraph (b)), or a deputy official receiver.

. . .

(2) In any case where a report is filed instead of an affidavit, the report shall be treated for the purposes of Rule 7.8(1) and any hearing before the court as if it were an affidavit.

E
(3) Any report filed by the official receiver in accordance with the Act or the Rules is prima facie evidence of any matter contained in it."

Mr Evans says that that shows that if it is intended to confer the privilege of putting evidence before the court by way of report rather than affidavit upon deputies, the rule-making body knows perfectly well how to do it and does it clearly and expressly, as r. 7.9(1)(a) shows. Further, he says that in the context of r. 7.9(1)(a) having so expressly

F
provided, the references to the official receiver in r. 7.9(3) omitting a deputy, must be taken to exclude a deputy. He comments (assuming his immediately preceding submission to be correct) that it would be odd if deputies could not report with the same consequences as an official receiver's report under the Insolvency Rules but could under the Disqualification Rules.

These three points, says Mr Evans, amount to sufficient for "the contrary intention"
G
to have appeared for the purposes of excluding from the Disqualification Rules the meaning of "official receiver" as given in the Disqualification Act. Hence, he says, it is only the official receiver who can use a written report within the meaning of r. 3(2) of the Disqualification Rules and, in turn, he argues that Mr Burns' document, whatever else it may be called, is not "a written report" and cannot have conferred on it the privileges attaching to a true report of being treated as prima facie evidence of any matter contained in it.

H
If that principal argument fails, Mr Evans raises a subsidiary point, namely that it is only where the applicant is the deputy that the deputy's report is to be treated as a written report. It will be remembered that here the applicant is not a deputy but is the official receiver.

I am unconvinced by these arguments. The least impressive is that based on the Insolvency Rules. There are obvious dangers in seeking to construe one body of

subordinate legislation, the Disqualification Rules, by referring to another and in any   A
event the legislature, or rule-making body, might well have thought it appropriate to
make different provisions as to deputies in the two quite separate situations.

As for the argument based on the express mention in r. 10 of the Disqualification
Rules of "deputy official receiver" and also the express definition of "the Companies
Act", it depends on the principle *expressio unius est exclusio alterius*. Lord *Hanworth*
in *Gregg v Richards* [1926] Ch 521 said at p. 527:   B

"It has been said by a succession of judges that this maxim, 'Expressio unius
exclusio alterius,' is one which is to be cautiously applied."

At p. 528 he cites *Lopes* LJ as having observed in an earlier case that:

"It is often a valuable servant, but a dangerous master to follow in the construction
of statutes or documents."

I thus approach the argument with caution.   C

The Disqualification Rules use, undefined, the terms "company", "director" and
"shadow director" — see r. 5(4) — each being a term defined in the Disqualification Act
— see sec. 22(2) for "company", sec. 22(4) for "director" and sec. 22(5) for "shadow
director". Whatever one might think of the need for a definition of "company" or
"director", says Mr Richards, the term "shadow director" is one to which no commonly
accepted meaning is clearly ascribed; it is a term which requires a definition. If Mr Evans   D
were right that a contrary intention had been demonstrated sufficient to displace the
otherwise automatic use in the Disqualification Rules of the definitions in the
Disqualification Act, this important term would, says Mr Richards, be left with no clear
meaning, and that, Mr Richards rightly says, is to be avoided.

I am far from sure that Mr Richards' argument thus far goes far enough. It shows only
that the meanings given by the Disqualification Act cannot have been intended to have
been excluded generally as a body from use in the Disqualification Rules. The answer to   E
it would be that the meanings in the Act are to apply in the rules, save to the extent, in
relation to any particular meaning, that a contrary intention was shown as to that
particular meaning. As there is no indication in the Disqualification Rules that the
Disqualification Act's meaning for "shadow director", for example, should not apply,
the Act's meaning should apply to that particular term. But that does not, of itself, assist
with the meaning of "official receiver".   F

However, Mr Richards then introduces r. 1(3) of the Disqualification Rules which
reads as follows:

"These Rules apply with respect to an application for a disqualification order
against any person ('the respondent'), where made—

(a) by the Secretary of State or the official receiver under section 7(1) of the
Company Directors Disqualification Act (on the grounds of the person's   G
unfitness to be concerned in the management of a company), or . . ."

It is beyond question that reference in sec. 7(1)(b) of the Disqualification Act to the
official receiver being able to make an application includes his deputy — sec. 21(1)
above. Unless r. 1(3)(a)'s reference to applications by the official receiver under
sec. 7(1) means also applications by deputies, the applications by deputies provided for
by sec. 7(1) would be left without any rules applying to them. They can only be brought   H
within the ambit of the Disqualification Rules by reading "the official receiver" in
r. 1(3)(a) as including deputies. I cannot think it intended that the rule-maker, having
seen that Parliament had carefully conferred an ability to apply on both official receivers
and their deputies, should then make rules that guided and regulated applications by
official receivers but left applications by their deputies entirely unguided and unregulated.
That would be truly absurd.

A
    In other words, the Disqualification Rules, having shown that there is no intention in them such as to exclude generally as a body the meanings given to terms by the Act, also show, in relation to the particular term "official receiver", that there is no total exclusion from the Disqualification Rules of the meaning, which is inclusive of deputies, given to the term by the Act. But, conversely, r. 10 of the Disqualification Rules seems to show that in such rules there is no total inclusion in the Disqualification Rules of deputies within the term "official receiver". If, then, there is neither a total exclusion from, nor

B
inclusion in, the Disqualification Rules of deputies as within the term "official receiver", the question becomes whether, in any particular use of the term, the particular sense is such that a contrary intention sufficient to exclude deputies appears. I put the question this way round as the way the Interpretation Act is framed the onus is on he who seeks to displace the meaning given by the principal Act not on he who would wish to incorporate it.

C
    Approaching the particular use of the term "official receiver" in r. 3(2), I see nothing in the sense of the subrules sufficient to exclude deputies. It is not possible, in my judgment, to discern any language in it such as to require that deputies who shall have been specifically enabled by the legislature to make disqualification applications and who have the same status and functions as official receivers should nonetheless be unable to make reports which are "written reports" for the purposes of r. 3(2). In my view Mr Evans fails to discharge the onus of showing the contrary intention which is

D
required of him.
    Rule 10 and the specific reference to "the Companies Act" in r. 1(2)(a) are shown, in the context of the Disqualification Rules as a whole, to be at worst inconsistencies or infelicities and not as having any force sufficient to disturb the ordinary importation of terms from the Disqualification Act which the Interpretation Act requires.
    I turn, then, to Mr Evans' subsidiary point. There is nothing in r. 3(2) that requires

E
the written report to be made by the official receiver. Rather it is that where the applicant is the official receiver, which therefore includes the case where the applicant is his deputy, there may be "a" (not "his") written report. Where there is a written report then a deeming provision operates in that it is to be treated "as if it had been verified by affidavit by him", the word "him" referring back to the official receiver (and thus again including his deputy). Thus, expanded as the Interpretation Act requires it to be, r. 3(2)

F
provides that where the applicant is the official receiver or his deputy, there may be a written report which shall be treated as if verified by the official receiver or his deputy. There is nothing in that expansion which rules out the case before me where the application was made by Mr Cramp but the written report was made by his deputy, Mr Burns. It would have been easy enough to provide that only the applicant could be the maker of the written report but I do not find that expressed and I see no necessity to imply it.

G
    Accordingly, in my judgment, Mr Evans' subsidiary point also fails. I thus find in favour of the Treasury Solicitor on the only points before me and, subject to discussion with counsel, the convenient course would seem to be, if a formal recording of my conclusions is desirable, for me to invite Mr Gillyon, as Mr Richards' junior, to prepare and circulate a minute for agreement. The matter can be restored to me should difficulties be encountered in agreeing its terms. As both the parties and I are conscious of other questions in and around r. 3 that have not been argued, and some, at least, of

H
which may be wished to be argued elsewhere by other parties concerned in the Homes Assured group, care will need to be taken to ensure that the minutes settle only the limited points that I have addressed.

(*Order accordingly*)

Re CCG International Enterprises Ltd.

Chancery Division (Companies Court).
Lindsay J.
Judgment delivered 30 April 1993.

Whether proceeds of insurance claim were subject to fixed charge in debenture.

This was an application by a contributory and former director (and perhaps creditor) of CCG International Enterprises Ltd ("the company"), which was in voluntary liquidation, to determine the proper destination of some insurance moneys received by the liquidator in respect of losses caused by a fire which occurred shortly before the voluntary liquidation began.

The applicant, who had guaranteed the company's indebtedness to the bank, argued that the proceeds were subject to a fixed charge in favour of the bank contained in a debenture given by the company to the bank. Under the debenture's principal charging clause, the company charged: "By way of assignment, by way of first fixed charge, all policies of assurance . . . ." A subsequent clause provided that: ". . . all moneys received under any such insurance [against loss or damage by fire] . . . shall, at the option of the bank, be applied either in making good the loss or damage in respect of which such moneys shall have been paid or in or towards the moneys hereby secured unless the bank shall otherwise consent in writing and in the meantime shall be paid into such account of the company with the bank as the bank may direct . . ." The liquidator argued that the insurance moneys were available to meet liquidation expenses and preferential creditors, being subject only to a floating charge in the debenture.

Held, directing payment to the bank:

1. The charge in the debenture on "policies of assurance" did not go beyond policies which either had or included death as the or as part of the triggering event and hence no part of the insurance moneys in respect of the fire was subject to that fixed charge.

2. The subsequent clause created a fixed charge, because the insurance moneys were not to be at the free disposal of the company. The possibility of the bank electing for reinstatement rather than repayment of the security did not preclude the charge from being a fixed one.

The following cases were referred to in the judgment:

Atlantic Computer Systems plc, Re [1990] BCC 859; [1992] Ch 505.
Atlantic Medical Ltd, Re [1992] BCC 653.
Bond Worth Ltd, Re [1980] Ch 228.
Brightlife Ltd, Re (1986) 2 BCC 99,359; [1987] Ch 200.
Cotton v Heyl [1930] 1 Ch 510.
Governments Stock & Other Securities Investment Co Ltd v Manila Railway Co Ltd & Ors [1897] AC 81.
Illingworth v Houldsworth & Anor [1904] AC 355.
Palmer v Carey [1926] AC 703.
Sinnott v Bowden [1912] 2 Ch 414.
Swiss Bank Corporation v Lloyds Bank Ltd & Ors [1982] AC 584.

Richard Ritchie (instructed by Ian Guyster & Co) for the applicant.

Philip Jones (instructed by Judge Sykes & Harrison) for the liquidator.

JUDGMENT

Lindsay J: I have before me an application by Harvey Edwin Mark Conroy, a contributory, former director and perhaps creditor of CCG International Enterprises Ltd ("the company"), which is in voluntary liquidation. Mr Conroy appears by

A   Mr Ritchie. The only respondent to the application is Mr Melvin Langley, the liquidator of the company in that winding up, who appears by Mr Philip Jones.

The application raises questions as to the proper destination of some insurance moneys received by the liquidator in respect of losses caused by a fire which occurred shortly before the voluntary liquidation began. However, before I go to the matters raised by the application it is convenient to set out the facts, which are not disputed.

B   On 3 July 1986 the company gave a debenture to Hill Samuel & Co Ltd ("the bank") in the bank's standard printed form. I shall come back later to some of its terms in more detail but the debenture was later supplemented, so far as concerned the bank, by a guarantee given to the bank by the applicant whereby Mr Conroy personally guaranteed to the bank payment of the whole of any sums at any time owing to the bank from the company. Mr Conroy and his wife, later still, charged their home to the bank with payment of Mr Conroy's indebtedness to the bank, including his indebtedness as surety.

C   In this way, as is common ground before me, Mr Conroy has come to have a keen interest in seeing that the company's debt to the bank is minimised and thus that every penny that might be paid by the liquidator to the bank should be so paid.

The bank itself, whilst knowing of this hearing, has not been required, nor has chosen, to take part in these proceedings. Presumably it is little concerned whether it recovers its indebtedness from the liquidator or from Mr Conroy or from Mr and Mrs Conroy so

D   long as it does recover. In the sense that Mr Conroy is concerned to maximise payments to the bank his interests and those of the bank in relation to the issues before me are identical and I have not thought it necessary to require the bank to be joined as a respondent.

I have not seen any evidence on the point but it is common ground that the particulars of the debenture were duly registered at the companies registry and that no points are available to the liquidator based on inadequate registration.

E   The company carried on business as installers and distributors of kitchen furniture from premises at Unit E, Eastway Commercial Centre, London E9. In 1984 or so, at the latest, it effected with insurers one or more wide ranging non-life policies which included cover against the risk of fire. From time to time thereafter the policy or policies were duly renewed. The liquidator has not been able to establish with certainty whether the relevant policies are one or more, nor its or their precise terms. It is common ground,

F   however, that whether it is one or more and what the precise terms were is unimportant for present purposes. What is important is that the policy or policies entitled recovery to be made in respect of the losses occasioned by the fire that occurred in June 1990 at the premises, Unit E. Shortly after the fire, on 13 June 1990, the company went into voluntary liquidation and Mr Langley became (as he remains) the liquidator. He instructed claims assessors in connection with the cover against fire risks and by 24

G   January 1991 they had received £108,000 in full and final settlement with the insurers of the claims under the policy or policies. Of that £108,000, £40,000 was payable and paid to the company's landlords at Unit E, who include Mr Conroy. No question is raised as to the propriety of that payment.

Of the remaining £68,000, £47,000 was attributable to "stock/fixtures and fittings" and £21,000 to "contractors all risks". It has not been argued that any of the £68,000 is payable to the landlords. Out of that £68,000 payable in the first instance to the liquidator

H   was taken the claims assessors' charges of £5,865, which left a balance of £62,135 which was received by the liquidator from the claims assessors in February 1991. No argument that it was wrong that the whole of the £5,865 should have been so deducted has yet been raised.

It is Mr Conroy's case that the £62,135 should have been paid without further deduction by the liquidator to the bank. It is the liquidator's case that the £62,135 is

available to meet proper liquidation expenses and preferential creditors before any part   A
is to be paid to the bank. I am told there are substantial preferential creditors. Indeed,
whilst I have no figures, the tone of the argument has been that the expenses and
preferential creditors are likely to be such that if the liquidator succeeds in his arguments
then none, or very little, of the £62,135 would find its way to the bank.

Just as Mr Conroy adequately represents the bank's interests, so also the liquidator
adequately represents the interests of preferential and general creditors and I have not
seen it necessary to require any representative creditor of any particular class or classes   B
to be joined.

I now turn to the terms of the debenture given to the bank on 3 July 1986. It is in "all
moneys" form. By cl. 2 the company, as beneficial owner, charged a series of different
descriptions of properties to the bank. Clause 2A(a) is a charge by way of first fixed
charge on all existing freehold and leasehold property of the company and on fixed plant
and machinery. Subclause (b) is a first fixed charge on all future freehold and leasehold   C
property of the company. Subclause (c) is a first fixed equitable charge on all the
company's present and future equitable interest in land or property or in the proceeds of
sale thereof, as there more fully set out. Subclause (d) is a first fixed charge on goodwill
and uncalled capital.

Clause 2A(e) is one to which particular reference was made and it reads as follows:

"(e) By way of assignment, by way of first fixed charge, all policies of assurance   D
and all stocks, shares and other securities now and from time to time hereafter of
the company and (so far as the law allows) the benefit of all licences."

At subcl. (f) there is a first fixed charge on book debts other than those which the bank
might exempt from a first fixed charge. At subcl. (g) there is a floating charge on other
book debts and, lastly, at (h):

"(h) By way of first floating charge all other, the undertaking and assets of the   E
company, whatsoever and wheresoever both present and future."

There are definitions of "the charged property", of "the equitable property" and of
"the charged assets". The definition which contains the largest body of charged assets is,
unsurprisingly, "the charged assets" and it is specifically required in cl. 2B that the
company shall have no power without the bank's written consent to deal with any part of
"the charged assets", except those assets charged by way of floating charge only, by way
of sale in the ordinary course of its business and for the purpose of carrying on the same,   F
save to the extent that there should be an express provision otherwise. "The charged
assets" consist of *all* property charged by the debenture and hence include property
thereby charged wherever the charging provision might appear in the debenture. There
is no restriction in the meaning of "the charged assets" to assets charged by what is
plainly the principal charging clause, cl. 2. Clause 4 of the debenture begins, "The
company hereby covenants with the bank". So far as material, subcl. (e), which relates
to insurance, reads as follows: G

"To insure and keep insured all the charged assets for the time being and from
time to time subject to this debenture against loss or damage by fire . . . in the full
reinstatement value thereof for the time being . . . all moneys received under any
such insurance and under any other insurance effected or maintained by the
company shall, at the option of the bank, be applied either in making good the
loss or damage in respect of which such moneys shall have been paid or in or
towards the moneys hereby secured unless the bank shall otherwise consent in   H
writing and in the meantime shall be paid into such account of the company with
the bank as the bank may direct. The name and address of the insurer shall be
noted on all policies of such insurance. The name and address of the bank shall be
noted on all policies of such insurance."

There is no evidence of the bank's name having been so noted.

A Subclause (f) of cl. 4 deals with other kinds of insurance, namely:

"insurance against risks and of liabilities to employees or third parties and contingencies arising under any statute or other legislation or of common law or in any other manner whatsoever."

Subclause (g) also refers to insurances and rights in relation to policies of insurance.

B It is against the background of the facts I have mentioned and the language of the debenture which I have described that Mr Ritchie raises Mr Conroy's case that the £62,135 should be paid without further deduction to the bank and he puts his case in a number of different ways which I shall deal with but in a different order to his.

First it is said that the assignment by way of first fixed charge of "all policies of assurance" in cl. 2A(e) is sufficient to carry the proceeds of the company's recovery from insurers for fire losses. Mr Jones accepts that if that is so then by reason of there C then being a fixed charge it would be right that the whole £62,135 should go to the bank but he argues that the policy, or policies, whatever their precise details may be, were not "of assurance".

Mr Ritchie referred me to p. 5 of Ivamy's *General Principles of Insurance Law* (1986) which includes the following quote:

D "The parties to a contract of insurance are the 'Assured' (or 'Insured') and the 'Insurers'.

The assured (or insured)

Any person who is capable of contracting may be the assured under a contract of insurance."

Mr Ritchie also referred me to the complete *Oxford English Dictionary,* which as to E the word "assurance", includes as the fifth meaning:

"The action of insuring or securing the value of property in the event of its being lost, or of securing the payment of a specified sum in the event of a person's death; insurance."

He argues that these references show that the terms "assurance" and "insurance" are interchangeable and that "assurance" cannot properly be limited only to life policies. F He does not argue that "insurance" is but a subcompartment, so to speak, of "assurance", rather that each term is as extensive as the other and that they are true alternatives. However, Mr Ritchie was not able to identify the edition of the *Oxford English Dictionary* which he had photocopied and it is to be noted that the *Oxford English Dictionary* from which Mr Ritchie quotes is not a recent supplement or fresh edition. I apprehend the quotation must have come, at the latest, from the reissue of August 1933 of the work, completed in 1928, which had begun around 1878. On the pages of G which photocopies were supplied to me there are no references to emerging meanings derived from this century, nor, in respect of the word "assurance" in its fifth meaning, to any reference later than 1883. This, of itself, does not, of course, suggest that the fifth meaning I have quoted is not a current usage but I put to counsel that "assurance" ordinarily means cover in respect of events, such as death, which are bound to happen, whereas "insurance" was against events which might or might not happen, such as fire or death before a certain age or whilst in service. Whatever meaning the word "assurance" H on its own might be, the word "assurance" in the debenture must take colour from its context, which in this case also includes the distinct references to "insurance" that I have referred to, each of which is at least consistent with "insurance" being the term intended to be used in respect of risks or events other than death and which might or might not occur. In context it is reasonable to suppose a distinction between the two terms was intended.

Mr Jones would, I think, be content with the meaning that I had suggested and he argues that, whether or not that be right, in context in cl. 2A(e) the word "assurance" refers to policies which he described as life policies, that is to say policies in which death was either the triggering event or part of the description of the triggering event and hence that cl. 2A(e) did not include policies against fire.

I need say nothing of instruments in which assurance alone is referred to but in relation to an instrument that refers to both "assurance" and "insurance" I see force in Mr Jones' definition. Moreover, if Mr Ritchie were right then there are difficulties in regarding the provisions of cl. 4(e) as appropriate. If the bank has a fixed charge on money under cl. 2A(e), why should there be need for the provision that the money recovered should be paid in or towards a secured debt as cl. 4(e) provides? Equally, if the money was duly charged by way of fixed charge under cl. 2A(e) could the bank, at its own election and without the consent of the chargor, as cl. 4(e) provides, require the money not to be paid towards a secured debt but in reinstatement?

The point is a short one but, in my judgment, a charge on "policies of assurance" in cl. 2A(e) of the debenture does not go beyond policies which either have or include death as the or as part of the triggering event (I need not decide which) and hence no part of the £62,135 has become subject to a fixed charge under cl. 2A(e).

Next Mr Ritchie relies on cl. 4(e) of the debenture. The clause is outside what is plainly the principal charging clause, cl. 2A, but he says — rightly in my view — that if the language of the clause is such as to create a fixed charge then that fact of itself is no matter. The bank, he says, has a choice either to require the £62,135 to be laid out in reinstatement or in repayment of the debt to the bank and that in the interim, until that election, the money is to be paid to "such account of the company with the bank as the bank may direct". There has been no such election, nor has any particular account of the company been designated by the bank to be the recipient of insurance moneys. But, says Mr Ritchie, this total control which the bank has over the money, which excludes the company from doing anything it might choose to do with it, amounts to a fixed charge. The company cannot use the money in its trade or take any other of the steps which would be open to it if the money was subject only to a floating charge.

He referred to *Re Bond Worth Ltd* [1980] Ch 228 at p. 248E where *Slade* J said:

> "In my judgment, any contract which, by way of security for the payment of a debt, confers an interest in property defeasible or destructible upon payment of such debt, or appropriates such property for the discharge of the debt, must necessarily be regarded as creating a mortgage or charge, as the case may be. The existence of the equity of redemption is quite inconsistent with the existence of a bare trustee-beneficiary relationship."

However, what is in issue before me is not whether there is a mortgage or charge — Mr Jones would, as I have understood him, concede there to be a floating charge by way of equitable assignment — but whether there was a fixed charge rather than the charge which, as created, was a floating charge: see sec. 251 of the *Insolvency Act* 1986. Mr Ritchie's citation from *Swiss Bank Corporation v Lloyds Bank Ltd & Ors* [1982] AC 584 at p. 613, where Lord *Wilberforce* quotes from *Palmer v Carey* [1926] AC 703, similarly goes to whether there is, in the relevant events, a valid equitable charge by way of equitable assignment without touching the question before me of whether the charge is fixed or floating.

Cotton v Heyl [1930] 1 Ch 510 is directed to whether there was a good equitable assignment and does not assist on the distinction between fixed and floating charges.

But when one comes on to the cases describing the characteristics of a floating charge there one finds more useful guidance. Thus in *Governments Stock & Other Securities Investment Co Ltd v Manila Railway Co Ltd & Ors* [1897] AC 81 at p. 86 Lord *Macnaghten* says:

A   "A floating security is an equitable charge on the assets for the time being of a going concern. It attaches to the subject charged in the varying condition in which it happens to be from time to time. It is of the essence of such a charge that it remains dormant until the undertaking charged ceases to be a going concern, or until the person in whose favour the charge is created intervenes. His right to intervene may of course be suspended by agreement. But if there is no agreement for suspension, he may exercise his right whenever he pleases after default."

B   I do not see the arrangements of cl. 4(e) as being of a floating security within that description. It is not that the company is able to do as it pleases with the proceeds or with the right to receive proceeds unless and until the bank intervenes, rather that the money is to be channelled exclusively as the bank directs from the moment of its receipt and that the right to receive the policy moneys cannot be alienated.

C   In *Illingworth v Houldsworth* [1904] AC 355, Lord *Macnaghten* returned to the subject at p. 358 where, on this occasion, he turns also to describing what is fixed security. The citation runs:

"With regard to the criticism which Vaughan Williams L.J. passed, not I think unkindly, on some words of mine in the *Manila Case*, I only wish to observe that what I said was intended as a description, not as a definition, of a floating security. I should have thought there was not much difficulty in defining what a floating

D charge is in contrast to what is called a specific charge. A specific charge, I think, is one that without more fastens on ascertained and definite property or property capable of being ascertained and defined; a floating charge, on the other hand, is ambulatory and shifting in its nature, hovering over and so to speak floating with the property which it is intended to affect until some event occurs or some act is done which causes it to settle and fasten on the subject of the charge within its reach and grasp."

E   Mr Jones says here that the charge does not fasten "without more" on the policy proceeds as before that happens the bank has to elect against a reinstatement. He would accept that if the terms of cl. 4(e) had been such that the proceeds were to be paid to the bank in reduction of the secured debt without the bank or anyone else being able to elect that the proceeds should be paid in reinstatement that would have created a fixed charge. But he says that the possibility of the bank electing for reinstatement rather than

F repayment of the security precludes the charge from being a fixed one. That seems to me to be too artificial. If the clause had provided in the way just suggested but the bank had then, by way of fresh agreement, agreed that the money received under the policy should be applied by way of reinstatement rather than repayment, that latter agreement would not, even on Mr Jones' view, have vitiated the charge's description as a fixed charge. Can it really matter that the bank has written into the charge in advance an alternative possibility whereunder, at its election, reinstatement could be permitted?

G In my opinion it cannot. The proceeds were not to be at the free disposal of the company. That ability, which *Hoffmann* J speaks of in *Re Brightlife Ltd* (1986) 2 BCC 99,359 at p. 99,363 as being the "badge of a floating charge", is absent. Indeed, on the thin evidence I have, it may even be that the only account which the company has with the bank is a (presumably) overdrawn one which Mr Conroy has guaranteed and hence that, even without and before any election repayment for the interim into that account

H pursuant to cl. 4(e) would necessarily effect a repayment, at least for the time being and pro tanto, of the secured debt.

    In my judgment, cl. 4(e) amounts to a fixed charge and hence Mr Conroy's argument succeeds. It may be thought unattractive that that should be so in that if there had been no fire the bank would have had only a floating charge on, for example, the stock lost in the fire. It might be thought attractive that a secured creditor should be no worse off nor

better off in relation to the proceeds of insurance than he would have been as to the A
assets destroyed. However, that is plainly not the common law. For example, apart from
special contract or the provision of statute, a mortgagee has no interest in the moneys
paid under a policy of insurance effected by the mortgagor on the mortgaged premises
— see *Sinnott v Bowden* [1912] 2 Ch 414 at p. 419. Moreover, it is a feature of modern
company charges both that there is a freedom to create by express language effective
specific charges outside the areas traditional for such charges and that events can move
property from being subject to a floating to being subject to a fixed charge independent B
of any activity on the part of the mortgagee. Thus, for example, the value of stock which,
whilst lying in the chargor's warehouse, is subject only to a floating charge, may find its
value has become effectively subjected to a fixed charge on its being sold and becoming
a book debt, even should it have continued to lie in the same warehouse. There is thus
nothing which offends any underlying principle in a chargee being the better off by
reason of an event he did not procure or control, nor in the value derived from insurance
ending up in a different pocket than would have the value of the subject-matter C
destroyed.

Next Mr Ritchie relies on sec. 108 of the *Law of Property Act* 1925 and in particular
subsec. (4) which reads as follows:

> "(4) Without prejudice to any obligation to the contrary imposed by law, or by
> special contract, a mortgagee may require that all money received on an insurance
> of mortgaged property against loss or damage by fire or otherwise effected under D
> this Act, or any enactment replaced by this Act, or on an insurance for the
> maintenance of which the mortgagor is liable under the mortgage deed, be applied
> in or towards the discharge of the mortgage money."

The terms "mortgagor", "mortgagee", "mortgage" and "property" are defined in
sec. 205 of the 1925 Act in terms such as to enable his argument to proceed further, with
"mortgagee" including a floating chargee. Mr Jones, however, argues that the opening
words, "Without prejudice to any obligation to the contrary imposed by law", include E
reference to the provisions in insolvency whereunder the liquidator's receipt should be
applied to the liquidator's expenses and preferential creditors ahead of a floating
chargee.

I am unclear as to the limits of that argument and it may, perhaps, prove too much in
the sense that if the words are invariably to have that effect then, even where the charges
are undoubtedly fixed, payment in full to the fixed chargee might be precluded. There F
are a number of authorities on sec. 108(4) to which I was not referred and, I am told, no
authority on the very point on sec. 108 which is now argued. As Mr Ritchie has already
succeeded on the express terms of cl. 4(e) I see the wiser course as leaving the effect of
sec. 108(4) to be determined in a case in which its effect is more material than it has now
become in this one.

Since writing this judgment I have had my attention drawn by Mr Ritchie, with
Mr Jones' consent, to the decision of *Vinelott* J in *Re Atlantic Medical Ltd* [1992] BCC G
653. I need say nothing about that case, save that, as I see it, the judge's reasoning and
conclusion is entirely consistent with the approach I had already arrived at and that
nothing in the authorities he cites, including *Re Atlantic Computer Systems plc* [1990]
BCC 859, requires me to reconsider my conclusion. I thus have not required the matter
to be relisted for further hearing.

As to the form of order I should now make, there will need to be further discussion H
with counsel and it seems to me inevitable that other questions will arise than merely the
proper destination of the £62,135. However, dealing simply with that, I hold that it
should be paid to the bank.

(Order accordingly)

A ## Stein v Blake.

Court of Appeal (Civil Division).
Balcombe, Staughton and Waite L JJ.
Judgment delivered 5 May 1993.

B
> *Bankruptcy — Mutual credit and set-off — Trustee in bankruptcy assigned claim against defendant back to bankrupt — Defendant had counterclaim and argued that there could be no assignment because statutory rules of set-off extinguished mutual debts — Whether after plaintiff's bankruptcy there could be no assignment until trustee had taken account in respect of mutual dealings — Insolvency Act 1986, sec. 323.*

This was an appeal from a judge's decision on the effect of sec. 323 of the Insolvency Act 1986 (mutual credit and set-off).

C
The plaintiff had commenced proceedings against the defendant in 1987. The defendant had a counterclaim. In 1990 the plaintiff was adjudicated bankrupt and a trustee of his estate was appointed. In 1991 the bankrupt, the trustee and a third party as surety entered into a deed of assignment whereby the trustee assigned to the bankrupt his claims in the action. After deductions for costs, any proceeds recovered by the bankrupt in the action would be split 51 per cent to the bankrupt, 49 per cent to the trustee. The bankrupt
D received legal aid to pursue the action.

The defendant then issued a summons to stay the action on the grounds that it was an abuse of the process of the court. Before the deputy master he contended that, after the plaintiff became bankrupt, his claims against the defendant and the defendant's counterclaim against the plaintiff fell to be dealt with in the bankruptcy and that until an account had been taken by the trustee under sec. 323 there was nothing to assign. In
E support of that contention the defendant relied upon the decision of Neill J in Farley v Housing and Commercial Developments Ltd (1984) 1 BCC 99,150. He succeeded in that contention both before the deputy master and, on appeal by the plaintiff, before the judge.

The question for the Court of Appeal was whether, after a bankruptcy but before a balance of account had been ascertained under sec. 323, a trustee in bankruptcy could assign to a third party the bankrupt's claims against a person who was entitled to avail
F himself of the statutory right of set-off. Ancillary to that question was whether Farley's case was rightly decided.

Held, allowing the plaintiff's appeal:

1. The account under sec. 323(2) did not have to be taken by the trustee in bankruptcy. All that the section provided was that some appropriate authority should take an account. It might be the trustee, or the court exercising bankruptcy jurisdiction under sec. 303(1),
G or any other judge exercising lawful jurisdiction.

2. Debts due to and from a bankrupt did not disappear on the making of a bankruptcy order. Section 323 was concerned only with the remedy that was available, and not with the existence of debts. The section drew a distinction between what was due (in subsec. (2) and (3)) and what was payable or recoverable (subsec. (4)). The separate causes of action (claim and cross-claim) remained due, and did not cease to exist, until the set-off had been
H completed by payment one way or the other. Farley's case was wrongly decided.

The following cases were referred to in the judgment of Balcombe LJ:

Cushla Ltd, Re [1979] 3 All ER 415.
Farley v Housing and Commercial Developments Ltd (1984) 1 BCC 99,150.
Forster & Ors v Wilson & Anor (1843) 12 M & W 191; 152 ER 1165.
Hanak v Green [1958] 2 QB 9.

M S Fashions Ltd & Ors v Bank of Credit and Commerce International SA & Anor   A
[1992] BCC 571.
M S Fashions Ltd & Ors v Bank of Credit and Commerce International SA & Anor
(No. 2) [1993] BCC 70; [1993] Ch 425.
National Westminster Bank Ltd v Halesowen Presswork & Assemblies Ltd
[1972] AC 785.
New Quebrada Co Ltd v Carr & Ors (1869) LR 4 CP 651.

  B

Philip Hoser (instructed by Bray Walker) for the appellant.

Michael Mark (instructed by Maislish & Co) for the respondent.

JUDGMENT

Balcombe LJ: This appeal by the plaintiff, with the leave of the judge, from an order
made on 11 June 1992 by Mr T Morison QC sitting as a deputy judge of the High Court   C
(Chancery Division) raises a difficult question as to the effect of sec. 323 of the
Insolvency Act 1986. I take the facts from the judgment below:

> "In February 1987 the plaintiff commenced proceedings against the defendant in
> the Queen's Bench Division. The essence of the claim was that the defendant had
> broken an agreement with the plaintiff to equalise his shareholding in various
> companies. The defendant put in issue the terms of the agreement and
> counterclaimed against the plaintiff for damages for misrepresentation. Separate   D
> proceedings were commenced by the plaintiff against the defendant in the Chancery
> Division in June 1988. In this action the plaintiff alleged that by the same
> agreement the defendant impliedly agreed to procure the various companies and/
> or their auditors to do certain things whereby the plaintiff would have been able
> to have received 25 per cent of the companies' net profits. It was further alleged
> by the plaintiff that, pursuant to the agreement, the defendant should have   E
> allotted or transferred to him a proportion of shares in a company which the
> defendant had caused to be incorporated. The defendant denied that the agreement
> had the effect contended for.

> In May 1989 the Queen's Bench action was transferred to the Chancery Division
> and in October 1989 the two actions were consolidated.

> On 16 July 1990 the plaintiff was adjudicated bankrupt and a trustee of his estate   F
> was appointed on October 19 1990. On 4 April 1991 the bankrupt, the trustee and
> a third party as surety entered into a deed of assignment whereby the trustee
> purported to assign to the bankrupt his claims in the consolidated action. After
> deductions for costs, any proceeds recovered by the bankrupt in the action would
> be split with the trustee: 51 per cent to the bankrupt, 49 per cent to the trustee.

> The bankrupt has received legal aid to pursue the action."

  G

The defendant then issued a summons to stay the action on the grounds that it was an
abuse of the process of the court. Before the deputy master he contended that, after the
plaintiff became bankrupt, his claims against the defendant and the defendant's
counterclaim against the plaintiff fell to be dealt with in the bankruptcy and that until an
account had been taken by the trustee under sec. 323 there was nothing to assign. In
support of that contention the defendant relied upon the decision of *Neill* J in *Farley v*
Housing and Commercial Developments Ltd (1984) 1 BCC 99,150. He succeeded in   H
that contention both before the deputy master and, on appeal by the plaintiff, before
the judge.

The question for our decision is whether, after a bankruptcy but before a balance of
account has been ascertained under sec. 323, a trustee in bankruptcy may assign to a
third party the bankrupt's claims against a person who is entitled to avail himself of the

A   statutory right of set-off. Ancillary to that question is whether *Farley*'s case was rightly
     decided.

     Section 323 of the *Insolvency Act* 1986 is in the following terms:

        "(1) This section applies where before the commencement of the bankruptcy
        there have been mutual credits, mutual debts or other mutual dealings between
        the bankrupt and any creditor of the bankrupt proving or claiming to prove for a
B   bankruptcy debt.

        (2) An account shall be taken of what is due from each party to the other in
        respect of the mutual dealings and the sums due from one party shall be set off
        against the sums due from the other.

        (3) Sums due from the bankrupt to another party shall not be included in the
        account taken under subsection (2) if that other party had notice at the time they
C   became due that a bankruptcy petition relating to the bankrupt was pending.

        (4) Only the balance (if any) of the account taken under subsection (2) is provable
        as a bankruptcy debt or, as the case may be, to be paid to the trustee as part of the
        bankrupt's estate."

     The section is similar in effect, although not in identical terms, to sec. 31 of the
     Bankruptcy Act 1914, which in turn replaced earlier provisions to the like effect —
D   sec. 38 of the *Bankruptcy Act* 1883; sec. 39 of the *Bankruptcy Act* 1869; sec. 171 of the
     Bankrupt Law Consolidation Act 1849 (12 & 13 Vict, c 106); 6 Geo 4, c 16, sec. 50;
     5 Geo 2, c 30, sec. 28; and 4 & 5 Anne c 17, sec. 11.

     In order to appreciate the purpose of the section it is necessary to look at it, as did the
     judge, in its statutory context. It forms part of Ch. IV of Pt. IX of the 1986 Act, the
     chapter title of which is "Administration by Trustee". The first section in the chapter is
E   sec. 305, which defines the general functions of the trustee, and of which the operative
     part is subsec. (2) which provides as follows:

        "The function of the trustee is to get in, realise and distribute the bankrupt's
        estate in accordance with the following provisions of this Chapter; and in the
        carrying out of that function and in the management of the bankrupt's estate the
        trustee is entitled, subject to those provisions, to use his own discretion."

F   If an asset of the bankrupt's estate is a cause of action (other than one of a personal
     nature) then that vests in the trustee in bankruptcy, and his statutory duty under
     sec. 305(2) is to realise that asset. One way in which he may do so is by assignment by
     way of sale. The discretion as to the manner of realisation belongs to the trustee and will
     not be interfered with by the court except on well-established principles (e.g. if the
     trustee has acted in bad faith). This is all trite law and was not the subject of contention
     before us.
G
     The next section to which I refer is sec. 322. This and the following ten sections are
     preceded by the subtitle "Distribution of bankrupt's estate". It provides, so far as
     relevant, as follows:

        "*Proof of debts*

        (1) Subject to this section and the next, the proof of any bankruptcy debt by a
H   secured or unsecured creditor of the bankrupt and the admission or rejection of
        any proof shall take place in accordance with the rules.

        . . .

        (3) The trustee shall estimate the value of any bankruptcy debt which, by reason
        of its being subject to any contingency or contingencies or for any other reason,
        does not bear a certain value.

(4) Where the value of a bankruptcy debt is estimated by the trustee under   A
subsection (3) or, by virtue of section 303 in Chapter III, by the court, the amount
provable in the bankruptcy in respect of the debt is the amount of the estimate."

"Bankruptcy debt" is defined by sec. 382:

"(1) 'Bankruptcy debt', in relation to a bankrupt, means (subject to the next
subsection) any of the following—

    (a) any debt or liability to which he is subject at the commencement of the   B
    bankruptcy,

    (b) any debt or liability to which he may become subject after the commencement
    of the bankruptcy (including after his discharge from bankruptcy) by reason
    of any obligation incurred before the commencement of the bankruptcy,
    . . .

(3) For the purposes of references in this Group of Parts to a debt or liability, it is   C
immaterial whether the debt or liability is present or future, whether it is certain
or contingent or whether its amount is fixed or liquidated, or is capable of being
ascertained by fixed rules or as a matter of opinion; and references in this Group
of Parts to owing a debt are to be read accordingly."

That being its statutory context, I turn to consider the purpose of sec. 323. Set-off in
bankruptcy rests on a different principle to the right of set-off between solvent parties.
The purpose of the latter is to prevent cross-actions, and the right is limited to the   D
categories listed in the well-known judgment of *Morris* LJ in *Hanak v Green* [1958]
2 QB 9 at p. 23. The object of set-off in bankruptcy is not to avoid cross-actions, but to
do substantial justice between the parties — see *Forster v Wilson* (1843) 12 M & W 191
at p. 204 — since it would be obviously unjust if the solvent party had to discharge his
debt to the bankrupt's estate in full while being left only with the right to prove, and
thereby receive only a dividend, in respect of the bankrupt's debt to him. In order to   E
achieve this object of substantial justice sec. 323 is not limited to the categories as
defined in *Hanak v Green*, but applies to all cross-claims provided that they are mutual
and are measurable in money terms. The operation of the section is mandatory in that it
cannot be excluded by agreement — see *National Westminster Bank Ltd v Halesowen
Presswork & Assemblies Ltd* [1972] AC 785.

The opposing arguments may be summarised as follows.   F

For the appellant plaintiff— Nothing in the wording of sec. 323 changes the *nature* of
set-off as it operates between solvent parties: it merely widens the categories of claim
capable of being, and which must be, set-off. The section contemplates a three-stage
procedure:

(1)   an ascertainment of what is due from A to B, and from B to A (the first part of
    sec. 323(2));
                                                                                   G
(2)   a setting-off of the sums found so to be due (the second part of sec. 323(2)); and

(3)   payment of, or proof for, the balance (sec. 323(4)).

The language of the section draws a distinction between what is *due* — which is the
word used in subsec. (2) and (3) — and what is payable or recoverable — as under
subsec. (4). The separate causes of action (claim and cross-claim) remain due, and do
not cease to exist, until the set-off has been completed by payment one way or the other.   H
It is also noteworthy that the section does not provide that only the trustee in bankruptcy
may take the account: subsec. (2) only states that "An account shall be taken". Certainly
the section contains no prohibition against the assignment to a third party by the trustee
in bankruptcy of a claim against a person who has a cross-claim against the bankrupt,
but it is accepted that any such assignment would be subject to all equities, so that the
assignee would take subject to the wide right of set-off created by sec. 323.

A   *For the respondent defendant* — The rules of set-off under sec. 323 are wholly
different, in nature as well as extent, from those which operate between solvent persons.
This is because sec. 323 is a part of the statutory code of procedure for the administration
of bankrupts' estates in a proper and orderly way: see *National Westminster Bank Ltd v
Halesowen Presswork & Assemblies Ltd* [1972] AC 785 at pp. 805D, 808E-809B and
824A. The 1986 Act requires the trustee to realise and distribute the bankrupt's estate
and where there are mutual dealings the trustee has a duty to take the account required
B   by sec. 323(2) as part of the process of ascertaining whether there is a bankruptcy debt.
That duty is non-delegable. The effect of the section is that as at the commencement of
the bankruptcy the claim and cross-claim cease to have any independent existence and
are replaced by the claim for the balance.

The authorities largely, but not entirely, support the arguments for the respondent
defendant.

C   In *Farley v Housing and Commercial Developments Ltd* (1984) 1 BCC 99,150 an
identical question arose in the liquidation of an insolvent company, to which the
provisions of sec. 31 of the *Bankruptcy Act* 1914 applied. *Neill* J accepted the arguments
of counsel for the respondent (who was in the same position as that of the respondent
defendant in the instant case) at pp. 99,155–99,156 that:

D   "the chose or choses in action represented by the debt or debts owed by the
respondents immediately before the liquidation for moneys due under the two
contracts ceased to exist and were no longer available to be assigned by the
liquidator in 1979."

—and at (p. 99,157) that:

"after the contractors went into insolvent liquidation the only relevant chose in
action which the contractors owned was the right to enforce a claim for the
E   amount, if any, which was due to the contractors after taking the account required
in accordance with sec. 31."

The decision is at first instance and is not binding on this court. For my part I find force
in the submissions of Mr Hoser, counsel for the appellant plaintiff, that the judgment of
Neill J manifests a confusion between the two distinct concepts of (1) a debt being due
(i.e. owed); and (2) a debt (which is ex hypothesi due) being payable or recoverable.
F   Thus he said (at p. 99,156):

"Accordingly, on 5 February 1975 the rights of the contractors and the respondents
inter se became subject immediately to the provisions of sec. 31. In accordance
with sec. 31 an account had then to be taken and the balance of the account and no
more became the sum thereafter *owing* to or from the respective parties."
(emphasis added)

G   —and later (at p. 99,157):

"It is clear that after the contractors went into insolvent liquidation in February
1975 an account should have been taken of what was due in respect of the mutual
dealings between the contractors and the respondents. It is apparent from the
pleadings in the arbitration that such an account would have disclosed that certain
sums were prima facie admitted to be due from the respondents to the contractors
but that the respondents were contending that they had cross-claims against the
H   contractors for an amount exceeding these admitted sums. At that stage the taking
of the account may well have involved arbitration proceedings to determine what
sums were *due* from the contractors to the respondents. Until such an account had
been taken, however, it would not have been possible to ascertain whether any
sum was *due* from the respondents to the contractors or vice versa. It is certainly
possible, and indeed in accordance with the contention of the present respondents,

that the taking of the account would have disclosed that no sum was *payable* from   A
the respondents at all." (emphasis added)

Neill J also cited, in support of his conclusion, a decision of *Vinelott* J in *Re Cushla Ltd* [1979] 3 All ER 415, which was not a case concerning (as was *Farley*'s case) the question of what was due from or to each party, to which question sec. 323(2)–(3) are directed, but with the question of what was payable by, or recoverable from, each party, to which sec. 323(4) is directed.

B

Although the judge in the present case said he agreed in full with the judgment of *Neill* J in *Farley*'s case, he obviously found some difficulty in accepting fully the reasoning of *Neill* J as appears from the following passage from the judgment below:

> "However, it seems to me that some misunderstanding of the ratio of *Neill* J's judgment in the *Farley* case may have been caused by the terms of counsel's submission which found favour with him. In that case, counsel submitted that on   C
> the bankruptcy the debts owed immediately before the bankruptcy 'ceased to have any independent existence' or 'to exist' and were no longer available to be assigned by the liquidator. It would seem to me that, on bankruptcy, the only chose in action which is capable of assignment is a right to such sum as is found to be due on the taking of the account. I would prefer to say that on bankruptcy the debts owed immediately before the bankruptcy ceased to be capable of assignment until after the statutory account has been taken under sec. 323. This is probably   D
> only a semantic difference, but it might meet the point made about a debt which vanishes and magically comes to life again after a bankruptcy is annulled. The debt itself does not vanish, it becomes non-assignable until the account is taken."

Farley's case is the only decision directly in point. However there are a number of other decisions or dicta which are material.

In *New Quebrada Co Ltd v Carr & Ors* (1869) LR 4 CP 651 a company made a call on   E
the three joint holders of shares. They pleaded set-off. The company's replication alleged lack of mutuality because after the commencement of the action and before the plea one of the three had been adjudicated bankrupt and his joint interest in the debt due from the company had thereby vested in his assignees. The shareholders argued that nothing passed to the assignees because of the bankruptcy, and that by virtue of the then equivalent of sec. 323 the bankrupt's share of the debt was automatically set off   F
against the company's claim for calls. The Court of Common Pleas held that there had been no bankruptcy set-off: the bankrupt's individual interest in a joint debt could not be set off against the three shareholders. However, *Brett* J went on to deal (obiter) with what the position would be if the set-off rule did apply and said (at p. 653):

> "I think its only effect is to transfer the claim to the assignees, subject, when they seek to enforce it, to a right of the plaintiffs to deduct their debt. It does not, I think, extinguish the mutual debts . . ."   G

That dictum clearly favours the appellant plaintiff.

In *M S Fashions Ltd v Bank of Credit and Commerce International SA (No. 2)* [1993] BCC 70, *Hoffmann* LJ (at p. 74D) describes the passage from which that citation is taken as "not altogether easy" but in my judgment the meaning is clear. The bankruptcy set-off does not, of itself, extinguish the mutual debts. The dictum of that very great judge who became Lord *Esher* MR is obviously entitled to considerable respect.   H

In *M S Fashions Ltd v Bank of Credit and Commerce International SA* [1992] BCC 571, this court (*Woolf* and *Scott* L JJ), on an interlocutory application, with limited argument and without the citation of any relevant case, expressed the view that the operation of r. 4.90 of the *Insolvency Rules* 1986 (which is the modern equivalent of sec. 323 in relation to insolvent companies) was:

A

". . . that the set-off operates as at the date of the winding up so as to leave simply the net amount claimable by the company in liquidation from the other party or, as the case may be, provable as a debt in the liquidation by the other party."

—per *Scott* LJ at p. 574D; and

B

"The rule operates as a matter of law upon the company going into liquidation. At that stage an account is required to be taken of what is due from each party to the other and there is then to be a set-off between them. Once there has been that set-off, to the extent of the amount which is set off, the company has been paid. That means that not only is the guarantor or joint principal discharged to the extent of the set-off, but so is any other debtor who is liable in relation to the same sum. That that is the position is made clear by the provisions of r. 4.90(4), where it states:

C

'(4) Only the balance (if any) of the account is provable in the liquidation . . .' "

—per *Woolf* LJ at p. 577A.

However, both *Scott* and *Woolf* L JJ made it clear that they were only expressing a provisional view and were not making a permanent ruling on the law. Further, it is by no means clear that *Woolf* LJ, at least, was suggesting that r. 4.90 operated to extinguish the mutual claims and cross-claims ab initio. Nevertheless, the trend of this decision is to support the respondent defendant.

D

Finally there is the decision of *Hoffmann* LJ (sitting as an additional judge of the Chancery Division) in *M S Fashions Ltd v Bank of Credit and Commerce International SA (No. 2)* [1993] BCC 70, to which I have already referred. That again was a case concerning r. 4.90 of the *Insolvency Rules* 1986. In the course of his judgment (at p. 73C) *Hoffmann* LJ set out three principles as being applicable:

E

"First, the rule is mandatory ('the mandatory principle'). If there have been mutual dealings before the winding-up order which have given rise to cross-claims, neither party can prove or sue for his full claim. An account must be taken and he must prove or sue (as the case may be) for the balance. Secondly, the account is taken as at the date of the winding-up order ('the retroactivity principle'). This is only one manifestation of a wider principle of insolvency law, namely, that the liquidation and distribution of the assets of the insolvent company are treated

F

as notionally taking place simultaneously on the date of the winding-up order (see *Oliver* J in *Re Dynamics Corp of America (in liquidation)* [1976] 1 WLR 757 at p. 762). Thirdly, in taking the account the court has regard to events which have occurred since the date of the winding up ('the hindsight principle'). The hindsight principle is pervasive in the valuation of claims and the taking of accounts in bankruptcy and winding up. A good example of the principle being applied outside the context of set-off is *Macfarlane's Claim* (1881) 17 ChD 337 in which

G

the value of a claim under a fire insurance policy was determined by reference to the loss suffered in a fire which occurred a month after the insurance company had been wound up."

With these principles as thus stated Mr Hoser does not seek to quarrel, and I express no comment. However, *Hoffmann* LJ then went on to express approval of the decision in *Farley*'s case in the passage immediately following that just quoted:

H

"In reading the cases, the interaction of these principles has to be borne in mind. Mr Neville Thomas QC, who appeared for BCCI, said that the right of set-off under r. 4.90 is procedural and that the mutual credits and debits of BCCI and the directors retain their separate existences until such time as the account is taken in the context of the director filing either a proof or a defence to a claim by the liquidator. This is of course true in the somewhat trivial sense that no account will

be taken until something happens which makes it necessary to apply r. 4.90 and   A
take one. But that cannot in my judgment affect the substantive rights of the
parties which, whatever the context in which the question may subsequently arise,
are treated as having been determined by an account taken at the date of the
winding up. This is a consequence of the mandatory and retroactivity principles.
Thus in *Farley v Housing and Commercial Developments Ltd* (1984) 1 BCC
99,150, Mr Farley was director of a building company engaged in erecting two
buildings for a developer. On 5 February 1975 the building company resolved to   B
go into creditors' voluntary winding up. At the date, the building company had a
claim for money owing under the contract but the developer said it had a cross-
claim for damages. Three years later, the liquidator of the building company
assigned the benefit of its claim to Mr Farley personally. He argued that he was
entitled to claim in full against the developer, leaving it to prove in his company's
liquidation for its damages. But *Neill* J rejected this submission. He said that on   C
the date of the winding up, sec. 31 of the *Bankruptcy Act* 1914 (in similar terms to
r. 4.90) immediately took effect and 'the balance of the account and no more
became the sum thereafter owing to or from the respective parties'.''

Again the decision was at first instance and the precise point which arises in this case
was not before the judge. However his clear approval of *Farley*'s case is significant.

Derham on *Set-off* (1987) at p. 73, 75 and 77 criticises the decision in *Farley*; Wood on   D
English and International Set-off (1989) refers to the decision without comment.
Whichever interpretation is accepted some anomalies will result.

(1) If *Farley* and the judge below are right:

(a) Wherever there is a claim by a bankrupt and a cross-claim against the bankrupt's
estate, the claim is unassignable: only the balance after the taking of the account
is assignable, and this may not be immediately possible. Mr Hoser suggests two   E
examples:

    (i) B commences proceedings for £100,000. No set-off or counterclaim is
        pleaded by A, the defendant. B seeks leave to amend the statement of claim
        and is given leave to do so on the usual terms, i.e. that the costs occasioned
        by the amendment are to be paid by him in any event. The amendment
        necessitates a slightly amended defence (though still no set-off or cross-
        claim is asserted). The costs of the amended defence are minimal — perhaps   F
        a few hundred pounds, but they will not be ascertained prior to taxation at
        the end of the action. B goes bankrupt. His trustee cannot assign the cause
        of action to him because there is a cross-liability (of a few hundred pounds).

    (ii) B claims against A £1,000 for goods sold and delivered. Some years earlier
        B had built a house for A. Damage is caused to A's house because of B's
        poor workmanship, but nobody yet realises that A has a cause of action.   G
        B goes bankrupt. His trustee assigns the cause of action against A. That
        assignment will have been ineffective because at the commencement of the
        bankruptcy A had (even if he did not then know it) a cross-claim against B
        arising out of a pre-insolvency mutual dealing (the housebuilding contract)
        and because there was accordingly nothing which the trustee could assign.

This could clearly inhibit the realisation by the trustee of the assets of the bankrupt   H
estate.

(b) If the bankruptcy is annulled before the balance of the claim and cross-claim has
been proved or paid, as the case may be, then:

    (i) Since the immediate effect of the bankruptcy was that the claim and cross-
        claim ceased to have any independent existence, and were metamorphosed

A   into a claim for the balance, then that metamorphosis remains valid upon annulment under sec. 282(4)(a) of the 1986 Act. Yet the precise amount of the claim or the cross-claim may not have been established before the annulment.

      (ii) If the balance is in favour of the bankrupt, that is an asset which will vest in him under sec. 282(4)(b).

B
      (iii) If the balance is against the bankrupt, that is all that can belong to the creditor, since his original claim will, possibly unbeknown to him, have ceased to exist.

(c)   It is an essential part of the respondent's case that only the trustee in bankruptcy of the bankrupt can take the account under sec. 323. But what if the original claimant against the bankrupt himself is, or becomes, bankrupt? Which trustee in bankruptcy is to take the account?

C

(d)   The rights of the claimant against the bankrupt are affected without his consent and possibly even without his knowledge since his debt, having ceased to exist, is also non-assignable. If the claimant himself becomes bankrupt, what is it that vests in his trustee in bankruptcy? Presumably only the balance, if in his favour, whenever that has been ascertained.

D

    (2) If the plaintiff is right then the anomalies are less obvious. One problem is that, on the facts of the present case, the defendant will not have lost his right to prove for his claim in the plaintiff's bankruptcy, but the plaintiff's trustee will not be able to set off the cross-claim, because he has assigned it away. But this is not the anomaly which it may at first sight appear to be. In any event it seems unlikely that the defendant would prefer to prove his debt in the plaintiff's bankruptcy, rather than use it in full as a set-off against the enforcement against him of the assigned claim. But if the trustee chooses to assign away the plaintiff's claim against the defendant — presumably for what he considers to be valuable consideration — it would hardly lie in his mouth to complain that he has thereby deprived himself of the ability to use that claim by way of set-off against the defendant. The defendant is in no worse a position since he both retains the right of set-off against the assignee, or the right to prove his claim in the plaintiff's bankruptcy, whichever he prefers.

E

F

    So although I do not find the question easy to answer, I have come to the firm conclusion that the plaintiff is right in his contentions and that the judgment below, and *Neill* J's decision in *Farley*, are wrong. The plaintiff's interpretation is not only consistent with the principle as stated by *Brett* J in *New Quebrada Co Ltd v Carr*; it avoids having to introduce into sec. 323(2) the requirement that the account can only be taken by the trustee in bankruptcy; it also avoids having to imply, as did the judge, a prohibition against assignment until the account has been taken.

G

    That is not to say that there may not be other grounds on which the defendant could attack the assignment which was made in this case. The defendant in his skeleton argument asserts that the assignment is an abuse of the legal aid system. I express no opinion on that assertion, but it was not the ground upon which the defendant relied before the deputy master or before the judge, and was not raised by a respondent's notice in the present case. This appeal is concerned only with the technical point I have mentioned, whose validity is independent of the fact that the plaintiff is in receipt of legal aid to prosecute the assigned claim.

H

    I would allow this appeal.

Staughton LJ: There were essentially two points discussed in this appeal. The first   A
was whether, upon a person becoming bankrupt where there have been mutual credits,
mutual debts or other mutual dealings, the obligations of the debtor and of the creditor
cease to exist, and are replaced by one obligation on the party who is a net payer in
respect of the balance. The second point was whether there is any enforceable obligation
to pay that balance until an account has been taken by the trustee in bankruptcy.

Mr Mark on behalf of the defendant relies on the second point. He submits that there   B
has not been an account taken by the trustee, and will not be if the present consolidated
action is allowed to proceed. There may be an account taken by the judge in that action.
But that, he says, will not do; it must be taken by the trustee. Hence the deputy master
and the judge were right to dismiss the action. It is of no significance and does not matter,
according to Mr Mark, whether the original debts remain alive or only the balance of an
account is payable.   C

I cannot accept that argument. It seems to me that when sec. 323(2) provides that "an
account shall be taken" it means just that — the taking of the account shall be conducted
by whoever is the appropriate authority in the circumstances. It may be the trustee; or it
may be the court exercising bankruptcy jurisdiction under sec. 303(1); or it may be any
other judge exercising lawful jurisdiction. All that the section provides is that some
appropriate authority shall take an account.   D

If the trustee does not wish the account to be taken otherwise than by himself and the
bankruptcy court, there are remedies available which will ensure that it does not happen
unless the interests of justice require it. And if the creditors are dissatisfied with a
decision of the trustee to allow such a situation to arise, they can ask the bankruptcy
court to review that decision under sec. 303.

There are two arguments of substance against that interpretation of sec. 323(2). The   E
first is that, under sec. 323(3), the trustee shall estimate the value of any bankruptcy
debt which, by reason of its being subject to any contingency or contingencies or for any
other reason does not bear a certain value. Can that power be exercised only by the
trustee? Or can it also be exercised by a judge who has jurisdiction to take the account?
Since it must in any event be exercisable by the bankruptcy court under sec. 303, I do
not see why it cannot also be exercised by a judge in an action between the trustee or his   F
assignee and the creditor.

The second argument is that inconvenience and multiplicity of proceedings may arise
if the amount owing to the creditor exceeds the amount owing to the bankrupt. That
may happen in the present case; and the assignee's action may fail because there is no
balance due to him. But the judge at trial may not find it necessary to decide how much
is still left owing to the creditor. Or if he does decide that, the trustee may wish to argue   G
that he is not bound by the judge's decision, since he was not a party to the proceedings.

Those consequences are theoretical possibilities; or at any rate the first of them is. But
in my opinion they are unlikely to arise in practice. If they do arise, one must face the
fact that difficulties and inconvenience do sometimes occur in insolvency proceedings,
for example when a creditor is partly secured in respect of his debt or has a remedy
against a guarantor which is contested.   H

Indeed it was argued that the creditor might choose not to rely on set-off against an
assignee, and choose to prove in the bankruptcy for the whole of his debt instead. I say
nothing as to whether a creditor would in law be entitled to take that course. It seems to
me very improbable that he would wish to do so; and the trustee would be likely to
enquire whether that was going to happen before he made any assignment.

A

    In my judgment Mr Mark's argument fails, and this appeal should be allowed. But I would add that I agree with the conclusion of *Balcombe* LJ that debts due to and from a bankrupt do not disappear on the making of a bankruptcy order. Section 323 is concerned only with the remedy that is available, and not with the existence of debts. So I agree that *Farley*'s case was wrongly decided.

    Waite LJ: I agree that the appeal should be allowed for the reasons given by *Balcombe* and *Staughton* L JJ, to which I do not feel it necessary to add anything.

B

(Appeal allowed)

C

D

E

F

G

H

Re Aldermanbury Trust plc.

A

Chancery Division (Companies Court).
Ferris J.
Judgment delivered 11 May 1993.

Disqualifying unfit directors after investigation of company — Whether court could properly adopt shortened form of procedure to avoid full hearing of disputed issues — Whether court could be satisfied that director was unfit and that particular period of disqualification was appropriate — Company Directors Disqualification Act 1986, sec. 8.

B

This was an application by the Secretary of State for Trade and Industry for a director disqualification order under the Company Directors Disqualification Act 1986, sec. 8 (disqualification after investigation of company).

The parties adopted a shortened form of procedure, in reliance upon the decision in Re Carecraft Construction Co Ltd [1993] BCC 336, to avoid a full hearing of all the disputed issues. On the basis of a schedule of agreed or non-disputed facts, the respondent, Mr Fulcher, accepted that his conduct had been such that the court was likely to find him unfit under sec. 8(2) of the Disqualification Act, and indicated that he did not argue strenuously against the making of a disqualification order for a period which was towards the lower end of the middle bracket of periods described in Re Sevenoaks Stationers (Retail) Ltd [1990] BCC 765 (at p. 771H).

C

D

Held, disqualifying Mr Fulcher as a director for seven years:

1. The court was satisfied that the facts stated and agreed were such as to make Mr Fulcher unfit to be concerned in the management of a company.

2. The court was also satisfied that it could properly proceed on the basis of the agreed or non-disputed facts, because if those issues on which there was no agreement were fought to a conclusion and the facts were ascertained by the court, it was unlikely that the conduct of Mr Fulcher would be shown to be of a different and greater order of seriousness than was implicit in the agreed or non-disputed facts.

E

3. The agreed or non-disputed facts revealed serious breaches by Mr Fulcher of the provisions of general company law, of certain provisions of Aldermanbury's own articles of association and of r. 9 of the City Code on Takeovers and Mergers. They also showed a lamentable failure on Mr Fulcher's part to recognise and either avoid or resolve conflicts of interest. They involved substantial breaches by Mr Fulcher of his fiduciary duty to the company, a failure to disclose proper information to shareholders who were being asked to approve certain important transactions, and what appeared to be seriously flawed commercial judgments in relation to transactions and valuations which went beyond mere commercial foolishness. The misconduct of Mr Fulcher was of quite a high degree of seriousness.

F

G

4. There was substantial mitigation: in relation to many of the transactions Mr Fulcher was advised by solicitors; the proceedings had been hanging over Mr Fulcher for a very considerable period of time (the events of which complaint was made took place in 1985–1987 and the proceedings were brought in 1989); Mr Fulcher had made no personal profit out of any of the transactions; and he was to be given credit for what was in effect a plea of guilty.

H

The following cases were referred to in the judgment:

Carecraft Construction Co Ltd, Re [1993] BCC 336.
Sevenoaks Stationers (Retail) Ltd, Re [1990] BCC 765; [1991] Ch 164.

Roger Kaye QC and Mark Cunningham (instructed by the Treasury Solicitor) for the Secretary of State.

A   Roydon Thomas QC and Ian Grainger (instructed by Bloom Camillin) for Mr Fulcher.

JUDGMENT

Ferris J: By the originating summons which is before me the Secretary of State for Trade and Industry seeks an order under sec. 8 of the *Company Directors Disqualification Act* 1986 that Mr Godfrey William Frederick Fulcher shall not without the leave of the court be a director or in any way, whether directly or indirectly, be concerned or take part in the promotion, formation or management of a company for such period as the court thinks fit.

An application may be made under sec. 8 if it appears to the Secretary of State from a report made by inspectors appointed under sec. 437 of the *Companies Act* 1985 or from information or documents obtained under sec. 447 or 448 of the Act that it is expedient in the public interest that a disqualification order shall be made against any person who is or has been a director or shadow director of any company. That is a matter on which the Secretary of State has to be so satisfied and the fact that he initiated and has carried through this application indicates that he is satisfied. It has not been suggested that in that respect he was wrong.

The court, however, has to make up its own mind. In particular, under sec. 8(2) of the Act, the court may only make a disqualification order if it is satisfied that the conduct of the individual in question in relation to "the company" makes him unfit to be concerned in the management of a company. The reference in subsec. (2) to "the company" clearly refers back to the company as to which the Secretary of State has to be satisfied under sec. 8(1). As I read those two subsections, it does not seem to me that it is limited to the company in relation to which the inspectors were appointed or in respect of which documents were obtained.

The circumstances leading up to the present application are somewhat complicated. They relate to a public company incorporated in England named Aldermanbury Trust plc. They relate also to two subsidiaries of that company. Those subsidiaries are a company which is conveniently referred to as KCP (its proper name is Key City Properties Ltd and it is incorporated in Gibraltar) and another company which started off as a subsidiary of KCP and became a subsidiary of Aldermanbury and which it is convenient to refer to as Cosita. I do not have its full name to hand, but it does not matter. That too is incorporated in Gibraltar.

In addition to being the recipient of a request for the production of documents under one or both of the sections I have referred to, Aldermanbury Trust plc has been the subject of an investigation under sec. 432 of the Companies Act carried out by Mr George Warren Staple and Mr Thomas Gregory James Tress. They delivered to the Secretary of State a detailed report on 11 December 1990. The matters alleged against Mr Fulcher are matters which are fully canvassed in that report which is admissible in evidence on this application. Had the hearing proceeded to a full trial of all the issues which arise, it would clearly have lasted a very considerable time. The estimate was I think 13–15 days and nothing which I have seen suggests that that was an underestimate.

In the event the parties have thought it possible to adopt a shortened form of procedure in reliance upon a decision which I gave in March of this year in a case called *Re Carecraft Construction Co Ltd* [1993] BCC 336. In that case I approved, subject to certain limitations, a method of disposing of applications under the Company Directors Disqualification Act, or at any rate under sec. 6 and 8 of that Act, which might avoid a full hearing of all the disputed issues.

What has happened here, as happened in the *Carecraft* case, is that the parties have prepared a schedule of facts which are either agreed or are facts alleged by one or other

of the parties, mostly by the Secretary of State, which the opposite party is content for   A
the purpose of this hearing not to dispute. On the basis of those agreed or undisputed
facts Mr Fulcher, through his representatives, accepts that his conduct has been such
that the court is likely to find him unfit to be concerned in the management of a company
for the purposes of sec. 8(2) of the Disqualification Act. Secondly, he has agreed not to
pursue two preliminary points of law which he otherwise wished to raise. Thirdly, he has
indicated that he does not argue strenuously against the making of a disqualification
order for a period which is towards the lower end of the middle bracket of periods   B
described in *Re Sevenoaks Stationers (Retail) Ltd* [1990] BCC 765 at p. 771H. In that
case the court of Appeal divided the possible period of disqualification (which is a
maximum of 15 years) into three brackets, one to five years being for the relatively
minor cases; 11–15 years being for the really serious cases involving a high level of
misconduct; and the middle bracket of from six to ten years being for cases which, whilst
still relatively serious, do not fall into the highest bracket.   C

I have already indicated to the parties that it seems to me that this is a case which I can
deal with by the procedure which I approved in the *Carecraft* case. In these circumstances
I think no useful purpose would be served by an attempt on my part to summarise the
relevant facts which, as I say, are quite complicated and the deployment of which in the
schedule of agreed or non-disputed facts runs to more than 20 pages with 131 separate
paragraphs. There should be treated as incorporated in this judgment the whole of the   D
schedule of agreed or non-disputed facts with its accompanying appendices dealing with
chronology.

On the basis of those agreed or non-disputed facts I have first to ask myself whether I
am satisfied of the requirement laid down by sec. 8(2), that is to say, whether I am
satisfied that the conduct of Mr Fulcher in relation to the company makes him unfit to be
concerned in the management of a company. The fact that this is accepted by Mr Fulcher
even though done on advice is not of course conclusive, nor is the fact that in relation to   E
the potential period of disqualification he accepts that this is not a case in the lowest
bracket. However, on this aspect of the matter there really is no doubt whatever in my
mind that the facts stated and agreed are such as to make Mr Fulcher unfit to be
concerned in the management of a company.

I have to say that I have had rather more anxiety about the next important question
which I have to consider, that is to say, whether it is satisfactory to proceed on the basis   F
of the agreed or non-disputed facts or whether if those issues on which there is no
agreement were fought to a conclusion and the facts were ascertained by the court, the
conduct of Mr Fulcher may be shown to be of a different and greater order of seriousness
than is implicit in the agreed or non-disputed facts. In that case it might be the duty of
the court to decline to allow the matter to be dealt with only on the agreed or non-
disputed facts. The matter has been fully canvassed before me. It does not appear to me
that there are other incidents or transactions which are not to a reasonable extent   G
covered by the agreed or non-disputed facts. In other words there are not whole areas or
transactions which are left unexplored. The aspects which have not been fully explored
relate mainly to such questions as Mr Fulcher's subjective outlook on the various
transactions, the degree of moral responsibility which he bears and matters of that kind.

It seems to me that, although a great deal of court time would be taken up if I were to
insist on going beyond the agreed or non-disputed facts, the court would be unlikely to   H
be in a very much better position to evaluate the conduct than it is on the basis of the
agreed or non-disputed facts. The prospect of the case appearing to be of a different
order of seriousness is not all that high.

Accordingly, I intend to proceed on the basis of the agreed or non-disputed facts.
I have to consider a number of charges which have been summarised in an affidavit

A sworn on behalf of the Secretary of State by Mr Osborne. I do not think that I need to go through those charges seriatim any more than I thought it necessary to go through the underlying facts.

I have to say that the picture which emerges from the agreed or non-disputed facts is one which reveals serious breaches on the part of Mr Fulcher of the provisions of general company law, of certain provisions of Aldermanbury's own articles and of r. 9 of the City Code on Takeovers and Mergers. The agreed or non-disputed facts also show a lamentable

B failure on Mr Fulcher's part to recognise and either avoid or resolve conflicts of interest. They involve substantial breaches on Mr Fulcher's part of the fiduciary duties which directors owe to the company of which they are directors, a failure to disclose proper information to shareholders who were being asked to approve certain important transactions and what appeared to me to be seriously flawed commercial judgments in relation to transactions and valuations which go beyond mere commercial foolishness.

C These commercial judgments had the result that transactions were carried out which ought not to have been carried out, as any director who had any reasonable appreciation of the duties which he owes to the company of which he is a director ought to have appreciated. In other words the misconduct of Mr Fulcher was of quite a high degree of seriousness.

I should say that I was at one time concerned as to the extent to which I could and

D should take into account the agreed or non-disputed facts which relate to Mr Fulcher's conduct as a director of KCP and to some extent Cosita, they being overseas companies. However, I have been satisfied that both KCP and Cosita are companies which fall within the purview of the Disqualification Act by virtue of the extended definition of the expression "company" contained in sec. 22(2)(b) of the Act. Moreover, even if I had felt inhibited in relation to KCP and Cosita, the fact remains that the affairs of Aldermanbury, KCP and Cosita were so interlocked on the relevant transactions that

E even if I had been obliged to leave on one side Mr Fulcher's conduct as a director of KCP and Cosita, his conduct as a director of Aldermanbury in relation to the very same transactions would have been something which would require the most serious consideration.

Having said all that and having indicated, as I have, that quite a high degree of seriousness is shown, I have to say that this is not a case which on any view falls into the

F highest category of misconduct which falls to be dealt with under the Disqualification Act. Nevertheless, in the absence of mitigation I would have been inclined to the view that the conduct is such as to merit a period of disqualification towards the upper end rather than the lower end of the middle bracket in the *Sevenoaks Stationers* case.

There is, however, substantial mitigation in this case. First and foremost, in relation to many of the transactions in which Mr Fulcher's conduct appears to me to be the most

G reprehensible, it is abundantly clear that Mr Fulcher was advised by solicitors. Indeed, in relation to one particular transaction, an agreement of June 1986 which was the final agreement under which Mr Fulcher acquired 90m shares in Aldermanbury Trust, the scheme (which is thoroughly objectionable) is said to have been devised by Mr Fulcher's solicitor. Moreover that scheme, if not given the approval, seems not to have attracted the positive dissent of at least one other firm of solicitors and other professionals.

H Mr Fulcher cannot of course escape his own responsibility for these matters because a director, whether he knows it or not, owes duties in relation to his company. But it seems to me to be quite clearly established that on a number of matters where one would have expected a competent legal adviser to advise Mr Fulcher in the most forthright terms that what was being proposed was simply improper, Mr Fulcher received no such advice. Moreover, that is not just something which Mr Fulcher says by way of mitigation. There is a high degree of corroboration of it both in the form of an affidavit sworn in these

proceedings by the solicitor himself and in the form of the account of the various   A
transactions which was given by the inspectors on the basis of evidence received by
them. It seems to me that that is most powerful mitigation of Mr Fulcher's conduct in
relation to many, if not most, of the more serious matters revealed by the agreed facts.

Beyond that it is an unfortunate fact that these proceedings have been hanging over
Mr Fulcher's head for a very considerable period of time. The events of which complaint
is made began in the year 1985 and most of them took place and were complete in the   B
year 1986 and to some extent 1987. The proceedings were brought in 1989 and they only
come on for hearing some four years later. That is not at all satisfactory. There are
explanations for it connected with the notorious ten-day notice point which has affected
a number of cases brought under this Act and which had to be resolved by the Court of
Appeal before this and other cases could proceed; and there have been, as I understand,
procedural delays on the part of both sides. It seems to me, however, that I ought to give
some credit for the fact that Mr Fulcher is now being brought to account under this   C
jurisdiction for matters which occurred a long time ago and he is being brought to
account in proceedings which have been hanging over his head for a considerable period
of time.

I must also take account of the fact there is no evidence of any real substance that
Mr Fulcher has made any personal profit out of any of these transactions. There were
suggestions that in some respects he either benefited or set up arrangements under   D
which he might benefit from the transactions, but these have either been brought to
nothing or have been reversed as a result of steps taken by Mr Fulcher himself. He has
made two substantial payments in respect of claims made against him. The first was a
payment to Aldermanbury in respect of Aldermanbury's money which he now recognises
was improperly applied in order to acquire certain Aldermanbury shares. The second
was a payment to KCP in respect of a claim by a KCP for moneys misappropriated.

There does not appear to be any doubt that Mr Fulcher himself has emerged from this   E
sorry series of transactions without employment and without assets. It is not a case
where he has in any respect been able to salt away sums of money for his own benefit.
He must also be given credit for what is in effect a plea of guilty.

In all the circumstances I think I can properly take the view that this case ought to be
dealt with by a period of disqualification towards the lower end of the middle bracket of
the *Sevenoaks* brackets. I do not feel able to go to the very bottom of that bracket, but I   F
think that justice will adequately be done and, perhaps more accurately, the public will
be sufficiently protected, if I impose a period of disqualification of seven years, which is
what I shall do.

(*Order accordingly. Mr Fulcher to pay the Secretary of State's costs to be taxed on the
standard basis, the order not to be enforced without the leave of the court. Legal aid
taxation of Mr Fulcher's costs. The disqualification order to take effect from   G
the date of judgment*)

A
Stanhope Pension Trust Ltd & Anor v Registrar of Companies & Anor.

Chancery Division (Companies Court).
His Honour Judge Weeks QC (sitting as a High Court judge).
Judgment delivered 17 May 1993.

B
Power of court to declare dissolution of company void — Landlord applied to have dissolution of original tenant avoided after tenant became insolvent — Original tenant would have claim against solvent assignees of underlease — Whether assignees should be joined as parties — Whether dissolution should be avoided — Companies Act 1985, sec. 651.

C
This was an appeal from two orders of the registrar, declaring the dissolution of a company void under sec. 651 of the Companies Act 1985 and refusing an application by the appellants to be joined as parties to the sec. 651 application.

The company was the lessee of premises which were subsequently assigned successively to the appellants, which were companies in the same group, and then to the Bank of Credit and Commerce International SA ("BCCI"). The company went into members' voluntary liquidation in 1988 and was as a consequence dissolved in 1992. BCCI was ordered to be wound up as insolvent in July 1991. The rent due in March 1992 was not paid and the liquidator disclaimed the leases involved in June 1992. The landlords then applied to have the original tenant's dissolution avoided: if that company was resurrected it could pursue its rights against the appellant assignees and the landlords could prove in its liquidation.

D

Held, ordering the appellants to be joined and dismissing the application to avoid the dissolution:

E
1. There was jurisdiction to add the appellants as parties under O. 15, r. 6(2)(b) of the Rules of the Supreme Court. Their presence was necessary to ensure that all matters in dispute in the case were effectually and completely determined in terms of the rule. First, because the appellants were the only source of funds to pay the landlords' proof, and the avoidance of the company's dissolution would directly affect them in their pocket. Secondly, if they did not argue against the avoidance no one would, because the defendants to the original application, that is the registrar and the liquidator, had indicated that they did not oppose the application.

F

2. The jurisdiction to avoid a dissolution ought not to be exercised to put the applicant for an order in a better position than he would have been in if the liquidation had been properly conducted and so to deprive third parties of benefits which had accrued to them during the course of the liquidation or thereafter. If the dissolution was avoided and the liquidation was reopened the landlords would not prove on the same basis as if they had proved in due time in the liquidation given that there were no arrears owing at the date of dissolution.

G

The following cases were referred to in the judgment:

Clarkson (H) (Overseas) Ltd, Re (1987) 3 BCC 606.
Gurtner v Circuit & Anor [1968] 2 QB 587.
H
House Property and Investment Co Ltd, Re [1954] Ch 576.
New Oriental Bank Corp, Re (No. 2) [1895] 1 Ch 753.
Portrafram Ltd, Re (1986) 2 BCC 99,160.
Servers of the Blind League, Re [1960] 1 WLR 564.
Spottiswoode, Dixon & Hunting Ltd, Re [1912] 1 Ch 410.
Workvale Ltd, Re [1991] BCC 109; [1991] 1 WLR 294.

Terence Etherton QC and James Ayliffe (instructed by Paisner & Co) for the   A
appellants.

Christopher Pymont (instructed by Jacques & Lewis) for the landlords.

JUDGMENT

His Honour Judge Weeks QC: It is now a notorious feature of English law that the
liability of a tenant to pay rent and to observe covenants persists during the continuance   B
of the lease, notwithstanding any assignment. When the current tenant fails to pay the
passing rent the landlord will often look to the original tenant, who will try in turn to
recover from the first assignee and so on down the chain. That is the situation in the
present case with two quirks. One is that the current tenant is in liquidation and the
liquidator has disclaimed the lease. The result is that the lease continues to exist until
the landlord chooses to forfeit or a vesting order is made, but the last tenant is under no
continuing liability to pay the rent. The other, and more important, unusual feature is   C
that the original tenant has gone into liquidation. The liquidation has been completed
and the company has been dissolved. The landlord therefore needs to have the dissolution
avoided in order to make a claim against the original tenant.

The matter comes before me on appeal from Mr Registrar *Buckley*, who made two
orders on 11 March 1993. By the first he refused an application by two intermediate
assignees to be joined as defendants. By the second he ordered the dissolution of the   D
original tenant to be avoided under sec. 651 of the *Companies Act* 1985. From those two
decisions the interveners appeal.

The original tenant is Forte's (Manufacturing) Ltd, a company incorporated under a
different name in 1896. On 31 December 1960 under its former name it took two
underleases of parts of 535, 537 and 539 Oxford Street, London W1 from Montague
Burton Ltd. The terms of those underleases will expire in the year 2002. The underleases   E
are registered at the Land Registry and the companies currently entitled to the reversion
are the respondents to this appeal, Stanhope Pension Trust Ltd and Custodian Holdings
Ltd.

On 28 January 1964, Forte's (Manufacturing) Ltd assigned both underleases to
another company in the Forte group, the first intervener, Post Inns Ltd, which also had
a previous name at the time. On 28 January 1967 Post Inns Ltd assigned both underleases
to the second intervener, which is now called Forte's Properties Ltd. On 4 February   F
1979, Forte's Properties Ltd assigned both underleases to Bank of Credit and Commerce
International SA ("BCCI"). All assignments were made with the consent of the current
lessor. After its assignment Forte's (Manufacturing) Ltd ceased to trade and became
dormant. The parent company decided to wind it up. A special resolution of Forte's
(Manufacturing) Ltd was passed on 27 October 1988, and on that date the company
went into members' voluntary liquidation. A declaration of solvency was made,   G
Mr Colin Bird was appointed liquidator, and the liquidation was duly advertised.
However, it is common ground that no specific notice was given to the landlords, and at
the time the liquidation did not come to their attention. On 8 November 1991 Mr Bird
filed his final report and three months later, on 8 February 1992, Forte's (Manufacturing)
Ltd was dissolved pursuant to sec. 201 of the *Insolvency Act* 1986.

In the meantime in January 1992 an order was made for the winding up of BCCI on a   H
petition presented to the High Court in July 1991. Until January 1992 the rent under
both underleases had been paid and there were no arrears owing, either at the date the
order was made for the liquidation of BCCI or at the date that Forte's (Manufacturing)
Ltd was dissolved. The liquidator of BCCI did not pay the instalment of rent which fell
due on the March quarter day, and on 10 June 1992 he disclaimed both underleases, so
terminating any further liability of BCCI.

A   On 17 December 1992 the landlords launched an application to avoid the dissolution of Forte's (Manufacturing) Ltd, and on 2 February 1993 the interveners applied to be joined on that application. Both applications came before Mr Registrar *Buckley* on 11 March 1993 with the result that I have mentioned.

The first issue I have to decide is whether the interveners should be joined to the application to avoid the dissolution. Their application is made under O. 15, r. 6(2) of the Rules of the Supreme Court which provides:

B

"Subject to the provisions of this rule, at any stage of the proceedings in any cause or matter the Court may on such terms as it thinks just and either of its own motion or on application—

. . .

C

(b)   order any of the following persons to be added as a party, namely—

(i)   any person who ought to have been joined as a party or whose presence before the Court is necessary to ensure that all matters in dispute in the cause or matter may be effectually and completely determined and adjudicated upon, or

(ii) any person between whom and any party to the cause or matter there may exist a question or issue arising out of or relating to or connected with any relief or remedy claimed in the cause or matter which in the opinion of the Court it would be just and convenient to determine as between him and that party as well as between the parties to the cause or matter."

D

Guidance in applying that subrule was given by the Court of Appeal in *Gurtner v Circuit & Anor* [1968] 2 QB 587. Lord *Denning* MR said at p. 595B:

E   "The relevant rule is the new R.S.C., Ord. 15, r. 6(2)(b), which says that the court may order any person to be added as a party

'whose presence before the court is necessary to ensure that all matters in dispute in the cause or matter may be effectually and completely determined and adjudicated upon.'

That rule is in substantially the same terms as the old R.S.C., Ord. 16, r. 11, and
F   nothing turns on the difference in wording. There were many cases decided on it. But I need not analyse them today. That was done by Devlin J. in *Amon* v. *Raphael Tuck & Sons Ltd.* [1956] 1 Q.B. 357. He thought that the rule should be given a narrower construction, and his views were followed by John Stephenson J. in *Fire Auto and Marine Insurance Ltd.* v. *Greene* [1964] 2 Q.B. 687. I am afraid that I do not agree with them. I prefer to give a wide interpretation to the rule, as Lord Esher M.R. did in *Byrne* v. *Brown* (1889) 22 Q.B.D. 657. It seems
G   to me that when two parties are in dispute in an action at law, and the determination of that dispute will directly affect a third person in his legal rights or in his pocket, in that he will be bound to foot the bill, then the court in its discretion may allow him to be added as a party on such terms as it thinks fit. By so doing, the court achieves the object of the rule. It enables all matters in dispute to 'be effectually and completely determined and adjudicated upon' between all those directly
H   concerned in the outcome."

At p. 596D Lord *Denning* said:

"It is thus apparent that the Motor Insurers' Bureau are vitally concerned in the outcome of the action. They are directly affected, not only in their legal rights, but also in their pocket. They ought to be allowed to come in as defendants. It would be most unjust if they were bound to stand idly by watching the plaintiff get

judgment against the defendant without saying a word when they are the people A
who have to foot the bill. I think that *Fire Auto & Marine Insurance Ltd.* v.
Greene was wrongly decided and should be overruled."

At p. 602G *Diplock* LJ said:

"Clearly the rules of natural justice require that a person who is to be bound by a
judgment in an action brought against another party and directly liable to the
plaintiff upon the judgment should be entitled to be heard in the proceedings in B
which the judgment is sought to be obtained. A matter in dispute is not, in my
view, effectually and completely '*adjudicated upon*' unless the rules of natural
justice are observed and all those who will be liable to satisfy the judgment are
given an opportunity to be heard. In the case of an ordinary insurer, this does not
arise in practice, since the standard terms of a third-party liability policy give to
the insurer a contractual right to conduct the defence of the running-down action
in the name of the assured. But as I read his judgment in the *Fire Auto & Marine* C
case, John Stephenson J. would have allowed an ordinary insurer to be added as a
party to a running-down action if the policy of insurance did not contain such a
term. And this, I think, would be right.

I do not think the rules of natural justice depend upon a technicality as to the
procedure by which the liability of a person who is bound to satisfy the judgment
obtained by the plaintiff in the running-down action is enforceable. So long as it is D
legally enforceable against that person either directly by the plaintiff or indirectly
by the Minister for the plaintiff's benefit under such a contract as exists in the
present case, the court has jurisdiction to add that person as a party and ought
normally to exercise its discretion by granting his application to be added. I think,
therefore, that the bureau is entitled to be added as a party to the present action
and to this extent, at any rate, this appeal should be allowed."

E
The rule was specifically applied to an application under sec. 651 of the Companies
Act by *Harman* J in *Re Workvale Ltd* [1991] BCC 109. *Harman* J did not refer to
his earlier decision in *Re Portrafram Ltd* (1986) 2 BCC 99,160 in which he appears to
have held that O. 15, r. 6 did not apply to an application under what is now sec. 653
of the Companies Act. I think it right therefore to treat the decision in *Re Portrafram
Ltd* as a decision under sec. 653 only. In so far as it is applicable to sec. 651, I prefer to
follow *Re Workvale*. I observe that in *Re H Clarkson (Overseas) Ltd* (1987) 3 BCC 606 F
Hoffmann J was referred to *Re Portrafram Ltd* but was prepared to assume for the
purposes of his case that there was jurisdiction under O. 15, r. 6 to join a party to a sec.
653 application.

I therefore hold that I have jurisdiction. I now have to decide whether the presence of
the interveners is necessary to ensure that all matters in dispute in the case may be
effectually and completely determined. I have no doubt that it is for two reasons: first, G
because the interveners are now the only source of the funds to pay the applicant's
proof, and the avoidance of Forte's (Manufacturing) Ltd's dissolution will directly affect
them in their pocket. The avowed purpose of the respondents in trying to resurrect
Forte's (Manufacturing) Ltd is to extract money from the interveners. Mr Prevett's
affidavit in support said in para. 7:

"It is the plaintiffs' contention that, if the dissolution of this company is declared
void, the company can pursue its own rights of action against the company to H
which it assigned the underleases under the indemnity provided by sec. 24(1)(b)
of the *Land Registration Act* 1925. This will enable funds to be available in the
liquidation from which a distribution can be made to the plaintiffs."

Secondly, if the interveners do not argue against the avoidance no one will, because
the defendants to the original application, that is the registrar and the liquidator, have

A indicated that they do not oppose the application. It would be unjust for the interveners to have to stand idly by, watching the landlords have the dissolution avoided and proving against Forte's (Manufacturing) Ltd when they are the people who have to foot the bill at the end of the day. Their interest appears to me similar to the insurer's interest in *Re Workvale Ltd*, and I do not think that decision should be read as limited to cases where the point is one of limitation.

B I therefore allow the first appeal and order the interveners to be joined as defendants.

It was common ground that there is no further evidence to be filed and that I should proceed to determine the second issue, namely whether the dissolution ought to be avoided. The jurisdiction arises under sec. 651(1) of the Companies Act, "Power of court to declare dissolution of company void", which reads:

C "Where a company has been dissolved, the court may, on an application made for the purpose by the liquidator of the company or by any other person appearing to the court to be interested, make an order, on such terms as the court thinks fit, declaring the dissolution to have been void."

I have no doubt that the applicants for the order, that is the respondents to the present appeal, are persons who "appear to the court to be interested".

There is no help in the Act itself and very little authority in law as to how the discretion D should be exercised. From what decisions there have been on sec. 651 and its predecessors, that is sec. 223 of the 1908 Act and sec. 352 of the 1948 Act, I can I think extract two principles. One is that generally the jurisdiction ought to be exercised to allow creditors to prove who, through no fault of their own, have had no earlier opportunity to prove, and so to prevent liabilities from being, whether intentionally or inadvertently, escaped by the process of liquidation. This was the situation which would have occurred if *Neville* J had not made the order which he did in *Re Spottiswoode, Dixon & Hunting Ltd* [1912] E 1 Ch 410.

The second principle is that exceptionally the jurisdiction ought not to be exercised to put the applicant for an order in a better position than he would have been in if the liquidation had been properly conducted and so to deprive third parties of benefits which have accrued to them during the course of the liquidation or thereafter. This principle I derive from *Re Servers of the Blind League* [1960] 1 WLR 564 where F *Pennycuick* J declined to make an order avoiding a dissolution of a company which was a beneficiary under the will of a testatrix who died after the dissolution was complete.

At first sight this case falls within the first general principle, but I have been persuaded by Mr Etherton for the interveners that in fact it falls within the second exceptional principle. If the landlords had proved in due time in the liquidation of Forte's (Manufacturing) Ltd they could then have proved only for the loss of the original G tenant's covenant, because the rent continued to be paid until December 1991. This loss could not have been passed on to the first assignee because the covenant implied by sec. 24 of the Land Registration Act, and for that matter the covenant implied by sec. 77 of the *Law of Property Act* 1925, is an indemnity covenant only, and no breach of that covenant occurred until the rent was not paid in March 1992. On the other hand, if the dissolution is avoided and the liquidation is now reopened the landlords will prove on one of three bases. Mr Pymont for the landlords accepts that there is no fourth basis on H which they could prove.

One of those three bases is for the loss of the tenant's covenant, valued now taking into account BCCI's financial position. This may well be the proper basis of proof having regard to *Re House Property and Investment Co Ltd* [1954] Ch 576 and the provisions of the Insolvency Rules, in particular r. 12.3, 13.12, 4.86 and 4.92, but I make no decision on that aspect. The important point is that again this is not a loss which could be laid at

A

the door of the interveners. There would be no point in restoring the company simply to allow a claim to be made which there were no assets to meet.

The second basis is for the rent due at the date of proof and a commuted sum for future rents. The third basis is for rent, again accrued due at the date of proof, with a reservation of a claim for future rents. Either of these bases may be consistent with the practice at least until the *Insolvency Act* 1986: see *Re New Oriental Bank Corp (No. 2)* [1895] 1 Ch 753. However, the important point is that a claim for rent is one which does fall within the scope of the indemnity covenant and which, if admitted, the first intervener would have to meet. That liability did not arise until March 1992 and would not have arisen in the ordinary course of winding up Forte's (Manufacturing) Ltd.

B

In the circumstances of the present case it seems to me that there will be no point in avoiding the dissolution unless the interveners are to be subjected to a liability which would not normally have arisen if the liquidation had pursued its usual course. In my judgment it would be unjust to the interveners if the dissolution were avoided, and that injustice outweighs the injustice to the respondents if the dissolution were not avoided. Accordingly, in my discretion I will allow the second appeal and dismiss the application to avoid the dissolution.

C

(*Order accordingly*)

D

E

F

G

H

A
Re Shoe Lace Ltd.
Power v Sharp Investments Ltd & Anor.
Court of Appeal (Civil Division).
Ralph Gibson and Nolan L JJ and Sir Christopher Slade.
Judgment delivered 20 May 1993.

B
> *Insolvency — Avoidance of floating charges — Whether advances were "at the same time as" creation of floating charge — Whether floating charge invalidated after commencement of winding up or only after winding-up order made — Whether clause in debenture charging assets by way of legal mortgage covered only immovable assets — Whether liquidator's case justified interim payment — Insolvency Act 1986, sec. 245.*

C
This was an appeal from an order of Hoffmann J (see [1992] BCC 367) for Sharp Investments Ltd to make an interim payment to the liquidator of Shoe Lace Ltd in respect of a claim by the liquidator that a debenture given by Shoe Lace to Sharp was invalid and for repayment of the proceeds of sale of Shoe Lace's business which were paid to Sharp after a petition was presented for the winding up of Shoe Lace.

D
Sharp was a Jersey company which held 80 per cent of Shoe Lace's issued share capital. Shoe Lace's directors resolved in March 1990, when the company had exhausted its banking facilities, to obtain further financial support from Sharp and give Sharp a debenture to secure past and future advances. Sharp then advanced £300,000 to the company on 3 April; £50,000 in May; £75,000 in June and a final payment of £11,500 on 16 July. The debenture was not executed until 24 July. The debenture contained fixed and floating charges.

E
A winding-up petition was presented in September 1990. Before the winding-up order was made the company sold all its assets and the proceeds were passed to Sharp as debenture holder.

The floating charge having been created at a relevant time within the meaning of sec. 245(3) of the Insolvency Act 1986, the main issue before the judge was whether the payments made by Sharp between 3 April and 16 July 1990 could be said to have been made "at the same time as" the creation of the charge under sec. 245(2)(a).

F
The judge first held on the construction of the debenture that a clause charging "all assets" by way of legal mortgage covered only immovable assets.

On sec. 245(2)(a), Hoffmann J applied a test of whether a businessman would say that the payments had been made at the same time as the execution of the debenture. He concluded that no businessman having knowledge of the kind of time-limits imposed by the Insolvency and Companies Acts and using ordinary language would say that the payments had been made at the same time as the execution of the debenture.

G
Hoffmann J then held that to obtain an interim payment under RSC, O. 29, r. 10 the liquidator had to show a case of a strength justifying judgment under O. 14, subject to O. 14A (disposal of case on point of law) and that the construction of sec. 245 was something which could be decided without a full trial of the liquidator's summons and whose determination would finally dispose of the question of the validity of the floating charge because it meant that even on the respondent's own evidence, the charge must be invalid. He accordingly made an order for interim payment.

H
Sharp appealed. In reliance on Re Columbian Fireproofing Co Ltd [1910] 2 Ch 120 and Re F & E Stanton Ltd [1929] 1 Ch 180, Sharp submitted that a payment made on account of the consideration for the security, in anticipation of its creation and in reliance on a promise to execute it, although made some days before its execution, was made "at the same time as the creation of the charge" within the meaning of sec. 245(2)(a).

Sharp submitted, in the alternative, that sec. 245 of the 1986 Act on its true construction took effect only from the date of the winding-up order (20 November 1990) and that accordingly the sale by Shoe Lace of its assets subject to the floating charge and payment of the sale proceeds to Sharp on 13 September 1990 were not avoided by sec. 245. This point was not argued before Hoffmann J.

Thirdly, Sharp submitted that the judge was wrong in holding that the proceeds of sale of various movable assets were not subject to the fixed charge provisions of the debenture, and were thus subject to the floating charge. Fourthly, it was submitted that the judge was wrong in holding that RSC, O. 14A, r. 1 was applicable since the issue under sec. 245(2) was a matter partly of fact and partly of law and not a question of law.

Held, dismissing Sharp's appeal:

1. The words "at the same time as, or after, the creation of the charge" in sec. 245 of the 1986 Act were clearly included by the legislature for the purpose of excluding from the exemption the amount of moneys paid to the company before the creation of the charge, even though they were paid in consideration for the charge. (Re Columbian Fireproofing Co Ltd [1910] 2 Ch 120 and Re F & E Stanton Ltd [1929] 1 Ch 180 not followed.)

2. In a case where no charge had been created by an agreement or company resolution preceding the execution of the formal debenture, then no moneys paid before the execution of the debenture would qualify for the exemption under the subsection, unless the interval between payment and execution was so short that it could be regarded as minimal and payment and execution could be regarded as contemporaneous.

3. Section 245 did not apply in the case of a compulsory liquidation until the winding-up order was made, but as soon as the order was made it related back to earlier transactions, and invalidated the charge from the commencement of the winding up, i.e. the date of presentation of the petition. (Mace Builders (Glasgow) Ltd v Lunn (1986) 2 BCC 99,532 applied.)

4. A number of factors strongly supported the judge's finding that the word "assets" in the charging clause meant only immovable assets.

5. The liquidator had shown a case which would justify judgment under RSC, O. 14A. There was no difficulty in formulating the relevant question of law; even on Sharp's own evidence as to the facts, the floating charge must be invalidated by sec. 245.

The following cases were referred to in the judgment of Sir Christopher Slade:

Columbian Fireproofing Co Ltd, Re [1910] 1 Ch 758; [1910] 2 Ch 120 (CA).
Fairway Magazines Ltd, Re [1992] BCC 924.
Jackson & Bassford Ltd, Re [1906] 2 Ch 467.
Mace Builders (Glasgow) Ltd v Lunn (1986) 2 BCC 99,532; [1987] Ch 191.
Margart Pty Ltd, Re; Hamilton v Westpac Banking Corp & Anor (1984) 2 ACLC 709.
Milbury Homes (North) Ltd v Arthur Young (unreported, 6 February 1992, Millett J).
Orleans Motor Co Ltd, Re [1911] 2 Ch 41.
Stanton (F & E) Ltd, Re [1929] 1 Ch 180.

John Briggs (instructed by McKenna & Co) for the appellant.

Daniel Serota QC and Paul Lowenstein (instructed by Fruhman Davies & Co, Manchester) for the liquidator.

JUDGMENT

Sir Christopher Slade: With the leave of the judge, Sharp Investments Ltd ("Sharp") appeals from an order of *Hoffmann* J made on 20 December 1991, whereby it was ordered, pursuant to the provisions of RSC, O. 29, r. 12 and O. 14A, that Sharp should

A   make an interim payment to Mr D J Power, as the liquidator of Shoe Lace Ltd ("Shoe Lace"), of the sum of £134,710 (see [1992] BCC 367).

Shoe Lace was incorporated in January 1989 and traded as a retailer and later as a mail-order supplier of shoes between April 1989 and September 1990. Sharp is a company registered in Jersey and holds 80 per cent of the issued shares in Shoe Lace. The other 20 per cent of the shares are held by Mr Barry Fox, who was until 28 August 1990 managing director of Shoe Lace.

B

Sharp itself is a Jersey registered company, which has at all material times been managed and run by offshore directors and has no place of business in the UK. Mr Mahtani, who is the second respondent to the original proceedings but is not represented on this appeal, is the protector of the Poppsy trust, which is alleged to be the owner of Sharp. He is a businessman who lives in Rantingen in Germany, where he acts as director of a footwear company called Teejoomals. It is alleged that he controls Sharp through the medium of the Poppsy trust and that he acted as a shadow director of Shoe Lace. Until he resigned on 3 September 1990, Mr Samuel Nolan, a chartered accountant resident in Jersey, was a director of Sharp. He was also a director of Shoe Lace.

C

Minutes of meetings of the directors of Shoe Lace, attended by Mr Nolan and Mr Fox, record that on 6 February 1990 it was resolved that Sharp should be approached "with a request to provide short term finance to meet the company's requirements for the next 3–6 months" and that "should it be a requirement of such finance, the company would be prepared to grant a debenture over its assets in favour of Sharp". They further record that on 20 March 1990:

D

> "It was agreed to obtain financial support from [Sharp] and give the requisite debenture. It was also agreed that in consideration of further time being given by [Sharp] for the repayment of the moneys advanced by [Sharp] the proposed debenture in favour of [Sharp] should also include and secure the moneys already advanced."

E

According to the evidence of Sharp's solicitor, Sharp, which had already made substantial advances to Shoe Lace, subsequently advanced to Shoe Lace £300,000 on 3 April, £50,000 in May, £75,000 in June and £11,500 on 16 July 1990.

At last, on 24 July 1990, the debenture was executed, signed by Mr Nolan on behalf of Shoe Lace and by Mr Nugent, a director of Sharp, on its behalf. Clauses 1 and 3 of this debenture, so far as material, read as follows:

F

> "1. Shoelace as beneficial owner and to the intent that the security created shall rank as a continuing security hereby charges with the payment or discharge of all moneys obligations and liabilities hereby covenanted to be paid or discharged . . .

> (i) by way of legal mortgage all assets (the legally mortgaged property) and/or the proceeds of sale thereof,

G

> (ii) by way of specific equitable charge all estates or interests in any freehold and leasehold property (except the legally mortgaged property) now and at any time during the continuance of this security belonging to or charged to Shoelace (the equitably charged property) and/or the proceeds of sale thereof,

H

> (iii) by way of specific charge all stocks shares and/or other securities now and at any time during the continuance of this security belonging to Shoelace in any of its subsidiary companies or any other company and all dividends and other rights in relation thereto,

> (iv) by way of specific charge all book debts and other debts now and from time to time due or owing to Shoelace,

　　(v)　by way of specific charge its goodwill and the benefit of any licences,　　　A

　　(vi)　by way of floating security its undertaking and all its property assets and rights whatsoever present and/or future including those for the time being charged by way of specific charge pursuant to the foregoing paragraphs if and to the extent that such charges as aforesaid shall fail as specific charges but without prejudice to any such specific charges as shall continue to be effective.　　　B

. . .

3. With reference to the legally mortgaged property and the equitably charged property Shoelace agrees:

　　(i)　to keep it in a good state of repair and condition and insured against such risks and in such office and for such amount as Sharp may require or approve and that failure to do so will entitle Sharp to do so at the expense of　　C Shoelace and as agent of Shoelace without thereby becoming a mortgagee in possession,

　　(ii)　that the statutory power of leasing and/or accepting surrenders of leases conferred on mortgagors shall not be exercised by Shoelace without the consent in writing of Sharp but Sharp may grant or accept surrenders of leases without restriction,　　　D

　　(iii)　not to part with the possession of it or any part thereof nor confer upon any person firm company or body whatsoever any licence right or interest to occupy it or any part thereof without the consent in writing of Sharp."

Clause 17 provided that the charge should be governed by and construed in accordance with English law.

While cl. 1 of the debenture created a charge to secure the payment of "all moneys　E . . . hereby covenanted to be paid", as the judge observed (at p. 368D):

"It is a curiosity of this document that it contains no covenant to pay anything, but the registered particulars describe it as an all moneys charge and I shall assume that, other things being equal, it could be rectified to correspond with this description."

The correctness of this assumption has not been challenged in this court. In this　F context, however, the judge continued:

"There is a fixed charge by way of legal mortgage over 'all assets . . . and the proceeds of sale thereof'. This looks like an improbable attempt to create a fixed charge over all assets including, for example, the stock in trade and the cash at bank and even in the till. But the covenants concerning the legally mortgaged property in cl. 3 are appropriate only to land and in my judgment 'all assets' means　G in context 'all immovable assets'."

The judge's conclusion that "all assets" in cl. 1 means "all immovable assets" is challenged on this appeal and I shall revert to this point.

On 13 August 1990, the debenture was registered pursuant to sec. 395 of the *Companies Act* 1985 ("the 1985 Act").

　　　　　　　　　　　　　　　　　　　　　　　　　　　　　　　　　　H

As the judge found, the trading history of Shoe Lace is difficult to reconstruct with accuracy because the liquidator has been unable to obtain its statutory books or accounting records and the directors have given him no assistance. The available evidence, however, shows that by February 1990 it had exhausted its banking facilities, by April 1990 it was hopelessly insolvent and its position thereafter became steadily worse.

A   On 3 September 1990, at a meeting of the directors of Shoe Lace, it was resolved that they should,

> "immediately attempt to dispose of the assets of the company in order to generate cash to meet the claims of all creditors."

At that meeting Mr Nolan resigned as a director of Shoe Lace with immediate effect. On 4 September 1990, a petition was presented for its compulsory winding up. It was served at the company's trading address on the same day and was duly served on its registered

B   office on 11 September 1990.

On 13 September 1990, Shoe Lace entered into a "sale of business agreement" ("the sale agreement") whereby it sold the retail part of its business, together with stock, fixtures, fittings and equipment to Shoe Hut Ltd, described by the judge as "another Channel Island company". The consideration for the purchase was £211,000 of which

C   £41,000 was expressed to be allocated to the immovable property and £5,000 to the goodwill. On completion of the sale agreement, on 13 September 1990, Shoe Hut Ltd paid direct to Sharp the sum of £180,710 in recognition of the rights asserted by Sharp as debenture holder. The balance was retained by Shoe Hut Ltd in respect of part of a stock of shoes to which a third party, named E F Clasters Ltd, claimed title.

On 20 November 1990, Shoe Lace was compulsorily wound up. On the next day,

D   Mr D J Power was appointed its liquidator. He instituted proceedings against Sharp and Mr Mahtani seeking (inter alia) a declaration that the debenture was invalid and also repayment of £180,710. On 15 February 1991, *Harman* J made an order freezing the £180,710 in Sharp's bank account. The liquidator then applied to *Hoffmann* J under RSC, O. 29, r. 10 for an interim payment in respect of the liquidator's claim for return of that sum. As the judge observed, that claim raised a number of issues with which for the purposes of the application before him he need not be concerned (at p. 368G):

E

> "So for example the liquidator says that Sharp, Shoe Lace and Shoe Hut were all controlled by Mr Mahtani. In an affidavit sworn in other proceedings Mr Mahtani admits to being a director of Shoe Hut but says that he had nothing to do with Sharp or Shoe Lace except to supply the latter with shoes. His solicitor however says that Sharp is owned by a standard Jersey discretionary trust in which Mr Mahtani is named as protector and which was intended to benefit his family

F

> . . . His lack of connection would make it difficult to explain such things as why the directors should in February 1990 have chosen to hold a meeting of the board in Rantingen. In my view there is a high probability that Shoe Hut is a phoenix company and that Shoe Lace was also controlled by Mr Mahtani."

Another significant issue raised by the liquidator's claim was an assertion that the debenture was a wrongful preference, in that it purported to create Sharp a secured

G   creditor of Shoe Lace in prejudice to the position of all other creditors of Shoe Lace. The judge, however, found it unnecessary to decide these other issues because the principal ground upon which the liquidator founded his application was that the floating charge created by the debenture was invalidated by sec. 245 of the *Insolvency Act* 1986 ("the 1986 Act"), of which the relevant parts read as follows:

> "(1) This section applies as does section 238 . . .

H

> (2) Subject as follows, a floating charge on the company's undertaking or property created at a relevant time is invalid except to the extent of the aggregate of—

>> (a) the value of so much of the consideration for the creation of the charge as consists of money paid, or goods or services supplied, to the company at the same time as, or after, the creation of the charge,

. . .

(3) Subject to the next subsection, the time at which a floating charge is created   A
by a company is a relevant time for the purposes of this section if the charge is
created—

> (a) in the case of a charge which is created in favour of a person who is
> connected with the company, at a time in the period of 2 years ending with
> the onset of insolvency,

> (b) in the case of a charge which is created in favour of any other person, at a   B
> time in the period of 12 months ending with the onset of insolvency . . .

(4) Where a company creates a floating charge at a time mentioned in subsection
(3)(b) and the person in favour of whom the charge is created is not connected
with the company, that time is not a relevant time for the purposes of this section
unless the company—

> (a) is at that time unable to pay its debts within the meaning of section 123 in   C
> Chapter VI of Part IV . . .

(5) For the purposes of subsection (3), the onset of insolvency is—
. . .

> (b) in a case where this section applies by reason of a company going into
> liquidation, the date of the commencement of the winding up.''

In the present case the winding up commenced on 4 September 1990, the date of   D
presentation of the petition: sec. 129(2) of the 1986 Act.

The judge held, and it is now common ground, that in the present case:

(1)   the floating charge created by the debenture dated 24 July 1990 was created within
       a period of merely two months before "the onset of insolvency" (4 September
       1990);
                                                                                        E
(2)   this floating charge was therefore created at "a relevant time";

(3)   at the date of creation, Shoe Lace was "unable to pay its debts" within the
       meaning of sec. 123 of the 1986 Act;

(4)   the floating charge was therefore invalid, except to the extent of,

> "the value of so much of the consideration for the creation of the charge as consists
> of money paid . . . to the company at the same time as, or after, the creation of   F
> the charge . . .''

In the circumstances, the judge said that the only real issue was whether any of the
payments alleged to have been made by Sharp between early April and 16 July 1990
could be said to have been made "at the same time as" the execution of the debenture.
He held that none of these payments could be so described. He concluded (at p. 371C):

> "For the purpose of obtaining an interim payment, the applicant must show a case   G
> of a strength justifying judgment under RSC, O. 14. This is subject to RSC,
> O. 14A, which enables the court to decide a question of law if it appears suitable
> for determination without full trial and such determination will finally determine
> 'the entire cause or matter' or will dispose of an issue in the cause. I think that the
> construction of sec. 245 is something which can be decided without a full trial of
> the liquidator's summons and that the determination will finally dispose of the
> question of the validity of the floating charge because it means that even on the   H
> respondent's own evidence, the charge must be invalid.

There remains the question of how much of the payment of £180,710 the liquidator
is entitled to recover. The sale agreement allocated £41,000 to the immovable
property and £5,000 to the goodwill. Both of these were subject to fixed charges
which, although possibly voidable on other grounds, do not fall within sec. 245.

A

This means that for the purpose of an interim payment, the sum which in my opinion it would be just to order to be paid to the liquidator out of the frozen funds is £134,710."

The judge so ordered. Mr Briggs, on behalf of Shoe Lace, presents his appeal to this court from this order on four grounds, which I will consider in turn.

The first ground of appeal

B

First and foremost, it is submitted that the judge erred in concluding that none of the payments alleged to have been made by Sharp to Shoe Lace between early April and 16 July 1990 can be said to have been made "at the same time" as the execution of the debenture, within the meaning of sec. 245 of the 1986 Act. Since the debenture was not executed until 24 July 1990, the judge's conclusion would, at first sight, appear difficult to challenge. As he recognised, however, two earlier authorities demonstrate or suggest

C

that a bare reference to the calendar may not necessarily provide the right answer to this crucial question of time. Since these two earlier cases formed the sheet anchor of Mr Briggs' argument on his first ground of appeal, I think it will be necessary to review in some detail both the decisions themselves and their legislative background.

A predecessor of sec. 245, namely sec. 212 of the *Companies (Consolidation) Act* 1908 ("the 1908 Act") provided:

D

"Where a company is being wound up, a floating charge on the undertaking or property of the company created within three months of the commencement of the winding up shall, unless it is proved that the company immediately after the creation of the charge was solvent, be invalid, except to the amount of any cash paid to the company at the time of or subsequently to the creation of, and in consideration for, the charge . . ."

The purpose of this provision was described by *Parker* J in *Re Orleans Motor Co Ltd*

E

[1911] 2 Ch 41 at p. 45 as being,

"to prevent companies on their last legs from creating floating charges to secure past debts or for moneys which do not go to swell their assets and become available for creditors."

It had to be read and applied alongside another provision in the 1908 Act which was designed (broadly) to prevent persons claiming to be secured creditors of a company on

F

its liquidation unless other creditors had been given the opportunity to acquire notice of the relevant charge by its registration. Section 93 of the 1908 Act provided that a charge created by a company and falling within various specified descriptions, including a floating charge, should, so far as any security on the company's property or undertaking was thereby conferred, be void against the liquidator and any creditor of the company unless the prescribed particulars of the charge were registered within 21 days after the date of its creation.

G

In *Re Jackson & Bassford Ltd* [1906] 2 Ch 467, *Buckley* J (at p. 477) drew an important distinction between two classes of case, namely,

(1)   an agreement to give security which was "so expressed as to create a present equitable right to a security" and was thus registrable; and

(2)   an agreement to give security which was so expressed as to be "merely an agreement that in some future circumstances a security shall in the future be

H

created" (which would not require registration).

As to class (1), it should be observed that in equity a floating charge is created by a contract evidenced in writing and for valuable consideration to execute, when required, a formal mortgage by way of floating charge (see *Halsbury's Laws of England* (4th ed.) vol. 32, para. 437 and 439). If the floating charge relates to a limited company's property or undertaking, it is registrable.

In *Re Columbian Fireproofing Co Ltd* [1910] 1 Ch 758, the directors of a company on 25 November 1909 accepted an offer by S to advance £1,000 upon the security of all the property of the company and passed a resolution that a debenture to be prepared by S should be executed at the next board meeting. S, relying on the resolution, then paid £350 and on 2 December 1909 a further £350 to the company on account of the £1,000. At the next board meeting, on 6 December 1909, the debenture was duly executed. S then paid the balance of £300 to the company and registered the debenture on 23 December 1909. The company went into liquidation in January 1910 and the liquidator disputed the validity of the debenture. His counsel, in the course of argument, referred to *Re Jackson & Bassford Ltd*. He submitted in effect that the debenture holder was on the horns of a dilemma. Either the resolution of 25 November created a present equitable charge, in which case, not having been registered within the due time, it was void against the liquidator under sec. 93 of the 1908 Act. Alternatively, if that resolution merely constituted an agreement that at some future time a charge would be given, then the two sums of £350 were advanced not "at the time of" but before the creation of the security. *Neville* J, in giving judgment, by necessary inference rejected the submission that the resolution created a present equitable charge. He expressly held that the whole £1,000 was advanced "at the time of the creation of the charge". He said (at p. 765):

> "I think whether any particular payment comes within these words must always be a question of fact depending upon the circumstances of the particular case. The word 'time' in this connection must always be to some extent indefinite, for the creation of the security and the payment of the money cannot be simultaneous . . ."

He went on to say:

> ". . . I think that a payment made on account of the consideration for the security, in anticipation of its creation and in reliance on a promise to execute it, although made some days before its execution, is made at the time of its creation within the meaning of the section."

The Court of Appeal ([1910] 2 Ch 120) endorsed *Neville* J's judgment without qualification, both as to the point based on sec. 93 of the 1908 Act and as to that based on sec. 212. In the latter context, *Cozens-Hardy* MR said this (at p. 123):

> "It was conceded by counsel for the appellant that the word 'at' does not mean contemporaneously with or immediately in exchange for the security or at the same moment as the security itself is created. It is a question of fact under all the circumstances of the case . . ."

Farwell LJ (at p. 123) said:

> "In my opinion it would be disastrous if we were to strain the words of a provision like this in order to invalidate bona fide honest transactions carried out in accordance with the usual course of business. It is plain to my mind that any cash paid to the company 'at the time' cannot mean on the stroke of the clock or even within the same twenty-four hours. As Neville J. has justly remarked, it is not a question of the clock; it is a question of what are the circumstances of each particular case . . ."

The *Columbian Fireproofing* case was one where the formal instrument was executed within 11 days from the date of the agreement and was registered 17 days after that. In some later cases, however, the delay has been much greater. In *Re F & E Stanton Ltd* [1929] 1 Ch 180, moneys were advanced in reliance on a promise to execute debentures creating a floating charge on the company's property by way of security. No less than 54 days elapsed after the first advance, and five days after the last advance, before the debentures were actually executed on 20 January 1926. The company went into liquidation

A

on 25 January 1926. *Maugham* J, in giving judgment, referred to *Re Columbian Fireproofing Co Ltd* and cited the second of the passages from *Neville* J's judgment quoted above. He continued (at p. 193):

> "I have not a doubt here, as I have already said, that the payments were made on account of the consideration and in anticipation of its creation and in reliance on a promise to execute, and the real difficulty is whether the lapse of time which took place between that promise and between the payments made in reliance on that promise and the actual date of the issue of the debentures is so long that I ought to hold that the exception in the section does not apply. In that matter I have two other cases which seem to help me to some extent. One is an Irish case of *In re Olderfleet Shipbuilding Co.*, and the other is an unreported case of *In re Nathan, Hope & Son, Ld.*, where the judgment of Romer J. was delivered on June 5, 1924. I have had the advantage of reading a shorthand note of the judgment in that case. In both of those cases there was a substantial delay between the dates of the payment in reliance on the promise to issue debentures and the date upon which the debentures were secured, and, in fact, in the case before Romer J., there was a delay of not less than sixty-seven days after the first advance and fifteen days after the last advance, before the issue of the debentures. In the present case the delay is serious, but not so serious as that . . .

B

C

> Now I am myself strongly of opinion that the exception in s. 212 in regard to cash advances at the time will not avail the debenture holder if the delay in the issue of the debenture is one which he has himself procured or suggested, or if the delay is one in which he has in any true sense acquiesced. I am not thinking of a delay such as would ordinarily be necessary for the passing of the resolution and the consideration of the form of the debenture and its actual execution, because the four or five days necessary in most cases to do those things is clearly not a delay which, according to the authority of the first case I have mentioned, the *Columbian Fireproofing* case, would be sufficient to invalidate the debentures if the cash had been or was being paid. But I think a delay greater than that requires explanation. In the present case I think there is sufficient explanation in the circumstances which I have mentioned, and I come to the conclusion as a fact that the delay was not acquiesced in by either [of the debenture holders]."

D

E

F

Maugham J concluded that, as a matter of fact, the sums in question were paid, within the true meaning of sec. 212 of the 1908 Act, "at the time of the creation of the charge and in consideration for the charge".

In the present case, *Hoffmann* J expressed his conclusions thus (at p. 369G):

> "There is no authority upon the meaning of 'at the same time as' in sec. 245. The degree of contemporaneity which such words connote must depend upon the context . . . In sec. 245, the context is commercial and regulatory. For example, it forms part of a scheme which includes the requirement that particulars of a floating charge must be delivered to the registrar of companies within 21 days of its creation. The question, I think, is whether a businessman having knowledge of the kind of time-limits imposed by the Insolvency and Companies Acts and using ordinary language would say that the payments had been made at the same time as the execution of the debenture.

G

> In my judgment no businessman would use such language of the payments made in this case. He would say (taking the respondent's evidence at face value) that the parties had agreed in March that a debenture should be granted, that a number of payments were made in consideration of that promise, but that for one reason or another, they did not get round to executing the debenture until afterwards. The respondent's solicitor Mr Pugh says that it was not executed earlier because

H

Mr Nolan, who was a director of both Sharp and Shoe Lace, was dilatory. He   A
thought that as Shoe Lace had agreed to grant the debenture, there was no
urgency about its execution. In other words, he had not read sec. 245."

Later in this judgment, after reference to the authorities, the judge said (at p. 371B):

"I mention these cases but I derive no principle from them except that stated by
the Court of Appeal in *Columbian Fireproofing*, namely that the question is one
of fact, or more precisely, whether the language of the statute appropriately   B
describes the facts of the particular case. So far as the language of sec. 245 of the
Insolvency Act 1986 differs from that of the 1908 Act, I think that the words 'at
the same time as' only emphasise that contemporaneity is an objective matter. If I
am wrong about this and need to look at the reasons for the delay, it seems to me
that Sharp (through Mr Nolan) acquiesced in the delay by Shoe Lace (through Mr
Nolan) in executing the debenture."

Mr Briggs submitted that *Hoffmann* J erred in his approach to the problem, and in his   C
conclusion. The new wording in sec. 245 of the 1986 Act "at the same time as, or after,
the creation of a charge" is not, in his submission, materially different from the old
wording "the amount of any cash paid to the company at the time of or subsequently to
the creation of . . . the charge" which appeared in sec. 212 of the 1908 Act and much
more recently in sec. 322(1) of the *Companies Act* 1948 ("the 1948 Act"); thus, he said,
the new wording does not represent an "emphasis on [objective] contemporaneity".   D
The judge, it was said, was wrong to take the relevant test as being how an informed
businessman would view the matter. The correct starting point in construing the relevant
wording is to prevent a valid charge being given to secure a past debt in respect of which
there has been no promise to give a charge and which does not go to swell the company's
assets. With this purpose in mind, the court must look at the real substance of the
transaction, and if the payment is, in *Neville* J's words, made,   E

"on account of the consideration for the security, in anticipation of its creation
and in reliance on a promise to execute it, although made some days before its
execution,"

it is made "at the same time as the creation of the charge" within the meaning of
sec. 245(2)(a) of the 1986 Act. Mr Briggs naturally relied strongly on the decisions of
Neville J and the Court of Appeal in the *Columbian Fireproofing* case. He also referred   F
us to *Re Fairway Magazines Ltd* [1992] BCC 924 where *Mummery* J, to whom the
decision of *Hoffmann* J in the present case had been cited, expressed the view (at p.
932A) that:

"although the language of sec. 245(2)(a) is different from the earlier provisions
the approach to be adopted is that adopted in the earlier cases."

Hoffmann J, as has already appeared, stated in his judgment that, if he were wrong   G
about the construction of the words "at the same time as" in sec. 245 and (in the light of
Maugham J's judgment in *Re F & E Stanton Ltd*) it was necessary to look at the reasons
for the delay, Sharp (through Mr Nolan) had acquiesced in the delay by Shoe Lace
(through Mr Nolan) in executing the debenture.

Mr Briggs sought leave to adduce to this court in evidence an affidavit sworn by
Mr Mahtani on 18 February 1993 (which we read de bene esse), the gist of which was
that Mr Nolan had no authority from Mr Mahtani or his brothers as effective controllers   H
of Sharp, to delay the execution of the debenture or to permit Sharp to advance moneys
before its execution. In broad terms, Mr Briggs submitted that the court should not
adopt a strict construction of sec. 245 which would make it more difficult for companies
to emerge from financial difficulties by raising money on security; that the sums in
question in the present case, when advanced, were new money which swelled Shoe

A Lace's assets and became available for its creditors; that since they were paid with the intention that the payment and the creation of the charge would be simultaneous, they must be treated as having been paid "at the same time as, or after, the creation of the charge" within sec. 245; and that if there was any delay in implementing that intention, the delay was on the facts excusable.

B Since the relevant wording of sec. 245 of the 1986 Act is different from that of its statutory predecessors, such as sec. 212 of the 1908 Act and sec. 322 of the 1948 Act, it is common ground that decisions relating to the wording of those predecessors are not binding on this court on this appeal. Nevertheless, I for my part can see little or no material difference between the words "at the time of or subsequently to the creation of" in the old sections and the words "at the same time as, or after, the creation of the charge" in the new section. If, therefore, the approach to the problem adopted by *Neville* J and the Court of Appeal in *Columbian Fireproofing* was correct in relation to

C the earlier sections, I could see no sufficient reason for declining to follow it in applying sec. 245.

In my judgment, however, with all due respect, that approach was wrong. As has been seen, it was based on the proposition that a,

D "payment made on account of the consideration for the security, in anticipation of its creation and in reliance on a promise to execute it . . . is made at the time of its creation within the meaning of the section."

As *Hoffmann* J observed, the proposition appears to treat the question whether the advance was in consideration for the charge as determinative of whether it was made "at the time of the charge". In my judgment, this cannot be correct. The words "at the time of or subsequently to the creation of . . . the charge" in sec. 212 of the 1908 Act (just as the words "at the same time as, or after, the creation of the charge" in sec. 245 of the

E 1986 Act) were clearly included by the legislature for the purpose of excluding from the exemption the amount of moneys paid to the company *before* the creation of the charge, *even though they were paid in consideration for the charge*; on any other construction these words would have been mere surplusage.

Though the distinction was brought to their attention in argument, both courts in *Columbian Fireproofing*, in my judgment, failed to pay due regard to the crucially important distinction between the two classes of case mentioned by *Buckley* J in *Re*

F *Jackson & Bassford*. In a case where the promise to execute a debenture creates a present equitable right to a security, and moneys are advanced in reliance on it, the delay between the advances and the execution of the formal instrument of charge is immaterial; the charge has already been created and is immediately registrable, so that other creditors of the company will have had the opportunity to learn of its existence; the temporal requirements of the relevant exemptions contained in sec. 212 of the 1908

G Act and sec. 245 of the 1986 Act will be satisfied. In a case where the promise to execute a debenture does *not* create any such present equitable right, the situation is quite different. In that situation the existence of the promise is, in my judgment, irrelevant for the purpose of applying sec. 245 of the 1986 Act and also the statutory provisions governing the registration of charges. In the latter situation, I do not, for my part, see how the relevant temporal requirements of the exemption contained in sec. 212 of the 1908 Act or sec. 245 of the 1986 Act can be satisfied if the making of the advance

H precedes the formal execution of the debenture by any time whatsoever, unless the interval is so short that it can be regarded as de minimis — for example a "coffee-break".

Maugham J in *Stanton* recognised that the requirements relating to time and consideration imposed by sec. 212 of the 1908 Act were separate requirements. In the passage from his judgment quoted above, however, he appears to have considered that a debenture holder could avail himself of the statutory exemption relating to cash

advances, even though they were made *before* the execution of the debenture, if either   A
(1) the delay in such execution was no more than "would ordinarily be necessary for the
passing of the resolution and the consideration of the form of the debenture and its
actual execution" or (2) the delay was not one which the debenture holder had himself
procured or suggested or in which he had in any true sense acquiesced.

As to (2), *Hoffmann* J commented (at p. 370H):

> "I find this reasoning puzzling because the section makes no distinction between   B
> excusable and inexcusable delay. It simply says that the advance must have been
> made at the time of the creation of the charge and I do not see how the answer to
> this question can be affected by whether the reasons for delay were good or bad.
> It is always open to the lender not to lend until the charge has actually been
> executed."

I entirely agree with these comments. Extraneous factors such as these cannot affect
the application of the statutory test. For these reasons I would refuse the application to   C
admit in evidence the affidavit of Mr Mahtani sworn on 18 February 1993 referred to
above, on which we have not yet formally adjudicated.

As to (1) above, the relevant interval of time, according to the wording of
sec. 245(2)(a) of the 1986 Act and its predecessor sections, is the interval between the
payment of the money and the "creation of the charge". In a case where no presently
existing charge has been created by any agreement or company resolution preceding the   D
execution of the formal debenture, then, in my judgment, no moneys paid before the
execution of the debenture will qualify for the exemption under the subsection, unless
the interval between payment and execution is so short that it can be regarded as
minimal and payment and execution can be regarded as contemporaneous. This is a
somewhat more rigorous (and possibly somewhat more certain) test than the test of "the
businessman" applied by the judge. However, as he commented, it is always open to the   E
lender not to lend until the charge has actually been executed; this must be the prudent
course.

In the present case it is not asserted that a charge was created by the resolution passed
by Sharp's board of directors or that the four sums paid in April, May, June and 16 July
1990 were secured by any charge at the time when they were advanced. If they were
secured at all, they can have been secured only by the debenture itself when it was
executed on 24 July 1990. I have no hesitation in agreeing with the judge that these   F
payments cannot be treated as having been made "at the same time as" the execution of
the debenture.

In the context of this first ground of appeal, I have thought it right to deal in detail
with the *Columbian Fireproofing* and *Stanton* cases because they are decisions of high
authority on which Mr Briggs' submissions were largely founded, and also to highlight
what seems to me the importance in this context of the statutory provisions for registration   G
of charges to which little reference has been made in earlier decisions. I would add that,
if Sharp's contentions were well-founded, it would follow that in respect of the advances
made by it between April and July 1990 it could claim priority over any unsecured
creditors who had advanced moneys to Shoe Lace during that period, but, presumably,
would have had no opportunity to learn of the existence of the floating charge until it
was registered on 13 August 1990.

                                                                                                   H
The second ground of appeal

The second, alternative, ground of appeal is one which was not argued before
Hoffmann J, but has been argued with leave in this court. It is submitted that, in the
alternative, sec. 245 of the 1986 Act on its true construction took effect not from the
date of the winding-up petition (4 September 1990) but from the date of the winding-up

A   order (20 November 1990) and that accordingly the sale by Shoe Lace of its assets subject to the floating charge and payment of the sale proceeds to Sharp on 13 September 1990 were not avoided by sec. 245. The steps in this argument, as presented by Mr Briggs, may be summarised as follows:

(1)   Section 245(1) provides that: "This section applies as does section 238 . . . ."

(2)   Section 238(1), so far as material, provides:

B

"This section applies in the case of a company where—

. . .

(b) the company goes into liquidation."

(3)   Section 247(2) provides:

C

"For the purposes of any provision in this Group of Parts, a company goes into liquidation if it passes a resolution for voluntary winding up or an order for its winding up is made by the court at a time when it has not already gone into liquidation by passing such a resolution."

(4)   The introductory words of sec. 245 of the 1986 Act, read together with the introductory words of sec. 238, are different from the introductory words of sec. 322 of the 1948 Act and of its successor, sec. 617 of the *Companies Act* 1985,

D   which sec. 245 replaced. Both the two last-mentioned sections began with the words: "Where a company is being wound up . . ."

(5)   In *Mace Builders (Glasgow) Ltd v Lunn* (1986) 2 BCC 99,532 the Court of Appeal held that in a case where sec. 322 of the 1948 Act applied, the charge in question was invalid as from the commencement of the winding up (the date of presentation of the petition), but not before that commencement. As Sir *John Donaldson* MR put it (at p. 99,534):

E

"The opening words are 'Where a company is being wound up . . .'. The section thus has no application unless and until the company is being wound up."

A little later he said (at p. 99,535):

". . . transactions effected . . . before the commencement of the winding up are unaffected by the section."

F

(6)   The change in the wording of sec. 245 of the 1986 Act from that of its statutory predecessors, it is submitted, is both material and deliberate. When sec. 245(1) of the 1986 Act is read together with sec. 238(1) and sec. 247(2), it can have no application unless and until the company passes a resolution for voluntary winding up or a winding-up order is made; transactions effected before the happening of either of those events (such as a sale of Shoe Lace's assets in the present case) will

G   be unaffected by the section. As Mr Briggs put it in the present case, any "cause of action" in relation to the invalidity of a floating charge only arises on the date of the winding-up order in the case of a compulsory liquidation.

(7)   Therefore, it is submitted, at the date of the sale of Shoe Lace's assets (13 September 1990) the debenture was not invalidated by sec. 245 and Shoe Lace could do no other than pay over the £180,710 to Sharp.

H   (8)   Section 127 of the 1986 Act provides:

"In a winding up by the court, any disposition of the company's property . . . made after the commencement of the winding up is, unless the court otherwise orders, void."

On the facts of the present case, the winding up of Shoe Lace by the court is deemed to have commenced at the time of the presentation of the winding-up

petition (sec. 129(2) of the 1986 Act). No order was made authorising the sale of
Shoe Lace's assets. That sale, however, it is submitted, was not caught by the
section because the holder of a floating charge has a beneficial interest in the
property covered by the charge and the word "disposition" in sec. 127 does not (it
is said) include the process by which a person with a beneficial interest in property
obtains that property or the proceeds of its realisation: see the decision of the
Supreme Court of New South Wales in *Re Margart Pty Ltd; Hamilton v Westpac
Banking Corp* (1984) 2 ACLC 709.

I have been impressed by Mr Briggs' argument on this second ground of appeal, but
in the end am not persuaded by it. It entirely rests on the proposition that there is a
material distinction between the effect of the opening words of sec. 245(1) of the 1986
Act and the opening words of sec. 322(1) of the 1948 Act (reproduced in sec. 617 of the
1985 Act). I am not convinced there is any material distinction.

It is true that the phrase "Where a company is being wound up" which appears in
sec. 322(1) at first sight appears to denote a period which begins at the commencement
of the winding up (namely, in the case of a compulsory winding up, the date of
presentation of the petition). In truth, however, as Mr Serota QC for the liquidator
pointed out, despite its wording, sec. 322(1) (like sec. 245 of the 1986 Act) was incapable
of applying in the case of a compulsory liquidation *until the winding-up order was
actually made.* (Until then, non constat that there would be a liquidation.) As soon as
the order was made (like sec. 245 of the 1986 Act) it would relate back to earlier
transactions. Like sec. 245, however, sec. 322 was silent as to how far in time it would be
capable of relating back. This last point in relation to sec. 322 was resolved in *Mace
Builders* by the decision that the section, as soon as it began to apply, related to any
transactions effected after the commencement of the winding up. I see no sufficient
grounds for placing a different construction on sec. 245, merely because the draftsman
of that section (more logically perhaps than the draftsman of sec. 322) has drafted the
relevant temporal phrase by reference to the point of time when the section begins to
take effect rather than the period over which it will relate back, as soon as it does take
effect.

I would therefore reject this second ground of appeal and hold that sec. 245 of the
1986 Act applies in the present case so as to preclude Sharp from claiming any right as
against the liquidator to the sums to which it claims title by virtue of the floating charge.
I would add that any other construction would in my view leave a serious lacuna in the
section when applied to facts such as those now before this court, which Parliament
could scarcely have intended.

The third ground of appeal

Thirdly, it was submitted that the judge was wrong in holding that the furniture,
fittings and equipment and motor vehicles or their proceeds of sale are not subject to the
fixed charge provisions of the debenture (and are thus subject to the floating charge).

The validity or otherwise of this point depends almost entirely on the meaning of the
word "assets" in cl. 1(i) of the debenture. In Mr Briggs' submission, the judge's
construction of the word does obvious violence to its true meaning; it is an all-embracing
word which includes movable, no less than immovable, property.

I would agree that the word "assets" is a word of wide import which, in a proper
context, is well capable of including both movable and immovable property. In the
context of this debenture, however, three factors in my judgment strongly support the
judge's construction of cl. 1. First, the "assets" charged by cl. 1(i) are defined thereby as
the "legally mortgaged property", and the estates and interests in freehold and leasehold
property (excepting the "legally mortgaged property") charged by cl. 1(ii) are defined

A   as "the equitably charged property". Under cl. 3, Shoe Lace entered into a number of covenants in relation to the "legally mortgaged property" and the "equitably charged property", most of which are obviously appropriate only to land.

Secondly, the phrase "charge by way of legal mortgage" is a well known term of art, introduced exclusively in relation to real property by sec. 87 of the *Law of Property Act* 1925.

B   Thirdly, it is prima facie inherently improbable that a company, such as Shoe Lace, which for the time being intended to continue trading, would intend to execute a mortgage which created a fixed charge on movable property such as all stock in trade and office furniture.

Recognising the difficulties caused by the last point, Mr Briggs accepted that the fixed charge created by cl. 1(i) did not attach to Shoe Lace's stock in trade. However, he

C   sought to adduce in evidence a further affidavit of Mr Pugh, sworn on behalf of Shoe Lace on the instructions of Mr Nolan, which asserted that it was the intention of both parties to the debenture that it should cover all assets, real and personal, including fixtures and fittings and the proceeds of stock in trade (though not stock in trade itself). It was suggested that, so far as necessary, the debenture would be rectifiable to reflect such intention of the parties. We read this evidence de bene esse but have not thus far given a formal ruling on the application to adduce it. I would refuse the application, if

D   only on the grounds that a court which hears a claim by a liquidator that a floating charge created by a debenture is invalidated by sec. 245 of the 1986 Act must proceed on the basis that the debenture means what it says, at least unless and until a formal application has been made for rectification of the instrument. I appreciate that in the court below, the liquidator took the point in argument that the floating charge was ineffective because the debenture contained no covenant to pay and that the judge, by an indulgence to Sharp, was prepared to assume in its favour that "other things being equal, it could be

E   rectified" so as to include an "all moneys" covenant. Without deciding the point, however, I think it possible that a covenant of that nature could be implied simply as a matter of construction of the debenture, without rectification.

I would reject the third ground of appeal.

F   **The fourth ground of appeal**

Finally, it was submitted that the judge was wrong in holding that RSC, O. 14A, r. 1 was applicable since the issue whether under sec. 245(2) of the 1986 Act a floating charge is invalid "except to the extent of . . . the value of so much of the consideration for the creation of the charge as consists of money paid . . . to the company at the same time as, or after, the creation of the charge" is a matter partly of fact and partly of law and not a question of law. The liquidator's application for interim payment is made under RSC,

G   O. 29, r. 10. The judge, in my opinion, correctly stated the test to be applied in such cases as follows (at p. 371C):

> "For the purpose of obtaining an interim payment, the applicant must show a case of a strength justifying judgment under RSC, O. 14. This is subject to RSC, O. 14A, which enables the court to decide a question of law if it appears suitable for determination without full trial and such determination will finally determine

H   'the entire cause or matter' or will dispose of an issue in the cause."

The judge concluded:

> "I think that the construction of sec. 245 is something which can be decided without a full trial of the liquidator's summons and that the determination will finally dispose of the question of the validity of the floating charge because it means that even on the respondent's own evidence, the charge must be invalid."

Mr Briggs referred us to an unreported decision in *Milbury Homes (North) Ltd v Arthur Young* (6 February 1992), where *Millett* J observed that O. 14A is not a substitute for O. 33, r. 3 and,   A

> "is intended to be available for cases in which the question is a relatively simple and straightforward one which can be easily identified by the court without great expenditure of time and effort in its formulation."

In the present case, questions of fact arose, he submitted, which would make it inappropriate for the court to apply O. 14A.   B

If, for the purpose of deciding the issues arising in sec. 245 cases, it were necessary for the court to consider whether the delay in executing the debenture was or was not excusable, I would be inclined to agree that they were not issues which could appropriately be determined under O. 14A, r. 1, since they would involve contentious issues of fact as well as issues of law. However, having held that this is not a relevant consideration, I see no difficulty in saying that the liquidator has shown a case which would justify judgment   C
under RSC, O. 14A. There is no difficulty in formulating the relevant question of law; and I share the judge's view that, even on Sharp's own evidence as to the facts, the floating charge must be invalidated by sec. 245.

Conclusion

For the reasons which I have given, despite Mr Briggs' able argument, I would dismiss   D
this appeal.

Nolan LJ: I too agree that this appeal must be dismissed. Subject to the reservation expressed below I concur completely with the judgment of Sir *Christopher Slade*. In particular, I agree that despite the contrary views expressed by this court and others on similar wording in previous Acts, the reference in sec. 245(2)(a) of the *Insolvency Act* 1986 to "money paid . . . to the company at the same time as, or after, the creation of   E
the charge" simply cannot cover money which by any reckoning has been paid a substantial period of time before the creation of the charge. From this it must follow that the charge which was created in the present case on 24 July 1990 is invalid in so far as it purports to secure the payments made to the company in April, May and June and on 16 July 1990.

It also follows that in the circumstances of the present case it is unnecessary to determine the precise points at which "before" changes into "at the same time as", and   F
"at the same time as" changes into "after". The position would be so much simpler if the legislature had omitted the words "at the same time as", and had confined the protection of sec. 245(2)(a) to money paid and goods and services supplied after the charge had been created: but the words are there, and no doubt a case will arise sooner or later when their applicability to the facts of the matter will have to be more closely studied. In the meantime I would prefer to leave the question open, but I feel bound to add that I   G
for my part see much force in the suggestion of *Hoffmann* J that (if I paraphrase him correctly) the question should be considered against the background of the time-limits which are to be found in the statutory context. It would seem to me that some degree of latitude might be permissible to take account of such matters as urgency, international transactions across different time zones and other factors which might make it difficult to determine at what precise time money was paid or a charge created.

Ralph Gibson LJ: I agree that this appeal should be dismissed for the reasons given   H
by Sir *Christopher Slade*. I agree with those reasons and have nothing useful to add to them.

The test for determining whether the sums in question were paid "at the same time as . . . the creation of the charge", within the meaning of sec. 245 of the 1986 Act, was stated by *Hoffmann* J (at p. 369H) as,

A   "whether a businessman having knowledge of the kind of time-limits imposed by the Insolvency and Companies Acts and using ordinary language would say that the payments had been made at the same time as the execution of the debenture."

Sir *Christopher Slade* has stated (at p.620D) that, in his judgment:

"In a case where no presently existing charge has been created by any agreement or company resolution preceding the execution of the formal debenture, then . . .

B   no moneys paid before the execution of the debenture will qualify for the exemption under the subsection, unless the interval between payment and execution is so short that it can be regarded as minimal and payment and execution can be regarded as contemporaneous."

I have hesitated before expressing my agreement to that more rigorous test. I have reached the conclusion that it is correct. I see no answer to the point that, as Sir

C   *Christopher Slade* has pointed out, the words "at the same time as, or after, the creation of the charge" in sec. 245 of the 1986 Act were clearly included by the legislature for the purpose of excluding from the exemption the amount of moneys paid to the company *before* the creation of the charge, even though they were paid in consideration for the charge. I can see no room for some less rigorous test which would permit to be included within the exemption money in fact paid before the creation of the charge. The only period of time, between the payment of the money and the creation of the charge, which

D   in my judgment can be ignored for this purpose is such that the law, as enacted, was not intended by Parliament to take notice of it, that is to say that it was de minimis.

(*Appeal dismissed*)

E

F

G

H

Re Leyland DAF Ltd.

A

Chancery Division (Companies Court).
Sir Donald Nicholls V-C.
Judgment delivered 28 May 1993.

Administrative receivership — Receivers of manufacturer sought repossession of vehicles from delivery company — Delivery company was creditor and refused to release vehicles — Whether there was agreement giving exclusive jurisdiction to Dutch courts — Whether appointment of receivers affected jurisdiction agreement — Materiality of proceeding under summary remedy for getting in company's property — Civil Jurisdiction and Judgments Act 1982, Sch. 1 (Brussels Convention), art. 17; Insolvency Act 1986, sec. 234.

B

These were proceedings by the administrative receivers of Leyland DAF Ltd ("Leyland") seeking an order under sec. 234 of the Insolvency Act 1986 requiring the respondent, Edcrest Ltd, to permit the receivers to enter Edcrest's premises and take back Leyland's vehicles, which were stored there pending delivery to customers. Edcrest was owed substantial sums of money by Leyland. Edcrest claimed that the arrangements between the parties were governed by Dutch law, by virtue of a term in the contract between Leyland and Edcrest's parent company (the "frame agreement"), and that under Dutch law it was not obliged to hand over the trucks and vans until it was paid, having, in effect, a lien.

C

D

Held, staying the receivers' proceedings, in favour of proceedings in the Dutch court, pursuant to art. 17 of the Brussels Convention:

1. So far as the parties to the frame agreement were concerned the governing law clause conferred exclusive jurisdiction on the Dutch courts pursuant to art. 17 of the Brussels Convention.

E

2. Edcrest had signed the agreement document in approval of its terms. By this means it evidenced its agreement. Having so agreed, Edcrest could not thereafter assert any greater rights against Leyland than those contained in the frame agreement. Nor, conversely, could Leyland assert against Edcrest any rights inconsistent with the terms of the frame agreement. There was no evidence to suggest that that analysis was inconsistent with Dutch law, if and in so far as the question was governed by that law. This was an agreement between Leyland and Edcrest satisfying the requirements of art. 17, whether or not there was a contract between Leyland and Edcrest for the storage and transport of Leyland's vehicles.

F

3. The use of the sec. 234 procedure did not affect the parties' substantive rights. If proceedings brought by the receivers by way of writ in the name of the company would be within art. 17, so also were proceedings brought by an office-holder in his own name under sec. 234. That was because the title on which they relied against Edcrest was Leyland's ownership of the vehicles, even though in commercial terms the receivers could be said to be acting in the interests of, and in that sense on behalf of, the debenture holder.

G

4. The appointment of the receivers did not automatically determine the jurisdiction agreement. Even though a receiver was in some respects in a better position than the company itself, repudiation of the agreement and of the jurisdiction clause by the receivers acting on behalf of Leyland achieved nothing if Edcrest was not prepared to accept that repudiation. This did not give Edcrest a priority to which it was not entitled over the debenture holder or over Leyland's unsecured creditors. All that the enforcement of the clause did was to hold Leyland to its agreement regarding the forum in which the dispute which had arisen should be determined. That agreement having been made, the mandatory provisions of the Brussels Convention applied thenceforth to disputes between

H

A   the parties to the agreement arising out of the agreement irrespective of the attitude taken
     by one of the parties when the dispute arose.

     The following cases were referred to in the judgment:

     Freevale Ltd v Metrostore (Holdings) Ltd [1984] Ch 199.
     Gomba Holdings UK Ltd & Ors v Minories Finance Ltd & Ors (1989) 5 BCC 27;
     [1988] 1 WLR 1231.
B   *Hemsworth v Brian* (1845) 1 CB 131; 135 ER 486.
     Johnson (B) & Co (Builders) Ltd, Re [1955] Ch 634.
     London Iron & Steel Co Ltd, Re [1990] BCC 159.
     Partenreederei MS Tilly Russ & Anor v Haven & Vervoebedrijf Nova NV & Anor
     [1985] QB 931.
     Robbie (N W) & Co Ltd v Witney Warehouse Co Ltd [1963] 1 WLR 1324.

C   Anthony Mann QC and Peter Arden (instructed by Wilde Sapte) for the administrative
     receivers.

     Mark Barnes QC and Fay Stockton (instructed by Barlow Lyde & Gilbert) for the
     respondent.

                                          JUDGMENT

     Nicholls V-C: Leyland DAF Ltd ("Leyland") and its Dutch ultimate parent van
D   Doorne's Bedrijfswagenfabriek DAF BV ("DAF") are both in severe financial difficulty.
     In February 1993 administrative receivers were appointed over Leyland by a debenture
     holder, and the Netherlands court appointed administrators of DAF. Both companies
     carried on business as manufactures of motor vehicles. DAF's business was centred on
     premises at Eindhoven. Leyland carried on its business in the UK. It assembled vans at
     Birmingham and trucks at Leyland, near Preston, in Lancashire. Spare parts were
E   stored at a depot at Chorley.

     Neither Leyland nor DAF had their own haulage facilities. For some years these were
     provided by a Dutch company, G M de Rooy & Zonen International Transport Bedrijf
     Eindhoven BV ("de Rooy") and its wholly-owned English subsidiary Edcrest Ltd. The
     relationship between de Rooy and DAF goes back many years. Edcrest operates from
     two sites. One is at Sittingbourne, Kent, and the other is a 30-acre compound forming
     part of Leyland's complex at Preston. When vehicles came off Leyland's production
F   lines they were parked and stored, pending delivery to customers, either in Edcrest's
     compound at Preston or at Edcrest's premises at Sittingbourne. The vehicles were then
     delivered as required either in this country or abroad, by the use of the transporter
     facilities provided in most cases by de Rooy or by Edcrest. That was the arrangement in
     operation from February 1991.

     When Leyland went into receivership almost all its finished vehicles were being stored
G   at one or other of these places. The vehicles were of considerable value: approaching
     £20m at Preston, and some £4m at Sittingbourne. The receivers wanted to sell them.
     They needed the money urgently to enable Leyland to continue to trade. The receivers
     are seeking to sell Leyland's business or parts of it as a going concern. However, there
     was a snag. Like many other companies which had been dealing with Leyland, de Rooy
     and Edcrest were owed substantial sums of money. They claimed altogether an amount
     of the order of £3.8m for transport facilities and other services provided. Edcrest was
H   not willing to deliver the vehicles as requested by the receivers, or to permit the receivers
     to retake possession of the vehicles, until they were paid. They claimed that the
     arrangements between the parties are governed by Dutch law, and that under Dutch law
     Edcrest is not obliged to hand over the trucks and vans until Leyland performs its
     contractual obligations and pays what it owes to Edcrest and de Rooy. In effect, Edcrest
     has what I may loosely refer to as a lien.

A

So on 16 February the receivers issued proceedings seeking an order requiring Edcrest to permit them to enter Edcrest's premises at Preston and at Sittingbourne and take back Leyland's vehicles. They seek a similar order in respect of some spare parts which were in course of delivery to customers and are now at Sittingbourne. Edcrest responded with an application for a declaration that the English court has no jurisdiction to determine this dispute over the existence of a lien. The relevant contract contains a clause under which the Dutch court has exclusive jurisdiction to determine any disputes. Edcrest seeks an order staying the receivers' application.

B

Many of the vehicles have now been released under arrangements made between the parties. Edcrest has retained vehicles and spare parts to the extent needed to provide security in the amounts which it claims.

The frame agreement

C

A document of prime importance in this case is an agreement in English, made between three parties: DAF and Leyland, referred to in the agreement as "the company", and de Rooy, called "the haulier". The agreement was headed "Operations agreement". It was described in a recital to the agreement as:

> "a frame agreement regarding transportation by transporter and/or storage of certain vehicles, produced by the company . . . such transportation/ storage to be performed by the haulier and/or its subsidiaries."

D

The agreement has been referred to throughout as "the frame agreement". Clause 1 provided that references to the haulier or to a party included references to subsidiary companies of the haulier. The haulier guaranteed due performance by its subsidiaries of obligations arising under the agreement. Clause 2 provided for the company to give written instructions to the haulier, which the haulier would accept, for the storage of vehicles or the transport of them by transporter. The agreement was to apply to every such instruction. The company was to pay the haulier for the services provided, at specified rates. The haulier was obliged to inspect the vehicles, to store them in good condition and provide adequate security pending receipt of delivery instructions, to carry out stock care procedures, to provide sufficient vehicles and equipment to fulfil its obligations under the agreement, and so forth. The agreement was to continue for five years from 1 January 1991. The haulier was not permitted to subcontract performance of its obligations without consent. Clause 22, the last clause in the agreement, was headed "Governing law". It provided that the agreement was to be governed by the laws of the Netherlands, and that the Dutch court should have exclusive jurisdiction to determine disputes. The clause read:

E

F

> "This agreement shall be governed by and construed in accordance with the laws of the Netherlands. All disputes and differences between the parties arising out of or in connection with this agreement shall ultimately be referred to and resolved by the Court of Justice of 's Hertogenbosch, the Netherlands."

G

The agreement was signed on behalf of DAF and Leyland. Mr de Rooy signed on behalf of de Rooy. The agreement was also signed by Mr de Rooy on behalf of Edcrest, under the rubric "for approval".

Jurisdiction under the frame agreement

H

In my view, so far as the frame agreement is concerned, it is clear that any dispute between the parties to that agreement on whether de Rooy or Edcrest is entitled to a lien over the vehicles stored at Edcrest's premises is a dispute over which the Dutch courts have exclusive jurisdiction. That is the effect of art. 17 of the Brussels Convention on jurisdiction and enforcement of judgments in civil and commercial matters, as made

A   part of English law by sec. 2 of the *Civil Jurisdiction and Judgments Act* 1982. Article 17 (as amended) provides:

> "If the parties, one or more of whom is domiciled in a Contracting State, have agreed that a court or the courts of a Contracting State are to have jurisdiction to settle any disputes which have arisen or which may arise in connection with a particular legal relationship, that court or those courts shall have exclusive

B

> jurisdiction. Such an agreement conferring jurisdiction shall be either—
>
> (a) in writing or evidenced in writing, or . . ."

The convention is concerned with the international jurisdiction of the courts of contracting states. This agreement is of an international character. It governs the relationship between two Dutch companies and the English subsidiary of one of them, and the subject-matter is in part the transport of goods internationally. Further, the agreement is in writing.

C

Edcrest's position

The principal thrust of the receivers' case was to draw a marked distinction between de Rooy and its wholly-owned subsidiary Edcrest. The receivers contended that there is no relevant contractual relationship between Leyland and Edcrest. The contract concerning the storage and transport of Leyland vehicles is between Leyland and de

D   Rooy. Edcrest's role was, in effect, no more than that of an authorised subcontractor. Edcrest stored and transported vehicles, but when doing so it was merely discharging de Rooy's obligations. As a matter of administrative convenience the instructions were given direct by Leyland to Edcrest. Furthermore, Edcrest normally invoiced Leyland for the cost of transporting vehicles within the UK. As a matter of law, however, Edcrest was no more than a bailee or sub-bailee of the vehicles. Leyland is now asserting its proprietary rights against Edcrest. In answer to that claim Edcrest is not entitled to rely

E   upon the choice of law or jurisdiction provisions in the frame agreement. Edcrest was not a party to the frame agreement, either initially or subsequently. Nor was it a party to an agreement impliedly incorporating cl. 22 of the frame agreement as one of its terms.

This submission leads to a highly unattractive result. It would mean that the terms governing the storage and transport of the vehicles are those set out in the frame agreement. Leyland's rights and obligations regarding vehicles handed over to Edcrest

F   for storage are those set out in the frame agreement. The frame agreement applies to every instruction given by Leyland to de Rooy or one of its subsidiaries to store or transport a vehicle. Nevertheless, vis-à-vis Edcrest, Leyland can ignore those terms. It can now reclaim the vehicles from Edcrest regardless of the terms of the contract pursuant to which it handed over the vehicles. By that means it can side-step the agreed terms of the frame agreement. It can do that, even though Edcrest is de Rooy's own

G   subsidiary, and even though there is no question of Edcrest asserting any rights to the vehicles independently of de Rooy. Edcrest's stance is only that the vehicles are held on the terms of the frame agreement.

In my view this contention is unsound. It would defeat the intention of all concerned. The frame agreement was intended to cover the storage and transport of vehicles, and it was intended to do so even when the operations were carried out by a subsidiary of de

H   Rooy, the haulier. That was expressly envisaged by the frame agreement. Further, the parties envisaged that after the signing of the frame agreement it would be Edcrest that would continue to provide storage and internal UK transport facilities. Still further, the parties intended *and agreed* that this participation by Edcrest would not detract from the arrangements agreed by the frame agreement. From the outset of the frame agreement, that was the position between Leyland and Edcrest. To this end Edcrest itself signed the frame agreement document in approval of its terms. By this means it evidenced its agreement. Having so agreed, Edcrest could not thereafter assert any greater rights against Leyland or DAF than those contained in the frame agreement. Nor, conversely, could Leyland assert against Edcrest any rights inconsistent with the terms of the frame agreement. I have seen no evidence to suggest that this analysis is inconsistent with Dutch law, if and in so far as this question is governed by that law.

In my view this agreement, direct between Leyland and Edcrest, is an agreement satisfying the requirements of art. 17. Whether or not there is a contract between Leyland and Edcrest for the storage and transport of Leyland's vehicles, Edcrest has agreed with Leyland in the manner I have described. The dispute which has now arisen concerns the parties' rights and obligations flowing from Edcrest's storage of the vehicles. The storage of vehicles was one of the matters embraced by the frame agreement. The storage of vehicles by Edcrest was not a departure from the scheme of the frame agreement: it was envisaged at the time. Edcrest approved the terms of the frame agreement. By this means it recognised and accepted that the terms of that agreement governed the storage of the vehicles so far as it was concerned as well as de Rooy.

In my view, even as between Leyland and Edcrest, there is a sufficient international element for this agreement to fall within art. 17. Edcrest and Leyland were each wholly owned subsidiaries of Dutch companies, and the subject-matter of the agreement by Edcrest was part and parcel of a larger arrangement which included transportation outside the UK. And Edcrest's written approval satisfies the requirement of art. 17 regarding the need for writing.

The receivers' position

The receivers advanced a further argument based on their position as administrative receivers. The proceedings are brought by them in their own names pursuant to sec. 234 of the *Insolvency Act* 1986. This section authorises the court to make an order requiring a person to hand over to an administrative receiver or other office-holder property in his possession to which the company appears to be entitled. The debenture holder is, or may be, bound by any lien Edcrest already had over the vehicles when the debenture holder's equitable charge crystallised on the appointment of the receivers. However, unlike Leyland, the debenture holder is not bound by any agreement made with Edcrest regarding the forum for the resolution of disputes between Leyland and Edcrest. The debenture holder was not a party to such an agreement, nor is it claiming under any such agreement. The debenture holder is relying on its proprietary interest in the vehicles. In bringing these proceedings the receivers are acting in right of the debenture holder which appointed them rather than in right of Leyland. This is so, even though the receivers are, at any rate for some purposes, the agents of Leyland. This agency is not an ordinary agency; it is primarily a device to protect the mortgagee or debenture holder, and the relationship is tripartite, involving the company, the receiver and the debenture holder: see *Gomba Holdings UK Ltd & Ors v Minories Finance Ltd & Ors* (1989) 5 BCC 27 at p. 29D. The receiver is a piece of administrative machinery designed to enforce a charge: see *N W Robbie & Co Ltd v Witney Warehouse Co Ltd* [1963] 1 WLR 1324 at p. 1338. Thus the courts have shown a readiness to have regard to the reality of a receiver's functions. His main purpose is to realise the property over which he is appointed for the benefit of the mortgagee: see *Re B Johnson & Co (Builders) Ltd* [1955] Ch 634 at pp. 644–646, 661–662.

I am not able to accept the conclusion for which the receivers contended. Section 234 is a procedural provision, enabling an office-holder to proceed summarily in the Companies Court rather than by issuing a writ in the name of the company. The history of this statutory provision was considered by *Warner* J in *Re London Iron & Steel Co*

A   *Ltd* [1990] BCC 159. The use of this procedure does not affect the parties' substantive rights. If proceedings brought by the receivers by way of writ in the name of the company would be within art. 17, in my view so also are proceedings brought by an office-holder in his own name under sec. 234.

Here the legal title being relied upon in the claim against Edcrest for delivery up of the vehicles is Leyland's title as owner. The vehicles belong to Leyland. The debenture did not pass legal title in the vehicles to the debenture holder. The debenture created an encumbrance on Leyland's title. By the debenture the vehicles were, on crystallisation of the floating charge, appropriated to discharge of the debts secured by the debenture. The debenture holder is entitled to look to the vehicles for repayment of the sums payable under the debenture in priority to the unsecured creditors and to the secured creditors ranking behind the debentures. The provisions of the debenture also furnish the receivers with authority to bring proceedings in the name of Leyland in respect of the vehicles: see, in this regard, sec. 42 of, and para. 1 and 5 of Sch. 1 to, the 1986 Act. That is the source of their authority to act for Leyland. But the position remains that the title on which they rely against Edcrest is Leyland's ownership of the vehicles, even though in commercial terms the receivers can be said to be acting in the interests of, and in that sense on behalf of, the debenture holder.

So much for the title being asserted against Edcrest. I turn to consider whether the receivers can rely on Leyland's title but at the same time shake themselves free from the agreement which lays down the terms on which the vehicles were handed over by Leyland to Edcrest. As to that, it is clear that before the appointment of the receivers the company itself could not have done so. A repudiation by Leyland of the terms of the agreement would not have enabled it to free itself from the effect of cl. 22 and art. 17 of the Brussels Convention. That is axiomatic. If that were not so, jurisdiction agreements would be singularly ineffectual. If Leyland had repudiated the agreement before the appointment of the receivers, and had sued in England for the return of the vehicles, there could have been no answer to Edcrest's riposte that the Dutch courts had exclusive jurisdiction to determine the dispute. Leyland could not have avoided the effect of cl. 22 and the Brussels Convention by the simple expedient of refusing to carry out the terms of the agreement. In such circumstances the court would give effect to art. 17 whatever the attitude of Leyland when the dispute arose.

Does the appointment of the receivers make a difference? I was referred to no authority on the point. In principle the appointment should make no difference. It does not automatically determine the jurisdiction agreement. The English courts have had to consider the analogous case of an arbitration clause. Bankruptcy does not itself revoke a submission to arbitration: *Hemsworth v Brian* (1845) 1 CB 131. Likewise, and this must surely follow, in the case of the liquidation of a company, or the appointment of an administrative receiver: these events do not in themselves determine an arbitration clause. In my view, by parity of reasoning the position is similar with a jurisdiction agreement.

I have in mind that, even so, in some respects a receiver is in a better position than the company itself. A receiver may repudiate an agreement made between a trader and the company, and leave the trader with a remedy in damages, often worthless, against the company. In my view, in the present case that course is not open to the receivers. True, it is not they who are seeking to rely on the agreement. They are not adopting the agreement. If they were, they could not at the same time renounce one of its terms. They could not blow hot and cold. They could not pick and choose in this way. What is happening is that they are being met with the terms of the agreement as a defence to the claim for delivery up of the vehicles.

A

I have already decided that Edcrest as much as de Rooy is bound to Leyland by the terms of the frame agreement, and vice versa. Accordingly the position is that the vehicles were delivered to Edcrest subject to those terms. If, on a proper construction of the agreement and the due application of Dutch law, Edcrest is entitled to retain the vehicles against payment of the debts owing to it and de Rooy, Edcrest can rely on the agreement as a defence to the proceedings. Edcrest can set up what I have referred to as a lien. That is so despite the appointment of the receivers. Likewise, in my view, with regard to cl. 22. That is another of the terms governing Edcrest's possession and retention of the vehicles. In defence to the claim by Leyland for delivering up of the vehicles, Edcrest can point to cl. 22 and say that also is binding on Leyland. The repudiation of that agreement and of cl. 22 by the receivers acting on behalf of Leyland achieves nothing if Edcrest is not prepared to accept that repudiation.

B

This approach does not result in Edcrest obtaining an untoward priority over the debenture holder. To enforce cl. 22 in response to a claim by Leyland brought through the receivers would not be to give Edcrest a priority to which it is not entitled over the debenture holder or over Leyland's unsecured creditors. All that the enforcement of cl. 22 does is to hold Leyland to its agreement regarding the forum in which the dispute which has now arisen should be determined. That agreement having been made, the mandatory provisions of the Brussels Convention apply thenceforth to disputes between the parties to the agreement arising out of the agreement irrespective of the attitude taken by one of the parties when the dispute arises. In principle the agreement remains enforceable against a contracting party as much after the appointment of a receiver as before. A specifically enforceable contract for the sale of land remains enforceable against a company despite the appointment of a receiver (see *Freevale Ltd v Metrostore (Holdings) Ltd* [1984] Ch 199). I do not see why an exclusive jurisdiction clause in an agreement should be any less effective.

C

D

I add that this conclusion conforms to the European Community jurisprudence on art. 17 of the Brussels Convention. In *Partenreederei MS Tilly Russ & Anor v Haven & Vervoebedrijf Nova NV & Anor* [1985] QB 931 the European Court of Justice held, regarding a jurisdiction clause contained in a bill of lading, that art. 17 applied between the carrier and a third party who succeeded to the shipper's rights and obligations upon acquiring the bill of lading. The present case is stronger. Despite the intervention of the receivers, the claimant is still Leyland, which was one of the parties to the agreement containing the jurisdiction clause.

E

F

Spare parts

The operative clauses of the frame agreement make no reference to the carriage of spare parts. The recitals and the operative clauses are concerned with vehicles. In fact, in addition to vehicles, de Rooy and Edcrest were already transporting spare parts for Leyland when the frame agreement was made. On 16 April 1991, some months before the agreement was signed, Mr van der Tempel, on behalf of Leyland, and Mr de Rooy had signed a document headed "Overview of prices transports de Rooy/Edcrest UK". The document set out the rates, as from 1 January 1991, payable for transporting spare parts. The document also made provision for the amount of compensation payable to Edcrest consequential upon use of Edcrest's vehicles for five days per week rather than six days as envisaged when the rates were calculated. That document was included as one of the documents forming annex 3, headed "charges", to the frame agreement. The frame agreement provided that the annexes should form an integral part of the agreement.

G

H

In my view the proper inference to be drawn from the inclusion of this document as part of annex 3 is that the parties intended that, so far as applicable, the terms of the frame agreement should apply to the transport of spare parts as well as the transport of

A   vehicles. That is hardly surprising. The only other explanation for the inclusion of this document in the annex is a mistake. I see no reason to think there was a mistake. The oral evidence I heard from those with first-hand knowledge of the contractual negotiations confirms this.

Conclusion

B   For these reasons I shall direct that the receivers' proceedings should be stayed, in favour of proceedings in the Dutch court, pursuant to art. 17 of the Brussels Convention.

(*Order accordingly*)

C

D

E

F

G

H

Scottish & Newcastle plc, Petitioners.

A

Court of Session (Outer House).
Lord Milligan.
Judgment delivered 9 June 1993.

> *Receivership — Floating charge — Whether properties had been released from charge — Companies Act 1985, sec. 419, 466; Insolvency Act 1986, sec. 63.*

B

This was a petition for directions under sec. 63 of the Insolvency Act 1986. The petitioners were the holders of a floating charge granted by the first respondents. The petitioners appointed the second respondents to be receivers of the first respondents. Questions then arose concerning the alleged release of a number of properties from the petitioners' floating charge in 1990 as part of a refinancing deal which involved the third respondents partially replacing the petitioners as lenders to the first respondents.

C

The petitioners submitted that the properties had not been released from the charge: there had been no instrument of alteration under sec. 466 of the Companies Act 1985 nor any memorandum of satisfaction under sec. 419. The second respondents adopted the submissions for the petitioners on this matter, and submitted that the first respondents averred only that the petitioners had consented to the release of the properties from the floating charge; they did not aver that they had actually been released.

D

The first respondents submitted that for there to be effective release it was not necessary for there to have been a registered instrument of alteration in terms of sec. 466 of the 1985 Act, or a memorandum of satisfaction within the terms of sec. 419 of the Act, or registration of such a memorandum. It was clear from the evidence that the petitioners acknowledged that they had released the properties from their floating charge.

Held, ruling that the properties were not within the floating charge at the date of appointment of the receivers (and declaring that the second respondents were receivers and not administrative receivers):

E

1. So far as competency of release without statutory registration was concerned, sec. 419 of the 1985 Act made it clear that release of the properties from the petitioners' floating charge could be effected competently and effectively by the petitioners without registration of any memorandum of satisfaction in terms of that section.

F

2. It was not suggested that in this case any attempt was made to execute an instrument of alteration in terms of sec. 466 of the Act but it was accepted that sec. 466 procedure was just one way of proceeding where properties were to be released from a floating charge.

3. In relation to the question whether the petitioners actually did release the properties, on the information on which the court was asked to decide the matter, they did so. In a matter where no formal deed was required, the petitioners' language was apt to convey to the first respondents and the third respondents acknowledgement that such release had been effected. Use of the phrase "consent to the release" rather than "release" was not inconsistent with this conclusion.

G

The following case was referred to in the opinion:

Ross v Taylor 1985 SC 156.

J E Drummond Young QC and J A Peoples (instructed by Morton Fraser Milligan) for the petitioners.

H

C S Haddow QC and D M MacNeill (Biggart Baillie & Gifford) for the first respondents.

G J B Moynihan (instructed by Gillam Mackie) for the second respondents.

J W McNeill QC (instructed by Dorman Jeffrey & Co) for the third respondents.

A

OPINION

Lord Milligan: The petition is for directions under sec. 63 of the *Insolvency Act* 1986. The petitioners are the holders of a floating charge granted by the first respondents. The floating charge was dated 29 March 1990 and registered in the register of charges on 12 April 1990. The floating charge bears to be granted over the whole property and undertaking of the first respondents to secure all sums due or that might become due to

B the petitioners by the first respondents and/or Anglo Scottish Leisure Investments Ltd. The charge contained a negative pledge in terms of sec. 464(1)(a) of the *Companies Act* 1985 and also a ranking clause in terms of sec. 464(1)(b) of that Act. No issue arises out of the terms of these clauses, which are in standard form. Following alleged failure by the first respondents to make due payment to the petitioners of sums outstanding, the petitioners, on 9 March 1993, made a written demand on the first respondents to pay £485,458.83. Upon failure by the first respondents to make the payment demanded, the

C petitioners, on 12 March 1993, appointed the second respondents to be receivers of the whole of the property and undertaking of the first respondents. The second respondents have since estimated that the first respondents have assets worth about £1,052,000 and liabilities, including sums due to the petitioners, of about £1,612,000 and accordingly believe that the first respondents are insolvent.

D The questions which have arisen concern alleged release of a number of properties from the petitioners' floating charge in late August/early September 1990. The properties concerned are 21 licensed premises. It is not in dispute that, the alleged release apart, these 21 properties would fall within the second respondents' receivership. I was informed by Mr Moynihan for the second respondents that, if they do so, they comprise about 90 per cent in value of the property falling into the receivership, the 21 properties being worth about £875,000. The petitioners' position is that the 21 properties do fall

E within the receivership and the second respondents' position is that, to the best of their knowledge, this is so. The first respondents' position is that the 21 properties did not fall into the receivership because of the release mentioned. The third respondents, being creditors of the first respondents and having security effective over the 21 properties in the event that they have not fallen into the second respondents' receivership, concur with the first respondents that the 21 properties were effectively released by the

F petitioners from their floating charge. I was invited by all parties to consider the question of whether there had or had not been effective release of the 21 properties from the petitioners' floating charge upon certain correspondence. Before recording the terms of the correspondence concerned, I record that it was recognised on behalf of all parties that this correspondence did not provide a full picture of communications between the parties concerned, it being clear that there were negotiations and discussions not fully recorded in the correspondence. Such missing material could be relevant to some,

G though not all, of the issues raised for my decision. While this was recognised on behalf of the parties, I was asked to determine such matters on the documentary material produced. It is appropriate at this stage to record the terms of the correspondence particularly founded upon.

On 17 August 1990, the petitioners' solicitors wrote to the first respondents' solicitors in the following terms:

H
> "*Scottish & Newcastle Breweries plc*
>
> *Ascot Inns Ltd*
>
> I refer to your letter and our telephone conversations of earlier this week. I understand that Mr Findlay and Mr Izatt have now met and that the following has been proposed:

(1) That forthwith your clients will pay our clients the sum of £1.5m to account of the purchase price. This is on the basis that your clients are unable to obtain funding from Hill Samuel for the whole price due at this time.

(2) Our clients will release from their security the properties previously agreed as being released with the exception of Wishes and the Alhambra which they require to have included in the subjects over which they have continuing security in view of the extent of the sums due by your clients.

(3) Your clients will continue to trade through all their outlets on a 100 per cent trade tie basis.

(4) Interest will accrue on the balance of the price due by your clients to which will be added the capitalised interest accrued on the whole price to date at two per cent above Bank of Scotland base rate until 31 October 1990 which will be the date on which the whole balances due to our clients shall be paid. In the event of failure to pay on or before 31 October 1990 interest will accrue on all balances due to our clients at five per cent above Bank of Scotland base rate.

(5) Immediately on payment of the interim capital sum proposed by your clients, your clients will instruct a direct debit from their bank of a monthly interest payment to meet the interest accruing on a daily basis on the balances due by your clients to our clients.

Please let me know if the foregoing proposals are agreed."

By letter also dated 17 August 1990, the first respondents' solicitors replied to the petitioners' solicitors as follows:

"*Ascot Inns Ltd*

Scottish & Newcastle Breweries plc

MMC disposals

I refer to our phone conversation this morning. Mr Findlay of my clients has confirmed the arrangements that the sum of approximately £1.5m will be repaid as soon as possible (I hope to effect this on Monday/Tuesday of next week). The balance together with the interest accrued to date will be capitalised and will remain secured on the other premises together with Wishes and the Alhambra Bar. There will be a full trade tie agreement. This arrangement will remain in force until 31 October 1990 and interest on the capitalised balance will be repayable monthly by direct debit. The interest rate will be two per cent above base rate until 31 October 1990 and if completion has not been effected in total the interest will be five per cent above base rate thereafter.

I hope to be in touch with you by telephone on Monday morning."

By letter dated 22 August 1990, the petitioners' solicitors wrote to the first respondents' solicitors as follows:

"Facsimile transmission

Scottish & Newcastle Breweries plc

Ascot Inns Ltd

MMC disposals

I have now had a telephone call from Gordon Izatt of Scottish & Newcastle with whom Mr Findlay has been discussing new arrangements for the repayment of the balances due.

I understand that because of Hill Samuel's demand that the Alhambra and Wishes be included in their security these properties are not available to my clients as continuing security. In the circumstances therefore I understand that Mr Findlay has agreed that in addition to paying the sum of £1,529,000 at this stage in exchange for discharges of certain of the existing securities he will also pay the sum of £100,000 to account of the accrued interest which has arisen on the loan to your clients. The balance of interest due is of course in excess of £100,000 and you have a note of the calculations and the daily rate.

I understand that the capital balance of £746,000 together with the balance of interest ascertained at the date when the sum of £1,629,000 is paid would be treated as a loan to your clients bearing interest at two per cent above bank base rate until 31 October 1990 when all sums due to our clients will be paid off except that by 30 September 1990 your client will have paid off the balance of the interest accrued on the loan up until the time that the sum of £1,629,000 is paid to our clients. Interest would accrue at five per cent above base rate on any balance due after 31 October 1990. Payment of interest will be made monthly by your clients. We understand that in security of the continuing loan our clients would hold the first and only charge securities over the Crown, Blackburn, the Cavalier, Falkirk, the County Bar, Carluke, Goodwins, the Rowantree, the Croft Hotel, the Ravenscraig and the Seafield.

The question of the full trade tie previously referred to in our correspondence would not be affected by these new arrangements. Please let me know if this now accords with your understanding of the arrangements between our clients and also let me know if you are now in funds and are in a position to settle."

By letter dated 27 August 1990, the first respondents' solicitors wrote to the petitioners' solicitors as follows:

"*Ascot Inns Ltd*

Scottish & Newcastle Breweries plc

MMC disposals

Thank you for your fax of 22 August and our subsequent phone conversations. I am pleased to confirm that Hill Samuel Bank Ltd remitted the sum of £1.629m direct to your clients' bank account on Friday and hopefully this will have been confirmed to you.

I enclose my firm's cheque for £2,484 in settlement of your firm's fee and shall be grateful if you would acknowledge receipt and in due course let me have a receipted invoice.

Please also let me have the executed discharges over the undernoted properties and also the various security deeds etc. back relative to Wishes and the Alhambra Bar.

In connection with the other 'joint venture' agreements which my clients are entering into with certain other tenants I have been requested to obtain a letter of non-crystallisation of the floating charges in favour of your clients and I shall be grateful if you would let me have appropriate letters as soon as possible to exhibit to the agents for the respective tenants involved."

This letter then contained a list of 19 properties, being all of the 21 properties listed in the letter of 7 September 1990 hereinafter referred to with the exception of the Winning Post in Broxburn and the Kenilworth Hotel in Airdrie.

By letter dated 7 September 1990, the company secretary of the petitioners wrote to the first respondents' solicitors as follows:

"We, Scottish & Newcastle Breweries plc ('the charge holder') considering that
the charge holder are creditors under floating charge granted by Ascot Inns Ltd
having its registered office at 364 Brandon Street, Motherwell ('the borrowers')
registered in the register of charges on 12 April 1990 hereby after due and diligent
enquiry certify and warrant (a) that no steps have been taken by us up to the date
of this letter or are about to be taken by us or, to the best of our knowledge and
belief by any third party, to effect a crystallisation of the floating charge or to
appoint administrators, receivers or liquidators thereunder, (b) that we have
given our consent to the release from the said floating charge of the subjects
owned by the borrowers at:

  (1) The Besom Inn, 75/77 High Street, Coldstream, Berwickshire;

  (2) The Office Bar, 6 Towerknowe, Hawick;

  (3) The Station Hotel, Station Road, Selkirk;

  (4) The Railway Hotel, Newton Street, Boswells, Roxburghshire;

  (5) The Royal Hotel, 3/9 Townfoot, Stow, Midlothian;

  (6) The Central Hotel, Bowhill, Cardenden, Fife;

  (7) The Auld Toll Hotel, Methilhaven Road, Methilhill, Fife;

  (8) The Rendezvous, La Porte Precinct, Grangemouth;

  (9) The Winning Post, 22 Main Street, Broxburn;

 (10) The Kenilworth Hotel, 2 Kenilworth Drive, Airdrie;

 (11) The Glenavon Inn, Carlisle Road, Birkenshaw, Lanarkshire;

 (12) The Welcome Inn, 2 Littlemill Road, Drongan, Ayrshire;

 (13) The Burns Inn, 55/57 Low Glencairn Street, Ayrshire;

 (14) London Arms Hotel, 69 Main Street, Newmilns;

 (15) The Royal Hotel, 67 New Street, Dalry, Ayrshire;

 (16) The Harbour Bar, 37 Knockcushion Street, Girvan;

 (17) The Crown Inn, 58 High Street, Sanquhar;

 (18) DG's, 23 English Street, Dumfries;

 (19) The Glebe Inn, 21 Market Street. Maxwelltoun, Dumfries;

 (20) The Alhambra Bar, 302/304 Main Street, Bellshill;

 (21) Wishes, 1 Main Street and 2 Caledonian Road, Wishaw; and

(c) we undertake that we shall take no steps or action to deprive or prevent the
borrowers granting a disposition or conveyance of the said subjects."

This correspondence reflected what was agreed to be a process of reorganisation of
the financing arrangements for the first respondents' borrowings, whereby the third
respondents were effectively partially taking over the position of lenders to the first
respondents from the petitioners, with appropriate effective transfer of securities from
the latter to the former as was to be expected in such a situation. It was not disputed that
this, at least, was the intention. What was in dispute was the consequences in law of what
actually happened.

The questions which I am asked to answer were presented at the hearing as being the
following:

"(1) Were the properties listed in the petitioners' letter of 7 September 1990
within the floating charge granted by these respondents in favour of the petitioners
as at the date of appointment of receivers?

A   (2) Have the said receivers been validly appointed as receivers of the whole property and undertaking of Ascot?

(3) What is the effect in law, if any, of the letter dated 7 September 1990 as regards the appointment of the said receivers?

(4) Has the said letter any effect as regards the ranking of S & N's floating charge and any subsequent floating charges or fixed securities in favour of Hill Samuel in relation to the disputed properties?

B   (5) Did the said letter have the effect of releasing the disputed properties from S & N's floating charge?

(6) *Esto* the receivers were validly appointed, is the petitioner bound, in a question with Ascot or otherwise, to execute and register with the registrar of companies a memorandum of satisfaction under sec. 419 of the *Companies Act* C   1985 in relation to the properties listed in said letter, and if so, what effect would such execution and registration have, on the appointment, powers and duties of the receivers *quoad* these properties?

(7) Are the petitioners obliged to release from their floating charge the properties listed in said letter, and if so, pending such release, how should the receivers act in relation to those properties and any income derivable therefrom?

D   (8) Upon a sound construction of the said letter does the reference to 'subjects' include subjects moveable as well as heritable?

(9) By virtue of the said letter and in the aforesaid circumstances were debts, in particular rent, due by tenants of Ascot who are occupying any of the disputed properties attached by S & N's said floating charge as at the date of appointment of the said receivers?

E   (10) By virtue of the said letter and in the aforesaid circumstances are the proceeds of a sale by the first respondents of any of the disputed properties attached by S & N's said floating charge?

(11) Who is entitled to the debts and proceeds referred to in 9 and 10?

(12) Who is entitled to any sums deposited by the said receivers in the said account with Hill Samuel?"

F   Mr Drummond Young, for the petitioners, submitted that the first question should be answered in the affirmative. The 21 properties had not been released from the petitioners' floating charge. There were two possible ways in which such release could be effected. The first such method involved an instrument of alteration in terms of sec. 466 of the *Companies Act* 1985. Section 466(1) provides:

> "The instrument creating a floating charge under section 462 or any ancillary
G   document may be altered by the execution of an instrument of alteration by the company, the holder of the charge and the holder of any other charge (including a fixed security) which would be adversely affected by the alteration."

In terms of this provision such an instrument of alteration would have required to have been executed by the first respondents and the petitioners in order to release the 21 properties from the petitioners' floating charge effectively by this method. There had been no execution by the first respondents and petitioners of any such instrument of H   alteration. Furthermore, in any event, in terms of sec. 410(2) of the Act, as applied to instruments of alteration by sec. 466(5),

> "Every alteration to a floating charge created by a company is, so far as any security on the company's property or any part of it is conferred by the charge, void against the liquidator or administrator and any creditor of the company unless the prescribed particulars of the charge, together with a copy (certified in

the prescribed manner to be a correct copy) of the instrument (if any) by which   A
the alteration is executed or evidenced, are delivered to or received by the
registrar of companies for registration in the manner required by this Chapter
within 21 days after the date of the execution of such alteration."

In the present case there had been no attempt to register any purported instrument of
alteration.

The other, and only other, method by which release of the 21 properties from the   B
petitioners' floating charge could have been effected was by means of a memorandum of
satisfaction in terms of sec. 419 of the 1985 Act. Section 419 provides,

"(1) The registrar of companies, on application being made to him in the prescribed
form, and on receipt of a statutory declaration in the prescribed form verifying,
with respect to any registered charge—

(a) that the debt for which the charge was given has been paid or satisfied in   C
whole or in part, or

(b) that part of the property charged has been released from the charge or has
ceased to form part of the company's property,

may enter on the register a memorandum of satisfaction (in whole or in part)
regarding that fact.

(2) Where the registrar enters a memorandum of satisfaction in whole, he shall,   D
if required, furnish the company with a copy of the memorandum.

(3) Without prejudice to the registrar's duty under this section to require to be
satisfied as above mentioned, he shall not be so satisfied unless—

(a) the creditor entitled to the benefit of the floating charge, or a person
authorised to do so on his behalf, certifies as correct the particulars submitted
to the registrar with respect to the entry on the register of a memorandum   E
under this section, or

(b) the court, on being satisfied that such certification cannot readily be obtained,
directs him accordingly.

(4) Nothing in this section requires the company to submit particulars with
respect to the entry in the register of a memorandum of satisfaction where the
company, having created a floating charge over all or any part of its property,   F
disposes of part of the property subject to the floating charge.

(5) A memorandum or certification required for the purposes of this section shall
be in such form as may be prescribed."

Mr Drummond Young submitted that in the present case there had been no attempt to
adopt the procedure available under sec. 419. The letter of 7 September 1990 was a
letter of non-crystallisation and had no greater significance for present purposes. It   G
necessarily followed that as at the date of the appointment of the second respondents no
steps had been taken effectively to release the 21 properties from the petitioners' floating
charge.

Mr Moynihan, for the second respondents, adopted the submissions for the petitioners
on this matter. He submitted that the first respondents averred only that the petitioners
had consented to the release of the properties from the floating charge. They did not
aver that they had actually been released. So far as the second respondents were   H
concerned, they lacked information on what had happened and could only take matters
as they found them. The statutory scheme for floating charges necessitated registration
of alterations as a matter of public record and the second respondents were faced with
an absence of registration of alteration of a floating charge which, in the absence of such
alteration, was accepted to cover the 21 properties. In this situation, and with the first

A   respondents averring only consent to release rather than actual release, the second
respondents had no alternative but to adopt the position of the petitioners on this
matter.

Mr Haddow, for the first respondents, submitted that for there to be effective release
it was not necessary for there to have been a registered instrument of alteration in terms
of sec. 466 of the 1985 Act or of a memorandum of satisfaction within the terms of
B   sec. 419 of the Act, nor registration of such a memorandum. It was clear from the terms
of the petitioners' letter of 7 September 1990 that they acknowledged that they had
already released the 21 properties there specified from the petitioners' floating charge.
Having regard to the terms of that letter it was unnecessary for the first respondents to
specify the particular date upon which such release had occurred. It sufficed that it was
clear that such release had taken place within the 2 weeks or so prior to the date of that
letter. The letter of 7 September 1990 was not, as Mr Drummond Young had suggested,
C   purely a letter of non-crystallisation. The letter recorded that the petitioners had given
their consent to the release of the 21 properties from their floating charge and also gave
an undertaking that the petitioners would take no steps or action to deprive or prevent
the first respondents from granting a disposition or conveyance of those properties. It
was unrealistic to suggest that that letter fell short of acknowledging that such release
had already been granted by the petitioners. The letter had obviously been obtained
from the petitioners for the specific purpose of satisfying the third respondents on
D   precisely that matter. It was clear that at the time all parties concerned regarded the 21
properties as having been released from the petitioners' floating charge by the time that
the petitioners' letter of 7 September 1990 was written. The petitioners had, prior to
7 September 1990, received in full the first tranche of repayment of borrowings by the
first respondents upon which repayment it was clear that the petitioners, the first
respondents and the third respondents were agreed that release of the 21 properties
E   from the petitioners' floating charge would occur. Release of 19 of these properties from
standard securities held by the petitioners had already occurred prior to 7 September
1990.

So far as the provisions of sec. 466 of the 1985 Act are concerned, it was not suggested
by the first respondents that they had proceeded by way of instrument of alteration
under that section. While this was so, it was to be noted that the wording of that section
F   showed that, even where such procedure was used, the effective date of alteration was
the date of the deed although the alteration might become void in certain circumstances
in terms of sec. 410 if it was not registered.

So far as procedure under sec. 419 of the Act is concerned, it is clear that no bilateral
deed is required to effect release of property from a floating charge. It was to be noted
that in terms of sec. 419(3)(b) the registrar could be directed by the court to enter a
G   memorandum of satisfaction in relation to release from a floating charge where such
certification cannot readily be obtained. This reinforced the point that all that was
required for the purposes of sec. 419 was unilateral consent to release on the part of the
creditor. What required acknowledgement in terms of sec. 419 was that property had
already been released and this in itself demonstrated that release could be effected
without resort to the formalities of either sec. 466 or sec. 419 with regard to registration.

H   Accordingly it was competent to release properties from a floating charge without
resort to the procedures set out in either of those two sections. Furthermore, in the
present case it was clear from the petitioners' letter of 7 September 1990 that they had
actually released the 21 properties from their floating charge. Accordingly, not only was
it clear that this is exactly what the petitioners, the first respondents and the third
respondents all expected and intended should happen but it was also clear that this is
what had actually happened. Therefore, not only was release competent outwith the

A

statutory procedures referred to but it had actually been effected in the present case so far as the 21 properties were concerned. Accordingly, the first question should be answered in the negative.

Mr McNeill, for the third respondents, adopted Mr Haddow's submission on this matter. He submitted that in order to understand the legal effect of the letter of 7 September 1990 it was necessary to understand the nature of dealings between the parties concerned and what their intentions were. It was clear that a refinancing deal was involved with the third respondents partially replacing the petitioners as lenders to the first respondents. Only such partial refinancing was to be achieved and accordingly both the petitioners and the third respondents would be left in a position where they had an interest to have security over properties of the first respondents. The correspondence made it clear that the petitioners were to be left after repayment of the first tranche of repayment of borrowing with eight identified properties as security. It was abundantly clear that release by the petitioners of the 21 properties from their floating charge was not only intended by all parties concerned but was an essential step in implementation of the refinancing deal.

B

C

It was to be noted that, while failure to register an instrument of alteration executed in terms of sec. 466 of the 1985 Act could lead to avoidance in a question with a liquidator or administrator or creditor of the company, there was no similar provision in sec. 419. It would be possible even now to proceed in terms of sec. 419 to achieve registration of a memorandum of satisfaction but that was not necessary. The important point was that sec. 419 referred to release which had already taken place and there was no statutory requirement for the form of such release.

D

In my opinion, the first question falls to be answered in the negative. I accept the submissions of Mr Haddow and Mr McNeill on this matter. So far as competency of release without statutory registration is concerned, I consider that sec. 419 of the 1985 Act makes it clear that release of the 21 properties from the petitioners' floating charge could be effected competently and effectively by the petitioners without registration of any memorandum of satisfaction in terms of that section. It is not suggested that in this case any attempt was made to execute an instrument of alteration in terms of sec. 466 of the Act but it is accepted that sec. 466 procedure is just one way of proceeding where properties are to be released from a floating charge. The terms of sec. 419 make it very clear indeed that the memorandum of satisfaction envisaged in that section is merely what it bears to be in terms of the section, namely a memorandum recording a prior release by the creditor of part of the debtor's property from the creditor's floating charge. Section 419(1)(b) in particular, in referring to part of the property charged "having been" released or "having ceased" to form part of the company's property, makes it clear, in my opinion, that this is so. Furthermore, the procedure under sec. 419(3)(b) for the court directing the registrar to enter a memorandum of satisfaction where this cannot readily be obtained reinforces this point. In contrast to the position of an instrument of alteration in terms of sec. 466 of the Act, there is no provision for failure to register under sec. 419 rendering the release void as against any party.

E

F

G

Not only is there no requirement, in my opinion, for registration of releases of properties from a creditor's floating charge to be registered in order to be effective, but I do not find it surprising that this is the position. The only party with an adverse interest to effectiveness of such a release is the creditor in a case such as the present. I suppose that in a sense a creditor of the creditor might have an interest to know what the creditor was doing but it is not suggested that that consideration is of any relevance in the present context. I envisage that a simple system of being able effectively to release properties from a floating charge is of commercial advantage to the creditor as well as to the debtor in expedition of dealings such as those involved in the present case. Nor does there

H

A   appear to be any sound reason why such registration should be required as a matter of public record. It is not as if there is any list of property covered by a floating charge over a company's whole property on public record to which recourse can be had to check the security being provided by a floating charge from time to time. Annual accounts go only a small way towards providing such detailed ongoing information. Property may be acquired and disposed of by the company without intimation to the registrar. In summary, it seems to me to be entirely reasonable that there is no requirement for

B   registration of a release of property from a floating charge. It also seems to me understandable that there are statutory mechanisms under sec. 466 and sec. 419 for formal registration where that happens to be sought in any particular case. However, what matters for present purposes is whether release is competent without such registration and, in my opinion, it is.

C   The other matter which arises in relation to the first question is whether the petitioners actually did release the 21 properties from their floating charge. In my opinion, upon the information upon which I am asked to decide this matter, they did so. It is clear that it was the intention of the petitioners, the first respondents and the third respondents that in return for capital repayments which had been made prior to 7 September 1990 the release concerned should be made. Indeed, it is inconceivable on such information as is available as to the dealings concerned that the third respondents would have agreed to

D   the involvement which they had in the matter unless there had been such release upon such repayment. That, of course, is not an end of the matter because one thing could be intended and another thing achieved. While this is so, I find it quite unrealistic to regard the petitioners' letter of 7 September 1990 other than as clear confirmation, to be shown to the third respondents, that release of the 21 properties there specified by the petitioners from their floating charge was not only agreed to in principle but had actually been effected prior to that date. In a matter where no formal deed is required, I find the

E   language of the petitioners' letter of 7 September 1990 apt to convey to the first respondents and the third respondents acknowledgement that such release had been effected.

    I am not persuaded that the use of the phrase "consent to the release" is inconsistent with this conclusion. In the context at least of a commercial dealing such as the present one, I find that no material distinction falls to be made between a creditor stating "I have

F   released . . ." and "I have given my consent to release . . .". I accept that the position might be otherwise if there was any sound reason to suppose that parties' intentions were to have some formal deed drawn up or some other formal step taken and that release should not be effective until this was done. I find reinforcement for the conclusion to which I have come in the terms of the undertaking given at the end of the letter of 7 September 1990, which I find consistent with that conclusion rather than the submission

G   made on behalf of the petitioners.

    It is agreed that the answer to the first question effectively provides the answers to questions (2)–(5) inclusive. Question (2) falls to be answered in the negative and I answer questions (3), (4) and (5) that the letter of 7 September 1990 is evidence of release of the 21 properties from the petitioners' floating charge prior to the date of the letter.

H   Questions (6) and (7) are superseded by my answer to question (1). It is right to record, however, that Mr Drummond Young submitted that, notwithstanding the petitioners' agreement prior to 7 September 1990 that the 21 properties should be released from their floating charge upon payment of the first tranche of capital, such agreement was part of a unitary contract with the first respondents. Essential conditions of this unitary contract included:

(1)   payment by the first respondents of the full balance of their indebtedness to the   A
       petitioners by 31 October 1990,

(2)   payment by the first respondents meanwhile of interest by direct debit, and

(3)   application of trade tie in respect of all properties concerned.

This submission became concentrated on the first of these points, in view no doubt of
the reference to payment of interest to be monthly in the petitioners' solicitors' letter of
22 August 1990 and the unchallenged submission that trade tie had in fact applied, being   B
Mr Haddow's responses to the second and third of these points. With regard to the first
point mentioned, Mr Drummond Young submitted that the contract between the
petitioners and the first respondents was unitary in nature, there being a presumption to
that effect (*Gloag on Contract* (2nd ed.) at p. 592–595). The first respondents being in
material breach of the essential condition for full payment by 31 October 1990 they
could not enforce any obligation on the part of the petitioners with regard to release of
the 21 properties from the petitioners' floating charge.   C

   In reply on this matter, Mr Haddow submitted that it was clear in the present case that
the petitioners' obligation to release the 21 properties from their floating charge in
exchange for payment of the first tranche of repayment of capital involved obligation
separable from the remainder of the contract between the petitioners and the first
respondents (*Gloag*, p. 594). Mr McNeill adopted Mr Haddow's submission on this
matter. In my opinion, Mr Haddow's submission is correct. As already recorded, I am   D
invited to determine the questions in issue on the basis of the correspondence lodged
and on that basis it seems to me clear that there was no intention in the contract between
the petitioners and the first respondents that the petitioners' obligation to release the 21
properties upon payment of the first tranche was dependent in any way whatsoever with
performance by the first respondents of their obligation to make payment of remaining
sums due by 31 October 1990. I record that Mr Moynihan specifically made no submission   E
on this matter.

   So far as question (8) is concerned, I am informed that the question is possibly
academic, and in any event at least virtually academic, in this case. This is because in the
case of only one property, the Alhambra, is there doubt whether the moveables are
owned by tenants. Mr Drummond Young referred to the use of the word "subjects" in
the petitioners' letter of 7 September 1990 and submitted that this should be interpreted   F
as covering only heritable subjects and not moveables. In submissions adopted by
Mr Haddow, Mr McNeill referred to *Erskine's Institutes*, Book II, Title I, para. 1 as
authority for the proposition that "subjects" comprise both heritage and moveables. He
submitted that the context should be looked at and, in context, there was no sound
reason why the reference to "subjects" should not include moveables in the present
context. Mr Drummond Young, in reply, referred to *Green's Glossary of Scottish Legal
Terms* (3rd ed., 1992) and Beaton's *Scots Law Terms and Expressions* (1982), where it is   G
stated respectively that "subjects", "usually" and "more commonly" refer to heritage
only although it could in appropriate context refer to moveables. Although the matter
was not very important in the present case "subjects" should be restricted to heritage in
the present context. On this matter, I agree with Mr Drummond Young. It seems to me
that ordinary commercial usage, at least, in a context such as the present would restrict
the meaning of "subjects" to heritage and exclude moveables. More generally, I have
no reason to doubt the accuracy of the glossary definitions referred to. Accordingly, I   H
answer question (8) in the negative.

   So far as questions (9) and (10) are concerned, Mr Drummond Young submitted that
these fell to be answered in the affirmative. He referred to the case of *Ross v Taylor* 1985
SC 156 and especially to what was said by the Lord President, giving the opinion of the
court, at p. 161. Mr Drummond Young pointed out that the legislation concerned was

A   now contained in sec. 53(7) of the *Insolvency Act* 1986 but that the material terms of the legislation involved in *Ross*'s case had not been changed. It is unnecessary to elaborate upon this matter as Mr Haddow and Mr McNeill did not contest Mr Drummond Young's submissions on this matter.

     With regard to questions (11) and (12), Mr Drummond Young submitted that the second respondents, as receivers, were entitled to these items for distribution in accordance with the terms of sec. 60 of the *Insolvency Act* 1986. In practical terms, the

B   petitioners would have a priority right over the third respondents so far as these items were concerned. Again, Mr Haddow and Mr NcNeill did not contest Mr Drummond Young's submission on this matter and I accordingly answer these questions in accordance with Mr Drummond Young's submissions.

     Mr Moynihan, for the second respondents, asked me to declare that they are receivers and not administrative receivers in terms of the *Insolvency Act* 1986 (sec. 29(2)(a) and

C   251) in the event of question (1) being answered in the negative. Having answered question (1) in the negative, I do so.

(Order accordingly)

Re D'Jan of London Ltd.

A

Chancery Division (Companies Court).
Hoffmann LJ (sitting as an additional judge of the Chancery Division).
Judgment delivered 17 June 1993.

> *Winding up — Summary remedy against delinquent directors etc. — Whether*
> *director was negligent in signing insurance proposal — Materiality of director's*
> *99 per cent ownership of company — Whether director had acted honestly and*
> *reasonably and ought fairly to be excused for negligence — Companies Act*
> *1985, sec. 727; Insolvency Act 1986, sec. 212.*

B

This was a summons by a liquidator under sec. 212 of the Insolvency Act 1986 against
"D", a former officer of the company. The company was insolvent with a deficiency as
regards unsecured creditors of about £500,000. D held 99 of the 100 issued ordinary
shares in the company, and his wife the other. He had proved as an unsecured creditor in
the sum of £102,913 and had been paid an interim dividend of 40p in the pound. The
liquidator had paid a further dividend of 20p but withheld payment to D pending the
resolution of the proceedings.

C

The liquidator's summons alleged that D was negligent in completing and signing a
proposal form for fire insurance, with the result that the insurers repudiated liability for
a fire at the company's premises in which stock said to be worth some £174,000 was
destroyed. D accepted that the wrong answer was given on the form, entitling the insurers
to repudiate. His evidence was that he did not fill in the form himself or read it before he
signed.

D

Held, declaring that D was liable to compensate the company for the loss caused by his
breach of duty in an amount not exceeding any unpaid dividends to which he would
otherwise be entitled as an unsecured creditor:

E

1. In failing even to read the form, D was negligent. Signing forms without reading
them was something a busy director might do, but that did not mean that it was not
negligent. A director did not always have to read the whole of every document which he
signed, but the proposal form was an extremely simple document asking a few questions
which D was the best person to answer. By signing the form, he accepted that he was the
person who should take responsibility for its contents.

F

2. The duty of care owed by a director at common law was accurately stated in
sec. 214(4) of the Insolvency Act 1986. Both on the objective test and on the subjective
test, D did not show reasonable diligence when he signed the form. He was therefore in
breach of his duty to the company.

3. It was no defence to argue that D and his wife as shareholders would probably have
ratified D's action if they had known or thought about it before the liquidation removed
their power to do so.

G

4. Although for the purposes of the law of negligence the company was a separate
entity to which D owed a duty of care which did not vary according to the number of
shares he owned, the economic reality of his 99 per cent shareholding could be taken into
account in exercising the court's discretionary power under sec. 727 of the Companies
Act 1985 to relieve a director from liability. His breach of duty in failing to read the form
before signing was not gross. It was the kind of thing which could happen to any busy
man. At that time the company was solvent and the only persons whose interests he was
foreseeably putting at risk by not reading the form were himself and his wife. D certainly
acted honestly. For the purposes of sec. 727 he acted reasonably and he ought fairly to be
excused for some, though not all, of the liability which he would otherwise have incurred.

H

A   The following case was referred to in the judgment:

Multinational Gas and Petrochemical Co v Multinational Gas and Petrochemical Services Ltd & Ors [1983] Ch 258.

Marion Simmons (instructed by Berwin Leighton) for the applicant.

Jonathan Russen (instructed by Ronald Fletcher Baker & Co) for the respondent.

B   JUDGMENT

Hoffmann LJ: This is a summons under sec. 212 of the *Insolvency Act* 1986 by a liquidator against a former officer of the company. This is a summary procedure which used to be called a misfeasance summons but has been extended to include breaches of any duty including the duty of care. The liquidator alleges that the respondent Mr D'Jan was negligent in completing and signing a proposal form for fire insurance with the

C   Guardian Royal Exchange Assurances plc. As a result, the insurers repudiated liability for a fire at the company's premises in Cornwall which had destroyed stock said to be worth some £174,000. The company is insolvent, having a deficiency as regards unsecured creditors of about £500,000. The liquidator therefore brings these proceedings for the benefit of the unsecured creditors.

Mr D'Jan signed the insurance proposal on 18 September 1986. It was headed

D   "Business insurances proposal". Mr D'Jan signed on the front page, under the words:

"I declare that to the best of my knowledge and belief all the statements and particulars made with regard to this proposal are true and I agree that this proposal shall be the basis of a contract of insurance to be expressed in the usual terms of the policy issued by Guardian Royal Exchange Assurances plc."

On the same page the form required certain information to be filled in and also asked

E   three specific questions, including:

"7. Have you or any director or partner . . . been director of any company which went into liquidation . . . ?"

The question was answered "No". Mr D'Jan admits that this was wrong. In the previous year, a company called Harleyshield Ltd, of which Mr D'Jan was a director, had gone into insolvent liquidation. And there had been a couple of other insolvencies

F   about five years earlier. The liquidator says that Mr D'Jan gave a wrong answer to another question as well, but as this involves construing the rather obscure language in which the question is phrased and as Mr Russen, who appeared for Mr D'Jan, realistically accepts that the wrong answer to question 7 was enough to entitle the insurers to repudiate, I need not say more about the other question.

Mr D'Jan says he realises — perhaps more clearly now than he did at the time — the

G   importance of giving correct answers on insurance proposals. But he says that he did not fill in the form himself or read it before he signed. It was filled in by his insurance broker, Tarik Shenyuz, who had been handling his personal and corporate insurance affairs for about five years. Mr D'Jan says that Mr Shenyuz had demonstrated his competence by obtaining good rates and recommending him to loss adjusters who had obtained satisfactory settlements on his claims. So he trusted Mr Shenyuz to fill in the form correctly.

H   Mr Shenyuz flatly contradicted this account of how the form came to be signed. He says that he simply delivered the form to Mr D'Jan's premises and took it away again, acting as no more than a messenger between the company and the firm of insurance brokers in Surrey for whom he was at the time acting as subagent. He says that Mr D'Jan's accountant Mr Ekrem was well versed in insurance matters and that the company would have needed no help in filling out the form.

Both Mr D'Jan and Mr Shenyuz are highly intelligent men who gave their evidence
with confidence and the conflict is not easy to resolve. But I prefer the evidence of
Mr D'Jan. He did not strike me as a man who would fill in his own forms. I think he
would have wanted Mr Shenyuz to earn his commission by attending to these matters
and I accept that he signed in the expectation that Mr Shenyuz would have completed
the form correctly.

Nevertheless I think that in failing even to read the form, Mr D'Jan was negligent.
Mr Russen said that the standard of care which directors owe to their companies is not
very exacting and signing forms without reading them is something a busy director might
reasonably do. I accept that in real life, this often happens. But that does not mean that
it is not negligent. People often take risks in circumstances in which it was not necessary
or reasonable to do so. If the risk materialises, they may have to pay a penalty. I do not
say that a director must always read the whole of every document which he signs. If he
signs an agreement running to 60 pages of turgid legal prose on the assurance of his
solicitor that it accurately reflects the board's instructions, he may well be excused from
reading it all himself. But this was an extremely simple document asking a few questions
which Mr D'Jan was the best person to answer. By signing the form, he accepted that he
was the person who should take responsibility for its contents. In my view, the duty of
care owed by a director at common law is accurately stated in sec. 214(4) of the
Insolvency Act 1986. It is the conduct of:

"... a reasonably diligent person having both—

    (a) the general knowledge, skill and experience that may reasonably be expected
           of a person carrying out the same functions as are carried out by that
           director in relation to the company, and

    (b) the general knowledge, skill and experience that that director has."

Both on the objective test and, having seen Mr D'Jan, on the subjective test, I think
that he did not show reasonable diligence when he signed the form. He was therefore in
breach of his duty to the company.

Mr Russen said that nevertheless the company could not complain of the breach of
duty because it is a principle of company law that an act authorised by all the shareholders
is in law the act of the company: see *Multinational Gas and Petrochemical Co v
Multinational Gas and Petrochemical Services Ltd* [1983] Ch 258. Mr D'Jan held 99 of
the 100 issued ordinary shares and Mrs D'Jan held the other. Mr D'Jan must be taken to
have authorised the wrong answer in the proposal because he signed it himself. As for
Mrs D'Jan, she had never been known to object to anything which her husband did in
the management of the company. If she had known about the way he signed the form
and it was too late to put the matter right, the chances are that she would also have
approved. She could hardly have brought a derivative action to sue her husband for
negligence because he could have procured the passing of a resolution absolving himself
from liability.

The difficulty is that unlike the *Multinational* case, in which the action alleged to be
negligent was specifically mandated by the shareholders, neither Mr nor Mrs D'Jan gave
any thought to the way in which the proposal had been filled in. Mr D'Jan did not realise
that he had given a wrong answer until the insurance company repudiated. By that time
the company was in liquidation. In my judgment the *Multinational* principle requires
that the shareholders should have, whether formally or informally, mandated or ratified
the act in question. It is not enough that they probably would have ratified if they had
known or thought about it before the liquidation removed their power to do so.

It follows that Mr D'Jan is in principle liable to compensate the company for his
breach of duty. But sec. 727 of the *Companies Act* 1985 gives the court a discretionary

A   power to relieve a director wholly or in part from liability for breaches of duty, including negligence, if the court considers that he acted honestly and reasonably and ought fairly to be excused. It may seem odd that a person found to have been guilty of negligence, which involves failing to take reasonable care, can ever satisfy a court that he acted reasonably. Nevertheless, the section clearly contemplates that he may do so and it follows that conduct may be reasonable for the purposes of sec. 727 despite amounting to lack of reasonable care at common law.

B   In my judgment, although Mr D'Jan's 99 per cent holding of shares is not sufficient to sustain a *Multinational* defence, it is relevant to the exercise of the discretion under sec. 727. It may be reasonable to take a risk in relation to your own money which would be unreasonable in relation to someone else's. And although for the purposes of the law of negligence the company is a separate entity to which Mr D'Jan owes a duty of care which cannot vary according to the number of shares he owns, I think that the economic

C   realities of the case can be taken into account in exercising the discretion under sec. 727. His breach of duty in failing to read the form before signing was not gross. It was the kind of thing which could happen to any busy man, although, as I have said, this is not enough to excuse it. But I think it is also relevant that in 1986, with the company solvent and indeed prosperous, the only persons whose interests he was foreseeably putting at risk by not reading the form were himself and his wife. Mr D'Jan certainly acted honestly. For the purposes of sec. 727 I think he acted reasonably and I think he ought

D   fairly to be excused for some, though not all, of the liability which he would otherwise have incurred. Mr D'Jan has proved as an unsecured creditor in the sum of £102,913. He has been paid an interim dividend of 40p in the pound and the liquidator has paid a further dividend of 20p but withheld payment to Mr D'Jan pending the resolution of these proceedings. In my view, having been responsible for the additional shortfall in respect of unsecured creditors, I do not think that he should be allowed any further

E   participation in competition with ordinary trade creditors. On the other hand, I do not think it would be fair to ask him to return what he has received or make a further contribution out of his own pocket to the company's assets. I therefore declare that Mr D'Jan is liable to compensate the company for the loss caused by his breach of duty in an amount not exceeding any unpaid dividends to which he would otherwise be entitled as an unsecured creditor.

F   (*Order accordingly*)

G

H

Secretary of State for Trade and Industry v Palmer.

Court of Session (Outer House).
Lord MacLean.
Judgment delivered 24 June 1993.

Disqualifying unfit directors of insolvent companies — Making of administration order — Whether interim order was administration order for purposes of disqualification application — Whether disqualification application was out of time — Insolvency Act 1986, sec. 8, 9(4); Company Directors Disqualification Act 1986, sec. 6(2), 7(2).

An interim order under sec. 9(4) of the Insolvency Act 1986 was not an administration order for the purposes of sec. 6(2)(b) of the Company Directors Disqualification Act 1986; and accordingly a disqualification application by the Secretary of State made more than two years after the court made interim orders under sec. 9(4) but within two years of the making of administration orders under sec. 8(3) was not out of time under sec. 7(2) of the Disqualification Act.

The following cases were referred to in the opinion:

Consumer & Industrial Press Ltd, Re (1988) 4 BCC 68.
Harris Simons Construction Ltd, Re (1989) 5 BCC 11; [1989] 1 WLR 368.
SCL Building Services Ltd, Re (1989) 5 BCC 746.

A R Dewar (instructed by the solicitor to the Secretary of State) for the Secretary of State for Trade and Industry.

Neil Davidson (instructed by Drummond Miller, for Friels, Uddingston) for the respondent.

OPINION

Lord MacLean: The first order in this petition, it is agreed, was made on 31 October 1991 when the court ordered intimation and service of the petition, and answers within 21 days thereafter. In this petition the Secretary of State for Trade and Industry, the petitioner, seeks a disqualification order in terms of sec. 6 of the *Company Directors Disqualification Act* 1986 against the respondent, Brian John Palmer.

The respondent was a director of Hinari Consumer Electronics Ltd (referred to as "Consumer") and Hinari Domestic Ltd (referred to as "Domestic"). On 3 October 1989 the directors of each company presented petitions to the court in terms of the *Insolvency Act* 1986 and on the same day in respect of each company the court pronounced orders in terms of sec. 9(4) of that Act. Section 9(4) provides that the court on hearing a petition may dismiss it, or adjourn the hearing conditionally or unconditionally, or make an interim order or any other order that it thinks fit. The orders it made in this case, it is accepted, were interim orders. On 1 November 1989 the court pronounced administration orders in respect of both companies in terms of sec. 8(2) of the 1986 Act. Section 8(1) of the Act provides that, if the court is satisfied that a company is or is likely to become unable to pay its debts within the meaning of sec. 123 of the Act and it considers that the making of an order under sec. 8 would be likely to achieve one or more of the purposes mentioned in subsec. (3), it may make an administration order in relation to the company. Subsection (3) sets out four purposes for whose achievement an administration order might be made. They are, (a) the survival of the company, and the whole or any part of its undertaking, as a going concern; (b) the approval of a voluntary arrangement made under Pt. I; (c) the sanctioning under sec. 425 of the *Companies Act* 1985 of a compromise or arrangement between the company and any such persons as are mentioned in that section; and

A (d) a more advantageous realisation of the company's assets than would be effected on a winding up.

Mr Dewar, who appeared for the Secretary of State, informed me that the orders pronounced on 1 November 1989 specified the purposes (a), (b) and (d), but that the orders pronounced on 3 October 1989 made no mention of these purposes.

B Section 7(2) of the *Company Directors Disqualification Act* 1986 (which in a number of respects specified in sec. 21 of the Act, falls to be read with the *Insolvency Act* 1986) provides that, except with leave of the court, an application for the making under sec. 6 of a disqualification order against any person shall not be made after the end of the period of two years beginning with the day on which the company of which that person is or had been a director, became insolvent. For the purposes of sec. 6 and 7 a company becomes insolvent, according to the terms of sec. 6(2), in three situations, one of which, provided for in sec. 6(2)(b), is when an administration order is made in relation to the

C company. The question is, what is comprehended in this context by the term "administration order"? Is it wide enough to include the orders pronounced in terms of sec. 9(4) of the *Insolvency Act* 1986 on 3 October 1989? Or, should it be restricted to the orders pronounced in terms of sec. 8(2) on 1 November 1989? On which date did the companies become insolvent? If on the former date, this petition is out of time and leave of the court would be required to permit it to proceed. If on the latter date, the petition is within time, because the first order in it was pronounced one day before the expiry of

D the two-year period provided in sec. 7(2). For the sake of completeness, but not, I think, relevancy, I should add that an order for the winding up of Consumer was made on 19 February 1991, and that for the winding up of Domestic was made on 15 May 1991.

Mr Davidson for the respondent submitted that an interim administration order was an order comprehended by sec. 6(2)(b) of the *Company Directors Disqualification Act* 1986. Such an order would only be granted on prima facie evidence that the company in

E question was insolvent. Finality was not of the essence because an administration order might be discharged. The purpose of such an order was to provide breathing space for a company facing insolvency. Its purpose was to allow the company to work its way out, short of liquidation. He pointed out that in terms of sec. 9(4) of the *Insolvency Act* 1986 an order, such as the initial order in this case, would be granted by the court only after a hearing. The language of sec. 8(1)(a) in its reference to "is or is likely to become unable

F to pay its debts" made it clear that there was to be no absolute finding of insolvency. So the court, under sec. 9(4), had a width of approach. It might take the view that the company was unable to pay its debts or was likely to become unable to pay them. The order granted by the court was, thus, not final. That was also to be seen from the terms of sec. 18 of the *Insolvency Act* 1986 which provided for a discharge or variation of the administration order. Indeed, sec. 18(3) provided inter alia that an administration order

G might be discharged, and an interim order made in its place. What was pronounced on 3 October 1989 was an order of the court. An order *ad interim* was still such an order and was nevertheless an administration order. If there was doubt, sec. 7(2) should be read strictly since it was in the nature of a punishment and imposed a restriction on the freedom of the individual.

Mr Dewar for the petitioner acknowledged that no decision on this matter had been reached either north or south of the border. No other test for insolvency was relevant

H except that which was provided in sec. 6(2). The *Company Directors Disqualification Act* 1986 was in tandem with the *Insolvency Act* 1986: see sec. 22(3) of the former and the definition in sec. 247 of the latter. If one read sec. 8–11 of the *Insolvency Act* 1986 it was plain that an interim order was not an administration order per se. With regard to the requirement in sec. 8(1)(a) of the Insolvency Act, namely that the court must be "satisfied" that a company is or is likely to become unable to pay its debts, it was unlikely

to be so satisfied at the stage when an interim order was pronounced. "Satisfaction"   A
meant more than a mere possibility. For the court to be satisfied there would have to be
documentation or at least a detailed submission. In the case of *Re Harris Simons
Construction Ltd* (1989) 5 BCC 11, *Hoffmann* J disagreeing with *Peter Gibson* J in *Re
Consumer & Industrial Press Ltd* (1988) 4 BCC 68, held that for a court considering
whether an administration order was likely to achieve one of the purposes set out in
subsec. (3), the degree of probability had to be such that there was a real prospect of
achieving one or more of these purposes. For that to be determined there would have to   B
be a full hearing. There had been none in this case. He referred also to *Peter Gibson* J's
further observations on this question in *Re SCL Building Services Ltd* (1989) 5 BCC
746. If an interim order was to be regarded as an administration order the level of
protection to the company under and in terms of sec. 10(1) of the *Insolvency Act* 1986
would be nil. On a fair reading of the provisions of both Acts there had to be an
administration order and nothing less for a company to become insolvent. I should repel   C
the first plea-in-law for the respondent and allow the petition to proceed.

In reply, Mr Davidson referred me to the *Insolvency Rules* 1986 (SI 1986/1925), Pt. 2,
r. 2.2(1). That made provision for the granting of an administration order on a report by
an independent person. That might be all that the court required before making such an
order. There did not have to be a full or elaborate hearing. Mr Dewar pointed out that
the rule merely allowed for documentation to be presented to the court and that it was
enabling only.   D

In my opinion the reference to an administration order in sec. 6(2)(b) of the *Company
Directors Disqualification Act* 1986 means just that — namely an administration order
granted in terms of sec. 8(1), (2) and (3) of the *Insolvency Act* 1986. When such an order
is pronounced the court has to fulfil the conditions in both sec. 8(1)(a) and sec. 8(1)(b),
and it must specify in its order which of the purposes in sec. 8(3) it considers would be
likely to be achieved by the making of the order. While it is not, I think, possible to   E
prescribe the kind of hearing necessary in any case for the court to fulfil its statutory
functions under sec. 8(1), it is of some significance in this case that when it pronounced
the interim order of 3 October 1989 the court did not regard itself as obliged to specify
any of the purposes under sec. 8(3) it thought was likely to be achieved. I do also think
that the language of sec. 18(1) and (3) indicates a distinction between an administration
order per se and an interim order. What further influences me towards this construction
is the point made by Mr Dewar that the protection afforded the company by the terms   F
of sec. 10 would be greatly reduced if not rendered nugatory, were the respondent's
construction to be preferred.

I shall therefore repel the respondent's first plea-in-law and allow the petition to
proceed.

(*Order accordingly*)   G

———————————

A # Re Baku Consolidated Oilfields Ltd.

Chancery Division (Companies Court).
Chadwick J.
Judgment delivered 2 July 1993.

Winding up — Distribution of surplus assets received 50 years after winding up
ordered — Position of those on register of members, personal representatives
B *and beneficiaries, and those in possession of share certificates.*

This was an application by the liquidator of Baku Consolidated Oilfields Ltd for directions as to the manner in which he should distribute a sum of £3,026,056 received from the Foreign Compensation Commission in respect of the company's claim for compensation for assets seized by the Soviet Government in 1920.

C The company was ordered to be wound up in 1943. Joint liquidators were appointed, the creditors were paid in full out of the available assets in England, and a modest distribution was made to the contributories. The joint liquidators obtained their release in 1954. The official receiver became liquidator in their place. A new liquidator was appointed by the Secretary of State in place of the official receiver in 1987.

D Those who could or might claim to be entitled to share in a distribution of the surplus assets of the company fell into three main classes: (1) those whose names appeared on the register of members of the company, (2) those who claimed through registered members, either as personal representatives or as beneficiaries entitled under a will, and (3) those who did not fall within either of those two classes but who were in possession of a share certificate issued by the company.

Held, giving directions:

E 1. The company's articles of association required the surplus assets on a winding up to be divided rateably amongst the members. There was no evidence, in relation to those who had been traced, to displace the statutory presumption that those whose names appeared on the register of members of the company were members of the company. Also, when giving directions as to the distribution of surplus assets in a winding up, it was right to treat as members those who would be entitled to have their names placed on the register.

F 2. Executors and administrators under an English grant of probate or administration were entitled to be recognised by the liquidator as the persons having title to the shares registered in the name of the deceased member in respect of whose estate they were appointed.

3. Persons claiming to represent a deceased member under a foreign grant of probate or administration, or persons claiming as beneficiaries under a will or intestacy, did not G enjoy the same recognition. If the liquidator was satisfied that such person would be entitled to obtain an English grant of probate or administration then he was at liberty to distribute the deceased member's share to that claimant without requiring the formality of a grant. In cases in which the liquidator did not think he could be sufficiently protected against liability by a suitable indemnity, he was entitled to insist on the protection of an English grant.

H 4. Possession of a share certificate made out in the name of another was no evidence against the company of any title in the possessor to the shares. Neither the company, nor the liquidator, was required to recognise the title of a transferee until he had complied with the articles' requirement to submit an instrument of transfer in the prescribed form for registration and had been registered. The liquidator ought not to distribute to a claimant whose claim was based solely on possession of a share certificate. He had to enquire into the circumstances. But he could distribute to a claimant who proved that he

was beneficially entitled, not merely to the certificate, but to the shares to which it related.   A
That claimant could compel the person registered in respect of those shares, or his
personal representative, to execute a proper instrument of transfer, and his case was
indistinguishable in principle from that of a beneficiary claiming under a will or intestacy.

The following cases were referred to in the judgment:

Bahia and San Francisco Railway Co, Re (1868) LR 3 QB 584.
New York Breweries Co Ltd v Attorney-General [1899] AC 62.   B
Reese River Silver Mining Co Ltd v Smith (1869) LR 4 HL 64.

Catherine Roberts (instructed by Norton Rose) for the liquidator.

JUDGMENT

Chadwick J: Baku Consolidated Oilfields Ltd was incorporated in 1919 under the
Companies Acts 1908 to 1917 for the purposes of acquiring and exploiting oil concessions   C
in the state of Azerbaidjan, in the southern part of what was then the Russian Empire.
The company never commenced trading. In 1920 the Russian assets which it had
acquired on incorporation were seized by the Soviet Government. The company lodged
a claim for compensation with the Russian Claims Department of the Board of Trade.
That claim did not bear fruit.

On 8 November 1943 it was ordered by *Bennett* J that the company be wound up   D
under the provisions of the *Companies Act* 1929. Joint liquidators were appointed, the
creditors were paid in full out of the available assets in this country, and a modest
distribution was made to the contributories. The joint liquidators obtained their release
in 1954. The official receiver became liquidator in their place.

Thirty years passed. On 15 January 1986 agreement was reached between Her
Majesty's Government and the Government of the Soviet Union for the payment of   E
Russian compensation claims. On 29 May 1987 Mr John Alexander, a partner in the firm
of KPMG Peat Marwick, was appointed liquidator of the company by the Secretary of
State in place of the official receiver under the provisions of the *Insolvency Act* 1986.
During 1990 the liquidator received from the Foreign Compensation Commission a total
sum of £3,026,056 in respect of the company's claim. By an application made on 9 July
1992 under sec. 112 of the 1986 Act the liquidator sought directions as to the manner in
which that sum ("the fund") should be distributed.   F

That application came before me in November 1992. On 16 November 1992 I made
an order in the following terms, so far as material:

"1 . . .

(i) that the applicant do distribute

(a) to registered members of the company who have been traced their   G
appropriate entitlement to the fund; and

(b) to the executors and administrators under an English grant of probate
of registered members who have been traced their appropriate
entitlement to the fund;

(ii) that the applicant have liberty to distribute their appropriate entitlement to   H
the fund to

(a) the executors and administrators of registered members under a
foreign grant of probate; and

(b) beneficiaries under a will whether English or foreign where there is
no English grant of probate; and

(c) persons having possession of a share certificate of the company in circumstances where the applicant is satisfied that they are beneficially entitled to the shares represented by the said share certificate;

(iii) that subject to para. (ii) the applicant do not distribute any part of the fund to persons whose names are not entered in the register of members of the company notwithstanding the fact that such a person may be in possession of a share certificate of the company . . ."

At the time when that order was made I indicated the reasons which had led me to give those directions; and I further indicated that I would set out those reasons in a formal judgment if it was thought that that would be of assistance. The liquidator was content, at that time, to proceed without a formal judgment. He has since taken the view that it would be of assistance to have a judgment which can be put before those who are affected by the directions given on 16 November 1992. It is in those circumstances that I now hand down this judgment.

Articles 135 and 136 of the company's articles of association require that, on a winding up, the assets remaining after payment of the liabilities of the company and the costs of liquidation ("the surplus assets") are to be divided rateably amongst the members of the company. Prima facie, the members of the company are those whose names are entered in the register of members — see sec. 25 and 102 of the *Companies Act* 1929 and, now, sec. 22 and 361 of the *Companies Act* 1985. The register is not, however, conclusive — see *Reese River Silver Mining Co v Smith* (1869) LR 4 HL 64, at p. 77 (Lord *Westbury*) and at p. 80 (Lord *Cairns*). The court can order rectification of the register as well after as before winding up. In my view the correct approach, when giving directions as to the distribution of surplus assets in a winding up, is to treat as members those who would be entitled to have their names placed on the register. It is, I think, unnecessary to insist on the formality of an application to rectify the register.

It can be seen from the directions which I gave on 16 November 1992 that those who could or might claim to be entitled to share in a distribution of the surplus assets of the company fell into three main classes: (1) those whose names appeared on the register of members of the company, (2) those who claimed through registered members, either as personal representatives or as beneficiaries entitled under a will, and (3) those who did not fall within either of those two classes but who were in possession of a share certificate issued by the company.

There is no difficulty in the case of the first category. I have seen no evidence, in relation to those who have been traced, to displace the statutory presumption that those whose names appear on the register of members of the company are members of the company.

The second category must be further subdivided. There is a relevant distinction between those who claim as personal representatives under an English grant, and those who claim as personal representatives under a foreign grant or as beneficiaries. That distinction arises from the terms of art. 14 of the articles of association of the company and the decision of the House of Lords in *New York Breweries Co Ltd v Attorney-General* [1899] AC 62. Article 14 provides, so far as material, that:

"The executors or administrators of a deceased member (not being one of several joint holders) shall be the only persons entitled to be recognised by the company as having any title to be registered in respect of the shares registered in the name of such member . . ."

It was held by the House of Lords in the *New York Breweries Co* case that "executors or administrators" in that context meant an executor or administrator acting under an English grant: see at p. 70 (Lord *Halsbury* LC) and at p. 77 (Lord *Davey*). It follows that the surplus assets ought to be distributed on the basis that executors and administrators under an English grant are entitled to be recognised by the liquidator as the persons having title to the shares registered in the name of the deceased member in respect of whose estate they were appointed. This is reflected in para. 1(i)(b) of my order of 16 November 1992.

Although the effect of art. 14, construed in the light of the decision of the House of Lords in the *New York Breweries Co* case, is that persons claiming to represent a deceased member under a foreign grant of probate or administration, or persons claiming as beneficiaries under a will or intestacy, are not persons who are entitled to be recognised by the company or its liquidator as having any title to be registered in respect of the shares registered in the name of that member, it does not follow that the liquidator is bound to ignore or disallow their claims. If the liquidator is satisfied, on the evidence put before him, that a claimant is a person who would be entitled to obtain an English grant of probate or administration to the estate of a deceased member, then, in my view, he may, if he thinks fit, distribute the deceased member's share of the surplus assets to that claimant without requiring the formality of a grant. To hold otherwise would oblige the liquidator to insist that, in all cases, the claimant must go to the trouble and expense of obtaining an English grant. There may well be cases in which the liquidator thinks it necessary, for his own protection, to take that course; but I think it would be wrong to give directions which required him to do so in cases in which he was satisfied that there was no appreciable risk of an adverse claim. Paragraphs 1(ii)(a) and (b) of my order of 16 November 1992 are intended to reflect this approach. The liquidator is to be at liberty to distribute to the claimants described in those paragraphs; but he is not directed to do so.

In deciding whether or not to exercise his power to distribute a deceased member's share of the surplus assets to a claimant who has not obtained an English grant of probate or administration, the liquidator will be wise to keep in mind that he may thereby become liable as an executor *de son tort* in respect of that share. In particular, he may become liable to account for any estate duty, inheritance or other tax which may be payable in respect of the death of the deceased member. This, of course, was the point at issue in the *New York Breweries* case. Nothing in the order which I made on 16 November was intended to affect, or could affect, the claims of the Revenue, of any other creditor or of any beneficiary to be paid out of assets forming part of the deceased member's estate. The liquidator may take the view that, in most cases — and, in particular, in cases where the amounts are small and the claimant appears to be a person of substance — he can be sufficiently protected against liability as an executor *de son tort* by a suitable indemnity. In cases in which he does not take that view, he is entitled to insist on the protection of an English grant.

The third category to which my order of 16 November 1992 was addressed comprises those who are in possession of a share certificate issued by the company. The company was, as I have indicated, incorporated under the *Companies (Consolidation) Act* 1908. Sections 22 and 23 of the 1908 Act are in these terms, so far as material:

> "22(1) The shares or other interest of any member in a company shall be personal estate transferable in manner provided by the articles of the company . . .
>
> 23 A certificate, under the common seal of the company, specifying any shares or stock held by any member, shall be prima facie evidence of the title of the member to the shares or stock."

Similar provisions are found in the *Companies Act* 1929 (sec. 62 and 68), the Act of 1948 (sec. 73 and 81) and the Act of 1985 (sec. 182 and 186).

The effect of sec. 23 of the 1908 Act and its statutory successors was explained in *Re Bahia and San Francisco Railway Co* (1868) LR 3 QB 584 — a decision on sec. 31 of the

A   *Companies Act* 1862 which was in similar terms. Sir *Alexander Cockburn* CJ described the position in these words, at p. 595:

> ". . . [the certificate] is a declaration by the company to all the world that the person in whose name the certificate is made out, and to whom it is given, is a shareholder in the company . . . with the intention that it shall be so used by the person to whom it is given, and acted upon in the sale and transfer of shares."

B   Possession of a share certificate made out in the name of another is, of itself, no evidence against the company of any title in the possessor to the shares to which the certificate relates.

Section 22 of the 1908 Act and its statutory successors require and enable shares to be transferred in the manner provided by the articles of association of the company. Article 11 is in these terms:

C
> "The instrument of transfer of any shares shall be executed both by the transferor and transferee, and the transferor shall, so far as the company is concerned, be deemed to remain the holder of such shares until the name of the transferee is entered in the register in respect thereof. The instrument of transfer shall be in the usual common form."

Article 13 requires that every instrument of transfer shall be left at the office of the D   company for registration, accompanied by the certificate of the shares to be transferred and such other evidence as the company may require to prove the title of the transferor or his right to transfer the shares. That article repeats the direction that the transferor shall be deemed the holder until the transferee is registered in respect of the shares transferred.

In the light of these provisions it is clear that neither the company, nor its liquidator, E   are obliged to recognise a person claiming title to shares as a transferee until an instrument of transfer in the prescribed form has been submitted for registration and has been registered.

It follows that it would be wrong to direct the liquidator to distribute any part of the surplus assets to a person whose only claim to a share in those assets was that he or she was in possession of a share certificate. The liquidator ought not to be directed to F   distribute to a person claiming as a transferee save in circumstances in which he could be required to enter the name of that claimant on the register. But it does not follow that there are no circumstances in which it would be sensible and appropriate for the liquidator, if he thinks fit, to recognise the claim of a transferee claimant. If the liquidator is satisfied, on the evidence before him, that a particular claimant who is in possession of a share certificate is beneficially entitled to the shares to which that certificate relates — so that the claimant would be able to compel the person registered in respect of those G   shares, or his personal representative, to execute a proper instrument of transfer — then the liquidator ought not to be obliged to put the claimant to the trouble and expense of perfecting his title. The position, in such a case, is indistinguishable in principle from that of a beneficiary claiming under a will or intestacy. The function of the liquidator — as sec. 143 of the *Insolvency Act* 1986 makes clear — is to secure that the assets of the company are got in, realised and distributed, to the extent of any surplus after the payment of the creditors, to the persons entitled to that surplus. Where the liquidator H   has satisfied himself that a claimant is entitled beneficially, it is not, as it seems to me, necessary to the proper discharge of his function that the liquidator insist that the claimant's title be perfected by a strict compliance with the formalities required by the articles of association. Claimants ought not to be put to expense unless that is unavoidable. It will be unavoidable if there is no other way in which the liquidator can obtain satisfactory protection from adverse claims; but, as I have already indicated, the

liquidator may properly be allowed to decide whether, and if so to what extent, he $\qquad$ A
requires protection in individual cases.

The principles upon which distribution may be made to those claiming as transferees
are reflected in para. 1(ii)(c) and 1(iii) of my order of 16 November 1992. In particular,
subpara. (iii) is intended to make it clear that the liquidator ought not to distribute any
part of the surplus assets of the company to a claimant whose claim is based solely on
possession of a share certificate. The liquidator must enquire into the circumstances in $\qquad$ B
which the claimant came into possession of the share certificate; and must satisfy himself
that the claimant is beneficially entitled, not merely to the certificate itself, but to the
shares to which it relates.

The evidence before me on the present application includes a substantial volume of
correspondence comprising the responses of claimants to inquiries made by the liquidator
for the purpose of ascertaining the circumstances in which they came into possession of
the share certificates which they now hold. It is clear from that correspondence that $\qquad$ C
some claimants purchased the share certificates as collectors or scripophilists; that is to
say, they purchased the certificate as a document having its own aesthetic or intrinsic
value. This is understandable in the circumstances (1) that, until 1986 or thereabouts
when the prospect that Russian compensation claims might be paid began to emerge as
a real possibility, the shares in companies whose assets had been confiscated by the
Soviet Government at the time of the Russian revolution were of little or no value, and $\qquad$ D
(2) that the share certificates themselves, which are elaborate and colourful documents,
may be thought to have aesthetic merit. At the least, it is possible to imagine that these
old certificates (unlike most certificates now issued) might have some ornamental value.
Be that as it may, the evidence suggests that there is an active market in old share
certificates and bonds which owes nothing to any value attributable to the underlying
obligations in respect of which those certificates or bonds were originally issued.

In my view the sale and purchase of a share certificate as a collector's item in the $\qquad$ E
circumstances and in the market which I have described is likely to lead to the conclusion
that the purchaser was not intended to, and did not, become beneficially entitled to the
shares to which that certificate relates. The absence of any attempt to provide, or to
obtain, a properly executed transfer — by the registration of which alone title to the
shares could be passed from vendor to purchaser — points towards that conclusion. I
have not, of course, considered or ruled upon individual cases. My order of 16 November $\qquad$ F
1992 gave liberty to apply to those within para. 1(iii) who might wish to persuade the
court that the view which I have expressed was wrong, either as a matter of principle or
in their own particular cases. Unless and until the court is so persuaded, the liquidator
ought to act on the basis that those who purchased share certificates as collectors did not
become beneficially entitled to the shares. As I explained at the time, that is the basis
upon which I made the order which I did.

$\qquad$ G
(*Order accordingly*)

———————————

$\qquad$ H

A **Midrome Ltd v Shaw.**

Court of Appeal (Civil Division).
Sir Thomas Bingham MR, Steyn and Hoffmann L JJ.
Judgment delivered 5 July 1993.

B
Appeals in insolvency proceedings — Appeals and reviews of court orders (winding up) — Whether appellant needed leave to appeal from decisions of High Court judge in insolvency proceedings — Insolvency Rules 1986 (SI 1986/1925), r. 7.47.

By virtue of r. 7.47 of the Insolvency Rules 1986 when the winding-up jurisdiction was being exercised by a county court, or by the registrar at the High Court, there was a single appeal without leave to a single judge of the High Court and thereafter a further appeal lay only with leave and not as a matter of right. Accordingly the appellant required leave
C **to appeal to the Court of Appeal against a High Court judgment that a winding-up order made by the registrar be affirmed.**

The following cases were referred to in the judgment of Bingham MR:

Busytoday Ltd, Re [1992] BCC 480; [1992] 1 WLR 683.
Calahurst Ltd, Re (1989) 5 BCC 318.

Nigel Ley (instructed by Finers) for the appellant.
D
Daniel Serota QC (instructed by Wallace & Partners) for the respondent.

JUDGMENT

Bingham MR: This matter concerns a company named Midrome Ltd which seeks to appeal against an order made by *Ferris* J on 5 February 1993. The issue which has come before the court for preliminary consideration is whether the company's appeal is one
E that it needs leave to make or whether it is an appeal it can make without leave as of right.

The facts giving rise to this issue are not of great significance but I shall recite them briefly in order to show how the problem arises. On 8 May 1992 a district judge sitting in the Willesden County Court ordered the company to pay the plaintiff in an action, Mrs Shaw, interim damages (inclusive of interest) amounting in total to £4,550. The company
F did not make that payment but instead on 13 May 1992 sought to appeal against the district judge's judgment. The appeal first of all came before the court on 3 December 1992 when it was adjourned part heard. Meanwhile, however, there were other developments. Mrs Shaw, as judgment creditor, petitioned for the winding up of the company on 9 July 1992 and after certain adjournments an order was made by Mr Registrar *Buckley* winding up the company on 9 December 1992. The company
G then applied to rescind that winding-up order. The application to rescind came before Mr Registrar *Buckley* on 16 December when he pointed out that evidence would be needed if he were to be persuaded to rescind the order and he adjourned the application to the judge for a hearing date of 18 January 1993. Meanwhile, he directed that the winding-up order should not be drawn up until 18 January.

On 18 January the matter came before His Honour Judge *Moseley* who for reasons that I need not go into adjourned the matter to 1 February. On 1 February it came before
H *Ferris* J and a further application was made to him for an adjournment. He was clearly reluctant to grant the adjournment but did grant a short adjournment until 5 February. Meanwhile the company had given notice of appeal on 11 January 1993 against the registrar's winding-up order.

Accordingly there were three matters that came before *Ferris* J on 5 February. First of all, there was a renewed application for an adjournment because the company sought a further adjournment despite the adjournment it had already had. Secondly, there was the application to rescind the order made by Mr Registrar *Buckley* on 9 December. Thirdly, there was an application that that order should be overruled. *Ferris* J heard the matter. He refused an adjournment. He refused to rescind the order and he ordered, for reasons which he set out in his judgment, that the winding-up order be affirmed. It is, as I say, that judgment which it is now sought to appeal.

Mr Ley, who appears on behalf of a director of the company and not apparently on behalf of the company itself, submits that leave is not necessary even in respect of the decision that the matter should not be adjourned and the decision that the order should not be rescinded. He bases himself primarily on O. 59, r. 1A(5)(d) of the Rules of the Supreme Court which provides:

"(5) Notwithstanding anything in paragraph (3), the following orders shall be treated as final—

. . .

(d) an order for the winding up of a company;"

Accordingly he submits that since, under sec. 18(1)(h) of the *Supreme Court Act* 1981, it is only interlocutory orders where as a general rule leave is necessary, an order for the winding up of the company is a final order for which leave is not necessary.

Plainly, O. 59, r. 1A(5)(d) gives him the basis of an argument so far as the winding-up order itself is concerned but it is relevant to draw attention also to O. 59, r. 1A(6)(w) which provides that among the orders to be treated as interlocutory are orders for, or relating to, the fixing or adjournment of trial dates.

It is further relevant to draw attention to O. 59, r. 1A(6)(bb) which similarly treats as interlocutory an order setting aside, or refusing to set aside, another judgment or order whether such other judgment or order is final or interlocutory. It would accordingly seem to me that at the outset it is obvious that the application for an adjournment, and the application refusing rescission, are orders for which leave is in any event necessary.

Even so far as the winding-up order is concerned, however, the matter does not in my judgment rest with the provisions of O. 59, r. 1A(5)(d) to which I have already drawn attention, because when one turns to the *Insolvency Rules* 1986, and in particular r. 7.47, one finds the following:

"(1) Every court having jurisdiction under the Act to wind up companies may review, rescind or vary any order made by it in the exercise of that jurisdiction.

(2) An appeal from a decision made in the exercise of that jurisdiction by a county court or by a registrar of the High Court lies to a single judge of the High Court; and an appeal from a decision of that judge on such an appeal lies, with the leave of that judge or the Court of Appeal, to the Court of Appeal."

Those two subrules seem to me to make it abundantly plain that when the winding-up jurisdiction is being exercised by a county court, or by the registrar at the High Court, there is a single appeal without leave to a single judge of the High Court and thereafter a further appeal only with leave and not as a matter of right. Mr Ley, however, submits that that is an incorrect reading of the rule and that in subr. (2) "that jurisdiction" does not refer to the jurisdiction to wind up, although that is a jurisdiction which is referred to as "that jurisdiction" in subr. (1), but to the jurisdiction to review, rescind or vary any order. That is to my mind an entirely ungrammatical and unsatisfactory reading of the rule and it seems to me that the meaning of "that jurisdiction" in r. 7.47(2) must be the same as that in subr. (1) which undoubtedly includes the jurisdiction to wind up.

I have accordingly for my part really no doubt at all in my mind that where a decision to wind up or any ancillary decision is made by a county court or by a registrar of the

A High Court and there is then an appeal to a single judge of the High Court any further appeal requires the leave either of that judge or of the Court of Appeal. That, I think, reproduces by analogy the effect of sec. 375(2) of the *Insolvency Act* 1986 which governs personal insolvency and it seems to me the inescapable meaning of these particular provisions.

B I am naturally fortified in that conclusion when I find that a similar conclusion clearly commended itself to *Harman* J in *Re Calahurst Ltd* (1989) 5 BCC 318 and in particular the passage at p. 319F; also to *Mummery* J in *Re Busytoday Ltd* [1992] BCC 480 and in particular the passage in his judgment at p. 484C–F. A similar conclusion is expressed in the current edition of *Palmer's Company Law* which simply says (at para. 15.203):

> "Appeals from decisions made in the exercise of insolvency jurisdiction by a county court or by a registrar of the High Court lie to a single judge of the High Court, and any appeal from a decision of that judge on such an appeal lies, with C the leave of that judge or of the Court of Appeal, to the Court of Appeal."

That very succinctly and accurately to my mind summarises the correct law on this subject. I would accordingly hold on this preliminary question that leave is required to appeal against each of the three paragraphs of *Ferris* J's judgment of 5 February.

Steyn LJ: I agree.

D **Hoffmann LJ:** I agree. Section 375 of the *Insolvency Act* 1986 and r. 7.47 of the Insolvency Rules were intended to establish a uniform system of appeal in personal and corporate insolvency actions. A litigant has one appeal as of right and any further appeal only with leave. If the decision is made by a High Court registrar, or county court judge, the appeal lies as of right to a judge of the Chancery Division and thereafter only with leave. If the decision is made by a judge of the High Court the appeal lies as of right to the Court of Appeal and then only with leave to the House of Lords.

E (*Order accordingly*)

F

G

H

Re Paramount Airways Ltd (No. 3).　　　　　　　　　　　　　A

Chancery Division (Companies Court).
Evans-Lombe J.
Judgment delivered 27 July 1993.

> *Administration orders — Debts and liabilities incurred under contracts of*
> *employment adopted by administrators — Administrators made employees*
> *redundant — Whether employees' claims were secured on company's assets in*　B
> *priority to administrators' remuneration — Whether administrators had adopted*
> *contracts of employment — Whether administrators could contract out of*
> *effect of adoption — Insolvency Act 1986, sec. 19(5).*

This was an application by the joint administrators of Paramount Airways Ltd
("Paramount") for directions whether the contracts of employment of former employees
of the company had been adopted by the administrators in the course of the carrying on　C
by them of their functions as administrators within the meaning of sec. 19(5) of the
Insolvency Act 1986; and/or whether certain sums claimed by the employees — for
holiday pay, pay in lieu of notice or by way of damages for wrongful dismissal, bonuses
under a bonus agreement, pension contributions and compensation for unfair dismissal
— were payable as expenses of the administration or otherwise; and if they were payable
when they should be paid.

The administrators were appointed on 7 August 1989. They caused Paramount to　D
continue trading with a view to seeking a buyer for its business as a going concern. On
14 August, the administrators wrote to the employees stating that they did "not and will
not at any future time adopt or assume personal liability in respect of your contracts of
employment". Attempts to find a buyer failed and the employees were made redundant
at the end of November.

One employee took proceedings for unfair dismissal in the industrial tribunal which　E
ordered that he be reinstated and awarded him compensation under sec. 69 of the
Employment Protection (Consolidation) Act 1978. The administrators declined to grant
leave for him to reapply to the industrial tribunal for an order under sec. 71 of the 1978
Act enforcing the sec. 69 orders. He then presented a petition under sec. 27 of the
Insolvency Act 1986 seeking leave under sec. 11(3)(d) of the Act to apply to the industrial
tribunal for an order under sec. 71 of the 1978 Act and an order requiring the administrators
to pay him on ceasing to be administrators out of the assets of Paramount under sec. 19(5)　F
the amount of the compensation for unfair dismissal which he would be awarded by the
tribunal and other sums said to be due to him in respect of salary in lieu of notice, bonus
payments and pension contributions. A petition was also presented by another former
employee of Paramount, who brought no claim for unfair dismissal and thus made no
sec. 11 application, but did allege unfairly prejudicial conduct of the administration and
claimed pay in lieu of two months' notice, unpaid holiday pay, two months' loyalty bonus,　G
and pension contributions, under sec. 19(5) of the 1986 Act. The petitioners were
respondents to the administrators' application for directions as to how they should deal
with the claims being advanced by the respondents as a result of their dismissal. The
directions sought were relevant to the claims of other employees.

Held, giving directions:

1. The word "adopted" in sec. 19(5) of the 1986 Act did not import personal liability　H
to the administrator.

2. The word "adopted" in sec. 19(5), and in sec. 44(1)(b), of the 1986 Act meant "has
procured the company to continue to carry out".

3. An administrator could contract out of the effect of adoption of contracts of
employment so as to prevent claims made in respect of liabilities incurred under such

A   contracts of employment from ranking in priority to his own remuneration and expenses under sec. 19(5).

4. The administrators' letter of 14 August was ineffective to exclude adoption of the contracts which the administrators had procured Paramount to continue to perform. In order to be effective as a contracting out, the letter of 14 August needed to make plain to its recipients what right of the employees the joint administrators were purporting to contract out of. The letter was suitable to exclude personal liability, but not to exclude the effect of adoption under sec. 19(5). To do that a letter had to be drafted specifically with that subsection in mind.

5. The joint administrators had adopted the contracts of employment of both respondents and accordingly liabilities incurred under those contracts of employment while the joint administrators were in office were charged on the assets of the company under sec. 19(5) in priority to the administrators' remuneration and expenses. The words, "debts or liabilities incurred, while he was administrator, under contracts . . . of employment adopted by him . . . in carrying out . . . his . . . functions" in sec. 19(5) meant debts or liabilities becoming due, for whatever reason, under the provisions of any contract of employment adopted by the administrator during the period that he was so acting.

6. Payment of the sum which became due on termination of an adopted contract of employment for remuneration for periods of holiday entitlement not taken, became secured under sec. 19(5) (notwithstanding that a substantial part of the entitlement resulted from employment predating the appointment of the administrators). Similarly, any obligation of the company to make a payment in lieu of notice was a debt or liability incurred under the relevant contract of employment which attracted the protection of sec. 19(5). The company's obligation to make payments to the pension scheme was a liability incurred under the contract of employment and extended to any period in respect of which the company would be liable to make payment in lieu of notice. The resulting debt attracted the protection of sec. 19(5).

7. The agreement to pay bonuses was a separate agreement made by the administrators with the employees after the commencement of the administration and could form no part of any contract of employment adopted by the administrators. Claims for compensation for unfair dismissal did not attract the protection of sec. 19(5) because they arose by reason of the provisions of the 1978 Act and not under the relevant contract of employment, albeit that compensation under that Act was calculated by reference to such contract.

8. Debts covered by sec. 19(5) were to be paid as the debt became due, i.e. forthwith.

9. Leave should be granted to the second respondent pursuant to sec. 11 of the 1986 Act to enable him to apply for a financial award under sec. 71 the 1978 Act in substitution for the award he had obtained under sec. 69 of that Act requiring him to be reinstated in his employment.

The following cases were referred to in the judgment:

Airlines Airspares Ltd v Handley Page Ltd & Anor [1970] Ch 193.
Astor Chemical Ltd v Synthetic Technology Ltd [1990] BCC 97.
Atlantic Computer Systems plc, Re [1990] BCC 859; [1992] Ch 505.
Botibol, Re [1947] 1 All ER 26.
Hartlebury Printers Ltd & Ors, Re [1992] BCC 428.
Specialised Mouldings Ltd, Re (unreported, 13 February 1987, Harman J).

Mark Phillips (instructed by Wilde Sapte) for the administrators.

Richard Snowden (instructed by Burrough & Co, Cardiff) for the respondents.

JUDGMENT

Evans-Lombe J: This is an application for directions by the administrators of Paramount Airways Ltd ("Paramount"). The application is dated 31 October 1991 and is made by the joint administrators, Roger Arthur Powdrill and Joseph Beaumont Atkinson, consequentially upon the presentation of two petitions under sec. 27 of the *Insolvency Act* 1986, the first, by Captain John Watson presented on 6 September 1991 and the second by Captain Anthony John Unwin presented on 10 September 1991. By order dated 25 November 1991 of *Hoffmann* J those petitions were adjourned to come on for hearing after the substantive hearing of the administrators' application for directions. The petitioners are two of a number of employees of the company who have been dismissed from their employment by the company in circumstances which I will shortly describe. The petitioners are made respondents to the application and the directions sought are designed to give guidance to the administrators as to how they should deal with certain claims being advanced by the respondents as a result of their dismissal. I am told that the directions which are being sought are relevant not only to the claims of the respondents but also to claims being made by a large number of other employees of the company. Accordingly, the respondents before me are, in that sense, representative respondents.

The application seeks:

"1. Directions whether:

   (1) The contracts of employment of the first and the second respondents were adopted by the applicants as administrators of Paramount Airways Ltd ('the company') in the course of the carrying on by them of their functions as administrators of the company within the meaning of sec. 19(5) of the *Insolvency Act* 1986 or otherwise: and/or

   (2) the following should be paid by the applicants to the respondents (together with interest or not) as employees of the company as expenses of the administration or otherwise:

      (a) sums due to the respondents in respect of holiday pay falling due by reason of cl. 8(f) of the respondents' contracts of employment;

      (b) sums payable in lieu of contractual notice under the respondents' contracts of employment or by way of damages for wrongful dismissal;

      (c) such bonuses (pursuant to an alleged agreement made between the applicants and the respondents) as would have been paid had notice of termination of employment been given in accordance with the respondents' contracts of employment;

      (d) pension contributions on such sums as may have been due under the contracts of employment at 15 per cent of earnings;

      (e) such sums as may have been awarded to the respondents in compensation for unfair dismissal pursuant to sec. 71(2) of the *Employment Protection (Consolidation) Act* 1978;

   (3) such of the sums referred to in (2) above as the court directs should be paid, should be paid to the respondents;

      (a) forthwith; or

      (b) on vacation of office by the administrators; or

      (c) on the discharge of the administration order; and/or

      (d) in priority to any remuneration paid or to be paid to the administrators;

A

(4) leave should be granted to the second respondent pursuant to sec. 11 of the *Insolvency Act* 1986 to enable him to apply for an award of compensation for unfair dismissal under sec. 71(3) of the *Employment Protection (Consolidation) Act* 1978."

Early in the hearing it emerged that, notwithstanding that cross-examination of deponents had been ordered, there was no issue between the applicants and the respondents on any of the material facts relevant to the application. Accordingly, I asked counsel to prepare a statement of agreed facts. This they have done and I read that statement verbatim into this judgment.

B

Paramount carried on business as a charter airline operating out of several airports in the UK. It was based in Bristol and also operated in Birmingham and Newcastle. It was an operating subsidiary of Paramount Holdings Ltd ("Holdings") which also owned Amber Airways ("Amber"). Holdings was a shell company which never traded in its own right, Paramount paid the salaries of all personnel.

C

Prior to December 1988, the employees had contracts of employment in the name of Paramount. After that date the employees had new contracts of employment in the name of Holdings. However, the employees continued to regard themselves as employed by Paramount which paid their wages. Although there was some initial uncertainty, the administrators concluded that in reality the employees had contracts of employment with Paramount.

D

The contracts of employment of the employees ("the contracts of employment") were in common form and contained clauses to the following effect:

"*Clause 8*

. . .

E

(c) Your holiday entitlement is 28 days plus eight associated days off per annum
. . .

(d) On termination of employment other than for misconduct, your holiday entitlement will be paid on the basis of one-twelfth of the annual entitlement for each full calendar month's service from the previous 1 April or, if you commenced employment after such date then your date of commencement, less any leave taken.

F

Clause 10

You may, if you wish, join Holdings' pension scheme on the applicable terms and conditions, whereupon you will become contracted out of the state earnings related pension scheme.

Clause 12

G

Notice of termination of employment to be given either by yourself or the company (as agent for Holdings) shall be in writing and as follows:

(a) during a probationary period comprising the first six months of your employment hereunder: two weeks,

(b) thereafter: two months,

H

where notice to be given by the company is stated to be less than 12 weeks, you are nevertheless entitled to one week's notice for each complete year of service from the fourth year of service up to a maximum of 12 week's notice, should this produce a greater result."

I interpolate that notwithstanding that the formal contracts of employment were between Paramount Holdings Ltd and each employee from December 1988 onwards, since both applicants and respondents asked me to treat Paramount as the employer

under those contracts, and since prior to December 1988 it was such employer and after
December 1988 it appears to have fulfilled the entirety of the role of employer, I will
treat Paramount as being the true employer and all provisions in the contracts of
employment applicable to the employer as applicable to the company. I now continue
with the statement of agreed facts.

Under the terms of Paramount's retirement pension plan, Paramount was obliged to
contribute five per cent of the employee's gross monthly salary. Additionally the
employees could increase their contribution by up to a further ten per cent (making a
total of 15 per cent) in which case Paramount would contribute 0.5 per cent for every
one per cent of increase. Both of the employees (the respondents) paid the increased
contributions to the maximum amount.

An order appointing as administrators Messrs Atkinson and Powdrill of Spicer and
Oppenheim (now merged with Touche Ross and Co) was made in respect of Paramount
on 7 August 1989 by *Warner* J. The purposes of the order were the survival of Paramount
and the whole or any part of its undertaking as a going concern; and the more
advantageous realisation of its assets than would be effected on a winding up.

Following the making of the administration order, the administrators caused Paramount
to continue trading during the crucial summer season with a view to seeking a buyer for
its business as a going concern.

On 14 August 1989, the administrators wrote to the employees in the following terms:

"I write to advise you that we were appointed joint administrators of the above
company by an order of the High Court dated 7 August 1989. Under the provisions
of the *Insolvency Act* 1986 the joint administrators act as agents of the company.

We are currently investigating the company's position but as yet we are uncertain
as to the true contractual position between yourself and the company.

Nothing in this letter is to be taken to affect the true identity of your employer,
however, we should like to take this opportunity of reassuring you that the
company will continue to pay your monthly salary during the interim period,
including that payable on 31 August 1989, together with any other sums which
you are contractually entitled to pursuant to the terms and conditions of your
contract of employment. We hope that we may have your co-operation during this
period.

We wish to make it clear that the joint administrators act at all times as agents of
the company and without personal liability. The administrators are not and will
not at any future time adopt or assume personal liability in respect of your
contracts of employment.

signed

R A Powdrill in his capacity as joint administrator of Paramount Airways Ltd
acting as its agent and without personal liability."

This letter was received by the respondents.

The administrators caused Paramount to continue to pay the salaries of the employees.

The pilots had been negotiating for pay rises for some time prior to the administration
order, being unhappy with the level of pay they were receiving which was below market
rates. Indications were given by pilots that they would consider leaving Paramount if a
pay rise was not forthcoming. The administrators wished to preserve Paramount's
workforce but not to increase salaries. Accordingly, and in response to a number of staff
resignations, the administrators agreed in September 1989 to pay a "loyalty bonus" in
order to encourage employees to remain in the employ of Paramount while attempts
were made to sell the business. The letter containing the offer of loyalty bonuses stated:

A   "Further to our meeting of 21 September 1989 . . . we would propose making the following additional payments to captains and first officers.

These payments would be made to all captains and first officers remaining in employment and working for Paramount as at 31 October 1989, or as at the date of a sale of business if earlier; and who have not tendered their resignation by such time . . .

B   If the administrators remain in office after 31 October 1989, this arrangement will continue on a monthly basis until further notice with each month end date being relevant for not having tendered resignations.

The administrators are not adopting any or all of the terms of any contracts of employment or service you have and act only as agents of Paramount Airways Ltd and without personal liability."

C   This letter was received by the employees.

I again interpolate that I was told in the course of argument that the bonus payments which were paid were paid monthly in arrears so that each employee received his bonus payment at the end of the month in respect of which it was payable. I continue with the statement.

At various junctures during the administration:

D   (1)   The administrators or their staff stressed that they acted as agents of Paramount without personal liability and that the administrators would not be personally liable on the contracts of employment.

(2)   The administrators and their staff made it clear that the employees were continuing to be employed under their existing contracts of employment with Paramount.

E   (3)   Salaries were paid in full during the course of the administration, and it was obvious to the pilots that this was an expediency measure in order to keep Paramount trading.

However, the question of what was meant by "adoption" of employment contracts was not mentioned or discussed in any conversations between the administrators and the employees.

F   The employees continued to work for Paramount until after the end of the summer season and continued to be paid by Paramount. They also received bonus payments in accordance with the bonus agreement.

The statutory creditors' meeting was held on 3 November 1989 at which proposals to seek a sale of Paramount as a going concern were approved. Attempts to find a buyer failed however and on 30 November 1989 a meeting was called by the administrators to inform employees that with the exception of a "wet lease" of a Boeing 737/300 aircraft G-PATB to a company called Ansett ("the Ansett wet lease") operations were suspended, G   and that the majority of them were accordingly to be made redundant with immediate effect. These decisions were confirmed by letter sent to all staff members dated 5 December 1989 which purported to terminate their employment with effect from 30 November 1989.

I interpolate again that in the course of argument I was told, and it was accepted on both sides, that all salary and bonuses due for periods actually worked were paid to H   those employees whose employment was terminated on 30 November. I continue with the statement.

After November 1989, Paramount continued to operate the Ansett wet lease. Captain Unwin considered that he ought to have been offered a position on the crew of this aircraft by reason of his seniority. He commenced industrial tribunal proceedings for unfair dismissal.

On 17 April 1990, Mr Roger Glogg, a manager with Spicer and Oppenheim, received   A
a call from the clerk to the Bristol industrial tribunal to enquire whether he had any
objection to a hearing on that day of a case brought by a former Paramount pilot,
Captain Anthony Unwin, for unfair dismissal. As a result of the report back to them by
the clerk following that conversation, the tribunal concluded that the administrators
had given their consent to proceedings against Paramount within the meaning of
sec. 11(3)(d) of the 1986 Act, and Captain Unwin was permitted to proceed.

   B

The tribunal decided that Captain Unwin's dismissal had been unfair on the grounds
that less long serving pilots had been retained to fulfil the Ansett wet lease and
consequently there had been a breach of Paramount's "last in, first out" redundancy
policy. Accordingly, pursuant to sec. 69 of the *Employment Protection (Consolidation)
Act* 1978 ("EPCA 1978"), the tribunal ordered (1) that Captain Unwin be reinstated by
1 May 1990; and (2) Paramount pay him £9,092.50 in respect of lost pay and benefits.

   C

The administrators were notified of the tribunal's decision on or about 23 April 1990.
They denied that they gave consent for the case to be brought. Following notification of
the award the administrators sought a review of the tribunal's decision under r. 10(1) of
the *Industrial Tribunals (Rules of Procedure) Regulations* 1985 on the grounds that the
administrators had not given their consent to the hearing under sec. 11(3)(d) of the
Insolvency Act 1986. That application was rejected on the ground that the tribunal did
not have jurisdiction to review on that ground. The administrators did not appeal the   D
decision, believing that Captain Unwin's award from the tribunal will rank simply as an
unsecured claim in Paramount's eventual liquidation. By a letter dated 25 June 1990,
Burrough & Co sought the administrators' consent for Captain Unwin to progress his
claim in respect of alleged unfair dismissal by reapplying to the industrial tribunal for an
order under sec. 71 of the EPCA 1978 for the enforcement of the original sec. 69 orders.
The administrators declined to grant leave.

   E

Captain Unwin consequently filed a petition under sec. 27 of the 1986 Act on 21
October 1991, seeking, inter alia:

(1)   the court's leave under sec. 11(3)(d) of the Act to apply to the industrial tribunal
for a sec. 71 EPCA 1978 order against Paramount in administration: and

(2)   an order requiring the administrators to pay to Captain Unwin on ceasing to be
administrators the amount of the compensation for unfair dismissal which he   F
would be awarded by the tribunal and other sums said to be due to him in respect
of salary in lieu of notice, bonus payments and pension contributions out of the
assets of Paramount under sec. 19(5).

A petition was also lodged on 21 October 1991 by another pilot formerly employed by
Paramount, Captain John Watson. Captain Watson has brought no claim for unfair
dismissal and thus makes no sec. 11 application. He does, however, allege unfairly   G
prejudicial conduct of the administration on the same grounds as Captain Unwin, and
claims payment of the following sums under sec. 19(5) of the 1986 Act:

(1)   pay in lieu of two months notice;

(2)   unpaid holiday pay;

(3)   two months' loyalty bonus; and

   H

(4)   pension contributions at 15 per cent of earnings.

Pursuant to sec. 14(3) of the 1986 Act (and in order to avoid a dispute about whether
or not, regardless of the merits of the underlying claims to payment, the administrators'
conduct was unfairly prejudicial to the pilots) the administrators issued this application
for directions.

A   On 25 November 1991, *Hoffmann* J ordered the administrators to pay the costs of Captains Unwin and Watson of this application as a cost and expense of the administration, such cost to be taxed on an indemnity basis if not agreed.

That concludes the statement of agreed facts.

I turn first to the question raised by para. 1(1) of the application: have the contracts of employment of the respondents, in existence prior to the appointment of the administrators, been "adopted" by them within the meaning of sec. 19(5) of the *Insolvency Act* 1986. This question subdivides into two questions, first, what is meant by "adopted" in the subsection and, second, have the respondents' contracts of employment been so adopted.

The material subsections of sec. 19 are subsec. (3), (4) and (5). These provide:

C
"(3) Where at any time a person ceases to be administrator, the next two subsections apply.

(4) His remuneration and any expenses properly incurred by him shall be charged on and paid out of any property of the company which is in his custody or under his control at that time in priority to any security to which section 15(1) then applies.

D
(5) Any sums payable in respect of debts or liabilities incurred, while he was administrator, under contracts entered into or contracts of employment adopted by him or a predecessor of his in the carrying out of his or the predecessor's functions shall be charged on and paid out of any such property as is mentioned in subsection (4) in priority to any charge arising under that subsection.

For this purpose, the administrator is not to be taken to have adopted a contract of employment by reason of anything done or omitted to be done within 14 days after his appointment."

E

These subsections are therefore dealing with one of the things which occur upon an administrator ceasing to act as such. He may do so as a result of death or retirement, alternatively he may do so at the conclusion of the administration when, if it has fully succeeded, the company simply continues to trade with its contracts of employment continuing in force, or, where the purpose set out in sec. 8(3)(a) — the survival of the whole or any part of the company's undertaking as a going concern — has either failed or only partly succeeded, the company is wound up.

The subsections provide for a charge on the company's assets:

(1)   securing the payment of debts or liabilities incurred by the company while in administration as a result of:

G
       (a)   new contracts, which could also be new contracts of employment, and

       (b)   existing contracts of employment which have been adopted by administrators;

(2)   on property of the company in his custody or control;

(3)   in priority to all other claims including claims by the administrator for his remuneration and expenses under subsec. (4).

H
This section is to be compared with sec. 44 of the 1986 Act which deals with the position of administrative receivers in a comparable area. That section provides:

"44(1)   The administrative receiver of a company —

       (a)   is deemed to be the company's agent unless and until the company goes into liquidation;

(b) is personally liable on any contract entered into by him in the carrying out   A
of his functions (except in so far as the contract otherwise provides) and on
any contract of employment adopted by him in the carrying out of those
functions; and

(c) is entitled in respect of that liability to an indemnity out of the assets of the
company.

(2) For the purposes of subsection 1(b) the administrative receiver is not to be   B
taken to have adopted a contract of employment by reason of anything done or
omitted to be done within 14 days after his appointment.''

There is no express provision in sec. 19 which equates with the provision in sec.
44(1)(a) expressly making the administrative receiver the company's agent until
liquidation, but a similar provision relating to administrators appears at sec. 14(5).

In sec. 44 there is an express provision for personal liability on new contracts and   C
"adopted" contracts of employment, see subsec. (1)(b). By contrast, there is no
provision in sec. 19 or otherwise expressly imposing personal liability on administrators.
By sec. 19(5) the charge on the company's assets is applied to new contracts made by the
administrator and his adopted contracts of employment.

The equivalent of the sec. 19(5) charge on the company's assets relating to
administrative receivers is the indemnity which the receiver is entitled to out of the   D
assets of the company provided for in subsec. (1)(c).

There is a similar provision for a 14-day breathing space in respect of both administrative
receivers and administrators, in the former case contained in sec. 44(2) and in the latter
case in the final paragraph of sec. 19(5).

It is submitted on behalf of the administrators that the word "adopted" when used in
sec. 19(5) means that the administrator has voluntarily assumed responsibility for the   E
employee's contract and thereby become personally liable on that contract either alone
or jointly with the company. Therefore, it is submitted, to adopt requires a clear
demonstration by the administrator of his acceptance that he is bound by the relevant
contract of employment. Merely continuing to pay the remuneration becoming due
under the existing contracts of employment does not have the effect of adoption, a
fortiori where, prior to any continuation of payment of remuneration, a letter has been   F
circularised to relevant employees in what may be known as *Specialised Mouldings* form
after the letter approved by *Harman* J in the *Re Specialised Mouldings Ltd* decision
(unreported, 13 February 1987). As the statement of agreed facts makes plain, such a
letter was circulated in this case which stated that the administrators do "not and will not
at any future time adopt or assume personal liability in respect of your contracts of
employment". It was further submitted, and the respondents accepted, that simply
doing nothing until the 14-day period of breathing space had expired could not by itself   G
amount to adoption.

My attention was directed to the case of *Re Botibol* [1947] 1 All ER 26. This was a
case which concerned the appointment by the court of a receiver in respect of a deceased
litigant of whose estate no personal representative had yet been appointed. The case
concerned an application to the court for leave to bring proceedings against him in
respect of liability for breach of contract under a contract which it was alleged he had   H
adopted. *Evershed* J at p. 28D said:

"As regards the question whether an action could possibly succeed, it may be
difficult to say that a receiver acting strictly as such can ever be sued in contract.
On the other hand, a receiver may, as I think counsel for the respondent concedes,
adopt as his own a contract and render himself liable as on a novation of it."

A I respectfully accept those words of *Evershed* J as applicable to both administrative receivers and administrators, but do not think that they assist in the proper construction of sec. 19(5). It is clear that both administrators and receivers can in appropriate circumstances so act as to make themselves personally liable on contracts entered into by the company in respect of which they have been appointed, notwithstanding that there may or may not be in the relevant legislation express provisions making them so liable in circumstances defined by that legislation.

B It was submitted on behalf of the respondents that sec. 19(5) does not import personal liability to the administrator in respect of contracts of employment which he may choose to adopt. I accept this submission. Both administrators and administrative receivers are expressly made agents for the company in respect of which they are appointed. It follows that unless made expressly liable by statute they are not, prima facie, so liable because they will be acting for a disclosed principal.

C It seems to me that the word "adopted" should have the same meaning in sec. 19(5) as it has in sec. 44(1)(b). If the word "adopt" in sec. 44(1)(b) implies personal liability then the express provision for personal liability contained in that subsection is surplusage. Indeed the whole of subsec. (1)(b) is probably unnecessary and all that would be required is that subsec. (1)(c) should give a right of indemnity to administrative receivers in respect of liabilities under contracts "adopted" by them.

D It seems to me also that the provision in sec. 19(5) that a succeeding administrator is bound by any adoption made by his predecessor militates against the word "adopted" being construed as importing personal liability.

I would accept that the use of the word "adopt" in sec. 19(5) and sec. 44(1)(b) is, perhaps, unfortunate having regard to the use of that word with relation to Companies Act receivers in the cases under old sec. 369 of the *Companies Act* 1948. Nonetheless, in
E my judgment, the word "adopted" when used in sec. 19(5) and also in sec. 44(1)(b) means "has procured the company to continue to carry out". In arriving at this conclusion I gratefully adopt the words used by *Vinelott* J in *Astor Chemical Ltd v Synthetic Technology Ltd* [1990] BCC 97 at p. 104, where the judge was discussing the judgment of *Graham* J in *Airlines Airspares Ltd v Handley Page Ltd* [1970] Ch 193, where that judge was using the word "adopt" with relation to the actions of a pre-Insolvency Act
F receiver appointed under a company's debenture. *Vinelott* J said:

> "It is clear that *Graham* J used the word 'adopt' in this context as meaning simply continue to carry out."

That the word "adopted" in sec. 19(5) does not import personal liability to the administrator is consistent with the judgment of *Nicholls* LJ in *Re Atlantic Computer Systems plc* [1990] BCC 859, where at p. 867D having quoted the section he says:

G > "There is a striking resemblance between the debts and liabilities to which this subsection applies in the case of an administrator, and the debts and liabilities in respect of which an administrative receiver is personally liable pursuant to sec. 44. Section 19(5) does not impose personal liability on the administrator. In that respect he is in a better position than an administrative receiver, even though his status resembles that of an administrative receiver in that in exercising his powers
H > he is deemed to act as the company's agent (sec. 14(5))."

—and also at p. 529, where he says:

> "This conclusion is consistent with sec. 19(5). If an administrator adopts an existing contract of employment, the liabilities arising under that contract are automatically payable as provided in that subsection. As to other existing contracts 'adopted' by an administrator, creditors have no automatic preference or priority."

I turn now to the second question, whether the respondents' contracts of employment have, in this case, been adopted within the meaning which I have just given to sec. 19(5), and also adopting gratefully the words of Professor Goode at p. 101 of his book *Principles of Corporate Insolvency Law* (1990) that adoption may be effected by,

> "any act or acquiescence (after expiry of the 14-day period) which is indicative of his intention to treat the contract as on foot."

It is accepted on both sides that this question is to be determined by the effect given to the letter of 14 August 1989 circulated to employees and, it is submitted on behalf of the administrators, to the effect to be given to the circular to captains and first officers circulated at the end of September 1989 and the material passages from which are set out in the statement of agreed facts.

I will deal with the effect of the circular first. It is no part of the statement of agreed facts nor is it suggested anywhere in the evidence that any employee of Paramount specifically accepted the circular as changing his status. Absent any such evidence it does not seem to me that the attempted exclusion contained in it could have any effect on the status of a contract of employment which had been "adopted" by the administrators by procuring Paramount to continue to perform its provisions since August of that year.

The question therefore becomes twofold, first, is contracting out of the effect of sec. 19(5) permitted by the Act, and secondly, if it is, did the 14 August letter combined with a continuation thereafter to perform the relevant contracts of employment have the effect that liabilities incurred under those contracts of employment were not charged on Paramount's assets pursuant to sec. 19(5).

I turn to deal with the first of these questions. My attention was drawn to the decision of *Harman* J in *Re Specialised Mouldings Ltd* on 13 February 1987. There is no proper report of the judgment but what appears to have occurred is that the judgment was given pursuant to an application under sec. 35 of the Insolvency Act by administrative receivers for directions that in the event of their circulating a letter in substantially the same form as the letter in this case of 14 August 1989, that that letter would have the effect of excluding their personal liability in respect of existing contracts of employment which might otherwise be treated as "adopted" by then within the meaning of sec. 44(1)(b) of the Act. *Harman* J concluded that it was possible for an administrative receiver to provide specifically that he did not adopt employment contracts and could, therefore, effectively contract out of any personal liability which might otherwise attach to him under sec. 44(1)(b).

This is a case of administrators attempting to contract out of the provisions of sec. 19(5). However, the respondents are driven to submit that *Re Specialised Mouldings Ltd* must have been wrongly decided, because if it is possible under sec. 44 to contract out of personal liability under subsec. (1)(b) there can be no reason why it should not be possible also to contract out of the effects of sec. 19(5).

In the *Specialised Mouldings* case it was submitted to *Harman* J that the presence in subsec. (1)(b) of sec. 44 of the words "except in so far as the contract otherwise provides" as qualifying new contracts entered into by him only, whereas there was no such qualification in respect of contracts of employment adopted by him, necessarily indicated that it was the intention of the legislature that in the latter case there should be no right to contract out. *Harman* J rejected that submission and held that an administrative receiver was able avoid personal liability by way of adoption provided he made his intention not to adopt or not to incur personal liability sufficiently clear within the 14-day grace period in respect of contracts of employment that he thereafter continued to perform.

I see the force of the argument which *Harman* J rejected. However, it is to be noted that the right to claim personally against an administrative receiver in respect of a

A contract of employment adopted by him is a private right conferred on employees by the effect of sec. 44 and which ought, without more, to be capable of being contracted out of. It must have been plain to the legislature that sec. 44 permitted at least two ways of getting round any statutory ban on contracting out. Thus sec. 44 would permit the dismissal of an employee and his re-engagement under a new contract of employment excluding personal liability. Alternatively, an administrative receiver might insist on a variation of the contract of employment as between the company and the employee to

B include such a term as a condition of his thereafter going on to adopt the contract of employment. It is therefore difficult to read into sec. 44 and, a fortiori, into sec. 19(5), where no similar qualification of new contracts only appears, any obvious public policy driving the court to the conclusion that the intention of the legislature was to exclude contracting out in respect of adopted contracts of employment. For these reasons I am not prepared to disagree with what seems to have been the conclusion of *Harman* J in

C *Re Specialised Mouldings Ltd.* In my judgment, the provisions of sec. 19(5) do not prevent an administrator from contracting out of the effect of adoption of contracts of employment so as to prevent claims made in respect of liabilities incurred under such contracts of employment from ranking in priority to his own remuneration and expenses. Such a conclusion seems to me consistent with what must be the general statutory purpose of the provisions as to administration in the 1986 Act which is, as far as possible,

D to keep companies alive without terminating the contracts of employment of employees so that the administration can achieve any one or more of the purposes set out in sec. 8(3) of the Act.

I now turn to the second question, namely, whether the circular letter of 14 August was effective to exclude the effect of adoption in this case.

In Bennion on *Statutory Interpretation* (2nd ed., 1992) at p. 37 the following passage appears:

E

> "*Facts must be fully known* Conduct by a person will not be taken to amount to the waiver of his statutory right unless it appears that he was aware of all the facts establishing the right. Waiver can arise only from presumed intention to give up a right. Conduct does not raise this presumption if it occurred in ignorance of relevant facts. In *Chapman v Michaelson* [1982] Ch 612 at 622 Eve J said the party

F renouncing must have been in a position 'to appreciate what his true legal rights were'."

In order to be effective as a contracting out, therefore, the letter of 14 August needed to make plain to its recipients what right it was of the employees which the joint administrators were purporting to contract out of.

It was submitted on behalf of the administrators that the final sentence of the letter

G which reads, "the administrators are not and will not at any future time adopt or assume personal liability in respect of your contracts of employment", was sufficient to do this. I disagree. It seems to me that whereas the final paragraph of the letter is entirely suitable when written by an administrative receiver seeking to exclude personal liability to effect that object, as *Harman* J has held, it is not suitable in the mouth of administrators to exclude the effect of sec. 19(5). To the uninstructed, which would include the vast majority of all employees at whatever level, this paragraph might well be read as only

H directed to excluding any personal liability which might attach to the administrators. The respondents concede that as a result of this letter they were entirely clear that there could be no personal claim against the joint administrators resulting from liabilities incurred under their contracts of employment. It seems to me that in order to be effective in the hands of administrators to exclude the effect of adoption under sec. 19(5) a letter must be drafted specifically with that subsection in mind and also bearing in mind

the difference between the effect of that subsection and sec. 44(1)(b). I do not propose   A
in this judgment to draft an appropriate form of words.

My conclusion therefore is that the joint administrators adopted the contracts of
employment of both respondents and that accordingly liabilities incurred under those
contracts of employment while the joint administrators were in office are charged on the
assets of the company in priority to the administrators' remuneration and expenses.

I now turn to consider para. (2) of the application and in particular whether payment   B
of the matters set out in subpara. (a)–(e) of that paragraph are secured by the charge
conferred by sec. 19(5). This turns on the meaning of the following words contained in
that subsection:

> "Any sums payable in respect of debts or liabilities incurred, while he was
> administrator, under . . . contracts of employment adopted by him or a predecessor
> of his in the carrying out of his or the predecessor's functions . . ."   C

It is submitted on behalf of the administrators that the only "liabilities incurred"
under contracts of employment which are protected by the charge, if the contract is
adopted within the meaning of sec. 19(5), are the costs of using the services of the
employee but not the rights incidental to each contract of employment. Thus remuneration
for periods of employment by the administrators should be paid but not payment in lieu
of contractual notice the length of which may result from substantial periods of   D
employment predating the appointment of the administrators. This submission places
stress on the words "while he was administrator" and invites the court to read the section
so that the words "liabilities incurred" are qualified by the words "by him . . . in carrying
out his . . . functions".

In my judgment this is not a legitimate reading of the subsection. It is plain that the
words "by him" qualify only the words "contracts of employment adopted".

It seems to me that the words of the section material to this issue are plain and   E
unambiguous and should be given their natural meaning. The words, "debts or liabilities
incurred, while he was administrator, under contracts . . . of employment adopted by
him . . . in carrying out . . . his . . . functions", mean debts or liabilities becoming due,
for whatever reason, under the provisions of any contract of employment adopted by
the administrator during the period that he was so acting.

I now turn to consider each of the specific subparagraphs in para. (2) of the application   F
and turn first to the claim for holiday pay.

The entitlement to holiday pay arises under cl. 8(c) and (d) of the contracts of
employment in respect of holiday entitlement accrued but not taken at the date of
termination. The liability to pay arises upon such termination. If, therefore, the
administrators, during their period in office, terminate the employment of an employee
whose contract of employment they have adopted, payment of the whole of the sum   G
becoming due for remuneration for periods of holiday entitlement not taken becomes
secured under sec. 19(5) notwithstanding that a substantial part of the entitlement
results from employment predating the appointment of the administrators.

Similarly, by cl. 12 the contracts of employment set out provisions for minimum notice
periods for termination of employment to be given by the company to its employees.
The minimum period of notice of two weeks is extended in accordance with those   H
provisions depending on the length of service of the relevant employee. It seems to me
that where the company terminates the employment of an employee without giving the
notice provided for in the contract of employment the company is nonetheless bound to
pay the remuneration of the employee which would otherwise have been paid during the
proper period of notice provided for in the contract. The resulting debt or liability is, in

A   my judgment, one which is incurred under the relevant contract of employment payment of which attracts the protection of sec. 19(5).

By contrast, it is plain that the agreement to pay bonuses was a separate agreement made by the administrators with the employees after the commencement of the administration and could form no part of any contract of employment adopted by the administrators. The bonus payments were to be paid monthly in arrears. I can see no

B   support for the submission on behalf of the respondents that there was an implied term in the contract to pay bonuses, that such payments would be made in respect of periods during which the employee was not employed by the company albeit that that employment had been unlawfully terminated without proper notice. To the extent, therefore, that any bonus payments remain unpaid for periods prior to the actual termination of the employee's employment the resulting debt is a liability attracting the protection of sec. 19(5). As I understand the position, all bonuses were fully paid up by the administrators

C   in respect of periods worked and accordingly no debts arise under this head which attract the protection of the subsection.

By contrast cl. 10 of the contracts of employment imposes on the company a duty to make payments to a pension scheme in respect of employees who assented to join the scheme. In my view this is a liability incurred under the contract of employment and extends to any period in respect of which the company would be liable by reason of

D   cl. 12 to make payment in lieu of notice. The resulting debt, in my judgment, attracts the protection of sec. 19(5).

Dealing finally with compensation for unfair dismissal, in my judgment, claims under this head do not attract the protection of sec. 19(5) because they arise by reason of the provisions of the *Employment Protection (Consolidation) Act* 1978 and not under the relevant contract of employment, albeit the compensation becoming due under that Act

E   is calculated by reference to such contract.

I recognise that my conclusions under para. (2) of the application mean that whether or not the relevant liability incurred under the contract of employment attracts the protection of sec. 19(5) will depend on whether the relevant employee had the "good fortune" to be dismissed from his employment by the administrator during the period of the administration. It is plain from the decision of *Morritt* J in *Re Hartlebury Printers*

F   *Ltd* [1992] BCC 428, that where an administration fails so that the employment contracts are terminated as a result of the ensuing winding-up order sums becoming due under those contracts of employment attract only the more limited protection of the provisions for the payment of preferential debts in the 1986 Act. In so far as such liabilities arise as a result of periods of employment prior to the appointment of the administrator there does not seem to be any logic behind this result.

G   Paragraph (3) of the application seeks determination of the time for payment and the priority of payment of the claims set out in subpara. (a)–(d) in para. (2) of the application. As to priority, those liabilities which I have found to attract the protection of sec. 19(5) take priority, as the subsection requires, over the claims for remuneration and expenses of the administrators. Where the administrator has effectively contracted out of the provisions of sec. 19(5) liability incurred under a contract of employment continued by him subject to such contracting out will fall into the provisions of sec. 19(4)

H   and be paid as an expense in the administration in priority to secured creditors.

Section 19(5) contains no provision as to when debts covered by the subsection should be paid by the administrators but simply confers upon those debts the protection of a charge over the assets of the company. It seems to me, therefore, that debts covered by sec. 19(5) should, like any other expense of the administration, be paid as that debt becomes due, that is, forthwith.

Finally, under this application I am asked to determine whether leave should be A
granted to the second respondent, Captain Unwin, pursuant to sec. 11 of the 1986 Act
to enable him to apply for a financial award under sec. 71(3) of the EPCA 1978 in
substitution for the award he has obtained under sec. 69 of that Act requiring him to be
reinstated in his employment by the company. The tribunal's finding that Captain
Unwin's dismissal was unfair stands. The administrators caused an application to the
tribunal to be made to review the tribunal's award which application did not succeed.
No appeal has been pursued against the tribunal's decision and the time for appeal is B
now past. If leave is given all that will happen is that the tribunal will substitute an
appropriate award in money to compensate Captain Unwin for the failure to reinstate
him. That award will form part of Captain Unwin's claim which will be payable by
Paramount if it survives or provable in any liquidation which follows after the
administration.

The court's power to grant leave under sec. 11 is discretionary. It was submitted to me C
on behalf of the administrators that the court should refuse leave because the
circumstances in which the original award were made were unsatisfactory in that had the
administrators been fully aware of what was going on they would have declined leave to
pursue the claim for unfair dismissal and it would never have reached the initial award
stage.

I cannot accept that this is a proper reason for refusing leave in this case. To do so D
would amount to the court refusing leave on the basis of submissions only, without being
shown the evidence which was before the tribunal and, in effect, acting as a Court of
Appeal from the tribunal in a case where the company acting by the administrators has
elected not to pursue an appeal through the normal route. In my judgment leave should
be granted.

(*Order accordingly*)

E

F

G

H

A   # Karella & Anor v Greek Minister of Industry, Energy and Technology & Anor (Joined Cases C-19/90 and C-20/90).

Court of Justice of the European Communities (Sixth Chamber).

G F Mancini, President of the Chamber, T F O'Higgins, C N Kakouris, F A Schockweiler and PJG Kapteyn JJ, G Tesauro, Advocate General.

B   Judgment delivered 30 May 1991.

Principles of Community law — Direct effect — Company law — Greek rules providing for adoption by administrative act of a decision to increase the capital of a company — Compatibility with Community law — Direct effect of specific provision of Community law providing that any increase in capital must be decided upon by the general meeting — Scope of provision —
C   *EC Directive 77/91 (second company law directive), art. 25, 41(1) (OJ 1977 L26/1).*

This was a reference by the Greek Council of State for a preliminary ruling under art. 177 of the EEC Treaty on the interpretation of art. 25, 41 and 42 of EC Directive 77/91 on co-ordination of safeguards which, for the protection of the interests of members and others, are required by member states of companies within the meaning of the second paragraph of art. 58 of the treaty, in respect of the formation of public limited liability companies and the maintenance and alteration of their capital, with a view to making such safeguards equivalent (the second company law directive).

The questions referred arose in two sets of proceedings between two shareholders in a company, on the one hand, and the Greek Minister of Industry, Energy and Technology and the Business Reconstruction Organisation, on the other. The Business Reconstruction Organisation was a public-sector body having the form of a public limited liability company which acted in the public interest under the control of the state. In 1983, by decision of the Greek Secretary of State for the Economy, the provisions of a national law were applied to the company, which was experiencing financial difficulties. Pursuant to that law, temporary management of the company was transferred to the Business Reconstruction Organisation. During that period of administration, the Business Reconstruction Organisation decided to increase the company's share capital substantially. That decision was approved by the Greek Secretary of State for Industry, Energy and Technology. The decision granting approval provided for the original shareholders to have an unlimited pre-emptive right which they had to exercise within one month of the publication of the decision.

Two shareholders in the company brought actions for the annulment of that decision before the Greek Council of State on the ground that it was contrary to the Greek Constitution and the second directive. The national court stayed the proceedings and made a reference to the Court of Justice seeking to ascertain, inter alia, whether, having regard to art. 41(1) of the second directive, art. 25(1) of the directive could be relied upon against the administration by individuals in the national courts, and whether art. 25(1), in conjunction with art. 41(1), was applicable with regard to public rules, such as those provided for in the national law at issue, which governed the exceptional cases of undertakings which were of particular economic and social importance and were undergoing serious financial difficulties.

Article 25(1) of the second directive provided that any increase in capital had to be decided upon by the general meeting, while art. 41(1) provided that member states could derogate from that provision to the extent that such derogation was necessary for the adoption or application of provisions designed to encourage the participation of employees, or other groups of persons defined by national law, in the capital of undertakings.

Held, ruling accordingly:

1. It was well established that wherever the provisions of a directive appeared, as far as their subject-matter was concerned, to be unconditional and sufficiently precise, individuals were entitled to invoke them against the state. Article 25(1) of the second directive was clearly and precisely worded and laid down, unconditionally, a rule enshrining the principle that the general meeting had the power to decide upon increases in capital. Its unconditional nature was not affected by the derogations laid down in art. 25(2) and 41(1) of the directive, in so far as those derogations were strictly limited to the cases provided for therein. Accordingly, art. 25(1) of the second directive could be relied upon by individuals against the public authorities before national courts.

2. As regards the scope of art. 25(1) of the second directive with respect to a law such as the national law in issue, it had to be noted that the aim of the second directive was to provide a minimum level of protection for shareholders in all the member states. That objective would be seriously frustrated if the member states were entitled to derogate from the provisions of the directive by maintaining in force rules, albeit rules described as special or exceptional, under which it was possible to decide by administrative measure, outside any decision by the general meeting of shareholders, to effect an increase in the company's capital which would have the effect either of obliging the original shareholders to increase their contributions to the capital or of imposing on them the addition of new shareholders, thus reducing their involvement in the decision-taking power of the company.

3. No provision which would allow the member states to derogate from art. 25(1) of the directive in crisis situations was provided for either in the EEC Treaty or in the second directive itself. Consequently, in the absence of such a derogation, art. 25(1) had to be interpreted as precluding the member states from maintaining in force rules incompatible with the principle set forth in that article, even if those rules covered only exceptional situations. To recognise the existence of a general reservation covering exceptional situations, outside the specific conditions laid down in the provisions of the treaty and the second directive, would, moreover, be liable to impair the binding nature and uniform application of Community law.

4. The derogation laid down in art. 41(1) of the directive could be applied to national rules only if, when applied in practice, they contributed to achieving the objective sought by that provision. In that regard that condition was not fulfilled merely because rules, such as those contained in the national legislation at issue, provided, as one of the means available of achieving their objective, for the possibility of the public restructuring body transferring shares to employees or to private individuals. Such a possibility was merely hypothetical and ancillary. Moreover, the reference in art. 41(1) of the second directive to other groups of persons referred to shareholding by private individuals and was not concerned with the transfer of shares to credit institutions or public-law bodies.

5. Accordingly, art. 25 in conjunction with art. 41(1) of the second directive precluded national rules which, in order to ensure the survival and continued operation of undertakings which were of particular economic and social importance and were in exceptional circumstances by reason of their excessive debt burden, provided for the adoption by administrative act of a decision to increase the company capital without prejudice to the right of pre-emption of the original shareholders when the new shares were issued.

The following cases were referred to in the judgment:

Becker v Finanzamt Münster-Innenstadt (Case 8/81) [1982] ECR 53.
Johnston v Chief Constable of the Royal Ulster Constabulary (Case 222/84) [1987] QB 129; [1986] ECR 1651.

Konstantinos Adamantopoulos, of the Athens Bar, and Philip Bentley, barrister of Lincoln's Inn, for the shareholders.

A   Panagiotis Milonopoulos, lawyer, legal adviser of the second class in the Department for Community Legal Affairs of the Ministry of Foreign Affairs, Konstantinos Stavropoulos, lawyer, also a member of that department, and Nikos Fragkakis, lawyer, acting as agents, for Greece.

Antonio Caeiro, legal adviser, and Maria Patakia, a member of its Legal Service, acting as agents, for the Commission.

B   Leonidas Georgakopoulos and Andreas Tsouderos, of the Athens Bar, at the hearing, for the Business Reconstruction Organisation.

REPORT FOR THE HEARING

I — Facts and procedure

1. *Relevant legislation*

C   (a) Second directive on company law

1. Article 54(3)(g) of the EEC Treaty provides that the Council and the Commission are to co-ordinate to the necessary extent the safeguards which, for the protection of the interests of members and others, are required by member states of companies or firms within the meaning of the second paragraph of art. 58 with a view to making such safeguards equivalent.

D   In pursuit of that objective, the Council adopted on 13 December 1976 the second directive (Directive 77/91) in respect of the formation of public limited liability companies and the maintenance and alteration of their capital (hereinafter referred to as "the second directive", OJ 1977 L26/1). Articles 25–29 thereof set out the provisions on increases in capital.

2. Article 25 provides as follows:

E   "1. Any increase in capital must be decided upon by the general meeting. Both this decision and the increase in the subscribed capital shall be published in the manner laid down by the laws of each Member State, in accordance with Article 3 of Directive 68/151/EEC.

2. Nevertheless, the statutes or instrument of incorporation or the general meeting, the decision of which must be published in accordance with the rules referred to in F   paragraph 1, may authorise an increase in the subscribed capital up to a maximum amount which they shall fix with due regard for any maximum amount provided for by law. Where appropriate, the increase in the subscribed capital shall be decided on within the limits of the amount fixed, by the company body empowered to do so. The power of such body in this respect shall be for a maximum period of five years and may be renewed one or more times by the general meeting, each time for a period not exceeding five years.

G   3. Where there are several classes of shares, the decision by the general meeting concerning the increase in capital referred to in paragraph 1 or the authorisation to increase the capital referred to in paragraph 2, shall be subject to a separate vote at least for each class of shareholder whose rights are affected by the transaction.

4. This Article shall apply to the issue of all securities which are convertible into H   shares or which carry the right to subscribe for shares, but not to the conversion of such securities, nor to the exercise of the right to subscribe."

3. Article 29(1) provides that whenever the capital is increased by consideration in cash, the shares must be offered on a pre-emptive basis to shareholders in proportion to the capital represented by their shares. Under art. 29(4), that right of pre-emption may not be restricted or withdrawn by the statutes or instrument of incorporation. This may,

however, be done by decision of the general meeting. The administrative or administration body is to be required to present to such a meeting a written report indicating the reasons for restriction or withdrawal of the right of pre-emption and justifying the proposed issue price.

4. It should further be observed that, under art. 41(1), member states may derogate from both art. 25 and art. 29 to the extent that such derogations are necessary for the adoption or application of provisions designed to encourage the participation of employees, or other groups of persons defined by national law, in the capital of undertakings.

5. Lastly, art. 42 states that, for the purposes of the application of the directive, the laws of the member states are to ensure equal treatment of all shareholders who are in the same position.

(b) Greek Law No. 2190/1920

6. Under art. 2 and 145 of the Act concerning the conditions of accession of the Hellenic Republic and the adjustments to the Treaties (OJ 1979 L291/17), the Hellenic Republic should have put into effect the measures to comply with the provisions of the second directive as from 1 January 1981. Such provisions, which were contained in Presidential Decrees No. 409/1986 and 498/1987, were not adopted until 1986 and 1987 (*Official Journal of the Hellenic Republic* No. 191 of 28/11/1986 and No. 236 of 31/12/1987). Those decrees amended Law No. 2190/1920 on public limited liability companies, which was codified by Royal Decree No. 174/1963 (*Official Journal of the Hellenic Republic*, 1963, I, No. 37). The codified Law contains provisions corresponding to art. 25(1) and (2) and to art. 29(1) and (4) of the second directive. The codified Law did not embody a provision corresponding to art. 41(1) of the second directive. However, the Greek legislation concerning the restructuring of undertakings does provide for the possibility of employees' participating in the capital of undertakings.

(c) Greek Law No. 1386/1983

7. Law No. 1386/1983 of 5 August 1983 (*Official Journal of the Hellenic Republic* No. 107 of 8/8/1983, p. 1926) sets up a public limited liability company whose capital was subscribed entirely by the state, known as Organismos Ikonomikis Anasinkrotisis Epikhiriseon AE (Business Reconstruction Organisation, hereinafter referred to as "the OAE"). Under art. 2 of that Law, the purpose of the OAE is to contribute to the economic and social development of the country through the financial rejuvenation of companies, the importation and application of foreign technology and the development of Greek know-how and through the establishment and operation of nationalised or mixed economy undertakings.

8. Article 2(3) provides, inter alia, that for the purpose of achieving its objects the OAE may in particular:

— take over the administration and day-to-day operation of undertakings undergoing rejuvenation or nationalised undertakings;

— participate in the capital of existing undertakings or undertakings which may be brought into being;

— grant loans of all kinds to undertakings in which it has a participatory interest and likewise provide guarantees for the security of such loans;

— acquire bonds issued by the state or by organisations controlled by the state and likewise bond issues by undertakings, organisations or banks;

— make over shares, in particular to employees or their representative bodies, to local government bodies or other legal entities governed by public law, to charitable institutions, to social bodies or to private persons.

A   9. Article 5(1) prescribes the conditions whereby undertakings are made subject to that Law. According to that article, undertakings undergoing serious financial difficulties may be made subject to the system established by the Law by decision of the Minister for the National Economy following the delivery of an opinion by a special advisory committee. This may also be done in the case of undertakings which are of interest to national defence or of vital importance in the exploitation of national resources or whose main aim is of public service, provided that they are in a state of manifest insolvency.

B   Undertakings making a request to that effect may also be made subject to the Law. Article 6 sets out the relevant procedure.

10. The substantive rules of the Law are set forth in art. 7–10. Under art. 7, the competent minister may decide to transfer to the OAE the administration of the undertaking subject to the Law, deal with the undertaking's indebtedness in order to secure its viability, by means of a compulsory increase in capital through new injections

C   of capital or the capitalisation of existing debts or by means of a restructuring of the debts, or wind up the undertaking under art. 9. However, capitalisation of debts may only be imposed on the state, legal entities governed by public law and state-controlled banks.

11. Article 8(1) on transferring the administration of the undertaking was amended by Law No. 1472/1984 of 3 August 1984 (*Official Journal of the Hellenic Republic*

D   No. 112 of 6/8/1984, p. 1273). The amended paragraph lays down the rules as to how the transfer is to be effected and governs relations between the persons appointed by the OAE to administer the undertaking and the undertaking's bodies. Accordingly, it provides that publication of the ministerial decision terminates the powers of the undertaking's administrative bodies and that the general meeting is to continue to exist but cannot terminate the appointment of the members of the administration appointed by the OAE or determine the amount of their remuneration or allowances. The

E   minister's approval is also essential for the distribution of profits and transfers to reserves. Under art. 8(4) the minister may also decide to suspend payment of the undertaking's debts and the corresponding execution measures.

12. Under art. 8(5), the OAE is to carry out, in the course of the provisional administration, a study of the viability of the undertaking and is to negotiate an agreement on the survival of the undertaking with the creditors and shareholders. The

F   validity of such an agreement is subject to the written agreement of a certain proportion of the creditors and 51 per cent of the undertaking's shareholders or members and to the agreement of the OAE. The agreement takes effect when it is approved by the minister. Under art. 8(6), publication of the ministerial decision brings the OAE's provisional administration to an end. If, however, no agreement is reached within a period prescribed by the OAE, the liquidation procedure provided for in art. 9 is carried out.

G   13. During its provisional administration, the OAE may also decide, by way of derogation from the provisions in force relating to public limited liability companies, to increase the capital of the undertaking concerned under art. 8(8). The increase, which has to be approved by the minister, may take the form of contributions in cash or in kind. The undertaking's capital may also be increased by set-off. However, the original shareholders retain their pre-emptive rights, which they have to exercise within a time-limit laid down in the ministerial decision granting approval.

H   14. Article 10 also deals with increases in capital. Unlike the measures contemplated by art. 8(8), those provided for in art. 10 do not come within the context of provisional administration by the OAE. The increase provided for in art. 10 is a definitive rejuvenation measure. Under that article, the minister may, in the cases covered by art. 7 and 8(5), decide to increase the undertaking's capital or to capitalise its debts to the state or other public bodies and undertakings. Article 10 does not give the original shareholders a

right of pre-emption in respect of the new shares. Nevertheless, the original shareholders   A
are not altogether unprotected. The minister has to fix the number and the price of the
newly issued shares on the basis of the undertaking's net worth, as determined in the
OAE's proposal. The ministerial decision may also provide for the possibility of issuing
the new shares to the original shareholders. The new shares may also be issued to the
creditors, the OAE, the undertaking's employees and local authorities.

15. In the event of the capitalisation of debts of public bodies, the decision determines   B
whether all or part of the shares will be issued to the creditors or to the OAE. In the
former case, the debts are extinguished. In the latter case, the OAE draws up and issues
a bond to the creditors representing all or part of their debts.

(d) Commission Decision 88/167

16. The Commission issued a decision in respect of Law No. 1386/1983 under the
procedure provided for in art. 93 of the EEC Treaty. In Decision 88/167 of 7 October   C
1987 (OJ 1988 L76/18), the Commission stated that it had no objections to the
implementation of Law 1386/1983 subject, inter alia, to the Greek Government's
amending the provisions concerning increases in capital so as to bring them into line
with art. 25 and 26 and 29 and 30 of the second directive. It appears from the decision
that individual interventions of the OAE under Law No. 1386/1983 have covered 45
undertakings, of which 22 have been put into liquidation.
                                                                                          D
(e) Other action by the Commission in respect of Law No. 1386/1983

17. On 7 March 1989 the Commission initiated the procedure provided for in art. 169
in respect of the Hellenic Republic's alleged failure to fulfil its obligations under the
second directive. On 9 February 1990 it notified the reasoned opinion to the Greek
Government. On 10 March 1990 the Greek Parliament adopted a law amending Law
No. 1386/1983 in order to bring it into line with the second directive (Law No. 1882/   E
1990, *Official Journal of the Hellenic Republic* No. A 43 of 23 March 1990).

2. *Background to the main proceedings*

18. The applicants in the main proceedings are shareholders in the company Klostiria
Velka AE. That company was subjected to the provisions of Law No. 1386/1983 by
decision of 14 December 1983 of the State Secretary for Industry, Energy and Technology
(Decree No. 2057, *Official Journal of the Hellenic Republic* No. 725 of 14/12/1983).   F
Under art. 7(1) of the Law, the OAE took over the administration of that company. On
28 May 1986 the OAE decided to increase its capital of Dr 222,399,800 by Dr 400m. The
said state secretary approved that decision, taken pursuant to art. 8(8) of Law No. 1386/
1983 by Decree No. 162 of 6 June 1986 (*Official Journal of the Hellenic Republic*
No. 374 of 10/6/1986). The decree provided that the original shareholders would have
an unlimited pre-emptive right which they had to exercise by written declaration within   G
one month of the publication of the decree in the *Official Journal of the Hellenic
Republic*. According to that same decree, in the event that the amount of the increase
was covered in full by the exercise of their pre-emptive rights by the original shareholders,
the shares had to be distributed proportionally to the number of shares held by each
shareholder. Lastly, the decree provided that the provisional administration of the OAE
would freely dispose of the shares which had not been taken up by the original
shareholders within the time-limit laid down and that it would certify that the undertaking's   H
new capital was covered and had been paid up and would amend the undertaking's
statutes to that effect in accordance with Law No. 2190/1920.

19. Marina Karella and Nikolaos Karellas brought an action for the annulment of
that decree in the Council of State, Athens, on the ground that it was contrary to the
Greek Constitution and the second directive.

A   3. *Questions referred for a preliminary ruling*

20. In its decisions of 25 May 1989, the fourth chamber of the Council of State held that the applicants' pleas in law seeking the annulment of the decree on the ground of its unconstitutionality were unfounded. In particular, it held that the decree did not infringe the constitutional principle of equal treatment. The national court did not consider that Decree No. 162 had to provide, in accordance with art. 10(2) of Law No. 1386/1983, for

B   the issue price of the new shares to be fixed on the basis of the undertaking's net worth and of the real value of the original shares. That article was concerned with cases different from those covered by art. 8(8), the provision at issue in this case.

21. As for the compatibility of art. 8(8) with the second directive, the national court took the view that Community law took precedence over national law providing to the contrary and that directives could have direct effect. More specifically, it considered

C   that art. 25 and 42 of the second directive set out rules which were sufficiently precise and did not depend on conditions which were left to the discretion of the member states in so far as they were not covered by the reservation set out in art. 41, and that art. 8(1) of Law No. 1386/1983 was incompatible with art. 25. It therefore asked whether the rules set out in art. 8(8) of the Law fell within the scope of the second directive. In its view, Law No. 1386/1983 constitutes rules justified by the public interest concerning specific factual situations of undertakings in difficulties, irrespective of their legal form.

D   Even if such specific rules fall within the scope of the second directive, it was appropriate to consider whether they were compatible with art. 25 of the second directive, regard being had to the derogation provided for in art. 41. The national court considers that the same considerations apply with regard to the compatibility of those rules with art. 42 of the second directive.

22. In that context, the fourth chamber of the Council of State decided to refer the

E   following questions to the Court of Justice for a preliminary ruling:

"1. Are the provisions of art. 25 in conjunction with art. 41(1) and art. 42 of Council Directive 77/91 of 13 December 1976 free of conditions which lie within the discretion of the member states and sufficiently precise that they can be relied upon against the state before a national court by an individual claiming that a provision of a law is incompatible with those provisions of the directive?

F

2. Does a legal provision come within the scope of art. 25 of Directive 77/91 where it does not permanently govern matters relating to increases in the capital of a limited liability company but is intended to deal with the exceptional circumstances of over-indebted companies which are of particular economic and social importance for society as a whole and provides, in order to ensure the survival and continued operation of those companies, for the adoption by

G   administrative act of a decision to increase the company capital, without prejudice, however, to the pre-emptive right of the existing shareholders when the new shares are distributed, and if so to what extent is it compatible with that provision in conjunction with art. 41(1) of the directive?

3. Is such a law compatible with the provisions of art. 42 of Directive 77/91 in view of the fact that it does not prescribe that the price of the shares is to be fixed by the

H   state on the basis of the objectively established net worth of the undertaking and the resultant inherent value of the old shares but leaves it to the discretion of the administration to fix the price so as to make possible the necessary immediate inflow of capital into companies which, because of their difficulties, have had confidence in them shaken, although it does safeguard the pre-emptive right of existing shareholders when the new shares are distributed?"

4. *Procedure before the court*

23. The national court's judgments were received at the Court Registry on 22 January 1990.

24. Written observations were submitted in accordance with art. 20 of the protocol on the statute of the court as follows:

— for Marina Karella and Nikolaos Karellas, by Konstantinos Adamantopoulos, of the Athens Bar, and Philip Bentley, barrister of Lincoln's Inn;

— for the Greek Government, by Panagiotis Milonopoulos, lawyer, legal adviser of the second class in the Department for Community Legal Affairs of the Ministry of Foreign Affairs, Konstantinos Stavropoulos, lawyer, also a member of that department, and Nikos Fragkakis, lawyer, acting as agents;

— for the Commission of the European Communities, by Antonio Caeiro, legal adviser, and Maria Patakia, a member of its Legal Service, acting as agents.

25. By order of 7 November 1990, the court decided to join Cases C-19/90 and C-20/90 under art. 43 of the rules of procedure.

26. Upon hearing the report of the Judge-Rapporteur, the court decided to open the oral procedure without any preparatory inquiry.

27. By decision of 7 November 1990, the court decided under art. 95(1) and (2) of the rules of procedure to assign the cases to the sixth chamber.

II — Summary of the observations submitted to the court

1. *Direct effect*

28. The *applicants in the main proceedings* observe that the court has consistently held that directives may be directly applicable in so far as their provisions are sufficiently precise and free of conditions which are left to the member states' discretion. They observe that the fact that the member states have a discretion is not sufficient to preclude the direct effect of a provision of a directive where that provision contains a concrete obligation which they cannot avoid (see, for example, the judgment of 12 June 1980 in Case 88/79 *Ministère Public v Grunert* [1980] ECR 1827; Common Market Reporter ¶8680).

29. According to the applicants in the main proceedings, the member states' obligation correctly to implement directives is not satisfied by the mere passing of national legislation to that effect. Article 5 of the EEC Treaty also requires such legislation to be effectively applied (judgment of 10 April 1984 in Case 79/83 *Harz v Deutsche Tradax GmbH* [1984] ECR 1921; Common Market Reporter ¶14,093). However, the fact that the legislation is not applied does not rule out the possible direct effect of provisions of the directive.

30. The applicants in the main proceedings take the view that art. 25(1) of the second directive satisfies the above conditions for direct effect. Consequently, the exception to the principle which is set out in art. 25(2) does not affect its direct applicability. Article 25(2) does not really derogate from art. 25(1) since they are both based on the will of the shareholders. Even allowing there to be a derogation, that derogation is clearly defined and does not leave member states any discretion capable of affecting the content of art. 25(1).

31. The same arguments apply to art. 41(1) of the directive. That article pursues the specific objective of the participation of employees and other clearly defined groups of person. It does not authorise the participation of persons who are not in a relationship of employment with the company concerned or of persons who have not been precisely

A determined beforehand by the national law. The member states are not entitled to invoke that provision unless they have effectively implemented it at the national level. Consequently, art. 41(1) merely introduces a derogation to art. 25(1) which has to be strictly interpreted and is sufficiently precise and clear.

32. In the applicants' view, art. 42 of the second directive also has direct effect. Although it leaves member states with a choice as to how to attain the objective sought, B it does not allow the member states to act contrary to that objective and to the content of that article. Consequently, they may not infringe the principle of the equal treatment of shareholders, which is unconditional, clear and, as a result, capable of giving rise to rights on the part of individuals.

33. The *Greek Government* states that Law No. 1386/1983 does not govern increases in the capital of public limited liability companies in a fundamental way, but provides for special measures in connection with the restructuring of undertakings which are in C difficulty. The rules in question are exceptional, their scope is not defined arbitrarily and they were introduced in order to protect the public interest. They were prompted by the need to ensure the survival of undertakings which are important for the national economy and to avoid labour unrest caused by mass redundancies. The Greek Government states that the undertakings subject to Law No. 1386/1983 employ 28,000 workers.

D 34. The Commission itself recognised the exceptional nature of the rules in question when it gave as a ground for its approval decision of 7 October 1987, cited above, serious disturbance in the economy of a member state within the meaning of art. 92(3)(b) of the EEC Treaty. The exceptional nature of the rules in question is also confirmed by the fact that the contested provisions of the Law were repealed by Law No. 1882/1990, cited above. In those circumstances, it is irrelevant whether or not art. 25 of the second E directive has direct effect, since that article is not concerned with the specific case of undertakings in difficulty. Law No. 1386/1983 governs matters falling outside that provision.

35. The Greek Government observes with regard to the relationship between art. 41 of the second directive and Law No. 1386/1983 that the Law and, in particular, art. 10(2) thereof are also designed to enable employees and other groups of persons, such as the OAE and credit banks, to participate in companies' capital.

F 36. The Greek Government further observes that, according to the court's judgment of 2 February 1988 in Case 24/86 *Blaizot & Ors v University of Liège & Ors* [1988] ECR 379; [1989] 1 CEC 392, pressing considerations of legal certainty may preclude any reopening of past legal relationships where that would retroactively upset the aims attained and the effects obtained through the application of Law No. 1386/1983.

G 37. The *Commission* considers that the first two paragraphs of art. 25 of the second directive are clear and provide and lay down, unambiguously, exclusive, mandatory rules which may be invoked by an individual and applied by the courts. Those provisions are unconditional and do not leave the member states with the possibility of making them subject to conditions or restricting their application. The possibility given the member states under art. 25(2) to authorise an increase in capital up to a maximum amount, does not affect the general principle of the competence of the general meeting H and does not detract from the binding nature of the other rules of art. 25.

38. Before drawing general conclusions as to the unconditional nature of art. 25(1) and (2), they should, in the Commission's view, be examined in relation to art. 41(1). That article seeks solely to foster the achievement of social policy objectives. It follows that the aforesaid paragraphs of art. 25 apply unconditionally to any increase in capital which does not pursue such social objectives. The Commission further observes that

Law No. 1386/1983, which is concerned with putting undertakings in difficulties to   A
rights, does not fall within the scope of art. 41(1).

39. The Commission concludes that the first two paragraphs of art. 25 may be invoked
against the Greek State in the national courts by individuals with a view to having the
ministerial decrees which were adopted in breach of the directive annulled.

40. The Commission considers that it is unnecessary in this context to consider
whether art. 41 of the directive has direct effect. That provision is not in point here,   B
since it does not prohibit the issue price of new shares from being lower than the net
worth of the undertaking concerned. The root cause of the damage suffered by the
shareholders in these cases is, moreover, the infringement of the rule to the effect that
the general meeting is to have exclusive powers and not unequal treatment of those
shareholders.

2. *Primacy*   C

41. The *applicants in the main proceedings* observe that the second directive is
intended to co-ordinate the safeguards required by member states in respect of the
formation of public limited liability companies and the maintenance and alteration of
their capital. A legal provision under which the capital of a public limited liability
company may be increased by administrative act consequently falls within the scope of
that directive, regardless as to whether or not the law in question essentially governs the   D
legal rules relating to the capital of public limited companies. The objective of co-
ordination and uniform application of the directive would be frustrated if the member
states were entitled to vary the degree of protection afforded to shareholders according
to their various laws.

42. In this case, art. 25(1) of the second directive clearly precludes an increase of
capital being decided by administrative act. The same is true of art. 25(2), which
expressly states that any increase in capital must be explicitly authorised by the statutes,   E
the instrument of incorporation or the general meeting. Article 41(1) merely pursues
aims of "industrial democracy" and therefore does not authorise an increase in capital
by administrative act which is not directly related to those aims.

43. According to the applicants, the incompatibility of Law No. 1386/1983 with those
provisions cannot be obviated on the ground that exceptional situations are involved.
Under Community law, it is not possible to derogate from provisions of Community law   F
unless specific provision has been made for a derogation. In this case, however, no
Community derogation has been provided for to cover the exceptional situations
covered by Law No. 1386/1983.

44. The *Greek Government* argues that these cases do not raise an issue in connection
with primacy, since Law No. 1386/1983 does not fall within the scope of the second
directive. It further observes that, in any event, Presidential Decree No. 409/86 adapted   G
the Greek legislation to comply with the provisions of the second directive.

45. In the *Commission's* view, the primacy of Community law is a fundamental,
absolute and unconditional principle which applies to all rules of national law and the
national courts must set aside any conflicting provision of national law (judgment of 9
March 1978 in Case 106/77 *Amministrazione delle Finanze dello Stato v Simmenthal
SpA* [1978] ECR 629; Common Market Reporter ¶8476). If in this way Community law   H
prevails over the constitutional provisions of the member states (judgment of 17
December 1970 in Case 11/70 *Internationale Handelsgesellschaft mbH v Einfuhr-und
Vorratsstelle für Getreide und Futtermittel* [1970] ECR 1125; Common Market Reporter
¶8126), a fortiori it prevails over ordinary legislative provisions, without its being
necessary to consider the reasons which induced the member state to adopt a derogation
to Community law in so far as those reasons are not based on Community law.

A   46. The Commission further observes that no derogation under primary or secondary Community law acts in favour of Law No. 1386/1983. The reservations expressed in its decision of 7 October 1987, cited above, and the initiating of proceedings under art. 169 of the EEC Treaty against the Hellenic Republic based on an infringement of the second directive confirm that that directive takes precedence over the exceptional rules of Law No. 1386/1983, Moreover, the recent amendment of that Law is tantamount to implicit recognition by the Hellenic Republic of the primacy of the second directive.

B
3. *The issue price of the new shares*

47. The *applicants in the main proceedings* consider that it is unnecessary to consider this issue in view of the answers which they suggest to the first two questions. If the court should nevertheless consider that the capital of a public limited liability company may be increased by an administrative act, the administration should make sure, in accordance with art. 42 of the second directive, that the issue price of the new shares is fixed on the
C   basis of the net worth of the company and on the real value of the original shares. The principle of equal treatment of all shareholders also applies to the relationship between the original and the new shareholders and therefore preclude the fixing of an issue price which is lower than the nominal value of the original shares if the new shares confer the same rights as the original ones.

48. In the view of the *Greek Government*, the determination of the undertaking's net
D   worth is not a question of law, but is covered by the assessment of the facts, which is a matter for the national courts. It observes with regard to those facts that, in the cases at issue, the company had no net assets at the time when its capital was increased, since its capital had evaporated on account of its debts.

49. The *Commission* considers that the national court's last question is otiose in so far as the facts underlying the main proceedings do not fall within the rules of art. 42 of
E   the second directive.

OPINION OF MR ADVOCATE GENERAL TESAURO
(30 January 1991)

1. In this case, the court is asked to interpret a number of provisions of the Second Council Directive 77/91 of 13 December 1976 on co-ordination of safeguards which, for the protection of the interests of members and others, are required by member states of
F   companies within the meaning of the second paragraph of art. 58 of the treaty, in respect of the formation of public limited liability companies and the maintenance and alteration of their capital, with a view to making such safeguards equivalent (OJ 1977 L26/1, hereinafter referred to as "the second directive").

2. I shall briefly summarise the relevant national legislation and the background to the main proceedings.

G   Greek Law No. 1386/1983 of 5 August 1983 (*Official Journal of the Hellenic Republic* No. 107 of 8/8/1983, p. 1926) set up the Organismos Ikonomikis Anasygkrotiseos Epicheiriseon AE (Business Reconstruction Organisation, hereinafter referred to as "the OAE"), a public limited liability company whose capital is entirely subscribed by the state and whose purpose is to contribute to the economic and social development of the country. To that end, the OAE may, inter alia, take over the administration and day-
H   to-day operation of undertakings undergoing rejuvenation or nationalised undertakings. Article 8(8) of Law No. 1386/1983 provides that, during its provisional administration of the undertaking subject to the system established by the Law, the OAE may decide, inter alia, by way of derogation from the provisions in force relating to public limited liability companies as regards the exclusive power of the general meeting, to increase the capital of the undertaking concerned. However, the original shareholders continue to have pre-emptive rights, which they must exercise within a certain period.

Law No. 1386/1983 was the subject of Commission Decision 88/167 of 7 October 1987   A
(OJ 1988 L76/18), which was adopted in the course of the procedure provided for in art.
93 of the EEC Treaty. In that decision, the Commission stated that it had no objections
to the implementation of the Law, provided that, among other things, the Greek
Government amended the provisions relating to capital increases in order to bring them
into line with art. 25, 26, 29 and 30 of the second directive. Subsequently, on 7 March
1989, the Commission initiated proceedings under art. 169 of the EEC Treaty on the
ground that the Hellenic Republic had failed to fulfil its obligations under the second   B
directive. Finally, on 10 March 1990, the Greek Parliament passed Law No. 1882/1990
(*Official Journal of the Hellenic Republic* No. A 43 of 23/3/1990) amending the previous
legislation as regards the point at issue in the way desired by the Commission.

3. The applicants in the main proceedings are shareholders in Klostiria Velka AE, a
company subjected to the provisions of Law No. 1386/1983 by decision of 14 December
1983 of the State Secretary for Industry, Energy and Technology (*Official Journal of the*   C
Hellenic Republic No. 725 of 14/12/1983). On 28 May 1986 the OAE, which had taken
over the administration of the company, decided to increase its capital of approximately
Dr 200m by Dr 400m under art. 8(8) of the Law. The decision was ratified by the Greek
authorities by Decree No. 162 of 6 June 1986 (*Official Journal of the Hellenic Republic*
No. 374 of 10/6/1986).

The Council of State, to which the applicants applied for the annulment of the decree   D
ratifying the increase in capital, which they claimed was unlawful on the ground that it
infringed the Greek Constitution and the second directive, dismissed as unfounded their
claims that the act was unconstitutional, but decided at the same time to stay the
proceedings and submit three questions to the court for a preliminary ruling on the
interpretation of the relevant Community legislation.

4. In its first question, the national court refers impliedly to the court's consistent case
law on the direct effect of directives and asks whether art. 25 in conjunction with   E
art. 41(1) and art. 42 of the second directive are free of conditions left to the discretion
of the member states and are sufficiently precise for individuals to rely on them against
the administration before the national courts, claiming that the rules set out in a
legislative provision are incompatible with them.

For the moment, I shall not consider the question of the direct effect, if any, of art. 42,
to which I reserve the right to return in the final part of my opinion. In contrast, as far as   F
art. 25 of the second directive is concerned, it must be observed that it lays down
extremely clearly and precisely a general principle concerning capital increases of public
limited liability companies in so far as the first paragraph states that "[a]ny increases in
capital must be decided upon by the general meeting". This precept does not appear to
be conditional on the provisions of the next paragraph, according to which the statutes,
the instrument of incorporation or the general meeting may authorise an increase in the   G
subscribed capital up to a maximum amount fixed by them with due regard for any
maximum amount provided for by law. In fact, art. 25(2) provides for an individual,
clearly defined derogation from the principle under which decisions to increase the
company's capital are to be reserved for the general meeting, which itself precludes a
national legislature from derogating from that principle above and beyond the cases for
which express provision is made. Consequently, the derogation provided for in
art. 25(2) is not such as to rule out the direct effect of art. 25(1).   H

5. The same applies to art. 41 of the second directive, under which the member states
may derogate from art. 25 if such derogation is necessary for the adoption or application
of provisions designed to encourage the participation of employees or other groups of
persons defined by national law in the capital of undertakings. Whilst it is true that the
provision does give the national authorities a discretion to derogate from the principle

A   set out in art. 25, it is also true that such a possibility appears to be strictly limited to the case provided for, namely that of encouraging popular participation in companies' capital by facilitating share purchase on the part of a number of groups of people, in particular employees.

Apart from the express reference to employees, the aim pursued by the provision is also apparent from the fact that it also enables derogations to be made from art. 9(1) and art. 26, under which shares issued for a consideration must be paid up at not less than 25 B   per cent of their nominal value. This is intended in fact to facilitate share purchase by social groups which normally do not dispose of substantial sums.

Consequently, art. 41 does not enable member states to limit *ad nutum* the scope of the principle set forth in art. 25, but merely lays down a precise derogation with a view to the achievement of a specific social aim. The very reference to "other groups of persons" must therefore be construed as referring to associations of employees or legal C   persons whose aim is in any event to foster popular shareholding and evidently not credit institutions or any entity governed by public or private law irrespective of the aims which they pursue. Consequently, the scope of art. 41 is not such as to preclude the direct effect of art. 25, apart from those cases for which express provision is made.

6. In its second question, the national court asks whether a legal provision comes within the scope of art. 25 of the second directive where it does not permanently govern D   matters relating to increases in the capital of a limited liability company but is intended to deal with the exceptional circumstances of over-indebted companies which are of particular economic and social importance for society as a whole and provides, in order to ensure the survival and continued operation of those companies, for the adoption by administrative act of a decision to increase the company capital, without prejudice, however, to the pre-emptive right of the existing shareholders when the new shares are E   distributed, and if so to what extent it is compatible with that provision in conjunction with art. 41(1) of the directive.

The first part of the question is concerned with the actual scope of art. 25 of the second directive. Indeed, as appears from the national court's order, the Greek Council of State is inclined to consider that art. 25 does not cover a national law which does not specifically govern increases in company capital but is intended to deal with exceptional situations in which some undertakings have found themselves on account of their over-F   indebtedness.

I shall say forthwith that I cannot agree with that view. The aim of the second directive consists in particular of ensuring minimum equivalence in terms of the protection afforded to shareholders. To concede that a member state was entitled, by means of special or exceptional legislation, to derogate from the provisions laid down at Community level to that end would considerably detract from the system of safeguards intended to be laid down by the directive and would therefore impair the uniformity of the minimum G   level of shareholder protection.

There is nothing in the wording or in logic to suggest that the Community legislature intended to restrict the scope of art. 25 to cases where undertakings are without difficulties, leaving the member states free to adopt special, exceptional provisions to cover crisis situations. On the contrary, the second directive expressly contemplates such situations but it does not mention any possible derogations from other provisions H   of the directive and merely provides that in the case of a serious loss of the subscribed capital a general meeting of shareholders must be called within the period laid down by national legislation to consider whether the company should be wound up or any other measures taken.

7. On the other hand, where the EEC Treaty itself seeks to allow the member states to adopt particular measures in order to safeguard vital interests, it makes express

provision for this and generally arranges for appropriate control mechanisms designed   A
to obviate abuses (see, in particular, art. 36; art. 48(3) and (4); art. 73(2); art. 92(3);
art. 100A(4); art. 108; art. 109; art. 223; art. 224; art. 226).

It is in fact obvious that if every provision of Community law were to be regarded as
being subject to a general reservation as regards exceptional events, this might impair
the binding nature of Community law and its uniform application (see to that effect the
judgment of 15 May 1986 in Case 222/84 *Johnston v Chief Constable of the Royal Ulster*   B
Constabulary [1986] ECR 1651 at para. 26; Common Market Reporter ¶14,304).

By way of confirmation of the legislative approach whereby any derogations are
expressly set out, I would point to the Third Council Directive 78/855 of 9 October 1978
concerning mergers of public limited liability companies (OJ 1978 L295/36), a special
provision of which provides that member states need not apply the directive in cases
where the company or companies which are being acquired or will cease to exist are the
subject of bankruptcy, composition or other similar proceedings (art. 1(3)).   C

The absence of similar provisions in the second directive must lead one to the
conclusion that the Community legislature intended to confer the greater scope on the
provision which reserves to the general meeting decisions on increases in capital,
precisely because of the major potential effects of such a change for the situation of the
company.

8. As for the view that the national legislation at issue may fall within the derogations   D
expressly provided for in art. 41 of the second directive, it must be observed that it
emerges from an examination of the wording of Law No. 1386/1983 that transfers of
shares, in particular to employees or their representative organisations, local authorities,
other public-law entities, charitable institutions or social organisations or private
individuals (art. 2(3)), constitutes just one of the possibilities and potential activities of
the OAE and is not the principal purpose of its operations. Consequently, the provision   E
is not such as to make the legislation at issue, taken as a whole, comply with the second
directive.

The fact that the Greek Government amended the legislation at issue as regards the
very point with which the court is concerned is further confirmation, albeit not decisive
in itself, of the observations which I have made in the foregoing.

9. The conclusions which I have reached regarding the interpretation of the provisions   F
in question release me from having to consider the question on the direct effect of art. 42
of the second directive as raised in the third question concerning the interpretation of
that provision (in its third question, the Council of State asked whether provisions of the
type embodied in Law No. 1386/1983 were compatible with the provisions of art. 42 of
the second directive (which provides that the member states are to ensure equal
treatment to all shareholders who are in the same position) in view of the fact that they
did not prescribe that the price of the shares was to be fixed by the state on the basis of   G
the objectively established net worth of the undertaking and the resultant inherent value
of the old shares but left it to the discretion of the administration to fix the price so as to
make possible the necessary immediate inflow of capital into companies which, because
of their difficulties, had had confidence in them shaken, although it did safeguard the
pre-emptive right of existing shareholders when the new shares were distributed).

10. Before concluding, I shall briefly dwell on the Greek Government's request to   H
the effect that the scope *ratione temporis* of the court's judgment should possibly be
limited.

In that connection, I would point out by way of preliminary that, according to the
court's case law, the interpretation which, in the exercise of the jurisdiction conferred
upon it by art. 177 of the Treaty, the Court of Justice gives to a rule of Community law

A   clarifies and defines where necessary the meaning and scope of the rule in question as it must or ought to have been understood and applied from the time of its coming into force. It follows that the rule as thus interpreted may, and must, be applied by the courts even to legal relationships arising and established before the judgment ruling on the request for interpretation, provided that in other respects the conditions enabling an action relating to the application of that rule are to be brought before the courts having jurisdiction are satisfied (judgments of 27 March 1980 in Case 61/79 *Amministrazione delle Finanze dello Stato v Denkavit Italiana Srl* [1980] ECR 1205 at para. 16; Common Market Reporter ¶8665 and Joined Cases 66, 127 and 128/79 *Amministrazione delle Finanze v Srl Meridionale Industria Salumi & Ors* [1980] ECR 1237 at para. 9; Common Market Reporter ¶8663).

It is only exceptionally that the court may, in application of the general principle of legal certainty inherent in the Community legal order and in taking account of the serious effects which its judgment might have, as regards the past, on legal relationships established in good faith, be moved to restrict for any person concerned the opportunity of relying upon the provision as thus interpreted with view to calling into question those legal relationships (judgment in *Denkavit Italiana*, cited above, para. 17; judgment in *Salumi*, cited above, para. 10).

The court has made use of that possibility in very specific circumstances, that is to say a risk of serious economic repercussions due in particular to the large number of legal relationships established in good faith on the basis of the legislation deemed to be validly in force together with the consideration that individuals and the national authorities were moved to act inconsistently with the Community legislation in view of an objective, substantial uncertainty relating to the scope of the Community provisions, which uncertainty may possibly have contributed towards other member states or the Commission adopting that same conduct (judgment of 17 May 1990 in Case 262/88 *Barber v Guardian Royal Exchange Assurance Group* [1990] ECR I-1889; [1990] 1 CEC 653 at para. 40–45, judgment of 2 February 1988 in Case 24/86 *Blaizot & Ors v University of Liège & Ors* [1988] ECR 379; [1989] 1 CEC 392 at para. 25–35, and judgment of 8 April 1976 in Case 43/75 *Defrenne v Société Anonyme Belge de Navigation Aérienne Sabena* [1976] ECR 455 at para. 69–75; Common Market Reporter ¶8346).

However, even in such circumstances, the court has made an exception for the rights of persons who brought court proceedings or took equivalent action before the date of the judgment.

In this case, there is no element — in relation to either the interpretation of the provision at issue or the number of persons concerned — such as to justify derogating from principle of the retroactive nature of the interpretative rulings. I therefore propose that the court should abide by the strict criteria which it has applied in its previous case law in this field and not limit the scope of its judgment *ratione temporis*.

11. In the light of the foregoing considerations, I propose that the questions referred by the Greek Council of State should be answered as follows:

1. Article 25 in conjunction with art. 41(1) of Council Directive 77/91 are unconditional and sufficiently precise, with the result that individuals may rely upon them before national courts as against the administration, claiming that rules set out in a legal provision are incompatible with them.

2. Article 25 in conjunction with art. 41(1) of Council Directive 77/91 must be interpreted as meaning that they preclude the application of national rules which, in order to regulate the administration of certain undertakings in crisis situations, provide for the adoption by administrative act, without a vote by the general meeting, of a decision to increase the company capital, without prejudice to the right of pre-emption of the original shareholders.

JUDGMENT
(30 May 1991)

A

1. By two judgments dated 25 May 1989 which were received at the court on 22 January 1990, the Symvoulio Epikrateias (Council of State) referred to the court pursuant to art. 177 of the EEC Treaty three questions for a preliminary ruling on the interpretation of art. 25, 41 and 42 of the Second Council Directive 77/91 of 13 December 1976 on co-ordination of safeguards which, for the protection of the interests of members and others, are required by member states of companies within the meaning of the second paragraph of art. 58 of the Treaty, in respect of the formation of public limited liability companies and the maintenance and alteration of their capital, with a view to making such safeguards equivalent (OJ 1977 L26/1, hereinafter referred to as "the second directive").

B

2. Those questions were raised in two sets of proceedings between two shareholders in the company Klostiria Velka AE, on the one hand, and the Minister of Industry, Energy and Technology and Organismos Anasygkrotiseos Epicheiriseon AE (Business Reconstruction Organisation, hereinafter referred to as "the OAE"), on the other. Those proceedings are concerned with an increase in that company's capital which was decided upon by the OAE and approved by the State Secretary for Industry, Energy and Technology.

C

3. The OAE is a public-sector body having the form of a public limited liability company which acts in the public interest under the control of the state. It was set up by Greek Law No. 1386/1983 of 5 August 1983 (*Official Journal of the Hellenic Republic* No. 107/A of 8/8/1983, p. 14). Under art. 2(2) of that Law, the purpose of the OAE is to contribute to the economic and social development of the country through the financial rejuvenation of undertakings, the importation and application of foreign know-how and the development of Greek know-how and through the establishment and operation of nationalised or mixed economy undertakings.

D

4. Article 2(3) of Law No. 1386/1983 lists the powers conferred on the OAE in order to achieve those objects. It may take over the administration and day-to-day operation of undertakings undergoing rejuvenation or nationalised undertakings; participate in the capital of undertakings; grant loans and issue or agree certain loans; acquire bonds; and make over shares, in particular to employees or their representative bodies, local government bodies or other legal entities governed by public law, charitable institutions, social organisations or private individuals.

E

5. Under art. 5(1) of Law No. 1386/1983, the Minister for the National Economy may make undertakings undergoing serious financial difficulties subject to the system established by the Law.

F

6. Under art. 7 of Law No. 1386/1983, the competent minister may decide to transfer to the OAE the administration of the undertaking subject to the system established by the Law, deal with the undertaking's debts so as to secure its viability or wind it up.

G

7. Article 8 of Law No. 1386/1983 contains provisions on transferring the administration of the undertaking to the OAE. Article 8(1), as amended by Law No. 1472/1984 (*Official Journal of the Hellenic Republic* No. 112/A of 6/8/1984, p. 1273) lays down the rules as to how the transfer is to be effected and governs relations between the persons appointed by the OAE to administer the undertaking and the undertaking's bodies. Accordingly, it provides that publication of the ministerial decision to subject the undertaking to the system established by the Law terminates the powers of the undertaking's administrative bodies and that the general meeting is to continue to exist but cannot terminate the appointment of the members of the administration appointed by the OAE.

H

8. Article 8(8) of Law No. 1386/1983 provides that, during its provisional administration of the company subject to the system established by the Law, the OAE may decide, by

A   way of derogation from the provisions in force relating to public limited liability companies, to increase the capital of the company concerned. The increase, which has to be approved by the minister, may take the form of contributions in cash or in kind. The undertaking's capital may also be increased by set-off. However, the original shareholders retain their pre-emptive rights, which they may exercise within a time-limit laid down in the ministerial decision granting approval.

B   9. By decision of 14 December 1983 the State Secretary for the Economy subjected Klostiria Velka AE to the provisions of Law No. 1386/1983 (Decree No. 2057, *Official Journal of the Hellenic Republic* No. 725/B of 14/12/1983). The OAE took over the administration of that company in accordance with art. 8 of the Law.

10. During its provisional administration the OAE decided, under art. 8(8) of Law No. 1386/1983, to increase the capital of the company subjected to the system established by the Law by Dr 400m. The State Secretary for Industry, Energy and Technology
C   approved that decision (Decree No. 162 of 6 June 1986, *Official Journal of the Hellenic Republic* No. 374/B of 10/10/1986). The decree provided that the original shareholders would have an unlimited pre-emptive right which they had to exercise within one month of the publication of the decision.

11. Marina Karella and Nikolaos Karellas, who are shareholders in Klostiria Velka AE, brought actions for the annulment of that decree in the Greek Council of State on
D   the ground that it was contrary to the Greek Constitution and the second directive.

12. In its judgments of 25 May 1989 the Council of State held that the applicants' pleas in law seeking the annulment of the decree on the ground of its unconstitutionality were unfounded. However, it decided that it should refer to the court for a preliminary ruling the following questions — identically worded in the two cases — on the interpretation of the second directive:

E   "1. Are the provisions of art. 25 in conjunction with art. 41(1) and art. 42 of Council Directive 77/91 of 13 December 1976 free of conditions which lie within the discretion of the member states and sufficiently precise that they can be relied upon against the state before a national court by an individual claiming that a provision of a law is incompatible with those provisions of the directive?

2. Does a legal provision come within the scope of art. 25 of Directive 77/91
F   where it does not permanently govern matters relating to increases in the capital of a limited liability company but is intended to deal with the exceptional circumstances of over-indebted companies which are of particular economic and social importance for society as a whole and provides, in order to ensure the survival and continued operation of those companies, for the adoption by administrative act of a decision to increase the company capital, without prejudice, however, to the pre-emptive right of the existing shareholders when the new
G   shares are distributed, and if so to what extent is it compatible with that provision in conjunction with art. 41(1) of the directive?

3. Is such a law compatible with the provisions of art. 42 of Directive 77/91 in view of the fact that it does not prescribe that the price of the shares is to be fixed by the state on the basis of the objectively established net worth of the undertaking and the resultant inherent value of the old shares but leaves it to the discretion of the
H   administration to fix the price so as to make possible the necessary immediate inflow of capital into companies which, because of their difficulties, have had confidence in them shaken, although it does safeguard the pre-emptive right of existing shareholders when the new shares are distributed?"

13. Reference is made to the report for the hearing for a fuller account of the facts in the main proceedings, the applicable legislation and the written observations submitted

A

to the court, which are mentioned or discussed hereinafter only in so far as is necessary for the reasoning of the court.

14. The national court's questions essentially raise two issues. The first is concerned with art. 25(1) of the second directive. The national court wishes to establish whether, having regard to art. 41(1) of the second directive, art. 25(1) may be relied upon against the administration by individuals in the national courts. It then asks whether art. 25(1), in conjunction with art. 41(1), is applicable with regard to public rules, such as those provided for in Law No. 1386/1983, which govern the completely exceptional cases of undertakings which are of particular economic and social importance for society and are undergoing serious financial difficulties.

B

15. The second issue is concerned with art. 42 of the second directive. The national court asks whether that provision may be relied upon by individuals and whether it has to be interpreted as precluding national rules of the type referred to above.

C

16. The court will initially consider the first issue, since, in the cases at issue in the main proceedings, the lawfulness of the increase in capital predominates over the question of the value of the issue price.

The direct effect of art. 25(1) of the second directive

17. As the court has consistently held, wherever the provisions of a directive appear, as far as their subject-matter is concerned, to be unconditional and sufficiently precise, individuals are entitled to invoke them against the state (see, in particular, the judgment of 19 January 1982 in Case 8/81 *Becker v Finanzamt Münster-Innenstadt* [1982] ECR 53; Common Market Reporter ¶8789).

D

18. Consequently, it should be examined whether art. 25(1) of the second directive, which provides that any increase in capital must be decided upon by the general meeting, satisfies those conditions.

E

19. It must be held in that connection that that provision is clearly and precisely worded and lays down, unconditionally, a rule enshrining the general principle that the general meeting has the power to decide upon increases in capital.

20. The unconditional nature of that provision is not affected by the derogation provided for in art. 25(2) of the second directive to the effect that the company's instrument of incorporation or the general meeting may authorise an increase in the subscribed capital up to a maximum amount which is to be fixed with due regard for any maximum amount provided for by law. That individual, clearly defined derogation does not leave member states any possibility of making the principle of the power of the general meeting subject to any exceptions other than that for which express provision is made.

F

G

21. The same applies to art. 41(1) of the second directive, under which member states may derogate from art. 25(1) and art. 9(1) and the first sentence of art. 19(1)(a) and (b) to the extent that such derogations are necessary to encourage the participation of employees or other groups of persons defined by national law in the capital of undertakings. That derogation, too, is strictly confined to the case provided for.

22. Moreover, the fact that the Community legislature provided for precise, concrete derogations confirms the unconditional character of the principle set forth in art. 25(1) of the second directive.

H

23. It is appropriate therefore to answer the national court by stating that art. 25(1) of the second directive may be relied upon by individuals against the public authorities before national courts.

A **The scope of art. 25(1) of the second directive**

24. As for the scope of art. 25(1) of the second directive with respect to a law, such as Law No. 1386/1983, it should be examined in the first place whether such a law falls within the field of application of the directive, since that legislation does not set out the basic rules on increases of capital and merely seeks to deal with exceptional situations. If that legislation falls within the field of application of the second directive, it should then be considered whether it can qualify for the benefit of the derogation provided for in art. 41(1) of that directive.

B

25. As far as the field of application of the second directive is concerned, it should be stated first of all that, in accordance with art. 54(3)(g) of the Treaty, it seeks to co-ordinate the safeguards which, for the protection of the interests of members and others, are required by member states of companies and firms within the meaning of the second paragraph of art. 58 of the Treaty with a view to making such safeguards equivalent. Consequently, the aim of the second directive is to provide a minimum level of protection for shareholders in all the member states.

C

26. That objective would be seriously frustrated if the member states were entitled to derogate from the provisions of the directive by maintaining in force rules — even rules categorised as special or exceptional — under which it is possible to decide by administrative measure, outside any decision by the general meeting of shareholders, to effect an increase in the company's capital which would have the effect either of obliging the original shareholders to increase their contributions to the capital or of imposing on them the addition of new shareholders, thus reducing their involvement in the decision-taking power of the company.

D

27. However, that observation does not signify that Community law prevents member states from derogating from those provisions in any circumstances. The Community legislature has made specific provision for well-defined derogations and for procedures which may result in such derogations with the aim of safeguarding certain vital interests of the member states which are liable to be affected in exceptional situations. Instances of this are art. 19(2) and (3), art. 40(2), art. 41(2) and art. 43(2) of the directive.

E

28. In this connection, it must be held that no derogating provision which would allow the member states to derogate from art. 25(1) of the directive in crisis situations is provided for either in the EEC Treaty or in the second directive itself. On the contrary, art. 17(1) of the directive provides expressly that, in the case of a serious loss of the subscribed capital, a general meeting of shareholders must be called within the period laid down by the laws of the member states to consider whether the company should be wound up or any other measures taken. Consequently, that provision confirms the principle laid down by art. 25(1) and applies even where the company concerned is undergoing serious financial difficulties.

F

G

29. The OAE further claimed at the hearing that the second directive could not apply to the special collective liquidation or rejuvenation procedures for companies incapable of meeting their commitments, since its field of application was confined to the normal operation of companies.

30. That objection cannot be accepted. The directive is intended to ensure that members' and third parties' rights are safeguarded, in particular in operations for setting up companies and increasing and reducing company capital. In order to be effective, that safeguard must be secured for members as long as the company continues to exist with its own structures. Whilst the directive does not preclude the taking of execution measures and, in particular, liquidation measures placing the company under compulsory administration in the interests of safeguarding creditors' rights, it nevertheless continues to apply as long as the company's shareholders and normal bodies have not been divested of their powers. Certainly, this is true where there is a straightforward

H

rejuvenation measure involving public bodies or companies governed by private law   A
where the members' right to the capital and to decision-making power in the company is
in question.

31. It follows that, in the absence of a derogation provided for by Community law,
art. 25(1) of the second directive must be interpreted as precluding the member states
from maintaining in force rules incompatible with the principle set forth in that article,
even if those rules cover only exceptional situations. To recognise the existence of a   B
general reservation covering exceptional situations, outside the specific conditions laid
down in the provisions of the Treaty and the second directive, would, moreover, be
liable to impair the binding nature and uniform application of Community law (see, to
this effect, the judgment of 15 May 1986 in Case 222/84 *Johnston v Chief Constable of
the Royal Ulster Constabulary* [1986] ECR 1651 at para. 26; Common Market Reporter
¶14,304).

32. As for the idea that rules comparable to those set out in Law No. 1386/1983 might   C
qualify under the derogation provided for in art. 41(1), it should be observed that that
provision pursues a precise, well-defined social-policy aim, namely to encourage private
individuals to hold shares. Like the exceptions provided for in art. 19(3) and art. 23(2)
of the second directive, it is intended solely to encourage, in an objective and concrete
manner, persons, such as employees, who generally do not have the means necessary to
do so under the normal conditions of company law in the member states, to participate   D
in the capital of undertakings.

33. Consequently, a national rule cannot take advantage of that derogation unless its
practical application helps to achieve the objective of art. 41(1) of the second directive.

34. In that connection, it should be made clear that that condition is not fulfilled
merely because rules, such as those contained in Law No. 1386/1983, provide for the
possibility, as one of the available means of achieving their objective, of the public   E
restructuring body's transferring shares to employees or to individuals. Such a possibility
is merely hypothetical and ancillary.

35. It should further be made clear, as stated by the Advocate General in para. 5 of
his opinion, that the reference in art. 41(1) of the second directive to other groups of
persons refers to shareholding by private individuals and is not concerned with the
transfer of shares to credit institutions or to public-law bodies.

36. Consequently, the answer to the national court's second question must be that   F
art. 25 in conjunction with art. 41(1) of the second directive must be interpreted as
meaning that they preclude national rules which, in order to ensure the survival and
continued operation of undertakings which are of particular economic and social
importance for society as a whole and are in exceptional circumstances by reason of their
excessive debt burden, provide for the adoption by administrative act of a decision to
increase the company capital, without prejudice to the right of pre-emption of the   G
original shareholders when the new shares are issued.

37. In view of the answers set out above there is no need to consider the national
court's third question or the part of the first question which is concerned with the direct
effect of art. 42 of the second directive.

Costs   H

38. The costs incurred by the Greek Government and the Commission of the European
Communities, which have submitted observations to the court, are not recoverable. As
these proceedings are, in so far as the parties to the main proceedings are concerned, in
the nature of a step in the proceedings pending before the national court, the decision
on costs is a matter for that court.

A   Ruling

On those grounds, the court (sixth chamber), in answer to the questions referred to it by the Symvoulio Epikrateias by two judgments dated 25 May 1989, hereby rules:

1. Article 25 of the Second Council Directive 77/91 of 13 December 1976 on co-ordination of safeguards which, for the protection of the interests of members and others, are required by member states of companies within the meaning of the second paragraph of art. 58 of the Treaty, in respect of the formation of public limited liability companies and the maintenance and alteration of their capital, with a view to making such safeguards equivalent, may be relied upon by individuals against the public authorities before national courts.

2. Article 25 in conjunction with art. 41(1) of the second directive must be interpreted as meaning that they preclude national rules which, in order to ensure the survival and continued operation of undertakings which are of particular economic and social importance for society as a whole and are in exceptional circumstances by reason of their excessive debt burden, provide for the adoption by administrative act of a decision to increase the company capital, without prejudice to the right of pre-emption of the original shareholders when the new shares are issued.

El Ajou v Dollar Land Holdings plc & Anor.

Chancery Division.
Millett J.
Judgment delivered 12 June 1992.

Knowing receipt of trust funds — Knowledge of company — Plaintiff victim of fraud sought to trace proceeds to company — Whether plaintiff could trace proceeds in equity through civil law jurisdictions — Whether company knew or should have known that money was proceeds of fraud — Whether knowledge of director and employee were attributable to company.

This was an action by the plaintiff, who was one of many victims of a massive share fraud carried out in Amsterdam by three Canadians between 1984 and 1985, claiming to be able to trace some of the proceeds of the fraud from Amsterdam through intermediate resting places in Geneva, Gibraltar, Panama and Geneva (again) to London, where they were invested in a joint venture to carry out a property development project in Battersea in conjunction with the first defendant, Dollar Land Holdings plc ("DLH").

The interest of the Canadians in the joint venture had been bought out by DLH. The plaintiff sought to recover from DLH the money which DLH originally received, alleging that DLH received it with knowledge that it represented the proceeds of fraud, or alternatively the value of the Canadians' investment, alleging that DLH acquired such knowledge before it bought them out. The plaintiff alleged that "F", DLH's chairman, and "S", who was not a director but was a shareholder and managed DLH's business and was managing director of one of its subsidiaries, possessed the necessary knowledge attributable to DLH that the funds represented the proceeds of fraud.

Subject to two points, DLH conceded that the plaintiff could successfully trace the money from Amsterdam to London. DLH submitted, first, that the plaintiff had not established that the money in an account in Geneva used to secure an advance to finance the project represented the proceeds of the fraud which had been remitted from Gibraltar to Panama; and secondly that the equitable tracing remedy depended on the continuing subsistence of the plaintiff's equitable title, and could not be invoked where the money was transferred to recipients in civil law jurisdictions like Switzerland and Panama which did not recognise the trust concept or the notion of equitable ownership. DLH further denied that it had any knowledge that the money which the Canadians invested in the project represented the proceeds of fraud, and in buying out their interest it claimed to have been a bona fide purchaser for value without notice.

Held, dismissing the action:

1. There was some evidence to support an inference that the money which reached the Geneva account represented part of the moneys which had previously been transmitted to Panama.

2. Foreign law was a question of fact which had to be pleaded and proved by expert evidence. The court could not take judicial notice of foreign law. In the absence of evidence, foreign law was presumed to be the same as English law. In the present case no question of foreign law had been pleaded, and no evidence of foreign law tendered.

3. In any event, any obligation on the part of DLH to restore to their rightful owner assets which it received in England was governed exclusively by English law, and the equitable tracing rules and the trust concept which underlay them were applicable as part of that law. There was no need to consider any other system of law.

4. On the issue of "knowing receipt" of trust moneys, the court assumed, without deciding, that dishonesty or want of probity involving actual knowledge (whether proved or inferred) was not a precondition of liability; but that a recipient was not expected to be

A   unduly suspicious and was not to be held liable unless he went ahead without further inquiry in circumstances in which an honest and reasonable man would have realised that the money was probably trust money and was being misapplied.

5. F's position as chairman and non-executive director of DLH was insufficient by itself to constitute his knowledge ipso facto the knowledge of DLH. Nor did F act as the agent of DLH in obtaining the money from the Canadians. F discovered that the Canadians were fraudsters and that their money had been obtained by fraud at a time when he was acting in his own interest and as a director of another company, and not as a director of DLH. In seeking finance on ordinary commercial terms, and in the absence of anything to put it on inquiry, DLH was not bound to inquire as to the source of the money it was offered and, that being so, F was under no obligation to tell DLH what he knew. At the time of the relevant transaction (in March 1988) F had ceased to be a director of DLH for nine months, and he had nothing to do with the transaction: even if F's knowledge should be attributed to DLH in 1986, it would be wrong to treat DLH as still possessing that knowledge in 1988.

6. It was not disputed that, in relation to the Canadians' investment in the project, the knowledge of S was the knowledge of DLH. Unless S knew (or possibly ought to have known) that the money had been obtained by the Canadians by fraud, DLH could not be made liable to restore it. S had no reason to suspect that the money had been obtained by fraud. He could not actually have known that the money had been obtained by fraud unless F told him. The court would not infer that F had told him.

The following cases were referred to in the judgment:

Agip (Africa) Ltd v Jackson & Ors [1991] Ch 547.
Chase Manhattan Bank NA v Israel-British Bank (London) Ltd [1981] Ch 105.
Cook Industries Inc v Galliher & Anor [1979] Ch 439.
Daly v Sydney Stock Exchange Ltd (1986) 160 CLR 371.
Diplock, Re [1948] Ch 465.
Eagle Trust plc v SBC Securities Ltd [1993] 1 WLR 484.
Ewing & Ors v Orr Ewing (1883) 9 App Cas 34.
Fenwick, Stobart & Co Ltd, Re [1902] 1 Ch 507.
Hampshire Land Co, Re [1896] 2 Ch 743.
Houghton (J C) & Co v Nothard, Lowe and Wills Ltd [1928] AC 1.
Lazard Bros & Co v Midland Bank Ltd [1933] AC 289.
Lipkin Gorman v Karpnale Ltd [1991] 2 AC 548.
Marseilles Extension Railway Co, Re (1871) LR 7 Ch App 161.
Montagu's Settlement Trusts, Re [1987] Ch 264.
Payne (David) & Co Ltd, Re [1904] 2 Ch 608.
Portarlington (Lord) v Soulby (1834) 3 Myl & K 104; 40 ER 40.
Tesco Supermarkets Ltd v Nattrass [1972] AC 153.

Michael Beloff QC, Roger Ellis and Sarah Moore (instructed by Bower Cotton & Bower) for the plaintiff.

Romie Tager (instructed by Kaufman Kramer Shebson) for the defendant.

JUDGMENT

Millett J: The plaintiff in this action, Mr El Ajou, is a wealthy Arab businessman resident in Riyadh. He was the largest single victim, though only one of many victims, of a massive share fraud carried out in Amsterdam by three Canadians between 1984 and 1985. He claims to be able to trace some of the proceeds of the fraud from Amsterdam through intermediate resting places in Geneva, Gibraltar, Panama and Geneva (again) to London, where they were invested in a joint venture to carry out a property development project in Battersea in conjunction with the first defendant, Dollar Land

Holdings plc ("DLH"). The interest of the Canadians in the joint venture has since been   A
bought out by DLH. The plaintiff seeks to recover from DLH the money which it
originally received, alleging that DLH received it with knowledge that it represented
the proceeds of fraud, or alternatively the value of the Canadians' investment, alleging
that DLH acquired such knowledge before it bought them out. There is an alternative
claim to damages for conspiracy, but that claim has not been pursued.

DLH is a public limited company incorporated in England and resident for tax   B
purposes in Switzerland. It is a holding company. Its principal activities, carried on
through its subsidiaries, are property dealing and investment. At the material time it
was in a substantial way of business. It denies that it had any knowledge that the money
which the Canadians invested in the project represented the proceeds of fraud, and in
buying out their interest it claims to have been a bona fide purchaser for value without
notice.

The second defendant, Factotum NV ("Factotum"), is a company incorporated in the   C
Netherlands Antilles. It has no assets, and has not been served with these proceedings.
It was the penultimate recipient of the money. The plaintiff alleges that it was a
subsidiary of DLH, but that is disputed.

The frauds
   D

The frauds were committed through the medium of two Dutch companies, Tower
Securities BV ("Tower") and BV Incassobureau B & K Zuidlaren, trading under the
name UC United Consultants ("United"). The persons who directed the operations of
Tower and United were three Canadian fraudsters, Allan Lindzon (or Levinson), Lloyd
Caplan, and Harry Roth ("the Canadians"). Tower and United carried on business as
stockbrokers in Amsterdam. They operated what are known in the trade as "boiler
rooms"; that is to say, they specialised in selling worthless or virtually worthless shares   E
at high prices to gullible investors who were subjected to high-pressure salesmanship,
usually over the telephone, by aggressive salesmen who would "hype" the shares, falsely
telling investors that the shares were about to be offered to the public at a higher price
and that a "quick killing" could be made if they acted without delay. In fact none of the
shares was ever quoted or capable of being quoted on a recognised stock exchange, or
was worth more than a tiny fraction of the price at which it was offered. The businesses
of Tower and United were closed down on 1 May 1986 when their premises and those of   F
other similar enterprises were raided by the Amsterdam police. Tower and United were
declared bankrupt by the local district courts on 7 October and 4 November 1986
respectively on the application of the public prosecutor on public interest grounds.
He characterised their dealings as involving fraud, deceit, embezzlement and forgery.
Mr Van Apeldoorn, a member of the bar of Amsterdam, was appointed trustee in
bankruptcy of both companies. He applied to be joined in the present action as a co-   G
plaintiff, but his application was refused by the master. He told me that, under Dutch
law, he has locus standi to recover the proceeds of the fraud for the benefit of the
creditors of Tower and United, including the victims of the fraud. The plaintiff has
concluded a formal agreement with him to share all moneys recovered in the present
action.

Tower was incorporated in the Netherlands on 7 February 1984. It appears to have   H
passed through three sets of beneficial owners. Initially it was owned by two Canadians,
Herbert West and Stephen Polon, through a Panamanian holding company, Catalytic
Ventures SA ("Catalytic"). On 22 October 1984 the shares in Tower were sold by
Catalytic to another Panamanian company, La Belle Capital SA ("La Belle Capital").
This marked the acquisition of Tower by the Canadians. Arrangements for the
incorporation of La Belle Capital were made by Mr David D'Albis, an American citizen

A resident in Geneva. He had recently been introduced to the Canadians by two associates of theirs, Mr Singer and Mr Goldhar, and had agreed to act as their fiduciary agent. This involved making arrangements to incorporate companies, attend to all necessary formalities, open and operate bank accounts, and transfer funds on the instructions of his principals. Mr D'Albis did not find it necessary or expedient to inquire into the background of his clients or the nature of their business activities. He took his instructions over the telephone. On 19 November 1984 La Belle Capital gave Mr D'Albis a general

B power of attorney and authorised him to open a bank account for the company at Compagnie de Banque et d'Investissements in Geneva ("CBI Geneva") and to be sole signatory on the account. In order to avoid disclosing the names of his principals, Mr D'Albis had to arrange for the account to be opened by a Swiss lawyer, who technically became a co-signatory; but she was not intended to operate the account and in practice Mr D'Albis was at all times sole signatory on the account.

C The documentation available in relation to United is more limited. It, too, was owned by a Panamanian holding company, Tulane Holding Corporation ("Tulane"). Tulane was registered on 25 October 1984. On 25 May 1985 Mr D'Albis was appointed by Tulane as one of the signatories on the account of United at Amro Bank NV in Amsterdam. A document found on Mr D'Albis' files when the contents of his office were later seized on the orders of the examining judge in Geneva records Tulane

D as belonging to the Canadians and one Waldi Steemers. Mr D'Albis told me that Mr Steemers dropped out at an early stage.

The Canadians took over an existing force of salesmen who operated from the companies' offices in Amsterdam. They were either self-employed or, more usually, employed by their own nominee companies incorporated in the Isle of Man with bank accounts in Geneva, and were paid commission at the excessively high rate of eight per cent. The Canadians did not, however, take over their predecessors' stock of worthless

E shares, but acquired their own. Nor did they make use of their predecessors' "vendor-clients". For this purpose Mr D'Albis arranged for the incorporation of two further Panamanian companies, Herron Holdings SA ("Herron") for Tower, and Wilmington Commercial SA ("Wilmington") for United. In the case of each company Mr D'Albis held a general power of attorney, signed a fiduciary agreement with the Canadians, and opened a bank account in the company's name at CBI Geneva on which he was the sole

F signatory. The fiduciary agreement in respect of Herron is dated 20 November 1984, and that in respect of Wilmington 23 November 1984. It was submitted on behalf of DLH that the Canadians must have acquired the stream of income due to Tower and resulting from sales made by their predecessors, but there is no evidence of this and it is unlikely. Tower acted as a broker only and accounted to its "vendor-clients" for the proceeds of the sales of shares (less only a commission at normal rates). Since West and Polon had

G used their own "vendor-clients", Tower ought to have accounted, and almost certainly did account, to them for the proceeds of sales made before, but which were received after, the takeover. The bank accounts of Herron and Wilmington show no moneys being received from Amsterdam until 11 February 1985, which is consistent with the proceeds of pre-acquisition sales continuing to be paid to West and Polon.

Mr D'Albis has confirmed the conclusion formed by Mr Van Apeldoorn from his examination of the companies' records that the Canadians' involvement with Tower and

H United lasted for 12 months, from about 19 November 1984 until about 19 November 1985. On the latter date La Belle Capital appointed a new attorney in place of Mr D'Albis. The accounts of Herron and Wilmington at CBI Geneva had by that date been run down to nominal sums, and were made available to the Canadians' successors by the simple expedient of altering the bank mandates. New powers of attorney and fiduciary agreements were, no doubt, entered into for the new owners, but they are not

available. Mr D'Albis confirmed that he no longer had anything to do with Herron or   A
Wilmington after November 1985.

Mr Van Apeldoorn has estimated that, during the whole period of the fraud, some
4,000 victims were defrauded of a total of more than US$43m, of which the Canadians
were responsible for approximately $20m during their year's tenure. (In this judgment
all dollars are US dollars.)

The only shares traded by Tower between November 1984 and November 1985 were   B
bearer securities in three companies, Goldseekers International Inc ("Goldseekers"),
Sprint Resources Ltd ("Sprint"), and European Computer Group ("ECG"); and the
only shares traded by United during the same period were bearer securities in Colt
Computer Holdings Ltd ("Colt"). None of the companies had any substance.
Goldseekers, for example, was a new company which Mr D'Albis caused to be
incorporated in Djibouti in February 1985 on the instructions of Mr Singer. Its share
capital consisted of 1.9m bearer shares of 10 cents each. Herron subscribed $100,000 for   C
shares, but within four days virtually all the money was paid away, mostly back to
Herron, leaving the company with a balance of $3,550 as its only asset. Its shares were
traded by Tower at over $6 each.

Shares in the other three companies were obtained with the assistance of another
Swiss fiduciary agent, Mr Sylvain Ferdman, the chairman of DLH and one of the
principal characters in the story, who now makes his appearance. Mr Ferdman had   D
worked for many years for the Bank of International Credit in Geneva. In 1972 he left
the bank and set up his own company, Société d'Administration et de Financement SA
("SAFI"). SAFI was owned jointly by Mr Ferdman and an old-established Swiss
cantonal bank of good reputation. In 1982 the bank relinquished its shareholding in
SAFI and Mr Ferdman became sole proprietor. Unfortunately, SAFI suffered a significant
loss from this transaction from which it never recovered. It ceased to trade in May 1988   E
and subsequently went into liquidation.

SAFI acted as a fiduciary agent for clients who did not wish their identities to be
disclosed. On this occasion its principals were Singer and Goldhar. In November 1984
Mr Ferdman arranged for the incorporation of a Panamanian company, Dunberry
Holdings SA ("Dunberry"), on their behalf and SAFI entered into a fiduciary agreement
with them. Mr Ferdman understood that his clients wished to buy and sell shares and to
subscribe for new issues both quoted and unquoted. He made no further inquiries. He   F
was accustomed to accept funds from clients without questioning their origin, and to act
for clients who were anxious to conceal their identity. He regarded the need to preserve
his clients' anonymity as paramount — without it he would have no business — and to
this end he was willing on occasion to present himself or SAFI as a beneficial owner and
to make false statements to this effect.

Sprint was a small and unsuccessful Canadian company of which Singer was president.   G
It was insolvent and loss making. It had over 3m common shares in issue. SAFI
subscribed for 300,000 shares on behalf of Dunberry at a few cents each. They were
traded by Tower at over $4 each. The proceeds were paid to Herron.

ECG was a Liechtenstein company. Its only asset was a 100 per cent shareholding in
an English company called PCML Ltd ("PCML"). PCML had previously been owned
by Mr Fuller, who was seeking a capital investment in his company. Early in 1985 Singer
and Goldhar introduced him to SAFI. They required PCML to become a subsidiary of a   H
Liechtenstein company to be formed for the purpose. Accordingly, ECG was formed
and Mr Fuller injected PCML into ECG in exchange for 6,500,000 shares in ECG. The
value of PCML was in the region of £150,000. SAFI, posing as a long-term investor and
pretending to be acting on its own account, subscribed $250,000 for 1m shares in ECG at
25 cents each, and had the right (which it exercised in October 1985) to subscribe for a

A further 1m shares at the same price; and another company run by Singer and Goldhar subscribed for 250,000 shares at one cent each.

Unknown to Mr Fuller SAFI in fact subscribed for the shares as nominee for Dunberry and on the instructions of Singer and Goldhar. The certificates were delivered to Tower and the shares were traded between $8 and $12 each. The proceeds were paid, not to SAFI or Dunberry, but to Herron. On occasion, the shares were sold by Tower before
B SAFI had subscribed for them.

Colt was acquired in similar fashion. An English company whose value cannot have been more than £100,000 was reversed into a new company formed in Liechtenstein in exchange for shares. SAFI subscribed for 500,000 shares at 25 cents each and had the right to subscribe for an additional 1.5m shares at the same price. The share certificates were delivered to United and the shares were traded at between $4 and $9 each. The proceeds were paid to Wilmington.
C

The plaintiff

In 1985 the plaintiff owned substantial funds and securities which were deposited with the First National Bank of Chicago in Geneva ("First National") and which were under the control of his investment manager, Mr Murad. Mr Murad's authority was strictly limited. Between December 1983 and May 1985, unknown to the plaintiff and without
D his authority, Mr Murad used his funds to invest on his behalf in shares traded by Tower and United. The limits of Mr Murad's authority were not known to Tower or United, and nothing turns upon the fact that he acted without authority. Nor is it clear whether Mr Murad was deceived as to the value of the shares which he bought on the plaintiff's behalf. What is beyond dispute is that he was bribed. He was involved before the Canadians came on the scene. Altogether, the plaintiff's account was debited with a
E total of $13,051,221.59. For the purposes of the present action, however, five separate transactions between February and May 1985 have been identified in respect of which Mr Murad paid to Tower and United a total of $10,653,100 of the plaintiff's money and received commissions totalling $1,217,500 paid by Herron or Wilmington.

The transactions and money movements are well documented. Mr Murad brought 500,000 shares in Colt at $5.15 per share, 350,000 shares in Goldseekers at $6.15 per share, and 1.5m shares in ECG at $8.15 per share; and sold the shares in Colt at $5.75
F per share and the shares in Goldseekers at $6.30 per share, as well as 200,000 shares in Sprint and 200,000 shares in a company called Clarendon at $4.50 and $4.75 per share respectively. (The circumstances in which the last two shareholdings were acquired are not known.) Each transaction resulted in a net payment to Tower or United. On each occasion Mr Murad gave the sale and purchase orders by telex to Tower or United, and gave instructions to First National to pay the net amount due to Tower or United against
G delivery of the shares. That sum was duly debited to the plaintiff's account at First National and credited to the account of Tower or United at its bank in Amsterdam. Within a day or two or its receipt, a corresponding sum less a small brokerage commission was debited to that account and credited to the account of Herron or Wilmington at CBI Geneva. Immediately on its receipt, Mr D'Albis gave written instructions to CBI Geneva for its disbursement. Within a few days, and in accordance with those instructions, a substantial sum was transferred out of the account in which it had been received and
H was credited to the account of Mr and Mrs Murad at Credit Suisse Geneva.

Of the $10,653,100 of the plaintiff's money paid to Tower and United, $10,591,312.75 was paid out to Herron and Wilmington. In addition to the commissions totalling $1,217,500 paid to Mr Murad out of moneys received by Herron and Wilmington $112,000 was paid to him direct by Tower. This probably represented commission earned by Mr Murad before the Canadians were involved.

The plaintiff was only one of many victims of the fraud, and his money was mixed with
that of many others. The total amount received by Herron and Wilmington from Tower
and United during 1985 was $18,595,492, of which $12,704,329 was received by Herron
and $5,891,253 was received by Wilmington. According to schedules submitted on
behalf of DLH the total amount credited to the accounts of Herron and Wilmington
during the relevant period was $19,374,000. The discrepancy, which is not material, is
largely accounted for by the fact that the schedules include moneys which came from
other sources, as well as circular payments and receipts (such as Herron's subscription
for shares in Goldseekers).

The money goes to Panama

The Canadians caused three Panamanian companies ("the first tier Panamanian
companies") to be formed in order to receive their individual shares in the profits
derived from their fraudulent activities, and a large part of the money received by
Herron and Wilmington was disbursed to these companies immediately after its receipt.
The first tier Panamanian companies were Bangor Corporation (Caplan), Egyptian
Seaway Inc (Roth), and Medallion Investments Inc (Lindzon). A fourth company,
Gemstone Capital Corporation ("Gemstone"), was also formed, probably for Mr
Steemers. Mr D'Albis held a general power of attorney for each company, opened a
bank account in its name at CBI Geneva on which he was sole signatory, and signed a
fiduciary agreement which identified his principal. In the case of Gemstone the fiduciary
agreement named all three Canadians as principals.

Of the $19,374,000 which was paid into the accounts of Herron and Wilmington,
$9,547,000 was paid out to the first tier Panamanian companies, $1,217,000 to Mr Murad
and $241,000 to Gemstone. Mr D'Albis identified a further $114,000 as representing his
own fees, and $1,878,000 as representing payments of commission to one of the
salesmen. A further $1,450,000 was paid to Zawi Resources SA ("Zawi"). This was
another Panamanian company which Mr D'Albis had formed for the Canadians and was
jointly owned by them. Mr D'Albis was unable to say for what purpose the money was
applied. The balance of $4,927,000 cannot be accounted for.

The correspondence of the dates and amounts involved means that the debits and
credits can easily be matched. On this basis (which is not necessarily correct as between
the plaintiff and other victims of the fraud) $6,673,440 of the money which was received
by the first tier Panamanian companies represented the plaintiff's moneys.

While the money was at the disposal of the first tier Panamanian companies,
Mr D'Albis arranged for it to be invested in short-dated American and Canadian
Treasury bills. Towards the end of 1985 and on the instructions of the Canadians Mr
D'Albis arranged for the formation of three new Panamanian companies ("the second
tier Panamanian companies") to hold their funds. The second tier Panamanian companies
were Panarea Investments Inc (Roth), Tirena Investments Inc (Lindzon) and Lipari
Investments Inc (Caplan). From November 1985, as the Treasury bills were redeemed,
the funds of the first tier Panamanian companies were transferred to the second tier
Panamanian companies. These companies maintained accounts in the books of Valmet
Investment Management Ltd of Gibraltar ("Valmet Gibraltar"), which banked with
Lloyds Bank, Gibraltar. Valmet Gibraltar was a subsidiary of Valmet SA ("Valmet
Geneva"), a financial institution in Geneva in which Mr D'Albis had become a partner.
Valmet Gibraltar maintained an account in the books of Valmet Geneva, which banked
with CBI Geneva. Appropriate money transfers were made so that, while the accounts
were held in Gibraltar, the money remained in Geneva and under the control of
Mr D'Albis in the accounts of Valmet Geneva at its own bank. The amounts actually
transferred were in US dollars, Canadian dollars and Swiss francs reflecting the

A   diversification of currencies in which investments were held. The total value of the moneys transferred at the rates then prevailing was $9,158,317. Thereafter the money was actively managed by Valmet Geneva on a discretionary basis and switched between various currencies. According to Mr D'Albis, the transfer from the first to the second tier Panamanian companies coincided with the return of the Canadians to Canada and the disposal of their interests in Tower, United, Herron and Wilmington.

B   The money did not stay for long in the second tier Panamanian companies. On 25 March 1986 a sum of £90,000 was transferred from each of the companies to the account of Grangewoods at the Royal Bank of Scotland, London. Grangewoods were the solicitors acting for DLH and the total of £270,000 represented the deposit payable in respect of the purchase of the site in Battersea.

A few days later, on 30 March and 1 April 1986, the accounts of the second tier Panamanian companies were closed and their funds were transferred to Panama. The C   arrangements were made by Mr D'Albis on Roth's instructions. The money was transferred in two stages. First, a total of $9,267,786 was transferred from Valmet Geneva to Valmet Gibraltar via Lloyds Bank, Gibraltar and (because the money was transferred in dollars) Lloyds Bank, New York. Next, a total of $9,267,500 was transferred in three tranches, two (of $5,000,000 and $2,667,500) to Banco Continental, Panama and one (of $1,600,000) to Bank of America, Panama. The difference of $286 probably D   represents bank charges.

And there the trail is lost.

The fraud is discovered

Mr Murad's purchases were brought to the plaintiff's attention in May 1985. He caused immediate inquiries to be made. By the time the fraud was uncovered, the E   plaintiff was the owner of 1.5m shares in ECG having an intrinsic worth of about $12,000 which had been bought at a cost of more than $13m. Mr Murad was confronted, arrested and thrown into gaol in Riyadh. He agreed to repay $1.5m to the plaintiff, and was released from prison. He has repaid $1,375,000. The plaintiff does not accept that he should give credit for this sum. The plaintiff also brought pressure on Tower to repurchase the shares which it had sold. Between August and November 1985 the plaintiff resold shares to Tower at prices at or near the prices paid for them and recovered F $2,382,000. The sales affirmed the corresponding purchases, and the plaintiff agrees to give credit for the sums realised.

In August 1987 the plaintiff commenced proceedings in Gibraltar to recover sums totalling $3,635,000 which had been transferred from Panama to Valmet Gibraltar in January 1987 and which had been frozen on the instructions of Valmet Geneva issued at the request of the Swiss authorities. The funds had been intended to be invested by G   Mr D'Albis on behalf of the Canadians who were proposing to use three further Panamanian companies for the purpose: Laxey Inc, Portan Holdings Inc and Unico Finance SA. Mr Van Apeldoorn was joined as a co-plaintiff in the Gibraltar proceedings in his capacity as trustee in bankruptcy of Tower and United. In 1991 proceedings were also commenced in Toronto by the plaintiff and Mr Van Apeldoorn against the Canadians, Singer and Goldhar. The Canadians made no pretence that they were not the persons behind the fraud. By this time, however, Lindzon had died, and the plaintiff and Mr Van H   Apeldoorn were given cause to believe that the Canadians had no significant assets in Canada and were judgment proof in that jurisdiction. The Gibraltar and Canadian proceedings were therefore compromised. The plaintiff and Mr Van Apeldoorn took 90 per cent of the money blocked in Gibraltar (which they divided between themselves in the proportions 75:25) and allowed ten per cent to be released to the Canadians. The plaintiff's share amounted to $2,773,817.

In addition, he has recovered a further £70,000 from Banque Scandinave en Suisse in Geneva ("Banque Scandinave") in circumstances which I shall describe later. The plaintiff has thus recovered a total of $6,495,817 and £70,000. He agrees to give credit for all but $1,375,000 of these sums.

In July 1985 the plaintiff's English solicitors sent a telex addressed to one of Mr Ferdman's fellow directors of SAFI seeking information. The telex disclosed the fact that in May 1985 Tower had sold the plaintiff 1.5m shares in ECG (for which, it will be remembered, SAFI had subscribed 25 cents a share) at $8.25 a share. In evidence to me Mr Ferdman admitted that he had been shown the telex and that it "probably" caused him some concern. On 16 October 1985 the plaintiff's Swiss lawyer, Mr Farina, wrote to SAFI making express allegations of fraud. Mr Farina gave many details and identified Goldhar (though not the Canadians) as being behind the fraud. He asked a number of detailed questions. Mr Ferdman took legal advice, and replied at length by letter dated 22 October. He gave particulars of SAFI's activities in relation to the impugned transactions, confirmed that SAFI was acting for a client (which he declined to identify), and denied all knowledge of the transactions entered into by Tower. Mr Ferdman's concern, which ought to have been increased by the terms of Mr Farina's letter, did not prevent him from writing on the very same day to his clients in Panama committing SAFI to a sale of a further 500,000 shares in ECG to Dunberry at 26 cents a share. In fairness to Mr Ferdman, it is possible, as he later told the examining magistrate in Geneva, that the shares had already been delivered to Tower and that his letter was merely regularising a fait accompli. Nevertheless, it must have been plain to him by now if not before that his clients were implicated in a fraud.

Mr D'Albis was a friend of Mr Ferdman's. Their offices were close, and from time to time they had lunch together, though they had had no business dealings with each other. According to Mr D'Albis, Mr Ferdman told him about Mr Farina's letter, and they discussed what they should do. Mr D'Albis told me that he had already become "uncomfortable" about his clients and had decided to withdraw from the association; though it is to be noted that neither his discomfort nor Mr Farina's letter was sufficient to prevent him from continuing to act for the Canadians in the management of their funds in Geneva and their eventual transmission to Panama.

Mr Ferdman did not dispute that as a result of the conversation with Mr D'Albis he became aware that the Canadians had been involved in the fraud. He comforted himself by the reflection that his principals were Singer and Goldhar, not the Canadians. But, as he frankly (though unavoidably) admitted to me, he knew perfectly well that the scheme was a fraudulent one; that Dunberry had been buying at 25 cents and selling at $8.25; that such transactions could not be honest; and that the Canadians were involved "with" Goldhar and Singer and not just "behind" them.

Mr Ferdman had already met Roth during a visit to Toronto in the summer of 1985, when he was introduced to him by Singer. Roth told him that he and associates of his were interested in investing in real estate in Europe, and asked him to look out for suitable opportunities for them.

In addition to bringing civil proceedings, the plaintiff made complaint to the fraud squad in Amsterdam, and caused criminal proceedings to be instituted in Switzerland. Mr D'Albis was arrested, charged and held in custody for some months before the charges were dropped. In 1988 he and Mr Ferdman were interrogated by the examining magistrate in Geneva. According to Mr Van Apeldoorn, the Canadians had prudently adopted a policy of not including residents of Canada or the Netherlands among their victims, and they have never been prosecuted.

Dollar Land Holdings

DLH is an English company which was formerly listed on the London Stock Exchange. In June 1985 its entire issued share capital was acquired by Keristal Investments &

A   Trading SA ("Keristal"), a Panamanian company beneficially owned by a Liechtenstein foundation. In the annual reports of DLH Mr Ferdman, its chairman, described himself as the beneficial owner of Keristal, but that was not the case. Mr Ferdman was, as usual, acting purely in the capacity of a fiduciary agent, and regarded his instructions to preserve the anonymity of his clients as justifying him in falsely describing himself as beneficial owner. His principals, the founders and beneficiaries of the Liechtenstein foundation, were two US citizens resident in New York ("the Americans"), whose
B   identity has been disclosed to me, but who the plaintiff is satisfied have no connection of any kind with the Canadians or their associates or any of the other persons involved in the fraud.

     DLH was acquired as a vehicle for the Americans' property dealings in the UK. Its business activities were under the direction of Mr William Stern, a property dealer who suffered a spectacular and well-publicised bankruptcy as a result of the 1974 property
C   crash. He was engaged in the business of identifying opportunities for property investment and introducing them to investors willing to pay him a fee or a share in the eventual profits. Mr Stern had lived in Geneva as a boy and was acquainted with Mr Ferdman. They became friends, though they lost contact with each other for some years. Mr Stern knew that he was a fiduciary agent and had established SAFI which he believed still to be jointly owned by Mr Ferdman and a reputable cantonal bank. From time to time he
D   suggested deals to Mr Ferdman and enquired of him whether he had any suitable investors among his clients.

     Mr Ferdman introduced the Americans to Mr Stern, who was able to recommend a successful investment in a UK property. The Americans were willing to make further investments in the UK, and Mr Stern suggested that he should look for a suitable English vehicle, if possible a quoted company, which they could acquire and use as a medium for further investment. Mr Stern found DLH, and Keristal acquired it as a pure cash shell in
E   June 1985. Mr Ferdman and Mr Favre and Mr Jaton, two fellow directors of SAFI, were appointed directors, and Mr Ferdman was appointed chairman. They were nominee directors representing the interests of the beneficial owners. They played no part in the conduct of DLH's business. That was carried on by Mr Stern in consultation with the Americans.

     Mr Stern was not a director of DLH, but he was appointed managing director of
F   Dollar Land Management Ltd, a subsidiary of DLH. He held no ordinary shares in DLH, but was allotted convertible deferred shares which could be converted into ordinary shares if the net asset value of DLH was doubled within a period of three years. Mr Stern succeeded in achieving the target, and his deferred shares were converted into ordinary shares in December 1986. The shares represented 24.5 per cent of the equity, and were held by Mr Stern and members of his immediate family.

     The board was strengthened by the appointment of Mr Babet, a Paris lawyer, in April
G   1987 and by Mr Fielding, the senior partner of Grangewoods, and Mr Herzka, a New York lawyer, in May 1987. Mr Ferdman, who had undergone open heart surgery in December 1986, resigned as director in June 1987 and Mr Fielding was appointed chairman in his place.

     DLH was in a substantial way of business, and was able to raise very large sums on the security of its assets. At the end of 1986 it had secured bank loans and other mortgage
H   creditors of more than £10m. By the end of 1987 that figure had risen to more than £30m.

The Nine Elms project

     The Nine Elms project was introduced to DLH in February 1986. It involved the speculative purchase of a piece of waste land in Battersea without the benefit of planning permission but with a view to residential development. Mr Stern asked Mr Ferdman if

he could find an investor willing to put up equity finance. This method of finance was   A
and still is normal practice for DLH. Mr Ferdman, who was to receive an introductory
commission of five per cent of the funds obtained, brought Roth to London in March
1986 and introduced him to Mr Stern. Together they inspected the site. It is possible that
Lindzon was also present. Mr D'Albis was not. Mr Stern was made aware that Roth was
acting for a consortium of three Canadians. Mr Stern provided Roth with a detailed
"Investment Proposal" which included a profit forecast.

          All negotiations were conducted between Roth and Mr Stern. Mr Ferdman played no   B
part. By a letter dated 20 March 1986 and addressed to Roth c/o SAFI in Geneva, Mr
Stern set out the terms which had been agreed between them. The contract for the
purchase of the site was to be signed by Dollar Land (London) Ltd ("DLH London"), a
subsidiary of DLH. Roth was to make a sum of £270,000 available by 24 March to enable
contracts to be exchanged, such sum to be paid into Grangewoods' client account at the
Royal Bank of Scotland and to be used exclusively for the payment of the deposit on   C
exchange of contracts. If contracts were not exchanged the money was to be returned.
Mr Stern recorded that it was DLH's intention, after exchange of contracts but before
completion, to enter into a joint venture with a builder of national repute under which
the builder would undertake the development at its own cost in return for a share of the
profits realised from the sale of completed units. Subject to such a contract being signed,
Roth was to make available a further sum of £1,030,000 two days before the contractual
date for completion, on receipt of which DLH was to complete the purchase of the site   D
for £2.7m. In return, Roth was to receive an "interest factor" together with 50 per cent
of the profits realised by DLH for the project.

          On 25 March Mr Ferdman copied the letter by telex to Mr D'Albis, who gave
instructions on the same day to Valmet Geneva's bank to transfer the sum of £270,000 to
the Royal Bank of Scotland for the account of Grangewoods. As I have already
mentioned, a sum of £90,000 was debited to the account of each of the second tier   E
Panamanian companies on the same day. Subsequently, Mr Ferdman sent a duplicate of
the telex in the form of a letter on DLH's headed paper but over his own signature,
dated 7 April, and addressed to Yulara Realty Ltd ("Yulara") in Panama. Yulara was
yet another Panamanian company owned by the Canadians. It had not been formed
by Mr D'Albis or Mr Ferdman and was not controlled by either of them, though
Mr Ferdman knew that it was a vehicle for the Canadians' investment in the Nine Elms
project. Mr Ferdman retained on his own files a copy of the letter countersigned by a   F
Panamanian lawyer on behalf of Yulara by way of acceptance, but he did not forward a
copy to Mr Stern until much later.

          The terms of Mr Ferdman's telex and subsequent letter differed from those of
Mr Stern's letter of 20 March to Roth in two respects. First, the Canadians' obligation to
provide £1,030,000 for completion was replaced by an obligation to provide "a global
guarantee of £1,3m": other terms of the telex show this to be an error for £1.03m.   G
Secondly, an additional term required Yulara to be given five days' notice to provide the
money. Mr Stern had nothing to do with the changes, which I infer to have been made at
the request of the Canadians.

          Contracts for the purchase of the site were exchanged on 26 March. The purchaser
was DLH London. The £270,000 which Grangewoods had received on the previous day
was used to pay the deposit. On 11 June 1986 DLH London assigned the benefit of the   H
contract to DLH for £100,000, and on the same date DLH entered into a contract for
the sale of the site to Regalian Properties (Northern) Ltd ("Regalian") for a purchase
price equal to 40 per cent of the aggregate gross proceeds of sale of the flats, garages and
parking spaces to be constructed on the site. Regalian was to pay £1.7m on account of
the purchase price immediately and the balance as the completed units were sold and

A   was to undertake the construction work. Completion took place on the same day. The purchase price of £2.7m was paid to the vendor and the site was transferred at the direction of DLH London to Regalian. The transfer records £1.7m of the purchase price as paid by Regalian and £1m as paid by DLH.

The funding of the project

B   On 6 May 1986 Yulara entered into an agreement with Keristal by which Yulara agreed to make $2.5m available to Keristal in order to obtain a bank guarantee of £1.3m in favour of DLH. Keristal undertook to use the funds "in order to make a joint venture in a certain real estate investment in London" and "to grant a bank guarantee of £1.3m to be issued in favour of [DLH] or another company owned by [DLH]". The word "grant" is obviously an error for "obtain". The wording of the agreement is consistent with Keristal being used as a vehicle for the Canadians to make their investment in the
C   project rather than as a vehicle for DLH to receive the funds. The agreement was signed on behalf of Keristal by Mr Ferdman and on behalf of Yulara by the Panamanian lawyer. On 12 and 16 May respectively two sums of $1,541,432 and $1,143,000, making a total of $2,684,432, were credited to an account of Keristal ("the Keristal no. 2 account") at Banque Scandinave. The account was operated by SAFI and was used exclusively for the purpose of funding the Nine Elms project. The sum of $1,541,432 is shown in the bank statement as having been received from the Bank of America. The source of the
D   other sum is not shown.

Pursuant to arrangements made by Mr Ferdman, Scandinavian Bank Group plc in London ("Scandinavian Bank") now agreed to advance £1.3m to Factotum. The advance was supported by a guarantee given by Banque Scandinave secured on the moneys in the Keristal no. 2 account.

E   £2,445,598.60 was required on completion, of which £2,430,000 represented the balance of the purchase price (£2.7m less the deposit of £270,000 already paid) and £15,598.60 represented interest for late completion. This was discharged as to £1.7m by Regalian and as to £745,598.60 out of moneys in Grangewoods' client account.

The whole of the loan from Scandinavian Bank to Factotum was drawn down and £1,030,000 was paid to Grangewoods on 29 May. £150,000 was remitted by Grangewoods in accordance with Mr Ferdman's instructions. According to Mr Ferdman, this sum
F   included his introductory commission of £65,000. The other £85,000 is not accounted for, but Mr Stern accepted that the whole of the £150,000 was used to discharge obligations of DLH. The balance of £880,000 was used to discharge the amount of £745,598.60 due on completion and to make various other payments at the direction of DLH.

The balance of the loan from Scandinavian Bank amounting to £270,000 was paid
G   by Scandinavian Bank direct to SAFI and was credited to the Keristal no. 2 account on 2 June. £209,655.43 was subsequently paid out of that account to Valmet Geneva, presumably for the benefit of the Canadians. It is not clear what happened to the balance.

Mr Ferdman's role

H   There is much confusion as to the capacity in which Mr Ferdman made the financing arrangements. He had, of course, more than one capacity. In effecting the introduction of the Canadians, he acted on his own account and earned commission for doing so. In copying and signing Mr Stern's offer he was acting on behalf of DLH, though he exercised no independent judgment or discretion of his own but acted on instructions and merely as a nominee or fiduciary agent. In substituting Yulara for Roth he was complying with a request from the Canadians. The financing arrangements with Banque

Scandinave and Scandinavian Bank were made at the insistence of the Canadians; they   A
did not wish to send money direct to London and evolved the alternative mechanism.
Mr Ferdman made the arrangements, but whether he did so as the agent of the
Canadians and on their behalf, or as chairman of DLH and on its behalf in order to
accommodate the Canadians' requirements, is impossible to determine: it is probably a
meaningless question.

According to Mr Ferdman, he was acting for DLH and Mr D'Albis was acting for the   B
Canadians. Mr D'Albis denied this; according to him, he had ceased to act for the
Canadians when he transmitted the money to Panama at the end of March, and he did
not become involved again on their behalf until they fell out with Mr Ferdman in 1987.
He thought that Mr Ferdman had taken over from him as fiduciary agent for the
Canadians. Mr Stern was not consulted about the financing arrangements, and was not
aware of them at the time. He denied that they had anything to do with DLH and
assumed that Mr Ferdman must therefore have been acting exclusively for the Canadians.   C
When the Canadians made the moneys available, Mr Ferdman told me, he ensured that
they were paid into an account which was under his own control so that he "could protect
the interests of DLH to whom the moneys were ultimately to be paid". Mr Stern was
extremely angry when, much later, he discovered that Mr Ferdman had called the
account "the Keristal no. 2 account", since in his view it was a SAFI account held for the
Canadians, and had nothing to do with DLH. This is supported by the terms of the
agreement of 6 May in accordance with which the money was provided to Keristal. But   D
whether Keristal received the money as principal or as agent for Yulara is immaterial; it
did not receive the money as agent for DLH and it has not been suggested that it did.

Factotum was a shelf company which Mr Ferdman had formed some time previously.
It had been intended by Mr Stern to use it to take title to the site, in which event it would
have become a subsidiary of DLH. In the event, Regalian objected, and the idea was
dropped. Mr Ferdman decided to make use of it as a convenient vehicle for channelling   E
the money to DLH. The terms of the agreement of 6 May between Yulara and Keristal
indicate that both Mr Ferdman and the Canadians regarded Factotum as part of the
DLH group. But in borrowing the money from Scandinavian Bank and making it
available to DLH it acted as principal and not as nominee. Whatever its status and
whatever the true nature of Mr Ferdman's role, its receipt of the money cannot be
treated as receipt by DLH, and the contrary has not been suggested.   F

The Canadians fall out with Mr Ferdman

By the end of 1986 SAFI was in serious financial difficulties and Mr Ferdman had
undergone major heart surgery. He was obliged to tell the Canadians that SAFI was
unable to repay $1m of their money which they had deposited with SAFI and which he
had misappropriated. The money had no connection with the Nine Elms project. It had
been placed with SAFI for investment. DLH did not know of the deposit which had no   G
connection with any of its affairs.

Not surprisingly in the light of this revelation the Canadians insisted that the money in
the Keristal no. 2 account should be transferred to an account outside SAFI's control.
In February 1987 the fund was transferred to the account of HRH, a Djibouti company
controlled by Mr D'Albis on behalf of the Canadians, but similarly hypothecated to
secure repayment of the loan to Factotum.   H

When the Canadians demanded the repayment of their money, Mr Ferdman sought
Mr Stern's advice. At first Mr Stern thought that Mr Ferdman would be able to sort out
his difficulties with them, but by February 1987 he realised that Mr Ferdman was not in a
position to repay the money, and understood that the Canadians were threatening to
report the matter to the Swiss police. Mr Ferdman begged Mr Stern to help him out, and

A   Mr Stern agreed to do so. He did so for several reasons, but his main reason was that it would be highly embarrassing to DLH for its chairman to be arrested and charged with stealing $1m from a client.

A meeting took place on 16 February 1987 at DLH's London office. It was attended by Mr Ferdman, Mr Stern, Mr D'Albis and two of the Canadians. This was the first and only occasion on which Mr Stern and Mr D'Albis met. Mr D'Albis was introduced to Mr Stern as a fiduciary agent who was acting for the Canadians. They demanded that B   they should be repaid their money. In Mr Stern's presence they repeated their threat to report the matter to the Swiss police. I find it impossible to judge whether the threat was genuine or whether the Canadians were bluffing; but I am satisfied that Mr Stern, who had no reason not to, took the threat seriously.

By the end of a two-hour meeting terms were agreed which Mr Stern confirmed by letter to Mr D'Albis the same day. By the letter DLH guaranteed repayment of C   Mr Ferdman's indebtedness to Mr D'Albis' clients limited to 15 per cent of DLH's beneficial entitlement in the Nine Elms project, and assigned to Mr D'Albis' clients a 15 per cent share in the project by way of security. The Canadians were far from happy with this. They pressed Mr Stern for more; but they had to be satisfied with what they got. Mr Stern did not consult the Americans, but he reported to them that same afternoon and obtained their approval.

D   The transaction was strongly criticised by counsel for the plaintiff, but I do not regard it as commercially incapable of justification. DLH was guaranteeing the repayment of a debt due from its own chairman. It would be extremely embarrassing to DLH if the debt were not discharged. It was not giving money away; if the guarantee was called on, Mr Ferdman would remain liable to reimburse DLH. DLH was paying substantial fees to Mr Ferdman, and Mr Stern saw his future earnings from DLH as a potential source of E   repayment.

In addition, Mr Stern had a personal interest in helping Mr Ferdman. He had persuaded the Americans to invest in DLH. He had introduced Mr Ferdman to them. They trusted Mr Stern, but their trust was not limitless. They did not make him a director. If Mr Ferdman had been arrested and charged with theft while still chairman of DLH, it would have severely damaged Mr Stern's relationship with the Americans.

F   Mr Ferdman resigned as chairman and director of DLH in June 1987. He did so primarily for health reasons. It is not clear whether Mr Stern had pressed him to resign, but his resignation was not unwelcome to Mr Stern, who was worried that Mr Ferdman's financial position might yet prove an embarrassment.

The Canadians are bought out

G   In December 1987 Mr Ferdman, who by then had no formal connection with DLH, telephoned Mr Stern and told him that the Canadians were anxious to withdraw from the joint venture without waiting for the completion of the sales programme. This suited Mr Stern very well, as he had discovered that for technical reasons DLH was unable to raise finance on the security of its interest in the project, and it enabled him to contemplate the possibility of selling out the whole investment to Regalian. Mr Ferdman H   gave Mr Stern no explanation for the Canadians' sudden desire to repatriate their funds, which may not have been unconnected with the freezing of their money in Gibraltar and the course of the criminal investigations in Geneva. But it was not in itself suspicious. There had been a sharp fall in stock market prices on both sides of the Atlantic on "black Monday" in October, the property market had turned flat, and there could well have been good commercial reasons for the Canadians wishing to realise their investment sooner rather than later.

Roth came to see Mr Stern on 18 December 1987, and Mr Stern agreed to arrange for   A
DLH to buy out the Canadians' interest in the Nine Elms project for the sum of £2m
payable no later than 31 January 1988 in return for the release of DLH from the
guarantee which it had given to assist Mr Ferdman. Mr Stern did not ask Roth why the
Canadians wanted to be bought out. He played "hard to get", and stressed that an early
pay out would be highly inconvenient to DLH. He was a tough negotiator and took full
advantage of his superior bargaining position to obtain a very good deal for DLH. As he
conceded in evidence, £2m was significantly less than the value of the expected return   B
on Yulara's investment discounted for early payment.

Grangewoods duly drew up formal documentation between DLH and Yulara to carry
this agreement into effect, but it was never signed. Meanwhile, Mr Stern opened
negotiations with Regalian for the sale to Regalian of DLH's 40 per cent interest in the
project. As soon as he was confident that Regalian would proceed, he met Roth in New
York and confirmed his willingness to complete the purchase of Yulara's interest. There   C
is no evidence that Mr Stern told Roth of his own negotiations with Regalian. Roth
undertook to reinvest part of the proceeds in another property deal in the UK which
Mr Stern was contemplating.

A few days before the expected completion with Yulara, Mr Stern received a telephone
call from Roth who told him that, owing to the sudden deterioration of the health of one
of his partners, the Canadians had decided to divide up their investment funds earlier   D
than expected and would not be reinvesting any part of the funds they were due to
receive from DLH. Mr Stern was furious, but he seized the opportunity to secure a
reduction in the amount payable by DLH to £1.75m. A formal agreement to this effect
was signed on 16 March.

The sum of £1.75m was paid by DLH on the same day. This was possible because on
9 March DLH had concluded the sale of its interest in the project to Regalian for £4.65m.   E
The £1.75m was paid direct to Yulara. The original financing arrangements by which
Yulara had provided its contribution to the project were allowed to unwind automatically.
Factotum was unable to repay the loan from Scandinavian Bank, which duly called upon
the guarantee of Banque Scandinave. Banque Scandinave in turn recouped itself from
the money in the HRH account. The balance in that account, amounting to approximately
£70,000, was eventually recovered by the plaintiff.

                                                                                            F
Tracing the money

In *Agip (Africa) Ltd v Jackson* [1991] Ch 547 at p. 566, *Fox* LJ restated the principle,
settled by *Re Diplock* [1948] Ch 465, that it is a prerequisite of the right to trace in equity
that there must be a fiduciary relationship which calls the equitable jurisdiction into
being. This makes it necessary to consider separately the common law and equitable
tracing rules. In the present case, it is manifestly impossible to follow the money at   G
common law. The international transfers of money were made electronically; the
plaintiff's money was mixed, not merely with the money of other victims or of the
fraudsters themselves, but with the money of innocent third parties in the accounts of
Valmet Geneva and Valmet Gibraltar, and passed on several occasions through the
clearing systems of New York and London; while the back-to-back financing arrangements
with Banque Scandinave and Scandinavian Bank would seem to present an insuperable
obstacle to the common law, even if it had not lost the trail long before. As counsel for   H
DLH properly concedes, however, none of these features creates a problem for equity.
Nor has the plaintiff any difficulty in satisfying the precondition for equity's intervention.
Mr Murad was the plaintiff's fiduciary, and he was bribed to purchase the shares. He
committed a gross breach of his fiduciary obligations to the plaintiff, and that is sufficient
to enable the plaintiff to invoke the assistance of equity. Other victims, however, were

A less fortunate. They employed no fiduciary. They were simply swindled. No breach of any fiduciary obligation was involved. It would, of course, be an intolerable reproach to our system of jurisprudence if the plaintiff were the only victim who could trace and recover his money. Neither party before me suggested that this is the case; and I agree with them. But if the other victims of the fraud can trace their money in equity it must be because, having been induced to purchase the shares by false and fraudulent misrepresentations, they are entitled to rescind the transaction and revest the equitable

B title to the purchase money in themselves, at least to the extent necessary to support an equitable tracing claim: see *Daly v Sydney Stock Exchange* (1986) 160 CLR 371 per *Brennan* J at pp. 387–90. There is thus no distinction between their case and the plaintiff's. They can rescind the purchases for fraud, and he for the bribery of his agent; and each can then invoke the assistance of equity to follow property of which he is the equitable owner. But, if this is correct, as I think it is, then the trust which is operating in

C these cases is not some new model remedial constructive trust, but an old-fashioned institutional resulting trust. This may be of relevance in relation to the degree of knowledge required on the part of a subsequent recipient to make him liable.

Subject to two points, counsel for DLH concedes that the plaintiff can successfully trace the money from Amsterdam to London. He submits:

(1) that the plaintiff has not established that the money which reached the Keristal

D no. 2 account on 12 and 16 May 1986 represented the money which was last seen leaving Gibraltar for Panama on 30 March and 1 April 1986; and

(2) that the equitable remedy depends on the continuing subsistence of the plaintiff's equitable title, and cannot be invoked where the money is transferred to recipients in civil law jurisdictions like Switzerland and Panama which do not recognise the trust concept or the notion of equitable ownership.

E I reject both submissions.

1. *Tracing through Panama*

It is, of course, beyond dispute that the money which was received in the Keristal no. 2 account was the Canadians' money. It is, however, true that the plaintiff is unable by direct evidence to identify that money with the money which Mr D'Albis had sent to Panama only a few weeks before. If the question arose in proceedings between the

F plaintiff and the Canadians, then, in the absence of evidence to the contrary, the court would draw the necessary inference against the latter, for they would be in a position to dispel it. But DLH is not; it is as much in the dark as the plaintiff.

Nevertheless, in my judgment there is sufficient, though only just, to enable the inference to be drawn. One of the two sums received in the Keristal no. 2 account was $1,541,432 received on 12 May 1986 from Bank of America. That corresponds closely with the sum of $1,600,000 transferred to Bank of America, Panama on 1 April 1986. In

G relation to the later transaction, Bank of America may, of course, merely have been acting as a correspondent bank in New York and not as the paying bank; and the closeness of the figures could be a coincidence. It is not much, but it is something; and there is nothing in the opposite scale. The source of the other money received in the Keristal no. 2 account is not known, but from the way in which the Canadians appear to have dealt with their affairs, if one sum came from Panama, then the other probably did

H so too.

The plaintiff points out that the deposit was paid out of funds held by the second tier Panamanian companies immediately before they were sent to Panama, and submits that it is a reasonable inference that the rest of the money came from the same source. If the Canadians had substantial funds elsewhere to invest in the project, the plaintiff asks, why did they not use them to provide the deposit? There is force in this submission.

Against it, DLH points out that, by the time the money was sent to Panama, Roth had   A
already struck the deal with Mr Stern, and the Canadians knew that another £1,030,000
would be needed in London within a few weeks. Why send it to Panama? Far simpler to
leave it in Geneva, especially when the Canadians had already decided to use it to
support a back-to-back guarantee, as the terms of Mr Ferdman's telex demonstrate.
There is force in this observation, too. But, in my judgment, any attempt to weigh the
Canadians' motives is too speculative to form the basis of any inference. They may have
decided to remove the funds at least temporarily from Geneva in order to conceal from   B
Mr D'Albis that they were transferring their allegiance to a different Swiss fiduciary
agent; or they may have decided to launder the money through Panama before making
any long-term investment in Europe. Their request to be given five days' notice before
coming up with the money is neutral; it may have had more to do with the time needed
to arrange the back-to-back guarantees than any additional time needed to bring back
funds from Panama.   C

But the fact remains that there is no evidence that the Canadians had any substantial
funds available to them which did not represent proceeds of the fraud. This is
acknowledged by counsel for DLH. For the source of the money he points to the $1.45m
received by Zawi and the payments totalling $4,927,000 made by Herron and Wilmington
which cannot be accounted for. But it has not been shown that any of these moneys were
still at the disposal of the Canadians in May 1986. They had many expenses to meet out   D
of moneys received by Herron and Wilmington (commissions to salesmen, for instance,
not already accounted for); and Singer and Goldhar would presumably need to be
looked after.

But, in my judgment, this is irrelevant. The money in the accounts of Herron and
Wilmington represented proceeds of the fraud. It can be traced in equity from those
accounts to the Keristal no. 2 account as well through Zawi or any other intermediate
recipient as through the first and second tier Panamanian companies. The victims of a   E
fraud can follow their money in equity through bank accounts where it has been mixed
with other moneys because equity treats the money in such accounts as charged with the
repayment of their money. If the money in an account subject to such a charge is
afterwards paid out of the account and into a number of different accounts, the victims
can claim a similar charge over each of the recipient accounts. They are not bound to
choose between them. Whatever may be the position as between the victims inter se, as   F
against the wrongdoer his victims are not required to appropriate debits to credits in
order to identify the particular account into which their money has been paid. Equity's
power to charge a mixed fund with the repayment of trust moneys (a power not shared
by the common law) enables the claimants to follow the money, not because it is theirs,
but because it is derived from a fund which is treated as if it were subject to a charge in
their favour.   G

Counsel for DLH, however, submits that in the present case the plaintiff is confined
by his pleading. In the statement of claim he has alleged that his money was paid to the
first and second tier Panamanian companies whence it eventually found its way to the
Keristal no. 2 account. Accordingly, counsel submits, he cannot now claim to trace it by
a different route. But the plaintiff's case has not changed. He still asserts that which he
must establish, viz. that the money in the Keristal no. 2 account was derived from the
moneys in the Herron and Wilmington accounts. It is still his case that it reached the   H
Keristal no. 2 account via the first and second tier Panamanian companies; but that is
not essential to his claim. DLH could not defeat the claim by proving that, although the
money in the Keristal no. 2 account was derived from the Herron and Wilmington
accounts, it had come by a different route. Still less can it defeat the claim by demonstrating
that it may possibly have done so.

A   In my judgment, there is some evidence to support an inference that the money which reached the Keristal no. 2 account represented part of the moneys which had been transmitted to Panama by the second tier Panamanian companies some six weeks previously, and the suggestion that it was derived from any other source is pure speculation.

2. *Tracing through civil jurisdictions*

B   Counsel for DLH next submits that the plaintiff's claim, whether personal or proprietary, depends on the continuing subsistence of his equitable title to the money, and cannot be established where the money had passed through the hands of recipients in civil law jurisdictions which do not recognise the concept of equitable ownership. In my judgment, this argument is not open to DLH. Foreign law is a question of fact. It must be pleaded and proved by expert evidence. The court cannot take judicial notice

C   of foreign law, though it be notorious: *Lazard Bros & Co v Midland Bank Ltd* [1933] AC 289 at p. 297. In the absence of evidence, foreign law is presumed to be the same as English law. In the present case no question of foreign law has been pleaded, and no evidence of foreign law has been tendered.

     But, even if the argument were open to DLH, I would reject it. In my judgment, it is misconceived. For technical reasons, the plaintiff's claim is brought in equity, where it is

D   of a kind generally described as a case of "knowing receipt". This is the counterpart in equity of the common law action for money had and received. Both can be classified as receipt-based restitutionary claims. The law governing such claims is the law of the country where the defendant received the money: see *Dicey & Morris on the Conflict of Laws* (11th ed., 1987), r. 203(2)(c); *Chase Manhattan Bank v Israel-British Bank (London) Ltd* [1981] Ch 105. Whatever money or property DLH received was received by it in England and, accordingly, the plaintiff's claim falls to be governed by English

E   law, including the principles of equity. It is not necessary to consider whether the concept by which equity gives effect to the claim by permitting the plaintiff to trace his money and identify it as his in the hands of the recipient is procedural or substantive, since on either footing it too is governed by English law, either as the *lex fori* or as the law of the restitutionary obligation.

     Although equitable rights may found proprietary as well as personal claims, it has

F   long been settled that they are classified as personal rights for the purpose of private international law. The doctrine was stated by Lord *Selbourne* LC in *Ewing v Orr Ewing* (1883) 9 App Cas 34 at p. 40 as follows:

     "The Courts of Equity in England are, and always have been, Courts of conscience, operating in personam and not in rem: and in the exercise of this personal jurisdiction they have always been accustomed to compel the performance of

G   contracts and trusts as to subjects which were not either locally or ratione domicilii within their jurisdiction. They have done so as to land, in Scotland, in Ireland, in the Colonies, in foreign countries . . ."

     In *Cook Industries Inc v Galliher* [1979] Ch 439, *Templeman* J entertained an action in which the plaintiff claimed a declaration that the defendants held a flat in Paris together with its contents in trust for the plaintiff, and made an order compelling the defendants to allow the plaintiff to inspect the flat. The fact that the subject-matter of

H   the alleged trust was situate in France, a civil law country, was no bar to the jurisdiction. DLH is, therefore, answerable to the court's equitable jurisdiction as regards assets situate abroad, even in a civil law country. A fortiori, it is amenable to the court's equitable jurisdiction as regards assets which were formerly in a civil law country but which it has received in England in circumstances which are alleged to render it unconscionable for it to retain them.

DLH's argument is based on the premise that, for the plaintiff to succeed in tracing his money in equity through successive mixed accounts, he must have been in a position to obtain an equitable charge against each successive account. Even if the premise were correct, however, it would not matter where the accounts were maintained. It would be sufficient (and necessary) that the account holders were within the jurisdiction. But, in my judgment, it is not correct. It is not necessary that each successive recipient should have been within the jurisdiction; it is sufficient that the defendant is. This is because the plaintiff's ability to trace his money in equity is dependent on the power of equity to charge a mixed fund with the repayment of trust moneys, *not upon any actual exercise of that power*. The charge itself is entirely notional. In *Lord Portarlington v Soulby* (1834) 3 My & K 104 at p. 108, Lord *Brougham* LC said:

> "In truth, nothing can be more unfounded than the doubts of the jurisdiction. That is grounded, like all other jurisdiction of the court, *not upon any pretension to the exercise of judicial and administrative rights abroad*, but on the circumstance of the person of the party on whom this order is made being within the power of the court." (emphasis added)

An English court of equity will compel a defendant who is within the jurisdiction to treat assets in his hands as trust assets if, having regard to their history and his state of knowledge, it would be unconscionable for him to treat them as his own. Where they have passed through many different hands in many different countries, they may be difficult to trace; but in my judgment neither their temporary repose in a civil law country nor their receipt by intermediate recipients outside the jurisdiction should prevent the court from treating assets in the legal ownership of a defendant within the jurisdiction as trust assets. In the present case, any obligation on the part of DLH to restore to their rightful owner assets which it received in England is governed exclusively by English law, and the equitable tracing rules and the trust concept which underlies them are applicable as part of that law. There is no need to consider any other system of law.

Knowing receipt

The plaintiff seeks a personal remedy based on "knowing receipt". As I have previously pointed out, this is the counterpart in equity of the common law claim for money had and received. The latter, at least, is a receipt-based claim to restitution, and the cause of action is complete when the money is received: see *Lipkin Gorman v Karpnale Ltd* [1991] 2 AC 548 at p. 572. So, in my judgment, is the former, unless arbitrary and anomalous distinctions between the common law and equitable claims are to be insisted upon. But it is necessary at the outset to identify the assets which DLH received, and the occasions upon which it received them. The plaintiff alleges that DLH received the sum of £270,000 in March 1986, and a further £1,030,000 in June 1986.

In my judgment, however, the position is somewhat more complicated than that. The sum of £270,000 was never received by DLH. It was paid into Grangewoods' client account, and their client at the time must be taken to have been DLH London. DLH London was not a nominee or agent for DLH. As had previously been agreed between Roth and Mr Stern, it was the intended contractual purchaser of the site, and the money was to be used exclusively for the payment of the deposit on exchange of contracts. In my judgment, DLH did not receive the money at all, and DLH London did not receive it beneficially but upon trust to apply it for a specific purpose. DLH London used the money, as it was bound to do, to pay the deposit on the site, and thereby acquired for its own benefit a corresponding interest in the site which it subsequently sold and transferred to DLH. The plaintiff can follow his money through these various transactions, but the relevant asset capable of being identified as having been received by DLH is an interest in the site corresponding to the payment of the deposit.

A   The sum of £1,030,000 was also paid into Grangewoods' client account, but by then their client had become DLH. The money was disbursed on the instructions and for the benefit of DLH. Only £745,598.60 was used to pay the money due to the vendor on completion, but this was the result of the arrangements which DLH had made with Regalian. So far as Yulara is concerned, the whole £1.3m must be taken to have been disbursed as agreed between them on the acquisition of a 40 per cent interest in the project. Moreover, in my judgment, on a proper analysis of the transaction between

B   Yulara and DLH, Yulara's money should be treated as having been invested in its share of the project, and not in or towards the acquisition of DLH's share.

     The investment proved highly successful. In itself it was not a breach of trust and caused the plaintiff no loss. Had he been able to intervene before the Canadians were bought out, he could have claimed the whole of Yulara's interest in the project; but whatever the extent of DLH's knowledge of the source of Yulara's funds, his claim

C   would have been confined to Yulara's interest in exoneration of that of DLH. In the events which have happened, the plaintiff is in my judgment bound to treat his money as represented by Yulara's interest in the project, and must rely exclusively on the transaction on 16 March 1988 when Yulara's interest was bought out by DLH.

     By that date Yulara's interest had (unknown to Yulara) crystallised into a 50 per cent share in a sum of £4.65m, which it sold to DLH (at an undervalue) for £1.75m. In those

D   circumstances the plaintiff can in my judgment either affirm the transaction and claim payment of the purchase price (£1.75m) for which DLH did not obtain a good receipt or repudiate the transaction and claim an account of its share of 50 per cent of the £4.65m (£2,325,000).

     On electing to repudiate the sale of Yulara's interest, the plaintiff could if he wished have an account of what DLH did with the £4.65m it received from Regalian, or the balance remaining after payment of the £1.75m to Yulara, in an attempt to identify it as

E   still in the possession of DLH with a view to asserting a proprietary claim against it to the extent of £2,325,000. The plaintiff has not sought to do so, seeing no advantage in the attempt. DLH is solvent and good for £2,325,000, and there is nothing to be gained by making a proprietary claim.

     All this, of course, is dependent on the plaintiff establishing that DLH possessed the requisite degree of knowledge at the time of its purchase of Yulara's interest. DLH

F   claims to be a bona fide purchaser for value without notice. Unfortunately, the nature of the knowledge required is highly controversial, at least where the recipient is a volunteer and the plaintiff brings a personal claim. In *Re Montagu's Settlement Trusts* [1987] Ch 264 at p. 285, Sir *Robert Megarry* V-C expressed the view obiter that, in such a case, dishonesty or want of probity involving actual knowledge or wilful blindness is required. In *Agip (Africa) Ltd v Jackson* [1991] Ch 547 at p. 567, *Fox* LJ expressed the view that

G   dishonesty is not required, and that knowledge of any circumstances which would indicate the facts to an honest and reasonable man, and knowledge of circumstances which would put an honest and reasonable man on inquiry, are sufficient.

     That was a case of knowing assistance, not knowing receipt, and it is not clear whether *Fox* LJ's remarks were intended to apply to the former. But they must at least cover the latter. In *Eagle Trust plc v SBC Securities Ltd* [1993] 1 WLR 484 at pp. 506–507,

H   *Vinelott* J based liability firmly on inferred knowledge and not on constructive notice. For my own part, I agree that even where the plaintiff's claim is a proprietary one, and the defendant raises the defence of bona fide purchaser for value without notice, there is no room for the doctrine of constructive notice in the strict conveyancing sense in a factual situation where it is not the custom and practice to make inquiry. But it does not follow that there is no room for an analogous doctrine in a situation in which any honest and reasonable man would have made inquiry. *Vinelott* J held that knowledge might be

inferred if the circumstances were such that an honest and reasonable man would have   A
inferred that the moneys were probably trust moneys and were being misapplied. He
left open the question whether a recipient might escape liability if the court was satisfied
that, although an honest and reasonable man would have realised this, through foolishness
or inexperience he did not in fact suspect it.

That question does not arise in the present case. In the absence of full argument I am
content to assume, without deciding, that dishonesty or want of probity involving actual   B
knowledge (whether proved or inferred) is not a precondition of liability; but that a
recipient is not expected to be unduly suspicious and is not to be held liable unless he
went ahead without further inquiry in circumstances in which an honest and reasonable
man would have realised that the money was probably trust money and was being
misapplied. That approach is in accordance with the preponderance of judicial authority
in this country and New Zealand, and is consistent with an analysis of the underlying
trust as a subsisting trust. Moreover, I do not see how it would be possible to develop   C
any logical and coherent system of restitution if there were different requirements in
respect of knowledge for the common law claim for money had and received, the
personal claim for an account in equity against a knowing recipient and the equitable
proprietary claim. In the present case, for example, it would be illogical and undesirable
to require the plaintiff to assert a proprietary claim he does not need in order to avoid
the burden of having to prove dishonesty or ask the court to infer it.   D

I turn, therefore, to the allegation that by June 1988, if not before, DLH possessed
the necessary degree of knowledge that Yulara's funds represented the proceeds of
fraud. DLH is a body corporate, and establishing knowledge on the part of an artificial
person involves identifying particular individuals and attributing their knowledge to it.
For this purpose, the plaintiff has singled out Mr Ferdman and Mr Stern as persons
alleged to have possessed the necessary knowledge at the relevant time.   E

Mr Ferdman's knowledge

I could not bring myself to describe Mr Ferdman as an honest man. He was deeply
implicated in the original fraud. He was willing to assist his clients by pretending that
SAFI was a long-term investor when he knew that it was nothing of the kind and that
Dunberry intended to market the shares as soon as it acquired them. He must have
realised that his clients' scheme was dishonest. He probably suspected the nature of the   F
fraud from the start. At first he thought that Goldhar and Singer were his clients; when
he was introduced to Roth in Toronto in the summer of 1985 he did not connect him with
the fraud. But he knew of the Canadians' involvement by the end of 1985. The service
which he gave his clients was to provide them with the means of concealment. He was
prepared to lie to the authorities rather than risk divulging a client's identity. He told me
that he was careful that SAFI should not charge substantial fees for its services because   G
he was afraid that, if it did so, it might be regarded as a participant in its client's
transaction. That was a highly revealing observation. He obviously realised that his
clients' transactions might be questionable. He preferred not to know why his clients
needed to keep their activities hidden from the light of day. As he admitted to me, he
could not function at all if he had to inquire what his clients were up to. Wilful blindness
was part of his job description. Despite all this, I have no hesitation in describing   H
Mr Ferdman as an honest and truthful witness. He was disarmingly frank. He did not
dissemble. He made no attempt to excuse his conduct. He freely admitted that he knew
that the persons who were providing the money for the Nine Elms project were the
persons who had been behind the fraud in Amsterdam; and that by 7 April 1986, when
he signed the letter to Yulara, he knew (or assumed) that the money which he would be
receiving into the Keristal no. 2 account was part of the proceeds of the fraud.

A   The plaintiff submits that Mr Ferdman's knowledge should be attributed to DLH because (1) he was the chairman of DLH, and (2) he was instrumental in obtaining the money for DLH and should be treated as the agent of DLH in relation to the very transaction in question. I reject both submissions.

    Since a company is an artificial person, the knowledge of those who manage and control it must be treated as the knowledge of the company: *J C Houghton & Co v Nothard, Lowe and Wills Ltd* [1928] AC 1; *Re Montagu's Settlement* (above) at p. 283.

B This is nothing to do with the law of agency. Those who "constitute the directing mind and will of the company" are the company for this purpose: *Tesco Supermarkets Ltd v Nattrass* [1972] AC 153 at p. 187. Their minds are its mind; their intention its intention; their knowledge its knowledge. Where the company is a one-man company, or all the directors possess the relevant knowledge, there is ordinarily no difficulty. Where the directors are merely nominees with no executive authority, or where only one of several

C directors has the necessary knowledge, different considerations come into play.

    DLH was not a one-man or nominee company. Unlike the other off-shore companies administered by a fiduciary agent which have featured in this narrative, it was not merely a vehicle for the concealment of the identity of the beneficial owners of moneys in a bank account. It carried on a substantial and genuine business. From April 1987 onwards it had an executive board of directors which met four to six times a year in Paris or Geneva.

D In 1986 its directors were all officers of SAFI, but they were merely nominee' directors representing the interests of the Americans. Mr Ferdman was a non-executive director. His only executive responsibilities were to act as a fiduciary agent, represent the interests of the Americans, and ensure that the necessary corporate documentation was in order. The witnesses agreed that, in the early days of DLH, Mr Ferdman played a bigger role than he did; but I do not think that that was due to any change in his role. He was always responsible for the formal paperwork, but not for the business. As the business expanded,

E so his relative importance diminished. Even in 1986, he played no part in business decisions. These were taken by Mr Stern in consultation with the Americans. In my judgment, Mr Ferdman's position as chairman and non-executive director of DLH was insufficient by itself to constitute his knowledge ipso facto the knowledge of DLH.

    It has not been alleged, still less established, that the other two officers of SAFI, who with Mr Ferdman constituted the board of DLH in 1986, shared Mr Ferdman's knowledge

F of the source of the Canadians' money, but in my judgment it would make no difference if they did. Like Mr Ferdman, they were merely nominee directors with non-executive responsibility. They had no authority to take business decisions. In relation to its business affairs in 1986, neither Mr Ferdman alone nor the board as a whole can realistically be regarded as the directing mind and will of DLH.

    Nor is it accurate to describe Mr Ferdman as having acted as the agent of DLH in

G obtaining the money from the Canadians. He introduced the Canadians to DLH as a potential source of finance, but he did so on his own account and for a commission — and not as agent for DLH. He played no part in the negotiations between the Canadians and DLH. These were conducted exclusively between Roth on the one hand and Mr Stern on the other. He was not responsible for the decision to accept the Canadians' money. That was made by Mr Stern, or by Mr Stern in consultation with the Americans. Once the decision had been taken, Mr Ferdman assisted in its implementation, but

H purely in an administrative capacity. He had formal authority only. He had no authority to commit DLH to a transaction without express instructions from Mr Stern or the Americans. It is true that it was his signature on the letter of 7 April 1986 that formally committed DLH to the transaction; but to fix DLH with his state of knowledge on this ground alone would elevate form over substance, and contravene the rule that to affect the principal with the knowledge of his agent, the knowledge must have been acquired

by the agent in the course of the same transaction. Knowledge acquired privately or in   A
the course of a previous transaction, however closely connected with the transaction in
which the question of knowledge is relevant, is not sufficient. Mr Ferdman knew that the
Canadians' money represented the proceeds of fraud, but he knew this before he
introduced them to Mr Stern, and he knew it because he had acted for their associates,
not because he was acting for DLH.

Moreover, even where the relevant knowledge is acquired by the agent in the course   B
of the same transaction, his knowledge will be attributed to the principal only if the
circumstances were such that it was his duty to communicate it to the principal. Where a
person is a common officer of two companies, therefore, it is not the law that any
knowledge which he has acquired as an officer of one of them is automatically to be
treated as the knowledge of the other: see *Re Marseilles Extension Railway Co* (1871)
LR 7 Ch App 161. Such knowledge will not be attributed to the other company unless he   C
owes a duty to the first company to communicate his knowledge to the second company,
as well as a duty to the second company to receive it: *Re Hampshire Land Co* [1896]
2 Ch 743; *Re Fenwick, Stobart & Co Ltd* [1902] 1 Ch 507.

Mr Ferdman acquired his knowledge in his capacity as a director of SAFI. He cannot
have been under any duty to SAFI to communicate information about SAFI's clients or
their associates to DLH without their authority. That would have been directly contrary
to SAFI's business interests. Its raison d'être lay in its willingness to maintain client   D
confidentiality. Moreover, the only result of passing Mr Ferdman's knowledge to DLH
would be to risk the rejection of the Canadians' money and the loss of SAFI's commission.
In the witness-box Mr Ferdman accepted that he had a moral obligation to tell Mr Stern
that he was being offered tainted money, an obligation which, he said, he did not
discharge because he knew that, if he did, Mr Stern would reject the Canadians' money
and SAFI would lose its commission. But this cannot have been an obligation owed to   E
SAFI; and in any case Mr Ferdman's moral (and possibly legal) obligation was different.
It was not to disclose what he knew to DLH, but to the authorities, or at the very least to
the plaintiff and his advisers, whose identity was known to him.

In my judgment, the facts of the present case are indistinguishable in any material
respect from those in *Re David Payne & Co Ltd* [1904] 2 Ch 608. In that case one
Kolckmann was a director of company A and was also interested in company B. At a   F
meeting of the directors of company B, at a time when he was acting in his own interest
and not as a director of company A, he learned of a proposal that company B should
borrow a sum of money for a purpose which was outside the scope of its business. He
recommended that an approach be made to company A to borrow the money and
effected the introduction. The money was advanced on the authority of the chairman of
company A. Kolckmann signed the cheque; and the board of company A later ratified   G
the transaction. The Court of Appeal refused to attribute to company A the knowledge
of the intended misapplication of the money which Kolckmann had acquired in the
course of the original meeting. In lending the money company A was not bound to
inquire as to the proposed application of the money and, that being so, Kolckmann was
under no obligation to tell company A what he knew.

This is essentially the converse case. DLH (company A) was seeking finance, not   H
lending it, and it was the source of the money, not its application, which was questionable;
but in all other respects the facts are closely similar. At a time when he was acting in his
own interest and as a director of SAFI, and not as a director of DLH, Mr Ferdman
discovered that the Canadians were fraudsters and that their money had been obtained
by fraud. In seeking finance on ordinary commercial terms, and in the absence of
anything to put it on inquiry, DLH was not bound to inquire as to the source of the

A money it was offered; and, that being so, Mr Ferdman was under no obligation to tell DLH what he knew.

In fact, the present case is stronger than this, for I have so far dealt with this question as if the relevant transaction were the establishment of the original joint venture in the Nine Elms project in March 1986. But, for the reasons I have stated, the relevant transaction, in my judgment, is the acquisition by DLH of Yulara's interest in the joint venture in March 1988. By then Mr Ferdman had ceased to be a director of DLH for
B nine months, and he had nothing at all to do with the transaction. Even if, contrary to my judgment, Mr Ferdman's knowledge should be attributed to DLH in 1986, it would be quite wrong to treat DLH as still possessing that knowledge in 1988. As Sir *Robert Megarry* V-C pointed out in *Re Montagu's Settlement* at p. 284, a natural person should not be said to have knowledge of a fact that he once knew if at the time in question he has genuinely forgotten all about it. In my judgment, where the knowledge of a director
C is attributed to a company, but is not actually imparted to it, the company should not be treated as continuing to possess that knowledge after the director in question has died or left its service. In such circumstances, the company can properly be said to have "lost its memory".

Mr Stern's knowledge

D Mr Stern was not a director of DLH but he was the moving force behind its business activities in general and the Nine Elms project in particular. It is not disputed that, in relation to the Canadians' investment in the project, the knowledge of Mr Stern was the knowledge of DLH.

To make a person liable on the basis of knowing receipt it must be established that he knew (or possibly ought to have known) not only that the money in question was trust money, but that its payment to him was a breach of trust. But the investment by the
E Canadians in the Nine Elms project was one which a trustee with sufficiently wide powers of investment could properly make. Unless Mr Stern knew (or possibly ought to have known) that the money was not that of the Canadians to invest but had been obtained by them by fraud, DLH cannot be made liable to restore it.

From Mr Stern's point of view there was nothing suspicious or untoward about the Canadians' initial investment in the project. There was nothing to make him suspect
F that the money had been obtained by fraud; nothing to put him on inquiry as to its source. The Canadians were introduced by Mr Ferdman who, so far as Mr Stern knew, was a reputable fiduciary agent of many years' standing whose business was partly owned by a Swiss cantonal bank (for Mr Ferdman had not told him of the termination of the association). The sum was not so large as to create suspicion. The terms of the deal were strictly commercial. Mr Roth conducted himself as a normal investor. He exercised "due diligence". He was provided with a detailed investment proposal complete with
G profit projections, and Mr Stern was required to report to him on a regular basis. There was nothing to suggest to Mr Stern that the Canadians were merely laundering their money and not investing it on commercial terms; and indeed I do not think that they were.

Mr Stern told me that he did not suspect for a moment that the money had been obtained by fraud. In my judgment, he had no reason to suspect it. The plaintiff's case
H must, therefore, fail unless Mr Stern actually knew that the money had been obtained by fraud. He cannot have known that unless Mr Ferdman told him. Both Mr Ferdman and Mr Stern denied that he did. Their evidence is not contradicted, and I accept it.

I was strongly pressed to infer that Mr Ferdman told Mr Stern about the Canadians from the length and closeness of their relationship. They had known each other for more than 40 years, and had dealt with each other for more than 25. When Mr Ferdman got

into financial difficulties, it was to Mr Stern that he turned for assistance, and Mr Stern   A
was generous in his help. But their relationship, though long, was intermittent and was
not particularly close. It was primarily a business relationship. They were not close
friends or confidants. In my judgment, the suggestion that Mr Ferdman would have
volunteered information about his clients or their associates (and by 1986 he knew that
the Canadians were associates of Goldhar and Singer) to Mr Stern is most implausible.
The maintenance of client confidentiality was a guiding principle of his business life. He
would not willingly have broken that principle. Even though he conceded in the witness-   B
box that strictly speaking he owed no duty of confidentiality to the Canadians because
they were not his clients in relation to the relevant transactions, I do not think that he
would have drawn such nice distinctions at the time in order to break the habits of a
lifetime.

Moreover, Mr Ferdman had no occasion to tell Mr Stern about the Canadians before
he introduced them to him and, when he did introduce them, he had an incentive not to   C
tell him. In the witness-box Mr Ferdman volunteered the information that he did not tell
Mr Stern that the Canadians had obtained the money by fraud because, had he done so,
Mr Stern would have rejected the deal and SAFI would have lost its commission. I found
this observation particularly illuminating, not only for what it said about Mr Ferdman
but for what it said about his perception of Mr Stern. Having seen and heard Mr Stern
subjected to a long and vigorous cross-examination, I find myself in complete agreement
with Mr Ferdman's perception. Mr Stern had suffered a major and well-publicised   D
bankruptcy. He was working his passage back to acceptance in the commercial world. The
last thing he would have wanted was to be associated with dirty money. It was not as
though he needed it. Finding equity finance for property development in the UK in 1986
was not particularly difficult. I accept Mr Stern's evidence that, had he known, or even
suspected, that the Canadians' money had been obtained by fraud, he would have had
nothing to do with it.   E

I was invited to infer that Mr Stern must have known that the Canadians were
fraudsters and that the money they had invested in the project was obtained by fraud
from the fact that he had been willing to help Mr Ferdman meet their demands in
February 1987. The terms of the transaction were exceedingly generous, and it was
suggested that this showed that Mr Stern was desperate to placate the Canadians rather
than risk exposure. Mr Stern described the suggestion as "unmitigated rubbish" and   F
I agree. As he himself said, had he known that the Canadians were fraudsters, he
would have "felt more comfortable", knowing that they could not go to the police. But
Mr Stern did not simply yield to the Canadians' demands. They asked for more and Mr
Stern refused. I am satisfied that the terms of the transaction were commercially
justifiable in DLH's interests, and are consistent with Mr Stern's ignorance of the
source of the Canadians' money. In my judgment there is not a scrap of evidence that   G
Mr Ferdman told Mr Stern anything to the discredit of the Canadians before they
invested in the project or, for that matter, before he resigned as chairman of DLH in
June 1987.

That, of course, is not an end of the matter for, as I have pointed out, the relevant date
is March 1988 when Yulara was bought out. In his witness statement Mr Stern volunteered
the information, which otherwise would have remained undiscovered, that in or about
February 1988 Mr Ferdman called him on the telephone and told him that Mr D'Albis   H
had been arrested in Geneva and was held in custody; that he himself was being
questioned by a magistrate; and that the matter related to the Canadians. According to
Mr Stern, he gave no details, but did make it clear that he himself was not guilty of
anything untoward. Mr Stern said that he did not wish to embarrass Mr Ferdman by
asking for any further information.

A   In the witness-box Mr Stern did not go beyond what he had said in his witness statement. What he remembered of the conversation was being told that Mr Ferdman had been called before an examining magistrate in Geneva in a case concerning the Canadians. He was familiar with Swiss legal procedures and knew that many cases which the English legal system would treat as civil claims were handled in Switzerland through the criminal justice system. He did not, therefore, assume that the Canadians were accused of engaging in what in England would be classified as criminal activity.

B   Mr Ferdman's telephone call, he told me, did not alert him to the possibility that the Canadians had been involved in a fraud, and the thought that the money they had invested in the Nine Elms project had been obtained by fraud did not cross his mind. Mr Ferdman did not mention the telephone conversation in his witness statement, though he confirmed it in the witness-box. He remembered very little of it, and did not recall mentioning the Canadians.

C   In my judgment, unless Mr Stern was told more than he was prepared to admit, what he learned from Mr Ferdman was nothing like sufficient to convey to the mind of an honest and reasonable man the probability that the money which the Canadians had invested in the project had been obtained by them by fraud. The most he could have understood was that they might have been implicated in some way in irregular and possibly criminal conduct, but there was nothing to indicate that they were accused of

D   fraud or to link the subject-matter of the Swiss proceedings with the money which the Canadians had invested in the project. Had Mr Stern already cause to suspect the truth, Mr Ferdman's information might well have been enough to turn the scales and make it unreasonable for him not to make further inquiry. But, in the absence of other cause for suspicion, I do not accept the plaintiff's submission that what Mr Stern learned from Mr Ferdman was enough to put him on inquiry. I accept Mr Stern's evidence that he still did not suspect that the money which the Canadians had invested in the project

E   represented the proceeds of fraud, and that his failure to press Mr Ferdman for further details was out of regard for his feelings and not from any wish not to know the truth.

    I was invited to find that Mr Stern was told more than he was prepared to admit, and to infer this from the terms on which he bought out the Canadians. They were very disadvantageous to the Canadians. They received only £1.75m for a half share in a project which Mr Stern had only just realised (without telling them) for £4.65m. It was

F   probably not a transaction which, as between ordinary partners, a court of equity would allow to stand.

    The transaction was negotiated in two stages. In December 1987 Mr Stern agreed to pay the Canadians £2m for their interest. This was before Mr Ferdman's telephone call in February 1988, but it was after he had learned from Mr Ferdman that the Canadians were anxious to realise their investment. With hindsight, this was obviously because

G   they knew that the net was closing in, and they wanted to repatriate their money as soon as possible. But hindsight was not available to Mr Stern, and there was nothing suspicious in itself about the Canadians' wish to realise their investment prematurely, and nothing sinister in Mr Stern's exploitation of the fact.

    At the second stage in March 1988, the consideration payable to the Canadians was reduced to £1.75m. Despite his denials, I think that Mr Stern was taking further

H   advantage of the financial pressure he knew that they were under. Perhaps he was also taking advantage, consciously or subconsciously, of his knowledge that they were in some kind of trouble in Switzerland. But I can see no ground for concluding that Mr Stern must have learned more from Mr Ferdman's telephone call than he was prepared to admit, or that he must have known that the Canadians' investment in the project represented the proceeds of fraud.

In cross-examination, Mr Stern was strongly pressed with a memorandum dated A
21 March 1988, just five days after completion of the purchase of Yulara's interest, and
which he addressed to Mr Favre at SAFI, who was still a director of DLH. It was in the
following terms:

"(1) Do consult with Sylvain on this matter as he personally handled the Factotum
end. As Factotum has got nothing to do with the Keristal/DLH I do not think its
affairs concern us in any way.

B

(2) Unless I missed a point, I do not see how and why Keristal could become
involved in Yulara's troubles. The completion of this transaction took place on 16
March and in a document which Dollar Land's solicitors have drafted and found
valid — backed by the usual opinion letters etc. — DLH has purchased back from
Yulara such right and interest as Yulara ever had in the Regalian development.
Accordingly, if Yulara were to be liquidated tomorrow and if Yulara's receiver
and liquidator were to address any claim to DLH/Keristal, DLH would simply C
reply that it no longer had any connection or dealing whatsoever with Yulara.

(3) The point I am not addressing and which you alone can help sort out is the
mess — in SAFI's own records — between Keristal and Factotum/Yulara. To the
extent that 'Keristal No. 2' has been used as a nom de plume for any of HR's
interests, it is essential that Sylvain should unwind that transaction and have the
records show the true situation which is that we never had anything whatsoever to D
do with either of these outfits, as far as ownership is concerned."

The memorandum was written in reply to a note from Mr Favre which stated:

"I don't remember the exact structure of this loan but it seems important to take
care of the following facts:

(1) Factotum was involved in this deal.

(2) Keristal is the mother of DLH and if Keristal is involved in Yulara's troubles E
it would be advisable to take some steps."

It was put to Mr Stern that "Yulara's troubles" was a reference to the proceedings in
Switzerland, and that the terms of his memorandum betrayed his anxiety to distance
DLH from Yulara because of his knowledge that the money which Yulara had invested
in the project represented the proceeds of fraud. Mr Stern denied this. He knew that the
Canadians were under financial pressure, he explained, and that was all that he understood F
or intended by "Yulara's troubles". This is confirmed by his reference in the memorandum
to the possibility of Yulara's liquidation. He had been concerned that DLH should not
have to pay out twice for Yulara's interest. He had instructed Grangewoods to satisfy
themselves that Yulara was entitled to give a good receipt for the money — a sensible
precaution, given that his own offer of a participation in the project had been addressed
to Roth, even though a copy of Mr Ferdman's letter to Yulara had subsequently reached G
his own files. Grangewoods had taken appropriate steps to satisfy themselves on this
point, and in the circumstances Mr Stern could not see how DLH could be affected by
the Canadians' financial difficulties. That was all he was intending to convey by the
second paragraph of his memorandum. In the last paragraph Mr Stern explained, he
was dealing with a different matter. He was furious when he discovered that, at a time
when, in his view, Mr Ferdman was acting for the Canadians, he had put their money in
an account bearing Keristal's name without his knowledge or that of the Americans. H

I accept Mr Stern's explanation. I think that he did want to distance DLH from
Yulara, but for understandable and proper reasons. He knew that the Canadians were
under financial pressure. He contemplated the possibility that Yulara might be put into
liquidation. He also knew, from Mr Ferdman's telephone conversation, that the Canadians
were in some kind of trouble in Geneva. No wonder he wanted to distance DLH and the

A   Americans from them. But to jump to the conclusion that he ought to have realised that they were probably fraudsters and that the money they had invested in the project probably represented the proceeds of fraud would in my judgment be quite unwarranted.

I have had the advantage of seeing Mr Stern in the witness-box and hearing him subjected to a long and rigorous cross-examination. I accept him as an honest and truthful witness. He knew that Yulara was a front for the Canadians; that they were investing offshore funds handled by a fiduciary agent; and that they did not want to be identified as the beneficial owners of the investment. But this was not a cause for

B suspicion; Mr Stern himself and the Americans were acting in a similar fashion in operating through Keristal and DLH. By the time the Canadians were bought out, he knew that they were under financial pressure and were anxious to realise their investment; and he had also learned from Mr Ferdman that they were involved in criminal proceedings in Geneva. In my judgment, and without the benefit of hindsight, this was not enough to

C convey to the mind of an honest and reasonable man that the Canadians were probably fraudsters and that the money they had invested in the project probably represented the proceeds of fraud. I accept Mr Stern's evidence that he did not know, and did not suspect, that this was the case; and that, had he done so, he would have taken legal advice before paying any money out to the Canadians.

Conclusion

D
It follows that the action fails. This makes it unnecessary to consider what the proper remedy would have been if it had succeeded, bearing in mind that the plaintiff was only one of the victims of the fraud and that he has not been appointed to represent the others. Counsel for DLH submitted that he could have recovered only a proportion of the value of the assets which DLH received. I doubt that I would have accepted that submission. The court would, of course, have been concerned to protect DLH from

E further claims by other victims, but that could have been achieved in a number of ways. Whether the agreement between the plaintiff and Mr Van Apeldoorn would have been sufficient by itself to prevent the risk of further claims is a matter which in the circumstances I need not explore.

I dismiss the action.

(*Order accordingly*)

F

G

H

Re a Company No. 0022 of 1993.

A

Chancery Division (Companies Court).
Knox J.
Judgment delivered 30 June 1993.

> *Winding up — Restraining presentation of petition — Petition debt bona fide*
> *disputed — Whether and when solicitors should have realised that debt was*
> *genuinely disputed and that presenting petition was abuse — Whether*
> *company's costs were "wasted costs" — Supreme Court Act 1981, sec. 51(6),*
> *(7).*

B

This was an application by Philex Ltd, by way of amendment to a successful application by Philex for an injunction restraining the presentation of a winding-up petition on the ground that the petition debt was bona fide disputed. The costs of the proceedings for the injunction were ordered to be paid by the prospective petitioner, "G", on the indemnity basis. Philex then applied for G's solicitors to pay those costs personally as "wasted costs" under sec. 51(6) and (7) of the Supreme Court Act 1981 (as amended by sec. 4 of the Courts and Legal Services Act 1990).

C

Held, giving judgment for the applicant:

Costs incurred by Philex after G's solicitors should have realised that the winding-up procedure was inappropriate and should not be followed because the debt was disputed were wasted costs and should be paid by the solicitors.

D

The following cases were referred to in the judgment:

Barrister, Re a (wasted costs order) (No. 1 of 1991) [1993] QB 293.
Company No. 0012209 of 1991, Re a [1992] 1 WLR 351.
Gupta v Comer [1991] 1 QB 629.
Holden & Co v Crown Prosecution Service [1990] 2 QB 261.
Myers v Elman [1940] AC 282.
Orchard v South Eastern Electricity Board [1987] QB 565.
Sinclair-Jones v Kay [1989] 1 WLR 114.

E

Julia Smith (instructed by Iliffes) for the applicant.

Andrew Sutcliffe (instructed by Berger Oliver & Co) for the respondent.

F

JUDGMENT

Knox J: This is an application by Philex Ltd introduced by way of informal amendment into a successful application by Philex for an injunction restraining the presentation of a winding-up petition by the original respondent, Mr S Golban, against Philex based on a statutory demand served by Mr Golban on 24 December 1992.

G

The application now thus made by amendment is against a firm of solicitors, Berger Oliver & Co, which has acted for Mr Golban, and the application is made under sec. 51(6) and (7) of the *Supreme Court Act* 1981, as amended by sec. 4 of the *Courts and Legal Services Act* 1990, that the costs of the proceedings for an injunction thus brought by Philex which were ordered to be paid by Mr Golban on an indemnity basis should be paid by his solicitors personally.

The relevant subsections of sec. 51 are, as I have said, (6) and (7) which read as follows:

H

> "(6) In any proceedings mentioned in subsection (1), the court may disallow, or
> (as the case may be) order the legal or other representative concerned to meet,
> the whole of any wasted costs or such part of them as may be determined in
> accordance with rules of court.

A   (7) In subsection (6), 'wasted costs' means any costs incurred by a party—

       (a)   as a result of any improper, unreasonable or negligent act or omission on
             the part of any legal or other representative or any employee of such a
             representative; or

       (b)   which, in the light of any such act or omission occurring after they were
             incurred, the court considers it is unreasonable to expect that party to pay."

B   The proceedings mentioned in subsec. (1) include proceedings in the High Court and
       therefore include the proceedings thus brought by Philex against Mr Golban.

       The relevant rules of court are in O. 62, r. 11 of the Rules of the Supreme Court.
       Counsel for the parties before me, that is to say Philex and Berger Oliver & Co, both
       accepted that I should take as my guide a passage in a practice note given by the Court of
       Appeal Criminal Division in relation to wasted costs (*Re a Barrister (wasted costs order)*
C   *(No. 1 of 1991)* [1993] QB 293 at p. 301G), although it is not in terms directly applicable
       since it was concerned with criminal rather than civil proceedings.

       The relevant paragraph in the Court of Appeal Criminal Division's guidelines is
       para. (iv) (it is set out at p. 57 of the third cumulative supplement to the *Supreme Court
       Practice 1993*) and it reads:

D   "A three stage test or approach is recommended when a wasted costs order is
       contemplated:

       (i)   Has there been an improper, unreasonable or negligent act or omission?

       (ii)   As a result have any costs been incurred by a party?

       (iii) If the answers to (i) and (ii) are yes; should the court exercise its discretion
              to disallow or order the representative to meet the whole or any part of the
E   relevant costs, and if so what specific sum is involved?"

       I was also referred to *Orchard v South Eastern Electricity Board* [1987] QB 565 in
       which Sir *John Donaldson* MR said at p. 572:

       ". . . this is a jurisdiction which falls to be exercised with care and discretion and
       only in clear cases. In the context of a complaint that litigation was initiated or
       continued in circumstances in which to do so constituted serious misconduct, it
F   must never be forgotten that it is not for solicitors or counsel to impose a pre-trial
       screen through which a litigant must pass before he can put his complaint or
       defence before the court. On the other hand, no solicitor or counsel should lend
       his assistance to a litigant if he is satisfied that the initiation or further prosecution
       of a claim is mala fide or for an ulterior purpose or, to put it more broadly, if the
       proceedings would be, or have become, an abuse of the process of the court or
G   unjustifiably oppressive."

       Miss Smith, for Philex, submitted that the reference to a solicitor being satisfied that
       proceedings constituted an abuse of process should be treated as extending to situations
       where a solicitor should, by objective standards, have been so satisfied. That submission
       was not in terms challenged on behalf of Berger Oliver & Co and is, in my judgment,
       correct because it is to be borne in mind that since *Orchard*'s case it is now clear, more
       especially after the amendments introduced by sec. 4 of the *Courts and Legal Services
H   Act* 1990, that the old law regarding the exercise of the common law jurisdiction of the
       court to discipline its officers, authoritatively stated in *Myers v Elman* [1940] AC 282,
       that gross negligence or misconduct had to be shown, is no longer applicable to the
       jurisdiction under sec. 51 as it now stands (see *Gupta v Comer* [1991] 1 QB 629 and
       Sinclair-Jones v Kay [1989] 1 WLR 114 rather than the dicta in *Holden & Co v CPS*
       [1990] 2 QB 261).

The test is therefore now one of negligence unvarnished by any pejorative adjective. Nevertheless a finding of negligence against a solicitor is not lightly to be made and there is a distinction between the degree of negligence which needs to be established and the degree of conviction that the court needs to feel before making such a finding. To that extent it seems to me that the changes in the law regarding the degree of negligence that needs to be established does not detract from the passage from Sir *John Donaldson* MR's judgment from which I have read a quotation.

Another proposition that was common ground between the parties was that it is an abuse of the process of the court to present a winding-up petition to secure payment of a debt concerning which there is a genuine dispute. *Hoffmann* J restated this principle in *Re a Company No. 0012209 of 1991* [1992] 1 WLR 351 at p. 354. He also said on the same page:

"In order to say that the respondent company is entitled to present a winding up petition I must come to the conclusion that that argument [that is the alleged debtor's challenge to the debt relied on] is either not put forward in good faith or that it has really no rational prospect of success."

Finally, so far as the law is concerned, in judging whether a solicitor has been negligent in involving himself in an abuse of the process of the court, there is no question of requiring the solicitor to assess his client's veracity or weighing one claim against another. What is required is an assessment whether or not there is a genuine dispute. The question is thus not who is right about the disputed debt but is there really a dispute about it?

I turn to the facts of this case. Philex purchased a property, 110/124 West Hendon Broadway, London, NW9 ("the property"). The evidence is to some extent conflicting regarding the price and the completion date but nothing turns on that conflict. The price was £370,000 or £380,000 and completion took place on 18 or 21 December. A statutory demand was served by Berger Oliver & Co on 24 December 1992 on Philex. The covering letter said:

"We enclose by way of service statutory demand signed by Mr S Golban."

There was a note below it saying:

"Christmas and New Year closing arrangements: these offices will close at 1.30pm on 24 December 1992 for the Christmas period. We will reopen on Monday, 4 January 1993 at 9.30am."

The particulars of the debt, which was given on the usual form 4.1 for a statutory demand, read as follows:

"The debt of £11,100 is in respect of commission due from the company to the creditor following the introduction by the creditor of the commercial premises known as 110–124 West Hendon Broadway, London NW9 in or about October 1992. As a result of the introduction the company acquired the premises for £370,000 on 21 December 1992, but refuses to pay the creditor his commission which had been agreed between the creditor and Mr M Sabourian on behalf of the company and which was payable to the creditor on completion of the purchase. The amount due at the date of this demand is £11,100."

The part of the form that requires there to be named any agent acting on behalf of the creditor (part A on the last page) named Mr Paul McAndrews of Berger Oliver & Co giving their address as the person to whom communications regarding the demand might be addressed and there is, of course, no doubt that it emanated from his office.

In fact that statutory demand had come hard on the heels of an invoice which was sent dated 22 December 1992, two days earlier, headed with the name of the property and addressed to Philex. It said:

"For introduction of the above property purchase from L & S Properties at purchase price £370,000 and completion taken place on 21 December 1992. Agreed commission of 3 per cent: £11,100."

I have corrected various spelling mistakes in that. The mathematics are rather better than the spelling.

That invoice had elicited a very prompt denial of liability in a letter from Philex dated 24 December, which presumably crossed with the statutory demand, and that letter from Philex said:

"We are in receipt of your invoice [giving the number] dated 22 November 1992 which we do not understand. So far as we are aware we have no liabilities outstanding to yourselves."

That was signed by Mr Torbati, the finance director of Philex. Philex then instructed its solicitors who wrote a letter on 31 December 1992. The solicitors said that they were instructed to write on behalf of Philex in connection with the statutory demand and continued:

"Our instructions are that, contrary to the particulars of the alleged debt stated on p. 2 of the statutory demand, no agreement was entered into between our respective clients for the payment of commission or of any sum, nor was your client engaged at any time by our client to perform any services on its behalf. Your client held himself out as, and our client understood him to be at all times acting as, agent for the vendors of the above mentioned property.

Our client is a solvent company. The reason that our client refuses to pay your client the sum claimed or any other sum is that your client has no entitlement to be paid. The alleged debt is disputed by our client and your client's statutory demand is an abuse of the process of the Companies Court. Unless we receive your client's undertaking by 4pm on Monday, 4 January 1993 that he will take no further steps in relation to the statutory demand and that he will not issue a winding-up petition in respect of it our client will make an immediate application to the Companies Court to restrain your client from presenting a petition and will apply for its costs on the indemnity basis in accordance with the principles laid down in *Re a Company. . .*"

—and then the reference to the decision of *Hoffmann* J from which I have read a short extract, is given. That is signed by Iliffes, the solicitors acting for Philex.

31 December 1992 was a Thursday. Friday, of course, was New Year's Day and Saturday and Sunday ensued. So the next working day was 4 January, a Monday, which was the day when the time for giving of the undertaking demanded by Philex's solicitors was due to expire. Miss Smith, for Philex, did not submit that Mr McAndrews, who had the conduct of the matter throughout at Berger Oliver & Co, was guilty of negligence in sending the statutory demand on 24 December 1992. She did, however, submit that the receipt of the letter of 31 December 1992 showed, or should have shown, to Mr McAndrews that there was a genuine dispute regarding the claim to commission. Mr McAndrews' evidence in the affidavit he has sworn is that he sent a copy of the letter of 31 December from Iliffes and a copy of *Hoffmann* J's decision referred to in that letter to his client. No particular date is given for this but the indications are that it was on 4 January when Berger Oliver & Co's offices were to reopen after Christmas and the New Year. In any event Mr McAndrews deposes that Mr Golban was abroad and he believes returned on 5 or 6 January 1993. In fact on 5 January, that is the day after the time limited for the giving of the undertaking not to present a winding-up petition had expired, an originating application returnable on 25 January was issued on behalf of Philex and served on Berger Oliver & Co under cover of a letter that stated that the affidavit in support of the application would be served shortly.

Mr McAndrews' evidence is that at this stage he felt unable to advise Mr Golban to   A
abandon the winding-up procedure until he, Mr McAndrews, had been able to consider
the affidavit in support. I do not consider that Mr McAndrews was guilty of negligence
at this stage. He could not give an undertaking on behalf of his client without instructions
and on the time-scale that Iliffes gave the issue of the originating application could not,
in my view, be laid at Mr McAndrews' door. I do not, of course, suggest that the order
for indemnity costs, which was later made on 25 January against Mr Golban, was not
entirely properly made in relation to the issue of the originating application as well as   B
the later hearings.

Abuse of the petition procedure is, as *Hoffmann* J observed, a high risk strategy and
it is the client who takes the risk. But the question of a solicitor's negligence in relation
to it has to be judged in relation to that solicitor's conduct and the practicalities of the
situation in which he found himself. In my view, Mr McAndrews was not given time
within which to procure his client's undertaking before the originating application was   C
issued, and I consider that he was not negligent in wanting to see the affidavit which he
was told was shortly to be served before giving definitive advice to his client with regard
to the request for an undertaking not to present a petition.

I should add that in reaching that conclusion I place very little weight upon ten pages
of copy letters and drawings which Mr McAndrews states in his affidavit were handed to
him by Mr Golban before the statutory demand was served. These documents show no   D
more than that Mr Golban was regarded by the architects, acting for Philex in connection
with the proposed purchase of the property and its conversion, as being connected in
some way with Philex's proposed purchase. They reveal nothing as to the capacity, if
any, in which Mr Golban was involved. A fortiori they reveal no support whatever for
the proposition that a commission had been agreed to be paid to Mr Golban on
completion.

The next critical date is 8 January 1993 when the promised affidavit in support sworn   E
by Mr Torbati, Philex's finance director, was served. That is a seven page affidavit which,
in my judgment, made it clear that Philex's case was that the property was originally
introduced to Mr Sabourian, Philex's managing director, by Mr Golban and that Philex
put offers to Mr Golban for him to transmit to the vendor and that, on finding that those
offers were not bearing fruit, Philex negotiated direct with the vendors L & S Properties
who were intending subpurchasers from the current owners, the East German Embassy,   F
and that eventually Philex exchanged contracts without any intervention from
Mr Golban in that behalf on 2 November 1992 and completed on 18 December of that
year.

Mr Torbati's affidavit contains the following. In para. 10 he says:

> "The purchase was completed on 18 December and subsequently Mr Sabourian
> told the respondent that the purchase had been completed. In my presence   G
> Mr Sabourian telephoned the respondent and said that he wished to give him
> some money for his introduction. He suggested that the respondent send the
> applicant an invoice for £2,000 for the introduction which would be paid at the
> beginning of January. Again, in my presence the respondent telephoned Mr
> Sabourian and objected to the sum that he had been offered. I pointed out to the
> respondent that he had kept on repeating that the deal would not go through and
> that he had told Mr Sabourian that his role was purely a friendly one and that he   H
> had not been expecting a fee."

A little later in para. 13 Mr Torbati says:

> "I have spoken to Mr Sabourian on the telephone and he informs me and I verily
> believe that he entered into no agreement with the respondent for him to act as
> the agent of the applicant and that, further, he at no time agreed to pay the

A   respondent any commission in respect of his introduction of the applicant to L & S Properties. Mr Sabourian mentioned that he had also discussed acquiring a private flat for himself personally with Mr Golban and he discussed a commission with him in relation to that transaction only. I understood that in inviting me to make an offer to him the respondent was in fact acting as the agent for L & S Properties. The applicant denies that it entered into any agreement with the respondent to pay him commission in respect of the purchase of 110/124 West
B   Hendon Broadway and the debt claimed by the respondent is disputed."

Obviously I am not concerned to decide where the truth lies with regard to whether there was an agreement to pay Mr Golban a commission. What I am concerned with is the different question whether on receiving and reading that affidavit Mr McAndrews should have appreciated that his client's claim to £11,100 commission was the subject of a genuine dispute. I would answer that question, yes. That conclusion is not detracted
C   from by the circumstance that Mr Torbati's evidence, regarding what Mr Sabourian had and had not agreed to otherwise than in Mr Torbati's presence, was hearsay from Mr Sabourian. Nor does the fact that there was an offer made to pay Mr Golban £2,000, which Mr Golban did not accept, detract from that conclusion.

I therefore conclude that once Mr McAndrews had read Mr Torbati's affidavit at all carefully he should have appreciated that there was a genuine dispute on foot.
D   Mr McAndrews, in his affidavit, states that he received Mr Torbati's affidavit on Friday, 8 January but read it only on the ensuing Monday, 11 January. I do not think he can be accused of negligence in taking that time. The events as related by Mr McAndrews thereafter were as follows. In para. 5 of his affidavit he says:

"The affidavit in support of the application was served, I believe, during the afternoon of Friday, 8 January. For the sake of expedition, I sent a copy forthwith
E   to my client without having considered it in any detail. I perused the affidavit on Monday, 11 January and on 12 January I sent my client a copy of the letter from Iliffes which I received that day. Although I have no attendance notes, I recall that my client gave me his comments on the affidavit of Mr Torbati during the week commencing 11 January, possibly on 13 January. Before I could consider these I received a telephone call from Mr Evered [he was the partner in Iliffes] on 14
F   January to which he refers in his affidavit at para. 9. An attendance note of this conversation is exhibited at p. 21. As I had to leave the office for a hearing in Basingstoke I was unable to speak to my client but on my return to the office I found the ex parte injunction."

That ex parte injunction was obtained by Iliffes on 14 January because of the unwillingness of Mr Golban, through Mr McAndrews, to say that the application on 25 January for an injunction to restrain presentation of a winding-up petition would not
G   be opposed. Indeed, Mr McAndrews said that his instructions were to press ahead with the statutory demand procedure. The attendance note of Mr McAndrews as regarding this telephone conversation with Mr Evered of Iliffes included the following:

"PM [McAndrews] attending Mr Evered of Iliffes who phoned to ask me whether we were intending to oppose the application of 25 January and I said that my instructions were to press ahead with the statutory demand procedure. He said
H   that the issue was crystal clear that where there was a genuine dispute as to a claim then it was inappropriate to use this procedure and the client should issue proceedings in the normal way and that he was therefore exposed to indemnity costs. I said that I had explained this to my client but he was adamant that he was owed the money and wanted to go ahead. Mr Evered asked me whether I would be issuing a petition because if we did this they would apply immediately ex parte

to injunct us from advertising it. I said that I would have to take instructions and get back to him on this point."

That attendance note is rather unspecific about the time when Mr McAndrews advised Mr Golban that where there was a genuine dispute it was inappropriate to use the winding-up procedure and that to do so would expose him to an indemnity order for costs. It is, of course, possible that when Mr McAndrews said, as I take him to have done as it is in his attendance note though not in Mr Evered's of the same conversation, that he had explained this to his client, he was referring back to the copy of *Hoffmann* J's decision which he sent on receipt of the letter of 31 December 1992. However that may be, Mr McAndrews' affidavit is less than clear on the important question when he advised Mr Golban that it would be an abuse of the process to present a winding-up petition. I infer that he did so on 15 January, since he says in his affidavit that on that day his client accepted his advice not to proceed with the statutory demand and that he had been unable to speak to him on the previous day, 14 January. In my view that was good advice, but it was not acted upon at all effectively until 19 January and even then in a distinctly half-hearted way. Mr McAndrews' affidavit in para. 6 says this:

"On the day following the service of the injunction, 15 January, my client accepted my advice not to proceed with the statutory demand and on that day I drafted a letter to Iliffes which was posted on 19 January. My client wished to keep alive his claim against the company and in order to preserve his position whilst conceding that the winding-up procedure was inappropriate, I submitted the draft letter to counsel for approval. For this reason the letter was not sent out until 19 January."

In the meanwhile, Iliffes, on behalf of Philex, had written as follows on 18 January by fax:

"On 31 December 1992 we wrote to you and informed you that the procedure adopted by your client and in respect of which you are acting was an abuse of the process of the court. Despite our letter and the service on you of Mr Torbati's affidavit setting out the basis for that view you have offered no undertaking on behalf of your client that he will desist from acting on the wholly misconceived statutory demand dated 24 December 1992 bearing your firm's name.

We have already made it clear that our client will apply for its costs on the indemnity basis in the event that it is successful on 25 January both in respect of that hearing and our client's ex parte application on 14 January which was necessitated by your client's failure to provide an undertaking prior to the expiry of the 21-day period specified in the statutory demand.

We believe that, notwithstanding his denial of the fact to you, your client is the same Tehrani Shahrdad Golban lately of Connolly Street, London W1 [and formerly of two other addresses] who was adjudicated bankrupt by an order dated 3 March 1992 . . . on the petition of solicitors Steel & Shamash . . . Under the circumstances it would appear that, even if our client is successful on 25 January in protecting its business and preventing your client's abuse of the process of the court, our client will stand very little chance of recovering any of its costs incurred as a result of the wholly misconceived statutory demand to which your firm has lent its name.

We place you on notice that unless terms can be agreed for the relief sought and payment of our client's costs prior to the hearing of the application on 25 January we shall seek an order to be made against your firm personally to pay our client's costs on the indemnity basis."

That was replied to by Mr McAndrews' letter, written it appears with the benefit of counsel's advice, though whether the latter had Iliffes' letter of 18 January must be at least doubtful. Mr McAndrews' letter of 19 January included the following passage:

A   "It appears from your client's affidavit that he has offered payment of £2,000 to
       our client in satisfaction of the claim. Whilst our client wishes to reserve his rights
       to pursue the full claim he is nevertheless prepared to accept payment of £2,000
       together with our reasonable costs if this can be agreed before 25 January. If not,
       our client intends to issue proceedings for the full amount of his claim and seeks
       your confirmation that the sum of £2,000 will be paid into court in such proceedings.

B   In spite of his reservations arising from the discrepancy between what you have
       stated on behalf of your client and what your client states in his affidavit our client
       accepts that the evidence contained in the affidavit establishes, prima facie, a
       dispute rendering inappropriate the continuation of the winding-up procedure
       and confirms that he does not intend to present a winding-up petition.

       We note your comments regarding our position and the alleged bankruptcy of our
       client. He has, as you know, denied to us that he is bankrupt and in view of your
C   persistence in asserting this we have made a search against our client which has
       disclosed that there are no subsisting entries. We are therefore unable to agree
       with your contention that we should be personally liable for costs and will certainly
       oppose any such application."

       There was a telephone conversation between the solicitors on 22 January in which a
without prejudice matter, of the details of which I have naturally no evidence, was
D   discussed. Mr Golban wanted an adjournment on the strength of this and that attitude
of seeking a four-week adjournment was only abandoned on behalf of Mr Golban at the
hearing on 25 January when the order I have already mentioned with indemnity costs
was made against Mr Golban.

       How far are the costs of Iliffes "wasted costs" within sec. 51(6) and (7) of the *Supreme
Court Act* 1981 must turn on whether they were incurred as a result of any improper,
E   unreasonable or negligent act or omission by Mr McAndrews. I have come to the
conclusion that it was unreasonable and indeed improper to use proceedings which by
11 January 1993 Mr McAndrews should have realised and did realise amounted to an
abuse of the process of the court as a vehicle to secure a compromise on the basis of the
£2,000 claim which at one stage was offered. Mr McAndrews did indeed, on his own
evidence, advise his client, Mr Golban, not to proceed with the statutory demand on
15 January. He should, and indeed may, have done so when Mr Golban gave Mr
F   McAndrews, on or about 13 January, his comments on Mr Torbati's affidavit. The fact
that Mr Golban continued to believe in the merits of his case for commission is not any
justification for not accepting that the winding-up procedure was inappropriate and
should not be followed.

       I therefore conclude that costs incurred by Philex after 13 January in these proceedings
were wasted costs within sec. 51(6) and (7) of the *Supreme Court Act* 1981 and should
G   be paid by the respondent firm. But credit should be given for such costs as would have
been incurred in obtaining a consent order in terms of the originating application,
because those costs would have been incurred in any event by reason of the issue of the
originating application for which I have already held Mr McAndrews bears no
responsibility on my view of the matter. It is important that solicitors should be free
fearlessly and energetically to advance their client's case. But it is also important that
they should not be parties to proceedings which constitute an abuse of the process of the
H   court.

                              (*Order accordingly*)
                        _____

Re a Company No. 005374 of 1993.

A

Chancery Division (Companies Court).
Harman J.
Judgment delivered 19 July 1993.

Administrative receivership — Private examination — Duty of confidentiality
— Whether receivers should disclose documents to bank which appointed
them — Insolvency Act 1986, sec. 236.

B

This was an application by administrative receivers for leave to disclose to the bank which appointed them information or documents, obtained under sec. 236 of the Insolvency Act 1986 or otherwise, relating to the receivership and to a claim by the receivers against the respondents.

Held, **ordering that the privilege which ordinarily attached to information obtained in confidence should be waived for the purpose of actions by the bank against the respondents or entities with which either of the respondents were connected:**

C

1. The duty of confidence imposed upon those who obtained information by the use of sec. 236 of the 1986 Act could be waived by the court, if it was satisfied that either it was for the purposes of the office which the office-holders who sought to disclose the information held, or was otherwise justified by the balance of considerations of how justice was properly to be attained. (Re Esal (Commodities) Ltd (No. 2) [1990] BCC 708 followed.)

D

2. The bank's claims appeared likely to be claims very closely analogous to the claims by the receivers on behalf of the company, claims which might lead to the company being relieved of liability and therefore for the benefit of the company. Further, there appeared to be dealings by the respondents of such a nature that justice could only properly be achieved if the information was made available to the bank which lent the money.

The following case was referred to in the judgment:

E

Esal (Commodities) Ltd, Re (No. 2) [1990] BCC 708.

Nicholas Harrison (instructed by Rowe & Maw) for the administrative receivers.

The first respondent appeared in person.

JUDGMENT

F

Harman J: I have before me an originating application issued on 16 June 1993 under No. 005374 of 1993. The applicants are the administrative receivers of a company called Salcrest plc; the respondents are Mr Anthony Peters and Mr David Goodman. Mr Peters is, I think, a director of Salcrest plc, or is at the very least closely associated with it. Mr Goodman is a solicitor of this court and has been acting as solicitor, so far as appears, for Salcrest plc and also for Mr Peters.

G

The application is for leave to the receivers to disclose to a bank, Gamlestaden plc, information or documents relating to (1) the receivership of Salcrest plc, and (2) a claim by them against the respondents in the course of the said receivership, whether the documents are obtained under sec. 236 of the Insolvency Act 1986 or otherwise, and in particular documents relating to a VAT receipt.

The story is a curious and quite complicated one which I will not recite at this time, but it involves the dealing with something over £250,000 of VAT refund due to Salcrest plc. That refund was dealt with in a manner which, on the face of it — although there may conceivably be explanations; I am unable at present to see them — is in flat breach of obligations binding upon Salcrest plc of which Mr Peters and Mr Goodman were both well aware. The £250,000 should have been paid into a special specific bank account. It was not; it was paid into a specially created bank account created at Mr Peters'

H

A application in the name of Salcrest plc. It was then paid away from that bank account to Mr Goodman as a solicitor. Although he was specifically to receive it on behalf of Salcrest as his client, he seems to have allowed it to be paid into his client account under the name of another client, also a company associated with Mr Peters and/or Mr Goodman, and thereafter to have dealt extensively with the moneys in that account. It does, on the face of it, look as if those dealings were entirely irregular and probably in breach of Mr Peters' fiduciary duty to Salcrest.

B The further dealings in this convoluted matter raise serious questions about the propriety of some of the activities that have gone on and, prima facie, point to attempts to avoid payment of debts when due. In those circumstances the duty of confidence imposed upon those who obtain information by the use of sec. 236 of the 1986 Act can, if the court is satisfied that either it is for the purposes of the office which the office-holders who seek to disclose the information hold, or is otherwise justified by the

C balance of considerations of how justice is properly to be attained, be waived by the court. That I base upon the decision of *Millett* J in *Re Esal (Commodities) Ltd (No. 2)* [1990] BCC 708, and in particular para. 1 and 2 of the headnote.

The claims here appear likely to be claims very closely analogous to the claims by the receivers, the office-holders, on behalf of Salcrest plc, all claims which may lead to Salcrest plc being relieved of liability and therefore for the benefit of Salcrest plc.

D Further, there appear to be dealings here of such a nature that, in my view, justice can only properly be achieved if the information is made available to the bank which lent the money, Gamlestaden plc. It seems to me that it is right to restrict the use of this information to use in the course of and for the purpose of actions by Gamlestaden plc or as they may properly direct against either Mr Peters, Mr Goodman or any of the entities with which either of them are connected by reason of being an officer in those companies. To my mind the overwhelming conclusion upon this case must be that the ordinary

E privilege which attaches to information obtained in confidence should for that narrow and specific purpose be waived. In my judgment it is right to allow Gamlestaden plc to apply for release from the undertaking which it will have to give in order to obtain the information in the terms which I have discussed with counsel, but allowing such an application for further leave to be made if occasion arises in the future. On that basis I shall grant the relief sought in this originating application in the terms of a minute which

F counsel will settle and which he will disclose to Mr Peters and upon lodging will be an order of the court.

(Order accordingly)

G

H

R v Institute of Chartered Accountants in England and Wales & Ors, ex parte Brindle & Ors.

A

Queen's Bench Division (Divisional Court).
Mann LJ and Sedley J.
Judgment delivered 27 July 1993.

> *Company auditors — Recognised supervisory bodies — Supervisory body*   B
> *placed auditors under enquiry — Whether enquiry should be adjourned*
> *pending outcome of litigation — Companies Act 1989, Pt. II.*

This was an application by a firm of chartered accountants for judicial review of a decision of the accountants' regulatory body, the Institute of Chartered Accountants in England and Wales, to proceed with disciplinary proceedings against the firm in relation to the firm's actions as auditors of BCCI Holdings (Luxembourg) SA and its subsidiaries.

C

The applicants' case was that to proceed with the enquiry, and not to adjourn it, before the determination of various pieces of litigation which were extant or pending, was productive of unfairness.

The respondents refuted unfairness and argued that to accede to the applicants' arguments would effectively abdicate the Institute's function as the principal regulator of auditors and would fail to deal with public concern at the audit of BCCI.

D

The handbook of the Institute's investigation committee stated that disciplinary proceedings must be deferred if they were likely to interfere with the course of justice, but also that even where there was a case for adjournment the investigation committee would press ahead with disciplinary proceedings where to fail to do so would be inconsistent or would appear to be inconsistent with its duties as a regulator or as a professional body, for example where the Institute was the prime regulator of the conduct in question.

E

Also, after the applicants had been placed under enquiry, the Institute adopted a new disciplinary scheme and the applicants sought to have the enquiry carried on under the new scheme, but were refused. The applicants challenged the decision not to agree to a transfer.

Held, refusing the application:

1. There was no real risk of injustice which would entitle the court to intervene so as to   F
prevent the performance in the public interest of an important investigative procedure which was part of a supervisory function underpinned by statute, especially as the procedure was to be performed in regard to a uniquely spectacular and serious banking failure.

2. The decision not to agree to transfer the enquiry to the new disciplinary scheme was not irrational.

G

The following cases were referred to in the judgment of Mann LJ:

Associated Provincial Picture Houses Ltd v Wednesbury Corporation [1948] 1 KB 223.
Conteh v Onslow-Fane (The Times, 26 June 1975, CA).
Currie & Anor v Chief Constable of Surrey [1982] 1 WLR 215.
Parry-Jones v Law Society & Ors [1969] 1 Ch 1.
Price Waterhouse v BCCI Holdings (Luxembourg) SA [1992] BCLC 583.   H
R v Panel on Takeovers and Mergers, ex parte Fayed & Ors [1992] BCC 524.
R v Panel on Takeovers and Mergers, ex parte Guinness plc (1988) 4 BCC 714; [1990] 1 QB 146.
Thames Launches Ltd v Trinity House Corporation [1961] Ch 197.
Tournier v National Provincial and Union Bank of England [1924] 1 KB 461.

A   David Oliver QC and Nigel Giffin (instructed by Herbert Smith) for the applicants.

Robert Carnwath QC and John Howell QC (instructed by Bates Wells & Braithwaite) for the respondents.

JUDGMENT

Mann LJ: There is before the court an application for judicial review for which leave
B   to move was given by *Tuckey* J on 21 May 1993. The applicants are the partners in Price Waterhouse, a well-known firm of chartered accountants, which in March 1991 became a registered auditor for the purposes of the *Companies Act* 1989. The purpose of the application is to restrain the further process of disciplinary proceedings against the applicants by their professional body. To that end various decisions are impuged.

Background
C

From June 1987 the applicants co-ordinated the worldwide audits and reviewed the consolidation of the accounts of Bank of Credit and Commerce International Holdings (Luxembourg) SA and its subsidiaries. One of those subsidiaries is Bank of Credit and Commerce International SA which operated as a bank in various countries including the UK. Another subsidiary is Bank of Credit and Commerce International (Overseas) Ltd which was also a bank and also operated around the world. The BCCI group collapsed
D   on 5 July 1991 when the Bank of England and other regulators withdrew its banking licences and orders were thereafter made in various jurisdictions, including England, putting the companies into liquidation.

The withdrawal of the licences followed upon a report by the applicants to the Bank of England under sec. 41 of the *Banking Act* 1987 which disclosed the applicants' discovery of widespread fraud in the affairs of BCCI. On 9 July the Chancellor of the
E   Exchequer and the Governor of the Bank of England appointed Lord Justice Bingham,

> "to inquire into the supervision of BCCI under the Banking Act; to consider whether the action taken by all the UK authorities was appropriate and timely; and to make recommendations."

The report was presented in July 1992 and in the covering letter Lord Justice Bingham stated that he had,
F

> "not attempted to evaluate the professional quality of the audits of BCCI's accounts conducted over the years . . . or to form a judgment whether irregularities in its business should have been discovered by the auditors earlier."

He did however pay tribute to the very high level of co-operation which he had received from, amongst others, the applicants. The applicants had submitted a 300-page memorandum and the six members of the firm most closely connected with the affair
G   had given oral evidence.

A number of actions have been commenced in various jurisdictions against the applicants which call in question the quality of their audit work in regard to BCCI.

There are in England the following proceedings:

(1)   An action in the Queen's Bench Division by Mr and Mrs Khasruzzanan who claim to be depositors with BCCI and who claim damages for deceit. The deceit is
H   alleged to arise from the audit report on the parent company's accounts for the year ending 31 December 1989.

(2)   Three actions in the Chancery Division commenced by the liquidators of the BCCI companies claiming damages for negligence and/or breach of duty and/or breach of contract and/or breach of statutory duty in connection with work done in respect of the audits of the BCCI companies for 1985, 1986 and 1987. The

A

claims are for large sums of money. The claim in respect of the 1985 audit is for in excess of $8 billion.

(3)   Two sets of proceedings between the applicants and their predecessors as auditors of the BCCI companies (Ernst & Young) in which each effectively claims contributions from the other.

There are in the USA the following proceedings:

B

(1)   In California there is a consolidated action which is based upon alleged violation of the US Racketeer-Influenced Corrupt Organisations Act. If this action comes to trial the plaintiffs are entitled to a jury. However at present the proceedings stand dismissed although there is an outstanding appeal to the United States Court of Appeals (ninth circuit) by the plaintiffs.

(2)   In New York there was a claim similar to the one in California but it has now been abandoned.

C

(3)   In Texas there are proceedings but it is not clear whether the applicants are defendants.

In other jurisdictions there are also actual or pending proceedings notably in the Cayman Islands and Luxembourg. There may also be further actions in England by the liquidators in regard to the audits for 1988 and 1989. It is of course possible that some or all of the claims will be withdrawn or settled, but it was suggested to us that in view of the large sums involved settlement may be difficult. In default of comprehensive settlement it seems very likely that the applicants will be involved in litigation at trial until the turn of the century and beyond. Any appellate process would postpone the date of conclusion.

D

Apart from their involvement in litigation the applicants will be required to provide witnesses for the prosecution in several pending criminal proceedings initiated by the Serious Fraud Office which allege conspiracy to deceive the auditors of BCCI companies.

E

Statutory background

The "main purposes" of Pt. II of the *Companies Act* 1989 are,

> "to secure that only persons who are properly supervised and appropriately qualified are appointed company auditors, and that audits by persons so appointed are carried out properly and with integrity and with a proper degree of independence."

F

(Section 24(1).)

In order to secure those objectives a person or firm is eligible for appointment as an auditor only if he is a member of a recognised supervisory body (sec. 25(1)). Such a body means a body established in the UK which maintains and enforces rules as to (a) the eligibility of persons to seek positions as company auditors and (b) the conduct of company audit work, which are binding on persons seeking appointment as or acting as company auditors (sec. 30(1)). The requirements for recognition as a supervisory body are contained in Pt. II of Sch. 11 to the Act. Paragraph 6(1) of the schedule provides that:

G

> "The body must have adequate rules and practices designed to ensure that the persons eligible under its rules for appointment as a company auditor are fit and proper persons to be so appointed."

H

Paragraph 7(1) provides that:

> "The body must have adequate rules and practices designed to ensure—
>
> (a)   that company audit work is conducted properly and with integrity . . ."

A   Paragraph 9 provides:

"The body must have rules and practices designed to ensure that persons eligible under its rules for appointment as a company auditor continue to maintain an appropriate level of competence in the conduct of company audits."

Paragraph 10(1) provides that:

B   "The body must have adequate arrangements and resources for the effective monitoring and enforcement of compliance with its rules."

Paragraph 12(1) provides that:

"The body must have effective arrangements for the investigation of complaints—

(a) against persons who are eligible under its rules to be appointed company auditor . . ."

C   The recognition of a supervisory body is a matter for (now) the President of the Board of Trade; and the Institute of Chartered Accountants in England and Wales, the Institute of Chartered Accountants of Scotland and the Chartered Association of Certified Accountants all received recognition. They are each bodies incorporated by royal charter. The applicant is a member firm of the English and Welsh institute.

The discipline scheme

D
A supplemental charter was granted to the English and Welsh institute on 21 December 1948. That charter gave effect to the bye-laws appended to the petition for the charter. Ch. VIII of the bye-laws makes provisions as to discipline and in particular for the constitution of an investigation committee. Under bye-law 79 it is the duty of the institute's secretary to bring to the attention of the investigation committee any facts or matters which indicate that a member firm may have become liable to disciplinary action

E   under the discipline scheme. If the investigation committee decides that in its opinion the matter is one which gives rise to or includes a question of public concern and considers that in all the circumstances it ought to be dealt with under the scheme then it shall refer the complaint to the executive committee provided for under the scheme.

The scheme referred to is the joint disciplinary scheme which was established by the three institutes, approved by the Privy Council and which had effect from 31 December

F   1986. The objectives of the scheme are,

"to promote the highest possible standards of professional and business conduct, efficiency and competence . . .

by providing a system for the investigation and regulation of the activities of . . . member firms so as to secure their adherence to all professional criteria including but not limited to all relevant recommendations and standards promulgated from

G   time to time by or with the approval of the councils of the participants."

The scheme is administered by an executive committee which is appointed for the purpose by the councils of the three institutes (para. 5(a)). Paragraph 6(a) provides:

"Whenever the executive committee receives a report from an investigation committee of any of the participants which concerns, or which in the opinion of the investigation committee may concern, the professional or business conduct, efficiency or competence of one or more members and/or member firms (whether

H   or not referred to specifically in the report) and the investigation committee making the report certifies that in its opinion the matter is one which gives rise to or includes questions of public concern, the executive committee shall as soon as practicable appoint a committee of inquiry to enquire into the matter and into such facts and circumstances arising in the course of the enquiry into the matter as the committee of inquiry considers appropriate."

Paragraph 6(f) provides that a committee of inquiry,

A

"shall have power to reach a finding on the professional or business conduct, efficiency or competence of every member under enquiry and of every member firm under enquiry . . ."

Paragraph 6(g) provides that before an adverse finding is made under para. 6(f) the committee is to give a member firm a reasonable opportunity to make representations.

Paragraph 5(d)(vii) of the scheme provides for the making of regulations as to the conduct and proceedings of committees of inquiry. Such regulations have been made. Regulation 8 provides that subject to the scheme and to the regulations,

B

"the conduct and proceedings of the enquiry shall be determined by the chairman in consultation with the other members of the committee of inquiry."

Regulation 9(a) provides that the committee shall give to each member or member firm under enquiry written notice that he or it is under enquiry. There then follow detailed provisions as to conduct of an enquiry. The procedure is essentially inquisitorial and there is no entitlement to cross-examination although such cross-examination may be allowed under the chairman's general discretion as to the procedure to be adopted.

C

The discipline procedures as applied to the applicants

On 19 March 1992 the secretary of the English and Welsh institute laid before its investigation committee certain facts and matters relating to the actions of the applicants as auditors of BCCI companies. In so doing he was acting under bye-law 79. On the same day the committee considered those facts and matters and decided to make a reference to the executive committee to be dealt with in accordance with the scheme. The certificate and reference were in these terms:

D

"*Certificate and reference by the investigation committee*

E

1. The investigation committee has considered facts and matters laid before it on 19 March 1992 by the secretary relating to the actions of Price Waterhouse as auditors of BCCI Holdings (Luxembourg) SA and its subsidiary companies. They are contained in the following documents:

    (a) Price Waterhouse evidence to the Treasury and Civil Service Committee of the House of Commons, contained in a memorandum of 5 February 1992.

F

    (b) A confidential Price Waterhouse draft report, dated 22 June 1991, addressed to the Bank of England under sec. 41 of the *Banking Act 1987*.

    (c) Press and television comment, in particular:

G

        i. a transcript of Channel 4 broadcast "Bandung File Special" on 13 August 1991;

        ii. an extract from the Independent of 10 July 1991;

        iii. an extract from the Financial Times of 11 July 1991.

    (d) Price Waterhouse letters and reports:

H

        i. addressed to the directors of BCCI Holdings (Luxembourg) SA, dated 18 April 1990;

        ii. addressed to the audit committee of BCCI Holdings (Luxembourg) SA, dated 3 October 1990;

    disclosed to the institute in confidence by the Bank of England.

A
2. The investigation committee having considered these facts and matters hereby certifies that in its opinion they give rise to or include matters of public concern and that in all the circumstances they ought to be referred to the executive committee to be dealt with in accordance with the joint disciplinary scheme.

3. The investigation committee therefore refers the above facts and matters to the executive committee to be dealt with in accordance with the joint disciplinary scheme."

B

The applicants by their application impugn the reference "if and so far as is necessary". In the event, I did not detect any argument which questioned the validity of the decision and in any event the application for relief (dated 15 March 1993) in respect of it was far too late.

C
The executive committee considered the reference and in pursuance of para. 6(a) of the scheme appointed a committee of inquiry. The committee comprises two experienced chartered accountants and a legally qualified chairman in Sir John Bailey who is a former Treasury solicitor. The firm of BDO Binder Hamlyn were appointed as investigating accountants. The decision to appoint a committee is impugned by the applicants, and the fourth to twelfth named respondents were the members of the executive committee when the decision was taken.

D
The investigating accountants made a number of enquiries of the applicants during the autumn of 1992. The applicants pointed out that to answer some of those enquiries would involve breach of confidence. In response to further enquiries they pointed out that the provision of information could be prejudicial to the applicants' position in the English and US litigation. I need not rehearse the correspondence but by 20 November 1992 there was a clearly expressed concern about confidence and prejudice and a doubt by the applicants as to whether the enquiry was necessary. Sir John Bailey responded to these concerns and doubts in a letter dated 16 December 1992 which I should read in full:

E

"As you would expect, BDO Binder Hamlyn have been keeping my committee fully informed about the correspondence and discussions they have had with you on this matter. Most recently the committee has seen your letter dated 20 November 1992 addressed to Richard Hall. It has also recently received documents and information from the Bank of England pursuant to its power to provide the same under sec. 85(1)(g) of the *Banking Act* 1987.

F

As you indicated in your letter of 20 November 1992, the investigation committee rejected your firm's case that there should be no JDS enquiry at this stage. This committee was therefore appointed in April 1992. Even assuming that the committee has the power to suspend its enquiry, it does not consider that, in all the circumstances, it should now do so in the light of the wider public interest.

G

In that context I would refer to the letter from Herbert Smith to the investigation committee of ICAEW dated 18 March 1992 which set out with some particularity the reasons why it was then submitted that it would be unfair to Price Waterhouse and inappropriate for the institute to commence an investigation at that stage. One of those grounds was that the Bingham inquiry was carrying out a major investigation and that any disciplinary enquiry should be deferred until after that inquiry had reported. That report has now been made and whilst it may be of considerable assistance to all concerned in considering the position of your firm, Lord Justice Bingham stated explicitly in the letter accompanying the report (fifth paragraph) that he had not attempted to evaluate the professional quality of the audits of BCCI's accounts or to form a judgment whether irregularities in its business should have been discovered by the auditors earlier. These are, of course,

H

issues which are apt for consideration by a disciplinary enquiry and which are   A
covered by my committee's terms of reference. Accordingly after carefully
considering your letter and discussing it with the committee's legal advisers, the
committee has decided that it ought now to put the UK firm of Price Waterhouse
formally under enquiry, and this letter is to give you notice to that effect in
accordance with reg. 9(a).

Your firm has already received a copy of the certificate and reference dated   B
19 March 1992. As required by reg. 9(a) I enclose a further copy herewith. The
principal areas of concern into which the committee believes it should enquire
are:

  (i) Whether the extent of the pervasive fraud within BCCI should have been
     detected earlier by your firm's audit work;

  (ii) Whether, in the light of the evidence of fraud which had already come to   C
     light by 30 April 1990 and the declared doubts which your firm had at that
     date concerning the authenticity and value of material assets stated in the
     balance sheet of BCCI at 31 December 1989, the form of your firm's audit
     report was adequate, notwithstanding the undertakings of support received
     from the principal shareholder;

  (iii) Whether assisting the management of BCCI with restructuring its operations,
     as well as advising the majority shareholder, adversely affected or was   D
     compatible with your firm's role as auditors.

As you will appreciate, it is quite possible that in the course of its work the
committee will decide to investigate other aspects of the affair. The above should
only be taken as giving an indication of its present principal areas of concern.

As mentioned above, the committee has received information and documents
from the Bank of England which it has taken into account in deciding to write this   E
letter. Copies of the documents which the committee has resolved to make
evidence in accordance with para. 1 of the scheme are being sent to you today by
the investigating accountants, as required by reg. 9(b).

I assume that all ex-employees and partners of Price Waterhouse who were
concerned with BCCI (e.g. Mr Cowan) will be apprised by your firm of the terms
of this letter and that there is no conflict of interest which would require me to   F
write to them individually. If that is not the case I should be grateful if you would
inform me by 21 December 1992.

The committee is anxious that its investigating accountants should pursue their
work with vigour immediately after the Christmas break. To that end Mr Hall
will, as envisaged in your exchange of correspondence with him, contact you in
the near future to arrange a meeting to discuss how progress can best be made, so   G
that you can respond to the initial list of questions from the investigating
accountants."

    The decisions embodied in this letter first, to place the applicants under enquiry and
second, to proceed with that enquiry, are now impugned by the applicants. The
members of the committee of inquiry are the thirteenth to fifteenth named respondents.

The new scheme   H

    On 21 January 1993 the Privy Council approved with effect from that date a new joint
disciplinary scheme. The new scheme provides for an executive committee as hitherto
but provides for the appointment of an executive counsel. His function is to investigate
references made to the executive committee with a view to ascertaining whether they
are fit for further enquiry. If so, they are referred to a joint disciplinary tribunal.

A   Proceedings before the tribunal are of an adversarial nature with rights of cross-examination. There is provision in the new scheme (para. 3) whereby enquiries in place on 21 January 1993 shall continue in accord with the old scheme. But if a member firm under enquiry and the executive counsel agree to a transfer then the enquiry can take place under the new scheme. The applicants perceived important advantages to themselves in the adversarial procedure and accordingly made an application to the newly appointed executive counsel (Mr Michael Chance) for his agreement to proceed
B   under the new scheme. On 17 June 1993 Mr Chance refused to agree. He wrote as follows:

> "I do not consent to the enquiry being taken over by me under para. 3 of the revised scheme. I would not wish to take over the work of a committee of inquiry which was appointed some time ago and which has already set about its task unless that appeared to me to be justified. No reasons are given in your letter why I
C   should agree to the proposed change of procedure. Having considered all the circumstances, however, I am not persuaded that my assumption of the enquiry is required for it to be fairly conducted and for it to reach proper conclusions on the basis of relevant material.

> I have borne in mind Sir John Bailey's indication that any requests in relation to the procedures which might apply at the committee's hearings will be considered
D   sympathetically. I have also had regard to the risk that material obtained from the Bank of England might not be available to me after the repeal of sec. 85(1)(g) of the *Banking Act* 1987.

> In all the circumstances, I am not willing to take over an enquiry for which a committee of inquiry was appointed over a year ago and which seems well equipped to discharge the task on which it has already embarked."

E   By an amendment to their application which was allowed without opposition at the start of the hearing, the applicants impugn the decision not to agree to a transfer. Mr Chance is the sixteenth named respondent.

The joint monitoring unit

The joint monitoring unit is an agent of the English and Welsh and Scottish institutes which investigates the competence of audit firms to be granted or retain registration
F   under the 1989 Act. The unit selects auditors for monitoring at random. In May 1992 the unit proposed to visit the applicants. Hitherto the practice department of the English and Welsh institute had written to the applicants requesting information about their "audit and quality control procedures" in particular in respect of regulated clients such as banks. The response to that request and the routine monitoring exercise seem to have been considered together by the unit. The investigation has now been completed and
G   the present position is that its final report has been sent to the applicants for their comment. The contents of the report are unknown to the court but we were informed that at the conclusion of the unit's examination the applicants were told that their quality assurance procedures were of the highest order. The respondents point out that it was no part of the unit's function to investigate the audits of the BCCI companies.

The arguments

H   The essential thrust of the applicants' case was directed not against the decision to put them under enquiry (unpalatable as that decision may be) but was against the decision to proceed with the enquiry before the determination of at least the trial stage of the various pieces of litigation which are extant or pending. The argument was that the decision to proceed was not a "proper" one in that it was productive of unfairness. If the applicants' argument is accepted by the court then the work of the committee of inquiry

will be postponed as will have appeared for many years. The respondents refute   A
impropriety and unfairness and point out that to accede to the applicants' arguments
would effectively abdicate the institute's function as the principal regulator of auditors
and would fail to deal with public concern at the audit of BCCI.

The decision to proceed with the enquiry is a decision not to adjourn. Such a decision
by a body such as is the committee of inquiry, is not to be judged by reference to the
Wednesbury principle of irrationality but by whether or not it is productive of a real risk   B
of prejudice or injustice. This appears from *R v Panel on Takeovers and Mergers, ex
parte Guinness plc* (1988) 4 BCC 714 and *R v Panel on Takeovers and Mergers, ex parte
Fayed* [1992] BCC 524. In the latter case the applicants sought leave to move for judicial
review of decisions of the Takeover Panel not to adjourn disciplinary proceedings
brought against the applicants pending the outcome of civil proceedings commenced by
a third party. The applicants argued that there was a substantial overlap between the   C
disciplinary proceedings and the action and that there was a risk of prejudice to the
conduct and trial of the action unless the disciplinary proceedings were stayed. The
application for leave was dismissed by the Court of Appeal. *Neill* LJ said at p. 531E:

> "It is clear that the court has power to intervene to prevent injustice where the
> continuation of one set of proceedings may prejudice the fairness of the trial of
> other proceedings. The existence of this power has been recognised in a number
> of cases including *Jefferson Ltd v Bhetcha* [1979] 1 WLR 898; *R v British*   D
> *Broadcasting Corporation, ex parte Lavelle* [1983] ICR 99; and more recently in
> the unreported decision in *R v Solicitors Disciplinary Tribunal, ex parte Gallagher*
> (30 September 1991). But it is a power which has to be exercised with great care
> and only where there is a real risk of serious prejudice which may lead to injustice.
> Thus there may be cases where the publicity given to the result of a disciplinary
> hearing might have a possible influence on a jury in a criminal trial which was   E
> about to start. In other cases publicity given to the evidence in one set of
> proceedings might lead to the fabrication of evidence in later proceedings; this
> was a fear which *Megaw* LJ had in mind in *Jefferson* at p. 905F.

> In the present case, however, the trial of the 1987 action will not take place until
> 1994 and it will be before a judge alone. There is no evidence whatever that
> witnesses would be interfered with. I have considered Mr Oliver's submissions on   F
> this aspect of the matter with care, but I can see no arguable case that there is any
> real risk to the conduct of the 1987 action or to the fairness of the trial of this
> action."

It is to be observed that in that case the applicants relied upon a passage in previous
statements by the Panel that it would "usually delay the commencement of its own
investigation until the outcome of litigation is known". In the present case Mr David   G
Oliver QC, appearing on behalf of the applicants, drew our attention to the investigation
committee's handbook which at para. 14.02 states "disciplinary proceedings *must* be
deferred if they are likely to interfere with the course of justice". Paragraph 14.07
provides by way of contrast:

> "Even where there is a case for adjournment under the preceding paragraph the
> investigation committee will press ahead with disciplinary proceedings where to   H
> fail to do so would be inconsistent or would appear to be inconsistent with its
> duties as a regulator or as a professional body, for example where the institute is
> the prime regulator of the conduct in question."

Mr Robert Carnwath QC on behalf of the respondents emphasised that it was the
view of the regulating body that this was a case such as was envisaged by para. 14.07.

A   Mr Oliver submitted that the harm which would be inflicted upon the applicants by proceeding with the enquiry now would be disproportionate to any end achieved by so proceeding. Particularly would this be so in the light of the joint monitoring unit's monitoring report. I do not consider this particular point to be of any weight because the unit is concerned with present standards whereas the disciplinary proceedings are in respect of a past performance. Contentment with present standards is one thing, anxiety about past performance is another.

B

Mr Oliver advanced a number of arguments as to harm. I shall deal with them separately.

(1)   Confidentiality. The applicants are concerned that they will not be able to defend themselves before the committee of inquiry unless they are enabled to break confidence. The applicants are in possession of a large number of documents some of which emanated from BCCI companies and some from customers of those companies. Documents originating with a BCCI company were doubtless supplied to the applicants subject to an implied term that the applicants could disclose them in disciplinary proceedings brought against them by their professional body. However, documents originating from BCCI customers were as between those customers and BCCI subject to an implication of confidence (see *Tournier v National Provincial and Union Bank of England* [1924] 1 KB 461 at pp. 473, 480 and 486). The applicants as recipients with notice of the confidentiality of the documents would be bound by the confidence. Mr Oliver submitted that the applicants would need orders of the court before the confidence could be broken and the documents disclosed to the committee of Inquiry. He referred us to *Price Waterhouse v BCCI Holdings (Luxembourg) SA* [1992] BCLC 583 where *Millett* J with some hesitation allowed an application to breach confidentiality for the purpose of production to Lord Justice Bingham's inquiry. Such applications he said might have to be numerous and would inevitably be expensive. Mr Carnwath recognised that there was a problem but suggested it had been exaggerated and was capable of being addressed from time to time as it arose. He mentioned the possibility of production under a subpoena issued under the Rules of the Supreme Court, O. 38, r. 14 (cp *Currie v Chief Constable of Surrey* [1982] 1 WLR 215), and the possibility of a confidence being overborne by the joint disciplinary scheme's provisions as to the production of documents underpinned as they are by statute (cp *Parry-Jones v Law Society* [1969] 1 Ch 1).

In my judgment Mr Oliver's perception of difficulty is one applicable to any auditor whose conduct is under investigation. The difficulty is an obvious one and will be apparent to the committee of inquiry. I do not see this inevitable difficulty as a ground for staying the enquiry until such time as the documents will have been produced in the various pieces of litigation. Production will destroy the constraint of confidence, but this uncertain future event is no ground for not proceeding now.

(2)   Production of material to the enquiry could constitute early disclosure of documents in the litigation. I am prepared to assume that this may be the case but I cannot see that there is a real risk of injustice to the applicants resulting from earlier revelation.

(3)   The result of the enquiry could prejudice the trial process. Mr Oliver did not suggest that a trial by judge alone could be affected by this consideration but submitted that an adverse conclusion could affect the deliberations of a jury. There is no prospect of a jury trial in England and there is not pending any such trial in the US. I do not regard the possibility of a jury trial in California or

A

(perhaps) Texas as being sufficient to found a present assertion of a real risk of injustice.

(4)   That the enquiry will generate documents which would be disclosable in subsequent litigation to the prejudice of the applicants. Some of those documents would possess legal professional privilege and would not give rise to difficulty. However, documents passing between the applicants and the committee of inquiry would not attract privilege. Sir John Bailey is conscious of this difficulty and has stated that the committee would claim public interest immunity in respect of such documents.

B

The outcome of a claim in this or any other jurisdiction cannot of course be anticipated, but in the light of the chairman's statement I do not at present see a real risk of injustice under this head.

(5)   The issues in the various pieces of litigation and those before the committee of inquiry are substantially the same. Unfairness can arise where two tribunals are contemporaneously considering the same issue and the occurrence of such unfairness can be restrained (see *Conteh v Onslow-Fane* (The Times, 26 June 1975) and *Thames Launches Ltd v Trinity House Corporation* [1961] Ch 197). Mr Oliver submitted that there was identity of issue in that the issue in both sets of proceedings was as to the competence of the audits. I accept that there is an overlap between the litigation and the issues before the committee, but the proceedings are essentially different in nature. The litigation is to determine what if any civil liability lies upon the applicants. The enquiry is an aspect of statutory supervision of the applicants which is undertaken in the public interest. That there is contemporaneity in process does not in my judgment give rise to a real risk of injustice to the applicants in either the litigation or in the enquiry procedure. While the data may in part be common to both proceedings, the purpose for which and the standard to which they will be appraised are quite different.

C

D

E

(6)   The strain upon the resources of the applicants which would be imposed by the enquiry. The applicants are a very large firm but plainly the litigation imposes a strain upon their resources which would be exacerbated by the enquiry. I am not impressed by monetary costs nor am I impressed by the diversion of human resources from other and perhaps more profitable activities. A large firm engaging in large enterprises must be prepared to accept the burdens which can arise from the enterprise. That said, I recognise that six people (one of whom is no longer employed by the applicants and is now working in Hong Kong) are bearing and will bear the principal burden in that they are the ones who were concerned with the BCCI audits. The strain upon them already has been great for apart from the litigation they have been concerned with the Bingham inquiry and with the investigation by the Trade and Industry Committee of the House of Commons. That an enquiry will be demanding upon the six individuals I do not doubt, but it has not been demonstrated that those demands give rise to a real risk of injustice.

F

G

I have discussed Mr Oliver's six heads separately if only because they cannot all be discussed at once. Mr Oliver submitted that it was the amalgam of heads rather than any individual one which was important. However, as I have concluded that none of the heads gives rise to a real risk of injustice an amalgam of the heads cannot produce a favourable result for the applicants.

H

In summary I find no real risk of injustice which would entitle this court to intervene so as to prevent the performance in the public interest of an important investigative procedure which is part of a supervisory function underpinned by statute. The more especially as the procedure is to be performed in regard to a uniquely spectacular and serious banking failure.

A   I turn to the challenge to the executive counsel's decision of 17 June 1993. A decision whether or not to consent to the transfer of an enquiry to the new scheme is a discretionary decision which is reviewable upon ordinary public law grounds. Mr Oliver submitted that the decision of 12 June 1993 was flawed because it had been based upon a misconstruction of sec. 82 of the *Banking Act* 1987. The relevance of the section is that on 20 November 1992 the committee of inquiry received from the Bank of England certain confidential documents which were released by the bank under sec. 85(1)(g) of the Act. That provision allowed the disclosure of information,

> "with a view to the institution of, or otherwise for the purposes of, any disciplinary proceedings relating to the exercise of his professional duties by an auditor . . ."

That provision was repealed as from 31 December 1992 (see *Banking Coordination (Second Council Directive) Regulations* 1992 (SI 1992/3218), reg. 40(1)). Had the provision not been repealed then there would have been no difficulty in the further transmission of the documents from the committee to the executive counsel. As it is, an ability to disclose depends on whether the original disclosure was to the institute and all its disciplinary organs whatever they from time to time are, or whether it was a disclosure specifically to the committee of inquiry. If the latter, then sec. 82(1) of the Act (which contains a general prohibition on disclosure) would prevent the committee from a further disclosure. The question is a nice one which may require investigation of facts. I find it unnecessary to determine the question (which I would be reluctant to do in the absence of the Bank of England) because all that the executive counsel stated was that there was a "risk" that the documents would not be available to him. That there is a risk is in my judgment undeniable and I cannot fault the executive counsel for having regard to it. Neither can I fault him for having regard to Sir John Bailey's indication that procedural requests would be considered sympathetically. Nor can I fault him for having regard to the volume of work which the committee of inquiry has already undertaken. The applicants point out that Sir John's sympathy is not as helpful as the procedure in the new scheme and that the volume of work already done is unquantified. However, there are no prescribed considerations and the matters to which Mr Chance had regard are not irrelevant to a decision upon transfer. It was for the executive counsel to attach the weight to them which he thought appropriate. It was for him to balance Sir John's sympathy against the virtues of the new scheme (with which it is reasonable to assume Mr Chance is familiar) and it was for him to assess the volume of work which had been done. I should add that upon the material before him and to which he had regard the executive counsel's decision does not come within measurable distance of being irrational. For what it is worth, my opinion is that the decision was eminently sensible in the circumstances.

Conclusion

This application for judicial review is refused.

Sedley J: I agree.

(Order accordingly)

Re Mixhurst Ltd.

A

Chancery Division (Companies Court).
Evans-Lombe J.
Judgment delivered 27 July 1993.

> *Power of court to declare dissolution of company void — Whether court could
> order that period between dissolution and restoration should not count for
> limitation purposes — Companies Act 1985, sec. 651.*

B

This was an application under sec. 651 of the Companies Act 1985 for an order
declaring the dissolution of a company void.

The applicants had issued proceedings against the company, amongst others, in July
and September 1992, but thereafter discovered that the company had been dissolved in
June 1992 (following a members' voluntary winding up which commenced in April 1990).

C

The applicants sought a further order that the period between the dissolution of the
company and the date of the order declaring the dissolution void should not count for the
purpose of any enactment as to the time within which proceedings against the company
must be brought (a "limitation override order").

Held, declaring the dissolution of the company to have been void:

1. There was no difficulty in making the declaration sought in the first part of the
application. The application was made within the necessary two-year period by a potential
creditor whose claim to be a creditor, on the material placed before the court, was
certainly more than a shadowy claim. (Re Wood and Martin (Bricklaying Contractors)
Ltd [1971] 1 WLR 293 applied.)

D

2. There was no jurisdiction under sec. 651(1) and (2) to make a limitation override
order. (Morris v Harris [1927] AC 252 applied.)

3. Section 651(6) conferred a power to make such an order in the limited circumstances
contemplated by subsec. (5). (Re Workvale Ltd [1992] BCC 349 applied.)

E

The following cases were referred to in the judgment:

General Rolling Stock Co, Re (1872) LR 7 Ch App 646.
Kenyon (Donald) Ltd, Re [1956] 1 WLR 1397.
Morris v Harris [1927] AC 252.
Vickers & Bott Ltd, Re [1968] 2 All ER 264.
Wood and Martin (Bricklaying Contractors) Ltd, Re [1971] 1 WLR 293.
Workvale Ltd, Re [1992] BCC 349; [1992] 1 WLR 416.

F

Nigel Davis QC and Nicholas Clifford (instructed by Cameron Markby Hewitt) for
the applicants.

Charles Falconer QC and Guy Philipps (instructed by Lawford & Co, Richmond,
Surrey) for certain contributories and insurers.

G

JUDGMENT

Evans-Lombe J: This is an application under sec. 651 of the *Companies Act* 1985 to
declare void the dissolution of a company under that section. It concerns a company,
Mixhurst Ltd, whose name was at all material times New Bridge Street Consultants Ltd
("the company").

H

On 12 September 1984 the company was incorporated. On 31 October 1984 it changed
its name to New Bridge Street Consultants Ltd. Its business was the giving of advice in
such things as share issues and pension schemes. At about the time of its change of name
the whole of its share capital became owned by the well-known firm of solicitors,
Clifford Turner. On 1 May 1987 those shares were transferred to the amalgamated firm

A   of Clifford Chance. On 28 April 1989, the company sold its assets to a sub-partnership of that firm, trading under the name of New Bridge Street Consultants. That partnership was offering the same services as the company had previously offered to the public. It was a feature of the contract of transfer of the assets that the liability in respect of pre-purchase matters was to remain with the company.

B   On 25 October 1989 the company changed its name to its present name, that is Mixhurst Ltd. On 5 April 1990 the members of the company resolved to place it in members' voluntary liquidation. That winding up was concluded on 5 March 1992 when the final meeting was held. Thereafter the registrar struck the name of the company off the register and it became dissolved on 5 June 1992.

Meanwhile, in 1986 negotiations had commenced for the takeover from British Airways of its helicopter subsidiary, British Airways Helicopters Ltd by the Maxwell group. The ultimate purchaser from the Maxwell group was a company called SDR

C   Helicopters plc. British Airways Helicopters had at this time approximately 500 employees including a number of pilots. The purchase by SDR Helicopters, it is common ground, would not have gone ahead if unions representing the workforce of British Airways Helicopters ("BAH") had not indicated their consent. It was those unions' concern that the BAH employees should, when they assumed employment from the purchaser, be in at least as good a position so far as their pensions were concerned as they had been when they were members of the British Airways pension scheme. The unions, accordingly,

D   played a substantial part in the negotiations and in that they took advice from Lovell White & King, the well-known firm of solicitors, from pension specialists, William Mercer Fraser Ltd and from the company.

On 23 September 1986 an agreement was entered into between British Airways and SDR Helicopters for the purchase of the BAH subsidiary. That agreement appears as part of an exhibit to an affidavit of Mr Hyman Wolanski. Clause 3(5) of the agreement

E   provides that:

> "The purchaser will use his best endeavours to procure that the purchaser's scheme will provide for and in respect of each transferring employee benefits in respect of his contributory service in the vendor's scheme before the pension transfer date on the basis set out in annexure 1 to this schedule, subject to the necessary consents being obtained from the Superannuation Funds Office and the

F   Occupational Pensions Board and that the purchaser's scheme shall assume the liabilities of the vendor's scheme under the *Social Security Pensions Act* 1975 in respect of the contracted out service of each and every transferring employee."

The schedule appears as a schedule to the agreement under the heading "Benefits to be provided on transfer to Mirror Group Pension Scheme". And at para. 3 under the heading "Warranty" at subpara. 3.2:

G   > "MGM agree that on any subsequent sale of BAHL"— that is the helicopter subsidiary — "that a transfer value will be offered to any purchaser calculated as an actuarial reserve based on the MGMS actuarial assumption including an allowance for future salary increases."

In the wake of the Maxwell crash, as is notorious, a number of deficiencies have been found in the Maxwell group pension fund. Accordingly, the plaintiffs in these proceedings are claiming against MGM for performance of the undertakings as to pensions contained

H   in the agreement of 1986. If such a claim should fail, however, they wish to pursue the present proceedings against Lovell White & King, William Mercer Fraser and the company for breach of duty and negligence arising from the advice given to the plaintiffs through their unions and before the September agreement was entered into.

Because any damage that could possibly have arisen as a result of any such negligence and breach of duty must have accrued at the time the agreement was entered into, it

A

accordingly became important, in order that limitation should not stand in the way of recovery, that the plaintiffs issued their proceedings before the end of September 1992. Accordingly writs were issued on 8 July, 10, 18 and 20 September 1992, inter alia against the company. All those proceedings together with proceedings against MGM were served on 3 November. It was thereafter discovered that the proceedings against the company must have at all material times been a nullity because during that time the company had been dissolved.

B

Thus, this application was made on 8 March 1993. Section 651, as amended by the *Companies Act* 1989, provides as follows:

> "(1) Where a company has been dissolved, the court may, on an application made for the purpose by the liquidator of the company or by any other person appearing to the court to be interested, make an order, on such terms as the court thinks fit, declaring the dissolution to have been void.

C

> (2) Thereupon such proceedings may be taken as might have been taken if the company had not been dissolved.
>
> . . .
>
> (4) Subject to the following provisions, an application under this section may not be made after the end of the period of two years from the date of the dissolution of the company.

D

> (5) An application for the purpose of bringing proceedings against the company—
>
>   (a) for damages in respect of personal injuries . . ."

There then follows a reference to certain statutes:

> "(b) for damages under the Fatal Accidents Act . . .
>
> may be made at any time; but no order shall be made on such an application if it appears to the court that the proceedings would fail by virtue of any enactment as to the time within which proceedings must be brought.

E

> (6) Nothing in subsection (5) affects the power of the court on making an order under this section to direct that the period between the dissolution of the company and the making of the order shall not count for the purposes of any such enactment."

The provisions of subsec. (7) are not material.

F

Mr Falconer appeared for certain parties: first, the contributories of the companies, nominees of the firm of Clifford Chance; and secondly, certain insurers of the company, not in fact to oppose the granting of relief under sec. 651 but to make certain comments which might guide the court in the exercise of its powers under that section. In actual fact he did advance, helpfully, comments on the extent of the jurisdiction that arises under that section. Those for whom he appears had not been made parties to the application. They had originally intended to oppose the application root and branch but their attitude was put forward as being one of neutrality at this stage.

G

I have no difficulty in making the declaration sought in the first part of the application. The application was made within the necessary two-year period by a potential creditor whose claim to be a creditor, in my judgment on the material placed before me, was certainly more than a shadowy claim. See the criteria established in *Re Wood and Martin* [1971] 1 WLR 293 at p. 297 in the judgment of *Megarry* J.

H

I then pass on to consider the second part of the order sought. By that an order is sought that:

> "the period between the dissolution of the above named company and the date of the order declaring the dissolution void shall not count for the purpose of any

A   enactment as to time in which proceedings against the above company must be brought."

In the course of argument such an order was referred to as a limitation override order and for the sake of brevity I will refer to it as such in this judgment, although of course there is no power to override the provisions of the Limitation Act.

B   This order is sought, it would seem, very much out of an abundance of caution. It is well established that on a dissolution being declared void, the company is restored to the state that it was in immediately prior to the dissolution becoming effective. In the case of the company therefore, this company would be restored to its state of being in the process of the liquidation shortly before it was dissolved. It is also well established, inter alia, by the decision in *Re General Rolling Stock Company* (1872) LR 7 Ch App 646, a decision of the Court of Appeal concerning a compulsory winding up, that periods of limitation cease to run once a winding up has commenced and the rights of those
C   claiming in the liquidation therefore crystallise at the commencement of the winding up. It is also well established by authority that the same principles apply to voluntary windings up. Therefore in this case any relevant period of limitation ceased to run on 5 April 1990 when the resolution to wind up this company was passed.

It follows that when by order the first part of the application takes effect and when a new liquidator is appointed he will prima facie be able to take proceedings such as are
D   contemplated in the amended statement of claim which I have been shown, free from any bar arising from limitation. Nonetheless it was submitted to me by Mr Davis that there remained a residual chance that what I have described as a well-established principle as to the application of periods of limitation in the winding up of companies, may be challenged and possibly challenged successfully, and it was accordingly against that background that he sought the order sought in the second part of the motion.

E   The provisions of sec. 651 are to be read in contrast with the provisions of sec. 653. That section reads as follows:

"(1) The following applies if a company or any member or creditor of it feels aggrieved by the company having been struck off the register.

(2) The court, on an application by the company or the member or creditor made before the expiration of 20 years from publication in the Gazette of notice under
F   section 652, may, if satisfied that the company was at the time of the striking off carrying on business or in operation, or otherwise that it is just that the company be restored to the register, order the company's name to be restored.

(3) On an office copy of the order being delivered to the registrar of companies for registration the company is deemed to have continued in existence as if its name had not been struck off; and the court may by the order give such directions and make such provisions as seem just for placing the company and all other
G   persons in the same position (as nearly as may be) as if the company's name had not been struck off."

Accordingly, by subsec. (3) the legislature has conferred on the court an express power to restore the position as near as may be to that which pre-existed the striking of the name off the register of companies. That power was first applied with relation to limitation periods and a limitation override order was first made in the case of *Re Donald*
H   *Kenyon Ltd* [1956] 1 WLR 1397. I will simply read the headnote by way of illustration:

"A petition for the restoration to the register, of a company which had not traded since 1940 and had been struck off in 1949 pursuant to section 353(6) of the Companies Act, 1948, and for its subsequent winding-up contained a statement: 'It is apprehended that all the debts of the company at the time of its dissolution have since become statute barred':—

A

Held, that there should be inserted in the order for restoration to the register a proviso that in the case of creditors who were not statute barred at the date of the dissolution, the period between that date and the restoration of the company to the register should not be counted for the purposes of any Statute of Limitations."

As I have said, there is no equivalent provision in sec. 651 and I was told that there has been no reported case in which that section, sec. 651, has been construed as conferring on the court a power to make a limitation override order. It was submitted to me that none the less there was such a power contained in the section for the following four reasons.

B

First, there was no reason in principle why if a power to make such an order existed under the provisions of sec. 653 there should be no power to make a similar order under sec. 651.

Secondly, that was so in particular because the words of subsec. (1) of sec. 651 were drawn in very broad terms and in particular the words that the court can make an order or make a declaration "on such terms as the court thinks fit".

C

Thirdly, it was submitted that the existence of such a power was consistent with the words used in subsec. (2) of the section where it says:

"Thereupon such proceedings may be taken as might have been taken if the company had not been dissolved."

D

—proceedings which would otherwise have been statute-barred.

Fourthly, it was submitted that the existence of such a power was clearly assumed by the provisions of subsec. (6) of sec. 651 which seems to be drawn on the assumption that there is a general power in the court under the section to make orders including such orders as were made in the *Donald Kenyon* case. It must be observed, however, that the provisions of subsec. (6) were added by amendment by the *Companies Act* 1989 and cannot be treated as expressing the intentions of the legislature when they re-enacted the earlier provisions of the section from previous company legislation.

E

My attention was drawn to the decision of the House of Lords in *Morris v Harris* [1927] AC 252. The House of Lords was here dealing with the case of an arbitration, the material parts of which had taken place after one of the parties to the arbitration, a company, had become dissolved. The application was made to declare that dissolution void under the provisions of sec. 223 of the *Companies (Consolidation) Act* 1908. That section is set out in the report of the case at p. 252 and it provided as follows:

F

"Where a company has been dissolved the Court may at any time within two years of the date of the dissolution, on an application being made for the purpose by the liquidator of the company or by any other person who appears to the Court to be interested, make an order, upon such terms as the Court thinks fit, declaring the dissolution to have been void, and thereupon such proceedings may be taken as might have been taken if the company had not been dissolved."

G

It will be seen, therefore, that the relevant section under which the House of Lords was proceeding repeats in precise terms the words of subsec. (1) and (2) of the *Companies Act* 1985, sec. 651. I turn to the speech of Lord *Sumner* in the case at p. 257, the top of the page, where he says:

H

"The next question turns on the language and effect of s. 223 of the Companies (Consolidation) Act, 1908. It deals with the case of a company which has been dissolved, and that at an ascertained or ascertainable date. It provides for an order, which it empowers a Court to make in all such cases, on such terms as the Court may think fit (and therefore also without terms, if the Court so thinks fit) 'declaring the dissolution to have been void.' Pausing here, I remark that the order is not expressed to be one setting anything aside or declaring that the dissolution is to be deemed not to have taken place and thus reversing the actual language of s. 195, or declaring the dissolution to be void. Nor, again, is the phraseology of s. 242 followed, whereby, when the registrar has reasonable cause to believe certain things and has taken certain action, ending in the erasure of the company's name from the register and a publication of the fact in the Gazette, the company thereupon 'shall be dissolved.' Under this section, when the Court intervenes by order to modify this result, 'the company shall be deemed to have continued in existence, as if its name had not been struck off,' and then the Court can give directions to replace the company and all parties affected in an 'as you were' position. The words 'to have been void,' in s. 223, appear, it is true, so far as they go, to have some retrospective effect, and tend to some extent to support the respondent's argument. On the other hand, the remaining words, which define the order, point rather to a declaration removing a bar to such action as might otherwise have been taken, than to one validating past proceedings, taken since the dissolution through ignorance or disregard of it and consequently invalid. The remaining words, 'and thereupon such proceedings may be taken, as might have been taken if the company had not been dissolved,' seem to me to point conclusively in the same direction. They describe an authority given to the parties concerned to do, 'thereupon' and accordingly thereafter, things which they might have done but obviously had not done theretofore, and, but for the order, could not have done after the dissolution. I think these words do not affect the validity or the contrary of steps taken during that interval. They must still depend on the facts existing and the rights arising before and independently of the order.

It is to be remembered what the scheme of the Act is. The statutory dissolution does not take place till three months have past from the time when the registrar has registered a return, made to him by the liquidator and stating that, having brought the liquidation to an end, he has embodied the results in a final winding-up account, which he has submitted to a general meeting. If the liquidator here had attended to matters himself, instead of 'delegating' them, as he calls it, to the directors of the new company, no doubt the winding up would have been complete, as the Act intended it to be, and proper provision of some kind would have been made for Mr. Harris's claim. Accordingly, the last three months of the life of the old company would have been, as they ought to have been under the statute, a period during which the company, stripped of its property and discharged from its debts, would have simply awaited dissolution. In case, however, of accidents there is a provision in s. 194, sub-s. 4, that the Court may make an order deferring the date at which the dissolution is to take effect.

My Lords, I think it follows that only in the rarest cases and always contrary to the contemplation of the Act is it possible for proceedings to have continued in fact during these three months when the company is moribund, and further that after dissolution, which is an event calculable by anybody from a date, of which public notice has been given, whatever is done is done at the actor's peril. The Legislature would never have bestowed on the Court a power to declare the dissolution void, without imposing terms, as by the section it certainly is empowered to do, if the effect of this order of avoidance might be to undo the reversion of freeholds to an original grantor or the acceleration of a reversioner's immediate title to leaseholds in the case of lands accidentally undisposed of in the winding up . . ."

Authorities are then cited:

". . . yet such would be the effect of the construction contended for, with a consequent avoidance of all dispositions made by such grantor or reversioner in favour of third parties, wholly innocent of any irregularity. This must be the result, if the judge's order simply puts back the clock and restores things, as though the dissolution had never been. Accordingly, I see no reason why the Legislature should be deemed to have had in its contemplation any intermediate proceedings. They must in any case be so rare and exceptional, that they might well either be passed over unconsidered or, if considered, be left by the Act to the ordinary operation of the law. The object of the provision was, I think, to give a fresh start to proceedings, which owing to the dissolution had been impossible and had not been taken, and thereupon it was to be open to those concerned to take them in the future as if the dissolution had not happened. In my opinion most of the proceedings in the arbitration in this case, and, above all, the award itself, are null, for they were taken and made against a company which did not exist, and no subsequent validity has been or could be given to them. The respondent must therefore prove his claim afresh in proceedings, to which the appellant will be a party."

In Lord *Blanesburgh*'s speech at p. 267, the following passage appears:

"First of all, a company treated as defunct by the registrar in the circumstance stated in s. 242, may by him be struck off"— and section 242 I point out is the equivalent of section 653 — " 'and the company will be dissolved.' It must be noted that in this case the dissolution takes place without any previous winding up and may be effected without any one interested in the company in fact being aware of it. Sub-s. 6 of s. 242 accordingly provides: 'If a company or any member or creditor thereof feels aggrieved by the company having been struck off the register, the Court on the application of the company or member or creditor may, if satisfied that the company was at the time of the striking off carrying on business or in operation, or otherwise that it is just that the company be restored to the register, order the name of the company to be restored to the register, *and thereupon the company shall be deemed to have continued in existence as if its name had not been struck off; and the Court may by the order give such directions and make such provisions as seem just for placing the company and all other persons in the same position as nearly as may be as if the name of the company had not been struck off.'*

My Lords, this section first appeared in company legislation in s. 26 of the Companies Act, 1900. It was before the Legislature when s. 223 was first enacted in 1907. It will appear in a moment how significant is the fact that the provisions of s. 242, sub-s. 6, which I have italicized, are not repeated in s. 223.

That section is concerned with a dissolution of a company following a winding up by the Court or one following a voluntary winding up the second and third of the events which may precede a dissolution. Sect. 172 regulates dissolution complementary to a compulsory liquidation. When the affairs of the company have been completely wound up the Court is to make an order that the company be dissolved from the date of the order, 'and the company shall be dissolved accordingly.' Sect. 195 regulates dissolution succeeding a voluntary winding up. The liquidator, as soon as the affairs of the company are fully wound up, convenes by advertisement a final meeting of the company and lays before it an account of the winding up. Within a week after the meeting the liquidator must make a return to the registrar of the holding of the meeting and its date; on receipt the registrar must forthwith register the return, and on the expiration of three months from that registration 'the company shall be deemed to be dissolved.' Sect. 223, which, as I have already indicated, did not appear in company legislation until the Act of 1907, applies equally but exclusively to a company which has been 'dissolved

A accordingly' under s. 172, and to a company which has been 'deemed to be dissolved' under s. 195, and an order under that section may be made at any time 'within two years of the date of the dissolution.'

In these circumstances, I cannot myself doubt that both the words of s. 223 empowering the Court to make an order 'declaring the dissolution to have been void,' and the following words expository of the result, 'and thereupon such proceedings may be taken as might have been taken if the company had not been

B dissolved,' were in each case designedly chosen to produce the precise result which my noble and learned friend has attributed to them. It is true that a declaratory order under the section unqualified in terms does, and it was in my judgment essential, if many difficulties which readily occur to the mind were to be avoided, that such an order should have the effect of restoring to the revived company its corporate existence as from the very moment of the dissolution thereby declared

C 'to have been void.' But the expository words which follow carefully and, as I think, advisedly refrain from adding that such an order is to have the effect of restoring to the company from the same moment, not its corporate existence only, but its corporate activity also. On the contrary, those expository words import, as I think, that it is only after the order has been made — it is 'thereupon' but not before — that any active consequences are to ensue.

D I think, my Lords, that the terms on which these consequences are described are exhaustive and emphatic. They are intended to show that an order under the section made, it may be, as long as two years after a dissolution which up to that moment was completely effective, is not at once and as of course to ratify acts done during the interval, which, if done at all, must necessarily have been acts of mere usurpation, by a liquidator or other pretended agent with no office knowingly done on behalf of a company which had no existence. On consideration, it

E appears, I think, clear that automatically to validate such acts as being the acts of a duly constituted officer on behalf of a duly incorporated company might involve consequences too disastrous to be even envisaged. These are avoided by the terms of the section. The company is restored to life as from the moment of dissolution but, continuing a convenient metaphor, it remains buried, unconscious, asleep and powerless until the order is made which declares the dissolution to have been

F void. Then, and only then, is the company restored to activity.

And now is made apparent the reason for the difference in phraseology and effect between s. 223 and sub-s. 6 of s. 242. A dissolution under s. 242, as I have said, is preceded by no winding up, and the section had to envisage a dissolution which might have taken place without the knowledge of any one concerned in the company. Hence the wide powers given to the Court by sub-s. 6. Sect. 223, on the other hand, is confined to cases where the dissolution succeeds the complete

G winding up of the company's affairs and cannot take effect at all except at the instance or with the knowledge of the liquidator, the company's only executive officer. The Legislature has not seen fit to make provision for validating any intermediate acts done on behalf of such a company so dissolved."

In their speeches the House of Lords in that case seemed to be construing sec. 223 as only bringing back the company for the purpose of proceedings for it or against it but

H commenced after the relevant declaration. The declaration did not validate anything happening during the dissolution. Further, the absence of an equivalent to subsec. (6) of sec. 242 from the provisions of sec. 223 meant that the court had not been given any power ex post facto to validate. I interpret that as meaning that the court had no powers to make orders restoring the status quo ante the dissolution. It seems to me that had the facts of the present case been before Lord *Blanesburgh* in 1926 he plainly would have

refused to make the second part of the order sought. I cannot discern anything in the
differences between the new legislation and the legislation which then existed to lead
me to the conclusion that Lord *Blanesburgh*, had he been looking at the case today,
would have come to a different conclusion. It is, it seems to me, also significant that
subsec. (6) which does appear to assume a power to make limitation override orders
retrospectively was added by amendment in 1989 and cannot be taken to represent the
intention of the legislature in re-enacting subsec. (1) and (2) in 1985. Subsection (6) by
itself cannot be construed as itself conferring a general power to make a limitation
override order. Indeed, that was not contended for. It can be construed, as it was
construed in *Re Workvale Ltd* [1992] BCC 349 by *Scott* LJ, as conferring a power to
make such an order in the limited circumstances contemplated by subsec. (5).

I was also referred to a case of *Re Vickers & Bott Ltd* [1968] 2 All ER 264. This is a
very short report and it is extremely difficult to discern from it what precisely it was with
which *Pennycuick* J was then dealing. It is possible that he was in fact referring to the
absence of any power to make a limitation override order under the then equivalent of
sec. 651, but it seems more probable that he was referring in his interlocutory comments
to the position as to the running of time for the purposes of limitation where companies
have been placed in winding up, to which I have already referred.

I conclude, therefore, reluctantly, that there is no jurisdiction under sec. 651 to make
what I have referred to as a limitation override order. I am slightly less reluctant in that
conclusion because I do not believe that that will have any material impact on the
prosecution of the litigation in this case.

I therefore return to the order which I will make. As I have said, I am satisfied that it
is an appropriate order to make. There is a letter from the Treasury Solicitor not
objecting on behalf of the Crown. There is also in evidence a letter from the liquidator
advancing no objection. Accordingly, I make the declaration declaring the dissolution
of Mixhurst Ltd to be void.

(*Order accordingly*)

A # Re Biddencare Ltd.

Chancery Division (Companies Court).
Mary Arden QC (sitting as a deputy High Court judge).
Judgment delivered 6 April 1993.

> *Liquidation — Directions — Costs — Proprietary claims against assets of company in liquidation — Proprietary claims might extend to all assets of company — Liquidators sought direction for costs of defending claims to be payable out of assets — Whether court should make prospective costs order — Whether liquidators' costs would be payable out of assets after trial if liquidators were unsuccessful.*

This was an application by the joint liquidators of Biddencare Ltd for a direction that their costs of investigating and dealing with certain proprietary claims against assets held by the company should rank as a charge on the company's assets in priority to the proprietary claims (but without prejudice to the ultimate incidence of the costs as between trust and other assets or as between proprietary claimants).

The liquidators' case was that tracing claims might be made against all the assets of the company, which was the parent of an insurance broker. Since they could not assume that any of the funds in the ownership of the company would be available to pay the expenses of the liquidation, they asked the court to make provision for their costs and expenses out of the funds, so as (inter alia) to enable them properly to consider and, if thought fit, defend the proprietary claims which had already been made.

Held, refusing the liquidators' application:

1. The pre-emptive costs order which was sought was unusual and could clearly result in injustice if the other party established a proprietary claim to assets which had been reduced by the payment of the costs of resisting his claim. It was the other creditors in the liquidation, and not the claimant, who should bear the burden of the costs of unsuccessfully defending the claim. There was no countervailing factor of sufficient weight to outweigh these factors. The balancing exercise which the court had to perform produced the clear answer that no pre-emptive order should be made.

2. If that was wrong, the court could not be satisfied that it was likely that an order would be made at trial for the payment of the liquidators' costs out of the assets subject to the proprietary claims, even if the liquidators were unsuccessful, because this was hostile litigation. (Re Westdock Realisations Ltd (1988) 4 BCC 192 applied.)

The following cases were referred to in the judgment:

Beddoe, Re [1893] 1 Ch 547.
Chandler v Church (unreported, Harman J).
Dallaway, Re [1982] 1 WLR 756.
Evans, Re [1986] 1 WLR 101.
Exchange Securities & Commodities Ltd & Ors, Re (No. 2) (1986) 2 BCC 98,932.
National Anti-Vivisection Society v Duddington (The Times, 23 November 1989).
PCW (Underwriting Agencies) Ltd v Dixon & Anor [1983] 2 All ER 158.
Westdock Realisations Ltd & Anor, Re (1988) 4 BCC 192.
Xylas v Khanna (unreported, 2 November 1992, CA).

Gavin Lightman QC and Philip Marshall (instructed by Ince & Co) for the applicant.

Michael Briggs (instructed by Elborne Mitchell) for the respondent.

JUDGMENT

Mary Arden QC: In these proceedings the applicant, Hartford Fire Insurance Co, seeks directions as to whether moneys held in three specified bank accounts are its

property or that of Biddencare Ltd (now in liquidation). The respondents to this
application are the joint liquidators of Biddencare, Mr Ian Bond and Mr Christopher
Hughes. The matter which has been argued before me, however, is merely an application
within those proceedings whereby the joint liquidators seek a direction that:

"... all proper fees and proper charges, costs, disbursements, expenses and
liabilities of and incurred by or on behalf of the joint liquidators in their capacity
as liquidators of Biddencare Ltd, including for the avoidance of doubt such fees,
charges, costs, disbursements, expenses and liabilities incurred in responding to,
investigating and (if thought fit) defending, compromising or complying with
proprietary claims against assets vested in Biddencare Ltd, do rank as a charge on
the assets held by or to the order of or reputedly belonging to or hereafter
recovered for Biddencare Ltd in priority to any proprietary claims but without
prejudice to the ultimate incidence thereof as between trust and other assets or as
between proprietary claimants."

The applicant has been represented by Mr Lightman QC and Mr Marshall. The joint
liquidators have been represented by Mr Briggs. Their application is supported by
evidence contained in two affidavits of Mr Alasdair Campbell Gillies, a partner in
Elborne Mitchell, the joint liquidators' solicitors. In the concluding paragraphs of his
second affidavit, Mr Gillies says:

"5. In my last affidavit, I referred to a concern on the part of the joint liquidators
that, having regard to the nature of Biddencare's activities, other proprietary
claims would probably be made of a type similar to the applicant's claim. I am
informed by the joint liquidators that a number of such claims have now been
made. Some of them have been expressed to be proprietary in nature, and the
facts relied upon in support of others of them suggest that a proprietary basis for
the claim, similar to that put forward by the applicant herein, could equally well
be made, and indeed may be made, in the future. Almost all of the claimants are
insurance companies and Lloyd's syndicates for which Biddencare and its
predecessors are alleged to have received money as agents.

6. Those claims may be summarised as follows . . ."

Then there is a table containing figures which shows that express proprietary claims are
in the amounts of £159,120, US$45,583 and Canadian $26,487; and in a separate column,
Mr Gillies shows the likely proprietary basis for the claim in the sums of £294,730 and
US$4,607,778.

"7. It will be apparent that the totality of the additional claims well exceeds the
funds reputedly the property of Biddencare (ignoring for the moment the
applicant's claim in the funds to which it relates). Furthermore, I am informed by
the joint liquidators and believe that such is the state of confusion and uncertainty
affecting the affairs of Biddencare and connected companies from which
Biddencare appears to have received funds that it is very likely that substantial
additional claims beyond those already received will be made.

8. In the circumstances, the joint liquidators are very concerned that they cannot
with confidence assume that any of the funds presently in the reputed ownership
of Biddencare will be available for the general purposes of its liquidation, including
of course the expenses of the liquidation. In the circumstances, I respectfully
request this court to make suitable provision for the joint liquidators' costs and
expenses out of the funds presently in the reputed ownership of Biddencare, so as
(inter alia) to enable them properly to consider and, if thought fit, defend this
application.

It is apparent that the form of direction now claimed extends beyond the assets in
which the applicant claims to have a proprietary interest and extends beyond solicitor

A   and client costs. It contains no limit in time or amount and confers no power on the court at the trial of this application to disallow any costs.

The applicant's claim in the proceedings is supported by a number of affidavits, including one by Michael MacBeth-Hepworth, an assistant solicitor with the applicant's solicitors. He sets out the background to the application. It appears that in about 1989 Biddencare became, first, a fellow subsidiary and later the parent company of a Lloyd's broker called Dewey Warren & Co Ltd. This company had acted as an intermediary under a reinsurance agreement between a company called Transatlantische Ruckversicherings ("Trans") and its reinsurers.

Biddencare took over the insurance balances of Dewey Warren & Co Ltd after it joined its group. A subsidiary of Biddencare, Derek Bryant Insurance Brokers Ltd, took over Dewey Warren's role under the reinsurance agreement as Dewey Warren had then ceased to be a Lloyd's broker. Biddencare also held the insurance balances of this company.

In 1987 the applicant acquired the rights and liabilities of Trans and the reinsurance agreement to which I have referred. Accordingly, it became entitled to receive sums collected under that reinsurance agreement, which became part of the insurance balances held by Biddencare. It is certain of these funds which the applicant says in the proceedings belong to it.

There are also affidavits sworn on behalf of certain of the reinsurers who state that, when making their payments, they never intended that their payments should form part of the general assets of Biddencare. I have not been concerned with the merits of the applicant's claim. The mere fact that an agent receives money for his principal does not mean that the agent holds that money on trust for his principal. However Mr Briggs accepts that the applicant has an arguable case, and that is the basis on which I have proceeded.

I now turn to the parties' respective submissions on the matter before me. Mr Briggs began by pointing out that it may be the case in this liquidation that tracing claims can be made against all the assets of Biddencare. He submits that this is a special circumstance which takes this case out of the general rule that a liquidator should get a fighting fund from creditors.

Mr Briggs submits that the court has jurisdiction to make the order sought, for three reasons:

(1)   He submits that where there is only a claim that assets belong to an applicant beneficiary, the court will conduct a balancing exercise between the potential injustice to the plaintiff if the court allows the defendant to use what may turn out to be the plaintiff's money against the potential injustice to the defendant if he cannot use his money to conduct the tasks which must necessarily be performed to enable the claim to be properly tested. Mr Briggs submits this principle originates in *PCW (Underwriting Agencies) Ltd v Dixon* [1983] 2 All ER 158. I will call this his "*PCW* argument".

(2)   Mr Briggs submits that the court has jurisdiction to make the order that he seeks under *Re Beddoe* [1893] 1 Ch 547. I will call this his "*Beddoe* argument".

(3)   He submits that, although ordinarily the liquidator must seek a fighting fund from creditors, the court will not require him to do so where special circumstances exist which justify his not approaching creditors. He based this submission on *Re Exchange Securities & Commodities Ltd (No. 2)* (1986) 2 BCC 98,932 and *Re Westdock Realisations Ltd* (1988) 4 BCC 192. I will call this his "*Westdock* argument".

The PCW argument A

In the *PCW* case, *Lloyd* J permitted a Mareva injunction, granted against the defendant, to be varied so that the defendant could pay his solicitors a sum on account of the costs of the action. The critical part of the judge's conclusion is at p. 164E and p. 165B–C:

> "The distinction between the ordinary Mareva plaintiff (to use Ackner LJ's phrase) and the case where the plaintiff is laying claim to a trust fund on the so-called wider ground, is thus clear. In the latter case the whole object is to secure the trust fund itself so that it should be available if the plaintiff should prove his claim. In the former case by contrast the plaintiff is not entitled to any security. The purpose of the jurisdiction, as is now clearly established, is not to provide the plaintiff with any form of pre-trial attachment. It is simply to prevent the injustice of a defendant removing or dissipating his assets so as to cheat the plaintiff of the fruits of his claim.
>
> Can the plaintiffs then bring the case within the wider jurisdiction? I have grave doubts. Both in *A v C* and *Chief Constable of Kent v V* the claim related to specific identifiable bank accounts. It is difficult to regard the whole of a man's assets as a fund in that sense, even though his assets may in part contain or be derived from money improperly come by. But even if I could regard the whole of the defendant's assets as a trust fund, I would be quite unwilling to uphold the ex parte order in the present case on that basis. All injunctions are, of course, in the end discretionary. I would regard it as unjust in the present case if the defendant were compelled to reduce his standard of living, to give up his flat or to take his children away from school, in order to secure what is as yet only a claim by the plaintiffs. I would regard it as even more unjust that he should be prevented from defending himself properly (for that is what it would amount to), merely because the plaintiffs say that in doing so he is using somebody else's money."

At p. 165B–C his Lordship said:

> "In my view justice and convenience require in the present case that the first defendant should be allowed the means of defending himself, even if it could be said that the plaintiffs had laid claim to the whole of his assets as a trust fund. Similarly justice and convenience require that he should be able to pay his ordinary bills and continue to live as he has been accustomed to live heretofore. So whether the case is put on the basis of the Mareva jurisdiction or the so-called wider jurisdiction to trace in equity I reach the same conclusion."

The sum involved in that case was a comparatively minor sum.

In the later, unreported case of *Chandler v Church*, the defendant applied for leave to use some £900,000 of the injuncted assets, of which he was alleged to be a trustee, to pay for his costs of defending the action. The injuncted assets were shares which the plaintiff sought to recover but which would have to be sold if the order sought was made. In reaching his decision, *Harman* J balanced the interests of justice on either side:

> "As it seems to me, I should approach the decision by saying that if the case is evenly balanced, what should be the exercise of my discretion? If I allow the application and the defendant wins, no injustice will in the end be caused. If I allow the application and the plaintiffs win, a very serious injustice will have been caused. The whole trust fund, including £450,000 already spent, will have been paid to the lawyers, leaving nothing for the beneficiaries. If I refuse the application and the defendant wins, either because Mr Church, who is plainly a very able chartered accountant and is thoroughly familiar with the web of companies, most of which he created, and with the complicated dealings, many of which he himself

negotiated, argues the case and gives evidence for himself, which is believed, or because the plaintiffs failed to discharge the heavy onus of proving serious dishonesty against a professional man, no injustice will have been caused. If I refuse the application and the plaintiffs win, the plaintiffs must have successfully discharged a very heavy burden of proof and convinced the trial judge. Although Mr Church will have been handicapped, it seems to me most unlikely that serious injustice will have been caused.

Trying to balance these matters as best I can, I conclude that the court's duty to preserve the possible trust fund overrides the difficulty in which Mr Church will be placed during the trial. I shall refuse to release the injuncted assets for the purpose of paying costs."

In the later, again unreported, case of *Xylas v Khanna* (2 November 1992) the Court of Appeal held that in these circumstances the court is required to carry out a balancing exercise and to reach a decision on the particular facts of the case in the exercise of its discretion.

The Beddoe argument

In support of his *Beddoe* argument, Mr Briggs referred not only to *Re Beddoe* itself but also to *Re Dallaway* [1982] 1 WLR 756. This was a case in which the executor of an estate was given leave to defend proceedings brought against the estate to enforce a contract, alleged to have been made by the testator prior to his death, to dispose of his principal asset in another way. Leave was given, subject to the trial judge ruling that he was not to be entitled to his costs out of the estate, even though the result of this order might well have been that the claimant if successful might find that the property had to be sold to meet the executor's claim to be indemnified as to his costs and even though there were adult beneficiaries who could have conducted the defence.

However, in a later case, *Re Evans* [1986] 1 WLR 101, cited by Mr Lightman QC, in which a claimant also claimed property in the estate in question, to the exclusion of the apparent beneficiaries on the deceased's intestacy, it was made clear by the Court of Appeal that the question whether a personal representative should be indemnified out of the estate for the costs of defending a claim against the estate or for pursuing a claim on its behalf regardless of the outcome, was a matter of discretion, to be exercised on the facts of the case. The court held that *Re Dallaway* was distinguishable on its facts, for a number of reasons, including the reason that there were serious grounds in that case for doubting the prospects of success of the claimant's claim. But the Court of Appeal held that where there are adult beneficiaries it would generally be just that they should bear the costs of defending the claim. In the words of *Nourse* LJ, with whom *Robert Goff* and *O'Connor* L JJ agreed (p. 107D):

"The injustice argument was summarised by Mr. Asprey, for the first plaintiff, in this way. He said that it would be most unjust if his client were to succeed in the action only to find that the farm and the house which ought to have been his must be sold in order to meet the unsuccessful party's costs of the action while, on the other hand, the deceased's other nephews and nieces, who were in truth the losers, would have started by risking nothing and would have ended by losing nothing. It seems that the master, who was very experienced in these matters, regarded that as a powerful argument. I am entirely of the same opinion. In my view, in a case where the beneficiaries are all adult and sui juris and can make up their own minds as to whether the claim should be resisted or not, there must be countervailing considerations of some weight before it is right for the action to be pursued or defended at the cost of the estate. I would not wish to curtail the discretion of the court in any future case but, as already indicated, those

considerations might include the merits of the action. I emphasise that these A
remarks are directed only to cases where all the beneficiaries are adult and sui
juris. The position might be entirely different if, for example, one of the
beneficiaries was under age.

We have not so far considered the evidence as to the merits of the action. It is
possible, although it seems unlikely, that it may be so strongly against the chances
of the plaintiff's success as to satisfy us that the order which was made by the
deputy judge was correct. If it does not go that far, I am of the opinion that his B
order cannot be sustained. I would think that, in adhering so close to the decision
in *In re Dallaway, decd.* . . the judge had misdirected himself, so that this court
could interfere with the exercise of his direction. Although I would fully understand
that it may, as a practical matter, have been difficult for him to distinguish that
decision, I would think that he ought to have done so.''

So analysed, it seems to me that this line of authority supports Mr Lightman's case C
rather than that of Mr Briggs.

The Westdock argument

In *Re Westdock Realisations Ltd* (1988) 4 BCC 192 there were two companies over
whom receivers had been appointed by a bank. The receivers had a substantial surplus
in their hands and wished to know whether they should pay this sum to the liquidators of D
the companies or to the export credit guarantee department who claimed to be subrogated
to the bank's rights against the companies. The liquidators were without a fighting fund.
Indeed, the companies had gone into liquidation some ten years previously and the
liquidators considered it unlikely that any creditor in the liquidation would be interested
in funding litigation against the receivers. The liquidators sought an order that they
should be indemnified as to their costs out of the surplus held by the receiver.

Sir *Nicolas Browne-Wilkinson* V-C, having rejected the argument that there was no E
jurisdiction to make an order for costs out of moneys which at the end of the day are
found to belong to some other person, considered that it would be appropriate to make
such an order in the case before him. At p. 197 he says:

"There being in my judgment jurisdiction to make the orders sought, is this an
appropriate case to make such order? In my judgment this depends on what would
be the appropriate order for costs to be made at the trial. Unless satisfied that F
after trial a judge would be likely to make an order that the costs of all parties are
to come out of the fund it cannot in general be right to make such an order at this
stage. I was initially surprised to discover that there is no general practice in the
Companies Court as to the correct order for costs in cases where receivers or
liquidators have taken out summonses to determine questions arising in the course
of their administration. In some cases the order is made that the costs follow the G
event and the unsuccessful claimant pays, in others the costs come out of the fund.

After hearing the argument I am satisfied that there is no fixed practice relating to
all cases. I am also satisfied that there cannot be any practice applicable as a rule
of thumb to all types of cases. The range of summonses which can be issued and
are heard raise such a wide range of issues that there can be no fixed rule.
However, in my judgment the proper approach is as follows. In general, claims H
arising for determination in such cases are, as Mr Moss submits, hostile claims in
which one or more parties are in dispute as to the ownership of property. It is
litigation between rival claimants. In those circumstances one would expect that
the costs would normally follow the event, the unsuccessful claimant paying not
only his own costs but also the other side's. However, there are many cases in
which it is essential for the due administration of the liquidator's or receiver's

duties to obtain a decision from the court. In such cases there are often large classes of creditors, contributories or other claimants, the exact membership of which class is often not easily established or even known, who will be affected by such decision. In such a case the liquidator or receiver joins a representative respondent to argue the point on behalf of the class. Frequently the sum at stake for the individual respondent joined does not justify him incurring the costs involved in litigating the matter. As a result, in order to ensure that the matter is properly determined the costs of the representative respondents are frequently paid out of the fund. An agreement to that effect is often made before the proceedings are heard; indeed on occasion the court orders it before trial. But in my judgment those are special cases in which it is necessary for the proper execution of the duties of the receiver or liquidator to have the matter determined and a pre-emptive order as to costs is a necessary prerequisite to that determination being obtained. This is not a rule applicable in all cases; it is simply in my judgment the right general approach to costs in these cases."

At p. 198 the Vice-Chancellor deals with the position of the Export Credits Guarantee Department (ECGD) which had originally said that the case in *Re Westdock* ought to be treated as a test case. The Vice-Chancellor continued:

"The ECGD has now changed its position and what it previously thought to be suitable for treatment as a test case is now no longer so regarded. The ECGD now says that the matter is clear. The result is likely to be that a number of other cases, where either exactly the same point or similar points arise, are likely to go undefended and unrepresented because the liquidators will never be in a position to put forward the argument in opposition to ECGD. For myself I find it unacceptable that a department of state, with all the resources of the state behind it and which itself thought the matter suitable for a test case, is now likely to take the moneys not only in this case but in other cases virtually by default since the argument to the contrary can never be put. I have considered whether the case is an appropriate one in which the receiver, in helping the court to reach a view, could put forward the appropriate arguments to enable the court to consider it properly. But I have reached the view that it is not such a case since, for reasons which I will seek to explain shortly, discovery will be necessary; it is not merely a question of putting forward legal argument. It seems to me therefore that if there is a real doubt whether the ECGD is entitled to the fund, and there are features common to this case and to others which call for investigation, a test case either in this or in some other case is necessary and desirable. There ought in my judgment to be a test case to determine the rights of the parties after argument, not by default."

Then at p. 199, the Vice-Chancellor says:

"Those special features demonstrate this is far from the straightforward simple case of subrogation by a guarantor to the rights of the principal creditor.

Mr Moss was anxious to address me, as he frankly said, at considerable length and with references to authority with a view to seeking to satisfy me that notwithstanding these special features there was here no arguable case at all. I declined to listen to submissions at such length on those issues of law. In my judgment it cannot be right on an application such as this to have a mini-trial on issues of law which are so complicated that they need to be developed at that length before the facts have been ascertained."

In conclusion the Vice-Chancellor says:

"I therefore propose, because of this very special 'test case' factor in this case, to make the order sought. However, I will direct the liquidators to apply ex parte

after the completion of pleading and discovery for directions whether they should
continue with the proceedings so that at that stage a judge having the relevant
material and a proper and full opinion from counsel before him, can determine
whether there is a real issue to be determined in which the liquidators have a
substantial chance of success. That I think will safeguard the ECGD against
endless, fruitless litigation."

It is thus clear that the court will only make an order of the kind made in the *Westdock*
case in very exceptional circumstances.

I was referred to a subsequent decision of *Mummery* J in *National Anti-Vivisection
Society v Duddington* (The Times, 23 November 1989). After reviewing the authorities,
Mummery J concluded that the factors which had featured in the decided cases as
relevant to the court's jurisdiction to make pre-emptive costs orders were (1) the merits
of the claims (see *Re Evans*); (2) the likely order for costs at trial (see *Re Westdock*);
(3) the justice of the case (see *Re Evans*); and (4) special factors as in the *Westdock* case.
It can thus be seen that the cases relevant to Mr Briggs' *Beddoe* and *Westdock* arguments
can thus be analysed as dealing with the same problem and as guided by similar
considerations. The cases on the *PCW* argument do not concern pre-emptive orders as
to costs but variations of Mareva injunctions in circumstances where it is said that the
party applying requires funds to pay his own legal costs. However, they do show that a
similar kind of balancing exercise is required.

Mr Briggs also relied on *Re Exchange Securities & Commodities Ltd (No. 2)* (1986) 2
BCC 98,932 in which *Vinelott* J held that the court could under its inherent jurisdiction
make a just allowance to the official receiver for his fees and costs and those of a special
manager out of assets ostensibly belonging to the companies in liquidation, even if it
should subsequently transpire that those assets did not belong to the companies. I do
not consider that I can follow that course here at this stage without evidence as to the
fees and costs in question and as to the assets out of which they might be paid. Moreover,
other creditors might have to be given notice of the application.

Vinelott J further held in the *Exchange Securities* case that it would be premature to
determine the apportionment of those fees and expenses to the trust or other assets.
It was that aspect of the decision which lay behind the formulation of the relief which
Mr Briggs sought, it being anticipated that other proprietary claims, if not already made,
would be made to the assets held by Biddencare. That point leads to the further question
(which I do not need to resolve) whether any creditors claiming to have proprietary
claims should be given notice of any proposed order in the liquidators' favour.

Mr Briggs properly accepted that special circumstances would have to be shown if the
court was to depart from the usual rule. He relies on two types of special circumstance in
this case, the first being the importance of the issue whether the applicant has a
proprietary claim or other like claim in the liquidation of Biddencare. He contends that
the present case is a test case within the liquidation of Biddencare. He points out that
Biddencare was apparently not in direct contractual relations with reinsureds, like the
applicant. However, whether reinsureds or other clients of Biddencare's broking
subsidiaries had proprietary claims is likely to depend on the facts relative to their
particular case, including the terms of their contract with that broker or other party.
Accordingly, the applicant's case on that issue is not, in my view, to be regarded as a test
case on the footing with the case proposed to be litigated in *Re Westdock*.

Mr Briggs also submitted that the question whether the assets to which proprietary
claims were established should be distributed pari passu to the claimants entitled or
whether each such claimant would have to trace his individual claim into the assets held
by Biddencare, would amount to a test case. In my view it would at least be premature

A   to form a view on this since no proprietary claims have yet been established nor are details of any claim, other than the applicant's, in evidence.

The second special circumstance on which Mr Briggs relied was this, namely that the position may be such that there are no unsecured creditors who do not have proprietary claims and who would be interested in defending the applicant's claim. In my view it would not be right for me to accept this as in fact the position, without evidence on the point. It may be the case that there is no one who has any commercial interest in

B   challenging the applicant's claim, but in my view that should be proved by evidence in the normal way.

Mr Briggs has properly accepted that he cannot say there is no prospect of obtaining a fighting fund. The statement of affairs dated 10 August 1992 shows unsecured claims of £4,143,914, including one creditor in the sum of approximately £2.5m. I would not go so far as to say that the court can never make a pre-emptive order as to costs where there

C   are creditors who could be asked to provide a fighting fund. However, following by analogy the approach of the Court of Appeal in *Re Evans*, it seems to me that countervailing considerations of some weight are required before the court could make such an order, even one limited to the legal costs of the specific application before it; *Re Westdock* illustrates the same point.

The courts have to bear in mind that a pre-emptive order is unusual and can clearly

D   result in injustice if the other party establishes his proprietary claim over assets which have been reduced by the payment of the costs of resisting his claim. It is the other creditors in the liquidation, and not the applicant, who should bear the burden of the costs of unsuccessfully defending the applicant's claim.

I do not see in this case any countervailing factor of sufficient weight to outweigh these factors. As it is, on the material which I have, in my judgment, the balancing exercise

E   which the court must perform in this case produces the clear answer that no pre-emptive order should be made. If I am wrong on that, I accept Mr Lightman's submission that the court cannot be satisfied that it is likely that an order would be made at trial for the payment of the liquidators' costs out of the assets the subject of the applicant's claim, even if the liquidators were unsuccessful. This is hostile litigation.

In *Westdock*, the Vice-Chancellor held that in general this factor, namely that it is not

F   likely that an order would be made at trial for the payment of the costs out of the assets, would be a bar to the court making a pre-emptive order. It has not been submitted by Mr Briggs that the statement of practice in *Re Westdock* at p. 197 should be read as modified or that the general bar would not apply in the present case.

I have heard submissions on the form of the proposed direction. In the circumstances, it is unnecessary for me to deal with these.

G   Finally, Mr Lightman helpfully accepted two matters that should be recorded:

(1)   that the applicant would not for its part object to the costs of reporting to creditors and asking them to put up a fighting fund being borne by the free assets of Biddencare, or, if none, its mixed funds pro rata; and

(2)   that the applicant would not seek an order for costs against the liquidators personally in this application if they took a purely neutral stand and would not

H   oppose the joinder to the application of an appropriate creditor of Biddencare.

(*Liquidators' application refused*)

Re Brooks Transport (Purfleet) Ltd.

A

Chancery Division (Companies Court).
John V Martin QC (sitting as a deputy High Court judge).
Judgment delivered 28 July 1993.

> *Disqualifying unfit directors of insolvent companies — Whether Secretary of State should have costs on indemnity basis — Company Directors Disqualification Act 1986, sec. 6.*

B

This was an application by the official receiver for his costs of a director disqualification application on the indemnity basis.

Held, making a disqualification order for seven years and awarding indemnity costs:

1. There was a valid distinction between the position of the Crown as applicant in director disqualification proceedings and the position of the ordinary litigant in hostile litigation. That distinction stemmed from the fact that the official receiver could be and had been directed by the Secretary of State to pursue proceedings and that the proceedings had at their foundation the principle that it was in the public interest that the privilege of limited liability should not be abused. (Re Godwin Warren Control Systems plc [1992] BCC 557 not followed; Re Synthetic Technology Ltd [1993] BCC 549 applied.)

C

2. The relevant consideration in deciding whether indemnity costs or standard costs should be awarded was whether, in the light of the conduct and nature of the defence and its outcome, it could be seen that the Crown had gone further than its public duty required it to do. In this case the vast majority of the complaints made by the official receiver were justified. It was a serious case, falling within the middle band as defined in Re Sevenoaks Stationers (Retail) Ltd [1990] BCC 765. In those circumstances the application in no way overstated the case and it followed that the appropriate award was indemnity costs.

D

E

The following cases were referred to in the judgment:

Bowen-Jones v Bowen-Jones & Ors [1986] 3 All ER 163.
Defence & Microwave Devices Ltd, Re (unreported, 7 October 1992, Nicholls V-C).
Godwin Warren Control Systems plc, Re [1992] BCC 557.
Moonbeam Cards Ltd, Re (unreported, 1 December 1992, Vinelott J).
Sevenoaks Stationers (Retail) Ltd, Re [1990] BCC 765; [1991] Ch 164.
Swift 736 Ltd, Re [1993] BCC 312.
Synthetic Technology Ltd, Re [1993] BCC 549.
Travers Shopfitters Ltd, Re (unreported, 13 May 1993, HH Judge Weeks QC).
Wedgcraft Ltd & Ors, Re (unreported, 7 March 1986, Harman J).

F

Stephen Moverley Smith (instructed by the Treasury Solicitor) for the official receiver.

M D Berkin (instructed by David Parry & Co, Grays) for the respondent.

G

JUDGMENT

John Martin QC: This is an application by the official receiver at the direction of the Secretary of State for Trade and Industry. What is sought is a disqualification order under the *Company Directors Disqualification Act* 1986 against Alan Raymond Brooks. The application is made under sec. 6 of the Act, which requires the court to make an order if it is satisfied about two things in relation to Mr Brooks. First, that he is or has been a director of a company which has at any time become insolvent. Secondly, that his conduct as a director of that company, taken alone or together with his conduct as director of another company or companies, makes him unfit to be concerned in the management of a company.

H

A   There is no dispute that the first of those things is satisfied in relation to a company called Brooks Transport (Purfleet) Ltd ("Purfleet"). The official receiver claims that the second is satisfied in relation to Purfleet and another company, Brooks Transport Ltd ("Transport").

Mr Brooks denies that his conduct as director of the two companies makes him unfit to be concerned in the management of a company. The issue therefore relates entirely to the second limb of sec. 6. Before I deal with that issue, I must set out the history of the companies. Except as to the amounts of the deficiencies I shall mention, none of what follows is disputed.

B

Transport was incorporated on 18 November 1981 and started trading in the same month. It carried on business as international road hauliers, carrying goods to continental Europe. Throughout its life its only directors were Mr Brooks and his wife. She played no part in its affairs and he accepts that he is solely responsible for the conduct of its business. Transport ceased trading in October 1988 and was compulsorily wound up a year later. Its liabilities exceeded its assets by a little over £150,000. Although there is broad agreement as to the figure, there is a dispute about its composition. I shall return to the nature and causes of the deficiency later.

C

Purfleet was incorporated on 7 October 1988 and began trading the following month. That was immediately after Transport ceased to trade. It too carried on business as international road hauliers; it too had Mr Brooks and his wife as its only directors, with Mr Brooks being solely responsible for the conduct of its business. It operated from the same premises as Transport, had the same telephone number and took over and refinanced Transport's vehicles. There is an obvious similarity in the names of the two companies. Purfleet ceased trading in December 1990, being compulsorily wound up on 12 December.

D

E

As I have said, it is common ground that Purfleet was insolvent, but there is a dispute as to the amount of the deficiency, the official receiver putting it at £247,000 and Mr Brooks at just under £49,000. As with Transport, that is a matter to which I shall return.

Against that background, I come back to the second limb of sec. 6 of the 1986 Act. In deciding whether or not Mr Brooks' conduct makes him unfit to be concerned in the management of a company, I am required by sec. 9 of the Act to have regard in particular to the matters set out in Pt. I and, because both companies became insolvent, Pt. II of Sch. 1 to the Act. I will therefore deal first with the criticisms of Mr Brooks' conduct which fall within the schedule.

F

The paragraphs of the schedule which are relevant are para. 4(a)–(e) inclusive, 5, 6 and 10(e) and (g). They are in the following terms. All of them are matters which, as I have said, I have to have regard to in deciding whether Mr Brooks is unfit to be concerned in the management of a company.

G

Paragraph 4 requires me to have regard to the extent of the director's responsibility for any failure by the company to comply with any of the following provisions of the Companies Act, namely:

H

    "(a) section 221 (companies to keep accounting records);

    (b) section 222 (where and for how long records to be kept);

    (c) section 288 (register of directors and secretaries);

    (d) section 352 (obligation to keep and enter up register of members);

    (e) section 353 (location of register of members) . . ."

Paragraph 5 requires me to have regard to the extent of the director's responsibility   A
for any failure by the directors of the company to comply with,

> "(a) section 226 or 227 of the Companies Act (duty to prepare annual accounts) . . ."

Paragraph 6 requires me to have regard to the extent of the director's responsibility
for the causes of the company becoming insolvent; and para. 10 directs my attention to
any failure by the director to comply with any obligation imposed on him by or under   B
any of the following provisions of the Insolvency Act:

> " . . .

> (e) section 131 (statement of affairs in winding-up by the court)

> . . .

> (g) section 235 (duty to co-operate with liquidator, etc.)."   C

Rather than deal with the paragraphs of the schedule in the order that I have just read
them, however, I will for ease of reference consider the official receiver's complaints in
the order in which they appear in the report prepared for the purpose of this application.

1. Failure to ensure that accounts were prepared and delivered to the registrar of
companies in accordance with sec. 226, 241 and 242 of the Companies Act (para. 5 of   D
Sch. 1). These complaints relate to both Transport and Purfleet.

In so far as Transport is concerned, audited accounts were due for filing with the
registrar as follows. In respect of the period ended on 31 March 1983, the accounts were
due on 21 September 1983. In respect of the period to 31 March 1984, they were due on
31 January 1985. In respect of the period to 31 March 1985, they were due on 31 January
1986. In respect of the period to 31 March 1986, they were due on 31 January 1987. In   E
respect of the period to 31 March 1987, they were due on 31 January 1988 and in respect
of the period to 31 March 1988, they were due on 31 January 1989. No accounts were
ever filed for the first or last periods. Those for the second, third and fourth periods were
not filed until 29 June 1988 and those for the period to 31 March 1987 were not filed until
31 March 1989.

Only one set of accounts was due from Purfleet, namely, that for the period to   F
31 March 1990, due for filing on 9 August 1990. It was never filed.

Mr Brooks admitted in evidence that he was aware of the need to file accounts. These
complaints are accordingly made out. Because of Mr Brooks' awareness of the need for
accounts, they are serious breaches of his duty as director. I do however bear in mind
that, although for unexplained reasons, there was a belated attempt to comply in 1988
and 1989.   G

2. Failure to maintain and preserve accounting records as required by sec. 222(4) of
the *Companies Act* 1985 (para. 4(a) and (b) of Sch. 1). The official receiver's complaints
under these heads relate to Purfleet alone.

In circumstances which I will describe later, original documents were produced by
Mr Brooks at the trial. Among them were four pages from a ledger completed in
manuscript covering the whole of 1990 and a few days either side. Mr Brooks' evidence   H
was that earlier pages from the ledger relating to 1989 and the ledger itself had been lost
or destroyed. That amounts to a breach of sec. 222(4) of the Companies Act before its
amendment by the 1989 Companies Act, which requires the retention of records for
three years. To that extent the complaint is made out. I make no finding as to the fate or
whereabouts of the other records specified in para. 91 of the report.

A   3. Failure to ensure that annual returns were delivered for filing in accordance with sec. 363 and 365 of the *Companies Act* 1985 (para. 4(f) of Sch. 1). These complaints relate to Transport and Purfleet. The dates on which returns were due are set out in para. 30 for Transport and para. 103 for Purfleet of the report together with the date of filing. Broadly speaking, they correspond to the pattern followed in the preparation and delivery of accounts.

B   Mr Brooks admitted in evidence that he was aware throughout the lives of both companies that returns were required. The element of knowledge again makes these serious breaches, although again I take into account the flurry of remedial activity in 1988 and 1989.

    4. Failure to give sufficient attention to the financial affairs of the companies (para. 6 of Sch. 1). These complaints relate to both companies. As I have said, original documents
C   were produced in court. The manuscript ledger extracts (together perhaps with the VAT record, which I have not seen) represent the nearest thing to financial information available to the companies. They are wholly inadequate for the purpose of extracting any assessment of the companies' financial status from time to time. Indeed, Mr Brooks admitted that he had made no assessments of the company's ability to pay its bills. He assumed that if he was able to send the lorries out, the companies were doing all right.
D   When it was put to him in cross-examination that the companies were living a day-to-day, hand-to-mouth existence, he replied: "Well, that's transport", meaning the transport business.

    I find that Mr Brooks made no attempt to monitor the financial position of either company and had no proper means of doing so had he wanted to. These complaints are therefore established. This again represents a serious breach of duty, although its
E   seriousness is to some limited extent reduced by the fact that the audited accounts of Transport produced in 1988 and expressly reliant upon statements made to the auditors by Mr Brooks showed that the company had been profitable up to 1986 and had then a surplus of assets over liabilities.

    5. Knowing continuation of Transport's business after a date when there was no reasonable prospect of creditors being paid (para. 6 of Sch. 1).

F   In answer to questions put to him by an insolvency examiner on 28 November 1989, which was soon after the liquidation of Transport, but a year after it ceased trading, Mr Brooks stated that Transport was insolvent from about 1987 and that he became aware of that fact when he realised that Transport could not pay certain fines imposed on it even if it wanted to. On the basis of those answers the official receiver complains that Mr Brooks knew of Transport's insolvency in 1987, but continued to trade until October
G   1988, incurring further liabilities.

    I am unable to accept that complaint in its entirety. In his evidence to me Mr Brooks tied his awareness of insolvency to a fine of £25,000. That fine in fact was imposed on 28 June 1988. I accept Mr Brooks' evidence on this point and find that it was not until the end of June 1988 that he became aware that Transport was unable to meet its liabilities. Trading continued thereafter until October 1988 and to that extent the complaint is
H   made out. I do not however regard this matter as particularly serious.

    6. Failure to maintain statutory records (para. 4(c)–(e) of Sch. 1). This allegation relates only to Transport. One of the documents produced in court was a blank record book. It had never been written up. This complaint is established.

    7. Failure to comply with obligations to supply information to the official receiver (para. 10(g) of Sch. 1). This allegation relates to Purfleet only.

Paragraphs 115 to 131 of the report set out a catalogue of missed appointments and   A
refusals to answer questions. There is little dispute about these matters and I find that
Mr Brooks has from time to time failed to supply the official receiver promptly with
information which he was obliged to supply. Despite the fact that the official receiver
has been hindered in his investigations, I do not regard this as a particularly serious
matter on its own. Having seen Mr Brooks in the witness-box, I am inclined to ascribe it
largely to an occasional natural truculence. There is nevertheless one connected area of
complaint about which I am quite unable to take the same view.   B

On 4 June 1991, Mr Registrar *Dewhurst* made an order on the application of the
official receiver requiring Mr Brooks to deliver to the official receiver: (1) a list of names
and addresses of customers and all letters, books of accounts or other documentation
relating to the company, which was Purfleet, within 21 days from service of the order;
and (2) a cash account covering the period from 7 October 1988 to 12 December 1990,
that account to be delivered within 56 days from the service of the order.   C

The application for the order was prompted in large part by undocumented cash
withdrawals of £134,000 made between 8 June 1990 and 3 December 1990. Nothing was
done to comply with that order until February 1993, when the official receiver was
notified that certain documents had been found by Mr Brooks. Photocopies were made
of parts of the documents which had been discovered and exhibited to an affidavit. That
affidavit was not itself provided to the official receiver until June 1993. Despite the   D
objection of the official receiver, I consented to read that affidavit and allow it to be
given in evidence on Mr Brooks' behalf. All the documents exhibited to it and the
originals which were produced in court were clearly subject to the order.

The explanation, if that is the proper word for it, that was provided for the late
production of these documents was that Mr Brooks had recently, but at a date which he
was unable to specify satisfactorily, found them in a tea chest at Purfleet's premises. The
documents largely consist of envelopes which contain an informal record of cash   E
expenditure, with vouchers for some recorded expenses. They go some, but by no means
the whole, way to explaining the £134,000 cash withdrawals.

I do not regard what has happened as a deliberate attempt by Mr Brooks to withhold
documents. As he himself said, if he had wanted to withhold them, he would not have
produced them now. It is however clear that no proper attempt was made to comply with
the order. When asked about this in cross-examination, Mr Brooks said: "I didn't look   F
too hard for them".

In relation to other areas of the order, in particular the list of names and addresses of
customers, Mr Brooks is still in default. These matters amount in my judgment to a clear
contempt of court and I am bound to regard it as a very serious matter.

8. Submission of a materially inaccurate statement of affairs for Purfleet (para. 10(e)
of Sch. 1).   G

The statement of affairs sworn by Mr Brooks in relation to the liquidation of Purfleet
disclosed a deficiency of assets amounting to £48,881. At his public examination on
26 April 1991, Mr Brooks maintained that there were no other debts than those which
he had disclosed in the statement of affairs. In fact that was wrong. At para. 58 of the
report there is a list of the creditors of Purfleet. A comparison between that list and the
statement of affairs shows on the face of it that the undisclosed creditors amounted in   H
value to just under £200,000. It is necessary for me however to comment in more detail
upon the composition of that figure.

The largest undisclosed debt is a debt due to the Customs and Excise in respect of
VAT. It is in the amount of £89,724. It was based on assessments resulting from the
overclaim of input tax. Mr Brooks' explanation was that he had not included it in the

A   statement of affairs because, so far as he was concerned, the company's VAT returns had been accurate and the Customs and Excise were wrong. This is a debt which should have been included.

The next highest undisclosed debt is a debt due to AIB Finance Ltd of just under £33,000. The origin of this debt was a hire-purchase agreement or agreements for vehicles operated by Purfleet. This debt was excluded by Mr Brooks from the statement

B   of affairs because it is a debt which he had guaranteed and in respect of which he is personally liable. It nevertheless remains a debt of the company and it should have been included.

There are two debts which I take together. They are a debt of just under £25,000 said to be due to a company called Kuhne & Nagel Ltd and a debt of £21,000-odd said to be due to a company called Metalimpex. It is likely that these debts arise out of the same transaction and it is entirely possible that there is some element of double counting.

C   Neither of them was included in the statement of affairs because Mr Brooks believed them to be unjustified. Indeed, there was a half-hearted attempt to include in the list of assets in the statement of affairs a cross-claim of £12,000 nevertheless said to be worthless. Although there is doubt, as I have said, as to the correct amount of these debts, some mention of them should nevertheless have been included in the statement of affairs.

D   The next item is unpaid fines of £12,960. Of these, only one for £970 can be shown to have been imposed before the winding-up order was made. The remainder are, or may be, unenforceable. Nevertheless, the figure I have mentioned, that is to say, £970, should have been included in the statement of affairs.

Finally, there is corporation tax of £1,250. This is based upon an assessment and should have been included. These complaints are established to the extent that I have

E   mentioned.

It will be convenient at this stage to deal with some of the comments made by Mr Brooks in relation to the deficiency in Transport. I stress that this is not the subject of any complaint by the official receiver and is not taken into account by me in deciding whether Mr Brooks is unfit to act as a director.

F   I have already mentioned that there is broad agreement between Mr Brooks and the official receiver as to the extent of the deficiency in Transport. In the statement of affairs which Mr Brooks swore, he put the deficiency at £157,000-odd. The official receiver says that the true figure is £154,000-odd. There is however a marked difference in the composition of the figures. The only creditors which Mr Brooks included in the statement of affairs were the debt of the petitioning creditor, a bank overdraft of £55,000 which, broadly speaking, corresponds to the figure accepted by the official receiver, and fines of

G   £100,000. No mention is made of three creditors: International Express Co Ltd, with a debt of £5,735; Mr Humphrey, with a debt of £5,633; and a liability to corporation tax of £23,950.

The reason for the failure to include the first two of those is that Mr Brooks' view is that they are unjustified. They are both however the subject of judgments and I must take the view that they are justly due. So far as corporation tax is concerned, no serious grounds are advanced for disputing this amount. The real discrepancy lies in relation to

H   the figure for fines. It is of itself remarkable that Mr Brooks should not merely not have known the accurate figure for fines, but should have acknowledged that they could be of the magnitude of £100,000. In fact, as I have said, their total was £58,453. Almost all of them – and they are listed in para. 41 of the report – arise out of failures, which I will mention in a moment, to have an operator's licence or a vehicle excise licence. At this stage I need do no more than remark upon the discrepancy between the figures.

9. Finally, when dealing with the complaints which fall within the schedule to the Act, I come to a complaint that there was no reasonable or probable ground for expectation that the business of Purfleet would succeed, in that Mr Brooks caused it to assume or continue without any significant change in the method of operation or financing the business which had been carried on by Transport and which had failed previously. I have already, when reciting the history of the companies, pointed to similarities between them. The same pattern of trading and the same pattern of ignoring licensing requirements was adopted in relation to Purfleet, despite its failure when adopted in relation to Transport. This complaint is established. I regard it as serious.

The matters I have already described are more than sufficient in themselves to justify a finding of unfitness. Collectively they amount to a serious and consistent dereliction of duty. In *Re Swift 736 Ltd* [1993] BCC 312, Sir *Donald Nicholls* V-C, giving judgment in the Court of Appeal, said at p. 315D:

> "Limited liability is a valuable tool in the promotion of trade and business, but it must not be misused. Those who make use of limited liability must do so with a proper sense of responsibility. The directors disqualification procedure is an important sanction introduced by Parliament to raise standards in this regard. Those who take advantage of limited liability must conduct their companies with due regard to the ordinary standards of commercial morality. They must also be punctilious in observing the safeguards laid down by Parliament for the benefit of others who have dealings with their companies. They must maintain proper books of account and prepare annual accounts; they must file their accounts and returns promptly; they must fully and frankly disclose information about deficiencies in accordance with the statutory provisions. Isolated lapses in filing documents are one thing and may be excusable, but not so persistent lapses which show overall a blatant disregard for this important aspect of accountability. Such lapses are serious and cannot be condoned even though, and it is right to have this firmly in mind, they need not involve any dishonest intent."

Before I express my conclusions, there are however four other areas of criticism of Mr Brooks' conduct which I must consider. They are his payment of remuneration to himself and his wife without deduction of tax, his failure to obtain a transport operator's licence for either company, his failure to ensure that excise licences were obtained for the company's vehicles and, largely as a result of those last two failures, his allowing the companies to suffer substantial fines. Although these complaints are important, I can deal with them relatively briefly. Indeed, the first of them is admitted in relation to both companies. It amounts to a breach of sec. 311 of the *Companies Act* 1985.

As to the remainder, it is common ground that both Transport and Purfleet required a licence to operate a haulage business. Neither of them ever had one. Mr Brooks himself had a licence until about 1982 or 1983, when it was revoked, and applications either to renew it or to obtain a licence for Transport failed. After a while, Mr Brooks gave up trying, but the companies carried on business regardless. Mr Brooks admitted in cross-examination that he knew that was illegal.

So far as the excise licences are concerned, Mr Brooks decided not to apply for them, because he felt it was wrong to have to pay road taxes both in the UK and in the European countries to which the lorries travelled. Again, he admitted in evidence that he knew that licences were required. Both failures persisted despite the prosecutions which led to the majority of the very large fines I have mentioned. Some of the fines also related to defects in the vehicles and, as director of the companies, Mr Brooks must take responsibility for those defects.

The matters I have considered lead inexorably to a finding of unfitness. I make that finding. I am obliged therefore to make a disqualification order and the remaining question is how long it should be.

A In relation to that, Mr Berkin, who has represented Mr Brooks in this matter, makes the following points. He says, and I accept, that Mr Brooks was honest in his evidence and honest in his dealings with the companies' affairs. He said that it was to Mr Brooks' credit that he had himself incurred personal liability in relation to some of the companies' debts. I accept that point to the extent that Mr Brooks' position was no better than if he had been trading without limited liability in those respects at least and to the extent that it means that Mr Brooks was himself not wholly unscathed by the collapse of the

B companies.

Mr Berkin points to the fact that Transport was apparently profitable until 1987. Again, I accept that, but I am dubious as to the quality of the information supplied by Mr Brooks on which the accounts were expressly based.

It was pointed out to me that in terms of company failures, this was relatively small,

C both as to amount and as to the number of companies with which Mr Brooks had been involved and which had failed. I see the force of that point, but the amounts are not in fact small amounts and although only two companies are involved, they represent the only two companies with which Mr Brooks has been involved over a nine-year period.

Lastly, Mr Berkin suggested to me that the true explanation for the failures that I have considered was that Mr Brooks carried on business in a manner which could be described at worst as incompetent or ham-fisted. At that point I part company with him. To my

D mind there is a consistent thread which runs through all the complaints which I have found to be established. It is this. Mr Brooks has persistently conducted the affairs of the companies in a manner which can be described at best as cavalier and at worst as a deliberate refusal to comply with legal requirements where he considered them inconvenient or an obstacle to the conducting of the business in the way in which he chose to conduct it. It is there as well as in the individual complaints, which are symptoms

E of the malaise I have just discussed, that the vice in this case lies.

I do not find myself helped in deciding what is the appropriate period of disqualification by considering the facts of other cases. Each case must turn on its own facts. I regard this case as falling within the middle bracket of the three described by the Court of Appeal in *Re Sevenoaks Stationers (Retail) Ltd* [1990] BCC 765, that is to say, the middle bracket of disqualification from six to ten years, which should apply to serious cases

F which do not merit the top bracket.

In all the circumstances I have come to the conclusion that the appropriate period of disqualification is seven years and I make an order to that effect.

Costs

I now have to rule on the question of costs of this application. As I understand it there

G is no dispute that the costs must be paid by Mr Brooks. The only question is whether those costs should be paid on the standard basis or on the indemnity basis.

Mr Berkin, understandably batting for the standard basis, draws my attention to a decision of Knox J in a case called *Bowen-Jones v Bowen-Jones & Ors* [1986] 3 All ER 163. He referred me merely to the headnote and it is sufficient for me to read that to explain what the case decided. It says:

H "RSC Ord 62, r 12, which provides by r 12(1) for the taxation of costs on the 'standard basis' in place of the 'party and party' and 'common fund' bases and by r 12(2) for taxation on the 'indemnity basis' in place of the 'solicitor and own client' basis, is a rationalisation of the different bases of taxation of costs rather than a complete restatement of the rules concerning awards of costs, and for the purposes of awarding costs on the standard basis under r 12(1) there is no reason

in principle to depart from the established practice that, save in exceptional
circumstances, the successful party in hostile litigation is not entitled to an
indemnity against expenses actually incurred but only to the lower, 'standard'
basis of taxation."

Mr Moverley Smith however, in batting for the indemnity basis, draws my attention
to a series of cases where the question of costs is decided in the context of applications
under the 1986 Act. The first of those cases, which is a case called *Re Wedgcraft Ltd &
Ors* was decided by *Harman* J on 7 March 1986. At p. 7A of the transcript in the
argument about costs the judge said:

". . . the usual practice has been to say, these are costs which fall upon the official
receiver as representing the public wholly because of what has now been held to
be misconduct of a serious sort . . . In the circumstances there does not seem any
reason why the public should have to pay for this application, which has been
brought for their protection; and indemnity costs has been the usual order made."

In that case, what the judge described as "the usual order" was indeed made.

Mr Berkin describes that decision as having been decided on what he called "the usual
order basis". I accept that submission to this extent only. The judge primarily bases his
decision upon the fact that it is usual to make an indemnity costs order in this sort of
case. I do not accept Mr Berkin's submission in its entirety, because it seems to me that
implicit in what the judge says is the proposition that the reason for the usual order is
that the official receiver represents the public, is fulfilling a statutory duty and to that
extent is to be placed in a more favoured position than an ordinary litigant.

Doubt was however cast upon the practice and indeed the justification for the practice
by *Chadwick* J in a case called *Re Godwin Warren Control Systems plc* [1992] BCC 557.
At p. 569G the judge said:

"As to the basis of costs, the Rules of the Supreme Court, O. 62, r. 12 provides
that on a taxation of costs on the standard basis there shall be allowed a reasonable
amount in respect of all costs reasonably incurred, whereas on the indemnity basis
all costs shall be allowed except in so far as they are of an unreasonable amount or
have been unreasonably incurred.

My attention has been drawn to a practice which I am told has grown up in this
division of ordering costs in these matters on an indemnity basis, apparently on
the ground that there is no reason why the public should have to pay for this
application which has been brought for their protection. It seems to me that there
is equally no reason why a defendant director . . ."

—and I stress the next words:

". . . who has conducted his defence properly and reasonably should be required
to pay more than a reasonable amount in respect of all costs reasonably incurred
on behalf of the public and, in particular, there is no reason why such a director
should be made subject to the burden of showing that costs incurred by the
Secretary of State are unreasonable.

It must be a matter of common occurrence that litigation is brought by the Crown
for the protection of the public in circumstances in which it is in the public interest
that such proceedings should be taken; but that does not, as it seems to me, justify
any general rule that Crown proceedings, if successful, should be marked by an
order for indemnity costs.

In my view the Crown should be treated in the same way as any other litigant in
this regard and, accordingly, I propose to order costs on the standard basis."

I note that because of the practice that had grown up, the judge gave leave to appeal,
which apparently was not taken up.

A   Despite the words that I have stressed there, "a defendant director who has conducted his defence properly and reasonably", it appears from the final sentence of the quotation that *Chadwick* J was rejecting as a justification for the practice the proposition that the Crown should be treated in any way differently from an ordinary litigant.

There then follow four cases, in all of which the *Godwin Warren* decision has been cited and, to a greater or lesser extent, an attempt made to explain what it decides. The first of those cases is a decision of Sir *Donald Nicholls* V-C on 7 October 1992 in a case called *Defence and Microwave Devices Ltd.* At p. 8G of the transcript the judge's attention was drawn to the *Godwin Warren* decision and at p. 9C counsel for the applicant, instructed by the Treasury Solicitor, said this:

> "My Lord, I do not think I can say much more other than that, with the exception of that decision"—meaning the *Godwin Warren* decision—"it has been the normal practice over a period for indemnity costs to be awarded and, my Lord, where there has been serious misconduct, such that directors have only themselves to blame for the proceedings, in my submission it is appropriate that indemnity costs are awarded."

The Vice-Chancellor then listened to a short submission from the director in person and finally at p. 9E said simply:

> "The right order to make here is that the respondents to the summonses pay the applicant's costs on an indemnity basis."

The most I think that can be drawn from that case is that the Vice-Chancellor took the view that there was no insuperable obstacle represented by the *Godwin Warren* case to the continuance of what had been described to him as "the usual practice".

The next case is a decision of *Vinelott* J on 1 December 1992 in a matter called *Moonbeam Cards Ltd.* At p. 2F of the transcript, counsel for the respondent drew the judge's attention to the *Godwin Warren* case, but before actually citing it to the judge, he accepted that there was a general practice that indemnity costs should be paid in applications of that sort and the judge said:

> "No doubt there are exceptional circumstances that justify departure from it."

That again to my mind indicates that that judge recognised that there was an existing practice. The *Godwin Warren* case was then cited to him and at p. 3E of the transcript the judge said:

> "I think the true position is that where the basis of taxation of costs is in issue, there is no inflexible or even prima facie rule. The courts must look at all the circumstances, including a particular position, the duty of the official receiver to take steps for the protection of the public, and weigh the gravity of the case in the way in which the defence is being conducted.
>
> In this case I think the costs that have been incurred have been largely unnecessary, in particular, the late service of expert evidence and the fact that every issue of fact has been contested and that the defendant has at no stage shown that he has any appreciation of the gravity of the charges that have been made. I think in all the circumstances, I shall order costs on the indemnity basis . . ."

Whether or not *Vinelott* J was intentionally picking up in the passage I have quoted the words that I stressed when considering the *Godwin Warren* case, it does appear that *Vinelott* J considered that two circumstances which were of primary importance were the position and duty of the official receiver and a balance between the gravity of the case and the method of conduct of the defence.

Similar ideas emerged from the penultimate case to which my attention has been A
directed, *Re Synthetic Technology Ltd* [1993] BCC 549, a decision of Mr *Evans-Lombe*
QC. He gave a formal ruling, at the end of which he made an order for costs on the
standard basis only, but it will be desirable for me to quote an extensive passage from
the ruling that he gave. It starts at p. 563F where the judge said:

"It has, as I know from my own experience, been the practice in this court until
recently that where the Secretary of State succeeds in an application to disqualify B
a director he obtains, save where exceptional facts occur, an order for costs against
that director on an indemnity basis."

Then after consideration of the *Godwin Warren* case and a reference to an apparent
decision of *Mervyn Davies* J following that case (to which I have not been referred) the
judge continued at p. 563H:

"It follows that I am confronted with two, perhaps, conflicting lines of authority, C
for one of which reasons are given and for the other of which no reason has
apparently been given.

It seems to me that the differentiation should be this. That where it can be shown
that a director has by defending the proceedings, albeit in the end unsuccessfully,
substantially reduced the charges made good against him, so that in the result the
case with which the court is confronted, albeit one justifying disqualification, is D
not as serious as that which was opened by the Secretary of State at the beginning
of the case, so that the court can take the view that the delinquent director's
defence was to that extent justified, then the order for costs should not be on an
indemnity basis. In each case, it seems to me it will be a matter of degree as to
whether the successful defence was justified in the sense which I have sought to
define."

E

The test there suggested is to my mind consistent with the passages I have emphasised
from the judgment of *Vinelott* J in the *Moonbeam Cards* case and, subject to the
qualification I have already expressed about the rejection of the principle, the words I
have emphasised in the passage in *Godwin Warren* itself.

The final case which I must mention is a decision of His Honour Judge *Weeks* QC,
sitting as a judge of the High Court, on 13 May 1993 in a case called *Travers Shopfitters* F
Ltd. After considering the *Godwin Warren*, *Microwave Devices* and *Synthetic Technology*
cases, the judge said at p. 27 of the transcript:

"It does seem to me that the distinction that Mr *Evans-Lombe* draws is not one
that really can be drawn from *Chadwick* J's judgment and that it is a question of
principle whether or not the Crown should be treated in the same way as any other
litigant in this regard. I propose to follow *Chadwick* J's judgment in that respect G
and, for that reason, I will order costs on the standard basis only."

In those circumstances I am faced, as Mr *Evans-Lombe* was, with conflicting decisions
as to the test I should adopt.

To my mind there is a valid distinction between the position of the Crown as litigant in
proceedings of this nature and the position of the ordinary litigant in hostile litigation.
That distinction stems from the fact that the official receiver can be, and in this case was, H
obliged by the Secretary of State to pursue proceedings and that the proceedings have at
their foundation the principle that it is in the public interest that the privilege of limited
liability should not be abused. To that extent I find myself unable to follow the judgment
of *Chadwick* J in *Godwin Warren*. I prefer the principle expressed by *Vinelott* J in the
Moonbeam Cards case and adopted, as in my judgment it was, by Mr *Evans-Lombe* in

A   the *Synthetic Technology* case. I consider that the relevant consideration in deciding whether indemnity costs or standard costs should be awarded is whether, in the light of the conduct and nature of the defence and its outcome, it can be seen that the applicant has gone further than its public duty requires it to do.

In the present case I have found that the vast majority of the complaints made by the official receiver were justified. I have categorised this as a serious case, falling within the

B   middle band as defined in the *Sevenoaks Stationers* case.

In those circumstances I cannot say that the application in any way overstated the case and it follows, on the basis of the principle that I have attempted to enunciate, the appropriate award is indemnity costs and I make that order.

(Order accordingly)

C

D

E

F

G

H

A

Barrett v Duckett & Ors.

Chancery Division (Companies Court).
Sir Mervyn Davies (sitting as a High Court judge).
Judgment delivered 29 July 1993.

B

Minority shareholder's action — Derivative action — Striking-out motions — Whether company prima facie entitled to relief claimed — Whether action fell within exception to rule in Foss v Harbottle — Whether plaintiff had another remedy — Whether plaintiff was proper person to bring action.

These were motions to strike out a derivative action by a fifty per cent shareholder in a company.

The plaintiff sued four defendants: (1) "D", the other fifty per cent shareholder in the company; (2) D's wife; (3) the company; and (4) another company owned and controlled by D and his wife. The plaintiff complained that the fourth defendant company was acquired by D and his wife for the purpose of acquiring assets rightly belonging to the company and diverting business from the company and that business had been diverted; that D had extracted cash from the company; and that D and his wife had paid themselves excessive remuneration. The plaintiff's case was that it was impossible for her to set the company in motion to bring the action because she had only an equal shareholding with D and D was the sole director.

C

D

The defendants argued that the action was not a permissible derivative action because the plaintiff had an alternative remedy. D had presented a winding-up petition. If a winding-up order was made the question of proceedings against D could be considered by the liquidator. The defendants also argued that the plaintiff was unlikely to be able to exercise independent and unbiased judgment when conducting an action on the company's behalf and was therefore not a proper person to bring the action. In particular it was said that while she had made claims against D and his wife she had made no claim against her daughter, although she was a director of the company at the time and had allegedly benefited from the misappropriation of money.

E

Held, refusing the striking-out motions:

1. There was plainly a prima facie case that the company was entitled to the relief claimed.

F

2. The plaintiff, although a fifty per cent shareholder, was a minority shareholder for the purposes of the exceptions to the rule in Foss v Harbottle (1843) 2 Hare 461. The exception to the rule usually known as "fraud on the minority" was wide enough to cover the plaintiff's case.

3. It was unreasonable to say that the plaintiff had another remedy in co-operating to wind up the company and then hope to see the wrongs done to the company made the subject of an action by the liquidator. First, the plaintiff's suggestion that the company had a future could not be wholly discounted because the fourth defendant was trading and it was claimed in the action that its assets and goodwill were held on trust for the company. Secondly, questions arose as to the willingness of the Companies Court to make a winding-up order at the suit of a contributory where the contributory alleged insolvency. Finally, there was no certainty that the liquidator would sue, and the plaintiff had no means of compelling him to sue.

G

H

4. The plaintiff was in no way unfitted to take action on behalf of the company. She had not knowingly benefited herself from the alleged misappropriations. No doubt there was ill-feeling between the plaintiff and D but that in itself could not debar the plaintiff.

The following cases were referred to in the judgment:

Daniels & Ors v Daniels & Ors [1978] Ch 406.
Edwards & Anor v Halliwell & Ors [1950] 2 All ER 1064.
Estmanco (Kilner House) Ltd v Greater London Council [1982] 1 WLR 2.
Fargro v Godfroy (1986) 2 BCC 99,167; [1986] 1 WLR 1134.
Foss v Harbottle (1843) 2 Hare 461; 67 ER 189.
Nurcombe v Nurcombe & Anor (1984) 1 BCC 99,269; [1985] 1 WLR 370.
Prudential Assurance Co Ltd v Newman Industries Ltd & Ors (No. 2) [1982] Ch 204.
Smith & Ors v Croft & Ors (No. 2) (1987) 3 BCC 207; [1988] Ch 114.
Williams and Humbert Ltd v W & H Trade Marks (Jersey) Ltd [1986] AC 368.

Paul Staddon (instructed by Seddons) for the plaintiff.

Philip Cayford (instructed by Harris Rosenblatt & Kramer, agents for Harvey Ingram, Leicester) for the first defendant.

Anthony Mann QC and Hugo Groves (instructed by Consolo International Lawyers) for the second and fourth defendants.

JUDGMENT

Sir Mervyn Davies: I have before me a number of notices of motion in this action. It is convenient first to deal with the strike-out motion dated June 1993 made by the second and fourth defendants and, as well, a motion to the same effect issued in the course of the hearing by the first defendant. The plaintiff appears by Mr Staddon. The plaintiff in the action is Mrs Elizabeth Ellen Barrett.

By a writ endorsed with a statement of claim issued on 11 March 1993, Mrs Barrett sues four defendants. They are (1) Christopher Francis Duckett; (2) Janet Francis Duckett, his wife; (3) Nightingale Travel Ltd ("Travel"); and (4) Nightingale Coaches Ltd ("Coaches").

Mrs Barrett is the widow of Albert Edward Barrett who died on 19 February 1983. The first defendant was married to Mrs Barrett's daughter, Carol, until the marriage was dissolved on 11 February 1991. The first defendant married the second defendant in or about July 1992. The statement of claim states that Mrs Barrett sues in a representative capacity on behalf of Travel and/or herself — that is to say, the action is a derivative action, that being,

"the convenient name to apply to an action by a member of a company who sues on behalf of the company to enforce rights derived from that company."

—see Sir *Robert Megarry* V-C in *Estmanco (Kilner House) Ltd v Greater London Council* [1982] 1 WLR 2 at p. 10A–B.

Travel's objects are to carry on business as vehicle hirers and proprietors of vehicles. It has been engaged in school bussing and in the operation of a few bus-routes. Travel has an issued share capital of £100 in £1 shares. Mrs Barrett owns 50 of those shares and Mr Duckett the remaining 50. Mrs Barrett has been a director and secretary of Travel, but she resigned both those offices on 31 December 1983. Her daughter Carol has also been a director and secretary, but she too has resigned, doing so on 21 August 1991. Mr Duckett has been a director of Travel since its incorporation in 1977. He remains a director and is in fact the sole director of Travel.

Mrs Barrett makes a number of complaints about the conduct of Travel's affairs. She says that Mr Duckett is not prepared to cause or authorise Travel to sue in respect of those complaints so that she is, she says, an oppressed minority shareholder entitled to bring an action on behalf of Travel. Travel itself has, as I have indicated, been made a defendant. The second defendant, Mrs Janet Duckett, has in recent years worked for Travel. In the statement of claim, it is said that she was appointed company secretary of Travel on 21 August 1991. It is also said that she has acted as a director of Travel but she has never been formally appointed.

The fourth defendant, Coaches, was incorporated on 13 July 1990. Its object is similar to those of Travel. Its issued capital is £2 in £1 shares. Mr Duckett owns one share, and Janet owns the other share. Mr Duckett was a director of Coaches from 11 December 1990 to 8 August 1992, on which date he resigned. Janet is now a director of Coaches, she having been so appointed on 8 August 1992. She is also the company secretary. I am told that she has a co-director in the person of Mr Duckett's father.

The principal complaint made by Mrs Barrett is that Coaches was acquired by Duckett and Janet for the purpose of acquiring assets rightly belonging to Travel, and for the purpose of acting as a medium by which Duckett and Janet could divert business from Travel. Other complaints made on Travel's behalf by Mrs Barrett are, put shortly: (1) that over the years 1986–90 Mr Duckett caused money belonging to Travel to be paid into a Post Office Giro Account in his own name, or in the name of himself and his then wife. The money in question exceeds £217,000 and is now said to be regarded as a sum owing to Travel on a director's loan account. The misapplication of this money has as well given rise to certain tax and penalty claims by the Revenue; (2) excessive remuneration is said to have been allowed to Mr Duckett as a director and, as well, to his present wife, Mrs Janet Duckett; (3) there are in para. 8 of the statement of claim some points about business diverted from Travel to Coaches and the misapplication of Travel's assets coupled with the claim that Coaches' assets are held on trust for Travel. It is said that Mr Duckett and Janet have conspired to defraud Travel.

There were before me many affidavits and their exhibits. There have been Mareva proceedings in the action. A petition is pending to wind up Travel and there are still current, as I understand, matrimonial proceedings between Mr Duckett and his former wife. The affidavits I read have been drawn from those proceedings other than the matrimonial proceedings and as well there are affidavits sworn for the purposes of the striking-out application.

I was referred to the following affidavits with some of their exhibits: 1 March 1993, Mrs Barrett in the Mareva proceedings; 18 March, Mr Duckett; 18 March, Mrs Janet Duckett; 25 March, Mr Duckett; 27 April, Mrs Janet Duckett; 1 June 1993, Mrs Barrett; 2 June 1993, Mrs Janet Duckett; with two further affidavits of Mrs Janet Duckett, the last being 28 June 1993. I have also seen a copy of the petition to wind up Travel and a copy of Mr Duckett's affidavit in support.

Mr Mann for Mrs Janet Duckett and Coaches, Mr Cayford for the defendant Mr Duckett, submit that the action should not proceed on the grounds the action is not a permissible derivative action. I was early of the view that I ought not to continue to hear the application. I have in mind the words of Lord *Templeman* in *Williams and Humbert Ltd v W & H Trade Marks (Jersey) Ltd* [1986] AC 368 at p. 435H.

> "My Lords, if an application to strike out involves a prolonged and serious argument the judge should, as a general rule, decline to proceed with the argument unless he not only harbours doubts about the soundness of the pleading but, in addition, is satisfied that striking out will obviate the necessity for a trial or will substantially reduce the burden of preparing for trial or the burden of the trial itself."

But Mr Mann persuaded me that those sentences are not appropriate when one has an application to strike out that is based on an attack on the locus standi of the plaintiff. He referred to *Prudential Assurance Co Ltd v Newman Industries Ltd & Ors (No. 2)* [1982] Ch 204 at p. 221A–C and *Smith v Croft (No. 2)* (1987) 3 BCC 207.

Strike-out applications are made under the Rules of the Supreme Court, O. 18, r.19 and under the inherent jurisdiction of the court. In considering such applications it is usually the duty of the court to consider whether or not there is made out a plain and

A   obvious case for striking out. There is recourse to striking out only in plain and obvious cases (see the *Supreme Court Practice 1993*, 18/19/3 (vol. 1, p. 332).

Having regard to *Prudential Assurance v Newman Industries* it seems to me that when a challenge is made to the right of the plaintiff to bring a derivative action, it is the duty of the court to decide as a preliminary issue the question whether or not the plaintiff is entitled to sue on behalf of the company. It is not enough for the court to say that there is no plain and obvious case for striking out and so, in consequence there should be no

B   striking out. I take that view in light of these words from the judgment of the court in the *Prudential* case at p. 221A. It says:

> "In the result it would be improper for us to express any concluded view on the proper scope of the exception or exceptions to the rule in *Foss* v. *Harbottle*. We desire, however, to say two things. First, as we have already said, we have no doubt whatever that Vinelott J. erred in dismissing the summons of May 10, 1979.

C
> He ought to have determined as a preliminary issue whether the plaintiffs were entitled to sue on behalf of Newman by bringing a derivative action. It cannot have been right to have subjected the company to a 30-day action (as it was then estimated to be) in order to enable him to decide whether the plaintiffs were entitled in law to subject the company to a 30-day action. Such an approach defeats the whole purpose of the rule in *Foss* v. *Harbottle* and sanctions the very

D
> mischief that the rule is designed to prevent. By the time a derivative action is concluded, the rule in *Foss* v. *Harbottle* can have little, if any, role to play. Either the wrong is proved, thereby establishing conclusively the rights of the company; or the wrong is not proved, so cadit quaestio."

See also *Smith v Croft* at pp. 214–217.

In these circumstances I follow the guidance given by *Megarry* V-C at p. 14H of the

E   *Estmanco* case:

> "It accordingly seems to me that even if Mr. Brodie were right in his main submissions of law (and I do not think that he is), as the evidence stands he has not got the necessary facts to support them. This is, of course, only a motion, and there has been no viva voce evidence or cross-examination on affidavits. It is clear from the decision of the Court of Appeal in *Prudential Assurance Co. Ltd.* v. *Newman Industries Ltd. (No. 2)* [1982] 2 W.L.R. 31 that it is right that a *Foss* v.

F
> *Harbottle* point should where possible be decided as a preliminary issue and not left for determination at the trial. On such an application the court has to do the best it can on the evidence and other material which the parties have chosen to put before it, even though further evidence and other material may well be put forward later, and perhaps lead to other conclusions."

So here I must do the best I can on the evidence the parties have put before me.

G   Mr Mann referred to a number of authorities bearing on the situation in which a derivative action is allowed. He drew attention to the rule in *Foss v Harbottle* (1843) 2 Hare 461 as explained by *Jenkins* LJ in *Edwards v Halliwell* [1950] 2 All ER 1064 at pp. 1066–1067.

> "The rule in *Foss* v. *Harbottle*. . . , as I understand it, comes to no more than this. First, the proper plaintiff in an action in respect of a wrong alleged to be done to a

H
> company or association of persons is *prima facie* the company or the association of persons itself. Secondly, where the alleged wrong is a transaction which might be made binding on the company or association and on all its members by a simple majority of the members, no individual member of the company is allowed to maintain an action in respect of that matter for the simple reason that, if a mere majority of the members of the company or association is in favour of what has been done, then *cadit quaestio*."

There are exceptions to the rule. The exceptions are mentioned in the *Halliwell* case
and are said to be summarised in *Palmer's Company Law* at para. 8.808. But whether or
not the exceptions there summarised are exhaustive is by no means clear. One notes
Megarry V-C in the *Estmanco* case as saying at p. 10G:

> "If the rule in *Foss* v. *Harbottle* had remained unqualified, the way would have
> been open for the majority to stultify any proceedings which were for the benefit
> of the minority and to the disadvantage of the majority. Accordingly, a number of
> exceptions from the rule have been established; and it is here that the difficulties
> begin. For convenience, I use the word 'exceptions' to embrace cases which are
> outside the true scope of the rule. It is far from clear just what the exceptions are,
> or what is the ambit of some of them. I do not think that it can simply be said that
> there is an exception from the rule whenever the justice of the case requires it.
> There are some dicta which support such a view (see, e.g. *Edwards* v. *Halliwell*
> [1950] 2 All E.R. 1064, 1067, *per* Jenkins L.J.), and this seems to have been part
> of the ratio in *Prudential Assurance Co. Ltd.* v. *Newman Industries Ltd. (No. 2)*
> [1981] Ch. 257; see at p. 327. But in the Court of Appeal in the latter case, the
> court . . . observed that this was 'not a practical test'; and I would respectfully
> concur. If it were the test, I feel no doubt that in this case the applicant would
> succeed."

The Vice-Chancellor goes on:

> "Although the concept of injustice is not the test, I think that it is nevertheless a
> reason, and an important reason, for making exceptions from the rule; yet the
> reasons for an exception must not be confused with the exception itself. If the test
> were simply justice or injustice, this would mean different things to different men;
> and the courts have in fact proceeded by way of formulating, not always with great
> clarity, a number of individual exceptions. The subject has, indeed, been gradually
> developing; and unless the remedy introduced by section 75 of the Companies Act
> 1980 inhibits that development, no doubt one day the courts will distil from the
> exceptions some guiding principle that is wide enough to comprehend them all
> and yet narrow enough to be practicable and workable. It may be that the test may
> come to be whether an ordinary resolution of the shareholders could validly carry
> out or ratify the act in question . . ."

In the *Prudential* case at pp. 221–222 it is stated that:

> ". . . whatever may be the properly defined boundaries of the exception to the
> rule [in *Foss v Harbottle*], the plaintiff ought at least to be required before
> proceeding with his action to establish a prima facie case (i) that the company is
> entitled to the relief claimed, and (ii) that the action falls within the proper
> boundaries of the exception to the rule in *Foss* v. *Harbottle*."

In this case it is in my view quite plain that the company is prima facie entitled to the
relief claimed. For the defendants, it was hardly denied but that the first defendant at
any rate had a formidable claim to meet as respects much of the relief claimed.

So one considers (ii) above; that is to say, whether or not the action falls within the
boundaries of the *Foss v Harbottle* exceptions. In this regard there are the words of
Templeman J in *Daniels v Daniels* [1978] Ch 406 at p. 414D:

> "The principle which may be gleaned from *Alexander* v. *Automatic Telephone
> Co.* [1900] 2 Ch. 56 (directors benefiting themselves), from *Cook* v. *Deeks* [1916]
> 1 A.C. 554 (directors diverting business in their own favour) and from dicta in
> *Pavlides* v. *Jensen* [1956] 2 Ch. 565 (directors appropriating assets of the company)
> is that a minority shareholder who has no other remedy may sue where directors
> use their powers, intentionally or unintentionally, fraudulently or negligently, in
> a manner which benefits themselves at the expense of the company."

A   I note the words there: "no other remedy". There are then the words of *Walton* J in
Fargro v Godfroy (1986) 2 BCC 99,167 at p. 99,168:

> "The situation therefore is that the defendants have taken the position that on the
> matters as pleaded in the statement of claim and as now refined by the evidence,
> that part of the action which constitutes a minority shareholders' action will not
> lie and that the rule in *Foss v Harbottle* . . . applies.

B   Now, as has been pointed out fairly recently in the Court of Appeal, *Prudential
Assurance Co Ltd v Newman Industries Ltd & Ors (No. 2)* . . . the rule in *Foss v
Harbottle*, although of course one applying more particularly to companies, is a
rule which applies generally in the sense that the proper plaintiff in every type and
sort of action is indeed the person in whom the cause of action is vested. So that
one starts from the position that as regards a claim such as is made in the present
C   action which, putting it very compendiously, is that the defendants (including the
third defendant, the other shareholder) have diverted assets and opportunity
belonging to the plaintiffs to their own use, the proper plaintiff is the fourth
defendant, the company . . . It is such because it is the company which has
suffered the loss. Now if that company had not been in liquidation, it is conceded
that the pleas contained in para. 8 and para. 28 of the statement of claim would
have laid a proper foundation for a minority shareholder's action because it would
D   have been impossible for the plaintiffs to have got the company to have taken any
action against its other shareholder or indeed the other defendants. That is quite
clearly because if the matter had been put to the board of the company the board
would have been equally split. There would therefore have been no resolution to
bring such an action. And if the matter had been carried to the shareholders in
general meeting exactly the same result would have followed.

E   Therefore, as a practical matter, it would have been totally impossible for the
plaintiff to set the company . . . in motion to bring the action and it is under those
circumstances that a minority shareholder's action will lie."

He goes on to refer to the situation that arises once the company goes into liquidation.

In the circumstances of this case it is impossible for Mrs Barrett to set the company in
motion to bring the action because she has only an equal shareholding with Mr Duckett
F   and, moreover, Mr Duckett is the sole director. Mr Duckett is, of course, unwilling to
put the company into action for the purpose of suing him, that is, Mr Duckett.

So I turn to Lord *Templeman*'s reference to the fact that the minority shareholder
may sue on behalf of the company if he, the minority shareholder, has "no other
remedy". I do not know of any remedy open to Mrs Barrett if she is to be denied in this
action the opportunity of seeking to redress the wrongs said to have be done to Travel.
G   Mrs Barrett is not, strictly speaking, a minority shareholder since she has 50 shares as
does Mr Duckett. Nevertheless she is, in my view, a minority shareholder for the
purposes of the exceptions to *Foss v Harbottle*. In the *Estmanco* case *Megarry* V-C said
at p. 15G:

> "As I have indicated, I do not consider that this is a suitable occasion on which to
> probe the intricacies of the rule in *Foss* v. *Harbottle* and its exceptions, or to
H   > attempt to discover and expound the principles to be found in the exceptions. All
> that I need say is that in my judgment the exception usually known as 'fraud on a
> minority' is wide enough to cover the present case, and that if it is not, it should
> now be made wide enough."

In the same way, I regard the exception to the *Foss v Harbottle* rule as being wide
enough to cover the present case, so that Mrs Barrett may sue on behalf of the company.

Mr Mann and Mr Cayford submitted that, contrary to my view, Mrs Barrett does have
another remedy in respect of the complaints which she makes. This submission arises
from the fact that on 13 November 1992 in the Leicester County Court, Mr Duckett
presented a petition for the winding up of Travel. A winding-up order is sought on the
grounds (1) that the company is unable to pay its debts; and/or (2) it is just and equitable
that Travel be wound up. I read from para. 6, 7 and 8 of the petition:

> "6. In support of ground (1) it is confirmed that an estimated statement of affairs
> of the company as at 29 October 1992 shows that whilst the book value of the
> company is £46,743 the forced sale value is (£192,097). The principal reason for
> this difference is the directors' loan account which stands at £239,000 and which is
> unlikely to be payable in full or at all and accordingly the value of the company's
> assets is less than the amount of its liabilities taking into account its actual and
> prospective liabilities. In addition the company ceased trading in August 1992 at
> which time the company's assets were sold at fair market value. Accordingly, the
> company is unable to pay its debts as they fall due.
>
> 7. In support of ground (2) the Articles of Association of the company have at all
> material times provided that at general meetings each shareholder should on a
> show of hands have one vote and on a poll one vote for each share held by him,
> and that the chairman should not have a casting vote at either general meetings of
> the company or meetings of the board of directors. The shares of Mr A E Barrett
> passed to his wife, Mrs Barrett, on his death. The petitioner is the only director of
> the company. Mrs Barrett has frequently blocked and obstructed the affairs of the
> company by voting against matters put forward by her fellow shareholder, the
> petitioner herein.
>
> 8. The petitioner called an extraordinary general meeting of the shareholders of
> the company at 29 October 1992 for the purpose of passing an extraordinary
> resolution that the company be voluntarily wound up. Mrs Barrett refused to
> consent to that resolution and the relations between the petitioner and Mrs
> Barrett have now broken down irretrievably. Accordingly the petitioner petitions
> the court that the company be wound up on the alternative ground that it is just
> and equitable to do so as the petitioner is unable to conduct the business of the
> company."

That is the end of the extract from the petition. The petition was on 18 May 1993
transferred to the High Court by *Vinelott* J and awaits a hearing date. At the hearing
Mrs Barrett intends to oppose the making of a winding-up order. Rightly or wrongly she
believes, so Mr Staddon says, that Travel has a future.

In this situation it is Mr Mann's submission that in all the circumstances of this case
including deadlock and the company's insolvency, and as he sees it, the company's poor
prospects for the future, it is right and proper to treat winding up as a genuine alternative
open to Mrs Barrett, that is an alternative to suing on behalf of the company in the
derivative action. As I understand, it is said that Mrs Barrett should join with
Mr Duckett in asking for a winding-up order. Mr Mann said it was to be borne in mind
that with a winding-up order made, the question of proceedings against Mr Duckett
would be considered by the liquidator. Mrs Barrett would doubtless urge such proceedings
and could, he said, apply to the court for directions should the liquidator be unwilling to
start proceedings.

I do not accept Mr Mann's submission. To my mind it is unreasonable to say that Mrs
Barrett, desiring to remedy a wrong done to Travel by way of a derivative action, has
another way of remedying those wrongs in that she can co-operate in steps to wind up
the company and then hope to see the wrongs done to the company made the subject of
an action by the liquidator.

A   I also take account of the following considerations put forward by Mr Staddon: (1) as I have mentioned, Mrs Barrett believes that Travel has a future. That suggestion cannot be wholly discounted because Coaches is, as I understand, trading and it is claimed in the action that the assets and goodwill of Coaches are held on trust for Travel; (2) questions arise as to the willingness of the Companies Court to make a winding-up order at the suit of a contributory and the contributory alleges insolvency (see *Palmer*, para. 15.228C). There is no certainty that the liquidator would sue, and Mrs Barrett has

B   no means of compelling him to sue.

     Another objection to the action being prosecuted by Mrs Barrett is derived from *Nurcombe v Nurcombe* (1984) 1 BCC 99,269. I read from the judgment of *Lawton* LJ at p. 99,273:

C   "It is pertinent to remember, however, that a minority shareholder's action in form is nothing more than a procedural device for enabling the court to do justice to a company controlled by miscreant directors or shareholders. Since the procedural device has evolved so that justice can be done for the benefit of the company, whoever comes forward to start the proceedings must be doing so for the benefit of the company and not for some other purpose. It follows that the court has to satisfy itself that the person coming forward is a proper person to do so. In *Gower's Principles of Modern Company Law* (4th ed., 1979) the law is

D   stated, in my opinion correctly, in these terms at p. 652:

     'The right to bring a derivative action is afforded the individual member as a matter of grace. Hence the conduct of a shareholder may be regarded by a court of equity as disqualifying him from appearing as plaintiff on the company's behalf. This will be the case, for example, if he participated in the wrong of which he complains.' "

E   Then in the same case at p. 99,274, *Lawton* LJ goes on:

     "My understanding of these judgments is that the court is entitled to look at the conduct of a plaintiff in a minority shareholder's action in order to satisfy itself that he is a proper person to bring the action on behalf of the company and that the company itself will benefit. A particular plaintiff may not be a proper person because his conduct is tainted in some way which under the rules of equity may

F   bar relief. He may not have come with 'clean hands' or he may have been guilty of delay."

     The suggestion was that Mrs Barrett is not a proper person to bring the action. This was asserted on a variety of grounds, most of which derive from the fact that Mrs Barrett is the mother of Carol, Mr Duckett's first wife; that mother and daughter get on well together and that the divorce proceedings have been acrimonious. In this situation it

G   was said, it was inherently unlikely that Mrs Barrett could exercise independent and unbiased judgment when conducting an action on Travel's behalf. In particular it was said that Mrs Barrett had disabled herself from suing because while she had made claims against Mr Duckett and Mrs Janet Duckett, she had made no claim against her daughter Carol, although it was manifest that Carol had benefited from the misappropriation of money referred to in ch. 6 of the statement of claim and that at a time when she, Carol, was a director of Travel complaint was also made concerning a house called "The

H   Noakes". "The Noakes" was, I understand, a second home of Mr Duckett and Carol. In the course of the matrimonial proceedings Mr Duckett proposed that "The Noakes" be transferred to Travel. Mrs Barrett at an extraordinary general meeting of Travel refused to sanction the transfer, although as I understand, she has been willing to see "The Noakes" sold and the proceeds of the sale paid over to Travel. In the events that have happened, that course has not been possible because I was told that, while "The

Noakes" has been sold, the proceeds of sale are held in an account under the control of the matrimonial court.

Mrs Barrett's unfittingness to sue was strongly urged upon me, but looking again at the affidavits read to me I cannot see that Mrs Barrett is in any way unfitted to act as a plaintiff on behalf of Travel. I am not in the least convinced that she ever knowingly benefited herself from misappropriations that are alleged in ch. 6 and 7 of the statement of claim. No doubt there is ill-feeling between Mrs Barrett and Mr Duckett but that in itself cannot debar Mrs Barrett, were it to do so most derivative actions would be frustrated.

Mr Staddon accepted that Carol should have been joined in the action at the outset. He applied at the hearing for her joinder. That being so, the failure to join her at the outset is not a reason for now holding Mrs Barrett as unfitted to sue.

Mr Mann submitted that Mrs Janet Duckett ought not to remain in the action as a defendant because Janet has never been either an appointed director or a de facto director of Travel. However that may be, the allegation that Janet has been a de facto director is pleaded and there are cheques drawn on Travel's bank account, signed by Janet, against the word "Director". Janet seeks to explain those signings in her affidavit sworn on 28 January 1993 where, however, she goes on to indicate that she took part "in trying to run the business of the third defendant". Whether or not Janet has acted as a de facto director can only be decided at the trial. She is, of course, a director of Coaches against which company relief is claimed.

Since I find that the action may proceed as a derivative action, I see no sound reason for removing Mrs Janet Duckett as a defendant. The strike-out motion asks in the alternative that the action be stayed until the hearing of the winding-up petition. I decline any such stay. The practical course is to list the action for hearing with the petition. An application may be made to the Companies Court to the effect that the petition be listed with the action. I make no order on para. 2 of the notice of motion of the second and fourth defendant.

(*Order accordingly*)

A

Re Bank of Credit and Commerce International SA & Anor.

Chancery Division (Companies Court).
Rattee J.
Judgment delivered 30 July 1993.

Insolvency — Co-operation between courts exercising jurisdiction in relation to insolvency — Company being wound up in Cayman Islands — Cayman Islands court sent letter of request to English court — Letter of request sought orders under Insolvency Act — No equivalent provisions in Cayman Islands law — Whether English court could apply UK insolvency law — Whether sufficient "matters specified in the request" — Whether court had discretion under letter of request in absence of equivalent Cayman Islands provisions — Insolvency Act 1986, sec. 426.

This was an application by respondents to an application by the liquidators of Bank of Credit and Commerce International (Overseas) Ltd ("Overseas") which was a Cayman Islands company being wound up by the Cayman Islands court.

The liquidators alleged that the respondents had participated and/or assisted in the fraudulent activities of the senior management of the BCCI group, and sought relief under sec. 212, 213, 214 and 238 of the Insolvency Act 1986. The liquidators of Overseas accepted that, because those sections applied only to a "company" within the meaning of the 1986 Act, which Overseas was not, the English court had no jurisdiction to entertain their application under the 1986 Act except to the extent, if any, to which such jurisdiction arose under sec. 426 of the Act. They submitted that the court did have and should exercise jurisdiction to make the orders sought under sec. 426. By virtue of a letter of request issued by the Grand Court of the Cayman Islands, the English court had jurisdiction to make such declarations as were requested by the letter of request, should the facts be found to justify them, notwithstanding that the court would otherwise have no power to make any such orders in relation to a foreign company being wound up abroad, and that the Grand Court would itself have no such power, because Cayman Islands insolvency law did not include provisions comparable with the sections of the 1986 Act under which the declarations were sought.

The respondents applied to strike out the claims by the liquidators of Overseas. They submitted that the court had no jurisdiction to make the declarations sought in relation to Overseas: first, because the power conferred on the court by sec. 426 of the Act was limited to applying English procedural law for the purpose of recognising and giving effect in England to decisions made by a relevant foreign court in the exercise of its own insolvency jurisdiction by the application of its own national insolvency law; and secondly because in any event the letter of request issued by the Grand Court was not a letter of request within the meaning of sec. 426 of the 1986 Act. The respondents objected to the letter of request because it did not specify the matters of fact on which the court's assistance was sought, but merely set out orders which the court was asked to make. They also argued that in the context of the terms of the letter of request the court had no discretion whether to apply English or Cayman Islands law, because there was no Cayman Islands law equivalent to the sections of the Act under which the letter of request sought declarations.

The respondents further argued that Mareva injunctions made against them should not be continued until trial or should be discharged for material non-disclosure on the ex parte application.

Held, refusing to strike out the claims by the liquidators of Overseas and continuing the Mareva injunctions until trial: A

1. Giving the words of sec. 426 of the 1986 Act their ordinary meaning there was no justification for restricting their effect in the manner urged on behalf of the respondents, namely to provisions of English law which were described as procedural as opposed to substantive. The effect of sec. 426 was to give the court a discretion (exercisable only for the purpose of carrying out its duty under sec. 426(4) to assist the courts having insolvency jurisdiction in other parts of the UK or any relevant country or territory) as to whether it should apply English insolvency law, whether procedural or substantive, or the law of the requesting court to matters specified in the relevant request from the foreign court.   B

2. Section 426(5) conferred a discretion on the requested court whether to apply its own law or the law of the requesting court to the matters specified in the request, and it was to that discretion that the "proviso" at the end of the subsection referring to the rules of private international law was directed.   C

3. To make a request within the meaning of sec. 426(5) the court of another part of the UK or a relevant country or territory had simply to ask the court to assist it. The words "any matters specified in the request" in subsec. (5) meant no more nor less than "any part of the subject-matter of the request".

4. If the declarations could have been made under Cayman Islands law then no doubt the Grand Court would not have been asking for the court's assistance in making them. The request having been made, the court had to consider how to respond to it. If the court decided to apply English law and to consider whether the declarations sought could properly be made under that law, that would involve an investigation of the relevant facts. That was a factor to be taken into consideration in exercising the discretion, and not a valid objection to the existence of the discretion in the terms of sec. 426(5).   D

5. The court should exercise its discretion in favour of giving the particular assistance requested by the Grand Court unless there was some good reason for not doing so. There was no good reason in the rules of private international law or elsewhere for the court not giving the assistance requested. On the contrary there were good reasons why the court should give the assistance sought by trying the claims by the liquidators of Overseas for declarations in the terms set out in the letter of request.   E

6. On the question of continuing the Mareva injunctions, the evidence disclosed a prima facie case that the respondents had assets both within and without the jurisdiction and that there was a real risk of dissipation or secretion of those assets. The liquidators had made out a good arguable case for the relief sought in their application. The court did not accept any of the respondents' objections to the form of the Mareva injunctions. There had been no breach of the duty of disclosure.   F

The following cases were referred to in the judgment: G

Bank of Credit and Commerce International SA, Re (No. 2) [1992] BCC 715.
Bishopsgate Investment Management Ltd, Re [1992] BCC 222; [1993] Ch 1.
Dallhold Estates (UK) Pty Ltd, Re [1992] BCC 394.
Debtor, Re a, ex parte Viscount of the Royal Court of Jersey [1981] Ch 384.
Derby & Co Ltd & Ors v Weldon & Ors [1990] Ch 48.
Derby & Co Ltd & Ors v Weldon & Ors (No. 3 & 4) [1990] Ch 65.
Galbraith v Grimshaw [1910] AC 508.
Hall v Woolf (1908) 7 CLR 207.
Osborn, Re [1931–32] B & CR 189.   H

Michael Crystal QC, Richard Sheldon and Susan Prevezer (instructed by Lovell White Durrant) for the liquidators.

A   William Blackburne QC, Matthew Collings and Richard Morgan (instructed by Nabarro Nathanson) for the first respondent.

Philip Heslop QC, George Bompas and Robert Miles (instructed by D J Freeman) for the second respondent.

William Stubbs QC, J Stephen Smith and Ian Peacock (instructed by Gouldens) for the third respondent.

B

JUDGMENT

Rattee J: These proceedings represent the latest instalment of litigation arising out of the collapse of the Bank of Credit and Commerce International ("BCCI").

Bank of Credit and Commerce International SA ("SA") was incorporated in Luxembourg on 21 September 1972. It was at all material times registered in England C   under Pt. XXIII of the *Companies Act* 1985 or its predecessors. It was ordered to be wound up by this court on 14 January 1992 pursuant to a petition presented on 5 July 1991 by the Bank of England. It is also the subject of winding-up proceedings before the court of Luxembourg.

Bank of Credit and Commerce International (Overseas) Ltd ("Overseas") was incorporated in the Cayman Islands on 25 November 1975. It has never been registered in this country. It was ordered to be wound up by the Grand Court of the Cayman Islands D   on 14 January 1992.

SA and Overseas were the principal operating subsidiaries of Bank of Credit and Commerce Holdings (Luxembourg) S.A. ("Holdings"). When carrying on business SA had 47 offices or branches in 13 different countries, 24 of which were in the UK. Overseas had 63 branches in 28 different countries, the largest number in any country being in Oman. As is now all too well known the companies went into liquidation E   hopelessly insolvent as a result of frauds perpetrated by persons entrusted with their management, with overall deficiencies estimated as being in excess of $10 billion, bringing financial ruin and misery on many of their erstwhile customers. So much appears from the judgment of *Dillon* LJ in *Re Bank of Credit and Commerce International SA (No. 2)* [1992] BCC 715 at pp. 720 et seq.

In those proceedings the court approved the liquidators of SA entering into, in F   particular, two agreements in the context of the liquidation of SA. One of those agreements (the contribution agreement) featured in the argument before me, and I shall have to say something more about it in due course. For the present it is sufficient to say that in essence it provided that the Abu Dhabi government would contribute $1.5 billion to the funds available for creditors of the companies, provided that there should be mutual releases of claims between the liquidators on the one hand and the majority shareholders of Holdings (including in particular the ruler, crown prince and government G   of Abu Dhabi) and certain other Abu Dhabi parties on the other hand, save that "the Abu Dhabi parties" should be admitted as creditors in the liquidations in the aggregate sum of about $1.9 billion.

The other agreement to which I have referred which was approved by the English court was a "pooling agreement" providing for the assets of the two companies, SA and Overseas, being pooled for the purposes of liquidation. As explained by Sir *Donald* H   *Nicholls* V-C (at p. 719F):

"... the affairs of BCCI SA and BCCI Overseas are so hopelessly intertwined that a pooling of their assets, with a distribution enabling the like dividend to be paid to both companies' creditors, is the only sensible way to proceed. It would make no sense to spend vast sums of money and much time in trying to disentangle and unravel."

The proceedings presently before me were commenced by an originating application A
issued on 10 December 1992 by the first four applicants named therein as the liquidators
of SA appointed in the winding-up proceedings in this court, and by the fifth, sixth and
seventh named applicants as the liquidators of Overseas in its winding up by the Cayman
Islands court. The application was described in an affidavit sworn by the first applicant,
Mr Christopher Morris, as:

"... part of a concerted worldwide effort by the liquidators ... to seek
compensation from the respondents for their participation and/or assistance in B
the fraudulent activities of the senior management of the BCCI group."

The respondents are:

(1) Khalid Salem bin Mahfouz, to whom I shall refer in this judgment as "Mahfouz",
as he is referred to in documents in the proceedings to which I shall have to refer.
He is a citizen of and resident in Saudi Arabia. He was a director of SA, Overseas
and Holdings between 4 September 1986 and 18 August 1989. C

(2) National Commercial Bank, Saudi Arabia ("NCB") is a bank incorporated in
Saudi Arabia which at all material times had a place of business in London.
According to Mr Morris's affidavit NCB was at all material times owned and
managed by members of the family of Mahfouz, its activities being under the
direction and control of Mahfouz.

(3) Haroon Rashid Kahlon, to whom I shall refer as "Kahlon", claims to be resident D
in Pakistan. According to Mr Morris's affidavit Kahlon at all material times
worked as an officer or employee of NCB under the supervision of Mahfouz. He
was also an employee of one or other of the companies in the BCCI group for
about three years prior to about May 1980.

By the originating application the applicants seek various forms of relief based on
alleged participation by the respondents in the wrongful activities of the senior
management of the BCCI group, and in particular of two persons by the names of Abedi E
and Naqvi. Some of the relief sought by the originating application is sought by the first
four named applicants as liquidators in the winding up by this court of SA, some by the
last three named applicants as liquidators in the winding up by the Grand Court of the
Cayman Islands of Overseas. The following claims are made by each set of liquidators.

(1) A declaration under sec. 213 of the *Insolvency Act* 1986 ("the 1986 Act") that
Mahfouz, NCB and Kahlon were knowingly parties to the carrying on of the
business of SA or Overseas, as the case may be, with intent to defraud creditors, F
and that accordingly the respondents are liable to contribute to the assets of the
company concerned, in the case of SA $5.9 billion and in the case of Overseas $4.6
billion (being in each case the amount of the current estimated deficiency of assets
of the company) or to make such contribution as the court thinks proper.

(2) A declaration under sec. 214 of the 1986 Act that Mahfouz knew or ought to have
concluded that there was no reasonable prospect that SA or Overseas, as the case G
may be, would avoid going into insolvent liquidation no later than 17 September
1986, alternatively April 1987, alternatively March 1988 or any time thereafter
and is accordingly liable to make a similar contribution to the assets of the
company as that sought under the first head of claim.

(3) A declaration under sec. 212 of the 1986 Act that Mahfouz was guilty of
"misfeasance and breach of fiduciary or other duty" in misapplying or causing or
permitting to be misapplied moneys of SA and/or Overseas amounting in the H
aggregate to some $1.33 billion.

(4) A declaration under sec. 212 that Mahfouz and/or NCB and/or Kahlon received
the moneys mentioned in head (3) of the relief sought on trust for SA or Overseas
as the case may be, and that they are liable to account for the moneys concerned
to SA or Overseas, as the case may be.

A   (5)   A declaration under sec. 238 of the 1986 Act that certain specified payments or transfers totalling $717,663,000 made to one or other of the three respondents within two years of the respective liquidations of the two companies constituted transactions at an undervalue and should be restored to the company concerned. All the payments or transfers specified under this head of claim are included in the payments amounting to $1.33 billion-odd included under head (3), to which I have referred.

B   (6)   Consequential orders for payment, interest, costs, etc.

     The originating application includes some ten pages of grounds on which the applicants seek the relief to which I have referred. The major part of these payments, such part amounting to over $1 billion, were, according to the liquidators' claim, made out of the assets of the company concerned as part of an allegedly fraudulent scheme involving the extraction of moneys from the insolvent companies by way of payments to purchase
C   from the recipients shares in Holdings itself or in a Netherlands Antilles corporation by the name of Credit and Commerce American Holdings NV ("CCAH"), itself the parent company of an American financial institution by the name of First American Bankshares Inc. According to the liquidators' claim the scheme was entered into at a time when NCB and/or Mahfouz knew that the BCCI group was in severe financial difficulties. Not only were BCCI funds thus misappropriated to the knowledge of the respondents to pay
D   Mahfouz or NCB under the scheme to buy back shares in Holdings and CCAH, but the misappropriations were concealed in the books of SA and Overseas by bogus or fictitious transactions which disguised the true financial position of the companies so as to allow them to go on trading to the disastrous detriment of future depositors and other creditors. This is in essence the basis on which it is sought by the liquidators to pursue the claims set out in the originating application. Mr Morris in his affidavit evidence explains how the liquidators enormously complex and lengthy investigations have led
E   them to the conclusions forming the basis for their claims, and how those conclusions are similar to conclusions reached by Price Waterhouse, former auditors of the companies in the BCCI group, and expressed in a draft report produced by them in June 1991 to the Bank of England pursuant to their appointment by the bank to investigate pursuant to sec. 41 of the *Banking Act* 1987.

     On the same day as the originating application was issued an ex parte application was
F   made on behalf of the liquidators to *Vinelott* J for Mareva injunctions and leave to serve the originating application out of the jurisdiction on Mahfouz and Kahlon. The judge gave leave to serve out of the jurisdiction as sought and a worldwide Mareva injunction against both Mahfouz and Kahlon. The injunction was subject to common form exceptions permitting payments for legal costs and $10,000 per week for ordinary living expenses. At the same time *Vinelott* J ordered that the aid of the Royal Court of Jersey be sought
G   by the issue of a letter of request to that court pursuant to sec. 426 of the 1986 Act requesting the Jersey court to make similar injunctions against Mahfouz and Kahlon. I shall have to return to consider sec. 426 in considerable detail later in this judgment.

     On the same day, 10 December 1992, the Royal Court of Jersey made a worldwide injunction in the terms sought by the letter of request issued pursuant to the order of *Vinelott* J. Also on the same day the District Court of the District of Columbia in Washington, USA, made a temporary restraining order restraining Mahfouz and Kahlon
H   dealing with assets in the US.

     On 22 December 1992 the liquidators' application for a continuation of the Mareva injunctions came before *Vinelott* J inter partes. He adjourned the application to a date to be fixed and continued the injunctions granted on 10 December over the adjourned hearing, with liberty to Mahfouz and Kahlon to apply on 48 hours' notice to vary or discharge the order. Also at the hearing on 22 December *Vinelott* J refused an application

made on behalf of Mahfouz and Kahlon to require the liquidators not to bring proceedings
against them abroad without the leave of the court.

On 21 January 1993 Kahlon issued one of the applications now before me, namely an
application for (inter alia) orders:

(1)   discharging the orders made by *Vinelott* J on 10 December, that is to say the
Mareva injunction and the leave to serve out of the jurisdiction, so far as those
orders related to Kahlon; and

(2)   setting aside the service of the originating application on him which had been
effected pursuant to the order of *Vinelott* J.

This application was said to be based on the proposition that England was not a forum
conveniens for the proceedings, as well as on the propositions that Mr Morris's affidavit
did not disclose a sufficient case to justify the orders made by *Vinelott* J, and that at the
hearing on 10 December the liquidators had failed to disclose to the court material facts
known, or which ought to have been known, to them.

On 25 January 1993 an application to set aside the Mareva injunction and the service
of the proceedings out of the jurisdiction was also made by Mahfouz. On the same day
Mr Sigler, Mahfouz's English solicitor, swore an affidavit in answer to the first affidavit
of Mr Morris. In that affidavit he said that Mahfouz had suffered a heart attack and was
not fit himself to swear an affidavit.

On 27 January 1993 the proceedings came before *Warner* J. He adjourned the
originating application and the applications by Mahfouz and Kahlon to which I have just
referred to a date to be fixed, and continued the Mareva injunction in the meantime.
The judge also gave directions in the originating application, including directions for the
service of points of claim. He further directed that Kahlon should swear an affidavit of
assets required of him by the order of 10 December by 17 February 1993, such affidavit
to be retained by his solicitors until further order after the determination of the
application made by Kahlon.

Points of claim with schedules thereto running in all to about 150 pages were served
by the liquidators on 24 February 1993. In these the grounds set out in the originating
application are expanded and elaborated upon with very great complexity. It is fortunately
not necessary for me to go into them in any detail for present purposes. They are the
subject matter of applications to strike out all or various parts of them which have been
launched on behalf of Mahfouz and NCB. Unfortunately the particular complaints
made of the points of claim were not disclosed by those respondents until the
commencement of the hearing before me, despite the liquidators' solicitors having
pressed their respective solicitors for some time for the grounds of the applications to
strike out, which were in fact issued in May 1993. The grounds now disclosed include a
great number of criticisms of the points of claim which, because they were (in my
judgment inexcusably) not disclosed to the liquidators prior to the beginning of the
hearing before me, the latter had had no opportunity to consider. In those circumstances,
not surprisingly, counsel for the liquidators was not willing to deal with them at the
hearing before me. I accordingly declined to deal with the applications to strike out
issued by Mahfouz and Kahlon in May.

On 28 May 1993 Mahfouz's solicitors notified the liquidators' solicitors that Mahfouz
no longer intended to pursue the parts of his application of 25 January which sought to
set aside the order of *Vinelott* J giving leave to serve him out of the jurisdiction and the
service on him made pursuant to that order. At a very late stage of the hearing before
me counsel for Kahlon indicated that he wished to abandon his attempt to set aside
service on him outside the jurisdiction and no longer sought to object to the court's
jurisdiction to entertain the claims made by the liquidators of SA as against him. He

A   maintains an objection to jurisdiction in relation to the claims by the liquidators of Overseas, but only on the ground that they do not fall within the jurisdiction conferred on this court by sec. 426 of the 1986 Act. A similar objection to jurisdiction in relation to the claims by the liquidators of Overseas is made on behalf of NCB by a summons issued in the course of the hearing before me so as to enable the arguments on sec. 426 of the 1986 Act to be decided as between the liquidators of Overseas and NCB as well as between those liquidators and Kahlon. For reasons no doubt best known to him or his

B   advisers, but which I understand to arise from the stance on jurisdiction being adopted by him in proceedings brought by the liquidators against the respondents to the originating application in Washington, USA, Mahfouz indicated by his counsel that he was not himself seeking to argue that this court has no jurisdiction in respect of any part of the originating application, though he may, of course, be the passive recipient of the benefit of any success his fellow respondents may have on the jurisdiction issue.

C   By the end of the hearing the issues to be decided by me had been resolved into the following:

    (1)   Does this court have jurisdiction to entertain the claims made in the originating application by the liquidators of Overseas?

    (2)   If it does, and has a discretion as to the exercise of that jurisdiction, how should it exercise that discretion?

D   (3)   Should the Mareva injunctions be continued until the trial of the originating application?

    (4)   Irrespective of the answer to question (3) should the Mareva injunctions made ex parte on 10 December 1992 be discharged on the ground of material non-disclosure by the liquidators?

E   **1. Jurisdiction**

      There is no doubt that this court has no jurisdiction to entertain the applications made by the liquidators of Overseas for orders under sec. 213 (para. 4 and 5 of the originating application), 214 (para. 6 of the originating application), 212 (para. 7, 8 and 9 of the originating application) and 238 (para. 10 and 11 of the originating application) of the 1986 Act except to the extent, if any, to which such jurisdiction arises under sec. 426 of

F   the Act. For each of those sections applies only to a "company" within the meaning of the 1986 Act, which Overseas is not. This was rightly accepted by counsel for the liquidators. He submitted, however, that in the circumstances of the present case the court does have and should exercise jurisdiction to make the orders sought in relation to Overseas by virtue of sec. 426 of the 1986 Act.

      It is, I think, convenient at this point to set out some parts of the sections of the 1986

G   Act to which I have referred:

Section 212

    "*Summary remedy against delinquent directors, liquidators, etc.*

    (1) This section applies if in the course of the winding up of a company it appears that a person who—

H   (a)   is or has been an officer of the company,

    (b)   has acted as liquidator, administrator or administrative receiver of the company, or

    (c)   not being a person falling within paragraph (a) or (b), is or has been concerned, or has taken part, in the promotion, formation or management of the company,

has misapplied or retained, or become accountable for, any money or other
property of the company, or been guilty of any misfeasance or breach of any
fiduciary or other duty in relation to the company.

. . .

(3) The court may, on the application of the official receiver or the liquidator, or
of any creditor or contributory, examine into the conduct of the person falling
within subsection (1) and compel him—

B

(a) to repay, restore or account for the money or property or any part of it, with
interest at such rate as the court thinks just, or

(b) to contribute such sum to the company's assets by way of compensation in
respect of the misfeasance or breach of fiduciary or other duty as the court
thinks just.

. . ."

C

Section 213

"*Fraudulent trading*

(1) If in the course of the winding up of a company it appears that any business of
the company has been carried on with intent to defraud creditors of the company
or creditors of any other person, or for any fraudulent purpose, the following has
effect.

D

(2) The court, on the application of the liquidator may declare that any persons
who were knowingly parties to the carrying on of the business in the manner
above-mentioned are to be liable to make such contributions (if any) to the
company's assets as the court thinks proper."

E

Section 214

"*Wrongful trading*

(1) Subject to subsection (3) below, if in the course of the winding up of a
company it appears that subsection (2) of this section applies in relation to a
person who is or has been a director of the company, the court, on the application
of the liquidator, may declare that that person is to be liable to make such
contribution (if any) to the company's assets as the court thinks proper.

F

(2) This subsection applies in relation to a person if—

(a) the company has gone into insolvent liquidation,

(b) at some time before the commencement of the winding up of the company,
that person knew or ought to have concluded that there was no reasonable
prospect that the company would avoid going into insolvent liquidation,
and

G

(c) that person was a director of the company at that time;

but the court shall not make a declaration under this section in any case where the
time mentioned in paragraph (b) above was before 28th April 1986.

H

(3) The court shall not make a declaration under this section with respect to any
person if it is satisfied that after the condition specified in subsection (2)(b) was
first satisfied in relation to him that person took every step with a view to
minimising the potential loss to the company's creditors as (assuming him to have
known that there was no reasonable prospect that the company would avoid going
into insolvent liquidation) he ought to have taken.

(4) For the purposes of subsections (2) and (3), the facts which a director of a company ought to know or ascertain, the conclusions which he ought to reach and the steps which he ought to take are those which would be known or ascertained, or reached or taken, by a reasonably diligent person having both—

  (a) the general knowledge, skill and experience that may reasonably be expected of a person carrying out the same functions as are carried out by that director in relation to the company, and

  (b) the general knowledge, skill and experience that that director has.

(5) The reference in subsection (4) to the functions carried out in relation to a company by a director of the company includes any functions which he does not carry out but which have been entrusted to him.

(6) For the purposes of this section a company goes into insolvent liquidation if it goes into liquidation at a time when its assets are insufficient for the payment of its debts and other liabilities and the expenses of the winding up.

(7) In this section 'director' includes a shadow director.

(8) This section is without prejudice to section 213."

Section 238

"*Transactions at an undervalue (England and Wales)*

(1) This section applies in the case of a company where—

  (a) an administration order is made in relation to the company, or

  (b) the company goes into liquidation;

and 'the office-holder' means the administrator or the liquidator, as the case may be.

(2) Where the company has at a relevant time (defined in section 240) entered into a transaction with any person at an undervalue, the office-holder may apply to the court for an order under this section.

(3) Subject as follows, the court shall, on such an application, make such order as it thinks fit for restoring the position to what it would have been if the company had not entered into that transaction.

(4) For the purposes of this section and section 241, a company enters into a transaction with a person at an undervalue if—

  (a) the company makes a gift to that person or otherwise enters into a transaction with that person on terms that provide for the company to receive no consideration, or

  (b) the company enters into a transaction with that person for a consideration the value of which, in money or money's worth, is significantly less than the value, in money or money's worth, of the consideration provided by the company.

(5) The court shall not make an order under this section in respect of a transaction at an undervalue if it is satisfied—

  (a) that the company which entered into the transaction did so in good faith and for the purpose of carrying on its business, and

  (b) that at the time it did so there were reasonable grounds for believing that the transaction would benefit the company."

The relevant time as defined in sec. 240 is, for present purposes, within two years of the commencement of the liquidation of the company concerned.

Section 426   A

"Co-operation between courts exercising jurisdiction in relation to insolvency

(1) An order made by a court in any part of the United Kingdom in the exercise of jurisdiction in relation to insolvency law shall be enforced in any other part of the United Kingdom as if it were made by a court exercising the corresponding jurisdiction in that other part.

(2) However, without prejudice to the following provisions of this section, nothing   B
in subsection (1) requires a court in any part of the United Kingdom to enforce, in relation to property situated in that part, any order made by a court in any other part of the United Kingdom.

(3) The Secretary of State, with the concurrence in relation to property situated in England and Wales of the Lord Chancellor, may by order make provision for securing that a trustee or assignee under the insolvency law of any part of the   C
United Kingdom has, with such modifications as may be specified in the order, the same rights in relation to any property situated in another part of the United Kingdom as he would have in the corresponding circumstances if he were a trustee or assignee under the insolvency law of that other part.

(4) The courts having jurisdiction in relation to insolvency law in any part of the United Kingdom shall assist the courts having the corresponding jurisdiction in   D
any other part of the United Kingdom or any relevant country of territory.

(5) For the purposes of subsection (4) a request made to a court in any part of the United Kingdom by a court in any other part of the United Kingdom or in a relevant country or territory is authority for the court to which the request is made to apply, in relation to any matters specified in the request, the insolvency law which is applicable by either court in relation to comparable matters falling within its jurisdiction.   E

In exercising its discretion under this subsection, a court shall have regard in particular to the rules of private international law.

. . .

(10) In this section 'insolvency law' means—

(a) in relation to England and Wales, provision made by or under this Act or   F
sections 6 to 10, 12, 15, 19(c) and 20 (with Schedule 1) of the Company Directors Disqualification Act 1986 and extending to England and Wales;

. . .

(d) in relation to any relevant country or territory, so much of the law of that country or territory as corresponds to provisions falling within any of the foregoing paragraphs;   G

and references in this subsection to any enactment include, in relation to any time before the coming into force of that enactment the corresponding enactment in force at that time.

(11) In this section 'relevant country or territory' means—

(a) any of the Channel Islands or the Isle of Man, or   H

(b) any country or territory designated for the purposes of this section by the Secretary of State by order made by statutory instrument."

The Cayman Islands were designated as a "relevant country or territory" by the *Co-operation of Insolvency Courts (Designation of Relevant Countries and Territories) Order* 1986 (SI 1986/2123).

On 7 December 1992 the Grand Court of the Cayman Islands, on an ex parte application made by the liquidators of Overseas, ordered that:

> "a letter of request do issue to the High Court of Justice, England to exercise its jurisdiction under sec. 426 of the *Insolvency Act* 1986 in the terms of the draft letter of request attached hereto."

The draft letter of request attached to the order, and therefore the letter of request which I treat as having been addressed to this court, is in the following terms:

"LETTER OF REQUEST

To the High Court of Justice, England

WHEREAS this court is a court exercising jurisdiction in relation to insolvency law in the Cayman Islands

AND WHEREAS a proceeding is pending in this court in respect of the winding up of Bank of Credit and Commerce International (Overseas) Ltd ("BCCI Overseas")

AND WHEREAS IAN WIGHT, ROBERT AXFORD AND MICHAEL MACKEY are duly appointed liquidators of BCCI Overseas

AND WHEREAS it appears to this court that it is desirable that the best possible realisation of the assets of BCCI Overseas (including claims) be achieved for the benefit of all its unsecured creditors

AND WHEREAS the said liquidators have shown to the satisfaction of this court that it is just and convenient that this letter of request should issue

THIS COURT HEREBY REQUESTS the High Court of Justice, England to exercise its jurisdiction under sec. 426 of the *Insolvency Act* 1986 to assist this court by making orders under the respective provisions referred to below in the form of and substantially in the form of the orders set out below if and in so far as the High Court of Justice, England considers it just and appropriate that such orders be made:

. . ."

The letter of request then repeats verbatim the prayer for relief contained in the originating application in so far as it relates to the claims thereby made in respect of Overseas for declarations under sec. 212, 213, 214 and 238 of the 1986 Act.

NCB filed affidavit evidence of Cayman law to the effect that that law has no statutory provision comparable to any of sec. 213, 214 or 238 of the 1986 Act, and that it does have a statutory provision (sec. 168 of the Companies Laws (Revised)) comparable to sec. 212 of the 1986 Act, save that under the Cayman section proceedings may only be brought against "any past or present director, manager, official or other liquidator or any officer" of the company in liquidation.

The liquidators submit that by virtue of the letter of request issued by the Grand Court of the Cayman Islands ("the Grand Court"), this court has jurisdiction by virtue of sec. 426 of the 1986 Act to make such declarations as are requested by the letter of request, should the facts be found to justify them, notwithstanding that this court would otherwise have no power to make any such orders in relation to a foreign company being wound up abroad, as is Overseas, and the Grand Court would itself have no such power, because its insolvency law does not include provisions comparable with the sections of the 1986 Act under which the declarations are sought.

NCB and Kahlon submit that this court has no jurisdiction to make the declarations sought in relation to Overseas, first, because the power conferred on this court by sec. 426 of the Act is limited to applying English procedural law for the purpose of

recognising and giving effect in this country to decisions made by a relevant foreign   A
court in the exercise of its own insolvency jurisdiction by the application of its own
national insolvency law, and secondly because in any event the letter of request issued
by the Grand Court is not a letter of request within the meaning of sec. 426 of the 1986
Act.

NCB and Kahlon submit that it would be quite wrong in principle that this court
should be in a position to apply its own substantive law to the liquidation of a foreign
company in a foreign jurisdiction. Section 426 of the 1986 Act should be construed with   B
this in mind. The legislature cannot have intended to enable a foreign liquidator of a
foreign company not otherwise subject to the insolvency jurisdiction of this court to seek
from this court orders subjecting a director of the foreign company to liability, including
criminal liability, for acts incurring no such liability under the law of the place of
incorporation of the company concerned. Otherwise, it was submitted, no one could
safely act as director of a foreign company without knowing what possible liabilities he   C
would be incurring not only under the law of the place of incorporation of the company,
but also English law, in the event of the company going into liquidation.

NCB and Kahlon rightly draw attention to the fact that provisions bearing some
resemblance to sec. 426 of the 1986 Act are to be found in earlier English bankruptcy
statutes.

Section 118 of the *Bankruptcy Act* 1883 was in these terms: D

"The High Court, the county courts, the courts having jurisdiction in bankruptcy
in Scotland and Ireland, and every British court elsewhere having jurisdiction in
bankruptcy or insolvency, and the officers of those courts respectively, shall
severally act in aid of and be auxiliary to each other in all matters of bankruptcy,
and an order of the court seeking aid, with a request to another of the said courts,
shall be deemed sufficient to enable the latter court to exercise, in regard to the
matters directed by the order, such jurisdiction as either the court which made the   E
request, or the court to which the request is made, could exercise in regard to
similar matters within their respective jurisdictions."

Counsel for NCB and Kahlon relied for support for the proposition that sec. 426 of
the 1986 Act does not permit the English court to apply its own substantive law in
relation to a foreign company not in liquidation in this country on dicta in the House of
Lords in *Galbraith v Grimshaw* [1910] AC 508 which, submitted counsel, show that the
House of Lords did not regard sec. 118 of the 1883 Act as enabling the English court to   F
apply English substantive law to a Scottish bankruptcy.

In *Galbraith v Grimshaw* the material facts were that, after a judgment creditor had
served a garnishee order nisi on a firm in England that owed a debt to the judgment
debtor, the estate of the judgment debtor was sequestrated under Scottish bankruptcy
law and was transferred to a trustee for creditors with power to recover all assets of the
judgment debtor. The question at issue in the proceedings that came ultimately before   G
the House of Lords was whether the English garnishee order took priority over the
rights under Scots law of the trustee. The House held that it did. Thus the House was not
concerned to apply, or even to construe, sec. 118 of the 1883 Act. However, in the
course of his speech Lord *Macnaghten* said (at pp. 511–512):

"It may have been intended by the Legislature that bankruptcy in one part of the
United Kingdom should produce the same consequences throughout the whole   H
kingdom. But the Legislature has not said so. The Act does not say that a Scotch
sequestration shall have effect in England as if it were an English bankruptcy of
the same date. It only says that the Courts of the different parts of the United
Kingdom shall severally act in aid of and be auxiliary to each other in all matters
of bankruptcy. The English Court, no doubt, is bound to carry out the orders of
the Scottish Court, but in the absence of special enactment the Scottish Court can

A   only claim the free assets of the bankrupt. It has no right to interfere with any process of an English Court pending at the time of the Scotch sequestration."

I do not find this dictum or anything else in the case of any real assistance on the effect of the request of a foreign court under sec. 426 of the 1986 Act. The House of Lords was not considering a case in which another court had requested its assistance pursuant to sec. 118 of the 1883 Act.

B   Another case in which the court considered sec. 118 of the 1883 Act and on which NCB and Kahlon particularly rely is an Australian case, *Hall v Woolf* (1908) 7 CLR 207. In that case there were bankruptcy proceedings in Queensland relating to a debtor resident there who subsequently left Queensland and ceased to be either resident or domiciled there. He later went to reside in Western Australia and became insolvent there. He had not obtained a discharge in the Queensland bankruptcy. His trustee in the Queensland bankruptcy obtained from the Supreme Court of Queensland an order

C   under sec. 118 of the Imperial Bankruptcy Act seeking aid from the Western Australia court to obtain possession of property of the debtor situate in Western Australia and an order that all property in the hands of the trustee in the Western Australia bankruptcy should be delivered to the Queensland trustee. The Western Australia court was thus being asked to apply Queensland law so as to pass the property concerned to the Queensland trustee in priority to the rights of the Western Australia trustee. The court of Western Australia refused. The High Court of Australia held that it rightly refused.

D   Thus the issue in that case was not whether the court receiving a request under sec. 118 could apply its own substantive law rather than that of the requesting state. On the contrary the court of Western Australia was being asked to apply Queensland law to the prejudice of creditors in its own bankruptcy proceedings. The case seems little help in relation to the question I have to decide. However the respondents rely on a dictum of *Griffith* CJ, who, in giving the judgment of the High Court of Australia, said (at p. 212):

E   "Sec. 118 of the English *Bankruptcy Act* 1883 does not create any new rights, but only creates new remedies for enforcing existing rights."

Given the context in which they were said these words really do not seem to me to assist in deciding the issue I have to decide.

Section 118 of the *Bankruptcy Act* 1883 was replaced by sec. 122 of the *Bankruptcy Act* 1914, which was in identical terms to sec. 118 of the 1883 Act. A case decided on

F   sec. 122 of the 1914 Act is *Re Osborn* [1931–32] B & CR 189. In that case a lady had been adjudged bankrupt by the Isle of Man court. There were no bankruptcy proceedings relating to her in England. The Isle of Man court ordered (see p. 190):

      "That the aid of the High Court of Justice, England . . . be sought pursuant to section 122 of the Bankruptcy Act, 1914, and in pursuance of such order a request is made to the said High Court of Justice . . . for declarations that the whole of the real and personal estate of the bankrupt situate in England . . . became vested in

G   the trustee . . . or that the same shall vest in the trustee from the date of the declarations now sought . . ."

In the course of his judgment *Farwell* J said at pp. 194–195:

      "I think it is clear that I am bound in a proper case under, section 122, to assist the Court in the Isle of Man in the bankruptcy which is the bankruptcy under that jurisdiction. I think under the section it is plain that this Court must give such

H   assistance as it can, but subject, of course, to the considerations which would arise if there was also a bankruptcy in this country, as to the rights of the creditors and other persons in this country. There not being any such conflict, I think this Court is bound to give all the assistance that it can. On the other hand, it is, in my judgment, a matter of discretion in this Court as to what assistance it ought to give in each case . . .

A

The question of making either a vesting order or a declaration that the property in this country has vested in the trustee in bankruptcy in the Isle of Man, seems to me to be one of considerable difficulty. In my judgment, it is not possible for me to make a declaration that 'all the rights and interests of the above-mentioned bankrupt in the following property', which includes freehold property, 'has vested in the trustee', because I do not think it has. In my judgment, the effect of the order made in the Isle of Man does not *ipso facto* vest the assets in this country in the trustee, but if the trustee desires to get those assets vested in him, or to get control over them, his only course is the course which has been adopted in this case of coming to this Court and obtaining the aid of this Court to enable him to get the control and possession of the assets.''

B

However, *Farwell* J went on to hold that he could not make the vesting declaration or order sought, because English law did not provide for the making of any such order, since under English law the property would have vested in an English trustee without any such order. Instead he appointed the trustee receiver in respect of the property concerned. In my judgment the case lends no support to the argument put forward on behalf of NCB and Kahlon. The reference made by *Farwell* J to the discretion conferred by sec. 122 is worth noting when I come a little later to consider the recent case of *Re Dallhold Estates (UK) Pty Ltd* [1992] BCC 394.

C

Another case cited on behalf of NCB and Kahlon decided in relation to sec. 122 of the 1914 Act was *Re a Debtor, ex parte Viscount of the Royal Court of Jersey* [1981] Ch 384. In that case the Royal Court of Jersey had commenced "en désastre" proceedings against a debtor, and had then requested the English court under sec. 122 of the *Bankruptcy Act* 1914 to appoint the Viscount (the principal executive officer of the Royal Court of Jersey) receiver of the debtor's movable property in England. *Goulding* J held that the désastre proceedings in Jersey were to be regarded as bankruptcy proceedings for the purpose of sec. 122 and made the order sought. He gave some consideration (at p. 404) to the question whether the Viscount's jurisdiction in Jersey extended to after acquired property. NCB and Kahlon in the present case rely on *Goulding* J's consideration of this point, because, they say, such consideration would have been unnecessary had the English court simply been able to apply its own substantive bankruptcy law. However, this point does not seem to have been argued and I do not think that the case really helps one way or the other on the issue I have to decide on sec. 426.

D

E

F

The only case cited to me which was decided under sec. 426 of the 1986 Act was *Re Dallhold Estates (UK) Pty Ltd* [1992] BCC 394. The company concerned was a company incorporated in Western Australia. The liquidator of its holding company applied to the federal court for an order that the company should be wound up. A significant asset of the company was a leasehold property in this country. The liquidator of the holding company was advised that a winding up of the company would have the effect of forfeiting the lease of the English property, and that a better result from the point of view of the holding company would be achieved by the making by the English court of an administration order in relation to the company under sec. 8 of the 1986 Act. However the liquidator was also correctly advised that the English court had no power under sec. 8 alone to make such an order, since the company (like Overseas in the present case), being a company incorporated abroad, was not a "company" within the relevant provisions of the 1986 Act. As a result the liquidator of the holding company asked the federal court to make a request to this court under sec. 426 of the 1986 Act to make an administration order in respect of the company. The federal court issued a letter of request to this court accordingly.

G

H

Chadwick J held that sec. 426 of the Act did confer on this court jurisdiction to comply with the letter of request and make an administration order in respect of the company

A
notwithstanding the fact that it was a company in respect of which this court would have had no such jurisdiction apart from sec. 426. In dealing with an argument that sec. 426 did not confer such jurisdiction which this court would not have had apart from sec. 426 *Chadwick* J said (at p. 398G):

B
"The two subsections, (4) and (5), read together envisage that assistance will be requested by a foreign court to the English court. If the English court were only to exercise the jurisdiction which it would have anyway in relation to the assistance requested, there would be no need for the provisions of subsec. (5).

It appears to me clear that the purpose of sec. 426(5) of the *Insolvency Act* 1986 is to give to the requested court a jurisdiction that it might not otherwise have in order that it can give the assistance to the requesting court which, by subsec. (4), it is directed to give.

C
The scheme of subsec. (5) appears to me to be this. The first step is to identify the matters specified in the request. Secondly, the domestic court should ask itself what would be the relevant insolvency law applicable by the domestic court to comparable matters falling within its jurisdiction. Thirdly, it should then apply that insolvency law to the matters specified in the request, which, on this hypothesis, are not matters which would otherwise fall within its jurisdiction, or may not be.

D
Also, of course, the domestic court is authorised to apply those provisions of the foreign insolvency law which the foreign court could apply to comparable matters falling within the jurisdiction of the foreign court; but that is not an issue in this case.

The result is that the English court can act on a request by the federal court by applying to the matters specified in the request provisions of English insolvency law, including the provisions of sec. 8 of the 1986 Act, which the English court could apply to comparable matters falling within the jurisdiction of the English court. Comparable matters for this purpose might, in my view, include matters in which all the facts were the same as those specified in the request, save that the company concerned was a company incorporated in England rather than a company incorporated in Western Australia.

F
I should perhaps add that it is my view that the proviso to subsec. (5) is directed towards the only discretion that can be exercised under subsec. (5), namely, the discretion of the requesting court in deciding whether or not to make a request. There is nothing in subsec. (5) which confers a discretion on the requested court."

I respectfully agree with that analysis by *Chadwick* J of sec. 426, save for the last paragraph which I have cited. It seems to me that subsec. (5) does confer a discretion on the requested court, namely a discretion whether to apply its own law or the law of the requesting court to the matters specified in the request, and it is to that discretion that what *Chadwick* J referred to as the proviso to the subsection referring to the rules of private international law is directed. With great respect for the contrary view expressed by *Chadwick* J, I do not think that by that "proviso" the legislature can have been intending to attempt to impose restrictions on the manner in which a foreign court should decide whether to ask this court for assistance.

H
Giving the words of sec. 426 of the 1986 Act their ordinary meaning I can see no justification for restricting their effect in the manner urged on behalf of NCB and Kahlon, namely to provisions of English law which are what counsel described as procedural as opposed to substantive. In my judgment the effect of sec. 426 is to give this court a discretion (exercisable only for the purpose of carrying out its duty under sec. 426(4) to assist the courts having insolvency jurisdiction in other parts of the UK or any relevant country or territory) as to whether it should apply English insolvency law,

whether "procedural" or "substantive", or the law of the requesting court to matters
specified in the relevant request from the foreign court. The objection raised on behalf
of NCB and Kahlon to this construction of the section, namely that it would expose, for
example, directors of foreign companies to potential liabilities under English law for
activities perfectly lawful under the law of the company's incorporation loses much of its
force when it is remembered that they would only be so exposed where both the court
having jurisdiction in relation to the company's insolvency and this court thought fit to
exercise their respective discretions to that effect. Section 426 confers no *right* on
anyone to have English law applied in relation to a foreign company. However, whatever
the strength of this objection, it cannot, in my judgment, prevail over the clear words of
sec. 426.

In the course of his submissions counsel for the liquidators warned me against taking
too much account, in considering the construction of sec. 426 of the 1986 Act, of the
arguments of counsel for the respondents based on earlier Acts and decisions in relation
thereto, and as authority for this warning he cited several dicta to the effect that the Act
should be construed as a new piece of legislation not necessarily reflecting similar
intentions on the part of the legislature to those embodied in earlier apparently
comparable provisions, the most recent of which dicta is to be found in the judgment of
Dillon LJ in *Re Bishopsgate Investment Management Ltd* [1992] BCC 222 at pp. 229–
230. However, in my judgment there is nothing in the authorities on earlier statutes cited
on behalf of the respondents, to some only of which I have referred in this judgment,
which is inconsistent with the conclusion which I have expressed in relation to the
construction of sec. 426 of the 1986 Act. Consequently there is, in my judgment, nothing
to be gained by the respondents from the argument also put on behalf of NCB and
Kahlon to the effect that in construing sec. 426 I should bear in mind that its purpose was
to implement the recommendation made in para. 1911 of the *Report of the Review
Committee on Insolvency Law and Practice* (1982, Cmnd 8558), chaired by Sir Kenneth
Cork to the effect that the "provisions for mutual aid" in sec. 122 of the *Bankruptcy Act*
1914 should be extended so as to be available in winding up proceedings.

I must now consider the alternative ground on which it was argued on behalf of NCB
and Kahlon that this court has no jurisdiction to entertain the application made by the
liquidators of Overseas, and that is that the letter of request issued by the Grand Court
is not a letter of request within the meaning of sec. 426 of the Act and accordingly this
court has no power to operate under that section.

The first objection made to the letter of request is that, so it is submitted, it does not
specify any matters on which it seeks this court's assistance. It states no facts, but merely
sets out orders which it asks this court to make. A letter of request within sec. 426 must,
it is said, specify facts to which the requesting court seeks the application by this court of
English law, and not, as does the Grand Court's letter of request in this case, ask, in
effect, this court first to investigate the relevant facts and then apply its law to the facts
so found.

This argument, in my judgment, has a superficial attraction, but is misconceived. To
make a request within the meaning of sec. 426(5) the court of another part of the UK or
a "relevant country or territory" has simply to ask this court to assist it (subsec. (4)).
The letter of request from the Grand Court in this case asks this court to assist it in
maximising the recoveries effected in the winding up of Overseas being carried out by
the Grand Court by considering whether it can properly make the declarations set out in
the letter of request, and, if so, by making those declarations. In my judgment the words
"any matters specified in the request" in subsec. (5) mean no more nor less than "any
part of the subject-matter of the request". Thus, in my judgment, the effect of
subsec. (5) in the context of the letter of request is to authorise this court — that is confer

A   jurisdiction upon it — to apply either English law or Cayman law in considering whether it can properly make the declarations sought by the Grand Court.

This leads to a consideration of the second objection to the letter of request as bringing sec. 426(5) into operation which was made on behalf of NCB and Kahlon, and that is that in the context of the terms of the letter of request this court can have no discretion whether to apply English or Cayman law, because there is no Cayman law equivalent to the sections of the Act under which the letter of request seeks declarations. Again, in

B   my judgment, this objection is misconceived. Of course the Grand Court would not ask this court to make declarations that could be made under Cayman law. If they could have been made under Cayman law then no doubt the Grand Court would not have been asking for this court's assistance in making them. The request having been made, this court must consider how to respond to it. It could decide to apply Cayman law in respect of the subject-matter of the request, in which case it would have to refuse to

C   make the declarations sought, because they are not available under Cayman law. Alternatively it could decide to apply English law and go on to consider whether the declarations sought can properly be made under that law. This would involve an investigation of the relevant facts, but that, in my judgment, is a factor to be taken into consideration by this court in exercising its discretion, and not a valid objection to the existence of that discretion in the terms of sec. 426(5).

D   Accordingly, in my judgment, this court does have jurisdiction to investigate the facts to see whether they would justify the making of all or any of the declarations sought by the letter of request if Overseas were a company within this court's insolvency jurisdiction, and, if they would, to make such declarations.

2. Should this court exercise the jurisdiction?

Subsection (4) of sec. 426 of the 1986 Act imposes an obligation on this court to assist

E   the Grand Court. As I have said, this court nonetheless does have a discretion as to how it should give such assistance. (Compare the similar approach of *Farwell* J to the application of sec. 122 of the *Bankruptcy Act* 1914 in the passage from his judgment in *Re Osborn* [1931–32] B & CR 189 which I have quoted earlier in this judgment.) In my judgment this court should exercise its discretion in favour of giving the particular assistance requested by the Grand Court unless there is some good reason for not doing so. As the concluding words of sec. 426(5) make clear one such reason could in some

F   cases be found in the rules of private international law, such as where the request is such that to comply with it would infringe the rule against enforcing another country's tax claims. In the present case, in my judgment, there is no good reason in the rules of private international law or elsewhere for this court not giving the assistance requested. On the contrary, on the facts of the case already apparent, there are, in my judgment, good reasons why this court should give the assistance sought. This court is inescapably

G   seised of claims by the liquidators of SA against the same respondents for the same declarations arising out of the same facts as those sought to be relied upon by the liquidators of Overseas in relation to the declarations sought by the letter of request. As is plain from the passage which I quoted early in this judgment from the judgment of *Nicholls* V-C in *Re Bank of Credit and Commerce International SA (No. 2)* [1992] BCC 715, the affairs of SA and Overseas are "hopelessly intertwined". In my judgment this is a classic situation in which it is desirable for the courts having insolvency jurisdiction in

H   respect of the two companies respectively to co-operate to the fullest extent possible.

Thus, in my judgment, this court should give to the Grand Court the assistance it has requested by trying the claims by the liquidators of Overseas for declarations in the terms set out in the letter of request. It follows that I decline to strike out the claims made in the originating application by Overseas on the grounds that this court either does not have or should not exercise jurisdiction to determine those claims.

3. Should the Mareva Injunctions be continued?

NCB is, of course, not concerned in this aspect of the case, since no injunction has been made or is sought against it. Both the other respondents, that is to say Mahfouz and Kahlon, resist the continuation against them of the injunctions originally granted against them by *Vinelott* J on 10 December 1992.

As has been said again recently by the Court of Appeal, there are three issues on which the court has to be satisfied before granting a Mareva injunction:

(1)   Has the applicant a good arguable case?

(2)   Has the applicant satisfied the court that there are assets within and, where an extraterritorial order is sought, without the jurisdiction?

(3)   Is there a real risk of dissipation or secretion of assets so as to render any judgment which the applicant may obtain nugatory?

(See *Derby & Co Ltd v Weldon* [1990] Ch 48 per *Parker* LJ at p. 57D–E.)

It is not necessary, before the court can grant an extraterritorial order, for the applicant to show that the respondent has assets within the jurisdiction of this court (see *Derby & Co Ltd v Weldon (No. 3 & 4)* [1990] Ch 65 per Lord *Donaldson of Lymington* MR at p. 79G–H).

As to questions (2) and (3), in my judgment the affidavit evidence of Mr Morris makes out a prima facie case that each of Mahfouz and Kahlon does have assets both within and without the jurisdiction and that there is a real risk of dissipation or secretion of those assets so as to render any judgment which the liquidators may obtain nugatory. Nothing in the evidence filed on behalf of the respondents rebuts this case, and indeed it is noteworthy that neither counsel for Mahfouz nor counsel for Kahlon made any submissions to the contrary. Neither made submissions as to why questions (2) and (3) should not be answered in the affirmative, as, in my judgment, they should.

Both counsel for Mahfouz and counsel for Kahlon did try at some length to persuade me that I should not be satisfied that the liquidators had shown a good arguable case for the relief sought in the originating application. In particular counsel for Mahfouz tried to take me to various selected bits of the voluminous documentation filed in these proceedings to support the argument that there were in fact perfectly innocent explanations for the transfers and payments relied on by the liquidators in the points of claim that have been delivered. Both counsel for Mahfouz and counsel for Kahlon raised arguments on the true extent of the court's jurisdiction to make orders such as those sought under sec. 212, 213, 214 and 238 of the 1986 Act. Throughout the hearing I have tried to bear well in mind the reminders given on more than one recent occasion both by the House of Lords and the Court of Appeal that the court should not on an interlocutory application, even on an application for a Mareva injunction, allow itself to be drawn into attempting to make a lengthy and detailed assessment of the strengths and weaknesses of the applicant's case at trial — see e.g. *Derby & Co Ltd v Weldon* [1990] Ch 48 at p. 58E–G, where *Parker* LJ said:

"It is to be hoped that in future the observations of Lord Diplock and Lord Templeman will be borne in mind in applications for a *Mareva* injunction, that they will take hours not days and that appeals will be rare. I do not mean by the foregoing to indicate that argument as to the principles applying to the grant of a *Mareva* injunction should not be fully argued. With a developing jurisdiction it is inevitable and desirable that they should be. What, however, should not be allowed is (1) any attempt to persuade the court to resolve disputed questions of fact whether relating to the merits of the underlying claim in respect of which a *Mareva* is sought or relating to the elements of the *Mareva* jurisdiction such as

A   that of dissipation or (2) detailed arguments on difficult points of law on which the claim of either party may ultimately depend."

In my judgment it is even more important than usual to bear this warning well in mind in the context of a case of such enormous factual complexity as the present, in which at least two eminent firms of accountants — I refer, of course to Price Waterhouse, the former auditors, who made reports to the Bank of England under sec. 41 of the *Banking Act* 1987 and Touche Ross, Mr Morris's firm — have spent very large resources on

B   investigating those facts over many months, and at the trial of which there seem certain to be wide-ranging issues of fact to be resolved by lengthy oral evidence and detailed examination of voluminous documentation. I was told by counsel that the trial could take up to a year, though I sincerely hope that that will prove to be a significantly over-pessimistic estimate. I should not, in my judgment, allow myself on this interlocutory application to be drawn into the sort of selective examination of what will be even more

C   massive documentation available at the trial on which counsel for Mahfouz would have had me embark.

I do not think it necessary or appropriate to say more on this part of the case than that I am satisfied on the evidence I have seen that the liquidators have made out a good arguable case for the relief sought in the originating application.

Accordingly, in my judgment the requirements to be satisfied for the grant of a

D   Mareva injunction are satisfied in the present case and, apart from the further submissions of Mahfouz and Kahlon which I shall mention shortly, it is, in my opinion, appropriate to continue the Mareva injunctions presently in force against each of those respondents until the trial of the originating application.

It was submitted by counsel for Mahfouz that even if, contrary to his primary submission, the court should (as I have decided it should) continue a Mareva injunction against Mahfouz, (1) that injunction should not have worldwide effect and (2) it should

E   not restrain dealings by Mahfouz with his assets to the extent that they exceed in value a figure of about $1.5 billion being the total of the allegedly wrongful payments specifically quantified in the originating application.

As to (1), of course I bear in mind that only in exceptional circumstances should the court grant a Mareva injunction restraining the respondent from dealing with assets anywhere in the world. I have no doubt that this is such an exceptional case, having

F   regard, in particular, to the complex international nature of the financial dealings in the past by both respondents and that both claim not to be resident in this country.

As to (2), the maximum claim made by the liquidators in the originating application against each of the respondents is the full amount of the presently estimated deficiencies in the liquidations of both SA and Overseas, on the basis that that is the maximum of the recoupment that can be ordered by the court under the discretion conferred on it by the

G   sections of the 1986 Act relied on. In these circumstances, as I indicated to counsel for Mahfouz, it seemed to me inappropriate to consider this argument unless and until there was some evidence before the court that a failure to limit the injunction to assets of $1.5 billion would have some practical effect, having regard to the assets actually owned by Mahfouz. At present there is no evidence whatever before the court as to his assets. I invited counsel to consider whether he wished to renew this argument in the light of some such evidence. He did not do so. In these circumstances it does not seem to me

H   appropriate to place any limit on the injunction in this respect.

Finally on this part of the case counsel for Mahfouz relied on what has been referred to during the hearing before me as "the Abu Dhabi factor" as something that should weigh heavily against the court's exercising its discretion in favour of continuing the injunction. "The Abu Dhabi factor" arises from the terms of the contribution agreement which I mentioned earlier in this judgment as one of the two agreements which this court

authorised the liquidators of SA to enter into on 12 June 1992. That agreement was
conditional upon (in the events which have happened) final approval being given to the
agreement on or before 30 June 1993 by the courts of Luxembourg, the Cayman Islands,
and this country. I understand that an appeal against such an order made by the
Luxembourg court is pending, with the result that this condition has not been fulfilled by
the time-limit specified in the contribution agreement and the whole agreement has
ceased to have effect. However, I was told by counsel for the liquidators that his clients
were optimistic that a renewal of the agreement might be negotiated between the
parties.

By virtue of the terms of the contribution agreement, which are complex, and into
which I need not go in any detail, one half of any moneys recovered by the liquidators
from any of the respondents in this litigation would have belonged to the government of
Abu Dhabi. The agreement contained provisions expressly relieving that government
from any obligation it might otherwise have been under to disclose to the liquidators any
documents the disclosure of which the government might consider to be adverse to its
interests.

Counsel for Mahfouz submitted that the result of any resurrection of the contribution
agreement such as counsel for the liquidators said was hoped for by his clients would
result in this litigation being conducted in an unfair manner as against the respondents,
in that a 50 per cent beneficiary of any success on the claims being made against the
respondents, namely the Abu Dhabi government, would be in a position to withhold
from the respondents and the court documents of which that government thought
disclosure might harm the liquidators' case. This potential unfairness, submitted counsel
for Mahfouz, should be a factor influencing this court against granting a Mareva
injunction the benefit of which would enure as to 50 per cent to the government of Abu
Dhabi.

I do not accept this submission. First, it does not seem to me to disclose a good reason
for refusing a Mareva injunction if it would otherwise be appropriate for the protection
of the claims by the liquidators which, even if the contribution agreement is resurrected,
will enure as to half for the benefit of the creditors of the companies, if successful.
Secondly there is at present no certainty that the contribution agreement will be
resurrected in its former terms. It has presently ceased to have any effect. Thirdly, even
if it is resurrected, the provision that the government of Abu Dhabi need not disclose
documents seems to me not to have any effect on the position which would obtain apart
from any such provision so far as these proceedings are concerned. The government of
Abu Dhabi is not a party to these proceedings and would be under no obligation to give
discovery of documents, quite apart from any question of sovereign immunity. In my
judgment this point is of no substance.

Counsel for Mahfouz also submitted that the fact that under the contribution
agreement, if resurrected, half the benefit of any success of the liquidators' claims would
be for the benefit of the government of Abu Dhabi (which, submitted counsel, had itself
been a party to part of the dealings by Mahfouz of which complaint is now made by the
liquidators) was itself a reason for the court not granting a Mareva injunction for the
protection of those claims. This I do not accept, given that the other half of the benefit
of the claims will be for the benefit of creditors of the BCCI companies and the
liquidators were authorised by this court to enter into the contribution agreement.

Accordingly, I do not accept any of the objections put on behalf of Mahfouz and
Kahlon to the grant of Mareva injunctions in the form previously granted by *Vinelott* J,
and I shall continue those injunctions until trial of the originating application or further
order.

A

4. Should the Mareva injunctions granted ex parte on 10 December 1992 be discharged on the grounds of material non-disclosure?

Counsel for Kahlon submitted that the injunctions granted ex parte should be set aside on the grounds of non-disclosure by the liquidators to *Vinelott* J of (1) the fact that the Abu Dhabi government would be the beneficiary of half of any success of the liquidators' claims by virtue of the contribution agreement and was in the position of being able to withhold material documents from the court and (2) a long list of what

B

counsel submitted were potential weaknesses in the liquidators' case.

Counsel rightly reminded me of the well established principle that a litigant seeking relief from the court on an ex parte application must make full and frank disclosure to the court of matters relevant to the application, and that in the case of a breach of this duty becoming apparent to the court the court may not only refuse further relief but may

C

discharge any order made on the ex parte application, notwithstanding that the court might well have granted the relief it did on the ex parte application even had the undisclosed matter been disclosed.

However, as to the alleged non-disclosure of "the Abu Dhabi factor", I have already explained why I do not consider that it is relevant to the liquidators' claim for Mareva injunctions. It follows that I do not consider that any failure to bring the significance of it to the attention of *Vinelott* J was any breach of the duty of full and frank disclosure

D

that I have mentioned. I have carefully considered the long list of other alleged breaches of this duty relied upon by counsel for Kahlon in his submissions. I think it unnecessary and inappropriate to say more on them than that I do not consider that any amounts to a breach of the duty referred to.

Accordingly I see no good reason to discharge any part of the order made by *Vinelott* J.

E

Finally I should say something of an application which was made during the hearing before me on behalf of Kahlon for an order for discovery of documents for the purpose of that hearing. By a summons issued on 25 June 1993 Kahlon sought production to the court of the following documents:

(1)   Documents relating to the application to the Grand Court which culminated in the issue by that court of the letter of request for the purposes of sec. 426 of the 1986 Act; and

F

(2)   The audited accounts of SA, Overseas and Holdings from 1977 onwards.

I refused the application because, in my judgment, it would have been wrong to make any such order for partial discovery unless I was satisfied that it was necessary for the purposes of doing justice to the other applications before me. I was not so satisfied, because, with regard to the documents before the Grand Court, I did not consider them likely to be of any relevance to the issues I had to decide, whether in relation to sec. 426

G

of the 1986 Act or otherwise, and with regard to the accounts of the BCCI companies, though they might well be relevant on a trial of the issues raised by the originating application relating to the financial state of the companies during that period, I did not consider that to look at those accounts in isolation from other documents that may well emerge on full discovery would be likely to assist the court in deciding the interlocutory matters before me.

H

(*Order accordingly*)

Re S N Group plc.

Chancery Division (Companies Court).
Jonathan Parker J.
Judgment delivered 11 August 1993.

> *Winding up — Appeals and reviews of court orders (winding up) — Company sought review by judge of registrar's refusal to rescind winding-up order — Whether judge could review registrar's decision — Whether rescission only available by way of appeal — Whether winding-up order should be rescinded — Whether winding up should be stayed — Insolvency Rules 1986 (SI 1986/ 1925), r. 7.47.*

This was an application for an order of the registrar dismissing an application to rescind a compulsory winding-up order made by him, to be reviewed and rescinded by the judge under r. 7.47(1) of the Insolvency Rules 1986. Alternatively, rescission of the winding-up order was sought by way of appeal under r. 7.47(2) from the registrar's refusal to order rescission. Alternatively, an order was sought staying further proceedings in the winding up.

Held, refusing the application:

1. The judge could not review the registrar's decision under r. 7.47(1). If the order was made by the registrar, it fell to be reviewed, if at all, by him.

2. If the court did have jurisdiction to review the registrar's decision, there were a number of reasons why it should not do so.

3. The jurisdiction of the court in relation to orders of the registrar was an appellate jurisdiction under r. 7.47(2). Such an appeal might take the form of either an appeal from the registrar's original decision, or of an appeal from a decision of the registrar to refuse to review his original decision. There were no grounds on which such an appeal could succeed.

4. The petitioning creditor opposed the grant of any stay and no proposals were made for payment of its debt. Given that a winding-up order had been made on a petition which was duly advertised, the court took the view that unless otherwise indicated the unsecured trade creditors (who did not appear) were not agreeable to such a stay being granted. In the circumstances the application for a stay was refused.

The following cases were referred to in the judgment:

Calgary and Edmonton Land Co Ltd, Re [1975] 1 WLR 355.
Debtor, Re a [1993] 1 WLR 314.
Ladd v Marshall [1954] 1 WLR 1489.
Lowston Ltd, Re [1991] BCLC 570.
Practice Note (Winding up order: Rescission) (No. 2) [1971] 1 WLR 757.
Telescriptor Syndicate Ltd, Re [1903] 2 Ch 174.

Stephen Atherton (instructed by Lee Lane Smith) for the applicant.

Lindsey Stewart (instructed by Denton Hall Burgin & Warrens) for the petitioning creditor.

The official receiver appeared in person.

JUDGMENT

Jonathan Parker J: On 30 June 1993, Mr Registrar *Buckley* made an order winding up S N Group plc ("the company") on the petition of Barclays Bank plc ("Barclays").

On 7 July 1993 the company applied to the registrar to rescind the winding-up order with a view to the winding up being replaced by an administration.

A   On 21 July 1993 following two adjournments sought, I am told, by the company the registrar refused that application.

Appearing for the company, Mr Atherton now applies to me in the vacation court for the following relief — and I quote from a written form of application which has been placed before me:

"1. An order that the order of Mr Registrar *Buckley* made on 21 July 1993
B   dismissing the application to rescind the compulsory winding-up order made by him in respect of the company on 30 June 1993 be reviewed and rescinded."

In the course of his submissions Mr Atherton made it clear that review or rescission was sought with a view to the presentation by the company of an administration petition.

"2. An order that the said winding-up order be rescinded.

3. An order that the winding-up petition presented to this honourable court on
C   19 April 1993 by Barclays Bank plc be dismissed.

4. An order that all copies of and references to the said winding-up order appearing in the company's file at Companies House be removed from the file and destroyed.

5. Alternatively, an order that all further proceedings in the winding up of the company be stayed."
D
And, once again, Mr Atherton made clear that a stay is sought with a view to the presentation of an administration petition.

"6. Further or other relief.

7. That the costs of this application be provided for."

In the course of his submissions Mr Atherton also invited me, notwithstanding that
E   the appropriate procedures had not been followed, to treat the application for rescission of the order as an appeal from the refusal of the registrar to order rescission.

The application is made ex parte. The hearing began at about 4 o'clock yesterday and has continued this morning. Barclays learnt of the company's intention to make the application in the course of yesterday, although it appears that no formal notice was given to Barclays and no documents were served upon it. Miss Stewart, however,
F   appears on this application for Barclays as the effective respondent to the company's application, and she opposes the application. I have also had the benefit of hearing Mr Bennett of the official receiver's office.

Mr Atherton submits that the registrar was wrong in law in refusing to order rescission. He makes this application, however, not by way of appeal from the registrar's decision under the provisions of r. 7.47(2) of the *Insolvency Rules* 1986, but rather, as he puts it, by way of "review" of the registrar's decision pursuant (as he contends) to r. 7.47(1) of
G   the Insolvency Rules. He seeks to proceed by way of review rather than by way of appeal in the light of what he contends is the urgency of the matter and he seeks a review by the vacation court rather than by the registrar himself who made the order because the registrar is not presently available (being on holiday) and also because any administration order would, in any event, have to be made by a judge and could not be made by the registrar.

H   This immediately raises the question whether this court could or should undertake a review of the registrar's decision. Mr Atherton's argument that I have jurisdiction to review the registrar's order proceeds as follows. In the first place, as I have already indicated, he points to r. 7.47(1) of the Insolvency Rules, which is in the following terms:

"Every court having jurisdiction under the Act to wind up companies may review, rescind or vary any order made by it in the exercise of that jurisdiction."

He then refers me to r. 7.6 (dealing with the hearing of applications before the registrar), para. (4) of which provides:

"Nothing in this Rule precludes an application being made directly to the judge in a proper case."

Mr Atherton submits that although an application to review the registrar's decision would in normal course be made to the registrar himself, nevertheless, in view of what he contends is the urgency of the matter and given the unavailability of the registrar, this is a proper case in which to make application to this court, pursuant to r. 7.6(4). He also indicated in the course of his submissions that another reason for seeking to take the route of review (if it be a route which is open to him) is that he wishes to place before the court additional evidence in support of the application for rescission of the winding-up order which, were he to proceed by way of appeal, he might not be allowed to adduce.

In my judgment, Mr Atherton's submissions on this aspect of the case are misconceived. Rule 7.47(1) gives the registrar the power to review orders which he has made but, in my judgment, it does not give this court the power to review orders which the registrar has made. The jurisdiction of this court in relation to orders of the registrar is an appellate jurisdiction (see r. 7.47(2)). Nor, in my judgment, is r. 7.6(4) of any assistance in this respect. In the first place, it is the practice of the Companies Court that an application for rescission of a winding-up order is made in the first instance to the registrar, as it was in this case. In the second place, r. 7.6(4), does not, in my judgment, enable an application to review an order made by the registrar to be made to this court. If the order was made by the registrar, in my judgment, it falls to be reviewed, *if at all*, by him.

At one stage in his submissions Mr Atherton went so far as to invite me, by way of an alternative to his primary invitation that I should review the order myself, to make an order directing the registrar to review the order; in effect, an order that the matter be remitted to the registrar for reconsideration. In my judgment, however, the jurisdiction to make such an order could only exist in the context of an appeal. Such an appeal might take the form of either an appeal from the registrar's original decision, or of an appeal from a decision of the registrar to refuse to review his original decision — compare the case of *Re a Debtor* [1993] 1 WLR 314, a decision of *Millett* J in the context of bankruptcy. But, as I have said, there is no appeal formally before me, nor has an application as yet been made to the registrar to review his decision. Accordingly, Mr Atherton's alternative submission is also, in my judgment, misconceived.

Even if I am wrong in my interpretation of the Insolvency Rules and in my conclusions as to jurisdiction, so that, contrary to my view on those matters, I have jurisdiction to review the registrar's decision, I decline to exercise that jurisdiction in this case for six reasons.

First, as a general observation, it seems to me undesirable that this court should be in the position of exercising two parallel but different jurisdictions; on the one hand, an appellate jurisdiction to the exercise of which the principles laid down in *Ladd v Marshall* [1954] 1 WLR 1489 will apply and, on the other, a review jurisdiction (assuming such a jurisdiction exists) to which such principles will not apply (see *Re a Debtor* [1993] 1 WLR 314, to which I referred a moment ago).

Second, if such parallel jurisdictions exist an applicant would be likely to choose review as being the easier option, as the company is seeking to do in the instant case, thereby avoiding the constraints placed upon an appellant by *Ladd v Marshall* in relation to the adducing of further evidence on appeal.

Third, the exercise of such parallel jurisdictions would, as it appears to me, produce the odd result that while appeals from a decision of the registrar subsequently reviewed by him would lie to this court, appeals from a decision of the registrar subsequently reviewed by this court would lie to the Court of Appeal.

A   Fourth, turning to the procedural circumstances of the instant case, the pressure on the vacation court to hear urgent applications is as everyone knows very great and I am extremely reluctant, to say the least, to allow the vacation court to be used as in effect a substitute for the registrar when he happens to be enjoying a well-earned holiday.

Fifth, turning to the facts of the instant case, I can see nothing in those facts to justify my taking what I would, in any event, regard as an exceptional course in undertaking a

B   review of, as opposed to hearing an appeal against, a decision of the registrar.

Sixth, Mr Kumar, who is a creditor and contributory of the company, for whom Mr Atherton also appears and who has made an affidavit which is before me, makes it clear in that affidavit that what he is in effect seeking is simply a second bite at the cherry, having decided to change his solicitors following the registrar's refusal of his original application. Thus, in para. 28 of his affidavit (which was sworn on 10 August — after the hearing before the registrar) he says:

C   "Following the making of the winding-up order on 30 June I sought urgent advice as to the company's position. I was advised that an application for rescission of the winding-up order should be made and that such an application had to be made within seven days. The matter accordingly came before the court on 7 July when it was stood over for a period of seven days. It came before the court again on 14 July and was stood over for a further seven days. Eventually the matter was

D   heard by Mr Registrar *Buckley* on 21 July and I understand that the application for rescission was turned down by him on that date summarily and without going into the essence of the merits. I was then advised that an application be lodged against the learned registrar's order. I was not however at all happy at the way in which the matter was being dealt with by the solicitors then acting, and therefore I decided that I should change solicitors. I first consulted my current solicitors on

E   26 July but their ability to take quick action was impaired because the previous solicitors were claiming a lien on the papers, and the court did not issue the order of 21 July until last week. Eventually my solicitors were able to obtain sufficient documentation from other sources and a conference was held with counsel on 4 August at which counsel advised making the current applications. Since then time has been spent on the preparation of this affidavit and the preparation of a

F   revised r. 2.2 report."

There are a number of comments which I should make on that paragraph. In the first place, Mr Kumar does not descend to particulars as to when precisely his new solicitors were able to obtain sufficient documentation. Secondly, I note that a conference with counsel was held on 4 August. Nevertheless, it appears that no notice of an intended application, despite the fact that counsel had advised the making of such application, was given to Barclays prior to the ex parte application which commenced yesterday

G   afternoon. As I have already said, Barclays by its own researches discovered that an application was going to be made and fortunately was able to be represented at the hearing of it. Thirdly, Mr Kumar, as I have quoted, refers to "time spent on the preparation of this affidavit and the preparation of a revised r. 2.2 report". Miss Stewart has in her possession a copy of the affidavit placed originally before Mr Registrar *Buckley* from which it appears that the additions made to this subsequent affidavit were

H   small. Similarly, there were, as it appears, only minor amendments made to the r. 2.2 report which Mr Kumar exhibits to his latest affidavit, which report is also dated 10 August — yesterday.

Given what Mr Kumar has said in para. 28 of his affidavit and in the light of the comments I have made, it seems to me that the case which Mr Kumar seeks to put forward does not begin to demonstrate that the order made by Mr Registrar *Buckley* refusing to rescind the winding-up order ought to be reviewed either by this court or, for that matter, by the registrar were he available to conduct such a review.

A

Accordingly, for those reasons I reject Mr Atherton's application for a review of the registrar's decision.

Mr Atherton then sought, in the alternative to a review, a permanent stay of the winding up of the company for the purpose of enabling an administration petition to be presented by the company. In this connection I was referred to sec. 8(4) of the *Insolvency Act* 1986, which provides so far as material as follows:

B

"An administration order shall not be made in relation to a company after it has gone into liquidation . . ."

Mr Atherton submitted that where an indefinite stay is granted on the operation of a winding-up order that is tantamount to rescission in the sense that it cannot then be said that the company has gone into liquidation for the purposes of sec. 8(4) of the Act. He referred me to a number of textbooks expressing the view that an indefinite stay is the equivalent of a termination, suggesting on the basis of that proposition that were a permanent or indefinite stay to be granted in the present case the proposal to present an administration petition would not fall foul of sec. 8(4) of the Insolvency Act.

C

I do not find it necessary for present purposes to decide this particular question, for reasons which will appear in a moment. Indeed, the vacation court may not be the appropriate place to give sufficiently mature consideration to what may be a difficult question of construction. I must say nevertheless (although I do not decide the matter today) that it seems to me as a provisional view that a company has gone into liquidation where there remains on the file a winding-up order which has not been rescinded. Only (as it seems to me on a provisional view) where there has been a rescission of the original winding-up order so that it is as if it had never been made can it be said that the company has not gone into liquidation for the purposes of that subsection. However, with those provisional comments and without deciding this particular question, I leave it.

D

E

The reason why it is not necessary for me to decide this question is that I am satisfied that even if I have jurisdiction to grant a stay indefinitely to enable an administration petition to be presented, this is not a case in which such a stay should be granted.

I have been referred to a number of cases relating to the grant of a stay where a winding-up order has been made. I refer, first of all, to the case of *Re Calgary and Edmonton Land Co Ltd* [1975] 1 WLR 355, a decision of *Megarry* J. At p. 360B the judge considered what matters ought to be taken into account where a stay is sought. He said:

F

"That brings me to the third point, that of the persons whose interests have to be considered on an application for a stay. These must, of course, depend on the circumstances of each case; but where, as here, there is a strong probability, if not more, that the assets of the company will suffice to pay all the creditors and the expenses of the liquidation and so leave a surplus for the members of the company, there are plainly three categories to consider. First, there are the creditors. Their rights are finite in that they cannot claim more than 100p in the pound. I cannot see that in normal circumstances any objection to a stay could be made on behalf of the creditors if for each of them it is established either that he has been paid in full, or that satisfactory provision for him to be paid in full has been or will be made, or else that he consents to the stay or is otherwise bound not to object to it."

G

H

He goes on to consider the position of the liquidator and his costs and expenses.

In the instant case, the material before the Court indicates that there are some £7,000 worth of unsecured trade creditors and Barclays itself has a debt of some £57,000. The

A
balance of the indebtedness of the company is, as it appears, represented by debts owed to contributories or associated parties. Barclays opposes the grant of any stay. No proposals have been made for payment of Barclays, save that, as I shall indicate in a moment, it is suggested that there is a prospect of profitable trading should an administration be ordered. Barclays, however, is not convinced, and opposes the grant of any stay.

B
So far as the unsecured trade creditors are concerned, none of them is before me and I have no indication as to what view such creditors might take. That being the position, it seems to me that, given that a winding-up order has been granted on a winding-up petition which was duly advertised, I must take the view that unless otherwise indicated trade creditors are not agreeable to such a stay being granted.

For those reasons, therefore, I am not satisfied that in any event this would be an appropriate case for a stay, based upon the extract of the judgment of *Megarry* J to which I have referred.

C
I was also referred in the same context to a decision of *Harman* J in the case of *Re Lowston Ltd* [1991] BCLC 570, which, although a different case on the facts, does indicate very clearly, in my judgment, the care which the court will take in seeing that creditors are so far as possible fully protected before any stay of winding-up proceedings will be granted in circumstances where it is proposed that the company continue to trade. At p. 572H, *Harman* J said:

D
> "In my view, the test I have to apply is still that laid down by Buckley J in *Re Telescriptor Syndicate Ltd* [1903] 2 Ch 174 that the court has to be satisfied that it is right to stay the winding-up proceedings, and, if there be matters as to which the court has doubts, it should not so stay. Megarry J was of the same view in *Re Calgary and Edmonton Land Co Ltd*. . ."

E
—the case to which I referred a moment ago.

The *Telescriptor* case itself has also been placed before me and, as is I think well known, *Buckley* J indicated in that case that it had to be proved to his satisfaction that a stay should be granted and he said (at p. 182) that he would:

> "decline to order a stay of these proceedings until it is proved to my satisfaction that the winding-up ought to be stayed."

F
He went on — and this is of some particular relevance in the present case:

> "That will not be proved to my satisfaction until it is shown to me that all the facts are as I hope they are — that the trading operations of this company have been fair and above-board."

On those authorities, and given the position as it appears to me today, and given in particular the opposition of Barclays to the application and the fact that there is no

G
immediate proposal for payment of Barclays, nor any other ground upon which (so far as I can see) it could be said that Barclays ought to consent to a stay, the application for a stay must, in my judgment, be refused.

That brings me to the final stage in Mr Atherton's submissions where, as I indicated earlier when referring to the application which he made, he invites me to treat this

H
application as being itself an appeal from Mr Registrar *Buckley*'s refusal to rescind the winding-up order. In normal circumstances I would have no hesitation in refusing that invitation, given that the proper procedures have not been complied with; no notice has been given, no grounds have been set out, no leave to appeal has been sought, no sufficient time has been provided to Barclays to prepare its case in opposition to the appeal. However, having been taken very carefully through the evidential material before the court, I am completely satisfied that there are no grounds upon which an

appeal could succeed. The burden of Mr Kumar's evidence is, as I have already

indicated, to the effect that there are a number of transactions which would fall to be
and which would be completed were an administration ordered, being as to five such
transactions, transactions by the company in respect of which it would on the figures
provided by Mr Kumar expect a substantial return and, as to the sixth, by a subsidiary of
the company. On the basis of the figures which he gives and what he described as his
"confidence" that all these matters will proceed according to plan, a cash-flow chart is
exhibited by Mr Kumar which indicates profitable trading by the company.

Mr Atherton naturally relies also very strongly on a r. 2.2 report prepared by Mr John
William Caley of Messrs Sterling Ford, being the report which I referred to earlier dated
10 August — yesterday. The r. 2.2 report has annexed to it an estimated statement of
affairs of the company as at 30 June 1993 showing estimated total assets available for
creditors of £5,000, as against creditors totalling some £141,000. As I said earlier, some
£57,000 of that sum is represented by Barclays' debt and a further some £7,000 by

unsecured creditors. Mr Caley in his r. 2.2 report deals with the various transactions
referred to by Mr Kumar in his evidence and proceeds on the basis that they will all be
completed in accordance with the expectations of Mr Kumar as set out in that affidavit.
It is, however, germane to note that Mr Caley has proceeded — and I make no criticism
whatever of him for so doing — on the basis of discussions that he and members of his
firm have had with Mr Kumar and Mr Kumar's colleagues. He says in particular in
para. 1.7 of his r. 2.2 report:

> "My firm have not been responsible for the preparation of the accounting
> information referred to in this report, although from discussions with Mr Kumar I
> am satisfied that the statement of affairs presents a reasonable reflection of SN's
> financial position and that the cash-flow forecast to the end of June 1994 reasonably
> reflects the likely cash movements and funds required for the purpose, during
> which it is proposed that SN will trade in administration for the purposes of
> completing the business referred to in para. 1.6 above."

That is a reference to the various transactions as to which Mr Kumar has given evidence.

In respect of the evidence as to these expected transactions and expected resulting
profits, I accept the submission of Miss Stewart that they are on the evidence purely
speculative transactions, they are not satisfactorily explained and there are a number of
respects in which one would wish to see very much greater detail. Moreover, I take the

point made by Miss Stewart that given the close trading relationship which Mr Kumar
emphasises at a number of points in his affidavit between the various parties to these
transactions, the availability of funds may be by no means certain given that the company
itself is, on the figures which I have quoted, hopelessly insolvent.

In my judgment, the evidence indicates no more than a possibility that the company
may make a profit on certain transactions, if such transactions in the event take place,
and amounts to no more than a prospect that such transactions may take place. That, in

my judgment, is by no means a sufficient ground for rescinding the winding-up order.

Moreover, there are other matters of which I must take account in my judgment.

The first is that it has been pointed out to me that the directors of the company,
particularly Mr Kumar, have not so far complied with the requirement in sec. 131(4) of
the Insolvency Act to submit a statement of affairs to the official receiver. I am told by
Mr Bennett of the official receiver's office that Mr Kumar acknowledged receipt of the

appropriate form on 12 July 1993 but no statement of affairs has been submitted
pursuant to subsec. (4) of sec. 131, notwithstanding that the period of 21 days stipulated
by that subsection has now expired.

A further matter to which I must briefly refer concerns the activities and connection
with the management of the company of Mr S Naidoo. Mr Naidoo is, it appears, a

A   bankrupt, having been made bankrupt on 29 August 1991. Despite that, Mr Kumar has exhibited a set of management accounts which form exhibit SK8 to his affidavit which are prefaced by a report of Ableman Shaw & Co (Chartered Accountants) and which is headed:

> "Accountants' statement to the management on the profit and loss account for the period from 1 August 1992 to 31 March 1993."

B   The statement of the accountants reads as follows:

> "The information which appears on the following page has been prepared for management purposes only. No audit work has been carried out in relation thereto, nor has any third party confirmation been obtained for the figures contained therein. Where necessary, information has been obtained from management to enable it to be included in these accounts."

C   That statement is dated 7 June 1993. When one then turns to the management accounts themselves one finds a set of consolidated financial statements for the year ended 31 July 1992 and following that statement there is a report of the directors signed by order of the board by Mrs A Yocoub as secretary on 24 February 1993. In the section of that report headed "Directors" one finds this:

> "The directors who have served during the year under review, together with their
D   interests in the ordinary share capital of the company, were as follows:
>
> S Naidoo, Esq . . ."

—and he is shown as owning 1,250 shares in the company and then three other gentlemen are also named. In these circumstances, it appears that Mr S Naidoo may have been concerned in the management of the company notwithstanding the bankruptcy order made, as I have said, on 29 August 1991.

E   Mr Atherton told me on instructions that since the making of the bankruptcy order Mr Naidoo has merely acted as a salesman abroad and has had no concern in the management of the company. I inquired as to when was the last board meeting which he attended and I was told by Mr Atherton on instructions that Mr Naidoo could not remember. In these circumstances, it may be — and I go no further than that — that there are matters which require to be investigated concerning Mr S Naidoo's participation in the management of the company following his being made bankrupt on 29 August
F   1991. That is a matter which may be investigated, if it is necessary to do so, in the course of the winding up.

So, for those reasons I take the view on the material which I have seen that there are no grounds on which an appeal against Mr Registrar *Buckley*'s refusal to order rescission could succeed. I accordingly accept Mr Atherton's invitation to treat this application as being such an appeal and I dismiss it.

G
Costs

So far as the costs of this application are concerned, I consider that it is an oppressive application, I think it was wrongly brought on, I think proper notice ought to have been given and in the circumstances it seems to me that the costs ought to be paid on an indemnity basis. As to the payees, I will make an order against Mr Kumar following the
H   practice direction to which I have been referred [*Practice Note* [1971] 1 WLR 757] . . . Mr Bennett, I will make an order for your costs on the usual basis and not on any different basis.

(*Appeal dismissed*)

Arab Bank plc v Mercantile Holdings Ltd & Anor.

A

Chancery Division.

Millett J.

Judgment delivered 29 September 1993.

Acquisition of own shares — Financial assistance by company or subsidiaries for purchase of own shares prohibited — Whether prohibition extended to foreign subsidiary — Whether giving assistance by subsidiary constituted assistance by parent — Companies Act 1985, sec. 151.

B

1. Section 151 of the Companies Act did not prohibit a company incorporated outside Great Britain which was a subsidiary of an English registered parent giving financial assistance for the purpose of the acquisition of shares in its parent company. The words "any of its subsidiaries" in sec. 151 had to be construed as limited to those subsidiaries which were English companies.

C

2. The mere giving of such assistance by the subsidiary did not ipso facto and without more necessarily also constitute the unlawful giving of financial assistance by the parent company contrary to sec. 151.

The following cases were referred to in the judgment:

Astor v Perry [1935] AC 398.

Drummond v Collins [1915] AC 1011.

IR Commrs v Collco Dealings Ltd [1962] AC 1.

D

International Tin Council, Re (1987) 3 BCC 103, [1987] Ch 419; (1988) 4 BCC 653, [1989] Ch 309 (CA).

Michael Briggs (instructed by Frere Cholmeley Bischoff) for the plaintiff.

Martin Mann QC and Elspeth Talbot Rice (instructed by Leslie Hyman) for the first defendant.

E

Alan Steinfeld QC and Adrian Francis (instructed by Ince & Co) for the second defendant.

JUDGMENT

Millett J: I will first give judgment under para. 1 of the originating summons.

F

This case illustrates the dangers which are inherent in any attempt to recast statutory language in more modern and direct form for no better reason than to make it shorter, simpler and more easily intelligible. It raises two questions:

(1) Whether sec. 151 of the *Companies Act* 1985 (which prohibits a company or any of its subsidiaries from giving financial assistance for the purpose of the acquisition of shares in the company) makes it unlawful for a company incorporated outside Great Britain ("a foreign subsidiary") which is a subsidiary of a parent company registered under the English Companies Acts ("an English company") to give financial assistance for the purpose of the acquisition of shares in its parent company.

G

(2) Whether the mere giving of such assistance by the subsidiary ipso facto and without more necessarily also constitutes the unlawful giving of financial assistance by the parent company contrary to sec. 151.

H

The facts

On 9 April 1990 the plaintiff, Arab Bank plc ("the bank") granted a loan facility of £15.4m to the second defendant Shelfco (No. 488) Ltd ("Shelfco") for the express purpose of enabling it to acquire the entire share capital of Queensbridge Estates

A Limited ("Queensbridge"). Queensbridge was the parent company and owned the entire share capital of the first defendant Mercantile Holdings Ltd ("Mercantile") which was the owner of a leasehold property, Queensbridge House and Queensbridge Quays, Upper Thomas Street in the City of London ("the property"). By a fixed and floating charge also dated 9 April 1990 Mercantile (inter alia) charged the property and, by a separate memorandum of the same date, it assigned the rental income of the property to the bank to secure the moneys advanced to Shelfco under the loan facility.

B Queensbridge and Shelfco are both companies incorporated in England and registered under the English Companies Acts. It is common ground that if Mercantile were also such a company, the security which it provided to the bank would constitute the unlawful giving of financial assistance contrary to sec. 151. Mercantile, however, was incorporated in Gibraltar. It maintains a place of business in Great Britain, and accordingly is an "oversea company" within the meaning of the 1985 Act: see sec. 744; but it is not a

C "company" within the meaning of the Act: see sec. 735. It is, however, a "subsidiary" of Queensbridge within the meaning of the 1985 Act, since the word "company" in sec. 736 (which sets out the circumstances in which one company may be deemed to be a subsidiary of another) includes any "body corporate"; and "body corporate" is defined by sec. 740 to include a company incorporated elsewhere than in Great Britain.

D The bank now wishes to realise its security by entering into a contract of sale to sell the property for £12m. The defendants, however, have long maintained that the bank's power of sale has not yet arisen and is not exercisable, and that its security is void as having been granted in contravention of sec. 151 of the 1985 Act. The purchaser has notice of these contentions and has refused to enter into a contract of purchase until the bank obtains a court order which will quieten the title. Hence the present application by originating summons, para. 1 of which seeks a declaration that the bank's power of sale has arisen and is now exercisable.

E I am satisfied on the evidence (and, for the purpose of these proceedings only, the defendants have conceded) that if the bank's security is valid, its power of sale has arisen and is exercisable. The only question, therefore, is whether the security was lawfully granted.

Both defendants received legal advice at the time of the granting of the security that Mercantile being a foreign subsidiary the transaction was not caught by sec. 151. They

F entered into the transaction honestly and in good faith in reliance on that advice. Now, however, it suits them to maintain that the transaction was in fact unlawful; and they have so contended before me.

The current legislation

Section 151 of the 1985 Act provides:

G "(1) Subject to the following provisions of this Chapter, where a person is acquiring or is proposing to acquire shares in a company, it is not lawful for the company or any of its subsidiaries to give financial assistance directly or indirectly for the purpose of that acquisition before or at the same time as the acquisition takes place.

. . .

H (3) If a company acts in contravention of this section, it is liable to a fine, and every officer of it who is in default is liable to imprisonment or a fine, or both."

"Financial assistance" is defined by sec. 152.

Section 153 exempts certain transactions from the operation of sec. 151. Subsection (1) opens with the words:

British Company Cases

"Section 151(1) does not prohibit a company from giving financial assistance for the purpose of an acquisition of shares in it or its holding company if . . ."

Some of the transactions listed in sec. 153 are transactions which could be entered into by a foreign subsidiary: for example, a transaction where the company's principal purpose in giving the assistance was not to give it for the purpose of the acquisition of the shares, or the giving of the assistance was only an incidental part of a larger transaction; or where it took the form of a distribution of the company's assets by way of a payment of a lawful dividend or was made in the course of the company's winding up. (This would involve reading the word "company" in the opening words of sec. 153 as including a foreign company, but if sec. 151 applies to such a company, so must sec. 153 so far as possible. The exemptions must, so far as possible, be co-extensive with the prohibition.) Other transactions, however, listed in sec. 153 could not be entered into by a foreign subsidiary: for example, where it involves a reduction of a company's capital confirmed by the court under sec. 137 of the 1985 Act, or a redemption or purchase of shares in accordance with Ch. VII of Pt. V of the 1985 Act.

Sections 155–158 relax the operation of sec. 151 for private companies provided that the provisions of those sections are complied with and the procedures there laid down are followed. The term "private company" is defined by section 1(3) of the 1985 Act and, unless the contrary intention appears, does not include a foreign company. The contrary intention does not appear in sec. 155–158. On the contrary, the provisions of those sections could not be complied with by a foreign subsidiary, even if it hived down its assets into an English sub-subsidiary.

The earlier legislation

The prohibition of a company from giving financial assistance in connection with the purchase *of its own* shares was introduced by sec. 45 of the *Companies Act* 1929. The prohibition was naturally limited to English companies. A corresponding provision in similar terms was enacted in Gibraltar in relation to companies incorporated there.

The prohibition was extended by sec. 73 of the *Companies Act* 1947 to the giving of financial assistance in connection with the purchase of shares in the company's holding company. It did so by enacting that sec. 45 of the 1929 Act should apply to shares in a company's holding company as it applied to shares in the company itself. No similar extension has ever been introduced into the law of Gibraltar.

Section 45 of the 1929 Act as amended by sec. 73 of the 1947 Act was repealed and replaced by sec. 54 of the *Companies Act* 1948. That section was in the following terms:

"(1) Subject as provided in this section, it shall not be lawful for a company to give, whether directly or indirectly . . . any financial assistance for the purpose of or in connection with a purchase or subscription made or to be made by any person of or for any shares in the company, or, where the company is a subsidiary company, in its holding company. . ."

The 1948 Act contained certain limited exemptions but it did not contain all those contained in sec. 153 of the 1985 Act, nor did it contain any provisions corresponding to the provisions of sec. 155–158 of the 1985 Act. It did, however, contain definitions of "company" and "subsidiary", which in all material respects were the same as those in the 1985 Act.

It is to be observed that the prohibition contained in sec. 54 of the 1948 Act, like that in the statutory provisions which it replaced, was directed to the company which provided the financial assistance ("the assisting company"). It was unlawful for that company to provide financial assistance in connection with the acquisition of its own shares or shares in its holding company. But the assisting company must be "a company".

A   In the absence of a context to the contrary, and there was none, the section did not
     extend to a foreign subsidiary of an English holding company. On the other hand,
     because of the definition of "subsidiary", it did extend to an English subsidiary of a
     foreign holding company (curiously, and probably inadvertently, the 1947 Act appears
     not to have done so).

Section 151 of the 1985 Act
B
         Section 54 of the 1948 Act was repealed and replaced by sec. 42–44 of the Companies
     Act 1981, which have in turn been re-enacted in similar terms by sec. 151–158 of the
     1985 Act. The language of sec. 54 of the 1948 Act has been completely recast. The whole
     perspective of the section has been altered. The prohibition is still directed to the
     assisting company. But the section no longer starts with the assisting company and
     prohibits it from giving financial assistance for the purchase of its own shares or shares in
C   its holding company. Instead, it starts with the company whose shares are to be acquired
     ("the target company") and prohibits it or "any of its subsidiaries" from giving financial
     assistance for the purchase of its own shares.

         It is difficult to believe that this change, which is primarily one of style, was intended
     to make any alteration in the substantive law, particularly when the opening words of
     sec. 153 refer back to sec. 151 as if it were still cast in the old form; and in an entirely
D   domestic situation it does not do so. But because of the statutory definitions of "company"
     (which prima facie means an English company) and "subsidiary" (which does not) it
     appears to have made at least one change and may have made two. Formerly, the
     assisting company had to be "a company", i.e. an English company; but the target
     company did not: it was sufficient if it was the assisting company's holding company.
     Now, however, it is the target company which has to be "a company"; the assisting
     company does not: it is sufficient if it is one of the target company's subsidiaries. The
E   new requirement that the target company must be "a company" means that the giving
     of financial assistance by the English subsidiary of a foreign parent company for the
     acquisition of shares in that company appears to be no longer prohibited. On the other
     hand, the removal of the former requirement that the assisting company must be "a
     company", coupled with the use of the words "any of its subsidiaries" instead of "any of
     its subsidiary companies", in place of the cumbersome and ungainly phrase "where the
     company is a subsidiary company", if taken literally, extends the prohibition for the first
F   time to the case where the prohibited act, i.e. the giving of financial assistance, is
     committed by a foreign company.

         Before considering whether it does so or not, I shall deal with the second of the two
     questions which has been argued before me.

Does the mere giving of financial assistance by the subsidiary ipso facto also constitute the giving of such assistance by the parent company?
G
         In my judgment the answer is plainly "no". The prohibition is, and always has been,
     directed to the assisting company, not to its parent company. If the giving of financial
     assistance by a subsidiary for the acquisition of shares in its holding company necessarily
     also constituted the giving of financial assistance by the holding company, sec. 73 of the
     1947 Act would not have been necessary. Moreover, sec. 153–158 of the 1985 Act are
     clearly predicated on the assumption that it is the conduct of the subsidiary alone which
H   needs statutory authorisation.

         This is not to say that the giving of financial assistance by the subsidiary may not
     involve unlawful conduct on the part of the parent. If the acts of the subsidiary are in
     breach of sec. 151, the conduct of the parent in procuring them will constitute an offence.
     And even if the section does not apply to foreign subsidiaries, the hiving down of an

British Company Cases

asset by an English company to such a subsidiary in order to enable it to be made
available to finance a contemplated acquisition of shares of the English company would
clearly contravene the section: it would constitute the indirect provision of financial
assistance by the English company.

**Does sec. 151 of the 1985 Act make it unlawful for a foreign subsidiary of an English
parent company to give financial assistance for the purpose of the acquisition of shares of
its parent company?**

Read literally and with the assistance of the statutory definition of "subsidiary",
sec. 151 clearly purports to make it unlawful for a foreign subsidiary of an English parent
company to give financial assistance for the purpose of the acquisition of shares of its
parent company. The result, however, is to give the section an extraterritorial effect
contrary to the general principles of private international law; for the capacity of a
corporation, the regulation of its affairs, the maintenance of its capital and the protection
of its creditors and shareholders are generally recognised to be matters for the law of the
place of incorporation. But there have been many cases in which the words of a statute
have been given a more limited meaning than they are capable of bearing where there is
a proper ground for concluding that this was the intention of Parliament: see, for
example, *Drummond v Collins* [1915] AC 1011 at p. 1017; *Astor v Perry* [1935] AC 398
at p. 417; *IR Commrs v Collco Dealings Ltd* [1962] AC 1; and *Re International Tin
Council* (1987) 3 BCC 103 at p. 114; (1988) 4 BCC 653 at p. 655 (CA). The consideration
that the more limited meaning is necessary in order to avoid the creation of a jurisdiction
wider than that generally recognised by international law has often been recognised as
such a ground.

The defendants submit that a literal construction is necessary in order effectively to
deal with the mischief which it is the object of the section to prevent. That mischief, it is
submitted, is by means of the forbidden assistance to circumvent the rule which forbids
an English company from distributing its assets to shareholders otherwise than by the
lawful distribution of profits, reduction of capital or distribution of surplus assets on a
winding up. Subsidiaries are included in the prohibition since the distribution of its
assets to the shareholders in its holding company is tantamount to a distribution of the
assets of the holding company itself. The same consideration applies whether the
subsidiary is incorporated in Great Britain or abroad. If foreign subsidiaries were
outside the prohibition, the defendants submit, a coach and horses could be driven
through the section by the simple expedient of always taking the precaution of always interposing
a wholly owned foreign subsidiary between a company and its assets.

I am not impressed by the "coach and horses" argument. As I have already observed,
the hiving down of the assets by an English company to a foreign subsidiary in order that
they may be available for the purpose of assisting in the financing of a contemplated
purchase of the parent company's own shares would, in my judgment, constitute the
indirect provision of financial assistance by the parent company; while the presence of
sec. 155–158 of the 1985 Act makes it unnecessary to interpose a foreign subsidiary in
advance as a matter of routine forward strategic planning. Bearing in mind that the
provision of financial assistance for the purchase will almost invariably be at the request
and instigation of the purchaser rather than the target company, and that it can easily
and lawfully be provided where this can be done without prejudice to the interests of
creditors and minority shareholders, the interposition of a foreign subsidiary where no
purchase was yet in contemplation would seem to require a combination of legal
acumen, foresight and dishonesty which is most unusual.

Nor am I satisfied that the mischief which the section is designed to prevent is the
extraction of the assets of the target company rather than those of its subsidiary. This

A   was not the case before 1981, when the prohibition was limited to English subsidiaries even when the target company was an English company. The defendants submit that if the mischief sought to be prevented was the extraction of assets from the subsidiary, then the section would have prohibited an English subsidiary of a foreign parent company from giving financial assistance for the purchase of shares of the parent company. This would be a formidable argument if I were persuaded that the failure to cover this case, covered in the 1948 Act, was deliberate; but I am not. The primary class

B   of persons which the section was designed to protect must, in my judgment, be the creditors of the assisting company; and they are equally prejudiced by the extraction of its assets for the purpose of financing the acquisition of shares in its parent company whether that parent company is English or foreign. I can see no possible reason or justification for excluding such a case from the prohibition and, if this was indeed the result of the recasting of the statutory language in 1981, I think that it must have been

C   inadvertent.

Whether the section is intended primarily for the protection of the creditors of the assisting company or for the protection of the creditors of its parent company, however, it is directed to the conduct of the assisting company. Where that company is a subsidiary, it is directed to the subsidiary, not to its parent company. The section operates by regulating the conduct of the subsidiary and depriving it of the capacity to enter into transactions of the kind specified. The capacity of a corporation, the regulation

D   of its conduct, the maintenance of its capital, and the protection of its creditors and shareholders are all matters for the law of the place of its incorporation, not the law of the place of incorporation of its parent company.

Conclusion

E   I have reached the firm conclusion that "any of its subsidiaries" in sec. 151 must be construed as limited to those subsidiaries which are subsidiary companies, that is to say, English companies. My reasons for this conclusion are as follows:

1. The recasting of the language of the section, and in particular the change from "subsidiary company" to "any of its subsidiaries", was almost certainly a matter of style and not intended to make a substantive change in the law.

F   2. There is a presumption that, in the absence of a contrary intention expressed or implied, UK legislation does not apply to foreign persons or corporations outside the UK whose acts are performed outside the UK. Some limitation of the general words of sec. 151 is necessary in order to avoid imputing to Parliament an intention to create an exorbitant jurisdiction which is contrary to generally accepted principles of international law.

G   3. In relation to the maintenance of the capital of a corporation and the protection of its creditors and shareholders the place where its assets are depleted or put at risk by the giving of the forbidden assistance is irrelevant. To limit the section to the giving of the forbidden assistance in the UK, as the defendants contend, would be misdirected legislation which would be wholly inadequate to protect the creditors of the subsidiary and would still be at variance with generally accepted principles of international law.

H   4. Section 151 is directed at the assisting company. It renders particular acts on the part of the assisting company unlawful. Whether the section is intended primarily for the protection of the creditors of the assisting company or for the protection of creditors of its parent company, where the assisting company is a subsidiary the section is directed at the subsidiary and not at the parent company. It operates by regulating the conduct of the subsidiary and depriving it of the capacity to enter into transactions of the kind specified.

A

5. The capacity of a corporation, the regulation of its conduct, the maintenance of its capital and the protection of its creditors and shareholders are all matters for the law of the place of its incorporation, not the law of the place of incorporation of its parent company.

6. Section 54 of the 1948 Act, which the 1981 and 1985 Acts replaced, did not prohibit a foreign subsidiary from providing financial assistance for the acquisition of shares in its parent company.

B

7. Section 151 does not prohibit a partly owned foreign subsidiary from providing financial assistance for the purchase of its own shares.

8. The penalties for contravention of sec. 151 do not extend to foreign subsidiaries or their officers.

9. A number of the more important exemptions in sec. 153 do not apply to a foreign subsidiary, which could not take advantage of the relaxation of sec. 151 provided by sec. 155–158. One would expect the exemptions and relaxations to be co-extensive with the prohibition.

C

10. If sec. 151 applies to foreign subsidiaries, such a subsidiary may be prevented from entering into a transaction which is lawful under the law of its incorporation, not only where that law is less stringent than our own, but even where it is in similar or even identical terms to our own. That cannot have been the intention of Parliament.

D

In my judgment sec. 151 does not prohibit a foreign subsidiary of an English parent company from giving financial assistance for the acquisition of shares in its parent company and I will so declare. I will also make a declaration under para. 1 of the originating summons that the power of sale has arisen and is now exercisable.

[The judgment under para. 3 of the originating summons which sought an order pursuant to sec. 91(2) of the *Law of Property Act* 1925 directing that the property be sold is not reproduced.]

E

(Declaration accordingly)

F

G

H

Re Dollar Land Holdings plc.

Chancery Division (Companies Court).
Sir Donald Nicholls V-C.
Judgment delivered 10 November 1992.

Winding-up petition — Striking-out application — Petitioner had provided security for company to obtain bank guarantee which was drawn on — Petitioner sought order for company to procure release of guarantee or damages — Whether petitioner had standing to petition — Whether contingent or prospective creditor — Materiality of company's inability to procure release of guarantee — Whether petitioner entitled to winding up on just and equitable ground — Insolvency Act 1986, sec. 124.

This was an application to strike out a creditor's winding-up petition on the basis that the petitioner, "W", was not a creditor of the company or that the petition was an abuse of process.

W had agreed, in exchange for a participation in a property being acquired by one of the operating subsidiaries in the company's group, to provide security which was used to obtain a bank guarantee. That guarantee was drawn on in the sum of £422,000, but the purchase of the property did not proceed to completion and W demanded the release of his guarantee.

W took proceedings seeking a mandatory order for the company to procure the release of the guarantee forthwith, and claiming liquidated damages of £422,000 for breach of contract. He also issued the winding-up petition against the company.

The company advanced a number of arguments to show that W had no standing to petition or that the petition was an abuse of process. Since W had not elected to abandon his claim for a mandatory order, he could not rely on the alternative and inconsistent remedy in damages. Secondly, it was not clear that W's claim for a mandatory order would succeed and W was not a contingent creditor in respect of his alternative damages claim because the fulfilment of the contingency was within W's own control. W's position was analogous to a person who had an option which he had not exercised and might never exercise against the company. Further, the petition was an abuse because W was suing the company in the action for certain relief and, on the other hand, had presented a winding-up petition which would make it impossible for the court to grant that relief. Finally, the evidence on the company's financial position was that although it had a deficiency on current account, overall it had a substantial surplus of assets over liabilities and, accordingly, the petition was bound to fail.

Held, dismissing the company's application:

1. W was a creditor, at least contingently or prospectively, on the basis of his claim to damages for breach of the obligation to procure the release of the guarantee. Further, he was, at least prospectively, a creditor in a substantial sum even if the claim was not one for liquidated damages in the sum of £422,000 (because the damages to which he was entitled by non-release of the securities might be less than £422,000).

2. The election point did not assist the company. Even while maintaining his claim for a mandatory order as the primary relief he sought, W was a contingent creditor in respect of his alternative claim for damages. The company was in breach of a contract made between it and W. All that remained open was which remedy W would pursue. The contingency on which the damages claim depended was the continuing non-performance by the company of its contractual obligation to W. W would only cease to be a contingent creditor if the company performed an obligation which it was unable to carry out.

3. The court had to ensure that a prospective or contingent creditor did not use the winding-up procedure oppressively. W's claim against the company was not geared to some remote or problematic contingency, nor was it prospective in any remotely distant sense. The company could not procure the release of the guarantee and was in breach of contract and had been so for a year or more. In respect of the damage flowing to W from that breach of contract, W had a good cause of action in a substantial sum.

4. The court in any event had a jurisdiction to make a winding-up order on the ground that it was just and equitable that the company should be wound up. As to that, the company could not carry out its obligation to obtain the release of the guarantee. That breach of contract carried with it an obligation to pay damages. The company had that damages claim hanging as a sword of Damocles over its head against which it was defenceless. At any moment the sword would fall. It would fall as soon as W abandoned, if he did, his attempt to obtain an order that the company specifically carry out its obligation to procure a release of the guarantee.

Gavin Lightman QC and Nicholas Harrison (instructed by Greenwood & Co) for the petitioner.

Romie Tager (instructed by Leslie Hyman) for the company.

JUDGMENT

Nicholls V-C: This is an application to strike out a creditor's winding-up petition on the basis that the petitioner, Mr Weiss, is not a creditor of the company, Dollar Land Holdings plc ("Dollar Land") and on the basis, further, that the petition is a misuse of the court's process.

Reduced to its barest essentials, the position between the parties is this. In July 1990 Mr Weiss reached an oral agreement with Mr Stern, a director of Dollar Land Management Ltd. Dollar Land Management Ltd is a company in the Dollar Land group responsible for the day-to-day management of Dollar Land and its operating and investment-holding subsidiaries. It seems that with regard to that agreement Mr Stern was, or may have been, acting as an agent on behalf of Dollar Land as an undisclosed principal. There is a dispute over some of the terms of the agreement but, suffice to say, pursuant to the agreement Mr Weiss provided security which indirectly had the result of a bank, Bank J Vontabel, guaranteeing, in one form or another, the liabilities of Dollar Land (106) Ltd to Bank Julius Bahr in the sum of £440,000. Against that guarantee the sum of £422,000 was subsequently drawn down from Bank Julius Bahr. Mr Weiss provided that security in exchange for a 25 per cent participation in a property, Magnet House, in Glasgow, which was in the course of being acquired by one of the operating subsidiaries in the Dollar Land group, namely, Dollar Land (106) Ltd. It was being acquired at the price of £4m. In the event, the purchase of Magnet House did not proceed to completion.

When Mr Weiss learned of this he demanded the immediate release of his guarantee. It is common ground that, subject to one point, Dollar Land is under a present obligation to procure the release of the guarantee provided by Mr Weiss.

On 1 July 1992 Mr Weiss issued a writ against Mr Stern, Dollar Land, Dollar Land (106) Ltd and others, claiming relief in respect of this transaction and in respect of another transaction of a similar nature concerning a property at Wimbledon Broadway. In that instance the purchase was completed, there by another subsidiary in the group, namely, Dollar Land (Broadway) Ltd. Mr Weiss provided security in the sum of £250,000. There, as in the case of Magnet House, the guarantee was agreed to be made available for a three-year period. In that instance the agreement was made in or about December 1989.

A   On 7 September 1992 three steps were taken by Mr Weiss. First, he served a statement of claim in the action. The relief sought included, regarding Magnet House, a mandatory order that Dollar Land do procure the release of the Bank J Vontabel guarantee forthwith, and a claim for liquidated damages for £422,000 for breach of contract. Secondly, Mr Weiss gave notice of motion seeking summary judgment in the action for the mandatory order and, further or alternatively, damages in the sum of £422,000 and interest. Thirdly, he issued the winding-up petition returnable on 25 November.

B   On 5 October Dollar Land responded with an application to the Companies Court seeking, under para. 1, an order that the petition should be struck out and, under para. 2, an injunction restraining advertisement. That application came before the court on, I think, 26 October. By agreement with the petitioner it was dealt with as follows. First, the petitioner agreed not to advertise the petition pending the hearing of para. 2 of the Dollar Land application, which was then adjourned to the present hearing before me. The further hearing of para. 1 of the application was adjourned to 11 December,

C that part of the application to come on at the same time as an application by Mr Weiss to continue a Mareva injunction and at the same time also as Mr Weiss's O. 14 application.

   This sundering of the Dollar Land application into two parts to come on on different days was, I think, unfortunate. Mr Lightman urged me to dispose of the O. 14 application as well as the whole of the Dollar Land application at this hearing. Mr Tager was unable

D to agree that I should decide everything at this hearing because his client, Dollar Land, wishes to put in further evidence before 11 December on its up-to-date financial position regarding discharge of the guarantee. However, he accepted that Dollar Land did not wish to adduce further evidence in support of para. 1 of its application and, further, that he was in a position to deal fully with that part of the application at this hearing as well as para. 2. Accordingly, and so as to avoid unnecessary duplication at two hearings and, hence, to avoid wasting costs, I proceeded to hear both paragraphs of Dollar Land's

E application. In truth, the two go hand-in-hand. Mr Tager accepted that, if and in so far as this method of proceeding may result in my determining any issue arising in the O. 14 proceedings then, for better or worse, that would happen. He was concerned only that Dollar Land should not be prejudiced on the matter on which Dollar Land wished to adduce further evidence. That evidence would only go to the form of relief, if any, to which Mr Weiss may be entitled on the O. 14 application.

F   The petitioner's case is a comparatively simple one. Mr Weiss is a present creditor of Dollar Land. Dollar Land has failed to carry out its obligation to procure the release of the guarantee, and it is liable in damages in the sum required by Mr Weiss to obtain that release, namely £422,000. Alternatively, Mr Weiss is a contingent creditor. Even if, for a reason I will mention, Dollar Land is not presently under an obligation to procure the release of the guarantee, Dollar Land is contingently liable to Mr Weiss in damages.

G Further, the prospect that in due course Dollar Land will procure the release of the guarantee, so that no claim for damages would ever arise, should be discounted. It should be discounted because it is clear that *at present* Dollar Land is unable to procure that release.

   The company has raised several objections to this simple approach. The points made by Mr Tager include the following. First, Mr Weiss has not elected to abandon his claim for a mandatory order. So long as that is so, he cannot, in effect, rely on the alternative

H and inconsistent remedy in damages. Second, it is not clear that Mr Weiss's claim for a mandatory order will succeed. Dollar Land has a ground of defence. It was an implied term of the agreement regarding the property at Wimbledon that Mr Weiss would make good a quarter of any loss sustained in respect of that property, namely, for present purposes, the shortfall between the income and the mortgage and other outgoings. There is such a shortfall, at present in a sum approaching £300,000. Until Mr Weiss pays

some £70,000-odd to Dollar Land or the Broadway company he is not entitled to a   A
mandatory order for the discharge of the Magnet House guarantee. Alternatively, the
court in its discretion should not make a mandatory order until that sum has been paid.
Further, the petition is an abuse because it does not spell out with sufficient clarity the
essential ingredients of Mr Weiss's claim to be a creditor. The petition is also an abuse
because, on the one hand, Mr Weiss is suing Dollar Land in the action for certain relief
and, on the other hand, he has presented a winding-up petition which would make it
impossible for the court to grant that relief. If a winding-up order were made on   B
25 November, there would be no question of a mandatory order or any award of
damages on 11 December. Still further, the evidence on Dollar Land's financial position
is that although the company has a deficiency on current account, overall it has a
substantial surplus of assets over liabilities and, accordingly, the petition is bound to
fail. That is a summary of the principal submissions made by Mr Tager.

This is not the hearing of the petition. I am concerned, primarily, with whether   C
Mr Weiss has standing as a creditor. Under sec. 124 of the *Insolvency Act* 1986 a petition
may be presented by a creditor, including a contingent or prospective creditor. Mr Tager
accepted, in my view rightly in view of the authorities, that a person with an undisputable
claim for unliquidated damages for more than a nominal amount qualifies as a prospective
creditor for the purposes of sec. 124. In my view, Mr Weiss is, and is at present, a creditor
within the meaning of that section. He is a competent petitioner.   D

First, I can see nothing in the evidence to support a case that it was a term of the
Magnet House agreement that Mr Weiss was not to be entitled to the release of his
guarantee until he had paid any money due from him in respect of the Wimbledon
property. Indeed, I did not understand Mr Tager to press that point.

That being so, secondly, I can see no answer to the argument based on Mr Weiss's
claim to damages for breach of the obligation to procure the release of the guarantee.
Mr Weiss is a creditor, at least contingently or prospectively. Further, he is, at least   E
prospectively, a creditor in a substantial sum even if the claim is not one for liquidated
damages in the sum of £422,000. I express no view on whether the damages would
inevitably be in that amount. I see force in Mr Tager's argument that, depending on the
nature and present value of the securities lodged, the loss Mr Weiss may suffer, and
hence the damages to which he is entitled by non-release of the securities, might be less
than £422,000. As to the present value of those securities, I have been shown a list of the   F
securities lodged but I really do not think that I have any very satisfactory evidence
regarding their present value.

Thirdly, even if Dollar Land has an arguable case that the agreement regarding the
Wimbledon property included an implied term that Mr Weiss was obliged to pay one-
quarter of the income shortfall, that would not touch Mr Weiss's entitlement to damages
for the non-release of the guarantee regarding Magnet House. At most it would   G
constitute a cross-claim. On the figures it would fall far short of extinguishing that claim.

Fourthly, I do not think the election point materially assists Dollar Land. Even while
maintaining his claim for a mandatory order as the primary relief he seeks, Mr Weiss is a
contingent creditor in respect of his alternative claim for damages.

Mr Tager submitted that is not so. He submitted that Mr Weiss is not a contingent
creditor because the fulfilment of the contingency is within Mr Weiss's own control.   H
Mr Weiss's position is analogous to a person who has an option which he has not
exercised and may never exercise against the company. I do not accept the analogy.
Dollar Land is already in breach of a contract made between it and Mr Weiss. All that
remains open is which particular remedy Mr Weiss will pursue. Here the contingency on
which the damages claim hangs is the continuing non-performance by Dollar Land of its

A　existing contractual obligation to Mr Weiss. Mr Weiss will only cease to be a contingent creditor if Dollar Land performs an obligation which currently it is unable to carry out.

I agree with Mr Tager that none of the detail regarding the matters I have referred to is spelled out in the petition. However, the petition does allege that Dollar Land has failed to procure the release of the guarantee. The underlying source of the complaint is clear, even though that is followed in the petition by a compendious incorporation by reference of everything set out in the lengthy statement of claim. Although this was an

B　unhelpful formulation of the petition, I do not think Dollar Land and its advisers could have been or can be under any misapprehension about the claim in respect of which Mr Weiss claims to be a creditor. The substance is sufficiently spelled out. Wisely, however, Mr Harrison today sought leave to amend the petition by setting out expressly the appropriate pleas from the statement of claim. Those amendments would dispose of this pleading point altogether. In any event, the dispute between the parties over this

C　petition does not turn on the precise wording of the petition. I do not think that the petition has been worded in a form which is embarrassing to Dollar Land, but so as to put the matter wholly at rest I will give leave to amend the petition as sought.

I add this. The weight to be attached to Mr Weiss's status as a creditor, whether contingent or otherwise, is a matter to be assessed when the petition comes on for hearing. The court will have regard to the up-to-date evidence then before it regarding

D　Dollar Land's financial position. That is a matter to be looked into and considered definitively at that stage.

In letting the petition proceed I have in mind that the very act of advertising the petition can cause substantial damage to a company and its business and its prospects of raising money. So the court must be astute to see that a prospective or contingent creditor does not use the winding-up procedure oppressively. In this case Mr Weiss's

E　claim against Dollar Land is not geared to some remote or problematic contingency, nor is it prospective in any remotely distant sense. Dollar Land at present cannot procure the release of the guarantee. It is *now* in breach of contract, and has been so for a year or more. In respect of the damage flowing to Mr Weiss from that breach of contract, Mr Weiss has a good cause of action in a substantial sum.

Further, the weight to be attached to the evidence from Dollar Land that it has an overall surplus of assets, and to the latest evidence about its prospects of being able to

F　discharge the guarantee, are matters which in this case should be determined when the petition is heard. Suffice to say, as matters stand, I am far from satisfied that on the evidence now before the court on the hearing of the petition, the petition will fail. Mr Weiss's claim may not qualify as a debt for the purpose of deciding whether Dollar Land is at present unable to pay its currently payable debts. I express no concluded view on that point. Certainly if Mr Weiss's claim for an order that the guarantee be released does not qualify to be taken into account as a debt when the court makes that assessment,

G　it would lead to an unattractive commercial result. It could lead to the result that a company is to be regarded as able to pay its debts currently due even though it is presently not able to discharge all its currently due financial obligations.

Be that as it may, the court in any event has a jurisdiction to make a winding-up order on the ground that it is just and equitable that Dollar Land should be wound up. As to that, as I have already observed, Dollar Land cannot presently carry out its obligation

H　to obtain the release of the guarantee. That breach of contract carries with it an obligation to pay damages. Dollar Land has that damages claim hanging as a sword of Damocles over its head against which it is defenceless. At any moment the sword will fall. It will fall as soon as Mr Weiss abandons, if he does, his attempt to obtain an order that Dollar Land specifically carry out its obligation to procure a release of the guarantee. In my view Mr Weiss is entitled to proceed with his petition.

Mr Tager finally pressed me, in effect, to be merciful and to restrain advertisement for
a short period to give the company more time to see if its present efforts to dispose of
certain property in Belgium fructify by the end of November. The company has
expressed every confidence that on completion of contracts, which it is hoped to
exchange this month, the company will be able to discharge all its commitments.
Mr Weiss's attitude is that in view of the past history he is unable to attach any credibility
to this latest proposal. In the circumstances, I do not think I ought to restrain
advertisement of the petition.

(*Order accordingly*)

A **Taylor, Petitioner.**
Cumming's Trustee v Glenrinnes Farms Ltd.
Court of Session (Outer House).
Lord Weir.
Judgment delivered 20 November 1992.

B *Winding up — Whether trustee of bankrupt contributory could petition for winding up without being registered as shareholder — Bankruptcy (Scotland) Act 1985, sec. 31; Insolvency Act 1986, sec. 124.*

Section 31(8) of the Bankruptcy (Scotland) Act 1985 enabled the trustee of a bankrupt contributory to present a winding-up petition under sec. 124 of the Insolvency Act 1986 without registering his title to the bankrupt's shares.

C The following cases were referred to in the opinion:

Bolton (H L) Engineering Co Ltd, Re [1956] Ch 577.
Morgan & Anor v Gray & Ors [1953] Ch 83.

Duncan Menzies QC and Andrew Smith (instructed by John G Gray & Co) for the petitioner.

Charles Macnair (instructed by Bennett & Robertsons) for the company.

D
JUDGMENT

Lord Weir: On 2 July 1992 the petitioner was appointed provisional liquidator of Glenrinnes Farms Ltd ("the company") and I have before me two motions for consideration. One is on behalf of the company for recall of that appointment and the other is at the instance of the petitioner in which the court is asked to grant the prayer of the petition.

E The company was incorporated in 1954 with the objects of carrying on business as farmers, farm retailers and associated trades and businesses. The principal shareholder is James Mitchell Cumming. His wife holds a significant number of shares and one share is held by Alastair George McOran-Campbell. The latter individual has lodged answers but was not represented at the hearing. The petitioner was appointed as trustee in sequestration on the estate of Mr Cumming in June 1992.

F The petitioner avers that upon carrying out investigations into the affairs of Mr Cumming he discovered that assets including Glenrinnes House, the home farm and other heritable property might not belong, as he believed, to Mr Cumming as an individual but may belong to the company. He makes averments to the general effect that the affairs and business of Mr Cumming on the one hand and the company on the other hand are intermixed. Moreover, in the absence of up-to-date accounts, the last available being three years old, it is impossible to ascertain what are the assets and liabilities of the company. On the strength of these averments it was submitted that it was just and equitable for the company to be wound up.

Section 124(1) and (2) of the *Insolvency Act* 1986 is in the following terms:

"(1) Subject to the provisions of this section, an application to the court for the winding up of a company shall be by petition presented either by the company, or
H the directors, or by any creditor or creditors (including any contingent or prospective creditor or creditors), contributory or contributories . . . or by all or any of those parties, together or separately.

(2) Except as mentioned below, a contributory is not entitled to present a winding-up petition unless either—

(a) the number of members is reduced below 2, or

(b) the shares in respect of which he is a contributory, or some of them, either   A
were originally allotted to him, or have been held by him, and registered in
his name, for at least 6 months during the 18 months before the
commencement of the winding up, or have devolved on him through the
death of a former holder."

The first submission of counsel for the respondents in support of the motion for recall
was that the petitioner did not come within the categories of those entitled to present a
petition for winding up. On the face of it, the petitioner bore to be acting as an individual   B
and in no other capacity. I consider this argument as a technicality and it can be
immediately disposed of. It is quite plain from the terms of the petition as a whole that
the petitioner was suing in his capacity as trustee upon the sequestrated estate of
Mr Cumming, one of the members of the company. The fact that this is not expressly
stated in the instance seems to me to be of no importance.

The second argument presented by counsel for the respondents is a substantial one.   C
In this connection it was not disputed that the petitioner had taken no steps to register
himself as owner of the shares of Mr Cumming in the company. The question is whether
a trustee of a bankrupt contributory is to be deemed himself a contributory so as to
entitle him to petition for the winding up of that company in terms of sec. 124 of the Act
of 1986.

It will be convenient if I refer to further relevant statutory provisions of the *Insolvency*   D
Act 1986.

Section 79(1)

"In this Act and the Companies Act the expression 'contributory' means every
person liable to contribute to the assets of a company in the event of its being
wound up, and for the purposes of all proceedings for determining, and all
proceedings prior to the final determination of, the persons who are to be deemed   E
contributories, includes any person alleged to be a contributory."

Section 82(1) and (2)

"(1) The following applies if a contributory becomes bankrupt, either before or
after he has been placed on the list of contributories.

(2) His trustee in bankruptcy represents him for all purposes of the winding up,   F
and is a contributory accordingly."

It will be seen that a contributory is not entitled to present a winding-up petition
unless either the number of members is reduced below two (which is not the case here),
or the shares in respect of which he is a contributory were held by him and registered in
his name for at least six months during the 18 months before the commencement of the
winding up. It was accepted that Mr Cumming would qualify as a contributory and I   G
understand it to be accepted that the petitioner would stand in his room provided he had
taken steps to register himself as a shareholder. If he did so then in terms of sec. 82(2) he
would represent the debtor for all purposes of the winding up and be a contributory. As
I have said, the question is whether it is necessary for the trustee to register as a
shareholder in order to be treated as a contributory and as someone entitled to present a
winding-up petition.

This problem has received some consideration in England in the context of the   H
provisions of the *Companies Act* 1948 which are for practical purposes to the same effect
as the provisions of the Act of 1986 which I have already narrated. It has been held that
a bankrupt remains a member of a company and is entitled to vote so long as he remains
on the register of the company (*Morgan v Gray* [1953] Ch 83 per *Danckwerts* J at p. 87).
It has also been held that the powers of a trustee to represent the debtor for all the

A   purposes of the winding-up can only come into effect after a winding-up order has been
    made and that a trustee who had not obtained registration of the bankrupt's shares in his
    own name has no locus standi as a contributory to present a petition (in *Re H L Bolton
    Engineering Co Ltd* [1956] Ch 577 per *Wynn-Parry* J at pp. 582–583).

        Counsel for the respondents founded on these decisions and submitted that applying
    in particular the ratio of the decision in *Bolton Engineering Co Ltd* it was clear that the
B   petitioner had no power in this case to present a petition for a winding-up order. Counsel
    for the petitioner recognising that the two judgments which I have referred to have
    stood unchallenged for many years, accepted that if the law remained as it then was, his
    client would have no title to seek a winding-up order. It is, therefore, unnecessary for
    me to comment on the law as expressed in the English cases. However, he submitted
    that the position was now different in view of the provisions of sec. 31(1) and (8) of the
    Bankruptcy (Scotland) Act 1985:

C   "(1) Subject to section 33 of this Act, the whole estate of the debtor shall vest as
        at the date of sequestration in the permanent trustee for the benefit of the
        creditors; and—

        (a) the estate shall so vest by virtue of the act and warrant issued on confirmation
             of the permanent trustee's appointment; and

D   (b) the act and warrant shall, in respect of the heritable estate in Scotland of the
             debtor, have the same effect as if a decree of adjudication in implement of
             sale, as well as a decree of adjudication for payment and in security of debt,
             subject to no legal reversion, had been pronounced in favour of the
             permanent trustee.

        . . .

E   (8) In subsection (1) above the 'whole estate of the debtor' means, subject to
        subsection (9) below, his whole estate at the date of sequestration, wherever
        situated, including—

        (a) any income or estate vesting in the debtor on that date; and

        (b) the capacity to exercise and to take proceedings for exercising, all such
             powers in, over, or in respect of any property as might have been exercised
F   by the debtor for his own benefit as at, or on, the date of sequestration or
             might be exercised on a relevant date (within the meaning of section 32(10)
             of this Act)."

        There is nothing in these provisions, in my view, which has the effect of treating the
    act and warrant as the equivalent of registration. So in a question concerning a trustee's
    title to the shares of a bankrupt in a company the necessary formality of registration
G   must be undergone before it can be recognised. That has always been the position and
    remains so.

        The question as to whether a trustee can present a petition without registering is,
    however, a different matter and in my opinion sec. 31(8) enables him to do so without
    first of all securing title to the bankrupt's shares. The powers given to a trustee in terms
    of sec. 31(8)(b) are very wide. He is given the capacity to exercise all such powers in
    respect of any property as might have been exercised by the debtor for his own benefit
H   as at the date of sequestration. As a member of the company the debtor in this case had
    powers including the power to vote and as a contributory the power to present a petition
    for a winding up. In my opinion in terms of sec. 31(8)(b) the capacity to exercise such
    powers vested in his trustee as at the date of sequestration. The position is now different
    from what it may have been before the coming into force of the *Bankruptcy (Scotland)
    Act* 1985.

A

For these reasons the petitioner is enabled, in my opinion, as from the date of sequestration to assume the debtor's powers in relation to the company and in particular to petition for the winding up of the company.

Counsel for the respondent finally submitted that the petitioner had failed to make averments to demonstrate that the company was solvent before a winding-up order could be made at the instance of a contributory. This argument is demonstrably unsound in view of an admission made by the respondents on record that the company was in fact solvent.

B

The motion for recall of the petitioner's appointment as liquidator accordingly fails.

The petitioner's motion was that the court should grant the prayer of the petition. The basis for the winding-up order was that the court had to be of opinion that it was just and equitable that the company should be wound up in terms of sec. 122(1)(g) of the *Insolvency Act* 1986. Counsel for the petitioner did not press that motion but moved for a proof before answer. On the other hand counsel for the respondents contended that the petitioner's averments were insufficient to disclose a case for enquiry. He founded also on the provisions of sec. 125(2) of the Act which gives the court the power to refuse to make a winding-up order if it is of opinion both that some other remedy is available to the petitioner and that he is acting unreasonably in seeking to have the company wound up instead of pursuing that other remedy.

C

I have no hesitation in allowing a proof before reaching a decision on this application. It is best that at this stage I should say as little as possible about the circumstances or about the merits of the submissions advanced by counsel for the petitioner and respondents respectively. However, from the averments of the petitioner and from certain other documentary material presented to me at the Bar, the petitioner has demonstrated to my satisfaction the existence of a prima facie case for a winding up. It appears that the affairs of the debtor, Mr Cumming, and the company are intermixed to a substantial degree and may be difficult to disentangle. The accounts for the company are hopelessly out of date and there is at present considerable uncertainty as to the ownership of the heritage and certain of the moveables and the extent to which, if at all, the heritage or part of it may be subject to an agricultural tenancy or tenancies. A question has been sufficiently raised in my opinion as to the solvency of the company to entitle the court to enquire into the matter.

D

E

(Order accordingly)

F

G

H

A # Re Seagull Manufacturing Co Ltd (No. 2).

Chancery Division (Companies Court).
Mary Arden QC (sitting as a deputy High Court judge).
Judgment delivered 7 April 1993.

B *Director disqualification — Disqualifying unfit directors of insolvent companies — Director resisted proceedings on basis of residence in Channel Islands — Whether director disqualification jurisdiction extended to foreigners abroad — Whether conduct complained of must be conduct within jurisdiction — Whether court had discretion not to order service out of jurisdiction — Company Directors Disqualification Act 1986, sec. 6, 22.*

C This was an application by the respondent to director disqualification proceedings for a declaration that the court had no jurisdiction to order service of the proceedings on him in the Channel Islands.

The respondent submitted that a limitation ought to be implied into the Company Directors Disqualification Act that the activities which were said to render the respondent unfit to be a director should either take place in the jurisdiction or be directed from abroad. Thus, the activities of a director would only be relevant to the extent that they D had some effect in the jurisdiction. The official receiver, on the other hand, submitted that sec. 6(1) of the Act applied to any person, whether a British subject or a foreigner, irrespective of their presence in the jurisdiction at the time of the proceedings or when the activities took place. He further argued that in the case of foreign persons the court retained a residual discretion under r. 5 of the Insolvent Companies (Disqualification of Unfit Directors) Proceedings Rules 1987 not to order service out of the jurisdiction if it was not satisfied that there was a good arguable case.

E *Held*, dismissing the respondent's application:

1. Section 6 of the Company Directors Disqualification Act contained no express statement of any jurisdictional requirement and no jurisdictional limitation was to be implied. Parliament must be presumed to have been legislating not simply for British subjects and foreigners who happened to be within the jurisdiction at the relevant time, F but also for other foreigners who were out of the jurisdiction at the critical time. Likewise, in relation to conduct, sec. 6 contained no territorial restriction. Accordingly, the conduct in question in sec. 6 did not have to be conduct which occurred within the jurisdiction. (Re Paramount Airways Ltd (No. 2) [1992] BCC 416 and Re Seagull Manufacturing Co Ltd [1993] BCC 241 applied.)

2. The court had a discretion not to order service out and should not do so where it was G not satisfied that there was a good arguable case on the requirements of sec. 6(1). (Re Paramount Airways Ltd (No. 2) [1992] BCC 416 applied.)

3. The evidence set out a number of grounds which could form the basis of a disqualification order if proved at trial (subject to any evidence on behalf of the respondent).

The following cases were referred to in the judgment:

H *Blain, Ex parte. Re Sawers* (1879) 12 ChD 522.
Clark (HMIT) v Oceanic Contractors Inc [1982] BTC 417; [1983] 2 AC 130.
Eurostem Maritime Ltd & Ors, Re [1987] PCC 190.
Levitt (Jeffrey S) Ltd, Re [1992] BCC 137; [1992] Ch 457.
Paramount Airways Ltd, Re (No. 2) [1992] BCC 416; [1993] Ch 223.
Seagull Manufacturing Co Ltd, Re [1993] BCC 241; [1993] Ch 345.
Sevenoaks Stationers (Retail) Ltd, Re [1990] BCC 765; [1991] Ch 164.

Nigel Davis QC (instructed by the Treasury Solicitor) for the official receiver.   A

Paul Teverson (instructed by Rose & Birn) for the respondent.

JUDGMENT

Mary Arden QC: These are proceedings brought by the official receiver for the disqualification as a director of the respondent, Colin John Slinn ("Mr Slinn"). Mr Slinn is a British subject but he is not resident in England. Accordingly, on 24 March 1992,   B
Mr Registrar *Buckley* made an order for service of the originating summons on him, out of the jurisdiction, pursuant to r. 5(2) of the *Insolvent Companies (Disqualification of Unfit Directors) Proceedings Rules* 1987 (SI 1987/2023).

By a summons dated 8 July 1992, Mr Slinn sought relief arising out of that order including by para. 3, the only paragraph with which I am concerned apart from possibly costs, a declaration that the court has no jurisdiction over Mr Slinn in respect of the   C
subject-matter of the proceedings or the relief or remedies sought in the proceedings. The only ground on which this application is now pursued is that of ground 3. The remaining grounds have been abandoned or, in the case of ground 4, reserved for a higher court. I should add that there is some dispute as to whether Mr Slinn can properly reserve ground 4.

Ground 3 reads: D

"The said order dated 24 March 1992 was made without jurisdiction since, at all material times, the respondent was resident and domiciled in Alderney."

On this summons Mr Teverson represented Mr Slinn. The official receiver has been represented by Mr Nigel Davis QC.

There is an affidavit of Mr Slinn in support of his summons. The only part to which I need refer is para. 11 in which Mr Slinn states that from January 1979 to July 1986 he was   E
resident in and domiciled in Alderney in the Channel Islands.

The application made for leave to serve out of the jurisdiction which culminated in the order of 24 March 1992, was supported by an affidavit of John Charles Udell, a solicitor employed by the Treasury Solicitor. Paragraphs 3 and 4 of that affidavit state as follows:

"(3) I am informed by the applicant and verily believe that the respondent was a   F
director of Seagull Manufacturing Co Ltd. That company was wound up on 4 April 1990 by order of the court upon the petition of the Secretary of State for Trade and Industry on public interest grounds. Since that time the respondent has resisted every effort of the official receiver to investigate the affairs of Seagull. He has refused to render up books and papers concerning the company in his possession before being compelled to do so by a court order obtained in Alderney.
He has failed to provide a statement of affairs. He has refused to provide   G
information to the official receiver and has sought to frustrate the official receiver by contending that he cannot be compelled to co-operate on the basis that he is resident outside the jurisdiction of the English court. The official receiver has been unable to trace the proceeds of a rights issue amounting to some £599,000.

(4) The Secretary of State has concluded that it is expedient in the public interest that the respondent be disqualified from holding office as a director of the   H
company and has directed the official receiver to make application to the court for such an order. It is my belief that the applicant has a good cause of action."

The arguments on which this application have been principally based revolved around sec. 1, 6 and sec. 22 of the *Company Directors Disqualification Act* 1986 and I will start by reading the relevant part of those sections.

A "1(1) In the circumstances specified below in this Act a court may, and under section 6 shall, make against a person a disqualification order, that is to say an order that he shall not, without leave of the court—

(a) be a director of a company, or

(b) be a liquidator or administrator of a company, or

(c) be a receiver or manager of a company's property, or

B

(d) in any way, whether directly or indirectly, be concerned or take part in the promotion, formation or management of a company,

for a specified period beginning with the date of the order."

I need not read the remainder of that section. I will read subsec. (1) and (2) of sec. 6.

"6(1) The court shall make a disqualification order against a person in any case where, on an application under this section, it is satisfied—

C

(a) that he is or has been a director of a company which has at any time become insolvent (whether while he was a director or subsequently), and

(b) that his conduct as a director of that company (either taken alone or taken together with his conduct as a director of any other company or companies) makes him unfit to be concerned in the management of a company.

D

(2) For the purposes of this section and the next, a company becomes insolvent if—

(a) the company goes into liquidation at a time when its assets are insufficient for the payment of its debts and other liabilities and the expenses of the winding up,

E (b) an administration order is made in relation to the company, or

(c) an administrative receiver of the company is appointed;

and references to a person's conduct as a director of any company or companies include, where that company or any of those companies has become insolvent, that person's conduct in relation to any matter connected with or arising out of the insolvency of that company."

F And sec. 22(2) states:

"The expression 'company'—

. . .

(b) elsewhere [i.e. elsewhere other than in sec. 11], includes any company which may be wound up under Part V of the Insolvency Act."

G There is no express statement in the Act of any jurisdictional requirements which must be satisfied before the court can make an order under sec. 6(1). For example, there is no statement as to whether the conduct complained of must have occurred in England. However, it is well established that English legislation is prima facie territorial (see *Ex parte Blain* (1879) 12 ChD 522). Accordingly, it was held in that case that an adjudication order in bankruptcy could not be made under the *Bankruptcy Act* 1869 against a foreigner who was neither resident nor domiciled here unless the act of bankruptcy which was relied upon occurred here. This was so notwithstanding that the *Bankruptcy Act* 1869 did not contain an express limitation to that effect. The court reached its decision by reference to the principle that legislation is prima facie territorial.

The principle in question was recently considered by two members of the House of Lords in *Clark (HMIT) v Oceanic Contractors Inc* [1982] BTC 417; [1983] 2 AC 130. The members of the House of Lords in question were Lord *Scarman* and Lord *Wilberforce*

with whom Lord *Roskill* agreed. After citing from the judgment of *Cotton* LJ in *Ex*   A
parte Blain, Lord *Scarman* said at p. 145D–E:

> "Put into the language of today, the general principle being there stated is simply
> that, unless the contrary is expressly enacted or so plainly implied that the courts
> must give effect to it, United Kingdom legislation is applicable only to British
> subjects or to foreigners who by coming to the United Kingdom, whether for a
> short or a long time, have made themselves subject to British jurisdiction. Two   B
> points would seem to be clear: first, that the principle is a rule of construction
> only, and secondly, that it contemplates mere presence within the jurisdiction as
> sufficient to attract the application of British legislation. Certainly there is no
> general principle that the legislation of the United Kingdom is applicable only to
> British subjects or persons resident here. Merely to state such a proposition is to
> manifest its absurdity. Presence, not residence, is the test."

At p. 152C–D, Lord *Wilberforce* put the matter thus: C

> "In my opinion this contention is erroneous, because it is based upon a mistaken
> application or understanding of the 'territorial principle'. That principle, which is
> really a rule of construction of statutes expressed in general terms, and which as
> James L.J. said a 'broad principle', requires an inquiry to be made as to the person
> with respect to whom Parliament is presumed, in the particular case, to be
> legislating.   D
>
> Who, it is to be asked, is within the legislative grasp, or intendment, of the statute
> under consideration? The contention being that, as regards companies, the statute
> cannot have been intended to apply to them if they are non-resident, one asks
> immediately — why not?"

From these passages it is clear that the question whether and, if so, what territorial
restriction applies to sec. 6 of the Company Directors Disqualification Act is a question   E
of construction. The general principle is that legislation applies only to British subjects
or foreigners who come to England. The general principle is subject to any express
enactment to the contrary or to any plain implication to the contrary. The court must
enquire as to the person with respect to whom Parliament is presumed in this particular
case to have been legislating.

I have been referred to two recent cases in which these principles have been applied   F
to the *Insolvency Act* 1986 and they are both of considerable assistance to me because,
as Mr Davis points out, that Act and the Company Directors Disqualification Act should
be treated as part of a single statutory scheme (see *Re Jeffrey S Levitt Ltd* [1992] BCC
137 at p. 148 per *Vinelott* J). The cases in question are *Re Seagull Manufacturing Co Ltd*
[1993] BCC 241, a decision of *Lloyd* and *Hirst* L JJ and *Peter Gibson* J delivered on
3 February 1993, and *Re Paramount Airways Ltd (No. 2)* [1992] BCC 416.

The former case concerned the question whether an order for public examination of   G
Mr Slinn could be served on him in Alderney. After citing *Ex parte Blain* and *Clark v
Oceanic Contractors*, *Peter Gibson* J with whom *Hirst* and *Lloyd* L JJ agreed, said at
p. 245A:

> "In considering Lord *Wilberforce*'s question as to who comes within the legislative
> grasp of the section, one must look to the policy of the legislature in enacting the
> section in question.   H
>
> Where a company has come to a calamitous end and has been wound up by the
> court, the obvious intention of this section was that those responsible for the
> company's state of affairs should be liable to be subjected to a process of
> investigation and that that investigation should be in public. Parliament could not
> have intended that a person who had that responsibility could escape liability to

A   investigation simply by not being within the jurisdiction. Indeed, if the section were to be construed as leaving out of its grasp anyone not within the jurisdiction, deliberate evasion by removing oneself out of the jurisdiction would suffice. That seems to me to be a wholly improbable intention to attribute to Parliament.

B   Further, sec. 133 must be construed in the light of circumstances existing in the mid-1980s when the legislation was enacted. By use of the telephone, telex and fax machines English companies can be managed perfectly well by persons who need not set foot within the jurisdiction. There is no requirement that an officer of an English company must live in England, nor of course need an officer of an overseas company which may be wound up by the court. Such a company is very likely to have offices not within the jurisdiction.

C   I would emphasise that the question before this court is one of the scope of the Act and we are not concerned with whether the order for public examination can be effectively enforced against a person out of the jurisdiction (cf. *Theophile v Solicitor-General* [1950] AC 186 at p. 195).

When Parliament enacted sec. 133, it is very likely that it did so against the background of what *Dillon* LJ in *Re Bishopsgate Investment Management Ltd* [1992] BCC 222 at p. 232G, described as:

D   'The public worry and concern over company failures on a large scale, and the need to safeguard the public against such failures . . .'

Both public and private examinations have a significant role to play in the investigation of a company failure. The particular purposes that can be served by public examination were instructively set out in the Cork Report . . ."

I will pause there and turn to the judgment of *Hirst* LJ at p. 249H:

E   "In my judgment the key to this appeal lies in the determination of the question who is within the legislative grasp, or intendment, of sec. 133 of the *Insolvency Act* 1986, per Lord *Wilberforce* in *Clark v Oceanic Contractors*. . . This section is headed 'Public examination of officers' and each class of persons referred to in subsec. 1(a)–(c) is or has been personally involved in that capacity in the direction or management of the company in liquidation.

F   The purpose of the public examination is to enable the official receiver in the fulfilment of his duty under sec. 132 to investigate inter alia the causes of failure of the company, and its business dealings and affairs, for which the officer in question is or may have been wholly or partly responsible, and therefore personally and directly accountable for what has gone wrong. The efficient and thorough conduct of such investigation by the official receiver is of great public importance, as several recent notorious cases have demonstrated. This process would be frustrated

G   if, for example, a director, who had with the aid of modern methods of communication run the company entirely from abroad, was immune from public examination as he or she would be if Mr Teverson's submissions were correct. The same applies to a director who has defrauded the company in England and then absconded abroad shortly before the liquidation. These are by no means fanciful illustrations in the world of the 1980s and 1990s, and many similar ones could be

H   given.

It follows that, in my judgment, all officers as described in sec. 133(1)(a)–(c), whether inside or outside the jurisdiction, are within the legislative grasp and intendment of sec. 133, which on its proper construction has no territorial limits."

Accordingly, the Court of Appeal held that sec. 133 of the *Insolvency Act* 1986 applied to persons such as Mr Slinn notwithstanding his absence from the jurisdiction.

The second case from which I have derived particular assistance is *Re Paramount Airways Ltd (No. 2)* [1992] BCC 416. In that case the question was whether a transaction with a bank in Jersey was justiciable under sec. 238 of the *Insolvency Act* 1986 as a transaction at undervalue. The relevant parts of sec. 238 as are as follows:

> "(2) Where the company has at a relevant time (defined in section 240) entered into a transaction with any person at an undervalue, the office-holder may apply to the court for an order under this section.
>
> (3) Subject as follows, the court shall, on such an application, make such order as it thinks fit for restoring the position to what it would have been if the company had not entered into that transaction."

The Court of Appeal held that it was not possible in construing the expression "any person" in sec. 238 to identify any particular jurisdictional limitation and accordingly that those words had to be given their literal and unrestricted meaning so as to apply to foreigners.

The Court of Appeal went on to hold that in the exercise of the discretion which the court had as to the relief to be given if a transaction at an undervalue was proved (see subsec. (3)) the court would need to be satisfied that the defendant was sufficiently connected with England for it to be just and proper to make an order against him despite the foreign element. There is no room for a similar exercise of discretion under sec. 6 of the Company Directors Disqualification Act, but it has not been suggested by counsel that that diminishes the assistance to be gained from the Court of Appeal's judgment in that case as to the question of construction of sec. 238.

The approach to that question of Sir *Donald Nicholls* V-C, with whom *Farquharson* and *Taylor* L JJ agreed, was as follows, starting at p. 421H:

> "It will be seen from the above summary that, on its face, the legislation is of unlimited territorial scope. To be within the sections a transaction must possess certain features. For instance, it must be at an undervalue and made at a time when the company was unable to pay its debts, the company must be in the course of being wound up in England or subject to an administration order, and so on. If a transaction satisfies these requirements, the section applies, irrespective of the situation of the property, irrespective of the nationality or residence of the other party, and irrespective of the law which governs the transaction. In this respect the sections purport to be of universal application. The expression 'with any person' merely serves to underline this universality. It is, indeed, this generality which gives rise to the problem.
>
> In these circumstances one is predisposed to seek for a limitation which can fairly be read as implicit in the scheme of the legislation. Parliament may have been intending to legislate in such all-embracing terms. Parliament may have intended that the English court could and should bring before it, and make orders against, a person who has no connection whatever with England save that he entered into a transaction, maybe abroad and in respect of foreign property and in the utmost good faith, with a person who is subject to the insolvency jurisdiction of the English court. Indeed, he might be within the sections and subject to orders even though he had not entered into a transaction with the company or debtor at all. Such an intention by Parliament is possible. But self-evidently in some instances such a jurisdiction, or the exercise of such a jurisdiction, would be truly extraordinary.
>
> The difficulty lies in finding an acceptable implied limitation. Let me say at once that there are formidable, and in my view insuperable, objections to a limitation closely modelled on the formula enunciated in *Ex parte Blain*, as explained Lord

A

Scarman in *Clark v Oceanic Contractors Inc.* The implied limitation for which Hambros Jersey contended is riddled with such serious, glaring anomalies that Parliament cannot be presumed to have intended to legislate in such terms.

B

In the first place, to treat presence of the other party within England and Wales as the factor which determines whether a transaction is within the ambit of the sections would be to adopt a criterion which would be capricious in the extreme. A transaction with a foreigner who is resident here would be outside the embrace of the legislation if he happened to be abroad, or chose to be abroad, at the time the transaction was effected. Conversely, a foreign national resident abroad would find that the transaction with him was within the Act if, but only if, he was physically present in this country at the time of the transaction. Secondly, this criterion would leave outside the scope of the legislation a transaction by a debtor with an overseas company wholly controlled by him. Siphoning money abroad in this way is a typical case to which the new legislation must have been intended to apply. Thirdly, this test would draw a distinction between the position of British subjects and others on a matter of substantive law affecting property transactions. It would be surprising if Parliament had such an intention today. Fourthly, this test would mean that there was no remedy under the Act in respect of a transaction with an overseas company, or a foreigner living here but abroad at the crucial moment, even if the subject-matter was English land. Mr Davis felt constrained to accept that such a case might be within the purview of the legislation. This concession betrays the weakness of the respondent's argument. If a transaction relating to English land is within the legislation regardless of the identity or whereabouts of the other party to the transaction, why should not this equally be so with regard to a transaction relating to shares in an English company? Or UK Government stocks? Or money in an English bank account? What this shows is that the physical absence or presence of the other party at the time of the transaction by itself bears no necessary relationship to the appropriateness of the transaction being investigated and made the subject of an order by an English court. As a sole touchstone it is useless.

C

D

E

The oddities do not end there. Hambros Jersey's contention, if correct, would mean that the jurisdiction of the English court under the sections would be much more restricted than the circumstances in which an individual may be adjudged bankrupt or a company may be wound up by the English court. Under sec. 265 the English court has jurisdiction, for example, over a debtor who is a foreign national who has never lived or been here so long as, at a time within the last three years, he was a member of a firm which carried on business in this country. As to companies, under sec. 221 the court has jurisdiction to wind up overseas companies, a subject to which I shall return. Given the width of the ambit of these basic provisions, it would be surprising if Parliament is to be taken to have intended to limit the sections now under consideration as the respondent contended. Particularly, perhaps, since English law provides for the distribution of the assets of the insolvent among all the creditors worldwide. English law does not erect a 'ring fence' so as to exclude creditors living abroad.

F

G

For completeness I would mention one further small pointer in the same direction, if one be needed. It is of a linguistic nature. As already seen, the sections make special provision for transactions with persons who are connected with the company or are associates of the debtor. For example, a company which has given a preference to a person connected with the company is rebuttably presumed to have been influenced by a desire to prefer that person. Under the statutory definitions one of the circumstances in which a person is connected with a company is where the person is a company which is under common control (see

H

sec. 249 and 435(6)). Section 435(11) provides that for this purpose 'company'
includes any body corporate, whether incorporated in England or elsewhere.
These provisions do not sit happily with the implied limitation for which the
respondent contended."

Then at p. 423E the Vice-Chancellor said:

"In the end I am unable to discern any satisfactory limitation. I am unable to
identify some other class. The case for some limitation is powerful, but there is no
single, simple formula which is compelling, save for one expressed in wide and
loose terms (e.g. that the person, or the transaction, has a 'sufficient connection'
with England) that would hardly be distinguishable from the ambit of the sections
being unlimited territorially and the court being left to display a judicial restraint
in the exercise of the jurisdiction. I mention, to dismiss, some examples of
unacceptable simple tests. One possibility might be that the section applies only
to transactions with persons who are available to be served with process in
England and Wales. Such a limitation would have similar defects to those discussed
above. Another possibility is that the transactions are confined to those governed
by English law. But the remedies given by the sections include personal remedies,
such as an order that the recipient of property transfer it back to the company, or
an order that the other party to a transaction pay a sum of money to the trustee of
the bankrupt's estate. It would be odd if a transaction were outside the section in
all circumstances solely because it was governed by a foreign law even though, for
instance, all the parties were in this country at all times. The same objection
applies to a third possibility, namely, that the sections apply only to dealings with
property, immovable or movable, situated in England and Wales at the relevant
time."

Then, lastly, at p. 424F, the Vice-Chancellor said:

"In my view the solution to the question of statutory interpretation raised by this
appeal does not lie in retreating to a rigid and indefensible line. Trade takes place
increasingly on an international basis. So does fraud. Money is transferred quickly
and easily. To meet these changing conditions English courts are more prepared
than formerly to grant injunctions in suitable cases against non-residents or
foreign nationals in respect of overseas activities. As I see it, the considerations
set out above and taken as a whole lead irresistibly to the conclusion that, when
considering the expression 'any person' in the sections, it is impossible to identify
any particular limitation which can be said, with any degree of confidence, to
represent the presumed intention of Parliament. What can be seen is that Parliament
cannot have intended an implied limitation along the lines of *Ex parte Blain*. The
expression therefore must be left to bear its literal, and natural, meaning: any
person."

In the present case, the positions taken by counsel in their submissions on jurisdiction
have been widely different. Mr Teverson, for Mr Slinn, while reserving, he said, the
right to argue elsewhere that the Company Directors Disqualification Act applied only
to directors present within the jurisdiction, submitted before me that the limitation
which ought fairly to be implied into the Company Directors Disqualification Act is that
the activities which it is said rendered him unfit to be a director should either take place
in the jurisdiction or be directed from abroad. Thus, the activities of a director would
only be relevant to the extent that they had some effect here.

Mr Davis, on the other hand, submitted that sec. 6(1) applied to any person, that is to
a British subject or a foreigner, irrespective of their presence here or at the time the
activities took place.

A   Section 6 of the Company Directors Disqualification Act contains no express statement of any jurisdictional requirement. Indeed, on its face it applies to any person and to any conduct. However, when it is analysed in a manner similar to that undertaken in *Paramount Airways (No. 2)* it is, in my judgment, clear that it too has no jurisdictional limitation as a matter of plain implication. The word "company" in sec. 6(1) includes any company which may be wound up under the Insolvency Act (see CDDA 1986, sec. 22(2)). In this way companies incorporated in other jurisdictions are included (see

B   sec. 220 and sec. 221 of the *Insolvency Act* 1986). In the case of foreign companies the likelihood is that some of the directors will not be persons resident here, or even foreigners present here, when the conduct relied upon as rendering them unfit takes place.

      Accordingly, in my judgment, Parliament must be presumed to have been legislating not simply for British subjects and foreigners who happened to be here at the relevant

C   time, but also for other foreigners who were out of the jurisdiction at the critical time. Likewise, in relation to conduct, sec. 6(1) contains no territorial restriction. Accordingly, the court must ask what is the conduct in respect of which Parliament must have been presumed to have been legislating?

      There are two factors which, in my judgment, indicate that the conduct in question in sec. 6(1) need not be conduct which occurred within the jurisdiction. The first such

D   factor is the definition of "company" to which I have already referred. This includes foreign companies and the acts of the directors of those companies are likely to have taken place abroad, and Parliament must have been presumed to have been legislating with that in mind.

      Secondly, in these days of modern communications a person may conduct himself as a director in such a way as to affect persons within the jurisdiction without himself ever entering the jurisdiction. Again, in my judgment, Parliament must be presumed to have

E   been legislating with this in mind and, accordingly, by plain implication to be taken to have been referring to conduct wherever committed.

      Were there a distinction in sec. 6(1) between foreigners based on presence, the results would be anomalous. For example, proceedings could be brought under that section against a director who from his office in London had caused a company to do acts in a foreign country which had no effect on the British public. Yet, on the other hand, a

F   director who was a citizen of another country and who conducted the company's business here from abroad could not be proceeded against under sec. 6(1) since his activities would be outside the scope of sec. 6. In my judgment, Parliament cannot have intended those anomalous results. They are significant because as *Dillon* LJ, with whom *Butler-Sloss* and *Staughton* L JJ agreed, said in *Re Sevenoaks Stationers (Retail) Ltd* [1990] BCC 765 at p. 773B, in a passage to which Mr Teverson referred me:

G   "It is beyond dispute that the purpose of sec. 6 is to protect the public, and in particular potential creditors of companies, from losing money through companies becoming insolvent when the directors of those companies are people unfit to be concerned in the management of a company."

      Accordingly, as a matter of construction, I prefer Mr Davis's approach to that of Mr Teverson. Moreover, it seems to me that Mr Teverson's construction would lead to

H   anomalous results. It would mean that disqualification proceedings could not be brought against a foreign director whose activities, which had been exclusively conducted abroad, had shown him to be unfit to be a director even though he might seek to expand his activities and to act as a director in England.

      Mr Davis submitted that as a result of an order under sec. 6(1) a director would be disqualified from acting as a director in any part of the world. I express no view upon this

proposition since I am not called upon to decide either the scope of an order under   A
sec. 1 or the acts which may be justiciable under sec. 13 which creates a criminal offence.

It was submitted to me that my conclusion in this case would be consistent with a
decision on sec. 300 of the *Companies Act* 1985 of *Mervyn Davies* J in *Re Eurostem
Maritime Ltd* [1987] PCC 190. However, in my view it is not clear from the report of that
case whether the director in question was within the jurisdiction when the conduct
complained of occurred.

                                                                                          B
Mr Davis submitted to me that there were limitations on the court's power under
sec. 6 which I accept have relevance in an enquiry as to Parliament's presumed intention
as to the persons to whom this section should apply. First, Mr Davis drew my attention
to the fact that the class of persons in respect of whom a disqualification order can be
made is limited to those mentioned in sec. 6(1)(a). Secondly, Mr Davis relied on the fact
that sec. 6 may only be invoked where the company has become insolvent. Thirdly, Mr
Davis relied on the fact that the application can be made only by the Secretary of State   C
or the official receiver: sec. 7(1). In my judgment, that is a particularly important point
since the official receiver is an officer of the court and responsible to the Secretary of
State and the Secretary of State is, in turn, responsible to Parliament.

Mr Davis also relied on a fourth limitation on sec. 6, namely, that in the case of foreign
persons the court retains a residual discretion in the context of deciding whether to give
leave to serve out. This involved the construction of r. 5 of the *Insolvent Companies*   D
(Disqualification of Unfit Directors) Proceedings Rules 1987. Mr Davis contended, but
Mr Teverson disputed, that that rule gave the court a discretion not to order service out
if it is not satisfied that there was a good arguable case.

In *Re Seagull Manufacturing Co Ltd* [1993] BCC 241, it was held that the discretion in
the parallel Insolvency Rule, r. 12.12(3) extended only to the time and manner of service
since the court could not refuse to make an order for public examination: see p. 249D.   E
In my judgment, where the court is ordering service of disqualification proceedings out
of the jurisdiction, the situation is different from where it is ordering public examination
because there are certain important conditions which must be fulfilled before an order
can be made and which are set out in sec. 6 itself.

However, in my judgment, the court has a discretion not to order service out and
should not do so where it is not satisfied that there is a good arguable case for satisfaction
of the conditions in sec. 6(1) (see *Re Paramount Airways Ltd (No. 2)* [1992] BCC 416 at   F
p. 426D–F).

Finally, on this aspect of the case, as I have already stated, Mr Slinn is a British
subject. He is, therefore, a person to whom sec. 6 applies on the *Ex parte Blain* test.
However, in my view, sec. 6 applies to anyone, British subject or not, and irrespective of
where the conduct occurs.

                                                                                          G
Mr Teverson submitted that there were no sufficient grounds for service shown in the
affidavit in support of the application for leave to serve out. I have already cited the
relevant passage of the affidavit of Mr Udell. In the light of my conclusion as to the
absence of a territorial limitation in sec. 6(1), I consider that that passage sets out a
number of grounds which could form the basis of a disqualification order if proved at
trial and subject, of course, to any evidence on behalf of the director sought to be
disqualified which that director seeks to place before the court.   H

Finally, Mr Teverson sought to rely on a charter of Queen Elizabeth I which had been
given to the people of Alderney and which provides in these terms:

> "Moreover, our royal pleasure is that we grant for ourselves our heirs and
> successors by these presents of the said bailiffs and jurists and all other inhabitants
> and sogenies in the said isles and maritime places that for the time to come none

A

of them be cited or summonsed or drawn by any lawsuit or forced in any manner
by any writs of process issued from any of our courts of the Kingdom of England
to appear and answer before any judges courts or other offices of justice out of
any of these islands and maritime places touching or concerning anything dispute
causes or matters in controversy whatsoever arising in the said islands."

B

However, the Court of Appeal dealt with a similar argument in *Re Seagull
Manufacturing Co Ltd* at p. 249E. There is no evidence before me as to the law of
Alderney or which shows that the matters arose within the islands. Accordingly, in my
judgment, Mr Slinn cannot rely on that charter in this court.

I should add that I have not dealt with Mr Teverson's submission based on the in-aid
procedure in sec. 426 of the *Insolvency Act* 1986, since Mr Teverson informed me that
he was merely reserving the right to argue that point elsewhere.

C

In the circumstances, I decline to make the declaration sought.

(*Order accordingly*)

D

E

F

G

H

Re Copecrest Ltd.

A

Chancery Division (Companies Court) and Court of Appeal (Civil Division).
Mervyn Davies J; Dillon, Evans and Hoffmann L JJ.
Judgment delivered 14 December 1992 and 23 July 1993.

Disqualifying unfit directors of insolvent companies — Leave to apply out of time — Materiality of respondent directors' responsibility for delay — Company Directors Disqualification Act 1986, sec. 7(2), (3).

B

This was an appeal from a judge's refusal to grant leave to the Secretary of State to commence director disqualification proceedings out of time under sec. 7(2) of the Company Directors Disqualification Act 1986.

The last insolvent company of which the respondents were directors was Copecrest Ltd which went into creditors' voluntary liquidation in March 1990. Copecrest's business had been sold to another company controlled by the respondents and the balance of the purchase price left outstanding. The statement of affairs showed only Crown debts and although the company could not pay them immediately its assets, i.e. the balance of the purchase price of the business, if paid, exceeded its liabilities. However, the balance of the purchase price was never paid and in January 1992 the liquidator reported the respondents' conduct to the Secretary of State. Disqualification proceedings were not launched by the March 1992 deadline and the application for leave was made in May 1992.

C

D

The judge concluded that no good reason had been shown for an extension of time, even though the applicant could not be blamed for the liquidator's delay in reporting and despite the fact that the complaints against the respondents were of a grave nature. The officers of the Secretary of State had failed to show that once they realised they were in difficulty as to time, they acted with all reasonable speed. The Secretary of State appealed.

Held, allowing the appeal:

E

1. The two-year period under sec. 7(2) had to be treated as having built into it a contingency allowance for unexpected delays for which the Secretary of State was not responsible. He was not entitled to assume that any period of delay for which he was not responsible would automatically be added by the court on to the two-year period. However, the judge had erred in not taking into account the respondents' own responsibility for the delay on the part of the liquidator, and consequent curtailment of the period available to the Secretary of State from 18 months to three weeks, by swearing a statement of affairs showing the company to be solvent and then stringing the liquidator along with promises of payment.

F

2. It was not unreasonable in all the circumstances for the Secretary of State to have decided that the proper route was not to attempt to get in an application by the March deadline, but to make an application for an extension. On the facts the progress made by the Secretary of State was not unduly dilatory.

G

3. Taking into account, as the judge did not, the directors' responsibility for the earlier delay and what the judge agreed to be the serious nature of the allegations being made against the directors, the balance clearly came down in favour of the grant of an extension.

The following cases were referred to in the High Court judgment:

Crestjoy Products Ltd, Re [1990] BCC 23.

H

Lo-Line Electric Motors Ltd & Ors, Re (1988) 4 BCC 415; [1988] Ch 477.
Probe Data Systems Ltd, Re (No. 2) [1990] BCC 21.
Probe Data Systems Ltd, Re (No. 3) [1992] BCC 110.

The following case was referred to in the judgment of Hoffmann LJ:

Probe Data Systems Ltd, Re (No. 3) [1992] BCC 110.

A   AWH Charles (in the Court of Appeal) and Stephen Moverley Smith (instructed by the Treasury Solicitor) for the Secretary of State for Trade and Industry.

Gregory Mitchell (instructed by Amhurst Brown Colombotti) for the respondents.

HIGH COURT JUDGMENT
(14 December 1992)

B   **Mervyn Davies J:** I have before me an originating summons dated 21 May 1992. It is headed "In the matter of Copecrest Ltd" ("the company") and "In the matter of the *Company Directors Disqualification Act* 1986". The applicant is the Secretary of State for Trade and Industry. The respondents are Mr F P McTighe and Mr J M Egan. In the summons the applicant asks for leave to commence proceedings against the respondents being proceedings in which disqualification orders under sec. 6 of the Act will be sought.

C   This application for leave arises from the terms of sec. 7(2) of the Act:

> "Except with the leave of the court, an application for the making under that section (section 6) of a disqualification order against any person shall not be made after the end of the period of 2 years beginning with the day on which the company of which that person is or has been a director became insolvent."

D   On 14 March 1990 the company went into creditors' voluntary liquidation and Mr MGV Radford was appointed the liquidator. In an affidavit sworn on 9 June 1992 Mr Radford says that the company commenced trading on 1 January 1987 as security specialists. There was a change of name from Barbican Security Specialists Ltd on 7 April 1989. Trading ceased on 5 March 1990. Throughout that time the respondents were the directors of the company. The issued share capital comprises 200,000 ordinary shares of 5p each. Mr McTighe owns 199,800 shares and Mr Egan the remaining 200. Mr Radford exhibits a statement of affairs dated 14 March 1990. It shows a surplus as

E   regards creditors of £129,846. The affidavit goes on to say that the company had ceased trading nearly one year before March 1990. During that period most of the company's liabilities had been discharged. The company's business had been sold to a company called Longdane Ltd. It appears from the statement of affairs that the balance of the price payable for the business was £1,170,741, to be paid by instalments. The respondents are the directors of Longdane.

F   Relying upon a letter dated 22 May 1990, Mr Radford expected to receive from Longdane on 31 March 1991 an instalment payment of £100,000. That payment was not forthcoming. On 31 May 1991 a statutory demand for that sum was served on Longdane. No result ensued.

An unsigned set of accounts of the company shows a balance sheet as at 20 March 1989 with an adverse balance of £568,500. Reviewing those accounts against earlier accounts of the company Mr Radford says that over the period December 1987 to March

G   1989, while there are reductions in the amounts owing to some classes of creditors, the amounts owing to the Revenue and other government creditors increased. In the result, as is disclosed in the statement of affairs, the company owed on 14 March 1990 £559,613 for PAYE, £464,996 to the Department of Social Security and £6,286 corporation tax, those sums totalling £1,030,895. Only two other creditors are shown. They were owed £10,000.

H   Mr Radford in his affidavit concludes that the respondents caused the company to conduct its business by funding its trading by the retention of substantial moneys owing to the Crown; and that the company discharged nearly all its other debts. There was, it is said, a policy of non-payment of Crown debts. As well as that, it is said that the respondents caused the company to dispose of its goodwill to Longdane in such a manner that creditors and particularly the Crown received no benefit. No security was

taken for the money to be paid to the company by Longdane. The statement of affairs
suggests that £1,170,741 was a balance owing for the sale of the company business. On
that footing the company could be considered as solvent. However it emerged that no
further payments would be made by Longdane. On that footing the company was of
course insolvent with its principal creditor by far being the Crown.

In his affidavit Mr Radford shows that the respondents have been concerned as
directors in another liquidation — that of Trigo Ltd (formerly Barbican Lock and Safe
Co). That company passed a resolution for voluntary winding up on 30 December 1985.
Mr Radford was the liquidator. The Trigo statement of affairs dated 30 December 1985
shows a deficiency of £212,651. Crown debts amounted to £218,842 with other creditors
totalling £53,203.

On the basis of the material to which I have referred above, Mr Gregory Mitchell for
the respondents accepted that, for the purposes of this application only, the applicant
has an arguable case for obtaining disqualification orders. From that starting point, I
now proceed to consider the circumstances in which the applicant failed to apply for the
orders within the two-year period specified in sec. 7(2). In this connection it was assumed
that the starting date of the two-year period was 14 March 1990, the date of the resolution
to wind up; and that despite the fact that the company was then on the showing of the
statement of affairs presumed solvent.

The circumstances to which I have referred require first that there be summarised
some correspondence of Mr Radford. The letter dated 22 May 1990 (already mentioned)
was an offer by Longdane to pay its debt to the company by yearly instalments running
from 31 March 1991–31 March 1996. There was no express acceptance of that offer.
Nevertheless, Mr Radford on 3 April 1991 wrote asking for payment of the first
instalment of £100,000. There was some pressing for payment, without success, in later
letters, and on 31 May 1991 the statutory demand was served. As I have said, no
payment resulted. Nor was there any immediate action by Mr Radford save in the way
of correspondence. In particular, there is a letter dated 25 September 1991, following a
discussion which Mr Radford had with the accountants who were advising Longdane.
However that may be, it seems that Mr Radford eventually concluded that no money
would be forthcoming from Longdane and in a letter dated 3 January 1992 he wrote to
the Department of Trade. It is a curious feature of this letter that whilst it is dated
3 January 1992, it is stamped as having been received at the Department of Trade on
20 February 1992. I read parts of the letter:

> "Whilst I realise that you like to receive forms D1 within a short period of the
> commencement of the winding up of a company, I delayed submitting it in this
> case for the very good reason that, on the evidence of the statement of affairs, the
> company was solvent, and thus, provided I received payment for the sale of the
> business, creditors would be paid in full and would not have a great deal to
> complain about, beyond the delay that had elapsed in receiving payment."

And:

> "There was an agreement between the company and the purchaser (Longdane)
> whereby the selling price would be paid by instalments over a period. Since I was
> appointed liquidator that period has been extended by agreement. I have, however,
> now reached the situation where it seems unlikely that any further payment will
> be made beyond the £5,000 that was provided to me at the outset. Clearly
> therefore the company is hopelessly insolvent and, as there is little or no prospect
> of funds being available for the creditors, I think that the attitude of the directors
> must be looked upon in different light."

A And:

> "It will be apparent from the enclosed forms and this letter that the directors have been running a chain of companies and, when one gets into difficulty, the assets are sold on to another which adopts the same, or a similar, name. The name of the original company is changed and it is then wound up."

So it is that the matter came to the attention of the applicant on 20 February 1992.
B Progress in the matter within the department is traced in the affidavit sworn on 23 June 1992 by Mr D H Henry, the chief examiner of the company directors disqualification unit. He says that the Radford letter was received in the disqualification unit on 25 February. On 26 February the case was reviewed and selected for action. For that purpose the papers were put before Mrs Helen Clements, a senior examiner. Mrs Clements considered the case and on 5 March recommended that there was a case for an application for disqualification but, as Mr Henry puts it, that:

C
> "as there was insufficient time to prepare the evidence in support of the substantive application before the limitation period expired on 13 March 1992, legal advice should be sought on the merits on an application to commence proceedings out of time."

The legal advice there referred to was sought on 12 March. In consequence of that advice the decision was made on 20 March to prepare evidence for a substantive
D application. Continuing this sequence of events, I now quote Mr Henry's affidavit:

> "Because of the high volume of work in the disqualification unit occasioned by the very high number of failures at this time, no officer was immediately available. In the normal course of events Mrs Clements would have dealt with the matter herself. Mrs Clements was however leaving the disqualification unit on 2 April 1992 on maternity leave and she had administrative duties to perform to ensure an orderly departure. In the event I prepared the draft of Mr Radford's affidavit on
E the substantive matters. This was dispatched to Mr Radford on 15 April which Mr Radford's assistant Miss S Williams agreed with me on 22 April. On 30 April I gave further instructions to the Treasury solicitor. The Treasury solicitor instructed counsel to advise on the leave application on 13 May. Counsel advised in conference on 20 May and on 21 May the summons for the hearing of the leave application was issued."

F
I turn now to the question posed in the originating summons, i.e. whether or not leave should be given pursuant to sec. 7(2). By way of general approach, there are the words of *Harman* J in *Re Crestjoy Products Ltd* [1990] BCC 23 at p. 29F:

> "It seems to me . . . that all I can do is try and assess the whole position here and consider whether I am satisfied that a good reason has been shown (and I adopt the words 'good reason' from Lord *Brandon*'s speech in the *Kleinwort Benson*
G case . . . by analogy) for an extension of time from 20 November to 14 March."

So one considers whether the court is satisfied that the applicant has shown good reason for being allowed an extension.

There are then the words of *Scott* LJ in *Re Probe Data Systems Ltd (No. 3)* [1992] BCC 110 at p. 118G:

> "In considering an application under sec. 7(2) for leave to commence
H disqualification proceedings out of time the court should, in my opinion, take into account the following matters: (1) the length of the delay; (2) the reasons for the delay; (3) the strength of the case against the directors; and (4) the degree of prejudice caused to the director by the delay . . ."

Another general consideration appears to me to be that, although the primary purpose of the legislation is not penal, disqualification involves a substantial interference with the freedom of the individual. The rights of the individual must be fully protected: see *Re Lo-Line Electric Motors Ltd* (1988) 4 BCC 415 per *Browne-Wilkinson* VC at p. 419.

There is the further point that on an application for leave, it is inappropriate for the respondent to oppose leave by rehearsing his defence: see *Re Probe Data Systems Ltd (No. 2)* [1990] BCC 21 at p. 22C–D.

With those general observations in mind, I look again at the words of *Scott* LJ above and in particular to (1) and (2) therein. At p. 119B, *Scott* LJ says that on a sec. 7(2) application for leave, delay over the period from the commencement of the winding up to the eventual application for leave should be taken into account. Thus it is that here one considers what delay there has been between 14 March 1990 (the date of the resolution to wind up) and 21 May 1992 (when the originating summons was issued).

I was taken through this period in four stages:

(1)   the period from 14 March 1990 up to 3 January 1992 when Mr Radford wrote to the Department of Trade;

(2)   the period from 3 January to 20 February 1992 when the Radford letter was in delay;

(3)   from 20 February until 14 March 1992 on which date the sec. 7(2) time-limit ran out; and

(4)   the period from 14 March until 21 May when the originating summons was issued.

As to period (1), Mr Mitchell said that a substantial contributory factor affecting the need to apply for leave consisted in Mr Radford having been laggard in reporting to the Department of Trade. It must have been obvious to him, he said, that, at any rate when there was no response to the statutory demand that was sent on 31 May 1991, the company was insolvent. By that time all the material facts were known to Mr Radford. And yet there was no report to the department until 3 January 1992.

It does not seem to me to be satisfactory to visit the Secretary of State with the consequences of the liquidator's tardy conduct. However that may be, and having in mind the words of *Scott* LJ at p. 119B referred to above, I am obliged to take into account that some of the delay has in this case been occasioned by the liquidator.

As to period (2), I take the view that Mr Radford's letter dated 3 January 1992 was received by the department on 20 February 1992 because the letter is so stamped. In an affidavit sworn on 22 June 1992, Mr Radford says that his letter was posted on 3 January. For the respondent, it was said that that evidence was inadmissible since it is not stated that Mr Radford himself posted the letter and there is then no compliance with RSC, O. 41, r. 5. The balance of probabilities was, it was said, that the letter was delayed in the office of Mr Radford. Be that as it may, it seems to me that one cannot say whether postal delay or carelessness in the Radford office caused the delayed delivery of the Radford letter. All one can say is that the reason for the delay in the delivery is not explained but that there is no compelling argument for saying that such delay should not work to the benefit of the respondents.

As to period (3), a striking feature of this period of delay is that Mrs Clements — a senior examiner — was aware of the time-limit on 5 March 1992. She knew that the two-year period ran out on 13 March. Yet no urgent action was taken. Instead there was the measured, I will not say unhurried, activity that is set out in Mr Henry's affidavit, including the words that I have quoted above. Mr Mitchell submitted that given the situation as known on 5 March, there was time to issue a substantive application for disqualification orders before 14 March, that is to say that an application in which leave was unnecessary could have been launched. In that regard I have in mind r. 3(1) of the

A   *Insolvent Companies (Disqualification of Unfit Directors) Proceedings Rules* 1987
     (SI 1987/2023). Rule 3(1) reads:

> "There shall, at the time when the summons is issued, be filed in court evidence in
> support of the application for a disqualification order; and copies of the evidence
> shall be served with the summons on the respondent."

     If that rule was to be regarded the department on 5 March faced a difficult task, bearing
B   in mind that there would have to be reference to solicitors and counsel. However that
     may be, I cannot suppose that it was beyond the competence of the department to act
     with the promptness that was required.

     That is not the end of the matter. Let it be assumed that the applicant (having in mind
     r. 3(1)) concluded that no substantive application could be made by 13 March. There
     were then other courses open to the applicant. First, consideration could have been
C   given to issuing an application for disqualification orders before 14 March and at the
     same time applying for an extension of time to file the evidence in support. In this
     connection one sees that r. 2 of the 1987 rules already referred to provides that the *Rules
     of the Supreme Court* 1965 apply to the proceedings, save where the 1987 rules make
     provision to inconsistent effect. So, it is said, an order to extend the time for service of
     the affidavit evidence could have been made by use of RSC, O. 3, r. 5(1). Even if such an
     order were refused, there could have been in readiness a brief affidavit supporting the
D   application on the footing that there would be a later application for leave to serve a
     further affidavit (see O. 28, r. 1A(6)). Secondly, the present application for leave could
     have been issued before 14 March. The 1987 rules do not apply to an application for
     leave so that such an application may be made by originating summons; as was eventually
     done in this case.

     As to period (4), the application for leave was made on 21 May, a date that is nearly
E   ten weeks after the expiration of the two-year time-limit on 14 March and 11 weeks after
     the imminence of the deadline was realised on 5 March. Thus, one cannot say that the
     application has been advanced with any speed.

     Having reviewed the four periods of time, I have to consider whether or not the
     applicant shows "good reason" (see *Crestjoy* above) why an application for
     disqualification orders should be allowed now when the Act lays down that the application
     should have been made before 14 March. Bearing in mind that one is considering quasi-
F   penal legislation, I conclude that no good reason has been shown. In my view "good
     reason" involves the officers of the Secretary of State in showing that once they realised
     they were in difficulty as to time, they acted with all reasonable speed. I have in mind
     principally what took place in periods (3) and (4). A senior examiner realised on
     5 March that time ran out on 13 March. Yet no immediate steps were taken to meet that
     deadline. I do not suggest that any official in the department would have been aware of
G   the intricacies of the 1987 rules and the Rules of the Supreme Court that I have
     mentioned. But one would suppose that legal advice would have been sought immediately
     and not left until 12 March; and that, when that advice was obtained, that there would
     have been a speedy application along the lines of one or other of the courses referred to
     in (3) above. Instead of that 11 weeks passed.

     I dismiss the originating summons. I do so with some hesitation because the applicant
H   cannot be blamed for the delay referred to in (1) above and there is then the fact that the
     complaints against the respondents are, on the one-sided evidence before me, of a grave
     nature. I add that there was a submission that the respondents have been materially
     prejudiced by the delay that has taken place and that that is another ground for refusing
     leave. In view of my findings on delay, it is not necessary to consider that submission.

                            (Application dismissed with costs)

COURT OF APPEAL JUDGMENT
(23 July 1993)

Hoffmann LJ: This is an appeal against the refusal of *Mervyn Davies* J to give the Secretary of State leave under sec. 7(2) of the *Company Directors Disqualification Act* 1986 to apply for disqualification orders under sec. 6 after the expiry of the two-year limitation period.

The last insolvent company of which the respondents were directors was Copecrest Ltd, which resolved to go into creditors' voluntary liquidation on 14 March 1990. The two-year period therefore expired on 13 March 1992. The application for leave was made by originating summons dated 21 May 1992.

Applications under sec. 6, which provides for mandatory disqualification on the ground of unfitness, must be made by the Secretary of State or at his direction by the official receiver. For this purpose it is obviously necessary that the Secretary of State should be properly informed of cases in which it appears from the conduct of the directors that the court may consider them unfit. If it appears to a liquidator that a director has shown himself unfit, he is required by sec. 7(3) to report the matter forthwith to the Secretary of State. Further, by sec. 7(4) the Secretary of State may require the liquidator to produce additional information. Then r. 4(5) of the *Insolvent Companies (Reports on Conduct of Directors) No. 2 Rules* 1986 (SI 1986/2134) requires a liquidator to send a report to the Secretary of State within six months of the resolution for creditors' voluntary winding up.

So the scheme of the Act and the rules envisage that the Secretary of State will ordinarily have at least 18 months in which to consider the information about the director's conduct, ask for any further information which he needs, decide whether to bring proceedings, and to prepare the necessary application and supporting evidence.

The chronology in this case is as follows. On 14 March — the date of the voluntarily liquidation resolution — Mr Michael Radford, an insolvency practitioner practising in Southampton, was appointed liquidator. On the same date Mr McTighe — one of the respondent directors — swore an affidavit exhibiting a statement of affairs. Copecrest Ltd had ceased to trade about a year earlier when it sold its security trading business to another company controlled by the respondents, called Longdane Ltd, for £1.4m payable over five years. Some of the money had been paid and used to pay off trade and certain other creditors, so that by the time of the liquidation the only substantial creditors were the Inland Revenue, who were owed £560,000 for PAYE, and the Department of Social Security who were owed £465,000. The only asset was the balance outstanding from Longdane for the purchase of the business, which was £1,170,741. This Mr McTighe swore to be fully recoverable. On this basis, although the company was unable to pay its debts as they fell due, because the money was payable over a five-year period and the debts to the Crown were owed immediately, its assets exceeded its liabilities and it could be expected eventually to emerge solvent.

In March or April 1990 Longdane paid Mr Radford £5,000. On 22 May 1990 Mr Egan, the other respondent, wrote saying that, although it was Longdane's intention to clear the outstanding liability "as quickly as cash flow allows", it would be more realistic to extend the period for payment. He suggested payment over six years commencing with a first instalment of £100,000 payable on 31 March 1991 — that is, just over a year after the date of winding up.

Mr Radford did not dissent from this proposal, but 31 March 1991 came and went without further payment. Mr Radford wrote to ask what had happened, and on 16 April Mr Egan replied saying that he was aware that the money was overdue, but that the company was:

A
"in the midst of a restructuring programme of our finances which we hope will be completed without undue delay. As soon as achieved, we will then be in a position to commence payments."

He went on to ask in business-like fashion whether payment should be made to Copecrest or to Mr Radford personally.

B
Despite further inquiries by Mr Radford in May, nothing materialised, and on 4 June Mr Radford raised the stakes by sending a statutory demand. He offered, however, a meeting to discuss the matter. On 11 June Mr Egan agreed to the meeting, and that took place in mid-September. On 25 September Mr Radford wrote saying that he was not satisfied with what he had been told at the meeting, and asked for firm proposals within two weeks. On 25 October, after a follow-up letter, Mr Radford was told that he would get a substantive reply "by the middle of next week." On 28 October Mr McTighe wrote saying that Mr Radford should "kindly indicate the amount he was looking for". This letter contained no concrete proposal, but ended "I look forward to hearing from you". On 26 November Mr Radford replied, saying that Mr McTighe knew perfectly well that what he wanted was payment of the debt.

C

Having heard nothing more, on 3 January 1992 Mr Radford wrote a letter reporting the matter to the Secretary of State. According to the rules, that letter should have been sent by 14 September 1990. Mr Radford apologised for being out of time, but he said:

D
". . . I delayed submitting it in this case for the very good reason that, on the evidence of the statement of affairs, the company was solvent and thus, provided I received payment for the sale of the business, the creditors would be paid in full and they would not have a great deal to complain about, beyond the delay that had elapsed in receiving payment."

Mr Radford's letter is dated 3 January 1993, but, whether on account of being held up in Mr Radford's office or delayed in the post, it was not received by the Department of Trade until 20 February 1992. The result was that, instead of having upwards of 18 months in which to consider the matter and prepare proceedings, the Secretary of State had precisely three weeks.

E

On 27 February 1992, Mrs Clements, a senior examiner in the department, took charge of the file and decided that the case ought to be progressed. There was a meeting on 5 March 1992 at which a decision was made that proceedings were warranted, but that there was not enough time to commence proceedings by 13 March.

F

The position then facing the Secretary of State was, first, that sec. 16(1) of the *Company Directors Disqualification Act* 1986 requires that a person against whom a disqualification order is sought should be given ten days' notice of the intention to apply. It would therefore be necessary for the Secretary of State to have made a decision to apply before 3 March, and by the time of the meeting on 5 March that was no longer possible. Secondly, r. 3(1) of the *Insolvent Companies (Disqualification of Unfit Directors) Proceedings Rules* 1987 (SI 1987/2023) says that the evidence in support of an application shall be filed at the time when the summons is issued. Both these provisions are directory. Failing to comply with them is an irregularity which the court may waive. Nevertheless, that is what the rules say, and that was the basis upon which the decision was taken. It was then also decided to seek legal advice as to whether this was a proper case in which to apply for an extension of time and, if so, to make the necessary application.

G

H
There followed what may have been something of a hiatus, because Mrs Clements was leaving on maternity leave on 2 April and had to hand over the file to someone else. The result was that the affidavit in support of the application for an extension was not sent to Mr Radford for his approval until 15 April, which was five weeks after the decision to make such an application.

Thereafter the proceedings took, if not a rapid, a fairly normal course. Mr Radford   A
approved the affidavit on 22 April; the Treasury solicitor was instructed on 30 April; he
instructed counsel on 13 May; counsel advised in conference on 20 May; and the
summons was issued on the following day.

The judge asked himself whether the Secretary of State had shown a good reason for
an extension. This seems to me a correct way of putting the question. The matter was
elaborated by *Scott* LJ in *Re Probe Data Systems Ltd (No. 3)* [1992] BCC 110 at p. 118   B
where he said:

> "In considering an application under sec. 7(2) for leave to commence
> disqualification proceedings out of time the court should, in my opinion, take into
> account the following matters: (1) the length of the delay; (2) the reasons for the
> delay; (3) the strength of the case against the director; and (4) the degree of
> prejudice caused to the director by the delay . . ."

C

The judge said that the Secretary of State could not have attributed to him any
responsibility for the delay before the receipt of Mr Radford's letter on 20 February.
Nevertheless, he said it had to be taken into account. I agree that it should be taken into
account in the sense that the two-year period must be treated as having built into it a
contingency allowance for unexpected delays for which the Secretary of State is not
responsible. He is not entitled to assume that any period of delay for which he is not
responsible will automatically be added by the court on to the two-year period. He must   D
take into account that such delays may curtail the period available to him.

What, however, the judge does not appear to have taken into account is the directors'
own responsibility for the delay on the part of the liquidator. The directors had sworn a
statement of affairs showing the company to be solvent and thereafter tried until
November to string the liquidator along with promises of payment. The respondents say
that the liquidator should have realised much earlier that the debt would never be paid,   E
but in my view it does not lie in the mouths of the directors to say that the liquidator
should have realised that they were only prevaricating. I regard the directors' responsibility
for the curtailment of the period available to the Secretary of State from 18 months to
three weeks as a very significant feature in this case.

The judge came to the conclusion that the Secretary of State had failed to show good
reason, because the action which he had taken after receipt of Mr Radford's letter was
not sufficiently urgent. It seems to me that the question really turns upon whether in all   F
the circumstances, and taking into account the responsibility for the earlier delay, it was
reasonable of the Secretary of State to take the decision in early March 1992 that it was
not practical to make an application before the expiry of the two-year period. Of course,
such an application was possible. As the judge points out, the Secretary of State could
have applied for leave to make the application without simultaneously filing the evidence.
He could have made the application and trusted to any irregularity being waived, and   G
the same could be said for the ten-day notice period.

The judge, referring to the rule which requires the evidence to be filed with the
application, said (at p. 849A):

> "If that rule was to be regarded the department on 5 March faced with a difficult
> task, bearing in mind that there would have to be reference to solicitors and
> counsel."

H

I agree. In my view it was not unreasonable in all the circumstances for the Secretary of
State to decide that the proper route was not to attempt to get in an application by
13 March, but to make an application for an extension. The application for an extension
was, of course, not subject to any particular statutory time-limit, but, given the situation
which occurred, it was obviously the duty of the Secretary of State to progress it with

A reasonable expedition. During the period following 13 March the Secretary of State was at risk that the respondents might suffer some prejudice which would make it unreasonable, even if the other questions were resolved in the Secretary of State's favour, for an extension to be granted. But on the facts of this case it does not appear to me that the progress made by the Secretary of State was unduly dilatory.

B If, therefore, one takes into account, as the judge did not, the directors' responsibility for the earlier delay and what the judge agreed to be the serious nature of the allegations being made against these directors, the balance, in my view, clearly comes down in favour of the grant of an extension. I think that if the judge had correctly directed himself on the importance of the directors' responsibility, he too would have come to that conclusion.

For that reason I would allow the appeal.

C **Evans LJ:** I agree, but I should like to emphasise that for my part I do not differ in any way from the judge's assessment of the delay which occurred here after the appropriate report was received by the officers of the Secretary of State. He said this (at p. 849F):

D "Bearing in mind that one is considering quasi-penal legislation, I conclude that no good reason has been shown. In my view 'good reason' involves the officers of the Secretary of State in showing that once they realised they were in difficulty as to time, they acted with all reasonable speed . . . A senior examiner realised on 5 March that time ran out on 13 March. Yet no immediate steps were taken to meet that deadline . . . But one would suppose that legal advice would have been sought immediately and not left until 12 March; and that, when that advice was obtained, that there would have been a speedy application (to the court). Instead of that 11 weeks passed."

E Section 7(2) imposes a time-limit upon such applications from the date of insolvency. There clearly are reasons of public policy why the Secretary of State does have the power to seek disqualification under sec. 6, but sec. 7(2) also makes it clear that the Secretary of State must act expeditiously within the time-limits laid down unless the time is extended. It follows that by definition the basic period of two years includes the time which will be taken by the liquidator to report to the Secretary of State.

F Here the report dated 3 January was apparently not received by the department until 20 February, for reasons which essentially remain unexplained save that there was evidence that it was not due to inaction on the part of the department. The report begins with an explanation as to why there was delay, and it begins too with express reference to the date of the liquidator's appointment on 14 March 1990. It was dealt with by a suitably qualified officer on 27 February, and, as I understand the position in matters of this sort, there would be no doubt but that any suitably experienced person reading this G letter on that date would immediately have heard alarm bells beginning to ring. There then followed what I would describe as a leisurely progress until this application was made on 21 May. That was the period of 11 weeks referred to by the judge, and I quote from p. 848H of his judgment. His description was "there was the measured, I will not say unhurried, activity . . ."

If this was a commercial context pure and simple, I would have little hesitation in H agreeing with the judge's conclusion that in these circumstances no extension should be allowed. An application could have been made including such supplementary applications as might be necessary for abridgment of time or waiver of rules before the two-year period expired. Instead of which a decision was taken to make the substantive application late, and no notice of any sort was given to the respondents let alone to the court. This is not entirely a commercial context and the public duty aspect may well have some relevance to the standards required, although it seems to me as at present advised t

those considerations lead merely to the conclusion that for some reason special allowance   A
should be made for the fact that a government department is involved.

However that may be, the position here is that there was a substantial period during
1991 which was accounted for by the attitude of the respondents to the liquidator. It
seems to me that that certainly should be taken into account and that the judge appears
not to have done so. It seems that the point was not clearly made until the matter came
before this court this morning. In those circumstances I do not dissent from *Hoffmann*
LJ's conclusion that in taking account of all the factors the balance weighs in favour of   B
the applicant.

Dillon LJ: I agree wholeheartedly with the judgment of *Hoffmann* LJ and I do not
share the reservations of *Evans* LJ. The key factor in this case is the responsibility of the
respondents for the delay before the department received the liquidator's report. That
the judge did not take into account, and this court is therefore entitled to review his
decision. I think much more would need to be known about the structure of the civil   C
service operations before any deeper analysis could be made of such delay as there was.
As I see it, in the circumstances they acted with reasonable dispatch. The receipt of the
letter on 20 February was, as I understand it, by the central registry of the department in
Birmingham, and it had to pass to the appropriate disqualification unit elsewhere. It was
then considered, and we have the outline.

We have been told a certain amount about the structure of responsibility in the   D
department, but the key factor to be taken into account is the responsibility for the delay
on the part of the respondents. In considering that, the answer to this case is in my
judgment clear.

Therefore, I too would allow this appeal.

(*Appeal allowed. Leave to issue summons within seven days. No order for costs below.*
Costs in appeal to be costs in disqualification proceedings)   E

F

G

H

A # Carr v British International Helicopters Ltd.

Employment Appeal Tribunal.
Lord Coulsfield, Mr G R Carter and Mr J Langan.
Judgment delivered 11 August 1993.

B
Administration orders — Effect of order — No proceedings against company without administrators' consent or leave of court — Appellant was made redundant by company in administration — Whether appellant needed consent or leave to complain to industrial tribunal — Whether complaint without consent or leave was a nullity — Insolvency Act 1986, sec. 11(3)(d).

1. Complaints and applications to industrial tribunals were "other proceedings" within sec. 11(3)(d) of the Insolvency Act 1986 and the appellant's complaint against a company in administration that he had been unfairly selected for redundancy required

C **the consent of the administrator or leave of the court. (Air Ecosse Ltd v Civil Aviation Authority (1987) 3 BCC 492 distinguished; MSF & Ors v Parkfield Castings (unreported, 14 April 1992, industrial tribunal) not followed.)**

2. An application made without prior consent was not a nullity. Further, it seemed likely that it would only be in rare cases that it would be appropriate for consent to be refused to the bringing of proceedings for unfair dismissal, or in respect of redundancy.

D **(Re Atlantic Computer Systems plc [1990] BCC 859 considered.)**

The following cases were referred to in the judgment:

Air Ecosse Ltd & Ors v Civil Aviation Authority & Anor (1987) 3 BCC 492; 1987 SLT 751.
Atlantic Computer Systems plc, Re [1990] BCC 859; [1992] Ch 505.
Jones v Secretary of State for Employment [1982] ICR 389.

E *MSF & Ors v Parkfield Castings, a division of Parkfield Group plc (in liquidation)* (unreported, 14 April 1992, industrial tribunal (Middlesbrough)).
Quazi v Quazi [1980] AC 744.
Ronex Properties Ltd v John Laing Construction Ltd & Ors [1983] QB 398.
Transport & General Workers' Union v Howard Rotovators (unreported, 21 October 1987, EAT).

F *Wilson v Banner Scaffolding Ltd* (The Times, 22 June 1982).

G C Bell QC (instructed by Allan McDougall & Co, Edinburgh) for the appellant.

J A Peoples (instructed by Dorman Jeffrey & Co, Edinburgh) for the respondents.

JUDGMENT

Lord Coulsfield: This is an appeal against a decision of an industrial tribunal, dated
G 3 March 1993, by which the appellant's complaint that he had been unfairly selected for redundancy was dismissed as incompetent.

During 1991, the respondents were found to be insolvent and, on 12 December 1991, the High Court in England made an administration order, and appointed administrators to the respondents. The company continued to trade while the administrators sought a buyer for it as a going concern. However, there was a reduction in work and certain contracts were lost and, following thereupon, on 31 July 1992, 62 staff, including the
H appellant, were made redundant.

On 6 October 1992 there was a meeting to discuss the appellant's redundancy, but by a letter dated 12 October 1992, which was not before the industrial tribunal, a representative of the administrators confirmed that the termination of the appellant's employment stood. The letter stated, inter alia, "I understand that you will wish to take this matter to an industrial tribunal". The appellant's application was lodged with the

industrial tribunal on 17 October 1992. The only remedy sought in the application was   A
reinstatement. The respondents notice of appearance, dated 9 November 1992, indicated
that the respondents proposed to contest the application but, at that stage, no question
of competency was raised. However, by letter dated 21 December 1992, it was intimated
that the respondents proposed to contend that the application was incompetent because
the appellant had not obtained either the consent of the administrators or leave of the
court, as required by sec. 11 of the *Insolvency Act* 1986, before raising the application.

The hearing before the industrial tribunal, which took place on 12 February 1993, was   B
a preliminary hearing concerned only with the question of competency.

It is convenient next to set out the relevant statutory provisions. Section 11(1) of the
Insolvency Act 1986 provides that:

> "On the making of an administration order—
>
> (a)   any petition for the winding up of the company shall be dismissed, and   C
>
> (b)   any administrative receiver of the company shall vacate office."

Subsection (2) deals with the case of a receiver appointed to part of the company's
property. Subsection (3) provides:

> "During the period for which an administration order is in force—
>
> (a)   no resolution may be passed or order made for the winding up of the   D
>   company;
>
> (b)   no administrative receiver of the company may be appointed;
>
> (c)   no other steps may be taken to enforce any security over the company's
>   property, or to repossess goods in the company's possession under any hire-
>   purchase agreement, except with the consent of the administrator or the
>   leave of the court and subject (where the court gives leave) to such terms as   E
>   the court may impose; and
>
> (d)   no other proceedings and no execution or other legal process may be
>   commenced or continued, and no distress may be levied, against the
>   company or its property except with the consent of the administrator or the
>   leave of the court and subject (where the court gives leave) to such terms as
>   aforesaid."
                                                                                        F
The question in the present case is whether a complaint to an industrial tribunal, on
the ground of unfair selection for redundancy, falls under the description of "other
proceedings", within the meaning of sec. 11(3)(d) of the 1986 Act.

It is therefore necessary to bear in mind the relevant provisions of the *Employment
Protection (Consolidation) Act* 1978. Section 54(1) provides:

> "In every employment to which this section applies every employee shall have the   G
> right not to be unfairly dismissed by his employer."

The circumstances in which a dismissal is to be considered unfair are defined in sec. 55–
66, and sec. 67(1) provides:

> "A complaint may be presented to an industrial tribunal against an employer by
> any person (in this Part referred to as the complainant) that he was unfairly
> dismissed by the employer."
                                                                                        H
The remaining provisions of sec. 67 deal with questions of the limits for the presentation
of complaints. Section 68 provides:

> "(1)   Where on a complaint under section 67 an industrial tribunal finds that the
> grounds of the complaint are well-founded, it shall explain to the complainant
> what orders for reinstatement or re-engagement may be made under section 69

A   and in what circumstances they may be made, and shall ask him whether he wishes the tribunal to make such an order, and if he does express such a wish the tribunal may make an order under section 69.

(2) If on a complaint under section 67 the tribunal finds that the grounds of the complaint are well-founded and no order is made under section 69, the tribunal shall make an award of compensation for unfair dismissal, calculated in accordance

B   with sections 72 to 76, to be paid by the employer to the employee."

Section 69 provides that an order may be made either for reinstatement or re-engagement, upon such terms as the industrial tribunal may decide, and defines the effect of such orders. Section 70 contains provisions supplementary to sec. 69. Section 71 deals with the enforcement of an order under sec. 69 and with compensation, and provides for compensation to be assessed and paid in cases in which an order for reinstatement or re-

C   engagement has been made but not complied with and, in certain circumstances, for an additional award of compensation to be made in such a case.

In the course of the debate in the present case, reference was also made to sec. 106 and 108 of the 1978 Act. Section 106(1) provides:

"Where an employee claims that his employer is liable to pay to him an employer's payment, and either—

D

(a) that the employee has taken all reasonable steps (other than legal proceedings) to recover the payment from the employer and that the employer has refused or failed to pay it, or has paid part of it and has refused or failed to pay the balance, or

(b) that the employer is insolvent and that the whole or part of the payment

E   remains unpaid,

the employee may apply to the Secretary of State for a payment under this section."

An "employer's payment" includes inter alia a redundancy payment. Section 106(3) provides that if the Secretary of State pays the relevant payment to the employee, the employee's rights and remedies vest in the Secretary of State. By subsec. (5)(c), a

F   company in respect of which an administration order has been made is to be taken to be insolvent for the purposes of the section. Subsection (7) provides:

"In this section 'legal proceedings' does not include any proceedings before an industrial tribunal, but includes any proceedings to enforce a decision or award of an industrial."

G   Section 108 provides:

"(1) Where on an application made to the Secretary of State for a payment under section 106 it is claimed that an employer is liable to pay an employer's payment, there shall be referred to an industrial tribunal—

(a) any question as to the liability of the employer to pay the employer's payment; and

H

(b) any question as to the amount of the sum payable in accordance with Schedule 7.

(2) For the purposes of any reference under this section an employee who has been dismissed by his employer shall, unless the contrary is proved, be presumed to have been so dismissed by reason of redundancy."

Provision for the enforcement of an order made by an industrial tribunal, requiring   A
payment of any sum of money, is made by para. 7 of Sch. 9 to the 1978 Act. Paragraph
7(1) and (2) provides:

> "(1) Any sum payable in pursuance of a decision of an industrial tribunal in
> England and Wales which has been registered in accordance with the regulations
> shall, if a county court so orders, be recoverable by execution issued from the
> county court or otherwise as if it were payable under an order of that court.
>
> B
> (2) Any order for the payment of any sum made by an industrial tribunal in
> Scotland (or any copy of such an order certified by the Secretary of the Tribunals)
> may be enforced in like manner as an extract registered decree arbitral bearing a
> warrant for execution issued by the Sheriff Court of any Sheriffdom in Scotland."

The industrial tribunal were referred to the decision of the Second Division in *Air
Ecosse Ltd v Civil Aviation Authority* (1987) 3 BCC 492; [1987] SLT 751, and to the   C
decision of an industrial tribunal in England (Middlesbrough) in *MSF & Ors v Parkfield
Castings, a division of Parkfield Group plc (in liquidation)* (Case No. 22180/90), in which
it was held that complaints to industrial tribunals did not fall to be regarded as
"proceedings" for the purposes of sec. 11(3) of the 1986 Act. The industrial tribunal, in
the statement of reasons for their decision, set out fully the submissions which were
made to them, and their assessment of the statutory provisions. Their conclusions are
set out as follows: D

> "The tribunal were of the view that proceedings before a tribunal were
> unquestionably proceedings of a legal nature even although they did not take
> place in a court of law. It is self-evident that the applicant's initial claim was a
> claim of a legal nature. It stemmed from his belief that he had been unfairly
> dismissed. He unquestionably has certain statutory rights within the provisions of
> the *Employment Protection (Consolidation) Act* 1978 and in exercise of these   E
> rights he initiated an application to the tribunal. Were he to succeed in his
> application either by way of his desired remedy of reinstatement being granted or
> by compensation being awarded, in either event in the end of the day he would
> obtain an order from the tribunal ordering his former employers to make payment
> to him of a certain sum of money. That order in the end of the day can be enforced
> by legal process. These features led the tribunal to the inescapable conclusion that
> tribunal applications came within the scope of proceedings. In the *Air Ecosse Ltd*   F
> case earlier cited reference was made to *R v Westminster Rent Officer, ex parte
> Rendall* [1973] QB 959. At p. 974 in that case Lord *Denning* MR stated
> "proceedings" covers any proceedings of a legal nature even though they do not
> take place in a court of law.
>
> The tribunal were satisfied that an application before a tribunal constituted
> proceedings within the meaning of sec. 11(3)(d) of the *Insolvency Act* 1986. To   G
> some extent the rights of an employee who has been unfairly dismissed (if that be
> the case) by an administrator are no different from the right of a subcontractor
> who did work for the company in administration but whose contract is unreasonably
> breached by the administrator. In that situation the subcontractor in question
> would in the normal course of events seek to enforce his legal remedies by suing
> the administrator. He is clearly prevented from doing so by the provisions of
> sec. 11(3)(d) of the *Insolvency Act* 1986. The rationale for the provisions of   H
> sec. 11(3)(d) are of course related to the purposes of the administration order
> subject to the overall protection that the order is in the first place granted by the
> court if the court is satisfied that such an order should be made. Later on after the
> order is made anyone who has a claim can make application to the court to seek
> authority for bringing that claim notwithstanding the fact that an administration

A   order is in place. In the present case the applicant clearly failed to make such application and it therefore follows that his application falls to be dismissed unless the tribunal feel able to grant the applicant's agent's request that the application be sisted pending a subsequent application to the court.''

In *Air Ecosse Ltd v Civil Aviation Authority* (1987) 3 BCC 492, a company which held air transport licences under the *Civil Aviation Act* 1982 was placed in administration, and thereafter an application was made for revocation of the licences held by the company. The company argued that the Civil Aviation Authority had no jurisdiction to deal with the application for revocation, but it was held that the hearing before the Civil Aviation Authority did not amount to ''proceedings'' for the purposes of sec. 11(3). The essential question before the court was whether the words in sec. 11(3)(d) fell to be given a wide construction, or whether they should be restricted by the application of the ejusdem generis rule to proceedings of a similar character to those dealt with in the rest of the section. The court held that the ejusdem generis rule did apply, and that a narrow meaning should be given to the words ''other proceedings'' in sec. 11(3)(d). The reasons for that conclusion were expressed by the Lord Justice-Clerk (*Ross*), at pp. 502–503, as follows:

''The vital question, however, is whether the words in sec. 11(3)(d) fall to be given a wide meaning or whether they fall to be given a restricted meaning. (Counsel for the petitioners) contended for the wide meaning whereas (counsel) for the first respondents and (counsel) for the second respondents argued for the application of what was in effect the *ejusdem generis* rule. Although the matter is not without difficulty, I have come to the conclusion that the submission for the respondents is well-founded. I agree with (counsel for the petitioners) that the matters referred to in sec. 11(3)(a)–(c) do not relate solely to rights of creditors. In so far as the Lord Ordinary appears to accept that they do, I am of opinion that he was in error. Section 11(3)(a) refers first of all to a resolution being passed for the winding up of the company. This is a clear reference to a members' voluntary winding up, and in such a situation there is no question of insolvency, and the remedy is not a remedy available to a creditor. Nonetheless the remaining matters in (a) and in (b) and (c) all relate to steps which are available to persons who are in some sense creditors of a company. In my opinion the whole flavour of sec. 11(3)(a)–(c) is that it is dealing with steps which may be taken by a creditor against a company. In my opinion, this colours the interpretation which falls to be placed upon the words, 'no other proceedings . . . may be commenced or continued . . . against the company', where these appear in (d). The situation might have been different if the word 'other' had not appeared, since (d) would then have contained a clear prohibition against any proceedings being taken against the company. However, the word 'other' does appear and effect must be given to it. The whole basis of the *ejusdem generis* rule is that the word 'other' falls to be read as if it meant 'similar' (*Quazi v Quazi. . .* per Lord *Diplock*). In my opinion the word 'other' in sec. 11(3)(d) falls to be read as if it meant 'similar'. That being so it is plain that what is prohibited by (d) is any proceedings against the company which are similar to those described in (a), (b) and (c). This would confine the prohibition to proceedings which might be taken by someone such as a creditor against the company and which was in some way related to a debt due by the company. That interpretation would be entirely consistent with sec. 8(3) which describes the purposes for which an administration order may be made. In my opinion, however, the prohibition in (d) does not extend to proceedings such as those which were before the first respondents on 23 April 1987. The hearing before the first respondents on 23 April 1987 may have constituted proceedings against the petitioners in the wide sense of these words, but, in my opinion, it did not amount to proceedings similar to those described in sec. 11(3)(a)–(c).''

The Lord Justice-Clerk went on to point out that the wider construction of the section
would lead to a serious infringement upon the powers of the respondents to deal with air
transport licences, and to express the view that had Parliament meant to infringe their
powers in that way, express provision would have been made. Lord *McDonald*, at
p. 495, said that, like the Lord Ordinary, he found little assistance in cases in which the
word "proceedings" had been interpreted in other statutes, and agreed with the Lord
Justice-Clerk's view that the words must be interpreted subject to the ejusdem generis
rule, and continued:

> "Adopting that approach it is my opinion, as already indicated, that sec. 11(3) of
> the Act of 1986 is confined to the activities of creditors of a company subject to an
> administration order. It does not extend beyond that to courses of action which
> may be open to persons who are not creditors, e.g. competitors, under a different
> statute. It seems to me that sec. 11(3)(a)–(c) disclose a genus, viz. creditors of a
> company subject to an administration order, whose rights as creditors are to be
> restricted, and the use of the word 'other' in sec. 11(3)(d) is simply to bring within
> that genus those species of creditor who complete the genus but who have been
> omitted in the earlier paragraphs."

Lord *McDonald* went on to agree with the Lord Justice-Clerk's observations upon the
probable intention of Parliament in relation to the powers of the Civil Aviation Authority.

In *MSF & Ors v Parkfield Castings*, an industrial tribunal, in England, considered the
question which arises in the present case, and came to the conclusion that sec. 11(3)(d)
of the 1986 Act did not apply to complaints or applications made to an industrial
tribunal. The grounds of the decision were, first, that, following the *Air Ecosse* case,
sec. 11 disclosed a genus of creditors whose rights as creditors were to be restricted, but
that the applicants in the case before them did not come within that category. The
industrial tribunal expressed the grounds for its decision as follows:

> "We further conclude that none of the applicants affected by this decision come
> within the category of a creditor within the terms of sec. 11(3) and none, in our
> view, is at this stage taking action in relation to the actual assets or property of the
> company. Here the applicants include trade unions claiming protective awards on
> behalf of their members and other employees affected by the redundancy,
> individual employees claiming they were unfairly dismissed for redundancy, and
> individual employees complaining that the respondents unreasonably refused to
> provide written reasons for their dismissal. They are essentially seeking from the
> industrial tribunal declarations that their complaints are well founded. It seems to
> us that until the industrial tribunal has ruled upon those complaints the applicants
> do not become creditors nor are they entitled to take enforcement proceedings
> against the assets of the company. In this context we think that Mrs Woods'
> reliance upon the interpretations of 'debt' and 'creditors' in the Insolvency Rules
> was misplaced. The principle at stake here, that these applicants should have
> unrestricted access to the industrial tribunal for speedy, inexpensive and informal
> resolutions of their complaints does not, it seems to us, in any way conflict with
> the purpose and effect of an administration order under sec. 8 of the Act."

In the present case, the appellants submitted that the industrial tribunal in *MSF v
Parkfield Castings* had correctly interpreted and applied the *Air Ecosse* decision and
reached the correct result. It was submitted that this was an application claiming unfair
dismissal and seeking reinstatement, which was a matter far removed from the matters
to which sec. 11 of the 1986 Act applied. An industrial tribunal which held that the
appellant had been unfairly selected for dismissal might order reinstatement or

A   compensation and, in order to enforce any award of compensation, it would be necessary
to apply to the sheriff for a warrant. Enforcement, in that sense, might require the
consent of a court, but the present application did not seek a decree for payment. The
administrator carried on the functions of the company, including its contracts of
employment. The administrator still had the duties of an employer, and the employee
had the rights of an employee, which would be severely restricted if consent from the
court, or the administrator, was necessary to the making of a complaint. In passing the

B   1986 Act, Parliament clearly intended that the administrator should not be hindered by
creditors taking proceedings to enforce debts, but the circumstances in which the court
would grant creditors leave to proceed were very different from anything that might
arise in employment cases. Whether the employee sought compensation or reinstatement,
he was entitled to establish his rights, even if proceedings for recovery of payment might
require leave. It would be surprising if Parliament had intended the rights of an

C   employee to be taken away, without express provision. Once the employee had a
decision in his favour by the industrial tribunal, if warrant to proceed was not granted,
the employee would have the benefit of sec. 106, and the opportunity to recover from
the Secretary of State.

For the respondents, it was submitted that the industrial tribunal were correct on the
principal issue in the present case. Section 11(3) of the 1986 Act might be draconian in
its effect, but that was what Parliament had enacted, and it was not necessary for the

D   respondents to justify a decision to refuse leave. Multiplicity of applications in employment
matters could be prejudicial to the rescue of a company which was the object of an
administration order. Time-bar was not a problem because it was clearly not practicable
for an employee who was refused leave or consent to make his complaint to an industrial
tribunal. It could not easily be said that there was no prejudice caused to the administration
by claims of this type, because there might be situations in which it was inappropriate to

E   allow a number of employees to pursue their claims, to the distraction of the proper
administration of the company. Section 11 did not take away employees' rights, but
merely restricted enforcement of them for a time. It was accepted that a person making
a claim under an ordinary contract would require leave to proceed, and there was no
distinction in principle between that and a compensation claim by a former employee,
although the basis of the claim might be statute as opposed to contract or duty of care in
other cases. All such claimants were creditors for the purposes of the distinction made

F   in the *Air Ecosse* case. The respondents did not accept the distinction made between an
award and a debt or claim, because an industrial tribunal could make a monetary award.
It was dangerous to read too much into sec. 106 because there was nothing to stop an ex-
employee making a claim against the Secretary of State without proceedings being taken
in the industrial tribunal and, as was demonstrated by *Jones v Secretary of State for
Employment* [1982] ICR 389, a claim could be made without joining the former

G   employer as a party, and industrial tribunal proceedings against the Secretary of State
did not require consent. Section 106 could, therefore, be read consistently with sec. 11.

In our opinion, the starting point for consideration of this case is that a complaint or
other application before an industrial tribunal must be regarded as falling within the
description "proceedings" in the ordinary sense of that term. As *Quazi v Quazi* [1980]
AC 744 shows, the word "proceedings" may encompass procedures which fall outwith
formal legal, or court, procedures or proceedings analogous to formal legal proceedings.

H   For the purposes of the present case, however, it is not necessary to extend the
meaning of the term so far. It is quite clear that the term "proceedings" covers not only
court procedures but also analogous procedures such as arbitrations. There is, in our
view, no reason why procedures before an industrial tribunal, whether initiated by
individuals or by organisations, should not fall within the meaning of the term. Such
procedures involve complaints or applications set out formally, although simply, seeking

A

specified remedies, to which the applicants claim to be entitled under law and which are pursued under definite rules of procedure. For the purposes of the present question, we do not think that distinctions can properly be drawn between the various categories of complaints or applications which may be made, under employment legislation, to the industrial tribunals. An application which seeks compensation for unfair dismissal, or an award of a redundancy payment, is an application making a claim to a sum of money to which the claimant believes himself entitled, and can be regarded as analogous to a claim in formal proceedings for a debt or damages. An application seeking reinstatement can be regarded as analogous to a claim in formal legal proceedings seeking an order *ad factum praestandum* and, if such an order is not obeyed, further proceedings will lead to an award of a sum of money. There is, perhaps, a less exact analogy between an application by a trade union for a protective award and ordinary proceedings in a civil court but, even in that case, the consequence of a successful application is a finding which determines personal rights under law; where a protective award is made, that award has consequences for the personal rights of individuals. Accordingly, in our view, complaints and applications to industrial tribunals, as a whole, fall within the description "other proceedings" in sec. 11(3)(d), and are subject to the conditions and limitations laid down by that section, unless they can be excluded by some other argument.

B

C

The *Air Ecosse* case was concerned with administrative proceedings, whose purpose was to bring under scrutiny a licence issued to an airline company under public legislation designed to regulate air transport. The court held that such proceedings did not fall under sec. 11, because they did not fall within the genus of proceedings with which sec. 11 was concerned. In order to reach that conclusion, it was necessary for the court to derive from the provisions of sec. 11 as a whole a genus which could be defined and which excluded the type of proceedings in question. The court did so by characterising the provisions of sec. 11 as a whole as concerned with claims by creditors as distinct from proceedings initiated by regulatory authorities dealing with matters of regulation by public law. The decision draws a broad distinction between claims by creditors, on the one hand, and administrative proceedings on the other, and it does not necessarily follow that all claims by "creditors" fall into the same category, or that no distinction can logically be made among them. However, to justify holding that industrial tribunal complaints do not fall within the scope of sec. 11, it would be necessary to derive from the provisions of the section a genus which is capable of definition and excludes industrial tribunal complaints. In our view, it is not possible to derive or define such a genus, and no definition of a genus which could be so derived or defined was suggested to us. As we read it, sec. 11 restricts, under various heads, the steps which may be taken to ascertain, define and enforce rights and claims against a company in administration. We can see nothing in the section which restricts either the categories of rights and claims, or the legal bases of such rights or claims, or the procedures by which they may be enforced, in such a way as to justify the exclusion of industrial tribunal proceedings. We have a great deal of sympathy with the argument that it seems very unlikely that Parliament really had it in mind to place limitations upon the ability of employees to make claims and enforce rights under the employment protection legislation, particularly having regard to the extent to which that legislation has sought to provide swift and informal means of establishing claims, and to require speedy presentation and processing of such claims. Nevertheless, we have to deal with the terms of the legislation as they are. It seems to us that there is no way of construing sec. 11 so as to exclude from its scope claims under the employment protection legislation, and, accordingly, that considerations of the kind which we have just mentioned must be relevant to the question whether, and on what basis, leave to proceed should be granted, rather than the question whether leave is required.

D

E

F

G

H

Two other arguments can be briefly disposed of. The first argument is that based on sec. 106, but we do not find sec. 106 of any assistance in the present question. In our

A   view, sec. 106(1)(a) is concerned to define the conditions under which an employee may recover a redundancy payment from the Secretary of State, and sec. 106(7) is merely designed to prevent any possible ambiguity in those conditions. If anything, subsec. (7) indicates that, without special provision, industrial tribunal proceedings might have been held to fall within the description of legal proceedings, and, therefore, reinforces the view which we have expressed that prima facie such provisions fall within the terms of sec. 11(3)(d) of the 1986 Act. The second argument is that a distinction can be drawn

B   between the proceedings with which sec. 11 is concerned and industrial tribunal proceedings, on the ground that enforcement of industrial tribunal orders, even for payment of money, is not possible without the taking of further steps. That point is founded on in the decision of the industrial tribunal in England in the *MSF* case. So far as Scotland is concerned, however, registration of an order makes the order equivalent to an extract registered decree arbitral with warrant for execution, and such registration

C   is an administrative step only, not requiring any positive intervention by the court. We are not aware precisely what the position is in England but, even on the assumption that orders of industrial tribunals cannot be enforced directly, without further procedure, we do not think that that feature is sufficient to remove them from the category of "other proceedings". "Other proceedings" certainly embrace arbitrations, to which the same arguments might be applied.

D   In all these circumstances, in our opinion, the industrial tribunal in the present case correctly interpreted sec. 11(3), and reached a correct conclusion on that part of the case. The remaining question is whether the effect of sec. 11(3) is to render a complaint to an industrial tribunal incompetent, as the present industrial tribunal held and as the respondents maintained, or whether, as the industrial tribunal held in the *MSF* case, the legislation is merely prohibitory, and the effect of sec. 11 is only to prevent steps being taken in prosecution of the proceedings until consent has been obtained. In the present

E   case, the industrial tribunal said:

> "The tribunal considered the question of a sist but they felt unable to sist the application because of the wording of sec. 11(3)(d) of the Insolvency Act. The wording of sec. 11(3)(d) is absolute namely 'no other proceedings . . . may be commenced or continued'. In the view of the tribunal those words did not permit the tribunal to consider sisting the application pending an application being made to the court. If the applicant now makes an application to the court and his
F   application is successful then it would then be open to the applicant having obtained that consent to then initiate proceedings before an industrial tribunal. Inevitably he will then face a fresh obstacle in relation to probable arguments regarding time-bar if the present application is dismissed. It is not appropriate for this present tribunal to express a view on any such probable arguments but the tribunal regrettably come to the conclusion that it is outwith their power to sist the present application knowing it is probable such an argument will be advanced in
G   the future. In reaching this view the tribunal considered the *Industrial Tribunals (Rules of Procedure) (Scotland) Regulations* 1985 fully but there seemed to the tribunal to be no rule that would entitle them to keep a plainly incompetent application 'live' pending an application being made to the court. The applicant's motion that the application be sisted pending the application to the court is accordingly refused. Given the tribunal's earlier determination on the issue of the
H   competency of the application it therefore follows that the application be dismissed."

The argument before the industrial tribunal on this point seems to have been brief, and the argument before us was also brief. It was submitted, on behalf of the appellants, that the purposes of the statute could be served without holding that an application, properly made, was incompetent, and that, on any other view, difficulties would arise in

relation to questions of time-bar, as the industrial tribunal pointed out. For the   A
respondents, it was submitted that there was an express statutory prohibition of bringing
proceedings without consent, and that that must go so far as to render the proceedings
incompetent. It was also submitted that no material difficulties over time-bar could
arise, given that it would not be reasonably practicable for an employee, who failed to
obtain the appropriate consent, to commence proceedings within the time-limit.

The industrial tribunal in the *MSF* case were referred to some authority including, in   B
particular, *Ronex Properties Ltd v John Laing Construction Ltd* [1983] QB 398. That
case was concerned with questions arising under the *Limitation Act* 1939, sec. 2 of which
provides, inter alia:

> "(1) The following actions shall not be brought after the expiration of six years
> from the date on which the cause of action accrued . . ."

Donaldson LJ pointed out at p. 404D that: C

> "it is trite law that the English Limitation Acts bar the remedy and not the right;
> and, furthermore, that they do not even have this effect unless and until pleaded."

Of course, the background to the English Limitation Acts is different from that to
sec. 11 of the 1986 legislation; but the significance of the case is that it demonstrates that
even the most express statutory prohibition of the bringing of an action is not necessarily
to be interpreted as rendering a purported action a nullity. The industrial tribunal in the   D
MSF case were referred to *Transport & General Workers' Union v Howard Rotovators*
(unreported, 21 October 1987, EAT), but that was a case in which the point was not
argued. The industrial tribunal were also referred to *Wilson v Banner Scaffolding Ltd*
(The Times, 22 June 1982) in which *Milmo* J held inter alia that a writ served on a
company, without leave, was a nullity. The report does not disclose any detailed
reasoning in support of the conclusion, and it does not appear that there was any
reference to *Ronex Properties Ltd.*   E

In the circumstances, we regard it as open to us to construe sec. 11 of the 1986 Act for
ourselves. In our view, the purposes of the insolvency legislation can quite well be served
without requiring that a summons served, or an application made, without prior consent,
should be considered to be a nullity or incompetent. The purpose of the legislation is, in
general terms, to prevent the liquidator's or administrator's task being made more
difficult, by a scramble among creditors to raise actions, obtain decrees or attach assets.
We cannot, however, see that there is any reason why it should be necessary for the   F
provision of such protection to treat any proceedings which may, for one reason or
another, be commenced without consent as null, and, therefore, incapable of proceeding
further. In the particular case of the application of sec. 11 to employment protection
proceedings, it seems to us that there are manifest practical advantages in treating
applications made without consent as not being nullities. As we have already observed,
industrial tribunal proceedings are designed to be quick and simple, and it is part of that   G
design that the procedure should be accessible to an individual, without legal or, indeed,
other representation. We do not think that, in the ordinary case, an individual affected
by unfair dismissal or redundancy is likely to be aware of the provisions of sec. 11, or of
the requirement of consent. It seems to us that it would be unduly burdensome, and
unduly restrictive of the statutory right to complain to an industrial tribunal, to require
such an individual to reapply after obtaining an appropriate consent: indeed, it would
be burdensome to require such an individual to keep in touch with the process of   H
administration and discover when his application may be presented.

Further, it seems to us to be likely that it will only be in rare cases that it will be
appropriate for consent to be refused to the bringing of proceedings for unfair dismissal,
or in respect of redundancy. The guidelines set out by the Court of Appeal in *Re Atlantic
Computer Systems plc* [1990] BCC 859; [1992] Ch 505 stress that the purpose of the

A   prohibition in sec. 11 is to enable the company to achieve the object for which the order was made, and the purpose of the power to give leave is to enable the court to relax the prohibition where it would be inequitable for the prohibition to apply, and that the court has to balance the interests of the parties concerned. However, the employment protection legislation is designed, in the main, for the protection of employees. One of the principal objects of the legislation is to secure the speedy presentation and disposal of employees' claims, and it is very hard to see that, in the ordinary case, it is likely to be

B   really prejudicial to the administration of the company that such matters should be so dealt with. That is perhaps particularly so in a case such as this, where the employee worked for the administrator for a substantial period after the administration order was made, and the administrator might well be regarded as having adopted his contract of employment. In the whole circumstances, therefore, we consider that the industrial tribunal were wrong in holding that the present application was a nullity, and that the

C   appropriate course would have been to sist the application in order to allow the applicant an opportunity to apply for consent for the proceedings to be brought, should the administrator persist in taking the point.

    We shall, therefore, allow the appeal to that extent, and remit the case to the industrial tribunal for further procedure.

(*Order accordingly*)

D

E

F

G

H

Re Olympia & York Canary Wharf Holdings Ltd & Ors.

A

Chancery Division (Companies Court).

Sir Donald Nicholls V-C.

Judgment delivered 19 October 1993.

Administration orders — Discharge and release of administrators — Whether court would approve scheme for restructuring companies in administration so that they ceased to be insolvent.

B

The court was asked to approve a scheme for the exit from administration of the Olympia & York companies responsible for developing Canary Wharf. The scheme was opposed by Ogilvy & Mather ("O & M") which had agreed to become a tenant of the development. O & M argued that under the administrators' proposals the future of the project was insufficiently clear and certain. The court should not approve the proposals unless satisfied that there was a reasonable prospect that the new landlord company would financially be able to perform its obligations. The views of the administrators and their advisers on the viability of the scheme were based on a number of assumptions which were not revealed in the evidence. The court ought not to sanction the scheme without these assumptions first being considered and tested.

C

Held, authorising the administrators to enter into the documents and agreements needed to carry through the proposed scheme:

D

1. Success of the scheme was far from assured. The administrators did not claim otherwise. But the scheme stood a fair chance of success and provided the best hope for the companies and their creditors generally.

2. O & M's objections were raised in other litigation between the parties and could not properly be taken into account on the application. O & M was not a creditor; it might never become one. The possibility that in future there might be breaches of the landlord's covenants was not a sufficient reason for, in effect, compelling the companies to go into liquidation by refusing to authorise the administrators to proceed with the scheme.

E

3. It was not necessary or appropriate to carry out, at O & M's request, an examination of the forecasts or assumptions on which the administrators and their advisers had reached their conclusion on the viability of the scheme.

Michael Crystal QC, Martin Pascoe and Robin Dicker (instructed by Allen & Overy) for the administrators.

F

John Higham QC and Mark Phillips (instructed by Allen & Overy) for the European Investment Bank and others.

Simon Mortimore QC and Antony Zacaroli (instructed by Freshfields) for London Regional Transport, London Underground Ltd and the Secretary of State for Transport.

Christopher Carr QC and Richard de Lacy (instructed by Nabarro Nathanson) for WPP Group plc and Ogilvy & Mather Ltd.

G

JUDGMENT

Nicholls V-C: Olympia & York is a privately owned world-wide group of companies. By 1991 it had become one of the largest developers of commercial property. The ultimate parent company is registered in Ontario, Canada. The UK arm, comprising many companies, has been much concerned with the development of Canary Wharf in London's docklands. As planned, the Canary Wharf development was to be one of the largest property developments in this country, with 11m square feet of high quality office accommodation in 32 buildings. The plan was to have offices of a higher standard than office accommodation generally in the City of London, but at a lower rent.

H

A   Of the five projected phases, only the first phase and part of the second had been completed when, in May 1992, administration orders were made in England in respect of 14 companies in the UK O & Y group. Early in June administration orders were made in Scotland in respect of another 14 companies in the group. The change in the market for office space in central London, in the late 1980s and early 1990s, had been so radical that, coupled with difficulties regarding the provision of adequate public transport to the Isle of Dogs, the end result was the foundering of the project.

B   The position now is that several banks are owed altogether sums exceeding £700m. Some or all of the loans are secured, but the present value of the Canary Wharf development is considerably less than the amounts owing to the banks on the security of the property. An early sale of all or part of the development would result in a significant deficit for the banks and, in addition, unsecured creditors whose debts total between £115 and £150m would receive nothing.

C   Over the last year or so the administrators and their advisers have prepared and put together a very elaborate package. This involves, as its vital elements, the extension of the Jubilee Line underground to the site and the provision by the banks of further loans of up to some £278m. In the administrators' view this is the most favourable option and it has a reasonable prospect of success. The proposal requires a high level of further funding, but it is the one which, with the completion of the Jubilee Line extension, offers

D   the best prospect of attracting tenants and higher rents.

For their part the banks are only willing to proceed down this route if the companies cease to be subject to administration orders. This, in turn, requires a substantial restructuring of the companies so that they cease to be insolvent. Further, there must be in place a landlord whose covenant will be sufficiently strong to attract tenants. Potential tenants need to be confident that the landlord's obligations to maintain and manage the estate and carry out many important functions will be duly performed throughout the

E   leases which they are being invited to take up.

There has now been prepared, with impressive professionalism, an overall scheme of very considerable complexity. I shall not attempt to summarise it beyond what I have already said, save to add this. First, what is envisaged is a new UK group structure, under which the banks will own the shares in the companies which hold the essential property interests in the Canary Wharf and the Heron's Quay sites, or which have essential functions to discharge in the construction or management of the sites. Second,

F   on 30 September voluntary arrangements were approved by creditors of five of the 14 companies, under which unsecured creditors will receive a dividend of between ten and 14 per cent in satisfaction of their debts, from a fund of £27m being provided by the banks for this purpose. Those five companies will be restored to solvency by the banks also rescheduling their debts. Third, it is proposed that the administration orders will be

G   discharged in respect of those five companies and a further three companies which have no significant debts. It is anticipated that the remaining six of the 14 companies in administration in England will in due course almost inevitably go into insolvent liquidation.

The scheme is opposed by WPP Group plc and its subsidiary, Ogilvy & Mather Ltd ("O & M"). O & M is in occupation of two floors of 10 Cabot Square, Canary Wharf, under an agreement for a 25-year lease. WPP received inducements totalling nearly £7m

H   to enter into this agreement. O & M has produced affidavit evidence setting out, clearly and cogently, its anxieties over the future of the project. Under the lease O & M will be required to pay, over the 25-year period, some £70m in rent and service charges. O & M is gravely concerned that under the administrators' proposals the future of the project is insufficiently clear and certain. The landlord's obligations are extensive, and in respect of unlet parts of the property the landlord will be receiving no income to assist financially

in the maintenance of the estate and its facilities. The scheme is built in part on the
receipt of rent from O & M; so the court, in the exercise of its discretion, should not
approve the proposals unless satisfied that there is a reasonable prospect that the
landlord company, in turn, will be financially able to perform its obligations under the
lease. As it is, the scheme envisages that within four years further funding, estimated at
£21m, will be needed, but surprisingly, it is said, no provision has been made yet for that
funding.

Against this background, O & M has launched a sustained attack on the adequacy of
the information provided in support of this application by the administrators. The views
of the administrators and their advisers on the viability of the scheme are based on a
number of assumptions on matters such as which premises will be let and at what rent,
and what inducements will be offered to prospective tenants. But these assumptions
have not been revealed in the administrators' evidence. The court is being asked to buy
a pig in a poke and it should decline to do so but should insist on first seeing the pig. The
court ought not to sanction this scheme without O & M having an opportunity to
consider and examine and test the assumptions. Failing this, the tenants' position ought
to be protected by, for example, the banks guaranteeing performance of the landlord's
covenants under the agreement, or the administrators agreeing to permit O & M to
rescind the agreement.

I am in no doubt that I should authorise the administrators to enter into the documents
and agreements needed to carry through the proposed scheme and should make orders
discharging the administration orders and releasing the administrators as asked. Success
of this scheme is far from assured. The administrators do not claim otherwise. But I can
see no reason to doubt that the scheme stands a fair chance of success and that it provides
the best hope for the companies and their creditors generally. It deserves to be given a
chance.

I understand the anxieties of WPP and O & M. When they entered into the lease
agreement they did not envisage that they would find themselves locked into a
development beset with such financial difficulties, with the adverse impact this is having
and may have hereafter on their occupation. They seek certainty. To enable them to
conduct their business properly, they need to be reasonably confident the landlord will
perform its obligations, in return for which they have agreed to pay some £3m rent each
year. As matters stand they do not wish to take up the lease. Indeed, they wish to end
their commitment, and in this regard there is already litigation on foot over a claim by
them that, by its conduct and by breaches of the landlord's covenants, O & Y has
repudiated the agreement. All these points seem to me to be matters to be pursued by
WPP and O & M in the existing litigation. O & M can raise these commercial concerns,
in addition to any other defences it may put forward, in answer to the claim for specific
performance of the agreement. It can seek to say that in the changed circumstances,
including the insolvency of Holdings, the proposed guarantor, it should not be compelled
to take up the lease. Whether these points will afford a good defence is not for me to say.
That is not an issue before me on this application today. If they do provide a defence, so
be it. But I do not think that, over and above that, the points raised by O & M should
properly have weight on this application. O & M is not at present a creditor; it may never
become one. It has to hand a means, in the other litigation, by which it can seek to
achieve its objective of not taking up the lease. The possibility that in future there may
be breaches of the landlord's covenants is a matter which O & M can seek to investigate,
and it is a matter in respect of which, if necessary and if appropriate, it can be protected
by the court in the other litigation. But that possibility is, in my view, not a sufficient
reason for, in effect, compelling these companies to go into liquidation by refusing to
authorise the administrators to proceed with the scheme or, indeed, requiring them to
agree that O & M should have the right to rescind the lease agreement.

A

In those circumstances I do not think it would be right for me on this application to carry out, at O & M's request, an examination of the forecasts or assumptions on which the administrators and their advisers have reached their conclusion on the viability of the scheme. That is not a necessary or appropriate exercise on this application.

I shall therefore make an order as asked by the administrators. That order will include similar directions in relation to the 14 Scottish companies, pursuant to the letter of request issued to this court by the Court of Session on 5 October.

B

Finality will not be achieved until 29 October, being the day after the expiration of the 28-day period for objections to the company voluntary arrangements ("CVAs"). The administrators are to mention the matter to the court again on that day, so that I can be informed of the up-to-date position generally and with regard to one or two remaining loose ends. In particular, I envisage that on that occasion the appropriate order will not be finalised by being drawn up and sealed until after the Secretary of State has given his approval later on that day to the construction of the Jubilee Line extension.

C

(*Order accordingly*)

————————————————

D

E

F

G

H

Radford v Samuel & Anor.

A

Court of Appeal (Civil Division).
Sir Thomas Bingham MR, Leggatt and Roch L JJ.
Judgment delivered 19 October 1993.

> *Body corporate not to carry on proceedings without legal representation —*
> *Whether sole director/majority shareholder could represent company — Rules*
> *of the Supreme Court, O. 5, r. 6(2); O. 12, r. 1(2).*

B

**This was an appeal by the sole director and 99 per cent shareholder of a company from
a judge's decision that the company should not be permitted to appear without legal
representation.**

Held, dismissing the appeal:

**There were no exceptional circumstances justifying departure from the rules of the
court requiring a company to litigate through legal advisers. (Arbuthnot Leasing
International Ltd v Havelet Leasing Ltd & Ors [1990] BCC 627 considered.)**

C

The following case was referred to in the judgment of Bingham MR:

Arbuthnot Leasing International Ltd v Havelet Leasing Ltd & Ors [1990] BCC 627;
[1992] 1 WLR 455.

The appellant appeared in person.

D

JUDGMENT

Bingham MR: This is an appeal by the defendant in an action against orders made by
Forbes J on 11 October 1993. The effect of the judge's order was that a corporate
defendant in the two actions, Freeway Classics Ltd, should not be permitted to appear
without legal representation by Mr Corry, a 99 per cent shareholder and sole director of
that company.

E

The history of the action is set out by *Forbes* J in the course of his judgment and it is
not necessary to go into much of the detail. The litigation arises, as it appears, out of a
contract made in November 1990 by which the plaintiff bought a substantial value of
antique or vintage MG motor cars and parts from the defendants. It is said, although I
am sure that this is in issue, that there were deficiencies in what was delivered in that
some of the parts which should have been delivered were missing. The result of that was
that on 16 July 1991 the plaintiffs issued proceedings against the defendants for breach
of contract, and *Gatehouse* J granted a Mareva injunction in relation to an MG motor
car with the registration number DOW 33. He also ordered disclosure of assets. It
appears that disclosure of assets was not made as ordered, and accordingly the matter
came on as a motion for contempt before *Saville* J. It was then undertaken on behalf of
the defendants, the company then being represented by leading counsel, that the
affidavit that was required would be sworn and delivered the next day. On that basis the
contempt application did not proceed. When, however, the affidavit was sworn it
transpired that the MG motor car, which was the subject of the first Mareva injunction,
had been transferred to Miss Samuel shortly before the injunction had been granted.
The result of that was that a second writ was issued challenging the transfer of the car to
Miss Samuel on the basis that it was transferred at an undervalue. In the course of these
further proceedings a second Mareva injunction was obtained on 4 October 1991 in
respect of an MG Coupe and some office equipment, and a third Mareva was granted in
relation to a small bronze model of an MG.

F

G

H

The present position, as we understand, is that the assets of the company which have
been frozen by the Mareva injunctions now in force are on the office equipment and the
MG Coupe that I have already referred to, and the bronze model of an MG, the value of
the goods, according to the judge who derived his evidence from Mr Corry, being some
£6,000.

A   One of the issues that has caused trouble throughout the history of this action is that
       since a relatively early stage the company, Freeway Classics Ltd, has not been represented
       by solicitors or counsel, but Mr Corry, as director and shareholder, has sought to act on
       its behalf. The plaintiff has resisted that, and on 22 July Master *Murray* made an order,
       the effect of which was to debar Mr Corry from acting on behalf of the company.
       Mr Corry challenged the master's order and he made a reference to the judge in
       chambers for determination of the issue as to whether Mr Corry should be allowed to
B   represent and act for the company or not. There was an abortive hearing before
       Popplewell J on 14 September but, for reasons that I need not go into, his order was set
       aside, and so it came before *Forbes* J on 11 October, just a week or so ago.

       Forbes J drew attention to O. 12, r. 1(2) of the Rules of the Supreme Court, which
       provides:

C   "The defendant to such an action who is a body corporate may acknowledge
               service of the writ and give notice of intention to defend the action either by a
               solicitor or by a person duly authorised to act on the defendant's behalf but,
               except as aforesaid or as expressly provided by any enactment, such a defendant
               may not take steps in the action otherwise than by a solicitor."

       That deals with the position of a corporation which is a defendant, and there is a
       corresponding provision dealing with plaintiffs to be found in O. 5, r. 6(2) of the Rules
D   of the Supreme Court, which provides:

               "Except as expressly provided by or under any enactment, a body corporate may
               not begin or carry on any such proceedings otherwise than by a solicitor."

       On a straightforward reading of those provisions they appear to be very clear
       legislative provisions requiring a limited company to pursue its litigation, other than to
       the limited extent of acknowledging service, through legal advisers. There is, however,
E   a limited gloss which has been put on those provisions in the cases, and the clearest and
       most succinct statement of the gloss is that given by *Scott* J in *Arbuthnot Leasing
       International Ltd v Havelet Leasing Ltd & Ors* [1990] BCC 627. In the passage of *Scott*
       J's judgment (at p. 633D) which *Forbes* J cited, one finds the following:

               "With the guidance given by those authorities, which collectively are of long
               standing, are consistent with one another and are, as (counsel) impressed on me,
F   of a character and weight such as to make it impossible for me to contemplate
               either overruling or ignoring them, the position seems to me to stand as follows.
               First, O. 12, r. 1 is of statutory effect and prohibits a body corporate from taking a
               step in an action otherwise than through a solicitor. Second, the courts have an
               inherent power to regulate their own procedure and a judge in an individual case
               has, as part of that inherent power, the power to permit an advocate to appear for
               a litigant if the exceptional circumstances of the case so warrant. No limit can be
G   placed on what might constitute sufficient exceptional circumstances. But third,
               subject to any exceptional circumstances that might require a particular individual
               in the interests of justice to be allowed to appear as advocate, the general practice
               of the court is that bodies corporate cannot appear by their directors but only by
               solicitors or counsel."

       Forbes J having cited that passage, then continued in this way:

H   "In my judgment, this case really reduces itself to a simple question, and it is this:
               Are there any exceptional circumstances in this case which require Mr Corry in
               the interests of justice to be allowed to appear as the advocate on behalf of the
               defendant company as an exception to the general practice of the court, which is
               that he should not be allowed to do so? I have considered everything that I have
               read in the papers, including two affidavits sworn by Mr Corry on 13 September

and 6 October 1993 and I am quite satisfied that there is nothing exceptional about
the circumstances of this case so as to require that he, in the interests of justice, be
allowed to appear as the advocate for the defendants. It is quite clear, in my
judgment, that the only circumstances in which those sort of exceptional matters
might arise are where there are substantial grounds for believing that some
application or step in the proceedings could not be brought or put fairly before the
court for some reason or other unless somebody on behalf of the company had an
opportunity to speak for the company. In very rare circumstances the court might
be able to recognise that it was necessary to allow a limited amount of address to
the court to be made by, for example, a director of the company and would take
steps appropriate to the circumstances to allow that to be done."

Then lower down in his judgment:

"To the extent the court would ever grant the sort of indulgence that *Scott* J had in
mind, it would be of a very limited nature in very special circumstances, sufficiently
special to justify being described as 'exceptional circumstances' requiring that sort
of indulgence to be granted in the interests of justice. There is no such circumstance
here. The Mareva injunctions which have been granted do not prevent the
defendant company from arranging finances so as to have the conduct of the
defence of these proceedings in the ordinary way through solicitors and, to the
extent needed, counsel. I am quite satisfied that Mr Corry has completely failed
to make out any basis for my coming to the conclusion that I should allow him to
do that which he wishes to do, in plain contradiction of the terms of O. 12, r. 1(2).
Accordingly, I am satisfied that the order sought by the plaintiffs in this matter
should be granted."

It is worthy of note that the provisions which I have cited from the rules which require
corporations to appear through solicitors are not merely rules for the sake of having
rules but rest on a basis of fairness and good sense which indeed, as I understand,
Mr Corry understood and accepted. A limited company, by virtue of the limitation of
the liabilities of those who own it, is in a very privileged position because those who are
owed money by it, or obtain orders against it, must go empty away if the corporate
cupboard is bare. The assets of the directors and shareholders are not at risk. That is an
enormous benefit to a limited company but it is a benefit bought at a price. Part of the
price is that in certain circumstances security for costs can be obtained against a limited
company in cases where it could not be obtained against an individual, and another part
of the price is the rule that I have already referred to that a corporation cannot act
without legal advisers. The sense of these rules plainly is that limited companies, which
may not be able to compensate parties who litigate with them, should be subject to
certain constraints in the interests of their potential creditors.

In this case Mr Corry challenges the judge's view that there are no exceptional
circumstances and urges that, indeed, there are a number of circumstances which are
exceptional and which require in the interests of justice that he should be allowed to
appear personally on behalf of the company. He urges that the company lacks the means
to instruct legal advisers. He says the company has a good defence to the plaintiff's
claim, and indeed goes so far as to say that the plaintiffs would have dropped their claim
had he been in a position to act for the defendants. He points out that if the order stands
the company's case will go by default since the company will be unable to be heard, and
that, he says, is contrary to justice. He makes certain criticisms of the plaintiff's
behaviour in the course of this action, or these actions, and he says that the giving of
judgment against the company will be damaging to him personally and to his business
reputation.

A   These are all points to which the court has paid attention but, speaking for myself, I find it quite impossible to dissent from the judge's view that there is nothing exceptional about them. It is indeed standard in these cases that the corporate defendant pleads that it has no means to seek legal advice. It is often said that there is a good defence and whether there is or not is something upon which one can reach no opinion. It is an inevitable effect of the rule that, where it applies, a corporation that is not legally represented cannot be heard. Whether the plaintiff's behaviour is subject to legitimate

B   criticism or not one is again in no position at this stage to decide, and also it is no doubt true that judgment against the company may be damaging to Mr Corry's personal and business reputation. That again is something that will very frequently be so and is in no way exceptional.

    In my judgment the rule which is ordinarily applied and which is rarely waived has a solid basis in fairness and common sense and I agree with the judge that there were no

C   exceptional circumstances which justify departing from it in this case.

    Reference has been made to the Mareva injunction, to the fact that it makes no allowance for the payment of legal expenses by the company, but that I think is because the company's bank balances, if any, are not subject to the injunctions. In any event, it is certainly open to Mr Corry to seek to make application for the release of funds with which to finance legal representation, but for whatever reason he has not up to now done

D   so.

    The issue for this court is whether the judge's decision that there were no exceptional circumstances justifying departure from the rules of the court was plainly wrong. Speaking for myself I am quite unable to say it was plainly wrong, and indeed I agree with it. It therefore follows that this appeal must be dismissed.

    Leggatt LJ: I agree.

E   **Roch LJ:** I agree.

(*Order accordingly*)

─────────────────

F

G

H

Re Witney Town Football and Social Club.

A

Chancery Division (Companies Court).

Morritt J.

Judgment delivered 21 October 1993.

> *Winding up of unregistered companies — Meaning of unregistered company — Whether club was "any association" — Whether club had attributes rendering it susceptible to statutory winding-up procedure — Insolvency Act 1986, sec. 220.*

B

This was an appeal by creditors from a county court judge's decision dismissing a petition for the compulsory winding up of Witney Town Football and Social Club on the ground that the club was not an unregistered company within sec. 220 of the Insolvency Act 1986.

The creditors relied on a number of the club's rules to show that the club was not simply a social club of a kind accepted not to be subject to the statutory winding-up procedure. Those rules provided that the club should exist solely for the purpose of professional association football (r. 2), that officials, members and supporters of visiting clubs could be honorary day members for the day of their visit (r. 13), and that on dissolution the assets should be devoted to association football and not distributed between the members (r. 17).

C

Held, dismissing the appeal:

D

1. The judge asked himself the right question, whether Parliament could reasonably have intended a club of this sort to be subject to the statutory winding-up procedure, and rightly decided that the answer must lie in the constitution of the club as provided for in its rules, rather than in the size or activity of the club. Accordingly, the remaining question was whether the club had legal attributes which rendered it not a club within the ordinary acceptation of the term. If that were the case, it would still be necessary to consider whether that attribute was one from which it should be inferred that Parliament must have intended that the court should have jurisdiction to wind up the club.

E

2. The purposes expressed in r. 2 did not have either of those results. A club within the ordinary acceptation of the term might exist for sporting purposes. Professional sports or games did not give rise to a material distinction. Likewise, r. 13 did not take the club out of the normal category. In relation to r. 17, the question was whether the club had the requisite legal attributes whilst it continued as a going concern. In so far as the rights of members on a dissolution were different from those of the members of a conventional members' club (assuming the rule to be valid) that distinction did not warrant any implication that Parliament must have intended this type of club to be capable of being wound up under the provisions of the Insolvency Act.

F

The following cases were referred to in the judgment:

G

Denby (William) & Sons Ltd Sick and Benevolent Fund, Re [1971] 1 WLR 973.
International Tin Council, Re (1988) 4 BCC 559, 653; [1989] Ch 309.
St James's Club, Re (1852) 2 De G M & G 383; 42 ER 920.
Wise v Perpetual Trustee Co Ltd [1903] AC 139.

Raquel Agnello (instructed by Linnells, Witney) for the appellants.

Donald Lambie (instructed by D A Borland & Co, Eynsham) for the club.

H

GROUNDS OF APPEAL

1. The judge erred in law in holding that the respondent was not an unregistered company within the meaning of sec. 220 of the *Insolvency Act* 1986 whereas the respondent is such an unregistered company inter alia because:

A   (i)   the respondent was not formed or set up to run as a small members club but was set up as a body for the purposes of professional association football;

     (ii)   the activities and facilities of the respondent were at no stage restricted or intended to be restricted for the benefit of members only, but instead provided access to its grounds for non-members by payment of a fee for the purpose of watching football matches; and

B   (iii)   by participation in professional association football the respondent was engaging in an activity which was not by its nature one restricted to its members and as such it was a commercially minded association and not a social club.

JUDGMENT

Morritt J: This is an appeal by the petitioner, Western Counties Construction Ltd, supported by four creditors with debts totalling approximately £30,000 from the judgment dated 11 August 1993 of His Honour Judge *Harris* QC, sitting in the Oxford County Court, whereby he dismissed a petition for the compulsory winding up of Witney Town Football and Social Club.

Since that decision the petitioner's debt has been paid, but not the debts of the supporting creditors nor the costs of the petitioner. Thus the point of principle raised on this appeal is not of only academic interest. That point is whether the club is an unregistered company within sec. 220 of the *Insolvency Act* 1986. The judge held that it is not and dismissed the petition.

The club was founded in 1885 and is now constituted and regulated by rules passed at a special general meeting held on 14 August 1969 as amended at subsequent general meetings. It has 500 members and owns property of considerable value. It is a member of the Football Association and the Southern Football League, known as the Beazer Homes League, and is affiliated to the Oxfordshire Football Association. It employs professional footballers.

The rules, as amended, provide for the club to have officers, trustees, a management committee, a membership paying subscriptions in exchange for which they may enjoy the facilities of the club subject to a power of the management committee to exclude a member for discreditable conduct, audited accounts and a power to amend the rules. The club, as constituted by the rules, is similar to many other social and sporting clubs, but there are three rules which are not usually found in the constitution of such clubs. They are r. 2, 13 and 17, which are in the following terms:

"2. The Club shall exist solely as a body for the purpose of Professional Association Football. The Club will also provide various Social amenities for its Members.

13. The Management Committee shall have the power to elect Honorary Day Members. Honorary Day Membership shall be open to Officials, Members and Supporters of Visiting Clubs for the days of the visit only.

17. The Club shall only be wound up by a resolution passed at a Special General Meeting called for that purpose and the assets of the Club shall be dispensed of, after repayment of all outstanding loans and dues, in accordance with the resolutions passed at such meeting. Upon dissolution of the Club all net assets of the Club shall be devoted to Association Football and not distributed between the Members."

In his judgment the judge considered the terms of sec. 220 of the *Insolvency Act* 1986, the provisions of the rules, and the decision of the Lord Chancellor in *Re St James's Club* (1852) 2 De G M & G 383; 42 ER 920 and of the Court of Appeal in *Re International Tin Council* (1988) 4 BCC 559, 653. He posed for his decision the question whether the words of sec. 220 "any association" indicate clearly that Parliament intended such a club to be subject to the winding-up jurisdiction of the court conferred

by the *Insolvency Act* 1986. In considering that question he decided that the answer
must lie in the constitution of the club as provided for in its rules, rather than in the size
or activity of the club. After quoting from the judgment of the Lord Chancellor in *Re St
James's Club*, he concluded:

> "I hold that a club like this is not an association within the meaning of sec. 220. I
> am confirmed in that view by an extract from *Halsbury* on the subject of clubs
> under the heading of 'Dissolution' at p. 88 in the current edition of *Halsbury's
> Laws* to which I have been referred."

The passage in *Halsbury's Laws of England* to which the judge referred deals with the
dissolution under the inherent jurisdiction of the court of unincorporated members'
clubs and includes the following sentence (4th ed., vol. 6 (1991 reissue), para. 256):

> "The court has jurisdiction under the Companies Act 1985 to wind up compulsorily,
> as an 'unregistered company', a working men's club which is not registered as a
> friendly society, but it has no such jurisdiction in the case of an unincorporated
> members' club."

The petitioner appeals on the basis that the judge was wrong in law in the conclusion
to which he came. It contends that the decision of the Lord Chancellor in *Re St James's
Club* on its face applies only to clubs "in the ordinary acceptation of the term" (see
p. 387; 922). It submits that this is not simply a social club but a body set up for the
purpose of professional association football as proclaimed by r. 2; that its facilities and
activities are not restricted to its members alone but extend to the members and
supporters of visiting clubs in the guise of honorary day members as provided for by
r. 13. It is pointed out that whether or not r. 17 is valid, the intention was that a member
should not have any interest in the assets of the club in the event of a dissolution.

The club submits that the judge was right for the reasons he gave; in particular, it is
submitted, he posed the right question and correctly looked to the constitution as
provided for in the rules for the answer. In reply it was accepted by the petitioner that
the answer must be found in the constitution rather than in the activities of the club, but
it was maintained that the rules showed that this club was not a normal members' club.

Ever since 1848 the statutory provisions conferring jurisdiction on the court to wind
up unregistered companies have defined an unregistered company as including "any
association and any company" subject to various exclusions which are not material (see
Re International Tin Council (1988) 4 BCC 653 at p. 655). Moreover, the various re-
enactments since 1852 have been made in the light of the decision of the Lord Chancellor
in *Re St James's Club* so that the apparently unlimited word "any" cannot be given its
literal meaning. The decision of the Court of Appeal in *Re International Tin Council*,
which is binding on me, establishes that the question is whether Parliament could
reasonably have intended a club of this sort to be subject to the statutory winding-up
procedure (see per *Nourse* LJ at p. 656). Thus the judge posed for himself the correct
question and correctly accepted that a club such as that with which the Lord Chancellor
dealt in *Re St James's Club* did not come within the words "any association" as used in
sec. 220 of the *Insolvency Act* 1986.

In *Re St James's Club* (1852) 2 De G M & G 383 at p. 387; 922 the Lord Chancellor
started his judgment by considering the nature and constitution of such clubs, namely
"clubs in the ordinary acceptation of the term". He said:

> ". . . they are, generally speaking (and there is nothing particular in this club) all
> formed on this principle: the candidate must be elected, he must then pay an
> entrance fee, and also an annual sum or subscription. In this club there was a rule
> under which, if the person elected did not pay the entrance fee and annual
> subscription, he ceased to be a member; there was also an express rule, that if a

A   member's conduct was objectionable out of the house, he might be dismissed from being a member. What, then, were the interests and liabilities of a member? He had an interest in the general assets as long as he remained a member, and if the club was broken up while he was a member, he might file a bill to have its assets administered in this Court, and he would be entitled to share in the furniture and effects of the club; but he had no transmissible interest, he had not an interest, in the ordinary sense of the term capital in partnership transactions; it was a simple right of admission to, and enjoyment of, the club while it continued."

B

In relation to the words in the statute "any association", he concluded at p. 389; 923:

"The words are very wide, no doubt; but still, I must give a reasonable construction to the Act, which is *in pari materia*, and incorporated with the Act of the preceding year. I cannot hold it to apply to every association or company. If I were to do so, I might be called upon to carry the application much lower than to such a club as that now in question. A cricket club, an archery society, or a charitable society, would come under the operation of the Act, and indeed every club would be included. Though 'associations' are mentioned, I cannot think that word is to be treated without regard to the particulars with which it is associated. I shall do as Lord Bacon did in treating of the Statute of Uses, when he said, 'The nature of a use is best discerned by considering what it is not' . . . so I will not say what associations are within the Acts; but, bearing in mind that the individuals who form a club do not constitute a partnership, nor incur any liability as such, I think associations of that nature are not within the Winding-up Acts. I find in all these Acts to which I have referred, that every provision is inconsistent with including such an association as this club is. If such had been the intention of the Legislature, why should not the word 'club' have been expressly mentioned? If, however, the Legislature has used ambiguous expressions, I will not extend their signification beyond their natural import. At first sight, the word 'association' would seem to include the case of clubs, but in looking at the context, I am clearly of opinion that it does not."

C

D

E

As was submitted for the club, it is plain that the members did not constitute a partnership, nor, under the rules, did they incur any liability as members except for their subscriptions (see *Wise v Perpetual Trustee Co Ltd* [1903] AC 139). Thus they do not come within either of the exceptions which the Lord Chancellor envisaged. Accordingly, the only remaining question is whether the respects in which the club has legal attributes other than those referred to by the Lord Chancellor, renders it not a club within "the ordinary acceptation" of the term. If that were the case, it would still be necessary to consider whether that attribute was one from which it should be inferred that Parliament must have intended that the court should have jurisdiction to wind up the club.

F

I do not think that the purposes expressed in r. 2 can have either of those results. The judgment of the Lord Chancellor in *Re St James's Club* in terms recognised that clubs of the type he was considering might exist for sporting purposes. He does not consider professional sports or games but I can see no reason why that should give rise to a material distinction. Likewise, I do not see how the provisions of r. 13 could take this club out of the category of club with which the Lord Chancellor was dealing. Certainly it provides no reason for thinking that Parliament must have intended a club of this nature to be susceptible of being wound up under the Insolvency Act.

G

H

Lastly, there is r. 17. Counsel did not argue for or against the validity of the final sentence. Both were prepared to proceed on the basis that, whether valid or not, it indicated that the members did not intend that they should share in any surplus assets on the dissolution of the club. But the essential question, it seems to me, is whether the club had the requisite legal attributes whilst it continued as a going concern. In that respect

A

the rights of the members are in all material respects the same as those of the members in the cases predicated by the Lord Chancellor.

In so far as the rights of members on a dissolution are different from those of the members of a conventional members' club, that is assuming the rule to be valid, I do not think that that distinction warrants any implication that Parliament must have intended this type of club to be capable of being wound up under the provisions of the Insolvency Act for, in appropriate cases, it could be wound up by the High Court under its inherent

B

jurisdiction without bringing in all the detailed provisions of the Insolvency Act and rules (compare *Re William Denby* [1971] 1 WLR 973).

In my judgment, the judge was right for essentially the reasons he gave. The remedy of the creditors lies against the individuals with whom the contracts were made. In the circumstances, I dismiss the appeal, and the consequential question of substituting another creditor as the petitioner does not arise.

(Order accordingly)

C

D

E

F

G

H

A # Re Normandy Marketing Ltd.

Chancery Division (Companies Court).
Morritt J.
Judgment delivered 22 October 1993.

B *Winding up — Winding up on public interest grounds — Winding up of unregistered companies — Secretary of State petitioned to wind up Northern Ireland company in public interest — Whether court had jurisdiction to entertain petition — Whether Northern Ireland company could be wound up as unregistered company — Whether definition of unregistered company "expressly related to companies incorporated elsewhere than in Great Britain" — Insolvency Act 1986, sec. 124A, 220, 221, 441.*

C This was an application by the company to strike out a winding-up petition on the ground that the court had no jurisdiction to entertain the petition because the company was incorporated in Northern Ireland, alternatively for advertisement of the petition to be restrained.

The petition was a public interest petition presented by the Secretary of State under sec. 124A of the Insolvency Act 1986. The Secretary of State accepted that by virtue of sec. 441(2) of the Insolvency Act it was necessary to find some provision in the Act D "expressly relating to companies incorporated elsewhere than in Great Britain" which authorised him to present the petition and the court to entertain it. He contended that sec. 220 was such a provision and that "any company" in the definition of an unregistered company in sec. 220 included companies incorporated elsewhere than in Great Britain.

Held, dismissing the application to strike out the petition and refusing to restrain advertisement:

E 1. The question on the striking-out application depended on the proper construction of the words "expressly relating to" in sec. 441(2). It was quite possible, as a matter of ordinary English usage, to have an express relation without an express reference. Thus the fact that sec. 220 did not refer expressly to companies incorporated elsewhere than in Great Britain was by no means conclusive.

2. The words "any company" in sec. 220 were unlimited and included companies incorporated elsewhere than in Great Britain and sec. 220 was a provision expressly F relating to companies incorporated elsewhere than in Great Britain notwithstanding that there was no express reference to such a company.

3. Section 220 was such a provision as was mentioned in sec. 441(2) and the consequence was that sec. 221(1) applied sec. 124A to such a company, thereby authorising the Secretary of State to present the petition. The court might in due course wind up the company under sec. 221(5) provided that it had a principal place of business in England G or Wales.

4. The company had not shown sufficient reason to depart from the normal practice and restrain advertisement.

The following case was referred to in the judgment:

Compania Merabello San Nicholas SA, Re [1973] Ch 75.

H Peter Griffiths (instructed by Lawrence Graham) for the company.

Richard Ritchie (instructed by the Treasury Solicitor) for the Secretary of State.

JUDGMENT

Morritt J: The company was incorporated on 25 October 1983 as a private company limited by shares under the Companies Acts (Northern Ireland) 1960–1982. On 26 February 1993 the Secretary of State for Trade and Industry authorised two of his officers, pursuant to sec. 447(3) of the *Companies Act* 1985, to require the company to produce to them such documents as they might specify. From the information and documents so obtained it appeared to the Secretary of State that it was expedient in the public interest that the company be wound up. On 9 September 1993 the Secretary of State presented a petition to this court seeking the compulsory winding up of the company on the just and equitable ground. The petition, which has not been advertised, is due to come before the court for the first time on 3 November 1993.

By the application before me the company seeks an order that the petition be struck out pursuant to O. 18, r. 19 or the inherent jurisdiction of the court on the ground that it discloses no reasonable cause of action and/or is otherwise an abuse of the process of the court. In the alternative, the company seeks a direction, pursuant to r. 4.11(1) of the *Insolvency Rules* 1986, that the petition be not advertised. Both applications are opposed by the Secretary of State. The latter application, but not the former, is supported by eight creditors of the company with debts totalling £237,000.

The basis of the first application is that, as the company contends, the Secretary of State had no power to present and the court has no jurisdiction to entertain the petition because the company was incorporated in Northern Ireland. The question is entirely one of law and depends upon the true construction of the *Insolvency Act* 1986.

By sec. 124A the Secretary of State is authorised to present a petition for the winding up of "a company" where it appears to him, from amongst other sources, information obtained under Pt. XIV of the *Companies Act* 1985 that it is expedient in the public interest that it should be wound up. The ground for making a winding-up order is that the court thinks it just and equitable that the company should be so wound up.

The relevant definition of the word "company" (see sec. 251 of the *Insolvency Act* 1986) is that contained in sec. 735(1)(a) of the *Companies Act* 1985 which is, "unless the contrary intention appears", "a company formed and registered under this Act, or an existing company".

"Existing company" is defined to mean a company formed and registered under the former Companies Acts which are also defined.

The *Insolvency Act* 1986, sec. 441 provides as follows:

"(1) The following provisions of this Act extend to Northern Ireland—

 (a) sections 197, 426, 427 and 428; and

 (b) so much of section 439 and Schedule 14 as relates to enactments which extend to Northern Ireland.

(2) Subject as above, and to any provision expressly relating to companies incorporated elsewhere than in Great Britain, nothing in this Act extends to Northern Ireland or applies to or in relation to companies registered or incorporated in Northern Ireland."

None of the exceptions referred to in subsec. (1) is material to the question I have to decide. Accordingly, the opening words of subsec. (2), "Subject as above", may be ignored. But the rest of subsec. (2) makes clear that the Secretary of State had no power to present the petition and the court has no jurisdiction to entertain it unless there is a "provision expressly relating to companies incorporated elsewhere than in Great Britain" enabling it. The company contends that there is no such provision. Counsel for the company referred to sec. 225 of the Insolvency Act and sec. 740 of the Companies Act to the like effect in connection with sec. 745 of the Companies Act as examples of such provisions. These sections refer in terms to "a company incorporated outside Great Britain" and "a company incorporated elsewhere than in Great Britain".

The Secretary of State accepted that it was necessary to find some provision expressly relating to companies incorporated elsewhere than in Great Britain which authorised

A him to present the petition and the court to entertain it. He contended that such provision is to be found in Pt. V of the *Insolvency Act* 1986 dealing with the winding up of unregistered companies, and in particular sec. 220 containing the definition of an "unregistered company".

The relevant provisions of Pt. V are as follows:

"220   *Meaning of 'unregistered company'*

B (1) For the purposes of this Part, the expression 'unregistered company' includes any association and any company, with the following exceptions—

   (a) . . .

   (b) a company registered in any part of the United Kingdom under the Joint Stock Companies Acts or under the legislation (past or present) relating to companies in Great Britain.

C . . .

221(1) Subject to the provisions of this Part, any unregistered company may be wound up under this Act; and all the provisions of this Act and the Companies Act about winding up apply to an unregistered company with the exceptions and additions mentioned in the following subsections.

D (2) If an unregistered company has a principal place of business situated in Northern Ireland, it shall not be wound up under this Part unless it has a principal place of business situated in England and Wales or Scotland, or in both England and Wales and Scotland.

. . .

(5) The circumstances in which an unregistered company may be wound up are as follows—

E (a) if the company is dissolved, or has ceased to carry on business, or is carrying on business only for the purpose of winding up its affairs;

   (b) if the company is unable to pay its debts;

   (c) if the court is of opinion that it is just and equitable that the company should be wound up."

F Section 225 provides that:

"Where a company incorporated outside Great Britain which has been carrying on business in Great Britain ceases to carry on business in Great Britain, it may be wound up as an unregistered company under this Act, notwithstanding that it has been dissolved or otherwise ceased to exist as a company under or by virtue of the laws of the country under which it was incorporated."

G Section 229 provides that:

"(1) The provisions of this Part with respect to unregistered companies are in addition to and not in restriction of any provisions in Part IV with respect to winding up companies by the court; and the court or liquidator may exercise any powers or do any act in the case of unregistered companies which might be exercised or done by it or him in winding up companies formed and registered under the Companies Act.

H (2) However, an unregistered company is not, except in the event of its being wound up, deemed to be a company under the Companies Act, and then only to the extent provided by this Part of this Act."

The response of the company is that none of the provisions of Pt. V, except sec. 225 which is irrelevant, is one "expressly relating to companies incorporated elsewhere than

in Great Britain" because such companies are not mentioned. In this connection,   A
reliance was placed on *Dicey and Morris on the Conflict of Laws* (11th ed.), pp. 1144
and 1145, which so far as relevant states:

> "Rule 176. — English Courts have no jurisdiction to wind up . . .
>
> (2) any company registered in Northern Ireland except one which has carried on
> business in Great Britain and which has ceased to carry on such business . . ."

In footnote 26 reference is made to "Insolvency Act 1986, ss. 441(2), 225." On p. 1145 it   B
is stated:

> "The definition of 'unregistered company' does not expressly relate to a Northern
> Irish company, and accordingly such a company cannot be wound up under
> section 221 of the Act. However, section 225 of the Act does expressly relate to
> companies incorporated outside Great Britain, and hence it is submitted that the
> courts have jurisdiction to wind up a Northern Irish company if that company has   C
> been carrying on business in Great Britain and has ceased to carry on that
> business."

It was submitted that if the Secretary of State were right, all companies incorporated
under the Northern Ireland Companies Acts were liable to be wound up in England,
contrary to the apparent intention behind sec. 441 of the Insolvency Act that they should
not be.   D

Reliance was also placed on the alteration to sec. 440 of the *Companies Act* 1985, the
statutory predecessor of sec. 124A of the *Insolvency Act* 1986 by the *Companies Act*
1989. Section 440 had authorised the Secretary of State to present a petition in respect
of a body corporate liable to be wound up under that Act, which was defined by sec. 740
as including a "company incorporated elsewhere than in Great Britain". The *Companies
Act* 1989 repealed sec. 440 of the *Companies Act* 1985, and replaced it by inserting
sec. 124A into the *Insolvency Act* 1986. But, in effecting that re-enactment, Parliament   E
changed "body corporate", as defined in sec. 740, to "company" as defined in
sec. 735(1)(a). It is submitted that such change was deliberate and intended to bring
petitions by the Secretary of State in respect of companies incorporated in Northern
Ireland (which on this basis would previously have been permissible) into line with the
petitions of creditors or contributories which previously would not have been possible.
Counsel emphasised that a company incorporated in Northern Ireland, which the
Secretary of State was authorised to investigate by sec. 453 of the *Companies Act* 1985,   F
could, if his submissions, were right, still be wound up in Northern Ireland because the
Secretary of State would be entitled to pass the information and documents to the
Department of Economic Development for Northern Ireland pursuant to sec. 449(1)(dd)
of the *Companies Act* 1985, which, it was to be assumed, had similar powers to present
a winding-up petition in respect of a company incorporated in Northern Ireland to those
of the Secretary of State in respect of a company incorporated in England conferred by   G
Order in Council made under sec. 214 of the *Companies Act* 1989.

In the end, the question depends upon the proper construction of the three words
appearing in sec. 441(2) of the *Insolvency Act* 1986: "expressly relating to". No doubt
the word "expressly" is to be contrasted with "impliedly". But the words "relating to"
are not the same as "referring to". The former includes but is not confined to the latter.
Thus, sec. 225 of the *Insolvency Act* 1986 and sec. 740 of the *Companies Act* 1985, which   H
the company relied on as provisions expressly relating to companies incorporated
elsewhere than in Great Britain, do so relate because they refer expressly to such
companies. But in my judgment it is quite possible, as a matter of ordinary English
usage, to have an express relation without an express reference. For example a provision
which referred expressly to citrus fruits would be a provision expressly relating to
oranges and lemons, even though they were not expressly mentioned in the provision.

A   Thus, in my judgment, the fact that sec. 220 of the *Insolvency Act* 1986 does not refer expressly to companies incorporated elsewhere than in Great Britain is by no means conclusive.

Section 220 of the Insolvency Act refers to "any company" as part of the definition of an unregistered company. Therefore, it is plain that the context of sec. 220 is one in which the definition of "company" in sec. 735(1)(a) of the *Companies Act* 1985 is inapplicable because that definition, in effect, confines the word "company" to a

B   registered company, which would be excluded by para. (b). Thus the words "any company" are unlimited and include companies incorporated elsewhere than in Great Britain. A company incorporated in Northern Ireland under the Companies Acts (Northern Ireland) 1960–1982 is not excluded from the definition by sec. 220(1)(b) because those Acts are not within the relevant definition of Joint Stock Companies Acts contained in sec. 735(3) of the *Companies Act* 1985, and the expression "Great Britain"

C   does not include Northern Ireland. In my judgment, sec. 220 is a provision expressly relating to companies incorporated elsewhere than in Great Britain notwithstanding that there is no express reference to such a company.

There are other provisions in Pt. V of the Insolvency Act which clearly point to the same conclusion. Thus the provisions of sec. 221(2) suggest that the draftsman considered that a company incorporated in Northern Ireland could be wound up in England as an

D   unregistered company because a company with a principal place of business in Northern Ireland would most commonly be a company incorporated there. But of more significance this provision disposes of the company's contention that the argument for the Secretary of State would, by a side wind, subject all companies incorporated in Northern Ireland to substantially all the provisions of the *Insolvency Act* 1986, when sec. 441 suggests that that should be the exception rather than the rule. Section 221(2) shows that only those companies incorporated in Northern Ireland which also have a principal place of

E   business in England and Wales are liable to be wound up in England.

Section 225 of the Insolvency Act was originally enacted to remove a doubt as to the court's jurisdiction which arose in connection with the dissolution of Russian Banks following the revolution in 1917. It did not confer any new power to wind up companies: see *Re Compania Merabello* [1973] Ch 75 at p. 86. It would be most surprising if a company incorporated in Northern Ireland might be wound up in England if it had

F   ceased to carry on business in England and had been dissolved in Northern Ireland, but not otherwise. This would be the consequence of the company's argument and of the view expressed in *Dicey and Morris* (to which I have referred).

Finally, the amendments introduced by the *Companies Act* 1989 on which the company relied did not remove an anomaly for none existed as both creditors and the Secretary of State were entitled to take steps to wind up a company incorporated in

G   Northern Ireland as an unregistered company provided that it had a principal place of business in England and Wales.

In my judgment sec. 220 is such a provision as is mentioned in sec. 441(2). The consequence is that sec. 221(1) applies sec. 124A to such a company, thereby authorising the Secretary of State to present the petition in this case. The court may in due course wind up the company under sec. 221(5) provided that it has a principal place of business in England or Wales. The company does not suggest that it does not have such a place of

H   business. Accordingly, I dismiss the application to strike out this petition.

I then turn to the second part of this application whereby the company seeks a direction pursuant to r. 4.11(1) of the Insolvency Rules that this petition be not advertised. Unless a direction is made as requested, the rule requires the Secretary of State to insert an advertisement in the *London Gazette* not less than seven days after service of the petition or before the day appointed for the hearing of the petition. The

advertisement must, amongst other things, indicate the venue fixed for the hearing of   A
the petition and state that anyone seeking to appear at the hearing must give notice of
his intention in accordance with r. 4.16. The rules contemplate that the persons responding
to the advertisement will be creditors of the company: see r. 4.16(2)(c) and 4.17(2). But
the practice of the court has been in its discretion to hear other interested persons in
order to hear what public grounds there may be for or against the making of an order:
see *Buckley on the Companies Acts* (14th ed.), vol. 1, p. 546.

    The company's application is not made on the basis that the petition of the Secretary   B
of State is bound to fail, rather that the advertisement of the petition would cause untold
damage to the company without any countervailing advantage to anyone else. The
nature of the company's business is adequately set out in para. 8 and 9 of the petition,
which state:

> "The company offers finance to other businesses using a method of invoice
> discounting which it describes as 'the Normandy concept'. The basis of the concept   C
> is that the company buys goods from a client at a small discount and resells them
> to the client's customer, paying the client immediately less a retention of 20 per
> cent. Upon receiving payment from the customer Normandy releases the retention
> to the client less interest charges.

> 9. The company is funded by 18 individuals and companies known as 'traders',
> who between them were owed some £395,981 at 1 October 1992, the last available   D
> figures. The traders each signed an agreement with Normandy allowing it to utilise
> their moneys to purchase and resell goods on their behalf accounting to them for
> the profits on those trades. The agreements contain a number of conditions which
> were designed to offer the traders a measure of protection including the provision
> of quarterly statements by the company showing the valuation of the traders'
> holding and identifying the trades in which they are involved."

Paragraphs 10–16 set out the conduct of the company on which the Secretary of State   E
relies. It is common ground that the victims of that conduct, if there be any, are primarily
the traders. Eight of the 18 traders referred to in para. 9 of the petition, with debts
aggregating £237,000 out of current total debts to traders of £425,000, have appeared by
counsel on this application and support it.

    The basis for the application is set out in para. 64 of the affidavit of Mr Leong Son, a
director of the company, sworn on 19 October 1993. In para. 3(2) and 62 he deposes that   F
the company proposes to make a fundamental change to the way the company is
financed, in consequence of which all traders' funds will be fully repaid to them in two to
three months so that the matters of which the Secretary of State complains will be
historic. He submits that it would be pointless to make a winding-up order and unfair to
subject the company and hence the traders to the considerable extra costs that a winding-
up order would involve. He also expresses concern that the company's customers would   G
not pay the amounts they owe the company, thereby giving rise to further loss and
expense. In para. 64 he states:

> "Finally, I turn to the consequences of this petition being advertised. If this
> petition is advertised, the company will obviously have to cease trading. There is
> also a considerable risk that customers will think that they can get away with not
> paying the company. It is a sad fact of life that whenever a company goes into   H
> liquidation its debtors try to avoid paying because they know a liquidator is
> unlikely to be as enthusiastic in trying to collect in all the debts as the existing
> management. If the petition is advertised, therefore, the customers will start
> inventing excuses justifying non-payment and that will destroy the business. That
> business is, however, a very valuable business and one that it is important to
> preserve. It will be destroyed if the petition is advertised and it will be pointless

A
defending the petition. Accordingly, I ask this court to direct that the petition be not advertised pending the hearing of the petition because otherwise, the mere advertisement of the petition, will result in the company going into liquidation without any hearing on the merits.''

As I have indicated, that is supported by eight traders with debts amounting to £237,000 of which counsel informs me four, with debts totalling £200,000, are entirely independent of the company or its directors. In addition, he asks for an opportunity for

B
his instructing solicitors to obtain instructions from the remaining ten traders.

The application is opposed by the Secretary of State. His counsel points out that the petition was presented because the Secretary of State considered it to be in the public interest that the company be wound up. He suggested that, in consequence, it should be brought to the attention of the public. He relied on the fact that, as counsel for the company had stated, the petition would take two days to hear so that an early resolution

C
of the dispute was unlikely. He contended that the court should not permit an unadvertised petition to lie on the file for any lengthy period. He submitted that the consequences to the company, if the petition is advertised, are no different in this case to all the many winding up cases which come before the court.

I consider that the efficacy of an advertisement in the *London Gazette* has been exaggerated by both sides. No doubt it alerts the company's bankers so that an order

D
under sec. 127 of the Insolvency Act may be required in order that the company may continue to trade. But I do not think that the *Gazette* is so widely read that an advertisement would alert ordinary trade creditors, who would not discover the existence of the petition by other means anyway. By the same token, the Secretary of State's concern that a petition presented in the public interest should be brought to the attention of the public is hardly allayed by advertising it in the *Gazette*. Nevertheless, the rules require advertisement unless the court otherwise directs. Thus it is for the company to

E
show sufficient reason to depart from the normal practice.

In the paragraph in the affidavit of Mr Leong Son, which I have quoted, he suggests that the business of the company will be destroyed if the petition is advertised. But he does not, in any of the passages in the affidavit to which I was referred, explain why that should happen, except by reference to the likely attitude of the company's customers. In that regard he does not seek to put forward any special case; he complains that

F
advertisement will lead customers to start inventing excuses justifying non-payment and that will destroy the business. This is described as a sad fact of life. But, if the value of the business is as great as he suggests, advertising the petition could not have the effect of destroying it. If the state of the company's business is so parlous as to be capable of being destroyed by advertisement in the manner suggested, that circumstance alone justifies advertisement to give an opportunity to creditors other than traders to express their wishes. Moreover, it would not be consistent with the normal practice of the court

G
to permit a petition to remain unadvertised for a lengthy period. If it be the case that the petition cannot be disposed of this year, then it should be advertised promptly.

In these circumstances, I see no reason to allow further time to enable the views of the remaining ten traders to be ascertained. If all of them supported the company's application, that would not discharge the onus on the company. Accordingly I refuse to direct that this petition be not advertised.

H
(Order accordingly)

Re Polly Peck International plc.
Secretary of State for Trade and Industry v Ellis & Ors.

Chancery Division (Companies Court).
Jonathan Parker J.
Judgment delivered 2 July 1993.

> *Disqualifying unfit directors of insolvent companies — Discovery — Secretary*
> *of State sought leave to commence proceedings out of time — Respondent*
> *sought production of documents referred to in evidence — Whether production*
> *necessary for disposing fairly of matter or for saving costs — Company*
> *Directors Disqualification Act 1986, sec. 7(2); Rules of the Supreme Court,*
> *O. 24, r. 10, 13.*

The court refused an application under RSC, O. 24, r. 10 for production of documents referred to in the evidence served by the Secretary of State in support of an application for leave to issue director disqualification proceedings out of time, on the grounds that production was not necessary either for disposing fairly of the matter or for saving costs.

The following cases were referred to in the judgment:

Probe Data Systems Ltd, Re (No. 3) [1992] BCC 110.
Tasbian Ltd, Re (No. 3) [1992] BCC 358.

Fernanda Pirie (instructed by the Treasury Solicitor) for the Secretary of State.

Jonathan Crow (instructed by Penningtons) for the respondent.

JUDGMENT

Jonathan Parker J: In August 1986 Mr David Stafford Fawcus was appointed a director of Polly Peck International. Subsequently he became finance director of that company. On 25 October 1990 an administration order was made in respect of the company. On 14 October 1992 the Secretary of State issued an originating summons seeking leave to commence proceedings against Mr Fawcus and four other directors of Polly Peck International, seeking disqualification orders under the *Company Directors Disqualification Act* 1986. The application was for leave to commence the proceedings out of time, bearing in mind that time was due to expire on 25 October 1992. The application, accordingly, was anticipatory in that time had not yet expired. On 30 November 1992 the Secretary of State was granted leave by *Knox* J to discontinue those proceedings.

On 5 February 1993 the Secretary of State issued a further originating summons, seeking similar leave (that is to say, leave to commence proceedings under sec. 6 of the *Company Directors Disqualification Act* 1986 out of time) and I am told that that application is due to be heard in October 1993. Shortly after the issue of the originating summons, the Secretary of State served his evidence in support of the application and, as may be expected, that evidence was very substantial.

On 10 May 1993 Mr Fawcus applied for disclosure under O. 24, r. 10, of the Rules of the Supreme Court of various categories of documents as being documents referred to in the evidence served by the Secretary of State in support of his application for leave to issue proceedings out of time.

There is no dispute as to the fact that the categories of documents listed in the application were referred to (for the purposes of the rule) in the Secretary of State's evidence. The issue before me is whether, in the case of each category of document, disclosure of those documents is "necessary either for disposing fairly of the cause or matter or for saving costs" (those words being taken, of course, from O. 24, r. 13(1)). And it is to be borne in mind that the cause or matter in question is the application by

A   the Secretary of State for leave to commence disqualification proceedings out of time. It is that application which is now before me and I have heard Mr Crow, who appears today for Mr Fawcus, and Miss Pirie, who appears for the Secretary of State.

Before turning to the specific categories of document in respect of which disclosure is sought, I must address the question of the appropriate approach of the court in the context of an application for leave to issue proceedings out of time under sec. 7(2) of the
B   Act.

Mr Crow submits that much of the evidence filed on behalf of the Secretary of State in support of the present application is partial in the sense that it does not give a fair and overall picture of what happened, and he directs my attention to the fact that the substance of the Secretary of State's case against Mr Fawcus is one of omission rather than commission. That being so, submits Mr Crow, it is appropriate at this stage and in
C   the context of this application by the Secretary of State that the court should look more widely at the relevant documentation in order that, as he would have it, a more balanced picture will emerge; and on that footing Mr Crow submits that disclosure of the categories of documents in question is essential to a fair disposal of the application for leave to commence proceedings out of time. He referred me, in support of his submissions in this respect, to the case of *Re Tasbian Ltd (No. 3)* [1992] BCC 358 and in particular to the passage at p. 364 in which the Court of Appeal approved the approach of *Scott* LJ in
D   *Re Probe Data Systems Ltd (No. 3)* [1992] BCC 110, where *Scott* LJ said at p. 118G:

> "In considering an application under sec. 7(2) for leave to commence disqualification proceedings out of time the court should, in my opinion, take into account the following matters: (1) the length of the delay; (2) the reasons for the delay; (3) the strength of the case against a director; and (4) the degree of prejudice caused to the director by the delay . . ."

E   He laid emphasis on number (3) in that list, the strength of the case against a director, and he submits that in the context of the present application, in order for the court to form a sensible view as to the strength of the Secretary of State's case against his client it is necessary that the court should have before it a wider picture on the documentation and in particular that the documents specified in his client's application should be disclosed.

F   He submitted that, in considering whether to grant leave, the court might find the question of the merits to be a crucial factor weighing in the balance and as dictating in the event whether leave is in fact granted. On that basis, he submits that, as I have indicated, the further documents in respect of which disclosure is sought are documents which the court should see at this stage in the context of the current application.

Miss Pirie, who appears, as I have said, for the Secretary of State, asserts a much
G   narrower test. She referred me to the case of *Re Probe Data Systems (No. 3)*. She directed my attention to the terms in which *Scott* LJ in fact dealt with the matter of the strength of the applicant's case on the facts of that particular case. Thus, at p. 119H, *Scott* LJ said:

> "This evidence, in my opinion, disclosed a well arguable case that Mr Desai [the respondent in question] was 'unfit to be concerned in the management of a
H   company'. . ."

And later *Scott* LJ said this (at p. 120E):

> "All of these points are, no doubt, relevant for the purposes of the disqualification proceedings themselves. None is so incontrovertible an answer to the case outlined in Mr Cummins' affidavit as to justify the conclusion at this stage that the case is too weak to warrant the grant of leave."

Miss Pirie submits that in the context of an application for leave to issue proceedings　A
out of time the only threshold which the Secretary of State has to cross is that of showing
an arguable case — a serious issue to be tried — by analogy with the approach of the
court in granting interlocutory relief. She submits that the application for production
and disclosure should be approached on that footing; and that so approaching the
application I should conclude that disclosure of these categories of document is not
necessary for the fair disposal of the application to issue proceedings out of time.

It seems to me that inevitably the court, in considering an application for leave to issue　B
proceedings out of time under sec. 7(2) of the Act, cannot attempt anything approaching
a substantial hearing, nor can it be expected to form anything approaching a final
assessment of the relative merits of the case of the applicant on the one side and the
respondent on the other. Plainly it is necessary that it should attempt some preliminary
assessment of the case against the director, but by definition that can only be on a prima
facie basis, not least because at that stage the evidence will be on affidavit and there will　C
be no cross-examination.

Moreover, on an application for leave to issue proceedings out of time, the defence of
the respondent may well not be fully before the court; indeed, normally it will not be.
Accordingly, in those circumstances, the scope for making any assessment of the merits
of the case against the director is very limited indeed. On the other hand, I accept that
where sins of omission are alleged there may be some scope — I emphasise "some" —　D
for further disclosure on the footing that a wider picture should be presented. But —
and this seems to me to be an important qualification on the comment which I have just
made — the mere possibility that there may be further evidence which may be relevant
to the issues to be raised at the substantive hearing could not, in my judgment, justify
disclosure at this stage.

It is therefore, as I see it, a question of degree, bearing in mind the scope and the
purpose of the present application, which is, of course, an application for leave to issue　E
the proceedings out of time. Accordingly, I propose to approach the various categories
of document listed in Mr Fawcus' application upon that basis.

I make one further general comment before doing so. Miss Pirie, on behalf of the
Secretary of State, has indicated that a considerable degree of selectivity was necessary
in formulating the evidence on behalf of the Secretary of State, given the massive
documentation which exists in relation to the matters potentially in issue if leave is　F
granted. That I can well understand, and the fact that such selectivity is obviously
necessary is a matter which I have to bear in mind when I consider the contention of
Mr Crow that the evidence is selective to the point of presenting an unbalanced picture.

With those general comments in mind therefore I turn to the specific categories of
document in respect of which production is sought. There are six such categories.
Category one refers to a number of documents referred to in an order of *Vinelott* J dated　G
28 January 1993, such documents comprising, as I understand it, transcripts or notes of
interviews with various individuals. Mr Crow submitted that this additional material,
which is not relied upon by the Secretary of State as matters stand today, may nevertheless
be useful to Mr Fawcus in demonstrating the weakness of the Secretary of State's case
against him. He submits that if the Secretary of State has such evidence, although he
may not at the moment be relying upon it, then his client should be entitled to see it in
case it helps him. And he submits, as I have said, that it is important that the full picture　H
(I use his words) be before the court, especially in a case such as this, where the
allegation is one of guilt by omission.

In my judgment, however, approaching the matter upon the basis which I attempted
to formulate earlier in this judgment, it seems to me that the production of such
documentation is not necessary for disposing fairly of the cause or matter (that is to say,

A   the application for leave to issue proceedings out of time). It seems to me, on the contrary, that to direct disclosure of such documentation would be tantamount to giving discovery in the context of the proposed substantive proceedings should leave be granted. It seems to me that it is not appropriate in the context of the present application, let alone necessary, that such documentation be disclosed.

B   The remaining categories (and there are five of them) I propose to take together, because it seems to me that, adopting the approach which I have described, the same comments will apply to each. In each case, the Secretary of State has exhibited certain documentation in support of specific allegations of what I may call "non-feasance" on the part of Mr Fawcus. He has not exhibited the entirety of the documentation which relates or may relate to those allegations. In other words, these are examples, as I see it, of the necessary selectivity which has had to be applied in the collation of the Secretary of State's evidence.

C   In each case Mr Crow submits in summary (and I hope I do his argument justice) that to refer only to part of the documentation of the type described is inevitably to present a selective and unbalanced picture, and that the court ought to have the opportunity of seeing the remainder of such documentation in order to have before it a balanced picture. In my judgment, however, given the approach which I have adopted, it would not be appropriate for such further documentation to be produced, let alone necessary for the fair disposal of the cause or matter. The Secretary of State has referred to those

D   documents on which he proposes to rely. He has not exhibited any further documents on which he proposes to rely. That is a matter for him and it is on the basis of the evidence which the Secretary of State has put forward that the strength of his case against the respondent has to be assessed. And when I say "assessed", I use that expression in the context of the comments which I made earlier as to the approach which I think it correct for the court to adopt. In my judgment, in relation to each of the remaining five

E   categories, production is not necessary for disposing fairly of the relevant cause or matter.

There is, of course, a further limb of O. 24, r. 13(1), namely "necessary for saving costs". Mr Crow submits that it is possible that, having seen such further documentation, were it to be disclosed, his client might take the view that further opposition to the application for leave should not be pursued; and if he were to take that course, costs

F   would inevitably be saved. With respect to Mr Crow, that sounds to me like a siren song and it is, in any event, pure speculation. As I see it, disclosure of the documentation in respect of which disclosure is sought would almost inevitably increase the costs of the present application and increase them very substantially indeed. Accordingly, I see no basis in the context of saving of costs for ordering production of these documents. Therefore, I refuse the application.

G   I would add that it seems to me that there is also a risk that if disclosure were made that might lead to further applications being made and thereby lead to an unacceptable escalation in the scale of this application, bearing in mind that it is an application limited to seeking leave to issue proceedings out of time. But I make it clear that I have not taken that factor into account in reaching my decision that this application should be refused.

H   (*Order accordingly*)

                          ————————————

Re Polly Peck International plc.
Secretary of State for Trade & Industry v Ellis & Ors (No. 2).

Chancery Division (Companies Court).

Lindsay J.

Judgment delivered 3 November 1993.

Disqualifying unfit directors of insolvent companies — Leave to apply for disqualification order out of time — Whether there was a good reason for extension of time — Whether applicant had to show only unfitness to be concerned in management "without leave of the court" — Meaning of unfitness to be concerned in management of "a" company — How past conduct led to finding of present unfitness — Whether applicant's evidence was hearsay and inadmissible — Whether there had been unreasonable delay — Materiality of strength of case against respondents — Whether respondents were prejudiced by delay — Company Directors Disqualification Act 1986, sec. 6(1)(b), 7(2).

This was an application by the Secretary of State for Trade and Industry under sec. 7(2) of the Company Directors Disqualification Act 1986 for leave to issue proceedings out of time for the disqualification under sec. 6 of the 1986 Act of four directors of Polly Peck International plc ("PPI").

The respondents were the finance director, another director based chiefly in the US from 1988, and two non-executive directors. The respondents did not represent a majority in number of the directors at any one time and were less than one-third of the directors who were directors at the date of the administration and did not include the company's chairman, Asil Nadir.

PPI went into administration in October 1990. In May 1991 the administrators made what they called an interim report under sec. 7(3) of the 1986 Act; the substantive report was not received until 1 June 1992. The Secretary of State issued proceedings on 14 October 1992 within the two-year period allowed under sec. 7(2) but those proceedings were withdrawn. The second originating summons seeking leave under sec. 7(2) was issued by the Secretary of State in February 1993.

The matters complained of in relation to the respondents' conduct were matters of omission. The Secretary of State alleged that they had failed (1) to institute adequate controls over the expenditure and transfer of moneys from PPI; (2) to ensure that adequate financial controls and reporting procedures were implemented and adhered to in respect of various subsidiaries; (3) to obtain appropriate responses to the question of the need of the subsidiaries for such substantial funding from PPI; and (4) to monitor, or set up proper procedures for monitoring, the actual expenditure incurred by the subsidiaries, the funds which had been provided to them and their ability to repay their indebtedness to PPI as and when required or at all. In evidence in reply, the Secretary of State's case was "not that they did not resign but that they failed as directors to procure that the omissions were rectified or to take the stance that 'enough is enough' and that they would resign if the omissions and the lack of knowledge and control of the board which arose therefrom and of which they were well aware were not rectified; and that after mid-1989 they continued as directors and thereby continued thereafter to be responsible in breach of their duties for the omissions and to rectify them."

A number of points on the 1986 Act were canvassed. The Secretary of State submitted that under sec. 6(1)(b) the conduct required for there to be a disqualification needed only to be such as to make the respondent unfit to be concerned in the management of a company without the leave of the court. Other questions were the meaning of "a" in "unfit to be concerned in the management of a company" in sec. 6(1)(b), and how the past conduct to be examined was properly to lead to a conclusion of present unfitness.

A   The respondents argued that much of the Secretary of State's evidence was hearsay and inadmissible as such.

Held, dismissing the Secretary of State's application for leave under sec. 7(2):

1. Section 6(1)(b) should not be read as if the words "without the leave of the court" were written in at the end. The subsection could easily have said so but did not say so, and where a provision, whilst not wholly or even primarily penal in intent, was nonetheless

B   plainly quasi-penal in effect, it would be wrong of a court, unless constrained to do so, to make the threshold which a complainant had to cross other than, and certainly not lower than, whatever Parliament had by its language provided.

2. The relevant unfitness to be determined under sec. 6(1)(b) was in relation to companies generally.

3. Evidence of past conduct within sec. 6(1)(b) which would justify a finding of past

C   unfitness to the required level would prove present unfitness to the same level, unless the respondent satisfied the court otherwise.

4. Hearsay was admissible by reason of the interlocutory character of the application. If that was wrong the material should be admitted leaving its weight at least and perhaps also its final admissibility to be argued over and ruled upon at any substantive hearing. (Re Rex Williams Leisure plc [1993] BCC 79 applied.)

D   5. In the period between October 1990 and February 1993 there were between three and a half and four months of unreasonable delay.

6. The failures alleged by the Secretary of State could not properly be regarded as breaches of duty by each individual respondent. The allegations confused the duty of the board as a whole with the duties of individual directors. A director who had not been individually charged by a board with the task of, for example, instituting adequate financial controls, might or might not be in breach of a duty to the company to use his best

E   endeavours to procure their institution but not, without more, with their absence. Were that not so, a director who had striven manfully to introduce them would be as much in breach as one who had resisted them.

7. In the circumstances it was impossible to regard as so serious a failure as to justify disqualification, the failure of any of the four individual directors, never a majority on the board at the time, to have cried "enough is enough" and to have threatened their

F   resignation, which, in the finance director's case, it was accepted could have caused the company a considerable loss in that ingredient of confidence so necessary to it and the effect of which upon Mr Nadir, in terms of bringing him to heel, was accepted as being speculative. The shortcomings alleged did not, in the light of indisputable facts and the Secretary of State's submissions, have the gravity required.

8. If the applicant's case was so weak that it could not lead to a disqualification the

G   application for leave should be rejected even before a balancing of all the factors was embarked upon. That initial threshold was not crossed. (Re Tasbian Ltd (No. 3) [1992] BCC 358 applied.)

9. If that was wrong and there was misconduct which could amount to a serious failure, there was nothing in the Secretary of State's evidence to suggest that such past failure would be the least likely to recur in any company of which any of the four was or was likely to become a director.

H   10. If the initial threshold was crossed, and it was necessary to consider the strength of the Secretary of State's case as part of the balancing exercise, it was at best speculative and very weak against each of the respondents. Furthermore, there was a case plainly arguable on the evidence as a whole that even if the respondents' shortcomings were seen as serious, they were not of a kind likely to recur in any company with which any of them would be likely to be associated except in the quite exceptional circumstances of PPI.

British Company Cases

11. By reason of the Secretary of State's failure to act within the time prescribed for the purpose by Parliament three of the respondents were certain to suffer some prejudice and more prejudice was likely to follow as to those respondents.

12. Balancing the factors of the delay, the reasons for it, the strength of the case and prejudice, there was no good reason for the extension sought in relation to three respondents. As for the other respondent, the initial threshold was not crossed and even if it had been the case against him was, on the evidence, threadbare to a degree and too weak to warrant the grant of leave. Moreover, as to all respondents, first, had there been any doubt the respondents would have to be given the benefit of it and, secondly, if no real likelihood of recurrence was shown, then the public interest was diminished in that the public, absent a likelihood of recurrence, did not need protection from the respondents.

The following cases were referred to in the judgment:

American Cyanamid Co v Ethicon Ltd [1975] AC 396.
Bath Glass Ltd, Re (1988) 4 BCC 130.
Cedac Ltd, Re. Secretary of State for Trade and Industry v Langridge [1990] BCC 555; [1991] BCC 148 (CA).
Copecrest Ltd, Re [1993] BCC 844.
Crestjoy Products Ltd, Re [1990] BCC 23.
Dawson Print Group Ltd & Anor, Re (1987) 3 BCC 322.
Godwin Warren Control Systems plc, Re [1992] BCC 557.
Lo-Line Electric Motors Ltd & Ors, Re (1988) 4 BCC 415; [1988] Ch 477.
Noble Trees Ltd, Re [1993] BCC 318.
Polly Peck International plc v Nadir & Ors [1992] 2 Lloyd's Rep 238.
Probe Data Systems Ltd, Re (No. 3) [1992] BCC 110.
Sevenoaks Stationers (Retail) Ltd, Re [1990] BCC 765; [1991] Ch 164.
Swift 736 Ltd, Re. Secretary of State v Ettinger [1992] BCC 93; [1993] BCC 312 (CA).
Tasbian Ltd, Re (No. 3) [1992] BCC 358.
Williams (Rex) Leisure plc, Re [1993] BCC 79; [1993] 3 WLR 685.

AWH Charles (instructed by the Treasury Solicitor) for the Secretary of State for Trade and Industry.

Michael Kennedy (instructed by Huggins & Co) for the first respondent.

Jonathan Crow (instructed by Penningtons) for the second respondent and (instructed by Theodore Goddard) for the third and fifth respondents.

The fourth respondent did not appear and was not represented.

JUDGMENT

Lindsay J: I have before me an application by the Secretary of State for Trade and Industry made under sec. 7(2) of the *Company Directors Disqualification Act* 1986. It is made by an originating summons dated 5 February 1993 and, as originally framed, it sought leave for the Secretary of State to issue proceedings out of time for the disqualification under sec. 6 of the 1986 Act of five directors of Polly Peck International plc ("PPI"). On the first day of the hearing Mr Charles, counsel for the Secretary of State, indicated he would not be seeking leave in respect of one of the five directors; so far as concerns the substance of the matter I have since then been concerned with only four. Leave is needed before the Secretary of State can proceed in respect of these remaining four because sec. 7(2) of the 1986 Act provides that except with the leave of the court an application for the making of a disqualification order under sec. 6 shall not be made:

"after the end of the period of 2 years beginning with the day on which the company of which that person is or has been a director became insolvent."

A   The date upon which, for the purposes of sec. 6 and 7 of the 1986 Act, the company "becomes insolvent" is fixed by sec. 6(2) and, in the case of PPI, it is common ground that that date was 25 October 1990, the date upon which an administration order was made in relation to PPI.

In the course of its life PPI has attracted attention, fame and, more recently, and particularly in relation to its chairman, Mr Asil Nadir, some notoriety. The making of the administration order on 25 October 1990 was a matter that attracted notice in the
B   press, both popular and financial. The four directors who are continuing respondents to the Secretary of State's originating summons do not include Mr Nadir and are by no means all or even a majority of the persons who were directors of PPI at the commencement of the administration. Indeed, the four were never, I think, a majority at any relevant time. I shall need to describe the lapse of time between the administration order on 25 October 1990 and the issue of the present application for leave on 5 February
C   1993 in more detail below, but I shall first briefly describe the respondents and then deal with a number of questions of law which have been canvassed before me.

The second respondent, Mr David Fawcus, for whom Mr Crow appears and whose case was argued first, is a chartered accountant. He joined PPI in August 1986 with a view to becoming its finance director, an office he then held until August 1990. Mr Mark Ellis, the first respondent, appears by Mr Kennedy. Mr Ellis is a barrister and was PPI's
D   joint managing director from 1983 to 1987. In the later stages he remained a director but was, from August 1988, based chiefly in the US, whereas PPI was run from London.

The third respondent, Mr Mills, was a non-executive director from April 1985 to January 1991. He had been a chairman of Sedgwick Group plc and a director of Midland Bank. He is the respondent in respect of whom the Secretary of State elected not to seek leave to proceed.

E   The fourth respondent, Dr Ulf Siebel, is a doctor of jurisprudence and a member of the Frankfurt bar. He was a non-executive director of PPI from August 1988 to January 1991. Amongst other offices he has held he has been, or is, I am told, deputy chairman of Hypothekenbank in Essen AG and a member of the admission board of the Frankfurt stock exchange. He lives out of the jurisdiction and was not represented before me. I am not told of any other English company of which he is an officer.

F   Lastly, the fifth respondent, Lawrence Tindale CBE, is a chartered accountant. He was a non-executive director from April 1985 to December 1990. He is or has been deputy chairman of 3i plc. He was not represented before me as to the substance of the case but only as to costs.

As for questions of law raised, the question to be asked by a court hearing an application under sec. 7(2) is one of an attractive but perhaps misleading simplicity: has the applicant, here the Secretary of State, shown a good reason for the necessary
G   extension of time? (See *Re Crestjoy Products Ltd* [1990] BCC 23 at p. 29F per *Harman* J; *Re Copecrest Ltd* [1993] BCC 844 at p. 847F per *Mervyn Davies* J, as approved in the Court of Appeal at p. 852A per *Hoffmann* LJ.)

The matters to be taken into account in answering that apparently simple question have been described in the Court of Appeal as follows:

H   "In considering an application under sec. 7(2) for leave to commence disqualification proceedings out of time the court should, in my opinion, take into account the following matters: (1) the length of delay; (2) the reasons for the delay; (3) the strength of the case against the director; and (4) the degree of prejudice caused to the director by the delay . . ."

per *Scott* LJ in *Re Probe Data Systems Ltd (No. 3)* [1992] BCC 110 at p. 118G, a judgment with which *Farquharson* LJ and *Parker* LJ concurred.

That list was adopted without comment by the Court of Appeal at p. 852B in the
judgment of *Hoffmann* LJ in *Copecrest*. The list is not in terms said to be exclusive of all
other matters but in most cases it is likely so to be. I will turn below to the four matters
separately but first I need to deal with other matters raised.

When each of those four matters has been looked at separately there then needs to
take place what Mr Charles calls a balancing exercise; all four are to be considered and
the court is to ascertain whether there then emerges from the exercise a good reason for
whatever extension is necessary.

I accept that approach qualified only to this extent; before the balancing exercise
there is a first stage. If the applicant's case is so weak that it could not lead to a
disqualification the application for leave should be rejected even before a balancing of
all four factors is embarked upon. If authority were needed for the proposition that
there would be no point in extending the time if the application were bound to fail, it is
to be found in *Re Tasbian Ltd (No. 3)* [1992] BCC 358 at p. 362C per *Balcombe* LJ in the
Court of Appeal. I shall deal with this possibility under the heading "Strength of case"
below but, to revert to the second stage, the "balancing exercise", calling it that confers,
as Mr Crow for the second respondent submits, a spurious exactitude on the operation;
the so-called balance involves matters which, if measurable at all, would be measurable
on different scales. I see sense in Mr Crow's suggestion that the four matters are best
considered as two pairs under which the longer the delay, the better need be the reasons
for it and in which the worse the prejudice to the respondent the stronger the case
against him needs to be. But even that pairing could obscure the position where, say,
despite well explained delay and a strong case against him there would be extreme
prejudice suffered by a respondent. In the event, the direction that I give myself is no
more specific than that I must have all four matters in mind and that the conclusion to be
drawn from them has been left by Parliament to the courts as a discretion which is
unfettered other than as is a necessary or reasonable inference from the very terms of
the subsection which confers it.

When I come to deal with the strength of the case against the directors I will need to
have in mind what an applicant needs to prove in disqualification proceedings under
sec. 6. It is common ground that disqualification is proper only on proof of serious
misconduct: see *Re Cedac Ltd* [1990] BCC 555 at p. 558E per *Mummery* J. The Court of
Appeal in *Re Sevenoaks Stationers (Retail) Ltd* [1990] BCC 765 at p. 779H specifically
approved a paragraph of the judgment of *Peter Gibson* J in *Re Bath Glass Ltd* (1988) 4
BCC 130 at p. 133 which began:

> "To reach a finding of unfitness the court must be satisfied that the director has
> been guilty of a serious failure or serious failures, whether deliberately or through
> incompetence, to perform those duties of directors which are attendant on the
> privilege of trading through companies with limited liability."

At the same time the Court of Appeal in *Sevenoaks*, whilst seeing it as understandable
that courts should attempt to give guidance as to what does or does not make a person
unfit, reminded readers of the dangers of treating such guidance as judicial paraphrases
of the statute which fell to be considered in lieu of the statute itself — see at p. 773F. The
Court of Appeal disapproved *in terms* of the guidance given by Sir *Nicolas Browne-
Wilkinson*'s passage in *Re Lo-Line Electric Motors Ltd* (1988) 4 BCC 415 at p. 419 only
to the extent that incompetence, which he had required to be total, need not be so. It
sufficed if it was to a very marked degree — see *Dillon* LJ at p. 780C. Nonetheless, in the
light of the warning in *Sevenoaks* as to the proper approach, it is not clear to me how
much the Court of Appeal intended should survive of the rest of the guidance given in
Lo-Line namely that:

A
> "Ordinary commercial misjudgment is in itself not sufficient to justify disqualification. In the normal case, the conduct complained of must display a lack of commercial probity, although I have no doubt in an extreme case gross negligence [or total] incompetence disqualification could be appropriate."

There is an echo of the *Lo-Line* reference to "a lack of commercial probity" in a later case in the Court of Appeal heard after *Sevenoaks*, namely, *Re Swift 736 Ltd. Secretary of State v Ettinger* [1993] BCC 312 at p. 315E. Sir *Donald Nicholls* V-C there refers to

B
"due regard to the ordinary standards of commercial morality" but there the reference is not so much the describing of a standard the failure to attain which is required in the proof of unfitness, but more as being something to which directors and others should pay due regard. A related difficulty is that in *Sevenoaks* the Court of Appeal, whilst disapproving of an approach other than to the words of the statute itself, could be taken, by endorsing the passage I have cited from *Peter Gibson* J, to be introducing a

C
qualification to the words of the statute, namely, that disqualification should spring from only those duties "attendant on the privilege of trading through companies with limited liability". The Act itself suggests no such qualification and, by making consideration of breach of *any* duty by a director, a matter to which regard is in particular to be paid by the courts (see sec. 9(1) of and Sch. 1, Pt. I, para. 1 to the 1986 Act) would seem to exclude it. There are duties, for example to apply the money of the undertaking only for the purposes of the undertaking, which would seem to me to be as applicable to, say, a

D
partnership as to a limited company and in any event the definition of "company" in the 1986 Act can include bodies not having limited liability — see sec. 22(2). I can think of few tasks less profitable in disqualification cases than an examination of whether a given shortcoming of a director could properly be said to be a consequence of or attendant upon the privilege of trading with limited liability; comments on the subject in *Bath Glass* and other cases are no more than remarks appropriate on the facts of the particular

E
cases and do not (and could not) prescribe a need for the examination I have mentioned.

In the circumstances I see the proper course on this application is for me first to pay close attention to the very words of the Act; as it is put in *Sevenoaks* (at p. 773C): "It is important to hold to those words in each case."

Secondly I should pay regard to the clear thread derived from the authorities that whatever else is required of a respondent's misconduct if he is to be disqualified, it must

F
at least be "serious", a conclusion which, authorities apart, could doubtless be fairly extracted from the Act itself which, under sec. 6, is such that proof of misconduct to the required degree leads inevitably, without any intervening discretion in the court, to disqualification and for a minimum of two years.

As for seriousness in relation to a breach of duty by a fiduciary such as a director, whilst there is authority in this context for the proposition that if the breach is designed

G
to benefit the director who owes the duty it is *always* to be regarded as serious, that citation itself and common sense suggest that where the breach is not so designed it may on the facts of a particular case be regarded as not sufficiently "serious" for this present purpose: see *Re Probe Data Systems Ltd (No. 3)* [1992] BCC 110 at p. 119D. So equally, again on the facts of the given case, imprudence or even impropriety may fall short of misconduct of the required seriousness: see *Bath Glass* at p. 139. Paying due attention,

H
as I am required to do, to the words of the statute, all I can derive from the Act as to the seriousness of the misconduct required (given that sec. 9 does not catalogue everything to which attention is to be paid) is that it must be such that in the view of the court it ought fairly to be visited with an automatic disqualification.

It is recognised too (and this is a fact which I will need to have in mind when I deal with the strength of the case against these directors) that in making or withholding a disqualification order the court is involved in an exercise that requires a balancing

between different and conflicting interests. There is a public interest, the serving and
protection of which was the primary purpose of sec. 6 of the 1986 Act, that the public
should be protected against the future conduct of companies by persons whose past
records as directors of insolvent companies has shown them to be a danger to creditors
and others: *Re Cedac Ltd* at p. 558H per *Mummery* J, citing from *Lo-Line* at p. 419.

It is not, of course, the case that sec. 6 is the only protection that the public has in
relation to the proper management of companies and in the provision of sufficient
information with regard to them. The public interest is served by means outside the 1986
Act and by means within the 1986 Act but outside sec. 6. Thus if, for example, a case
were to be made against any of the four respondents that they have been in breach of
duty to PPI and that thereby PPI has suffered loss, they would be vulnerable to
misfeasance or similar proceedings, proceedings which have a merit not present under
the 1986 Act that there may thereunder be recovery for the creditors of PPI. So also
where a director has been convicted on indictment of what one might call a company
offence (CDDA, sec. 2) or has been persistently in default as to the provision of company
material required by statute (sec. 3) or has been guilty of fraudulent trading or a
company fraud (sec. 4) or repeated lesser company offences (sec. 5), the public interest
in relation to him can be protected by disqualification at the discretion of the court under
the Act. It is thus very far from the case that refusal of leave under sec. 7 necessarily
leaves the public interest bereft of protection or the directors free from proceedings.

As against public interests of that kind the courts recognise that, on the other hand,
the making of a disqualification order represents a substantial interference with the
liberty of an individual: *Lo-Line* cited in *Cedac* at p. 558D. As put in *Cedac (Secretary
of State for Trade and Industry v Langridge)* on appeal [1991] BCC 148 at p. 153G:

> "While a disqualification order is not of itself penal, it is clearly restrictive of the
> liberty of the person against whom it is made and its contravention can have penal
> consequences under sec. 13."

As disqualification can have such consequences, it is proper to give a director the
benefit of any reasonable doubt, an example of that approach being *Re Swift 736 Ltd*
[1992] BCC 93 at p. 95B per *Hoffmann* J (in part of his judgment which I do not see as
affected by the Court of Appeal's view that the period of disqualification he had ordered
was too short — see [1993] BCC 312; the appeal was, so to speak, only against sentence,
whereas the observation I have quoted was, as it were, as to conviction).

Turning to a different point, Mr Charles submits that under sec. 6(1)(b) the conduct
required for there to be a disqualification needs only to be such as to make the
respondent unfit to be concerned in the management of a company *without the leave of
the court*. I do not agree. The subsection could so easily have said so but does not say so.
Where a provision, here sec. 6(1)(b), whilst not wholly or even primarily penal in intent,
is nonetheless plainly quasi-penal in effect, it would, in my view, be wrong of a court,
unless constrained to do so, to make the threshold which a complainant has to cross
other than, and certainly not lower than, whatever Parliament shall by its language have
provided. Nothing in sec. 9, which directs the court to the matters to which, in particular,
it is to have regard, indicates any justification for the introduction of the words which
Mr Charles admits he seeks, in effect, to write in. Consistently, as I see it, with my view
of the section, the *Insolvent Companies (Disqualification of Unfit Directors) Proceedings
Rules* 1987 (SI 1987/2023) contain no reference which supports Mr Charles' submission.
Nor can the submission be based on the fact that if the court makes a disqualification
order it is an order that the person against whom it is directed shall not be a director of a
company etc. *without the leave of the court*. It might in other circumstances have been
arguable that if that is the prospective consequence of a disqualification then unfitness
to that degree is what is to be expected to need to be proved; there must have been

A   intended (the argument would be) a direct relationship between the requirements stipulated before the order can be made and the effect of the order. However, quite apart from the answers that I have already given, it is plain that there is no such direct relationship; sec. 6(1)(b) provides that if a director's specified conduct makes him unfit to be concerned in the *management* of a company then it is not only from the management of a company from which he is (without leave) barred but also, because the provisions of sec. 1(1)(a) to (d) are cumulative (the "or" which joins them is plainly intended to be

B   conjunctive) from being a liquidator, an administrator, a receiver or manager of a company's property or concerned in the promotion or formation of a company.

     Another difficulty that has been the subject of argument has been the meaning of unfitness "to be concerned in the management of *a* company". This use of the indefinite article does not, in my view, require the court to look at unfitness with respect to any particular identified or identifiable company or even to a company which is, or is (if such

C   a thing could be discerned) of the same type as, the company of which the respondent director shall have been director and which has become insolvent. It is, on the one hand, no escape, for example, for a respondent to urge against the applicability of sec. 6(1)(b) that he would be fit to be concerned in the management of, say, a small or private company or of a company which, for example, did not receive deposits from the public or which by its memorandum was able to trade only on cash terms. If that was the case disqualification would be virtually unattainable and no public interest would be served

D   by the section; even a respondent with an appalling track record could escape disqualification by calling into existence a company in respect of which his particular shortcomings would, on the face of things, be effectively denied further life. Nor, on the other hand, does the use of the indefinite article have the effect that the applicant merely has to show that in respect of *a* company, some ascertained or ascertainable company, the respondent is unfit. An applicant is not able to point to the existence of some

E   company in which the duties falling upon a director would be unusually onerous and to say that in respect of *a* company — that is to say that company — the respondent would be unfit to be concerned in its management. Thus, although unfitness to be concerned in the management of companies generally is admittedly a somewhat nebulous concept, that, I apprehend, is what Parliament has intended to be required under sec. 6(1)(b), just as "*a* company" in sec. 1(1)(a), (b), (c) and (d) is equally intended to be a general reference.

F   Mr Charles asks rhetorically, by way of opposing a construction involving unfitness as to companies generally, how, if unfitness has to be in relation to companies generally, could leave have ever be given under sec. 17 immediately after a disqualification, thus permitting a disqualified director to be or remain, for example, a director of specified companies, a practice which is not unusual. One answer is that the court can alleviate the general disqualification by imposing terms, not otherwise exigible, such as would be

G   intended to make a person fit upon those undertakings, notwithstanding his general unfitness otherwise. That terms can be required or imposed when leave is given under sec. 7 is shown by *Re Godwin Warren Control Systems plc* [1992] BCC 557 at p. 569. Whilst I would not have wished to end up with so nebulous a concept, I do not see Mr Charles' argument as displacing my view that the relevant unfitness is as to companies generally.

H   As to proof of a respondent's unfitness to be concerned in the management of companies generally, it is plainly intended to be proved and must be taken to be capable of proof from the *particular* instances to which sec. 6(1)(b) directs regard:

       ". . . his conduct as a director of *that* company (either taken alone or taken together with his conduct as a director of any other company or companies) . . ." (emphasis added)

Turning to a different point, and accepting that the statute requires that unfitness as   A
to companies generally is capable of proof from proof of particular cases, the Act gives
no guidance as to the circumstances in which the particular conduct permitted to be
examined under the Act and Rules — necessarily in the past — is properly to lead to a
conclusion as to a *present* general unfitness. It is notable that in sec. 6(1)(b) it is the
present tense "makes him unfit" that is used and not a past tense. The conduct proved,
if it is to justify a disqualification order, must therefore have at least these next two
characteristics. First, that it is such that from the respondent's conduct as director of   B
only one company or a number of companies having a relevant nexus between them (see
Godwin Warren at p. 567E) it is right to move to a conclusion as to unfitness in relation
to management of companies generally. Secondly, that the past conduct must be such as
to satisfy the court of a present unfitness.

There plainly can be cases, including cases where the respondent's defaults do not fall
outside Sch. 1 to the 1986 Act, where the only reasonable present inference from the   C
respondent's defaults in the past is that he is at present unfit to be concerned in the
management of "a company", that is to say, of companies generally. The man who, for
example, has a past record of breaches of duty involving dishonesty may have so
comprehensively forfeited any confidence a court might otherwise have had in his
reform that no conclusion could fairly be reached other than that he remained unfit. But
difficulties (referred to in argument as the recurrence or repetition problem) may arise   D
where, for example, no dishonesty is alleged and no irredeemable or insuperable
incompetence or where the past defaults are wholly or in part explicable by reference to
past circumstances that are unlikely to recur.

Suppose, to take a rather lurid illustration, that a man's defaults, after an earlier
blameless career as a director, consisted of his failing to see that his company's accounting
records were duly kept and lodged within sec. 221 of the Companies Act, but that such
defaults had occurred only whilst, and were referable to, a short and past period of   E
extreme distress whilst his wife or child was suffering from a lingering and terminal
illness. Could it fairly be held that his past conduct as a director was such as to lead to a
finding of *present* unfitness? Could it be a fair answer to say, even if an authorised
complainant was misguided enough to proceed for his disqualification and a court
misguided enough to disqualify him, that it mattered not that his past defaults made him
vulnerable to sec. 6 because some court might be wise enough to give him leave under
sec. 17? A better conclusion, in my view, would be that that man could never have been   F
described as unfit within sec. 6(1)(b) in the first place.

The courts are, I think, entitled to be cautious if not cynical about a respondent's
reform and sceptical as to the attribution of defaults to circumstances said to be unlikely
to recur. It would be all too easy for a man to swear to, and very difficult to test the truth
of, his reform. It may often be easy for a man to point to conduct (within the bounds of
what can be looked at within sec. 6(1)(b)) that apparently supported his proposition that   G
(at all events whilst proceedings impended) he had reformed. It would not serve the
public interest were unsupported evidence as to the unlikelihood of recurrence to be
lightly accepted. In the absence of guidance from other cases I see it as right to carry the
caution or scepticism I have mentioned into an approach such that evidence of past
conduct within sec. 6(1)(b) which would justify a present finding of past unfitness to the
required level may, unless the respondent otherwise satisfies the court, be taken by the
court also to prove a present unfitness to that same required level. It may be that such an   H
approach has been so far accepted, albeit tacitly, in the cases, as would explain the
absence of earlier discussion on the point save for the passing mention in *Re Dawson
Print Group Ltd* (1987) 3 BCC 322 at p. 325 per *Hoffmann* J, which, whilst not needing
to deal with the point, is at least not inconsistent with the approach to which I have
referred.

A   Mr Charles sought to resist the conclusions that past unfitness did not necessarily prove present unfitness and that present unfitness could be rebutted even if past unfitness was proved by referring to *Bath Glass* and to what he called the "tunnel vision" imposed by the Act whereunder I may, as to unfitness, look only at the conduct specified in sec. 6. However, *Bath Glass* at p. 132 underlines that what has to be looked for is whether, as the matter appears at the hearing, the respondent *is* unfit. I do not see the case as otherwise dealing with the point with which I am concerned, nor, in my judgment,

B   does any "tunnel vision" as to what is to be looked *at* preclude the view I have formed as to what is to be looked *for* and as to what needs to be found.

     Another attempt to find a route out of the recurrence problem was one in which Mr Charles argued that because sec. 6(1)(b) is to be read, as he submits, as if the words "without leave of the court" were found at its end, questions such, for example, as to whether the respondent had learned his lesson or whether the circumstances were

C   otherwise such that further defaults were unlikely, do not arise unless and until application is made for leave under sec. 17. However, as I have already held for the reasons I have given that the subsection cannot be treated as if those words were written in at its end, I cannot see this submission as assisting with the recurrence problem.

     I shall shortly turn to the four matters I listed earlier to which, upon an application for leave under sec. 7(2), the court should pay regard, but before I do that I should mention

D   that notwithstanding that in February 1991 the Court of Appeal made it plain that service of a ten-day notice under sec. 16(1) of the 1986 Act, whilst not mandatory, was something that was strictly required, none was served in this case: compare *Re Cedac Ltd. Secretary of State v Langridge* [1991] BCC 148 at p. 152C. However, little was made of this point before me because, as *Langridge* shows, the absence of the ten-day notice is a procedural irregularity and on the particular facts of this case, including the October 1992 proceedings to which I shall shortly refer, little could be made of the

E   irregularity. I now turn to the four matters.

(1) Length of the delay

     The administration order was made on 25 October 1990. The Secretary of State issued *some* proceedings during the two-year period; on 14 October he issued an originating summons and an ordinary summons against the present four continuing respondents

F   plus three others. Those proceedings were a hybrid in that they asked for leave to proceed under sec. 7(2) against all seven respondents but, in the alternative, for a disqualification of all seven, and, in effect, in the further alternative, either for directions extending the time for filing evidence in the disqualification application until 23 January 1993 (which was then considered by the Secretary of State to be a deadline he could meet) or a standing-over generally until after that date. Those applications were met by applications by three of the seven then respondents that the Secretary of State's then

G   proceedings should be struck out. On 22 October 1992, still within the two years, all those applications (which I shall together call "the October 1992 proceedings") came before *Knox* J when, by consent, the Secretary of State's applications were withdrawn, save as to costs, "without prejudice to the applicant's right to make a further application under sec. 7(2) . . .", and the respondents' applications were the subject of no order material for present purposes save as to costs.

H   On 5 February 1993 the present originating summons for leave under sec. 7(2) was issued by the Secretary of State as an inter partes matter but by then directed to only five of the earlier seven. The Secretary of State's evidence-in-chief on the present application under sec. 7(2) was sworn on 4 and 5 February and served with the originating summons.

     On 3 March 1993, at a hearing attended only on behalf of the Secretary of State, directions were given for evidence, the respondents being given to 1 May 1993 and the

Secretary of State's reply to be by 1 June 1993. The estimated time for the hearing was A
between four and five days. In the event it took ten.

Preparation of the respondents' evidence was delayed by an unsuccessful application
by one respondent as to discovery to *Jonathan Parker* J and, he having refused it (see
[1993] BCC 886), for leave to appeal to the Court of Appeal. Once that delay was passed
the respondents' evidence was completed and in late September the Secretary of State
filed evidence in reply. The hearing began on 1 October 1993; it is doubtful it could have
been heard earlier even had the original time for evidence been honoured. B

Against that background, what is the length of the delay? There would inevitably be
some delay in the sense that it could not reasonably be expected that disqualification
proceedings would be launched on the very day of the administration order. To call the
elapse of time in that circumstance "delay" is unfair to the Secretary of State, but he
does accept that things done and not done within the two-year period to 24 October 1992
are properly to be taken into account in the assessment of the Secretary of State's C
conduct. It is common ground that, so far as concerns delay and the reasons for it, time
stopped when the Secretary of State's full body of evidence-in-chief was served on or
about 5 February 1993 (service on one of the respondents was later as he was out of the
jurisdiction). Thus the time in relation to which the Secretary of State's conduct is to be
scrutinised for delay is from 25 October 1990 to early February 1993.

(2) The reasons for the delay D

If, as is clear from the authorities I have mentioned, sec. 6 of the 1986 Act is intended
to serve a public interest, it becomes important that publicity should be given to its
existence and exercise. The business community needs to have matters drawn to its
attention from time to time — consider *Ettinger* [1993] BCC 312 at p. 315G. PPI was
and is a high profile administration. If ever there was a case in which it would be
appropriate for the Secretary of State, if minded at all to move to disqualify, to move in E
good time, this would surely be such a case. The joint administrators appointed on
25 October were Mr Christopher Morris of Touche Ross & Co and Mr Jordan and
Mr Stone of Coopers & Lybrand Deloitte, men of extensive experience in administrations
and in insolvency generally and partners in firms with considerable resources. PPI itself
was far from without the funds remaining sufficient to finance a proper investigation and
inquiry; by November 1992 professional and other fees paid and the administrators' fees
amounted to over £25m. Mr Charles accepts that by the end of 1990 it could be seen by F
the Secretary of State that disqualification proceedings might be appropriate. As
Mr Charles put it, alarm bells would have been ringing in the disqualification unit.

The very size of the matter, though, suggests that time would need to be taken in
sorting the wheat from the chaff. Mr Morris's staff (he having been charged by an order
of 30 October 1990 with investigation of any claims PPI might have against Mr Nadir
and others) have by now amassed some 17,000 files and whilst, no doubt, the vast G
majority are irrelevant to disqualification of the four individuals with whom I am
concerned, the task of reporting to the Secretary of State would plainly have been a task
involving prolonged research and inquiry. Section 7(3) of the 1986 Act requires that if it
appears to an administrator that the conditions of sec. 6(1) are satisfied in respect of a
person who is or has been a director of the company in administration, then the
administrator shall *forthwith* report the matter to the Secretary of State. Without his
waiting for, and irrespective of the contents of, any such report, the Secretary of State H
can by sec. 7(4) require the administrator to give him information as to a director's
conduct or to produce or permit inspection of papers relevant to his conduct in the light
of the discretion which the Secretary of State has should it appear to him that it is
expedient in the public interest that a disqualification order should be made against a
person (see sec. 7(1)).

A   The *Insolvent Companies (Reports on Conduct of Directors) No. 2 Rules* 1986 (S 1986/2134) provide at r. 4 that where the company concerned appears to the administrator to have become insolvent within sec. 6(2) of the 1986 Act then as a matter of express duty a return in specified form must be made to the Secretary of State by the administrator during the first six months of the administration. The rules go on at r. 5 to deal with the case where the Secretary of State has required information or the production or inspection of documents under sec. 7(4); the Secretary of State is entitled to apply to the

B   court that it should direct compliance by the administrator within such period as may be specified and the rules provide also that an administrator may in such a case be required to pay all the costs of such an application. I would expect any responsible administrator (and the administrators in this case are plainly within that description) to be at pains to avoid the making of such an order and even the making of such an application which, costs apart, would be likely to be harmful to his own and to his firm's reputation.

C   There was no return made within the specified six month period. That failure inspired no application by the Secretary of State under sec. 7(4) for the provision of information nor as to documents and, upon there having been no calling for the same under sec. 7(4), there could be no direction from the court on the point under r. 5.

     Not later than 30 April 1991 the administrators had reason to regard PPI as a company not in any sense solvent; on that day its then finance director swore a statement of affairs disclosing a deficiency as to creditors of £551m.

D   On 1 May 1991 the Joint administrators made what they called an interim report under sec. 7. It has not been shown to me or to the respondents, but it is said that it stated that sufficient information was not then to hand to enable a substantive report to be filed and that it would be some time before the administrators could report fully. The Secretary of State did not use sec. 7(4) to ensure that he could be examining documents in the meantime nor did he take any other step until over a month later on 10 June 1991

E   when there was a meeting with the administrators' staff. I have not seen any notes of the meeting, but it is said that Mr Morris indicated that whilst he "anticipated" (as it is said) submitting a detailed return "in time" outlining various allegations of misconduct against some or all of PPI's directors, he was unable to determine the precise nature and scope of the matters on which he anticipated reporting or the identity of the persons concerned.

F   Still sec. 7(4) was not deployed by the Secretary of State and nothing appears to have been for over a month until, on 15 July 1991, the disqualification unit requested a further meeting. I have not seen that request but it cannot have been expressed in terms of any urgency as the meeting did not take place for a further three weeks. The meeting, on 5 August 1991, did not advance matters. Nothing was done for a further two months until on 8 October 1991, the unit wrote to the administrators. I have not seen that letter.

G   There is no suggestion that the letter excited any response until well over two months later, the administrators on 2 January 1992 told the unit that work had commenced on a full return. That the contents of any return would be likely to fall far short of anything that could quickly be turned into admissible evidence for the purposes of a disqualification application must surely have been known to the unit, just as they would have known also, if only because of the bulk of the papers involved in PPI, that application against directors of PPI was likely to be an exceptionally burdensome application if application

H   were to be made. Indeed, the Secretary of State's evidence states that the preparation of the evidence in support proved to be an immense task; I do not understand it to be said that that could not have been foreseen. If alarm bells had begun to ring by the end of 1990, by now, 2 January 1992, one could expect in the unit a sense that a great deal might need to be done in what could prove to be a dangerously short period before the two years were to expire. Nonetheless, nothing was done until over a month later, on

February 1992, when, in terms neither I nor the respondents have seen, the unit wrote requesting a submission of the "final return" which had been said to have been already in the course of preparation some six weeks earlier.

On 20 February 1992 the joint administrators said they expected to report within four weeks, namely by 9 March 1992. Even were it right, as it may be, to have allowed the joint administrators to have proceeded thus far without the Secretary of State using sec. 7(4) and without the Secretary of State having insisted on a timely compliance with the rules as to returns, any toleration of delay beyond the indicated 19 March would, given the very leisurely pace so far adopted, surely run the risk (as would no doubt have been seen by the unit itself) of being inexcusable.

For all that, 19 March 1992 came and went. In the evidence-in-chief in the October 1992 proceedings there is no explanation beyond this:

"In the event the substantive report was not received until 1 June 1992."

In the evidence-in-chief in the present proceedings there is added, in respect of the period from 20 February 1992:

"During this period there was little contact between the unit and the joint administrators."

At my invitation, Mr Charles amplified "little contact"; he said there was no contact on which the Secretary of State could rely. There has been no attempt to explain the delay between 19 March and 1 June 1992 which I hold to have been inordinate and unreasonable. Only a few days short of two and a half months were thus wasted.

The report received from the joint administrators on 1 June 1992 came with a good deal of associated material which needed perusal and which itself suggested that further material and enquiries would be needed. By now, and upon its seeing the bulk of the matter, one would have expected a real urgency to have infused the unit having regard to the October deadline and the beginning of the season of holidays, including the long vacation. The unit had discussions with the Serious Fraud Office and obtained transcripts from it. It sought and obtained board minutes from the joint administrators. It considered the material it had and what further material it might need. The timetable for June and July 1992 is given in the Secretary of State's evidence with such lack of detail that it is difficult to be sure whether, for example, the steps next after the receipt of the report on 1 June 1992 were taken with the urgency I have said could be expected, but I am not prepared to hold June and July to have been the occasion of any unreasonable delay. In particular, I cannot assume from the fact that any particular documents or class of documents have not found their way into the Secretary of State's evidence that it was unreasonable for the unit to seek them or unreasonable for the unit to have waited for their production and to have spent time perusing them.

In early August 1992 (before 5 August it would seem) the Secretary of State formed the view that it was expedient in the public interest that disqualification orders should be made against a number of the directors of PPI including the present respondents:

". . . and thus that the unit should proceed with the preparation of evidence to support an application for such an order."

A Conference was arranged with experienced junior counsel on 5 August 1992. It was decided to instruct a more junior counsel to embark on the drafting of the evidence that would be required and a nomination for her so to act on behalf of the Secretary of State was obtained. The plan was that she would be able to do the bulk of the initial preparation before going on her holidays in early September. However, a misunderstanding occurred; counsel (and this is hardly unusual) had been awaiting formal instructions before starting work and the Treasury Solicitor and the unit were unaware that that was the case. Counsel went on holiday in early September without the

A   drafting having even been embarked upon. Mr Charles accepts that criticism can fairly be made of this spell. I hold that the delay, of the order of a month, from early August to early September, whilst explained, has found no satisfactory explanation and that the month's delay was unreasonable.

In early September a difficulty arose. One of the reasons for selecting the more junior of the counsel intended to be used in the drafting was that she had been previously instructed on behalf of the joint administrators in proceedings against Mr Nadir and

B   hence had come to know a good deal about PPI and its history and affairs. At first the joint administrators' solicitor had not objected to her being used by the Secretary of State in the drafting of the disqualification proceedings. The Treasury Solicitor's view was that instructing her would not lead to difficulties but rather would expedite matters in that whatever material the joint administrators would be likely to have supplied to her when she was acting for them and which could be of relevance to her drafting on the

C   instructions of the Treasury Solicitor, would in any event have been properly open to the Secretary of State for use by him in the prospective disqualification proceedings. However, by early September 1992 the joint administrators' solicitors had taken the point that the material obtained by them by the use of sec. 235 and 236 of the *Insolvency Act* 1986 and other material obtained by them on a confidential basis could not properly be available, at least without the directions of the court in that behalf, in the disqualification drafts.

D   The decision still to persist with the junior counsel who had previously acted for the joint administrators was unwise and further time was lost by reason of it, but I do not regard the decision as in any way unreasonable at that stage. The Treasury Solicitor's view that he could properly have access to the material as to the disclosure of which the joint administrators had real doubts was later upheld by *Vinelott* J in January 1993 and the Treasury Solicitor could well have thought that he might overcome the joint

E   administrators doubts without awaiting a full hearing for directions. In the result the drafting was left undone; it would have been wiser forthwith to instruct counsel untainted by knowledge from other sources. Time was lost in September. The deadline was looming.

By 24 September 1992 it was recognised by the Treasury Solicitor that the deadline could not be met. On that day the Treasury Solicitor wrote to the court. He then felt that

F   if the deadline was extended by three months to 23 January 1993 the necessary evidence could be prepared. This three-month extension was not dictated to the Treasury Solicitor, but was then regarded by him as the period he would need.

On 14 October 1992 the October 1992 proceedings were launched as I have earlier described and were heard on 22 October 1992. No sec. 16 notice had preceded them.

At the end of October 1992 Mr Charles was instructed (but not, I think, to draft the

G   evidence) and the idea of persisting with junior counsel who had previously acted for the joint administrators was at last abandoned. That decision could have been made earlier; it could have been realised that the joint administrators' doubts would not easily be overcome, that the joint administrators would be unlikely to accede to the Treasury Solicitor's views without obtaining the court's directions and that persisting with the counsel initially chosen could needlessly delay matters. However, there *could* perhaps have been a saving of time if counsel already familiar with PPI matters could have been

H   used and the joint administrators' solicitors *could* have dropped their objections. Things were delayed but not, in my view, unreasonably.

In early November a fresh junior counsel who was in a position to proceed was at last instructed to prepare a first draft of the evidence. The Treasury Solicitor had had in mind a two-tier plan under which the incoming counsel would prepare a first draft which would next be worked upon by a more experienced junior. Two weeks were lost in very late December because the more experienced counsel had other commitments and could not turn to the drafts the incomer had prepared. Given that even the extra three months which the Treasury Solicitor had sought was by then running out and that the need to instruct more senior counsel assuredly able to work on the papers had been foreseen from early November at the latest, I hold that this loss of a further two weeks in late December was unreasonable.

Eventually drafts were prepared and were considered by the Treasury Solicitor, the disqualification unit and by the joint administrators. I see no ground for complaint in the time thus taken up.

On 28 January 1993 *Vinelott* J ruled in what was effectively the Secretary of State's favour in the joint administrators' direction proceedings. There were consequential further meetings between the unit and the joint administrators and on 5 February 1993 the originating summons for leave under sec. 7(2) which is now before me was issued and the voluminous evidence on behalf of the Secretary of State was sworn. For present purposes the period needing to be examined then ceased. The fact that the further material from the joint administrators obtained only after the order of *Vinelott* J provided little or no further matter that has found its way into the evidence, provides no ground of itself for saying that it was unreasonable to press for it and to await its arrival.

In sum, therefore, over the whole period I have found between three and a half and four months to be represented by unreasonable delay. None of it is any way sought to be attributed to any of the respondents. As *Vinelott* J pointed out in *Re Noble Trees Ltd* [1993] BCC 318 at p. 322A–B, dispatch is required in the public interest; it is wrong that a person whom the Secretary of State considers unfit should be left free to concern himself in the management, formation or promotion of companies any longer than is necessary. Even in this complicated matter, given the resources of the joint administrators, the powers available to the Secretary of State, the fact that almost from the outset it had been seen as a case in which disqualification proceedings might be appropriate and the other circumstances I have described, the sec. 6 proceedings could have been launched within the time prescribed by Parliament had only the matter been attended with a sense of purpose and, later, of urgency with which it should have been marked.

(3) The strength of the case

This third of *Scott* LJ's four matters requiring to be considered can conveniently be divided, as I have mentioned above, into two parts. First, is it the case that if the matter relied on by the Secretary of State were taken to be proved as alleged it could lead to a disqualification? Could that matter, assuming it to be so proved, amount to a failure so serious as fairly to be visited with a disqualification? If that relatively low threshold, which is principally related to the gravity of the misconduct alleged, is crossed by the Secretary of State then the strength of the case needs further to be examined so that it can be evaluated for the purposes of being considered alongside the other three factors in the so-called balancing exercise. If that low threshold is not crossed then, as it seems to me, the balancing exercise never needs to be embarked upon; as I have mentioned, it would be pointless to allow to proceed a case which could not succeed.

(a) The initial threshold

At this stage of the case I should treat the Secretary of State's case as if matters of fact therein are to be taken to be true and as sufficiently proved without regard to anything said to counter it in the evidence in answer filed by the respondents. Although the exercise is different, because I am considering affidavits rather than a pleading, there are some similarities to the assumptions made where a party moves to strike out a pleading as disclosing no cause of action. Thus, whilst I shall accept the Secretary of

A   State's evidence as sufficiently proving the matters it alleges, I shall not, for the purposes
of considering whether the initial threshold is crossed, speculate on how far that
evidence might be improved were there to be a sec. 6 hearing. Just as, on a strike out, a
plaintiff's pleading is to be considered as it stands unless and until an amendment is
specifically put up for consideration, so also here I should at this stage consider the
Secretary of State's case as it is, except to the extent that some particular likely or
possible improvements are canvassed. In the event, none was canvassed and, indeed,
B   Mr Morris's affidavit is described within itself as being the evidence which will be
deployed by him on the substantive application itself. It is thus hard to see from the
present evidence how the Secretary of State's case could attain a greater strength than it
will have upon the assumptions I am here making.

As to whether those assumptions are too favourable to the Secretary of State,
Mr Crow and Mr Kennedy asked me to bear in mind that much of the Secretary of
C   State's evidence is hearsay. They urge, too, that this application is final rather than
interlocutory in the sense that whichever way my decision goes the originating summons
under which the application is made will be completely disposed of. On that basis I am
invited to treat much of the Secretary of State's evidence as inadmissible. Mr Charles
draws attention to one possible escape from that and, without enthusiasm on his part,
does not dissent from another possible escape, one which I raised in the course of
D   argument. That was that although, in the sense which I have described, the present
application is final, it has an interlocutory character: see per *Scott LJ* in *Probe Data
Systems (No. 3)* at p. 120B. I am bound to say, first, that it seems to me extremely
technical to describe as interlocutory a proceeding the sole purpose of which is the
seeking of leave out of time for the launch of other proceedings, they being other
proceedings which would be certain to follow forthwith if only that leave were to be
given. Secondly, to expose parties to the extra costs and delays inherent in an insistence
E   upon the reception of only direct evidence on all points (notwithstanding that in the
nature of things neither an office-holder nor the Secretary of State is likely to have direct
personal knowledge of many relevant events) would, in my judgment, be to make even
more and unnecessarily burdensome a leave-seeking process which I would think, to
judge from the total absence of guidance which it gave, that Parliament foresaw as being
both simple and cheap. I would therefore have been disposed to accept hearsay at this
F   stage notwithstanding the technically final nature of the present application, but the
alternative ground Mr Charles urges is derived from *Rex Williams Leisure plc* [1993]
BCC 79 per Sir *Donald Nicholls* V-C, who had before him an application by respondents
to disqualification proceedings raising three issues, one of which was that the Secretary
of State's evidence in that case was hearsay and should be struck out. In that case the
Secretary of State was relying upon a report made under sec. 447 of the *Companies Act*
G   1985 and the papers which had been collected in connection with that report, including
incomplete drafts. When the Vice-Chancellor said at p. 84E:

"The general relaxation of [RSC, O. 41, r. 5] for affidavits used in interlocutory
proceedings is not applicable here, because this disqualification application is not
an interlocutory proceeding."

—he was referring not to the strike-out application but to the substantive disqualification
H   application. The sentence cited does not therefore deter me from the view I have
expressed as to sec. 7(2) having an interlocutory character. But, more importantly, the
Vice-Chancellor went on at pp. 85–86 to allow into evidence the contents of the sec. 447
report by way of an analogy with cases in which inspectors' reports were admitted in
winding-up petitions. Further, of the drafts and other material received under sec. 447
he said, at p. 87D:

"Here also I do not think I should strike out the criticised material. The Secretary   A
of State must be entitled to put such documents in evidence, for what they may be
worth. At the hearing of the summons there may be argument about their
evidential significance or even their relevance, but that does not mean they should
be struck out from the affidavit evidence at this stage as inadmissible. Those are
matters to be looked into properly at the hearing of the disqualification application."

Were I to be wrong in taking the view that hearsay is admissible by reason of the
interlocutory character of the present application, I would in any event have admitted   B
the material under the approach adopted in *Rex Williams*, leaving its weight at least and
perhaps also its final admissibility to be argued over and ruled upon at any substantive
hearing. For present purposes I have therefore ruled none of the Secretary of State's
evidence to be inadmissible at this stage.

It is necessary at this point to say something as to PPI's business and its banking
arrangements. Soon after Mr Nadir became chairman of PPI, the company acquired   C
Unipac Packaging Industries Ltd, a company operating in Northern Cyprus. It was very
profitable and its profits fuelled a massive rise in PPI's own share price in 1981 and 1982.
No doubt encouraged by this experience, PPI expanded further in the Near East. PPI
became very dependent on the success of its Near East subsidiaries; as late as 1989,
when acquisitions and diversifications had begun to reduce the proportion, the profits of
the Middle and Near East subsidiaries still represented 67 per cent of the profits of the   D
group. PPI's investment in the Middle and Near East led to a very substantial outflow of
funds in that direction. By 31 December 1989 its Near East subsidiaries owed PPI over
£650m and were themselves building up large reserves at banks in Turkey and Northern
Cyprus, reserves which, at the end of June 1990, amounted to £300m. By 25 October
1990 PPI's nominal ledger showed £1,466.9m as owed by its subsidiaries worldwide to
PPI.

Of that overall indebtedness something like £371m represented money paid to   E
Northern Cyprus and Turkish subsidiaries between September 1987 and October 1990
out of PPI's accounts by Mr Nadir personally (in the sense that the actual transfers were
authorised at point of transfer only by him).

In August 1990 PPI had successfully renewed facilities with its bankers, but then
Mr Nadir made public an offer of his to acquire the whole share capital of PPI. This led
to considerable speculation in the press. The offer was withdrawn on 17 August and the
shares plunged in price. PPI then came under considerable pressure from its bankers of   F
whom some who had earlier lent on the security of PPI shares began to sell their security.
The shares fell from 418p at the beginning of August 1990 to 108p when dealings in them
were suspended on 20 September, a day after the SFO had visited offices of a company
associated with Mr Nadir. Mr Nadir continued to assure the board of PPI that funds
would be remitted back from Turkey to ease PPI's position. On 24 September 1990 the
board resolved to appoint Coopers & Lybrand Deloitte to carry out a review of the   G
group. A standstill was arranged with PPI's bankers; its difficulties were seen as ones of
cash flow rather than insolvency. If only the Middle and Near East subsidiaries had
repaid sums owing to PPI or even had repaid parts of those debts then, as Mr Morris
asserts, it would seem PPI would not have needed to be put into administration.
Mr Nadir was confident money would be received but creditors lost patience.

The administration petition was presented on 25 October 1990 and the order was
made on the same day. To date, as I understand Mr Morris's affidavit, PPI's recovery on   H
intercompany loans has been nil and the administrators' investigations have been
severely hampered by injunctions obtained by various parties in the courts of Northern
Cyprus. The administrators have obtained judgments in default against Mr Nadir and
others in respect of £370m although Mr Crow and Mr Kennedy for the second and first
respondents assert, correctly in my view, that it cannot be taken as proved against these

A   respondents that such sums were taken out either by way of misappropriation at all or by way of misappropriation from PPI (for which the respondents would be directly responsible) rather than from one or more subsidiaries (for which their responsibility would only be indirect).

Throughout PPI's life Mr Nadir not only had a considerable degree of control on movement of funds within the group, but was a signatory, with power to act as sole signatory, on PPI's principal bank accounts. Although, in time, dual signatories were

B   required for the dealings of subsidiaries and were approved by PPI's board for its own accounts, Mr Nadir remained to the end able to move sums from PPI's accounts on his sole signature.

To revert to what I have called "The initial threshold", the 1987 proceedings rules provide at r. 3(2) in respect of the substantive application itself that the evidence shall include a statement of the matters by reference to which the respondent is alleged to be

C   unfit to be concerned in the management of a company. The Secretary of State's evidence includes such a statement even though at this stage it is not the substantive application that is yet made. The need for the applicant clearly to state his case is underlined by *Rex Williams* at p. 87B. Each of the matters complained of is a matter of omission and, lumping the respondents together, it is said as follows:

> "(i) They failed to institute adequate controls over the expenditure and transfer

D   of monies from PPI;

> (ii) They failed to ensure that adequate financial controls and reporting procedures were implemented and adhered to in respect of the Near East subsidiaries;

> (iii) They failed to obtain appropriate responses to the question of the need of the Near East subsidiaries for such substantial funding from PPI;

> (iv) They failed to monitor, or set up proper procedures for monitoring, the

E   actual expenditure incurred by the Near East subsidiaries, the funds which had been provided to the Near East subsidiaries and the ability of the Near East subsidiaries to repay their indebtedness to PPI as and when required or at all."

It will be remembered that the four continuing respondents do not represent a majority in number of the directors at any one time and, indeed, were less than a third of the directors who were directors at the date of the administration and do not in any event include the company's chairman. I cannot see that the failures as framed by the

F   Secretary of State in the above statement can properly be regarded as breaches of duty by each individual respondent of the four respondents. As I have quoted them, these allegations seem to me to confuse what is the duty of the board as a whole with what are the duties falling to each individual respondent director. An individual director who has not been individually charged by a board with the task of (for example) instituting adequate financial controls, might or might not be in breach of a duty to the company to

G   use his best endeavours to procure their institution but not, without more, with their absence. Were that not so, a director who had striven manfully to introduce them would be as much in breach as one who had resisted them. The omissions specified (if intended, as it seems to me they are, to be alleged breaches of duty within Sch. 1, Pt. I, para. 1 to the 1986 Act) are, as framed, in my judgment misconceived.

If the Secretary of State were to be confined to those specified omissions with the

H   rigidity appropriate to consideration of a pleading, then his case against all four respondents would, in my judgment, necessarily fail. I should add that whilst I can see that a director might well be at risk for not posing appropriate questions, I cannot see (as to omission (iii)) how he can be arraigned for a failure "to obtain the appropriate responses". However, the Secretary of State's evidence further developed the four omissions and the alleged shortcomings of the respondents were reframed until, in reply, the Secretary of State said this in his evidence:

"The heart of the case against the respondents is not that they did not resign but that:

  (a) they failed as directors to procure that the omissions were rectified or to take the stance that 'enough is enough' and that they would resign *if* the omissions and the lack of knowledge and control of the board which arose therefrom and of which they were well aware were not rectified; and

  (b) after mid-1989 they continued as directors and thereby continued thereafter to be responsible in breach of their duties for the omissions and to rectify them."

This case, which Mr Charles accepts represents "new territory" amongst disqualification cases, needs to be put into the context of PPI's position and the role within it of Asil Nadir. Mr Nadir acquired a controlling interest in PPI by way of one of his companies in 1980, his interest later diminishing but remaining above 25 per cent. He had considerable personal interest in the success of PPI. The company developed under his chairmanship into being a holding company of a major international group with over 200 subsidiaries, including some 80 trading subsidiaries. So far as its accounts disclose, it developed under his charge from having net assets of £10m or so to over £845m and it grew to having a turnover of over a billion pounds per annum. In August 1988 it became one of only 145 companies awarded alpha stock status at the London Stock Exchange and in 1989 it entered the FT-SE 100. Its growth throughout the 1980s was outstanding. Mr Nadir was responsible for the overall strategy of the PPI group and its implementation and retained executive control over a number of its subsidiaries. Especially did Mr Nadir retain such control over subsidiaries in Northern Cyprus and Turkey where his influence and connections were of considerable importance to PPI. Mr Charles accepts as applicable to this case the observations of *Scott* LJ in *Polly Peck International plc v Nadir & Ors* [1992] 2 Lloyd's Rep 238 at pp. 244–245. Those passages were, of course, based on different evidence but they are accepted as being applicable here. What was there said was this:

"It is important in this regard to bear in mind that it is common ground, for present purposes at least, that at the relevant time Mr Nadir was a man of unblemished commercial reputation and integrity. He had achieved quite staggering commercial success over a relatively short period. He loomed, in Northern Cyprus, like a colossus over the local economy and over the commercial prospects and fortune of the country."

I interpose that it is not said that had the alleged omissions not occurred, then the perception of Mr Nadir as a man of "unblemished commercial reputation and integrity" would have been, or would have been likely to have been, dismantled or would have been known to the board to be false, nor that any misappropriations made by him (none is here proved) would have not occurred or would have been likely to have been avoided. In asserting Mr Nadir's "unblemished commercial reputation and integrity" the respondents are not said to be profiting from their own shortcomings.

PPI's growth had been financed by borrowings from banks, the issue of loan stocks and bonds and through rights issues; towards the end it acted as banker for the whole group. It was by 1989 and 1990 a company which depended heavily on the confidence of its banks and of the Stock Exchange and whose reputation was likely to be inextricably linked with the chairman who had presided over its spectacular growth (as was illustrated by the failure in August 1990 of Mr Nadir's offer to acquire the whole share capital of PPI and the consequential plunge in its share price).

Of the "heart of the case" as put by the Secretary of State, a number of things need to be said. All of the continuing respondents are men of some commercial experience and three have professional qualifications. It is disavowed that there is anything dishonest

A   alleged in their conduct, nor is any complicity in or covering up of or blindness to fraud
      suggested. It is not said that the omissions alleged were designed to or did benefit
      themselves or any of them. None of the specific statutory requirements to which
      particular attention is drawn in the schedule to the 1986 Act is alleged in terms to have
      been broken. It is accepted by Mr Charles that the duties alleged to have been breached
      are not such as to which any guidance is to be found in the authorities or in textbooks. It
      is not said that PPI's auditors, an international firm, suggested to the board generally or
B   to these directors in particular that there were gaps in the information or control
      procedures which needed plugging but which were left unplugged. It is not said that the
      "due diligence" needed to have been shown by PPI and its various advisers on the
      several rights issues disclosed weaknesses which were drawn to the attention of these
      directors but which they yet persisted in. It is not said that Mr Nadir was left totally
      unsupervised and beyond enquiry; at one point some directors acted upon a disquieting
C   report of advantages being taken by Mr Nadir's family and the purchase of some gaming
      machines in suspicious circumstances. The directors who received the report (one of
      whom was Mr Tindale) discussed it with the auditors who later came back to say that
      they had looked at their audit files and could not see any evidence. The matter was thus
      not taken further.

          It is not said that the respondents did nothing to raise the subject of further and better
      financial information; on the contrary Mr Morris's evidence itself sets out steps repeatedly
D   taken by various members of the board and by Mr Fawcus in particular as financial
      director to improve PPI's state of information and control. That evidence also shows
      Mr Nadir's apparent tractability in some areas as to financial information and control
      but also his reluctance (sometimes assisted by directors other than these four) to accept
      a curtailing of his private influence in the particular areas covered by the four alleged
      omissions. It was not as if Mr Nadir answered the board with unreasoning refusals. PPI,
E   as Mr Charles accepts, was, even in 1990, still at what has been described as an
      entrepreneurial stage. Investment by PPI in Turkish and Northern Cyprus subsidiaries
      had served it well and when Mr Nadir said he could not be responsible for their
      profitability unless he had personal control over the movement of funds the board was
      entitled to have his entrepreneurial successes in mind and to recognise that his ability
      speedily to take advantage of investment opportunities could be to PPI's advantage.

          In the circumstances it was realistically accepted by Mr Charles that the problem
F   facing the board (let alone four of the individuals within it) was "a difficult one", but it is
      said that it was serious misconduct on the part of each of the respondents not to have
      brought matters to a head in 1989 with a view to the repair of the alleged omissions.
      Mr Charles accepts that resignation of any of the four would not of itself have mended
      any of the four omissions. He expressly accepted that it could be that Mr Fawcus's
      resignation as financial director could have caused a considerable loss of confidence in
      PPI and that equally it was speculative whether the threat of his resignation would have
G   brought Mr Nadir to heel. It is not said the four should have taken any steps to procure
      or threaten Mr Nadir's removal as a director. It is notable that the evidence shrinks from
      asserting that if only these four or any of them had cried "enough is enough" and had
      threatened resignation the least good would or even might have been achieved. The
      only resignation that is held up as an example in the Secretary of State's evidence is that
      of Mr Reading, but it is not said that PPI's controls or information were thereby
H   improved one jot. It is not said that strict use of a "joint-signatory" policy in PPI would
      have prevented any misappropriations, nor is it said that if it had been introduced it
      would have been unlikely that Mr Nadir could have found willing second signatories
      from other members of the board.

          The matter, as *Dillon* LJ emphasises in *Sevenoaks*, is one of fact, but, having regard
      to the whole spectrum of misconduct from, say, a single oversight or delay in the

ovision of minor accounting material at one end to repeated fraud or dishonesty for   A
ersonal gain at the other, in the circumstances I have described (none of which is
controvertible by the Secretary of State on his evidence and submissions) it is in my
judgment quite impossible, even allowing the Secretary of State to go outside his four
stated omissions, to regard as so serious a failure as to justify disqualification the failure
of any of these four individual directors, never a majority on the board at the time, to
have cried "enough is enough" and to have threatened their resignation, which, in
Mr Fawcus's case, it is accepted could have caused the company a considerable loss in   B
that ingredient of confidence so necessary to it and the effect of which upon Mr Nadir, in
terms of bringing him to heel, is accepted as being speculative.

The shortcomings alleged do not, in the light of indisputable facts and the Secretary
of State's submissions, have the gravity required. The initial threshold is not crossed if,
as *Bath Glass* at p. 133 suggests in the paragraph approved by the Court of Appeal, the
serious failure has, on one alternative, to be "deliberate". A fortiori the initial threshold   C
is not crossed if the guidance given by Sir *Nicolas Browne-Wilkinson* V-C in *Lo-Line* as
to a lack of commercial probity survived *Sevenoaks*, as there is no hint of its lack in this
case.

If I am right as to the recurrence problem then even if I am wrong as to the place of the
four omissions (as amplified) in the spectrum of misconduct and if, therefore, they *could*
amount to a serious failure, it is still to be noted that nothing in the Secretary of State's   D
evidence suggests that such past failure would be the least likely to recur in any company
of which any of the four is or is likely to become a director. However, on the approach I
have adopted as to the recurrence problem (involving a burden being on the respondents
to satisfy the court), any requirement as to recurrence is unlikely to come into play until
after the initial threshold has been crossed by the applicant, which is the assumption
upon which, contrary to my decision so far, I shall next proceed.
                                                                                          E
(b) *Strength of case generally*

I shall here suppose that my conclusion under (a) is wrong and that I now have to
assess the strength of a case in which the allegations are of a sufficient gravity to be able
to lead to a disqualification. At this stage regard can be had to the respondents' evidence:
see *Probe Data (No. 3)* at p. 120B per *Scott* LJ. Mr Charles invites me to form a present
view as to the strength of the applicant's case as it would be likely to be at a substantive   F
hearing. I can only do that on the basis of the evidence now put in front of me although,
of course, in any particular case the present evidence may itself suggest that the evidence
at the hearing could be different.

However, in this particular case I have not been addressed as to areas in which the
evidence of the Secretary of State at a substantive hearing would be likely to differ from
that already collected. As I have mentioned, Mr Morris's present evidence will be his   G
evidence at any substantive hearing and the respondents can fairly comment that with
three years and (as the evidence shows) some £25m and more already spent as professional
and other costs and remuneration in the administration, the circumstances should be
such that one can reasonably expect the case to be already fully collected.

Although I can now take into account the respondents' evidence I cannot, of course,
decide any disputes of fact. But what is a dispute of fact? Mr Charles invites me to treat
everything said in the respondents' evidence which is not clearly admitted in the   H
Secretary of State's evidence or submissions as if it were disputed. That is not, in my
judgment, a correct approach to evidence. The Secretary of State has had the opportunity
to reply to the respondents' evidence and I am not disposed to accept comments in that
reply that the respondents' evidence is not to be taken to be *agreed* as of themselves
giving rise to a dispute as to such facts. Where the respondents' evidence is not in any

A way countered by anything said on the Secretary of State's behalf I can receive it, in my view, as undisputed.

In *Probe Data (No. 3)* at p. 120E *Scott* LJ spoke of some matters in the respondents evidence in that case as not being "incontrovertible", but that was, it would seem, in relation to evidence sought to be put in for the first time, late, in the Court of Appeal and presumably therefore not answered by the Secretary of State. Different considerations

B plainly apply in such a case to those applicable where, as here, there has been a full opportunity to file evidence in reply.

As for the strength of case needed to be shown at this stage, different authorities have described the strengths found in their particular respective cases. In *Cedac* at p. 565B it was held a "prima facie case" had been shown. In *Tasbian (No. 3)* at p. 362C a "fairly arguable case" was spoken of. In *Probe Data (No. 3)* at p. 119H the case was "well

C arguable"; and in *Copecrest* at first instance, p. 846C, the case was "arguable". None in terms purports to describe a necessary *minimum* threshold as opposed to their giving a description of each respective case. Once the initial threshold is crossed, the court's task is to weigh the strength of case for the purpose of then moving on to the so-called balancing exercise.

Turning to the respondents' evidence, what can I glean from it as undisputed and as relevant to the strength of the Secretary of State's case? Here it is convenient to look

D chiefly at Mr Fawcus's evidence. In practical terms the case against the others is unlikely to be stronger than the case against the finance director; if an honest and apparently competent and qualified finance director could be excused for not crying "enough is enough", a fortiori could the others be excused? The evidence, says Mr Crow on Mr Fawcus's behalf, shows a finance director who introduced a whole series of improvements in PPI's financial systems, whose efforts at improvements were generally

E rewarded and who could thus reasonably form the view that nothing beneficial to PPI would be generated by the staging of a confrontational crisis of the kind which the Secretary of State would seem to have preferred. Further, Mr Fawcus says that some important steps could not be forced by him upon Mr Nadir as the board as a whole would, in a confrontation, be likely to support Mr Nadir and not the finance director and hence that his gentle and steady approach was more conducive to an improvement in

F PPI's systems than the alternative possible strategy suggested by the Secretary of State.

The improvements which on evidence accepted by Mr Charles as undisputed can be attributed to Mr Fawcus's efforts include a restructuring of PPI's finance department, the recruitment of better staff in his department, and the preparation of a finance manual to set standards expected of a public company of PPI's size. That alone took nine months. He introduced budgets, monthly reporting by subsidiaries and daily returns made by PPI's treasury department showing the daily flow of funds in and out of

G London on a daily basis. Dual signatory control was introduced and was, as Mr Fawcus understood things, operational in all subsidiaries (albeit not in PPI itself so far as concerned Mr Nadir). Mr Fawcus saw to it that regular finance reports were presented to the board, including reports on deficiencies in information. He required all auditors to provide management letters to the board of the company being audited, letters identifying any matters relating to the systems, controls or commercial decisions of the

H company and any opportunity for or appearance of fraud. Mr Charles accepts Mr Fawcus worked long and hard to achieve improvements in PPI's administration.

The first part of Mr Crow's argument — that here there was a responsible finance director steadily and successfully introducing improvements — is in my judgment completely made good. Mr Fawcus was not put on guard by the auditors who not only delivered unqualified audit reports, but who made no adverse comments either in the course of their special investigations in relation to the rights issues in 1988 and 1989 or in any management letter from auditors of the kind Mr Fawcus had required.

As for Mr Fawcus's inability sometimes to carry board members with him if confrontation with Mr Nadir loomed, that is illustrated by the board's failure in June 1989 to implement his and another director's suggestion that PPI should ask Coopers & Lybrand to carry out an investigation into PPI's financial systems. Mr Morris describes this matter as having been put to the board, but the better view is that it was put rather to a committee of the board, the chairman's committee. Another example was when Mr Fawcus was interested in setting up a separate bank account for cash deposits accumulating in the Near East, an account which was to be under control of London *only*. It was at that stage that Mr Nadir said he could not be responsible for the profitability of the Near Eastern subsidiaries if he did not have control of funds and if control passed to the treasury department and Mr Fawcus. Typically, Mr Nadir gave a reason for his view: immediate decisions were frequently necessary. The non-executive directors backed down from their support of Mr Fawcus's position and the subject went off for a later report. It was not as if Mr Fawcus deliberately delegated matters to Mr Nadir or chose to allow him free rein; it was more that it proved a long task to remove from Mr Nadir the power that had doubtless been more appropriate when PPI had been a smaller undertaking.

I have already said that I cannot find the "deliberate" failure that *Bath Glass* suggests, as one alternative, is necessary, but I go on to add, having regard to the totality of the undisputed evidence, that I cannot find the other alternative either, namely failure through "incompetence", let alone incompetence which, as *Sevenoaks* suggests, has to be to a very marked degree (p. 780C). Mr Morris exhibits without adverse comment evidence in which Mr Fawcus says "it was a constantly improving position" and "It was progressive; we were getting there." It is not said Mr Fawcus did not honestly hold such views. I shall not go into the evidence at greater length but, as to Mr Fawcus, his perception that things were steadily improving and that, with a stronger and more independent board to support his efforts, things would continue to improve, seems to me, on the basis of undisputed evidence, not only to be a perception he held but one that could reasonably be formed. Others in his place may conceivably have acted differently, but I cannot see Mr Fawcus as a danger to creditors or others (to echo *Cedac* (at p. 558) and when I add to my reading of the undisputed evidence the weaknesses in the Secretary of State's case which I described under the heading "The initial threshold", I cannot see a case based on any failure by Mr Fawcus to discharge his duties as being other than highly speculative and very weak.

Turning to Mr Ellis, he raises issues as to his knowledge of shortcomings in the financial systems of PPI. At the most material times he was away in the USA running that part of PPI's operations. He had himself pressed for improvements in the company's financial information. I would be prepared to assume against him that he did sufficiently know of, or was sufficiently put on notice as to, deficiencies, but, quite apart from the fact that if he had discussed matters with Mr Fawcus he could well have been put at rest and have adopted Mr Fawcus's view that matters were steadily improving, there is another weakness in the case against him. Rightly or wrongly he was being marginalised in PPI's affairs; there were moves to get rid of him. The Secretary of State provides no evidence of how Mr Ellis' pressing matters to an issue, if necessary to a resigning issue, would have been greeted by the board, but in the light of the evidence of a wish to be rid of him I cannot see it as being other than a reaction of relief. Certainly I have no material which suggests a threat of his resignation or his resignation would have in any way served the cause of improving PPI's financial controls or information.

So also with Mr Tindale; again the Secretary of State's evidence does not condescend to particulars as to just what he should have done and when he should have done it, but I

A   have no evidence to suggest, even had he seen it right to make or threaten to make better financial controls and information a resigning issue, that PPI's position would have improved. His resignation could, for example, have been attributed to his age or health; his replacement, to be voted in by a general meeting at which 25 per cent or more votes would be within Mr Nadir's control, might have been more not less compliant.

As for Dr Siebel, he is barely mentioned in the evidence at all.

B   I shall shy away from terms such as "an arguable case" or a "prima facie case" which, as Lord *Diplock*'s analysis in *American Cyanamid* shows, mean different things to different people and in any event are not necessary to use once the initial threshold is crossed, but I do conclude that on the undisputed evidence the Secretary of State's case is and will remain at best speculative and very weak against each of these respondents. Moreover, that is my conclusion without bringing the recurrence problem into consideration. If it is brought into play, then the Secretary of State's case can only be

C   weakened further. There is a case plainly arguable on the evidence as a whole that even if the respondents' shortcomings were seen as serious, they are not of a kind likely to recur in any company with which any of them would be likely to be associated except in the quite exceptional circumstances (applicable in PPI) of better information and controls being thwarted or delayed by "a man of unblemished commercial reputation and integrity" who was widely seen as responsible for the company's success and who had retained a substantial stake in it as a shareholder. In other words, the respondents

D   would have a good prospect of satisfying a court, even assuming against them that a present finding of past unfitness was justified, that the court should, on the particular facts, see that such past unfitness did not permit a jump to a finding of a present unfitness. Nor have I brought into play in the respondents' favour the notion that unfitness is to be shown in relation to companies generally; again, and corresponding to the recurrence position, it is arguable on the evidence that even if there were to be unfitness in these

E   respondents, it was not in relation to companies generally but only in respect of companies in which the quite exceptional conditions met with in PPI would be likely to be met.

(4) Prejudice

   Under sec. 7(2) it is the leave of the court that is required if there are to be

F   disqualification proceedings launched outside the two-year period. By contrast with, say, proceedings for a striking out for want of prosecution, it is not open to the parties to waive delay and by their own choice to proceed after all. Furthermore, on the approach adopted by the Secretary of State (which is that full evidence-in-chief is needed even for a sec. 7(2) application and that there is contemplated as appropriate evidence from the respondents in answer and a reply from the Secretary of State) an application under

G   sec. 7(2), especially in a matter with voluminous papers or several parties, is itself likely to take some time. Simply obtaining a hearing for such an application would itself involve a lapse of some time. In such circumstances it seems to me that except where it can be seen that a respondent's opposition is unreasonable or unreasonably prolonged, it is wrong, when examining prejudice, to look only at that represented by the delay between the expiry of the two years and the date when full evidence on the application launched under sec. 7(2) is served. That would not adequately recognise that the

H   eventual hearing of the sec. 6 application, were there to be one, would inevitably be delayed by far longer than by that interval. Thus, in the present case, the delay (some three and a half months) from 24 October 1992 to 5 February 1993 has inevitably led to a delay in the hearing under sec. 6, if there is to be one, of the order of at least a year.

I arrive at the year because Mr Charles, invited to estimate how the case under sec. 6 would have proceeded had it been duly launched in time, indicated that after its

upposed launch in October 1992 he would have expected a considerable contest as to   A
discovery. I think he is justified in that hypothesis; even though the present application
is not the trial, there has been a hearing before *Jonathan Parker* J and an application to
the Court of Appeal for leave to appeal in respect of discovery. On that basis Mr Charles
would have expected, not unreasonably in my view, that it would only have been about
October 1993 that a timely sec. 6 application would have been ready to be set down with
its evidence complete, probably on an estimate of at least four weeks for the hearing
itself. As it is, that supposed October 1992 start cannot be replaced with a start earlier   B
than November 1993 and there is no good reason why the year to setting down which
Mr Charles contemplated had there been an October 1992 start, should not apply to a
start in November 1993. Hence there will be at least a year's postponement. It is not, in
one sense, the fault of the Secretary of State that the initial three and a half month's
delay to 5 February should be magnified to a delay of a year or so, but it is an almost
inevitable consequence of that three and a half months that any sec. 6 hearing would be   C
likely to be put back about a year. It cannot be said here that the respondents' opposition
has been in any way unreasonable or that they have been tardy.

I cannot be sure when a four to five week case with witnesses and cross-examination
set down in October 1993 would come on for hearing, nor when one would come on
were it to be set down in October 1994. It is, I think, agreed that the hearing would need
to be a fixture rather than to float. Average figures are not necessarily a guide and doing
the best I can to be realistic, I shall take it that the beginning of such sec. 6 hearings   D
would be respectively February 1995 and February 1996. On this basis the question as to
prejudice becomes this: what, if any, prejudice is suffered or is likely to be suffered by
each respondent respectively if a sec. 6 application against him were to be heard in
February 1996 rather than in February 1995?

I recognise that in taking this view of what is the material period to be looked at for
the purposes of ascertaining prejudice I am, in effect, giving the word "delay" a different   E
meaning in the fourth of *Scott* LJ's four matters to that which it bears in the first and
second, but I do not regard his judgment as precluding this present approach.

As to the contrast between February 1995 and February 1996, Mr Charles says that
the mere fact that the stress and unease caused by sec. 6 hanging as a possibility over a
respondent for longer than it might otherwise have done cannot of itself be a reason for
withholding leave under sec. 7(2) as, were that so, leave could never be granted.   F
However, stress or unease are not constant from one respondent to another and it
cannot be asserted that their mere prolongation may not, on suitable facts, be taken to
represent so serious a prejudice as to bar an extension. Moreover, on any view such
things are capable of being factors, amongst others, such as with those others may bar
an extension. The question of prejudice requires me to look separately at each of the
respondents.
                                                                                                G
Whatever "tunnel vision" there is in connection with what can be looked at for
disqualifications under sec. 6, there is none imposed as to what can be looked at on the
subject of prejudice for the purposes of sec. 7(2). It is therefore appropriate to say
something of each respondent separately.

Mr Fawcus, the second respondent, is now aged 60. He has a degree in law and
economics and is a chartered accountant. He remained with Unilever for 23 years where
for nine years he was board member with responsibility for accounting, purchasing,   H
planning, distribution and export. He spent two years as financial officer to the overseas
committee, assisting the chairman to control a turnover of about £2bn in 30 countries.
In 1984 he moved to Guinness Overseas as finance/commercial director in charge of a
business with a turnover of some £500m. In 1986 he was "head-hunted" and joined PPI
as its financial director. The Secretary of State's own evidence shows that the very fact

A   that Mr Fawcus remained as financial director of PPI was a matter which, in the eyes of the press, helped to preserve confidence in the company, which was no doubt one of the factors that led Mr Charles to accept that Mr Fawcus's resignation could have caused PPI considerable loss. Mr Fawcus deposes that third parties will be reluctant to employ him as a director if there remains any risk of him being disqualified and he gives a concrete example of that reluctance. At 60 and in industry he has, he says, only a limited number of years left in which to earn a living and to provide for his retirement. As to

B   that, his pension from PPI, as it transpired, was underfunded to the order of about £200,000, but his claim in that regard has been settled for only £30,000. He has remained a director of some relatively small companies, but in relation to his likelihood of employment at any level commensurate with his qualifications and experience, the year's postponement represents, at his age, he says, a real prejudice.

     Added to that, he refers to the unavoidably speculative effect of the passage of time in

C   that year on the strength of the evidence he would be able to adduce. He is looking for support from at least three other directors of PPI and in the light of the board minutes, in particular, being incomplete and sometimes altered (as is common ground) he says that his case would not be one reliant only on documents, but reliant also upon the recollections of directors not as to one single memorable event, but as to events over a period. As the most relevant events are likely to be those of 1989 and 1990, the events are already at least three or four years old. In addition to the ordinary effect of the lapse

D   of time on memory, he refers to the age and health of the co-directors on whom he would wish to rely. There is a threat that evidence available in, say, early 1995 will be unavailable or weakened by February 1996. As to one of the co-directors, Mr Halpin, a chartered accountant, and non-executive director, he is now aged 80. I have been given a doctor's report as to another, Mr Mills, who is aged 70, which describes him as a sick old man whose age is beginning to affect him with impairment of his memory.

E   Mr Charles rightly says that Mr Halpin's and other evidence could already have been put into affidavit form, but in a matter where cross-examination is likely, perhaps even inevitable, that answer is far from a complete answer to the possibility of the year's postponement materially weakening Mr Halpin's and Mr Mills' evidence. Another co-director intended to be relied on is the respondent Mr Tindale, who is now 72. I have been given a medical report as to his health and I see a real risk of his case giving rise to a prejudice similar to that said to exist in relation to Mr Halpin's and Mr Mills' evidence.

F   The fairness of any hearing of proceedings against Mr Fawcus is put at real risk. There are other factors Mr Fawcus asserts as likely instances of prejudice, but I need look no further than the two heads I have mentioned. Taken together (and a fortiori were an inevitable prolongation of stress and worry to be added) they show, in my judgment, a prejudice already being suffered and a very real risk of material further prejudice being occasioned to Mr Fawcus by the Secretary of State's failure to have started his proceedings

G   in time.

     As to Mr Ellis, he is 40 years of age. He read law at university and was called to the Bar in 1977. After working at a merchant bank he joined the board of PPI. Although, at his age, a prolongation of a year may not be as serious to him as it would be likely to be in Mr Fawcus's case, it is nonetheless a real present prejudice to Mr Ellis. He, too, (in addition to the other defences deriving from his absence abroad and his claimed lack of day-to-day involvement in or knowledge of the financial arrangements of PPI's

H   headquarters) asserts the potentially prejudicial effect of a postponement on the evidence of the co-directors he would wish to call. The totality of prejudice which he is likely to suffer is not as grave as that of Mr Fawcus, but I have no doubt but that he is already prejudiced and threatens to be further prejudiced by the Secretary of State's delay.

     As to the fourth respondent, Dr Ulf Siebel, he is not represented before me and no evidence has been sworn on his behalf. As he lives and works out of this jurisdiction

and, (if I may speculate from his CV) is unlikely to depend on a British reputation for his   A
livelihood, the effect of proceedings being possible or impending for an extra year is
likely to be far less significant to him than it would be to the others. How far he would be
intending to rely on the evidence of co-directors whose health is at risk or whose
attendance at such a delayed hearing would be threatened, I cannot judge. I have no
material to suggest he will be materially prejudiced by delay, but if I am right as to the
strength of the case against him, the absence of demonstrated prejudice is hardly
significant.   B

As for Mr Tindale, he is now 72 or 73. I have touched on the subject of his health when
considering him as a witness whom Mr Fawcus and Mr Ellis will wish to rely upon. His
health is poor. He has not been represented before me in the general argument and his
evidence consists of no more than the exhibition of a solicitor's letter. I shall not go into
detail in his case, but in the light of the medical evidence I have received I believe I
should regard the postponement or prolongation of proceedings as likely to occasion   C
substantial prejudice to him.

(5) The balancing exercise

Lest I am wrong in the conclusions I have arrived at under the heading of "The initial
threshold", I need now to exercise the discretion given to me by sec. 7(2) with regard to
the matters under the four main headings I have referred to. I bear in mind that the
Secretary of State's delays include periods which I have found to represent unreasonable   D
delay. Even supposing the initial threshold to have been crossed, I have found the
Secretary of State's case to be at best speculative and very weak. I have found that by
reason of the Secretary of State's failure to act within the time prescribed for the purpose
by Parliament the respondents Mr Fawcus, Mr Ellis and Mr Tindale are certain to suffer
some prejudice and that more prejudice is likely to follow as to those respondents.
Mr Charles accepts the onus is on his client.

I conclude as to those three respondents that there is no good reason for the extension   E
sought. I would therefore not have given leave for the Secretary to State to launch
proceedings out of time against those three respondents even were I to be wrong in my
earlier conclusion that the case ought not to be proceeded with on the ground that it
could not succeed.

As for Dr Siebel, although, in the absence of evidence or argument from him on the
subject, I have found no significant prejudice in his case, the initial threshold was not   F
crossed as to him and even if it had been the case against him is, on the evidence,
threadbare to a degree. The case against him is, to use the language of *Probe Data (No.
3)* at p. 120E, "too weak to warrant the grant of leave". Moreover, as to all respondents,
first, had I been left in doubt I would have had to give the respondents the benefit of it
for the reason I have mentioned and, secondly, I comment that if no real likelihood of
recurrence is shown, then the public interest is diminished in that the public, absent a   G
likelihood of recurrence on the facts of this case, hardly needs protection from these
particular respondents.

(6) Conclusion

I should mention that detailed criticisms of Mr Morris's evidence was made by
Mr Kennedy and Mr Crow. It is the case that in some rare instances Mr Morris's citations
from or inferences from board or other minutes or papers have been, unwittingly I am   H
sure, less than just to the respondents or even mistaken and one or two have been so
accepted by Mr Charles. However, the accepted errors are by no means of a weight such
as to vitiate or weaken his evidence generally and that being so, I do not think it
necessary to go further into this subject save to say that I have not taken the remaining
disputes of fact thus emerging as resolved in the respondents' favour.

A   I would wish to add that I am not intending to prescribe less onerous or different duties for individual directors should they have amongst them a commanding figure such as Mr Nadir, one closely associated with their company and its growth and reputation. Nor am I saying that directors, non-executive or executive, need not stand up to such a man. However, where there is such a figure it can be that the steps which a director might reasonably consider to be the best to take in seeking to discharge his duties in what is accepted by the Secretary of State to be a difficult situation will be different to the steps

B   required in other and simpler cases. The shortcomings to be required of a director before his conduct can reach the level of misconduct required by sec. 6(1)(b) need to recognise that difference.

In the outcome, for the various reasons I have given, there has not been shown to be a good reason for the necessary extension of time and I decline to give leave to the Secretary of State to proceed out of time.

C
Costs

As to costs, first of all, I give liberty to Mr Halpin and Mr Doshi to apply specifically as to the costs of the October 1992 proceedings should that become necessary. It would seem unlikely, but, still, that is the liberty I grant them.

So far as concerns Mr Mills' costs, by consent there will be no order as to his costs

D   either of these present proceedings or of the October 1992 proceedings.

In so far as concerns Mr Fawcus, Mr Ellis and Mr Tindale, I award them their costs of these proceedings and of the October 1992 proceedings to be paid by the Secretary of State.

The only remaining issue is the level of taxation of those costs, should it be standard or should it be on an indemnity basis? I have no doubt but that I may order indemnity

E   costs should I so choose. I have no doubt also that I am not bound to award costs on an indemnity basis. The respondents, Mr Fawcus, Mr Tindale and Mr Ellis take the point that here there is, so to speak, a double default in the sense that not only have the proceedings been lost by the Secretary of State, but they were occasioned by his own default in not commencing with the two-year period. I bear that in mind, but I do not take the view that that, which is the strongest point they can urge, is sufficient to displace the ordinary disposition of the court to order costs on a standard basis. So as to the

F   taxation, I order that it should be on the standard basis.

(*Order accordingly*)

G

H

CASES CITED

This table lists alphabetically all cases referred to in judgments of the courts reported in British Company Cases in 1993. References are to the first page of the relevant case.

LEGISLATION FINDING LIST

The following Legislation Finding List covers all cases reported in British Company Cases 1993. References to legislative provisions are to section numbers unless otherwise stated. References are to the first page of the relevant case.

TOPICAL INDEX

References are to the first page of the relevant case.

© **1993 CCH Editions Limited**

BCP BCP$$$$197